BACKCOUNTRY ADVENTURES

NORTHERN CALIFORNIA

Warning: While every effort has been made to make the backcountry trail descriptions in this book as accurate as possible, some discrepancies may exist between the text and the actual trail. Hazards may have changed since the research and publication of this edition. Swagman Publishing, Inc., and the authors accept no responsibility for the safety of users of this guide. Individuals are liable for all costs incurred if rescue is necessary.

Printed in Korea.

Publisher's Cataloging-in-Publication
(Provided by Quality Books, Inc.)

Massey, Peter, 1951-
Backcountry adventures. Northern California: the ultimate guide to the backcountry for anyone with a sport utility vehicle / Peter Massey and Jeanne Wilson. —1st ed.
p.cm.
Includes bibliographical references and index.
ISBN 1-930193-08-4

1. Automobile travel—California, Northern—Guidebooks. 2. Four-wheel drive vehicles. 3. Trails—California, Northern—Guidebooks. 4. Ghost towns—California, Northern—Guidebooks. 5. Plants—California, Northern—Identification. 6. Animals—California, Northern—Identification. 7. California, Northern —Guidebooks. I. Wilson, Jeanne (Jeanne Welburn), 1960- II. Title. III. Title: Northern California

GV1024.M37 2002 917.9404'54
QBI02-200503

BACKCOUNTRY ADVENTURES

NORTHERN CALIFORNIA

THE ULTIMATE GUIDE TO THE
BACKCOUNTRY FOR ANYONE
WITH A SPORT UTILITY VEHICLE

PETER MASSEY AND JEANNE WILSON

SWAGMAN
PUBLISHING

Acknowledgments

Many people and organizations have made significant contributions to the research and production of this book. We owe them all special thanks for their assistance.

The production of the book has been a team effort, and we would especially like to thank the following people who have played major roles in its production.

Project Editor:	**Timothy Duggan**
Senior Field Researchers:	**Donald McGann, Maggie Pinder**
Researchers:	**Chris Munden, Angela Titus**
Copy Editing and Proofreading:	**Sallie Greenwood, Alice Levine**
Graphic Design and Maps:	**Deborah Rust**
Finance:	**Douglas Adams**
Office Administration:	**Peg Anderson**

We received a great deal of assistance from many other people and organizations. We would like to thank Donna M. Powell, Karen Rhoden, and Linda McPhail of Sierra National Forest; Mike Bradshaw, Dorothy Riddell, and Roy Morris of Stanislaus National Forest; Donna A. Day, assistant forest archaeologist at Tahoe National Forest; Melanie-Sue Bowers and the Alpine Sportsman's Club for history and local information; Scott J. Lawson, director, and staff of the Plumas County Museum; Deborah Tibbetts, district archaeologist at Lassen National Forest; Bev Way, Bill Tierney, Jami Nield, Nancy Gardner, and Gerald R. Gates of Modoc National Forest; staff at the BLM information center in Briceburg; Sue Hirschfeld for consulting on the geology section.

Staff at many offices of the National Forest Service also provided us with valuable assistance.

The book includes more than five hundred photos, and we are most thankful to the following organizations and people who have helped to research photographs or allowed us to publish the wonderful photographs they have taken: Lori Swingle and Coi Gehrig, Denver Public Library; Linda Fisk and Ken Hedges, San Diego Museum of Man; Dace Taube, University of Southern California; Carrie Burroughs and Karren Elsbernd, California Academy of Sciences (CalPhotos); Barbara Pitschel, Strybing Arboretum & Botanical Gardens; Jim Gratiot, CalFlora; Tanya Hollis, Abby Bridge, and Crissa Van Vleck, California Historical Society; Professor Ron Olowin, Department of Physics and Astronomy at Saint Mary's College and curator of the Alfred Brousseau Collection; staff at Denver Botanical Gardens; staff at Tucson Botanical Gardens; Alison Sheehey, James Cokendolpher, Earle Robinson, Doug Von Gausig, Don Baccus, Lauren Livo, Steve Wilcox, and Paul Berquist.

For maintaining our vehicles, we would like to thank Dave's European, Denver, Colorado, and Tina Niksic and Matt Sokolowski of Trek Outfitters, Redondo Beach, California.

We would like to draw our readers' attention to the website (www.bushducks.com) of our senior researchers, the Bushducks—Donald McGann and Maggie Pinder. It provides information on current 4WD trail conditions and offers their valuable assistance to anyone who is planning a backcountry itinerary.

Publisher's Note: Every effort has been taken to ensure that the information in this book is accurate at press time. Please visit our website to advise us of any changes or corrections you find. We also welcome recommendations for new 4WD trails or other suggestions to improve the information in this book.

Swagman Publishing, Inc.
P.O. Box 519, Castle Rock, CO 80104
Phone: (303) 660-3307
Toll-free: (800) 660-5107
Fax: (303) 688-4388
www.4WDbooks.com

Contents

The North Coast Region

Appendix: Trail Lists

Introduction

From the fog-cloaked bluffs of the Pacific Coast and bustling metropolis of San Francisco Bay to the jagged, snow-capped summits of the Sierra Nevada and volcanic peaks of the southern Cascades, Northern California is one of the most geologically diverse regions in the United States. Yosemite's Half Dome and El Capitan, giant granite formations tucked in the Yosemite Valley; Lake Tahoe on the eastern slopes of the Sierra Nevada, one of the largest and highest natural reservoirs of its kind; and the coastal redwood forests, home to some the world's tallest trees, are area icons all with distinct climates and home to unique wildlife and natural resources.

Mountains, deserts, and ocean created a formidable natural boundary around California for centuries. Because of this relative isolation, many species of plants and animals that thrive in Northern California exist nowhere else on earth. Towering redwoods and ancient bristlecone pines dot the edges of many trails in this book. A lucky traveler might also spot an elusive mountain lion or a majestic bald eagle. In spring and summer, much of California's backcountry is covered in dazzling swathes of wildflowers.

Rich and diverse Native American cultures originally populated Northern California. Evidence of their daily lives is apparent along the coast, where they formed huge mounds of seashells from meals of countless generations. In other areas, elaborate rock paintings and carvings communicate cultures now lost forever. Life for many of California's Indian tribes changed irrevocably when Spanish explorers and priests began to colonize the region in the late 1700s. Their lives were further disrupted by the influx of gold-hungry settlers in the 1850s.

The discovery of gold near Sutter's Fort in January 1848 transformed California. In fact, the rush for riches sparked the largest mass migration in American history. In a few short years, immigrants streaming into the state along the Oregon and California Trails created bustling mining camps on sites previously unexplored by Europeans. Miners settled the remote and rugged banks of the Trinity and Klamath Rivers, areas that might have remained undeveloped except for the determination of prospectors to tap into California's rich mineral deposits. News of California's gold circled the globe, prompting an immigration of Chinese that would further diversify the new state's culture.

Some communities that sprang up around mining claims, such as Auburn and Oroville, remain population centers today. But many, like Coloma and Bodie, faded when the mineral wealth was depleted. Often, a backcountry driver may stumble upon the remains of a mining operation or abandoned settlement without warning. Discovering these dilapidated buildings and hidden adits conjure images of a youthful state far removed from modern California.

We have selected 152 of our favorite unpaved roads and 4WD trails to take you off the highways and into the wild backcountry where much of Northern California's most interesting history has taken place. Our trails often retrace the routes taken by gold rush era emigrants as they completed long journeys into the state. Other trails follow old wagon roads, abandoned train lines, and disused mining roads. We have included descriptions of historic points of interest as well as the region's other important settlements—large and small, existing and ghosted—all influenced by the Indians, explorers, and settlers who played a part in establishing the Northern California we know today.

All the trails in this book are within the capabilities of stock sport utility vehicles, allowing you to escape into remote wilderness in the same car that you take to work and to the grocery store. The trails range in difficulty from unpaved scenic drives with easily negotiated obstacles to exciting routes that provide a challenge for experienced off-highway drivers. Many SUV owners are unaware of the opportunities their vehicles offer. With this book, readers will discover the immense rewards of backcountry touring. We are certain that you will get the same enjoyment we have as you travel through the most remote, scenic, and historic locations in Northern California.

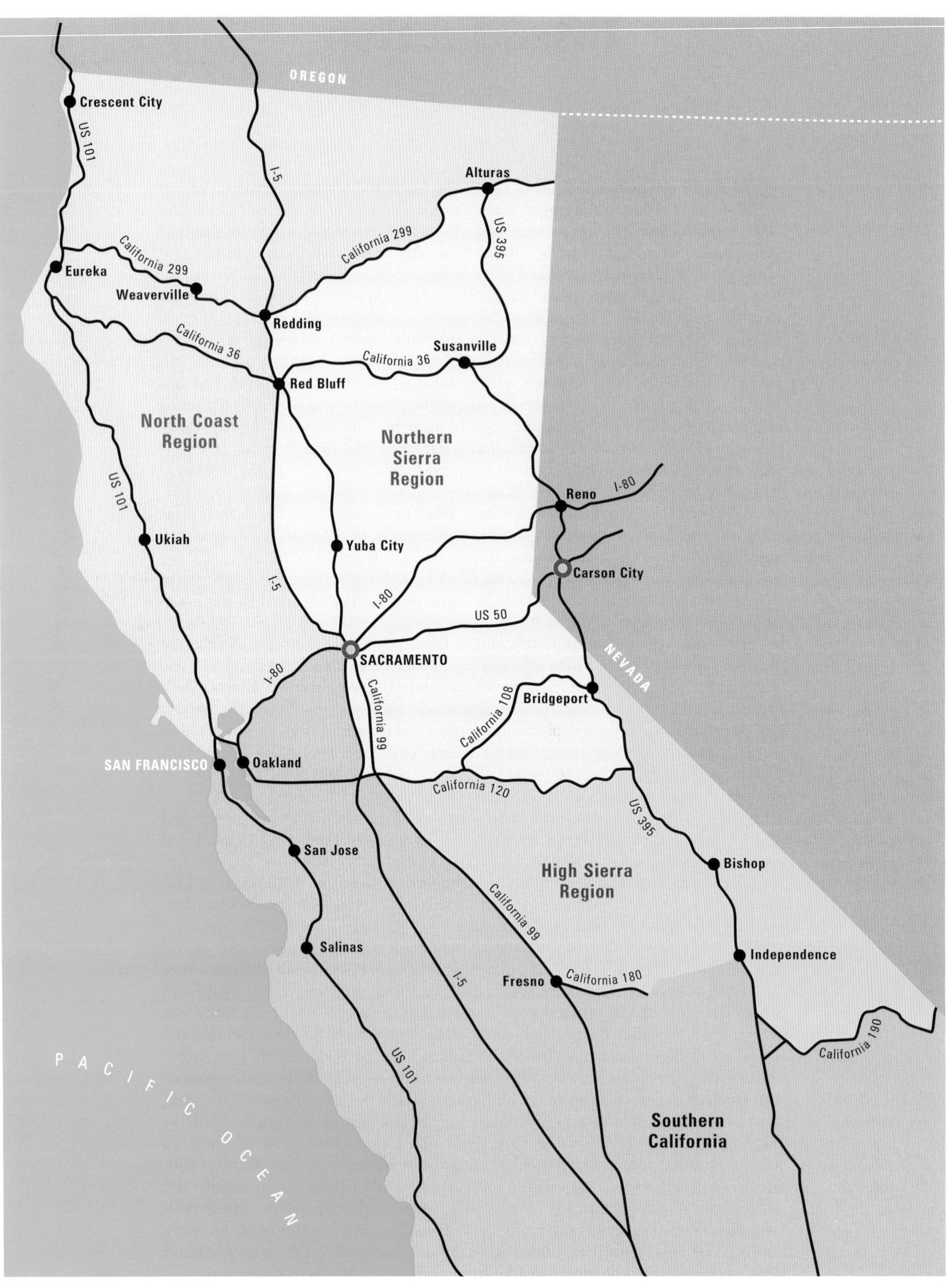

OREGON
NEVADA
PACIFIC OCEAN
North Coast Region
Northern Sierra Region
High Sierra Region
Southern California
Crescent City
Eureka
Weaverville
Redding
Alturas
Susanville
Red Bluff
Ukiah
Yuba City
Reno
Carson City
SACRAMENTO
Bridgeport
SAN FRANCISCO
Oakland
San Jose
Salinas
Bishop
Independence
Fresno
US 101
I-5
California 299
California 36
US 395
I-80
US 50
California 99
California 108
California 120
California 180
California 190

Before You Go

Why an SUV Does It Better

The design and engineering of four-wheel-drive SUVs provide them with many advantages over normal cars when you head off the paved road:

■ improved distribution of power to all four wheels;

■ a transmission transfer case, which provides low-range gear selection for greater pulling power and for crawling over difficult terrain;

■ high ground clearance;

■ less overhang of the vehicle's body past the wheels, which provides better front- and rear-clearance when crossing gullies and ridges;

■ large-lug, wide-tread tires;

■ rugged construction (including underbody skid plates on many models).

If you plan to do off-highway touring, all of these considerations are important, whether you are evaluating the capabilities of your current SUV or looking to buy one; each is considered in detail in this chapter.

In order to explore the most difficult trails in this book, you will need a four-wheel-drive SUV that is well rated in each of the above features. If you own a two-wheel-drive SUV, a lighter car-type SUV, or a pickup truck, your ability to explore the more difficult trails will depend on conditions and your level of experience.

A word of caution: Whatever type of SUV you drive, understand that it is not invincible or indestructible. Nor can it go everywhere. An SUV has a much higher center of gravity and weighs more than a car, and so has its own consequent limitations.

Experience is the only way to learn what your vehicle can and cannot do. Therefore, if you are inexperienced, we strongly recommend that you start with trails that have lower difficulty ratings. As you develop an understanding of your vehicle and of your own taste for adventure, you can safely tackle the more challenging trails.

One way to beef up your knowledge quickly, while avoiding the costly and sometimes dangerous lessons learned from on-the-road mistakes, is to undertake a four-wheel-drive course taught by a professional. Look in the Yellow Pages for courses in your area.

Using This Book

Route Planning

Regional maps at the beginning of each section provide a convenient overview of the trails in that portion of the state. Each trail is highlighted in color, as are major highways and towns, helping you to plan various routes by connecting a series of backcountry trails and paved roads.

As you plan your overall route, you will probably want to utilize as many 4WD trails as possible. However, check the difficulty rating and time required for each trail before finalizing your plans. You don't want to be stuck 50 miles from the highway—at sunset and without camping gear, since your trip was supposed to be over hours ago—when you discover that your vehicle can't handle a certain difficult passage.

You can calculate the distances between Northern California towns by turning to the Northern California Distance Chart at the end of this chapter.

Difficulty Ratings

We utilize a point system to rate the difficulty of each trail. Any such system is subjective, and your experience of the trails will vary depending on your skill and the road conditions at the time. Indeed any amount of rain may make the trails much more difficult, if not completely impassable.

We have rated each trail on a scale of 1 to 10—1 being passable for a normal passenger vehicle in good conditions and 10 requiring a heavily modified vehicle and an experienced driver who expects to encounter vehicle damage. Because this book is designed for owners of unmodified SUVs—who we assume do not want to damage their vehicles—most of the trails are rated 5 or lower. A few trails that rate as high as 7 are included, while those rated 8 to 10 are beyond the scope of this book.

This is not to say that the moderate-rated trails are easy. We strongly recommend that inexperienced drivers not tackle trails rated at 4 or higher until they have undertaken a number of the lower-rated ones, so that they can gauge their skill level and prepare for the difficulty of the higher-rated trails.

In assessing the trails, we have always assumed good road conditions (dry road surface, good visibility, and so on). The factors influencing our ratings are as follows:

- obstacles such as rocks, mud, ruts, sand, slickrock, and stream crossings;
- the stability of the road surface;
- the width of the road and the vehicle clearance between trees or rocks;
- the steepness of the road;
- the margin for driver error (for example, a very high, open, shelf road would be rated more difficult even if it was not very steep and had a stable surface).

The following is a guide to the ratings.

Rating 1: The trail is graded dirt but suitable for a normal passenger vehicle. It usually has gentle grades, is fairly wide, and has very shallow water crossings (if any).

Rating 2: High-clearance vehicles are preferred, but not necessary. These trails are dirt roads, but they may have rocks, grades, water crossings, or ruts that make clearance a concern in a normal passenger vehicle. The trails are fairly wide, so that passing is possible at almost any point along the trail. Mud is not a concern under normal weather conditions.

Rating 3: High-clearance 4WDs are preferred, but any high-clearance vehicle is acceptable. Expect a rough road surface; mud and sand are possible but will be easily passable. You may encounter rocks up to 6 inches in diameter, a loose road surface, and shelf roads, though these will be wide enough for passing or will have adequate pull-offs.

Rating 4: High-clearance 4WDs are recommended, though most stock SUVs are acceptable. Expect a rough road surface with rocks larger than 6 inches, but there will be a reasonable driving line available. Patches of mud are possible but can be readily negotiated; sand may be deep and require lower tire pressures. There may be stream crossings up to 12 inches deep, substantial sections of single-lane shelf road, moderate grades, and sections of moderately loose road surface.

Rating 5: High-clearance 4WDs are required. These trails have either a rough, rutted surface, rocks up to 9 inches, mud and deep sand that may be impassable for inexperienced drivers, or stream crossings up to 18 inches deep. Certain sections may be steep enough to cause traction problems, and you may encounter very narrow shelf roads with steep drop-offs and tight clearance between rocks or trees.

Rating 6: These trails are for experienced four-wheel drivers only. They are potentially dangerous, with large rocks, ruts, or terraces that may need to be negotiated. They may also have stream crossings at least 18 inches deep, involve rapid currents, unstable stream bottoms, or difficult access; steep slopes, loose surfaces, and narrow clearances; or very narrow sections of shelf road with steep drop-offs and potentially challenging road surfaces.

Rating 7: Skilled, experienced four-wheel drivers only. These trails include very challenging sections with extremely steep grades, loose surfaces, large rocks, deep ruts, and/or tight clearances. Mud or sand may necessitate winching.

Rating 8 to 10: Stock vehicles are likely to be damaged and may find the trail impassable. Trails with these difficulty ratings are for highly skilled, experienced 4-wheel drivers only.

Scenic Ratings

If rating the degree of difficulty is subjective, rating scenic beauty is guaranteed to lead to arguments. Northern California contains a spectacular variety of scenery— from its coastal cliffs and redwood forests to the towering peaks of the Sierra Nevada. Despite the subjectivity of attempting a comparative rating of diverse scenery, we have tried to provide a guide to the relative scenic quality of the various trails. The ratings are based on a scale of 1 to 10, with 10 being the most attractive.

Remoteness Ratings

Many trails in Northern California are in remote mountain country; sometimes the trails are seldom traveled, and the likelihood is low that another vehicle will appear within a reasonable time to assist you if you get stuck or break down. We have included a ranking for remoteness of +0 through +2. Prepare carefully before tackling the higher-rated, more remote trails (see "Special Preparations for Remote Travel," page 12). For trails with a high remoteness rating, consider traveling with a second vehicle.

Estimated Driving Times

In calculating driving times, we have not allowed for stops. Your actual driving time may be considerably longer depending on the number and duration of the stops you make. Add more time if you prefer to drive more slowly than good conditions allow.

Current Road Information

All the 4WD trails described in this book may become impassable in poor weather conditions. Storms can alter roads, remove tracks, and create impassable washes. Most of the trails described, even easy 2WD trails, can quickly become impassable even to 4WD vehicles after only a small amount of rain. For each trail, we have provided a phone number for obtaining current information about conditions.

Abbreviations

The route directions for the 4WD trails use a series of abbreviations as follows:

SO CONTINUE STRAIGHT ON
TL TURN LEFT
TR TURN RIGHT
BL BEAR LEFT
BR BEAR RIGHT
UT U-TURN

Using Route Directions

For every trail, we describe and pinpoint (by odometer reading) nearly every significant feature along the route—such as intersections, streams, washes, gates, cattle guards, and so on—and provide directions from these landmarks. The abbreviations to the right of the mileages tell you which way to go at each point. Odometer readings will vary from vehicle to vehicle, so you should allow for slight variations. Be aware that trails can change quickly. A new trail may be cut around a washout, a faint trail can be graded by the county, or a well-used trail may fall into disuse. All these factors will affect the accuracy of the given directions.

If you diverge from the route, zero your trip meter upon your return and continue along the route, making the necessary adjustment to the point-to-point odometer readings. In the directions, we regularly reset the odometer readings—at significant landmarks, popular lookouts, or spur trails—so that you won't have to recalculate for too long.

Most of the trails can be started from either end, and the route directions include both directions of travel; reverse directions are printed in blue below the main directions. When traveling in reverse, read from the bottom of the table and work up.

Route directions include cross-references whenever two trails included in this book connect; this allows for an easy change of route or destination.

Each trail includes periodic latitude and longitude readings to facilitate using a global positioning system (GPS) receiver. These readings may also assist you in finding your location on the maps. The GPS coordinates are given in the format dd°mm.mm'. To save time when loading coordinates into your GPS receiver, you may wish to include only one decimal place, since in Northern California, the first decimal place equals about 150 yards and the second only about 15 yards.

Map References

We recommend that you supplement the information in this book with more-detailed maps. For each trail, we list the sheet maps and road atlases that provide the best detail for the area. Typically, the following references are given:

- Bureau of Land Management Maps,
- U.S. Forest Service Maps,
- *California Road & Recreation Atlas,* 2nd ed. (Medford, Oregon: Benchmark Maps, 2000)—Scale 1:300,000,
- *Northern California Atlas & Gazetteer,* 5th ed. (Yarmouth, Maine: DeLorme Mapping, 2000)—Scale 1:150,000,
- Maptech-Terrain Navigator Topo Maps—Scale 1:100,000 and 1:24,000,
- *Trails Illustrated* Topo Maps; National Geographic Maps—Various scales, but all contain good detail,

We recommend the *Trails Illustrated* series of maps as the best for navigating these trails. They are reliable, easy to read, and printed on nearly indestructible plastic paper. However, this series covers only a few of the 4WD trails described in this book.

The DeLorme atlas is useful and has the advantage of providing you with maps of the entire northern part of the state at a reasonable price. While its 4WD trail information doesn't go beyond what we provide, it is useful if you wish to explore the hundreds of side roads.

The Benchmark atlas provides two sets of maps of the entire state. The "Recreation Guides" give excellent information about a region's parks, recreation opportunities, and points of interest. The "Landscape Maps" provide detailed road and topographical information. This is a wonderful atlas and very useful in getting the most out of any backcountry adventure.

U.S. Forest Service maps lack the topographic detail of the other sheet maps and, in our experience, are occasionally out of date. They have the advantage of covering a broad area and are useful in identifying land use and travel restrictions. These maps are most useful for the longer trails.

In our opinion, the best single option by far is the Terrain Navigator series of maps published on CD-ROM by Maptech. These CD-ROMs contain an amazing level of detail because they include the entire set of 2,815 U.S. Geological Survey topographical maps of California at the 1:24,000 scale and all 116 maps at the 1:100,000 scale. These maps offer many advantages over normal maps:

- GPS coordinates for any location can be found, which can then be loaded into your GPS receiver. Conversely, if you have your GPS coordinates, your location on the map can be pinpointed instantly.
- Towns, rivers, passes, mountains, and many other sites are indexed by name so that they can be located quickly.
- 4WD trails can be marked and profiled for elevation changes and distances from point to point.
- Customized maps can be printed out.

Maptech uses 14 CD-ROMs to cover the entire state of California, which can be purchased individually or as part of a two-state package at a heavily discounted price. The CD-ROMs can be used with a laptop computer and a GPS receiver in your vehicle to monitor your location on the map and navigate directly from the display.

All these maps should be available through good map stores. The Maptech CD-ROMs are available directly from the company (800-627-7236, or on the internet at www.maptech.com).

Backcountry Driving Rules and Permits

Four-wheel driving involves special driving techniques and road rules. This section is an introduction for 4WD beginners.

4WD Road Rules

To help ensure that these trails remain open and available for all four-wheel drivers to enjoy, it is important to minimize your impact on the environment and not be a safety risk to yourself or anyone else. Remember that the 4WD clubs in California fight a constant battle with the government and various lobby groups to retain the access that currently exists.

Although many vehicle manufacturer advertisements depict high-speed rally-style driving as proof of the automobile's off-highway abilities, these commercials are misleading—such driving techniques would only result in vehicle, occupant, and environmental damage. For all concerned, this style of driving is best left to professionals in controlled driving events. The fundamental rule when traversing the 4WD trails described in this book is to use common sense. In addition, special road rules for 4WD trails apply:

- Vehicles traveling uphill have the right of way.
- If you are moving more slowly than the vehicle behind you, pull over to let the other vehicle by.
- Park out of the way in a safe place. Blocking a track may restrict access for emergency vehicles as well as for other recreationalists. Set the parking brake—don't rely on leaving the transmission in park. Manual transmissions should be left in the lowest gear.

Tread Lightly!

Remember the rules of the Tread Lightly!® program:

- Be informed. Obtain maps, regulations, and other information from the forest service or from other public land agencies. Learn the rules and follow them.
- Resist the urge to pioneer a new road or trail or to cut across a switchback. Stay on constructed tracks and avoid running over young trees, shrubs, and grasses, damaging or killing them. Don't drive across alpine tundra; this fragile environment can take years to recover.
- Stay off soft, wet roads and 4WD trails readily torn up by vehicles. Repairing the damage is expensive, and quite often authorities find it easier to close the road rather than repair it.
- Travel around meadows, steep hillsides, stream banks, and lakeshores that are easily scarred by churning wheels.
- Stay away from wild animals that are rearing young or suffering from a food shortage. Do not camp close to the water sources of domestic or wild animals.
- Obey gate closures and regulatory signs.
- Preserve America's heritage by not disturbing old mining camps, ghost towns, or other historical features. Leave historic sites, Native American rock art, ruins, and artifacts in place and untouched.
- Carry out all your trash, and even that of others.
- Stay out of designated wilderness areas. They are closed to all vehicles. It is your responsibility to know where the boundaries are.
- Get permission to cross private land. Leave livestock alone. Respect landowners' rights.

Report violations of these rules to help keep these 4WD trails open and to ensure that others will have the opportunity to visit these backcountry sites. Many groups are actively seeking to close these public lands to vehicles, thereby denying access to those who are unable, or perhaps merely unwilling, to hike long distances. This magnificent countryside is owned by, and should be available to, all Americans.

Remember that you are sharing the road with other users. It is courteous to slow down when you encounter travelers on foot, mountain bike, or horseback, and also sensible for safety reasons and to prevent a dust hazard. Pulling over and turning off your vehicle—whether it is a 4WD, ATV, or motor bike—is a simple gesture appreciated by those with horses. Offering water to people on foot or mountain bike is a small act of generosity that may be much valued by those engaged in physically demanding activities in remote locations.

Special Preparations for Remote Travel

When traveling in remote areas, you should take some special precautions to ensure that you don't end up in a life-threatening situation:

- When planning a trip into remote areas, always inform someone as to where you are going, your route, and when you expect to return. Stick to your plan.
- Be sure your vehicle is in good condition with a sound battery, good hoses, spare tire, spare fan belts, necessary tools, and reserve gasoline and oil. Other spare parts and extra radiator water are also valuable. If traveling in pairs, share the common spares and carry a greater variety.
- Keep an eye on the sky. Flash floods can occur in a wash any time you see "thunderheads"—even when it's not raining a drop where you are.
- Test trails on foot before driving through washes and sandy areas. One minute of walking may save hours of hard work getting your vehicle unstuck.
- If your vehicle breaks down, stay near it. Your emergency supplies are there. Your car has many other items useful in an emergency. Raise your hood and trunk lid to denote "help needed." Remember, a vehicle can be seen for miles, but a person on foot is very difficult to spot from a distance.
- Leave a disabled vehicle only if you are positive of the route and the distance to help. Leave a note for rescuers that gives the time you left and the direction you are taking.
- If you are stalled or lost, set signal fires. Set smoky fires in the daytime and bright ones at night. Three fires in a triangle denote "help needed."
- A roadway is a sign of civilization. If you find a road, stay on it.
- If hiking in remote areas, equip each person, especially children, with a police-type whistle. It makes a distinctive noise with little effort. Three blasts denote "help needed."
- Avoid unnecessary contact with wildlife. Some mice in California carry the deadly Hanta virus, a pulmonary syndrome fatal in 60 to 70 percent of human cases. Fortunately the disease is very rare—only 33 cases have been reported in California and 283 nationwide—but caution is still advised. Other rodents may transmit bubonic plague, the same epidemic that killed one-third of Europe's population in the 1300s. Be especially wary near sick animals and keep pets, especially cats, away from wildlife and their fleas. Another creature to watch for is the western black-legged tick, the carrier of Lyme disease. Wearing clothing that covers legs and arms, tucking pants into boots, and using insect repellent are good ways to avoid fleas and ticks.

Obtaining Permits

Backcountry permits, which usually cost a fee, are required for certain activities on public lands in California, whether the area is a national park, state park, national monument, Indian reservation, or BLM land.

Restrictions may require a permit for overnight stays, which can include backpacking and 4WD or bicycle camping. Permits in some areas may also be required for day use by vehicles, horses, hikers, or bikers.

When possible, we include information about fees and permit requirements and where permits may be obtained, but these regulations change constantly. If in doubt, check with the most likely governing agency.

Assessing Your Vehicle's Off-Road Ability

Many issues come into play when evaluating your SUV, though most of the four-wheel-drive SUVs on the market are suitable for even the roughest trails described in this book. Engine power will be adequate in even the least powerful modern vehicle. However, some vehicles are less suited to off-highway driving than others, and some of the newest, carlike SUVs simply are not designed for off-highway touring. The following information should allow you to identify the good, the bad, and the ugly.

Differing 4WD Systems

All 4WD systems have one thing in common: the engine provides power to all four wheels rather than to only two, as is typical in most standard cars. However, there are a number of differences in the way power is applied to the wheels.

The other feature that distinguishes nearly all 4WDs from normal passenger vehicles is that the gearboxes have high and low ratios that effectively double the number of gears. The high range is comparable to the range on a passenger car. The low range provides lower speed and more power, which is useful when towing heavy loads, driving up steep hills, or crawling over rocks. When driving downhill, the 4WD's low range increases engine braking. It is recommended that only SUVs with low range attempt trails rated 4 and above.

Various makes and models of SUVs offer different drive systems, but these differences center on two issues: the way power is applied to the other wheels if one or more wheels slip, and the ability to select between 2WD and 4WD.

Normal driving requires that all four wheels be able to turn at different speeds; this allows the vehicle to turn without scrubbing its tires. In a 2WD vehicle, the front wheels (or rear wheels in a front-wheel-drive vehicle) are not powered by the engine and thus are free to turn individually at any speed. The rear wheels, powered by the engine, are only able to turn at different speeds because of the differential, which applies power to the faster-turning wheel.

This standard method of applying traction has certain weaknesses. First, when power is applied to only one set of wheels, the other set cannot help the vehicle gain traction. Second, when one powered wheel loses traction, it spins, but the other powered wheels don't turn. This happens because the differential applies all the engine power to the faster-turning wheel and no power to the other wheels, which still have traction. All 4WD systems are designed to overcome these two weaknesses. However, different 4WDs address this common objective in different ways.

Full-Time 4WD

In order for a vehicle to remain in 4WD all the time without scrubbing the tires, all the wheels must be able to rotate at different speeds. A full-time 4WD system allows this to happen by using three differentials. One is located between the rear wheels, as in a normal passenger car, to allow the rear wheels to rotate at different speeds. The second is located between the front wheels in exactly the same way. The third differential is located between the front and rear wheels to allow different rotational speeds between the front and rear sets of wheels. In nearly all vehicles with full-time 4WD, the center differential operates only in high range. In low range, it is completely locked. This is not a disadvantage because when using low range the additional traction is normally desired and the deterioration of steering response will be less noticeable due to the vehicle traveling at a slower speed.

Part-Time 4WD

A part-time 4WD system does not have the center differential located between the front and rear wheels. Consequently, the front and rear drive shafts are both driven at the same speed and with the same power at all times when in 4WD.

This system provides improved traction because when one or both of the front or rear wheels slips, the engine continues to provide power to the other set. However, because such a system doesn't allow a difference in speed between the front and rear sets of wheels, the tires scrub when turning, placing additional strain on the whole drive system. Therefore, such a system can be used only in slippery conditions; otherwise, the ability to steer the vehicle will deteriorate and the tires will quickly wear out.

Some vehicles, such as Jeeps with Selec-trac™ and Mitsubishi Monteros with Active Trac 4WD™, offer both full-time and part-time 4WD in high range.

Manual Systems to Switch Between 2WD and 4WD

There are three manual systems for switching between 2WD and 4WD. The most basic requires stopping and getting out of the vehicle to lock the front hubs manually before selecting 4WD. The second requires you to stop, but you change to 4WD by merely throwing a lever inside the vehicle (the hubs lock automatically). The third allows shifting between 2WD and 4WD high range while the vehicle is moving. Any 4WD that does not offer the option of driving in 2WD must have a full-time 4WD system.

Automated Switching Between 2WD and 4WD

Advances in technology are leading to greater automation in the selection of two- or four-wheel drive. When operating in high-range, these high-tech systems use sensors to monitor the rotation of each wheel. When any slippage is detected, the vehicle switches the proportion of power from the wheel(s) that is slipping to the wheels that retain grip. The proportion of power supplied to each wheel is therefore infinitely variable as opposed to the original systems where the vehicle was either in two-wheel drive or four-wheel drive.

In recent years, this process has been spurred on by many of the manufacturers of luxury vehicles entering the SUV market—Hummer, Porsche, Mercedes, BMW, Cadillac, Lincoln, Acura, and Lexus have joined Range Rover in this segment.

These higher-priced vehicles have led the way in introducing sophisticated computer-controlled 4WD systems. While each of the manufacturers has its own approach to this issue, all the systems automatically vary the allocation of power between the wheels within milliseconds of the sensors detecting wheel slippage.

Limiting Wheel Slippage

4WDs employ various systems to limit wheel slippage and transfer power to the wheels that still have traction. These systems may completely lock the differentials, or they may allow limited slippage before transferring power back to the wheels that retain traction.

Lockers completely eliminate the operation of one or more differentials. A locker on the center differential switches between full-time and part-time 4WD. Lockers on the front or rear differentials ensure that power remains equally applied to each set of wheels regardless of whether both have traction. Lockers may be controlled manually by a switch, a lever in the vehicle, or they may be automatic.

Manual lockers are the most controllable and effective devices for ensuring that power is provided to the wheels with traction. However, because they allow absolutely no slippage, they must be used only on slippery surfaces.

An alternative method for getting power to the wheels that have traction is to allow limited wheel slippage. Systems that work this way may be called limited-slip differentials, positraction systems, or in the center differential, viscous couplings. The advantage of these systems is that the limited difference they allow in rotational speed between wheels enables such systems to be used when driving on a dry surface. All full-time 4WD systems allow limited slippage in the center differential.

For off-highway use, a manually locking differential is the best of the above systems, but it is the most expensive. Limited-slip differentials are the cheapest but also the least satisfactory, as they require one wheel to be slipping at 2 to 3 mph before power is transferred to the other wheel. For the center differential, the best system combines a locking differential and, to enable full-time use, a viscous coupling.

Tires

The tires that came with your vehicle may be good enough to take off-road, but many SUVs are fitted with passenger-car tires. These are unlikely to be the best choice because they are less rugged and more likely to puncture on rocky trails. They are particularly prone to sidewall damage as well. Passenger vehicle tires have a less aggressive tread pattern than specialized 4WD tires, providing less traction in mud.

For information on purchasing tires better suited to off-highway conditions, see "Special 4WD Equipment" below.

Clearance

Road clearances vary considerably among different SUVs—from less than 7 inches to more than 10 inches. Special vehicles may have far greater clearance. For instance, the Hummer has a 16-inch ground clearance. High ground clearance is particularly advantageous on the rockier or more rutted 4WD trails in this book.

When evaluating the ground clearance of your vehicle, you need to take into account the clearance of the bodywork between the wheels on each side of the vehicle. This is particularly relevant for crawling over larger rocks. Vehicles with sidesteps have significantly lower clearance than those without.

Another factor affecting clearance is the approach and departure angles of your vehicle—that is, the maximum angle the ground can slope without the front of the vehicle hitting the ridge on approach or the rear of the vehicle hitting on departure. Mounting a winch or tow hitch to your vehicle is likely to reduce your approach or departure angle.

If you do a lot of driving on rocky trails, you will inevitably hit the bottom of the vehicle sooner or later. When this happens, you will be far less likely to damage vulnerable areas such as the oil pan and gas tank if your vehicle is fitted with skid plates. Most manufacturers offer skid plates as an option. They are worth every penny.

Maneuverability

When you tackle tight switchbacks, you will quickly appreciate that maneuverability is an important criterion when assessing the capabilities of an SUV. Where a full-size vehicle may be forced to go back and forth a number of times to get around a sharp turn, a small SUV might go straight around. This is not only easier, it's safer.

If you have a full-size vehicle, all is not lost. Most of the trails in this book are suitable for full-size SUVs. That is not to say that some of these trails wouldn't have been easier to negotiate in a smaller vehicle! We have noted in the route descriptions if a trail is not suitable for larger vehicles.

In Summary

Using the criteria above, you can evaluate how well your 4WD will handle off-road touring, and if you haven't yet purchased your vehicle, you can use these criteria to help select one. Choosing the best 4WD system is, at least partly, subjective. It is also a matter of your budget. However, for the type of off-highway driving covered in this book, we make the following recommendations:

- Select a 4WD system that offers low range and, at a

minimum, has some form of limited slip differential on the rear axle.

■ Use light truck, all-terrain tires as the standard tires on your vehicle. For sand and slickrock, these will be the ideal choice. If conditions are likely to be muddy, or traction will be improved by a tread pattern that will give more bite, consider an additional set of mud tires.

■ For maximum clearance, select a vehicle with 16-inch wheels, or at least choose the tallest tires that your vehicle can accommodate. Note that if you install tires with a diameter greater than standard, the odometer will undercalculate the distance you have traveled. Your engine braking and gear ratios will also be affected.

■ If you are going to try the rockier 4WD trails, don't install a sidestep or low hanging front bar. If you have the option, have underbody skid plates mounted.

■ Remember that many of the obstacles you encounter on backcountry trails are more difficult to navigate in a full-size vehicle than in a compact SUV.

Four-Wheel Driving Techniques

Safe four-wheel driving requires that you observe certain golden rules:

■ Size up the situation in advance.

■ Be careful and take your time.

■ Maintain smooth, steady power and momentum.

■ Engage 4WD and low-range gears before you get into a tight situation.

■ Steer toward high spots, trying to put the wheel over large rocks.

■ Straddle ruts.

■ Use gears and not just the brakes to hold the vehicle when driving downhill. On very steep slopes, chock the wheels if you park your vehicle.

■ Watch for logging and mining trucks and smaller recreational vehicles, such as all-terrain vehicles (ATVs).

■ Wear your seat belt and secure all luggage, especially heavy items such as toolboxes or coolers. Heavy items should be secured by ratchet tie-down straps rather than elastic-type straps, which are not strong enough to hold heavy items if the vehicle rolls.

California's 4WD trails have a number of common obstacles, and the following provides an introduction to the techniques required to surmount them.

Rocks

Tire selection is important in negotiating rocks. Select a multiple-ply, tough sidewall, light truck tire with a large-lug tread.

As you approach a rocky stretch, get into 4WD low range to give maximum slow-speed control. Speed is rarely necessary, since traction on a rocky surface is usually good. Plan ahead and select the line you wish to take. If a rock appears to be larger than the clearance of your vehicle, don't try to straddle it. Check to see that it is not higher than the frame of your vehicle once you get a wheel over it. Put a wheel up on the rock and slowly climb it, then gently drop over the other side using the brake to ensure a smooth landing. Bouncing the car over rocks increases the likelihood of damage, as the body's clearance is reduced by the suspension compressing. Running boards also significantly reduce your clearance in this respect.

It is often helpful to use a "spotter" outside the vehicle to assist you with the best wheel placement.

Steep Uphill Grades

Consider walking the trail to ensure that the steep hill before you is passable, especially if it is clear that backtracking is going to be a problem.

Select 4WD low range to ensure that you have adequate power to pull up the hill. If the wheels begin to lose traction, turn the steering wheel gently from side to side to give the wheels a chance to regain traction.

If you lose momentum, but the car is not in danger of sliding, use the foot brake, switch off the ignition, leave the vehicle in gear (if manual transmission) or park (if automatic), engage the parking brake, and get out to examine the situation. See if you can remove any obstacles, and figure out the line you need to take. Reversing a couple of yards and starting again may allow you to get better traction and momentum.

If, halfway up, you decide a stretch of road is impassably steep, back down the trail. Trying to turn the vehicle around on a steep hill is extremely dangerous; you will very likely cause it to roll over.

Steep Downhill Grades

Again, consider walking the trail to ensure that a steep downhill slope is passable, especially if it is clear that backtracking uphill is going to be a problem.

Select 4WD low range and use first gear to maximize braking assistance from the engine. If the surface is loose and you are losing traction, change up to second or third gear. Do not use the brakes if you can avoid it, but don't let the vehicle's speed get out of control. Feather (lightly pump) the brakes if you slip under braking. For vehicles fitted with ABS, apply even pressure if you start to slip; the ABS helps keep vehicles on line.

Travel very slowly over rock ledges or ruts. Attempt to tackle these diagonally, letting one wheel down at a time.

If the back of the vehicle begins to slide around, gently apply the throttle and correct the steering. If the rear of the vehicle starts to slide sideways, do not apply the brakes.

Sand

As with most off-highway situations, your tires are the key to your ability to cross sand. It is difficult to tell how well a particular tire will handle in sand just by looking at it, so be guided by the manufacturer and your dealer.

The key to driving in soft sand is floatation, which is achieved by a combination of low tire pressure and momentum. Before crossing a stretch of sand, reduce your tire pressure to between 15 and 20 pounds. If necessary, you can safely go to as low as 12 pounds. As you cross, maintain momentum so that your vehicle rides on the top of the soft sand without digging in or stalling. This may require plenty of engine power. Avoid using the brakes if possible; removing your foot from the accelerator alone is normally enough to slow or stop. Using the brakes digs the vehicle deep in the sand.

Air the tires back up as soon as you are out of the sand to avoid damage to the tires and the rims. Airing back up requires a high-quality air compressor. Even then, it is usually a slow process.

Slickrock

When you encounter slickrock, first assess the correct direction of the trail. It is easy to lose sight of the trail on slickrock, as there are seldom any developed edges. Often the way is marked with small rock cairns, which are simply rocks stacked high enough to make a landmark.

All-terrain tires with tighter tread are more suited to slickrock than the more open, luggier type tires. As with rocks, a multiple-ply sidewall is important. In dry conditions, slickrock offers pavement-type grip. In rain or snow, you will soon learn how it got its name. Even the best tires may not get an adequate grip. Walk steep sections first; if you are slipping on foot, chances are your vehicle will slip too.

Slickrock is characterized by ledges and long sections of "pavement." Follow the guidelines for travel over rocks. Refrain from speeding over flat-looking sections, as you may hit an unexpected crevice or water pocket, and vehicles bend easier than slickrock! Turns and ledges can be tight, and vehicles with smaller overhangs and better maneuverability are at a distinct advantage—hence the popularity of the compacts in the slickrock mecca of Moab, Utah.

On the steepest sections, engage low range and pick a straight line up or down the slope. Do not attempt to traverse a steep slope sideways.

Mud

Muddy trails are easily damaged, so they should be avoided if possible. But if you must traverse a section of mud, your success will depend heavily on whether you have open-lugged mud tires or chains. Thick mud fills the tighter tread on normal tires, leaving the tire with no more grip than if it were bald. If the muddy stretch is only a few yards long, the momentum of your vehicle may allow you to get through regardless.

If the muddy track is very steep, uphill or downhill, or off camber, do not attempt it. Your vehicle is very likely to skid in such conditions, and you may roll or slip off the edge of the road. Also, check to see that the mud has a reasonably firm base. Tackling deep mud is definitely not recommended unless you have a vehicle-mounted winch—and even then, be cautious, because the winch may not get you out. Finally, check to see that no ruts are too deep for the ground clearance of your vehicle.

■ When you decide you can get through and have selected the best route, use the following techniques to cross through the mud:

■ Avoid making detours off existing tracks to minimize environmental damage.

■ Select 4WD low range and a suitable gear; momentum is the key to success, so use a high enough gear to build up sufficient speed.

■ Avoid accelerating heavily, so as to minimize wheel spinning and to provide maximum traction.

■ Follow existing wheel ruts, unless they are too deep for the clearance of your vehicle.

■ To correct slides, turn the steering wheel in the direction that the rear wheels are skidding, but don't be too aggressive or you'll overcorrect and lose control again.

■ If the vehicle comes to a stop, don't continue to accelerate, as you will only spin your wheels and dig yourself into a rut. Try backing out and having another go.

■ Be prepared to turn back before reaching the point of no return.

Stream Crossings

By crossing a stream that is too deep, drivers risk far more than water flowing in and ruining the interior of their vehicles. Water sucked into the engine's air intake will seriously damage the engine. Likewise, water that seeps into the air vent on the transmission or differential will mix with the lubricant and may lead to serious problems in due course.

Even worse, if the water is deep or fast flowing, it could easily carry your vehicle downstream, endangering the lives of everyone in the vehicle.

Some SUV owner's manuals tell you what fording depth the vehicle can negotiate safely. If your vehicle's owner's manual doesn't include this information, your local dealer may be able to assist. If you don't know, then avoid crossing through water that is more than a foot or so deep.

The first rule for crossing a stream is to know what you are getting into. You need to ascertain how deep the water is, whether there are any large rocks or holes, if the bottom is solid enough to avoid bogging down the vehicle, and whether the entry and exit points are negotiable. This may take some time and involve getting wet, but you take a great risk by crossing a stream without first properly assessing the situation.

The secret to water crossings is to keep moving, but not too fast. If you go too fast, you may drown the electrics, causing the vehicle to stall midstream. In shallow water (where the surface of the water is below the bumper), your primary concern is to safely negotiate the bottom of the stream, avoiding any rock damage and maintaining momentum if there is a danger of getting stuck or of slipping on the exit.

In deeper water (between 18 and 30 inches), the objective is to create a small bow wave in front of the moving vehicle. This requires a speed that is approximately walking pace. The bow wave reduces the depth of the water around the engine compartment. If the water's surface reaches your tailpipe, select a gear that will maintain moderate engine revs to avoid water backing up into the exhaust; and do not change gears midstream.

Crossing water deeper than 25 to 30 inches requires more extensive preparation of the vehicle and should be attempted only by experienced drivers.

Snow

The trails in this book that receive heavy snowfall are closed in winter. Therefore, the snow conditions that you are most likely to encounter are an occasional snowdrift that has not yet melted or fresh snow from an unexpected storm. Getting through such conditions depends on the depth of the snow, its consistency, the stability of the underlying surface, and your vehicle.

If the snow is no deeper than about nine inches and there is solid ground beneath it, crossing the snow should not be a problem. In deeper snow that seems solid enough to support your vehicle, be extremely cautious: If you break through a drift, you are likely to be stuck, and if conditions are bad, you may have a long wait.

The tires you use for off-highway driving, with a wide tread pattern, are probably suitable for these snow conditions. Nonetheless, it is wise to carry chains (preferably for all four wheels), and if you have a vehicle-mounted winch, even better.

Vehicle Recovery Methods

If you do enough four-wheel driving, you are sure to get stuck sooner or later. The following techniques will help you get back on the go. The most suitable method will depend on the equipment available and the situation you are in—whether you are stuck in sand, mud, or snow, or are high-centered or unable to negotiate a hill.

Towing

Use a nylon yank strap of the type discussed in the "Special 4WD Equipment" section on page 19. This type of strap will stretch 15 to 25 percent, and the elasticity will assist in extracting the vehicle.

Attach the strap only to a frame-mounted tow point. Ensure that the driver of the stuck vehicle is ready, take up all but about 6 feet of slack, then move the towing vehicle away at a moderate speed (in most circumstances this means using 4WD low range in second gear) so that the elasticity of the strap is employed in the way it is meant to be. Don't take off like a bat out of hell or you risk breaking the strap or damaging a vehicle.

Never join two yank straps together with a shackle. If one strap breaks, the shackle will become a lethal missile aimed at one of the vehicles (and anyone inside). For the same reason, never attach a yank strap to the tow ball on either vehicle.

Jacking

Jacking the vehicle allows you to pack under the wheel (with rocks, dirt, or logs) or use your shovel to remove an obstacle. However, the standard vehicle jack is unlikely to be of as much assistance as a high-lift jack. We highly recommend purchasing a good high-lift jack as a basic accessory if you decide that you are going to do a lot of serious, off-highway four-wheel driving. Remember a high-lift jack is of limited use if your vehicle does not have an appropriate jacking point. Some brush bars have two built-in forward jacking points.

Tire Chains

Tire chains can be of assistance in both mud and snow. Cable-type chains provide much less grip than link-type chains. There are also dedicated mud chains with larger, heavier links than on normal snow chains. It is best to have chains fitted to all four wheels.

Once you are bogged down is not the best time to try to fit the chains; if at all possible, try to predict their need and have them on the tires before trouble arises. An easy way to affix chains is to place two small cubes of wood under the center of the stretched-out chain. When you drive your tires up on the blocks of wood, it is easier to stretch the chains over the tires because the pressure is off.

Winching

Most recreational four-wheel drivers do not have a winch. But if you get serious about four-wheel driving, this is probably the first major accessory you should consider buying.

Under normal circumstances, a winch would be warranted only for the more difficult 4WD trails in this book. Having a winch is certainly comforting when you see a difficult section of road ahead and have to decide whether to risk it or turn back. Also, major obstacles can appear when you least expect them, even on trails that are otherwise easy.

Owning a winch is not a panacea to all your recovery problems. Winching depends on the availability of a good anchor point, and electric winches may not work if they are submerged in a stream. Despite these constraints, no accessory is more useful than a high-quality, powerful winch when you get into a difficult situation.

If you acquire a winch, learn to use it properly; take the time to study your owner's manual. Incorrect operation can be extremely dangerous and may cause damage to the winch or to your anchor points, which are usually trees.

Navigation by the Global Positioning System (GPS)

Although this book is designed so that each trail can be navigated simply by following the detailed directions provided, nothing makes navigation easier than a GPS receiver.

The global positioning system (GPS) consists of a network of 24 satellites, nearly 13,000 miles in space, in six different orbital paths. The satellites are constantly moving at about 8,500 miles per hour, making two complete orbits around the earth every 24 hours.

Each satellite is constantly transmitting data, including its identification number, its operational health, and the date and time. It also transmits its location and the location of every other satellite in the network.

By comparing the time the signal was transmitted to the time it is received, a GPS receiver calculates how far away each satellite is. With a sufficient number of signals, the receiver can then triangulate its location. With three or more satellites, the receiver can determine latitude and longitude coordinates. With four or more, it can calculate altitude. By constantly making these calculations, it can determine speed and direction. To facilitate these calculations, the time data broadcast by

GPS is accurate to within 40 billionths of a second.

The U.S. military uses the system to provide positions accurate to within half an inch. When the system was first established, civilian receivers were deliberately fed slightly erroneous information in order to effectively deny military applications to hostile countries or terrorists—a practice called selective availability (SA). However on May 1, 2000, in response to the growing importance of the system for civilian applications, the U.S. government stopped intentionally downgrading GPS data. The military gave their support to this change once new technology made it possible to selectively degrade the system within any defined geographical area on demand. This new feature of the system has made it safe to have higher-quality signals available for civilian use. Now, instead of the civilian-use signal having a margin of error between 20 and 70 yards, it is only about one-tenth of that.

A GPS receiver offers the four-wheeler numerous benefits:

- You can track to any point for which you know the longitude and latitude coordinates with no chance of heading in the wrong direction or getting lost. Most receivers provide an extremely easy-to-understand graphic display to keep you on track.
- It works in all weather conditions.
- It automatically records your route for easy backtracking.
- You can record and name any location, so that you can relocate it with ease. This may include your campsite, a fishing spot, or even a gold mine you discover!
- It displays your position, allowing you to pinpoint your location on a map.
- By interfacing the GPS receiver directly to a portable computer, you can monitor and record your location as you travel (using the appropriate map software) or print the route you took.

However, remember that GPS units can fail, batteries can go flat, and tree cover and tight canyons can block the signals. Never rely entirely on GPS for navigation. Always carry a compass for backup.

Special 4WD Equipment

Tires

When 4WD touring, you will likely encounter a wide variety of terrain: rocks, mud, talus, slickrock, sand, gravel, dirt, and bitumen. The immense variety of tires on the market includes many specifically targeted at one or another of these types of terrain, as well as tires designed to adequately handle a range of terrain.

Every four-wheel driver seems to have his or her own preference when it comes to tire selection, but most people undertaking the 4WD trails in this book will need tires that can handle all of the above types of terrain adequately.

The first requirement is to select rugged, light-truck tires rather than passenger-vehicle tires. Check the size data on the sidewall: it should have "LT" rather than "P" before the number.

Among light-truck tires, you must choose between tires that are designated "all-terrain" and more-aggressive, wider-tread mud tires. Either type will be adequate, especially on rocks, gravel, talus, or dirt. Although mud tires have an advantage in muddy conditions and soft snow, all-terrain tires perform better on slickrock, in sand, and particularly on ice and paved roads.

When selecting tires, remember that they affect not just traction but also cornering ability, braking distances, fuel consumption, and noise levels. It pays to get good advice before making your decision.

Global Positioning System Receivers

GPS receivers have come down in price considerably in the past few years and are rapidly becoming indispensable navigational tools. Many higher-priced cars now offer integrated GPS receivers, and within the next few years, receivers will become available on most models.

Battery-powered, hand-held units that meet the needs of off-highway driving currently range from less than $100 to a little over $300 and continue to come down in price. Some high-end units feature maps that are incorporated in the display, either from a built-in database or from interchangeable memory cards. Currently, only a few of these maps include 4WD trails.

If you are considering purchasing a GPS unit, keep the following in mind:

- Price. The very cheapest units are likely outdated and very limited in their display features. Expect to pay from $125 to $400.
- The display. Compare the graphic display of one unit with another. Some are much easier to decipher or offer more alternative displays.
- The controls. GPS receivers have many functions, and they need to have good, simple controls.
- Vehicle mounting. To be useful, the unit needs to be placed where it can be read easily by both the driver and the navigator. Check that the unit can be conveniently located in your vehicle. Different units have different shapes and different mounting systems. If you are considering attaching a GPS unit to the dashboard of your vehicle be sure not to obstruct the safe deployment of air bags. A GPS unit could cause serious bodily harm to an occupant of the vehicle at the speed at which air bags deploy.
- Map data. More and more units have map data built-in. Some have the ability to download maps from a computer. Such maps are normally sold on a CD-ROM. GPS units usually have a finite storage capacity, so the ability to download maps covering a narrower geographical region means that the amount of data relating to that specific region can be greater. Some units accept memory expansion cards. Maps can be downloaded to the memory cards instead of the built-in memory, allowing for quick changeover of maps when traveling from one region to the next.
- The number of routes and the number of sites (or "waypoints") per route that can be stored in memory. For off-highway use, it is important to be able to store plenty of waypoints so that you do not have to load coordinates into the machine as frequently. Having plenty of memory also ensures that you can automatically store your present location without fear that the memory is full.

■ Waypoint storage. The better units store up to 500 waypoints and 20 reversible routes of up to 30 waypoints each. Also consider the number of characters a GPS receiver allows you to use to name waypoints. When you try to recall a waypoint, you may have difficulty recognizing names restricted to only a few characters.

■ Automatic route storing. Most units automatically store your route as you go along and enable you to display it in reverse to make backtracking easy.

■ After you have selected a unit, a number of optional extras are also worth considering:

■ A cigarette lighter electrical adapter. Despite GPS units becoming more power efficient, protracted in-vehicle use still makes this accessory a necessity.

■ A vehicle-mounted antenna, which will improve reception under difficult conditions. (The GPS unit can only "see" through the windows of your vehicle; it cannot monitor satellites through a metal roof.) Having a vehicle-mounted antenna also means that you do not have to consider reception when locating the receiver in your vehicle.

■ An in-car mounting system. If you are going to do a lot of touring using the GPS, consider attaching a bracket on the dash rather than relying on a Velcro mount.

■ A computer-link cable and digital maps. Data from your GPS receiver can be downloaded to your PC; maps and waypoints can be downloaded from your PC; or if you have a laptop computer, you can monitor your route as you go along, using one of a number of inexpensive map software products on the market.

Yank Straps

Yank straps are industrial-strength versions of the flimsy tow straps carried by the local discount store. They are 20 to 30 feet long and 2 to 3 inches wide, made of heavy nylon, rated to at least 20,000 pounds, and have looped ends.

Do not use tow straps with metal hooks in the ends (the hooks can become missiles in the event the strap breaks free). Likewise, never join two yank straps together using a shackle.

CB Radios

If you are stuck, injured, or just want to know the conditions up ahead, a citizen's band (CB) radio can be invaluable.

CB radios are relatively inexpensive and do not require an FCC license. Their range is limited, especially in very hilly country, as their transmission patterns basically follow lines of sight. Range can be improved using single sideband (SSB) transmission, an option on more expensive units. Range is even better on vehicle-mounted units that have been professionally fitted to ensure that the antenna and cabling are matched appropriately.

Winches

There are three main options when it comes to winches: manual winches, removable electric winches, and vehicle-mounted electric winches.

If you have a full-size SUV—which can weigh in excess of 7,000 pounds when loaded—a manual winch is of limited use without a lot of effort and considerable time. However, a manual winch is a very handy and inexpensive accessory if you have a small SUV. Typically, manual winches are rated to pull about 5,500 pounds.

Electric winches can be mounted to your vehicle's trailer hitch to enable them to be removed, relocated to the front of your vehicle (if you have a hitch installed), or moved to another vehicle. Although this is a very useful feature, a winch is heavy, so relocating one can be a two-person job. Consider that 5,000-pound-rated winches weigh only about 55 pounds, while 12,000-pound-rated models weigh around 140 pounds. Therefore, the larger models are best permanently front-mounted. Unfortunately, this position limits their ability to winch the vehicle backward.

When choosing between electric winches, be aware that they are rated for their maximum capacity on the first wind of the cable around the drum. As layers of cable wind onto the drum, they increase its diameter and thus decrease the maximum load the winch can handle. This decrease is significant: a winch rated to pull 8,000 pounds on a bare drum may only handle 6,500 pounds on the second layer, 5,750 pounds on the third layer, and 5,000 pounds on the fourth. Electric winches also draw a high level of current and may necessitate upgrading the battery in your vehicle or adding a second battery.

There is a wide range of mounting options—from a simple, body-mounted frame that holds the winch to heavy-duty winch bars that replace the original bumper and incorporate brush bars and mounts for auxiliary lights.

If you buy a winch, either electric or manual, you will also need quite a range of additional equipment so that you can operate it correctly:

- at least one choker chain with hooks on each end,
- winch extension straps or cables,
- shackles,
- a receiver shackle,
- a snatch block,
- a tree protector,
- gloves.

Grill/Brush Bars and Winch Bars

Brush bars protect the front of the vehicle from scratches and minor bumps; they also provide a solid mount for auxiliary lights and often high-lift jacking points. Additionally, they are an ideal place to fit a tall whip-antenna with a brightly colored flag atop, something that reduces safety concerns on trails with restricted visibility. The level of protection brush bars provide depends on how solid they are and whether they are securely mounted onto the frame of the vehicle. Lighter models attach in front of the standard bumper, but the more substantial units replace the bumper. Prices range from about $150 to as much as $1,000 for stainless steel models.

Winch bars replace the bumper and usually integrate a solid brush bar with a heavy-duty winch mount. Some have the brush bar as an optional extra to the winch bar component. Manufacturers such as Warn, ARB, and TJM offer a wide range of integrated winch bars. These are significantly more expensive than standard brush bars, starting at about $650.

Remember that installing heavy equipment on the front of the vehicle may necessitate increasing the front suspension rating to cope with the additional weight.

Portable Air Compressors

Most portable air compressors on the market are flimsy models that plug into the cigarette lighter and are sold at the local discount store. These are of very limited use for four-wheel driving. They are very slow to inflate the large tires of an SUV; for instance, to reinflate from 15 to 35 pounds typically takes about 10 minutes for each tire. They are also unlikely to be rated for continuous use, which means that they will overheat and cut off before completing the job. If you're lucky, they will start up again when they have cooled down, but this means that you are unlikely to reinflate your tires in less than an hour.

The easiest way to identify a useful air compressor is by the price—good ones cost from around $200 to as much as $400. Viair and Quickair both manufacture an extensive range of portable and hard-mount compressors. These pumps draw between 10 and 45 amps. Those drawing more than 10 amps should not be plugged into the cigarette lighter socket.

Auxiliary Driving Lights

There is a vast array of auxiliary lights on the market today, and selecting the best lights for your purpose can be a confusing process.

Auxiliary lights greatly improve visibility in adverse weather conditions. Driving lights provide a strong, moderately wide beam to supplement headlamp high beams, giving improved lighting in the distance and to the sides of the main beam. Fog lamps throw a wide-dispersion, flat beam; and spots provide a high-power, narrow beam to improve lighting range directly in front of the vehicle. Rear-mounted auxiliary lights provide greatly improved visibility for backing up.

For off-highway use, you will need quality lights with strong mounting brackets. Some high-powered off-highway lights are not approved by the Department of Transportation for use on public roads.

Roof Racks

Roof racks can be excellent for storing gear, as well as providing easy access for certain weatherproof items. However, they raise the center of gravity on the vehicle, which can substantially alter the rollover angle. A roof rack is best used for lightweight objects that are well strapped down. Heavy recovery gear and other bulky items should be packed low in the vehicle's interior to lower the center of gravity and stabilize the vehicle.

A roof rack should allow for safe and secure packing of items and be sturdy enough to withstand knocks.

Packing Checklist

Before embarking on any 4WD adventure, whether a lazy Sunday drive on an easy trail or a challenging climb over rugged terrain, be prepared. The following checklist will help you gather the items you need.

Essential

- ❐ Rain gear
- ❐ Gloves
- ❐ Small shovel or multipurpose ax, pick, shovel, and sledgehammer
- ❐ Heavy-duty yank strap
- ❐ Spare tire that matches the other tires on the vehicle
- ❐ Working jack and base plate for soft ground
- ❐ Maps
- ❐ Emergency medical kit, including sun protection and insect repellent
- ❐ Bottled water
- ❐ Blankets or space blankets
- ❐ Parka, gloves, and boots
- ❐ Spare vehicle key
- ❐ Jumper leads
- ❐ Heavy-duty flashlight
- ❐ Multipurpose tool, such as a Leatherman
- ❐ Emergency food—high-energy bars or similar

Worth Considering

- ❐ Global Positioning System (GPS) receiver
- ❐ Cell phone
- ❐ A set of light-truck, off-highway tires and matching spare
- ❐ High-lift jack
- ❐ Additional tool kit
- ❐ CB radio
- ❐ Portable air compressor
- ❐ Tire gauge
- ❐ Duct and electrical tape
- ❐ Tire-sealing kit
- ❐ Tire chains
- ❐ Chainsaw or Wyoming saw (or similar)
- ❐ Binoculars
- ❐ Firearms
- ❐ Whistle
- ❐ Flares
- ❐ Vehicle fire extinguisher
- ❐ Gasoline, engine oil, and other vehicle fluids
- ❐ Portable hand winch
- ❐ Electric cooler

If Your Credit Cards Aren't Maxed Out

- ❐ Electric, vehicle-mounted winch and associated recovery straps, shackles, and snatch blocks
- ❐ Vehicle-mounted off-road or driving lights
- ❐ Locking differential(s)

Northern California Distance Chart

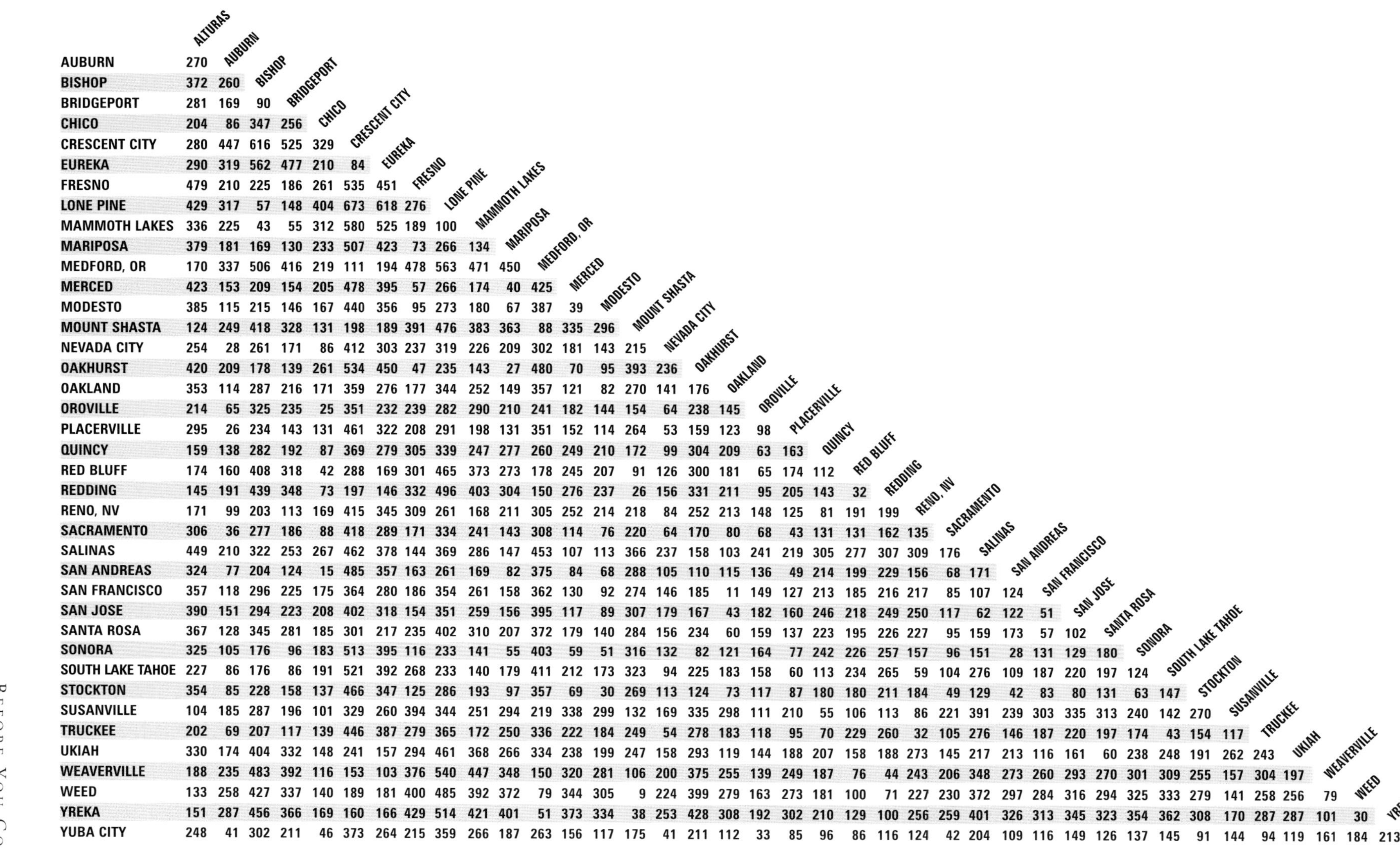

	ALTURAS	AUBURN	BISHOP	BRIDGEPORT	CHICO	CRESCENT CITY	EUREKA	FRESNO	LONE PINE	MAMMOTH LAKES	MARIPOSA	MEDFORD, OR	MERCED	MODESTO	MOUNT SHASTA	NEVADA CITY	OAKHURST	OAKLAND	OROVILLE	PLACERVILLE	QUINCY	RED BLUFF	REDDING	RENO, NV	SACRAMENTO	SALINAS	SAN ANDREAS	SAN FRANCISCO	SAN JOSE	SANTA ROSA	SONORA	SOUTH LAKE TAHOE	STOCKTON	SUSANVILLE	TRUCKEE	UKIAH	WEAVERVILLE	WEED	YREKA
AUBURN	270																																						
BISHOP	372	260																																					
BRIDGEPORT	281	169	90																																				
CHICO	204	86	347	256																																			
CRESCENT CITY	280	447	616	525	329																																		
EUREKA	290	319	562	477	210	84																																	
FRESNO	479	210	225	186	261	535	451																																
LONE PINE	429	317	57	148	404	673	618	276																															
MAMMOTH LAKES	336	225	43	55	312	580	525	189	100																														
MARIPOSA	379	181	169	130	233	507	423	73	266	134																													
MEDFORD, OR	170	337	506	416	219	111	194	478	563	471	450																												
MERCED	423	153	209	154	205	478	395	57	266	174	40	425																											
MODESTO	385	115	215	146	167	440	356	95	273	180	67	387	39																										
MOUNT SHASTA	124	249	418	328	131	198	189	391	476	383	363	88	335	296																									
NEVADA CITY	254	28	261	171	86	412	303	237	319	226	209	302	181	143	215																								
OAKHURST	420	209	178	139	261	534	450	47	235	143	27	480	70	95	393	236																							
OAKLAND	353	114	287	216	171	359	276	177	344	252	149	357	121	82	270	141	176																						
OROVILLE	214	65	325	235	25	351	232	239	282	290	210	241	182	144	154	64	238	145																					
PLACERVILLE	295	26	234	143	131	461	322	208	291	198	131	351	152	114	264	53	159	123	98																				
QUINCY	159	138	282	192	87	369	279	305	339	247	277	260	249	210	172	99	304	209	63	163																			
RED BLUFF	174	160	408	318	42	288	169	301	465	373	273	178	245	207	91	126	300	181	65	174	112																		
REDDING	145	191	439	348	73	197	146	332	496	403	304	150	276	237	26	156	331	211	95	205	143	32																	
RENO, NV	171	99	203	113	169	415	345	309	261	168	211	305	252	214	218	84	252	213	148	125	81	191	199																
SACRAMENTO	306	36	277	186	88	418	289	171	334	241	143	308	114	76	220	64	170	80	68	43	131	131	162	135															
SALINAS	449	210	322	253	267	462	378	144	369	286	147	453	107	113	366	237	158	103	241	219	305	277	307	309	176														
SAN ANDREAS	324	77	204	124	15	485	357	163	261	169	82	375	84	68	288	105	110	115	136	49	214	199	229	156	68	171													
SAN FRANCISCO	357	118	296	225	175	364	280	186	354	261	158	362	130	92	274	146	185	11	149	127	213	185	216	217	85	107	124												
SAN JOSE	390	151	294	223	208	402	318	154	351	259	156	395	117	89	307	179	167	43	182	160	246	218	249	250	117	62	122	51											
SANTA ROSA	367	128	345	281	185	301	217	235	402	310	207	372	179	140	284	156	234	60	159	137	223	195	226	227	95	159	173	57	102										
SONORA	325	105	176	96	183	513	395	116	233	141	55	403	59	51	316	132	82	121	164	77	242	226	257	157	96	151	28	131	129	180									
SOUTH LAKE TAHOE	227	86	176	86	191	521	392	268	233	140	179	411	212	173	323	94	225	183	158	60	113	234	265	59	104	276	109	187	220	197	124								
STOCKTON	354	85	228	158	137	466	347	125	286	193	97	357	69	30	269	113	124	73	117	87	180	180	211	184	49	129	42	83	80	131	63	147							
SUSANVILLE	104	185	287	196	101	329	260	394	344	251	294	219	338	299	132	169	335	298	111	210	55	106	113	86	221	391	239	303	335	313	240	142	270						
TRUCKEE	202	69	207	117	139	446	387	279	365	172	250	336	222	184	249	54	278	183	118	95	70	229	260	32	105	276	146	187	220	197	174	43	154	117					
UKIAH	330	174	404	332	148	241	157	294	461	368	266	334	238	199	247	158	293	119	144	188	207	158	188	273	145	217	213	116	161	60	238	248	191	262	243				
WEAVERVILLE	188	235	483	392	116	153	103	376	540	447	348	150	320	281	106	200	375	255	139	249	187	76	44	243	206	348	273	260	293	270	301	309	255	157	304	197			
WEED	133	258	427	337	140	189	181	400	485	392	372	79	344	305	9	224	399	279	163	273	181	100	71	227	230	372	297	284	316	294	325	333	279	141	258	256	79		
YREKA	151	287	456	366	169	160	166	429	514	421	401	51	373	334	38	253	428	308	192	302	210	129	100	256	259	401	326	313	345	323	354	362	308	170	287	287	101	30	
YUBA CITY	248	41	302	211	46	373	264	215	359	266	187	263	156	117	175	41	211	112	33	85	96	86	116	124	42	204	109	116	149	126	137	145	91	144	94	119	161	184	213

Distances are calculated using major highways.

Along the Trail

Towns, Ghost Towns, and Interesting Places

Alleghany

Alleghany is one of the few Mother Lode towns still producing gold. Local newspapers still report gold strikes, and many residents enjoy hunting for the treasured metal.

Placer mining began in the vicinity in the early gold rush days, though a mining camp didn't develop on the site until the late 1850s. The settlement took its name from the nearby Alleghany Mine—established in 1853 and named for Pennsylvania's Allegheny River. The mine's richest gold vein was discovered in October 1855. The Alleghany area had many rich gold mines, with several claims producing more than a million dollars a year. Perhaps the most famous mine was the Sixteen-to-One Mine, established by Thomas J. Bradbury in 1896. He named it for then-presidential candidate William Jennings Bryan's 1893 proposed ratio of silver to gold, "sixteen-to-one." "Original" was added to the name of the Sierra County mine to distinguish it from a Sixteen to One Mine in Nevada County. Bradbury operated on a small scale until consolidating with the Tightner Mine in 1916. It turns out that the two mines were working the same vein. The Original Sixteen-to-One was an economic powerhouse, producing more than $26 million worth of gold before it closed in 1965.

Alleghany is not easy to get to. It is 17.5 miles south of Downieville off California 49 and reached only by negotiating one of several winding unpaved roads. For this reason, it remains a small community, with houses precariously gripping steep hillsides. Unfortunately, fires, a common occurrence in gold camps, have destroyed much of the town. The last conflagration, in 1987, damaged much of the downtown area. Today, Alleghany has a general store and a tavern.

GPS COORDINATES: N39°28.32' W120°50.54'
TRAIL: Northern Sierra #26: Alleghany Trail
MAP: Page 389

Alleghany quartz mine, circa 1861

Altaville

Situated at the junction of California 49 and California 4 in Calaveras County, just a mile south of Angels Camp, Altaville has always been an important supply center and travel stop. It was known initially as Forks in the Road or Forks of the Roads. Settled in 1852, it became known as Low Divide, then Cherokee Flat, and then at an 1857 town meeting, as Altaville. *Alta* is Spanish for "high" or "upper."

Several of Altaville's buildings survive from its days as a mining camp. The stone Prince and Garibaldi Store, constructed in 1857, is the most significant landmark, and a red brick grammar school, erected in 1858, was used until 1950.

Altaville, circa 1857

D. D. Demarest established California's first iron foundry here in 1854. The foundry produced most of the mine equipment used in the surrounding area, as well as the workings of several stamp mills.

Altaville is perhaps most famous for a gold country hoax. A human skull was discovered in a mine shaft on nearby Bald Mountain in 1866 and was pronounced by no less a figure than California state geologist Josiah D. Whitney as the skull of a man from the Pliocene period, perhaps five million years old. Others, including writer Bret Harte, were dubious, as were miners who knew that a skull was missing from a local doctor's office. Harte mocked the affair with his poem "To the Pliocene Skull." In the early 1900s, scientists concluded that the skull was part of a relatively recent Native American burial. No one ever admitted to perpetrating the hoax.

GPS COORDINATES: N38°05.03' W120°33.59'
NEAREST TRAIL: Northern Sierra #5: Crandall Peak Trail

Alturas

Alturas, located at the confluence of the North and South Forks of the Pit River, is the largest town in Modoc County. This region of the Modoc Plateau, at the western edge of the Warner Mountains, was the ancestral home of the Achomawi

Train station at Alturas, circa 1914

band of Pit River Indians. Kosealekte, an Achomawi village, was near present-day Alturas. Some Achomawi still live on the Alturas Rancheria and the XL Ranch Indian Reservation. The 2000 Census counted about 1,500 Achomawi, the same number as before a 1921 smallpox epidemic that severely reduced tribal numbers. Alturas's Modoc County Historical Museum has an excellent collection of Native American artifacts, including many arrowheads.

James Dorris and his family settled here and ran a cattle ranch. They built a wooden bridge over the Pit River in 1869 and had a cabin where travelers could find lodging. By 1874, a hamlet known as Dorris's Bridge formed on the Dorris Ranch, and when Modoc County was created in 1874 from a portion of Siskiyou County, Dorris's Bridge (also known as Dorrisville) became the county seat. Residents changed the town's name to Alturas, Spanish for "heights," on June 1, 1876. In 1906, the U.S. Fish and Wildlife Service purchased much of the original Dorris Ranch to include its wetlands in the Modoc National Wildlife Refuge. Deer, antelope, sandhill cranes, Canada geese, and other birds and animals live on the refuge.

In 1908, the Nevada-California-Oregon Railway began operating between Reno and Alturas. Over the next few years, the line was lengthened until it reached Lakeview, Oregon. The Western Pacific bought 107 miles of the Nevada-California-Oregon in 1917, and the company moved its headquarters from Reno to Alturas. The railroad benefited Alturas greatly. Ranchers from across Modoc County came to town to sell their livestock and produce and purchase supplies. The Nevada-California-Oregon continued to run until 1945, and parts of its line are still used by the Great Western Railroad. An excellent collection detailing the company's history is at the Alturas Railroad Museum.

Because US 395, the main north-south thoroughfare in northeastern California, runs through Alturas, the town of 4,500 is a commercial center. In addition to cattle, the area also produces potatoes and alfalfa. Buildings of note are the Modoc County Courthouse, built in 1914, the N-C-O Office Building, built in 1917, and the Sacred Heart Catholic Church, completed in 1910. Alturas's motto is "Where the West Still Lives."

GPS COORDINATES: N41°29.25' W120°32.50'

NEAREST TRAIL: North Coast #41: Fairchild Swamp Trail

Arcata

A captain sailing for the Russian-American Company discovered the entrance to Humboldt Bay in 1806. However, it remained for Josiah Gregg, who had been commissioned by the U.S. government to follow the Trinity River to its mouth, to rediscover in 1849. A member of Gregg's party, L. K. Wood, founded a town on the site of present-day Arcata in 1850 and called it Uniontown, which became the seat of Humboldt County in 1853.

The town became a staging area for pack trains carrying supplies to mining camps such as Yreka, French Gulch, Happy Camp, Weaverville, Helena, and Ingot along the Trinity and Klamath Rivers. In 1855, the Union Plank Walk Railtrack and Wharf Company constructed the first functioning railroad in California, later known as the Arcata & Mad River Railroad. The limited system consisting of a horse-drawn rail car connected the wharf and the Jacoby storehouse, expediting the shipment of supplies. By 1856, the region's timber industry superseded the declining mining industry, and Eureka, with its deepwater port on the south side of Humboldt Bay, replaced Uniontown as the county seat.

Bret Harte, who would write such popular short stories as "The Luck of Roaring Camp" and "Outcasts of Poker Flats," wrote for the *Californian* newspaper from 1857 until 1860. When he publicly denounced the 1860 Indian massacre at Indian Island, the violent minority who disagreed with him forced him to leave Arcata.

For years, the Jacoby Building on Eighth and H Streets, built in 1857, was home to firms that supplied mining camps. It was also used as a fortress during Indian attacks in its earliest years. In 1860, Uniontown was renamed Arcata in order to avoid confusion with a Uniontown in El Dorado County. The new name derived from a Yurok word meaning, "where there is a lagoon."

Also in the vicinity, near Korbel on California 299, is the Arrow Tree. The first European accounts of the tree, now a redwood snag, noted that it looked like a giant porcupine because it had hundreds of arrows protruding from its trunk 30 to 40 feet above the ground. The tradition of shooting an arrow into the tree apparently originated during a war between two coastal and hill country Indian tribes. After the hill country Indians' defeat, the tribes met near the tree, which was from then on treated as the border between the two Indian territories. Traditionally, Chilula and Wiyot Indians left an arrow in the tree's trunk whenever they were nearby. As years

Arcata, circa 1857

passed the original meaning of the tree faded, and the site was used more for general worship and prayer; people began to leave sharpened sticks in the trunk rather than arrows.

Arcata, on Humboldt Bay's Arcata Bay, is in the heart of redwood country. The town of more than 16,500 attracts visitors on their way to Redwood National Park, 25 miles to the north. In the 575-acre Arcata Community Forest and Redwood Park, hikers, bikers, and horseback riders have access to miles of trails. Arcata Marsh and Wildlife Sanctuary, formerly a 75-acre landfill now developed as a marshland, is a scenic destination for birders. Trails on the campus of Humboldt State University, founded in 1913 to train elementary school teachers, parallel the scenic Redwood Highway.

GPS COORDINATES: N40°52.16' W124°05.14'

NEAREST TRAIL: North Coast #17: Bald Hills Road

Auburn

Like many Mother Lode towns, Auburn, just off of I-80 east of Sacramento, can be found on California 49. It is one of the largest of the gold country towns.

Claude Chana, a Frenchman, discovered gold while camping in Auburn Ravine and founded the town in May 1848. A statue in downtown Auburn celebrates Chana's discovery. A mining camp quickly grew around the ravine, at first called Rich Dry Diggings, then North Fork Dry Diggings. By early 1849, the settlement was known as Woods Dry Diggings after John S. Woods, a soldier who had staked a profitable claim along the present-day western city limits. Many of the early claims in the area were extremely rich, but not easy to work because the gold was some distance from streams and loads of dirt had to be hauled to the water in order to wash out the gold.

Auburn's Sacramento Street, circa 1861

Among the early settlers in the mining camp were members of a volunteer regiment from New York state who had arrived in California in 1846. In August 1849, Samuel W. Holladay, a member of the regiment and alcalde (a position similar to mayor) of the settlement, renamed the camp Auburn after his hometown in New York. Auburn became the first county seat of Sutter County in 1850 when an election in which the votes exceeded the county's population decided the issue. Subsequently, Placer County was formed from a portion of Sutter County on April 25, 1851, and Auburn was made the seat of government of the new county. Auburn became a city in 1860, but voted to become unincorporated in 1866 to avoid payment on railroad bonds for the transcontinental railroad, which was being built toward the east. The town reincorporated in 1888 and was a significant stop along the Lincoln Highway (US 40) before I-80 was built.

Auburn became a prominent transportation center; a network of pack-mule trails connected the settlement with surrounding camps. In the 1850s and '60s, toll roads replaced trails, and pack trains gave way to sturdy horse- or mule-drawn stagecoaches. Widening and extending narrow mule trails was often difficult and costly. Construction of the 20-mile toll road along Foresthill Divide cost more than $60,000 and necessitated carving a winding route into canyon walls. These freight routes continued to function even after the Central Pacific Railroad reached Auburn. The first passenger train entered town May 13, 1865. In the early years of the railroad, a number of wagon roads were built into Auburn, which was one of the few towns in the region connected to a rail line.

The oldest fire department in the West has operated in Auburn since 1852

Auburn's jail hosted a number of outlaws, including Rattlesnake Dick Barter. By the 1870s, Auburn was quite a social center; its clean air and cooler temperatures than those of the Central Valley attracted visitors in search of rest and relaxation. Today, Auburn's location on California 49 and Interstate 80 means that it continues to be a transportation center and a convenient stop for travelers heading to Reno, Sacramento, or San Francisco. Old Town Auburn is south of the interstate and west of California 49. Several buildings remain from the early 1850s, including California's oldest operating post office, established on July 21, 1853. The Auburn Hook and Ladder Fire Company, founded in 1852, has much to do with the town's survival. The company claims to be the "oldest volunteer fire department this side of Boston." Company Fire House Number Two, built in 1893, is a distinctive feature of historic Auburn. Overlooking the old part of town is the Placer County Courthouse, built in 1894 solely with materials extracted from the county.

GPS COORDINATES: N38°53.93' W121°04.17'

NEAREST TRAIL: Northern Sierra #14: Slate Mountain Trail

Bear Valley

Bear Valley, south of Coulterville on California 49 in Mariposa County, should not be confused with the ski area on California 4 in Alpine County. This settlement, originally known as Haydensville after three brothers who began placer mining operations here in 1850, later became Biddleville for miner William C. Biddle, then Simpsonville for storeowner Robert Simpson, then Johnsonville for John F. Johnson. In 1858, it

Frémont sits atop a stage outside the Wells Fargo depot in Bear Valley

became Bear Valley, taking the name of the valley to the south of town, which was named by John C. Frémont in 1848.

Frémont purchased a 44,000-acre land grant, Rancho Las Mariposas, from Juan Bautista Alvarado for $3,200 in 1847. The rancho's boundaries were vague, and as the gold rush began, Frémont resurveyed his property to include some of the richest mining country. Miners, some of whom had been working claims for several years, protested Frémont's boundaries, and a virtual war ensued between Frémont's workers and angry miners. Several of Frémont's most profitable diggings were jumped, and about 50 armed men laid siege to his Pine Tree Mine. The dispute was resolved when California's governor threatened to send in the state militia.

Between 1858 and 1861, Frémont owned a large stone mansion in Bear Valley called La Mariposas Estate. Indians referred to it as the "Little White House," perhaps because of Frémont's unsuccessful 1856 campaign as the Republican Party's first presidential candidate. Jesse Frémont, the explorer's wife, moved to the estate from Washington, D.C., in 1858. However, she left for San Francisco after just one year. Frémont turned out to be a better explorer than businessman, and he was forced to sell off his indebted Mariposa property in 1863.

Looking at Bear Valley today, it is hard to imagine that 3,000 people lived there during the gold rush. Quartz mining continued in the vicinity until about 1900, but the stamp mill closed in 1902. Today, Bear Valley has only a few residents. A number of old buildings remain, including the gold rush era Odd Fellows Hall, now a museum, and the 1862 stone Simpson and Trabuco store, which retains traces of its original cut block façade and is still open for business.

GPS COORDINATES: N37°34.14' W120°07.10'

NEAREST TRAIL: High Sierra #26: Merced River Road

Big Pine

The area of Big Pine in the high desert of northern Inyo County is part of the ancestral homeland of Paiute Indians. Americans began to develop the rich agricultural lands of the Owens Valley in the 1860s, which conflicted with the interests of the Mono, a band of Northern Paiute. A series of incidents took place between settlers and Indians, including a fight at Bishop Creek on April 6, 1862, in which three settlers and dozens of Indians were killed. Hostilities abated somewhat when army troops were posted at nearby Camp Independence in July 1862. A plaque near California 168 north of Big Pine marks the Bishop Creek battle site.

Big Pine is on Big Pine Creek, 2 miles east of the Owens River. The town was apparently named for a large pine tree on its outskirts, which has long since disappeared. Today, a tall sequoia marks one entrance into town. By 1870, Big Pine had a post office, and the Owens Valley was a flourishing agricultural and lumber region. In the early 1900s, unbeknown to Owens Valley residents, the burgeoning metropolis of Los Angeles purchased rights to water from the Owens River. Construction of a 233-mile-long aqueduct to drain water from the Owens River and carry it to Los Angeles began in 1908 and was completed in 1913. The project effectively changed the nature of the Owens Valley, rendering once rich farmland dry and unworkable. The issue remains contentious to this day.

Big Pine, at the intersection of US 395 and California 168 in the Owens Valley, currently has a population of about 1,500. This makes the town an ideal stop for visitors heading west into the Sierra Nevada or east into Inyo National Forest. It is the closest town to the 28,000-acre Ancient Bristlecone Pine Forest, part of Inyo National Forest. Some of the bristlecone pines in the forest are thought to be the oldest living things on earth, with specimens as old as 4,600 years. The ancient trees are protected today.

GPS COORDINATES: N37°09.98' W118°17.31'

TRAIL: High Sierra #45: Saline Valley Road

MAP: Page 274

Bishop

Bishop, at the northern end of the Owens Valley, is the largest town in the region. This area is the ancestral home of the Mono Indians. Petroglyphs a few miles north of Bishop attest to native peoples' long habitation of the valley. The Bishop petroglyphs make up the largest collection of Indian rock art in California and include representations of deer, snakes, insects, as well as handprints and geometric designs. The exact meaning of these petroglyphs is not entirely clear, nor are the artists known. Today, many Native Americans live at the Bishop Paiute Reservation, the largest in the Owens Valley. The Owens Valley Paiute–Shoshone Cultural Center on the reservation celebrates the area's native history and current cultures. The center is located east of High Sierra #41: Coyote Creek Trail's starting point.

Samuel Bishop, for whom the town was named, was among the first American settlers in the Owens Valley. He arrived in California in 1840 and moved to what became Inyo County in 1861 with his wife, three herders, 50 horses, and 600 head of cattle. By August 1862, he had built two cabins along the creek that now bears his name as headquarters for the Saint Francis Ranch. A town began to develop along Bishop Creek, 3 miles northeast of Bishop's ranch headquarters, in the mid-1860s. At first, the settlement was called Bishop Creek, and by 1870 it had a post office. In 1889, the post office relocated, and the town's name was shortened to Bishop.

Another small settlement, originally known as Bishop Station, arose to the east of Bishop. Established in 1883 as a depot along the new Carson & Colorado Railroad, the town later known as Laws served as a supply center for Bishop. Laws Railroad Museum and Historical Site exhibits what remains of the defunct settlement, including a doctor's office, carriage house, and old locomotive.

Bishop remained a small farming community until it incorporated in 1903, which enabled it to finance sewage and water systems, and from 1903 to 1910 its population more than doubled from 540 to 1,190. A variety of crops were grown around Bishop, including alfalfa, celery, corn, figs, potatoes, wheat, fruits, and nuts.

Bishop is now the most populous community in Inyo County with 3,800 residents in town and about 11,000 more in the surrounding area. The town prides itself as a gateway to backcountry activities in the Sierra and high desert. It holds the Blake Jones Opening Sierra Trout Derby in March and claims to have some of the best fall colors this side of New England in the Inyo National Forest.

GPS COORDINATES: N37°22.18' W118°23.67'
TRAIL: High Sierra #40: Casa Diablo Road
MAP: Page 261

Bodie

In 1859, Waterman S. Body was digging a wounded rabbit out of a hole when he discovered gold. Body and his partner, E. S. Taylor, built a cabin near the discovery but Body died before he realized any wealth from the diggings. By 1862, a mining camp known as Bodie (its spelling reflecting the pronunciation of Body's name) grew near Taylor Gulch, the site of Body and Taylor's cabin.

Bodie languished when miners turned their attention to gold strikes at nearby Aurora, Nevada. Following the boom and bust cycle of gold mines, two prospectors bought one of Bodie's first mines, the Standard, in the mid-1870s for just $950. In 1876, a cave-in at the Bunker Hill Mine revealed a rich vein of ore. Two years later, rival operations at the Bodie Mine also made a huge strike, extracting $1 million worth of gold in less than two months. Between 1878 and 1881, about $20 million of ore was brought up from beneath Bodie, and the town's population shot up to more than 10,000.

In its heyday, Bodie had more than 600 wooden structures. Some buildings, salvaged from towns that had gone bust, were transported piecemeal to Bodie because finding lumber for new buildings was not easy. At an elevation of 8,375 feet, the town is in a high desert area with few trees. The growing population required wood not only for building but also for heating in winter and as fuel for the stamp mills.

Hauling wood by wagon from forests south of Mono Lake was very expensive, so in 1881 mine operators pooled their resources to build a railroad line. The Bodie & Benton Railway ran between Bodie and the small lumber camp of Mono Mills, but Bodie's boom ended before the line was completed to Benton, which would have connected Bodie to the rest of the world via the Carson & Colorado Railroad. So Bodie remained an isolated mining town high in the eastern Sierra.

Bodie's rich diggings attracted an assortment of lawless characters. Shootings became commonplace, especially along "Virgin Alley," a facetiously named district of brothels and saloons. Claim jumping was also common in and around Bodie. Three breweries and more than 60 saloons fueled those with a proclivity for illegal activity. Robbers held up stages, and in one instance, two bandits wounded a Wells Fargo guard, who in turn killed one while the other escaped. When the wounded Wells Fargo guard sought help at a nearby house, the second thief returned and rode off with the unguarded loot. Bodie's citizens took the law into their own hands, and lynch mobs enforced a justice the courts could not. Aurora newspapers transcribed the prayers of one young girl after being notified by her parents of an imminent relocation to Bodie as: "Goodbye, God! We're moving to Bodie."

Bodie's story is characteristic of many western mining camps—when the ore played out, the people moved on. By 1882, the town had fewer than 1,000 residents. One resident who chose not to leave was Canadian-born James Stuart Cain. Cain, who had come to Bodie in 1875, gradually bought almost every building in Bodie. In order to revitalize the area, he introduced cyanide processing of old tailings, telephone lines, and electricity to run the cyanide plants. Cain's power lines, from a hydroelectric station about 13 miles away, were the first to carry electricity over such a long distance. The technology was so new that the people stringing the lines thought they had to be in a straight line so that the power wouldn't get lost on any sharp bends. Cain kept Bodie alive even when no more gold could be extracted from tailings and no new strikes were made. He kept the Bodie Bank open on weekdays until 1932,

Bodie's main street, circa 1920

despite a conspicuous absence of customers. A fire that year destroyed much of what remained of Bodie, and Cain, then in his 70s, moved to San Francisco after hiring a watchman for the town.

More than 150 buildings still stood when Bodie became a state park in 1962. The structures are kept in a state of arrested decay—no attempts are made to restore buildings, though some are braced from within. Although only about five percent of the original town survives, Bodie is probably California's best-preserved and most authentic ghost town.

GPS COORDINATES: N38°12.74' W119°00.79'
TRAIL: High Sierra #31: Bodie Ghost Town Trail
MAP: Page 237

Mono County Courthouse, circa 1930

Bridgeport

In the 1850s, farmers and ranchers from New England settled Bridgeport, which was originally called Big Meadows after the large grassy fields in the area. Located along the East Walker River at the intersection of US 395 and California 182, the town became the seat of Mono County in 1864 when the Sage Brush Survey revealed that Aurora, the seat of government at the time, was actually in Nevada. Bridgeport's post office opened the same year. The town thrived during the peak mineral-yielding years of surrounding mining settlements, such as Dogtown (the site of the first gold discovery in the eastern Sierra), Monoville, Bodie, and Aurora.

The ornate Mono County Courthouse, now the second oldest continuously operating courthouse in the state, was constructed in 1881 and remains one of the only buildings that showcases the New England–influenced Victorian architecture of the original town. An old cannon that once rested in front of the courthouse was said to be a repository for liquor during prohibition.

In 1924, the Walker River Irrigation District constructed the Bridgeport Reservoir, which in addition to providing water to farms and ranches is a good place for trout fishing, camping, hiking, and boating. Bridgeport is also home to the Travertine Hot Springs, which developed during Pleistocene volcanic activity. The travertine, or calcium carbonate, has been excavated from the site and sold as a decorative stone.

The Mono County Museum in Bridgeport is home to a collection of Paiute baskets and artifacts from Bodie, Masonic, and other historic mining towns. Bodie State Historical Park, Sonora Pass, and the mine tailings of Dogtown are notable historic sites in the area.

GPS COORDINATES: N38°15.50' W119°13.61'
TRAIL: High Sierra #31: Bodie Ghost Town Trail
MAP: Page 236

Burney

In 1857, Scottish immigrant and trapper Samuel Burney settled in the Shasta County valley that would bear his name. Burney built a small farm a mile north of the present-day town and lived peacefully with the Indians—even learning their language—until they killed him two years later. Locals called the area tucked between Mount Shasta and Lassen Peak "the valley where Burney was killed." On December 6, 1872, Burney Valley Post Office opened in the Bunker Hill building, which served as a stage stop, trading post, and saloon. The town's name was shortened to Burney in 1894.

The McArthur family settled in the valley in the 1860s, and obtained thousands of acres of wetlands under the Swamp Lands Act. They built McArthur, which consisted of the headquarters of their cattle ranch and a mercantile store. When the Pacific Gas & Electric Company formed in 1917 and threatened to claim land and water rights in the Burney Falls area, Frank and Scott McArthur bought 160 acres of land that encompassed the falls and presented it to the state as McArthur-Burney Falls Memorial State Park in 1920.

McArthur-Burney Falls Memorial State Park is 6 miles north of Burney on California 89; it is open daily for a small fee. The 910-acre park and the land surrounding it are layered with porous black volcanic rock; rain and snowmelt drain through the rock and collect in a giant underground reservoir. This water, about 100 million gallons a day, flows through springs to create the majestic 129-foot Burney Falls. The park has a boat launch, campsites, and hiking trails that connect with the Pacific Crest Trail.

Burney, a stopping point for through-hikers on the Pacific Crest Trail, lies in a corridor between national forest lands. It also serves as a supply center for smaller towns in the area such as Johnson Park, Cassel, Hat Creek, and Old Station. Logging and tourism continue to play a big role in the town's economy and culture.

GPS COORDINATES: N40°52.91' W121°40.17'
TRAIL: Northern Sierra #48: Burney Mountain Trail
MAP: Page 470

Camptonville

In 1850, J. Campbell built a hotel called the Nevada House on the road (now California 49) from Marysville and Nevada City to Downieville. Campbell's hotel was a regular stop for pack mule trains supplying the Mother Lode country. Gold discoveries attracted a blacksmith named Robert Campton, who was among the first to arrive at the diggings in 1852. His name was given to the mining camp in 1854.

Camptonville remained a small village until hydraulic mining became widespread in the 1860s. By 1866, Camp-

Camptonville's main street, circa 1875

tonville had a population of 1,500 and more than 30 businesses. Hydraulic operations were producing more than $500,000 a year, and Camptonville had to relocate twice so that runoff from the operations wouldn't wash it away. Fires eventually destroyed much of the town, so hardly any buildings from its heyday remain. One of the last standing is a small wooden structure marked "Jail."

The site of Camptonville honors two of its citizens. Ohio native Lester Pelton revolutionized dredging with his invention of a highly efficient waterwheel in the 1870s. A large plaque and miniature waterwheel at the west end of town commemorate his invention. An adjacent monument honors William "Bull" Meek, the only regular Wells Fargo driver in the northern Mother Lode never to be held up.

GPS COORDINATES: N39°27.15' W121°03.01'

TRAIL: Northern Sierra # 21: Henness Pass Road

MAP: Page 364

Cedarville

Cedarville, just east of the Warner Mountains, was originally called Surprise Valley when it was settled in the early 1860s because its lush green vegetation was so unexpected by travelers who had crossed Nevada's Black Rock Desert.

Cattle drive through Cedarville, circa 1910

Cedarville's name is not indicative of any local abundance of cedar trees. Resident John H. Bonner suggested it in 1867 to honor his hometown in Ohio. Bonner and his partner, William T. Cressler, operated a trading post in a small cabin built by James Townsend in 1865. Townsend's widow sold the building to Cressler and Bonner after Indians killed her husband. The store, then in Siskiyou County, was the first in the newly organized Modoc County in 1874. Migrants entering California via Cedar Pass (originally Cedarville Pass) stopped at the store, and some chose to stay in the area. The trading post served new arrivals and sold their lumber and produce. Today, the Cressler and Bonner Trading Post is Modoc County's oldest structure. It is located in the center of Cedarville and surrounded by a grove of cottonwoods planted by James Townsend.

Cedarville got its first post office in 1869, the same year John Bonner organized construction of a road from Cedarville to Alturas. The road quickly became a major stage and freight route. Bonner helped maintain the road until Siskiyou County took over its maintenance in 1871. The Bonner Grade on California 299 honors the pioneer road builder.

During the 1900s, Cedarville's economy was based on logging and agriculture. Today, the town attracts tourists and travelers because of its location near Modoc National Forest and its position on California 299, 23 miles east of Alturas.

GPS COORDINATES: N41°31.78' W120°12.25'

NEAREST TRAIL: Northern Sierra #55: Payne Peak Trail

Chico

Chico, in Butte County, is 80 miles north of Sacramento. Much of the city is built on what was John Bidwell's Rio Chico Ranch. In 1849, Bidwell, one of the organizers of the first emigrant wagon train to arrive in California, bought land that included present-day Chico from William Dickey. The land had been granted to Dickey in 1844. Bidwell also bought land from Edward A. Farwell to consolidate his holdings. The Chico Post Office was established in 1851, but it was not until 1860 that county surveyor J. S. Henning laid out the town. John and Annie Bidwell gave generously to the new town, donating land for churches and public schools. In 1887, they donated the land for the Northern Branch Normal School, now Chico State University.

An avid agriculturalist, Bidwell grew every species and variety of fruit he could adapt to the region before his death in 1900. On July 10, 1905, Mrs. Bidwell gave the city of Chico a nearly 1,900-acre tract of land, which contained some of the most beautiful portions of Rio Chico Ranch, including Oak Forest and Iron Canyon. The land was named Bidwell Park, and upon Mrs. Bidwell's donation of an additional 301 acres in 1911, the park became the second largest in the state (behind Los Angeles' Griffith Park) and the third largest in the nation.

Located 4 miles northwest of downtown Chico in Bidwell Park is the site of the famous Hooker Oak, named after English botanist Sir Joseph Hooker, who visited Bidwell's ranch in 1877. The tree, a valley oak, measured 100 feet tall and 28 feet around its base. Lightning severely damaged the tree in 1962, and it finally fell in 1977. This area was part of the set used during the filming of the 1938 version of *Robin Hood.*

Today Chico's population is nearly 65,000, and it thrives as an agricultural center and university town. Historic highlights include the Masonic Hall, which dates from 1871. The square

Chico's main street, circa 1910

outlined by Broadway and Main Streets and by Third and Fourth Streets is the location of Bidwell's original land donation to the city. Local legend says Bidwell himself planted the elms on this site. There are two cemeteries of note in Chico, although some of the older graves are no longer marked. The Mechoopda Indian Tribal Cemetery, which was established with the Indian church by Annie Bidwell in the 1870s, is still used and maintained by the Mechoopda Tribal Association. The Chico cemetery, originally established in 1860 as the Bidwell family plot, is the site of General and Mrs. Bidwell's graves and is now the city burial ground.

The original 26-room, 3-story, Victorian stucco mansion that Bidwell built on Rio Chico Ranch is maintained and open for tours for a small fee in the Bidwell Mansion State Historic Park. At the time of its construction in 1865 the pink-plastered brick home had the most modern plumbing and gas lighting systems in existence.

On East Seventh Street, Shubert's Ice Cream & Candy, owned and operated by the same family, has served sweets since 1938. Stroll or bike the streets of the picturesque town, voted most "bike friendly" in the nation.

GPS COORDINATES: N39°43.92' W121°50.46'

NEAREST TRAIL: Northern Sierra #42: Ponderosa Way

Chinese Camp

Chinese Camp, at the junction of California 49 and 120 in Tuolumne County, was a placer mining camp occupied by Chinese at the beginning of the gold rush. The first Chinese residents may have been a ship's crew, who with their captain abandoned their vessel in San Francisco Bay, or they may have been Chinese hired to work for Americans. In any case, at one time an estimated 5,000 Chinese lived here. The town's name commemorates the Chinese immigration; before the gold rush, in 1847, there were fewer than 400 Chinese in California. By 1850, there were 25,000, and over the next 30 years, 300,000 Chinese arrived in California.

In 1856, Chinese Camp was the scene of a war between tongs—Chinese fraternal organizations. About 1,200 Sam Yap members confronted 900 Yan Wo members after a large rock rolled into one or the other's camp. They battled each other with a crude assortment of weapons, mainly shovels and picks, but also one or two firearms. When fighting ended, four men lay dead and a dozen more were injured. Local authorities arrested about 250 participants.

Post office and general store in Chinese Camp, circa late 1800s

At its peak, Chinese Camp had several hotels and general stores, a bank, an express office, a Masonic Lodge, and a church. Several stone and brick buildings remain from the gold rush era; the restored St. Francis Xavier Catholic Church dates from 1854.

GPS COORDINATES: N37°52.24' W120°25.93'

NEAREST TRAIL: Northern Sierra #2: Lumsden Bridge Road

Coloma

On January 24, 1848, James Wilson Marshall spotted gold in a sawmill's tailrace on the South Fork of the American River, 45 miles northeast of Sutter's Fort. Ultimately, this find triggered the gold rush. The mining camp and village of Coloma grew up near the sawmill and was large enough to have a post office by January 1851.

Coloma's main street, circa 1856

Gold fever peaked in Coloma, located on present-day California 49, 18 miles south of the I-80 exit for Auburn and 9 miles northwest of Placerville, in 1849, bringing more than 5,000 fortune-seekers from all over the world. Although this was not the first gold discovery in California, it was the first in a series of hundreds of strikes in a short period of time that started a population migration unmatched in American history. The state's population increased from 14,000 in 1848 to 300,000 in 1860. During Coloma's heyday, its merchants charged unprecedented prices for supplies, including a flat rate of $1 per pound for food. Shovels and picks sold for at least $50 and boots for $25 to $50 a pair. One enterprising Coloma woman charged $1 an item for laundry service; she earned twice as much as her husband earned as a miner in a four-week span.

Coloma's population dwindled as soon as the mines played out. An 1851 visitor called the settlement "the dullest mining town in the whole country." By 1870, the "Queen City of the Mines" had only 200 residents. Today, the 300-acre Marshall Gold Discovery State Historic Park, open daily for a modest fee, covers most of Coloma and preserves the town's history. The park features the Gold Discovery Museum, a visitor center, and several original and reconstructed buildings, including a reproduction of Sutter's Mill with a path leading 100 yards upstream to its original location. There is also a reproduction of Marshall's cabin, and a monument stands over his grave, indicating the site of his historic discovery. A few other gold rush era buildings survive: Robert Bell's Brick Store, the Coloma School House, Emmanuel Episcopal Church, and St. John's Church.

GPS COORDINATES: N38°48.04' W120°53.43'
NEAREST TRAIL: Northern Sierra #14: Slate Mountain Trail

Columbia

"Gem of the Southern Mines," Columbia is another Mother Lode town on California 49, in Tuolumne County, between Sonora and San Andreas. Dr. Thaddeus Hildreth discovered gold while camping in the vicinity in 1850 and a mining camp, Hildreth's Diggings, soon formed. The gravel around Hildreth's Diggings was extremely rich and it was not long before the settlement grew quite large. For a time, it was known as American Camp before prominent citizens of the town decided on Columbia in 1882. Unlike many mining camps, Columbia did not have ready access to a water supply. Initially, water was hauled in by wagon, but by 1852, a ditch from Five Mile Creek had been dug by 200 workers. By that year, the town had a population in excess of 15,000 and boasted 4 banks, 3 express offices, 8 hotels, 3 theaters, 2 fire companies, 17 general stores, and more than 40 saloons. Columbia was the biggest settlement in the Mother Lode; it incorporated in 1854, the same year a fire destroyed many of its buildings. Another blaze in 1857 convinced residents to rebuild using fire-resistant materials. Many of the buildings are brick rather than the local marble and limestone. Occasionally buildings would be torn down, the brick reused elsewhere, and the site mined. Quite a few of the buildings date from the post-1857 reconstruction.

Approximately $87 million worth of gold was mined from 640 acres on the edge of Columbia—more than in any other comparable area in the Western Hemisphere. Hundreds of rich deposits were found in the gravel, but 20 to 60 feet of topsoil had to be removed. By the 1860s, however, placer mining was all but finished near Columbia. An observer passing through in 1867 described "an almost total desertion" of the once bustling town.

Old stage stop in Columbia, circa 1925

The old Wells Fargo office still stands in Columbia

Despite its dramatic change in fortune, Columbia was never completely abandoned. The town site is now a state historic park, a very different one from Bodie State Historic Park, California's other major mining camp park. Bodie (see High Sierra Trail #31: Bodie Ghost Town Trail, page 234) is preserved as a ghost town, but Columbia has been restored to an 1850s gold rush town. The Wells Fargo Building was built in 1858, and the City Hotel, dating from 1856, still offers accommodations, as does the Fallon House Hotel and Theater, which dates from 1859. The brick schoolhouse, built in 1860, is also a charming structure.

GPS COORDINATES: N38°02.17' W120°11.77'
NEAREST TRAIL: Northern Sierra #5: Crandall Peak Trail

Coulterville

A small Mexican mining camp was on the site of today's Coulterville when Pennsylvania-born George W. Coulter arrived to open a store in 1849. In 1850, George Maxwell opened a store, and Coulter flew a small Stars and Stripes above his emporium to distinguish it from Maxwell's, prompting Mexicans to call the settlement Banderita, meaning "little flag." From 1852 until 1872, the post office name was Maxwell Creek and then changed to Coulterville. Tradition has it that Coulter and Maxwell drew lots to decide the town's name. Maxwell lost, but his name survives on Maxwell Creek, which flows through town. Nelson Cody, Buffalo Bill Cody's brother, was one of Coulterville's early postmasters.

Coulterville became an important trading center for the southern Mother Lode. At its peak, it had 5,000 residents, of whom 1,500 were Chinese, and boasted 10 hotels, 25 saloons, a Wells Fargo office, and several general stores. The Jeffrey Hotel, now restored, dates from 1851 and still offers hospitality. Ralph Waldo Emerson and President Theodore Roosevelt supposedly were guests there. An antique store is one of the few remnants of the town's once extensive Chinatown. The Sun Sun Wo store was constructed in 1851, and the old adobe residence next door was once a popular bordello.

The Northern Mariposa County History Center opened in the early 1980s around the ruins of the 1850s Coulter Hotel. The museum houses an impressive collection of antiques. The town's hanging tree is just outside its doors, and it also has an eight-ton Porter narrow-gauge locomotive. The train, known as Whistling Billy, was put into service in 1897 on the 4-mile winding grade from the Mary Harrison Mine to the Black Creek Potsoi stamp mill. The grade was called the "Crookedest Railroad in the World." The Mary Harrison Mine, south of town, operated from the 1860s to 1903 and had 15 miles of tunnels; one shaft went down 1,200 feet.

Coulterville's Jeffrey Hotel

Like many Sierra Nevada mining towns, Coulterville suffered from several devastating fires. The conflagration of 1899 led to one of the most peculiar gold rushes in California history. When a gutted stone building was razed and used to fill potholes in the town's streets, someone found a fortune in gold coins in the building's walls. Town residents hurried to dig up the filled-in holes, leaving Coulterville's streets an impassable mess.

Coulterville's population numbers just over 100 souls today, many fewer than in its heyday. It is at the junction of California 49 and CR J132, which winds through Stanislaus National Forest to meet California 120 on its way to Yosemite National Park.

GPS COORDINATES: N37°42.65' W120°11.77'

NEAREST TRAIL: High Sierra #28: Old Coulterville Road

Crescent City

Crescent City is on a picturesque portion of the Pacific Coast, just 20 miles south of the Oregon border. This land of redwoods, rivers, and rugged mountains was Tolowa and Yurok Indian country prior to the arrival of Euro-Americans in the 1850s. A Tolowa village survived here until the late nineteenth century. Today, many descendents still live in the vicinity on the Smith River and Elk Valley Rancherias.

Gold strikes along the Klamath and Smith Rivers attracted prospectors to northwestern California. Crescent City was laid out on an arc of a bay in 1852–53; the bay made an excellent harbor for ships with supplies for inland mining camps. The town's first post office opened in 1853, and the town incorporated the following year. That same year, Crescent City became the Klamath County seat and citizens lobbied for the town to become California's capital. Sacramento, however, won out in February 1854. Twenty years later Klamath County ceased to exist; its area was parceled out into Siskiyou, Del Norte, and Humboldt Counties, and Crescent City became county seat of the newly organized Del Norte County.

Gold mining—even beach sands were worked as placer mines—and supplying goods to mines over wagon roads dominated Crescent City's early days. Timber, however, played a longer lived role. Machinery for the town's first mill arrived by boat in 1853, and by 1854, more than 300 homes and businesses had been built. Timber from the seemingly endless redwood forests quickly became a cornerstone of the town's economy and remained so for more than 100 years.

The town depended on shipping for its connection to the outside world. Railroads never penetrated the rugged Coast Ranges or Klamath Mountains of Del Norte County. Ships often fell prey to the rocky coastline and heavy fog; more than 50 ships wrecked along the Del Norte coast. The Battery Point Lighthouse was built in 1856, but it failed to prevent the June 30, 1865, sinking of the side-wheeler *Brother Jonathan* on St. George Reef with 200 passengers. The dead are buried at a cemetery, now a park, near town. The 140-foot-tall St. George Reef Lighthouse was eventually built at a cost of more than $700,000. The light operated from 1891 to 1974, when it was decommissioned. Its 18-foot-high Fresnel lens is now at the Del Norte County Historical Society Museum. Another tragedy occurred on December 20, 1941, just two weeks after the attack on Pearl Harbor. The SS *Emidio* was torpedoed by a Japanese submarine and foundered on rocks near Crescent City. Salvaged pieces of the tanker's hull are displayed on the waterfront.

The stone house and stubby tower of the Battery Point Lighthouse is now a nautical museum, accessible only by a causeway at low tide. The light ceased to operate in the early 1900s, but it reopened again in 1982. A 20-foot wall of water destroyed much of Crescent City's downtown March 28, 1964. The tsunami was the result of a major earthquake that

Crescent City, circa 1855

caused a great deal of damage in Anchorage, Alaska, and other Pacific coastal towns on that Good Friday. Floods later that year destroyed other parts of Crescent City.

The town has since rebuilt and has a population of 8,800. Approximately 15,000 of Del Norte County's 26,000 residents live in the greater Crescent City area. The city has an information center for Redwood National Park, and Smith River National Recreation Area and Del Norte Redwood State Park are within easy driving distance.

GPS COORDINATES: N41°45.49' W124°11.81'

NEAREST TRAIL: North Coast #14: Howland Hill Road

Dinkey Creek

In August 1863, a dog named Dinkey took on a grizzly near an unnamed creek to protect its owners. The owner named the creek after the dog. Rancher Jack Ducey built the popular Camp Ducey Summer Resort in 1925 at the confluence of Dinkey and Rock Creeks, about 60 miles northwest of Fresno off California 168. The lively camp was a retreat for families to escape the summer heat of the San Joaquin Valley. The resort eventually included a two-story hotel, but early vacationers camped in furnished tents that had cots, tables, and chairs.

Truman and Beulah Parker bought the hotel in 1948 and managed the well-loved retreat during the height of its popularity. The Parkers welcomed guests as if they were family and created fond memories for their summer visitors. They offered weekly movies on an open pavilion overlooking Dinkey Creek. Price of admission was a quarter. On Saturday nights, vacationers gathered on the open-air dance floor. On Sunday mornings, church services were held there. Guests feasted on venison, baked beans, garlic bread, and coleslaw at the traditional end-of-the-season barbeque while savoring the last days of summer. The hotel deteriorated when it changed hands. It finally met its end in 1981, during the cleanup after a fire.

Dennis Beard, owner of the Dinkey Creek Inn, caters to visitors who come for solitude and outdoor recreational activities. The Sierra National Forest surrounds Dinkey Creek, with recreational opportunities at Dinkey Lakes Wilderness, McKinley Grove Botanical Area, Shaver Lake, the Sierra Summit Ski Area, and access to the John Muir Wilderness on the Sierra Crest.

GPS COORDINATES: N37°04.04' W119°09.34'
TRAIL: High Sierra #1: Dinkey-Trimmer Road
MAP: Page 165

Downieville

Downieville is nestled at the confluence of the Downie and North Fork of the Yuba Rivers. A party led by a Scot, "Major" William Downie (the "major" was likely a title of respect rather than his military rank), camped in this wooded amphitheater in November 1849. They built several log cabins and named their settlement The Forks. While at The Forks, members of the party prospected for gold with good results.

News of their success spread, and by the following spring scores of miners came to the settlement. Miner James Calloway suggested the name of Downieville, and it was adopted. Placer claims in the vicinity proved extremely rich. A nugget weighing 25 pounds was found at Gold Flat, 2 miles from town, and one group of miners took $12,900 in 11 days from a claim of just 60 square feet. By 1851, the town's population reached 5,000, and the following year, when Sierra County was created from a portion of Yuba County, Downieville became the seat of its government.

In 1851, Downieville was the scene of one of the most infamous lynchings of the gold rush. On the night of July 4, a drunken Australian miner named Jack Cannon attempted to break into the house of a Mexican woman named Juanita. She stabbed Cannon to death, probably in self-defense. Anti-Mexican feelings were running high and Juanita was tried by a kangaroo court and hanged. As she was being strung up, she claimed she was pregnant. Her death sparked an outrage across the United States and even as far as Europe. The gallows still standing in Downieville date from 1885. They were used only once, to hang a criminal named James O'Neal.

Downieville retains much of its gold rush atmosphere, but it has only about a tenth of its 1851 population. The Sierra County Museum houses its collection in an 1852 building.

Downieville, after the flood of 1861

The Hirschfelder house, now a store, and the nearby Craycroft House, both on Main Street, also date from 1852. The town's Catholic and Methodist churches are also remnants of the 1850s. Evidence of gold mining abounds with piles of tailings, displaced boulders, and mining equipment scattered around the area. Nearby Heritage Park displays a stamp mill and other machinery.

GPS COORDINATES: N39°33.63' W120°49.63'
TRAIL: Northern Sierra #30: Poker Flat OHV Trail
MAP: Page 405

Eureka

Founded in 1850 by the Mendocino Exploring Company and the Union Company, Eureka was intended to be a port for gold mines along the Klamath River. Surveyor James Ryan supervised construction of the new town. Eureka's name was adopted in May 1850. "Eureka!" is California's motto, meaning "I've found it" in Greek. Located on Humboldt Bay, the town is in the ancestral home of Wiyot Indians. Although the Wiyot were peaceful, other Indians were less welcoming and Fort Humboldt was established in 1853 to protect settlers.

In 1854, Captain Ulysses S. Grant was stationed at the post for four months. Apparently the post drove him to drink; he

Rider parading his saddle horse down Eureka's main street

resigned from the army and only resumed his career at the outbreak of the Civil War, rising to command the Union Army and, eventually, to become president. Attacks by white settlers, including a horrific 1860 massacre of all of a village's women and children while the men were away hunting, wore on the resilience of local tribes. By 1864, when the nearby Hoopa Valley Indian Reservation was established, disputes between Indians and whites were generally over. Fort Humboldt was abandoned in 1870, and the property became Fort Humboldt State Park in 1955.

Uniontown (now known as Arcata) initially attracted more trade than Eureka, which was farther from the Klamath River mines. When mining in the Trinity River region increased and a wagon road was built, Eureka's fortunes improved. But it was the logging industry that enabled it to surpass Arcata and replace it as the Humboldt County seat in 1856. Logging continues to be important to Eureka and Humboldt County's economy, although the issue is contentious as environmentalists urge preservation of old-growth forests. Eureka protects a grove of redwoods in centrally located Sequoia Park.

Eureka's economy diversified with commercial fishing for crab, salmon, shrimp, and albacore as the twentieth century progressed. Humboldt Bay Maritime Museum displays maritime artifacts from Eureka's fishing history as well as relics from the wreck of the USS *Brooklyn*, which sank in 1930. Other attractions include a cruise around Humboldt Bay in a 1910 ferry, the Clarke Memorial Museum, with its collection of Native American baskets, and the renovated Victorian Old Town.

GPS COORDINATES: N40°46.84' W124°08.30'

NEAREST TRAIL: North Coast #21: Hennessy Ridge Road

Fall River Mills

Explorer John C. Frémont named the Fall River for its rapids (known locally as falls) when he passed through this region in 1846. The flow of the Fall, Tule, and Pit Rivers is now controlled by dams, which create a number of reservoirs throughout the region. Timber brought the first settlers to the Fall River Valley in 1855. Two men, Bowles and Rogers, brought mill machinery by ox team from Yreka, a settlement to the north, and began cutting trees. Indians killed them as well as William Lockhart, who had followed them to the valley. A fourth settler, Sam Lockhart, spent the winter in Yreka and was attacked by Indians upon his return to the mill in the spring. He fought for five days, until men from Yreka arrived unexpectedly and chased off the attackers.

The old jail still stands in Fall River Mills

Sam Lockhart eventually built a ferry just below the mouth of Fall River where the California-Oregon stage road crossed the Pit River. In 1857, the U.S. Army built an outpost named Camp Hollenbush on the Fall River. The fort had a 12-foot-high pine-pole barricade that enclosed a number of log buildings. A young army lieutenant, George S. Crook, who would go on to fight Indians, including Cochise, Crazy Horse (who defeated him), and Geronimo, was stationed here. The post's name was later changed to Fort Crook. The fortress closed in 1869, and troops were transferred to Fort Bidwell.

In 1871, William Henry Winter established a flour mill at the site that would become Fall River Mills. A hamlet grew up around the mill, and by 1886, the population was about 300 and businesses included two hotels, a blacksmith shop, three stores, two saloons, Winter's flour mill, and a door and sash factory.

The Fort Crook Museum, open from May through October, has exhibits of the area's history. An 1884 one-room schoolhouse and an 1860s log cabin have been relocated to the museum's grounds. Agricultural equipment used by the vicinity's first settlers is also on display.

GPS COORDINATES: N41°00.26' W121°26.23'

NEAREST TRAIL: Northern Sierra #49: Popcorn Cave Trail

Forbestown

Forbestown, about 15 miles east of Oroville, is surrounded by Plumas National Forest. Considered to be in the northern part of the Mother Lode, the town began to grow in September 1850 around a general store run by Wisconsin native Ben F. Forbes. By 1855, the settlement had about 900 residents and supplied nearby mines. In its heyday the town boasted a private academy, an assembly hall used for lectures during the week and church services on Sundays, and a post office.

Forbestown, circa 1897

The South Fork of the Feather River and its tributaries supported many profitable placer claims in the 1850s, and lode mining continued into the twentieth century. Fires destroyed many of the town's businesses in 1860 and 1861, but citizens rebuilt and continued to work in the mines during the shift from placer to lode mining. Harry P. Snow's Gold Bank Mine employed 50 miners at its peak and produced $2 million worth of gold between 1888 and 1904.

By the 1930s, mining had ended and much of the population moved away; by 1940 only about a dozen people remained. In recent years, several houses have been constructed on the outskirts of the former mining camp, and the post office, which closed in 1925, has reopened. The deserted part of town is now known as Old Forbestown. The most significant structure from its mining days is the Masonic Lodge, which dates from the 1850s. The Forbestown Museum, located in the new part of town, contains artifacts from the mining era.

GPS COORDINATES: N39°31.16' W121°16.49'

NEAREST TRAIL: Northern Sierra #32: Forbestown to Feather Falls Trail

Forest

Forest, in Sierra County, is on the northern slope of Pliocene Ridge, just up the road from Allegheny. The site has had a number of names over the years. Tradition attributes the first name, Brownsville, to sailors mining on Oregon Creek in 1852, who named it for the owner of a sawmill, I. E. Brown. It was also known as Elizabeth and as Yomana, an Indian name for a nearby bluff. When a post office was established in 1854, the name was changed to Forest City, after journalist Mrs. Forest Mooney, who used Forest City as her byline in Marysville newspapers.

Forest, circa 1863

In October 1855, news of a major gold strike came from Alleghany, on the southern slope of Pliocene Ridge. Most Forest City residents deserted the town for Alleghany, but a few returned. Timber became a steady source of income. Logs from the vicinity were used in the covered bridge built at Bridgeport in 1862. Forest City's mining fortunes rose again in the 1880s with large drift mining operations. In what must have been a case of déjà vu for old-time residents, the second boom faded when more profitable quartz mines, like the Sixteen-to-One, were discovered closer to Alleghany.

The post office officially dropped the "City" from the town's name in 1895, but the change does not seem to be generally accepted by Forest's residents. The hamlet has never been abandoned, and a small population continues to live there. Several old buildings remain, although most are either ruins or private residences. The dance hall was built after an 1883 fire and the 1874 Forest City Schoolhouse was in use until the 1930s. Another feature of interest is Forest's Mountain House Cemetery, with many headstones from the 1870s and 1880s. Visitors might also spot a weathered rock dotted by small holes left from miners' core-drilling contests.

GPS COORDINATES: N39°29.37' W120°51.14'

NEAREST TRAIL: Northern Sierra #26: Alleghany Trail

Fort Bidwell

The northeastern-most town in California, Fort Bidwell began as an army encampment established between 1865 and 1866 to deter hostile Indians in northeastern California, southern Oregon, and northwestern Nevada from attacking emigrants. Originally called Camp Bidwell, the post was several miles north of the present location. It was moved to its current position in 1879. It was named after John Bidwell, leader of the first wagon train into California and later a general in the state militia.

A civilian settlement grew up around the post. Apparently, target practice occasionally turned into less innocuous marksmanship and the army claimed livestock it had "accidentally" shot. Troops stationed at Fort Bidwell saw action as early as 1866, when they attacked a village in Guano, Nevada, killing 96 Indians, including 15 women and children. They also fought with George Crook at the 1867 Battle of Infernal Caverns, and during the Modoc War in 1872-73. They also participated in the Bannock and Nez Percé campaigns.

The need for a military presence had ended by 1892, and the fort was decommissioned. The buildings were used as a boarding school for Native American children. The school was closed in 1930 and much of the fort was dismantled. Today, the remains of the post, including the cemetery and chapel, are part of the Fort Bidwell Indian Reservation. A general store built in 1874 continues to do business as Krober's Dry Goods Store.

GPS COORDINATES: N41°51.84' W120°09.05'

TRAIL: North Coast #45: New Pine Creek to Fort Bidwell Trail

MAP: Page 615

French Gulch

In 1849 or 1850, French miners discovered large gold deposits while exploring a gulch 1.5 miles from the settlement of Morrowville, just west of Redding. Mines and streams in this region of Shasta County eventually yielded more than $28 million in gold. By 1852, the town boomed, and the gold frenzy peaked. Local legend tells of some miners tearing down their houses to follow veins that ran beneath them. Two water-driv-

Freight wagon outside French Gulch's Feeney Hotel, circa 1890

en stamp mills existed in the town in 1851, and by 1900, 11 mills were processing ore. When the post office was established in 1856, settlers officially named the town French Gulch after the first prospectors.

The current community of 200 residents fervently protects the town's heritage, and some still mine for gold. On the western slopes of the Trinity Mountains, French Gulch is still an important lode mining area and a good location for placer mining. Some original buildings still stand, including the 1854 E. Franck and Company Store (now Fox Store), Odd Fellows Hall, and the French Gulch Hotel built in 1885, where visitors can still stay. The town's much-photographed icon, St. Rose's Catholic Church built in 1898, burned down in 1999.

GPS COORDINATES: N40°41.87' W122°38.25'
TRAIL: North Coast #24: Deadwood Road
MAP: Page 555

Georgetown

A party of Oregonians mined along Oregon Creek and Hudson's Creek in 1849. George Ehrenhaft established a mining camp at that time, though it is uncertain whether it was named for him or George Phipps, a sailor who arrived in the vicinity in 1850. The settlement became known as Growlersville, possibly a nickname given for the sound nuggets found in placer gravels made in mining pans.

By late 1850, Georgetown was a center known especially for seam mines that followed gold-bearing quartz veins interspersed with slate. One such claim, the Nagler Mine (or French Mine), produced at least $4 million worth of gold between 1872 and 1885.

At first, Georgetown was a tightly packed tent city, but after a photographer's flash ignited a devastating fire in 1852, the town rebuilt with wide streets and alleys. Main Street is 100 feet wide. The settlement flourished, and by 1855 it had a population of 3,000 and boasted a school, church, theater, town hall, Masonic Hall, three hotels, and more than a dozen

Looking across Main Street to a hotel in Georgetown, circa 1903

stores. The Odd Fellows Hall dates from 1859 and was previously a hotel and opera house. The U.S. Armory on Main Street was constructed in 1862. The impressive Georgetown Hotel was built in 1896 on a site used for hostelries since 1856. Georgetown's oldest private residence is the Shannon Knox House, dating from 1864. Because of Georgetown's cultural attractions and beautiful setting, many refer to it as the "Pride of the Mountains." Georgetown is on California 193 (Georgetown Road), north of Placerville, at the western edge of Eldorado National Forest.

GPS COORDINATES: N38°54.33' W120°50.32'
NEAREST TRAIL: Northern Sierra #14: Slate Mountain Trail

Graniteville

Graniteville, an old mining camp in northern Nevada County, lies between the Middle and South Forks of the Yuba River. It was founded in 1850 as Eureka, then Eureka

Graniteville, circa 1908

South, and finally Graniteville in 1867, to distinguish it from other Eurekas. Unfortunately, the placer claims could not be worked without a steady water supply and nearby streams generally dried up in summer. So from a winter population of 500, Graniteville's summer population would dwindle to 20 to 30 residents.

Graniteville's first mining boom ended by 1858 when the placer deposits played out. Hydraulic mining on the San Juan Ridge southwest of Graniteville revitalized the town, beginning in 1866. Within three years Graniteville boasted five saloons, two hotels, a blacksmith's shop, a carpenter's shop, and a post office, and over the next decade, a brewery and a bakery opened.

Hydraulic mining was banned in 1884, due in part to complaints about the silt and debris from San Juan Ridge. Mountainsides that weren't destroyed by high-pressure water jets were deforested to provide lumber for the flumes. Time has restored much of the area's beauty, but a visit to the Malakoff Diggins State Historic Park will give an idea of the process.

Graniteville is in the Tahoe National Forest, and residents supported an effort by the Yuba Nation to prevent logging in a 2,000-acre forest in the Marsh Mill Timber Harvest Plan in October 2000. Yuba Nation activists staged a successful seven-day tree sit to force a logging company from the forest.

Except for a few old houses and its cemetery, Graniteville shows few signs of its mining heyday. Several dozen residents live along its main road, the number probably decreasing during the harsh snowy winters. Poet Gary Snyder is the town's most famous resident.

GPS COORDINATES: N39°26.35' W120°44.49'

TRAIL: Northern Sierra #25: North Bloomfield to Bowman Lake Trail

MAP: Page 385

Grass Valley

The businesses and homes of Grass Valley, east of Marysville on California 20, now extend to the boundaries of its one-time rival, Nevada City. In August 1849, five men led by a Dr. Saunders established the first camp in the vicinity of the present-day town. A month later, a second party, led by Reverend H. H. Cummings, set up camp nearby at what became known as Boston Ravine.

Miner George Knight of Boston Ravine stumbled over a rock one moonlit night in October 1850 while looking for a stray cow. Knight noticed the distinct glint of metal. He had accidentally found gold-bearing quartz, and his find caused the first quartz mining rush in California.

Quartz mines required heavy machinery and much capital investment. The Gold Hill Mining Company operated between 1850 and 1857, producing $4 million worth of gold. Other rich mines included the Pennsylvania, North Star, Idaho-Maryland, and one of the most profitable gold mines in the world, the Empire. In July 1851, the first post office was established for Centerville, which became Grass Valley in August 1852.

A large percentage of the hard-rock miners in Grass Valley (an estimated 85 percent in 1890) came from Cornwall, a tin-mining region of southwestern England. The Cornish brought many useful techniques with them, including Cornish pumps to keep deep mines free of water. They also brought their traditional miners' fare: pasties—a savory pastry shaped like a half moon, filled with meat and vegetables, and baked without a dish. Some restaurants still serve them.

Grass Valley attracted its share of characters, including Lola Montez and Lotta Crabtree. Lola Montez was born in Ireland as Maria Dolores Eliza Rosanna Gilbert in 1818 and became a theatrical sensation in Europe during the 1840s. She was friends with some of the foremost figures of the time, including George Sand, Victor Hugo, and Alexander Dumas. She had an affair with King Ludwig I of Bavaria and was eventually exiled. She arrived in California in 1851, and after being critically acclaimed in San Francisco, toured the gold country. She settled in Grass Valley and befriended a precocious six-year-old girl, Lotta Crabtree, and taught her to be an entertainer. Lola left California in 1855 and died in New York in 1861, but her young apprentice went on to stardom, first in the Mother Lode, later in San Francisco, New York, and internationally. She received accolades for her performances in adaptations of Dickens' novels and other plays. She retired in 1891. She left an estate of $4 million to charity upon her death in 1924. Lotta Fountain on San Francisco's Market Street was built using her donations.

Other famous residents and visitors included Mark Twain, Bret Harte, Black Bart, and George Hearst. Writer, philosopher, and historian Josiah Royce was born here in 1855, and novelist and illustrator Mary Hallock Foote, subject of Wallace Stegner's *Angle of Repose* (1971), spent her last 30 years here. Most prominent visitors to Grass Valley spent at least a portion of their time at the Holbooke Hotel, built in 1862 and recently restored. A plaque in the hotel commemorates the stays of four U.S. presidents.

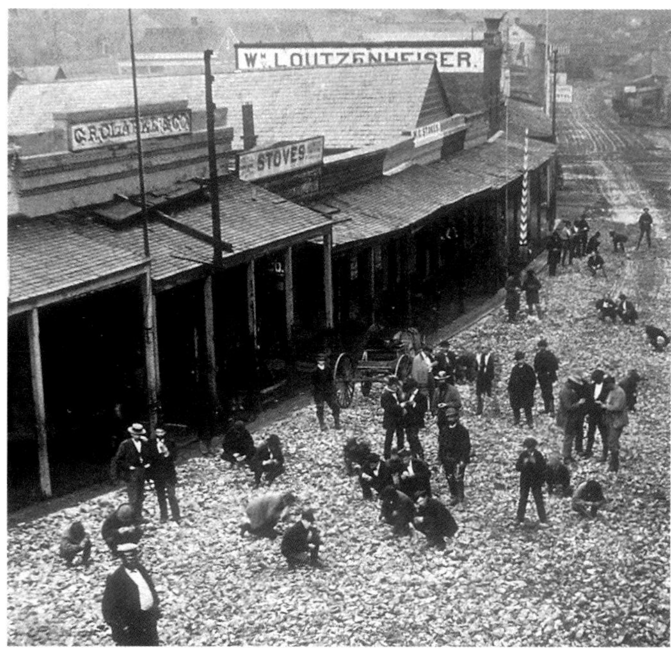

Townspeople searching for gold in the rocks used to macadamize Grass Valley's Mill Street, circa 1873

Mining continued in Grass Valley until the 1950s when the fixed price of gold precluded profit-making. Hundreds of miles of tunnels have been dug in the area; the Empire Mine alone totals more than 350 miles, reaching an inclined depth of 8,000 feet and a vertical depth of 4,000 feet. From 1850 until 1956, 5.8 million ounces of gold were extracted from the mine. Visitors today can learn about the workings of the mine at the Empire Mine State Historic Park. The park includes Bourn Cottage, former residence of William Bourn, Jr., owner of the Empire.

Another attraction near Grass Valley, the North Star Mining Museum and Pelton Wheel Exhibit, displays an array of mining artifacts. It is the site of the world's largest Pelton wheel, a turbine waterwheel used to power mining equipment. The waterwheel, which dates from 1896, is 30 feet in diameter.

GPS COORDINATES: N39°12.98' W121°03.61'

NEAREST TRAIL: Northern Sierra #25: North Broomfield to Bowman Lake Trail

Harrison Gulch

W. H. Harrison staked a claim on the North Fork of Cottonwood Creek in 1852. He later became the first judge of Shasta County, one of the state's 27 original counties. Harrison Gulch Mining District had a number of mines including the Midas Mine, which was established in 1894. The Midas Gold Mining Company operated the site until a fire destroyed the main shaft in 1914; the mine produced an estimated $7 million in gold. Mining activity within the region was so great, that some considered building a railroad through the district. A post office opened in Platina on California 36, possibly named for platinum ore found in the region.

The town of Knob was the center of the mining district's activity. The town's population soared to nearly 2,000 residents, some of whom ran the school and a number of hotels, stores, and saloons. The town was a social center, hosting theatrical performances and sporting events. The recent discovery of a piece of a slot machine dated 1898 confirms the lively and social nature of the town. People left when the mines closed in 1914, and little remains at the site of Knob, except a rock tower, mine remnants, and an abandoned house.

GPS COORDINATES: N40°23.32' W122°59.14'
NEAREST TRAIL: North Coast #11: Knob Peak Trail

Highgrade

The Highgrade Mining District, in the Warner Mountains northwest of Fort Bidwell on CR 2, was the site of Modoc County's most significant gold rush. A young sheepherder named Hoag discovered gold here in 1905. A settlement was named for him, and it boomed from 1905 to 1913. Northern Paiute once mined obsidian here for arrowheads, knives, and other tools. Hoag had a post office, restaurant, bar, and hotel. William Wrigley of chewing gum fame was an investor. The Highgrade district is still occasionally mined, but less than $100,000 in gold has been extracted. Ruins in the vicinity include a log cabin and a collapsed mill with several iron boilers left behind by the organization of miners called Klondyke Group. Farther down the road a roofless log cabin remains from the Lodge Pole Mining Claim.

GPS COORDINATES: N41°50.66' W122°35.03'
NEAREST TRAIL: North Coast #47: Highgrade Trail

Hoopa

The Hupa populated the Trinity River Valley long before the Spanish or other Europeans arrived in California. Nearly 1,000 Hupa lived peacefully in 13 villages along the Trinity River. Now the town of Hoopa, the Yurok name for Hupa, due north of Willow Creek in Humboldt County, is the largest town on the 93,000-acre Hoopa Valley Indian Reservation, established on August 12, 1864, when the Hupa and the U.S. government signed the Treaty of Peace and Friendship, which secured Hupa rights to nearly 90 percent of their ancestral land.

Although the tribe has successfully maintained its territory in the Trinity and Klamath River Valleys, people still struggle to maintain their cultural and spiritual heritage. In 1891, President William Henry Harrison joined the Hupa and Yurok reservations by signing an executive order, and soon after troops left the reservation. The U.S. government introduced schools, land titles, paved roads, and modern clothing, greatly influencing Hupa culture. In 1911, the tribe created the first modern Hupa Tribal Council, but it wasn't recognized until 1933 when a constitution was written. The reservation's economy picked up in the 1950s during a timber boom when seven sawmills flourished in the valley. Profits were distributed to individual tribal members. Logging continues on the reservation today only in restricted areas where trees are replanted. In 1988, Ronald Reagan signed a treaty that recognized the Hoopa Valley Reservation as a sovereign territory and ended the union of the Hupa and Yurok reservations. Hupa celebrate the event as Sovereign Day every year during the second week of August.

The Hoopa Valley Reservation is a 12-mile by 12-mile square with a tract in Humboldt County that extends northwest into Del Norte all the way to the coast, along the Klamath River corridor. The reservation currently has nearly 3,000 residents who maintain a delicate balance between their cultural identity and influences of the outside world. The Hoopa Valley Tribal Museum and ancient Indian villages preserve the tribe's rich history, dating back 10,000 years. Exhibits contain Hupa, Yurok, and Karuk artifacts, including tools, baskets, and ceremonial garments. The museum also conducts tours of the traditional village of Takimildiñ.

GPS COORDINATES: N41°03.18' W123°40.55'
NEAREST TRAIL: North Coast #17: Bald Hills Road

Independence

Charles Putman set up his trading post at this site in the Owens Valley in 1861. Two years later, Putman sold the store to Thomas Edwards, who completed platting a town site in 1866. Inyo County was formed that same year from parts of Mono and Tulare Counties, and Independence became the county seat.

Edwards named the town for the cavalry post north of the site that had been established July 4, 1862, during a period of Indian unrest. Lieutenant Colonel George S. Evans and troops of the Second Cavalry of the California Volunteers were to protect settlers from Indian raids and to act as a buffer against possible attacks by Confederate sympathizers in Arizona and Nevada. Camp Independence, later Fort Independence, survived until 1877 when its buildings were sold at auction. Before the fort was dismantled, the commanding officer's quarters, called the Commander's House, were moved from the post to the corner of Edwards and Main Streets. The site has been Fort Independence Indian Reservation since 1915.

When gold was discovered in the Inyo Mountains in 1862, Independence flourished as the supply center for the rich mining district. When the gold played out, many miners switched to agriculture. The Owens Valley was a thriving agricultural region until the 1900s when the Los Angeles Aqueduct project essentially dried up the Owens River. In 1917, local businessmen opened the Mount Whitney Fish Hatchery and specialized in propagating California's state fish, the golden trout. Its attractive buildings and spacious grounds continue to attract as many as 60,000 visitors a year. The hatchery is located 2 miles north of Independence off US 395.

During World War II, thousands of Japanese-Americans were interred just south of Independence at Manzanar, one of ten relocation centers in the western United States. Previously the site of a Paiute village and a settlement of American fruit growers, Manzanar is now a national historic site. More than 10,000 people of Japanese ancestry were housed at the 6,000-acre facility. Little remains today; a sign at the entrance reads, "May the injustices and humiliation suffered here as a result of hysteria, racism and economic exploitation never emerge again."

The Eastern California Museum in Independence displays

artifacts from Manzanar and other articles relating to the region's history. The Commander's House and Independence's oldest structure, the 1865 Edwards House, are also administered by the museum. In addition to these historical attractions, Independence is a gateway to the east side of the Sierra Nevada and Inyo National Forest. Other nearby attractions include the John Muir Wilderness and the Ancient Bristlecone Pine Forest.

GPS COORDINATES: N36°48.16' W118°11.92'

TRAIL: High Sierra #49: Mazourka Peak Trail

MAP: Page 286

Jackson

For centuries, the vicinity of present-day Jackson in Amador County was home to Miwok Indians, who collected acorns for food from the abundant oaks. Indian Grinding Rocks State Historic Park, northeast of town, preserves a large limestone outcropping with mortar holes used to grind acorns and seeds; the park also preserves petroglyphs. The Miwok lost their lands in the Mother Lode when the gold rush began.

The town of Jackson began at a spring used by passing miners who discarded bottles there. Mexican and Chilean miners, who arrived in 1848, named their camp Bottileas (Bottles). The camp was renamed the following year for Alden M. Jackson, a New England lawyer and respected resident, and by July 1851 Jackson's post office opened.

Overview of Jackson in its early days

The placer mines around Jackson were not especially rich by gold rush standards, but the camp grew quickly because of its convenient location on roads from Sacramento and Stockton (now California 88 and California 49) to the southern gold country mines. Prosperity arrived, however, when quartz mines, the Argonaut in 1850 and the Kennedy in 1856, began producing. Both mines operated intermittently until 1942. The Argonaut Mine yielded an estimated $25 million in gold. One shaft reached a staggering vertical depth of 5,570 feet. The mine was the site of California's deadliest mining disaster. In August 1922, a fire in the mine trapped 47 men. Frantic rescue efforts continued for more than a week, but the miners, when located, were all dead.

The Kennedy often operated at a substantial loss. At other times, it produced massive wealth, yielding, in 1949 prices, approximately $45 million worth of gold. Its deepest shafts reached a vertical depth of 5,912 feet and workings underground totaled about 150 miles. Two large tailing wheels dating from 1912 are still visible at the Kennedy Tailing Wheels Park just outside Jackson.

Jackson has many historic buildings from the 1850s and 1860s. Many of the earliest buildings burned in 1862 and were replaced by brick structures. The I.O.O.F. (Independent Order of Odd Fellows) Hall, one of the tallest three-story structures in the world, was built that year. Other remarkable buildings include the 1894 Serbian Orthodox Church, the mother church for the denomination in the United States, and the Amador County Museum, another nineteenth-century structure. Jackson was also once the site of the only Jewish synagogue in the Mother Lode. A plaque at the corner of Church and North Streets marks the spot where the building once stood. Another marker celebrates a salubrious, if not delayed, claim to fame for Jackson—it was the last city in California to make prostitution illegal.

Initially, Jackson was in Calaveras County and served as that county's second seat of government after residents orchestrated a switch from Double Springs (now a ghost town) in July 1851. Several men from Jackson roughed up the county clerk at a tavern in Double Springs while others went to the courthouse, took the county archives, and hurried them back to Jackson. Mokelume Hill beat Jackson in an election for the county seat in April 1852, but Jackson was chosen as the county seat of Amador County when the jurisdiction was created in 1854 from parts of Calaveras County.

GPS COORDINATES: N38°20.80' W120°41.82'

NEAREST TRAIL: Northern Sierra #9: Calaveras Dome Trail

Johnsville

Johnsville, once the company town of the Plumas-Eureka Mine, is now on the edges of the Plumas Eureka State Park, about 5 miles west of Grangeville in Plumas County. Placer mining in the area began on Jamison Creek in the spring of 1851. Prospectors who explored the creek upstream found rich veins of gold, and 36 men involved in the enterprise formed the Eureka Company, California's first mining corporation. Initially, they worked their claim with arrastras and chili wheels, crude but efficient small-scale tools used to break up gold-bearing rock. By 1856, the operation was sufficiently profitable to build a 12-stamp mill. Other mines sprang up in the area—the Mammoth, Washington, and Rough-and-Ready. The principal settlement for the region was the hamlet of Jamison Creek.

Immigrants from many countries, including Switzerland and Austria, prospected in the district, and some brought snowshoes and skis with them as well as a long tradition of getting around in the snowy Alps in winter. A few of these prospectors organized a ski race near La Porte, perhaps the first in North America. In 1872, the Sierra Buttes Gold Mining Company, Limited, of London purchased all of the mining operations in the area, consolidated their operations, and introduced modern technology to the workings. The result was a highly successful enterprise—the Plumas-Eureka Mine.

Johnsville was laid out as the company town in 1876 and named after William Johns, the mine's manager. Originally called Johnstown, the name was changed to Johnsville in 1882, the year the post office opened. Operations at the Plumas-Eureka continued profitably until the early 1890s. When mines became less profitable, the London company sold off individual claims. Some of these were worked into the 1940s.

The Plumas Eureka State Park, established in 1959, incorporates much of the area of old mines and has an impressive collection of old wagons and mining equipment. The park's headquarters and museum are located in a renovated mining-era boardinghouse just outside Johnsville. An imposing 48-stamp mill is currently being restored within the park.

Johnsville today is a somnolent mountain village. Heavy annual snows weather its buildings. Most buildings, including the 1908 Johnsville Hotel, are now private residences. Nevertheless, the town remains one of the best-preserved wooden mining camps in the Mother Lode, having escaped the devastating fires that destroyed other settlements.

GPS COORDINATES: N39°45.42' W120°41.82'
TRAIL: Northern Sierra #29: Gold Valley Trail
MAP: Page 398

Klamath

Klamath, a Del Norte County village with a population of about 200, is near the coast, where a bridge on US 101 spans the Klamath River. Two bear statues on the bridge were originally painted gray by the state, but locals repainted them gold. The state restored the gray color, but soon after the bears would sport a fresh coat of shiny gold paint. Finally, after a decade or so, the state accepted the bears' gold color. Initially, Klamath was a fishing village that began in the late 1800s. Another village, Klamath City, was several miles nearer the mouth of the river, but survived only a year after its start in 1851 as a mining supply port.

Yurok Indians lived on the lower Klamath River, and the U.S. Army established an armed presence at Fort Ter-Wer in October 1857. The fort was abandoned in 1862; its site is on California 169 east of Klamath. To the east, north, and south of Klamath is Redwood National Forest, excellent for backcountry activities. An attraction near California 169 outside Klamath allows visitors to drive through a living 700-year-old redwood. Strangely formed redwoods can be seen at the Trees of Mystery Park, 4 miles north of Klamath.

GPS COORDINATES: N41°31.59' W124°02.23'
NEAREST TRAIL: North Coast #15: Redwood National Park Coastal Trail

La Porte

Placer mining began along Rabbit Creek, a tributary of the Slate River, in 1850. Prospectors called a camp on the stream Rabbit Creek. Its name changed to Rabbit Town when a post office opened in 1855. Two years later, it became La Porte, after the Indiana hometown of Frank Everts, a local banker.

La Porte claims to be near the site of the first organized ski competition in the Western Hemisphere (and perhaps the world). Frequent races were held starting in the 1860s. The town was the birthplace of Lotta Crabtree. She and her family moved to Grass Valley, and Lotta became an acclaimed child performer under the tutelage of Lola Montez. La Porte boomed in the 1860s and 1870s as a commercial center for the 50 hydraulic mining sites in operation by 1857. The region yielded perhaps $93 million worth of gold, but the fortunes of La Porte faded when the Anti-Debris Act of 1884 was enacted to curtail hydraulic mining.

Postcard of La Porte, circa 1859

Today, La Porte is a quiet Mother Lode village. The Union Hotel began serving customers in 1855, and the present building dates from 1905. Stone ruins near the hotel remain from an old general store, once used as Wells Fargo offices. Other historic towns on the road from Oroville to La Porte include Strawberry Valley, Woodleaf, and Forbestown.

GPS COORDINATES: N39°41.00' W120°59.14'
TRAIL: Northern Sierra #30: Poker Flat OHV Trail
MAP: Page 405

Lee Vining

Lee Vining overlooks Mono Lake and is on U.S. 395 at the turnoff for the Tioga Pass entrance to Yosemite National Park. It is named for Leroy Vining, a prospector who moved from Indiana to California in 1852. Vining scoured the Mono Basin in search of gold but was generally unsuccessful. He settled along the creek that now bears his name and built a lumber mill. Vining's mill proved very profitable when nearby Bodie began to boom after the big gold strikes of 1877.

Swiss settlers populated Lee Vining in the early 1900s. By 1925 it had a school, and by 1928 a post office. For many years the town was too small to support a high school, and students had to go to Bodie. Several buildings in Lee Vining date from the 1930s, when the town was a camp for workers on the Los Angeles Aqueduct, which changed the nature of the lake. The Mono Basin National Forest Scenic Area is headquartered in Lee Vining, and many lakefront hotels offer accommodation. The Tioga Lodge is a particularly attractive resort.

GPS COORDINATES: N37°57.45' W119°07.15'
NEAREST TRAIL: High Sierra #31: Bodie Ghost Town Trail

Lewiston

Named for B. F. Lewis, the town of Lewiston started in 1853. One of the first in Trinity County, the Lewiston Post Office was established on May 24, 1854. The town's founder operated a ferry until 1901, when a one-lane bridge was constructed on the site. The bridge is one of the last of its kind operating in the state. Stages stopped at the Lewiston Hotel during the days of gold mining, and it still caters to residents and visitors today.

It is estimated that 10,000 miners worked the Brown Bear Mine in Deadwood, just 7 miles east of town. One of the many mines rumored to have been robbed by Black Bart, the mine saw activity as late as 1974. Remains at the ghost town of Deadwood include an old stamp mill, bunkhouse, dining hall, school house, supply store, smelting shack, tailings pile, and stables. The tracks of the ore carts lead to the mine, which has since filled with water.

The buildings of the National Historic Gold Mining town of Lewiston, 34 miles west of Redding off California 299, stretch along the Trinity River, where the historic Lewiston Hotel and charming antique store, Country Peddler, welcome visitors. The tourism and timber industries support the town's 1,300 residents.

The damming of the Trinity River in 1950 created Lewiston and Trinity Lakes, which attract hikers, bikers, boaters, and anglers. Wildlife thrives in and around Trinity Lake, the state's third largest, from bald eagles to hummingbirds and gray foxes to otters. Populated with salmon and trout, the Trinity River sees numerous fly fisherman and adventurous rafters during the summer. The 120-mile Trinity Heritage National Scenic Byway climbs 4,500 feet as it winds through the county from Weaverville to Mount Shasta along an early wagon route.

GPS COORDINATES: N40°45.12' W122°48.56'
TRAIL: North Coast #24: Deadwood Road
MAP: Page 554

Lone Pine

The Inyo County town of Lone Pine was settled in the 1860s as a supply point for miners. Its first cabin was built in 1862, and a post office was established in 1870. When mining slowed at Cerro Gordo and Darwin, Lone Pine catered to farmers and ranchers. Lone Pine was named for a solitary pine tree that grew at the entrance to Lone Pine Canyon, until felled by a storm in 1876.

The beautiful Alabama Hills, just west of Lone Pine, were discovered by Hollywood in the 1920s. Many Westerns and war movies have been filmed here, with the hills as a backdrop. TV shows, feature films, and commercials continue to be filmed in the vicinity. It is not uncommon to see camera crews in Lone Pine, capturing the ambience of a typical western town. Movie stars stayed at the Lone Pine Hotel while making movies, and an annual film festival pays homage to the movie industry's history in the area.

Lone Pine ruins after the earthquake of 1872

Lone Pine's biggest attraction is its backcountry. Within a two-hour drive one can reach the base of Mount Whitney, the highest point in the continental United States (14,496 feet above sea level), or the lowest point, Badwater Basin (246 feet below sea level) in Death Valley National Park. Each March there is a 100-mile bike race over two days from Stovepipe Wells in Death Valley to the Mount Whitney trailhead. The overnight stop is in Lone Pine.

The hundreds of dirt roads through Owens Valley make the area perfect for backcountry driving. Anglers also enjoy the region, which is well known for its trout fishing, some of the best in the eastern Sierra. Fishing season begins the first Saturday in March, earlier than in most areas.

Lone Pine has no municipal government, but the town's Chamber of Commerce organizes community events and promotes the surrounding area. The chamber occupies the old Lone Pine Hotel, completed in 1918. Lone Pine's population was 2,257 in 2000.

GPS COORDINATES: N36°36.30' W118°03.71'
NEAREST TRAIL: High Sierra #49: Mazourka Peak Trail

Mammoth Lakes

The resort of Mammoth Lakes takes its name from the Mammoth Lode, a rich gold strike made in 1877, and mined by the Mammoth Mining Company, organized June 3, 1878. Several settlements arose around the claim, and Mammoth City, with a population of 2,500 and a 12-stamp mill, was the largest. The heyday lasted only three years, ending in 1881. The town, at an elevation of 9,000 feet, was one of California's highest settlements. Little remains of Mammoth City today, just a few sunken foundations and stone ruins. Nearby Mill City and Pine City are likewise deserted. Remains of the 1927 Mammoth Consolidated Mine are somewhat more extensive.

In the 1930s, ski enthusiasts began to set up rope tows on Mammoth Mountain. The first permanent tow was installed after World War II and the first chairlift in 1955. Dave McGee, an accomplished ski racer and skiing enthusiast, was instrumental in guiding Mammoth Mountain's growth as a major ski area. Today, the mountain has more than 30 lifts and 2 gondolas. In the summer, visitors can bike extensive trails on the mountain. Mammoth Lakes serves as a resort town for year-round tourists.

Even before skiing became popular, the Mammoth area was drawing outdoorsmen. The first highway to the area was completed in 1937, and soon hotels and summer cabins dotted the banks of Mammoth Creek. Fishing, hunting, hiking, camping, and horseback riding are all popular in the region on the east side of the Sierra and within easy reach of Devils Postpile National Monument and national forests.

GPS COORDINATES: N37°38.09' W118°57.97'
TRAIL: High Sierra #37: Deer Mountain Trail; High Sierra #38: Laurel Lakes Trail
MAP: Page 254

Mariposa

Mariposa means "butterfly" in Spanish. Padre Pedro Muñoz, who accompanied Gabriel Moraga's 1806 expedition from San Juan Bautista into the San Joaquin Valley, used the name for a stream, perhaps Mariposa Creek. In 1844, Mexican authorities gave Juan B. Alvarado a land grant called Rancho Las Mariposas. John C. Frémont acquired the ranch in 1847 for just $3,200. The original grant had prescribed the ranch's area but not its specific borders, so after gold was discovered in the area Frémont moved his ranch several miles to the north to ensure that his holdings included the mountainous mining region. A lengthy court battle ensued, but ended in victory for Frémont. For several years afterwards, he operated profitable mining operations in the hills.

Mariposa County was one of California's original 27 counties. In 1850, the jurisdiction covered 30,000 square miles, one-fifth of the state, with boundaries stretching as far as Los Angeles County. Between 1850 and 1880, ten present-day counties were formed from its area. Today, the county covers just 1,455 square miles. Agua Fria, now a ghost town, was the first county seat. The town of Mariposa succeeded its fading neighbor in September 1851. Mariposa was founded in 1849 on John Frémont's ranch after gold was discovered on Mariposa Creek. The richest area claim was the Mariposa Mine, established in 1849 by Alex Goody and Kit Carson. The mine remained in operation until well into the twentieth century. The Princeton Mine, located to the north of Mariposa, produced more than $4 million in gold.

Much remains from Mariposa's mining days. The Mariposa County Historical Center has an eclectic collection of artifacts including Native American art, mining objects, and furniture once owned by the Frémont family. The California State Mining and Mineral Museum is south of town and has impressive holdings of rocks, gems, minerals, and fossils. The museum also features a 150-foot-long mine tunnel and other gold-related exhibits. The Mariposa County Courthouse, built in 1854, is the oldest continually used courthouse in California, and its tower clock has been running since 1866. The Trabucco Warehouse and Store, I.O.O.F. Hall, Schlageter Hotel, Jones house, Counts house, St. Joseph's Catholic Church, and an old stone jail building on Jones Street all date from the 1850s or 1860s.

Overview of Mariposa, circa 1908

The Chamber of Commerce building on Jones and Ninth Streets is the original home of the *Mariposa Gazette*. The weekly newspaper claims not to have missed an issue since January 10, 1854.

Mariposa is at the intersection of California 49 and California 140. California 140, also known as the All-Year Highway, winds into the Sierra along the Merced River and is the principal route to the El Portal entrance to Yosemite National Park. The route passes a number of historical sites and is a good starting point for a number of High Sierra trails. California 49, the Mother Lode Highway, meanders north through the Sierra Nevada gold country from Madera County in the south to Plumas County in the north. Until 1969, Mariposa was the southern terminus of the Mother Lode Highway, but the famous route now continues to Oakhurst.

GPS COORDINATES: N37°29.24' W119°58.02'

NEAREST TRAIL: High Sierra #24: Ferguson Ridge Trail

Marysville

John Sutter received a Mexican land grant in 1841 that encompassed a large portion of Central California in the vicinity of present-day Sacramento. Sutter owned the mill where gold was discovered in January 1848, sparking the gold rush. The grant was larger than Mexican law allowed, so Sutter leased portions of it to other settlers. In 1842, a Prussian immigrant named Theodore Cordua leased the area around present-day Marysville, where the Yuba and Feather Rivers meet. Cordua operated a ranch on this land and built an adobe house, with a trading room, at what is now the foot of D Street in Marysville. Cordua called his ranch Honcut, for a Maidu village, but others referred to it as New Mecklenburg (after Cordua's birthplace) or Cordua's Rancho. He hoped to attract more German settlers to the vicinity.

In 1848, Frenchman Charles Covillaud purchased a half-share in Cordua's ranch. By the following year, he controlled the entire ranch and sold quarter shares to José Ramirez, John Sampson, and Theodore Sicard. Covillaud and Company convinced John Sutter to sell the ranch outright. In the winter of 1849–50, the men commissioned French surveyor Auguste Le Plongeon to plat a town. The settlement was to be named Yubaville, but it may have been confused with nearby Yuba City. Other possible names included Sicardoro, Circumdoro, and Norwich. In January 1850, settlers agreed to call the new town Marysville after Mary Murphy Covillaud, a survivor of the ill-fated 1846 Donner Party and wife of a leading landowner. Marysville became the seat of government for Yuba County, one of the original 27 counties, when it was organized later that year.

Marysville became an important commercial center for the northern mines of the Mother Lode, principally because it was head of navigation on the Feather River. Very quickly trails and roads into the Mother Lode were crowded with pack trains, wagons, and stagecoaches from Marysville. The wealth of the gold mines passing through the town enabled the settlement to grow exponentially in the early years. In 1857 alone, $10 million worth of gold passed through the town.

Several buildings remain from the 1850s. The Bok Kai Temple, on Front Street, is one of the oldest Chinese tem-

Marysville, during the flood of 1867

ples in the United States, and it is the only temple in the nation celebrating the water god Bok Kai. The building once overlooked the Feather River, but the view is now obstructed by a levee. Another historic building, known as The Castle, is at 220 Fifth Street. The elaborate structure was once the residence of town founder José Ramirez and later occupied by W. T. Ellis, creator of Marysville's levee system and namesake of Ellis Lake in the center of town. The Mary Aaron Memorial Museum at 704 D Street is in a building constructed in 1856. Despite the scattering of historic buildings, most of the structures in Marysville date from the latter half of the twentieth century.

Marysville has a number of arches initially part of the town's electric trolley system built along D Street in 1911. The arches were dismantled in 1925; however, one arch survives on Rio Linda Boulevard. In the 1990s, Marysville decided to reconstruct the arches, and the first of these was completed in April 1996 at the intersection of Fifth and D Streets.

At one time, Marysville residents could watch boats and side-wheelers on the Feather River from Front Street. However, sediments washed down from hydraulic mining that began in the 1860s raised the beds of the Feather and Yuba Rivers. The sediments ended navigation on the Feather to Marysville and led to periodic flooding, necessitating the construction of levees. W. T. Ellis directed the levee construction, and the dredging of Ellis Lake was begun in 1924. The lake, on the site of a slough, was finished in 1939; funds and labor were provided by the New Deal's Works Progress Administration.

Yuba City, the seat of Sutter County, is across the Feather River from Beale Air Force Base, southeast of Marysville. The base is on the site of Camp Beale, organized in 1942 to hold German prisoners of war during World War II. Camp Beale was named after Edward F. Beale, who figured prominently in California's history during the war with Mexico. The Edward F. Beale Museum on the air force base houses a military history collection from the 13th Armored Division, which was stationed there, ready to ship out to Japan when the war ended, and the 100th and 9th Bomb Groups.

GPS COORDINATES: N39°08.63' W121°34.93'

NEAREST TRAIL: Northern Sierra #32: Forbestown to Feather Falls Trail

Masonic

Masonic, now a ghost town in Mono County, was founded when members of a Masonic lodge mined on what they called Masonic Mountain in 1862. The ore produced was not particularly high quality; most miners moved to richer goldfields, notably at Aurora, just across the state line in Nevada. Some hardy prospectors continued to work their Masonic claims, and others returned when the gold played out elsewhere.

The first big strike came on July 4, 1902. J. S. Phillips, one of the discoverers, named his claim the Pittsburg-Liberty, to celebrate his hometown and the date of discovery. Between 1902 and 1910, the Pittsburg-Liberty produced about $700,000 worth of gold, most of it during its last few years of existence.

By 1906, Masonic was a sprawling conglomeration of three settlements in the high desert—Upper Town, Middle Town, and Lower Town—about half a mile apart along the road on the north slope of Masonic Mountain. The three clusters boasted a combined population of about 500 and had a post office, a hotel, several general stores, and a newspaper—*The Masonic Pioneer*—but no Masonic lodge.

Mining continued in Masonic until the 1920s, but the town dwindled after the Pittsburg-Liberty closed in 1910. Remains of the Pittsburg-Liberty Mill and Cyanide Plant, with foundations dug into the mountainside, are Masonic's most prominent landmarks today. Other features of the ghost town include a few log cabins, one stone house, and some rubble.

GPS COORDINATES: N38°22.00' W119°07.07'

TRAIL: High Sierra #32: Masonic Trail

MAP: Page 240

McCloud

Hudson's Bay Company explorers, led by Alexander Roderick McLeod, originally scouted the river valley to the south of Mount Shasta in 1829. No significant settlement existed at present-day McCloud, 9 miles east of Interstate 5 on California 89, until 1829 when A. F. Friday George built a lumber mill, which quickly failed because of the difficulty of transporting lumber. In 1897, William VanArsdale and George W. Scott established the mill town of McCloud by creating the McCloud River Railroad Company. The railroad solved the lumber transportation problem and guaranteed the success of the McCloud River Lumber Company.

The lumber company established a dairy, a hospital, and power plant (among other institutions) for its workers. Known as "Mother McCloud," the mill provided heating and electricity for residents' homes. One third-generation native recalled that when a light bulb burned out or a faucet leaked, "you'd just call Mother McCloud and a crew would be over to fix it for you."

The situation changed in 1963 when U.S. Plywood bought the lumber company and began to privatize the lumber-dependent town. Utilities, fire and police protection, library services, and road maintenance were turned over to the McCloud Community Services District, and houses were sold to their residents. In the early years of privatization, the wealthy and famous, including Jean Harlow, Herbert Hoover, and the Hearst family, reportedly retreated to McCloud. Although the new lumber company attempted to provide a secure economic future for the city, new requirements placed on the diminishing logging industry caused the gradual erosion of the economy. In 1979, the mill closed and

Lumbermen from the McCloud River Lumber Company cutting logs

the railroad faced adversity as well. In 1980, the economy turned around when P&M Cedar Products reopened a state-of-the-art mill to supply custom-home builders and home supply centers across the nation with premium lumber products. Today the P&M McCloud mill employs more than 150 residents and works with local land management companies as a steward of the region's forests.

McCloud experienced a resurgence of tourism and, in 1990, the downtown square was established as a nationally registered historic district. Visitors enjoy the quaint district's turn-of-the-century architecture and other original buildings, such as the McCloud River Inn and the McCloud Hotel, which have both been restored and reopened. Although the McCloud Railway is still a commercial freight line, the Shasta Sunset Dinner and Excursion Trains cater to passengers. Preserving McCloud's history, the Heritage Junction Museum exhibits a century's worth of artifacts and photographs.

Recreation areas include McCloud River, McCloud Lake, and Mount Shasta Ski Park. The river has world-class trout fishing and three impressive waterfalls with short hikes, swimming areas, and campsites nearby. The ski park provides year-round recreation; downhill skiing, cross-country skiing, snowboarding, and sledding are popular in the winter, and mountain biking, hiking, and rock climbing in the summer.

GPS COORDINATES: N41°15.19' W112°08.47'

NEAREST TRAIL: North Coast #33: Mount Shasta Loop

Modesto

Modesto is the closest big city to the geographical center of California. It was founded in 1870 as a stop on the Southern Pacific Railroad. The railroad intended to name the station Ralston after William C. Ralston, a San Francisco banker and director of the Central Pacific. When the financier declined the honor, his modesty (*modesto* in Spanish) was recognized instead. Modesto is in the San Joaquin Valley, on the banks of the Tuolumne River. The railroad gave it an edge over other towns and Modesto became the major commercial center for Stanislaus County, much of which is in the Sierra above the valley. In 1871, it became the county seat, the fifth and final town to receive that honor.

When trains first rolled into Modesto on November 8, 1870, the settlement consisted of 25 buildings, many of them hastily transferred from elsewhere. When the county government began its duties in town, its offices were dispersed in boardinghouses and the back rooms of stores.

In its early days, Modesto had a reputation as a "Wild West" town, and vigilantism was a common form of law enforcement. Gradually, though, the rich trade in agricultural produce fueled by the railroad stabilized the town. By the early 1900s, Modesto supported a population in excess of 3,000. Farms spread across the surrounding region, and Modesto itself was often called "Garden City" or "Rose City," for its beautiful rose bushes and manicured gardens. The city's most famous landmark—the Modesto Arch was completed in 1912. The arch spans 75 feet across I Street at the intersection of 9th Street and is 25 feet high. The Modesto Business Men's Association commissioned the arch and had a contest to determine the slogan to be emblazoned with electric lights on the iron monument. One suggestion that was almost inadvisably chosen was "Nobody's Got Modesto's Goat." Sam Harbaugh, however, received $3 for the winning slogan: "Modesto: Water, Wealth, Contentment, Health," now the town's motto.

Modesto grew steadily through the twentieth century. In addition to its agricultural base, canning, packing plants, wineries, stores, and factories fueled this expansion. Its population in 2000 was 188,856, more than three times that of 1970. Modesto is on California 99, one of the state's major north-south highways, where it intersects California 132 and California 108. Modesto is on routes to the gold country and Yosemite National Park. Residents include the wine-making visionaries Ernest and Julio Gallo, Olympian Mark Spitz, and

Modesto, circa 1910

Star Wars director George Lucas. Lucas set and filmed his breakthrough movie *American Graffiti* in Modesto.

GPS COORDINATES: N37°40.11' W120°57.40'

NEAREST TRAIL: High Sierra #28: Old Coulterville Road

Mono Mills

In the 1870s, the booming Mono County town of Bodie was producing massive amounts of gold ore but faced a dire lumber shortage. For years, Chinese immigrants, deterred from mining, had collected wood from surrounding mountains to fuel and build the burgeoning settlement. However, timber found near Bodie was inferior and was soon short in supply.

With Bodie using 45,000 cords of wood each year as fuel for stamp mills, lumber for buildings, and timbers as mine supports, an alternative source was essential. A planned community and mill was constructed south of Mono Lake in the heart of good timber forests. Trees were milled at Mono Mills, then freighted to Bodie. However, it was extremely expensive to freight timber over the mountains.

In 1881, construction began on an ambitious railroad project to connect Bodie to Mono Mills and eventually to other railroad lines. The Bodie & Benton Railway began operating from Bodie to Mono Mills in November 1882, but by that time Bodie's halcyon days were numbered. Mono Mills might have survived as a supplier of lumber to other areas, but the track was never laid. The town's fortunes were inextricably tied to Bodie's. Service continued intermittently along the Bodie & Benton until 1917, but Mono Mills was never more than a tiny lumber camp. In the twentieth century, the elements and excavators ravaged Mono Mills. Today, little remains of the camp that enabled Bodie to thrive—some timbers, a few stone blocks, a concrete foundation, and a lonely historical marker.

GPS COORDINATES: N37°40.02' W118°57.58'
TRAIL: High Sierra #34: Mono Craters Trail
MAP: Page 245

Monoville

Before the mid-1850s, there were no settlements on the east ern side of the Sierra Nevada in the Great Basin region in California. In 1857, Mormons began mining along Dog Creek, calling their camp Dogtown. The placer mines attracted miners from the overworked Mother Lode in the Sierra. In July 1859, a prospector named Cord Nost made a rich strike several miles from Dogtown, attracting even more miners. At first, the area was known as Mono Diggings. Soon there was a bustling town of 700 residents called Monoville, for nearby Mono Lake.

Monoville's population was large enough in 1863 for the town to be a candidate for the Mono County seat after citizens realized that Aurora, county seat since 1861, was in Nevada rather than California. Bridgeport won out, and by 1864, Monoville was in decline; its post office had been discontinued in 1862. By 1870, the town was mostly deserted. Little remains today of Monoville except the Sinnamon Cut, a hydraulic mining venture operated by James Sinnamon. Using water diverted from Virginia Creek, Sinnamon extracted more than $90,000 worth of gold from the cut and left a scar on the landscape that is still evident.

GPS COORDINATES: N38°05.77' W119°08.78'
NEAREST TRAIL: High Sierra #31: Bodie Ghost Town Trail

Mount Shasta

Originally, the vicinity southwest of the snowcapped Mount Shasta was called Strawberry Valley. Today's city of Mount Shasta is on Interstate 5 surrounded by the Shasta-Trinity National Forests, 60 miles north of Redding. The first post office was established in 1870, when the town was named Berryvale; it became Sisson in 1888, to honor John H. Sisson, who donated some of his property to re-establish the city along the Central Pacific's new railroad near Berryvale. It became Mount Shasta City in 1924.

The towns neighboring Sisson along the railway were company-owned and restricted drinking and other leisure activities in order to increase productivity in the lumber mills. The residents of those towns were mainly men away from home and family from spring until winter snows prevented logging. They often visited Sisson on weekends to take advantage of independent establishments along Whiskey Row; Sisson had one bar for every 40 residents during the lumber industry's heyday. Little remains of the original town because it burned down several times. In 1922 residents voted to change the town's name to Mount Shasta, and with the state's lumber industry in decline, the town has become a tourism center.

Visitors from all over the world come to Mount Shasta. Mountaineers approach the mountain by the Everitt Memorial Highway, which begins in Mount Shasta and dead-ends just past Burney Flats at the former Mount Shasta Ski Bowl at 6,900 feet. Not far from the Bunny Flat trailhead is Horse Camp, an old Sierra Club lodge that serves as a base camp for many climbers attempting the peak. The most popular of the 17 routes to the 14,162-foot summit is Avalanche Gulch. For those interested in hikes that do not involve crampons and ice axes, Black Butte offers a 2.5-mile trail that climbs nearly 2,000 feet to its summit at 6,325 feet. The trailhead is located a short distance off Everitt Memorial Highway, south of the Shasta Valley on Interstate 5. Challenging backpacking segments of the Pacific Crest Trail can be accessed from Parks Creek, South Fork Road, Whalen Road, and Castle Crags State Park. The Mount Shasta Ranger District (530-926-4511) supplies wilderness permits and maps.

The headwaters of the Sacramento River are in Mount Shasta City Park where icy spring waters that originate deep inside Mount Shasta surface from a lava tube and flow into Cold Creek. The creek is the northernmost feeder of the Sacramento River, which meanders about 320 miles south, ultimately reaching Suisun Bay, an extension of San Francisco Bay. There are stunning views of the Sacramento River Canyon, Lake Siskiyou, and Mount Shasta at Box Canyon Dam on W. A. Barr Road from Old Stage Road, west of Interstate 5. Water sports include boating, fishing, swimming, kayaking, canoeing, and windsurfing on Lake Siskiyou in summer months. Spelunkers also come to the region to explore caves at Lava Beds National Monument, the Medicine Lake complex, and Pluto Caves.

Trout fishing is good in the Sacramento and McCloud Rivers. The Mount Shasta Fish Hatchery, the oldest and first successful hatchery in California, is open to the public free of charge. The hatchery produces 3 to 5 million rainbow and brown trout fingerlings for release in nearby rivers as well as other Northern California streams, rivers, and lakes. The Sisson Hatchery Museum (open daily March through December and free to the public) is on the grounds of the hatchery off Interstate 5 at the Old Stage Road exit. Its exhibits feature Mount Shasta's lively local as well as natural history. In the winter Mount Shasta Ski Park offers 21 ski runs for downhill

skiing and snowboarding, 25 kilometers of groomed cross-country ski trails, a ski school, equipment rentals, and a lodge. Summer ski park attractions include mountain biking, scenic chairlift rides, and concerts.
GPS COORDINATES: N41°18.78' W112°18.57'
TRAIL: North Coast #33: Mount Shasta Loop
MAP: Page 578

Napa

Napa Valley was the ancestral home of the Wappo Indians, and the word Napa may have been the name of a Wappo village. A Spanish party passed through the vicinity in 1823 while looking for a suitable place to establish a mission and found it to be densely populated by Indians. The Napa River flows through the valley to San Pablo Bay. Mexican soldier Nicolas Higuera obtained the Rancho Entre Napa grant in 1836. Part of the region also belonged to Salvador Vallejo, and in 1848 Nathan Coombs, who had moved to California from Massachusetts, bought land from Vallejo. That year, Coombs proceeded to plat a town called Napa.

Napa grew tremendously in the early years of the gold rush; many miners from the Mother Lode country in the Sierra spent winters in the Napa Valley. Some stayed to work on ranches or in the growing lumber business or just to spend their earnings from mining. Lumber from Napa's sawmills provided wood used to build San Francisco. Napa County was organized as one of the state's original 27 counties in 1850, and Napa became its seat. By the mid-1850s, Napa was a bustling city; its streets, hotels, and saloons were consistently crowded, and it even boasted an opera house. Silver was discovered in Napa Valley in 1858, creating a small-scale mining rush. During the 1860s, quicksilver (mercury) mining also boosted the economy. Robert Louis Stevenson and Fanny Osbourne, his American-born wife, spent a summer near the Silverado Mine on Mount St. Helena. Stevenson wrote *The Silverado Squatters* (1883), based on his experiences there.

Hotel Alexandria, Napa

Napa is the commercial and governmental center of Napa Valley, and two industries dominate the valley: wine and wine tourism. Vineyards had been planted elsewhere in Alta California, and Charles Krug produced wine in Napa in 1859. It was evident that the region had an ideal climate and soil for grape production. Recent decades have seen a substantial growth in the demand for California wines and particularly those of the Napa Valley. Many excellent wineries dot the valley and make some of the world's best wine. Robert Mondavi, owner of a major vineyard, supported recent redevelopment of Napa's downtown district and its opera house, built in 1880. Mondavi was also instrumental in the creation of the American Center for Wine, Food, and the Arts, which is on First Street.
GPS COORDINATES: N38°16.91' W122°17.94'
NEAREST TRAIL: Northern Sierra #14: Slate Mountain Trail

Nevada City

One of the earliest of the northern Mother Lode towns, Nevada City is named for the majestic mountains surrounding it, not the state to the east. A prospector named Hunt established a camp known as Deer Creek Dry Diggings in 1849. The site was later known as Caldwell's Upper Store, after a business operated by Dr. A. B. Caldwell, to distinguish it from Caldwell's second store, 7 miles downstream on Deer Creek. A settlement at the northwestern end of present-day Nevada City, called Coyoteville, was established in early 1850. "Coyoteing" was a mining method that involved digging small shafts to extract pay dirt from deep within ancient riverbeds. Nevada City's Coyote Street also alludes to the practice.

Nevada City Courthouse, circa 1868

The city of Nevada was incorporated in March 1851. When Nevada County was organized from parts of Yuba County the next month, Nevada, with "City" informally added to distinguish it from the county, became the county seat. The area around Nevada City was extremely rich in gold; in just two years, $8 million was taken from the Coyoteville settlement alone. Even the streets of Nevada City were dug up in search of gold. An oft-recounted tale tells of a store merchant who confronted a miner digging in the middle of the street. The miner countered that there was no law preventing him from doing so. "Then I'll make a law," retorted the merchant, pulling out his revolver, thus bringing the practice to an abrupt halt.

The South Yuba Canal Building dates from 1855. It was used as a general store and as the headquarters for the first company to supply water for hydraulic mining. The Miner's Foundry, opened in 1856, now houses a museum and a winery. The first Pelton wheel was cast at the foundry in 1878. The Nevada Theatre, built in 1865, is the oldest theater building in the state.

Nevada City suffered a series of devastating fires in its early days. Residents formed several fire companies after a fire in 1856. The Museum of the Nevada County Historical Society is now housed in Firehouse Number One, built on Main Street in 1861. Firehouse Number Two, also constructed in 1861, still stands on Broad Street.

Nevada City was home to several Californian celebrities. The playwright Richard Walton Tully was born there in 1877. Acclaimed opera singer Emma Nevada was so enamored by her birthplace that she changed her surname from Wixom to commemorate it. Nevada City retains much of its historic charm, even though a freeway divided the downtown in 1960. Citizens were outraged, but "progress" prevailed when the stretch of California 49 through the middle of town was widened.

GPS COORDINATES: N39°15.74' W121°00.92'

TRAIL: Northern Sierra #25: North Bloomfield to Bowman Lake Trail

MAP: Page 384

New Almaden

New Almaden is the site of the oldest mine and mining town in California. Andrés Castillero located mercury, or quicksilver, deposits there in 1845. The Ohlone Indians had known about the site before and had used the reddish cinnabar, a form of mercury sulfide, for war paint and other decorations.

At first the mine was worked for gold and silver, but mercury soon became the most important content. The gold rush increased the need for quicksilver because it was used in smelting gold and silver ore. Forty-niners had reason to be thankful for the mercury discoveries in California; without them, smelters would have had to rely on foreign quicksilver deposits. The mine was originally known as the Santa Clara, but by 1848 the mine and the surrounding camp was called New Almaden, for the Almadén, a rich mercury mine in Spain whose deposits are still not depleted despite being worked for more than 2,000 years.

Today, New Almaden has an excellent mining museum in a two-story brick mansion built in 1854. The mansion was once the home of the New Almaden Mine manager. At the museum, visitors can pick up a brochure for a walking tour through town. Sites include many structures from the 1860s, St. Anthony's Church from 1899, several mining shafts, and some old cemeteries.

GPS COORDINATES: N37°10.66' W121°48.99'

NEAREST TRAIL: Northern Sierra #2: Lumsden Bridge Road

New Almaden, circa 1879

North Bloomfield

The virtually deserted town of North Bloomfield is within the boundaries of Malakoff Diggins State Historic Park, northeast of Nevada City. Three prospectors first discovered gold near Humbug Creek in 1851. By 1853, the hamlet of Humbug had sprung up along the creek. When Humbug's population merited a post office in 1857, residents decided to change the image of their town with a new name. They voted June 1, 1857, and chose Bloomfield. The post office added "North" to the name to distinguish it from a Sonoma County settlement of the same name.

North Bloomfield hotel

Before long, North Bloomfield had some 1,700 residents, eight saloons, five hotels, two breweries, two churches, a daily freight service, and a variety of other services. The Malakoff Mine was North Bloomfield's economic base, and it used hydraulic mining to extract gold. Entire hillsides were blasted away with high-pressure streams of water, turning dirt and rock into muddy, debris-filled streams that were directed through sluices, which caught the gold. The rest of the mud was carried through an 8,000-foot tunnel and dumped into the South Yuba River. Operated by the North Bloomfield Gravel Mining Company, the Malakoff Mine was the largest hydraulic mining operation in the world. Its gigantic operation created a huge canyon, which can now be seen in the Malakoff Diggins State Historic Park.

In order to manage its operations, the North Bloomfield Gravel Mining Company aided in the construction of the world's first long-distance telephone line, stretching from French Corral through North Bloomfield to Bowman Lake.

Hydraulic mining was extremely profitable, but proved devastating to streams, filling them with sediment, and burying cropland. The process was banned in 1884, and the end of hydraulic mining was also the end of North Bloomfield. People abandoned the town, and today it is the headquarters for the state park and residence for a number of park employees. Several of its mining era buildings, including the schoolhouse, are still standing, and others have been reconstructed. The pharmacy, saloon, and general store have been refurbished and appear to be ready for business. A museum has exhibits illustrating the town's history. The Malakoff Diggins State Historic

Park also has picnic areas and campgrounds, hiking trails, and a beautiful reservoir.
GPS COORDINATES: N39°22.08' W120°53.95'
TRAIL: Northern Sierra #25: North Bloomfield to Bowman Lake Trail
MAP: Page 384

Oakhurst

Oakhurst, when it was first settled in the mid-1850s, was known as Fresno Flats. The town, in Madera County, was renamed Oakhurst for the abundance of oak trees in its vicinity, and since 1964 has been the southern start of California 49, the Mother Lode Highway. California 41 from Fresno goes through Oakhurst, into the south entrance of Yosemite National Park. The area of present-day Madera County (created in 1893 from a portion of Fresno County) was never as rich in gold as other regions of the Mother Lode. Nevertheless, prospectors scoured the Fresno River and its tributaries in search of the precious metal. Oakhurst began as a mining camp for these placer miners. Quartz mining succeeded placer mining by the 1870s, but no major quartz mines were established near Oakhurst. The closest was the Enterprise Mine, 5 miles downstream on the Fresno River. The Oakhurst area instead became well known for its granite, and much of it was quarried during the rebuilding of San Francisco after the 1906 earthquake and fire.

Some of the buildings from Oakhurst's early days are preserved at Fresno Flats Historical Park, including a log cabin built in 1867, an old farmhouse, schoolhouse, courthouse, jail, and blacksmith shop. There is also a collection of old wagons. Other attractions near Oakhurst include the Sierra Mono Indian Museum, southeast of Oakhurst in North Fork, and the Wassama Round House State Historic Park, northwest of the city in Ahwahnee. Sierra Mono Indian Museum exhibits Mono Indian artifacts. The Wassama Round House is a 1975 reconstruction of an 1860s Miwok structure, and it is open on weekends.
GPS COORDINATES: N37°19.67' W119°38.81'
NEAREST TRAIL: High Sierra #17: Central Camp Road

Oakland

Paleo-Indians lived in the vicinity of Oakland, as evidenced by huge shell mounds, remains of past meals over scores of generations. Spanish explorers found these when they first came to the area in the late 1770s. In 1820, Luis Maria Peralta received a grant that stretched along 13 miles of San Francisco Bay shoreline and included the site of present-day Oakland. He called it Rancho San Antonio. The Peralta family's ownership was challenged at the end of the War with Mexico and the gold rush. American squatters disregarded their ownership.

In 1850, Horace W. Carpentier, Edson Adams, and Andrew J. Moon commissioned Julius Kellersberger to lay out a town for them. Carpentier, who chose the name Oakland because of the surrounding oak groves, became the first mayor and reserved a large tract of waterfront property for himself. The town incorporated in 1852. The nearby towns of Clinton, San Antonio, and Brooklyn also developed in the 1850s and were later annexed to Oakland.

The first Central Pacific Railroad train rolled into Oakland on November 8, 1869, the line's western terminus. Ferries had started running to the burgeoning area starting in 1850. With the combination of railroads and shipping, both passenger and freight, and shipbuilding, Oakland became an important transportation center, which was further enhanced when it became a U.S. Army Port of Embarkation and a Navy Supply Depot. The San Francisco–Oakland Bay Bridge was completed in 1936, ending much of the ferry traffic to San Francisco.

Oakland grew as an industrial center during World War II, with shipbuilding, machinery, and chemicals as its major industries. The industrial boom increased Oakland's African-American population, and cultural diversity is celebrated with various events and festivals.

As Oakland grew, it sprawled onto the wooded hills to the east, and a number of wildfires have burned the city over the years. A fire in 1923 destroyed 584 homes, and a terrible blaze in 1991 destroyed 2,700 structures, killed 25 people, and caused almost $1.7 billion in property damage. Although Oakland, with a population of 399,484, is part of the greater

Oakland, circa 1869

San Francisco metropolitan area, it retains an identity of its own. Downtown attractions include Jack London Square (London was a resident of Oakland in his younger years), the Oakland Museum of California, and Lake Merritt. Lake Merritt, a 160-acre bird sanctuary in the heart of the city, is named for Dr. Samuel B. Merritt, mayor of Oakland from 1868 to 1869. Merritt urged that a dam be built to impound coastal tidewaters, and the area was designated a wildfowl refuge—the first in the United States. In 1909, the city of Oakland began to develop Lakeside Park, which now offers boat rentals, sailing lessons, and bowling greens. It also includes Children's Fairyland, a kid's attraction featuring rides, puppet shows, and depictions of various fairy tales and nursery rhymes.
GPS COORDINATES: N37°48.25' W122°16.25'

Orick

Oo'rekw was a Yurok village at the mouth of Redwood Creek. The town of Orick (the English version of the Yurok name) was established as a lumber town in 1887. Area mills processed redwood trees, prized for their durability and resist-

Orick, circa 1930

ance to fire, for mining towns along the coast. In recent years Orick's population has dwindled as a result of its struggle to find an economic base other than the timber industry.

Located on US 101, 35 miles north of Eureka, Orick is among units of Redwood National Park and several state parks. Phoebe A. Hearst donated an area of original growth redwoods as Basin Redwoods State Park in 1902. In years following, the Sierra Club and the Save-the-Redwoods League mounted a campaign to save the virgin stands of redwoods. President Lyndon B. Johnson created Redwood National Park in 1968, and the size of the park was increased by 48,000 acres in 1978. Parks in the vicinity of Orick include Prairie Creek State Park, Del Norte State Park, Jedediah Smith State Park as well as Redwood National Park.

The tallest known tree in the world, at 367.8 feet, stands within the Tall Trees Grove of Redwood National Park. A trek to the grove requires a permit, which can be obtained at the Redwood Information Center south of Orick on US 101, a drive down Bald Hills Road, and a one-mile hike. The giant redwoods aren't the only attraction in the park, which also encompasses a long stretch of rugged coastline of cliffs and beaches, and prairies with spring wildflowers and abundant wildlife. In addition to hiking trails, there is first-rate paddling on the Klamath River, a biking trail on Enderts Beach Trail, and campgrounds in the three state parks.

GPS COORDINATES: N41°17.24' W124°03.49'
NEAREST TRAIL: North Coast #17: Bald Hills Road
MAP: Page 538

Oroville

Prior to the intrusion of gold seekers in the mid-nineteenth century, the area around present-day Oroville was home to a band of Native Americans known as the Yahi. After their culture was precipitously destroyed by disease and violence, a few Yahi survived in the mountains near Oroville, living an isolated tribal lifestyle. The last survivor of the tribe, a middle-aged Indian named Ishi, revealed himself to the world in 1911 near Oroville. He lived his remaining years in San Francisco under the care of two University of California anthropologists.

Prospectors arrived at the site of Oroville in 1849. A year later, the mining camp of Ophir City had grown near the confluence of the North and Middle Forks of Feather River. Ophir City, named for Ophir, the land of gold in the Old Testament, had to change its name when the post office opened in 1855 to avoid confusion with Ophir in Mariposa County and Ophirville in Placer County. Judge J. M. Burt coined the name Oroville, preserving the reference to gold (*oro* means "gold" in Spanish).

Oroville displaced Bidwell's Bar as Butte County seat in 1856, and the town became an important commercial center. Marysville, downstream from Oroville, siphoned off much of the steamer traffic, and boats to Oroville ceased after devastating floods on the Feather River in 1862.

A Chinese population of perhaps 10,000, second only to San Francisco, once resided in the town, and they built a temple in 1863 on Broderick Street. The temple is open for tours, but little else remains of the once-thriving Chinese community.

Hydraulic mining, which used high-powered streams of water to wash gold away from mountainsides, proved highly profitable, and millions of dollars worth of gold was obtained from the Oroville area. Hydraulic mining enabled companies to extract gold from previously mined placer deposits, but the process devastated the landscape, clogged streams, and created much pollution. It was made illegal in 1884, but canals, flumes, and scarred hills remain from that era.

Dredging also became a method to mine for gold in streams, with as many as 35 dredges working in the region that produced about 2 million ounces of gold. One dredging company even offered to pay to relocate the whole town so it could dredge the site. Much of the construction material for the Oroville Dam, completed in 1968, came from hydraulic tailings. The 770-foot dam is the tallest in the United States, and it formed Lake Oroville, which covers 24 square miles and has a 160-mile shoreline. Tourism and water recreation

Oroville, circa 1880

are now leading industries for the town. Historic attractions include the Chinese Temple, the 1856 Lott Home, and the 1911 Ehmann House, headquarters of the Butte County Historical Society. Oroville is a thriving agricultural processing center, for the region's olives, citrus, and other fruits.

GPS COORDINATES: N39°30.92' W121°32.84'
NEAREST TRAIL: Northern Sierra #32: Forbestown to Feather Falls Trail

Placerville

Placerville is just 10 miles from the site of James Wilson Marshall's January 1848 discovery of gold. By the summer of 1848, prospectors had flooded the vicinity of Marshall's find. Miners on Hangtown Creek called their camp Dry Diggings because of the scarcity of water necessary to wash gold from the dirt. William Daylor was credited with finding the first gold in the vicinity; Daylor and two companions took $17,000 in gold from their claim in just one week. Richard Mason, the military governor of California until February 1849, mentioned the site in his official report to Washington on gold deposits, published in August 1848.

The camp was bustling by the beginning of 1849 with gold seekers and some criminals. With no established legal system, residents of camps such as Dry Diggings would resort to vigilante justice. On January 22, 1849, Dry Diggings became the site of the first gold rush era lynching in California. Three men caught robbing a Frenchman were also recognized as suspects of an attempted murder in a neighboring town. A drunken mob strung them from a tree. Legend has it that Dry Diggings became known as Hangtown. Placerville's name, which dates from 1850, was suggested because streets were almost impassable because of placer mining holes.

By the mid-1850s, Placerville was one of the most populous and wealthy settlements in California. Approximately $25 million worth of gold was extracted from regional placer mines alone. The area of Coon Hollow, just south of Placerville, was particularly rich, with at least $5 million of gold obtained from about 5 acres of land. Spanish Hill and Tennessee Hill, mining areas on the same ridge, were equally profitable. Mining continued around Placerville until the 1930s.

Placerville replaced Coloma as the county seat of El Dorado County in 1857. It was a stop on the Overland Route, Pony Express, and the Overland Mail; for a time its population rivaled San Francisco and Sacramento. It recovered from several fires over the years, and the 1859 discovery of silver at Comstock, Nevada, brought new life to the town as a gateway to the diggings east of the Sierra.

Many of Placerville's historic buildings date from this period, however the Placerville Hardware Store, constructed after an 1856 fire, predates the renewal era and is one of the oldest continuously operating hardware stores in California. The old City Hall was originally built in 1860 as a firehouse. Cary House, at 300 Main Street, is on the site of a Wells Fargo Office; Wells Fargo ran a stage line to Comstock, and an estimated $90 million worth of minerals passed through the Placerville office.

Placerville, then known as Hangtown, in 1849

Placerville attracted entrepreneurs: Philip Armour became the meatpacking king of Chicago; John M. Studebacker operated a wheelbarrow business in town; and Mark Hopkins and Collins P. Huntingon, two of the Big Four businessmen who later built the Central Pacific Railroad Company, worked here. Placerville was a stop on the Central Pacific line when it was completed in 1869.

US 50 links Placerville to Sacramento and the resorts on Lake Tahoe, and California 49 connects it to gold country north and south. Placerville's streets wind and turn because they follow old wagon roads. Several museums celebrate Placerville's past; the Gold Bug Mine run by the city, for example, offers visitors the chance to explore an old mining shaft.

GPS COORDINATES: N30°43.99' W120°46.93'

NEAREST TRAIL: Northern Sierra #14: Slate Mountain Trail

Red Bluff

Peter Lassen of the Lassen Emigrant Trail obtained a 25,000-acre Mexican land grant and founded the town of Benton City, just south of the future site of Red Bluff in 1843. Benton City's residents abandoned their town for the Mother Lode at the beginning of the gold rush. Charles W. Wilson and Sashel Woods returned to Lassen's site in 1850 to plan a town at "the Bluffs," or Red Bluffs, on the Sacramento River, about 30 miles south of Redding. Initially, the town was known as Leodocia; it became Red Bluff in 1854.

The town thrived as a transportation center (much as it does today on Interstate 5). River traffic on the Sacramento began in the early 1850s and railroads arrived in 1871. Boats traveling up and down the Sacramento River supplied Red Bluff, which in turn supplied pack trains headed to the mining towns in the Shasta and Trinity regions.

Before the end of the Civil War, in 1864, Red Bluff welcomed the widow of abolitionist John Brown, who had led the 1859 raid on the arsenal at Harpers Ferry, Virginia, and was subsequently hanged for treason. Citizens purchased a home for Mary Ann Brown and her daughters, who lived there until 1870. The house has been designated a Registered Historic Landmark by the state.

Today more than 13,000 Red Bluff residents celebrate their heritage by preserving the city's Victorian homes, historical buildings, and museums. The Kelley-Griggs Museum, in a home built in 1885, has exhibits of Indian artifacts. The William B. Ide Adobe State Historic Park along the Sacramento River includes a restored adobe from the 1840s or 1850s, a carriage shed, and small corral. This was also the site of a ferry that operated from the 1840s until 1876.

A unit of the Lassen National Forest 20 miles east of town includes the 41,339-acre Ishi Wilderness Area, designated by Congress in 1984 to honor Ishi, a Yahi Yana who survived alone until 1911. Within the rugged canyon lands of the Southern Cascade foothills, the landscape is covered with basaltic ledges, caves, and unusual lava formations. Evidence

Red Bluff, circa 1900

of the Yahi Yana's decades of life in the wilderness also exists. A number of trails, which were originally Indian travel ways, are accessible for a stroll or a challenging hike.

GPS COORDINATES: N40°10.72' W122°14.07'

NEAREST TRAIL: Northern Sierra #43: Hogsback Road

Redding

Major Pierson B. Reading obtained a 26,000-acre land grant at the northern end of the Sacramento Valley in 1844 and called it Rancho Buena Ventura. Reading had come overland to California in 1843 and participated in the Bear Flag Revolt in 1845. He explored lands to the north and discovered and named the Trinity River. With John Bidwell, he contributed to settling parts of present-day Shasta County. The town of Redding is on Reading's grant. The California & Oregon Railroad arrived in the vicinity of the present-day town in 1872 and built a station named for Benjamin B. Redding, land agent for the Central Pacific. The town grew up around the station. Redding was the end of line, but track was laid farther north, eventually reaching Portland, Oregon, in 1887. Some residents wanted to keep the memory of Major Reading, who had died in 1868, alive. In 1874, citizens changed the town's name to Reading, but the railroad company refused to recognize it, and by 1880, Redding was again the official name.

Redding became an important transportation hub and milling center for the region's lumber industry. In 1888, the Shasta County seat was moved from Shasta City to Redding.

Redding, circa 1904

The county had a brief copper boom in the early 1900s, but ranching and farming are its principal industries. The Central Valley Water Project to provide irrigation, flood control, and hydroelectricity began in 1935. Shasta Dam, one of several dams built during the 20-year life of the project, impounded the Sacramento, Pit, and McCloud Rivers, to form the 29,500-acre Shasta Lake, which was completed in 1945. The Whiskeytown-Shasta-Trinity National Recreation Area manages camping and recreation sites for Shasta Lake and other reservoirs near today's Redding, with its population of 85,000.

GPS COORDINATES: N40°35.25' W122°23.49'

NEAREST TRAIL: North Coast #25: South Shore Drive

Sacramento

California's capital since 1854, the area of Sacramento was part of a 50,000-acre land grant given to John Sutter in 1839. Prior to becoming part of Sutter's ranch, the land was home to Miwok Indians. A horrific smallpox epidemic in 1833 killed an estimated 20,000 Indians in the region; the remaining population was further marginalized by the hordes of gold rush settlers who came to the area in the wake of James Wilson Marshall's discovery of gold at nearby Coloma in 1848. Sacramento's State Indian Museum, a major tourist attraction for the town, celebrates Native American history.

Despite owning much of the land to which forty-niners came in droves, John Sutter soon found himself bankrupt. Workers at his various enterprises deserted to the goldfields, and squatters settled on his land and stole his livestock. In order to save himself from creditors, Sutter transferred much of his ranch to his son, John Sutter, Jr., who had recently arrived from Switzerland. Sutter, Jr. and Captain William A. Warner laid out a town not far from Sutter's Fort, and by June 1849, there were more than a hundred buildings in the new settlement.

Samuel Brannan established a hugely profitable store that supplied miners heading to the Mother Lode and called it the Sacramento, after the river. Sutter and Warner adopted the name for their town. Spanish explorer Gabriel Moraga had named the river Sacramento, for the Holy Sacrament, in 1808.

Sacramento's location as gateway to the goldfields and on the navigable river, was an economic benefit: The town's population was just under 7,000 in 1850 and 10,000 shortly thereafter. Much of the gold from the mining camps left the Mother Lode via Sacramento, and a network of trails allowed goods brought to the town by boat to be distributed throughout gold country. However, the river was also a constant threat. Floods devastated Sacramento in 1850 and 1852 and fires added to the city's woes. An ambitious proposal to raise much of the town and construct a series of levees was sidelined in 1853, but accepted after another serious flood in 1862.

Sacramento County was one of California's original 27 in 1850, and its boundaries have been only slightly altered to reflect the changing banks of the Sacramento and Mokelumne Rivers. Sacramento has always been the county seat, but it was not chosen as the state capital until 1854. The capitol building itself (a converted courthouse) was destroyed by fire not long after the first legislative session, and another building was constructed on the same site. Foundations were laid at the present location as early as 1860, only to be washed away by a flood the

Sacramento waterfront, circa 1856

following year. Today's gold-domed building was finally completed in 1874, although the government occupied the unfinished building as early as 1869. California's state capitol building reflects the neoclassical architecture of the U.S. Capitol in Washington, D.C. The building underwent a $68 million renovation between 1975 and 1982. It houses both the legislature and an interesting museum. The 33-acre Capitol Park in the shadow of the capitol's 237-foot-high dome, has a remarkable collection of plants from around the world; 3 acres are dedicated to California flora. The California State Library and State Archives are also located in Capitol Park.

Throughout its history, Sacramento's economy has been tied to transportation. Sacramento was the terminus of California's first railroad, the 22-mile-long line to Folsom, completed in 1856. It was also the western terminus for the Pony Express, the famous transcontinental mail service that ran between April 1860 and October 1861. Sacramento was also the start of the Central Pacific Railroad, the first transcontinental railroad, which was completed in 1869.

Many important business magnates built extravagant residences in Sacramento. Examples of stately homes from the late 1800s include: the building that houses the Crocker Art Museum, the Old Governor's Mansion—built in 1877 for Albert Gallatin and the home of 13 California governors—and the structure that houses the Leland Stanford Museum.

The business center of Sacramento gradually moved east from the riverfront toward the capitol until the original downtown became a slum. Some residents suggested the modernized slum buildings should be demolished, but in the 1960s a large-scale project was undertaken to revive the old quarter. Restored Old Sacramento is now a national landmark and a portion of it is a state historic park. The area now attracts 5 million visitors a year and hosts a popular annual jazz festival. Excursion boats leave the public dock and offer excellent dining opportunities. Town residents recently voted Old Sacramento the best place for a first date.

In 2000, Sacramento's population was 407,018, with a total of 1.8 million people residing in the greater metropolitan area. The town remains a transportation center. Its biggest business is state government, and tourism is becoming increasingly important.

GPS COORDINATES: N38°34.78' W121°30.42'

San Andreas

Mexican miners founded San Andreas in the early days of the gold rush, naming the settlement for Saint Andrew. By 1850, Americans had displaced the Hispanic residents and were working the rich placer deposits around San Andreas. Chinese emigrants later reworked the tailings to glean a small fortune from sand and gravel abandoned by others.

San Andreas's first post office opened in 1858, and the town became the Calaveras County seat in 1866. It was quite lively in the gold rush days; today only a cluster of gold rush era buildings survive on Main Street. The Fricot Building and the I.O.O.F. Hall both date from the 1850s. The Calaveras County Museum and Archives Building was once the Courthouse and Hall of Records and now houses an impressive collection of county history, including Miwok Indian artifacts. Below the courthouse a marker in a jail cell reads "Black Bart slept here." Black Bart Bolton plagued the Mother Lode region between 1877 and 1883. He was held in San Andreas during his highly publicized trial and was sentenced to six years at San Quentin prison.

Just outside town is the Pioneer Cemetery, used since at least 1851, making it the county's oldest. A few headstones remain, but the site has suffered from much vandalism. The Sheep Ranch Mine once owned by tycoon George Hearst, father of William Randolph Hearst is nearby. Before it closed in 1942, a series of tunnels had been dug to a depth of more than 3,000 feet, and it had produced more than $8 million in gold.

GPS COORDINATES: N38°11.78' W120°40.79'

NEAREST TRAIL: Northern Sierra #5: Crandall Peak Trail

Metropolitan Hotel in San Andreas, circa 1885

San Francisco

Costanoan Indians lived for centuries in the vicinity now incorporated as the coextensive city and county of San Francisco. In 1769, a scouting party from Gaspar de Portola's expedition, which had started in San Diego, stumbled onto the bay. José de Ortega and his men became the first Europeans to see the bay. The entrance to the bay, named Golden Gate by John C. Frémont in 1846, would not be located until the next year, 1770, by Pedro Fages.

San Francisco's waterfront crowded with boats, circa 1849

The first settlement within the present-day boundaries of the city was the Presidio de San Francisco, established by Juan Bautista de Anza in September 1776. Father Junípero Serra lobbied for a mission at the presidio, and the San Francisco de Asis was established in 1776. A mass celebrated the event on June 29, 1776, the day now considered San Francisco's birthday. The mission was known as Mission Delores, after a little stream that once flowed near it. The surviving church, not far from the original mission site, was dedicated in 1791.

In 1835, William A. Richardson began the English-speaking settlement of Yerba Buena, which forms the core of present-day San Francisco. *Yerba buena* (Spanish for "good herb") remained a small village until 1848 when Samuel Brannan and 238 Mormon settlers arrived by ship from New York; they almost doubled the population of the town.

The gold rush brought thousands of emigrants to California from all over the world and by land and sea. San Francisco was transformed: thousands of tents crowded its hills; ships abandoned in its harbor were converted to hotels, warehouses, and a prison. Eventually, these makeshift establishments were replaced by more permanent structures. Distinct ethnic neighborhoods began to take shape, the 10-block Chinatown being the largest and most famous. Sand from coastal dunes was used to reclaim land from the shallow bay. Today, markers on Market and Montgomery Streets denote the previous shoreline.

San Francisco became a major city before it had an adequate legal system to deal with ruffians. In response to a growing sense of lawlessness, prominent citizens formed several Vigilance Committees. The 1856 committee lynched several accused murderers and committed itself to cleaning up corruption in the city government.

Fires repeatedly destroyed large areas of San Francisco in its early days. The most devastating was the aftermath of the powerful 1906 earthquake. Four-fifths of the city—28,000 buildings—was destroyed by the conflagration. Many San Franciscans made do with temporary housing in Golden Gate State Park. The city quickly rebuilt; much of its present-day beauty is a result of urban planning following the fire. An international exhibition celebrated San Francisco's renewal in 1915.

In the early 1900s, San Francisco began to lose its primacy of population to Los Angeles. Its relatively small area—just 29,056 acres, surrounded on three sides by water—has limited San Francisco's growth. Although the city's population growth slowed, that of its environs surged. The Golden Gate Bridge and the San Francisco–Oakland Bay Bridge, both completed in the 1930s, enabled residents from Marin County and East Bay cities to commute to San Francisco without having to rely on ferries.

San Francisco Bay's Alcatraz Island was the site of one of America's most infamous federal prisons. Begun as an army prison in 1859, the island was ceded to the Justice Department in 1933. From 1934 until 1963, it housed a maximum-security federal penitentiary. Native Americans occupied Alcatraz in November 1968 to bring attention to their treatment by the government. Today, Alcatraz is one of San Francisco's most popular tourist attractions. Regular ferries take visitors from Fisherman's Wharf to the island.

Perhaps the most famous landmark in San Francisco is its trolley system. Begun in 1873, it is the last of its kind in the United States. Grips under the trolley cars grasp a perpetually moving cable, and the cars travel across town until the cable is released. Early design faults in the system sometimes led to a car being stuck on the underground cable and dragged around the city until the entire system was halted. At its peak, the trolley system consisted of eight lines. The three remaining lines were designated a national landmark in 1964.

Voices of the 1950s Beat generation such as Allen Ginsberg and Jack Kerouac were heard here. The City Lights Bookstore (still in business), run by Laurence Ferlinghetti, was a popular gathering place for these young writers. As the Vietnam War escalated in the late 1960s, universities in San Francisco and the University of California at Berkeley became centers of protest and the hippie movement. The house band for wild parties known as Acid Tests, The Warlocks (which later changed its name to The Grateful Dead) played long improvisational jams. The Dead, tie-dyed and longhaired, captured the psychedelic spirit of the confused generation. In later years, the band evolved into a national institution on the touring circuit. The Haight-Ashbury section of San Francisco where The Dead lived was known for a time as a focal point for the hippie movement. Now a major tourist hotspot, the

The intersection of Market and Jones Streets in San Francisco after the 1906 earthquake

area has lost much of its 1960s atmosphere.

San Francisco is a vibrant, cosmopolitan city. Residents call it "The City," and its cultural diversity, moderate climate, and its strong economic base make it one of America's most liberal and pleasing cities to live in. The city's population in 2000 was 776,773; however, the statistical metropolitan area, which includes Oakland and San Jose, has a population in excess of 7 million.

GPS COORDINATES: N37°46.87' W122°23.73'

San Jose

José Joaquin Moraga established the Pueblo de San José de Guadalupe in 1777 on the banks of the Guadalupe River. Named for Saint Joseph, San Jose (the accent on the "e" was dropped in the mid-nineteenth century when American settlers began to outnumber Spanish-speakers) was the first pueblo (city or town) in Alta California. Earlier settlements had been established as presidos, or forts, and missions. Two missions were established in the vicinity, Mission Santa Clara de Asis, in 1777, and San Jose, in 1797, about 15 miles northeast of the pueblo by Father Fermin Lasuén. The San Jose mission was one of the most successful agricultural ventures of the time in all of California. More than 350,000 cattle grazed its extensive lands, it produced more olive oil than any other mission, and its agricultural output was second only to Mission San Gabriel. The mission lands were secularized in 1833 and many of its buildings were used as storehouses during the gold rush. In the 1850s, the Roman Catholic Church regained control of the mission. Restoration in the 1980s refurbished the old mission church. At one time, the pueblo of San Jose had hundreds of adobe houses. Over the years, these were destroyed, and only two remain today. The Peralta Adobe at 184 West St. John Street, built in 1799, is the second oldest building in the Bay Area, after Mission Delores in San Francisco. The Suñol Adobe, built around 1836, stands at 770 Lincoln Avenue and now houses law offices.

By 1848, San Jose had about 700 residents, most of whom were farmers. It grew dramatically in the early days of the gold rush as a supply center for miners. San Jose's population was more than 3,000 at the time of its incorporation in 1850. When California became a state in 1850, San Jose was its capital as well as seat of government for Santa Clara County. The first legislative session was called the Legislature of a Thousand Drinks because sessions frequently adjourned to the local saloon. The capital moved briefly to Vallejo in 1851. The oldest educational institution in California, the University of the Pacific, was established in San Jose in 1851; it has since relocated to Stockton. California State University at San Jose, founded in 1857, is California's oldest state college. Prestigious Stanford University, located in adjacent Palo Alto, completes the area's impressive academic reputation.

The Santa Clara Valley developed as a fertile agricultural region. Fruit orchards, vineyards, cattle ranches, and vegetable fields spread across the area, making San Jose an important packing, canning, and shipping city. The town grew steadily through the early 1900s and saw a surge in growth following World War II. From 1945 to 1975, the population increased by about tenfold. In the past few decades, Santa Clara Valley's economic base has changed from agricultural to emerging technologies. San Jose is the center of Silicon Valley, as the region has become known. Many computer-related firms have chosen to make a home in the area.

Because San Jose underwent much of its growth in the automobile era, it is a sprawling community of suburban housing and businesses. Even its city hall was moved from downtown in 1958, although it is due to be relocated back to the city center. Still, San Jose offers several attractions for the tourist—Rosicrucian Egyptian Temple and Planetarium, Winchester Mystery House, Municipal Rose Gardens, and the Tech Museum of Innovation. The 2000 census counted San Jose's population as 894,943, making it the eleventh largest city in the United States and the third most populous in California after Los Angeles and San Diego.

GPS COORDINATES: N37°19.43' W121°54.12'

Santa Rosa

Santa Rosa, in Sonoma County, stands on land once inhabited by Pomo, Miwok, and Wappo Indians. In 1837, the Rancho Cabeza de Santa Rosa was granted to Mexican General Majariano Vallejo's mother-in-law, Maria Ignacia Lopez de Carrillo. She lived in a brick home on the south side of Santa Rosa Creek where one building remains. Tradition has it that the vicinity was named in the late 1820s after Father Juan Amorosa baptized a young Indian girl on the banks of a creek on the feast day of Santa Rosa de Lima. The creek, valley, and girl were given the saint's name. A monument on the north side of the creek, across from the Carrillo adobe, commemorates the baptism. Many settlers who came to California following the end of the Mexican War and for the gold rush discovered the fertile valley in Sonoma County. In 1853, Carrillo's son, Julio, obtained a section of his mother's grant near Santa Rosa Creek and built a home on what is now Santa Rosa's Second Street. Hoen & Company, owned by Berthold "Barney" Hoen, Feodor Gustav Hahman, and William Hartman, bought the property adjoining Carrillo's, and the four men agreed to develop the town of Santa Rosa by selling lots for $25 a piece. In 1854, Barney Hoen successfully lobbied for the county seat to be moved from the town of Sonoma to Santa Rosa. Hoen and Carrillo donated land for the courthouse and downtown plaza. Santa Rosa incorporated in 1868, and a railroad through the valley in 1870 ensured the city's growth.

In 1871, Luther Burbank, a 21-year-old horticulturalist influenced by Darwin's theory of natural selection, bought 17 acres near Lunenberg, Massachusetts. He developed the Burbank potato to which he sold the rights, and in 1875, he moved to Santa Rosa. He built an experimental farm, nursery, and greenhouse that became world famous; he experimented on millions of plants, using hybridization and selection. Creating the plums now widely grown in the state, he tested as many as 30,000 varieties. All told he produced more than 800 new varieties of flowers, fruits, vegetables, and grains, including the Shasta daisy, the forefather of the Idaho potato, and new plants such as plumcots, blackberries without thorns, and cactuses without spines. Published in 1914 and 1915, his book, *Luther Burbank, His Methods and Discoveries and Their*

Practical Applications, preserved some of the extensive knowledge and data that was lost upon his death on April 11, 1926. His widow bequeathed the care of most of the farm (with the exception of an orchard she established on one section) to the Stark Brothers Nursery in the form of a lease, which expired in 1957. The property deteriorated until 1974 when local historians formed the Western Sonoma County Historical Society to preserve Burbank's heritage. In 1978, the Burbank home was listed as a National Historic Landmark, and 3 acres of the original farm was established as the Burbank Home and Gardens. Since 1983, the group has maintained the property, including his home and varieties of his plants.

Thomas Lake Harris began Fountain Grove, a utopian community in 1875, on 400 acres just north of Santa Rosa. He built an ornate three-story Victorian dwelling, "The Commandery," and then planted extravagant gardens around the mansion. Harris gradually added more than 1,000 acres to the community's property. His theory of a new way of life blended socialism and mysticism, and new members relinquished their possessions to the community and joined the Brotherhood of New Life. Dr. John Hyde helped Harris establish a successful winery, which shipped 200,000 gallons annually to support Fountain Grove. Accused of adultery by a *San Francisco Chronicle* reporter, Harris left the settlement and put the community in the hands of his adopted son, Kenaye Nagasawa. The winery continued to be successful, and Nagasawa constructed a round barn, a present-day historical landmark. Luther Burbank also contributed to the community's landscape. Nagasawa died in 1934, and the property was sold.

Another notable site in Santa Rosa is the Church of the One Tree, constructed in 1873. A 275-foot-tall redwood tree (18 feet in diameter) growing near Guerneville was felled and produced 78,000 feet of lumber from which the church was assembled. The church was made famous in the newspaper feature "Believe It or Not," created by Robert L. Ripley who was born in Santa Rosa in 1893. The first feature appeared in 1918, and it continued uninterrupted for 30 years during which time Ripley traveled to 198 countries in search of the bizarre. Ripley also established himself as a radio broadcast pioneer and a television personality, befriending such public figures as Ed Sullivan and Lou Gehrig. Following his death in 1949, the Church of the One Tree became a tribute to the adventurer: the Robert L. Ripley Memorial Museum. Another Santa Rosa attraction, Snoopy's Gallery & Gift Shop, boasts the world's largest collection of Snoopy and Peanuts cartoon paraphernalia; the items were contributed by Santa Rosa's late cartoonist, Charles Schulz. With nearly 150,000 residents, Santa Rosa is the largest city in Sonoma County.

GPS COORDINATES: N38°25.88' W122°42.86'

NEAREST TRAIL: Northern Sierra #25: North Bloomfield to Bowman Lake Trail

Shasta

The hamlet of Shasta lies 5 miles west of Redding on California 299. Shasta, in Shasta County, is not to be confused with the town of Mount Shasta in Siskiyou County, 60 miles north of Redding. Shasta started as a tent city named Reading's Diggings, following Major Pierson B. Reading's 1848 discovery of gold in Clear Creek. His find prompted a gold rush to this vicinity. Reading retrieved $800 of gold a day from placers along the creek. The name of the town was changed to Shasta City in 1850, and when a post office opened the following year it was shortened to Shasta. As a gateway to rich backcountry mining camps and the expanding Oregon frontier, Shasta thrived throughout the 1850s and '60s as a supply center. For 5 years, mule trains packed supplies to isolated gold camps along the Trinity River and returned with $100,000 in gold each week. One night as many as 100 mule trains stopped to re-supply. Shasta's population grew to several thousand, and in 1857 it was the fifteenth largest city in the state.

Shasta's riches attracted gamblers and crooked characters, some of whom ended up on the gallows behind the courthouse. One of the most famous residents, Rattlesnake Dick Barter, fled from Auburn where he had been wrongfully accused of stealing a mule. He maintained a low profile in Shasta, but when visitors from Auburn spotted him and spread rumors of his alleged crimes he hit the trail as an outlaw. He teamed up with several highwaymen for a particularly high-profile heist of an $80,000 Wells Fargo shipment coming from Yreka. Rattlesnake Dick's part in the robbery was to bring mules to carry the spoils, but he was arrested and jailed in Auburn while stealing mules for the robbery. His partners pulled off the theft without mules to pack the load; half the gold was buried somewhere in the Shasta vicinity. Authorities shot or apprehended all the perpetrators, and the robbers who knew the location of the spoils died in jail. The gold has never been found.

The Central Pacific began to build a railroad between San Francisco and Portland in 1886. The line bypassed Shasta for the town of Redding, 6 miles to the east, and Shasta began to fade. Once the largest settlement between Sacramento and the Oregon border, the town became deserted almost overnight. In 1888, placer mines became less productive and the county seat was moved to Redding. In the late 1940s, Native Sons of the Golden West obtained a large portion of the town and donated it to the state for preservation and restoration.

Shasta State Historic Park, open Wednesday through Sunday for a small fee, currently maintains one of the state's best-preserved ghost towns. This long row of brick buildings was constructed in 1853 after a fire razed much of the town, and these have since been reinforced with masonry and steel. The courthouse is now a museum, housing a Western art collection, implements belonging to Chinese emigrants, and collections of rifles, revolvers, and pocket watches. The four-cell jail in the lower level is close to the gallows out back. A store and a few other buildings were restored and are open for visitors today. Two cemeteries within the park have headstones that date from 1850.

GPS COORDINATES: N40°35.94' W122°22.47'

NEAREST TRAIL: North Coast #25: South Shore Drive

Shasta Lake

The city of Shasta Lake, 9 miles north of Redding on Interstate 5, developed after the U.S. Bureau of Reclamation proposed the construction of a large dam in the summer of 1937. Government officials conceived the project, named

Central Valley Project, in 1921, hoping to control the yearly flooding of valuable farmland in the Sacramento Valley and to provide irrigation water to farmers in the drier San Joaquin Valley. Job-hopefuls flocked to the area to wait for construction to begin. Future dam workers camped in tents, trailers, or cars along a new road off Highway 99 (a predecessor of Interstate 5). As construction began late in 1938, businesses took root along Shasta Dam Boulevard, creating the Project City, Central Valley, and Summit City areas of commercial and residential growth. Summit City, home to most of the bars, dance halls, and other evening recreation spots, including the popular Charley's Place, Mint Pool Hall, and The Round-Up, attracted crowds of dam workers after hours.

The commercial centers soon had grocery stores, tobacco shops, restaurants, and general stores, and families continued to move to the new settlements. In need of a school, the community came together to build one in record time. The Bureau of Reclamation donated the land, Pacific Constructors, Inc. (the contractor for the dam), donated the materials, and dam workers provided the manpower for construction of Toyon School. New students finished the job by mounting shelves, cabinets, and putting up a fence. When the school opened, record numbers of children attended—as many as 70 students per class.

The town's renaissance lasted until 1941, when the onset of World War II diverted many workmen to the military, and others relocated to more lucrative wartime employment elsewhere. Population declined until war veterans started returning to the city in 1945. The Main Lumbering Mill and the Rocky Mountain Lumbering Mill recharged the economy. After Shasta Dam's completion in 1944, workers commuted to build Keswick Dam, just northwest of Redding. The three separate areas of development near Shasta Dam were incorporated on July 3, 1993, establishing the city of Shasta Lake, home to 9,008 residents in 2000.

Shasta Dam, the creator of Shasta Lake, impounds the Pit, McCloud, and Sacramento Rivers to store extra runoff, control flooding, prevent salt from contaminating inland waterways, and produce electricity. Completed over the span of six years and nine months, it is the second largest dam in the United States. During its construction, Columbia Construction Company built a 9.5-mile-long, 36-inch-wide conveyor belt from the town of Redding where they broke rocks into aggregate. The belt transported 1,100 tons of material per hour used to make concrete for the dam. More than 12 million tons of crushed rock traveled on the conveyor belt.

The finished dam is made up of nearly 7 million barrels of concrete, enough to construct a 3-foot-wide sidewalk around the world at the equator. The structure is 602 feet tall, 3,460 feet long, 883 feet thick at its base, and 30 feet thick at the top. A temperature control device was added to the dam in 1997 to aid salmon by releasing colder water from the bottom of the reservoir during summer.

Shasta Lake, which has 360 miles of shoreline, contains nearly 1.5 trillion gallons of water, making it the largest man-made reservoir in California. That volume equals about 10,000 gallons of water for each U.S. resident. Boating, hiking, camping, fishing, birding, water skiing, hunting, and spelunking are popular activities around the lake. The forest service provides six public access boat ramps and numerous campsites on the lake. Shasta Caverns are open for year-round tours. The free 45-minute Shasta Dam tour is also a popular attraction.

GPS COORDINATES: N40°40.90' W122°22.47'

NEAREST TRAIL: North Coast #27: Backbone Road

Sheep Ranch

The town of Sheep Ranch, in Calaveras County west of San Andreas, was just that—a sheep ranch—where a rich lode deposit of gold was discovered in 1866. The workings were named Sheep Ranch Mine after the nearby sheep corral, and the settlement that grew around the mine became known as Sheep Ranch. A post office was established in the town in 1877.

In 1874, George Hearst, father of media magnate William Randolph Hearst, acquired the Sheep Ranch Mine, one of his several very profitable investments. By the time George Hearst died in 1891, while serving his second term as Democratic U.S. senator for California, the Sheep Ranch had yielded more than $4 million worth of gold. The Hearst family sold the mine in 1893, and it temporarily ceased to operate. Between its reopening in 1899 and its final closure in 1942, the Sheep Ranch produced another $3 million in gold. When operations concluded, the mine's tunnels reached 3,100 feet in depth. Today, a plaque placed by E Clampus Vitus commemorates the profitable mine.

Stamp mill at Sheep Ranch, circa 1920

In a national effort to simplify place names, postal authorities changed the town's appellation to Sheepranch in 1895, but it continues to appear today as two words. The hamlet has scattered remnants of its heyday. The cemetery on Armstrong Road contains about 40 graves, some of them quite old. Sheep Ranch's principal attraction is the two-story Pioneer Hotel. Built in the Mountain Ranch area, the hotel was moved to Sheep Ranch in 1868. The one-story hotel was expanded in 1899. Instead of removing the roof and building a new floor above the first, the entire building was jacked up and a ground floor added under the existing one. The Pioneer Hotel, now a private residence, remains an attractive structure, with beautiful porches on all sides.

Other buildings of note include a red schoolhouse, built in 1911 and used until 1955. The boarded-up general store and post office are also quite old, and a nearby brick structure no longer in use may have been a powder-house or vault. Several old wooden residences also dot Sheep Ranch's Main Street; most of these are vacant. One definite sign of modern occupation is the new volunteer fire department building—proof that Sheep Ranch lives!

GPS COORDINATES: N38°12.55' W120°27.80'

NEAREST TRAIL: Northern Sierra #5: Crandall Peak Trail

Sierra City

Sierra City is one of the many historic mining towns along California 49. Located in the northern Sierra Nevada, Sierra City and the county in which it lies—Sierra County—were named after the towering mountain range. The region had numerous Indian camps and rancherias at the time of the gold rush. The inhabitants were displaced, killed, or died of diseases against which they had no resistance. P. A. Haven and Joseph Zumwalt camped on the site, on the North Fork of the Yuba River, in 1850. An avalanche in the winter of 1852 wiped out the mining camp that had grown at the site. No permanent settlement was established again until 1858; avalanches hit the town again in 1888 and 1889 and caused many fatalities.

In August 1860, the second largest gold nugget in California history was discovered near Sierra City at the Monumental Quartz Mine. The nugget weighed 1,596 troy ounces and was valued at more than $25,000. Several structures in Sierra City survive from gold mining days. The Zerloff Hotel was constructed in the 1860s and is still operated by heirs of the original owners. The refurbished Busch Building, once a Wells Fargo office, dates from 1871.

The Ancient Order of E Clampus Vitus was established in Sierra City in 1857, principally as a joke, making fun of the proliferation of Masonic lodges and the I.O.O.F. The leader of E Clampus Vitus (the name is meaningless) was called the Grand Noble Humbug. The organization performed hoaxes, jokes, and charitable acts. They were especially kind to widows and orphans and were well respected throughout the Mother Lode. Reestablished in 1931 as E Clampus Vitus Redivivus by historian Carl I. Wheat, the society is still committed to fun, but also focuses on preserving gold rush lore and placing plaques on historic gold country buildings.

The Kentucky Mine Museum, at the site of the Kentucky Mine that operated from the 1850s until 1953, is one of the best mining museums in the Mother Lode. The museum is located on the east side of the city and includes a restored blacksmith shop, miner's cabin, and the mine's 10-stamp mill, still in working order. An impressive collection of gold rush artifacts and an assortment of Chinese and Native American artwork is also exhibited. Outdoor concerts are held at the park on Fridays during the summer.

Sierra City's main street

In addition to tourism, Sierra City's economy survives on logging and livestock. It is the northernmost major town on California 49, the Mother Lode Highway, before the road ends in the tiny settlement of Vinton.

GPS COORDINATES: N39°33.96' W120°22.70'

NEAREST TRAIL: Northern Sierra #27: Sierra Buttes Trail

Soda Springs

Located near the headwaters of the North Fork of the American River, Soda Springs is less than 10 miles from Donner Pass. It is west of Truckee and Lake Tahoe off Interstate 80, which was the original route of US 40, a segment of the Lincoln Highway. Several small mining operations existed in the area during the gold rush; Leland Stanford and Mark Hopkins developed Soda Springs as a summer resort in the 1860s along the route of the Central Pacific Railroad. Stanford and Hopkins were two of the Big Four businessmen who provided capital to construct the western portion of the first transcontinental railroad. They called the settlement Hopkins Springs; then, from 1867 to 1873, it was known as Tinker's Station, after local teamster J. A. Tinker. The name was changed to Soda Springs in 1875 when the town opened a post office.

Soda Springs, circa 1882

The present-day town of Soda Springs is north of Mark Hopkins's estate, which is now in ruins. A few stone buildings and log cabins remain, and a small mineral water spring, apparently the inspiration for Soda Springs's name, is inside one of the cabins. The Soda Springs Winter Resort, founded in 1935, features snow tubing as well as skiing, snowboarding, sledding, and snowshoeing.

GPS COORDINATES: N39°19.41' W120°22.70'

TRAIL: Northern Sierra #20: Soda Springs Road

MAP: Page 357

Sonora

Known as the Queen of the Southern Mines, Sonora is on California 49 near the southern end of gold country. First settled by miners from the Mexican state of Sonora in 1848, the town was called Sonorian Camp; nearby Jamestown was then

Sonora, circa 1905

known as American Camp. The abundance of pay dirt around Sonora soon attracted a flood of Yankee miners who quickly outnumbered their Hispanic counterparts. Tensions rose between the two groups and sporadic violence hit the town. In mid-1850, following California's admission as a state, a prohibitive $20 monthly tax was imposed on all foreign residents of Sonora. Mexicans and Chileans decided to abandon the settlement, and almost overnight Sonora's population shrank from 5,000 to about 3,000. Local business suffered until the tax was repealed in 1851 and Hispanic miners began to return.

In 1850, Sonora became seat of government for Tuolumne County, one of the original 27 counties of California. The town's name was briefly changed to Stewart for Major William E. Stewart, but the change lasted only two months.

Chilean gold seekers discovered the Big Bonanza Mine, the richest pocket mine (a mine that yields a large amount of gold in a small area) in the Mother Lode. In 1871, the mine was sold cheaply to three partners. The men patiently worked the mine for several years before suddenly encountering a body of almost solid gold. The next day, they extracted $160,000 worth of the precious metal. Within a week, they had sent $500,000 of gold to the San Francisco Mint.

The Big Bonanza was not the only profitable strike near Sonora. An estimated $41 million worth of gold was removed within a two-mile radius of the town. Although its population dwindled after the gold rush, Sonora saw something of a renewal when the railroad reached town in 1898. The impressive Tuolumne County Courthouse dates from that year. Other historic buildings include the Gunn House, the oldest residence in Sonora, and the Tuolumne County Museum, the town's jail from 1865 until 1961. The oldest part of the Gunn House is an adobe, begun in 1849; it was a family home from 1851 to 1861, when it was converted into a hospital. It once again became a private residence in 1899 and is now a charming hotel, though much of the original structure has been altered. St. James Episcopal Church, built in 1859, is one of the oldest Episcopalian churches in California. Nearby stands the Street-Morgan Mansion, a well-preserved Victorian home. Numerous other historic buildings in Sonora make it one of the most picturesque towns in the Mother Lode.

GPS COORDINATES: N37°58.99' W120°22.89'
NEAREST TRAIL: Northern Sierra #1: Clavey Bridge Road

South Lake Tahoe

Washoe Indians used Lake Tahoe in much the same way that Californians do today—as a summer retreat. Artifacts found along the lake's shore indicate that humans have inhabited the area for at least 10,000 years. The name Tahoe comes from the Washoe word for the lake: *dá'wa*. The first explorers to see the lake were members of John C. Frémont's expedition in 1844. At 6,229 feet above sea level, Lake Tahoe is the highest lake of its size in the United States. The lake has a shoreline of 71 miles, 42 of which are in California. South Lake Tahoe is at the southern end of the 22-mile-long lake close to the Nevada border.

American settlers generally ignored the Tahoe Basin until 1859, when silver was discovered in Comstock, Nevada. Comstock's demand for lumber led to massive deforestation around Lake Tahoe. Lake House, the first lakefront hotel, was built in 1859 and burned down in 1865. Mark Twain passed the lake on his way West and observed in *Roughing It* (1872) that "three months of camp life on Lake Tahoe would restore an Egyptian mummy to his pristine vigor, and give him an appetite like an alligator."

US 50 links Placerville and South Lake Tahoe, and tourist traffic increased dramatically after lumber tycoon Duane L. Bliss completed his railroad from Truckee in 1897. By the early 1900s, it was increasingly evident that tourism was the Tahoe Basin's most viable industry. Al Tahoe Hotel was constructed near the old Lake House, and a community known as Al Tahoe grew around the hotel. Soon many luxurious estates and hotels dotted the shore. The Tallac Historic Site, north of South Lake Tahoe on California 89, allows visitors to view several historic twentieth-century estates. Lake Tahoe Historical Society Museum, on US 50, also celebrates the area's past.

The world came to Lake Tahoe when the winter Olympics were held at Squaw Valley in 1960. In 1965, the community of Al Tahoe incorporated with several neighboring settlements as South Lake Tahoe. Heavenly Valley is the closest world-class resort to South Lake Tahoe. The southern shores of the lake attract visitors interested in Nevada's casinos. Exponential growth in the 1960s began to threaten the lake. In 1969, the legislatures of California and Nevada, in conjunction with the U.S. Congress, created the Tahoe Regional Planning Agency. Today, South Lake Tahoe is the largest settlement in the Tahoe Basin, with more than 20,000 residents and thousands of seasonal visitors. It is accessible via California 89, which runs along the western shore of Lake Tahoe, and US 50.

GPS COORDINATES: N38°56.05' W119°58.63'
NEAREST TRAIL: Northern Sierra #16: Angora Lakes Road

Stockton

Charles M. Weber, a German immigrant who had arrived in California with John Bidwell in 1841, bought a 49,000-acre ranch in 1845. In 1847, he organized Tuleburg, named for the tule wetlands and sloughs of the site, where the Calaveras River flows into the tidal waters of the San Joaquin. Many of the settlement's early houses had tule roofs. Weber changed the settlement's name in 1849 to honor Commodore Robert F.

Stockton, a major figure in the U.S. seizure of California during the Mexican War.

Stockton's location at the head of a navigable channel less than a hundred miles from San Francisco Bay made it a major supply center for the southern mines of the Mother Lode. The first steamboat arrived from San Francisco in November 1849, and by 1850 the town had a population of more than a thousand. Many forty-niners passed through Stockton on their way to the goldfields, and the settlement quickly became the staging point for dozens of freighting businesses. To keep up with the demand for produce by the influx of miners, hundreds of farms sprang up around Stockton, taking advantage of the temperate climate and rich soil. Gradually, Stockton evolved into an agricultural supply center.

Stockton became a deepwater port when the 75-mile-long Stockton Deepwater Channel to San Francisco Bay was completed in 1933. The channel enabled Stockton to adapt to the requirements of modern ships. Major crops grown near Stockton include asparagus, cherries, tomatoes, walnuts, almonds,

The bustling Stockton wharf in 1852

and grapes. Some good wine is produced to the north of town. Stockton was also a major supplier of agricultural equipment. The first treaded tractors were produced here in the early 1900s at the Holt Tractor Works, ultimately the Caterpillar Tractor Company. During World War II, the San Joaquin County Fairgrounds were used as an internment camp for 4,271 Japanese Americans.

Stockton incorporated in 1850 and became the San Joaquin County seat. Many of the town's historic 1850s buildings were destroyed during an urban renewal project in the 1960s. Stockton is home to the oldest university in California, the University of the Pacific. Established in 1851, the college moved from San Jose to Stockton in 1924; the San Francisco forty-niners use some of UOP's sports facilities. The Haggins Museum exhibits San Joaquin County history.

More than 1,000 miles of navigable waters make excellent boating and fishing opportunities, surprising given Stockton's location in the heart of the Central Valley. The city has undergone an astounding surge: In 1970, the population was 107,644; by 2000, it had more than doubled to 243,771.

GPS COORDINATES: N37°59.05' W121°16.99'

NEAREST TRAIL: Northern Sierra #5: Crandall Peak Trail

Early view of Strawberry Valley

Strawberry Valley

The hamlet of Strawberry Valley, not to be confused with the valley below Mount Shasta, is on California 120, east of Oroville. Its name may or may not be because of berries in the vicinity. It may be that roadhouse owner Berry understuffed his straw mattresses, causing customers to demand: "More straw, Berry!" Another apocryphal origin is that roadhouse owner "Straw" Berry was the name teamsters gave him because he fed their horses straw instead of hay. Yet another suggestion claims that the name was derived by combining Berry's surname with that of a local miner, Mr. Straw.

The town, on the South Fork of the American River, is at the northern end of the Mother Lode, and placer mines were established here in 1850. By 1855, Strawberry Valley had a post office and thrived as a supply center for mines in the vicinity. Dozens of stores and residences lined its busy streets. When the gold played out, however, the population dwindled.

The Strawberry Valley Cemetery, still in use, has graves dating from the 1850s. The Strawberry Valley General Store opened in 1852 and still sells goods, and nearby is the three-and-a-half story Columbus Hotel, built in 1900.

GPS COORDINATES: N39°33.85' W121°06.37'

NEAREST TRAIL: Northern Sierra #40: Poker Flat OHV Trail

Susanville

Marylander Isaac Roop arrived in this area of Northern California, then Plumas County, in 1853 and established a trading post—Roops Fort—the following year. In 1855, California pioneer Peter Lassen arrived at the post with a prospecting party, which found gold in Honey Lake Valley. A settlement grew around Roops Fort to accommodate the miners. At first

Isaac Roop's 1854 cabin, Fort Defiance

it was called Rooptown, but eventually it was renamed Susanville in 1857 after Roop's daughter.

Meanwhile Roop, Lassen, and the other settlers refused to acknowledge that they lived in California; they proclaimed the Territory of Nataqua—and at one time declared a republic that survived from 1856 to 1857. The boundary between California and the Territory of Nevada, established in 1861, was vague. Roop served as Nevada's first provisional governor and later U.S. senator, claiming he lived in Nevada rather than California. In 1863, a government survey found Susanville to be well within California's border. Susanville residents were enraged, and they defied California law, represented in the person of the sheriff of Plumas County. Residents congregated at Roop's cabin, called Fort Defiance and prepared for a fight. On February 15, 1863, the only battle of the Sagebrush War took place: A posse led by the Plumas County sheriff had a daylong gunfight with the rebels, who reluctantly acquiesced. Susanville got some consolation when it was made the seat of newly created Lassen County in 1864.

Lassen County's economy relied on livestock, poultry, and logging, and tourism has become increasingly important. The Nevada-California-Oregon Railroad reached Susanville in 1899, providing transportation to outside markets, and the town incorporated in 1900.

By 1990 the population was 7,279, and a decade later the town had increased to 17,023. Geographically, Susanville is in

Roop's cabin today

the Basin and Range province, east of the Cascade Range. Nearby attractions include Lassen Volcanic National Park and units of the Lassen and Plumas National Forests. Isaac Roop's cabin survives, and exhibits include artifacts from its early days. The Pioneer Saloon, open since 1862, claims to be the oldest continuous business in Northern California.

GPS COORDINATES: N40°24.93' W120°38.88'

NEAREST TRAIL: Northern Sierra #37: Thompson Peak Trail

Sutter Creek

Sutter Creek in Amador County was named for the stream on which John A. Sutter had a mining camp, beginning in 1848. The camp was almost abandoned when several large deposits of gold-bearing quartz were discovered nearby in 1851, but the camp survived to become a supply center for the mines,

Sutter Creek's main street

including the Eureka, and three mines—Wildman, Mahoney, and Lincoln—which eventually became the Lincoln Consolidated Mine. John Sutter saw little or no return from the area, but Leland Stanford invested in the Lincoln mine, which yielded some $2.2 million. With these profits he became one of the Big Four investors in the transcontinental railroad and established Leland Stanford, Jr. University in Palo Alto. He also ran successfully for governor and U.S. senator.

Sutter Creek's post office opened in 1852 and the village had at least 200 residents when it incorporated in 1854. The town's Methodist Church has architectural elements dating from the 1860s, and the Sutter Creek Grammar School was first used in 1870. The Knight Foundry, built in 1873, is now the only operating water-powered foundry in the United States and offers tours. The Monteverde Store, built in 1898, is open as a re-created general store and has a museum.

GPS COORDINATES: N38°23.67' W120°48.16'

NEAREST TRAIL: Northern Sierra #9: Calaveras Dome Trail

Tahoe City

Tahoe City, in Placer County, is on the northwestern shore of Lake Tahoe. The town site was surveyed in 1863 and named Tahoe. William Pomin built the Tahoe House in 1864, and in 1870, Colonel Alexis Von Schmidt built a log structure across the Truckee River just downstream of its outlet in an attempt to regulate the river's flow. Tahoe's post office was established in 1871, but it wasn't until 1949 that the town's name was changed to Tahoe City.

By the 1890s the logging industry, which had virtually deforested the woods around Lake Tahoe, was in decline. As a result, the Bliss family developed Tahoe City with a plan to stimulate tourism by building a grand resort. To ensure the hotel's success, the first stage of construction involved securing rail transportation. By 1900, a spur of the Central Pacific extended from Truckee to Tahoe City. Water and electricity infrastructures were established during construction of the resort, thereby ensuring future development, and the Tahoe Tavern opened for business in 1902. The retreat's popularity was unsurpassed until it closed 1964; arsonists subsequently burned the structure.

The second Truckee River Dam, located closer to the outlet than the original, was built in 1913 to regulate Lake Tahoe's water level. Record high water levels overcame the original wooden structure in 1907. The physical raising and lowering of the lake's water level still takes place here with the original hand-turned winch system. In 1986, control of Tahoe's water level was turned over to the Federal Water Master's Office in Reno, Nevada.

Lake Tahoe is one of California's most popular resort destinations. During summer, visitors enjoy fishing, boating, and hiking in the surrounding national forests. In winter, skiers and snowboarders flock to the slopes at Squaw Valley, site of the 1960 Winter Olympics, and to other resorts at Alpine Meadows and Granlibakken. Tahoe City is less metropolitan than South Lake Tahoe and Stateline, Nevada, towns on the lake's southern shores. It retains a pleasant rural atmosphere despite its tourist appeal.

Tahoe City has the distinction of being home to the first snowboard halfpipe, built by Mark Anolik in 1979 on Tahoe-Truckee Sanitation Company land. The Tahoe City Pipe helped spark the sport's popularity, which is now a Winter Olympic event.

GPS COORDINATES: N39°10.32' W120°08.30'
TRAIL: Northern Sierra #19: Mount Watson Trail
MAP: Page 353

Tahoma

Tahoma is a pretty lakeshore resort on the western shore of Lake Tahoe, near the boundary between El Dorado and Placer Counties. Settlers built cabins near the present-day town as early as the 1860s. An 1870s cabin is preserved in Sugar Pine Point State Park, which also includes the Ehrman Mansion, a two-story Queen Anne–style house built in 1902. The mansion, home of the Hellman-Ehrman family, is a fine example of the summerhouses that were built in the Tahoe Basin in the late 1800s and early 1900s as retreats for wealthy Californians.

The town of Tahoma was laid out in 1916 as a resort whose name combines the words "Tahoe" and "home." Tahoma has about 500 permanent residents, but many more seasonal visitors. In addition to water sports, tourists can enjoy the wilderness areas in the Tahoe and Eldorado National Forests. The Pacific Crest Trail stretches along the Sierra Crest to the west, and many backcountry roads travel through the region. Tahoma is situated on California 89, south of Tahoe City and Homewood. Homewood Ski Resort is just a short drive away.

GPS COORDINATES: N39°04.23' W120°08.36'
TRAIL: Northern Sierra #17: McKinney Creek Trail
MAP: Page 349

Truckee

Truckee, the town and river, are on one of the great routes westering emigrants used beginning in the 1840s. The California Trail passed this way, crossing the Sierra at Donner Summit. Interstate 80, the current road across the Sierra, closely follows the route of the California Trail. A Paiute named Winnemucca, grandfather of Sarah Winnemucca, an advocate for Native American rights, may have directed explorer Frémont or Elisha Stevens to the Truckee River in 1844, saying *"Tro-kay,"* which meant "okay," or "everything is all right." Thinking this was his name, they named the Truckee River for the Paiute.

In 1862, as the Civil War raged, Congress passed the Pacific Railroad Act in July authorizing the construction of the first transcontinental railroad. The final survey selected Donner Pass as the crossing for the Sierra Nevada. In 1863, Joseph Gray built a home, known as Gray's Station, on the proposed route. As one engineering problem after another was solved while work progressed on the railroad, a settlement called Coburn Station, named after a saloonkeeper, grew as a supply point. Coburn Station burned to the ground in 1868, and residents rebuilt and named the town Truckee, after the river. Truckee was not incorporated until 1993.

A logging mill built in 1867 marked the beginning of a healthy lumber industry. The following year, Central Pacific trains began rolling through town, and by 1869, the transcontinental railroad had been completed. By then Truckee had a reputation as a lawless lumber and railroad town, a reputation now belied by this tranquil mountain village that retains much of its historic atmosphere. Trains still pass through town, and the streets are lined with nineteenth-century buildings. The White House, former home of banker C. B. White, dates from 1889 and now houses a restaurant and Victorian museum. The old Truckee jail, built in 1875 from local stone, is also a museum.

Truckee residents took advantage of long Sierra winters and their elevation at 5,800 feet to harvest ice. From the 1860s until the invention of electric refrigeration in the 1920s, hundreds of ice ponds dotted the banks of the Truckee River. Ice was cut, packed, and shipped to much of California.

Snow is also crucial to Truckee's big industry today—tourism. By the 1890s, visitors were already flocking to Truckee to see ice palaces, go ice-skating, enjoy sleigh rides, or participate in the growing sport of skiing. In 1960, the Winter Olympics were held at Squaw Valley, just 10 miles south of Truckee on California 89. The highway follows a railroad grade, dating from 1897, when a railroad was built between Truckee and Lake Tahoe.

GPS COORDINATES: N39°19.43' W120°10.00'
TRAIL: Northern Sierra #19: Mount Watson Trail
MAP: Page 352

Early Truckee

Tulelake

Originally the land of the Modoc Indians, the present-day site of Tulelake, 52 miles north of Canby on California 139, first saw European pioneers in the early 1800s. Settlers established agricultural communities on the fertile land around the California-Oregon border and the dry bed of Tule Lake. For years, strife and conflict escalated as colonists attempted to drive the Indians from their land. The first battle of the Modoc War took place on November 30, 1872, on the Lost River in southern Oregon. Greatly outnumbered, the Modoc took refuge in the lava beds (now Lava Beds National Monument), where they defended themselves for months. Today, many historic battle sites and points of interest around Tulelake are marked, including Canby's Cross at the southern end of Tule Lake.

After the surprise attack on Pearl Harbor, which initiated U.S. involvement in World War II, discrimination against Japanese Americans reached an all-time high. On February 19, 1942, President Roosevelt signed an order that would relocate people of Japanese descent from their homes in Arizona, California, Oregon, and Washington to concentration camps for the duration of the war. On May 27, 1942, the Tule Lake Relocation Center opened, imprisoning nearly a quarter of the country's 120,000 Japanese Americans. In 1943, prisoners at each of the 10 concentration camps were questioned about their loyalty to the United States. Those determined by the government to be traitors were moved to the Tule Lake camp, which had become a center for the most troublesome inmates. The U.S. Army declared marshal law on the camp after a prisoner uprising in November 1943, which resulted from camp authorities' poor handling of a farming accident and ensuing strike. Normal functioning resumed in February 1944. Following the war, nearly 4,500 prisoners requested to return to Japan, while the rest re-integrated. The camp closed on March 20, 1946. Little remains of the camp, which is now closed to the public, except for a historical marker 7 miles southeast of the city on California 139.

Just south of Tulelake, the 460,000-acre Lava Beds National Monument contains 430 caves and other lava formations as well as site markers from the Modoc War. The Tule Lake Petroglyphs are also located within the lava beds. This series of deep carvings, now protected by a fence, stretches hundreds of yards across a smooth sandstone bluff. The Modoc deny any knowledge of the mysterious petroglyphs origin, but some believe the last of the Rock Indians carved them. The Modoc, who allegedly exterminated the Rock Indian tribe in the 1850s, were awed by the carvings and told stories about them. The Tule Lake National Wildlife Refuge, established west of the city in 1928, is home to bald eagles and pelicans, among millions of migrating and wintering waterfowl and other wildlife.

Tulelake, known as the horseradish capital of the world, is a small agricultural community of 1,020 residents.

GPS COORDINATES: N41°57.26' W121°28.62'

NEAREST TRAIL: North Coast #39: Tule Lake National Wildlife Refuge Trail

Ukiah

Mendocino County was made up of three Mexican land grants, the Yokayo, del Norte (also known as Garcia grant), and the Sanel, or Felix, grants. In 1845, Mexican Governor Pío Pico gave the Yokayo, in the Russian River Valley, to Cayetano Juarez, a militia captain and native Californian. The city of Ukiah takes its name from the phonetic pronunciation of Yokayo, which is Pomo for "deep valley."

State Street, Ukiah, circa 1930

In 1856, Samuel Lowry built a log cabin on the site, now 60 miles north of Santa Rosa on US 101. The first post office was established in 1858, and once Ukiah had a sufficient population, the town became the Mendocino County seat. Until then, the county, one of the original 27, had been administered from Sonoma.

Harrison Standley, the first postmaster, built a hotel in 1858, and the *Mendocino Herald* began publication in 1860. Property prices surged in 1889 when a railroad reached the town. A fire burned much of the Ukiah in 1917, then a town of nearly 2,000 people. The Parducci Winery opened in 1931 and was for many years the northernmost winery in the state. Ukiah, amid great redwoods, thrived in the late 1940s and early 1950s as a logging town. Now the area has numerous wineries, such as Fetzer, vineyards, pear orchards, and wood product plants. Ukiah's population has topped 15,000.

The Grace Hudson Museum and Sun House, once the home of artist Grace Hudson and her physician husband and amateur anthropologist, John Hudson, has a large collection of artifacts, Grace Hudson's paintings, Pomo Indian baskets, and historic photos. The house, built in 1911, is of redwood and is a classic of the California Craftsman style.

US 101, a principal north-south highway, brings hundreds of tourists to the region to enjoy nearby Lake Mendocino and the Cow Mountain Recreation Area.

GPS COORDINATES: N39°08.62' W123°12.32'

NEAREST TRAIL: North Coast #3: Bartlett Springs Road

Vallecito

Daniel and John Murphy discovered gold along Coyote Creek in 1848. The supply camp that arose near their placer claims was known as Murphy's Diggings and later as Murphy's Old Diggings to distinguish it from Murphy's New Diggings, now the town of Murphys. Mexican miners who controlled the site until 1852 named the site Vallecito, "little valley" in Spanish. When a post office was established in 1854, the name was misspelled Vallecita, an error not corrected until 1940.

The major discovery at Vallecito was made in 1852. Gold was also taken in large quantities from the Central Hill Channel, an ancient streambed between Murphys and Vallecito. By 1860, most people had left town. Vallecito was never completely deserted, and today it is a sleepy community 6 miles east on California 4 from Angels Camp.

Several buildings remain from Vallecito's boom days. In front of the old Union Church is a stone monument with a large bell. Originally, the bell, brought to the camp by a traveling preacher, hung from an oak tree, which blew over in 1930. Ruins of the 1854 Wells Fargo office stand nearby, and the Dinkelspiel Store, built in 1851 as Cohen and Levy's Store, is still open for business. The Cuneo Building, built of blocks of rhyolite tuff, also dates from 1851.

GPS COORDINATES: N38°05.24' W120°28.33'
TRAIL: Northern Sierra #5: Crandall Peak Trail
MAP: Page 310

Weaverville

The seat of Trinity County, Weaverville was named for gold miner George Weaver, who built the site's first cabin in 1849. Although not as rich as the Mother Lode, Trinity County, one of the state's original 27 counties, had good gold mining opportunities. Profitable placer mines attracted prospectors during the gold rush, but hydraulic mining produced the best yield in the vicinity of Weaverville. The La Grange Mine, 4 miles northeast of town, was one of the best-producing hydraulic mines in all of California. Although hydraulic mining was banned in 1884, the practice at the La Grange Mine continued until sometime during World War I.

Indians resented the arrival of hundreds of Yankee settlers and their destructive ways, and raids on settlements became commonplace. After Indians killed a rancher in 1852, Weaverville residents organized a large posse. They came upon a large village at Bridge Gulch in Hayfork Valley and attacked, slaughtering 153 men, women, and children. Only two young girls survived the massacre.

Weaverville attracted a large population of Chinese workers in the early 1850s, and at one time, Chinatown occupied two blocks of Weaverville's Main Street. Two groups of Chinese (members of different tongs) faced off during an 1852 battle, involving perhaps 600 of the town's 2,000 Chinese.

Weaverville, circa 1930

Matters were resolved with fists, tools, and knives on a flat near Five Cent Gulch. The Chinese presence is recalled at the state's oldest Chinese temple, Joss House State Historic Park.

Apart from Joss House, Weaverville's Chinatown and much of the rest of its early days was destroyed by fires in 1853, 1855, and 1905. What remains was built in the late 1850s out of fireproof brick and iron. Trinity County Courthouse, originally a saloon, was built about the same time. Weaverville remains a small county town, but it is no longer as isolated as it was in the 1850s. California 299 and California 3 connect Weaverville to Eureka, and Redding, and to units of the Shasta-Trinity National Forests, and the Whiskeytown-Shasta-Trinity National Recreation Area. Weaverville's population is now about 3,000, significantly down from the heady gold rush days.

GPS COORDINATES: N40°44.00' W122°56.33'
NEAREST TRAIL: North Coast #22: Hobo Gulch Trail

Weed

In 1897, Maine-born Civil War veteran Abner E. Weed bought the Siskiyou Lumber and Mercantile Company and 280 acres of surrounding land for $400 and founded the Weed Lumber Company. The lumber town of Weed is 7 miles north of Mount Shasta at the intersection of US 97 and Interstate 5. Mr. Weed's company had only 28 employees at first. By 1960, the mill employed 1,500 people to construct plywood, doors, lumber, and other products from 90 million board feet of logs per year. Weed's economy slowed as limitations were placed on the timber industry.

The town, on the rugged western slopes of Mount Shasta, has unlimited access to lakes, national forests, and the arid Modoc Plateau. Siskiyou County's public community college, the College of the Siskiyous, is an important part of the town's economy. The indomitable spirit and the strong sense of community of young northwestern lumber towns lives at the Weed Historic Lumber Town Museum. Exhibits include antique logging tools, a fully operational 1923 La France fire truck, tools from a blacksmith shop, and a still used to make whisky and brandy during Prohibition.

Lake Shastina, north of Weed, attracts water skiers, windsurfers, boaters, and and jet skiers. A Robert Trent Jones 18-hole championship golf course and a 9-hole executive course are also located on its shores. Also north of Weed on California 97, the Vietnam veteran and sculptor Dennis Smith has created the Living Memorial Sculpture Garden as a memorial to those who fought in the Vietnam War.

GPS COORDINATES: N41°25.58' W122°23.23'
NEAREST TRAIL: North Coast #33: Mount Shasta Loop

Whiskeytown

Established in 1849, the mining camp may have gotten its name when a mule loaded with two whiskey kegs lost its footing on a narrow pass and the precious cargo crashed into a ravine where it emptied into the stream below. Almost in tears, the miner leading the mule cried, "This is sure one hell of a whiskey creek now." The stream became known as Whiskey Creek and the camp, Whiskeytown. Refusing to accept Whiskeytown as a legitimate name, the town's post office was

Whiskeytown Hotel, circa 1930

named Blair in 1881, Stella in 1885, and Schilling in 1917. Finally, in 1952, Whiskeytown residents could receive mail with Whiskeytown as an address.

Jedediah Smith passed this way in 1826, and prospectors following his trail to Oregon some 30 years later found nuggets of gold in the gravel. The rich gold deposits were more important to prospectors than the difficulty of getting to the camp. The town, as the name implies, grew into a free-spirited place that produced great wealth, which was typically spent without restraint. The vicinity's mines and streams are estimated to have yielded $25 million in gold.

In order to create Whiskeytown-Shasta-Trinity National Recreation Area, the Bureau of Reclamation diverted the Trinity River in 1963, submerging the old Whiskeytown beneath the icy 200-foot-deep Whiskeytown Lake. Old Whiskeytown was located east of Weaverville and west of Redding off California 299. New Whiskeytown sits on the banks of the lake. The post office from old Whiskeytown was relocated to the lake's eastern shore before the original settlement site was flooded.

GPS COORDINATES: N40°38.08' W122°33.62'

NEAREST TRAIL: North Coast #25: South Shore Drive

Yreka

In 1851, a party of Oregonians traveling south rested at Yreka Flats. Abraham Thompson was astonished to see gold flakes among grassroots pulled up by his hungry mules. Thompson and his companions camped at the site, and within weeks, a bustling tent city of 2,000 had sprung up. At first the camp was called Thompson's Dry Diggings and then Shasta Butte City. But to avoid confusion with Shasta City, residents decided on Yreka, an Anglicized version of an Indian name for Mount Shasta. When Siskiyou County was organized in 1852, Yreka was designated the county seat.

Yreka, circa 1851

Yreka lay in the heart of Pit River Indian territory. The Pit River tribes resented the intrusion of white settlers onto their land, and conflicts were commonplace. Stagecoaches were vulnerable to attack not just by Indians, but on several occasions by gangs passing as Indians. The Modoc and Klamath tribes were also threats to settlers. In 1852, frustrated Americans resorted to treachery, inviting a delegation of Modoc to a peace talk and then slaughtering them all.

Yreka expanded rapidly; by 1852, it had a population of 5,000. Yrekans took mining matters seriously. The Greenhorn "war" of 1855 arose when miners on Lower Greenhorn Creek diverted ditch water heading to claims on Yreka Flats. The Yreka Flats Ditch Association took the matter to court. The judge enjoined the Greenhorn miners against further diversion of the ditch and threw one of their party in jail when he ignored the injunction. The prisoner's friends raided the Yreka jail while most of the town's residents were attending the opening ceremony for a newly constructed church. Alerted to the jail break, Yreka men abandoned the ceremony and took on the Greenhorn bunch. One man died and several were wounded in the ensuing shootout.

Yreka's mining days faded, and the town moved on to logging, which sustained the area economy for many years. Today, Yreka is a charming town, one of Northern California's largest and prettiest. Near the town's center is a historic old section, which survived an 1871 fire that destroyed much of the city. The Siskiyou County Museum has exhibits about Native Americans, mining, and lumbering. Siskiyou County Courthouse also has interesting displays on gold mining.

GPS COORDINATES: N41°43.86' W122°37.93'

NEAREST TRAIL: North Coast #36: Klamath River Road

Historic Trails

California Trail

The overland route to California in the 1840s began at the Missouri River town of Independence. The Oregon Trail, which led pioneers to the Willamette Valley in Oregon, had been used as early as 1840; the California Trail followed it as far as Fort Hall, on the Snake River in present-day Idaho. The trails parted, with the California Trail leading southwest across lands unorganized since their acquisition in 1804 (as part of the Louisiana Purchase) into Mexican territory. The trip took at least five months. The trails were not laid out as roads, but general routes heading west, converging only when geography dictated—at river crossings or mountain passes.

The Oregon Trail was relatively well established by 1841 when a small party organized by John Bidwell and John Bartleson pioneered the route to California. They joined an Oregon-bound party leaving St. Louis in May 1841. The group of 77 people, led by mountain man Thomas "Brokenhand" Fitzpatrick included Jesuit missionary Pierre-Jean De Smet. Half of the party followed Fitzpatrick into Oregon, but 32 people completed the journey to California. They headed

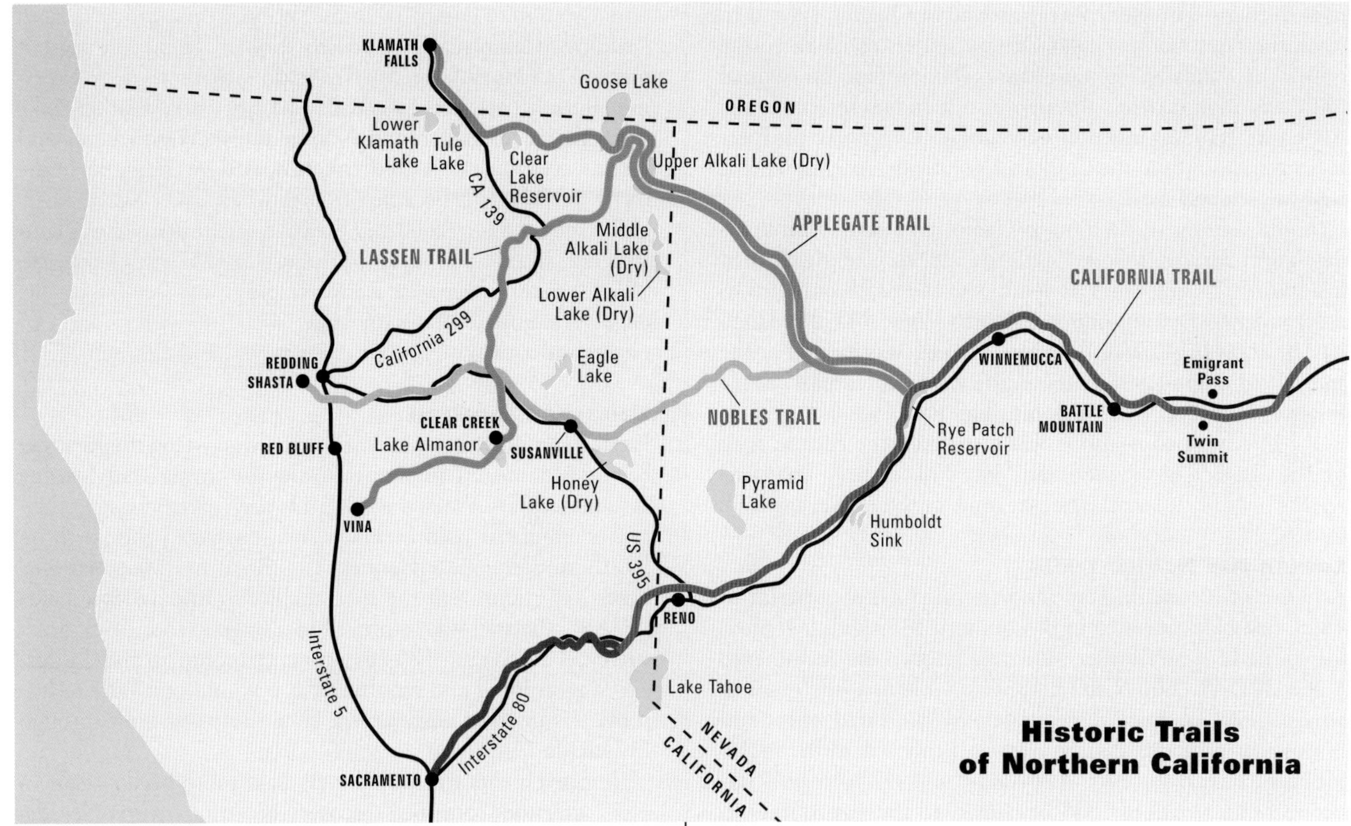

across the Great Plains toward Fort Williams, later called Fort Laramie on the North Platte River, crossing the Rockies at their low point of South Pass, and continued to Fort Hall.

At Fort Hall, the southwest-bound party set out in nine wagons to California. Forced to abandon their wagons in dry northern Nevada, the group headed south eventually to cross the Sierra Nevada at Sonora Pass, arriving in the Central Valley in November. Later groups generally chose to cross the mountain farther north at Carson Pass, Donner Pass, Henness Pass, or Emigrant Gap, among others. The first party to make it to California without losing their wagons was led by Elisha Stevens. In 1844, the Stevens Party crossed the Sierra Nevada at what would become known as Donner Pass with five wagons. One member of the party, Moses Schallenberger, was left for dead by the group, but became the first emigrant to survive a winter in the mountains by himself. The 87-member Donner-Reed Party of 1846 lost 41 people to the Sierra Nevada winter. Some who survived had resorted to cannibalism.

The routes of the California Trail were refined after the experiences of Bartleson and Bidwell in 1841, but the parties headed west were still few. The Sacramento Valley had perhaps 3,000 settlers by mid-decade. This changed dramatically in 1849, following the January 1848 discovery of gold near Sutter's Fort. Travel over the trail increased 50-fold between 1848 and 1849. In 1850, an estimated 30,000 to 45,000 took the California Trail. The Pony Express and its successor, the transcontinental telegraph, followed much of the route, too, as did the transcontinental railroad, completed in 1869. For the men, women, and children who traveled in covered wagons, the journey was arduous indeed. One wonders at the motivation of those who crossed the vast plains into the arid Great Basin and through the Sierra Nevada.

Applegate Trail

The Applegates, from western Missouri, were farmers facing difficult times when they sold their land and set out for the Oregon frontier in 1843. Following a particularly treacherous section of the Oregon Trail across the Columbia River, two young family members drowned in the swift river's rapids. While mourning the deaths of the children, the Applegate patriarchs swore to establish a faster and safer route to Oregon. After settling in Oregon, Jesse and Lindsay Applegate and 13 other men began blazing an alternate route on June 22, 1846. They headed south through the Willamette Valley on a route mirrored by Interstate 5. After fording the Rogue River, they traveled past what would become Medford and Ashland, Oregon, and crossed the Klamath Basin, heading south around Goose Lake, through the Warner Mountains, and into northwestern Nevada. They proceeded southeast across the moonscape of the Black Rock Desert to meet the California Trail on the Humboldt River, which they followed to Fort Hall.

On August 9, 1846, Jesse Applegate convinced a wagon train of nearly 100 emigrants to leave the Oregon Trail at Fort Hall and try the new route. The wagon train encountered harsh conditions along the new route. There was little forage for their livestock and many waterless miles through desert. Overworked and worn down by disease, weak and dying livestock forced the party to stop in California just beyond Surprise Valley at Goose Lake. They sent a messenger ahead to Oregon, and the Applegates brought fresh livestock and supplies to them. The party finally arrived in Oregon, excited to reach their destination. Later Oregon settlers condemned the trail for its hardships because it was longer than the original route and took travelers through hostile Indian territory. The Applegate Trail was much more useful for Oregonian prospectors rushing south to the California goldfields. After 1849, the trail was scarcely used.

Some sections of the trail in California are still visible today. From Alturas, follow California 299 to Cedarville, then head north 19 miles on CR 1 into the Warner Mountains to the Fandango Pass summit (see North Coast #44: Fandango Pass Trail on page 610). A historic marker was erected at the summit to commemorate the journey, and the trail is visible on the mountain's eastern slopes. The Fort Crook–Fort Bidwell Military Road is also visible just under the current road on the east side of the mountain. In 1866, soldiers constructed this road to replace the steeper route of the Applegate Trail.

Lassen and Nobles Trails

A native of Denmark, Peter Lassen emigrated to America in 1829, first blacksmithing in Boston until 1839 and then moving to the Oregon frontier. When he reached the Sacramento Valley in 1844, John Sutter helped him obtain a land grant in what is now Tehama County, where he cultivated wheat and grapes. To promote Benton City, a proposed town on his property, Lassen traveled to Missouri in 1847 to recruit settlers. On his return in 1848 he convinced the wagon train to use the Applegate Trail to Goose Lake and then led them southwest through Devil's Garden to the Pit River, 4 miles west of the future site of Alturas. Lassen and his party followed the Pit River, crossing it for the first time just south of Canby, and made their way west through Stone Coal Valley where they met up again with the Pit River. Led south by the river, Lassen forded the rocky waterway several times before finally crossing it 10 miles north of Lookout. They reached Lassen's ranch in the Sacramento Valley after wandering for two months. Prospectors from Oregon rescued the party and put them on the right route to the Sacramento Valley.

Although the trail was arduous, as many as 8,000 emigrants followed the Lassen Trail into gold country in 1849. The trail was referred to as "Lassen's Death Route," among other nicknames, because it took a month longer to travel than other emigrant trails, the terrain was rough, and there were hostile Indians along the way. Portions of the trail are still evident today in Pit River Canyon. From the intersection of California 299 and California 139 in Canby, take 299 southwest to the Canby Bridge. Travel 4 miles west on Forest Road 84 to where the Pit River turns south; a trail marker is located here. From the primitive campsite just up a short dirt road, follow the trail heading south along the banks of the Pit River to a site along the original Lassen Trail.

Supported by businessmen from the town of Shasta, William H. Nobles raised $2,000 to find an alternative to the Lassen Trail in 1851. Nobles' cutoff left the Humboldt River at Rabbit Springs, Nevada, and entered California near Honey Lake. The trail passed through present-day Susanville and crossed the Cascade Range north of Lassen Peak through Nobles Pass, now on California 89 near the Manzanita Lake entrance station to Lassen Volcanic National Park. From Viola to Redding, California 44 parallels Nobles Trail. The trail is marked at Honey Lake, Shaffer Station, Willow Creek Crossing, Roop's Fort, the Susanville County Park, Feather Lake (intersection of Lassen and Nobles Trails), Poison Lake, and Butte Creek. The trail was frequently used by emigrants in the early 1850s, but it became obsolete when other Sierra passes and wagon roads opened and the subsequent railroad was constructed. In one period, from August 2, 1857, to October 4, 1857, a record keeper at Roop's trading post (see Susanville, page 59) counted 99 wagon trains, with 306 wagons and carriages, and a total of 1,479 men, women, and children.

Henness Pass Trail

Patrick Henness may or may not have discovered the pass that bears his name, an alternative to the California Trail crossing at Donner Pass. After the 1846 Donner party disaster, California emigrants used Henness Pass (farther to the north on Northern Sierra #21: Henness Pass Road in Tahoe National Forest) to circumvent the rugged cliffs around Truckee Lake. In 1852, the trail was improved to a wagon road. D. B. Scott surveyed the road in 1855 as a potential route for the California Wagon Road and reported that it would cost little to improve. Ultimately, however, the state route was built through El Dorado County to the south.

Improvements to the Henness Pass route began again in 1859 after the Comstock discovery in Virginia City, Nevada, then in the Utah Territory. Road builders, David Wood and Thomas Freeman, began scouting the pass to upgrade it to a wagon road from North San Juan near Nevada City to the Comstock mines in Utah Territory. The team found a viable 92-mile route between North San Juan (now a ghost town on California 49 north of Nevada City) and Virginia City. The Henness Pass Turnpike Company began construction of a wagon road west from Virginia City toward Graniteville in November 1859. At the same time, the Truckee Turnpike Company started to build an improved road from Marysville to the Comstock mines. Both routes were planned to follow the Middle Yuba River through Jackson Meadows, now the site of Jackson Meadows Reservoir, and then briefly parallel the Little Truckee River. From the river, the trail would diverge and head east into Dog Valley to the town of Verdi and continue farther east into the Utah Territory. The two companies collaborated to complete the route, which would be called the Henness Pass Road.

The well-constructed, 15- to 18-foot-wide road was banked, had drainage ditches, low elevation grades, and a surface that could support wagons carrying loads as heavy as 11,000 pounds. The Henness Pass Road connected to the steamboat ports on the Sacramento River at Marysville, which made it possible to transport goods to and from Virginia City by boat and wagon as far as San Francisco.

Freight wagons along the trail were pulled by six to ten animals. In order to reduce the possibility of wagons or stagecoaches meeting at narrow places on the road where one or the other would have to back up (downhill vehicles had the right of way), freight wagons used the road during the day and stagecoaches ran at night. Occasionally, wagons would meet, and the one heading uphill would have to be taken apart for the downhill rig to pass. The horses and mules that drew loaded wagons were well trained, waiting patiently on grades when unhitched for other wagons to pass. Eventually, the transcontinental railroad replaced the freighters and eliminated the need for wagon roads such as Henness Pass. Today, Henness Pass Road is paved in some stretches and unimproved in others, but it still provides stunning vistas over the Sierra Nevada. The 1860s Webber Lake Hotel, north of Truckee off California 89 on Webber Lake, is still in use today. Henness Pass Road joins California 89, 9 miles east of Sierraville.

Rubicon Trail

The Maidu Indians of the northern Sierra followed the Rubicon River Valley into the Sierra Nevada to Lake Tahoe to trade with the Washo tribe of western Nevada. George Ehrenhaft established a camp at what became Georgetown, just south of the river, in 1849; George Phipps, a sailor, arrived at about the same time, and it is not clear which George the site is named for. Georgetown is 10 miles northeast of Coloma, where James Marshall first discovered gold in 1848. Georgetown is the western start of the Rubicon Trail, which travels east to Lake Tahoe.

In 1864, a black trapper and trader built a cabin on the Rubicon, a site called Uncle Tom's Cabin, which is now a favorite stop of trail riders and hunters. Miners John and George Hunsucker built a cabin at Rubicon Springs in 1867 and began bottling spring water in 1880 to sell to visitors. The Rubicon Soda Springs Resort opened on the site of the brothers' cabin and catered to health-seeking vacationers. Its two-story hotel collapsed during the winter of 1953. The site is now the largest campground along the trail and a place for jeepers to swap trail stories.

Ranchers moved livestock along the trail to graze in mountain pastures from the 1880s to the 1940s. The El Dorado County Board of Supervisors ensured unlimited access to the trail by declaring it a public highway in 1887.

The first automobiles took to the trail in the 1920s, using ropes and planks to negotiate the hairiest obstacles. Tales of derelict and destroyed cars littering the trail served to warn drivers of its hazards. In 1952, Georgetown residents organized the first Jeepers Jamboree, and on August 29, 1953, 55 vehicles traversed the trail in two days. The annual event is still held the last weekend in July. Four-wheel drive manufacturers test their newest designs on the trail, considering it the ultimate test for prototypes. They swath their vehicles in canvas to hide cutting-edge designs. A successful negotiation of the Rubicon Trail means the 4WD is suitable to drive anywhere.

The Rubicon River was likely named for the river in northern Italy crossed by Caesar in 49 B.C. on his way to overthrow Pompey and gain control of Italy. Crossing the Rubicon means reaching the point of no return, an appropriate phrase for this extreme 4WD trail, which should only be attempted in its entirety by experienced four-wheel drivers with vehicles modified for extreme backcountry conditions.

The trail is most commonly traveled from west to east starting at Georgetown, on California 193, 20 miles east of Auburn. The pavement ends at mile 24 and Uncle Tom's Cabin is passed just after mile 30. Beyond mile 38, the trail intersects paved Ice House Road, which joins US 50 at Riverton. A little more than 40 miles from Georgetown, the trail follows Loon Lake's shoreline to its staging area where the terrain gets rough for the first time.

The trail crosses Ice House Road again at the turnoff to Wentworth Springs. Because of the challenges of the road ahead, the next portion of the trail, from Wentworth Springs to Rubicon Springs, is named Devil's Playground. Just before the trail reaches Rubicon Springs, about 60 miles from Georgetown, it crosses the Rubicon River Bridge. The original log bridge was built in 1860, and it has been replaced by a steel structure and refurbished several times since. From Rubicon Springs the trail follows the river north. About 20 miles from trail's end at Lake Tahoe, the body of an old LaSalle marks Cadillac Hill, the beginning of the final extreme section. From Observation Point, where there is a noteworthy view of the Rubicon River Gorge and trail back toward Georgetown, the

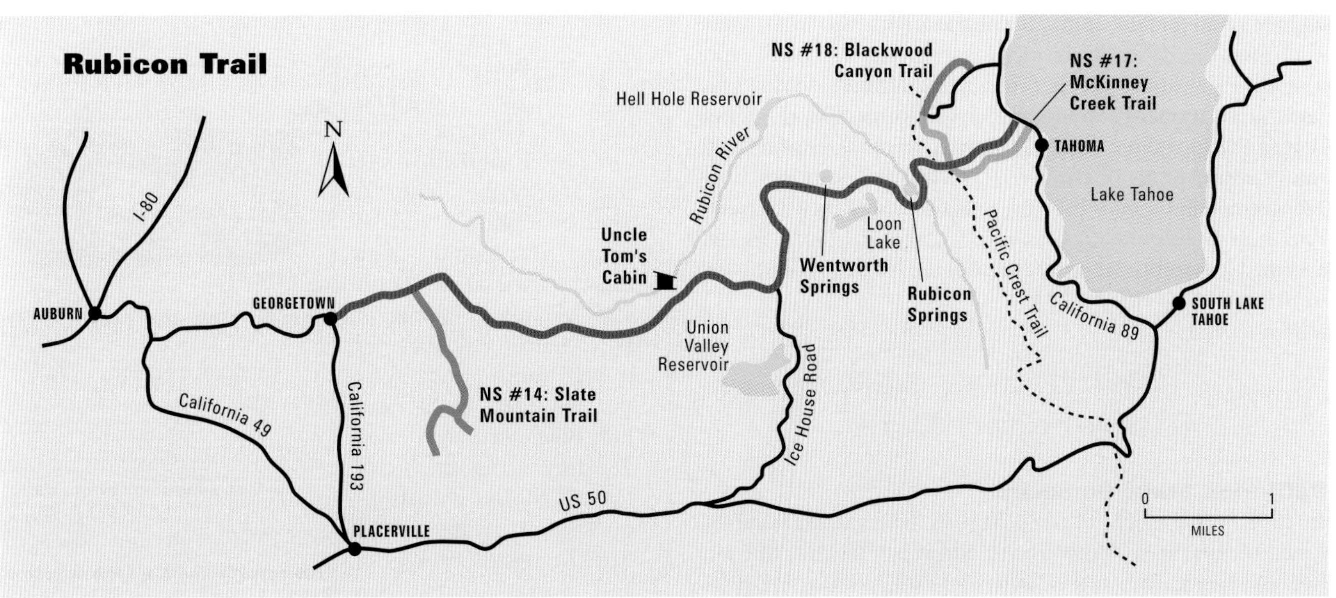

trail evens out. At Barker Pass, the route's highest elevation at 7,115 feet, the Pacific Crest Trail intersects the Rubicon Trail. The Rubicon ends just over 5 miles beyond this point.

Pacific Crest Trail

The Pacific Crest National Scenic Trail was established by the National Trails System Act, signed into law in 1968. The route, still under development at the time, became the second of two national scenic trails, the other being the Appalachian Trail that runs from Maine to Georgia. The California segment of the Pacific Crest Trail, which ultimately extends from Canada to Mexico, was not completed until just before the dedication ceremony on June 25, 1993.

The idea for a hiking route that traversed the entire West Coast of the United States was suggested at least as early as 1926. By then there were already several short trails in the mountains of California and Oregon. In the 1930s, Clinton C. Clarke, who formed and headed the Pacific Crest Trail System Conference, proved the feasibility of a connected border-to-border route. Teams of volunteers explored the proposed route under the guidance of a YMCA secretary, Warren L. Rogers. Clarke and Rogers continually promoted the idea of a Pacific Crest Trail. In the 1960s, the suggestion gained public support, and the Pacific Crest Trail was finally designated in 1968, but it was left to a citizen advisory council to work out the complete route.

The biggest problem facing the committee was the parcels of private land along the proposed route. It often took years to negotiate a right of way with private landowners, and sometimes permissions were never granted and the trail had to be re-routed. When the route was finalized, the 1993 ceremony was meant to emulate the 1869 celebrations at Promontory Point, Utah, where the tracks of the transcontinental railroad were joined.

Composed of the Southern California, Central California, Northern California, Oregon, and Washington sections, the 2,650-mile trail runs through 24 national forests and 7 national parks. In the Central California segment, the corridor dips through lush canyons and climbs to Forester Pass (the highest point on the trail). It connects with the John Muir Trail near the Kings River in Kings Canyon National Park. The hike continues north through Tuolumne Meadows in Yosemite National Park and crosses California 108 at Sonora Pass. The Northern California portion traverses breathtaking snow-capped peaks of the Sierra Nevada and southern Cascades, crossing Donner Pass just south of Interstate 80, Lassen Peak near California 89, Interstate 5 south of Mount Shasta, and the Oregon border on the crest of the Siskiyou Mountains in Rouge River National Forest.

Mail Routes and Stagecoach Lines

California Stage Company

In 1849, at the height of the gold rush, James E. Birch established the first stage company in California. His small line ran between Sacramento and Coloma and was a popular means of transportation into the goldfields. Soon several other companies had lines from Central California to the mining districts. In 1854, Birch and fellow New Englander Frank Stevens consolidated many of the lines into the California Stage Company. From their base in Sacramento, the two partners soon dominated more than 80 percent of stage travel in California. Most of the routes were associated with the gold rush in Northern California.

By 1858, the company owned 134 coaches and more than 1,000 horses. It ran 28 daily stage lines over nearly 2,000 miles, making it one of the largest stage services in the nation. Lines to the Mother Lode ran from Sacramento, Oakland, San Francisco, and Monterey. Isolated mining camps relied on the California Stage Company for mail and other supplies. Many of the routes were poorly developed and passenger stage travel in 1850s and 1860s California was notoriously uncomfortable and at times treacherous. Most of the roads were privately built. Only in 1859 did the state begin to fund road construction.

In 1860, the California Stage Company obtained a contract to deliver mail to and from Portland and Sacramento. For the next several years, the company dominated travel in Northern California, but began to sell interests south of Sacramento. The California Stage Company continued to flourish until the 1870s, when railroads made stage lines obsolete.

Butterfield Overland Mail

> Remember, boys, nothing on God's earth must stop the United States mail.
>
> —*John Butterfield*

On March 3, 1857, John Butterfield and his business associates received a contract from Congress subsidizing a transcontinental stagecoach line, thus giving birth to the Butterfield Overland Mail. One of Butterfield's associates was William G. Fargo, who would later play a key role in stagecoach history. Butterfield Overland Mail was not the first long-distance stagecoach line; that title belonged to the San Antonio and San Diego Mail Line, also known as the Jackass Mail. Butterfield built onto the ailing San Antonio and San Diego.

Time was of the essence; Butterfield had only one year to organize his route. He chose to follow a more southerly route than that of the California Trail because it would be open year-round. The route started at St. Louis and Memphis, joining at Fort Smith, Arkansas, to travel south and west through Texas to El Paso, Fort Bowie in New Mexico Territory, across the Sonoran and Mojave Deserts into California, and on to San Diego and Los Angeles and north up the San

1866 advertisement for the Overland Stage

Overland Mail stage

Joaquin Valley to San Jose and San Francisco.

Butterfield hired Indian-friendly frontiersmen to work for the company. He avoided using way stations by paying farmers along the route to room and board passengers and drivers. In the sparsely settled Southwest, he built sod houses as way stations. Drivers were stationed along the route. Each one had to memorize his 60-mile route because they would drive the stagecoach during day and night. A conductor who had to make a 120-mile run would ride along with the driver.

On September 15, 1858, the first Butterfield stage left from San Francisco to make its way overland. The stagecoach arrived in St. Louis 23 days, 23 hours, and 30 minutes later. Regular mail service had finally been provided across the continental United States. A ticket for a passenger from St. Louis to San Francisco cost $200. The trip from San Francisco to St. Louis was a bargain at $100 because hardly anyone was leaving California at the time. Meals were not provided, so passengers either had to pack food for the more than three-week trip, or buy it at the way stations and farmhouses along the way. Passengers were also obligated to help drivers in case of trouble, which ranged from getting stuck in sand or mud to an Indian attack. The coach's speed depended on the smoothness of the road and ranged from three-and-a-half to nine miles an hour.

For those who were hardy, the trip was exciting. For weaker souls, the trip was a grueling nightmare. One traveler remarked that he knew what hell was like because he'd just spent 24 hours there. Waterman L. Ormsby, a reporter for the *New York Herald*, made the trip and reported that during the ride he had subsisted on beans, salt pork, and black coffee. He slept very little, constantly inhaled trail dust, and lived in fear of an Indian attack. Indian attacks rarely occurred, though.

In 1860, John Butterfield left the Butterfield Overland Mail after a successful career. William B. Dinsmore replaced him. In the 1860s, William G. Fargo's Wells, Fargo & Company took an interest in the mail route. Fargo's stagecoaches carried mail and gold across the continent and gradually came to dominate the express business. Butterfield Overland Mail was then absorbed into Wells, Fargo & Company.

Wells, Fargo & Company

In March 1852, this great freighting and banking firm was established in New York City by two experienced expressmen, Henry Wells and William G. Fargo. Wells, Fargo & Company established its main office in San Francisco and began transporting mail and freight to the booming mining camps of California and to the East. The company bought up many smaller express companies, and by the 1860s, it had a monopoly on California's express business. For a brief time, Wells Fargo also operated a passenger line between San Francisco and Sacramento.

In 1866, Wells, Fargo & Company combined with several interstate stage companies and for the next few years it ran a transcontinental express service. While work continued on the transcontinental railroad, Wells Fargo connected the lines with stagecoaches. The railroad's completion in 1869 rendered the express line superfluous.

Because the most important freight shipped from California was gold, Wells, Fargo & Company branched into banking quite early in its career. At first, the chief enterprise was dealing in gold dust, which could be bought in mining camps for less than it could be sold to the U.S. mint. Soon the company extended its operations into general banking. A banking crisis in California in 1855 led to the collapse of many rivals, and the

Concord stagecoaches featured pinstriping and retractable window covers, circa 1885

company emerged as the leading financial institution in the West. The bank separated from the express business in 1905 and continues to operate today. The headquarters has a small museum at its California Street location in San Francisco.

The Pony Express

On April 3, 1860, the first riders of the Pony Express set out across the West; one rider headed east from Sacramento, the other headed west from St. Joseph, Missouri. Opened and run by the firm of Russell, Majors and Waddell, the Pony Express lasted only a brief 19 months. Although the prospect of a mail system that could cross the country in 10 days (rather than three weeks by stagecoach) excited the public, lack of government subsidies and increasing debts soon forced the new postal system out of business. Also, the transcontinental tele-

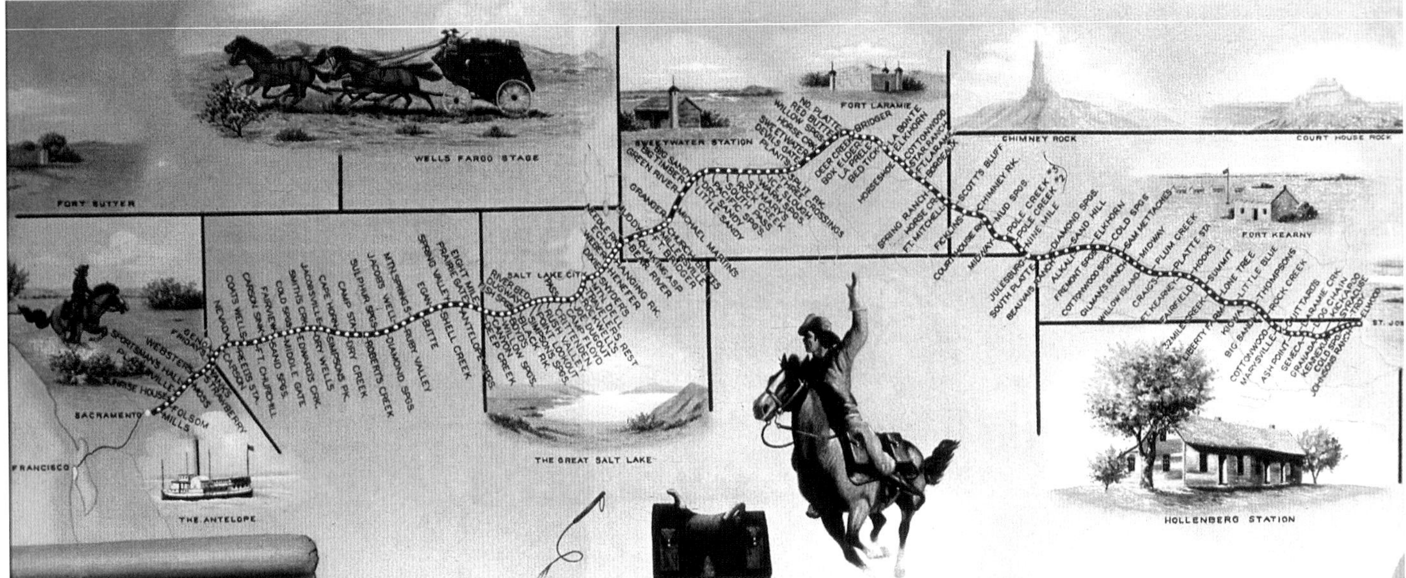

Map of the Pony Express route

graph line completed in April 1861 contributed to the demise of the Pony Express.

The Pony Express had 190 stations between St. Joseph and Sacramento. About 80 riders and 400 horses carried news to the people of California and provided them with a means of communication with the East.

The Pony Express succeeded because of the extraordinary efforts of riders, stationmasters, and hands. Riders weighing 120 pounds or less were hired because horses could carry only a relatively light load. They were equipped with a knife, revolver, horn, and some jerky. The land traversed by these boys (the company advertised for "young, skinny, wiry fellows, not over 18 … Orphans preferred,") was some of the most desolate terrain in the country, and the riders would travel 100 to 125 miles daily (and nightly), braving Indian attacks and rough weather. One rider, William F. "Buffalo Bill" Cody, is credited with a continuous ride of 384 miles.

Because of weight restrictions, the mail carried by the Pony Express was extremely expensive; one ounce cost $10 when service began. As a result, much of the correspondence sent by the Pony Express was government or business related. Eventually, the expense of the operation outran income, and when no government subsidies came through, the Pony Express was forced to shut down with losses of about half a million dollars. Still, the company proved the viability of a transcontinental route through the nation's center. The route was similar to that used by the Central Pacific and Union Pacific and, eventually, Interstate 80.

Railroads

Central Pacific Railroad Company and the First Transcontinental Railroad

Prior to May 10, 1869, there were three options for individuals wishing to travel from one coast of the United States to the other. They could journey six months via boat around Cape Horn and the length of South America; they could walk, a grueling experience that could take six months; or they could take a very bumpy and expensive 24-day stagecoach ride. However, after the fateful day when two trains met at Promontory, Utah, travelers could buy a first-class ticket on the Union Pacific and Central Pacific Railroads for $100 and make the journey in four comfortable days.

In 1862, Congress approved a venture to create the first coast-to-coast railroad in the United States. Two railroad companies were authorized for its construction: the Union Pacific Railroad in the east and the Central Pacific in the west. After delays due to disagreements over financing, Congress passed the Railroad Act of 1864, which allowed larger land grant offerings and 30-year loans to the companies. Pleased with the deal, the railroads began construction in late 1865.

The Central Pacific had been conceived and incorporated in 1861 by Theodore D. Judah, who served as its chief engineer until his death in 1863. Its major investors were Charles Crocker, Mark Hopkins, Collis Huntington, and Leland Stanford—known collectively as the Big Four (see page 85). The four were prominent Sacramento businessmen when they heard Judah's idea for a western railroad route. Even before it received federal funding, the company began to survey a route through the Sierra Nevada and to purchase adjacent lands.

The Civil War was coming to an end and the California gold

Conness locomotive no. 6, Central Pacific Railroad, circa 1865

rush was still on when construction commenced. The railway companies were faced with a labor shortage, so they hired large numbers of immigrants. Union Pacific hired more than a thousand Irishmen, while Central Pacific shipped in 15,000 Chinese laborers to work for just $30 a month. Once the Civil War ended, German and Italian immigrants, war veterans, and ex-slaves also became railroad employees.

Construction in the east began in Omaha, Nebraska, with Union Pacific workers laying an average of one mile of rail per day over the rolling Nebraska plains. The Central Pacific began in Sacramento. Its employees experienced a much different and challenging job of laying rail through the rugged Sierra Nevada. Each company had the same goal: to lay more rails in less time than its competitor. The population of the traversed land was sparse, and temporary shantytowns were built

C.P. Huntington, **the original Central Pacific engine no. 3, circa 1864**

to accommodate workers along the way. Following in their wake were gamblers, saloon owners, and merchants. Towns were settled, but when the tracks outdistanced the town, workers deserted, leaving economic ruin behind them.

As the two railways grew closer, competition became even fiercer. Congress allowed the companies to send their respective graders up to 300 miles ahead of the end of the track. At one point, the Union Pacific and Central Pacific graders actually passed each other and created parallel grades for 200 miles. Most of the parallel grades can still be observed today. Realizing the wastefulness, Congress ended this competition and set the official meeting place at Promontory Summit, Utah. In addition to the railroad, a second transcontinental telegraph was simultaneously constructed. This enabled workers to keep in constant communication with their headquarters. Near the end of construction, Union Pacific workers boasted to their competitors that they had put down an extraordinary 8 miles of rail in one day. Never to be outdone, the Central Pacific waited until the distance between the two was too short for Union Pacific to defeat them again and laid 10 miles and 56 feet in one incredible day. What makes this almost inconceivable is the fact that each 28-foot section of rail weighed approximately 522 pounds.

Although the railroad was actually completed on May 8, 1869, the commemorative ceremony was not held until two days later. Seven years after the railway's initial planning, Leland Stanford drove in a solid gold spike to mark the completion of the first transcontinental railroad. Two trains, Central Pacific's *Jupiter* and Union Pacific's *119*, triumphantly came together, facing each other, joining two oceans and a world of individuals across what had previously been a daunting space. From that moment on, the Great West would no longer be such a mystery to the rest of the nation. Engraved on the famous gold spike were the words, "May God continue the unity of our country as this Railroad unites the two great oceans of the world." The transcontinental railroad would not only unite two oceans but would change the lives of Americans forever. Much of the route through California is still used by railroad companies today and is generally mirrored by Interstate 80.

In later years, the Central Pacific extended the railroad to San Francisco. The Big Four acquired the rival Southern Pacific in 1868, and the tracks of these two corporations made up much of the early infrastructure in California. In 1899, the companies were joined as one as the Southern Pacific Company, which was purchased the following year by the Union Pacific. This merger was later reversed and government regulations preserved the Central Pacific as a corporate entity until 1959.

Western Pacific Railroad

In the early 1900s, the Southern Pacific had a near monopoly over rail travel in California. The Denver & Rio Grande had tracks as far as Salt Lake City, but no route into the Golden State. When the Western Pacific Railway was incorporated in 1903 to build a line from San Francisco to Salt Lake City, the Denver & Rio Grande underwrote $50 million for its construction. The proposed route followed the Feather River and crossed the Sierra Nevada via Beckwourth Pass. It would provide the first serious Northern California competition to the Southern Pacific.

The Western Pacific took its name from a subsidiary line of the Central Pacific that ran between Sacramento and Oakland. This line opened in 1869 and was later absorbed into the Southern Pacific. The new Western Pacific began service in 1909 after the last spike was driven in at Keddie, north of Quincy. In California, the main line from San Francisco passed through Oakland, Stockton, Sacramento, Marysville, and Oroville before crossing into Nevada and winding to Salt Lake City. A lack of branch lines quickly caused financial difficulties for the young railroad. The Western Pacific Railway succumbed to bankruptcy in 1915. The Denver & Rio Grande sold its interests in the company in 1916 and it was reorganized as the Western Pacific Railroad.

The new, independent company set about to purchase smaller companies. In 1917, the Western Pacific purchased the Tidewater Southern, an interurban railroad based in Stockton. The same year, it bought a branch line that connected to Reno, Nevada. Other purchases brought more

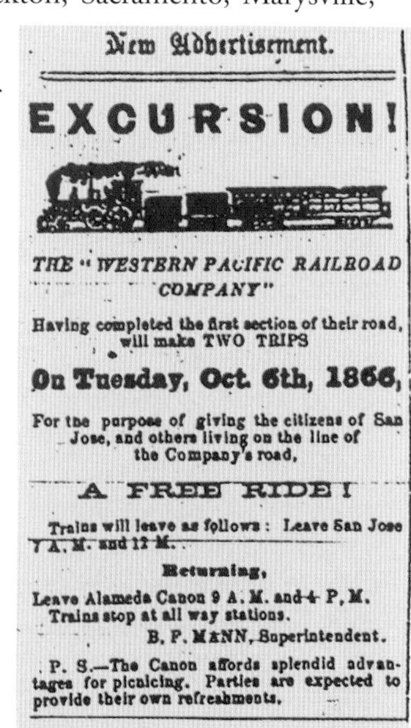

New Advertisement.

EXCURSION!

THE "WESTERN PACIFIC RAILROAD COMPANY"

Having completed the first section of their road, will make TWO TRIPS

On Tuesday, Oct. 6th, 1866,

For the purpose of giving the citizens of San Jose, and others living on the line of the Company's road,

A FREE RIDE!

Trains will leave as follows: Leave San Jose 7 A. M. and 12 M.

Returning,

Leave Alameda Canon 9 A. M. and 4 P. M.

Trains stop at all way stations.

B. P. MANN, Superintendent.

P. S.—The Canon affords splendid advantages for picnicing. Parties are expected to provide their own refreshments.

Advertisement in the *San Jose Evening Patriot* for the new Western Pacific Railroad

traffic to the Western Pacific line. A 1926 agreement gave the company access to the Great Northern Railway station in Bieber, southwest of Adin. The main line of the Great Northern ran from Seattle, Washington, to St. Paul, Minnesota. The new connection established the Western Pacific as an important carrier from the northwestern states into California.

The company suffered during the Depression and was placed in receivership for several years in the 1930s. The economic boom that began with World War II revitalized the Western Pacific. In 1949, it teamed up with the Burlington Northern and Denver & Rio Grande Railroads to operate the *California Zephyr*, a luxury passenger train from Chicago to San Francisco. The train exploited the beautiful scenery along the Western Pacific's tracks, operating until 1970. During the 1970s, the company focused on its regional lines, resisting takeover bids from larger competitors. The Western Pacific ceased to exist as a separate entity in 1982 when it became the Fourth Operating District of the Union Pacific Railroad.

Nevada-California-Oregon Railway

The Nevada-California-Oregon Railway was founded in 1880 as the Nevada & Oregon Railroad Company. It was the brainchild of John T. Davis, a San Francisco businessman. Davis wanted to build a line from Reno, then an important shipping center, to the California-Oregon border. Before the company was incorporated on April 25, 1881, Davis had a falling out with his associates and returned to San Francisco. Service began under new management on October 2, 1882. The original 30 miles of track ran from Reno, Nevada, to Oneida, California. Service was suspended after just three months while the sole locomotive was overhauled in Carson City. The train began running again in June 1883.

In 1884, the company was sold to the Moran brothers, who renamed it the Nevada & California Railroad, a more apt name because the line terminated more than 200 miles from the Oregon border. The Morans bought rolling stock—cars and locomotives—for the railroad and resumed construction of the line in 1888. Track reached Amedee, California (named for Amadee Moran), in November 1890, for a total length of 70 miles.

On January 1, 1893, the company was reorganized as the Nevada-Oregon-California Railway. In 1899, track construction started again after a 10-year hiatus. By 1908, the line reached as far north as Alturas, and in January 1912, it finally reached Lakeview, Oregon. Trains now ran from Reno, Nevada, 275 miles to Lakeview, Oregon. The company had also acquired a 36-mile subsidiary line—the Sierra Valleys Railway.

In 1917, the Western Pacific bought 104 miles of track from the Nevada-California-Oregon. Because the N-C-O no longer owned track in Reno, the company moved its head offices to Alturas the following year. In 1926, the Southern Pacific Railroad Company bought the entire railway. The Nevada-California-Oregon continued to run as a subsidiary of the larger corporation until 1945, when service was discontinued. Portions of the old line are still operated: trains of the Great Western Railway run from Alturas to Lakeview, Oregon; trains of the Union Pacific Railroad Company (the UP purchased both the Western Pacific and the Southern Pacific) run from Reno, Nevada, to Reno Junction, California, and from Wendel to Alturas in California.

Sugar Pine Railway

The first segment of the Sugar Pine Railway was completed in 1903. It ran from Standard to Ralph Station (near Tuolumne). The railroad, owned and operated by the Standard Lumber Company, transported lumber to the Sierra Railroad, on which it could be carried throughout California. By 1907, the main line was finished, running 15 miles from Standard to Lyons Dam. The first steam-powered train ran on its tracks on July 9, 1906. At its peak, the Standard Lumber Company transported more than 75 million board feet of pine and fir annually on the Sugar Pine Railway.

The Pickering Lumber Company bought the logging enterprise in 1911, and ownership of the railroad was likewise transferred. By 1915, the two logging companies had invested $1.3 million in the railway. In addition to the 25 miles of main track, dozens of spur grades connected to the line. Four locomotives and 70 freight cars ran on the Sugar Pine. The main track was abandoned in 1922, though parts of the line were in use for decades afterwards.

A section of the original track has been restored and operates as the Yosemite Mountain Sugar Pine Railroad. Visitors can experience authentic early 1900s rail travel, although the original Sugar Pine carried only freight. The restored track parallels the Middle Fork of the Stanislaus River in Sierra National Forest. It passes evidence of logging before ending at a magnificent standing trestle.

West Side Lumber Company Railroad

William H. Crocker founded the West Side Lumber Company in 1898. Crocker purchased 50,000 acres of ponderosa and sugar pine forest outside the present-day town of Tuolumne. After building a mill in Tuolumne, Crocker began construction of a railroad originally called the Hetch Hetchy and Yosemite Valley Railroad; trains began running on March 23, 1900. He envisioned the narrow-gauge railway meandering through the forest with the dual purpose of transporting timber from the vicinity of Yosemite National Park and carrying tourists to Yosemite Valley. The tourist trade never really took off; in addition to its seven locomotives, an equipment roster from 1906 shows the company owned 150 logging cars but only one passenger car. The harsh winters prevented trains from running for several months a year. Nevertheless, so much lumber was transported during the summer that the company mill in Tuolumne ran year-round.

The West Side Lumber Company was bought by Pickering Lumber Company in 1925. In total, 250 miles of spur tracks were laid along the West Side route. Operations continued on parts of the line until 1965. Several of the Lima Shay locomotives used on the route are now restored and carry passengers on two reconstructed railroads—the Georgetown Loop between Georgetown and Silver Plume in Colorado, and the Yosemite Mountain Sugar Pine Railroad in Sierra National Forest, California. Sections of the original West Side track remain, and railroad enthusiasts fight to preserve this historic site. The West Side Lumber Company Model Railroad Club, based in Michigan, has won awards for its miniature re-creation of the California railroad.

Bodie & Benton Railway

The Bodie & Benton Railway is unique among California's railroads because it is connected to no other line. Its track, which was completed in November 1881, terminated just south of Mono Mills, 30 miles from the nearest line, the Carson & Colorado Railroad. Incorporated in February 1881 as the Bodie Railway & Lumber Company, the railroad was formed with the sole purpose of providing Bodie with wood. Bodie, which was founded in 1859 by Waterman S. Body, experienced a population explosion in the late 1870s as thousands of dollars worth of gold was excavated from its mines. The cost of hauling lumber to build and heat houses and stores and fuel mills proved astronomical. There was little suitable wood in the surrounding area, but the forests south of Mono Lake would be an excellent lumber source. A railroad to these forests seemed a logical proposition.

Grading commenced on May 23, 1881, along various stretches of thc proposed line. Most of the workers were Chinese, a fact that caused temporary resentment in Bodie. Drunken miners congregated at the Miners Union Hall and resolved to confront the unfortunate Chinese. However, the railroad's management hastened their Asian employees aboard a steamboat on Mono Lake. The workers were provided with a month's worth of food and supplies and transported to Paoho Island in the middle of Mono Lake. When the angry mob reached the town, they found it deserted. A proposed siege of Paoho Island dissipated when the mob's liquor began to wear off.

When completed, the southern terminus of the railroad was at Mono Mills, a planned community devoted to the lumber trade. Eventually, spur lines extended the tracks several miles south of the milling center and into the surrounding forest. The railroad's name was changed to Bodie & Benton Railway & Commercial Company in January 1882. The change reflected the intention of Thomas Holt, the company owner. Holt envisioned a lengthened line running all the way to Benton, which was a stop on the newly constructed Carson & Colorado Railroad. Grading proceeded on this venture but halted several miles short of Benton. Future attempts to connect Bodie to the greater railroad network also faltered. (The company name reverted to Bodie Railway & Lumber Company in 1893.)

Even as the railroad was being completed, the town of Bodie was entering decline and the demand for lumber dropped accordingly. The trains ran for only a few months every summer and sometimes not at all. A gold bonanza at nearby Aurora and improved mining techniques in the 1890s helped to sustain the ailing corporation (as did demand for wood as a result of a devastating 1892 fire), but in 1908 it was leased to a private individual. When Bodie's most productive mine, the Standard, closed in 1914, it became apparent that the town's, and the railroad's, days were numbered. On September 6, 1917, the California Railroad Commission approved abandonment of the line. The tracks were pulled up and sold. Bodie suffered another awful fire in 1932 and became a California State Historic Park in 1964. It remains a beautifully, if only partially, preserved ghost town. Mono Mills gradually disappeared, blown away by the wind or picked apart by scavengers. Today, only a forest service sign marks its location.

The Friends of Bodie Railway & Lumber Company is a nonprofit group fighting to reestablish the old railroad along 14 miles of its original right-of-way. Evidence of the railroad's grade is still visible along the eastern shores of Mono Lake and in the Mono Basin.

San Joaquin & Eastern Railroad Company (Big Creek Railroad)

The San Joaquin & Eastern Railroad was built, beginning in 1915, as part of the ambitious Big Creek Hydroelectric Project northeast of Fresno. (See High Sierra #9: Big Creek Railroad Grade Trail, page 179.) The project was conceived to provide the burgeoning metropolitan areas of Southern California with electricity produced from the flowing streams of the Sierra Nevada. To harness the necessary power from a relatively small amount of water, a series of dams needed to be built. Because the steep mountain terrain precluded the use of mules or wagons, construction could not begin before railroad tracks were laid down to ferry supplies.

The San Joaquin & Eastern was built with amazing speed. The entire 56 miles of track were laid in just 157 days. Known as the "crookedest railroad in the world" (one of several California rail lines to merit that nickname), the San Joaquin & Eastern had 1,073 curves, 43 wooden trestles, and 225 steep grades. At 5.3 percent, the grade near Webstone was the steepest in the world. One of the curves was 60 degrees—a conductor could entertain his passengers by hopping off the front of a train before the curve and reboarding after it. Completed without the use of power machinery, the construction employed up to 1,200 workers. In all, the railroad alone cost more than a million dollars.

In addition to supplying material for the hydroelectric project, the railroad transported dam workers and summer tourists. Travelers dubbed the San Joaquin & Eastern (SJ&E) the Slow, Jerky & Expensive; the trip from Fresno to Big Creek took at least 5 hours and cost 10 cents a mile, 8 cents more than standard contemporary rail lines. It was the only passenger service to use geared engines for its cars because its grade was so steep.

As construction of the hydroelectric project neared completion, the railroad was used less and less. By 1929, only three round-trips ran each week. Soon, buses and automobiles rendered the San Joaquin & Eastern irrelevant as a passenger service as well. In 1933, the railroad was abandoned, but not before it had made a major contribution to the lives of millions of Californians.

Yosemite Valley Railroad

Although Yosemite Valley was designated a state park in 1864, and the surrounding area was incorporated into the national park system in 1890, the area remained very difficult to reach. The few visitors arrived by stagecoach and by horseback. The Yosemite Valley Railroad, completed in 1907, made the trip much easier. The line ran 79 miles from Merced to El Portal, through the Merced River Valley. Roundtrip service to the park cost $18.50 in 1907, and the cost eventually dropped to just $10.25.

The Yosemite Valley Railroad Company was incorporated in 1902 with John S. Drum as its president. Its expressed purpose was to carry passengers to the beautiful valley, but the railroad was quick to exploit freighting opportunities and developed a significant business transporting lumber, limestone, and barium lead. By 1923, the railroad owned 8 passenger cars and 182 freight cars.

In the early 1920s, construction of the Exchequer Dam east of Merced Falls necessitated relocating 17 miles of the original track. The new section included four concrete tunnels and five bridges. The 1,600-foot-long steel bridge over Lake McClure was the largest of its kind in the West.

Passenger travel peaked on the Yosemite Valley Railroad in the years immediately preceding the completion of the All-Year Highway in 1927, now California 140. Competition from the automobile route, combined with declining freight business due to the Great Depression and World War II, meant that the railroad was no longer able to earn a profit. Service ended on August 24, 1945. Ironically, the following years saw a remarkable increase in visitation to the park. In 1990, environmentalists dismayed with the heavy motor traffic in the valley re-formed the Yosemite Valley Railroad Company. Their aim is to rebuild the old line and offer passenger service. As it is, parts of the railroad grade are accessible to motor vehicles and make for a scenic and historically significant backcountry drive.

People

Explorers, Mountain Men, and Surveyors

Juan Rodriguez Cabrillo

Born in Portugal around 1495, Juan Rodriguez Cabrillo sailed for Spain. He served with Hernan Cortés during the conquest of Mexico in 1521, but he is best known for being the first European to visit California.

Cabrillo set sail from Navidad on the Pacific coast of Mexico in June 1542 to search for the fabled Northwest Passage to the Atlantic along the continent's Arctic coast. He landed at San Diego Bay on September 28, the first white man to set foot in present-day California. The expedition continued north to the Channel Islands where Cabrillo fell and broke his arm. The voyage continued north as far as the vicinity of Point Arena, when bad weather forced them to return to San Miguel. Cabrillo died on January 3, 1543, likely from an infection resulting from his broken arm.

Juan Rodriguez Cabrillo

Cabrillo instructed his pilot, Bartolomé Ferrelo, to continue the expedition. Ferrelo sailed as far as the modern Oregon-California border before turning back because he was short of supplies. The expedition returned to Navidad on April 14, 1543.

Cabrillo named many of the islands and bays he visited during the voyage, but a later Spanish explorer, Sebastian Vizcaíno, renamed them 60 years later. Today, Point Cabrillo in Mendocino County and Cabrillo Point in Monterey County honor him, and Cabrillo National Monument on San Diego Bay marks the probable site of his first landing on California soil.

Friar Junípero Serra

Junípero Serra, often called the founder of California, was born November 24, 1713, on the Spanish Mediterranean island of Majorca. Christened Miguel José Serra, he changed his name to Junípero when he joined the Franciscan order at age 17.

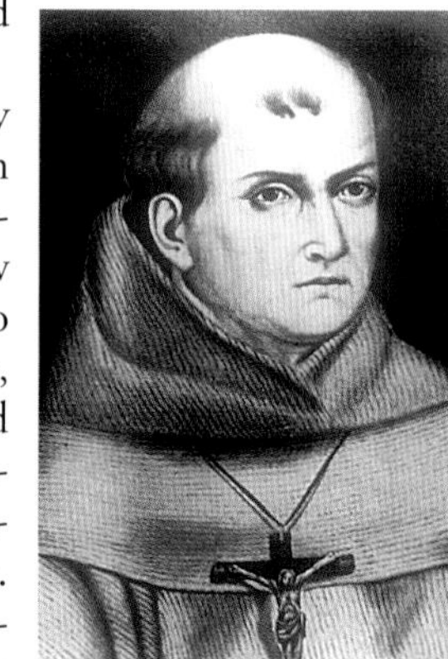
Friar Junípero Serra

In 1749, he was sent as a missionary to New Spain, as Mexico was known in the Spanish Empire, landing at Veracruz on December 7. Within a few years of his arrival, Jesuit monks, who had accompanied the conquistadors, were expelled from New Spain, and their missions were given to the Franciscans. In 1768, Serra was made president of the missions in Baja California.

From the Baja Peninsula, Serra traveled north to Alta, or Upper, California (as the Spanish called California). Spanish authorities at the time feared Russian and British encroachment along the Pacific Coast and sought to further establish their control of the empire's northern dominions. On July 16, 1769, Serra founded the mission of San Diego de Alcalá. He waited there while his party, under the command of Gaspar de Portolá, continued north, discovering the natural harbor of San Francisco Bay.

When Portolá returned to San Diego in January 1770, spirits and supplies were low. Portola urged a return to Mexico, but at Serra's insistence he agreed to stay for nine days of prayer. While the group waited, a supply ship appeared and Spanish presence in California was assured. Serra sailed to Monterey and established a second mission in Carmel. He lived in Carmel for most of his remaining years, though he traveled much, despite suffering a severely ulcerated leg. He either founded or co-founded 9 of the 21 missions in California, including Mission Delores in San Francisco.

Serra baptized thousands of Indians during his time in California. Although the Franciscans and subsequent European settlers are widely blamed for the disease epidemics that ravaged native populations, Serra himself treated the converts well. Once he trekked all the way to Mexico City to plead on their behalf. He also introduced cattle, which became the foundation of California's herds for years to come. Today, his bust is one of two chosen to represent the state in the Capitol's Statuary Hall in Washington, D.C., and he is often suggested as a candidate for sainthood. A significant step toward that was taken in 1988 when the Vatican beatified Serra. Junípero Serra died near Monterey on

August 28, 1784. He is buried at the Mission San Carlos Borroméo in Carmel.

Jedediah Smith

Jedediah Smith was born January 6, 1799, in New York State. Smith answered an ad in the *St. Louis Gazette and Public Advertiser* in 1822 that called for young men who wanted to explore the West. He soon became part of William Ashley's great fur-trapping and exploration venture.

On one of Smith's first expeditions he was attacked by a grizzly bear that ripped off one ear and part of his scalp. Undeterred, he commanded a companion to sew him up, and he returned to the trail after just 10 days. For the rest of his life, he wore his hair long to conceal his wounds.

In 1824, while searching for the fabled Buenaventura River, Smith and his party became the first Americans to cross overland into California. Following his arrival in the Mexican mission of San Gabriel, he was taken to the authorities in San Diego. The Mexican governor feared American intrusion into the area and ordered the party to leave California immediately. Instead of leaving, Smith entered the San Joaquin Valley via Tejon Pass and headed north. At the Stanislaus River, he left most of his party and crossed the Sierra Nevada on his way back to Utah, becoming the first American to do so. Upon returning to the group in California, Smith again ran into trouble with authorities while attempting to trade for supplies in San Jose. After a stint in a Monterey jail, he was released with strict orders to leave California immediately. This time Smith obeyed, and his party trekked north, following the Sacramento River into Oregon.

Jedediah Smith

In Oregon, Smith's party was attacked by Indians, one of many such encounters that the great mountain man faced in his short career. The survivors made their way to Fort Vancouver, and eventually they were able to regain some of the goods taken during the attack. Smith was preparing to retire in 1831 when Comanche Indians attacked him and he was slain in the ensuing fight. He died before publishing an autobiography. A highly religious and strong-willed man, Jedediah Smith is remembered as one of the most important figures in the opening of the American West.

Ewing Young

Ewing Young was born in 1792 in Tennessee. A third generation frontiersman, he received training as a carpenter. Soon, however, the lure of the American wilderness took him west. As a mountain man, Young was persistent and single-minded in acquiring wealth from trapping. By the time he was 30, he had traveled to Santa Fe and was trapping beaver along the Pecos River.

Young reached Los Angeles with a group of 36 men in 1832. After a failed trip hunting sea otters, the party traveled north to trap Kings River and the Sacramento River. They made it all the way into Oregon before returning south, where Young chose to settle. Two years later, he decided to migrate to Oregon with livestock, including 50 horses. The Mexican governor of California, José Figueroa, sent word to Oregon officials that the horses were stolen. The accusations were likely false, but Young's new life was made more difficult by the wild claims. It was a hard time for northern settlers, and there was an acute shortage of cattle. To rectify the situation, Young returned to California to buy 650 head. His journey overland with the herd predated the great cattle drives of the 1880s by more than 40 years and established Young as a prominent rancher and an important figure in early Oregon history. His many Californian expeditions also demonstrated the accessibility of the state to future emigrants. He is credited with improving trails from California to New Mexico and Oregon. Ewing Young died in 1841.

Joseph Reddeford Walker

Joseph Reddeford Walker was born December 13, 1798, in eastern Tennessee's Roan County. Soft-spoken, disciplined, and never a braggart, Walker stood 6 feet tall. For four years he served as a sheriff in Jackson County, Missouri, before heading west. Here, on the frontiers, he established his reputation as one of the greatest figures of American expansion.

Joseph Reddeford Walker

In 1832, Walker met Captain Benjamin Bonneville, who was planning a trapping expedition in the Rocky Mountains. Walker joined Bonneville's party as it moved west toward the Green River. After wintering on the Salmon River, Walker and a group of 40 men left the main party and headed to California. The motives for the trip are unknown, but the exploration was a resounding success. The group found the Humboldt River, in what is now Nevada, crossed the Sierra Nevada, and made its way to the Pacific Coast. On the way, they passed through the Yosemite Valley and its huge sequoia trees. It was along Walker's route that many of the forty-niners reached California during the gold rush.

Once rested in the Mexican mission of San Juan Bautista (near present-day Monterey), the group moved down the San Joaquin Valley and through the mountains at Walker Pass, before heading north to reconnect with Bonneville's party. California 178 retraces his steps today.

Walker returned to California many times, often as a guide to emigrants from the East, and notably as a member of John Frémont's expeditions. He mined gold in the state for several years. A prospecting trip to southern Arizona in the 1860s yielded much wealth and sparked a gold rush to the area around present-day Prescott. In 1867, Walker retired to his nephew's ranch in Contra Costa County. The old pathfinder died in 1876 at the age of 77. By then, his trailblazing had helped open California to many Americans.

William Brown Ide

A little-known figure in California's early history, William Brown Ide was born in Massachusetts in 1796. Growing up he learned carpentry and politics from his father, who struggled as a tradesman and ultimately became a statesman in Vermont's legislature. Ide married Susan G. Haskell in 1820, and the couple had six children. In 1845, Ide began moving west in search of new experiences. He moved his family to Kentucky, Ohio, and Illinois where he bought a farm, which he immediately sold when he heard about the Oregon frontier. With proceeds from the sale, he bought wagons and livestock and hired hands who would help the family reach the West. In Independence, Missouri, the family joined a wagon train and set out for the Oregon Trail. Joe Meek and John Grigsby, the leaders of the train, appointed Ide to the position of chief herdsman when they learned of his farming experience. By the time the party reached Fort Hall, Idaho, it was known as the Grigsby-Ide Party.

At Fort Hall the party met Caleb Green, a colorful mountain man and an agent of John Sutter who convinced some members of the Grigsby-Ide party to travel the newly blazed California Trail and settle on Sutter's land. Determination, spirit, and calm judgment helped the party successfully navigate the grueling route, which would claim the lives of 40 members of the Donner Party the following year. On November 1, 1845, the Grigsby-Ide party arrived at Sutter's Fort, where Peter Lassen invited Ide to settle on his ranch and begin construction of a sawmill. Unfortunately for the well-traveled Ide family, Lassen returned to his ranch and displaced them. R. H. Thomes who owned a ranch on the Sacramento River allowed Ide to build a log cabin there, where the family passed a long harsh winter. In the following spring of 1846, Ide met Josiah Belden, a settler and ranch owner in search of someone to care for his livestock. Ide accepted Belden's offer of half-interest in his ranch to oversee it for three years.

Just as the family's luck was finally turning around, news began spreading along the frontier that Mexican General José Castro was planning to clear his government's territory of American settlers. A group of the new emigrants besieged Captain John C. Frémont for protection. Quickly realizing Frémont would not act on their behalf, the incensed settlers organized an informal garrison that included Ide and Grigsby. The militia made several successful raids against the Mexican army, including the capture of General Vallejo's fort at Sonoma. When Mexican troops left the fort, the group took over and began the process of establishing California as an independent republic and preparing for the retaliation of Mexican forces. The flag they fashioned was a piece of white muslin decorated with a grizzly bear, a red star, and the words, "California Republic." Next, the "Bear Flaggers" penned a formal declaration of the territory's independence and arranged its administration with William Ide as its governor and commander. With war between the United States and Mexico imminent, Frémont arrived with troops to fortify the volunteer army. Word arrived at Sonoma that America had officially declared war, and Frémont assumed leadership of the forces. Commodore Stockton swore the "Bear Flaggers" into the U.S. Army in Monterey and Ide served honorably throughout the remainder of the war.

Far from home with little money at the end of the war, Ide bargained with a captain to work as a carpenter on his ship to pay his way back to San Francisco and home to Belden's ranch. During the trip, Commodore Stockton brought Ide's true identity to the captain's attention; he immediately relieved Ide of his duties and provided him with the best accommodations the ship had to offer. Ide made his way home and bought part of the Red Bluff Ranch, but he promptly left it to participate in state government. When gold was discovered in Coloma in 1848, he rushed in and made enough money to buy more land for his ranch. It is on this portion of his property that Ide is presumed to have built an adobe where a ferry (known at the Adobe Ferry) across the Sacramento River operated for 30 years. Today, the adobe is preserved as part of the William B. Ide State Historic Park in Red Bluff. Susan Ide died in the late 1840s. William Ide held several state government offices, including judge of Colusa County. He died in Monroeville, 30 miles south of his ranch, in December 1952 after catching smallpox.

Edward Fitzgerald Beale

Regarded as "Mr. California," Edward Beale played many successful roles throughout his life. Born in 1822, he had a variety of professions, ranging from naval officer and prominent explorer to bureaucrat and politician. Those who knew him described him as a thin, wiry man who was outspoken and very frank. Status, wealth, and a thirst for adventure seemed to drive Beale in his many exploits.

Beale first gained prominence in the Mexican War of 1846–48. He and Kit Carson slipped through enemy lines at San Pasqual (see Mexican War, page 102) and fetched relief for the embattled American troops led by Stephen Kearny. During and after the war, he made a series of transcontinental journeys with dispatches to and from Washington. On one trip he carried the first sample of California gold to the East Coast, helping inspire the gold rush of 1849. Beale married Mary Edwards in Chester, Pennsylvania, later in 1849. He also carried a copy of a draft of the California State Constitution to the nation's capital that year.

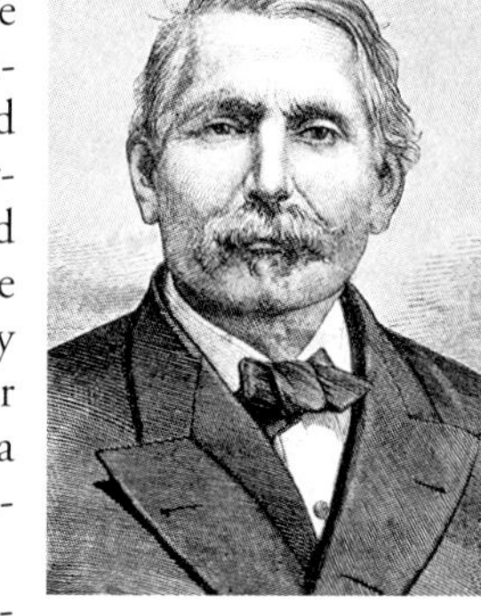
Edward Fitzgerald Beale

After reaching the rank of lieutenant, Beale left military service in 1851. Earnings from a Mariposa County freighting enterprise enabled him to bring his family to California in the spring of 1852. Earlier that year, he had entered politics as California's first superintendent of Indian affairs. He used the post to promote humanitarian solutions in disputes with Native Americans, but also connived to purchase some Indian lands for himself at a greatly reduced price. In 1853, he was given a concurrent assignment as brigadier general of the California state militia in order to give him greater leverage in his struggle to protect Indian rights.

Beale resigned from both positions in 1856 and served briefly as sheriff of San Francisco. Soon, however, he turned his attentions to the problem of transporting goods from the East to the West. He proposed the formation of a camel corps to better supply forts across the dry deserts of the Southwest.

In 1857, he accepted a job as superintendent for a transcontinental wagon road. This led to the creation of the Beale Wagon Road and the introduction of camels in the American Southwest. When the State Department sold the animals, Beale relocated them to his ranch near Bakersfield. He spent the Civil War in the West as surveyor general of California and Nevada. During the war, he used his political influence to dissuade President Lincoln from enforcing the draft in California, helping to prevent a potential revolt by Confederate sympathizers.

Beale stayed in politics through his later years and was active in the Pennsylvanian movement for African-American suffrage. During the 1870s, he climbed the Republican political ladder and soon became one of President Ulysses S. Grant's personal friends, serving a year as ambassador to Austria-Hungary. Beale first met Grant in 1852, while the future president was stationed with the army in San Francisco. On April 21, 1893, after attending a reception committee meeting for Grover Cleveland's inaugural ball, Edward F. Beale died at the age of 71. His remarkable contributions to California history are commemorated today by street names in Bakersfield and San Francisco and by Beale Air Force Base, near Marysville in Yuba County.

James P. Beckwourth

Probably the most noteworthy African-American mountain man of the old west, James Pierson Beckwourth was born in Fredericksburg, Virginia, on April 26, 1798. He was the son of Sir Jennings Beckwith, a white revolutionary war hero, and Beckwith's black slave, Miss Kill. Young James was never a very good speller, and his commonly accepted surname of Beckwourth may have been an error of illiteracy or a conscious attempt to distance himself from his father.

When Beckwourth was eight, his father, Miss Kill, and their large family moved west to an area near the confluence of the Missouri and Mississippi Rivers. At that time, this area was considered the far west. Life was tough; Beckwourth worked in the fields among his father's slaves. At age 14, he was sent to St. Louis to be a blacksmith's apprentice. After five years in the blacksmith's shop, Beckwourth got in a brawl with his employer over a girl and left the shop. He got a job as a hunter for a lead mine and he became friends with local Indians, who showed him the prime hunting grounds. Throughout his life, Beckwourth discovered that his mixed-race skin color garnered the trust of Native Americans, who trusted him more than his white compatriots.

By 1824, Beckwourth was using his wilderness skills as a beaver trapper. He roamed the West in trapping parties, working along the Platte and Yellowstone Rivers and running with such famous mountain men as Jedediah Smith and James Bridger. Much of the American West was hostile territory in these days, and Beckwourth was caught in Indian attacks on more than one occasion. In 1829, in order to preclude disputes with the Crow Indians, a companion of Beckwourth's told the tribe that James had been stolen from the Crow as a baby. One Crow woman became convinced that Beckwourth was her long lost son. Beckwourth decided to join the tribe. He spent some years with the Crow, eventually becoming one of their leaders, marrying several Indian women, and leading raids on neighboring tribes.

By 1836, Beckwourth had left the Crow to work for the American Fur Company. In 1837, he served briefly as a captain in the U.S. Army during Florida's Seminole Wars. Later, he ran his own trading company, helping to found Fort Pueblo, now Pueblo, Colorado. During this time, he took a Mexican wife named Louisa Sandoval and became acquainted with Kit Carson and John Frémont.

Beckwourth first came to California in 1840 on a horse raid. Beckwourth's group, led by Thomas "Peg Leg" Smith, took 5,000 horses in just three days. Beckwourth returned to California as a trader in 1844 and became embroiled in the civil dispute between Governor Micheltorena and Juan Alvarado, taking the side of the rebels. As war between his Mexican allies and the United States approached, he left California, taking more than 1,000 illegally obtained horses with him. He sold the horses in Utah and returned to California for his wife. He found her remarried, so he left for Santa Fe, where he bought a small hotel. In his preparations for war in California, General Stephen Kearny stayed in Beckwourth's hotel. Although he didn't accompany the general to the west coast, Beckwourth did contribute his services to the U.S. war efforts, helping to quell the Taos insurrection.

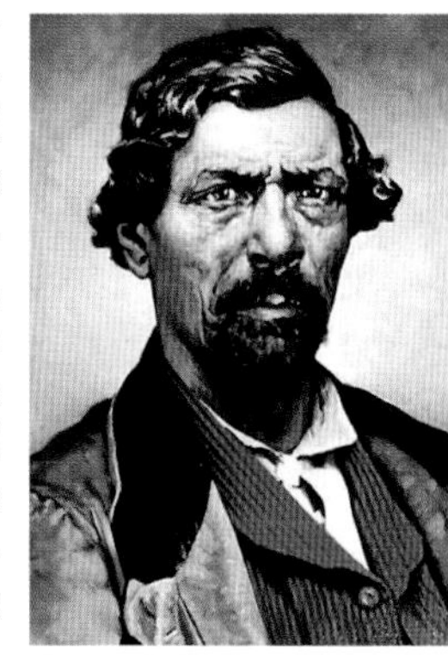

James P. Beckwourth

In 1848, news began to spread through the West of James Wilson Marshall's discovery of gold. Beckwourth rushed to the Mother Lode. He was not a very successful prospector, but did well as a supplier to miners and blazer of new wagon trails. In 1851, the intrepid mountain man discovered Lassen County's Beckwourth Pass. The following year he began dictating his memoirs to Thomas D. Bonner, a former journalist. Published in 1856, *The Life and Adventures of Jim Beckwourth* was an international success, though historians consider it too full of inaccuracies and fabrications to be a reliable source.

For a time, Beckwourth operated a hotel and trading station on the western side of his pass. He left California in the

Beckwourth's trading post, established in 1852, now a museum located 2 miles west of Beckwourth

late 1850s; some accounts claim he was driven out for horse theft. In 1859, he settled in Denver and married Elizabeth Ledbetter. When Elizabeth left him, he took an Indian wife named Sue.

In 1866, Beckwourth left Colorado and returned to the Crow nation to pursue negotiations for the U.S. Army. While staying with his old tribe, Beckwourth died, perhaps of poison. He was buried as a Crow Indian. In addition to Beckwourth Pass, the names of a mountain and a town in California commemorate his remarkable life.

Lawmen, Gunfighters, and Outlaws

Joaquin Murrieta

Joaquin Murrieta (also spelled Murieta) was probably the most famous of the gold rush era outlaws. His legend is so clouded in myth that many historians dispute his very existence. Nevertheless, several recent researchers have meticulously pieced together a few definite facts about his life.

Church records indicate the birth of a Joaquin Murrieta in 1830 near Alamos in Sonora, Mexico. After marrying Rose Feliz, Murrieta followed the northern exodus of 1848 in search of gold. His wife, half-brother, and three brothers-in-law, including the outlaw Claudio Feliz, accompanied him on his migration to California. The group settled in the tent city of the gold camp at Sonora, in Tuolumne County.

Legend says that Murrieta was forced from his claim by a group of Americans who lynched his brother and raped his wife. Though this story is likely a fabrication, it is probable that Murrieta was mistreated by Anglos and developed a dislike for them. By 1850, Claudio Feliz was leading a murderous outlaw gang that committed a series of thefts and killings around San Jose. Murrieta's involvement in these crimes is unknown, but according to legend he was in a gunfight on April 5, 1852, which led to the serious wounding and arrest of his wife's brother.

Three weeks after Feliz's imprisonment, Murrieta led a group of outlaws in the murder of a young farmer named Allen Ruddle. Ruddle's family was wealthy and offered a large reward for Murrieta's capture. Respected lawman Harry Love gathered a posse to hunt for the outlaw, but it would be some time before he was successful. In the meantime, Murrieta's reputation grew. He was blamed for a multitude of robberies and murders across the Mother Lode. By January 1853, his gang was considered to be the bloodiest and most feared of the gold rush. They would ride into mining camps—often Anglo, but also Chinese and Hispanic—and steal all the gold in the town and kill those who resisted.

Joaquin Murrieta

In May 1853, the state legislature formed the California Rangers, headed by Harry Love, to capture the "five Joaquins," as the gang was known. Love arrested another of Murrieta's brothers-in-law, Jesus Feliz, who led the Rangers to the outlaws' hideout. On July 25, 1853, Love's men awakened the gang and shot Murrieta dead in the ensuing firefight. His head and the hand of a companion, Bernardino "Three-fingered Jack" Garcia, were removed and paraded around the state as evidence of their deaths.

In 1854, John Rollin Ridge published *The Life and Adventures of Joaquin Murieta, the Celebrated California Bandit,* a highly fictionalized account of Murrieta's violent career, and a movie, *Robin Hood of El Dorado,* was made about him in 1934. His myth grew and he was portrayed as avenging injustice in the Old West. In 1967, Chilean poet Pablo Neruda wrote a play about the outlaw. As accounts of Murrieta's life grew increasingly fictionalized, historians began to question whether he had ever really existed. Recent works have helped restore a historical view of the bandit, but his legend persists.

Harry Love

Harry Love was born in Vermont in 1810. In his youth, Love served as a scout in the Seminole wars in Florida and the Blackhawk War of 1832. He also worked as a seaman before serving as an express rider in the Mexican War of 1846–48. Love arrived in California in December 1850 and began mining. None of his mining projects succeeded, but Love was recognized as a capable lawman, becoming deputy sheriff of Santa Barbara and Los Angeles. He was living in Mariposa County when Joaquin Murrieta's gang murdered Allen Ruddle in April 1852. On May 17, 1853, the state legislature authorized the formation of the California State Rangers to catch the Mexican bandits. Love was asked to command the 20-man group.

The Rangers tracked Murrieta across Mariposa County. The gang members refused to lie low—they continued to commit daring robberies, even as the law closed in on them. Love successfully captured several of the bandits, but his real break came when Murrieta's brother-in-law Jesus Feliz was brought into custody. On July 25, 1853, the Rangers were able to confront Murrieta. The outlaw was killed in a firefight. Love ordered his men to decapitate Murrieta's body. The detached head and the hand of another gang member, Bernardino "Three-fingered Jack" Garcia, were displayed at towns across the Mother Lode.

For his efforts, Harry Love and his Rangers received a reward of $6,000. With his share of the money, Love bought a sawmill near Santa Cruz. In 1854, he married the sawmill's previous owner, a wealthy divorcee named Mary Bennett. The marriage was not happy, and bad luck seemed Love's fate: the mill was flooded out, farming was unprofitable, his home burned down, and he lost a race for justice of the peace. On July 29, 1868, Love tried to fire Christian Eiverson, a German handyman hired by his wife. Eiverson refused to leave, saying only Mrs. Love could fire him. Love, armed with a pistol and shotgun, confronted the hired man. Eiverson drew his pistol and wounded Love in the right arm. Love died after surgery to amputate his arm. He was buried in the Santa Clara Mission Cemetery.

Richard A. "Rattlesnake Dick" Barter

Richard Barter was born in Quebec, Canada, in the early 1830s, a son of a British army officer. Dick moved to California in 1850 with his elder brother and settled on the North Fork of the American River in the mining camp of Rattlesnake

Bar. A contemporary described Rattlesnake Dick, as he came to be known, as "nearly six feet in height, ... about 160 pounds, slight of build, but ... very muscular." Other sources testify to his handsome appearance. Rattlesnake Dick's first encounter with the law was in 1853 when he was arrested, and then acquitted, for stealing clothes from a shop. The following year he was convicted of stealing a mule and sentenced to a year at San Quentin.

During his imprisonment Dick met highwayman Tom Bell; Dick joined Bell's outlaw gang and participated in a string of horse thefts, robberies, and killings in mining country. Following Bell's death in 1856, Rattlesnake Dick took control of the gang's surviving members. Under Dick's guidance, the gang burgled a Wells Fargo safe in Fiddletown, Amador County, in February 1857. From May 1858 to January 1859, the gang held up three stagecoaches to the tune of more than $30,000 in gold. Huge rewards were offered for the arrest of the bandits, but the gang evaded the law.

Rattlesnake Dick was captured and brought to justice several times, but he managed to escape custody with some regularity. In August 1858, for example, he was caught trying to break out of the Auburn jail while awaiting trial. Reluctant to return to San Quentin, Dick repeatedly filed for a continuance and before the trial could take place, he successfully escaped! Once free, the outlaw sought to avenge his capture. He lurked all night outside the house of lawman John Boggs. The constable was absent and did not return until the following morning. He found a petulant note from the outlaw: "Have been waiting for you nearly all night."

Time was short for the bandit, however. On July 11, 1859, a posse caught up with Dick and a companion on a stage road north of Auburn. The outlaws shot their way out of the ambush, killing one posse member, but not before Dick was severely wounded. Rather than be imprisoned once more, he finished the job with a self-inflicted shot to the head.

Tom Bell

One of California's most successful outlaws, Tom Bell was born Thomas J. Hodges around 1825 or 1830 in Rome, Tennessee. From a good family, he was educated and had some medical training. As a volunteer with a Tennessee regiment, he served as a hospital orderly during the Mexican War. Bell arrived in California in 1849 or 1850 and soon ran afoul of the law. He was convicted of grand larceny in 1851. He served time aboard an abandoned ship at Angel Island, where he worked in a quarry. The stone was for the state prison being built at San Quentin in Marin County. He escaped briefly while being treated for an illness at a facility in San Francisco. Once recaptured, he was among the first prisoners to be incarcerated at San Quentin. Bell and several other convicts broke out on May 12, 1855.

Bell then organized a group of 30 or so outlaws to conduct robberies in the northern mining region. The group included Rattlesnake Dick Barter as well as several escapees from San Quentin, including Bill Gristy, Jim Smith, Cherokee Bob Talbot. The gang's crimes ranged from holding up individual travelers to robbing well-armed pack trains and coaches. Dispersed and diverse, many members of the gang did not know each other and were only connected through Bell's organizational genius.

One of the outlaws' most lucrative robberies was of a Rhodes & Whitney pack train on March 12, 1856. The gang held up the mule train as it made its way south from Yreka to Shasta and made off with leather bags of gold dust valued at some $17,000. A huge manhunt followed, and several of Bell's accomplices were arrested or shot.

On the run from the law and dissatisfied with the meager pickings that travelers provided, Bell decided to rob a stagecoach. He learned of a coach that was to run between Comptonville and Marysville on August 11, 1856, and to carry more than $100,000. Though he knew the coach would be heavily guarded, he set up an ambush. The driver refused to stop for Bell's gang, and passengers and guards alike defended themselves with gunfire. The coach escaped, but the gang inadvertently killed an unarmed woman in the fighting. Her murder caused a public outcry, and efforts to capture Bell and his companions intensified.

Bell then decided that ranching could be an alternative to highway robbery, though robbery could also support the ranch. He chose a ranch site along the San Joaquin River and stocked it with stolen livestock. His career as a rancher, however, was short lived. Lawmen pieced together information as gang members were captured and questioned. Charley Hamilton, a member of his gang, agreed to lead Sheriff John Boggs to the outlaw. A posse confronted Bell and two others on the night of September 30, 1856. One outlaw was killed in the shootout, but Bell managed to escape. He was discovered four days later, on October 4, 1856, and surrendered to two young posse men, George Belt and Robert Price. Belt and Price gave Bell a few hours to write some letters. He penned a note to his mother and one to Elizabeth Hood, an accomplice, in which he lamented: "I have but a few moments to live.... I have been most foully betrayed." Bell's captors, fearing that he would escape or be rescued if they held him for too long, decided to hang him. So as dusk approached, Tom Bell was hanged from a sycamore tree along the San Joaquin River.

John C. Boggs

John Boggs, the "outlaws' nemesis," was born in Greencastle, Pennsylvania, October 18, 1825. He left for California after the first news of gold strikes reached Pennsylvania. Following the long sea journey around South America, Boggs arrived in San Francisco in September 1849. He went to Auburn in the Sierra northeast of Sacramento and had some small success in placer mining, but gave it up to be the town's first night watchman in 1853. Soon he was promoted to deputy sheriff of Placer County. With most of the readily available gold already gone, the California mining regions were awash with violent criminals. Boggs had his hands full capturing villains.

One of the most notorious outlaws to hit the Mother Lode was a young Tennesseean who called himself Tom Bell. Bell had escaped from San Quentin with a handful of criminals and organized the escapees into a violent gang. The Bell gang committed robberies around Placer County. Public outcry against the outlaws peaked after a Jewish peddler was murdered in a robbery and a woman was killed during a stage holdup. Boggs and his fellow deputies embarked on a vigorous campaign to capture Bell and his gang. In exchange for a pardon, Charley Hamilton, a member of the gang, agreed to help the law find Bell. On September 30, 1856, Boggs received a telegram from Hamilton saying that Bell was at Folsom. The deputy sheriff organized a posse and sped from Auburn to meet his informant. As they rode through the night, they heard a gunshot and hid to see Hamilton and his companion Joe Burrows rush through the woods. Hamilton informed the lawmen that Bell and two other outlaws were camped close by, but that they might have been alerted when Burrows shot a coyote. The posse split into three groups and hurried toward the camp. Boggs, Hamilton, and Burrows, riding atop an embankment above the road were traveling so fast that they failed to see the outlaws below them until they had passed. Quickly turning around, Boggs cautioned the criminals to surrender. Instead, Hill and the others jumped behind their horses and started shooting. Bell escaped, but Boggs managed to kill Hill's companion, Ned Conway, with a gunshot through the heart. Bell was captured and lynched four days later.

John Boggs

While Boggs had been instrumental in breaking up the Bell gang, other outlaws remained to take their place. One former associate of Bell's, Rattlesnake Dick Barter became a feared gang leader himself. Rattlesnake Dick's band perpetrated highway robberies in Placer and Nevada Counties, and Boggs pursued the gang relentlessly, earning Dick's bitter enmity. Dick even lurked outside of the lawman's home for a night, intending to kill him when he returned. Fortunately, Boggs stayed out until the next morning, at which time he found a petulant note form the outlaw: "Have been waiting for you nearly all night."

Boggs captured Dick several times, but the latter managed to escape from the Auburn jail. Dick finally met his end on July 11, 1859. A three-man posse met Dick as he rode south on the stage road just north of Auburn. A gunfight ensued in which one lawman was killed. Dick was shot, but escaped on horseback. Boggs found him the next morning, dead from a gunshot to the head, apparently self-inflicted. Dick, thinking that the lawman shot the night before was Boggs, left a note: "Rattlesnake Dick dies, but never surrenders.... If J. Boggs is dead, I am satisfied."

But Boggs was alive and well. He survived to capture and kill a multitude of criminals. Despite being in an alarming number of gunfights, Boggs always escaped unscathed. For a time, he worked as a special detective for the Central Pacific Railroad. During his stint with the company, he solved a gruesome series of murders. Unfortunately, the revelation that the killers were Chinese led to intense persecution of this minority, including burnings of Chinese camps. Even though all the Chinese were driven from the area, Boggs refused to let his Chinese servant be a victim of abuse.

Boggs was elected sheriff of Placer County in 1879. In 1881, the first train robbery in California took place within his jurisdiction. Boggs pursued the robbers and captured the first one within a few weeks. All four were eventually caught and convicted, though Boggs was severely embarrassed when one of the perpetrators escaped his custody. Boggs retired from law enforcement in 1883 and later served as postmaster of Newcastle. He died there on May 28, 1909, and was buried in the Newcastle cemetery.

Tiburcio Vásquez

One of the most feared and notorious outlaws in California history, Tiburcio Vásquez was born in Monterey on August 11, 1835. He apparently came from a respectable family and was bilingual at an early age. Nevertheless, Vásquez found himself an outlaw at just 19 years of age after he was involved in the killing of a police constable. In 1857, he was convicted of horse theft and sentenced to five years at San Quentin, where he was treated roughly because of his ethnicity. He participated in the mass escape of June 1859 but was recaptured and sentenced again the following year.

Upon his release in 1863, Vásquez moved on to more serious crime, killing an Indian butcher in a robbery attempt. By 1871, he was head of a bandit gang that included Procopio Bustamente, the nephew of Joaquin Murrieta. The group proceeded to rob a couple of stages. Vásquez and Procopio used their proceeds for a debauched stay in rural Mexico. They soon tired of the "quiet" life, however, and Vásquez returned to California once more. Over the next several years his gang conducted a series of daring and well-publicized heists. Although numerous murders were committed during the course of the robberies, Vásquez was reportedly reluctant to take lives. His civilized character is further revealed in an incident that took place in a bank raid. Vásquez ordered a lady's watch returned, stating that they didn't rob women. Indeed, the outlaw was quite a ladies' man, and was almost as famous for his many spurned female partners as for his bold thefts. On at least one occasion, a member of his band turned informer after finding Vásquez in a compromising situation with his wife.

Tiburcio Vásquez

The band's exploits increasingly angered state law enforcement. At times, Vásquez would rob entire towns, shop by shop. By 1874, there was a reward of $8,000 on his head and a multitude of posses scouring Central California on his trail. The vigilante atmosphere took its toll on California's Mexican community, whose members were frequently hassled just for looking "suspicious." But instead of retiring from his life of crime, Vásquez continued to conduct audacious raids even as he was being pursued. His luck ended on May 14, 1874. A posse learned of his whereabouts near Los Angeles, in the area now known as Hollywood, and surrounded the house in which he was staying. The outlaw tried to shoot his way out, but was wounded by a reporter's buckshot. He was tried in San Jose, convicted of three murders committed in Tres Pinos in 1873, and hanged March 19, 1875.

Tomas Procopio Bustamente

Procopio was born in the Mexican state of Sonora around 1840. His mother, Vicenta Bustamente, was an older sister of famed outlaw Joaquin Murrieta. She was widowed in 1852 when Indians killed her husband, so she and her son joined Murrieta in California. Murrieta was killed the following year, and Procopio's mother married a member of Murrieta's gang.

Procopio left home when still a teenager, and his first brush with the law was in 1862 when he and others were detained during an investigation of the murder of rancher John Rains near San Bernardino. Procopio was released because of a lack of evidence against him, and within a month he and two others were implicated in killing rancher Aaron Golding and his family in the Livermore Valley. Again, lawmen lacked sufficient evidence to arrest him. That was not the case in 1863, when Procopio and a companion stole a herd of cattle in Alameda County. He was arrested as he sold the livestock to a butcher in Alvarado and was sentenced to nine years in San Quentin.

After his release in March 1871, Procopio resumed his career. That August he stole two steers but fled before he could be captured. Procopio joined highwayman Tiburcio Vásquez, and with others committed several robberies before fleeing to Mexico. Procopio returned to San Francisco in April 1872 and was arrested, convicted of the 1871 cattle theft, and sentenced to seven years in San Quentin.

Paroled in June 1877, after serving five years of his sentence, he led a gang of bandits in raids around Fresno, Grangeville, and Caliente after only five months of freedom. Gang members were captured near Tejon Pass, and five were lynched in Bakersfield. Procopio escaped and assembled another band of outlaws within a week to rob a store in Hanford. A posse surprised Procopio a few days later while he was sleeping, but he managed to shoot his way out of trouble, killing one deputy in the process. Other posses chased him, but none seemed willing to corner him again.

Details about Procopio's later life are vague, contradictory, and nonexistent. He may have returned to Sonora, Mexico, where he may have been killed in 1882 or as much as a decade later.

Charles E. "Black Bart" Boles

Charles Boles, or Bolton, arrived in California at about age 20 from Jefferson County, New York. His parents had moved from England to New York in 1830 with their two-year old son. He worked in the mines and eventually went back East, married, and settled in Decatur, Illinois. During the Civil War he served in a Union infantry regiment. Rather than return to a quiet life in Decatur, Boles roamed the mining camps of Idaho, Montana, and Utah before returning to California. In 1875, as Black Bart, he began a career as a stagecoach robber when he held up a Wells Fargo stagecoach on the run between Sonora and Milton. Working alone and always on foot, he held up at least 28 coaches in Northern California with his cry, "Throw down the box!"

Charles "Black Bart" Boles

Black Bart never stole from passengers and he never killed. Indeed, it is reported that he carried an unloaded shotgun. After two of his robberies, he left a brief verse:

> I've labored long and hard for bred
> For honor and for riches
> But on my corns too long you've tred
> You fine haired Sons of Bitches.

The poem was signed Black Bart, the Po-8. Wells Fargo agents collected as much information as possible about Bart, but clues were sparse. He was careful to always wear a flour sack over his head. During what was to be his final holdup he was interrupted mid-robbery and dropped several items, including a handkerchief with a San Francisco laundry mark. A persistent and tenacious private detective hired by Wells Fargo finally tracked Black Bart down. He had been passing himself off as a prosperous mining engineer living in San Francisco. On November 17, 1883, Charles Boles was sentenced to six years at San Quentin. Upon his release, he disappeared. Rumors placed him elsewhere in the West and even as resuming his former career. His wife moved to Hannibal, Missouri, and by 1892 listed herself as his widow.

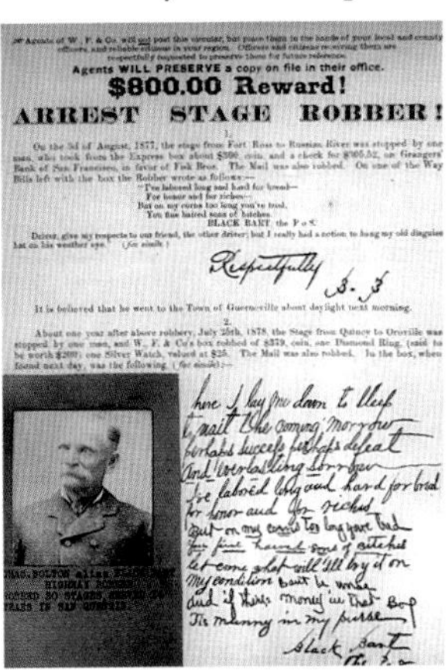
$600.00 Reward!
ARREST STAGE ROBBER!

Reward poster for Black Bart

Leaders, Ranchers, Settlers, and Other Colorful Characters

John A. Sutter

Swiss John Augustus Sutter was born in February 1803 in Kandern, Germany, and raised in Switzerland. He married Annette Dubeld in 1826, and she bore him five children. In order to support his family Sutter joined the Swiss army, where he achieved the rank of lieutenant. However, Sutter was not as successful in civilian life. For several years he ran a dry-goods business that his mother-in-law set up for him, but it was soon crippled by debts. He liquidated the business and departed for America, leaving his family in Europe.

Landing in New York in 1834, Sutter quickly headed west; for a while he lived as a trader in Missouri. He arrived in California in 1839, having traveled the Oregon Trail to the Pacific Northwest, and then by ship to Hawaii and Alaska before finally sailing to Monterey. While in Monterey he persuaded the Mexican governor, Juan Alvarado, to give him permission to establish a settlement called Nueva Helvetia (New Switzerland). If the settlement was successful, he would apply for Mexican citizenship and be eligible for a grant of land.

The settlement on the American River soon flourished as Indian and Hawaiian workers cleared fields, planted crops, irrigated vast meadows for livestock, and artisans made trade goods. In 1840, he began construction of a huge high-walled adobe fort, built to protect his interests from Indians and Mexican authorities. By the time Sutter's Fort was completed in 1844, New Helvetia was a bustling community. Granted Mexican citizenship, Sutter was appointed *alcade*, or chief law enforcement officer, for his 50,000-acre land grant. His wealth and stature grew enormously, and he was known to be a compassionate host when emigrant trains and exhausted explorers like John Frémont arrived from their arduous journeys.

John A. Sutter

Around this time Sutter became entangled in a small-scale civil war between allies of the penultimate Mexican governor, General Manuel Micheltorena, and his successor, Pío Pico. Sutter had gathered a force to fight for Micheltorena. When Pico took control of the government and relocated the capital from Monterey to Los Angeles, Sutter was imprisoned, tried, and eventually freed.

Sutter met and hired a young millwright and carpenter from New Jersey named James Wilson Marshall in 1845. Soon, however, he was embroiled in another conflict. U.S. forces under John C. Frémont took control of the fort during the Mexican War. In the course of the war many of the fort's workers, including Marshall, left to fight with Frémont.

When Marshall returned in 1847, Sutter commissioned him to construct a water-powered lumber mill. Now partners, Marshall selected a site on the South Fork of the American River, in the Cullomah Valley, about 45 miles from the fort, and took a group of workers to build the sawmill. On January 24, 1848, the mill was nearing completion when Marshall discovered several gold nuggets in the tailrace. He hurried back to the fort with samples for Sutter. They consulted an encyclopedia and conducted several tests on the metal before being satisfied that the samples were indeed gold.

Though Sutter was excited at the discovery, he feared that his workers would flee in search of gold if word got out. He urged Marshall to finish work on the mill, telling the laborers that they could prospect in their free time. The men agreed and the mill began sawing logs in March. Nevertheless, rumors about the discovery were beginning to spread and migrants flooded the area. All of John Sutter's fears were realized as his workers deserted their jobs to mine gold, leaving crops in the ground, stealing livestock, and leading him to financial ruin.

He was forced to sell Sutter's Fort and to move to a farm on the Feather River. Slowly, Sutter sold his other real estate interests. Much of present-day Sacramento is built on plots of land auctioned by him during the gold rush, and Sutter's Fort, now reconstructed, is a state historic park in the city's midtown.

Sutter brought his estranged family over from Europe after a 16-year separation. He served in California's constitutional convention in 1849 and lost a close race for governor of the new state. He was appointed general in the state militia in 1850. Creditors hounded Sutter. A fire on his farm in 1865 demoralized him, and he chose to relocate to Lancaster County, Pennsylvania. He spent years petitioning the U.S. Congress to reimburse losses incurred when Frémont took over his fort in 1846. He died on June 18, 1880, in Washington, D.C., and was buried in Lititz, Pennsylvania.

John Bidwell

John Bidwell, born in 1819 in New York, was raised in Pennsylvania and Ohio. After a brief stint as a teacher, he moved to Missouri where he claimed land for a farm, but lost it to a claim jumper in 1840. Bidwell helped organize the Western Emigration Society, and he spent the winter of 1840-41 preparing for an expedition to California. In May 1841, a group of 77 people, including Jesuit missionary Pierre-Jean De Smet, led by mountain man Thomas Fitzpatrick, set out from St. Louis. Half of the party followed Fitzpatrick into Oregon, but 32 people completed the journey to California.

The Bartleson-Bidwell party (John Bartleson was the nominal leader) was the first emigrant party to traverse overland from the Missouri River to South Pass in what is now Wyoming, north of the Great Salt Lake, and through the Sierra Nevada. No one in the group was an experienced trailsman and they only knew to head west. They negotiated numerous rivers, crossed stretches of desert, and endured rain, dust, and wind, and had little success hunting. They decided to abandon their wagons after passing the Great Salt Lake and had to resort to eating their livestock. It was not until November 1841 that the exhausted pioneers completed their journey. Their route came to be known as the California Trail.

John Bidwell

Once in California, Bidwell worked for John Sutter. In 1844, he became a Mexican citizen and gained a large land grant at today's Rio Vista. He joined in the Bear Flag Revolt of 1846 and marched with John C. Frémont's volunteers from Sonoma to Monterey, eventually returning to work again for Sutter in 1847.

The gold discovery in 1848 led Bidwell to prospect successfully for gold at Bidwell's Bar on the North Fork of the Feather River. By 1849, he was able to purchase a 28,000-acre ranch in the vicinity of Chico. Bidwell established himself as one of the state's finest agriculturists and his 26-room mansion in Chico is now a state historic park. He embarked on a political career and served in the House of Representatives, from

1865 to 1867; he made an unsuccessful bid for the Presidency on the Prohibition Party ticket in 1892.

Bidwell recounted his pioneer experiences in a series of articles titled "Echoes of the Past" in the popular *Century Magazine* in 1890 and 1891; he died in 1900.

John Charles Frémont

A native of Savannah, Georgia, John Frémont was born in 1813 to Charles Fremon (the family later added a "t" to the surname) and Anne Whiting Pryor. He grew up in Charleston, South Carolina, where he attended the College of Charleston until he was expelled in 1831. He taught math for a few years at a prep school and worked on a survey project with the U.S. Corps of Topographical Engineers. In 1838, he was hired, with the rank of second lieutenant, as a member of the expedition that surveyed the Louisiana Purchase.

John Charles Frémont

It was during this time that Frémont met Missouri Senator Thomas Hart Benton, a man who would have great influence in the young explorer's life. Frémont also met and fell deeply in love with the senator's 16-year-old daughter, Jessie Benton. Despite the couple's 11-year age difference, they happily eloped and were married in October 1841. After each of his many explorations, Frémont returned home to his wife and energetically dictated his tales to her. Her elaborate stories became national best sellers and even caught the attention of members of Congress, who were impressed by Frémont's organizational and topographical abilities.

Frémont arrived in California for the first time while on a mapping expedition during the winter of 1844-45. He found a welcome at Sutter's Fort. He returned to California during the summer of 1845 on an expedition during which he named the Humboldt River in what is now Nevada. In January 1846, Frémont became embroiled in political tensions between Mexico and the United States. Although ordered by Mexican authorities to leave California, he remained in the vicinity, continuing explorations farther north. American settlers began a revolt on June 10, 1846, and captured Sonoma. Frémont supported the rebels and returned to occupy Sutter's Fort. The rebellion became known as the Bear Flag Revolt after the symbols on the flag created by the Americans. President James Polk had declared war against Mexico in May 1846, and U.S. Navy Commander John D. Sloat raised the Stars and Stripes over Monterey, declaring California a U.S. possession on July 7. Frémont joined Sloat's forces at Monterey, and Sloat's replacement, Commodore Robert Stockton, appointed Frémont military governor of California. Stockton and Frémont went south to occupy San Diego and Los Angeles successfully. General Stephen Watts Kearny, meanwhile, had been ordered to capture New Mexico and California. He arrived in California with a weary force of dragoons and lost a battle at San Pasqual. Once reinforced, however, with U.S. control established in the area, Kearny and Stockton became embroiled in a power struggle. Eventually Kearny replaced Stockton, and Frémont was court-martialed in 1847. Although acquitted, Frémont resigned from the army and returned to California to run a ranch near Mariposa. With the discovery of gold, California quickly became a state, and Frémont served as a senator. He ran for president in 1856 as the first candidate on the Republican Party ticket. Frémont's fortune dwindled in his later years; he served as governor of the Arizona Territory from 1878 to 1883, and he died a virtual pauper in 1890.

James Wilson Marshall

Born October 8, 1810, James Wilson Marshall was raised in Lambertville, New Jersey, where his childhood home stands today. His father died in 1834 and much responsibility fell on the young man's shoulders. Marshall bolted for the West when he was jilted. He wandered to western Missouri, where land had recently been opened to homesteading. By 1837, he had built a cabin, started to farm, and fell in love again; however, the girl married another man. Marshall picked up and moved to Oregon in 1844. Dissatisfied with the weather, Marshall joined an emigrant party and reached the Sacramento Valley in 1845.

A skilled millwright and woodworker, he sought employment with John A. Sutter at Sutter's Fort. Marshall soon established his own ranch nearby.

When American settlers revolted against Mexican rule in 1846, Marshall volunteered to march with Captain John C. Frémont. He served as chief military carpenter before his discharge early in 1847. Upon returning to his ranch, he found it plundered. Again he looked to Sutter for work. Sutter sent Marshall to build a sawmill on the banks of the South Fork of the American River, in the Cullomah Valley, about 45 miles northeast of the settlement.

James Wilson Marshall, circa 1848

On January 24, 1848, James Marshall was tweaking the flow in the mill's tailrace when he saw pieces of a shiny metal glistening in the sunlight. Seizing a small nugget, he placed it on the ground and began pounding it with a rock. Instead of shattering like fool's gold (pyrite), the nugget thinned under the beating. Convinced he had found gold, Marshall rushed to tell his colleagues. Four days later he traveled back to the fort to consult with Sutter. The pair conducted a series of tests until they felt convinced that the metal was gold.

Sutter urged Marshall to keep the discovery a secret until work on the mill was complete. However, by mid-March when the mill began sawing logs, rumors had already spread and another strike had been made at Mormon Island. When Samuel Brannan announced the discovery, first shouting it on the streets of San Francisco and then in his newspaper, prospectors rushed to the valley.

Soon the mill's vicinity became the bustling town of Coloma. Marshall kept sawing logs and only dabbled in gold mining. When he tried to extract a percentage from other miners, he was nearly driven from town. By 1850, the mill's operation was crippled by lawsuits; litigation would eat away Marshall's wealth, eventually forcing him to sell the last of his real estate.

The rest of Marshall's life was spent in the shadow of the gold discovery. He tried his hand as a vintner at Coloma; his grapes even won prizes at the state fair. Bad luck dogged him: In 1862, his cabin burned down, destroying valuable papers and perhaps a historically priceless diary. He became a little too keen on drink and quit the wine business. In 1872, the state legislature granted him a small pension, but it was not extended when it was discovered that the money was spent mostly on booze. Nevertheless, the allowance did enable Marshall to establish a small blacksmith shop in Kelsey, a town not far from Coloma. The man who started the world's greatest gold rush was squeaking out a living in this little shop when he died peacefully on August 10, 1885. A charitable group, The Native Sons of the Golden West, built a statue of Marshall on a hill overlooking his original discovery. The Marshall Gold Discovery State Historic Park in Coloma preserves the site and honors him as well.

Kientopoos (Captain Jack)

Kientopoos, also known as Kintpuash, was a Modoc born around 1839 near the village of Wa'chamshwash, situated on Lost River on the California-Oregon border. During his adolescence, his village and tribe faced increased encroachments by American settlers into their homeland. Kientopoos's father, a village chief, advocated retaliation against the settlers, but his young son spoke out against this. Kientopoos got on well with some of the local miners. One gave him a military jacket that he often wore. Settlers took to calling the friendly Indian Captain Jack.

Kientopoos (Captain Jack)

In 1864, Kientopoos, who succeeded as chief after settlers killed his father, was leader of a Modoc band when the tribe was forced by treaty to move to a reservation shared with their traditional enemies, the Klamath, in Oregon. The Modoc left the reservation in 1865, partly because of the Klamath's hostility toward them. They returned for a short time in 1869, but some 300 fled permanently, returning to the vicinity of Lost River in 1870. Camping along Lost River, his small band caused inconvenience to whites who grazed cattle in the area. The settlers persuaded the government to force Kientopoos and his people back to the reservation.

In November 1872, U.S. cavalry troops confronted the Indians at their camps. Eight Modoc and seven soldiers were killed in the gunfights that ensued. The retreating Modoc killed several settlers as they fled to their traditional sanctuary called "The Stronghold" among the lava beds south of Tule Lake, an area now encompassed by national forests and Lava Beds National Monument.

Kientopoos's band included just 50 to 90 warriors, and the group resisted repeated attacks by regular army and volunteer troops. Kientopoos wanted to negotiate a settlement with the army, but a majority of warriors rejected this approach. Kientopoos met with General Edward Canby, the leader of the American peace party, and other white men over a period of months. Finally, warriors, in a direct challenge to his leadership, persuaded Kientopoos to kill Canby, who had continued to bring reinforcements to the field throughout the negotiations. Within days, in April 1873, the army besieged the Modoc, who fled south.

As conditions worsened, Indians began to defect from Kientopoos's band. One leader, Hooker Jim, who had been the most eager to kill General Canby, surrendered to U.S. forces. He then guided the troops to Kientopoos, now deeply entangled in a conflict that he had never wanted and that he had resisted escalating. He proved adept at eluding the superior forces; he was now outnumbered by more than 20 to 1, and his position was untenable. Knowing that his surrender would mean death, Kientopoos laid down his arms on June 1, 1873.

Kientopoos and five other Indians were put on trial for the murder of General Canby. Hooker Jim, an instigator in the killing, testified against them. The trial was a farce—none of the Indians were fluent in English and no counsel was assigned to their defense. All six were sentenced to death, but President Grant reduced two sentences to life in prison. On October 3, 1873, Kientopoos and three others were hanged for murder. The chief's body was interred at Fort Klamath, but it was dug up and sent to Washington, D.C., where it was displayed for a dime a view. Eventually, the skeleton was given to the Surgeon General's office, where it was kept as a specimen of Indian anatomy. The few remaining Modocs were sent to Indian Territory, as Oklahoma was called. Many perished from diseases that spread through the unhygienic Indian camps, but two of Kientopoos's wives survived him by several years.

Samuel Brannan

Samuel Brannan, born in Maine in 1819, moved as a teenager to Ohio with his sister and her husband. Apprenticed to a printer, he learned the trade, eventually setting up a business with his older brother in New Orleans. He returned to Painesville, and in 1842 converted to the Mormon faith and married. His marriage was unhappy, and he spent much time away from home as a missionary. He relocated to Connecticut, where he met his second wife. In 1844, the Mormon Church paid him to go to New York and set up a printing press. He, with the younger brother of Mormon founder Joseph Smith, published *The Prophet*.

Samuel Brannan

On February 1, 1846, a proclamation by the Illinois governor forced Mormons to leave that state. Now led by Brigham Young, the colony decided to head to California. Brannan was designated to lead Mormons from New York to San Francisco Bay. He chartered a vessel and had it configured for some 250 passengers, supplies, and cargo. He was to purchase land and prepare for the arrival of the main body of the church. The émigrés arrived in California only to discover that the Mexican province had been seized by U.S. forces. Undeterred, Brannan established the state's first flour mill and first daily newspaper, *The California Star.*

He thought that Brigham Young might prefer the isolation of the Great Basin as the site of the new Mormon settlement. Brannan rode east through Truckee Pass in April 1847 to meet Young and to try to persuade the religious leader to come to California. He was unsuccessful.

Brannan returned to California, stopping at Sutter's Fort in September. Several Mormons were working there, and Brannan visited quite often. He was present shortly after James Marshall told John Sutter of his discovery of gold in January 1848. It is unlikely that Brannan was told about the gold at this time, but he was soon aware of the metal's presence in the region. An astute businessman, Brannan cornered the market on mining equipment and supplies and opened a store at Mormon Island, another gold strike site. He then sent 2,000 copies of his newspaper confirming gold's discovery to the East in April. In May he stood on a San Francisco street corner with a glass bottle of the shiny metal shouting, "Gold! Gold from the American River!" Within a few days the small town was almost deserted as its inhabitants rushed to the mines.

Hordes of migrants began arriving in California. Brannan made a fortune selling them necessary supplies and providing transportation to the goldfields. He was excommunicated by the Mormon Church for not paying tithes. However, he became a prominent citizen of San Francisco. He helped organize the Committee on Vigilance, a vigilante group to combat the city's growing crime, and established a land commission to address the confusing and complex ownership arrangements. Brannan's marriage was increasingly strained, partly because of his earlier marriage, but also because of his heavy drinking and adultery; the relationship eventually ended in divorce. The settlement left Brannan, who was frequently land rich and cash poor, with heavy debts from which he never recovered. California's first millionaire died lonely and destitute on May 5, 1889, in Escondido in San Diego County.

The Big Four

Collis P. Huntington, Mark Hopkins, Leland Stanford, and Charles Crocker financially backed and managed the construction of the Central Pacific (and later the Southern Pacific) Railroad. Theodore D. Judah came from New York in 1854 to supervise construction of the Sacramento Valley Railroad. He lobbied for government backing of a transcontinental railroad in the form of the Pacific Railroad Act of 1862 and discovered a viable route through the Sierra Nevada in the same year. His projections of the profits of a railroad that crossed the continent convinced Collis P. Huntington and his associate Mark Hopkins to invest in the venture.

Historians have written that Huntington, who was born in 1821 in Harwinton, Connecticut, was the most important of the Big Four. Enticed by the gold rush of 1849, he moved from New York City to San Francisco where he established a mining supply business. In partnership with Mark Hopkins, he ran a flourishing wholesale supply business, Huntington & Hopkins, which by 1856 became the most profitable on the West Coast. Huntington then turned his attention to the Central Pacific Railroad project; he had learned to lobby the government for funds from Judah. Huntington also recruited the other half of the Big Four, Leland Stanford and Charles Crocker, to invest in the venture. The successful passage of the Pacific Railroad Act of 1864, more generous than the previous bill, was the result of his efforts. He also campaigned for corporate funds, and his skillful and vigilant management of the risky operation kept the railroad debt-free and afloat during the depression of the 1870s. With the Central Pacific line completed, the four partners started construction on the Southern Pacific, which ran south from San Francisco into Los Angeles and San Diego and east to El Paso, Texas. Huntington managed the southern line with the same skill that ultimately assured the financial success of both railways. He usurped the presidency of both railroads in 1890. While Huntington spent most of his time in New York after the railroad's completion, his nephew, Henry Edwards Huntington, who became successful in the railroad business as a result of his uncle's support, resided in the Los Angeles area. There he developed an intra-urban railroad system and an extensive collection of western history books and art, which was the foundation for the Huntington Library Art Collections and Botanical Gardens in San Marino.

Collis P. Huntington

Mark Hopkins

Mark Hopkins, who also moved from New York to California in 1849, met and started the supply company with Huntington. Upon organization of the Central Pacific, Hopkins became its treasurer. He was described by contemporaries as, "one of the truest and best men that ever lived," and the Big Four trusted his judgment in business matters unconditionally, giving him final say on all matters. Hopkins oversaw the day-to-day railroad administration and was given power of attorney by the other members of the Big Four to conduct business in their absence.

Leland Stanford, born in 1824 in Watervliet, New York, relocated with his wife in 1852, migrating to El Dorado County to work with Leland's brothers in their grocery store. With new wealth from a lucky find in a Northern California mine, Stanford became a prominent citizen of the new state and, with his background in law, launched a successful bid for governor in 1861. In this role he helped keep California in the Union as the Civil War erupted in the East. As a result of his growing power and popularity, Huntington invited him to invest in the Central Pacific project. As president of the Central Pacific, he drove the final spike (which he missed on his first attempt), connecting the line to the Union Pacific on May 10,

Leland Stanford

Charles Crocker

1869, at Promontory Point, Utah, thus completing the transcontinental railroad. It was his political clout that helped smooth the way for the railroad's construction. He remained president of the Central Pacific throughout his life and held the same title with the Southern Pacific Railroad Company from 1885 to 1890.

Stanford developed other interests after the Central Pacific's completion. In 1885, he was appointed senator for California. Stanford was not a great senator. During his first term he gave much of his attention to the endowment of a new college, the Leland Stanford Junior University. Named after his only son, who died of typhoid fever in 1884 at age 15 in Florence, Italy. Stanford University opened in 1891 and today is arguably the West Coast's finest educational institution. Stanford was also an agriculturist. He bought half a million acres of farmland on which vast vineyards grew. His favorite ranch in Palo Alto, where he kept horses, became the site of the university. To settle a bet with a friend on whether all four legs ever left the ground during a horse's movement, he commissioned Eadweard Muybridge to take a series of photographs of a galloping stallion. Muybridge's study, when viewed through an invention called a zoopraxiscope, proved that all four legs do leave the ground. The invention became the basis of the motion picture.

Born in 1822 in Troy, New York, Charles Crocker ran a successful forge in Indiana before leading an overland expedition to California in 1850. After mining for gold for two years, Crocker found his fortune selling dry goods to the exploding population of San Francisco. Within a few years he was one of the wealthiest men in the city. Elected to the state legislature in 1860 by the Republican Party, he left office after only one term and gave up his dry-goods business in order to concentrate on the construction of the Central Pacific Railroad. As superintendent of construction, he overcame the obstacles of too few workers, delayed shipment of supplies from the East (which traveled all the way around Cape Horn), and winter storms of the High Sierra. He completed the railway seven years ahead of deadline, setting many long-standing construction records in the process. After the Central Pacific, Crocker moved on to manage the construction of the Southern Pacific. Later he began investing heavily in Bay Area real estate and irrigation projects, and he established the Crocker Bank. He also helped develop the area around Merced, California.

After realizing the railroad's profits, the Big Four constructed ornate mansions on San Francisco's Nob Hill overlooking the booming bay. Stanford constructed the first residence in 1876. Hundreds of workers labored to build the largest private residence in the state, which included a 50- by 14-foot porch (supported by 16 Corinthian columns), 25 bedrooms, an elevator, and an art gallery. In 1878, Hopkins outdid Stanford on the neighboring lot by building a $2.5 million 40-room gothic estate, which he didn't live to see completed. On Nob Hill, Crocker is most famous for building a 40-foot "spite fence" around a nearby house. The fence, which successfully blocked most of the light from his neighbor's windows, was revenge for his neighbor's refusal to sell his property to Crocker when the latter was buying up the entire block. The neighbor, an undertaker, retaliated by mounting a coffin on his roof facing the Crocker estate. Huntington was the last to arrive on the hill. For $250,000, he bought the residence of David Colton, attorney for the Central Pacific Railroad, after his death.

In 1906, the great earthquake's fires destroyed the ostentatious structures of the Big Four. In 1915, Huntington's widow donated the property of the burned home to the city for present-day Huntington Park, which is said to be one of the finest pieces of property in the city. Grace Cathedral was built on the sight of Crocker's manor and today the Mark Hopkins Intercontinental Hotel stands on the site of the former gothic mansion. All that remains of the original structures are a medieval turret from the Hopkins residence and the stone posts of the Stanford estate's entrance gate near the Stanford Court Hotel.

William Randolph Hearst

Born in San Francisco on April 29, 1863, William Randolph Hearst was the only son of George and Phoebe Hearst. George Hearst came to California during the gold rush and made a fortune in mining. He represented California in the U.S. Senate in the 1880s. In 1887, George gave control of the *San Francisco Examiner* to his son. William Randolph Hearst soon became known for his sensationalist editorial style. Hearst and his paper prospered, and soon he owned a chain of dailies and weeklies around the nation. Hearst used his newspapers to press his own political agenda, which included extreme nationalism. He helped secure a second presidential term for Theodore Roosevelt and gave excessive coverage to the sinking of the battleship *Maine*, an event that helped spark the Spanish-American War (1897–98). Hearst was also accused of racism. His papers often published diatribes against minorities, including Japanese and Filipinos. He seems to have felt particular animosity toward Mexicans, portraying them as marijuana-smoking job stealers. His isolationism during World War II was criticized by many but praised by others as patriotic.

William Randolph Hearst

Hearst maintained a home in California, but for a while his principal residence was in New York City. He served as a congressman of New York from 1903 to 1907, and he ran unsuccessfully for mayor of New York City and governor of that state. In addition to his political interests, Hearst expanded his business empire to include magazines, motion picture studios, radio stations, and real estate. His eccentric and lavish lifestyle was the basis of Orson Welles's classic film *Citizen Kane*, released in 1941.

Hearst's greatest love was movie star Marion Davies. The two spent many years together at Hearst's vast estate at San Simeon, on the California coast just north of Cambria. The estate, now a state park, had a zoo, an airport, a private theater, and several opulent guesthouses. William Randolph Hearst died on August 14, 1951, in Beverly Hills.

The Hearst family came into the national spotlight again in 1975 when a fringe terrorist group calling themselves the Symbionese Liberation Army kidnapped the heiress to the family fortune, Patricia Hearst. The story took a strange twist when Patty sided with her captors in staging a bank robbery. The group was later cornered and caught after a bloody shootout. Patty was released from custody and still resides in California today.

Hiram Warren Johnson

Hiram W. Johnson, born in Sacramento in 1866, attended the University of California at Berkeley and continued his studies in the law offices of his father, a state legislator and supporter of the powerful railroad companies. Hiram defied his father when he joined the growing anti-railroad movement.

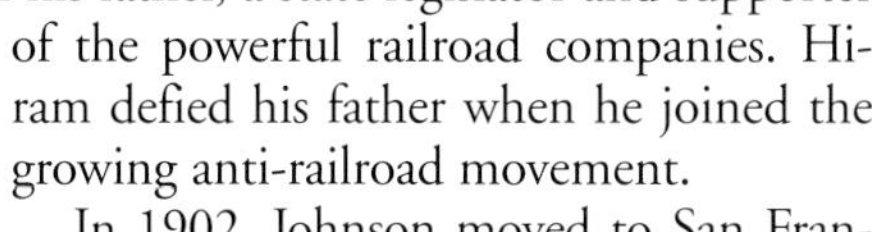

Hiram Warren Johnson

In 1902, Johnson moved to San Francisco, where he helped prosecute the defendants in the city's graft trials. When Francis J. Henry, the lead attorney was shot, Johnson took over the case and secured the conviction of political boss Abe Ruef. The trial brought the young lawyer much public attention. He ran for governor in 1910 on the Progressive Party ticket and won. During his seven years in office, he decreased the political power of the Southern Pacific Railroad, enacted some of the nation's first conservation statutes, and introduced the initiative and referendum process—tools that still shape the state's politics. Teddy Roosevelt selected him as his vice president for his Bull Moose Party in 1912. The pair lost the election to Woodrow Wilson, but carried California and four other states, becoming the only third party ticket to place second in a twentieth-century presidential campaign.

Johnson was elected to the U.S. Senate as a Republican in 1916. He declined Warren Harding's offer of the vice presidency in 1920 and lost the Republican presidential nomination to Calvin Coolidge in 1924. He served in the Senate for another 20 years, his politics moving slowly to the right. As an isolationist, he opposed Wilson's League of Nations, supported anti-Japanese legislation to limit the rights of Asian immigrants and citizens, attacked Franklin Roosevelt's New Deal aimed at easing the economic depression of the 1930s, and opposed the U.S. joining the United Nations. By the time Hiram Johnson died in 1945, the once powerful California Progressive movement had perished, too.

Ishi

Known as the "last of the Yahi," Ishi was introduced to the American public in 1911. For at least 40 years, he and a small band of Indians had lived in the Sierra near Oroville. Ishi was born in about 1860. By this time, the Yahi—a subtribe of the Yana—had already seen their traditional life destroyed by settlers who rushed to their homeland in search of gold. The newcomers stole Yahi land and depleted the wild plant and animal stocks upon which the Yahi depended for survival. Resistance against the settlers was met with harsh reprisal. The major Yahi village on Mill Creek was raided in 1865 and its residents massacred. Three years later, the surviving Yahi were cornered in a cave and slaughtered; only about a dozen escaped.

The small group survived in the mountains, hiding all traces of their existence. They lived off the land, capturing game with the same weapons their ancestors had used for generations. Only occasionally did they raid ranches and mining camps for supplies. In 1908, the group—which now numbered only four—was sighted in Deer Creek Canyon. Ishi lost all his companions as they fled from their white discoverers. In 1911, starvation forced him to make contact with the modern world.

Ishi walked to the settlement of Oroville, where he was taken into custody by the sheriff. His appearance caused great interest among Californian ethnologists. He had no knowledge of modern customs or of the English language, and other Indians were also unable to communicate with him. Alfred Kroeber, an anthropologist in San Francisco, recognized Ishi as the sole survivor of the Yahi, until then thought to be extinct. Kroeber brought him to the anthropological museum of the University of California where Ishi could be studied.

Ishi related his story to Kroeber, but refused to give his real name. Kroeber decided to call him Ishi, "man" in the Yahi language. Ishi had no desire to return to the wilderness. He slowly learned English and adopted modern clothing and habits. He showed anthropologists a variety of traditional skills, including how to make arrowheads, bows, and nets and how to catch deer and start a fire. All knowledge about Yahi mythology and culture comes from Ishi's recollections.

In 1916, Ishi died of tuberculosis. With him, the Yahi also died. Kroeber's wife later published a biography of Ishi, calling him "the last wild Indian of North America." Most of Ishi's body was cremated according to his wishes, but his heart was sent to the Smithsonian Institution in Washington. Recently, California Indians have requested that it be returned to them for proper burial.

John Steinbeck

John Steinbeck, arguably California's most revered novelist, was born in Salinas in 1902. He studied at Stanford University and worked as a farmhand and fruit picker before publishing his first novel, *Cup of Gold*, in 1929. This work romanticized the life of a seventeenth-century Welsh buccaneer, Sir Henry Morgan.

John Steinbeck

Steinbeck's most remembered writings were set against a contemporary California backdrop and generally dealt with people who depended on the soil for their livelihood. The critically acclaimed novelette *Of Mice and Men*, published in 1937, focuses on two itinerant farm workers yearning for some land of their own. Two years later he published the Pulitzer Prize–winning *The Grapes of Wrath.* Probably his most famous novel, *The Grapes of Wrath* chronicles the migration to California of the Joads, a farming family escaping the Oklahoma dust bowl. The work, now an American classic, highlighted the exploitation of migrant workers on California ranches.

Steinbeck's later writing was somewhat inconsistent. Among his best works, *Cannery Row,* published in 1945, depicts idlers associated with the Monterey sardine-packing industry. *The Pearl* (1948) is an excellent novelette, an allegorical story about a young Mexican fisherman who discovers an enormous pearl. *East of Eden* (1952) and *The Winter of Our Discontent* (1961), for which he was awarded a Nobel Prize for literature, are also considered classics. Steinbeck was the first Californian to receive the Nobel Prize for literature. He took a road trip around the United States with his standard poodle, Charley. *Travels with Charley* (1961) recounts his adventures, including driving down the California coast and revisiting Monterey and Salinas. Steinbeck died in 1968.

Indians of Northern California

People likely first arrived in the area of present-day California 8,000 to 15,000 years ago; however, earlier peoples from Asia may have migrated along the coastline. Historians, anthropologists, and archaeologists are learning more and more about early people living in what we now know as California. It is likely that Indians in the area were generally cut off from any major interaction beyond occasionally trading with people who lived inland beyond the mountains and deserts. Isolated, tribes developed lifestyles that fit their environment. The diverse climate and geography of California meant that many different cultures developed. Classification of the different California tribes has always been extremely complicated; most communities were organized by village, and allegiance to a larger tribal entity varied greatly. European settlement further confused the issue as bands were lumped together into a mission or vanished because of diseases. Names for tribal units are also vague. Often the tribal name was taken from the Indians' word for "people."

Before the arrival of Europeans, life for native Californians was fairly idyllic. Life expectancy in the area in 1700 was probably higher than in Europe at the same time because of an absence of disease. Game and edible plants, most notably the acorn (a primary food source for nearly all the tribes), were plentiful. Often, the acorn gathering festival in fall was an important ritual for the village community. Some tribes developed elaborate storage baskets, and most carved grinding bowls into stones. Evidence of these mortars can still be found today. Many Northern California tribes ate salmon, and hunters used a variety of tools—bows and arrows, antler-tipped spears, and hemp snares. The pleasant climate and abundant resources meant that Northern California had the densest population of Native Americans in North America. Fully one-tenth of Indians north of Mexico lived within California's present-day borders. (Interestingly, about the same proportion of Americans live in the Golden State today.)

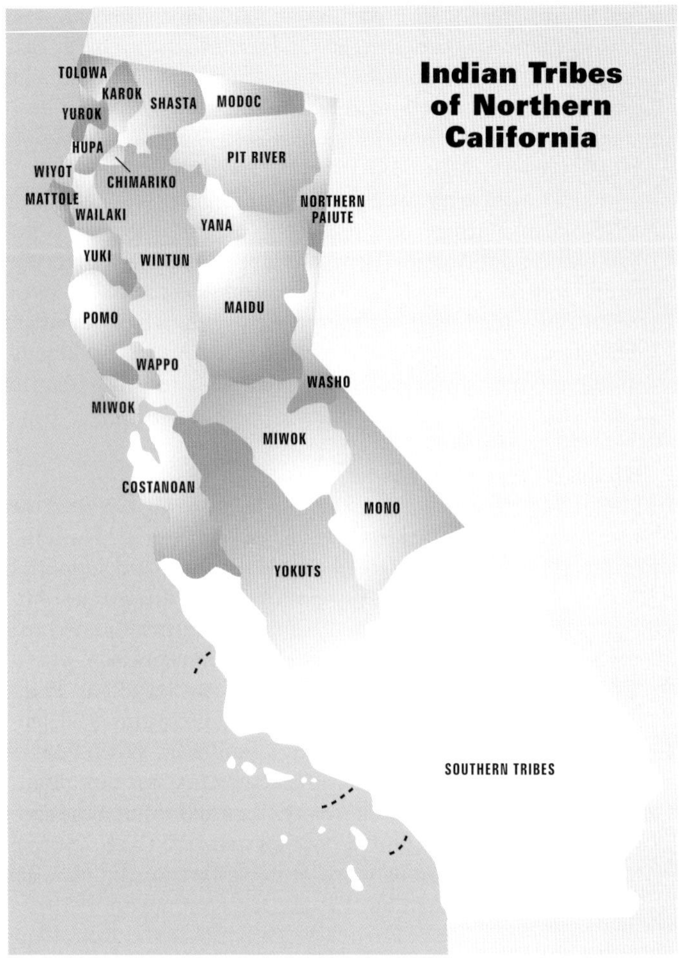

Generally, native people in the area did not practice agriculture but they did prune plants to encourage growth and burn forests and grasslands to clear debris and open areas for hunting. These controlled burns also reduced the risk of dangerous wildfires, an occurrence now much feared throughout the western United States. The plant most commonly cultivated among aboriginal residents was tobacco, which was used to induce sleep and as a painkiller.

Many Indians in Northern California used beads or shells as currency, and trade between tribes was not uncommon. Deerskins, obsidian, baskets, and other manufactured goods were among the most regularly traded items. They wore few clothes; footwear was almost unheard of, and simple deerskin robes and skirts were the most common outfit. Hats and fiber skirts were also worn.

Life for Indians in California changed drastically with the arrival of Europeans and Americans. The population was decimated: in 1500 the population is estimated to have been about 300,000, and by 1900 it was one-tenth of that. Illness, starvation, and murder had killed thousands.

The eradication of native peoples took place in two waves. The first began in 1769, when Junípero Serra established the first of 21 Franciscan missions at San Diego de Alcalá. The elaborate mission system, which extended along the coastal regions of Southern California north to Napa Valley, sought to spread Christianity to pagan inhabitants and eventually incorporate the Indians into the society of the Spanish Empire. The second aim failed; the first succeeded in varying degrees. Still, the missions changed the lives of the coastal Indians irrevocably. Spanish priests and soldiers sent to protect them brought diseases against which the natives had no immunity. Smallpox and measles killed thousands, and syphilis, often spread by forced sexual contact, resulted in the deaths or sterilization of many more.

The missions also altered the coastal environment by turning vast tracts of land into farms, which served to supply the missionaries and Indians living at the missions. Surpluses went to soldiers and were traded with foreign visitors. Indeed, the constant supply of food helped draw many Indians into the missions. However, huge herds of cattle and sheep now occupied land on which they had hunted game. Fields of corn and wheat took the place of native plants upon which the Indians had depended. Inhabitants in the vicinity of missions were often left with little choice but to enter the religious communities. Once there, residents were forever indentured to the missions. Escapees were pursued with force. And although forbidden to do so, bands of soldiers often brought back additional prisoners as well as the fugitives, at times killing those who refused to come.

The second wave of outside intrusion began with the discovery of gold in 1848. The next few years saw an amazing influx of emigrants, mostly from the eastern states. The forty-niners, who settled in the gold-rich regions of Central and Northern California, encountered Indians who had been largely ignored and untouched by the Spanish and Mexicans. But now they had to face white encroachment at its worst. Again, disease ravaged the population—one smallpox epidemic around Nevada City destroyed one-fifth of the region's native population. Despite California's admittance into the Union as a free state in 1850, Indians were often used as forced labor in the mines. In other instances, Indians of Central California were seen as an unwanted nuisance, and violence against them was largely condoned. Settlers and miners stripped Indians of their traditional homelands without compensating them.

California's Indians presented little organized opposition to the white settlers, perhaps because the tribal groups were not unified and because change came so quickly. The Modoc War in the northeast corner of the state lasted from 1872 to 1873 and involved fewer than a hundred warriors, and the Mariposa War of 1851 took place on an even smaller scale. Instead, centuries-old cultures vanished silently from the California landscape. In a relatively short span of time, some of the most diverse and distinct aboriginal populations in the world disappeared, and others lost much of their unique identity.

Only a few large reservations were established for the displaced Indians. Hoopa Valley and Round Valley Indian Reservations are quite large, but most Indian land is confined to small, disunited rancherias. Tribes have struggled to preserve their traditional character. In 1969, a group of Native Americans calling themselves the Indians of All Tribes seized the abandoned federal prison on Alcatraz Island in San Francisco Bay, bringing the plight of native peoples national attention. The current population of California Indians has survived much and endures to this day. In 1980, California passed Oklahoma as the state with the highest population of Native Americans.

Tolowa

The Tolowa held a stretch of the Pacific Coast from the mouth of Klamath River north to the present-day California-Oregon border. They also controlled a tract of land inland, but most Tolowa villages of redwood houses were on the coast, while the interior was used mostly for hunting. The name Tolowa was given to the tribe by the Yurok. The Tolowa had no name for the whole tribe because loyalty was to a village rather than the tribe; it was not uncommon for Tolowa villages to fight one another. At times, though, they combined to face a common enemy, usually the Yurok. For the most part, the Tolowa were peaceful and thrived on trade. They supplied the seashells from Vancouver Island that were used as currency throughout much of Northern California.

Tolowa elk-horn spoons

Salmon and game were prominent in the Tolowa diet. They built redwood canoes, some of which were quite large; Tolowa were not averse to lengthy sea journeys, although they generally kept within sight of the coast.

The first American contact with the tribe came in 1824, when Jedediah Smith met them while traveling through California to Oregon. At that time, their population was spread among eight villages and numbered somewhere between 800 and 2,400 individuals. European diseases such as cholera and smallpox reduced this number to about 200 by 1870. The population dropped even lower, but it has rebounded considerably in recent years. Today, more than 500 people claim Tolowa ancestry, and most Tolowa live on the Siletz Indian Reservation in western Oregon, where tribal pride is flourishing. Youngsters are learning the Tolowa language and tribal customs, which were once in danger of disappearing entirely.

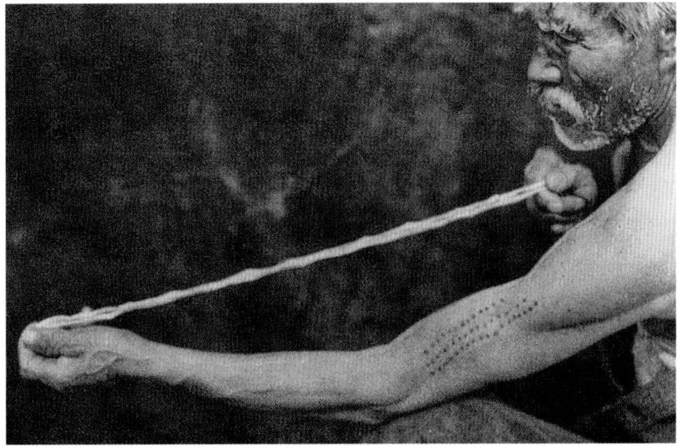

A Tolowa displays a cord used to measure shell money

Karok

The Karok inhabited an inland area of Northern California along the Klamath River, on what is now the California-Oregon border. In the tribe's Hokan dialect, *karok* means "upstream." *Yurok*, the Karok word for downstream, has been used to designate a neighboring tribe. The Karok, who had no word to describe their tribe, only used these words as adjectives.

Karok culture was almost identical to that of the Yurok and the Hupa, but all three tribes spoke completely different languages. The Karok dialect was related to that of the Shasta and the Chimariko, part of the diverse Hokan language family. The Karok traded with their neighbors, swapping excess acorns, baskets, and canoes for obsidian (used to make knives or arrowheads), furs, and other goods. The Karok were especially known for their basketry. They used a twining technique in which horizontal strands were wrapped between vertical supports. They applied basketry to make storage containers as well as clothing, including hats.

The Karok, Hupa, and Yurok are distinguished by their adherence to the World Renewal religion, a religion centered on two major ceremonies believed to stabilize the world and to encourage bountiful harvests of fish, acorns, and other foods. The Deerskin Dance, whose length varied from three to ten days, involved carefully prescribed rituals performed by participants dressed in rare albino deer furs. The Jumping Dance was performed in costumes made from red woodpecker feathers.

In Karok society, as in many of the other aboriginal societies of Northern California, women were shamans and healers. The initiation ceremony for females was quite important. Girls fasted for 10 days and were kept awake at night by ritual dances, generally performed by the men of the village. Each man would dance with the young female as she shook a deer hoof rattle.

A Karok woman making acorn mush

Children among the Karok did not receive names until they were several years old. Even after that, Karok would be unwilling to say their name or those of their family members out loud. To speak the name of the dead was forbidden. Other Karok beliefs included faith in a mischief-making near-deity, the Coyote. Many narrative stories were told about the Coyote, including a myth that told how he created the salmon of the rivers.

The Karok were largely untouched by American or European influence until about 1850. The mining rush into their area was short-lived and on a small scale, but still destroyed the tribe with diseases and indiscriminate violence. The Karok recovered and remain a distinct tribal entity with populations on the Orleans Karok Reservation, Quartz Valley Rancheria, and scattered around northwestern California.

Shasta

The origin of the name Shasta, which refers not only to an Indian tribe but also to a mountain, river, county, city, lake, national forest, and wilderness area, is obscure. Most likely it was the name of an important chief, prominent around the time trappers began to operate in areas that are now Oregon and California. Shasta territory ran from Mount Shasta in Northern California to Mount Pitt in Oregon and included a stretch of the Klamath River and many of its southern tributaries. Despite a large homeland, the Shasta population was quite sparse, probably never numbering more than 2,000, spread across approximately 50 villages.

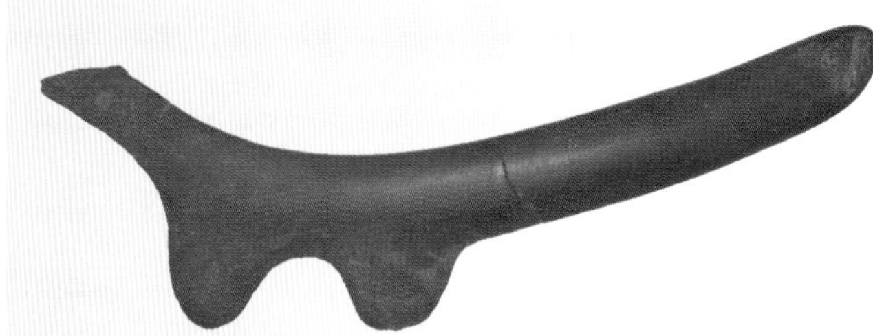

Polished Shasta stone club referred to as a "slave killer"

The Shasta language was related to that of the Karok, and Shasta culture was similar to the Karok's. Their religious ceremonies were not as elaborate, and their houses, rectangular wooden structures, were simpler. As in Karok society, shamans were almost always women. The title of village chief, however, was hereditary and was generally given to the male head of the richest family. His role was one of arbitrator in the various disputes that arose in tribal life. Separate war leaders were chosen for infrequent military action. Most tribal members appeared to be shorter in stature than their neighbors.

The homeland of the tribe provided a wealth of food. Salmon and game were abundant, and oak trees provided ample acorns. The first salmon catch of the season was greeted with celebration. Acorn harvest was also an important time of the year. The Shasta created large acorn granaries—leaf-lined holes in the ground covered with pine bark—to store nuts through the winter. Deer hunting was an important social activity, and they traded deerskins; rare albino furs were especially treasured. Special songs were sung before each hunt. Their aim was to make the hunt successful and to ward off rattlesnakes and much-feared grizzly bears.

The Shasta's fate was similar to most other California tribes—a rapid decline after American settlers entered their homeland. The 1910 census counted just 250 tribal members, and their descendants live at the Quartz Valley Rancheria and several other small reservations in Northern California and southern Oregon.

Modoc

This proud tribe of Northern California Indians is best known for its armed resistance to reservation life—which became known as the Modoc War in 1872-73 (see page 107). The Modoc fought for the right to live on land upon which their ancestors had dwelled for centuries. This ancestral homeland encompassed part of northeast California in the vicinity of Lower Klamath Lake and Tule Lake, and to the east, extending into Oregon. The Modoc were semi-nomadic, moving across their territory in a seasonal hunt for food. In spring, when salmon made their way upriver to spawn, the Modoc camped by streams in mat-covered tents to catch the large fish with spears and nets. In summer, they roamed the forests, collecting roots and hunting game. As fall came, they picked berries and other fruits. With the onset of winter, they retreated to permanent villages of earth-covered homes, where they spent the cold months.

Their homeland was sacred to the Modoc. They believed the Sky Chief created it when he came down to earth onto Mount Shasta and moved down the mountain, making trees and streams. The Modoc have a colorful mythology, with many different characters and stories. One recorded narrative told the story of mankind's creation at the hands of Kmukamch. Other mythological characters include Kmukamch's son, Aishish, and the tricky hero Silver Fox.

Modoc culture was more similar to tribes in the Pacific Northwest than to tribes in California. Unlike adjacent tribes to the south, the Modoc cremated their dead, and the deceased's family practiced a ritual purification in a sweathouse. They also bound their infants' heads to deform their skulls. Modoc men wore fitted deerskin shirts and pants.

Modoc culture was severely threatened when settlers arrived in the 1850s. Ranches and farms impinged on the tribe's traditional life of moving with the seasons. Forced to leave their homeland, the Modoc were relocated to a reservation in southern Oregon to be shared with the Klamath, a larger band considered to be bitter enemies by the Modoc. The Klamath pressured the Modoc to flee the reservation. Led by Kientopoos, a small band of Modoc returned to the Lost River area, near the California-Oregon border. When they refused settlers' demands to leave, an armed struggle known as the Modoc War began (see page 107). After their defeat, many Modoc were forced to relocate to Indian Territory (Oklahoma). Today, Modoc descendants live there (on the Quawpaw Reservation) and on the Klamath Reservation.

Pit River Indians (Achomawi and Atsugewi)

The Achomawi and the smaller but culturally indistinguishable Atsugewi were known collectively as the Pit River Indians. Both were related to the neighboring Shasta, and some sources consider them an offshoot of that tribe. They inhabited a narrow stretch of land along the Pit River in the northeastern part of the state, just west of the Nevada boundary. They hunted over a larger area without settling in it.

Achomawi mother and child

Food was scarcer in the Achomawi's arid territory than in coastal California. Salmon rarely made it far up the tribe's streams and acorn-providing oak groves were almost nonexistent. Deer populations were also relatively low. To catch large game, the Achomawi dug concealed holes in the ground; hence, early trappers and traders called them Pit Indians. Rabbits, ducks, and a variety of plants made up the rest of their diet. They also knew about the therapeutic properties of plants, knowledge that continues to attract interest today.

Achomawi summer hut

The Achomawi believed the world was created by a god they called Quan, which translates to "silver fox." The benevolent creator also made laws by which the Indians lived. Quan's dictates encouraged selflessness and forbade killing without cause. Another tribal myth was the legend of Thakilmasi, a wicked humanoid monster who stole children. His rumored appearance is reminiscent of the Big Foot character. In later years, the Pit River Indians adopted the Ghost Dance, imported from the Paiute of Nevada.

The Achomawi and the Atsugewi were federally recognized as the Pit River Nation. The nation is based on the Susanville Rancheria, located near Lassen National Forest.

Northern Paiute

The Paiute Indians, one of the Shoshonean tribes, included many bands scattered over the vast area from present-day Arizona to Oregon. They are generally studied as two separate groups, the Northern and Southern Paiute. The Southern Paiute lived along the Colorado River, in an area that is now southern Utah, Nevada, and northwestern Arizona. The bulk of Northern Paiute territory was in Nevada, but their homeland stretched to Oregon, Idaho, and northeastern California.

Survival in the generally arid region of the Great Basin necessitated constant movement in search of food. Men chased small game, singing individual religious songs as they hunted. Women collected wild plants for food. Because they had to dig for roots and bulbs, the Paiute earned the derogatory appellation Digger Indians.

Because of the Paiute's nomadic life, their dwellings were temporary. Their architecture was similar to that of Apache wickiups—huts of brush spread over pole frames. A village consisted of up to 10 of these houses. Each band elected its own leader; the tribe had no overall chief.

Religion and ceremonies were important to the Paiute. Funerals could last up to four days, with mourning rituals continuing for up to a year. Both sexes adorned themselves with tattoos and piercings. The Round Dance, the most important religious ceremony for the Northern Paiute, was held three

A Northern Paiute brush dwelling

times a year, when whole bands were collected in one place for a major food harvest. During the ritual, men and women danced around either a pole or a male singer, celebrating tribal unity. The dance also mentally prepared them for the upcoming pine-nut harvest, rabbit drive, and fishing season.

The California Trail, the major route to California for westbound emigrants (see page 64), ran through Northern Paiute territory. At first, eager to trade furs and clothing, the Indians welcomed travelers; however, the mass of forty-niners streaming across their land during the gold rush angered the Paiute. Raids on wagon trains and mining camps sparked a series of conflicts between whites and Indians. One dispute, the Paiute War (or Pyramid Lake War), began in 1860 when traders kidnapped and raped two Paiute women near the California-Nevada border. A group of Northern Paiute warriors killed five Americans in the course of rescuing the girls. A force of California and Nevada volunteers attempted to subdue the band, but was outmaneuvered near the Truckee River. A larger force tracked the Paiute to Pinnacle Mountain, where the Indians were defeated.

Today, Northern Paiute are scattered across a series of small reservations in Nevada, Oregon, and California.

Yurok

The Yurok occupied a stretch of the Pacific Coast about 40 miles long and an area of the interior along the Klamath River to its tributary, the Trinity River. Their name survives in the town of Yurok, on the coast in Del Norte County. They spoke an Algonquin language similar to the Wiyot but were culturally more like the Hupa and the Karok.

A Yurok man paddling a canoe

Yurok houses were very much like those of the Hupa—rectangular structures with a three-pitch roof and a circular entrance. They were generally made of cedar planks or slabs, which acted as a natural insect repellant.

Religious practices by the Yurok were similar to the Hupa. Both tribes performed World Renewal ceremonies, including the Deerskin Dance. Other dances included the Jumping Dance and the Brush Dance, which male singers used to heal sick children. In the late 1890s, some Yurok followed the messianic Ghost Dance ritual, a widespread movement among Native Americans who thought the ritual would return them to their former ways of life. Whites feared that it was a war dance and tried to ban it.

A Yurok fisherman

Other Yurok beliefs included stories of a bearded dwarf who carried acorns on his back and was thought to be the master of the plant world. The Yurok also believed in an afterlife. They thought the dead crossed an underground river to enter.

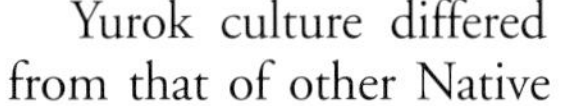

Yurok culture differed from that of other Native Americans in that the tribe respected property rights. Most tribes did not understand the idea of land ownership, but the Yurok could own, buy, and sell land and other properties. This created an upper class in Yurok society, which enjoyed special rights, including feasting on the first fish caught each season. In return, they were expected to provide for those less fortunate.

Females were respected in Yurok society. Usually only women were permitted to be shamans. In some tribes, menstruation was viewed as a curse, while the Yurok regarded it as a highly spiritual time. For its duration, women would bathe and meditate, gathering spiritual energy.

Because most Yurok villages were situated along water, fish was the most important part of their diet. The Yurok word for food, *nepu,* was the same as the word for salmon. When American settlers entered Yurok land in the late 1800s, they tried to force the people onto reservations and to farm. The Yurok refused. Today, they retain fishing rights along the Klamath River on an extension of the Hoopa Valley Indian Reservation.

Hupa

The Hupa were one of the most influential tribes of northwestern California. Though they controlled a relatively small area of land in the vicinity of the Trinity River, their influence was felt by all of their neighbors. The Hupa dialect (part of the Athapascan language family) was known throughout the region. Two Indians who spoke not a word of the other's language might have been able to converse in Hupa much as two

A Hupa sweat house

English-speakers could today. The dominance of the Hupa culture seems to have been due to their military prowess. They resisted white settlement and, in 1864, they were granted a 144-square-mile reservation called the Hoopa Valley Indian Reservation, which today straddles California 96 in Humboldt County.

The Hupa tribal identity has largely survived because of the success of this reservation, and quite a lot is known about their culture. Hupa religion centered on the World Renewal ceremonies. Two biannual ceremonies, lasting several weeks each, are still performed by Hupa descendants today. The Hupa believed these ceremonies were necessary to ward off earthquakes and other natural disasters and to encourage acorn harvests and an abundance of salmon—in other words, to maintain and renew the world. The ceremonies consisted of various rituals and dances. The most important dance was probably the Deerskin Dance in which participants dressed in skins of rare albino deer and followed exact rituals preserved for many generations.

Aboriginal Hupa culture made many distinctions between males and females. Generally, only females were allowed to be shamans. The two sexes usually slept separately, even husband and wife. Villages camped together during late summer and early fall, and this is when most procreation took place. Men who committed adultery were severely punished—one eye was pricked so that its fluid slowly dripped out, rendering it useless. Punishment for adulterous women was less cruel and generally left to the husband.

Hupa baskets

The Hupa took great pride in their houses, and their sturdy structures of sweet-smelling cedar planks often lasted many generations. Roofs were flat-topped, and there was just one entrance—a small circular opening in one wall—and cobblestone porches surrounded the houses. Traditional structures can still be seen on the Hoopa Valley Reservation.

Salmon was a staple of the Hupa diet, making up perhaps one third of their caloric intake. Acorns were important, as were eels and other fish. Tobacco was the only plant that the Hupa cultivated before they moved onto reservations.

The Hupa have adapted to reservation life remarkably well. Today, Hoopa Valley is the largest and most populous reservation in California, supporting more than 2,000 Indians. It boasts a museum, motel, post office, tribal law enforcement and a court system, several fisheries, a restaurant, and a radio station. A thriving logging industry ensures the reservation's prosperity.

Chimariko

The Chimariko were one of the smallest distinct tribes in all North America. They spoke a Hokan-dialect not unlike several other Northern California tribes, but different enough for scholars to conclude that they had been isolated for many centuries. The Chimariko homeland consisted of a small 20-mile stretch on either side of the Trinity River.

The principal source of food for the Chimariko was the river. Salmon were so abundant that the Chimariko invited other tribes to fish their waters. This situation changed when miners polluted tributaries to the Trinity River, killing the fish. Hungry Indians were forced to steal miners' mules and supplies, and these thefts were punished harshly.

Chimariko culture may not have been as complex as that of some of their neighbors, the Hupa and the Wintun. The tribe did not participate in World Renewal ceremonies or the Kuksu cult. Chimariko houses were small wooden structures with a two-sided roof and were less sturdy and elaborate than those of their neighbors.

The population of the tribe in 1850 was only about 250; by 1906 only two elderly Chimariko remained. Today, the tribe is extinct, although some Californians are probably descended in part from the vanished people.

Wiyot

The Wiyot were a small tribe who lived along the 35-mile coast of Humboldt Bay, in the vicinity of Eureka and Arcata. They spoke a variant of the Algonquin language used extensively by Native Americans in the east, from North Carolina to northern Canada and in the Great Lakes region. How the Wiyot and their neighbors the Yurok (also Algonquin speakers) came to be separated by such distance from their common ancestors is unknown.

Every Wiyot village was located on the coast, along Humboldt Bay or on a coastal stream. The Pacific shoreline in Wiyot territory is relatively shallow and sandy, and is not made up of rocky cliffs. The ocean provided most of the Wiyot's food, including clams, a principal part of their diet. Some villages hollowed out canoes from coastal redwood trees and practiced both salt- and fresh-water fishing.

Information about much of the Wiyot culture has been forever lost; however, narrative storytelling seems to have been important to the tribe's religion. One spiritual being, Gatswokwire, was a common character in Wiyot stories. Gatswokwire was portrayed as an itinerant god who wandered the earth attempting to satisfy his unquenchable erotic impulses. He was believed to have taught humans their various ritual dances and to have given them an important food, the salmon. Wiyot shamans were generally female, and the initiation ceremony for girls was more important than that for boys.

The Wiyot numbered about 800 when Americans entered their homeland in the 1850s. European diseases and persecution diminished their numbers rapidly. By 1900, only a handful of full-blooded Wiyot remained.

Mattole

The Mattole were one of several Athapascan tribes of northwestern California. Their homeland was centered along the banks of the Mattole River, in what is now southwestern Humboldt County. The origin of their tribal name is unknown; they called themselves *bedool.* Possibly Matol was the name of one of the tribe's villages.

Although they resided along the coast of the Mattole River, the Mattole depended less on fish than other coastal Northern California tribes. Instead, they hunted game and collected various edible plants. The rugged terrain they inhabited and their hearty diet made them strong and fearsome fighters, able to resist all attackers with the exception of the white man. The Mattole often disagreed with their neighbors. All tribal members knew the exact boundaries of Mattole land and would attack any intruders. When American settlers arrived, the Mattole robbed only settlers who lived within the domain of their enemies. White posses would take revenge on neighboring tribes instead of on the Mattole.

Nevertheless, the Mattole suffered greatly because of American settlement. Diseases ravaged their population, and American attacks killed countless more. For this reason, very little is known of Mattole customs. It is known that they believed in a single creator, the Big Man, and had a myth of a great flood similar to the biblical story of Noah's ark. The Mattole cremated their dead and believed in an afterworld somewhere over the ocean. People who were bad did not go to the afterworld, but instead returned to earth as grizzly bears, a symbol of evil to the Mattole.

By 1900, the Mattole were extinct as a tribal entity, although descendants survive today on the Round Valley Indian Reservation in Mendocino County and elsewhere in California.

Wailaki

The Wailaki were part of the Athapascan family of tribes (the Navajo of Arizona also belong to this group). Their culture was somewhat like that of their neighbors, the Wintun, and some sources describe them as an offshoot of that larger tribe. However, their language is distinct from the Penutian dialect of the Wintun, and the Wailaki thought of themselves as a separate entity. They called themselves the Kenesti. *Wailaki* was the Wintun phrase to describe them.

Wailaki man

The Wailaki inhabited part of the Eel River Valley, including most of the North Fork. In winter, they fished for salmon, and they were such skilled fishermen that other tribes bought nets and harpoons from them. They built conical wigwams as shelter during cold weather, and in spring they would move farther into the hills to gather edible plants. In autumn, like many California tribes, they celebrated the acorn harvest. Wailaki also hunted deer and elk by running them down. One runner would chase a deer toward another hunter who would take up the chase to the next sentry. This continued until the animal was exhausted, at which time it was killed. They hunted bears less frequently, and a bear kill was marked by ritual dancing and celebration.

Well-worn trails connected the various Wailaki villages, and settlers followed these paths when they cut wagon routes. Wailaki trails usually crossed the high points in order to get a good view of surrounding territory, and they also followed streams and mountain ridges.

The Wailaki probably never exceeded a thousand people. Their survival after settlers commandeered their land would have been precarious, but surviving tribal members relocated to the Round Valley Indian Reservation in northeastern Mendocino County, where their descendents live today.

Yuki

The Yuki inhabited Round Valley—the drainage basin of the Eel River south of the North Fork—and a small stretch of the Pacific Coast. They share a common language family with the southerly Wappo, but otherwise Yukian is an isolated speech group. It is different from all others in California and North America, rather like the Basque language in Europe. Between 2,000 and 5,000 Yuki lived in California prior to European arrival. Their name is from their neighbors to the east, the Wintun, whose word *yuki* means "stranger" or "enemy." The Yuki often went to war with the Wintun and their southern neighbors, the Pomo, although they apparently had friendly relations with the Wailaki to the north. The Yuki had no word for the entire tribe. Instead, they identified themselves by where they lived; for example, *Ukhoatnom* means "on the ocean."

Yuki woman

The tribe was organized into several villages of about 200 people. Their houses, known as *han,* were circular and earth covered and had a conical roof supported by a forked central pole. Villages often had a dance house with a similar design but on a larger scale. Temporary structures for various religious ceremonies were also common. The villages were generally inhabited only in winter, and summers were spent in the mountains where the people built brush structures for shelter.

Yuki religion was similar to that of other Northern California tribes. It was based on belief in a single creator, Kuksu, who taught humans how to hunt and cook and gave them their laws. One verse spoken by Yuki shamans captures this belief: "This rock did not come here by itself./ This tree does not stand by itself./ There is one who made all this,/ Who shows us everything." They also had many religious ceremonies and dances. These included initiations for both girls and boys and an annual acorn dance to encourage a rich harvest. Different types of shamans conducted different ceremonies.

In addition to the ubiquitous acorn, venison was a staple in the Yuki diet. Their lands were well populated with the animals. Most Yuki clothing and blankets were made from deerskins. They fished for salmon and hunted bear. Reportedly, they also had a favored delicacy—rich and oily worm soup.

The Yuki regarded the Pomo as their traditional enemies, but the appearance of the white man caused them to change their tactics. A party of Yuki leaders met with the Pomo and requested a combined attack on their common enemy. Instead, the Pomo betrayed the Yuki and troops were sent to preclude a Yuki offensive. Yuki villages were destroyed and warriors fled through the valleys. The dispute ended when a band of 40 Yuki was surrounded on a large granite boulder now known as Bloody Rock in Mendocino County. Instead of surrendering, the Indians committed mass suicide by jumping off the cliff.

By 1910, there were fewer than 100 people in California with Yuki blood. Today, the surviving Yuki are centered on the Round Valley Indian Reservation in northeastern Mendocino County.

Pomo

Pomo territory was on the Pacific Coast, about 50 miles north of San Francisco Bay, and extended some distance inland and along the shoreline, encompassing most of present-day Sonoma, Lake, and Mendocino Counties. It included almost the entire drainage basin of the Russian River, and the greatest concentration of Pomo villages was along the Russian River and around Clear Lake.

To describe the Pomo as a single tribe is somewhat misleading. About 8,000 Pomo were spread among 75 or so settlements over a large area of coastal California. At least seven major dialects of the Pomo language existed and some were mutually incomprehensible. Leadership within the Pomo was based on kinship—each extended family unit had a head. Chiefs were chosen from among the heads of various families, and a chief may have had authority over several villages. Each village had a large assembly hall where residents would meet to discuss tribal issues.

The Pomo were the most skilled basket makers in California. Unlike most tribes, men as well as women made baskets.

Pomo summer camp

They used coiling and twining techniques to produce diverse styles and functions. Simple and utilitarian, the baskets were used to capture fish, to carry water and supplies, and to cook in. The same techniques were used to create complex and decorative mats and hats. Pomo baskets are now collectors' items.

Clamshells were a major form of currency among Indians—and the Pomo were quite wealthy because shells were easily found along the coast. They polished, rounded, and strung clamshells, and Pomo traders exchanged the shell beads for tools, weapons, and furs.

Pomo food supplies were also quite rich. Acorns were a staple of the Pomo diet, but they used a variety of other plants as food. The Pomo believed that a spirit Blue Jay, who planted nuts during his travels, brought acorns to the world. Other religious beliefs focused on the Kuksu cult. According to legend, Kuksu and Marumba, two other spirits, were supposed to have created the world. Cult members practiced many different rituals to placate the spirits.

Pomo dancer

The two sexes were fairly equal in social stature, and there were initiation ceremonies for both young men and women. Women could become chiefs, and inheritance was sometimes matrilineal. Wives were not purchased, although betrothed families exchanged gifts.

The Pomo suffered greatly at the hands of settlers. Ranchers and miners often enslaved them. In 1850, Pomo workers killed two ranchers in response to their inhumane treatment. In retribution, a contingent of U.S. Army troops raided a Pomo village on Clear Lake and massacred about 135 men, women, and children. Another massacre of 75 Pomo on the Russian River took place at around the same time.

Resilient Pomo began to acquire land; the first purchase was of 120 acres in 1881. These acquisitions, combined with grants from the government, are now organized into a number of reservations. The largest Pomo reservation is the Hopland Rancheria in Mendocino County.

Wappo

The Wappo gained their name from Spanish troops led by General Mariano Vallejo. The troops, never able to subdue the fierce tribe, dubbed the Indians *guapo,* "brave." The tribe called themselves the Ashochimi, and their homeland stretched from the Geysers, southwest of Clear Lake, to the headwaters of the Napa River. Most of their land was mountainous. The tribe controlled two natural wonders of California: the Geysers and the hot springs at what is now called Calistoga. They valued these sites for their therapeutic powers and defended them fiercely. They believed parts of the Geysers to be haunted and never visited them. The Wappo probably never numbered more than a thousand people, and the 1910 census recorded only 73 members.

Because the northerly Yuki speak a dialect similar to the Wappo and a Wappo subtribe held land on Clear Lake, in the midst of Pomo territory, it is thought that the tribe once controlled a large area of Northern California before being pushed into the hills by other migrating groups. Even when the Spanish arrived in California, the Wappo were considered fearsome, and other Indians shied from them. Despite this, the Wappo traded with their neighbors, including the Pomo and the Miwok. Tribal members prided themselves on being able to converse with other tribes in their tongue. Old Colorado, the Wappo chief who led his people to victory against the Spanish, was said to speak 14 different dialects.

Wappo woman

Only a few traditions of the Wappo can be identified today. Wappo society was patriarchal and a suitor had to visit a maiden's father to ask for her. Marriage was considered permanent. If a husband left his wife, the wife was permitted to use any means within her power to get him to return. Infanticide was sometimes practiced when a family could not provide for a child, but this was rare.

Little is known of Wappo religion, but several accounts indicate they worshiped two birds—the owl and the hawk. When an owl arrived in a village, it was seen as an omen of death. Only by wearing owl feathers and offering gifts to the nighttime visitor could an owl be placated. If the offerings were unsuccessful and a member of the tribe died, the body was cremated. Wappo believed that the ashes would reform in the spirit world.

Wintun

The Wintun lived on the west side of the Sacramento River. The Penutian-speaking tribe is often divided into three subtribes: the Wintu (northern), Nomlaki (central), and the Patwin (southern). The groups shared a common language and culture, although minor differences distinguished the bands. The subtribes were further divided into individual village units, with perhaps several satellite villages. Each village had its own chief, whose duties were varied, but often included giving an inspiring morning speech instructing tribal members on how to live their lives. The pre-European Wintun probably exceeded 12,000. It is difficult to make sweeping claims about the tribe's culture because surviving evidence is scarce. Wintun villages close to Pomo may have adopted cultural practices of that tribe, whereas villages near the Maidu might have been similar to those neighbors. The Wintun lived in different types of houses—from conical wigwam structures to earth-covered domes.

Their territory supported edible plants, including acorns, hazelnuts, bracken ferns, raspberries, grapes, and wild onions. They cultivated tobacco by clearing small plots of land with controlled burns and planting seeds in the ashes. They smoked tobacco, using clay pipes or pipes with wooden stems and stone bowls. Tobacco was generally used as a sedative. Game, too, was plentiful. Antelope, elk, and deer were abundant, and Wintun hunters would sometimes dress in buckskins to attract these animals. They trapped smaller game, such as rabbits and squirrels, in snares made out of hemp or human hair and fished for salmon, trout, and eel. Wintun basketry was quite advanced, and styles between villages varied. Northern Wintun made elaborate baskets of pine root and maidenhair fern, woven so tightly as to make them watertight.

Most Wintun villages had members of Kuksu cult, an exclusive religion that encouraged worship of a single supreme being. Not all tribal members attended Kuksu ceremonies, but the whole village did celebrate some religious dances and rituals, including initiations for males and females and seasonal dance cycles.

The Wintun did not suffer initially from European occupation, but their lands were in Mother Lode country so that they were overrun during the gold rush. Many died of diseases against which they had no resistance. Settlers killed others indiscriminately. At times, posses attacked entire villages, slaughtering as many inhabitants as they could and herding the survivors to reservations. Often, the Indians, who were accustomed to surviving off the land, could not adapt to farming. At least once, Wintun were even pushed off the rancherias onto which they had been forced. Today, Wintun descendants live mainly on small rancherias—Grindstone Rancheria in Glenn County, Cortina and Colusa Rancherias in Colusa County, and Rumsey Rancheria in Yolo County. Wintun also live on the Round Valley Indian Reservation in Mendocino County with other Native Americans.

Yana

The Yana, like the Chimariko, were a small tribe in Northern California. They lived east of the Sacramento River, with volcanic Lassen Peak, which the tribe called Yana Wahganupa, as a prominent landmark. Together, the four subtribes of the Yana, each of which spoke a slightly different dialect, totaled about 1,500 individuals in the years prior to the gold rush. The small linguistic variations among the groups was further confused by differences in speech between males and females. Each sex spoke a distinct variation of their local dialect. During conversations between sexes, the female dialect was used.

Despite the diminutive size of the Yana people, they were feared as fighters. When salmon were scarce in their rivers, Yana warriors would raid Wintun villages to steal food and to capture women and children as slaves. Generally though, the tribe was able to subsist on resources found within its homeland. Wild raspberries and grapes grew abundantly, and acorns and salmon—staple foods for many Northern California Indians—were easily found in Yana territory.

The gold rush dramatically altered the tribe's way of life. American and European migrants came in droves to seize land the Yana considered theirs. The settlers killed or drove away deer and elk, game that the Indians depended on for survival. Runoff from mining operations polluted rivers, killing salmon and other fish. Livestock brought by the newcomers grazed on plants and acorns, further depleting Yana food supplies. When starving Indians raided mining camps, angry miners responded in force. At times, whole villages were wiped out, every resident either killed or captured.

Because Yana culture was destroyed within just a few decades, little was recorded about their way of life. Almost nothing is known of their religious beliefs. Narrative myths of gods manifested in the form of a rabbit, a squirrel, and a lizard survive today but their significance is not recorded. Some sexual taboos seem to have been observed by the Yana, but their exact nature is unknown. Certainly, a child born out of wedlock was considered socially inferior.

Though the destruction of Yana society as a whole is tragic, the story of its southernmost band, the Yahi, is even more so. Until 1911, the Yahi were thought to be extinct—victims of disease and settlers' aggression. After 45 years of hiding in the wilderness northeast of Oroville, the sole survivor of the band presented himself at a farmhouse. Ishi, as the man became known, spoke no English and knew only traditional Indian ways. He and a small band of Yahi had escaped a murderous raid on their camp in 1865 during which most of the band had been killed. The survivors camped in the woods, hiding all traces of their existence, and only occasionally coming out of hiding to steal food and supplies from ranches and mining settlements. When he became separated from the last of his companions, Ishi was forced out of hiding by hunger, although he probably expected to be killed when he did. Instead, he became the subject of great public and scientific interest. He spent the final years of his life at the anthropological museum at the University of California in San Francisco, where he died in 1916 of tuberculosis. (For more on Ishi, see page 87.)

Maidu

The Maidu were one of Northern California's largest tribes, numbering about 9,000 before European and American contact. Their territory was south of the Northern Paiute. The Maidu had no single leader or tribal identity. Instead, bands of up to 500 held stretches of territory that encompassed several villages. The bands were united into three geographic divisions, each speaking a slightly varied form of the Maidu language. The mountain group lived on the western side of the Sierra Nevada in the drainage area of North and Middle Forks of Feather River. The foothills group occupied an area to the west and south of the mountain group in the foothills of the Sierra Nevada and part of the Sacramento Valley. The valley group, who called themselves Nisenan, inhabited a large area of the Sacramento Valley, including the drainage basins of the American, Bear, and Yuba Rivers. The valley group was the most numerous of the three divisions.

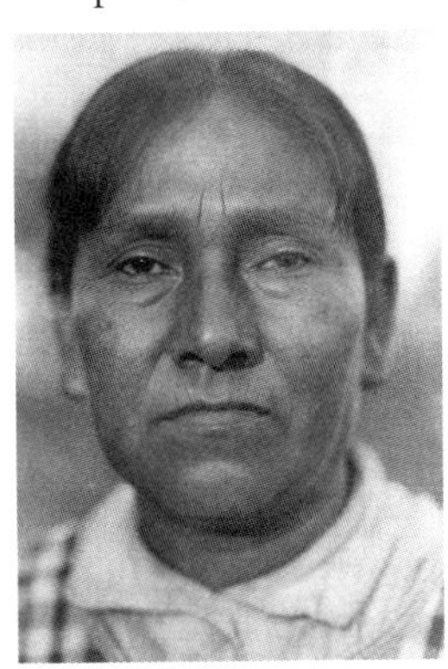

Portrait of a Maidu woman

Maidu territory had abundant resources and a generally pleasant climate. Oak groves provided ample acorns, and gathering them was an important time in tribal life, with whole villages participating in the harvest. Acorns must be processed to remove tannin, a harmful toxin, before being eaten. The nuts were ground into powder in hollows chiseled into rocks, called nutting stones, which can still be found today. They also collected other plants. Farming was unnecessary, although tobacco was sometimes grown in small plots. The Maidu also hunted small and large game. Several animals—grizzly bears, coyotes, and owls—were considered sacred and never killed.

Maidu houses were domed wooden-framed structures, partially buried in the ground and covered with earth, which provided excellent insulation. They wore few clothes, and generally only young women wore more than a minimum.

Baskets were important to the Maidu. The twined, often conical containers were used for storage, carrying loads, dining, and even cooking. They dropped hot stones into large watertight baskets to heat acorn mush and water.

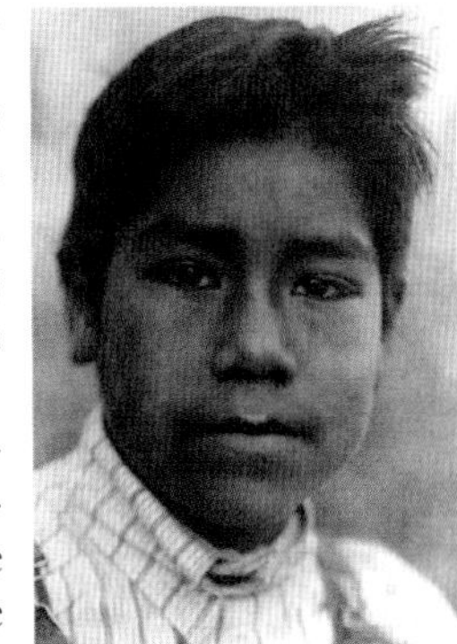

Portrait of a Maidu boy

The Maidu followed the religious cult of Kuksu. The secret, selective religion held special rituals for the initiated. Members dressed in elaborate costumes and impersonated a variety of spirits during ceremonial dances.

Mourning ceremonies were important to all Maidu. They cremated individuals with their belongings, and if the death occurred in a home, the house was abandoned and burned, too. Mourning ceremonies were held annually to commemorate those who had died during the previous year. The Maidu believed that death liberated the soul and that the soul might enter an owl, a coyote, or a lizard and travel over the Milky Way to an idyllic afterlife, where constant feasting and games replaced work. A bad soul, however, would be reincarnated as a rock or a bush.

Maidu society was devastated by contact with Europeans and Americans. A malaria epidemic in 1833 killed an estimated 75 percent of the tribe, and the gold rush reduced them even more. In 1849, miners raided a Maidu village, raped the women, and killed the men who tried to stop them. When Maidu warriors retaliated by attacking a mining camp, the miners raided the village again, killing anyone they found. Such occurrences were not uncommon. By 1900, the Maidu population was about 1,000. Farmers and ranchers had carved up most of the Indians' land and tribal society was irrevocably changed. The remaining Maidu control Berry Creek and Enterprise Rancherias in Butte County and share the Susanville Rancheria and the Round Valley Indian Reservation with other tribes.

Washo

Eastern California, in the Lake Tahoe vicinity, was once home to a small band of Indians who called themselves Washo. The tribe's territory was situated between distinct cultural regions: California areas—and the Great Basin, an area now marked by the present-day boundary between California and Nevada. Washo speech was unlike that of other Great Basin tribes. For many years, linguists believed it was an isolated language, but similarities have since been found with other dialects in California, including that of the Karok. The linguistic links lead some experts to think that the Washo once resided on the western side of the Sierra Nevada. What might have caused them to relocate is unknown.

When American traders first passed through Washo territory in the 1820s, the tribe had been living in the area for many centuries. Each summer, bands of Washo would meet at Lake Tahoe, where they fished for trout in nearby streams. Another important food for the Washo was pine nuts. Bowl-shaped grinding stones have been discovered in several places around Lake Tahoe, and these were used to grind the nuts into a coarse powder for cakes or soup.

Before the pine-nut harvest—and before other seasonal food gathering—Washo would perform ritual dances to request an abundant yield. Like tribes in the heart of the Great Basin, the Washo would move several times a year, following their food supply. Although they did not practice agriculture, Washo sometimes pruned plants to encourage growth and penned up antelope, killing the animals only as needed.

Because the Washo were semi-nomadic, their houses were temporary and somewhat crudely built. They built a conical pole frame bound at its apex, covering it with cedar bark, pine, or manzanita and leaving a small smoke hole at the top. The houses were generally inhabited only during winter months.

Washo were skilled in basketry, using willow, black fern root, and redbud for color and pattern. Washo basketry continues today. When tourist resorts began replacing Washo camps on the banks of Lake Tahoe, the Indians exploited the change by selling baskets to the visitors. Some Washo crafters,

Washo cradle baskets

such as Dat-So-La-Lee, became renowned for their work.

The Washo probably numbered around 1,500 prior to American contact. When settlers began usurping Washo lands in the 1850s, they disrupted the Indians' seasonal migrations. The Washo adapted to accommodate the newcomers and were able to coexist peacefully with settlers. Although violence and disease did deplete their population, the tribe was never as affected as those elsewhere in California. Today, the federally recognized Washo control nine parcels of land near Lake Tahoe, ranging in area from 11 to 2,000 acres. Despite dropping to as few as 800 members, the Washo have rebounded. Today almost as many people claim Washo descent as in 1850.

Miwok

The Miwok lived in Central California, predominantly in the western foothills of the Sierra Nevada. They also had relatives to the northwest, even as far as the Pacific Coast north of San Francisco Bay. The name Miwok merely means "people" in

Miwok woman cooking

their Penutian dialect. The tribe was spread over more than a hundred villages and numbered, in precontact times, approximately 9,000 souls. There was no overall tribal leader and the society was apparently decentralized.

Like many other tribes in California, the Miwok valued acorns as food source. They supplemented them by collecting other plants and hunting small game and fish. The usual Miwok house consisted of a pole frame covered with grass or brush. Each village had an earth-covered assembly chamber where religious rituals and performances were held. The Miwok celebrated their beliefs with a variety of ceremonial dances performed to the accompaniment of a large foot drum. Each dance had a different cast of characters, with performers dressing in feather costumes, animal skins, or paint. One common character was the *Wo'ochi*, a type of clown who would appear at interludes to shout "*woo!*"

Until the gold rush brought hordes of outsiders into their homeland, the Miwok had little interference from Europeans. Their relationship with the Spanish was peaceful; the colonists never attempted to incorporate the tribe into the mission system. After the discovery of gold, however, the Miwok suffered. They had no immunity to European diseases, and many died as a result. Miners exploited the land upon which the surviving Miwok depended, and some prospectors, accustomed to the warlike tribes of the Great Plains, shot innocent Indians on sight. Eventually, the Miwok became so enraged that they resisted the newcomers with force. Their uprising was known as the Mariposa War (see page 107).

Miwok now inhabit three small reservations in California—Jackson Rancheria, Sheep Ranch Rancheria, and Tuolomne Rancheria.

Costanoan

The Costanoan occupied a large area of the Central California coast from San Francisco Bay south to Point Sur. Their name, derived from Spanish *costaños*, means "coast people." Most of the tribe's villages were near the ocean shore or along inland rivers. Some settlements had thatched assembly houses that could seat up to 200 people and large ritual dance enclosures surrounded by a circular brush fence. Men generally wore no clothes; women wore a short deerskin skirt. Facial tattooing in the form of a row of dots was customary for females.

The Pacific Ocean was an important resource for the Costanoan. Early explorers saw tribal members navigating the waters of San Francisco Bay on small tule rafts. They collected oysters, clams, mussels, crabs, and other shellfish from the shore. Shell middens, the debris of centuries of feasts, up to 30 feet high can still be seen along the Central California coast.

The Costanoan diet included small game and edible plants. As was the case for many California Indians, the staple food was the acorn. The Costanoan calendar was based on counting the number of months, or "moons," since the autumn acorn harvest and anticipating the number of months until the next one. The harvest was the central event in Costanoan life. Several villages would camp together in the oak groves while gathering the nuts. The whole population worked from sunrise to sunset. Young boys would climb trees to shake acorns down and the smallest children would join in collecting them. At night, they held dances and feasts, and the men would trade and gamble. The harvest festival was also important for adolescent courtship, and many marriages were arranged during this brief time.

The pre-colonial Costanoan population was probably about 7,000. The population was greatly reduced during the Spanish mission period. Five Franciscan settlements were established on Costanoan land, and eventually the whole tribe was subject to Christian conversion. Soldiers would hunt down runaways from the missions and often forced other Indians to join against their will. European disease killed thousands of Coastanoan, and by the time the Mexican government finished secularizing the missions in 1834, many Costanoan had died and their way of life was lost forever.

Yokuts

The Yokuts occupied the San Joaquin River Valley and the western Sierra Nevada foothills. They were organized into at least 50 "tribelets," divided into several villages rather than having a centralized structure. The small tribes were united by a common language, culture, and religion, although disagreements between groups could lead to intratribal warfare at times. The population probably never exceeded 15,000.

The Yokuts diet was fairly opportunistic. They ate a variety

Yokuts baskets

Yokuts utensils

of small game, including skunks, which many tribes shunned. They fished and collected edible plants, most importantly the acorn. They were also adept at catching birds. A Yokuts prayer, invoked before killing an eagle, has been recorded: "Do not think I will hurt you/ You will have a new body/ Now turn your head northward and lie flat." One crop planted was tobacco, which was smoked as a painkiller, as a sedative, or in rituals. The Yokuts interacted with neighboring tribes, exerting cultural influence over the Salinan and Tubatulabal in Southern California and trading melons, pigment, tobacco, herbs, and salt with the Chumash.

The Yokuts are generally recognized as superb artisans. Their basketry is exemplary, they drew elaborate pictographs on rocks, and they fashioned tule rafts on which they explored rivers. One Yokuts band, the Choinimni, built huge floating barges, 50 feet in width, upon which whole families could live for long expeditions. Other bands constructed large thatch buildings, 35 feet long and 12 feet high, the largest of their kind in North America. In summer, villagers might construct tule shade mats; sometimes mats would cover the entire settlement.

The Yokuts were quite religious. Mourning ceremonies would last a week. A prayer invoked during cremation was: "You are going to another land/ You will like that land/ You will not stay here." After the ceremony, it was forbidden to speak the name of the deceased. Young men were initiated into adulthood in a *toloache*-drinking ritual, during which they drank hallucinogenic jimson weed.

Yokuts culture was largely unaffected by Spanish missions, but it was devastated by the gold rush. Much of the Yokuts territory was part of the Mother Lode in the Sierra Nevada, the area richest in precious metal. Prospectors stole Yokuts land, plundered the natural resources, and at times enslaved Yokuts as laborers. In 1850, together with the Miwok, the Yokuts fought in one of the few California Indian wars, the Mariposa War (see page 107). The combined bands attacked mining camps and trading posts in Central California before a volunteer battalion quashed the uprising.

Today, surviving Yokuts live on two reservations—the Santa Rosa Rancheria and the Tule River Indian Reservation. Tribal members still come together annually for traditional ceremonies.

Mono

The Mono Indians of California were part of a larger group known as the Northern Paiute. Northern Paiute Indians ranged over northwest Nevada, eastern Oregon, southern Idaho and parts of eastern California. The Northern Paiute of Central California were known as Mono; the origin of this name is unknown.

The Mono probably numbered about 6,000 before the gold rush. Most lived in the Great Basin around Mono Lake and the Owens Valley. Others lived in the Sierra Nevada of Central California. The Mono were probably relatively new to California compared to other tribes; they moved into the region from farther east, in present-day Nevada.

Mono shelter

Mono Indians in the Owens Valley and around Mono Lake lived a nomadic life. They moved constantly in search of seasonal foods such as pine nuts and grass seeds. Their possessions were light and portable—carrying baskets, bows and arrows, and rabbit blankets. The Mono hunted creatures ranging in size from insects to bighorn sheep.

Little was recorded of aboriginal Mono culture, although evidence suggests it was influenced by the neighboring Yokuts tribe. Pottery and baskets similar to that of the Yokuts have been excavated in Mono territory.

Mono in the Sierra Nevada suffered persecution during the gold rush, but the Mono population has never been endangered because the inhospitable conditions of their territory prevented colonization. Sizeable numbers of present-day Californians still identify themselves as Mono. The tribe has given its name to a county and a lake in California. Those of Mono descent reside on Big Sandy, Cold Spring, and North Fork Rancherias in central California.

Events

Era of the Spanish and Mexican Missions and Presidios

By 1769, Spain had claimed California as part of New Spain, its Mexican empire, for more than two hundred years. Despite this, no Spaniards had visited the province they knew as Alta, or Upper, California since Vizcaíno's voyage in 1602. But when Russian and British trappers and traders began to visit North America's Pacific shores in search of furs, Spanish officials decided that they needed to establish a visible presence in the area. Partially in response to this reasoning, Franciscan Father Junípero Serra and his civilian counterpart, Governor Gaspar de Portolá, were sent from Mexico to establish settlements along the territory's coast. Spanish colonization was a process of establishing three institutions: the pueblo, the mission, and the presidio. Pueblos consisted of a number of Hispanic civilians charged with maintaining food stores for the colony. At the missions, native laborers farmed, ranched, and crafted supplies to supplement the efforts of the pueblos. Finally, presidios were the military and civil centers, protecting as well as administering the governmental, social, and economic functions of the settlement.

Two land parties and two sea parties left La Paz on Mexico's Gulf of California coast and arranged to meet at San Diego Bay. In July 1769, after months of hard traveling, the four parties met. Of the 219 men who had left Baja California, only about one hundred had survived, and many were exhausted and sick. Undeterred, on July 16, 1769, Father Serra erected a tall wooden cross on a hill overlooking the bay. In doing so, he established San Diego de Alcalá, the first of an eventual 21 missions in California. By the time Serra built his first brushwood church, Portolá was already marching north in search of Monterey Bay. His expedition failed to find the bay, but instead stumbled farther north to reach San Francisco Bay, becoming the first Europeans to see it.

When Portolá returned to San Diego after six months, the new mission was in dire straits. Serra's attempts to befriend the local Indians had failed. He had tried handing out food and beads, but this only encouraged them to raid the vulnerable settlement. Food and supplies were running dangerously low, 19 graves had already been filled, and not a single Indian had been persuaded to convert to Christianity. Portolá's men were also suffering after their long, unsuccessful trek. The governor wanted to return to Mexico; Serra persuaded him to wait for a supply ship. On the very last night before they were due to depart, the *San Antonio*'s sail appeared on the horizon; the Franciscan presence in Alta California was assured.

Leaving Father Jayme in charge of the Mission San Diego, Serra sailed north in search of Monterey Bay. Portolá reached the bay first, by land, and this time recognized it. He began construction of a presidio where soldiers would be stationed to protect the nearby mission and secure Spanish claim to the land. Two more presidios were eventually built in California at Santa Barbara and San Francisco. Serra decided to build the second mission a few miles from the bay in the Carmel Valley. San Carlos Borromeo was officially established on June 3, 1770. It was here that Serra would spend the majority of his time as the leader of the California missions until his death in 1784.

Serra went on to establish another seven missions and traveled thousands of miles along the El Camino Real (the Kings Highway, the name given to the trail that connected the missions). By the time of his death, many of the settlements had begun to flourish. The Spanish were becoming accustomed to the climate and growing cycles. Indians began to come to the missions, encouraged by the ready supply of food, and gradually sturdy adobe buildings replaced crude brushwood structures. Settlements were established at San Luis Obispo (1772), San Juan Capistrano (1776), and Los Angeles (1781). Another four were added after Serra's death.

In June 1776, Captain Juan Bautista de Anza established El Presidio de San Francisco on San Francisco Bay in order to ex-

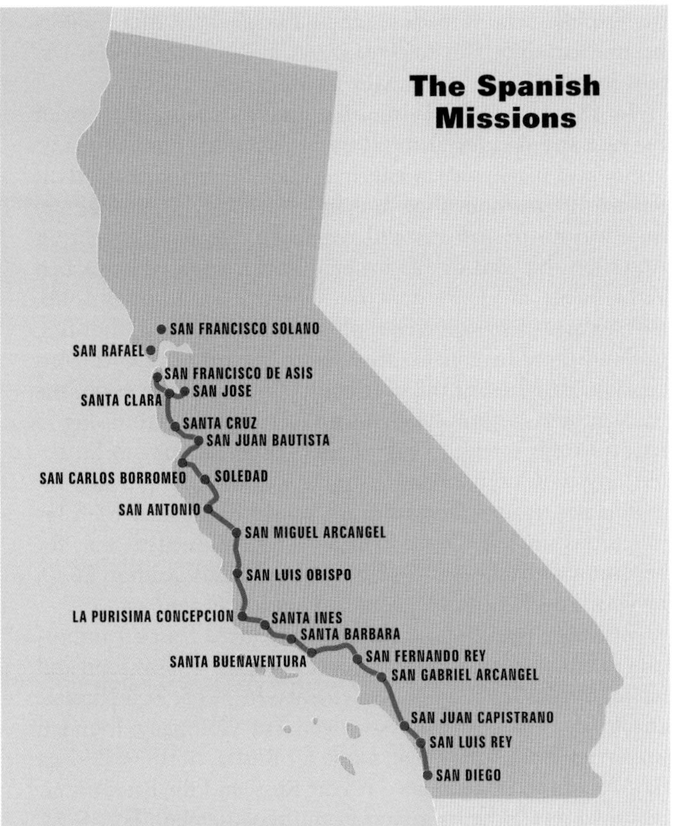

tend Spanish presence farther north. Largely undersupplied and ignored, residents of the fringe settlement faced hard times under Spanish rule. In 1822, the presidio came under Mexican rule, but little changed. The dilapidated fort lacked basic resources and was plagued with internal strife. In 1834, Mariano Guadalupe Vallejo, new commander of the presidio, abandoned the hopeless base for a new and stronger settlement farther north at Sonoma.

Life at the missions was often hard. Supply ships were infrequent, and the settlements were forced to be self-sufficient. Workdays were long and hard, especially for Indians who were pressed into agricultural labor. Discipline was strictly enforced by whippings, daily life was rigorously regimented, and any neophyte (as Indian converts were called) who attempted to escape was tracked down and returned to the mission. Sanitation was a problem, and many Indians, with no immunity to European ailments, died of imported disease. Soldiers treated neophytes harshly to the dismay of most priests. Rape of Indian women was not uncommon.

Recently, historians have criticized the Franciscan mission system for quashing native culture and oppressing the neophytes. Although it is true that the Spanish viewed neophytes with condescension, it should be remembered that most priests were genuinely concerned about their charges' welfare. And although their treatment of the native Californians was abhorrent when viewed through modern eyes, flagellation, poor sanitation, and cultural elitism were standard practice in the eighteenth century. Also, most Indians entered the mission system voluntarily, and some settlements, notably San Gabriel Arcángel, near Los Angeles, developed quite large populations. Nevertheless, the missions indisputably devastated coastal Indian tribes, much as the gold rush would destroy inland tribes decades later. Traditional practices were forgotten, populations were obliterated, and at least one cultural group, the Esselen, was lost forever.

The breakup of the mission system, which began during the last days of Spain's rule over Mexico, only exacerbated the Indians' problems. The Franciscans were to be replaced by nonorder clergy, and Indians who lived within the mission system were to receive land and livestock. Mexican governors issued secularization orders in the period between 1824 and 1836. Unfortunately, Indians, with little concept of land ownership, were taken advantage of and most lost their land to settlers. Some Indians worked on the new Mexican ranchos, often as virtual slaves; others returned to the wilderness from which they had come.

For years, the buildings of the missions decayed. Some, such as the Mission Santa Barbara, were continuously inhabited by Franciscan priests, but most were abandoned. On July 9, 1846, American forces claimed the San Francisco presidio, which Mexican soldiers abandoned in 1839. The military repaired the base and it became an important post during the subsequent military conflicts of the Civil War, Spanish-American War, World Wars I and II, and the Korean War. The fort that became known as Fort Mason was the oldest operating military base in U.S. history until 1994 when the National Park Service assumed ownership. Remnants of the old artillery guns remain at the southwest end of the Golden Gate Bridge. Many other missions are now ruins, but a few have been restored and can be visited. The Mission Delores in San Francisco remains a tourist attraction. Other missions in Northern California include San Rafael, San José, Santa Clara, and Santa Cruz.

Mexican Land Grants

On February 21, 1821, revolutionaries took control of Mexico City and declared independence from Spain. While Spanish priests, soldiers, and settlers had continued to be an imperial presence in this far-flung province, California had become part of a new nation. Mexican rule was uneasy; political rivalry was rife in a province accustomed to paternalistic authority, and governors changed frequently. Still, it was during this period that the region saw its most far-reaching land reform: the land grant, or rancho.

A few land grants were bestowed during the Spanish era as early as 1784, but the crown retained title to the lands. After 1821, the Mexican governor could give land outright. Any one who was a Roman Catholic and a citizen of Mexico could petition to receive a holding of up to 11 square leagues (48,400 acres). At first, land grants were uncommon, but after the Franciscan missions were secularized in 1834, land was readily granted. The mission Indians sometimes retained small holdings, but much of the mission land became privately owned. The Indians attempted to resist this process with force, but in the end could not prevail.

Life on the ranchos was simple. Manufactured goods were as scarce as natural produce was abundant. More than half of each land parcel was devoted to cattle. Cowhides were pro-

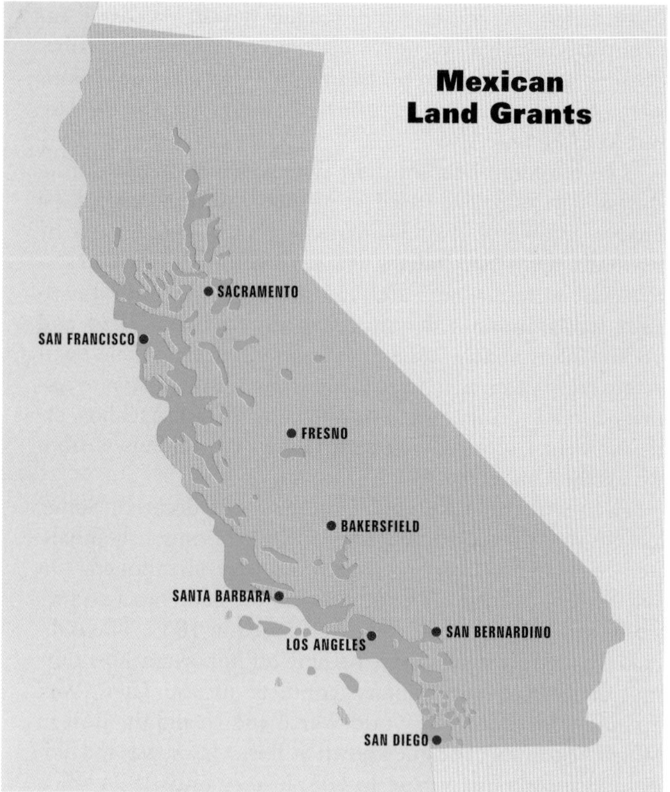

duced in great quantities and were a valuable trading commodity as was tallow, the rendered fat of cows. From a herd of just 200, brought to California by Gaspar de Portolá, in 1769, and supplemented by Juan Bautista de Anza a few years later, the province's stock had mushroomed. Although ranchers held many roundups (*rodeos* in Spanish), some cattle were left to run wild. Ranchos on the old mission lands relied on agriculture and were generally self-supporting.

By 1846, there were some 700 ranchos, many of them concentrated around San Francisco and Monterey Bays. The last Mexican governor, Pío Pico, made dozens of grants. At the time of American conquest, his family held 532,000 acres of California. Non-Mexicans, like John Sutter (see page 81), often became naturalized citizens and accepted Catholicism in order to be eligible for land grants. The rancho boundaries were often vague, however, and many of the larger grants were broken up when California became a state in 1850. The federal commission set up to adjudicate disputed claims approved grants totaling about nine million acres. Even to this day many land titles are based on Mexican grants made when California was a different place indeed.

Russian Settlement in California

Beginning in the 1720s, Danish-born explorer Vitus Bering, in the service of Czar Peter the Great, began to explore the North Pacific for Russia. Russians pursued a lucrative fur trade along Alaskan shores and established an outpost at Sitka. It was partially a response to the threat of Russian encroachment in California that led Spain to establish missions, presidios, and pueblos along the coast, beginning in San Diego in 1769. Russians with the Russian-American Fur Company ignored the Spanish, who forbade trade by foreigners in Alta California and continued to trap sea otters in North American waters, moving farther south with each season.

In 1805, Nicholai Petrovich Rezanov, a representative of the czar and partner in the Russian-American Fur Company, inspected Russian settlements in Alaska. He found residents at Sitka to be malnourished and suffering from scurvy because they had no fresh fruits and vegetables. Rezanov bought an American ship and set sail for Spanish California. He reached Yerba Buena, as San Francisco was then called, in spring 1806, and his arrival was greeted with suspicion by the authorities. Rezanov saved his mission by wooing 15-year-old Doña Concepción, daughter of the port commander. In May 1806, the Russian left California with a ship full of goods, promising to return for his intended wife. Letters from Rezanov to St. Petersburg indicate the relationship may have been pursued for diplomatic reasons, but his death several months later left his intentions unclear. Doña Concepción continued to wait for her suitor until she was finally informed of his death in 1850, by which time she had become a Dominican nun.

Rezanov's mission to California convinced Russian authorities to establish a southern outpost at which to grow food and make supplies for Alaskan settlements. In 1812, Ivan Kuskov, an officer in the Russian-American Fur Company, founded Rossiy, an antiquated Slavic name for Russia, north of Bodega Bay. American traders called it Fort Ross, and the Russians established several farms inland from the settlement. Fort Ross, now a state historic site, is located on California 1 in Sonoma County.

California's waters supported a large sea otter population, which was almost completely exterminated by the Russians between 1812 and 1840. Fort Ross never supported more than 400 residents and it relied on funds from the Russian government. In 1841, the fur company sold its land, buildings, cattle, and machinery to John Sutter who relocated much of the material to Sutter's Fort. Russians continued to maintain a presence in California, especially during the gold rush years. The United States ended the Russian presence in North America in 1867, when it purchased Alaska. California remembers Russian settlements in the names of Sonoma County's Russian River and San Francisco's Russian Hill, among others.

Mexican War (1846–1848) and the Bear Flag Revolt

The U.S. annexation of Texas in 1845 set the stage for war between Mexico and the United States. Continued border disputes fueled anger between the two nations, until Mexico severed relations in March 1845. President James Polk would not be refused. He sent John Slidell on a secret mission to Mexico City. His orders were to settle U.S. claims and to purchase California and the New Mexico territory for $30 million. Slidell's mission wasn't a complete secret. Mexican officials knew he was coming and would not negotiate with him. President Polk ordered General Zachary Taylor to occupy the disputed territory between the Nueces and Rio Grande Rivers in Texas. Mexican troops crossed the Rio Grande and fired on American soldiers, killing 16. Polk declared that Mexico "invaded our territory and shed American blood on American soil." On May 11, 1846, Congress overwhelmingly supported a declaration of war.

As Taylor began his march into the heart of Mexico, Colonel Stephen Kearny (later brigadier general) was to march across some Mexican territory and take New Mexico and California. Kearny's march through the Southwest went without a hitch. Mexican citizens generally welcomed him, and only a few resented the change in governments. Hearing reports that the American flag was flying throughout California, Kearny left two thirds of his force in Santa Fe and proceeded toward Los Angeles with only 100 men.

Fighting had been going on in California for several months when Kearny arrived. Even before the United States declared war on Mexico, volunteers among the 500 or so Americans living in California had organized into the California Battalion under the guidance of explorer John Charles Frémont (see page 83), son-in-law of Thomas Hart Benton, the chairman of the Senate Committee on Territories. The unpaid battalion captured Mexican General Mariano Vallejo and raised its distinctive flag over California towns, declaring a Californian Republic. The banner depicted a grizzly bear and the uprising became known as the Bear Flag Revolt.

Even as the Bear Flaggers were conquering Sonoma, Commodore John Drake Sloat was sailing with 250 troops to California. On July 7, 1846, he landed in Monterey and raised the Stars and Stripes above the provincial capital. By the time Commodore Robert F. Stockon arrived to replace Sloat a week later, the American flag was flying over Yerba Buena (San Francisco), Sutter's Fort, Sonoma, and Bodega Bay.

Commodore Stockton organized the Bear Flaggers under the U.S. banner and entered Los Angeles, conquering the town and leaving a force of 50 to guard it. However, the occupying force soon angered the Californios, and on September 23 they surrounded the Americans, forcing the troops to flee. Reinforcements arrived two weeks later, but the Angelenos rebuffed these too.

Meanwhile, General Kearny was having problems of his own. At San Pasqual, near present-day Escondido, Californios trapped Kearny. For four days the besieged Americans resisted, and of the hundred or so troops, 21 were killed and 18 wounded. Kit Carson and Edward F. Beale (see page 76) crossed through enemy lines to request reinforcements from Commodore Stockton in San Diego. Together, Stockton, Kearny, and Frémont planned to retake Los Angeles with a combined force of 1,000 men. On January 13, 1847, Mexican commander Andrés Pico surrendered to Frémont; his brother, Pío Pico, the last Mexican governor, had already fled. The war in California was won.

The conflict in Mexico, however, raged on. General Zachary Taylor was confronted several times in his march through Mexico. His troops emerged victorious, but their march south was slow. President Polk decided to send General Winfield Scott with an army by sea to capture the seaport of Veracruz. After a three-week siege, the city fell, opening the way for Scott's occupation of Mexico City, which he took on September 14, 1847.

On February 2, 1848, just days after the discovery of gold near Sutter's Fort, Mexico and the U.S. signed the Treaty of Guadalupe Hidalgo. Mexico relinquished control over the huge parcel of land that now comprises New Mexico, Texas, and California as well as parts of Utah, Nevada, Arizona, and Colorado. For this vast territory—about 1.2 million square miles—the United States paid just $15 million.

Although the United States gained considerable territory, the acquisition nearly propelled the nation into civil war. Discussions raged over whether the new states should be slave states. The separation between North and South grew, but the Compromise of 1850 settled the immediate argument. This agreement also allowed California to enter the union as a free state.

Gold Rush

The greatest mass migration the United States had ever seen, and the defining moment in California history, began rather inconspicuously one morning in 1848. On Monday, January 24, James Wilson Marshall was inspecting the flow in the newly constructed tailrace of an isolated sawmill on a branch of the American River in the foothills of the Sierra Nevada. He spotted several flakes of yellow nestled on the floor of the race. Collecting them, Marshall hurried to Sutter's Fort to show John Sutter. Together they established that the yellow flakes were gold.

Prospector posing with his gear

Despite Sutter's best efforts to keep the strike secret until he could bring in crops and supplies, news of the find began to spread. As Sutter feared, his workers abandoned their posts to pan for the precious metal. In May, entrepreneur Samuel Brannan, who had a store at Sutter's Fort, purchased as many mining supplies as he could and walked through the streets of San Francisco carrying a jar of gold dust shouting, "Gold! Gold! Gold from the American River!" Within two weeks, the port of San Francisco was deserted as residents abandoned their daily lives to go to the goldfields and soldiers deserted to seek riches. Ships carried newfound gold to Hawaii and Mexico, Asia and South America, and to Europe. Ranchers streamed down from the Oregon Territory. By the end of 1848, there were about 10,000 men mining in California.

Letters began to arrive in the East, telling of California's wealth. At first the news was treated with great suspicion, but when President James Knox Polk mentioned the gold mines in his address to Congress on December 5, 1848, gold fever became international. Young men across the world dreamt of easy wealth and began to plan how to get to California. Forty-niners (as the emigrants became known) from the eastern United States had three options. Most chose one of two routes by sea: either a ship all the way around South America and Cape Horn or a ship to Panama with a treacherous wagon trip across the Isthmus and a trek north to California by ship. The trip around Cape Horn could take as long as a year, depending on winds. Travelers who crossed Panama began arriving as early as February 1849. Less expensive, but no less difficult was the overland route across the midwestern plains and through the Sierra Nevada. This involved careful timing in order to reach California before winter snows blocked mountain passes.

Before the gold rush, California's non-native population was small, around 25,000. By 1850 it was 115,000, and in the first census of the state, in 1860, it had skyrocketed to more than 300,000. This population included thousands of foreigners. Chinese came to the land they called Gold Mountain in great numbers, although they faced much discrimination when they arrived. Mexicans and Latin Americans also flocked to the goldfields, where their superior mining knowledge was resented. Frenchmen and Englishmen also arrived by the boatload.

Marshall standing in front of Sutter's Mill, circa 1850

People en route to the Mother Lode were said to be "going to see the elephant," a popular expression of the time. (The phrase was common during the gold rush; it indicated forty-niners' anticipation of finding gold. It was derived from a story about a farmer going to a circus to see the elephants. On his way the farmer ran into the circus train led by an elephant. The strange creature caused his horses to buck, overturning his wagon, but the farmer was unperturbed. "I don't give a darn," he said, "I have seen the elephant.") Soon gold country was full of hopeful prospectors. Although it was rich in placer mines, the scores of newcomers found most of the best claims taken. Many decided to make a living serving the miners—as blacksmiths, saloonkeepers, wagoneers, or farmers. Some left California dejected, but others spread out into new areas of the state in search of gold.

New prospectors found conditions far different from what they had envisioned. Few roads had been constructed, and the ones that did exist were poorly developed and generally ran along the coast instead of inland to the goldfields. Almost all supplies had to be brought by ship, and prices were astronomical, even for basic goods. And the gold, though plentiful, required more hard work and good luck to find than many had been led to believe.

Occasional solitary miners made fortuitous strikes. One prospector tied his mule to a stake overnight and when he took the stake out in the morning he found a rich deposit of gold in the hole. Another, a discouraged fellow, kicked a rock in anger, rolling it aside to expose a large nugget. But for the majority of forty-niners, especially those who arrived after the initial rush, riches were scarce. The inexperienced young men who did stumble upon a good placer often wasted their wealth on gambling, liquor, and women. Sometimes supplying the miners was most lucrative. Food, alcohol, and entertainment fetched a good price in gold rush California. Young women flocked to the mining camps and often made a small fortune, plying the world's oldest trade.

Soon the streams and rivers were played out. The "easy pickings" were gone. Mining increasingly became a corporate industry. Newcomers found that they could extract more gold by pooling their resources, and some of these conglomerations became large companies. Corporate mining further ravaged the already damaged environment. Entire mountains were torn-up, rivers were diverted, and huge hydraulic machines tunneled into the earth, leaving gaping holes in their wake. (For more information on mining techniques, see pages 114-116.) Streams were poisoned, forests felled to provide fuel, and hastily constructed shantytowns spread across the California mountainsides.

The native populations in the mining districts suffered. Prior to the gold rush, Indians living beyond the coast generally had little contact with white men because the Spanish missionary influence did not extend much inland and was mostly in the south. The large ranches, some in the Central Valley, had only a small impact on the largely peaceful bands of Indians. Their experience with the new settlers who invaded their homeland en masse was unfavorable. Their lands were stolen, the natural resources upon which they depended destroyed, and their way of life irrevocably altered. Some unfortunate tribal members were virtual slaves in mining enterprises. Still others were used as target practice by bored prospectors. Entire groups of people who had lived in the foothills and mountains for centuries became extinct over the course of a single decade. From the first European settlement in 1769 to 1860, a decade after the gold rush, the indigenous population dropped from an estimated 300,000 to about 30,000. For the most part, the 105 or so tribes and bands did not offer any organized resistance like the Plains Indians and Arizona's Navajo.

Lawlessness flourished in the mining camps. In the predominantly male society, traditional moral compasses were absent. Rowdy young men often became embroiled in brawls, which sometimes escalated into knife or gun fights. Theft was rare when gold was plentiful, but rampant when mines became less productive. Several bandits became legendary: Joaquin Murrieta, Black Bart, and Tiburcio Vasquez were famous outlaws of the day. In the absence of an established judicial system, crime was often combated by vigilantism. Lynchings were at times as common as murders. Still, the majority of miners were law abiding, and most towns had a church in addition to several saloons.

Though many unlucky prospectors returned to their homes poor and disillusioned, most chose to stay in California. When the mining camps declined, the miners flocked to cities. Although the metropolitan population of Southern California remained small, villages like San Francisco and Sacramento became cities overnight. Ranches were established across California, and immigration continued into the new state. The person who sparked the gold rush, James Wilson Marshall, died a pauper. John Sutter saw his fort ruined and his dreams destroyed. But their discovery had changed California, and the United States, forever.

Chinese Immigrants in California

Chinese were the first Asian group to enter the United States en masse. In 1849, a large number migrated to California from the Pearl River Delta, located on China's southern coast, where political upheaval and a burgeoning population was making it nearly impossible to support a family. Hearing of California's riches, many had visions of crossing the Pacific and quickly collecting enough gold to return home and comfortably support their families. Reportedly, stories of California, which the Chinese called *Gam Saan,* or "Gold Mountain," were so alluring that Chinese towns would have been empty if everyone who wanted to go could have afforded to. The voyage to "Gold Mountain" was expensive, and most traveled on the credit-ticket system. Under this agreement, a company would loan the emigrant money for passage, and the worker would repay the amount, with interest, from his earnings in America.

Records indicate that more than 300 Chinese immigrants were in California in 1849, mostly mining for gold in remote camps. Groups of Chinese immigrants effectively placer mined their claims along the Yuba River and its tributaries. By 1852, more than 20,000 Chinese immigrants were in California and the governor was quoted as calling the Chinese "one of the most worthy classes of our newly adopted citizens—to whom the climate and character of these lands are peculiarly suited." Signs of shifting public opinion began in May 1852 with the passage of a foreign miners tax of three dollars a month on those who did not become citizens. The tax was aimed at the Chinese who could not become citizens due to the Naturalization Law of 1790 (the law wasn't changed until 1952) that stated American citizenship was only granted to "whites." By the time the Civil Rights Act of 1870 repealed the tax, California had collected nearly $5 million, or a third of the state's total income, from the tax.

Discrimination grew based on the fear that Chinese workers would take jobs away from white Americans because they were generally underpaid for their efficient and dependable work. In 1854, when two immigrants testified against a white man who had murdered a Chinese man, the white man was not convicted of the crime because his lawyer cited a law that stated, "No black or mulatto person, or Indian, shall be permitted to give evidence in favor of, or against, a white person." The Chinese thus faced much the same discrimination as American Indians and blacks. In many cases, Americans despised the Chinese even more because they were seen as smarter and more competitive than other minorities.

Employers, however, sought out Chinese labor. In 1865, the Central Pacific Railroad began hiring Chinese workers because they were more reliable than white laborers. By 1867, the railroad employed an estimated 12,000 Chinese, totalling 90 percent of its entire workforce. Without the Chinese, America's first transcontinental railroad likely could not have been built. The Central Pacific organization saved significant sums of money employing the motivated and dependable workers who arduously labored to lay rail through California's most extreme terrain, the rugged Sierra Nevada. Although underpaid, Chinese railroad workers were motivated by their minimal salaries of $31 a month, 10 times what they could make in China. In 1866, aware of the injustices that were imposed on them under such harsh working conditions, the laborers went on strike for a wage increase of $14 a month. Charles Crocker, chief of construction for Central Pacific, cut off their food supply and coerced them to accept a meager $4 a month increase.

With the railroad project complete and the gold mines played out, many Chinese relocated to California's cities where they entered boot, shoe, wool, tobacco, cigar, and sewing factories. As a result, industry in urban areas boomed. Although companies realized the important contribution of Chinese workers, wage discrimination continued. In the agricultural community, the Chinese, with a background of farming southern China's Pearl River Delta, taught Californians how to cultivate fruits and vegetables rather than simply wheat and grains. The Chinese transformed the landscape, building irrigation systems like those that were well established in their homeland. Their alterations increased the new farmland's value from $28 an acre in 1875 to $100 an acre in 1877. Hoping to farm the land for themselves, some immigrants attempted to enter the agricultural industry through tenant farming, still a difficult and low-paying lifestyle.

Chinese emigrants arriving in port on their way to the goldfields

Riots broke out during one economic downturn, and unemployed white workers blamed the Chinese. Throughout the state they were beaten, shot, and driven onto railroad cars. In 1882, when the Chinese population in America numbered almost 100,000, Congress passed the Chinese Exclusion Act, banning the immigration of Chinese workers. It was an attempt to appease the working class, which blamed the woes of the American economy on the hapless immigrants.

Facing these grim conditions, the Chinese opened their own stores, restaurants, and especially laundries. By 1900, one out of every four Chinese immigrants worked in a laundry. Chinatowns, which had been in existence since the 1850s, thrived in San Francisco, or *Dai Fou* ("Big City") and Sacramento, or *Yee Fou* ("Second City"). Havens for the overworked, underpaid, and poorly treated immigrants, the towns reflected Chinese culture. Colorful traditional festivals were held and theater productions were staged. *Tongs* ("secret societies") ran the opium, gambling, and prostitution rackets in the towns while *fongs* ("village associations") maintained clubhouses for gatherings, temples for worship, as well as police and garbage services for the towns. The district associations, each made up of Chinese from a specific region of China, helped new immigrants find employment and housing and managed the credit-ticket system.

Later, the associations merged into the Chinese Six Companies to provide education and health care for workers. This group, made up of merchants who dealt with the white community, advanced Chinese interests by recruiting influential American officials to advise and speak for them. The Chinese Six Companies also lobbied Congress for Chinese civil rights. Finally in 1943, Congress repealed the Chinese Exclusion Act of 1882 as a gesture of goodwill toward a new wartime ally. Subsequent changes aided Chinese immigration and the Chinese have gradually been accepted in American society.

The Donner Party

In the spring of 1846, a party of pioneers led by Jacob and George Donner and James F. Reed left Springfield, Illinois, bound for California. In July 1846, after resting at Fort Bridger, Wyoming, the small group decided not to take the well-known California Trail. Instead, they chose to risk the shorter and less-traveled wagon trail recommended by Lansford Hastings in his book, *The Emigrant's Guide to Oregon and California.* (Although he was an experienced trailblazer, Hastings himself had never completed the route he recommended.) Hastings was willing to guide parties to California for a fee, but when the Donners reached Fort Bridger, they found that the guide had already departed with another group. He left a letter indicating that he would mark the trail so the Donner Party decided to follow his route. A mixture of poor judgment and bad luck made their journey disastrous.

Hastings advised the wagon train to journey from Fort Bridger through the Wasatch Mountains, to the south of the Great Salt Lake, and across the Great Salt Desert. The trip through the Wasatch Mountains proved extremely arduous. The group waited for eight days, hoping Hastings would double back to show them a suitable route. James Reed eventually went ahead to find the guide; he returned with instructions but without Hastings. In all, the party took a month instead of the expected week to reach the Great Salt Lake. Tired, yet eager to continue on the next leg of its journey, the Donner party hurried past the lake region and headed into the Great Salt Desert on August 30, 1846.

Due to unusually soft ground, the typical two-day trip turned into a six-day nightmare. The party lost two of its best men in the alkaline flats after John Snyder inadvertently bullwhipped James Reed's wife. Reed responded by stabbing Snyder to death, for which he was banished from the party. Two men were sent ahead to fetch much-needed supplies and the rest of the group drove on continuously until they reached the Sierra Nevada. As they climbed the mountains, it became increasingly obvious that winter was coming. Still, the group decided to wait again before attempting passage over the Sierra. One member of the party reached them with provisions from Sutter's Fort. In late October, just before the party was set to depart, the first snows made crossing the mountain range impossible, and the group was trapped for the winter.

By mid-December, it became obvious that the group would starve to death, so 15 of the strongest pioneers set off in search of civilization. The volunteers faced a horrific journey. They were forced to eat their dead. Two Indian guides who refused to eat human flesh were themselves shot and eaten. After 32 days, seven survivors arrived at an Indian village.

The first rescue party reached the survivors of the main group on February 19, 1847; three more parties followed, including one led by the banished Reed. Reed arrived to find his wife and four children alive, but like others in the party, in an awful state. Survivors had been forced to commit cannibalism in order to live. Only 45 of the 89 people who had left Fort Bridger had survived the ordeal. Among the dead were both Donner brothers, Jacob and George. One of the last to perish was George's wife, Tamsen Donner. Tamsen had refused to leave her dying husband with any of the rescue parties. When the last rescuers arrived, they found Tamsen dead. It was commonly thought that Lewis Keseberg, another survivor, had killed her for fresh meat. Keseberg spent the rest of his life trying to live down the accusations. Other members of the ill-fated party became heroes and symbols of strength in the young Californian state.

California Statehood

U.S. forces took Alta California from Mexico in 1846 and treated the former Mexican province as a military district, subject to military law. However, with the end of the Mexican War in 1848 and the huge migration into California that followed the discovery of gold, it became clear that bringing California into the Union was necessary. Although there had been talk of establishing a California Republic, most residents—there had been only about 500 American traders and ranchers living in California at the time of the Bear Flag Revolt—felt allegiance to the United States. Although President James Polk had pressed for territorial status, his successor, Zachary Taylor, thought that the residents, not Congress, should decide on their status. Even before Taylor took office, Californians called for a constitutional convention in Monterey in September 1849 to draft a state constitution to submit to Washington. The delegates had to decide whether or not to allow slavery, a practice allowed in 15 states. Delegates chose to enter the Union as a free state. They also had to draw boundaries for the new state. Some argued that California should include the desert east of the Sierra Nevada, perhaps even as far as Salt Lake City, then newly settled by Mormons. Eventually, delegates decided a smaller California would be more palatable to congressional lawmakers and its present boundary lines were drawn, just east of the mountains. California became the nation's thirty-second state September 9, 1850.

Where to locate the capital was another contentious issue. Several cities presented proposals, including San Francisco and Monterey, the province's seat of government during Spanish and Mexican rule. The first legislature was held in San Jose in December 1849, but in 1851, it seemed as though Vallejo might become the capital when the government moved its archives there. The legislature did not follow, and in 1853 Benicia became California's third state capital, only to be superseded permanently by Sacramento the following year.

From the beginning of European settlement in California, a rivalry has existed between residents in the north and residents in the south. Following the Mexican revolution against Spain, the more populous south sought to move the provincial capital from Monterey to Los Angeles. During the gold rush and in years following, the huge population growth was mostly in the north. In 1859, Andrés Pico, a state senator from Los Angeles, proposed a plan to split California in two. Though the proposal won the approval of the state Senate, it died in a Congress preoccupied by the nation's slip toward civil war. The 1880s saw another southern proposal for partition when unfavorable water laws and corporate hegemony angered separatists. By this time, however, Southern California was booming and beginning to catch the north in terms of population. Fearful of an expanding Los Angeles, it was the northerners' turn to request separation, but the bill was quashed in 1915.

In 1926, the legislature decided that the Assembly should be based on population and that state senators should represent districts based on area. In 1964, the U.S. Supreme Court further jolted northerners with a ruling that effectively handed control of the state legislature to the now more populous south. The last bid for partition came as recently as 1978, when northern lawmakers proposed an "Alta California" state north of the Tehachapi. Although most Californians today still hold strong regional affiliations, few actively support a separation of the state.

Mariposa Indian War

When miners began searching for gold in the southern Sierra Nevada of Central California, they found themselves in a region occupied by a large Indian population. The valleys and Sierra foothills were lush with oak groves and wildlife that supported several tribes, including bands of Yokuts, Mono, and Miwok. Unfortunately for the indigenous people, the rivers and streams, with excellent fishing, were rich in gold. Soon, miners and settlers had overrun the area, much to the Indians' chagrin.

James D. Savage, who had come to California in 1846 and fought in the California Battalion during the Mexican War, was one settler who had managed to establish close relations with the Indians. After the war, Savage worked at Sutter's Fort, where he was staying when the first gold was discovered on the American River. Using Indian labor, he made a fortune by placer mining. He secured his ties with local tribes by marrying as many Indian women as he could, generally the daughters of the village chiefs. One writer claimed Savage had 33 wives, ranging in age from 10 to 22. Somehow, Savage's activities angered his Indian friends. In December 1850, a band of warriors attacked his trading post, killing three men. Some historians have conjectured that the attack was not aimed at Savage personally, but rather against the hordes of white settlers invading Indian land.

Attempts to apprehend the Indians were unsuccessful, so Governor John McDougal organized the Mariposa Battalion. Savage was elected major of the unit. The campaigns against the Indians brought out many of the resentments held by both the tribes and the settlers. A federal Indian commission sought a peaceful resolution to the tensions. On March 19, 1851, six tribes concluded a treaty with the commissioners. However, two groups, the Chowchilla and the Yosemite, both subtribes of the Miwok, did not sign the treaty. Three companies of civilians pursued the tribes through the mountains. Little blood was shed on either side. The Chowchilla surrendered to whites after their chief was killed. The Yosemite were captured at Lake Tenaija, now Tenaya Lake in Yosemite National Park, on May 22, 1851. Both bands were forced onto reservations.

Modoc Indian War

Indians in California suffered greatly from the white intrusion into their traditional homelands. Despite this, the Golden State had few of the conflicts that characterized Indian relations elsewhere in the west. An exception lasted over a short period when bands of Modoc in Northern California resisted U.S. Army troops in the 1870s.

Disagreements between the Modoc Indians and American settlers began as early as 1852, when a group of Modoc warriors who were accused of slaughtering a small party of whites were invited to a peace parley and then massacred. In response, the tribe ambushed a wagon train at Bloody Point and killed 65 settlers. Hostilities continued until 1864, when the Modoc agreed to move to a reservation in Oregon shared with their traditional enemies, the Klamath. The tribe found it impossible to coexist there, and in 1870, they left the reservation for good.

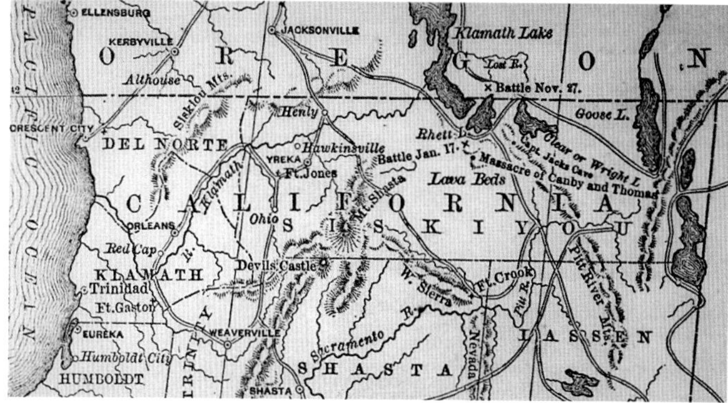

Map of events published during the Modoc War

On November 29, 1872, a Modoc band was camping on the Lost River, a traditional site for them, when the U.S. Army tried to force them back to the reservation. The Indians fled, murdering more than a dozen settlers along their escape route. Led by Chief Kientopoos (known to whites as Captain Jack), the tribe retreated to the Stronghold, lava beds that formed an impenetrable fortress. A force of only 50 to 90 Modoc warriors resisted more than a thousand U.S. troops. On one attempt to dislodge the tribe from its hideout, the U.S. Army lost 35 men and inflicted no Indian casualties.

Negotiations between the government and Kientopoos continued through the winter. On April 11, 1873 (Good Friday), the Modoc demanded their own reservation along Lost River. When General Edward Canby once again refused this request, Kientopoos shot him. Hawkish warriors who had convinced the chief that the Americans would depart if their leader were killed probably coerced Kientopoos into this act. General Canby was the highest-ranking American soldier killed in any of the Indian wars. His death forced the army to redouble its efforts against the Modoc. They laid siege to the Stronghold, depriving the Indians of food and water. However, Kientopoos led his people to safety before the troops entered the rocky fortress. Despite reaching refuge, the Modoc were suffering from the long siege and many warriors began to defect. An unsuccessful ambush of an army unit on May 10, 1873, further weakened Kientopoos's force. Nevertheless, he was able to lead 33 Modoc out of a trap set by more than 300 troops at Big Sand Butte. The same Modoc warriors who had convinced Kientopoos to kill General Canby had defected, and now guided the defectors.

Outnumbered, hungry, and betrayed by his people, the resourceful chief surrendered on June 1, 1873. He and three fellow warriors were hanged for killing the general. The remaining Modoc were transported to the Indian Territory in present-day Oklahoma. There diseases virtually eradicated the band. To preserve space to graze cattle, settlers and the army had wiped out a culture that had existed in Northern California for centuries.

Vigilantism

The gold rush brought thousands of newcomers to California before an effective and efficient law enforcement agency and a court system were established. Some forty-niners were scoundrels fleeing their homeland for the easy pickings of the mining regions. Theft and murder became rampant, especially as gold became scarce. With no effective justice system, Californians resorted to vigilantism. Individuals who considered themselves to be law abiding came together to form commit-

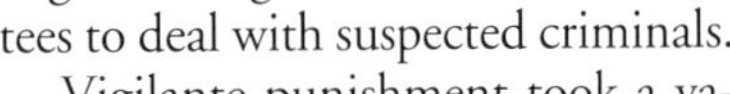

tees to deal with suspected criminals.

Vigilance Committee badge

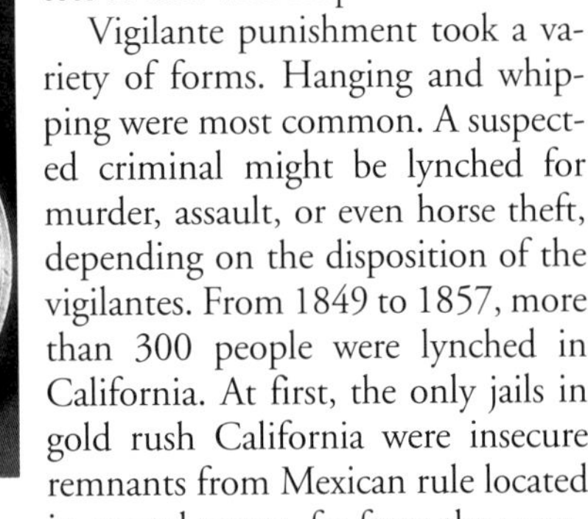

Vigilante punishment took a variety of forms. Hanging and whipping were most common. A suspected criminal might be lynched for murder, assault, or even horse theft, depending on the disposition of the vigilantes. From 1849 to 1857, more than 300 people were lynched in California. At first, the only jails in gold rush California were insecure remnants from Mexican rule located in coastal towns, far from the populous mining camps. Punishment was therefore quick and final. More often than not, a criminal was lynched the day he was captured. If the crime were less severe, the suspect would generally be lashed, usually at least 15 times, and often 10 times after that. Other less common punishments were ear cropping, head shaving, and branding to mark thieves as such.

Depiction of a San Francisco vigilante lynching

Vigilantism was often racist. Latinos, blacks, and especially Indians were particularly subject to hanging. Chinese and Mexicans were often driven from rich placers for the supposed actions of one of their fellows. Indian villages were sometimes destroyed in retribution for simple theft by one of their residents.

One mining town gained a special reputation for its vigilante justice. Dry Diggings, in El Dorado County, was the site of the first gold rush era lynching. On January 22, 1849, three men were hanged by a drunken mob after they were caught stealing $600. At first, they were flogged and released, but someone recognized them as suspects in a robbery and attempted murder that occurred some months earlier. The three men were recaptured and hanged from a tree, the first of many lynchings carried out in the town. Dry Diggings, later renamed Placerville, became known briefly as Hangtown.

Vigilantism was not confined to mining camps. In 1851, law-abiding residents of San Francisco formed a Vigilance Committee to deal with the unrestrained crime plaguing the city. Two groups, the Regulators, also known as the Hounds, and the Sydney Ducks, escapees or ex-convicts from the British penal colony in Australia, wreaked havoc on the town, looting, robbing, burning, and killing. The Regulators were mainly Mexican War veterans who persecuted Latino residents in the name of law and order, once carrying out a murderous looting raid on the Little Chile section of town.

Two Sydney Ducks—John Jenkins and "English Jim" Stuart—became notorious criminals, and the Vigilance Committee was formed in part to punish these men. William T. Coleman, a successful merchant who became known as the Lion of the Vigilantes for his fierce prosecution of criminals, headed the committee. John Jenkins was the first bandit to be hanged by the committee. He stole a strong box from a shipping office and defied anyone to capture him. The Vigilance Committee took up his challenge, and within a few hours Jenkins was hanging from a scaffold in Portsmouth Square. "English Jim" Stuart, known to be a murder, was caught and hanged not long afterwards.

Vigilance committees disbanded when an official justice system began to function more effectively. However, when the courts were unable to stop a rising tide of murders in San Francisco, Coleman reformed San Francisco's Vigilance Committee in 1856. The new committee attracted thousands of members and formed its own police department. Although they did lynch several murderers, Coleman and his supporters were now more interested in combating government corruption. The committee published a list of criminals and corrupt politicians. Several of the blacklisted people were deported and others fled; eventually, the committee reconfigured, becoming a legitimate and powerful political party.

Slowly, a criminal justice system arose even in the most remote mining camps. Jails and courthouses became fixtures of established settlements. Occasionally, mobs of angry citizens would mete out their own crude punishments, but soon the lynchings and whippings of gold rush California were things of the past.

San Francisco Earthquake

The 1906 earthquake and the resulting fire was a cataclysmic event in San Francisco's history. It is remembered as the most significant natural disaster ever to hit the United States. The first tremors were felt at 5:12 A.M. on April 18, 1906. The main shock lasted 45 to 60 seconds and caused ruptures along a staggering 290 miles of the San Andreas Fault. At some points along the fault, the Pacific and North American Continental plates had slipped 20 feet. Modern estimates place the shock at 8.3 on the Richter scale. The tremors were centered just off the coast, near Pacifica, but were felt as far away as Oregon and central Nevada. Aftershocks continued all day.

The earthquake razed many structures in San Francisco, especially in poorer areas of the city where building safety standards were nonexistent. More damaging than the earthquake, though, were the fires it caused. Within a few hours of the first shock, at least 52 fires had erupted in various parts of the city. San Francisco's fire department was relatively modern and well organized, but it faced a daunting task. The earthquake had destroyed water pipes, rendering fire hydrants useless. Old cisterns dotted San Francisco, but only senior department officials knew their locations and communications had been cut. Fire Chief Dennis T. Sullivan had emergency action plans in place, but he was mortally wounded in the original tremors.

The city was in disarray as frightened citizens crowded its streets. By nightfall on the first day of fires, more than 100,000 people out of a population of 400,000 were homeless. In the next few days, that number climbed to 225,000. Hundreds of people were trapped in buildings after the earthquake and perished in the fires. Survivors fled the city. On the first day, residents streamed to the waterfront hoping to fill departing ferries. The streets filled with people trying to escape the fires. As they fled, buildings fell around them and debris rained from the sky, killing many. Along Mission Street, a herd of longhorn steers stampeded, trampling people in its path. The stampede was halted when a building collapsed on most of the herd. On April 20, the USS *Chicago* evacuated 20,000 San Franciscans by sea; this was the largest sea rescue in history until Dunkirk 34 years later. Law enforcement officials were disorganized and preoccupied by the fire. Looting was prevented when the mayor issued an order declaring that looters would be shot on sight.

Raging fires caused by the 1906 earthquake

Gaping trench created by the quake along a cobblestone city street

Meanwhile, firefighters fought desperately to control the blaze engulfing the city. At one point, the various fires combined into one and were burning along a 3-mile front. Smoke from the blaze blocked out the sun. Cistern after cistern was drained, often to no avail. Attempts were made to create a fire wall by destroying whole city blocks with dynamite; at times, this merely started new fires.

Rain on the night of April 20 slowed the blaze and by the next morning the fire was extinguished. Firefighters, some of whom had worked without sleep for several days, were assisted by thousands of volunteers. The final toll on the city was devastating; 498 deaths were confirmed in San Francisco, with almost 200 more outside the city. The actual number is thought to be closer to 3,000, but most bodies were incinerated in the fires, making an accurate count impossible. Over 28,000 buildings were destroyed and many others were damaged. Whole stretches of San Francisco were reduced to rubble and ash. The army quickly supplied food and tents to feed and house the thousands of homeless and relief poured in as the rest of the nation heard of the catastrophe. The cost to the city was in excess of $400 million in 1906 dollars. Valiant efforts had saved much of the Old City, but massive rebuilding was necessary elsewhere.

Even today, San Francisco's history is divided into two periods—before and after the earthquake. Gradually, San Francisco reestablished itself as the West Coast's major metropolis. Greater attention was paid to building safety and earthquake risk. The quake taught scientists much about seismology, then a field of study in its infancy. Today, experts think an earthquake of such a magnitude probably occurs just once every 200 years or so. The chance of a similar incident in the next few decades is small.

Geology

The Geological Timeline

The geologic history of California is long and complex. Northern California's most stunning features—the Sierra Nevada, Coast Ranges, Klamath Mountains, and the Central Valley—have their origins in the magisterial collisions between tectonic plates. California lies on two tectonic plates: the continental North American plate and the oceanic Pacific plate. About 200 million years ago, the Pacific plate, with its covering of sedimentary layers, was overridden by the North American plate. The underside of the continental plate melted because so much heat was generated by the friction. Over the millennia, this pool of molten rock—magma—cooled deep beneath the surface and became granite. Over time, the granite rocks were uplifted and exposed by erosion, creating the dramatic range of the Sierra Nevada. With the magma came minerals, most famously gold, that would shape so much of California's more recent history. The movements of the plates also caused the North American plate to scrape rocks off the ocean floor as it overrode the Pacific plate. The results, in part, are the crumpled coastal mountains, the Coast Ranges that extend north from Santa Barbara County to the Oregon border. About 25 million years ago, the direction of the plates changed. Instead of colliding, they now slide by one another. The change in movement created the San Andreas Fault. The Pacific plate now grinds northward, past the North American plate. Sometime between two million and three million years ago, huge glaciers—during multiple ice ages—carved into the Sierra Nevada, Cascades, and Klamath Mountains, further sculpting the landscape. When the glaciers retreated once and for all, the land began to assume the form we know today. Worldwide, the freezing and melting of glacial ice caused sea levels to fall and rise, and the coastline of California reflects these climatic changes.

Humans, Paleo-Indians, may have come to California from Asia by raft or boat along the coast during the Ice Age, when the shoreline was wider. Evidence of their passing may be beneath the ocean. Other sites, found inland, suggest a migration from Asia occurred some time after the last ice age, 10,000 to 15,000 years ago. Humans, whenever they came, have continually altered the natural surroundings.

Since the arrival of Spanish settlers at the end of the eighteenth century, the region has lost 80 percent of its woodlands, 99 percent of the native grasslands, 94 percent of the coastal wetlands, and streams and rivers have been diverted, dammed, channeled, and dried up. The gold rush beginning in 1849 brought a huge influx of people into the region. Today one in ten Americans resides in California, and an estimated 2,000 immigrants arrive daily. Nevertheless, California is still a land of immense and varied natural beauty, a sampling of which you can experience by following the trails in this book.

The Regions

Northern California can be divided into four geologic regions: the Coast Ranges; the Central Valley; the Sierra Nevada, which includes some regions of the Great Basin; and the North, which includes the Cascades, Klamath Mountains, and Modoc Plateau.

Coast Ranges

California 1 sweeps north from Monterey in Northern California and contours the Pacific Coast into Mendocino County. Farther north, US 101 snakes along to the Oregon border. The mountains and hills rising above the Pacific along these spectacular roads are the Coast Ranges, formed as a result of the continental North American plate scraping sediments off the upper portion of the oceanic Pacific plate.

Seals and sea lions bask on the shores, and hundreds of species of birds thrive here. Miles of sandy beaches, many protected as state and federal parks, encourage long walks, but only the hardy swim in the cold Pacific waters. In the north, redwood forests thrive in ocean mists. Sea otters once more play in bays and inlets, their population still recovering from large-scale hunting by trappers and traders in the early 1800s.

Central Valley

The Sacramento Valley in the north and San Joaquin Valley to the south compose California's great Central Valley. Nearly 75 miles wide and 430 miles long, the valley lies between the Coast Ranges to the west and the Sierra Nevada to the east. The Sacramento River, navigable as far as the state's capital, and the northwest-flowing San Joaquin River form a vast watershed, and where the rivers join, they create the Sacramento–San Joaquin Delta, before flowing into San Francisco Bay.

With irrigation from groundwater and natural streams, the Central Valley supports much of California's agriculture. Perhaps more fruits, nuts, grains, and vegetables are grown here than in any other valley in the world. Many cattle are also raised here, and the soil in the delta region is especially rich for asparagus, tomatoes, rice, and alfalfa.

The foothills of the Sierra Nevada, at the edge of the San Joaquin and Sacramento Valleys, were also the site of the Mother Lode, the rich gold mining area of the 1850s. Both the San Joaquin and Sacramento Rivers once supported runs of salmon. Although pollution, irrigation, and dams have diminished some of their populations, good fishing remains.

Sierra Nevada

John Muir, the nineteenth-century Scottish-born naturalist, once called the Sierra Nevada the Range of Light; its name in Spanish means white, or snowy, mountains. The 400-mile range begins just south of Lassen Peak in the north and extends to the Tehachapi Mountains in the south; the mountains form the lush eastern slope of the Central Valley and the arid western buttress above the Great Basin.

Perhaps the prime destination for recreation in the state, the Sierra Nevada has 11 peaks over 14,000 feet, including the tallest in the continental United States, Mount Whitney, which towers at 14,494 feet. The range encompasses 8 national forests, 3 national parks, 14 wilderness areas, and many more state parks, historical sites, and recreation areas. Rivers fed by snowmelt, such as the Feather, American, and Yuba, are perfect for kayaking and whitewater rafting. The Sierra's deep valleys are also home to numerous waterfalls, including the 2,425-foot-tall Yosemite Falls in Yosemite National Park.

The mountains are granitic and metamorphic rock formed from molten rock—magma—that intruded into overlying rock some 185 to 65 million years ago when the North American plate overrode the oceanic Pacific plate. Over geologic time, these rocks have been uplifted and eroded to expose the granite. The rock has been shaped by rivers and glaciers and weathered into the spires and domes we know today.

The range is home to the largest living thing on earth—the sequoia. Though the related redwood trees grow taller, and one species is wider, none have the same weight or volume. Some of the magnificent sequoia trees are protected in Sequoia and Kings Canyon National Parks and Giant Sequoia National Monument. The largest of the large is a tree named General Sherman, which is 275 feet tall, with a base diameter of 36 feet, a weight of about 2.7 million pounds, and an estimated age of 2,300 years.

The Sierra Nevada has several life zones determined by elevation, precipitation, and soil. Plants and animals live in predictable zones based on these three factors. For example, trees do not grow in the highest elevations where the weather can be arctic in the winter, with heavy snowfall and cold temperatures, and animals, such as pikas and marmots, have adapted to the harsh conditions. Coyotes and jackrabbits flourish in the warmer temperatures at lower elevations, and mountain lions and black bears survive in middle elevations.

Part of the Great Basin to the east of the Sierra is in this region, including the high deserts of the White Mountains and the northern reaches of the Owens Valley as far south as Lone Pine, on US 395.

The North

California north of the Sierra Nevada and Coast Ranges becomes a different state. The volcanic, snow-covered dome of Mount Shasta rises above the north end of the Central Valley. Mount Shasta, like Lassen Peak, is part of the Cascade Range, mountains associated more with Oregon and Washington. Then, to the west of the Cascades, the heavily forested Klamath Mountains have a complex geologic history contrasting with that of the Modoc Plateau, which stretches to the Oregon-Nevada border in the extreme northeast part of the state.

National forests and wildlife refuges cover much of the region and some of the best bird-watching in Northern California is here at refuges centered on Lower Klamath Lake and Tule Lake.

The rugged, complex Klamath Mountains have vegetation influenced by the mixed elements of Pacific moisture and arid inland conditions. Geologically, they are a domain of ancient tectonic plate collisions.

Famous Geological Features of Northern California

San Andreas Fault

Active faults, fractures in the earth's crust, occur in California because the state is at the boundary between two tectonic plates: the continental North American plate and the oceanic Pacific plate. Earthquakes occur when the plates shift and grind along faults. The San Andreas Fault System and its branches are the most significant faults in the state. The San Andreas extends for nearly 700 miles, from Cape Mendocino in the north, south to San Francisco, and inland, west of San Jose, continuing through the Coast Ranges into Southern California. In Northern California, much of the fault is along the coast. The fault is visible at Tomales Bay in Marin County where California 1 runs right along its edge.

The fault dramatically revealed itself in the San Francisco earthquake of April 18, 1906. The powerful earthquake that struck that day, and the fires that followed, took the lives of at least 700 people. Land along the fault moved as much as 21 feet. Approximately 20 million people now live in the vicinity of the San Andreas Fault, named for the San Andreas Valley in San Mateo County. The fault causes hundreds of small earthquakes each year, and its presence and the potential for another catastrophic earthquake are part of everyday life for millions of Californians.

Lassen Peak

Lassen Volcanic National Park, east of Redding, includes Lassen Peak, the southernmost peak of the Cascade Range. Between 1914 and 1921, the volcano exploded in a series of eruptions. Lassen sent a 7-mile-high cloud of steam and ash into the stratosphere during the climax event in 1915. Lassen's eruption was the most recent volcanic activity in the lower 48 until Washington's Mount St. Helens erupted in 1980.

Lassen is but one vent of a huge volcano, called Mount Tehama. Mount Tehama was most active about 600,000 years ago, and its main vent was probably at what today is called the Sulphur Works, near the southwestern entrance to the park. Tehama's huge caldera was more than 11 miles wide and either collapsed or eroded over the millennia.

Lassen is a plug dome volcano, and it is the largest of its kind in the world, rising 2,000 feet from its base at about 8,000 feet, to an elevation of 10,457 feet. Cinder Cone, another volcanic feature in the park, was active as recently as the 1850s.

Lava Beds

The volcanic rocks in Lava Beds National Monument were formed about 1,100 years ago, so recently that they appear fresh and unweathered. Soil is forming and collecting very slowly on the lava flows. The lava beds are composed of basalt, the most common volcanic rock in the monument, and can appear smooth or rough and bubbly.

Cinder cones are another volcanic feature in the monument. The cones formed when lava erupted explosively, spewing molten rock over large areas. Lava tubes, a third volcanic feature, formed when molten rock drained from under a flow's surface after the top of the flow cooled and hardened, leaving openings. In some places in the Lava Beds National Monument, the ceilings of tubes have collapsed, creating depressions and troughs. Lava bridges, remnants of tube ceilings, span the troughs. Drips in the tubes formed when still molten lava dripped from the tube's ceiling.

Medicine Lake, south of the national monument, is also the result of relatively recent volcanic activity. Some of the volcanic rock at Medicine Lake is obsidian, a hard shiny rock that fractures into sharp fragments. Indians shaped tools such as arrowheads and knives from it.

Mono Lake

Mono Lake, east of Yosemite National Park, lies in the Great Basin, below the eastern buttress of the Sierra Nevada. The lake has existed for at least a million years. At one time, it held much more water and had a much higher shoreline than it does today. Although freshwater streams feed the lake, its long existence, high rate of evaporation, and the fact that it has no outlet means that its salt content is extremely high. Mono Lake is far saltier than the ocean, and its salinity has increased dramatically over the last century.

In 1941, the Los Angeles Department of Water and Power began diverting water from four of the five streams that feed Mono Lake; aqueducts carried the diverted water nearly 300 miles across deserts and mountains to the southern metropolis. Between 1941 and 1994, when legislation partially curtailed the diversions, the lake lost half its volume and its surface dropped 45 feet. The loss of water and increased salinity drastically affected Mono Lake's ecosystem. Although the salt content is too high to sustain fish, brine shrimp thrive in the lake waters. A large population of California gulls breed on the lake's two islands, and their primary food is shrimp.

Shrimp numbers have dropped as salinity levels increase, thus threatening the gulls' food supply. The lower water level means coyotes and other predators can now cross from the shore to Negit Island and ravage the breeding colony. After one or two disastrous breeding seasons, gull populations have stabilized.

Great horned owls, kestrels, and northern flickers nest in the vicinity of Mono Lake, and Wilson's phalaropes arrive in summer to feed on alkali fly larvae. Alkali flies generated the lake's name: *Mono* is from the Yokuts word for fly eaters, the name Yokuts gave to the Indians that inhabited the region.

The lower water levels of the lake reveal dazzling, cathedral-like formations of calcium carbonate deposits (tufa). Tufa forms when springs under the lake provide nutrients for blue-green algae, which, in turn, promote precipitation of calcium carbonate. The receding shoreline has also left expanses of white salts.

The two islands in the lake, Negit and Paoha, are recent volcanic creations. Paoha Island is believed to be less than 300 years old. Additional evidence of volcanic activity is just south of Mono Lake, at the dormant Mono Craters, formed within the last 600 to 35,000 years.

The Mono Basin National Forest Scenic Area Visitor Center, just north of Lee Vining, on US 395 is a good place to find information about the lake.

Mount Shasta

The splendid snowcapped summit of Mount Shasta, at an elevation of 14,162 feet, is visible for more than 100 miles on a clear day. This volcanic mountain, one of the largest volcanoes in the Cascades, began to form around 590,000 years ago. The mountain is a stratovolcano, or stratocone, made up of four overlapping volcanic cones, which formed on remnants of an older stratocone, toppled more than 300,000 years ago by an immense landslide estimated to have been 20 times greater than the slide created by the eruption of Mount Saint Helens in 1980. Each of the cones that form Mount Shasta had independent volcanic activity, although they are not all individually recognizable.

Sargents Ridge, Misery Hill, Shastina, and Hotlum Cone compose Mount Shasta. The oldest cone, Sargents Ridge, formed when a now-extinct vent erupted about 50,000 years ago. The cone's size increased with frequent eruptions over hundreds to thousands of years. The cone's activity continued through two major glaciations, and glaciers and streams eroded its slopes. During this period, vents formed on the north, west, and south sides of Sargents Ridge.

Misery Hill, north of Sargents Ridge, erupted about 130,000 years ago and almost buried the cone of Sargents Ridge. This cone makes up most of what we recognize as Mount Shasta today. The volcanic episode that established today's Misery Hill occurred when thick hot lava filled the interior of the cone and pushed upwards to create a lava dome supported by a ridge of the eroded cone's rim.

The most individually recognizable cone is Shastina, which grew from a vent on the western slope of Misery Hill between 9,700 and 9,400 years ago. Shastina Cone developed in the relatively short span of 300 years, after the close of the Ice Age.

Hotlum Cone, the fourth cone, is slightly younger than Shastina and forms the north and northwest flank of Mount Shasta. Layers of lava on the north side of the mountain indicate that Hotlum's formation began during Shastina's period of volcanic activity, but most of what we recognize as the cone today developed from eruptions within the last 6,000 years. The remaining heat from such recent activity has created steam vents, sulfur deposits, and a hot spring just below the summit. French navigator Jean La Pérouse may have witnessed Hotlum Cone's most recent volcanic explosion in 1786.

Slopes of Mount Shasta

Black Butte is another distinct feature associated with Mount Shasta. It is at the foot of the mountain's western slope and formed about 9,500 years ago as a group of overlapping domes. As lava cooled on the exterior of Black Butte, the interior lava continued to rise, shattering the surface into angular boulders. Part of Black Butte collapsed sending large volumes of volcanic ash and debris down its south and west slopes. The towns of Weed and Mount Shasta are built on that debris.

Yosemite Valley

Yosemite Valley's 7 square miles include the dramatic geologic icons of Half Dome and El Capitan and dazzling Yosemite Falls. The valley has been protected as part of Yosemite Na-

Yosemite Valley

tional Park since 1890. Towering granite walls, waterfalls, a U-shaped valley, and the Merced River compose the essential geologic character of today's Yosemite Valley. The features we see today are the result of time, uplift, and glaciation.

The Sierra experienced a period of uplift beginning about 15 million years ago. At that time the landscape had rolling hills, meandering streams and rivers, and widespread hardwood forests. After the uplift, accompanied by a general steeper rise in the west, the Merced River cut a canyon. During the Ice Ages that began about eight million years ago, glaciers filled the canyon until as recently as 250,000 years ago. The rivers of ice deepened and widened the canyon cut by the Merced, creating today's U-shaped gorge, with its hanging valleys and waterfalls. As the Ice Age came to an end 10,000 years ago, the remaining glaciers melted in the valley leaving behind terminal moraines, or rock debris, which walled off one end of the valley to form 7-mile-long Yosemite Lake. Sediment gradually filled the lake to form the flat floor of the present-day valley. Just as Yosemite Lake became Yosemite Meadows, sediments are quickly transforming Mirror Lake, at the north end of the valley, into a meadow.

Lake Tahoe

The Lake Tahoe Basin began to form five to ten million years ago as a result of pull-apart faulting, which was so severe that it caused the earth's crust to break into massive blocks to the east and west of today's Tahoe Basin. The Sierra Nevada block to the west was uplifted and today includes Freel Peak at 10,891 feet and Monument Peak at 10,067 feet, on the basin's rim. The blocks uplifted to the east formed the Carson Range in Nevada. The blocks between the two ranges dropped to create a deep valley. Over time, rain, snowmelt, and run-off filled the valley's south end.

An estimated two million years ago, andesite lava flows from several volcanoes including Mount Pluto, north of the lake, cooled and dammed the northeastern end of the valley. Water collected in the enclosed basin. As the water level rose, it overflowed the lava dam and cut an outlet that became known as the Truckee River, which flows north and northeast to Pyramid Lake in Nevada. During the Ice Age, the vast snowpacks on the Sierra Nevada peaks froze to form glaciers that flowed down the mountain slopes. Glaciers also dammed the lake, raising its water level 800 feet above today's level. The terraces of sediments at the basin rim are evidence of the lake's higher levels.

Glaciers melted leaving piles of debris, or terminal moraines, that formed Emerald Bay, Cascade Lake, and Fallen Leaf Lake. The water level waned after the glaciers melted, and a long drought caused shores to recede below their present level. Scientists have discovered tree trunks as much as 40 feet below today's surface, and studies revealed the trees were about a century old when they were drowned.

The lake's eastern shore is composed almost entirely of granite from the Sierra Nevada. Some volcanic rock can be found at Glenbrook Bay and Cave Rock. Between Crystal Bay and Tahoe City, the rock is volcanic, part of the lava flow that originally dammed the lake. Sediment covers the north shores, smoothing the landscape. The peaks of Carson Range to the east of the lake are smooth granite because the mountains, in the rain shadow of the towering Sierra Nevada, did not accumulate enough snow to create glaciers.

Lake Tahoe's deepest point is 1,645 feet near Crystal Bay. Its average depth is 989 feet, and it is the third deepest in North America, behind Oregon's Crater Lake (1,930 feet) and Canada's Great Slave Lake (2,010 feet), and tenth deepest in the world. Measuring roughly 22 miles long and 12 miles wide, Lake Tahoe holds 39 trillion gallons of water within its 71 miles of shoreline. Spread out, that volume would cover a flat area the size of California with 14 inches or supply each resident of the United States with 50 gallons daily for 5 years. The amount of water that evaporates from its 191-square-mile surface in 24 hours is enough to supply Los Angeles for one day. At 6,225 feet above sea level, it is the highest lake of its size in the United States. Thirty inches of average annual precipitation supplies Lake Tahoe, and 63 streams filtered by the granite-filled soil provide 300,000 acre-feet of water each year. Snowmelt keeps the lake cool, and it does not freeze because of its significant circulation. The surface temperature drops to 40 degrees during the winter and reaches nearly 70 degrees in the summer. Below 700 feet the temperature is constant at 39 degrees.

Although Lake Tahoe is clear to depths of up to 75 feet, the survival of its pristine waters is threatened. New development near the lake has increased the amount of sediment entering the water. These sediments carry nutrients into the lake that stimulate algae growth, which threaten to cloud its waters. Likewise, treated sewage water released into the lake stimulates algae growth. As a result, the waste from towns and businesses around the lake is treated and diverted from flowing directly into the lake. Lake Tahoe is also particularly susceptible to pollution because of its large volume and limited drainage. This means the lake can harbor pollutants for centuries before they circulate out. A dam in Tahoe City, at the outlet of the Truckee River, regulates its water level.

Seasonal temperature swings within the Tahoe Basin in the subalpine life zone have created flora and fauna unique to the region. For example, *Clarkias,* a member of the sunflower family, and buckwheat grow nowhere else on earth. Ponderosa, lodgepole, sugar pine, and Sierra juniper are a few of the tree species here. Wildlife includes black bears, pine martens, mule deer, and marmots. And likely birds to be seen are Calliope and broad-tailed humming birds, pygmy nuthatches, and western tanagers. The kokanee salmon is an interesting Lake Tahoe resident. Unlike most salmon, which migrate to the ocean to spawn, this fish lives its entire life within the lake, spawning nearby in its shallow tributaries.

Mining

Gold Mining

California achieved statehood in the wake of the biggest mass migration in American history—the gold rush. The cause of this huge surge to the west was the discovery of gold near Sutter's Fort in January 1848. For years, Spanish colonists and Mexican settlers were unaware of the vast fortunes that lay in Alta California's hills and riverbeds. Gold had been found now and again, but it fell to New Jersey native James Wilson Marshall working for John Sutter to start the rush (see page 83). Mining has since played an elephantine role in California's history. In addition to gold, the state has silver, copper, zinc, borax, and petroleum operations, to name a few. Still, it is from the shiny yellow metal that the Golden State takes its name.

The Mother Lode region, as the western Sierra Nevada from Mariposa County to El Dorado County is known, was by far the richest source of gold. Geologically, though, the Mother Lode is a mile-wide belt from the vicinity of Mariposa in the south to Georgetown, in El Dorado County, in the north. From an estimated $250,000 extracted from the Mother Lode in 1848, yields jumped to about $80 million in 1852, the peak year of the gold rush. Small tent cities popped up along riverbanks and on mountainsides. Some of these faded as soon as the gold played out, but others—such as Oroville, Auburn, Placerville, Sonora, and Mariposa—remain vibrant communities today.

Oregonians moving south into California discovered deposits in the northern mountain ranges, especially along the Klamath and Trinity Rivers as early as 1848. The Klamath Mountains were second only to the Mother Lode and remained productive into the 1930s. Gold mining peaked in 1894 with a yield of $3 million. A revival during the Great Depression brought production back up to $5 million a year by 1940. World War II forced most mines to close, but geologists think that large quantities of rich ore remain buried in northwestern California. In total, more than $150 million worth of gold has been extracted from northwestern California, and while logging has replaced mining as the chief income producer, gold remains a significant aspect of the region's economy, with small-scale mining continuing today.

Minor discoveries have also been made in the foothills near the outskirts of the Central Valley. Great quantities of gold were extracted from just a few areas of Sacramento County. Yolo and Tehama Counties also had small mining districts. Even Napa and Sonoma—known today more for wine than gold—yielded hundreds of thousands of dollars' worth of gold. The Modoc Plateau, though generally devoid of gold, had at least one major mine—the High Grade west of Fort Bidwell.

Mining for Other Minerals

California has also been the world's leading source for other minerals, such as diatomite, gypsum, molybdenum, borax, and tungsten. Tungsten is a hard white metallic element used in light filaments and to strengthen steel. Inyo County is home to the largest tungsten mine in the world, on Mount Morgan, northwest of Bishop.

Mexican settlers mined mercury in Northern California. Also known as quicksilver, mercury is a liquid metal important in the extraction of gold and silver from ore deposits. Without this native source of mercury, English investors, who previously dominated the quicksilver market, might have controlled gold mining in the state. The discovery of mercury in the Coast Ranges at the New Almaden Mine near San Jose in 1845 was extremely fortuitous. San Benito County's New Idria Mine was also an important source of mercury.

Black gold, oil, was the most significant resource for California during the twentieth century. Native Americans caulked boats with pitch and Spanish and Mexican settlers sealed their roofs with crude oil. The world's first commercial oil well was drilled near Pittsburgh in 1859 encouraging oil exploration in other states, but the first well in California had been dug in 1835. The San Joaquin Valley, in Southern California, was the state's leading oil producer, but the San Francisco Bay area has many refineries, as do Calaveras and El Dorado Counties. Oil has proved far more profitable to the state than gold. In the 1920s alone, the value of petroleum produced in California exceeded by 20 percent the total value of gold extracted throughout California's history.

Many other minerals have been mined in California—antimony, arsenic, copper, feldspar, lead, manganese, potash, quartz crystal, silver, talc, uranium, and zirconium. Copper found in southwestern Calaveras County led to the establishment of Copperopolis. The northern Sierra Nevada foothills have also seen substantial copper operations.

Silver was often discovered during gold rush mining, but it was largely ignored in favor of gold. Interest peaked after 1859, when large deposits of silver were found in Comstock, just over the Nevada border. Silver from the Comstock Lode generally came through San Francisco, allowing Californians to profit from the silver mines. Southern California's Death Valley saw some major silver strikes. In Northern California, Alpine and Napa Counties were the most productive.

Placer Mining

Miners found gold in two environments: either as placer deposits in streams or ancient streambeds or as lode deposits in rock formations, usually of quartz. Gold deposits are ultimately the result of the collision of tectonic plates, over millions of years, which formed magma that contained precious metals. Gold deposits formed when the magma was forced into cracks in overlying rock. In the case of gold, the host rock is quartz. Uplift exposed gold-bearing deposits, and over time, weathering and erosion broke down the rock, freeing the gold in its pure form.

When water washed gold along streambeds, it could be found as nuggets, scale, shot, grains, and dust. These deposits are called "placers" when the gold is found in streambeds or

Gold dredge

along stream banks. Gold still contained in a rock formation is called a "lode," and it requires different mining techniques. Because placers are relatively easy to find, they are normally the first gold deposits discovered in any area. Miners typically followed placers upstream to their source, the mother lode. Placer mining involves separating nuggets, dust, and grains from a stream's gravel, sand, or mud by panning, literally with a pan, or sluicing by shoveling stream debris into a box and funneling water over it to wash away the debris, leaving the heavier gold to catch in riffles in the box's bottom.

Placer mining, "poor man's mining," could be done with very little capital. Despite the stereotypical image of solitary miner with a gold pan and a burro, most placer mining involved several prospectors with at least some machinery. Imagine spending hours wading in fast-flowing streams fed by snowmelt. The work was cold, dirty, and only occasionally rewarding. Every year, spring melts renew placer deposits in the Sierra Nevada and Klamath Mountains; it is still possible to find gold in California's streams.

Hydraulic mining was developed when prospectors realized that gold could be found in the loose gravel of ancient riverbeds. Devised at American Hill north of Nevada City by Connecticut native Edward E. Matteson in 1853, the process of directing a high-pressure stream of water at sedimentary deposits revolutionized placer mining, but was appallingly destructive.

Sluicing for gold in California

The process required a steady water supply, as much as 30,000 gallons a minute, to be held in a reservoir and then released through a penstock to a canvas hose with a nozzle. The high-pressure stream would be aimed at a gravel bank to undercut it so it would collapse. The gravel and dirt was then washed down the hillside to be collected in huge sluice boxes, with graduated riffles to catch the gold. A blast from a hose could kill a man 100 feet away.

By 1867, there were almost 5,500 miles of canals and nearly another thousand miles of ditches with wooden flumes and viaducts built across the Mother Lode. While the technique proved to be extremely profitable, it devastated huge areas of Mother Lode country. Malakoff Diggins State Historic Park in Nevada County shows the result of one hydraulic operation.

Hydraulic mining deposited massive amounts of mud into rivers, clogging streams and flooding farmlands; silt even discolored San Francisco Bay. Eventually, the 1884 Anti-Debris Act, one of the world's first pieces of environmental legislation, banned the process. New regulations enacted in the 1890s allowed hydraulic mining under special circumstances. Tailings from hydraulic operations often contained gold washed away with debris. New technology, such as cyanide leaching, can yield substantial wealth from hydraulic tailings.

In the late 1890s, dredging replaced hydraulic operations on the Yuba, American, and Feather Rivers, among others. A chain of buckets was mounted so that it would dig up a streambed from a platform on a barge. The advantage was that large volumes of streambed materials could be processed. By the 1940s, single buckets could hold 18 cubic feet and dig more than 100 feet below the surface of the water.

Hard-Rock Mining

Frontier guide and explorer Kit Carson discovered the Mariposa Mine in the spring of 1849. By July, Carson and his partners had built likely the first stamp mill in California. Farther north, gold-bearing quartz was found on Gold Hill in June 1850 at what would become Grass Valley. By that August, the first claims were made in Amador County. In this labor-intensive process, hard-rock miners dug ore-bearing rock out of the ground and then had to separate the gold from the rock, usually quartz, surrounding it. Miners tunneled under a vein or sank a shaft. Rocks blasted or drilled from the face would either be hauled out by carts on rails pulled by mules or winched to the surface. Hand-drilling and black powder, used in the early days, were replaced by air drills and dynamite in 1868. Once mined, the gold had to be separated from its host rock. At first, miners used an arrastra, a simple mule- or horse-powered rock crusher developed by Mexicans. Arrastras were replaced by stamp mills, a technique used at gold mines in the eastern U.S. to crush rock. Stamp mills are large structures that processed rock in stages, and they required water and a downhill slope. Milling progressively crushed the rock, which was then processed chemically to extract the precious metal. Mine workers brought the ore into the mill and fed it into a stamper, which weighed up to a ton. The stamper crushed the

Rock crusher in Ventura, California

host rock; the resulting slurry of crushed rock and water was fed over a series of mercury-coated amalgamation plates, which captured the precious metal.

Steam engines were used to power mining operations, but soon gave way to hydropower. Fuel had become scarce and water was at hand. Innovations such as the Pelton waterwheel, developed in the goldfields by Lester Pelton, were efficient and eventually used to generate electricity.

Because hard-rock mining required substantial capital, only large mining corporations normally undertook this kind of operation. The men who worked the mines were employees of the larger corporations. They often received little for the immense wealth they extracted. More unscrupulous mine owners even used Indian slave labor in their operations.

Northern California's Lost Mines

Lost Cement Mine

High in the Sierra Nevada, northeast of Mammoth Mountain, a small fortune in gold nuggets rests in a peculiar dark conglomerate rock resembling cement. The site gave rise to the legendary Lost Cement Mine (for more information on the location of the Lost Cement Mine, see High Sierra #37: Deer Mountain Trail, page 252). Several prospectors have discovered this wealth only to die mysterious deaths not long afterwards, leading observers to conclude that the treasure is cursed.

The first victim of the "curse" was an unnamed miner who died in 1857. The miner had discovered a strange outcropping of rock while prospecting with a partner. The dark vein contained a scattering of peanut-size gold nuggets. Despite protests from his companion that the nuggets were worthless fool's gold, the miner worked at the site for several days. After filling a small sack with samples, the miner told his partner he was heading to San Francisco to have it assayed. The night before he left, the prospector was wracked by fits of coughing. Nevertheless, he set out on the arduous two-week journey across the Sierra to San Francisco.

Leaving his samples at an assay office, the sick man went to a physician named Dr. Randall. While the assayer confirmed the miner's dreams—that he had discovered a rich gold deposit—Dr. Randall confirmed his worst fears—that he had tuberculosis and was dying. The unfortunate prospector related the story of his newfound wealth as he lay in Randall's office. He paid Randall from his sack of nuggets, lived one more restless night, and died the following day. He had given Dr. Randall a crude map to his rich find.

Dr. Randall quickly organized an expedition that became a nightmare. Randall's party was caught in a severe snowstorm and three members froze to death in crude shelters. Randall became obsessed, making 17 trips in as many years to find the site, but the miner's map was too vague. On what was to be his final expedition, in 1874, Dr. Randall and a dozen men led by Gid Whiteman were nearing Deadmans Pass when a band of Indians slaughtered all but one member of the poorly armed party.

Randall's obsession attracted other searchers. Before he perished with the doctor, Whiteman had gone on numerous treks in search of the mine. Mark Twain described Whiteman's commitment to his search in his 1872 journal, *Roughing It.* Twain claims that that the indefatigable prospector carried around a piece of dark red cementlike rock given to him by a German miner. Three German brothers had apparently discovered the mine in the 1860s and extracted quite a sizeable quantity of gold-laden rock before leaving the site. Two of the brothers died in the trip out of the mountains, and the third, when he arrived at a settlement, could not be induced to return to the unlucky mine.

Twain himself went out on a nighttime expedition in search of the lost treasure and encountered miners working a cementlike vein. He decided that the lost mine had been found so his party retired for a week's camping on the shore of Mono Lake.

A year after Randall's death, in 1875, a prospector named Farnsworth was panning the streams near the Owens Valley when he found an outcropping with a dark vein that appeared to have been mined previously. Farnsworth was delighted to discover nuggets embedded in the rock. As one account goes, he went to Sacramento with some of the gold and returned with a Mr. Creighton, a former partner. The pair worked the vein for several weeks until they had all the gold that their pack animals could carry. The evening before they planned to leave for San Francisco, the miners got into a heated argument that ended with Farnsworth shooting Creighton in the head. After burying his murdered companion, Farnsworth set out through the mountains. On a narrow cliffside trail, one of the pack animals panicked and kicked Farnsworth off the cliff to his death.

In 1877, a man named Kent rediscovered the Cement Mine while hunting for deer. He came across a reddish outcrop with mining tools scattered beneath it. Kent worked the mine on his own for several months. He then traveled to San Francisco with several burros weighed down by nuggets. He converted his gold to cash and went out with friends to celebrate. That night, as he was leaving a tavern, Kent collapsed, dead from a heart attack.

The Lost Cement Mine is still in the Sierra Nevada. But, with more than a dozen deaths among those who found it, the superstitious would be well advised not to seek its wealth.

Lost Lake of Gold

Another of Northern California's most famous treasure stories involves a small lake high in the Sierra Nevada. Rumors abounded in the early days of the gold rush of a mountain lake with nuggets scattered on its shore and bottom. Several mining camps, including Downieville and Placerville, boomed because the lake was supposed to be in their vicinity. Traders also started rumors that the golden pond lay nearby so that they could sell supplies to expeditions searching for it.

In 1849, guide and trapper Caleb Greenwood claimed to know where the pool of gold was. He made a map for his son John, who led a party of 13 to search for it. Greenwood became hopelessly lost in the mountains above Placerville. Though he found several mountain lakes, none contained any trace of precious metal.

A year later, a Scandinavian miner named Lingard was prospecting in Grass Valley when he decided to search upstream for the source of the placer deposits. He followed the stream to its source high in the Sierra Nevada. One afternoon, while camping by a lake, he noticed a glimmer below the surface, reached for the sandy bottom, and pulled a gold nugget out of the water. In just half an hour, he collected 6 pounds of gold from the lakeshore.

Lingard hurried to Downieville to find partners to work the treasure-filled lake. When news of his discovery spread through town, hundreds of men followed the small group Lingard had put together to mine the gold. Unfortunately, Lingard became lost while trying to shake the trailing horde and was unable to find the lake. His partners deserted him after threatening to hang him. Lingard searched the mountains for years, trying to find his golden pond. Others tried to find the lake with similar results; eventually, locals came to doubt that it existed.

Prospector Thomas R. Stoddard claimed that he and a companion found the lake while bear hunting, but Indians attacked them before they could pick up any gold. Stoddard's friend was killed, and Stoddard wandered the mountains for months before finally reaching Downieville in the winter of 1851. When he recovered from his ordeal, Stoddard led a party to search for the lake. When they arrived at where Stoddard thought the body of water was, they found no sign of a lake at all and abandoned the search. Stoddard gave information about the lake's site to a mining engineer named Roberts in 1853. When Roberts reached the site, he too found no lake, but he observed that there had recently been a landslide. The engineer looked at the edges of the slide and found gold. He concluded that the lake was buried by tons of rock and that it would be impossible to bring in the heavy equipment needed to uncover the gold at such a remote location. Similarly, attempts to dynamite the slide would probably just cause more landslides. Now, the Lost Lake of Gold is lost forever. There is a Gold Lake in Plumas County, which has no gold, but like this lost lake has its own myth.

Lost Bell Treasure

Somewhere in the vicinity of Shelter Cove in Humboldt County lies a cache of gold. A mining company's ship, which was transporting a fortune in gold to the San Francisco Mint, ran aground at Shelter Cove. Instead of aiding the crew, wreckers stole the cargo.

Because the gold was very heavy, the thieves found they could not carry their loot very far. They took as much as they could and buried the rest under a tree on a flat near the shore. They marked the spot by hanging the ship's bell in a tree. Some days later, the bandits returned to recover the gold, but a squad of soldiers sent to look for the ship confronted them. A firefight ensued, and the looters were killed. Women associated with the wreckers refused to disclose the location of the gold. Years later, an old woman finally revealed the story about the ship's bell. Unfortunately, deer hunters, unaware of the bell's significance, had removed it a long time ago. To this day, no one has admitted to finding the buried treasure. It probable still lies hidden somewhere near Humboldt County's Shelter Cove.

Captain Dick's Mine

The legend of Captain Dick's lost mine pervades the folklore of northeastern California's Warner Mountains as thoroughly as the Lost Cement Mine permeates that of the Mammoth Lakes area of the Sierra Nevada. Despite the distance between the locales of these two treasures, some suggest they are one and the same.

Captain Dick, an Indian, lived on Owl Creek near Middle Alkali Lake in Modoc County in the 1850s. Captain Dick would leave his mountain retreat now and again to visit nearby settlements. He paid for his goods with large gold nuggets. Excited townspeople urged him to reveal the source of his treasure, but Captain Dick refused. Frustrated, two miners followed him as he wandered into the hills. When the men failed to return, Captain Dick was arrested, jailed, and accused of murdering them.

Although beaten and hung by his thumbs, Captain Dick remained silent. Angry townspeople broke into the jail and lynched him.

Captain Dick's wife received many marriage proposals from prospectors eager to learn the secret of Captain Dick's wealth, but she refused them all. When she died, many assumed that knowledge of the cache died with her. But one man had apparently seen Captain Dick enter his mine. A herder drunkenly told a friend that he had seen an Indian emerge from a small cave and cover the entrance with a large rock. The shepherd removed the stone and entered the tunnel after the Indian had departed; he found a rich vein of gold-bearing rock and the decomposed heads of two men. The herder decided not to return to the cave until he heard that the Indian and his wife were both dead.

Sometime after Captain Dick's widow passed away, the herder came to town wearing a new suit and spending money freely. When his money ran out, he returned to the mountains and came back with gold. This continued for several months, until the herder failed to return from one of his trips out of town. Acquaintances attempted unsuccessfully to find the missing shepherd or the source of his mysterious fortune. Since then, rainbow chasers in Modoc County and beyond have tried to find Captain Dick's cave but it has eluded discovery for more than a hundred years. Similar stories about Indians coming to town with gold nuggets or dust from undisclosed locations abound throughout the West. Locals in Oroville tell of an Indian who came there in the late 1900s with nuggets, claiming he had enough to last a lifetime. He too hid his mine every time he left it. Interestingly, the Indian claimed his treasure was to the north.

Rattlesnake Dick's Hidden Gold

Northern California teems with tales about caches of loot buried by fleeing outlaws. One such story involves the infamous bandit Richard Barter, known to the world as Rattlesnake Dick (see page 78). In the late 1850s, Rattlesnake Dick and his daring gang terrorized stagecoaches of the northern Mother Lode. Prior to his gold country banditry, the outlaw had lived a relatively law-abiding life near Redding in Shasta County. When Dick heard that a mule train carrying a fortune in gold would be traveling from Yreka to Redding, he decided to intercept the shipment.

Dick put together a gang to help him hold up the mule train and headed north to intercept the shipment. Just before the heist was to commence, an informant told the outlaws that the mules were branded and could be identified as mining company property. Dick and a companion hurried to steal other pack animals and instructed the gang to proceed with the robbery, hide their take, and scatter the branded mules.

The gang successfully held up the mule train and waited for him to return. However, unbeknown to the outlaws, Dick had been captured by his nemesis Sheriff John Boggs. After a day's wait, the robbers decided to leave the vicinity lest a posse find them. They took as much gold as they could carry and buried the rest—perhaps $50,000 worth. With their portion of the heist, they headed to Rattlesnake Dick's ranch outside of Folsom. Sheriff Boggs was expecting them. As the outlaws approached, his men opened fire. All but one of the bandits was killed, including the man who had hidden the gold. The only survivor was sent to prison, where he died soon afterwards.

Although Rattlesnake Dick escaped to continue his life of crime, all those who knew the location of the hidden loot had passed away. A fortune in gold remains buried in the woods somewhere in the mountains, approximately 12 miles south of Clear Creek.

Animals

Mammals

Badger

Badgers measure about two feet long, have short legs, claws, and shaggy gray-brown coats. A white stripe reaches from midway on their pointy snouts back to their shoulders, and they have bushy, short, yellowish tails. Found in open grasslands, sagebrush, and brushy areas, badgers use their powerful legs and front claws to dig out ground squirrels and other rodents. They are most active at night and make their homes in burrows.

Badger

Beaver

Beavers, North America's largest rodents, have thick, waterproof brown fur, chunky bodies, short legs, rounded heads, small rounded ears, yellowish orange front incisors, webbed hind feet, and flat, hairless, paddle-shaped tails. They range in weight from 30 to 60 pounds. Beavers live in lakes, streams, ponds, and rivers and eat bark and twigs. Because they do not hibernate, they cache twigs and branches to eat in their lodges during the winter. Their thick layers of fat and waterproof fur prevent icy waters from bothering them. Skin flaps close over their ears and nostrils when they are submerged, and webbed feet aid in swimming. A clear membrane covers their eyes, enabling them to see under water and protecting their eyes from floating debris. A beaver can remain submerged for up to 15 minutes.

Beaver

Beavers gnaw down trees, strip the bark, chew them into small sections, and weave them into dams built across streams and slow rivers. They hold the logs and branches in place with mud. The lodges they build have one or more entrances below the water and a living chamber well above the waterline. Beavers may live as long as 20 years and mate for life. In the spring, furry beaver kits are born in the lodges with their eyes open.

The beaver population was almost exterminated during the nineteenth century because of extensive trapping for their fashionable fur (used primarily for hats). However, the population has recovered and is thriving in the northern two-thirds of California, especially on the Sacramento–San Joaquin Delta.

Bighorn Sheep

Bighorn sheep are grayish brown with yellowish white rump patches and short brown tails. Some have whitish fur around their muzzles, eyes, bellies, and legs. They have muscular bodies and thick necks. Ewes weigh about 150 pounds, and rams may range from 150 to 250 pounds. Both males and females have horns that grow continually and never shed. The ram's horns are massive and curl in a C and may be up to 40 inches long. The ewe's horns are thin and only slightly curled—no more than a half curl.

Bighorn sheep

Bighorn sheep are active by day on mountain slopes, cliffs, and rolling foothills feeding on grasses and shrubs. Rams challenge each other in butting contests in which they charge each other simultaneously. Their combined speed can be more than 40 miles per hour just before impact, and their foreheads meet with a *crack* that can be heard a mile away. These contests can last for as long as 20 hours. Horn size determines a ram's status, but butting contests establish hierarchy among rams with horns of similar size.

The bighorn population dwindled in the twentieth century from hunting, habitat fragmentation, and diseases contracted from domestic livestock. Reintroduction programs and habitat protection have increased their populations but they are still endangered. Today, bighorn sheep can be seen in the southern Sierra Nevada and on the Modoc Plateau at elevations above 10,000 feet.

Black Bear

Black bears can actually be black, brown, or cinnamon. Their bodies are powerful and densely furred, with small rounded ears, small close-set eyes, and five dark, strongly curved claws on their front paws. Females range in weight from 120 to 200 pounds, and males range from 200 to 400 pounds. Nocturnal and solitary, black bears prefer forested habitats throughout the year, although they can sometimes be seen on open slopes searching for greens and sometimes even on the beaches of northwestern California. They usually make their dens in tree cavities, under logs, in brush piles, or under buildings; the dens are lined with leaves or grass. Black bears are omnivorous, and their diet includes grasses, sedges, berries, fruits, tree bark, insects, honey, eggs, fish, rodents, and garbage. In the fall they go into a feeding frenzy to gain as much weight as possible to get them through their winter hibernation, often adding a four-inch layer of fat to keep them warm and nourished. At hibernation, black bears crawl into their dens, and their bodies go dormant for the winter; they do not eat, drink, urinate, or defecate during their long sleep. Their kidneys continue to make urine, but it is reabsorbed into their bloodstream. They awaken by an internal clock in the spring and wander out in search of food.

Black bear

The black bear has a lumbering walk and can travel up to 30 miles per hour in a bounding trot. Black bears are powerful swimmers, able fishers, and agile tree climbers. They breed in the summer; the females undergo a phenomenon in which the fertilized egg passes into the uterus but changes very little until late fall, when it implants, and then begins to grow quickly. Females commonly give birth to a litter of one to five cubs in January or February.

Despite its appearance on the state flag, the grizzly bear has been extinct in California since 1922, and the black bear is the only bear encountered in the state. Black bears range widely through the Sierra, and campers should be careful to keep food stored out of sight and in airtight containers, if possible. Some campgrounds may have bear boxes; if so, use them.

Bobcat

Bobcats are reddish brown (grayer in winter) with dark spots on their buff-colored bodies and legs. Their ears are slightly tufted. Bobcats get their name from their short, stubby tails, which have three horizontal dark stripes. Females range in weight from 15 to 25 pounds, and males range from 20 to 35 pounds. The most common wildcat in North America, bobcats live in virtually every habitat below 10,000 feet—from dry, rocky mountainsides to forests to brushy, arid lands.

Although more gregarious than mountain lions, bobcats are still secretive and are seldom seen or heard. When threatened, they make a cough-bark sound, and during mating season, they yowl. Bobcats are efficient predators with keen eyes and ears to help them locate prey in poor light. When hunting, they stalk and move at blinding speed for short distances, then pounce, and make the kill. Their diet includes rabbits and hares, ground squirrels, mice, birds, insects, lizards, and frogs. Generally solitary animals, bobcats come together mainly for mating. Litters of two or three kittens are born in April and May in maternity dens constructed in hollow logs or under rock ledges or fallen trees and lined with dry leaves. The bobcat population is stable, although trapping once nearly eradicated the species.

Bobcat

Chipmunk

A number of species of these small rodents are common in Northern California, eight of which are in the Sierra Nevada. They share similar characteristics and are not easily distinguished from one another. Ranging in color from chestnut to yellowish gray to light gray, chipmunks have dark and light stripes on their faces, and dark stripes line their backs from their necks to the base of their tails, with white stripes running parallel on the back only. The palest chipmunks tend to be found in the deserts. They measure about 3 to 6 inches long, with 3- to 4-inch tails, and weigh a mere 1 to 4 ounces.

Chipmunks are most active during the day. Their diet includes seeds, leaves, fruits, flower parts, and other plants. They have large fur-lined cheek pouches used for carrying food. Chipmunks stow away much of their food; instead of relying on stored body fat to sustain them during hibernation, they awaken periodically throughout winter and early spring to eat from their caches. They dig burrows underneath rocks, logs, and roots and line them with grass. These burrows become the nests where they have their young. Babies are born blind and naked after a gestation period of about 30 days.

Chipmunk

Cottontails (Rabbits)

Cottontails are very similar in appearance and behavior to jackrabbits. However, they tend to be smaller and have shorter ears, smaller feet, and shorter hind legs. They do not turn white in winter. Nuttall's cottontails, also known as mountain cot-

Cottontail

tontails, are grayish, with a white belly and black-tipped ears. They inhabit rocky, wooded, or brushy areas, often with sagebrush, throughout the higher elevations of California. They use dense vegetation for shelter or, when that is not available, burrows and rocky crevices.

Similar, but smaller, brush rabbits are common in the western Sierra Nevada, Cascade Range, and coastal mountains. They usually remain in dense brushy areas, rarely moving far from cover. Audubon's cottontails are more commonly sighted in open areas, generally in shrub-covered parts of Central California. Northern California is also home to the smallest rabbit in North America, the pygmy rabbit.

Because they are so vulnerable at birth, cottontails are born in maternal nests, which the pregnant female finds and prepares about a week before giving birth. She locates a suitable spot, where brush or high grass provides protection, and makes a saucerlike depression in the ground, lining it with her own downy fur, soft grasses, and leaves. In a good habitat, a doe may have three or four litters per year. Unlike hares, cottontails are born naked with their eyes closed.

Coyote

Coyotes look like leggy dogs. They are grayish brown with rusty or tan fur on their legs, feet, and ears and have pointed muzzles and bushy tails. They range in weight from 30 to 50 pounds. Their tracks look much like those of a dog, but they are in a nearly straight line; hind feet usually come down in foreprints, with four toes per print. Coyotes rarely seek shelter and remain in dens only when they have pups. Their opportunistic diet includes rabbits, mice, squirrels, birds, frogs, snakes, grasshoppers, fruits, berries, and occasionally sheep and other livestock. In winter they often eat carrion of larger animals, especially deer, which is an important food source.

Coyote

They are vocal, and their call—typically, a series of barks and yelps followed by a prolonged howl and short yaps—is commonly heard at dusk or dawn. Coyotes communicate with one another; one call usually prompts other coyotes to join in, resulting in a chorus audible for significant distances. They are speedy runners and can cruise at 25 to 35 miles per hour, making leaps as high as 14 feet. They hunt singly or in pairs and may act as a relay team to chase and tire their prey.

The animals are monogamous, often mating for life. Females usually establish dens under large boulders or in caves. Sometimes they dig them into hillsides or in river embankments. The openings, or mouths, of these dens usually measure several feet wide and are often marked by a mound of earth and tracks. A coyote might use the same den from year to year unless it is disturbed. Coyotes breed in February, March, and April and give birth to a litter of four or more pups by May.

Elk

There are two elk species native to California: tule, the smaller of the two, and Roosevelt elk. Elk from the Rocky Mountains have been introduced and are only in the vicinity of Shasta Lake

Tule elk males grow much larger than females, but neither sex regularly exceeds 5 feet in height. Because of their size, uncharacteristically small for elk, they have also been known as dwarf elk. Tule elk have buffy brown backs; males often have a grayish brown mane of long throat hairs. They feed on grasses, herbs, twigs, and bark.

Roosevelt elk

Tens of thousands of tule elk once roamed the grasslands of California. Their natural habitat has been reduced and excessive hunting during the gold rush depleted the population. The population has been protected. Now there are about 20 separate herds in the wet grasslands of the Central and Owens Valleys.

Roosevelt elk are found only in a small area of northwestern California. They are readily found in Redwood National Park, near Orick, and a herd can usually be found in a meadow next to US 101 in Prairie Creek Redwoods State Park. The animals are large with brown bodies, tawny-colored rumps, thick necks, and sturdy legs. Cows range in weight from 500 to 600 pounds. Bulls range from 600 to 1,000 pounds and average about 6 feet in height. Only males have antlers, which they shed each year. They remain in herds throughout the year and feed on grasses, shrubs, and trees. During rutting season, in late summer and early fall, bulls thrash bushes and bugle, a sound that begins as a bellow, changes to a shrill whistle or scream, and ends with a series of grunts. This vocalization broadcasts a bull's presence to other bulls and calls to cows. Bulls become territorial, establish harems of up to 60 cows, and mate as the cows come into heat while keeping other bulls at a distance. Bulls often clash antlers in jousts for harems, but they are seldom hurt. Calves are born in the late spring after a gestation period of about nine months. Elk calves are primarily brown with light spots until the early fall of their first year.

Tule elk

Foxes

Gray foxes, the most common native fox in Northern California, have a salt-and-pepper gray coat, rust-colored legs and feet, white throat and belly, black-tipped tail, and dark streak down the spine. Red foxes exist as well, but they are not native to the state, and kit foxes live in the deserts in the southern part of the state.

Gray fox

A gray fox weighs 7 to 13 pounds and is about 22 to 30 inches long with a 10- to 15-inch tail. The animal prefers heavier cover and is nocturnal, so it is rarely seen. Found in the Central Valley, it prefers wooded and brushy slopes. It is the only fox that commonly climbs trees and has been known to rest, hide, or escape into them. Gray foxes sometimes raise their young in large hollow trees, some of which have entrance holes as high as 20 feet above the ground. More often, dens are located among rocks, in cliffsides, or in hollow trees or logs. Because the gray fox's pelt is undesirably bristly, it has never been heavily hunted or trapped for its fur. Like other foxes, its worst enemies are humans.

Red foxes are rusty red in color, with white underparts, chins, and throats. Their tails are very bushy, long, and red with white tips. Their lower legs and feet are black. The red fox weighs 8 to 12 pounds and measures about 2 feet long with a 15-inch tail. Red foxes are primarily nocturnal, elusive animals, making them difficult to spot. Their favorite foods are voles and mice, followed by almost anything that is available—including rabbits, birds, reptiles, fruits, berries, eggs, insects, and carrion from larger animals. An adult red fox can eat up to a hundred mice per week. Red foxes have keen hearing and can listen for burrowing or gnawing animals under ground and then dig into the soil or snow to capture them. They continue to catch food even when they are full, burying the excess in the dirt or snow for later. The native distribution of red foxes in California includes all of the Sierra Nevada and the Klamath Mountains. An introduced species of red fox from the Great Plains now inhabits a large area of the Sacramento Valley.

Red fox

Agricultural development and poison coyote baits have drastically reduced the kit fox population within the state, although small numbers remain in Contra Costa County and open arid regions. This fox is much smaller than the red fox with uniformly gray coloration except for a black-tipped tail. Their longer legs differentiate the kit fox from the gray fox. Its food source includes kangaroo rats, brush rabbits, mice, small squirrels, lizards, insects, and berries of wild shrubs. Mating in winter, their three to five offspring are born in February or March.

Jackrabbits (Hares)

Jackrabbits, also known as hares, are very similar in appearance to cottontails, but are larger and have longer ears, bigger feet, and longer hind legs. They may have been named jackrabbit because their large ears resemble those of jackasses. California has several species of jackrabbits.

Black-tailed jackrabbits live mostly in desert country. Their fur is mottled gray and brown, grizzled with black, and their tail has a black stripe above, which extends onto the rump, and a white border. Their very long ears are brown with black tips. Does (females) are larger than bucks (males), which is unusual in mammals. The hare's weight varies from 4 to 8 pounds.

White-tailed jackrabbits are slightly larger, with longer hind legs and a distinctive white tail and live in the higher elevations in the southern Sierra and in the Great Basin. The two species of jackrabbit are rarely found in the same area. A third species of jackrabbit, the slightly smaller snowshoe hare, has shorter ears and large feet and is common in the northern Sierra Nevada to about 8,000 feet. It turns white in winter, making it difficult to see.

Black-tailed jackrabbit

In summer, jackrabbits eat mostly green plants, such as clover and flowers. In winter, they rely more on shrubs and dried vegetation. Their ears are so sensitive that they can detect the muted sound of a coyote as its fur brushes against the grass. When threatened, they first freeze, laying their ears back to be less conspicuous, and rely on camouflage. If this fails, they can move from a hiding place like lightning, running at speeds up to 35 miles per hour and changing direction instantly. If they are running at moderate speeds, every fourth or fifth leap is higher so they can get a broader view of their surroundings. Unlike cottontails, young hares are born fully furred with their eyes open. The female places each young hare into an individual form, or depression, in the ground, thereby decreasing a predator's chance of taking her entire litter. She keeps her distance by day and nurses several times during the night so that she attracts less attention.

Kangaroo Rat

Kangaroo rats, named for their upright hopping gait, their huge hind legs and feet, and a long furry tail on which they balance, generally have buff-reddish or blackish color above with white underparts and a 6- to 8-inch-long tail. Their large eyes enable them to see in minimal light. Kangaroo rats can survive in desert country without ever consuming water because of several amazing features. Their nasal passages are elongated to cool outgoing breath and recapture moisture; their kidneys concentrate salts and urea from 10 to

Kangaroo rat

20 times before eliminating them; and their feces are concentrated to contain 50 percent less water than similar rodents.

These nocturnal creatures spend their days in underground burrows with the opening sealed, so as to maintain a stable temperature. Kangaroo rats eat seeds and when out foraging can store up to a teaspoon in their cheeks for later caching. As defense against rattlesnakes, owls, badgers, skunks, foxes, and coyotes, kangaroo rats kick dirt into the face of their attacker. When pursued, the kangaroo rat speeds off in a zigzag pattern, changing course quickly, using its tail as a rudder—sometimes leaping as far as 10 feet. Adults live a solitary existence except during mating, when males compete for females. The reproductive season is concurrent with rainfall and new vegetative growth. California kangaroo rats inhabit north-central California beyond the Sacramento Valley. Ord's kangaroo rats are found in far eastern regions of the state, including the Modoc Plateau.

Mink

Minks are weasel-like rodents found in watercourses mostly in the forests of northwestern California. They have rich dark brown coats with a white chin patch, pointed muzzles, small ears, and bushy tails. Their den is usually close to water, and minks like to swim. They eat fish, rodents, frogs, birds, and crayfish. Minks mate in late winter and females give birth to three or more young in May or June.

Mink

Mink fur is highly prized, and pelts continue to fetch $10 to $20 each. The species seems to have survived extensive trapping remarkably well. They are common in the wild in Northern California but in some areas are farmed for their fur. Similar species include American martens and weasels.

Mountain Lion

Also known as cougars or pumas, mountain lions have brown fur shaded gray, yellow, or red, with buff on their bellies, necks, and faces. They have long heavy legs, padded feet, retractable claws, long black-tipped tails, small round heads, short muzzles, small rounded ears, and supple, strong bodies. Females range in weight from 80 to 150 pounds, and males range from 120 to 180 pounds. Mountain lions are good climbers and jumpers, able to leap more than 20 feet. The state paid a bounty on mountain lions from 1907 to 1964, after which there were fewer than 600 animals remaining. The population has since recovered, but the animal's habitat is threatened.

Mountain lion

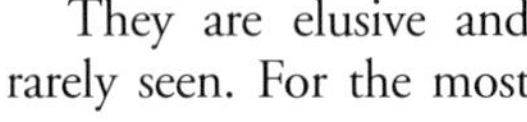

They are elusive and rarely seen. For the most part, they are territorial loners that live in wilderness throughout the mountains, foothills, and canyons. Carnivores, they prey on deer and elk as well as on porcupine, mice, rabbits, and grouse. The big cats stalk their prey, slinking forward close to the ground, then springing onto the animal's back, holding and biting its neck. They may bury the leftovers of a large kill and return one or more times to feed.

Females with young may stay together. Each mountain lion has its home range and rarely ventures outside it. Mountain lions breed every other year, and although there is no fixed breeding season, it often occurs in winter or early spring. The lions' maternity dens are lined with vegetation and may be in caves or thickets, under rock ledges, or in similarly concealed places. Two to four spotted kittens are born in maternity dens from May to July.

Mule Deer

This medium-size deer has a stocky body and long, slim, sturdy legs. In summer its gray coat changes to reddish brown. Its most distinguishing characteristic is its large mulelike ears that it moves constantly. Some have a whitish throat and rump patch, and their tails are either black-tipped or black on top. Does range in weight from 100 to 180 pounds, and bucks range from 150 to 400 pounds. Only the buck has antlers; he sheds them in the winter and begins to grow another set in the spring.

Summers are spent in mountain pastures, alpine meadows, and sometimes logged areas. The onset of winter drives them to lower slopes, where browse is more abundant. Summer forage includes grasses, sagebrush, serviceberry, and chokecherry. In winter they eat twigs, shrubs, and acorns. Mule deer are mostly active in the mornings, evenings, and on moonlit nights. A social group generally consists of the doe and her fawn or twins; bucks often remain solitary. During the November breeding season, bucks become increasingly active and intolerant of one another, sometimes engaging in vigorous fights during which each tries, with antlers enmeshed, to force down the other's head. Injuries are rare, and usually the loser withdraws. Mule deer breed in mid-November; fawns usually arrive in June, July, and August, with spotted coats for camouflage. A doe giving birth for the first time normally produces a single fawn, whereas an older doe tends to have twins. Together with the similar, but smaller, black-tailed deer that lives mostly in the coastal ranges, the mule deer is the primary big game animal in California.

Mule deer

Opossum

An introduced species that is now plentiful along the coast of California, from San Diego to Oregon, opossums are the on-

Opossum

ly pouched mammals in the United States. They have grayish black furred bodies with a ratlike, hairless tail and thin, black, hairless ears. Their snouts are long and pointed. Most opossums range from 25 to 40 inches long, including the tail, and weigh between 4 and 14 pounds. Opossums make their nests in hollow trees, logs, brush piles, and under houses. They are known to hang upside-down from trees with their tails wrapped around the branches. Their diet includes fruit, vegetables, nuts, insects, bird eggs, and carrion. They pretend to be dead when frightened and when approached by a predator. Nocturnal and solitary, opossums do not hibernate but they are considerably less active in winter and may remain in the den for several weeks to wait out cold weather. Opossums have one to two litters per year and have a unique birthing process; 1 to 14 embryos (which are collectively small enough to fit on a teaspoon) crawl out of the womb and somehow find their way into the mother's pouch. There, they nurse for approximately two months; only about half of the infants survive to the juvenile stage. After detaching themselves, the young venture out of the mother's pouch and may be seen riding on her back.

Pika

These small rodents, also know as coneys, have short, dense, gray brown fur, round bodies, short legs, large heads, short rounded ears, and no visible tail. They are mouselike and are about 8 inches long and weigh 4 to 7 ounces. Pikas live in colonies in rocky fields, talus slopes, and meadows above the tree line. They feed on grasses, sedges, and forbs, and spend their summers gathering huge quantities of vegetation and storing it for winter. They take bits back to rockpiles, where they spread it out to dry in the sun. If rain threatens before the stacks are cured, the pika carries its harvest one mouthful at a time to the shelter of a rocky burrow. It is not uncommon for one pika to store as much as four bushels.

Pika

When not foraging, pikas find a safe perch near an escape route and keep an eye out for predators. Active during the day, they blend with the rocks, yet their characteristic squeak gives them away every time. You can often hear a pika before you see it, although it is usually difficult to tell the direction from which the sound comes. Uttered at the first sign of danger, the call is picked up by other pikas and echoed throughout the colony. Pikas are active all year, and in winter they move around in tunnels dug through the snow, living off the caches of food gathered in the summer. Pikas usually mate in the early spring, producing a litter in May or June; a second litter may arrive in late summer.

Porcupine

Porcupines are gray-brown, with chunky bodies, high arching backs, and short legs. Yellowish guard hairs cover long quills on their backs, rumps, and tails. These rodents measure up to 2 feet in length, have an 8-inch tail, and range in weight from 10 to 28 pounds. After the beaver, they are the largest rodents in California. Found mostly in northern mountains—the Klamath and the Cascades—porcupines are active year-round. They are slow moving and have poor eyesight. They have thousands of barbed quills as protection against predators. When they brush against an attacker, the quills release from the porcupine. The barbs at the end of each quill make pulling them out painful. Porcupines spend much of their time in trees feeding on bark, needles, or leaves. They make dens in logs or caves and use them for sleeping and birthing. Kits are born in May and June, after a gestation period of seven months. They are born headfirst, with quills aimed backward.

Porcupine

Pronghorn

Pronghorns are pale or reddish tan in color on the upper body and outer legs, with two white bands across their throat, a white rump patch, white chest, white lower sides, and white inner legs. Bucks have vertical black markings from eyes to nose and on the cheeks. Does range in weight from 75 to 110 pounds, and bucks range from 110 to 130 pounds. Both sexes have sets of horns; the doe's horns are seldom longer than three or four inches, but a buck's horns can grow as long as 20 inches, curving back and slightly inward. Horn sheaths are shed each year.

Pronghorns once roamed the Central Valley and eastern California in great numbers, on open rolling plains and grasslands. Their numbers decreased dramatically following the gold rush and spread of agriculture, so that they were rare by 1875. Today the population is mostly in the northeast, on the Modoc Plateau.

Pronghorn

The animals are active night and day, alternating sleep with watchful feeding on grasses and forbs in summer and sagebrush and other shrubs in winter. They are the fastest animal in the Western Hemisphere and have been clocked at 80 miles per hour, although 45 miles per hour is more usual. Pronghorns run with their mouths open, not from exhaustion but to gasp extra oxygen. When it senses danger, a pronghorn snorts and erects the white hairs on its rump (twice as long as the body hairs), creating a flash of white as it flees, warning other pronghorns of danger. If an attack forces a pronghorn to fight rather than flee, it uses its sharp hooves, which can effectively drive off a coyote.

Adult bucks establish territories in March and hold them through the September breeding season. Throughout the spring and summer, nonterritorial bucks gather into bachelor herds, while does and fawns drift on and off the territories. By late September, territorial bucks attempt to hold groups of does and fawns in their territories for breeding and keep other bucks away. These territories are abandoned after the breeding season, horns are shed, and all ages and both sexes congregate on the winter range. The young are usually born in April, May, and June.

Raccoon

The raccoon's most distinguishing mark is its masked face. Their bodies have a salt-and-pepper coloring, and they have black-and-white ringed tails. They are about 2 feet long with a 10-inch tail, and they appear slightly hunchbacked. They range in weight from 10 to 25 pounds. Raccoons live near water, and their dens are in hollow trees, logs, rock crevices, or ground burrows. They feed mostly along streams, lakes, and ponds, and their favorite foods include fruits, nuts, grains, insects, eggs, and fish. They appear to wash their food before eating it by either dipping it in water or rubbing it in their paws. Why they do this is a mystery, but it may be that they moisten their food because they are so used to getting it from water. Another theory is that they are feeling for the edible parts. Raccoons do not hibernate in winter, although they may sleep for several days during cold weather. Raccoons give birth in April and May to litters of two to seven young. Raccoons have adapted well to life near humans.

Raccoon

Ringtail

Members of the raccoon family, the ringtail, also called ringtail cat, is named for the black and white rings encircling its bushy, 15-inch-long tail. Their catlike bodies are yellowish brown or gray, with whitish buff below. Their heads resemble those of foxes, with big eyes and pointy ears and snout. They inhabit mostly arid rocky areas, canyons, and large trees with hollows, generally in lower mountain forests. Solitary and nocturnal, ringtails spend their days in a den—usually a crevice in rocks, padded with grass, moss, or leaves. They emerge at night to hunt insects, scorpions, lizards, snakes, birds, eggs, and small animals. Despite their short legs, ringtails are excellent tree climbers and they have the traction to scale rock walls. They are particularly nimble on rock ledges and can turn around with a surefooted hop if the ledge runs out. When threatened, ringtails will scream at their predator and they might secrete a foul-smelling liquid. Females typically give birth to three or four young in May or June in their dens. They are born white, fuzzy, and stubby-tailed. Ringtails were once called miner's cats because of their propensity for catching and eating mice in and around mines.

Ringtail

River Otter

Dark brown in color, with silvery fur on their underparts, river otters have long cylindrical bodies; small rounded ears; large noses; small beady eyes; long whiskers; and thick furry tails. These terrestrial animals, cousins of sea otters (see page 127) live mostly along streams in the northwestern part of the state.

They are about 3 feet long, with 10- to 18-inch tails; they range in weight from 10 to 25 pounds. They feed primarily on fish, frogs, and aquatic invertebrates. River otters can stay under water for two to three minutes because their pulse slows and skin flaps close over their ears and nostrils. They have powerful feet and webbed toes to propel them through the water. Stiff whiskers help them hunt by feel under water. Cold water does not bother them because their dense fur and oily underfur do not allow water to reach their skin. River otters tend to use beaver and muskrat burrows as their own. They are very playful animals that spend much time frolicking and chasing each other. Pups are born—furry, blind, and helpless—in litters of one to four in March, April, and May.

River otter

Skunks

There are two species of skunk, members of the weasel family, resident in California: Striped skunks and spotted skunks.

The striped skunk has a black coat, with two broad white stripes on its back that meet at the head and tail. It also has a narrow vertical stripe on its forehead, a white cap, and bushy tail, which can range from black to varying amounts of white. Striped skunks are typically 2 feet in length, with 9-inch tails.

The western spotted skunk has a smaller body, approximately 16 inches in length, with a 9-inch tail. Their bodies are black with small horizontal white stripes on the neck and shoulders and irregular stripes and spots on their sides.

A skunk's boldly patterned black and white fur advertises its presence to potential predators that it is an animal to beware of. If its appearance fails as a deterrent, a skunk will face a potential predator, arch and elevate its tail, chatter its teeth, and stomp the ground with its front feet in a show of aggression. If the predator ignores these signals, the skunk will emit an oily, foul-smelling sulfurous spray from its anal glands. The irritating substance causes a temporary loss of vision if it sprays

Striped skunk

into the antagonist's eyes. Great horned owls are the principal predator.

Both the striped skunks and spotted skunks are omnivores with a widely varied diet, ranging from insects, small mammals, and eggs to seasonal fruits. They are primarily nocturnal and live in underground burrows that they have either dug themselves or taken over from other animals. Young are usually born in the spring to fiercely protective mothers. Skunks are currently the main carriers of rabies in the United States.

Squirrels

Many different species of squirrels inhabit Northern California. Members of the squirrel family include chipmunks, marmots, and prairie dogs; there are also ground squirrels, tree squirrels, and flying squirrels. The most common in the state is the native California ground squirrel. It prefers open oak forests and lives throughout the state except in the southern deserts. It rarely climbs trees, and it avoids tall grass. With an appearance and body shape much like a chipmunk, ground squirrels are generally brown and have a tail that is not very bushy. Not all ground squirrels have stripes on their bodies.

Most ground squirrels consume seeds, berries, woody plants, tubers, and even road-kill. They will also scurry into campsites to chew through packs, plastic bags, and tents to get to food. They have well-developed cheek pouches, in which they carry food to their dens. In the Sierra, dens are usually a system of tunnels up to 100 feet long.

Golden-mantled ground squirrels have brownish gray backs, and their heads and shoulders are coppery red, forming the "golden mantle." Bellies are white or buff. They have one white body stripe bordered by black stripes on each side. Also called copperheads, these little squirrels live in moist forests, on mountains, and sometimes in sagebrush country or rocky meadows. They hibernate through winter, putting on a layer of fat in the fall. Another common ground squirrel whose habitat is desert is the antelope squirrel. Like the pronghorn, it holds its tail vertically to expose the white underparts when it flees. Other types of ground squirrels in Northern California include Townsend's ground squirrels and Belding's ground squirrels.

Flying squirrel

Tree squirrels tend to be larger than ground squirrels and have larger ears and eyes. They also have longer, bushier tails to help balance on tree limbs. Tree squirrels include chickarees (red squirrels), western gray squirrels, and Douglas' squirrels. Chickarees are the smallest of the tree squirrels in Northern California, and they are very active, especially in their prime habitat in lodgepole pine and fir forests. They are rusty red with a black line that separates the reddish back from its whitish belly. They are similar in appearance to the Douglas' squirrel, except the Douglas' squirrel is duller red with grayish or orangish underparts. Western gray squirrels are the largest gray squirrels in Northern California (measuring about 23 inches). They have silver-gray bodies with numerous white-tipped hairs that give a grizzled salt-and-pepper appearance. Their bellies are whitish to buff-colored. Western gray squirrels prefer oak forests in the foothills.

Red squirrel

Golden-mantled ground squirrel

The mountains of Northern California are habitat for northern flying squirrels. They are small brown-gray tree squirrels whose limbs are joined by a web of skin that spreads when they extend their legs, enabling them to glide from tree to tree. They occur mostly in forests on the west side of the Sierra, and because they are nocturnal, they are difficult to see. They build nests of shredded bark in hollow tree cavities. Northern flying squirrels are ground foragers with a diet that consists of lichens and fungi, nuts, berries, birds' eggs, and insects. Their fondness for birds made them targets for early trappers who used traps baited with martens to lure the squirrels for their velvety fur.

Wolverine

The wolverine is the largest and fiercest terrestrial member of the weasel (*Mustelidae*) family. It has a somewhat bearlike appearance and is powerfully built, with a heavy body. Unlike a bear, wolverines have an arched back, shorter legs, and a long, bushy tail. They have five toes on each foot and walk on the soles of their feet, like bears and humans. This plantigrade posture allows the animal to move easily through soft, deep snow. The wolverine's head is broad and rounded, with small eyes and short rounded ears. Wolverine fur is typically thick, glossy, and dark brown. Males are generally 30 to 40 percent larger than females and can grow up to 4 feet long, including their tail, and weigh more than 70 pounds.

These elusive creatures communicate through vocalizations and scent markings. Like skunks, they have anal musk glands, which produce a foul-smelling scent that they use as a defense mechanism. Wolverines are efficient and agile predators; they have one of the mam-

Wolverine

mal world's most powerful jaws, enabling them to crush through bones in a single bite. Their long claws allow them to climb trees or tear food. Wolverine diets include ground squirrels, mice, beavers, birds, larvae, eggs, and berries. In winter they may become opportunistic scavengers and feed on carcasses, which can result in encounters with other predators.

Wolverines become reproductively active from May to August, when pairs will remain together for several days. As habitat, they prefer large areas of remote wilderness and make their dens in the ground or in crevices. Although not commonly sighted, wolverines in California may live in the High Sierra south of Lake Tahoe and in Humboldt, Del Norte, and Trinity Counties at elevations above 3,000 feet.

Wood Rat

Also known as the pack rat, wood rats are brownish gray above, with tawny-colored sides. Their feet, bellies, undersides of tail, and throats are white. They measure about 12 inches in length and have a 4- to 6-inch tail. They are called pack rats because the animal accumulates all sorts of objects, such as cow pies, newspaper, aluminum cans, coins, and jewelry. They have a particular fondness for shiny objects and line their dens with a collection of treasures, which serve as insulation to maintain consistent internal temperatures. Their nests are bulky, approximately five feet wide by two feet tall, and constructed of various materials, mostly stacks of cacti, twigs, and cow droppings. Often the nests are built at the base of a cactus, the needles of which are used by the wood rat to cover its entrance. Only one adult inhabits each nest. Badgers are the only animals that tear wood rat nests apart, and other predators include snakes, coyotes, owls, ringtails, and weasels. Wood rat diet includes prickly pear, juniper, yucca, cholla, and leafy plants. They obtain water from the plants they consume. Wood rats may communicate by drumming their hind feet. Females give birth to two to four litters per year, usually yielding two or three young per litter. In Northern California, the dusky-footed wood rat inhabits the western woodlands, whereas the bushy-tailed wood rat is found primarily on the more arid eastern slopes of the Sierra Nevada.

Desert wood rat

Yellow-bellied Marmot

A high country resident at tree line or above, yellow-bellied marmots are large ground-dwelling squirrels, ranging in weight from 5 to 10 pounds and measuring 1 to 2 feet in length (with 5- to 7-inch tails). Their coloration ranges from russet grizzled brown to yellowish brown with yellowish bellies. Marmots have heavy bodies with short legs, small ears, and bushy tails. They live in colonies and feed on grass and other plants. Habitats vary from talus slopes to meadows with large boulders. Sunbathing on rocks is a favored pastime; while the group enjoys the activity, at least one marmot stays alert to warn others of danger. When danger approaches, the sentry lets out high-pitched chirps so that the group can scurry to safety.

Yellow-bellied marmot

Marine Mammals

Porpoise

Eleven of the world's more than 50 species of porpoises, also called dolphins, have been spotted in California's coastal waters. Members of the family vary in size from an orca, or killer whale, which can reach 25 feet in length, to the small bottle-nosed dolphin at 9 feet in length. Bottle-nosed dolphins regularly ride in the bow waves of coastal ships. Other porpoise in California waters include the Pacific white-sided dolphin and the northern right-whale dolphin. Porpoise eat fish and squid. They often feed in large herds, sometimes comprising several different species. They are highly intelligent creatures and are also quite playful. They can be spotted leaping out of the water all along the California shoreline.

Porpoise

Seals

Seals bodies are more compact and their limbs are smaller than sea lions. This makes them better swimmers, but more awkward and slower on land. The two common types of seals in California waters are the large northern elephant seal and the harbor seal. Male northern elephant seals weigh as much as 5,000 pounds and reach lengths as long as 16 feet, while females are about two-thirds that size. They are brown or gray with a lighter-colored underbelly. Males have a distinct pendulous snout, which earn the species its name. They are excellent hunters, feeding on fish, squid, and octopus. They can remain submerged for up to 80 minutes. In breeding season, males fight over the best beaches and build up harems. The seals depart for the open ocean after winter breeding season. Point Reyes National Seashore is a good place to see them.

Northern elephant seal

The smaller harbor seals mainly inhabit shallow coastal waters along the entire California shore, but breed on the Channel Islands. They are playful and curious, though somewhat shy. They range in color from pale to gray to dark brown and have a cute doglike face. They grow to about 5 feet in length. Breeding season is late summer, and females give birth to one pup in April or May.

Sea Lions

Sea lions are generally larger than seals and are distinguished by their external ear flaps and divided rear flippers. They breed on the Channel Islands but can be seen along the entire California coast. California sea lion males are about 7 feet in length and dark brown in color. Females are about a foot shorter and lighter in color. Although they sometimes become entangled in the nets of salmon fishers, their numbers have increased in recent years. Females give birth to a single pup in June. The dominant males form harems, leaving younger, weaker males with no mate. The species is familiar to circus goers. The northern sea lion is larger and heavier than the California sea lion. Males grow to about 10 feet in length, females to about 7 feet. They are buff-colored and shy. Northern sea lions are less commonly sighted than California sea lions because they generally stay in deep ocean water, but breeding colonies can be seen along the California coast from Santa Cruz to Oregon.

Sea lion

Sea Otter

Nineteenth-century traders and trappers came to the California coast from as far away as Russia and Britain to hunt sea otters and pushed the animal to the brink of extinction. By 1900, the known population was thought to have been just 14 animals in the vicinity of Point Sur. Fortunately, with protection and the discovery of other populations, their numbers now exceed 2,000 in California.

Sea otters are larger than river otters and have larger and blunter heads. Their fur is long and brown, and insulates them from the cold. Their front paws are webbed and their back paws are almost flipperlike. They eat, sleep, and give birth at sea, hunting sea urchins, crabs, mussels, and fish. Sea otters are one of the few animals to use tools; they balance rocks on their chests to break open mollusks. They are readily seen at Point Lobos and can be spotted farther north along the coast.

Sea otter

Whales

Several species of whales can be seen along the California coast, including the largest mammal ever to exist, the 90-foot-plus blue whale. Other commonly spotted species include gray whales, fin whales, and humpback whales. Nineteenth-century whaling destroyed much of the worldwide whale population, but it is recovering somewhat today. Whales feed on plankton and sometimes small fish. They breed infrequently, often only biannually. Individual whales have distinct markings on their tails, and marine biologists can identify individuals by these markings.

Whale

Reptiles and Amphibians

Alligator Lizards

California has two species of alligator lizards, the northern and southern alligator lizard. Both species can be found in forests of the Sierra Nevada and Coast Ranges. The lizard may have been named for its resemblance to a miniature alligator.

Alligator lizard

The southern alligator lizard has a long slender body, up to 7 inches long, and small legs. The lizards can shed their tails if attacked by predators. The tail regenerates and may be shorter and a different color than the previous appendage. An individual that has never lost its tail may have one nearly twice the length of its body, perhaps up to 21 inches, making it a formidable looking animal.

Adult lizards have dark crossbands, and the scales on their backs are large, giving their skin a rough appearance. Males have large, triangular shaped heads that, combined with their size, make them look intimidating. The lizards will fight if caught, and bite. Active during the day, they feed on insects and small animals. Like a snake, they shed their skin in one piece.

Frogs

California has three species of true frogs: native red-legged frogs and yellow-legged frogs, and the East Coast import, the bullfrog. Escapee bullfrogs in the early 1900s proliferated, to compete successfully with native species, particularly the red-legged frog, for habitat and food.

California red-legged frogs, now becoming scarce because of habitat loss and bullfrogs, are about 4 inches in length, and can jump as much as 3 feet in

California tree frog

Pacific tree frog

Bullfrog

one leap. They are brown in color, with red bellies, sides, or legs. They live where there are slow moving streams or ponds. During breeding season, a female frog may deposit up to 4,000 eggs at one time. Mark Twain celebrated red-legged frogs in his 1865 story "The Celebrated Jumping Frog of Calaveras County." Each May, Angels Camp holds a frog-jumping contest to reenact the story.

Foothills yellow-legged frogs are about 2½ inches in length, with yellow legs and sides. They live along rivers and streams to about 6,000 feet of elevation in the mountains. Mountain yellow-legged frogs, rarely more than a jump or two from water, live near ponds and streams between 6,000 and 12,000 feet. This is a dark brown frog with black spots, and it lacks the ability to vocalize, unlike the foothill yellow-legged frog, which makes a deep guttural noise.

Tree frogs live in aquatic environments, too. The Pacific tree frog, about 1½ inches in length, is actually a ground dwelling frog that lives at elevations from sea level to 11,000 feet. Generally green, it can change to shades of brown and red in a few minutes. Pacific tree frogs and gray California tree frogs are common throughout the state, except in the southern deserts. They emit a recognizable, high-pitched, *kre-eek.*

Bullfrogs grow to about 6 inches, which is large for a frog. They are yellowish green above, with dark mottling; bellies are pale yellow. Their legs are long and dark-banded, ending in webbed feet. They make a distinctive *jug-o-rum* call, often repeated throughout the night. They prey on other frogs, crayfish, and small fish.

Garter Snakes

There are three common species of garter snakes in California. Common garter snakes occur in the Coast Ranges, and western terrestrial garter snakes are in the Sierra Nevada to about 8,000 feet. The western aquatic garter snake, as its name suggests, prefers ponds and rivers and lives in most habitats except for desert region.

Adult garter snakes have moderately slender bodies and range from 24 to 45 inches in length. Common garter snakes, the most colorful, have red on their sides, with blue-green below. Other species have light stripes down the sides of their bodies, with a distinctive light stripe down the back of some individuals. The color between the stripes is brownish, marked with dark spots. Underneath they are brownish, bluish, or gray, with reddish blotches. These snakes feed on fish, tadpoles, frogs, earthworms, snails, lizards, small mammals, and occasionally insects, birds, and carrion. Unlike other snakes, garter snakes give birth to live young. When threatened, they emit a foul-smelling fluid from vent glands.

Garter snake

Horned Lizard

A member of the iguana family, horned lizards can be found in arid regions and other parts of the state, with the exception of the damp and humid northwestern corner. The coast horned lizard has sharply pointed horns along the back of its head and is often referred to as a horned toad.

Short horned lizard

About 3 or 4 inches in length, horned lizards have squat, somewhat flat bodies and can be brown or bluish gray, with the color matching the local soil. Their sides and quite short tails are edged with whitish spines. They inhabit rocky and sandy open areas, remaining active throughout warm days, but restrict their activity to mornings when it is hot. Although other lizards rely on speed and breakaway tails to avoid predators, the horned lizard is slow and sluggish and relies on its camouflage and the ability to inflate itself like a blowfish as defense. These lizards are far from an easy meal for its predators—their spikelike scales make them difficult to swallow. Horned lizards feed on insects—primarily ants—but also eat small snakes. Females give live birth of up to 30 offspring.

King Snake

The king snake is a nonvenomous member of the Colubridae family, which includes gopher snakes, garter snakes, and whip snakes. The king snake earned its name because it eats other snakes—including rattlesnakes—and is immune to their toxic venom. They also eat lizards, birds and their eggs, small mammals, turtles, and frogs. They will even climb trees in pursuit of prey. King snakes use their keen sense of smell to locate prey at night, then quickly bite and constrict the victim with suffocating coils. They swallow their prey whole, while it is still alive. Generally regarded as a gentle snake, a king snake will hiss, strike, and vibrate its tail when threatened. If attacked, king snakes roll into a ball with their heads in the center and smear attackers with musk and feces. Females lay up to 20 eggs in the spring or summer; once the eggs are laid, she shows no further interest.

King snake

Common king snakes, found in lowland and coastal areas, vary in pattern and color. Although most have a pattern of alternating black and white bands, these colors may vary to brown, white, cream, or pale yellow, depending on the region. Some individuals have black bellies, while others are nearly all black. Mature adults are 3 to 4 feet long.

California mountain king snakes can be found in elevations to about 8,000 feet. Their bodies are banded with wide red, narrow white, and black rings, and their heads are black. They are slightly smaller than common king snakes, reaching lengths of about three feet. Because they are active during the day, California mountain king snakes are not an uncommon sight in the Sierra Nevada and Coast Ranges.

Newts

Newts, members of the same family as salamanders, are small amphibians that must live around water. Three species live in Northern California: Coast Range newts, red-bellied newts, and the rough-skinned newt. Generally newts' skin is rough and moist, and they have slender snouts, blunt, rounded heads, long bodies and tails, and short legs. They lay their eggs in fresh water and young newts live in the water. Later in life, they spend much of their time on land. Although they are active during the day, newts are most commonly sighted at night, when they congregate to mate or lay eggs.

Redbelly newts live in coast redwood forests, usually in decaying logs, in northwestern California. Adults are dark above and red below and measure about 7 inches from the tip of their nose to the end of their tail.

California newt

Coast Range newts are about the same size as redbelly newts. They are found in the central and southern coastal regions of California and throughout the lower elevations of the western Sierra Nevada. Adult Coast Range newts are brown above and yellow or orange below. They live in riparian areas of conifer and oak forests.

Rattlesnake

There are six species of rattlesnake in California, all of which are dangerous to humans. The most commonly found rattlesnake in Northern California is the western rattlesnake. They are typically gray (although individual colors will vary, depending on how long it has been since the last molt), with darker blotches along the back. The tail is ringed with black and white bands. They have a triangular head, narrow neck, and grow to lengths as long as 4 feet, including the rattle. In hot summer weather, they usually hunt at dusk and during the night. Pores in their heads pick up scents and heat to help detect prey. The snake kills its prey by injecting it with venom through hollow fangs that snap downward and forward as the snake strikes. To human beings, a rattler's bite is painful and should be treated at a hospital as soon as possible. They are relatively docile snakes—most frequently they lie still and allow danger to pass, only coiling and rattling if they sense a threat. Even then, they often do not rattle. If left alone, they crawl away and seek a hiding place. Rattlesnakes inhabit scrubby areas, from the coast to deserts. Exercise caution in tall grass, rocky areas, and around prairie dog towns, especially in the mornings, evenings, and after summer thunderstorms. They use burrows of California ground squirrels, and females give birth to as many as 15 live young in late summer.

Rattlesnake

Salamanders

Salamanders, in the same family as newts, have moist, smooth skin instead of scales and just four toes. They invariably live close to water, in decaying logs, among tree roots, or in soil. Salamanders eat insects, earthworms, and even small frogs. They are active both day and night.

Pacific giant salamander

Northern California is habitat to one of the largest species of salamanders in the world—the Pacific giant salamander. Pacific giant salamanders grow to lengths of about one foot. Their backs are brown, sometimes with a hint of purple. Their bellies are a lighter color. They live in the wet redwood forests of northwestern California and burrow into stream gravels.

California tiger salamanders are smaller, about 8 inches from head to the end of the long tail. Their bodies are shiny black with yellow or white spots and a large head. They live in open woodlands and pond areas of Central California.

Ensatinas are a species of lungless salamanders; they breathe through their skin and capillaries in their throats. They are about 5 inches in length, and their coloration varies. *Ensatinas* range throughout California except the Central Valley and the southern deserts. In the northwestern portions of the state they are brown with yellow dots; along the central coast they are reddish orange. Elsewhere in the state they might be brown or black with orange spots. Unlike most salamanders, *Ensatinas* lay their eggs on land and do not spend much time in the water. Females lay 25 eggs in spring.

Skinks

Skinks are shiny-skinned, small-legged reptiles with a long tail and a fondness for water. They generally feed on insects. Two species of skink are common in California: Gilbert's skink inhabits the woodland streams of the central and southern mountains, and the western skink is common in coastal regions and inland as far south as Lake Tahoe. Gilbert's skinks are pale brown; the head is pink in breeding seasons. The tail is pinkish or

Skink

sometimes blue. Their average length is about 10 inches. Western skinks are slightly smaller, about 8 inches in length. They have brown, tan, black, or red-brown stripes running the length of their bodies.

Toads

Toads, unlike frogs, are generally terrestrial animals with rough skin, and they walk, not hop. California has several species. The western spadefoot is a medium-small toad that grows to 3 inches. Its color is dusky brown, green, or gray, and its eyes protrude and have vertical elliptical pupils. Spadefoot toads are named for their built-in digging tools—a black sickle-shaped spade on each hind leg, which they use to "swim" through mud. When handled, the toads emit a foul-smelling liquid. Their vocalizations resemble the sound of fingers rubbing along a comb.

Spadefoot toad

The western toad is grayish green or brown with a bold yellow stripe along its back. It lacks the ability to vocalize except for small peeps, and it is common in the low mountains, where it is active during the day. In warmer regions, it is predominantly nocturnal. Western toads feed on insects, shooting out a long sharp tongue to capture them.

Whiptail

Western whiptails are slender lizards found throughout most of California, except for high mountains and the northwest coast. They are yellow to grayish brown, sometimes with dark markings. Underbellies are white or yellow. Adult males have a black throat and chest. Predators include birds, snakes, and small mammals. For protection, whiptails dig burrows that provide a safe retreat. Their agility and speed help them escape danger; they can travel up to 15 miles per hour. In addition, they have breakaway tails, which help them elude capture. Whiptails are constantly in motion—almost hyperactive. They are known to run upright on their hind legs, swiveling their head rapidly from side to side, sniffing the air with their forked tongue as they forage ceaselessly for spiders, termites, and other insects. Some all-female species of whiptail lizard do not reproduce sexually but by parthenogenesis, which means that all of their offspring are female. Their eggs require no fertilization, and the offspring are exact and complete genetic duplicates of the mother.

Whiptail

Invertebrates

Ant Lion

Ant lion larvae are sometimes called doodlebugs because they have a clumsy backward motion that leaves doodling tracks in the sand. When larvae hatch, they immediately begin digging individual ant traps with their sickle-shaped jaws. After they reach the bottom of their pitlike trap (approximately 2 by 2 inches), they open their jaws and wait for ants to slip on the edge of the pit and tumble inside—right into the ant lion larvae's mouth. Victims are then injected with venom and eaten. Eventually, the larvae spin cocoons and metamorphose to emerge in late summer as winged dragonfly-like creatures with one single mission—to mate. Adults die almost immediately after mating, but not before females lay their eggs directly onto the soil surface, where her larvae will hatch and repeat the life cycle. Ant lions range throughout the Sierra Nevada, the Central Valley, and Central California's Coast Ranges.

Ant lion larvae

Ant lion

Ants

Ants are related to wasps and bees. They are social creatures, found in colonies with populations ranging from a few dozen to millions of members. All colonies have a queen—a large, fertile female—in addition to numerous, sterile, wingless females. The queen is the only one to reproduce. The cycle of a colony begins when the queen lays eggs that are both male and female. The eggs hatch into winged ants, which leave the nest and mate. The males die and the females go on to become new queens, which build nests, lay eggs, and begin the cycle again. Individual ants can live as long as 5 years; queens live up to 15 years. Only old workers leave the nest.

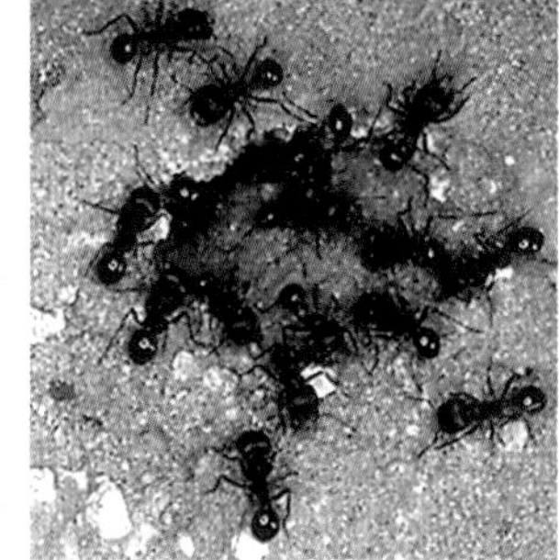
Harvester ants

When a harvester ant, common in arid regions of California, is killed, a defensive scent is emitted that draws others from the colony to attack the killer of the worker. They will inject venom that produces a painful sting. Most creatures will not eat harvester ants because of their venom. An exception is the horned lizard, which has an antitoxin in its blood specific to harvester ants. Harvester ants get their name because a colony can collect as many as 7,000 seeds in one day. Some plants, such as datura, rely on harvester ants to gather and scatter their seeds before rodents eat them from the vine. Harvester ants do not eat datura seeds because of their thick coating. The California harvester ant is reddish, with a large head.

Other ants in the state include the red mound ant, a rusty red ant with a painful stinger. Red mound ants are common in woodlands of the Sierra Nevada and Coast Ranges. They build domelike nest mounds, which they will protect in droves if disturbed. Argentine ants, which were introduced from South America in coffee shipments, have also thrived in California, especially in residential areas.

Banana Slug

An interesting creature of redwood forests, the banana slug is a large bright yellow gastropod without an external shell. Its body is soft, cylindrical, and about 4 inches in length. The yellow skin is sometimes covered with black dots. Banana slugs have two eyes on stalks and a large breathing hole. They are often spotted on the moist floors of redwood forests and enjoy a symbiotic relationship with the large trees by providing nutrition for young trees while eating debris on the forest floor. Slugs emit slime as they move. This helps traction and deters predators (they taste bad!). Banana slugs are hermaphrodites, so any two can mate with each other. Before mating, they eat each others slime. After mating, the large relative size of the banana slug's penis often makes post-coital separation difficult. In such instances, the slug will gnaw off the stuck organ. The banana slug is the school mascot of the University of California at Santa Cruz.

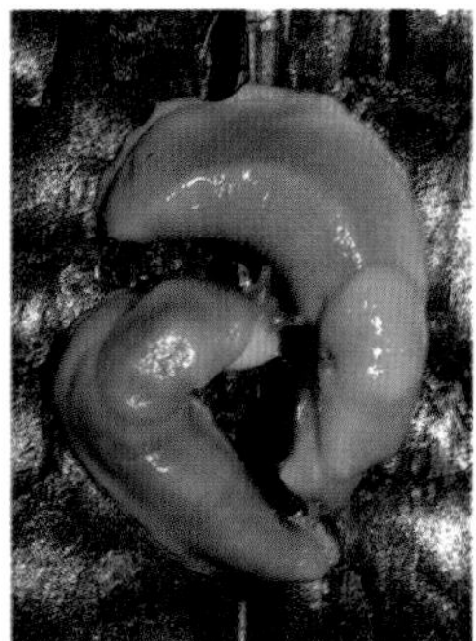
Banana slug

Butterflies

There are many species of butterflies in California, some of which, like the California tortoiseshell and the beautiful California sister, are rarely found elsewhere. Dependent on plants for their survival, butterflies lay eggs on host plants, which then become food for the caterpillars after they hatch. Mature caterpillars spin cocoons on the host plants. After weeks or months, a butterfly emerges to mate, sip flower nectar, lay eggs, and die.

Hairstreak butterflies are small and have cobalt blue wings with black borders dotted red and white. Hairstreaks fool predators into attacking a false head on their hind wings, which they rub up and down. Birds will bite the false head, allowing the butterfly to escape with minimal damage. Monarch butterflies have striking reddish-brown wings with black veins and black borders with two rows of white dots. The wingspread may reach 4 inches. When monarch caterpillars feed on milkweed plants, they accumulate a poisonous substance in their bodies that makes them distasteful to birds and other predators. Birds learn to recognize the butterflies' bright pattern and avoid them.

Monarch

Swallowtail butterflies are named for the long "tails" on their hind wings, which look a bit like the long pointed tails of swallows. With wingspans of 4 to 6 inches, the giant swallowtail is the largest butterfly in the United States. Their forewings have a diagonal band of yellow spots, and their tails are edged with black and filled with yellow. The caterpillars, sometimes called orangedogs, feed mostly on citrus and prickly ash. Tiger swallowtails are yellow with black stripes and have black wing margins. Some females are all black with a bluish iridescence. When it is very young, the caterpillar is camouflaged to look like bird droppings. Later, it develops distinctive eyespots that make it look like a snake, which scares off some predators.

Tiger swallowtail

Acmon blue

California sister

Edith's checkerspot

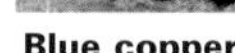
Blue copper

Pipe vine swallowtail

Mourning cloak

Damselfly and Dragonfly

Damselflies and dragonflies belong to the order Odonata. These insects have biting mouthparts, short antennae, and very large eyes. Their legs are attached to the body just behind the head. This makes walking almost impossible but greatly facilitates gripping. Damselflies have broad heads with widely spaced eyes; dragonflies have rounded heads with eyes that are closer together. Damselflies have two similar pairs of wings, which they hold above their bodies and fold together when at rest. Dragonflies' hind wings, which they hold outstretched when at rest, are broader than their forewings. In both insects, the powerful wings move independently. Damselflies sit and wait for prey; dragonflies actively pursue their prey in air. Both creatures lay their eggs on aquatic plants in the water.

Flame skimmer dragonfly

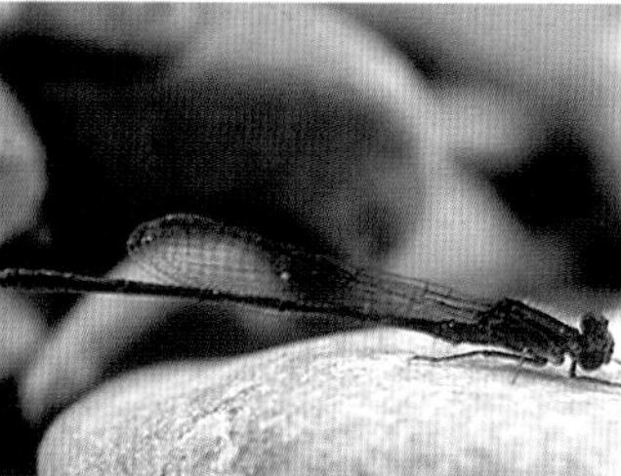
Damselfly

Scorpion

Found in arid regions, scorpions are venomous relatives of spiders, mites, and ticks and belong to the class Arachnida. They look like miniature lobsters, with elongated bodies, four pairs of legs, pincers, and a segmented tail (actually the abdomen), which is tipped with a stinger. A scorpion stings by thrusting its "tail" forward over its head and impaling the prey held in its pincers. Scorpions are covered with several layers of wax in order to conserve body water. Most scorpions are nocturnal

Scorpion

and predatory, and their diets include crickets, spiders, centipedes, other scorpions, snakes, and mice. They locate prey by sensing vibrations. The primary purpose of a scorpion's venom is to capture prey—self-defense is secondary. A scorpion would much prefer to be left alone or to retreat than sting. Exercise caution when camping or participating in other outdoor activities; be sure that scorpions have not crawled into footwear, clothes, or sleeping bags. First aid for a scorpion bite should include cleaning the site with soap and water, applying a cool compress, elevating the affected limb to approximately heart level, and ingesting aspirin or acetaminophen as needed for minor discomfort. Children or anyone experiencing severe symptoms from a bite should be taken to a health care facility immediately.

Silk Moth

Distinguished by its pretty rose-brown wings, the silk moth is a large moth—wingspan is 4 to 5 inches. Markings include black edged lines and large comma-shaped white marks. The silk moth caterpillar is green and yellow. Food plants include the California buckthorn, California coffeeberry, and willows. Silk moths thrive in Northern California woodlands and chaparral in spring and early summer. They are nocturnal, so look for them by campfire lights.

Giant silk moth

Sphinx Moth

Sphinx moths are also known as hummingbird moths for their ability to hover in front of flowers and sip the sweet nectar with an extremely long proboscis (feeding tube) tongue. They sound like hummingbirds, too, because of noise made by the rapid beating of wings. Sphinx moths are stout-bodied with long, narrow forewings and shorter hind wings; wingspans range from 2 to 8 inches. Sphinx moths emerge at dusk from their hiding places and begin feeding on the nectar of flowers. Many species pollinate flowers such as orchids, petunias, and evening primroses while sucking their nectar with a proboscis, which exceeds 10 inches in some species. Caterpillars of this group are known as hornworms because of a sinister-looking barb on the rear; they are the culprits that eat all the leaves in tomato and petunia gardens. Sphinx moth larvae change into adult moths underground and then dig their way to the surface to mate. Females lay up to a thousand eggs on the underside of food plants; the eggs hatch within a few days. Sphinx moth males and females die after they have completed the reproductive process. Two types of sphinx moths in California are the white-lined sphinx moth and Cerisy's sphinx moth (also known as the eyed sphinx moth). Other moths common in the state are California tent caterpillar moths, whose caterpillars build silken tents in willows and oaks; polyphemus moths; and the brightly colored ceanothus silk moth. Moths are distinguished from butterflies in several ways: Butterflies fly only during the day, whereas moths come out both day and night; moths' antennae lack the clubbed tip of butterfly antennae; and moths rest with their wings angled or outstretched while butterflies rest with their wings held vertically, like a sail.

Sphinx moth

Spiders

Spiders are not insects, but like scorpions, are arthropods, meaning they have jointed bodies, and like scorpions they are arachnids. California is habitat for numerous species of spiders of various sizes and habitats. Spiders have two body sections, eight legs, and eight eyes. Most spiders weave webs. They can extrude up to four types of silk: for cocoons, for lowing themselves, for the structure of their webs, and for trapping prey in the webs. Spiders kill their prey by injecting a paralyzing venom into them. The venom also breaks down tissue, much as digestive juices do. Most of the spiders in California are not harmful to humans, though the bite of a black widow is poisonous.

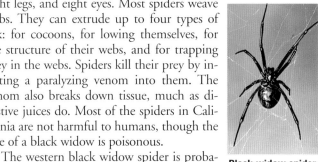

Black widow spider

The western black widow spider is probably the most feared in the state. They are called black widows because females will generally kill males after mating. The males are much smaller than the females and appear grayish. Females are black with a red hourglass on their abdomen.

Common orb weavers have fairly large hairy bodies, about 3/4 of an inch in length. The oval bodies are brown with hints of purple and dotted with yellow spots; legs are paler with dark bands. Between spring and fall, their large wheel-shaped webs are common in gardens and shrubby areas. If you look closely in the spring, it is possible to see small crab spiders climbing in the heads of flowers. Crab spiders do not weave webs, instead they ambush their prey.

Birds

American Coot

The American coot can be found throughout California except at the highest elevations and southeast deserts. In summer, it rests on freshwater lakes and ponds; in winter, it also comes to coastal bays and inlets. Similar to a duck, the American coot is distinguished by its smaller size (15 inches), dark coloring, white chicken-like bill, and white and red frontal shield. Coots are expert swimmers, propelling

American coot

themselves with wide lobed toes. They feed by diving underwater or foraging near the shore. Coots are gregarious birds and are often seen gathered in rafts (flocks). They vocalize with a variety of harsh clucks, cackles, and grunts. Their nests, shallow platforms of dead plant matter, are usually secured to reeds on the water. Females lay 8 to 10 pinkish eggs with brown spots.

American Kestrel

The American kestrel, a falcon, is a commonly seen bird of prey once called the sparrow hawk. Kestrels can be spotted hovering in search of prey in open country and less dense woodlands. The American kestrel is identified by two distinctive facial stripes. The male has a rusty back with blue-gray wings and crown. The female has a rusty back and rusty wings. The female's tail is rusty with black banding and the male's is solid rust with a black tip. At about 8 to 12 inches long, the American kestrel is the smallest, most common falcon in Northern California. It is similar to a robin in size but fiercely preys on insects, small rodents, reptiles, and amphibians. It has a loud voice and when excited lets out a shrill *killy, killy, killy*. Kestrels make their nests in the cavities of saguaros or trees, or in abandoned cavities of flickers. American kestrels from Northern California often migrate to the south for the winter months, returning to normal breeding areas in the spring.

American kestral

Bald Eagle

Bald eagles can be sighted near the lakes of the Klamath Basin in winter, and in summer they may also be seen along rivers, lakes, the coast, and marshes in the rest of the state. They are large birds—their beak-to-tail length approaches 3 feet and their wingspan is often 7 feet. Young birds are often mistaken for golden eagles; their heads do not turn a distinctive white color until age four or five. Adult birds are brown except for their white head, tail, and wing linings, and yellow eyes, beak, and feet. Their flight is graceful and controlled, using slow wingbeats and flat-winged glides. Eagles are noted for their strength and keen vision. They have large heavy hooked bills and strong sharp claws called talons. They make their nests, or aeries, high in trees or on rocky ledges out of reach of other animals because the young are helpless for a long period. Each year, the nesting pair will add new material to the same nest. The largest nest ever measured was 20 feet deep and nearly 10 feet wide.

Bald eagle

Like other raptors, bald eagles declined with the widespread use of eggshell-thinning DDT. Prior to DDT's use in the late 1940s, California was the winter home to several thousand bald eagles. By the late 1960s, only about twenty breeding pairs remained. (Eagles mate for life.) Today, the population has rebounded to about a thousand birds.

Band-tailed Pigeon

A common bird in Northern California's oak woodlands, band-tailed pigeons are larger than the domestic pigeons, rock doves. Immature birds are all gray, and adults have a white crescent on the back of their neck and purplish underparts. Band-tailed pigeons feed on acorns. They build loose twig nests in trees, where females lay one white egg. In winter, they migrate from higher mountain forests (up to 8,000 feet) to lower elevations. Many band-tailed pigeons have now become urban birds, although they are generally shy and unapproachable. Their voice resembles that of an owl.

Band-tailed pigeon

Blackbirds

Red-winged blackbirds are about 8 or 9 inches long. Males are black with crimson shoulder patches, while females are mottled brown, with heavily streaked underparts and a faint red shoulder patch. The red coloration serves as a flag in courtship and also in aggression. In an experiment, males whose red shoulders were painted black soon lost their territories to rivals they had previously defeated. These birds inhabit marshes, wetlands, and open fields. Their nests—woven of dried grass and soft materials—are found among grasses or cattails. Another species, the tricolored blackbird, is unique to California. Similar in appearance to the red-winged blackbird, tricolored blackbird males have a white slash below their crimson shoulder patch. Brewer's blackbirds and yellow-headed blackbirds are also found in the state. The yellow-headed blackbird is more closely related to meadowlarks than to blackbirds and is distinguished by its yellow head and throat and a white patch near the bend of its wings. Male Brewer's blackbirds, a cousin of grackles, are almost entirely black with hints of purple; females are grayish brown.

Red-winged blackbird

California Gull

Found along the coast and in western inland valleys, the adult California gull reaches 18 to 23 inches in length. California gulls tend to nest on islands, and Negit Island in Mono Lake has the largest breeding colony in the state. They need very little cover because the open water keeps them safe from terrestrial predators. Nests are often on open beaches or shorelines in a shallow hole lined with plants, grass, feathers, and small sticks.

California gull

Similar in appearance to other gulls, California gulls are mostly white with gray wings and backs and black tails. Their legs and beak are yellow.

The California gull is, paradoxically, the state bird of Utah. They are credited with saving Mormon pioneers in that state by eating insects during the locust plague of 1848. The California gull is one of several types of gull found along California's shoreline.

California Quail

The California quail, adopted as California's state bird June 12, 1931, is found in the foothills, often near rivers or lakes. Males have a brown crown and buff forehead with a bluish brown scaled belly. Females' markings are less bold. Both sexes have distinct topknots. During the mating season, birds pair to mate and build nests on the ground beneath low shrubs. Females lay from 12 to 16 cream-colored eggs. Because of their vulnerability in ground nests, on average more than half the youngsters die within their first year. The adult cry is distinctive. It sounds like *chi-ca-go*, with an emphasis on the middle note. Whole families will take to trees for breeding. After breeding, they become quite gregarious, often grouping in city parks and gardens.

California quail

Chickadees

The chickadee is a small, energetic bird that sings its name: *chick-a-dee-dee-dee*. Identified by their black cap and bib, black eye line, white cheek, and gray underparts and tail, Mountain chickadees grow to about five inches and must consume nearly their body weight in seeds and insects each day because of their amazingly fast heart rate of 500 beats per minute. During cold weather, it puffs out its feathers so that it resembles a fluffy ball with a beak. Nests are usually in natural cavities or abandoned woodpecker nests.

Black-capped chickadees are occasionally found in extreme northwestern California. As their name suggests, they are distinguished by a more predominant black cap. Side feathers are pale yellow. Chestnut-backed chickadees are more common in Northern California than black-capped chickadees. They are fairly common in coastal mountains and may also be seen in the lower Sierra Nevada. Their *chick-a-dee* call is somewhat shriller and faster than that of the mountain chickadee. Crown and throat is brown, back and sides are chestnut, tail is grayish, and other parts are white. Chestnut-backed chickadees rest and feed high in coniferous or oak trees.

Black-capped chickadee

Clark's Nutcracker

This jay has a light gray body, white tail feathers, and black wings. A gregarious and bold bird, it grows to 12 or 13 inches. It was named for Captain William Clark, of the Lewis and Clark expedition, who collected the first specimen. He mistook the bird for a woodpecker because of its large, straight black bill. Despite the corrected name, this bird cracks more conifer cones than nuts. They hammer the cones with their bills and store food for winter. They also eat insects. Clark's nutcrackers construct twig-and-stick platforms lined with grass and strips of bark as nests on horizontal limbs (see jays, page 136).

Clark's nutcracker

Cliff Swallow

These small birds grow to 6 inches. They have a square tail; blue-gray head and wings; cream-colored rump, forehead, and breast; and rusty cheeks, nape, and throat. Cliff swallows build gourd-shaped all-mud nests on rocky cliffs as well as under many low-elevation bridges. They consume enormous quantities of bugs, entirely during flight. The most common of the five swallow species in California migrates from the south. A colony once arrived at Mission San Juan Capistrano with such regularity that it was used as a calendar reference.

Cliff swallow

Common Raven

The common raven is entirely black and looks a bit like the American crow, but is much larger. Common ravens are 20 to 27 inches long with thick black bills that are heavier than most birds of similar size. They have a wedge-shaped tail and shaggy throat feathers. When in flight, they often soar like hawks. Common ravens have an opportunistic diet, ranging from berries and other birds' eggs and nestlings to small vertebrates; they frequently feed on road kill along highways. They inhabit cliffs and canyons, where they build large nests of sticks or bones, lined with fur or plant materials, on steep cliffs or in tall trees. Females usually lay four to seven eggs, which are green with brown spots.

Common raven

Dipper

Also known as water ouzel, American dippers are plain gray birds about 8 inches in length with short tails and stubby bills. They are invariably found near cold, clear, swiftly flowing mountain streams. Dippers often nest on ledges behind tumbling waterfalls but also under man-made structures such as bridges or small dams—any sheltered nest site near running water. Dippers have specially adapted features to survive near water. A third eyelid closes over the eyes to enable them to see underwater without risking damage from floating debris; large preen glands coat dippers with water-repellent oil; and a flap of skin closes over the nostrils to keep out water.

Dipper

Dippers are remarkable birds to watch. They are comfortable on the land, in the air, and under the water. They fly over streams, then suddenly submerge to walk along the streambed or swim, flapping their wings as though in the air. Dippers are found throughout Northern California's mountains.

Golden Eagle

Golden eagles are truly magnificent birds, ranging in length from 30 to 40 inches with a wingspan of 6 to 8 feet. Males and females are similar in appearance, with brown bodies that have a golden tint, especially on the neck and head. Their feet are yellow and their hooked bills are dark. Golden eagles swoop down onto prey, which includes ground squirrels, marmots, and grouse. They are also capable of killing young goats, sheep, and deer. Normally they build nests of sticks, branches, and roots atop a cliff that overlooks an open area with a reasonable population of small mammals. While golden eagles are year-round residents, they are not seen very often.

Golden eagle

Great Blue Heron

The great blue heron stands nearly 5 feet tall with blue-gray feathers, a long curving neck, and a straight yellow bill. Great blue herons are occasionally mistaken for cranes because of their similarity in size and proportion, but in flight, cranes hold their necks outstretched while herons fold their necks back onto the shoulders. These birds are adept at catching aquatic fauna with their spearlike bill. Great blue herons nest in trees in flimsy to elaborate stick-and-twig platforms that are added to over the course of many years. These nests can be up to 4 feet in diameter to accommodate the heron pair as they incubate three to seven blue-green eggs.

Great blue heron

Hawks

Hawks, like eagles and kites, are powerful raptors common throughout Northern California. These birds perch in trees and on telephone poles overlooking open meadows and grasslands with a sit-and-wait hunting technique; then they swoop down on their prey, ripping it apart with their hooked beak and sharp talons. They also dive on prey. Their diet ranges from small rodents to medium-size birds, amphibians, and reptiles.

Red-tailed hawk

Golden Gate National Recreation Area, north of San Francisco, is a good place to see large numbers of hawks, especially during fall migration, September to October.

Male harrier

The red-tailed hawk is a large bird that reaches lengths of about 24 inches and has a wingspan more than twice its length. The red-tailed hawk goes through several color phases, which can make identification difficult. Generally, the bird has dark upperparts, light underparts, and a red tail. Females are larger than males. Red-tailed hawks like open country, fields, and mixed woodlands. Red-tailed hawks normally make their nests in trees; bulkily constructed with sticks, the nests are usually added to each year. Both parents incubate the eggs but only the female raises the young.

Female harrier

Northern harriers are slender hawks with long tails and wings and range from 16 to 24 inches in length. The male is gray with black wingtips; the female is larger and brown with a streaked underside. They both have white rump bands at the base of the tail and a disc-shaped ruff of feathers that give an owl-like face. This facial disc, like that of some owls, serves as a sound-gathering system to assist in the pursuit of prey. The northern harrier actively hunts, flying close to the ground, looking for motion and listening for the squeak of mice and other small animals in the ground cover below. In fact, because of this behavior, the harrier may be the easiest hawk for novices to identify because no other hawk routinely flies so close to the ground. It cruises over fields and meadows, seemingly grazing the grasses with its belly. Northern harriers are found in almost any type of open country—including open fields, wet meadows, marshes, and alpine meadows. They nest on raised mounds on the ground in tall vegetation, with shelters made of grass and sticks.

Cooper's hawk

Cooper's hawks are also fairly common in Northern Cali-

Red-shouldered hawk

Sharp-shinned hawk

fornia, especially when migrants from outside California winter over. They are grayer in color and smaller than red-tailed hawks, with a rounded tail. They prefer woodlands. The largest hawk in California is the red-shouldered hawk, primarily found along the coast. From tip of the beak to the end of the tail, red-shouldered hawks can measure more than 3 feet. The back and head are pale brown, underparts are orange with buff bars, wings are black and white, and the tail is black with white bands. Another hawk of Northern California is the sharp-shinned hawk, a smaller raptor with rounded wings and a long tail. Both hawks have gray backs and heads and rusty bellies and faces.

Hummingbirds

The name hummingbird originated from the noise the birds' wings make while in flight. Hummingbirds, only a few inches long, are the smallest of all birds. A number of species are present in California, including black-chinned, Anna's, Allen's, Costa's, and rufous. The most common are Anna's hummingbirds, recognizable by the red hood of the males. Hummingbirds feed mainly on nectar; they also regularly consume small insects. They obtain nectar by inserting their bills and tongues

Costa's hummingbird

Rufous hummingbird

Anna's hummingbird

into a flower, accumulating pollen on their bills and heads; this pollen is then transferred from flower to flower. Hummingbirds are strong fliers and have exceptional flight characteristics for birds: They can hover and fly backward. The extremely rapid beating of their wings can reach 80 beats per second. Some hummingbirds save energy on cool nights by lowering their usually high body temperature until they become sluggish and unresponsive—a condition termed torpor. In contrast, during daylight hours, hummingbirds are often very active and can be highly aggressive, sometimes attacking much larger potential predators, such as hawks and owls.

Jays

The Steller's jay is the only western jay to have a crest. Because of its large size (10 to 12 inches), blue coloration, and crest, the Steller's jay is quite distinct. Male and female Steller's jays look similar: The head and upper breast are brownish or grayish black to jet black. The underparts below the breast are greenish blue, turning brighter blue under the tail. Wings are bright purplish blue to sky blue with narrow black barring; the rump and tail are bright blue with black barring that becomes more prominent toward the end. Under the wings and tail, the body is gray. The Steller's jay prefers conifer forests in the mountains of California. Like other jays, the Steller's jay consumes a variety of foods, including small vertebrates, seeds, berries, nuts, and especially acorns and pine seeds when available. They commonly take the eggs and nestlings of small birds, and they have even been observed attacking and eating adult birds. Normally a shy and wary bird, the Steller's jay can become accustomed to humans at campgrounds and picnic areas. They build bulky nests of sticks and twigs, which are lined with mud, grass, and conifer needles. The nests are found in conifer trees. Females typically lay four eggs.

Steller's jay

The western scrub jay is found throughout California. This 11- to 12-inch jay has no crest; it has sky blue upperparts, a long tail, and grayish buff underparts. It is found in scrubby grasslands and oak woodlands. The western scrub jay is aggressively intolerant toward the Steller's jay and drives it away.

Pinyon jays, smaller than western scrub jays, prefer pinyon forests, but will traverse a variety of habitats in search of food. They store pine nuts for winter and spring. Pinyon jays tend to gather in flocks. Adults are almost completely dull blue with a black beak. Their tails are somewhat shorter than those of other jays. In Northern California, they are resident on the eastern slopes of the mountains, on the Modoc Plateau, eastern Cascades and Sierra.

Mountain Bluebird

These beautiful sky-blue birds are found in Northern California at elevations above 5,000 feet. They normally take over nests abandoned by woodpeckers because their beaks are not strong enough to hollow out their own cavities. Their survival is becoming more difficult, as the logging industry cuts down many standing dead trees that the birds would normally use as homes. They readily adapt to whatever homes they can find, including chipmunk burrows, abandoned car bumpers, and fence posts in open areas. When not nesting, mountain bluebirds are often spotted in sizable flocks. They hunt by flying slowly, low to the ground, and swooping down to catch insects and spiders.

Mountain bluebird

Western bluebirds, distinguished by chestnut colorings on their bodies, are found at most elevations.

Mourning Dove

Mourning doves are one of the most common wild doves native to North America. They range throughout California with the exception of the deserts and highest mountains. They are members of the same family as pigeons but are grayish brown, with thinner pointed tails. Their outer tail feathers have white tips with a black marking midway, so that the tail is edged with a black and white stripe. The male and female mourning doves look alike but females have more of an overall brown coloring. Mourning doves are named for their sad-sounding long calls most often heard in the mornings. This melancholy song has been compared to a person mourning the loss of a loved one. Mourning doves produce up to six broods per year—the most of any native bird. Typically, two eggs are laid in a nest made in an evergreen tree, although a wide variety of nest sites are used, including clumps of grass.

Mourning dove

Northern Flicker

The northern flicker, a woodpecker, can be identified in flight by a flash of salmon red under its wings and tail. Viewed at rest, the northern flicker has a brown crown, a brownish body, and a red streak behind its bill. Northern flickers are the most terrestrial of North American woodpeckers because they feed on ants, and they can be found anywhere from tree line to sea level. They are occasionally spotted bathing in dusty depressions, as dust particles absorb oils and bacteria from their feathers. Northern flickers use their powerful beaks to create nesting holes in dead or dying deciduous trees and line the cavity with wood chips.

Northern flicker

Northern Mockingbird

Northern mockingbirds are long streamlined gray birds reaching up to 10 inches in length, with white undersides and flashy white wing patches and outer tail feathers. The males and females look alike. Of all North American birds, the mockingbird is most famed for vocal imitations—its repertoire has been known to include more than 40 different sounds. These birds can also mimic sounds such as those of a barking dog, squeaky hinges, notes from a piano, and even a cackling hen. During the mating season the male will mark his territory with song. Mockingbirds sing incessantly, both night and day, hopping from one song post to another. They are known to be aggressive when defending their nests and territories. However, if you see them jumping up and down in the air, they may be catching a few insects. Although they breed and nest in Northern California, mockingbirds often winter farther south.

Northern mockingbird

Nuthatches

Nuthatches are small birds, only about 4 to 6 inches in length. They are the only tree-climbing birds that descend headfirst. While foraging on a tree trunk, a nuthatch might pause in mid-descent, arch its head, and call out noisily. Nuthatches clasp the trunk, gripping with their feet, which are equipped with a back claw to help them traverse the undersides of branches. They nest in natural cavities in trees or in abandoned woodpecker nests. They line the nests with bark, grass, fur, and feathers. Females lay five to eight eggs and incubate them for up to two weeks. California has three species of nuthatches. The white-breasted nuthatch has bluish gray coloring on its back and a white breast; males have a black crown. This nuthatch, the only one with an entirely white face, lives throughout the forests of Northern California. The red-breasted nuthatch is primarily found at higher elevations, whereas pygmy nuthatches reside mainly in yellow pine forests. The habitats of the three species rarely overlap.

White-breasted nuthatch

Red-breasted nuthatch

Orioles

Orioles are members of the blackbird family. The brightly colored hooded oriole is commonly found in California. Its breeding range spans along the coast from Sonoma County to Monterey County and through the entire Central Valley. The male's head and underparts are bright yellowish-orange; it has a black back, tail, and throat. Females are olive gray with greenish-yellow underparts. Another oriole, Bullock's, also migrates to Northern California in the spring and summer from Mexico and Central America. Bullock's oriole males are very brightly colored orange and black—distinguishable from other black and orange orioles by their black eye line. It is closely related to the Baltimore oriole common in the eastern states. Baltimore orioles are rarely spotted in California.

Hooded orioles

Orioles create beautifully woven hanging nests of plant fibers, suspended pouchlike from the very tips of tree branches. They eat insects, fleshy fruits, berries, nectar from hummingbird feeders, and nectar that they probe from flowers.

Osprey

These distinctive black-and-white raptors can be seen flying low over Northern California lakes. They are large birds, 2 feet in length, with a wingspan more than twice that. Also known as fish hawks, ospreys search for fish over

Osprey

open water. Sighting prey, they make a steep dive. If the dive is successful, they maneuver the fish into a forward-facing position during flight. They are recognizable by black streaks over the eyes and black wrist patches on otherwise white underbelly.

Ospreys suffered heavily from DDT and other pesticide pollution in the 1950s and 1960s, but their population is making a steady recovery.

Owls

California is host to a number of owl species from the large and imposing great horned owl to the diminutive burrowing owl. Owls are truly unique birds, characterized by their large heads; round, penetrating eyes; acute hearing and eyesight; generally nocturnal hunting habits; and slow, silent flights. They accomplish their quiet movement using specially adapted serrated feathers that allow air to pass through them slowly. Owls also have a wide range of vision; in some species the neck can rotate nearly 180 degrees. They are equipped with excellent night vision. Many owls make a distinctive "hooting" sound and often respond to imitations of their call. Around the nests of owls one can find regurgitated pellets, revealing the bones of the predator's last meal.

Great horned owl

Saw-whet owl

Barn owl Great gray owl

Screech owl Short-eared owl

The great horned owl is the largest of Californian owls. It reaches heights of up to 2 feet, with a $4^1/_2$-foot wingspan. The "horns" are actually feathered tufts. Great horned owls are usually found in woodlands but can be seen occasionally in more suburban areas. Also common is the barn owl, which has a recognizable heart-shaped facial disc and white- or cream-colored plumage. Barn owls are very beneficial to man because they primarily eat rodents; but as humans have urbanized increasingly large areas of California, barn owls have lost much of their habitat. They can still be spotted in rural areas, where they earn their name nesting in farmyard barns.

Western screech owls are small owls that inhabit woodlands in Northern California. They nest in natural cavities or abandoned woodpecker holes. They are quite numerous in the state, but like other owls, they are nocturnal and thus infrequently seen.

Other owls sometimes spotted in Northern California include the northern saw-whet owl, the great gray owl, the short-eared owl, and the northern pygmy owl.

Some California owls have become endangered in recent years. An increasingly uncommon owl is the northern spotted owl, whose plight has attracted the attention of environmentalists, much to the chagrin of logging companies and developers. Its habitat is mainly in the Coast Ranges and the Klamath Mountains, among redwoods and Douglas firs. The loss of dense woodland habitat has also robbed the long-eared owl of its primary breeding ground.

Owls often played a part in Native American spirituality. They were viewed alternatively as a bringer of fortune, an omen of evil, or a harbinger of death. Owls commonly appear in popular culture as a symbol of wisdom. They are difficult to see in nature because they are nocturnal. Still, backcountry travelers should be alert for the opportunity to see these beautiful raptors.

Prairie Falcon

Prairie falcons, found in much of Northern California, are medium-size birds with pale brown upperparts, a pale face, and creamy white and heavy brown spotting below. Their crown is streaked. Found in open treeless areas and canyons throughout California, prairie falcons are stealthy fliers and utilize a high-speed strike and kill method, swooping down on ground squirrels, chipmunks, waterfowl, grouse, songbirds, and other vertebrates. Young birds, when learning to fly, tend to make many attempts—with many crash landings. Prairie falcons typically seek shelter in rocky cliffs or outcroppings and sometimes in trees, usually without nesting material.

Prairie falcon

Sandhill Crane

This native of northern Canada migrates south to winter in California's Sacramento–San Joaquin Delta at the north end of San Francisco Bay. Sandhill cranes are very tall birds, up to 4 feet, with long legs and neck. Coloring is mostly gray, though the cheeks and throat are white and the forehead is

Sandhill cranes

red. Young birds are a paler gray-brown color. Sandhill cranes emit a distinctive *goroooo-ah-ah-ah* call, often when in flight. The birds glide in flight and flap with a rapid upstroke of the wings. Northeastern California is the southernmost area of their breeding area. Sandhill cranes can be spotted there from March to October.

Sparrows

Sparrows are small fast birds with a rounded head and a stout neck. Generally about 6 inches from beak to tail, sparrows come in a variety of colors, most commonly rusty or gray with black markings. Sparrows use their conical bills to crush seeds. During warmer months they supplement their diet with insects.

California is habitat to numerous species of sparrows. White-crowned sparrows arrive in large flocks during fall; some reside as far north as Alaska. White-crowned sparrows range from 6 to 7 inches in length. This bold, colorful, and vocal bird has a white crown ringed with black stripes, a white eyebrow, black eye line, gray face, gray back streaked with brown, and gray underparts. White-crowned sparrows scratch the ground to expose insects and seeds, although they also eat berries.

Chipping sparrow

Chipping sparrows, slightly smaller than white-crowned sparrows, have chestnut caps, white eyebrows, and black eye lines. Chipping sparrows prefer woodland areas in the mountains. The largest sparrow in the state is the fox sparrow, which migrates to California from elsewhere in North America. Lark sparrows are resident throughout the year and are known for their lovely songs and beautiful plumage. They nest on the ground, concealed by dense vegetation. The English sparrow is also common in the state, having been introduced from Europe in the 1800s.

Swifts

These remarkable little birds spend most of their lifetime in flight; they feed, drink, bathe, and even mate while flying! In foul weather, flocks of swifts may fly hundreds of miles until they find more favorable conditions. The white-throated swift is a 6- or 7-inch long bird with a long forked tail and a black upper part with white below that tapers down the belly. One of the fastest birds in the world—and certainly one of the fastest in California, white-throated swifts like open habitat, mainly in the Coast Ranges in Northern California, where they feed almost entirely on flying insects. They build nests within cracks or crevices of cliffs. The smallest swift in California is Vaux's (rhymes with hawks) swift, about 4 inches in length. It is brown with light undersides. Vaux's swift builds its nest in hollow trees. Larger black swifts breed in Northern California and nest in cliff or canyon walls. Like other California swifts, black swifts winter in the tropics.

Tanagers

The male western tanager is brightly colored, with a red head, yellow body, black back, wings, and tail. The female's coloring is more subdued, yellow-green above with yellow below. Both males and females have horizontal bars on their wings; the top one is thin and yellow and the bottom one is white. They eat insects and fruit and grow to about 7 inches in length. Found in coniferous mountain forests, the western tanager migrates into the state from the south. Western tanagers build frail cup nests, made of twigs, grass, or other plant materials, on horizontal branches or in the fork of high trees. The summer tanager, another of the four species found in Northern California, rarely though beyond the Coast Ranges in Humboldt County. The male has a rose-red color. The female is olive-green with yellow underparts. The tanager's song is similar to that of the American robin, a series of short fluty phrases. Tanagers migrate to the tropics for the winter.

Summer tanager

Western tanager

Thrashers

Several species of thrashers are found here, including the California thrasher, sage thrasher, and brown thrasher. The pictured curve-billed thrasher is most common in desert regions and is similar in appearance to other species. Adult thrashers measure about a foot from the tip of the beak to the end of the tail, but this length is somewhat misleading; they have very long tails and long curved bills. Adults are mostly grayish brown with buff breasts and black patches on the chin and around the eyes. Relatives of mockingbirds, thrashers have similar, but harsher, *chuck* calls. They are also expert mimics. The California thrasher feeds mainly on the ground in dense thickets and chaparral, while the Sage thrasher eats harmful insects and fruits and vegetables from gardens. It uses its deeply curved bill to turn over leaves and dig in the earth looking for insects and other invertebrates. Females lay two to five pale blue-green speckled eggs in nests built from sticks and roots in the thick of low shrubs.

Curve-billed thrasher

Towhees

The California (or brown) towhee, spotted towhee, green-tailed towhee, and rufous-sided towhee are all found in Northern California. These birds range from approximately 7 to 8 inches in length and are in the same family as sparrows. Towhees scratch the ground vigorously for insects and seeds. They nest low in a bush, on the ground under cover, or in a brushy pile in a cup nest made of leaves, grass, and

Spotted towhee

bark shreds. California towhees, small gray birds, are often seen in suburban gardens, especially along the coast. They prefer heavily brushed areas, and their range does not extend far beyond the state borders. Spotted towhees, slightly less common than California towhees, are more brightly colored, with red sides, white underparts, black backs, and white spots on their black wings. The green-tailed towhee, common in more arid mountains, has olive wings and tail, gray neck and sides, a red crown and a white chin. The rufous-sided towhee is mostly black with bright red sides and a whitish belly and can be found on the eastern slope of the Sierra Nevada.

Turkey Vulture

Also known as a buzzard, this scavenger bird is predominantly black, with a featherless red head. Its legs and feet are orange and its hooked beak is yellow. Turkey vultures are large birds with bodies to 32 inches and wingspans to as much as 72 inches. They soar over open areas, seldom flapping their wings, in search of carrion they locate by keen sight and smell. To conserve energy, they ride on rising columns of warm air known as thermals. They gather for communal roosts on fence posts or in dead trees at night. Instead of building nests, turkey vultures lay their eggs in logs or under protective ledges. They are mostly seen in spring or fall.

Turkey vulture

Western Kingbird

Western kingbirds are 8 or 9 inches long, gray above, and white, gray, or yellow below, with whitish edges on the outermost tail feathers, and a blackish mask through the eye. They have a red spot (usually concealed) on the crown, which is flared in courtship displays or during confrontation with rivals. Western kingbirds are somewhat social since two or more pairs have been found nesting in the same tree, but they will attack hawks, crows, ravens, and other birds that fly near their nest; they will even ride on the larger bird's back and peck at its head. The western kingbird is mostly found in the summer months in open country around ranches and towns. A large flycatcher, it perches upright on tall weeds, exposed branches, or wires before sweeping forward to catch insects in midair. Western kingbirds occasionally eat berries. An entertaining tumble-display takes place during courtship when males fly to about 60 feet, then stall and tumble, free-falling toward the ground. Kingbirds build nests in cottonwood, oak, sycamore, and willow trees, on utility poles, water towers, and barns. Made of weed stems, twigs, and string, the nests are lined with sheep's wool, cotton, hair, and feathers. Four eggs are laid between April and July; incubation is usually 12 to 14 days. Fledglings can usually fly about two weeks after hatching.

Western kingbird

Western Wood-Pewee

This 5- or 6-inch-long bird is a member of the flycatcher family. It is dark olive brown on the upperparts and has a lighter belly. It has a distinct voice; calls include a harsh, slightly descending *pee-yew*, which it calls persistently throughout the day. Found mainly in open woodlands, these birds perch on high tree branches during the day and launch down to forage upon flying insects. Western wood-pewees build camouflaged nests of plant fibers that resemble a bump on a horizontal limb, which they defend fiercely, chasing away hawks, jays, and chipmunks.

Western wood-pewee

White-faced Ibis

These birds stand about 2 feet tall and have dark chestnut plumage, a long down-curved bill, and long dark red legs. They are common in summer in the marshes and farmlands of the Central Valley and Klamath Basin lakes, where they feed on aquatic invertebrates, amphibians, and other small vertebrates. White-faced ibis fly in long wavering lines to and from their roosts, which are typically in bulrushes or other vegetation. They build deep nests of coarse materials lined with plant matter.

White-faced ibis

Wilson's Phalarope

Wilson's phalaropes are shorebirds that have long thin bills, chestnut throats, bold blackish stripes on the face, and light gray underparts. They are unlike most bird species in that the female has bolder coloring and usually mates with several different males. This role reversal continues during breeding, since it's the male who incubates the eggs and the female who defends the nest. Nests are usually built near water in a depression lined with grass and vegetation. Thousands gather at Mono Lake during their molt in summer.

Wilson's phalarope

Woodpeckers

California is home to 17 species of woodpecker. Woodpeckers bang their strong bills on trees and utility poles, generally as a way of establishing territory and probing for insects in the barks of trees. They have thick chisel-like bills, and long tongues for this purpose. The male's plumage is similar to the female's, but the male often has a patch of red on his head. Acorn woodpeckers have dark wings and back, white face and belly, and a red cap. They live in oak forests and eat

Acorn woodpecker

Gila woodpecker

Downy woodpecker

acorns, which they sometimes store in holes in tree trunks for later consumption. For other woodpeckers, diets consist mostly of insects, seeds, and berries. Woodpeckers make holes in trees for their nests, which are used for just one season before being appropriated by other birds, often owls. Females lay three to five eggs; the young can fly in about a month. Nuttall's woodpecker is perhaps the most common, living mostly west of the Cascades and Sierra Nevada. It is a small bird that usually nests in woodlands with streams. Lewis's woodpecker is larger—up to a foot from the tip of the beak to the end of the tail—and more darkly colored. The hairy woodpecker is named for its fluffy feathers. It has black wings with a few white spots, a white or pale brown back, a long beak, and a red neck (in males).

Pileated woodpecker

The largest woodpecker in North America (now that the ivory-billed woodpecker is thought to be extinct) is the pileated woodpecker. About the size of a crow, it is found in the Klamath and Coast Ranges. The pileated woodpecker is black with white neck stripes and wing linings. It is distinguished by a prominent red crest, similar to that of Woody Woodpecker, of cartoon fame.

Other woodpeckers in Northern California include the red-breasted sapsucker, with its distinctive red head, and the downy woodpecker, a small bird colored white and black with a red cap. The northern flicker is also found here (see page 137).

Wrens

California has eight species of wrens. Bewick's wren grows to about 5 inches and is brown with white underparts. It has a long full tail with white corners. It usually holds its tail high up over the back. The bill is fairly long and pointed. It has a white eyebrow stripe. Bewick's wren is a very common bird and is frequently seen in Northern California's Sierra Nevada.

Canyon wren

The canyon wren, about 6 inches, is brown and buff with a long down-curved bill. It can be identified by its flight pattern, which consists of a quick raising and lowering of its hindquarters every few seconds. The agile canyon wren also has a slightly flattened body shape, which allows it to navigate through narrow crevices. Canyon wrens are usually found on open cliffs, in canyons, and on rocky slopes foraging for food—even throughout the hottest parts of the day—scanning ledges and crevices for insects and spiders. Canyon wrens nest on ledges, in crevices under rocks, or inside caves in cup-shaped nests of moss, twigs, and spider silk, lined with fur and feathers. They are found throughout Northern California with the exception of the Central Valley, the immediate coast, and the high Sierra.

The winter wren is small—about 6 inches from beak to the end of its tail. It is dark brown with fine black bars on its sides, wings, and tail, and a buff throat. It is resident in northwest California and the Sierra Nevada. It spends summers at higher elevations and moves downslope in winter months.

Yellow-billed Magpie

The yellow-billed magpie, a California native, is common in the Central Valley and the Coast Ranges south of San Francisco to Santa Barbara County. Magpies' black-and-white coloration and long tails make them easy to identify. This bird is distinguished, as its name suggests, by its yellow bill. Magpies are big, flashy, boisterous, and loud birds with a reputation for raiding the nests of other birds, picking sores on cattle, and attacking the eyes of injured animals. Their sturdy nests, made of mud and reeds, are used from year to year; they also mate with the same partners from year to year. They can often be seen in parks and picnic areas feeding on food scraps. In northeastern California, the black-billed magpie is the more common variety. With the exception of the bill, this bird has the same coloring as the yellow-billed magpie.

Yellow-billed magpie

Plants

Wildflowers

American Brooklime

The shiny oval 2-inch-long leaves with sometimes-toothed edges dwarf the tiny quarter-inch flowers, which grow in vibrant blue, violet, or white masses and have red-purple markings. The bloom is made up of four petals—three small ones along the bottom and one much larger (actually two petals fused together) on top—two stamens, and one pistil (between the stamens). The plant's stems are long, but flowers grow close to the water source, near the ground. The flower thrives in damp areas and will grow in dense patches in slow-moving streams or pools of water. Typically found in the Lake Tahoe region, the plant grows below 10,500 feet in wet, grassy fields or on the banks of slow-moving streams. Height: 4 to 40 inches.

American brooklime

Baby Blue-Eyes

One of the most well known wildflowers in Northern California, baby blue-eyes is an annual found in grasslands, meadows, canyons, wooded foothills, and on roadsides. Baby blue-eyes is a low plant with slender branched stems. The blue bowl-shaped flowers bloom singularly on the ends of hairy stalks. Flowers are about 1 inch wide and have five petals; coloring is paler near the center. Flowering occurs between March and June. Baby blue-eyes is endemic to California and southern Oregon, but is often included in wildflower mixes and has been cultivated in England for more than a century. Height: to 1 foot.

Baby blue-eyes

Bindweed

Bindweed is a twining plant found throughout North America. Common bindweed and field bindweed were introduced from Europe. Bindweed is related to morning glory, and its white or cream-colored flowers resemble those of that vine. In California, it is often found in gardens, fields, roadsides, and waste areas. Many people consider it a weed and its deep root system makes it difficult to eradicate. Length: 1 to 3 feet.

Field bindweed

Blue Dicks

In bloom from March to May, this flower of the lily family is also called wild hyacinth or common brodiaea. The electrifying pink- to blue-purple blooms have six petals each. The six stamens are difficult to locate because they are often hidden by a forked appendage that grows from the bloom's center. On top of the weak, commonly bent stem, anywhere from two to fifteen flowers are tightly clustered. The plant has grasslike leaves that grow from $^1/_2$ to 2 feet in length and often wilt before the flower appears. Blue dicks will grow below 6,000 feet on plains, grasslands, hillsides, or clearings within wooded areas. The flowers grow from Oregon to Mexico, sometimes in dense clusters that create blankets of purple. Height: 1 to 3 feet.

Blue dicks

Butter-and-Eggs

Also called johnny-tuck or toadflax from the shape of the bloom, this member of the snapdragon family has blooms $1^1/_2$ inches tall composed of three yellow sacs with white bases. Two upper petals protrude from the flower's base, slightly above the lower petals, and resemble pointed purple beaks. Growing in dense groupings as large as an acre in size, it has narrow grayish green leaves of up to 4 inches long. Butter-and-eggs grows below 4,000 feet from California's lowlands and Sierra Nevada into the Coast Ranges of southwest Oregon. Height: 1 to 3 feet.

Butter-and-eggs

California Poppy

The California poppy is the state flower, and it is a common sight throughout California. It can be a perennial (surviving for several years) or an annual (completing its life cycle in one year). Flowers start to bloom in February or March and continue to form until September. They are usually deep orange in color, but are often pale yellow by the end of summer. The flowers are bowl-shaped and about 2 inches in height. They often close at night or during bad weather. The preferred habitat for the California poppy is open grassy areas. Height: 18 inches.

California poppy

Chicory

This wildflower is a member of the sunflower family. It has tall wiry branched stems with a few small leaves on their upper parts. Leaves near the base are larger—4 to 8 inches long. The leaves are edible and make a good spinach substitute when young. The plant is sometimes grown for its roots, which can be roasted and added to or substituted for coffee. Chicory blooms between April and October. Flowers are pale blue (rarely pink or white), wheel-shaped, and scattered along the stem. Chicory is often found in disturbed places such as fields or roadsides. Height: to 6 feet.

Chicory

Chinese Houses

Chinese houses are beautiful and charming spring wildflowers. The central stem of a Chinese houses plant is erect and slender. Leaves form in pairs and are sparse. Flowers are slightly less than an inch long and two-lipped. The upper lip has two erect white lobes; the lower lip has three drooping purple lobes. The flowers cluster in widely spaced whorls near the top of the stem. Flowering takes place between March and June. When in bloom the plants resemble a colorful Chinese pagoda tower. Chinese houses are common in Central California at elevations below 3,000 feet. Height: 1 foot.

Chinese houses

Chuparosa

Chuparosa means "rose sucker," or "hummingbird" in Spanish, and this wildflower is indeed a favorite for hummingbirds. The birds help pollinate the plant as they feed from it. Chuparosa blooms between February and June. Flowers are about an inch long and look like narrow red tubes. The shrub itself is densely branched, wide, and tall. Leaves are scarce and, when flowerless, the plant has a dull gray-green appearance. Height: to 5 feet.

Chuparosa

Common Mullein

Also known as flannel mullein, blanketweed, woolly mullein, and velvet plant, common mullein is a naturalized weed from Europe. It is an erect, stout, woolly biennial with matted layers of short starlike hairs that cover the entire plant. Leaves form a rosette on the ground in the first year, from which the stem arises in the second year. Its large woolly stem is very leafy. Greenish yellow flowers, which bloom from June to September, are crowded on a tall thick spike at the top of the plant, 1 to 3 feet long and 3/4 to 1 1/2 inches thick. Egg-shaped seedpods contain numerous tiny, dark brown seeds. Common mullein grows in dry disturbed soil in waste places or fields and along roadsides, railroad embankments, and old dwellings. This widespread plant has no value as forage. Colonists and Native Americans lined their footwear with the leaves of this plant for warmth. Height: 2 to 6 feet.

Woolly mullein

Common Sunflower

Common sunflowers are tall robust branched annuals with coarse, rough stems. Hairy leaves are heart-shaped and pointed at the tip; the edges are usually toothed. Sunflowers have large 2- to 5-inch flower heads that bloom from March to October or November. Flower heads follow the sun as it moves across the sky during the day. The sunflower was introduced in California and is native to the Great Plains. This showy and somewhat ornamental plant is abundant in moist soils throughout most of the state along roadsides and in waste places, abandoned fields, lowlands, and barren spots. It can be a pest near cultivated crops. Birds, rodents, and humans eat sunflower seeds. Native Americans have been known to make purple and black dye from the seeds and yellow dye from the flowers. Height: 3 to 7 feet.

Common sunflower

Cream Cups

A member of the poppy family, cream cups ranges in color from pale cream to yellow; some have a reddish cast. The stem is covered with soft hairs and droops when in bloom. The plant's buds are pink. Each stem has one flower from 1/2-inch- to 1 1/2-inches-wide with six petals and numerous stamens. The flower's narrow leaves grow low around the bottom of the plant and reach up to 3 inches in length. The plant thrives in sandy or clayey soil in open areas or burns below 3,000 feet. It ranges from Oregon south through most of California into southwestern Utah and central Arizona. Cream cups blooms during spring. Height: 4 to 12 inches.

Cream cups

Elegant Brodiaea

Ranging from northern Oregon to southern California, elegant brodiaea can be seen blooming between April and July. The plant prefers the dry soils of plains or grassy mountainsides. The stem of elegant brodiaea is erect. Long narrow leaves generally wither by late spring when flowering begins. The violet flowers are funnel-shaped, about 1 inch long, and have six petals. Several other similar varieties of brodiaea also grow in Northern California. Height: to 16 inches.

Elegant brodiaea

Farewell-to-Spring

Farewell-to-spring is a late bloomer. Flowering does not begin until June and continues through August. Found on dry grassy slopes and in open woods in coastal Northern California, farewell-to-spring has a slender branched stem. Flowers are showy and poppylike with four pink petals and a maroon blotch near the center. They close at night and reopen in the morning. Height: 2 to 3 feet.

Farewell-to-spring

Fiddleneck

Fiddleneck is a common annual found in open disturbed areas such as roadsides and fields. Part of the forget-me-not family, fiddleneck was named because its curved flower spike resembles the head of a violin. The orange-yellow flowers grow in a cluster at the end of bristly coiled branches that sprout from a long erect stem. As the flowers bloom, the coil opens. Blooming generally occurs in April and May. Height: 1 to 3 feet.

Fiddleneck

Golden Fairy Lantern

Golden fairy lantern, also known as yellow globe lily, is found exclusively in Northern California. Leaves near the base are long and thin; those on the stem are much smaller. Flowers droop in an open-branched cluster at the end of the stems. They are quite beautiful—egg-shaped and deep yellow. Blooming occurs between April and June. Golden fairy lantern prefers shaded rocky places and dry open woods. Height: to 20 inches.

Golden fairy lantern

Goldenrod

Also known as yellowweed, goldenrod is a member of the sunflower family. It typically has a slender unbranched stem with short-stalked or stalkless leaves and small yellowish flower heads in complex clusters. It is one of the later-blooming plants, usually flowering from July to September. Medicinal applications of this plant include use as an astringent and as a diuretic for kidney stones. In powder form it has been used for cicatrization of ulcers. Height: 1 to 5 feet.

Goldenrod

Golden Yarrow

Golden yarrow is found in dry open areas of Northern California, including oak woodlands and coastal scrub. It is a shrubby plant with many erect stems and clusters of small golden yellow flowers. The stems are branched and leafy. Stems and leaves are both woolly. Flowers are small, about $^1/_2$ inch long, and form rounded clusters at the end of the stems. Blooming occurs from early spring to late summer. Height: to 2 feet.

Golden yarrow

Goldfields

Goldfields are small annuals that thrive throughout California and range from northern Baja California to Oregon. When there is adequate moisture, they can cover entire slopes or fields with a golden yellow hue. Goldfields bloom from March to May. Flowers are a little more than 1 inch wide with about 13 pale-tipped petals spreading from the central disc. Height: to 6 inches.

Goldfields

Hyacinth Brodiaea

This delicate member of the lily family, also known as white brodiaea, has a cluster of anywhere from 10 to 40 brilliant white blooms radiating from its central stem. The six-petal flower flares out from the stem into a bowl formation. The white petals contrast strikingly with dark green or black midveins, and its six stamens are white, yellow, or pale lilac. Blooms are generally $^1/_2$ inch wide. Its leaves are long, narrow, and grasslike. This wildflower reaches higher elevations than most of its relatives, growing below 6,500 feet mainly in the Sierra's wet meadows and forest clearings. It ranges from the Sierra Nevada north through the Cascades and into Canada. Height: 10 to 28 inches.

Hyacinth brodiaea

Indian Paintbrush

Indian paintbrush flowers are small modified leaves called bracts, which have colorful tips of fiery orange, pink, maroon, red, or yellow, giving the appearance of a dipped paintbrush at the end of the stems. The roots of these plants are partially parasitic and steal food from other plants. Found most often in habitats with dry open soil, sometimes with sagebrush, this plant blooms from May to September. Height: 1 to 3 feet.

Indian paintbrush

Indian Pink

Indian pink, also known as catchfly or campion, is one of Northern California's showiest wildflowers. Found in brushy or rocky wooded areas, Indian pink is quite widespread, though generally not abundant in any one area. In May and June, it blooms bright red flowers with numerous pointed teeth. Flowers are 1 to 2 inches wide. Leaves are 3 inches long and ovate. Height: 6 to 16 inches.

Indian pink

Marsh Marigold

Members of the buttercup family, also known as elk's lips, marsh marigolds grow high in the mountains in small pools and lakes that are often the result of early spring runoff. Each stem has a single flower at its tip with seven to ten white petals and many yellow stamens. The distinctive fleshy green leaves are heart-shaped. Sometimes marsh marigolds push up through the snow very early in the season. They are typically found in marshy places throughout the Sierra from 4,000 to 10,000 feet. Height: 3 to 10 inches.

Marsh marigold

Miner's Lettuce

Miner's lettuce is a common green annual found throughout Northern California at elevations below 6,500 feet. Pairs of leaves that grow together to form a circular cup about 2 inches wide interrupt the slender stems. Clusters of small white flowers grow from the center of these cups. Blooming occurs from early spring to early summer. Miner's lettuce prefers loose, moist soil in shady places. As its name indicates, the leaves of miner's lettuce are succulent and edible. Height: to 8 inches.

Miner's lettuce

Miniature Lupine

One of several types of lupine found in Northern California, miniature lupine is distinguished by its diminutive size and multicolored flowers. Miniature lupine grows in open areas at low or moderate elevations and is often found in conjunction with California poppies. Together, the two species often blanket entire fields. Small blue and violet flowers are arranged in whorls around the hairy branching stem. White pealike flowers add color to the plant. Miniature lupines bloom between March and May. Leaves are small (about 1 inch long) with five to seven leaflets arranged like wheel spokes. Height: to 14 inches.

Minature lupine

Mission Bells

Spanish priests thought these dark purple-brown and yellow drooping flowers resembled church bells and named them mission bells. Their preferred habitats are open woodlands and grassy areas. Mission bells' stems are very long and erect. The leaves separate in a circle around single points along the stalk, generally occurring more toward the top of the stem. Flowers bloom between February and July. Height: 1 to 4 feet.

Mission bells

Monkeyflower

Monkeyflowers are extremely variable plants characterized by trumpet-shaped flowers. This plant is also called wild lettuce because Native Americans and early settlers ate the bitter leaves. In Northern California, monkeyflowers appear in a variety of colors including yellow, scarlet, magenta, and orange. The Douglas monkeyflower rarely exceeds 2 or 3 inches, while Kellogg's and yellow-and-white monkeyflowers can grow to a foot. There is also a shrub variety with orange flowers called bush monkeyflower, which grows from 2 to 4 feet. Height: 2 inches to 4 feet.

Monkeyflower

Yellow monkeyflower

Douglas monkeyflower

Monkshood

This creamy white and bluish violet flower has two tiny petals under a hood. Monkshood is poisonous and was once used as a medicine to reduce fevers. It grows in meadows and other moist areas and normally blooms in mid or late summer. Monkshood occurs in wet areas through the Sierra from 4,000 to 9,000 feet. It typically can be found on creek banks near Grass Lake in the Sierra Buttes and Lakes Basin areas. Height: to 6 inches.

Monkshood

Mule's Ears

This beautiful flower, a relative of the sunflower, is found throughout the American West. Mule's ears grow on open hillsides and woods. Leaves are long (up to 2 feet) at the base and shorter on the stem. The entire plant has a resinous appearance. Long stalks end in several deep yellow flowers. The central flower is the largest—often 5 inches in width. Each flower has dozens of petal-like bracts surrounding a disc of smaller petals. Blooming takes place between May and July. Height: to 2 feet.

Narrowleaf mule's ears

Owl's Clover

The Spanish name for owl's clover is *escobita*, which means "little broom," referring to the broomlike flower cluster. The clusters range in color from cream to a deep magenta, increasing in hue toward the top. The leaves are 1 to 2 inches long and are divided into a few narrow segments. Owl's clover is very common after a wet spring, when it blankets whole fields. After blooming, which occurs between March and May, the plant forms a small fruit. Height: 4 to 16 inches.

Owl's clover

Pine Drops

A distinctive slender plant, pine drops is a root parasite of conifers. In California, it is often associated with ponderosa pine. The hairy red-brown stems are leafless, but covered with small yellowish brown egg-shaped flowers that hang down from the stalk. Stems often grow in clusters. Blooming occurs between June and August. Pine drops live for just one year, but remain as dry stalks for several years afterwards. Height: to 3 feet.

Pine drops

Purple Nightshade

This woody member of the nightshade family is a sticky glandular perennial. Purple nightshade is a native subshrub with deep purple starlike flowers that have a crinkly appearance and a small cluster of yellow stamens in the center. Leaves are hairy and dark green. All parts of the plant are toxic. Purple nightshade grows in several habitats, including chaparral and oak woodlands. Height: 3 to 5 feet.

Purple nightshade

Red Columbine

Columbines are beautiful two-colored flowers. The blue and white variety is the state flower of Colorado; the red and yellow species is the most common in California. Red columbine is found throughout the state in open woods and along rivers. The stems branch a lot, forming a bushy plant. Leaves repeatedly divide into rounded leaflets. Handsome flowers droop from the end of the stem. Five petal-like sepals spread as a frame for five tubular yellow petals. Height: to 2 feet.

Red columbine

Redwood Sorrel

Redwood sorrel forms large carpets in the shaded undergrowth of California's redwood forests. Redwood sorrel is a low plant, and its flowers and leaves are attached at ground level. Redwood sorrel is related to the shamrock, and its leaves resemble those of its Irish relative. They have three heart-shaped leaflets with a pale blotch in the middle. Leaves fold up in rain or bright sun. Flowing occurs between February and August. Flowers are about $1^1/_2$ inches wide and have five white or pinkish petals with red veins. Height: to 5 inches.

Redwood sorrel

St. John's Wort

Also known as Klamath weed, St. John's wort is not native to California. It was first identified near the Klamath River around 1900. In the next few decades it spread across thousands of acres of ranchland, rendering them worthless. Since 1945, beetles imported from Europe have controlled its growth. It is still quite common on roadsides of Northern California. Each plant has several erect branched stems, quite leafy near the top. The stems support clusters of star-shaped yellow flowers, sometimes with black dots near the tips. Blooming begins around June 24, the feast day of Saint John the Baptist. The plants have a reputation for warding off evil spirits and therapeutic qualities exploited by modern herbal medicines. Height: to 5 feet.

St. John's wort

Salsify

Also called goat dandelion, this member of the sunflower family looks much like a tall large dandelion after it goes to seed. Its yellow flowers bloom in the morning and close by noon. (There is also a purplish variety.) The plants are found in meadows, fields, waste areas, and roadsides. Salsify was brought by European settlers to use as a garden vegetable; roots were soaked to remove the bitterness, then peeled and eaten raw or stewed. Their flavor is similar to that of oysters. In our research, we have found many recipes for salsify dishes on the Internet. Height: 1 to 4 feet.

Salsify

Scarlet Gilia

These showy little wildflowers are members of the phlox family. Primarily biennials, these flowers produce a small clump of leaves the first year, followed by flowering stems the next year. The bright red trumpet-shaped flowers are mottled with yellow and are $^3/_4$ to $1^1/_2$ inches long. Scarlet gilias are frequently visited by hummingbirds, which thrust their bills down the tube to reach nectar at the base. The little bird's head becomes covered with pollen during this process, which it deposits at the next flower. Gilia plants may have a skunklike odor. They are found on dry slopes through the Sierra Nevada from 4,000 to 10,000 feet. Height: 12 to 36 inches.

Scarlet gilia

Scarlet Penstemon

Members of the snapdragon, or figwort, family, many species of penstemon grow in California. Scarlet penstemon grows in forest openings and on scrubby slopes south of the Tahoe area from 5,000 to 9,000 feet. It extends into the southern Sierra and desert mountains and east to Colorado. Penstemon means "five stamens." Some of the plants are called beardtongue, which refers to the fact that one of the stamens is different from the rest. The

Scarlet penstemon

odd stamen is covered with fine hairs and appears to have a beard. It does not develop any pollen itself, but it probably helps to attract insects into the center of the flower where pollen from other stamens can cover their bodies and be carried to the next flower. The flowers fall into two groups, each designed to accommodate their pollinators: One group produces brilliant red or scarlet narrow tubular flowers to attract and feed hummingbirds; the other group has pale lilac flowers that are better shaped for bees' bodies. Penstemon's fruit is a dry many-seeded capsule. Leaves are gray-green and oblong. Height: to 4 feet.

Shooting Star

Also known as birdbill, shooting star is a member of the primrose family. In appearance, shooting star resembles a colorful rocket. It has a yellow circle in the center with backward-curving magenta petals that point down to form the nose. A rosette of leaves circles the base of the stalk. Elk and deer browse on the young shoots and cattle graze on them too. The young shoots grow in rich soil and partial shade along streams and in wet meadows. Height: 6 to 16 inches.

Shooting star

Sky Pilot

These plants, also known as skunkweed, emit a skunklike, musky odor that comes from the leaves and woody stems when they are crushed. The deep bluish purple flowers actually have a sweet, pleasant smell. Bell-shaped flowers grow in crowded clusters around the head, blooming from June to August. They are only found growing on rocky slopes at or near the summit of the Sierra's highest peaks at elevations from 10,000 to 13,000 feet. Height: 4 to 12 inches.

Sky pilot

Subalpine Buttercup

This pretty wildflower can be seen on high mountain meadows and rocky slopes. There are more than 20 varieties of buttercup in California, including the endemic California buttercup. All have shiny yellow flowers and are hard to distinguish. Subalpine buttercup can be identified by the high elevations at which it is found (California buttercup occurs at elevations below 8,000 feet). Most of the plant's smooth oval leaves grow at its base. Between June and August these are hidden by a profusion of five-petaled brilliant yellow flowers. Height: to 10 inches.

Subalpine buttercup

Thistle

Several species of thistle grow in California, all members of the sunflower family. The most common is probably yellow star thistle, an extremely invasive nonnative plant found in most of California outside the deserts. It is characterized by long yellow thorns below the flower. These spines are painful to touch. Another common thistle is the creeping thistle, a pink-flowered tall plant that blooms all summer. The Latin name for thistle, *Cirsium,* means "a swollen vein," for which the plants were thought to be a remedy. Height: 2 to 4 feet.

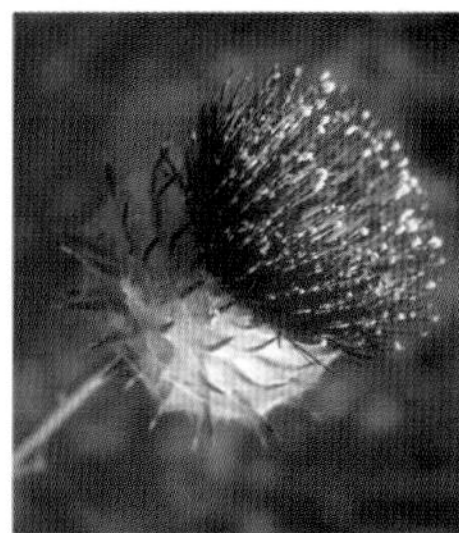

California thistle

Tidytips

A pretty Northern California wildflower, two-toned tidytips grow west of the Sierra Nevada. They are tall erect plants with narrow leaves. Tidytips bloom from March to June. Flowers are yellow with white three-lobed tips. Tidytips are found in a variety of habitats, but they prefer grassy areas. Height: to 2 feet.

Tidytips

Western Trillium

Western trillium is a low plant similar to a lily. It is found along stream banks or on the floor of moist redwood or mixed evergreen forests. The stalk is short, ending in a single three-petaled white flower. Between the petals alternate three small green leaves. Three larger, broader leaves frame the flower. Western trillium is also known as western wake robin because it starts to bloom in early spring as robins return to the forests. Blooming continues until early summer. Height: to 1 foot.

Western trillium

Trees, Shrubs, and Ferns

Bigleaf Maple

As their name implies, bigleaf maples have the largest leaves of all maple trees, often 8 inches long. Bigleaf maples thrive in the woodlands of Northern California and the Pacific Northwest, especially along stream banks. They grow to heights between 30 and 80 feet. The broad rounded crown of drooping branches and large leaves provides good shade and beautiful autumn colors. Their wood is the only western maple used commercially. Native Americans used it to fashion canoe paddles.

Bigleaf maple

Bishop Pine

Found almost solely in coastal regions of Northern and Central California, Bishop pine was identified in 1835 near the

Spanish mission of San Luis Obispo. San Luis Obispo is named after Saint Louis, Bishop of Toulouse; the common name of the species refers to this bishop. Bishop pine grows to heights between 40 and 80 feet. The trunk is often long and bare, with a conical, rounded, or irregular crown at the top. Dull green needles are stiff, about 5 inches long, and arranged in bundles of two. Cones are about 3 inches long, conical or egg-shaped. They remain closed for many years. Bishop pines prefer low hills and plains in foggy areas of coastal California and the Channel Islands.

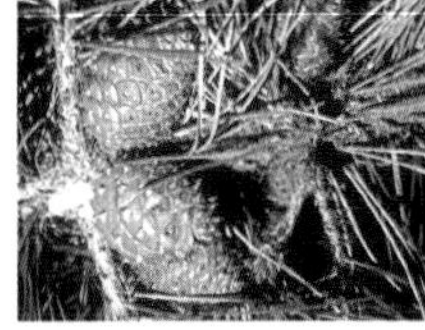

Bishop pine cones

Bishop pine

Black Hawthorn

Common along stream sides and in the valleys of northwestern California, black hawthorn is a pretty thicket-forming shrub or small tree. Its small 1- to 3-inch-long leaves are ovate, glossy, and sharply saw-toothed. Twigs are shiny red. Miniature white flowers with pink stamens and five white petals appear in clusters in early summer. Shiny black fruit follows. Large animals eat the leaves and birds consume the berries. Black hawthorn is called Douglas hawthorn after its discoverer, Scottish botanist David Douglas.

Black hawthorn

Blue Blossom

Blue blossom flowers decorate the roadsides of coastal Northern California every year between February and April. Blue blossom occurs as a shrub or a small tree less than 20 feet in height. Its flowers resemble lilacs; another name for the plant is California lilac. Blue blossom is an evergreen, with shiny green oblong or elliptical leaves about 2 inches long. Bark is red-brown and twigs are pale yellow-green. The flowers are tiny and, as its name suggests, light to dark blue. Small three-lobed fruits mature in summer after the flowers have died.

Blue blossom

Bristlecone Pine

Bristlecone pines in eastern California's Inyo National Forest are thought to be more than 4,600 years old, making them the oldest living trees in the world. Despite their superannuated age, bristlecone pines rarely grow taller than 40 feet. Close to timberline, they may even be low shrubs. The crown of a bristlecone pine forms very irregularly; branches twist and hang from the trunk. Short, blunt needles crowd in bundles of five into a mass that has been likened to a foxtail. Bark is gray or red-brown, furrowed, and scaly. The species takes its common name from the bristles that form on each scale of the reddish, cylindrical cones. In Central California, bristlecone pines occur at elevations between 7,000 and 12,000 feet. High Sierra #43: White Mountain Road travels to the Ancient Bristlecone Pine Forest in Inyo National Forest, home to some of the oldest bristlecones in the world.

Bristlecone pine

Bristlecone pine cones

California Black Walnut

California black walnuts come in two varieties: the Southern California black walnut and the Northern California black walnut. The Southern variety is more widespread and bears smaller fruits than the Northern. Most natural stands of Northern California black walnuts have been associated with locations of early Native American camps. The trees provide good shade and occur naturally along moist stream banks and valleys, often near willows and sycamores. Some Northern California cities have lined their streets with these walnut trees.

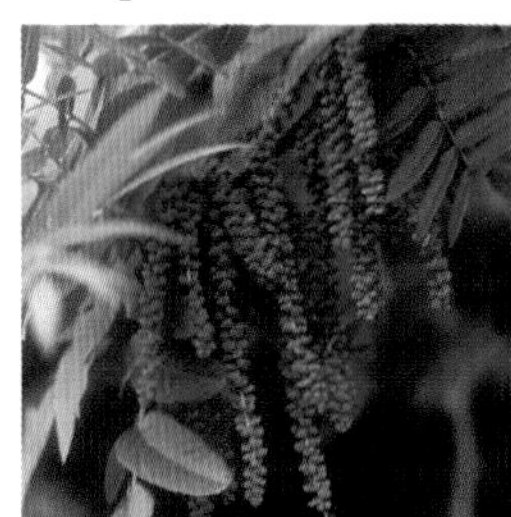

California black walnut

California Buckeye

California buckeye grows as a shrub or small tree with a broad rounded crown. Its range is confined to California in the coastal ranges and Sierra Nevada to 4,000 feet. It prefers moist soils in canyons or oak woodlands. Leaves are generally arranged into five pointed leaflets. In spring and early summer, many showy pink or white flowers bloom on California buckeye branches. Fruits mature in late summer. Each fruit has one or two poisonous seeds. Native Americans would drop the seeds into pools of water, making fish easy to catch, or leach the toxins out of the seeds to make crude flour. Chipmunks and squirrels are immune to the poison, but the flower nectar is believed to kill bees.

California buckeye flower

California buckeye

California Fremontia

Also known as flannel bush, California fremontia occurs as a shrub or small tree throughout California at elevations between 1,000 and 6,500 feet. Although it is also found in parts of Arizona and Baja California, its range is mostly confined to the Golden State. California fremontia prefers dry rocky mountain or canyon slopes and is often found in oak-pine woodlands, sometimes forming a dense thicket of undergrowth. Leaves are three-lobed and evergreen. Yellow five-petal flowers bloom in May or June.

California fremontia

California Laurel

Found only in California and southern Oregon, California laurel is also known as California bay. Fully mature trees are usually between 40 and 80 feet tall. Their short thick trunks fork close to the ground to form a broad rounded dense crown. The evergreen leaves are thick and pointed, shiny on their top surface and rougher gray-green below. The leaves and the twigs exude a pleasant odor when crushed. Although often planted as a street tree or ornamental, California laurels occur naturally in Northern California's coastal ranges and Sierra Nevada below 6,000 feet. They prefer moist soils, especially mountain canyons and valleys. In early spring, the trees bloom with numerous pale yellow flowers clustered at leaf bases. The flowers give way to small olivelike fruit colored green to purple. The wood of California laurels is used as a veneer for furniture, cabinetry, and interior trim.

California laurel

California laurel leaves

California Redbud

An elegant shrubby tree often planted as an ornamental, California, or western, redbud occurs naturally on the slopes of Northern California's mountains. It is more common on the western side of the Sierra Nevada and the eastern side of the coastal ranges. About 16 feet in height, California redbud has a rounded crown of spreading branches. Bark is gray and smooth. The round leaves are dark green early in the season and later turn red. In early spring, before the leaves appear, California redbud blooms in a magnificent display of small red or pink flowers, which give the plant its name. Native Americans used the flexible wood to make bows.

California redbud

California Red Fir

Almost pure forests of this remarkable conifer can be found on the western slopes of the Sierra Nevada; it can also be found on the Sierra's eastern slopes and in the mountains of northwestern California. It prefers a high mountain habitat, growing at elevations up to 9,000 feet. The fir is distinguished by its characteristic thick red bark and aromatic odor. In the right conditions, locations with dry summers and snowy winters, California red firs can reach heights of about 120 feet. Its evergreen needles are bluish, blunt, and about 1 inch long. Cones are 7 inches long, purplish brown, and upright on the highest branches. California red fir is a common tree in Yosemite National Park.

California red fir

California Rhododendron

Also known as California rose-bay or Pacific rhododendron, California rhododendron is a pretty evergreen shrub that ranges from Southern California to Canada. It grows as a gnarled shrub in moist shaded forests below 4,000 feet and is often associated with pines, redwoods, and Douglas firs. Its leaves are 8 inches long, leathery and elliptical, and the edges roll under in summer. Flowers are more than an inch long, pink to pinkish purple, and bell-shaped. They bloom in broad rounded clusters between April and August.

California rhododendron

California Sycamore

These large pretty trees thrive in the valleys of California at elevations below 6,500 feet. They have large stout trunks. The trunk often forks early and branches separate into picturesque shapes. The bark is mottled and distinctive, and the leaves are light green and star-shaped. The fruit forms small bristly red-brown balls grouped in stalks of three to seven. Its range is almost exclusively confined to California.

California sycamore

California Torreya

California torreya

Also called California nutmeg for the aromatic resemblance of its seeds to nutmeg spice, California torreya is found only in the Golden State. Other parts of the tree have a different, disagreeable odor. California torreya reaches heights between 15 and 70 feet. Its slender branches spread into a conical crown. Needles are evergreen and arranged in two rows. Each sharp spike is about 2 inches in length. Fruit is small, green, and olivelike. The seeds and male pollen cones are found on separate trees. California torreya grows in the coastal ranges and on the western slopes of the Sierra Nevada. It grows among conifers and along mountain streams at elevations from sea level to 6,500 feet.

California torreya branch

California White Fir

California white fir is a very large conifer, growing to heights up to 160 feet. Its whitish coloring can be seen throughout the tree. The bark is light gray and deeply furrowed near the base. Twigs are gray-brown. The evergreen needles are light blue-green with whitish lines. California white fir can be found in pure and mixed stands in Northern California's mountains and throughout the Sierra Nevada at elevations between 3,000 and 10,000 feet. During the holiday season, it is used as a Christmas tree.

California white fir

Chamise

Chamise is the most common shrub of the California chaparral. It is also known as greasewood because of its oily, stringy wood. Chamise grows as an erect shrub or small tree to heights of about 10 feet. The leaves are needlelike and evergreen. It is most prominent in May and June, when it blooms in dense clusters of tiny white flowers. It is common in all of Northern California except the extreme northwest.

Chamise

Cinquefoils

California is home to Pacific cinquefoils and shrubby cinquefoils, also known as yellow rose. These shrubs both have yellow flowers that measure about 1 inch across, with five petals each. Cinquefoils keep their leaves in winter; some animals eat them when food is scarce, although they don't seem to enjoy the taste. Cinquefoils are found during the summer in open woods and meadows.

Cinquefoil

Coulter Pine

The species Coulter pine, found only in California, was identified in 1831 by Irish botanist Thomas Coulter. It is often known as bigcone pine because of the extraordinary weight of the cones, which often have a mass of 4 to 5 pounds. The needles are evergreen and come in bunches of three. The shape of the tree is similar to a Christmas tree. The wood is often used as rough lumber and as firewood. Native Americans collected the large, elliptical seeds for food; they are also a favorite for squirrels.

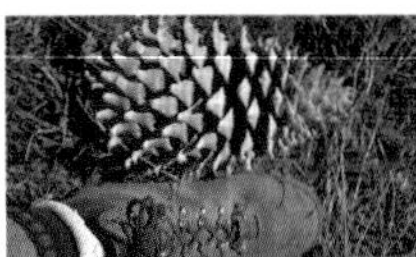
Coulter pine cone

Coulter pine

Dogwood

Dogwood grows throughout Northern California's mountains to elevations of about 6,500 feet. Its dense, conical, or rounded crown often reaches as high as 50 feet. Bark is reddish brown, and either smooth or scaly. Leaves are shiny green on top, paler and hairy below. Dogwood is grown as an ornamental tree because of its beautiful white flowers. Blooming occurs in spring and early summer; sometimes a second blooming occurs in September. Flowers are made up of four to seven petal-like bracts around a dense cluster of tiny flowers.

Dogwood

Douglas Fir

Douglas fir, also known as red pine, is a conical evergreen with flattened needlelike leaves that are yellow-green or blue-green. Trees are pyramid-shaped when young, but the crown becomes irregular with age. The bark is dark red-brown and smooth on young trees; it becomes thick, furrowed, and corky on older trees. At the end of the twigs there is usually one, though sometimes more than one, cone-shaped, sharp-pointed, reddish brown, oblong cone with three-pronged tongues sticking out

Douglas fir

between the cone scales. The cones are 3 to 4 inches long. Douglas firs are long-lived conifers that grow in vast forests, often in pure stands, in well-drained soil at elevations from sea level to 9,000 feet. They are also found in canyons below 6,000 feet. Among the world's most important timber trees, Douglas firs are often used for reforestation. In California, height ranges from 60 to 180 feet.

Douglas fir pine cones

Ferns

California is host to myriad species of fern. Ferns thrive in shady forests and valleys, where they often make up much of the undergrowth. Ferns are seedless plants; they reproduce by releasing spores from tiny sacks on the underside of leaves. In spring, small young ferns sprout as fiddleheads. They are called fiddleheads because their coiled heads resemble the end of a violin. Fiddleheads of some species are considered delicacies, but only experts can distinguish the edible varieties from poisonous look-alikes. The most common fern is called bracken. It is a deep green plant with long triangular leaflets. Most other ferns bear a general resemblance to bracken.

Bracken fern

Deer fern

Fremont Cottonwood

Cottonwoods are deciduous members of the poplar family. The Fremont cottonwood is named for John Charles Frémont, an early explorer of the West prominent in California's early history. Frémont found these trees useful throughout his expeditions because their presence indicated nearby water and provided shady resting spots. They are short-lived, fast-growing trees that produce an abundance of seeds. Male and female flowers bloom on separate trees in clusters of tiny petal-less flowers (catkins) in spring before leaves appear. The cotton-haired seeds, produced in small capsules, are carried to new locations by the wind. In suburban areas, this tree is sometimes prohibited because of the mess caused by the amount of "cotton" it yields. Fremont cottonwood foliage is dark shiny green above and paler below, and turns dull yellow in the fall.

Fremont cottonwood

Sometimes confused with aspens, the Fremont cottonwood is distinguished by larger, coarser, more deeply toothed triangular leaves; the trees are also larger than aspens and have coarser bark, except when young. The bark is whitish and smooth on young trees and thick, rough, and light gray or brownish on mature trees. Found along streams and in moist places below 6,000 feet, Fremont cottonwoods are important to riparian areas and coniferous forests. Mule deer and cattle often browse the twigs and foliage. Frémont referred to it as "sweet cottonwood" because his horses could eat its inner bark. This handsome hardwood usually reaches a height between 40 and 90 feet. Its cousin, black cottonwood, reaches similar heights.

Giant Sequoia

The giant sequoias of California are among the largest and oldest living things on earth. Almost all of these magnificent giants, remnants from the age of dinosaurs, are protected in Sequoia, Kings Canyon, and Yosemite National Parks. The trees have a tall, bare, reddish brown trunk; the diameter at the base sometimes exceeds 20 feet. The leaves are evergreen and scalelike, and the cones are pinelike. Sequoias grow to astonishing heights: usually between 150 and 250 feet tall. The largest of the species is a tree in Kings Canyon National Park named General Sherman, which is 275 feet tall, with a base diameter of 36 feet, a weight of about 2.7 million pounds, and an estimated age of 2,300 years. Rings on other trees imply ages more than 3,200 years old. Many of these ancient trees were irresponsibly felled in earlier times, and now the wood is no longer used as lumber.

Giant sequoia

The trees were named after a Cherokee Indian, Sequoya, the only inventor of a tribal alphabet in North America. Sequoya was the grandson of George Washington's personal guide, Christopher Gist.

Hemlock

Two species of hemlock, the mountain hemlock and the western hemlock are found in Northern California. Hemlocks are evergreen conifers. They have long trunks and narrow crowns of horizontal or drooping branches. Western hemlock is the largest North American hemlock, reaching heights of 150 feet. Its thick bark is reddish or grayish brown. Its 1-inch-long oval cones hang down from its branches. Although it is one of the most common trees in the Pacific Northwest, western hemlock's range extends only to the extreme northwestern corner of California, where it is found at elevations below 2,300 feet.

Mountain hemlock

Mountain hemlock cones

Mountain hemlock is smaller than the western variety; mature trees are between 30 and 100 feet tall. Mountain hemlock bark is darker and its cones are larger—2 inches long. Its habitat is the moist subalpine zone of Northern California's mountains—elevations from 4,000 feet to tree line. Toward tree line, trees are smaller and shrubbier.

North American hemlock is not related to the poisonous European and Asian plant.

Incense Cedar

Found throughout California at elevations between 1,000 and 8,000 feet, incense cedar is named for its aromatic wood. The tree is felled for a variety of purposes, including clothes, chests, and closets. It is also a leading source of pencil wood because it is soft but does not easily splinter. It is recognizable by its red-brown deeply furrowed bark and dense foliage crown. Long scalelike leaves end in hanging oblong cones composed of six flattened scales. The thick bark of mature trees enables them to survive forest fires.

Incense cedar

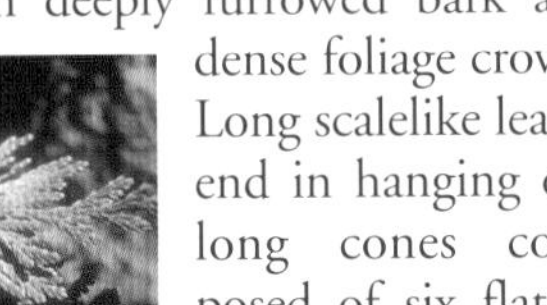

Incense cedar foliage

Jeffrey Pine

Also known as western yellow pine or bull pine, Jeffrey pine was named after the man who identified the species, John Jeffrey, a nineteenth-century Scottish botanist. Jeffrey pine is found almost solely in the state of California, most commonly on the eastern slopes of the Sierra Nevada at elevations between 6,000 and 9,000 feet. It grows to heights of 130 feet. The long evergreen needles come in bundles of three, and the cones are egg-shaped or conical. They are 5 to 10 inches long and end in a sharp bent-back prickle. The bark is purplish or reddish brown and furrowed into scaly plates. When crushed, both the bark and the twigs give off a pleasant odor that is commonly likened to vanilla or lemon.

Jeffrey pine

Jeffrey pine cone

Junipers

Members of the cypress family, western junipers and California junipers are found throughout plateaus, plains, foothills, and the pinyon-juniper belt. Similar in appearance, they grow from 10 to 40 feet tall with rounded crowns. These trees often have several branches that are as large as the main stem extending from ground level. The yellowish green foliage is scale-shaped and is pressed tightly against the twigs. Bark ranges from gray-brown to gray, growing whiter as the tree ages. It is fibrous and tends to shred in long strips. California junipers have coppery cones, about 1/2 inch in diameter, covered with a bluish waxy substance. The branches of one-seed junipers arise from the base of the trunk, giving the tree a globular appearance. All juniper berries serve as an important food source for some birds and small wildlife.

California juniper

California juniper

Knobcone Pine

Knobcone pine is distinguished from other pines by its closed knobby cones. The 4-inch, yellowish cones occur in bunches. These bunches often become embedded in an expanding branch or trunk. If a forest fire sweeps through a stand of knobcone pines, decades old cones are revealed and open to shed their seeds, replanting the stand. Found in Northern California at elevations around 1,000 or 2,000 feet, knobcone pine adapts well to rocky mountain soils. Its needles are evergreen, 3 to 7 inches long, and arranged in bundles of three. Bark is gray and gets darker as the tree ages. Knobcone pines grow to heights between 30 and 80 feet.

Knobcone pine

Knobcone cones

Lodgepole Pine

The bark of lodgepole pine trees is thin and loosely scaly. The foliage is yellow-green. Needles are 1 to 3 inches long and grow in pairs. The trees have yellow-brown egg-shaped cones that range in length from 3/4 to 2 inches. These resin-sealed cones remain on the trees for many years. In the event of a forest fire, the resin melts away, causing the cones to open and distribute the seeds to regenerate the species. These trees vary enormously in size, from 15 to 90

Lodgepole pine

Lodgepole cones

feet high. The Pacific variety is generally small with a broad rounded crown; the variety in the Sierra Nevada is usually tall with a narrow conical dense crown. The taller trees look like fields of evenly spaced telephone poles with little separating them but fallen needles. They grow smaller at higher elevations, where winds twist them into gnarled, bent shapes. Lodgepole pines can grow at elevations between sea level and 11,500 feet, depending on the climate.

Manzanita

Manzanita is a California peculiarity. There are about 40 species of this native shrub, mainly found in the north of the state. A few of the species, including the common manzanita, grow to the size of small trees (often 20 feet or more). Botanists disagree on whether the common manzanita should be classified as a tree or a shrub. The contention is that manzanitas branch near the ground and thus lack the single trunk that characterizes a tree.

Manzanita

Manzanita is a Spanish word that means "little apple." The fruit is enjoyed by a variety of wildlife and was also eaten by Native Americans, who often fermented a manzanita cider. Manzanita's dense foliage provides a refuge for birds and small mammals; it is very unpleasant to hike through dense growths of the shrub. Its reddish brown branches twist into aesthetically pleasing shapes; they are termed "mountain driftwood" and are often trimmed into collectors' items.

Manzanita fruit

Mountain Mahogany

Two types of mountain mahogany—curl-leaf and birch-leaf—are found in Northern California. Mountain mahogany is not related to true mahogany, the tropical tree that yields valuable furniture wood, but its heartwood has a similar reddish brown color. Both varieties of mountain mahogany in California grow as large shrubs or small trees. Their fruit, which occurs in summer, is also similar—seedlike, with long white hairy tails. The fruit gets carried for long distances by the wind, or in the coats of wild animals. Flowers are also alike—small, yellowish, and funnel-like. Both varieties bloom in early spring, birch-leaf slightly earlier than curl-leaf.

Mountain mahogany

Despite their similarities, the two types of mountain mahogany are easily distinguished by (as their names suggest) their leaves. Birch-leaf mountain mahogany, prominent on the dry rocky slopes of the northwestern coastal ranges below 6,500 feet, has elliptical evergreen leaves reminiscent of birch trees. It is also known as hardtack because of its ability to survive drought or fire. Curl-leaf mountain mahogany, found most commonly in the Sierra Nevada between 4,000 and 9,000 feet, has small, narrow evergreen leaves with rolled edges. Deer browse on the leaves of both varieties year-round.

Mountain mahogany leaves

Oaks

California has 20 species of oak, more than half of which can be found nowhere else in the world. Oak trees are prominent throughout the state. The acorn was a staple of aboriginal Californians' diets; it was ground and rinsed to remove tannin, then prepared as a bread or in soup. Most Central California Indians celebrated some sort of acorn harvest ritual. Oak is an important hardwood, prized as a timber source.

California black oaks

The largest of California's oaks is probably the valley oak (or California white oak), which grows in wooded inland foothills. It reaches heights over 100 feet. By contrast, California scrub oak rarely exceeds 10 feet. A particularly recognizable species of oak is the blue oak, whose bluish foliage can be

California scrub oak and acorns   Canyon live oak and acorns

Valley oak

picked out from a distance. Perhaps the most beautiful of the varied oak species found in California is the canyon live oak, whose crown spreads out into broad picturesque shapes. The oak most valued for commercial use is the Oregon white oak, which is used for everything from furniture to fuel. Native Americans prized the acorns of the Oregon white oak for their sweet flavor. Other common species include the interior live oak and the California black oak. The different oaks occur in pure stands and in mixed forests. Certain species have suffered heavily from disease in recent years and efforts are now underway to replenish them.

Valley oak leaves

Oregon Ash

Oregon ash is found along streams and in shaded canyons of mountainous Northern California below 5,000 feet. Mature trees grow 60 to 80 feet tall. Oregon ash leaves are large—5 to 12 inches long—and split from twigs in opposite pairs with a single leaf at the twig's end. Bark is gray and furrowed into forking ridges. Oregon ash blooms in early spring before leaves appear. The light brown flowers are 1 to 2 inches long.

Oregon ash

Oregon ash is the only western ash important for commercial purposes. Some of its uses include furniture, flooring, boxes, and fuel. Velvet ash, endemic to California, is found more in the south of the state, but occurs locally in northern mountains.

Oregon ash leaves

Pacific Madrone

This 40- to 100-foot tree varies widely in shape and height. Trunks can be straight or crooked and distinctive features include peeling bark, evergreen leaves, and a rather sparse look. It bears small white bell-shaped flowers in the spring that mature into red or orange berries in late summer. These berries are a favorite food source to small animals and birds, particularly the band-tailed pigeon. Pacific madrone has a beautiful and distinctive tree bark. In early summer, most of the bark peels, leaving a smooth and pale green surface that soon becomes a rich red-brown color, and the trunk often acquires an interesting gnarled form. The thick leathery leaves are dark green on top and the undersides are pale green. Native Americans brewed a medicinal tea from the bark or leaves, which they used to treat colds and stomach ailments. Pacific madrone is usually found as a single tree or in small groves in dry areas from the Cascade or Sierra foothills to the Pacific, at elevations to 6,000 feet.

Pacific madrone

Pacific madrone bark and leaves

Pacific Yew

Northern California is the southernmost habitat of the Pacific yew, found in coastal regions as far north as southeastern Alaska. It is an evergreen that grows to heights of 40 or 50 feet. Its crown is broad and irregular, its trunk is often angled, and its bark is purplish brown and thin. Pacific yews often form an understory of coniferous forests. In Northern California, they survive in elevations up to 7,000 feet. All parts of Pacific yew are poisonous and possibly fatal if eaten by humans. Birds eat the juicy cup outside seeds. The strong wood was used by Native Americans to manufacture bows and canoe paddles. It is still utilized by some carpenters, but its small range limits use.

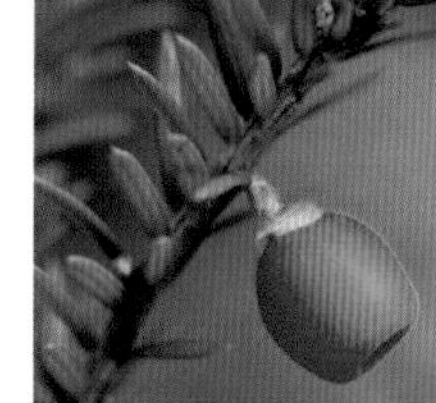
Pacific yew

Ponderosa Pine

Also called western yellow pine, the ponderosa pine has long needles—4 to 11 inches—which grow in clusters of three from a single point. The bark of young trees is yellowish brown to cinnamon; older trees develop orange flaky bark. The spiky red-brown cones are about 3 to 6 inches long. Seed cones provide an important food source for wildlife. Ponderosa pines can grow 60 to 125 feet tall and are usually found at elevations of 6,000 to 8,500 feet. The species was named in 1826 by Scottish botanist David Douglas for its ponderous (heavy) wood. Ponderosa pine is the most common and widely distributed pine in North America, and its wood is often used for doors and window frames.

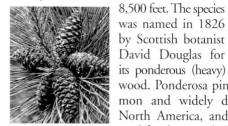

Ponderosa pine

Ponderosa pine cones

Port Orford Cedar

Port Orford cedar occurs naturally only in a narrow coastal belt encompassing part of northwestern California and

Port Orford cedar

southwestern Oregon. It is grown as an ornamental and shade tree in other countries. Dwarf and drooping varieties of Port Orford cedar have been cultivated. Named after Port Orford, Oregon, the species requires wet winters and foggy summers to survive—it is well adapted to its climate.

Port Orford cedars are large evergreen trees that grow from 70 to 200 feet tall. Their trunks are enlarged at the base, with diameters of 6 or more feet at the bottom not uncommon. Leaves are scaled and branch in opposite pairs. Bark is thick, furrowed, and reddish brown, though silvery red when stripped. Cones are small—about 1/2 inch in diameter—and found in clusters. Not a true cedar, Port Orford cedar is actually a member of the cypress family.

Port Orford cedar leaves

Quaking Aspen

Quaking aspen have smooth cream-colored bark with green heart-shaped deciduous leaves that turn brilliant gold in fall. Older trees are dark at the base. The aspens grow from 40 to 70 feet tall and are 1 to 2 feet in diameter. In California, they are normally found at elevations between 6,000 and 10,000 feet in dry, cool places, often close to clean, flowing water. Groves of these trees allow sunlight to penetrate to the forest floor, thus encouraging diverse plant growth and providing food and shelter for numerous wildlife species. They are called quaking aspen because they shake at the slightest breeze.

Quaking aspen

Redwood

Northern California's most famous tree, the redwood is the world's tallest. The tallest of the tall was measured at 368 feet, and most mature trees reach at least 200 feet. Redwood bark is thick, reddish brown, very tough, and fibrous. Leaves are evergreen and needlelike, though shorter and scalelike on the highest shoots. Redwood cones are relatively small—only about an inch long. They are reddish brown spheres, hanging from twigs. Redwood trunks taper upward from a large base; base diameters are usually between 10 and 15 feet, though sometimes larger. Redwoods, in contrast to their massive sequoia cousins, appear to be slim. Redwoods generally live for 400 to 500 years, but one felled tree was judged to be 2,200 years old by the annual rings of its stump. Often, young redwoods will grow from the stump of an old tree.

Redwood foliage

Redwoods are found solely in a coastal strip from southwestern Oregon to Monterey County; only a small fraction of the pre-Euro-American settlement redwood population remains. They are protected in many state parks, including Redwood National Park and along the Redwood Highway, but earlier logging destroyed many dense pure redwood forests. Selective logging continues today.

Sitka Spruce

Sitka spruce is an evergreen. Its needles are short (less than an inch in length), dark green, and flattened, and they cover twigs. Cylindrical cones 2 to 4 inches in length hang down from the branches. The cone scales are very thin. The tree's bark is gray and thin; in older trees the bark becomes dark purplish brown and forms scaly plates.

With a usual height of about 160 feet, Sitka spruce is the largest spruce in the world. It is the most important timber tree in Alaska, and northwestern California is the southernmost extent of its range. Products made from Sitka spruce include piano sound boards, boats, and wood pulp. Sitka spruce grows in cold areas that have high annual rainfall, often in moist soils near coastal river mouths. It is found in pure stands and in conjunction with western hemlocks. In California it rarely occurs above 1,200 feet.

Sitka spruce

Sugar Pine

Sugar pine, an evergreen, is named for the sweet resin that oozes from cuts. Found in mixed coniferous forests throughout Northern California's mountain ranges, sugar pine is recognizable by its large cylindrical cones that often measure 18 inches in length, the largest of any conifer. It is a fairly tall tree, regularly reaching heights of more than 100 feet, and it has been recorded being as tall as 241 feet. The trunk diameter is also impressive—often 8 feet or more. The sugar pine is quite beautiful. Its large trunk extends very high before it branches, and the branches are long and almost horizontal. The long straight trunk makes it an important lumber source. Its needles occur in bundles of five. Its bark is red-brown or grayish and furrowed into irregular ridges. Its size and beauty, coupled with its gigantic cones, have led some to call it the "king of the pines."

Sugar pine

Sugar pine cones

Settlers used sugar pine extensively—as firewood and to build houses, fences, and panning flumes, among other things. Native Americans ate the large sweet seeds.

Tanoak

Although their acorns closely resemble those of oaks, botanists place tanoaks in a separate genus. However, the trees are often found interspersed in oak forests. Tanoaks are distinguished by their oblong leaves, which lack the ridge pattern of true oaks and instead resemble chestnut leaves. Tanoak bark is grayish brown, and it was once the main commercial source of tannin in the West. Tanoaks prefer moist valleys and mountain slopes. They are concentrated in northwestern California but are also found in the northern Sierra Nevada and the coastal ranges as far south as Ventura. Native Americans used tanoak acorns similarly to true oak acorns by grinding them into flour, steeping the flour in water to remove the tannin, and preparing them in various food dishes.

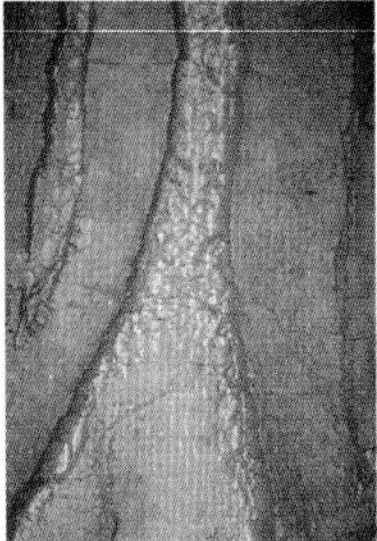

Tanoak bark and leaves

Two-petal Ash

Two-petal ash is a small tree common in the inner coastal ranges of Northern and Central California and the foothills of the Sierra Nevada. It grows to heights of about 15 feet. Two-petal ash is a native of the state and is rarely found elsewhere. It is recognizable by its snowy white flowers, and it is often planted as an ornamental shrub. The petals of this ash are divided into two at the end of a narrow lobe. Leaves are dark green, about 5 inches long, with $1^1/_2$-inch leaflets.

Two-petal ash

Two-petal ash flowers

Western Azalea

Ranging from Southern California to southwestern Oregon, western azalea is a large deciduous shrub. From April to August, large clusters of white or pinkish flowers bloom at the ends of its stems. The flowers are very fragrant. Leaves are 1 to 3 inches long and elliptical. Western azalea is generally found in moist or shaded areas below 7,500 feet. It grows to heights between 3 and 17 feet.

Western azalea

Western Poison Oak

Western poison oak is a shrub or climbing vine that can cause great discomfort if it touches bare skin. The leaves are recognizable by three shiny ovate leaflets that often have a reddish green or crimson color. The flowers are very small and greenish white. Berries come in clusters of tiny whitish balls. Beware! Western poison oak is common in Northern California's oak woodlands.

Western poison oak leaf

Western White Pine

Western white pine ranges from Central California to Canada. It is one of the tallest pines in North America, and one tree in southern Oregon was recorded to be 239 feet tall. In Northern California, it is found in the snowy upper montane and subalpine areas below 9,000 feet. Needles come in bunches of five; like other white pines with this characteristic, the western white pine has been hit by white pine blister rust, which is caused by an introduced fungus. Its cones are long, curved, and cylindrical and hang down, ending in a small point. Western white pine is an important timber tree; it is of a uniformly high grade and rarely has knots or twists.

Western white pine bark and cones

White Fir

White fir, also known as balsam fir or silver fir, grows to 130 feet tall and 4 or 5 feet in diameter. The ashy gray-brown bark has deep fissures and can be 4 to 6 inches thick. Bark on the upper branches is smoother and more silvery white in color. White fir has longer needles than most firs (2 to 3 inches); they are flat, bluish green, and grow directly from the branch. These needles generally curve upward from the bottom of the branches, although those on lower branches may be more horizontal with less curvature. White fir foliage tends to be extremely dense with a somewhat scraggly and irregular appearance. Oblong purplish green cones (3 to 5 inches long) sit on the top of the upper branches and fall apart when they mature.

White fir

White fir cone

In Northern California, white firs are found on moist mountain slopes throughout the Sierra, often in pure stands (but also mixed forests), at elevations ranging from 3,000 to 10,000 feet.

Whitebark Pine

Whitebark pine grows in dry rocky soils of subalpine forests, which in Northern California is between 8,000 and 12,000 feet. At tree line, it forms dense shrubs or thickets, and its grayish white bark and purplish egg-shaped cones distinguish it from other pines. One bird—Clark's nutcracker—rips open the cones to eat the seeds. Otherwise, the cones do not open until they decay. Whitebark pine crowns are irregularly shaped and widely spread; trees sometimes have multiple trunks. Its evergreen needles grow in bundles of five, and they are light green or yellowish green.

Whitebark pine

Whitebark pine needles

Winter Fat

Winter fat is also called white sage, sweet sage, or winter sage, although it is not related to sage at all. The plant has many erect woolly branches that arise from a woody base. It has flowering clusters that when gone to seed fluff out to look like cotton balls. The plant has a fuzzy, white, and hairy appearance because of the densely woolly leaves that cover the entire plant. Leaves are dry in the fall but remain on the plant throughout winter. Winter fat serves as an important winter food source for wildlife and livestock.

Winter fat

The High Sierra Region

Trails in the High Sierra Region

- HS1 Dinkey-Trimmer Road *(DR: 1; 26.7 miles; page 162)*
- HS2 Sycamore Springs Trail *(DR: 3; 9.2 miles; page 165)*
- HS3 Kings River Trail *(DR: 2; 6.7 miles; page 168)*
- HS4 Sawmill Flat Road *(DR: 1; 10.1 miles; page 170)*
- HS5 Granite Gorge Overlook Trail *(DR: 3; 4.4 miles; page 172)*
- HS6 Spanish OHV Route *(DR: 7; 5 miles; page 174)*
- HS7 Bald Mountain OHV Route *(DR: 5; 3.4 miles; page 176)*
- HS8 Brewer Lake OHV Route *(DR: 5; 4.3 miles; page 178)*
- HS9 Big Creek Railroad Grade Trail *(DR: 1; 12.8 miles; page 179)*
- HS10 Balloon Dome Overlook Trail *(DR: 2; 23.1 miles; page 182)*
- HS11 Mount Tom Fire Lookout Trail *(DR: 3; 2.7 miles; page 186)*
- HS12 Bear Diversion Dam OHV Route *(DR: 4; 2.3 miles; page 187)*
- HS13 Onion Spring OHV Route *(DR: 4; 5.7 miles; page 189)*
- HS14 Peckinpah Road *(DR: 2; 20 miles; page 191)*
- HS15 Whisky Ridge Trail *(DR: 4; 4 miles; page 194)*
- HS16 Browns Meadow Trail *(DR: 4; 5.1 miles; page 196)*
- HS17 Central Camp Road *(DR: 1; 17.8 miles; page 198)*
- HS18 Shuteye Peak Trail *(DR: 5; 6.6 miles; page 201)*
- HS19 Fresno Dome Road *(DR: 2; 15.3 miles; page 202)*
- HS20 Quartz Mountain Trail *(DR: 2; 9.2 miles; page 206)*
- HS21 Iron Lakes Trail *(DR: 5; 3.1 miles; page 208)*
- HS22 Sugar Pine Road *(DR: 3; 8 miles; page 209)*
- HS23 Miami Trail *(DR: 3; 28.6 miles; page 211)*
- HS24 Ferguson Ridge Trail *(DR: 2; 12.7 miles; page 216)*
- HS25 Hite Cove Road *(DR: 6; 5.1 miles; page 219)*
- HS26 Merced River Road *(DR: 1; 4.9 miles; page 221)*
- HS27 Burma Grade Trail *(DR: 3; 15.4 miles; page 223)*
- HS28 Old Coulterville Road *(DR: 1/3; 31.4 miles; page 226)*
- HS29 Crocker Ridge Trail *(DR: 3; 4.1 miles; page 230)*
- HS30 Trumbull Peak Trail *(DR: 3; 7.9 miles; page 232)*
- HS31 Bodie Ghost Town Trail *(DR: 2; 26.6 miles; page 234)*
- HS32 Masonic Trail *(DR: 2; 14.3 miles; page 238)*
- HS33 Mono Lake Trail *(DR: 3; 12.5 miles; page 242)*
- HS34 Mono Craters Trail *(DR: 3; 9.1 miles; page 244)*
- HS35 Sawmill Meadow Road *(DR: 2; 29.4 miles; page 246)*
- HS36 Kelty Meadows Trail *(DR: 3; 15.6 miles; page 250)*
- HS37 Deer Mountain Trail *(DR: 3; 11.3 miles; page 252)*
- HS38 Laurel Lakes Trail *(DR: 4; 8.7 miles; page 256)*
- HS39 Convict Lake Overlook Trail *(DR: 3; 4 miles; page 258)*
- HS40 Casa Diablo Road *(DR: 1; 23.5 miles; page 259)*
- HS41 Coyote Creek Trail *(DR: 3; 16.2 miles; page 262)*
- HS42 Coyote Flat Trail *(DR: 4; 8.6 miles; page 264)*
- HS43 White Mountain Road *(DR: 1; 22 miles; page 266)*
- HS44 Silver Canyon Trail *(DR: 3; 11.1 miles; page 269)*
- HS45 Saline Valley Road *(DR: 2; 91.4 miles; page 271)*
- HS46 Papoose Flat Trail *(DR: 4; 16.3 miles; page 277)*
- HS47 The Narrows Trail *(DR: 3; 14.1 miles; page 280)*
- HS48 Harkless Flat Trail *(DR: 5; 6.3 miles; page 283)*
- HS49 Mazourka Peak Trail *(DR: 2; 16.1 miles; page 285)*
- HS50 Sierra View Trail *(DR: 5; 14.3 miles; page 288)*

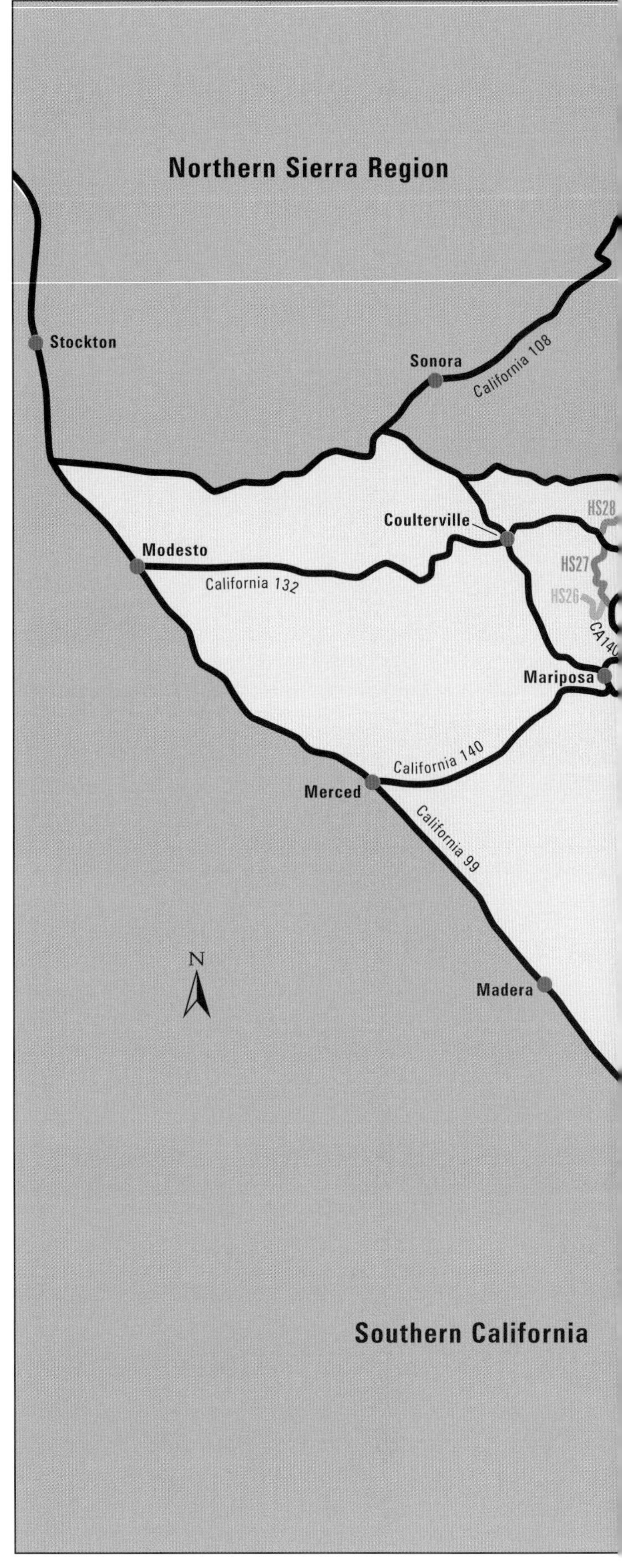

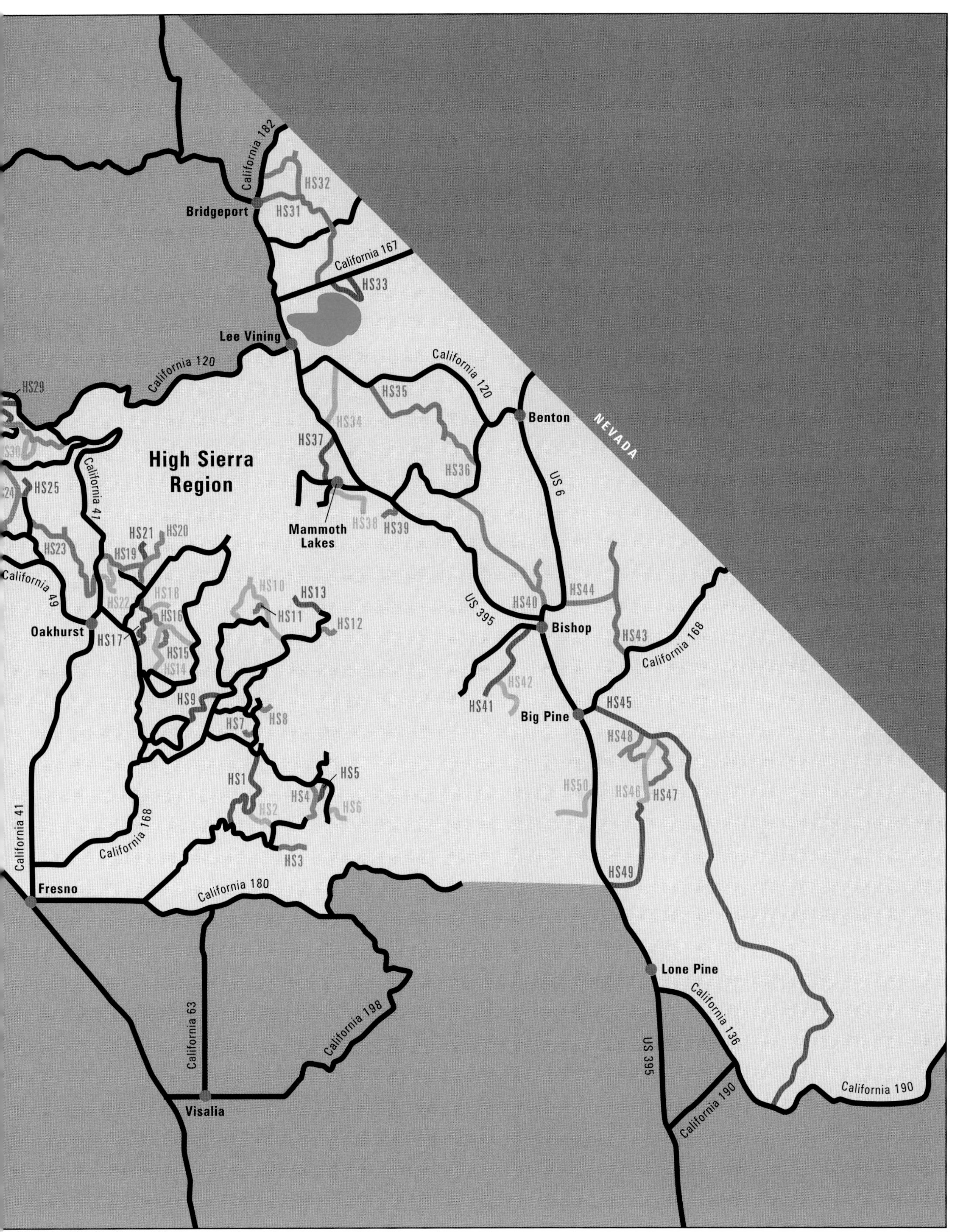

High Sierra Region
Bridgeport
Lee Vining
Mammoth Lakes
Benton
Bishop
Big Pine
Lone Pine
Oakhurst
Fresno
Visalia
NEVADA
California 182
California 167
California 120
California 41
California 49
California 168
California 180
California 63
California 198
California 136
California 190
US 6
US 395
HS1
HS2
HS3
HS4
HS5
HS6
HS7
HS8
HS9
HS10
HS11
HS12
HS13
HS14
HS15
HS16
HS17
HS18
HS19
HS20
HS21
HS22
HS23
HS25
HS29
HS31
HS32
HS33
HS34
HS35
HS36
HS37
HS38
HS39
HS40
HS41
HS42
HS43
HS44
HS45
HS46
HS47
HS48
HS49
HS50

HIGH SIERRA #1

Dinkey-Trimmer Road

Starting Point:	**Trimmer Springs Road, 7.9 miles east of Trimmer**
Finishing Point:	**Dinkey Creek Road, 0.9 miles west of Dinkey Creek**
Total Mileage:	**26.7 miles**
Unpaved Mileage:	**26.7 miles**
Driving Time:	**2.5 hours**
Elevation Range:	**1,000–6,000 feet**
Usually Open:	**May to November**
Best Time to Travel:	**Dry weather**
Difficulty Rating:	**1**
Scenic Rating:	**9**
Remoteness Rating:	**+0**

Special Attractions

- Swimming holes along Big Creek.
- Boating, fishing, and camping at Pine Flat Reservoir.
- Long trail that travels through oak and pine forests.

History

Dinkey Creek was named for an unfortunate hunting incident in the summer of 1863. Hunters camped near the then unnamed creek encountered a grizzly bear, an experience not uncommon at the time. Their little dog, Dinkey, was all too quick to defend them and lost the battle. Though undocumented, it is unlikely the grizzly survived either.

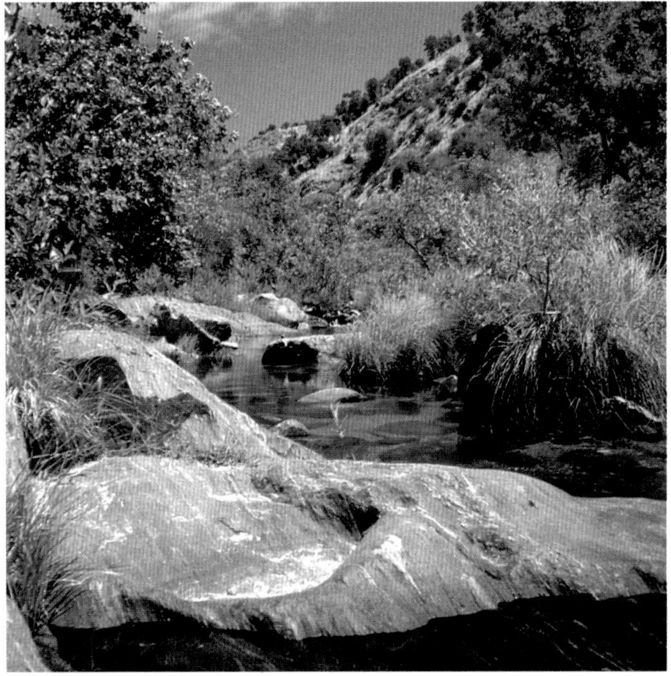

Gentle Big Creek attracts wildlife and has excellent swimming holes for hot summer days

Dinkey Creek's population is somewhat seasonal because it is largely a resort town. Local rancher Jack Ducey founded Camp Ducey as a mountain resort in 1925. It became popular with folks wishing to escape the sweltering summer heat of the nearby San Joaquin Valley. In its early days the camp had tents and outdoor dining areas. The resort changed hands over the years, and new owners made improvements, eventually adding a two-story hotel and dining room. The Buckhorn Café, a bar, a general store, a post office, and a service station were added in time. Open-air movies, large group barbecues, and live music played for dances held on an outdoor dance floor all contributed to the warm, welcoming atmosphere that became a tradition for many families.

The Dinkey Creek Fire of 1981 brought an end to the aging Camp Ducey. Today, the Dinkey Creek Inn caters to campers, travelers, and seasonal visitors. It is hard to re-create the homey atmosphere that developed over many years at the old camp.

Dinkey Creek Road passes through the Walter Watkins Plantation, which was named for the man responsible for revegetating this area after the Haslett Fire of 1961. Watkins served the Kings River Ranger District of Sierra National Forest from 1960 to 1984.

Trimmer, near the southern end of the trail, was named after Morris Trimmer, who developed Trimmer Estates.

Description

Dinkey-Trimmer Road is one of the major forest roads connecting Pine Flat Reservoir with Dinkey Creek and the heart of Sierra National Forest. The trail leaves Pine Flat Reservoir and enters Sierra National Forest, heading north on an easy graded road that travels along Big Creek. Big Creek has some excellent swimming holes with big boulders perfect for lying out in the sun. The creek is shaded in places by oaks and pines.

After FR 9 leaves to the north, Dinkey-Trimmer Road narrows to a single track, but it remains suitable for passenger vehicles in dry weather. It travels along a shelf road on the side of a mountain, offering great views east over Haslett Basin, Cats Head Mountain, and Eagle Peak.

After the turnoff to High Sierra #2: Sycamore Springs Trail, Dinkey-Trimmer Road swings away from the North Fork of the Kings River Valley. The main trail continues to climb, leaving behind the oaks and manzanitas of lower elevations to enter forests of pines and firs. A side trail leads 2 miles up to the Fence Meadow Fire Lookout. This is one of the few in the region that is still periodically manned. The gate to the tower will be open if someone is occupying it.

The final part of the road travels through privately owned forest. Although you can drive through, no camping or fires are allowed on the private property. Campers will find some good backcountry sites along the rest of the trail and developed campgrounds at Dinkey Creek and Trimmer. Note that the USFS campgrounds shown on the Sierra National Forest Map at Pine Flat Reservoir—Sycamore Flat No. 1 and No. 2 and Lakeview—are closed.

An old weir on Big Creek

The road is closed during winter to prevent surface erosion. Opening dates given above are approximate. Check with the forest service if in doubt.

Current Road Information

Sierra National Forest
High Sierra Ranger District
PO Box 559
Prather, CA 93651
(559) 855-5360

Map References

BLM Fresno, Shaver Lake
USFS Sierra National Forest
USGS 1:24,000 Sacate Ridge, Dinkey Creek
1:100,000 Fresno, Shaver Lake
Maptech CD-ROM: Central Coast/Fresno
Southern & Central California Atlas & Gazetteer, pp. 24, 25
Northern California Atlas & Gazetteer, p. 121
California Road & Recreation Atlas, p. 78

Route Directions

▼ 0.0 From Trimmer Springs Road, 7.9 miles east of Trimmer, zero trip meter and turn northwest on graded dirt FR 9 (10S69), following the sign to Haslett Basin. Turn is immediately west of the road bridge over Big Creek at the Sierra National Forest sign.
4.6 ▲ Trail ends at intersection with paved Trimmer Springs Road. Turn left for Balch Camp; turn right for Trimmer and Fresno.

GPS: N36°54.56′ W119°14.56′

▼ 2.8 SO Cattle guard; then track on right to campsite alongside creek.
1.8 ▲ SO Track on left to campsite alongside creek; then cattle guard.

GPS: N36°56.58′ W119°14.22′

▼ 3.2 SO Old weir on right.
1.4 ▲ SO Old weir on left.

GPS: N36°56.81′ W119°14.13′

▼ 4.1 SO Track on left and track on right to campsite.
0.5 ▲ SO Track on right and track on left to campsite.

GPS: N36°57.49′ W119°13.81′

▼ 4.6 SO Track on left; then second track on left is 10S04 marked to Soaproot Saddle. Zero trip meter.
0.0 ▲ Continue to the southeast on FR 9 (10S69), following sign to Pine Flat Reservoir.

GPS: N36°57.82′ W119°13.92′

▼ 0.0 Continue to the northwest on FR 9 (10S69), following sign to Haslett Basin.
2.8 ▲ SO Track on right is 10S04 marked to Soaproot Saddle; then second track on right. Zero trip meter.

▼ 0.2 SO Cross over Big Creek on bridge.
2.6 ▲ SO Cross over Big Creek on bridge.

▼ 1.0 SO Track on right; then track on left.
1.8 ▲ SO Track on right; then track on left.

▼ 1.8 SO Cattle guard.
1.0 ▲ SO Cattle guard.

▼ 2.8 SO Haslett Basin. Graded road on left is continuation of FR 9 to Blue Canyon. Zero trip meter.
0.0 ▲ Continue to the southwest and join FR 9, following sign to Pine Flat Reservoir.

GPS: N36°58.17′ W119°12.96′

▼ 0.0 Continue to the northeast onto 10S69, following sign to Dinkey Creek.
4.9 ▲ SO Haslett Basin. Graded road on right is FR 9 to Blue Canyon. Zero trip meter.

▼ 0.6 SO Track on left; then cross over Nutmeg Creek on bridge.
4.3 ▲ SO Cross over Nutmeg Creek on bridge; then track on right.

▼ 0.7 SO Track on right.
4.2 ▲ SO Track on left.

▼ 0.8 SO Cattle guard.
4.1 ▲ SO Cattle guard.

▼ 1.8 SO Track on left.
3.1 ▲ SO Track on right.

▼ 2.6 SO Track on right.
2.3 ▲ SO Track on left.

▼ 3.6 SO Track on right.
1.3 ▲ SO Track on left.

▼ 3.7 SO Cattle guard.
1.2 ▲ SO Cattle guard.

▼ 4.7 SO Seasonal closure gate.
0.2 ▲ SO Seasonal closure gate.

GPS: N36°56.18′ W119°12.30′

▼ 4.9 BL Track on right is High Sierra #2: Sycamore Springs Trail (11S02). Zero trip meter.
0.0 ▲ Continue to the northwest.

GPS: N36°56.08′ W119°12.18′

▼ 0.0 Continue to the northeast and pass through seasonal closure gate.
4.6 ▲ BR Seasonal closure gate; then track on left is High Sierra #2: Sycamore Springs Trail (11S02). Zero trip meter.

▼ 1.1 SO Track on left.
3.5 ▲ SO Track on right.

▼ 1.9 SO Track on right.
2.7 ▲ SO Track on left.

▼ 2.6 SO Cattle guard; then track on left to campsite.
2.0 ▲ SO Track on right to campsite; then cattle guard.

GPS: N36°56.82′ W119°11.00′

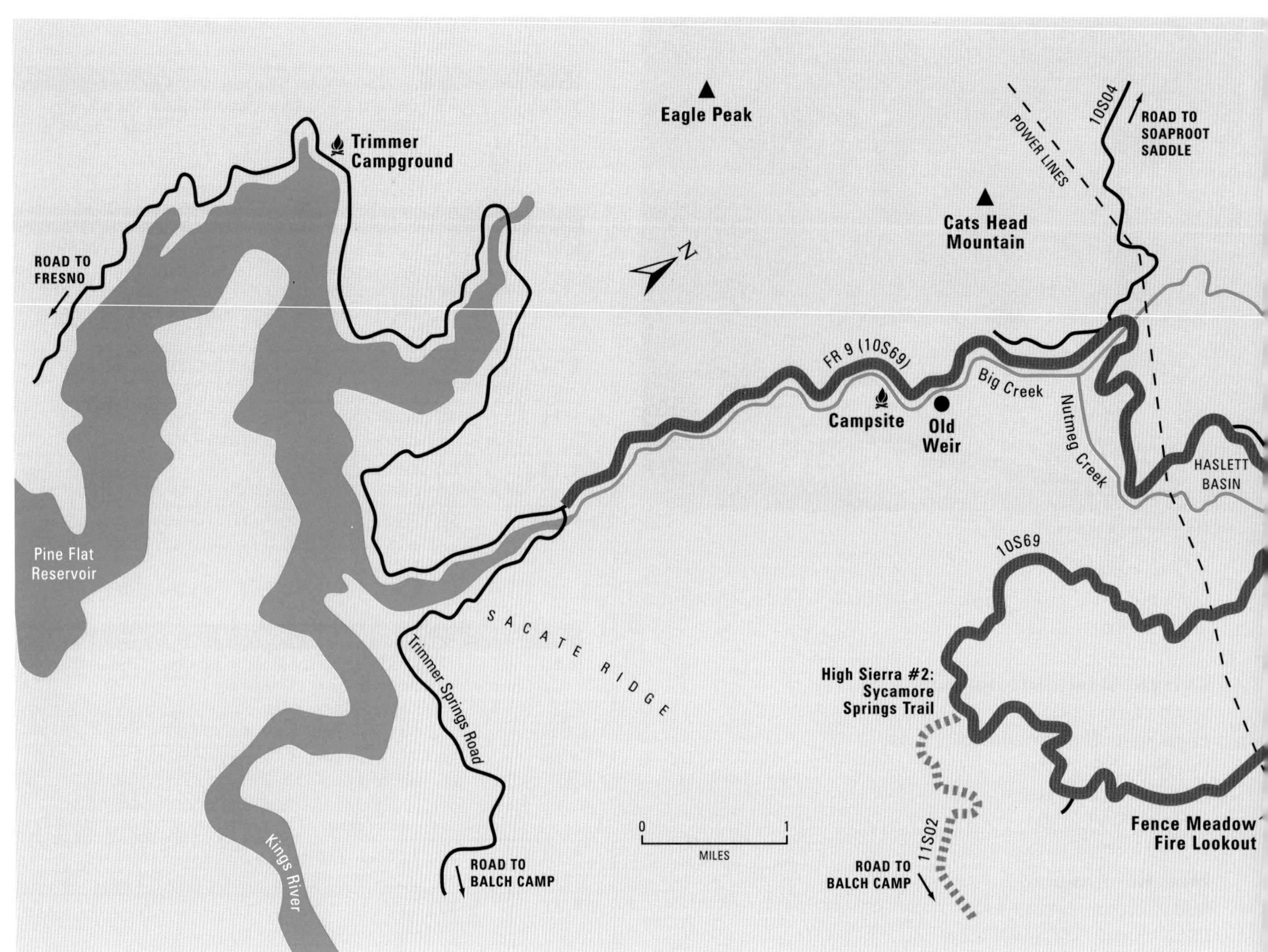

▼ 3.5	SO	Pass under power lines.
1.1 ▲	SO	Pass under power lines.
▼ 3.6	SO	Track on right.
1.0 ▲	SO	Track on left.
▼ 4.6	SO	Track on right is 11S08, which goes 2 miles to Fence Meadow Fire Lookout. Zero trip meter.
0.0 ▲		Continue to the south.
		GPS: N36°58.36′ W119°10.64′
▼ 0.0		Continue to the north.
3.5 ▲	SO	Track on left is 11S08, which goes 2 miles to Fence Meadow Fire Lookout. Zero trip meter.
▼ 0.6	SO	Track on right is 11S69.
2.9 ▲	SO	Track on left is 11S69.
		GPS: N36°58.74′ W119°10.57′
▼ 2.7	BL	Track on right gives access to Bear Meadow Creek.
0.8 ▲	SO	Track on left gives access to Bear Meadow Creek.
		GPS: N36°59.64′ W119°09.64′
▼ 3.2	SO	Track on left.
0.3 ▲	SO	Track on right.
▼ 3.5	SO	Track on left; then Nutmeg Saddle (4,827 feet). Track on right is Ross Crossing Road (10S67) to Oak Flat. Zero trip meter and continue straight ahead on 10S69, following sign to Dinkey Creek.
0.0 ▲		Continue to the east. Track on right.
		GPS: N36°59.65′ W119°10.37′
▼ 0.0		Continue to the northwest. Marker for Walter Watkins on left.
2.3 ▲	SO	Marker for Walter Watkins on right; then Nutmeg Saddle (4,827 feet). Track on left is Ross Crossing Road (10S67) to Oak Flat. Zero trip meter and continue straight ahead on 10S69, following sign to Fence Meadow.
▼ 1.1	SO	Track on right is 10S69A.
1.2 ▲	SO	Track on left is 10S69A.
▼ 2.1	SO	Track on left.
0.2 ▲	SO	Track on right.
▼ 2.3	SO	Road on right is 11S91. Zero trip meter.
0.0 ▲		Continue to the south.
		GPS: N37°00.63′ W119°11.57′
▼ 0.0		Continue to the north and enter private forest through seasonal closure gate—no camping or fires permitted.
4.0 ▲	SO	Exit private forest through seasonal closure gate; then road on left is 11S91. Zero trip meter.
▼ 1.4	SO	Track on left.
2.6 ▲	SO	Track on right.

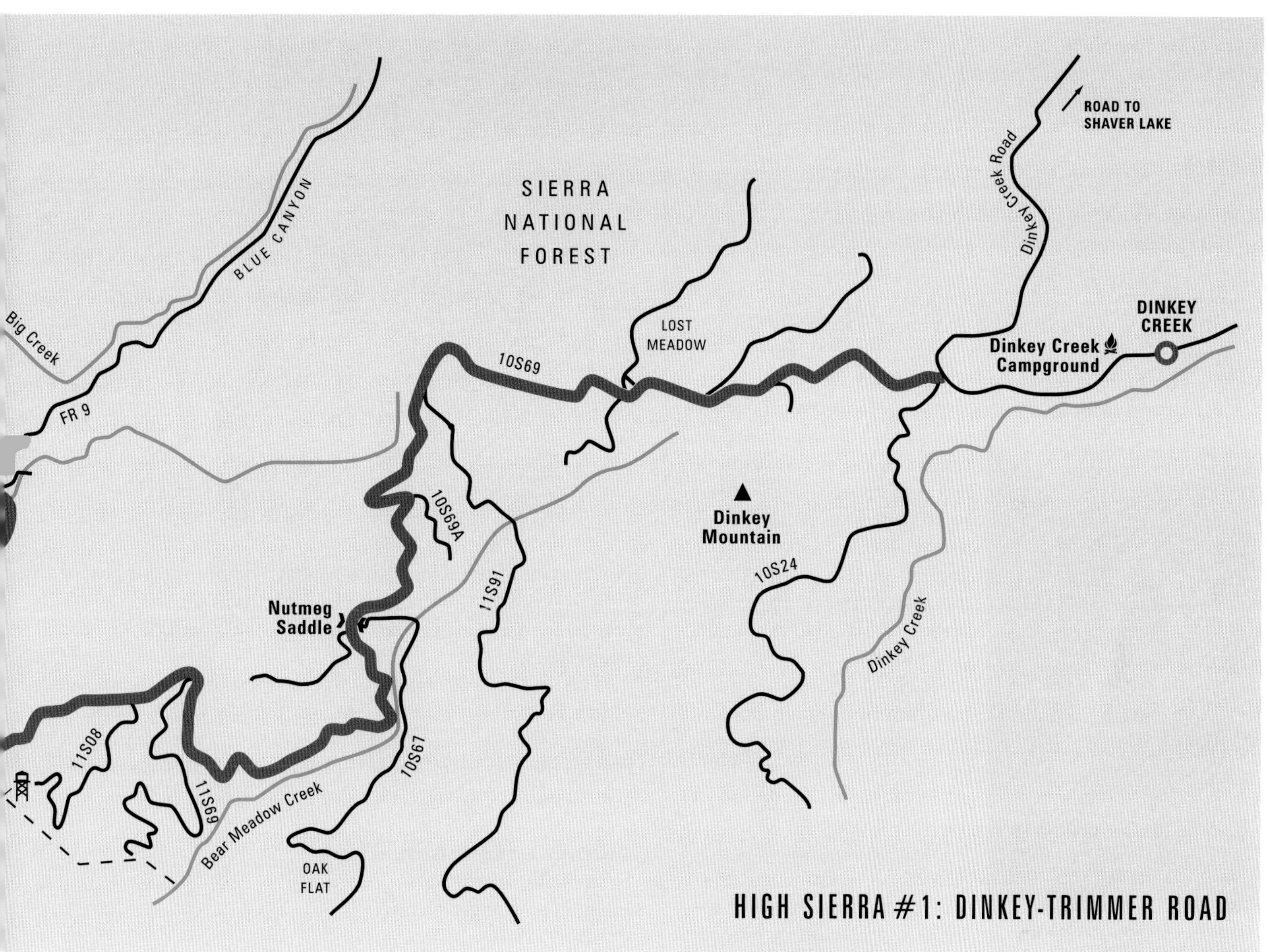

▼ 1.6	SO	Track on right; then two tracks on left to Lost Meadow.
2.4 ▲	SO	Two tracks on right to Lost Meadow; then track on left.
		GPS: N37°01.61' W119°10.83'
▼ 2.2	BR	Track on left.
1.8 ▲	SO	Track on right.
		GPS: N37°02.00' W119°10.53'
▼ 2.6	SO	Track on right.
1.4 ▲	SO	Track on left.
▼ 3.0	SO	Track on left.
1.0 ▲	SO	Track on right.
▼ 3.4	SO	Exiting private forest. Track on left.
0.6 ▲	SO	Track on right. Entering private forest—no camping or fires permitted.
▼ 4.0		Road on right is 10S24; then seasonal closure gate. Trail ends at T-intersection with paved Dinkey Creek Road. Turn right for Dinkey Creek; turn left for Shaver Lake.
0.0 ▲		Trail commences on Dinkey Creek Road, 0.9 miles west of Dinkey Creek. Zero trip meter and turn south on small paved road at sign for Fence Meadow and Pine Flat Reservoir. Immediately bear right onto 10S69. Road on left is 10S24. Road was once paved.
		GPS: N37°03.24' W119°09.84'

HIGH SIERRA #2

Sycamore Springs Trail

Starting Point:	**High Sierra #1: Dinkey-Trimmer Road (10S69), 12.3 miles northeast of Pine Flat Reservoir and 4.9 miles south of the intersection with FR 9**
Finishing Point:	**Black Rock Road at Balch Camp**
Total Mileage:	**9.2 miles**
Unpaved Mileage:	**9.1 miles**
Driving Time:	**1.5 hours**
Elevation Range:	**1,400–3,600 feet**
Usually Open:	**May to November**
Best Time to Travel:	**Dry weather**
Difficulty Rating:	**3**
Scenic Rating:	**9**
Remoteness Rating:	**+1**

Special Attractions

- Long winding shelf road.
- Unparalleled views of Patterson Bluffs and the North Fork of the Kings River Valley.

History

Balch Camp, at the eastern end of this trail, was named for prominent Southern California utility magnate A. C. Balch. In 1899, Balch and fellow businessman W. G. Kerkoff purchased the bankrupt forerunner of the San Joaquin Light and Power Company.

Balch Camp evolved as the employees' settlement during construction of the Kings River Hydroelectric Project in the 1920s. The remote camp had a one-room wooden schoolhouse that was heated by a wood stove. The spectacular view from the school was down the canyon to the west. Eventually it was replaced with a two-room building, and a residence was added for the teacher. To this day, educational facilities remain a challenge for this small mountain community.

A steel bridge crosses the North Fork of the Kings River

Balch Powerhouse, 2 miles upstream from the hydroelectric camp on the North Fork of the Kings River, was built in 1927 with a capacity of 34,500 kilowatts.

Situated high above Balch Camp, the prominent Patterson Bluffs were named for John A. Patterson, a pioneer cattle rancher. A Georgia native, Patterson moved west as a young man during the gold rush of 1849. Unlike many miners, he made money and invested in cattle in 1852. He moved to the Kings River region where he remained for the next 14 years, becoming the first to raise cattle in the area. Patterson played a major role in organizing the construction of the Fresno County courthouse.

Description

Sycamore Springs Trail is a lightly used trail that connects the easier High Sierra #1: Dinkey-Trimmer Road with the North Fork of the Kings River Valley. Just past the trail's well-defined start is a corral and stock tank used by cattle during summer. Past the corral, the trail is faint and little used as it gradually descends along a shelf road. However, it quickly turns into a formed trail that winds down the mountainside, offering panoramic views to the south and southwest. The trail is lumpy in places, with enough rough spots to make 4WD advisable. Some sections become extremely muddy after rain, and it is best avoided in wet weather. Oaks and pines line the trail, and some sections are brushy, especially for wider vehicles.

The trail crosses over a saddle and continues to descend to the southeast, with views toward Rodgers Ridge and the

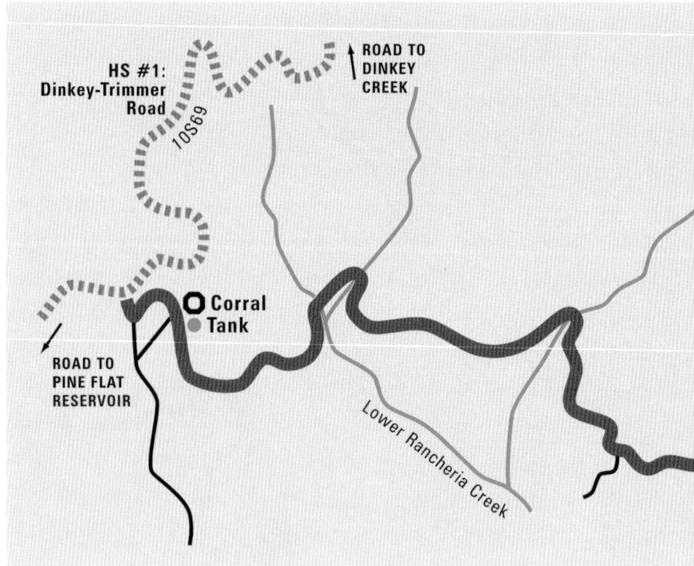

North Fork of the Kings River Valley. The prominent face of Patterson Bluffs, visible to the east, dominates the landscape as you descend toward Dinkey Creek and the North Fork of the Kings River.

The trail ends at Balch Camp, near the confluence of the North Fork of the Kings River and Dinkey Creek. Typically the trail closes at the end of bear-hunting season, around December 1, and re-opens April 1; exact dates vary from year to year.

Current Road Information

Sierra National Forest
High Sierra Ranger District
PO Box 559
Prather, CA 93651
(559) 855-5360

Trail provides spectacular views of Patterson Bluffs and the North Fork of the Kings River

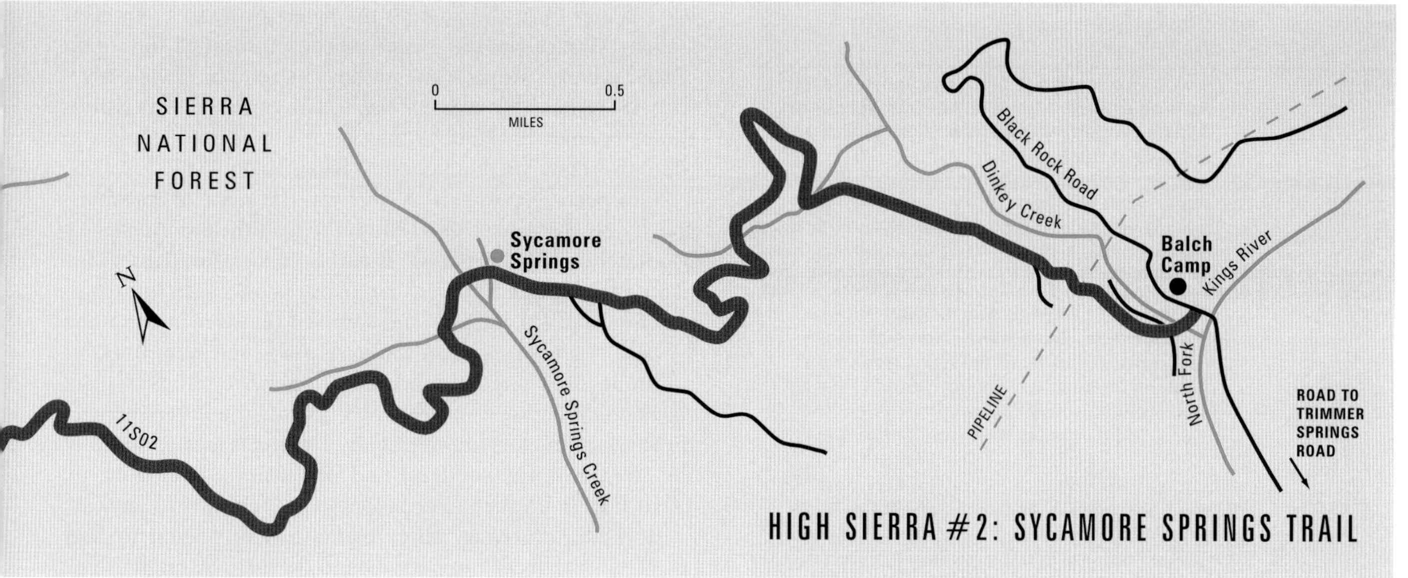

Map References

BLM Fresno
USFS Sierra National Forest
USGS 1:24,000 Sacate Ridge, Patterson Mt.
1:100,000 Fresno
Maptech CD-ROM: Central Coast/Fresno
Southern & Central California Atlas & Gazetteer, pp. 24, 25
California Road & Recreation Atlas, p. 78

Route Directions

▼ 0.0			From High Sierra #1: Dinkey-Trimmer Road (10S69), 12.3 miles northeast of Pine Flat Reservoir and 4.9 miles south of the intersection with FR 9, zero trip meter and turn south on well-used dirt road marked 11S02. Immediately track on right, which travels along Sacate Ridge.
	9.2 ▲		Track on left, which travels along Sacate Ridge; then trail ends at the intersection with High Sierra #1: Dinkey-Trimmer Road (10S69). Turn right for Dinkey Creek; turn left for Pine Flat Reservoir and Fresno.
			GPS: N36°56.08' W119°12.18'
▼ 0.3		SO	Corral and tank on left and track on right. Trail appears faint as it continues straight ahead, but it quickly becomes more defined. Start to descend shelf road.
	8.9 ▲	SO	End of shelf road. Corral and tank on right and track on left. Trail improves in standard.
			GPS: N36°55.96' W119°12.09'
▼ 0.6		SO	Cross over creek.
	8.6 ▲	SO	Cross over creek.
▼ 0.9		SO	Track on right.
	8.3 ▲	SO	Track on left.
▼ 1.1		SO	Cross through Lower Rancheria Creek. Spring up creek on left.
	8.1 ▲	SO	Cross through Lower Rancheria Creek. Spring up creek on right.
			GPS: N36°55.88' W119°11.64'
▼ 1.3		SO	Cross through creek.
	7.9 ▲	SO	Cross through creek.
▼ 2.1		SO	Cross through creek.
	7.1 ▲	SO	Cross through creek.
▼ 2.5		SO	Track on right.
	6.7 ▲	SO	Track on left.
			GPS: N36°55.24' W119°11.00'
▼ 3.1		SO	Cross over creek.
	6.1 ▲	SO	Cross over creek.
▼ 3.4		SO	Cross over creek.
	5.8 ▲	SO	Cross over creek.
▼ 3.9		SO	Track on right on saddle.
	5.3 ▲	SO	Track on left on saddle.
			GPS: N36°54.69' W119°10.14'
▼ 5.1		SO	Cross over creek.
	4.1 ▲	SO	Cross over creek.
			GPS: N36°54.83' W119°09.51'
▼ 5.5		SO	Cross over creek.
	3.7 ▲	SO	Cross over creek.
			GPS: N36°54.95' W119°09.41'
▼ 5.6		SO	Cross over Sycamore Springs Creek.
	3.6 ▲	SO	Cross over Sycamore Springs Creek.
			GPS: N36°55.05' W119°09.32'
▼ 5.8		SO	Cross over creek. Sycamore Springs on left.
	3.4 ▲	SO	Sycamore Springs on right. Cross over creek.
			GPS: N36°55.01' W119°09.18'
▼ 6.0		SO	Track on right.
	3.2 ▲	SO	Track on left.
			GPS: N36°54.88' W119°09.00'
▼ 6.1		SO	Track on right.
	3.1 ▲	SO	Track on left.
▼ 6.8		SO	Track on left.
	2.4 ▲	SO	Track on right.
▼ 7.2		SO	Cross through creek.
	2.0 ▲	SO	Cross through creek.
▼ 8.0		SO	Cross through creek.
	1.2 ▲	SO	Cross through creek.
▼ 8.6		SO	Seasonal closure gate; then track on right goes 0.2 miles to pipeline.
	0.6 ▲	SO	Track on left goes 0.2 miles to pipeline; then seasonal closure gate.
			GPS: N36°54.53' W119°07.70'
▼ 8.8		SO	Pass under pipeline.
	0.4 ▲	SO	Pass under pipeline.

▼ 9.0		SO	Cattle guard.
	0.2 ▲	SO	Cattle guard.
▼ 9.1			4-way intersection at private property. Paved road on right and track on left both lead into private property. Continue straight ahead and join paved road.
	0.1 ▲	SO	4-way intersection at private property. Paved road on left and track on right both lead into private property. Continue straight ahead on dirt road, following sign for Sycamore Springs.
			GPS: N36°54.20' W119°07.39'
▼ 9.2			Cross over Dinkey Creek on bridge; track on right; then trail finishes at T-intersection with paved Black Rock Road at Balch Camp. Turn right for Trimmer; turn left for Wishon Reservoir.
	0.0 ▲		Trail commences on paved Black Rock Road at Balch Camp, 5 miles northeast of Kirch Flat USFS Campground, 3.1 miles north of the Kings River Bridge, and immediately north of a road bridge over the North Fork of the Kings River. Black Rock Road is the continuation of paved Trimmer Springs Road, which runs north along the side of the Pine Flat Reservoir. Zero trip meter and turn southwest on paved road signed for Sycamore Springs Road. Immediately track on left; then cross over Dinkey Creek on bridge.
			GPS: N36°54.22' W119°07.29'

HIGH SIERRA #3

Kings River Trail

Starting Point:	**Trimmer Springs Road, 1.6 miles east of Kirch Flat USFS Campground**
Finishing Point:	**Kings River National Recreation Trailhead**
Total Mileage:	**6.7 miles (one-way)**
Unpaved Mileage:	**6.7 miles**
Driving Time:	**45 minutes (one-way)**
Elevation Range:	**1,000–1,500 feet**
Usually Open:	**Year-round**
Best Time to Travel:	**Year-round**
Difficulty Rating:	**2**
Scenic Rating:	**9**
Remoteness Rating:	**+0**

Special Attractions

- Trout fishing in the Kings River.
- White-water rafting on the Kings River.
- Many camping opportunities along the river.
- Access to the Kings River National Recreation Trail for hikers and equestrians.

History

The earliest recorded sighting of the Kings River was January 6, 1806, the Day of the Epiphany on the Roman Catholic calendar. This day commemorates the visit of the Three Wise Men, Kings from the East, to the newborn Jesus. Lieutenant Gabriel Moraga was leading an expedition through the region when his party camped close to the river, refreshing themselves with its waters. Moraga named the river Río de los Santos Reyes (Spanish for "Holy Kings River") after the feast day; in time, the name was anglicized to Kings River.

This particular stretch of river was the scene of enormous activity in the late 1800s. Hiram T. Smith and Austin D. Moore founded the Kings River Lumber Company (later named the Sanger Lumber Company) in 1889 after purchasing some 30,000 acres of land south of the river in the Sierra Nevada. A growing nation was in need of increasing amounts of lumber, and these mountains held massive stands of giant redwoods. The town of Millwood became the hub of activity for this gigantic logging operation. The site is located south of the river, past the southern end of Central Mountains #3, Davis Flat Trail (*Backcountry Adventures: Southern California*).

By 1890, the Kings River Flume had been built to float rough-sawn timber from Millwood to the railhead and finishing mill at Sanger. The flume, an impressive engineering feat in this mountainous terrain, stretched 62 miles, making it the longest of its kind in the world at the time. It emerged from the dense mountain forest to join the river at Mill Flat, the site of today's Mill Flat Campground, on the south side of Kings River.

Estimates suggest that loggers harvested close to 200 million board feet, the equivalent of approximately 7,500 redwoods, from this pristine old growth forest. Sadder still is the fact that most of the 2,000-year-old trees were left to rot because they were too difficult to transport. Possibly only 25 to 30 percent of the felled trees made it to the milling yard.

Description

The Kings River Trail exists primarily as an access road to the Kings River National Recreation Trailhead and the raft put-ins at Garnet Dike and Hermit Hole. However, for the casual driver, it offers a beautiful short trail that meanders alongside the very scenic Kings River. For the backcountry camper, it offers many undeveloped riverbank campsites set in the shade of large oak trees. The road alternately follows alongside the riv-

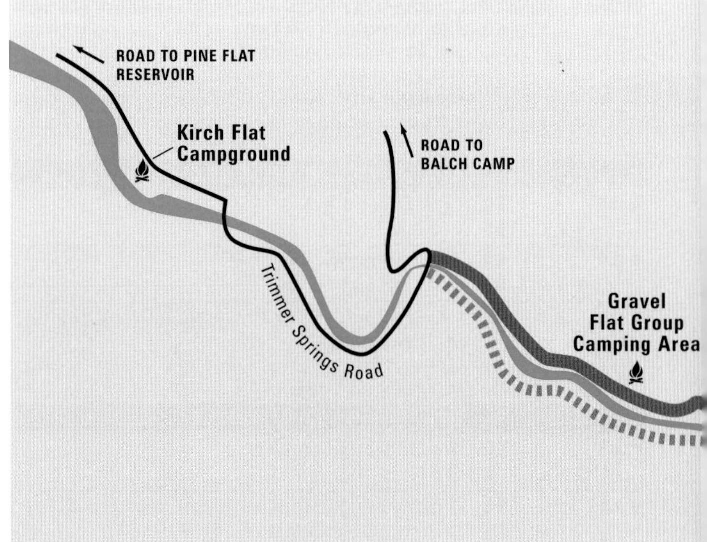

er or climbs high above it on a shelf road. Most of it is smooth and well graded, but some wash crossings are rough enough that high-clearance is necessary.

The Bear Wallow Hiking Trail departs from the main vehicle trail and climbs to the top of Rodgers Ridge. The trail is very steep and the 1.5-mile hike to the ridge and back takes about half a day. If you want a longer hike, the trail continues along Rodgers Ridge for some distance.

The vehicle trail ends at the Kings River National Recreation Trailhead. From here, retrace your steps to the Trimmer Springs Road.

Kings River is a designated wild-trout stream from Pine Flat Reservoir to the western boundary of Kings Canyon National Park. It is managed purely for wild trout and is not stocked. There is a catch limit of two trout, and catch and release fishing with a single-point, barbless hook or a bent down barbed hook is encouraged.

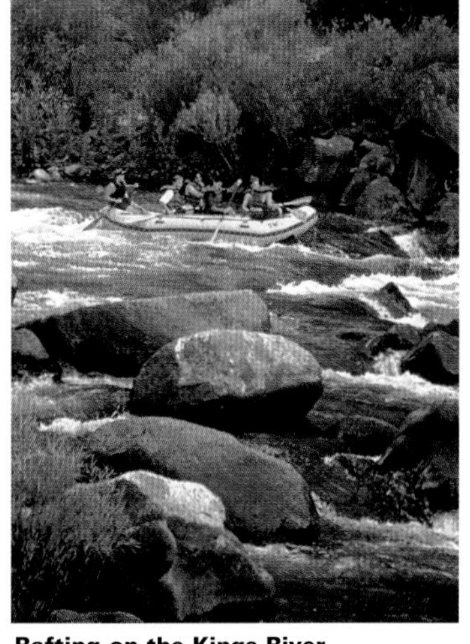

Rafting on the Kings River

The Kings River is one of the most popular stretches of white water in California. Upstream, the river has been designated a wild and scenic river. The 10-mile stretch from Garnet Dike, at the end of this trail, downstream to Kirch Flat Campground boasts some class III and class IV rapids. The rafting season generally runs from late April to mid July with the highest water usually between late May and early June. Guided tours are available, and tour companies operate a base camp near Kirch Flat during the rafting season. Private individuals do not need a permit to raft the Kings River, but some large groups or non-commercial guided trips may. The Kings River Ranger District office can answer questions. There is currently no fee for the campgrounds or undeveloped campsites along this trail.

Current Road Information

Sierra National Forest
High Sierra Ranger District
PO Box 559
Prather, CA 93651
(559) 855-5360

Map References

BLM Fresno
USFS Sierra National Forest
USGS 1:24,000 Luckett Mt., Verplank Ridge
1:100,000 Fresno
Maptech CD-ROM: Central Coast/Fresno
Southern & Central California Atlas & Gazetteer, p. 25
California Road & Recreation Atlas, p. 78

Route Directions

▼ 0.0		From the eastern end of Trimmer Springs Road, proceed north on the bridge over the Kings River and zero trip meter. Turn northeast on graded dirt road signed to Garnet Dike and Kings River Trailhead and pass through closure gate. Immediately south of the bridge is Central Mountains #3: Davis Flat Trail.
		GPS: N36°52.29' W119°07.82'
▼ 1.0	SO	Pass through Gravel Flat—undeveloped group camping area. There is a pit toilet but no other facilities.
		GPS: N36°51.65' W119°07.05'
▼ 1.9	SO	Track on left.
▼ 2.2	SO	Bear Wallow Hiking Trail on left for hikers and horses.
		GPS: N36°51.67' W119°05.98'
▼ 2.4	BL	Track on right to Bear Wallow—undeveloped group camping area. Bear left at pit toilet.
▼ 2.7	SO	Track on right gives river access.
▼ 3.4	SO	Bay Horse Flat. Two tracks on right to camping area.
▼ 3.5	SO	Track on right to camping area.
▼ 3.6	SO	Cross through wash.
▼ 3.8	SO	Track on right to camping area.
▼ 5.1	SO	Cross through wash.
▼ 5.4	SO	Track on left.

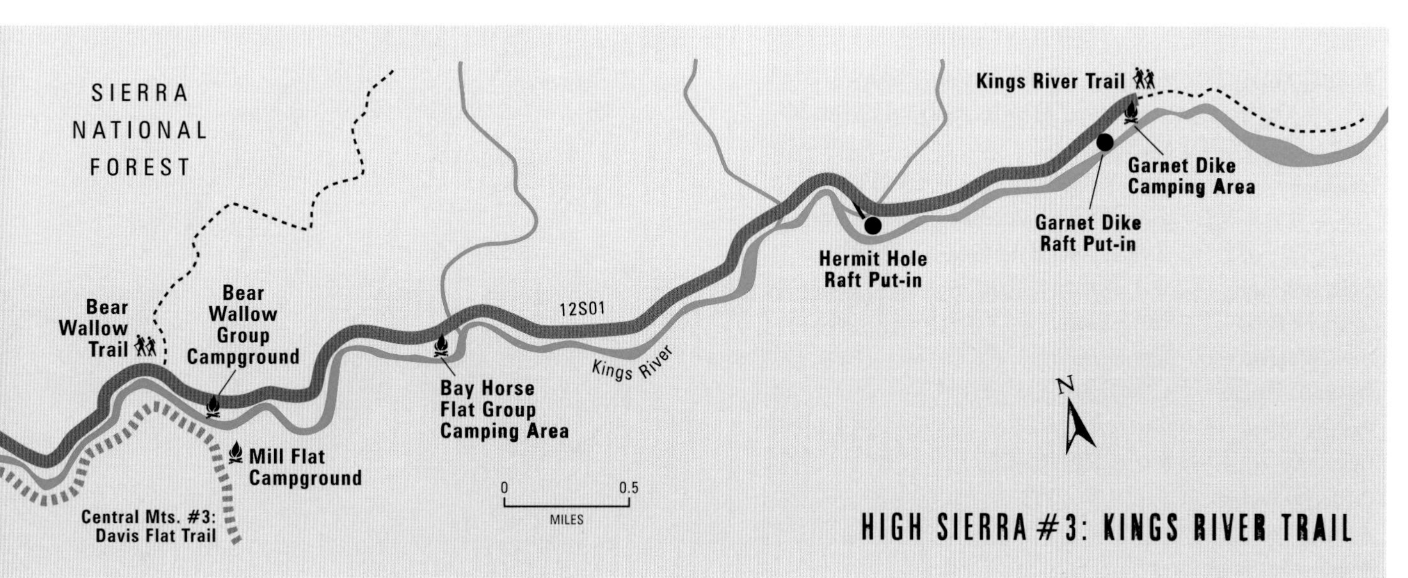

In places, the trail becomes a shelf road above the Kings River

▼ 5.5	SO	Track on right to Hermit Hole Raft Put-in (Winfrey Mine)—no overnight parking or camping.
		GPS: N36°51.76' W119°02.87'
▼ 5.6	SO	Cross through wash; then track on right to camping area.
▼ 6.2	SO	Track on right to camping area. Track on left goes to stone tiered walls and ruins.
▼ 6.5	SO	Parking area for Garnet Dike Raft Put-in.
		GPS: N36°51.81' W119°01.75'
▼ 6.6	SO	Garnet Dike Camping Area.
		GPS: N36°51.85' W119°01.63'
▼ 6.7		Kings River National Recreation Trailhead and parking area at the end of vehicle trail.
		GPS: N36°51.87' W119°01.57'

HIGH SIERRA #4

Sawmill Flat Road

Starting Point:	**Black Rock Road, 11.5 miles north of Balch Camp and 1.6 miles north of Black Rock Station**
Finishing Point:	**McKinley Grove Road (FR 40), 3.8 miles west of Wishon Reservoir and 1.2 miles west of Courtright Reservoir Road**
Total Mileage:	**10.1 miles**
Unpaved Mileage:	**10.1 miles**
Driving Time:	**1.25 hours**
Elevation Range:	**4,800–7,200 feet**
Usually Open:	**May to November**
Best Time to Travel:	**May to November**
Difficulty Rating:	**1**
Scenic Rating:	**10**
Remoteness Rating:	**+0**

Special Attractions

- Views of Rancheria Creek Falls on east side of the North Fork of the Kings River Valley.
- Easy winding trail with excellent views over the North Fork of the Kings River Valley.

History

Haas Powerhouse, near the southern end of this trail, was constructed in 1958. This underground facility, part of the Helms Hydroelectric Project, is driven by water from Wishon Reservoir passing through the Haas Tunnel some 500 feet below the mountainside. This was the first large underground hydroelectric generator of its kind in the United States.

Teakettle Experimental Area, midway along the trail, has been an ecological study area since 1930. The Civilian Conservation Corps built an office, dwelling, and storage facility when the size of the area was increased and officially designated as the Teakettle Experimental Area in 1938. Studies included comparing sediment runoff to annual precipitation and growth patterns until World War II interrupted the operation.

Field studies resumed in 1957 to determine what timber harvesting methods would allow maximum water yield in the Central Valley. In the 1960s, the studies altered somewhat—to measure actual water flow based on varying weather patterns. By the 1980s, funding for the studies dwindled and all but bird observation activities came to a halt. Vegetation studies were carried out in the 1990s, and the twenty-first century promises additional experiments in timber harvesting methods.

McKinley Grove Botanical Area, northwest of the trail, has an undisturbed stand of giant sequoias, protected as a re-

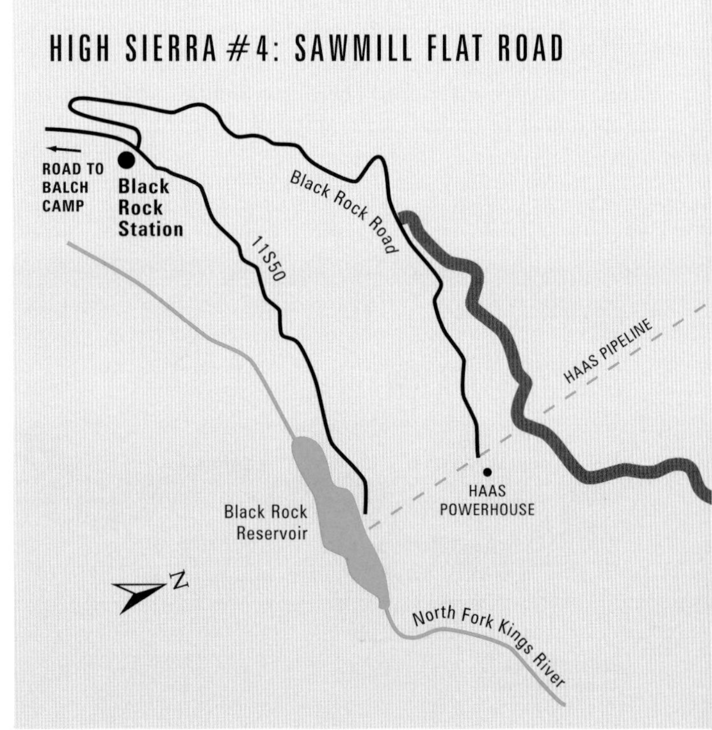

serve since 1893. This particular forest was undisturbed simply because trails were late in coming through this remote mountainous area.

Description

Sawmill Flat Road is an easy graded road that travels from the Haas Powerhouse, along the edge of the North Fork of the Kings River Valley, to McKinley Grove Road. The trail winds up a single-lane shelf road, climbing steadily along the edge of the canyon. The southern end of the trail offers glimpses of Black Rock Reservoir, about a thousand feet below in the valley. The landscape is an eye-catching mixture of huge granite domes, boulders, and sheer rock faces. After 6.7 miles, High Sierra #5: Granite Gorge Overlook Trail leaves to the north; this trail follows more closely along the edge of Granite Gorge.

Rancheria Creek Falls on the far side of Kings River Valley's North Fork

Sawmill Flat Road leaves the valley and winds through pines and firs, passing Sawmill Flat Campground and various other dirt roads to finish at McKinley Grove Road. This is a good trail for glimpsing bobcats, coyotes, and deer; in summer, the air is alive with darting hummingbirds.

The trail is rated 1 for difficulty and is generally suitable for passenger vehicles. It is not suitable for RVs or trailers because of its narrow and winding route. In addition, access from the south via Balch Camp and Black Rock Road, although paved, is similarly narrow, twisting, and equally difficult for large vehicles. It is, however, a spectacular addition to this route. The trail is usually closed from December 1 to late April, although exact dates vary.

Current Road Information

Sierra National Forest
High Sierra Ranger District
PO Box 559
Prather, CA 93651
(559) 855-5360

Map References

BLM Fresno
USFS Sierra National Forest
USGS 1:24,000 Patterson Mt.
1:100,000 Fresno
Maptech CD-ROM: Central Coast/Fresno
Southern & Central California Atlas & Gazetteer, p. 25
California Road & Recreation Atlas, p. 78

Route Directions

▼ 0.0		From paved Black Rock Road, 11.5 miles north of Balch Camp and 1.6 miles north of Black Rock Station, zero trip meter and turn north on graded dirt road following sign to Sawmill Flat and Wishon Reservoir. Pass through seasonal closure gate. The paved road continues 0.8 miles east to Haas Powerhouse.
	5.3 ▲	Seasonal closure gate; then trail ends at intersection with paved Black Rock Road. Turn left

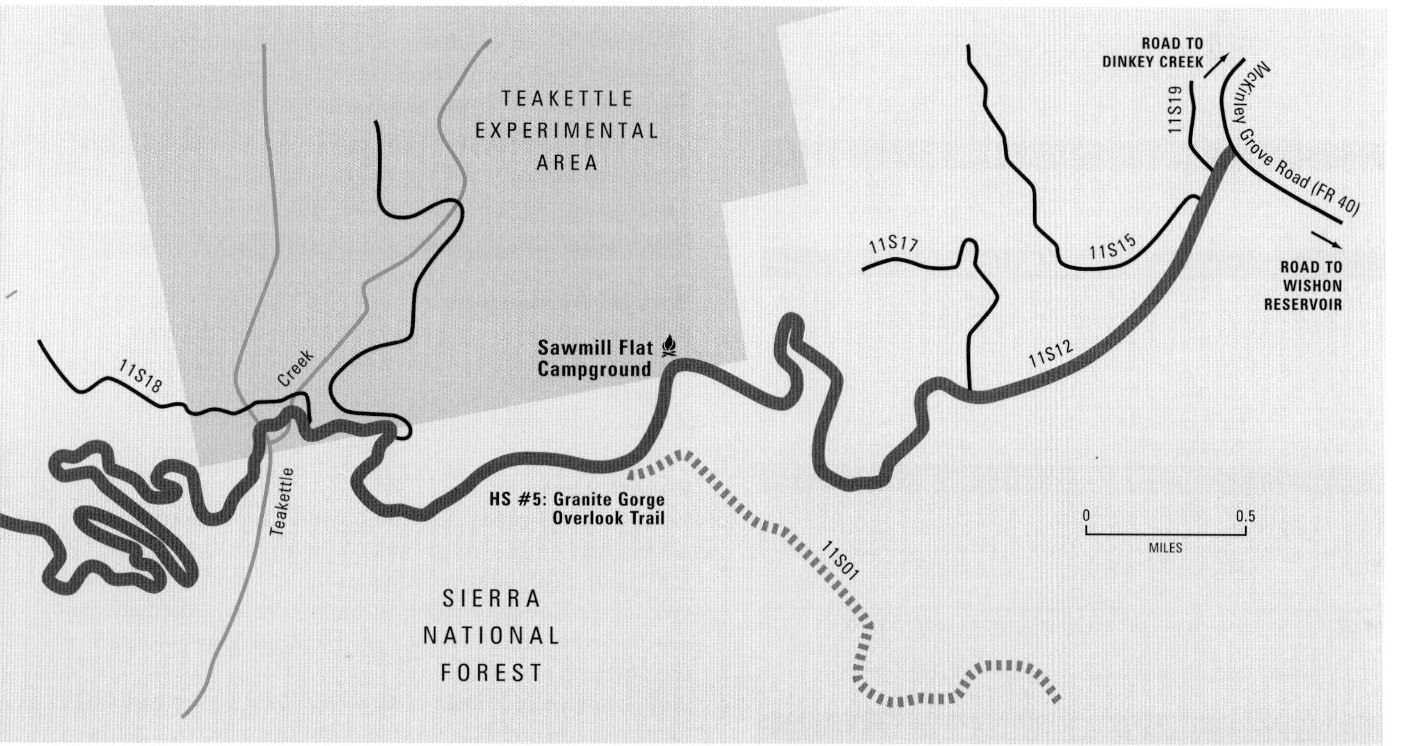

Spectacular sheer granite rocks along the North Fork of Kings River Valley

		to visit Haas Powerhouse; turn right for Balch Camp and Pine Flat Reservoir.
		GPS: N36°55.55′ W119°02.00′
▼ 0.9	SO	Pass under Haas Pipeline.
4.4 ▲	SO	Pass under Haas Pipeline.
▼ 2.4	SO	Campsite and viewpoint over Rancheria Creek Falls on right.
2.9 ▲	SO	Campsite and viewpoint over Rancheria Creek Falls on left.
▼ 5.1	SO	Cross over creek.
0.2 ▲	SO	Cross over creek.
		GPS: N36°57.04′ W119°01.00′
▼ 5.2	SO	Cross over Teakettle Creek.
0.1 ▲	SO	Cross over Teakettle Creek.
▼ 5.3	SO	Graded road on left is 11S18. Zero trip meter.
0.0 ▲		Continue to the southwest.
		GPS: N36°57.15′ W119°00.93′
▼ 0.0		Continue to the north.
1.4 ▲	SO	Graded road on right is 11S18. Zero trip meter.
▼ 0.3	TR	Track on left goes through gate and enters Teakettle Experimental Area.
1.1 ▲	TL	Track straight ahead goes through gate and enters Teakettle Experimental Area.
		GPS: N36°57.37′ W119°00.89′
▼ 1.4	BL	Track on right is High Sierra #5: Granite Gorge Overlook Trail (11S01). Zero trip meter.
0.0 ▲		Continue to the south.
		GPS: N36°57.94′ W119°00.64′
▼ 0.0		Continue to the northwest, following sign for Wishon Reservoir and Sawmill Flat Campground.
3.4 ▲	SO	Track on left is High Sierra #5: Granite Gorge Overlook Trail (11S01). Zero trip meter.
▼ 0.4	SO	Sawmill Flat USFS Campground on left.
3.0 ▲	SO	Sawmill Flat USFS Campground on right.
		GPS: N36°58.19′ W119°00.93′
▼ 0.5	SO	Track on right.
2.9 ▲	SO	Track on left.
▼ 2.1	SO	Track on left.
1.3 ▲	SO	Track on right.
▼ 2.2	SO	Track on left; then graded road on left is 11S17.
1.2 ▲	SO	Graded road on right is 11S17; then track on right.
		GPS: N36°58.88′ W119°00.65′
▼ 3.2	SO	Unmarked graded road on left is 11S15.
0.2 ▲	SO	Unmarked graded road on right is 11S15.
		GPS: N36°59.64′ W119°01.14′
▼ 3.3	SO	Track on left is 11S19 and track on right.
0.1 ▲	SO	Track on right is 11S19 and track on left.
▼ 3.4		Trail ends at T-intersection with McKinley Grove Road (FR 40). Turn right for Wishon Reservoir; turn left for Dinkey Creek.
0.0 ▲		Trail commences on McKinley Grove Road (FR 40), 3.8 miles west of Wishon Reservoir, 1.2 miles west of Courtright Reservoir Road, and 12 miles east of Dinkey Creek. Zero trip meter and turn south on graded dirt road at the sign for Sawmill Flat Campground and Pine Flat Reservoir.
		GPS: N36°59.73′ W119°01.28′

HIGH SIERRA #5

Granite Gorge Overlook Trail

Starting Point:	**High Sierra #4: Sawmill Flat Road (11S12), 0.4 miles south of Sawmill Flat Campground**
Finishing Point:	**McKinley Grove Road (FR 40), 0.2 miles west of Lily Pad USFS Campground and 0.7 miles west of the western end of Wishon Dam**
Total Mileage:	**4.4 miles**
Unpaved Mileage:	**4.3 miles**
Driving Time:	**1 hour**
Elevation Range:	**6,400–6,800 feet**
Usually Open:	**May to November**
Best Time to Travel:	**May to November**
Difficulty Rating:	**3**
Scenic Rating:	**10**
Remoteness Rating:	**+0**

Special Attractions

- Wishon Reservoir near the northern end of the trail.
- Pretty lily pond and swimming hole on Long Meadow Creek.
- Spectacular views into Granite Gorge.

Description

Granite Gorge Overlook Trail winds high above Granite Gorge, part of the North Fork of the Kings River Valley, before passing through the forest to finish near Wishon Reservoir. The 3-difficulty rating is due to a short, extremely narrow, twisting section of shelf road and the uneven surface at the northern end of the trail.

The trail, also known as Crabtree Road, leaves easy High Sierra #4: Sawmill Flat Road and immediately starts to travel

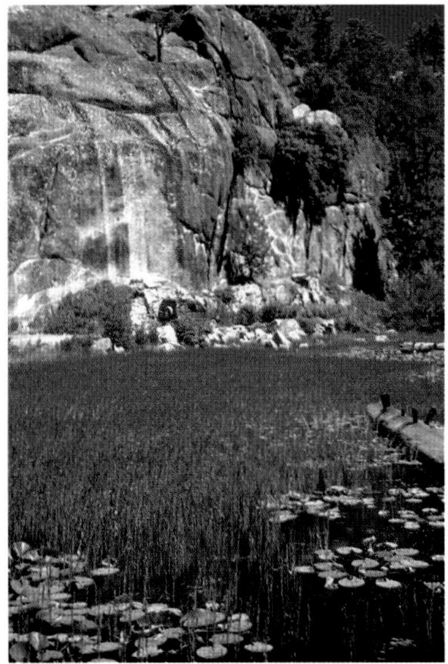

Birds flock to this lake covered with reeds and water lilies near Long Meadow Creek

around the edge of the valley. The single-track road hugs the sheer granite walls of the canyon. There are some passing places along this section. The narrowest part is a 0.5-mile-long stretch that is a tight squeeze for full-size vehicles in places. There are spectacular views down along Granite Gorge, which lives up to its name with rounded granite rock faces and cliffs studded with pine trees.

The road leaves the edge of the canyon and travels along a rough, lumpy trail through pine forest. At Long Meadow Creek, a small pool at the bottom of a series of small waterfalls makes for a lovely place to cool off on a hot day. There are campsites nearby, but campers and bathers should have a good supply of insect repellent—mosquitoes and other biting insects abound. A small reservoir, covered with reeds and yellow pond lilies in early summer, lies 0.1 miles farther along the trail.

The trail finishes near Wishon Reservoir, a popular destination for boaters and anglers. Two developed campgrounds—Lily Pad and Upper Kings—can be found near the north end of the trail.

Current Road Information

Sierra National Forest
High Sierra Ranger District
PO Box 559
Prather, CA 93651
(559) 855-5360

Map References

BLM Fresno, Mt. Whitney
USFS Sierra National Forest
USGS 1:24,000 Patterson Mt., Rough Spur, Courtright Reservoir
1:100,000 Fresno, Mt. Whitney
Maptech CD-ROM: Central Coast/Fresno; Kings Canyon/Death Valley
Southern & Central California Atlas & Gazetteer, p. 25
Northern California Atlas & Gazetteer, p. 122
California Road & Recreation Atlas, p. 78
Other: Sierra National Forest OHV Guide

Route Directions

▼ 0.0		From High Sierra #4: Sawmill Flat Road (11S12), 0.4 miles south of Sawmill Flat USFS Campground, zero trip meter and turn northwest on graded dirt road marked 11S01. There is a sign for Sawmill Flat Campground at the intersection.
4.4 ▲		Trail ends at intersection with High Sierra #4: Sawmill Flat Road (11S12). Turn right for Wishon Reservoir; turn left for Balch Camp.
		GPS: N36°57.94' W119°00.64'
▼ 0.2	SO	Track on left.
4.2 ▲	SO	Track on right.
▼ 0.6	SO	Track on right is 11S01B.
3.8 ▲	SO	Track on left is 11S01B.
▼ 0.9	SO	Start of shelf road.

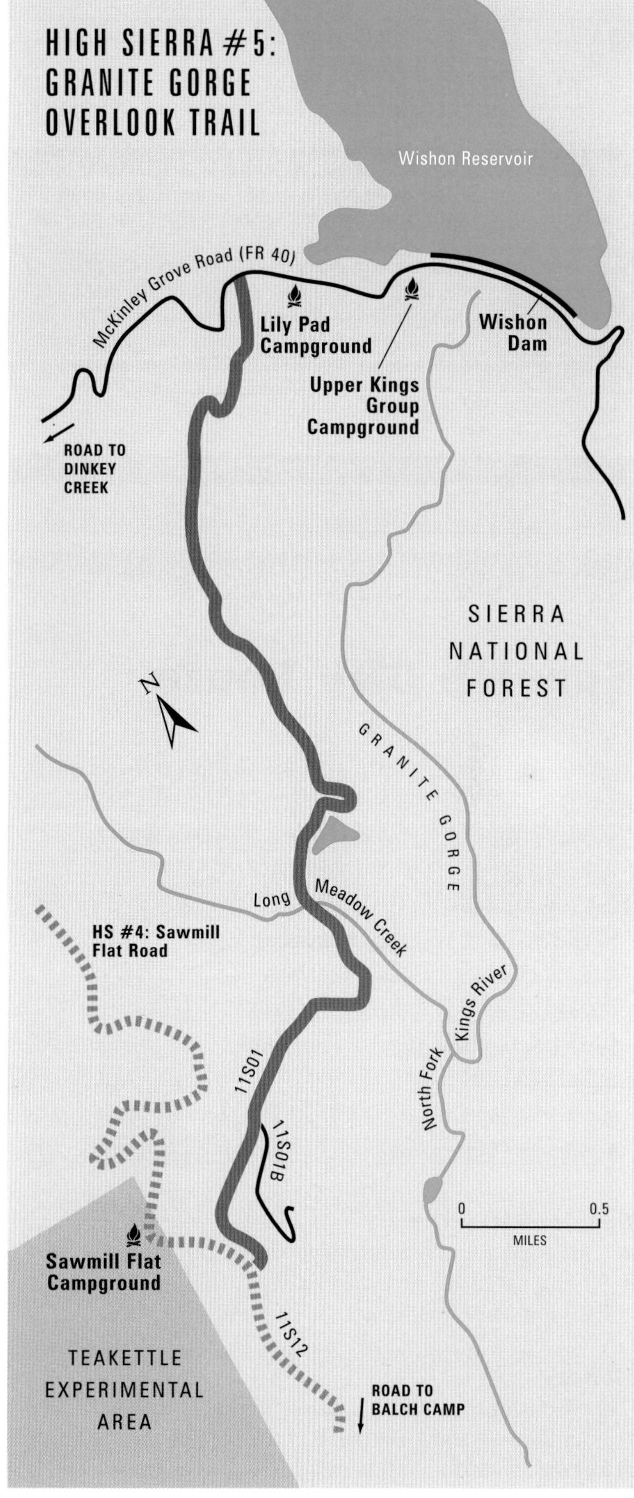

	3.5 ▲	SO	End of shelf road.
▼ 1.4		SO	End of shelf road.
	3.0 ▲	SO	Start of shelf road.
▼ 1.8		SO	Cross over Long Meadow Creek.
	2.6 ▲	SO	Cross over Long Meadow Creek.
			GPS: N36°58.81' W118°59.79'
▼ 1.9		SO	Small reservoir on right.
	2.5 ▲	SO	Small reservoir on left.
			GPS: N36°58.97' W118°59.64'
▼ 2.7		SO	Wishon Reservoir Dam visible on the right.
	1.7 ▲	SO	Wishon Reservoir Dam visible on the left.
▼ 4.3		BL	Bear left onto paved road. Immediately track on left opposite shed.
	0.1 ▲	BR	Track on right opposite shed; then immediately bear right onto second unmarked, formed dirt trail.
			GPS: N37°00.53' W118°58.85'
▼ 4.4			Trail ends on paved McKinley Grove Road (FR 40). Turn right for Wishon Reservoir; turn left for Dinkey Creek.
	0.0 ▲		Trail commences on paved McKinley Grove Road (FR 40), 0.2 miles west of Lily Pad USFS Campground and the marked turn to Helms Headquarters, and 0.7 miles west of the western end of Wishon Dam. Coming from the west, it is 1.9 miles east of Courtright Reservoir Road. Zero trip meter and turn southwest on unmarked paved road.
			GPS: N37°00.58' W118°58.81'

HIGH SIERRA #6

Spanish OHV Route

Starting Point:	**11S07, 1.7 miles south of intersection with FR 40**
Finishing Point:	**Boundary of the John Muir Wilderness**
Total Mileage:	**5 miles (one-way)**
Unpaved Mileage:	**5 miles**
Driving Time:	**2 hours (one-way)**
Elevation Range:	**6,600–9,000 feet**
Usually Open:	**July to November**
Best Time to Travel:	**July to November**
Difficulty Rating:	**7**
Scenic Rating:	**7**
Remoteness Rating:	**+1**

Special Attractions

- Challenging trail for most high-clearance SUVs.
- Hiking access to Little Spanish Lake and Spanish Lake in the John Muir Wilderness.

History

The Spanish OHV Route leads high into Sierra National Forest. Statham Meadow, northeast of the trail, lies on the boundary of the John Muir Wilderness and was once the site of a few houses. Albert H. Statham ranged sheep between Dinkey and Deer Creeks, to the west of today's Wishon Reservoir, beginning in 1871. In later years Albert ran sheep on a large tract of land that included the meadow now bearing his name.

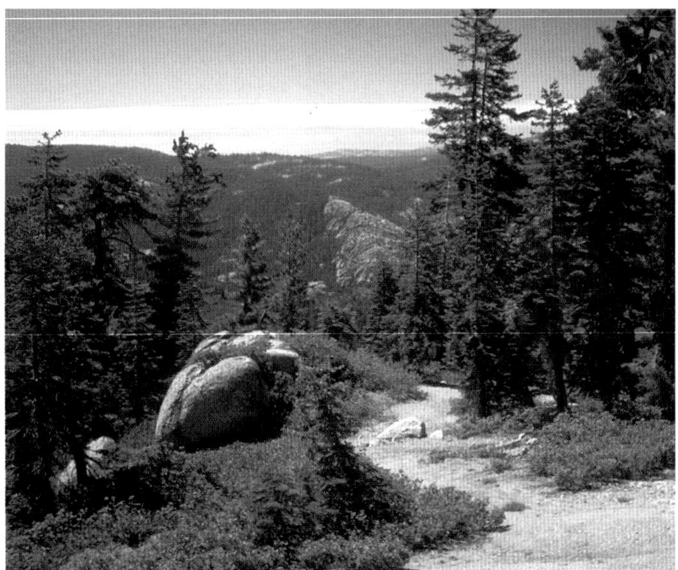

Distant view of Granite Gorge from the Spanish OHV Route

The trail climbs the slopes of Spanish Mountain to a trailhead for Little Spanish Lake and Spanish Lake, named for legendary Spanish mines hidden in these rugged mountains. The exact location of the mines remains a mystery.

The John Muir Wilderness encompasses more than half a million acres in Inyo and Sierra National Forests. Established by the 1964 Wilderness Act, the area now covers more than 580,000 acres. This exquisite wilderness stretches nearly a hundred miles along the crest of the Sierra Nevada.

Description

Spanish OHV Route is one of a series of designated OHV routes in Sierra National Forest. It is described as "more difficult" by the forest service, and it is not considered suitable for full-size vehicles because of some tight maneuvering between standing and fallen trees.

The marked trail leaves 11S07 and gradually climbs through pine forests on the western slopes of Spanish Mountain. After crossing a small creek, the trail becomes more difficult. Careful driving is needed because there is often little clearance between the trees. In dry weather the trail is extremely dusty, with a loose, sandy surface. It should be avoided in wet weather.

Sections of the OHV route are rocky, loose, and steep

The trail starts to climb more steeply as it nears Lost Meadow Ridge; this section may be troublesome to some drivers. The very loose, powdery surface offers little traction, and the slight off-camber slope can cause vehicles to slip sideways. Embedded rocks require careful wheel placement to avoid underbody damage. The trail continues to climb; some short pinches reach slopes of 25 degrees.

The final 1.5 miles of the trail are the rockiest, with large embedded boulders to negotiate. There are a few campsites along the ridge and a few before Garlic Meadow. From the end of the trail it is a steep mile-long hike into the wilderness to reach Little Spanish Lake and a short distance farther to Spanish Lake.

The trail is usually open from July to November depending on conditions. It sometimes opens earlier. Check with the National Forest Service for details. A permit is required to stay overnight in the John Muir Wilderness.

Current Road Information

Sierra National Forest
High Sierra Ranger District
PO Box 559
Prather, CA 93651
(559) 855-5360

Map References

BLM Mt. Whitney
USFS Sierra National Forest
USGS 1:24,000 Rough Spur
1:100,000 Mt. Whitney
Maptech CD-ROM: Kings Canyon/Death Valley
Southern & Central California Atlas & Gazetteer, p. 25
California Road & Recreation Atlas, p. 78 (route not shown)
Trails Illustrated, Sequoia & Kings Canyon National Parks (205)
Other: Sierra National Forest OHV Guide

Route Directions

▼ 0.0		From FR 40, at the southeastern end of the Wishon Dam spillway bridge, zero trip meter and continue south for 2.7 miles on paved FR 40. Turn right onto 11S07, following the sign for Spanish Lake OHV Route. Proceed 1.7 miles on 11S07 to the start of the trail. Zero trip meter and turn left (northeast) on formed dirt trail marked Spanish OHV Route and pass through seasonal closure gate.
		GPS: N36°57.05′ W118°57.98′
▼ 0.6	SO	Cross through a tributary of Rancheria Creek.
		GPS: N36°57.10′ W118°57.51′
▼ 1.7	SO	Trail starts to climb steeply.
▼ 2.1	SO	Top of Lost Meadow Ridge. Viewpoint on right.
		GPS: N36°56.74′ W118°56.50′
▼ 2.4	TL	Trail turns sharp left and climbs up granite rock.
		GPS: N36°56.56′ W118°56.72′
▼ 2.5	SO	Track on right to campsite and viewpoint over Pine Flat Reservoir, Granite Gorge, and the San Joaquin Valley.
		GPS: N36°56.50′ W118°56.73′
▼ 3.5	SO	Finger Rock visible through the trees to the left.
		GPS: N36°55.97′ W118°56.04′
▼ 4.1	SO	Meadow on right.
		GPS: N36°55.57′ W118°55.78′
▼ 4.2	SO	Garlic Meadow off to the right.
▼ 5.0		Trail ends at boundary of the John Muir Wilderness.
		GPS: N36°55.38′ W118°55.11′

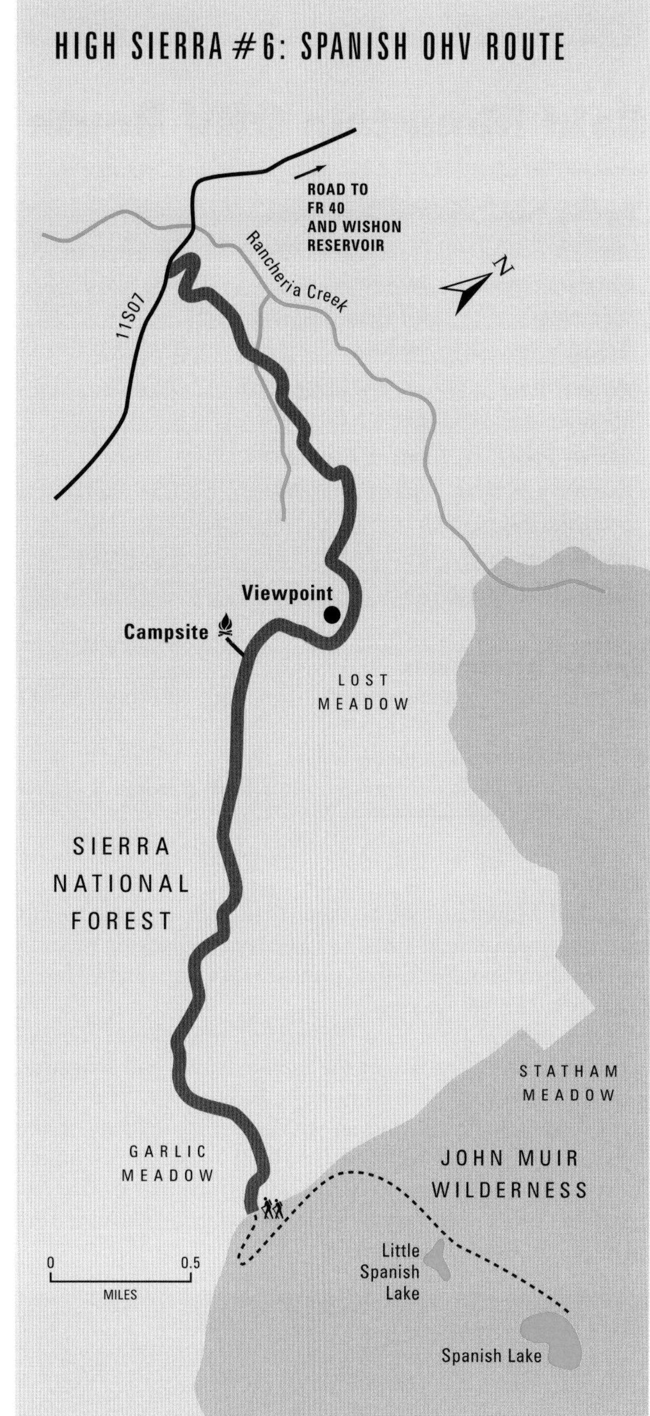

HIGH SIERRA #7

Bald Mountain OHV Route

Starting Point:	**Rock Creek Road, 3.3 miles north of Dinkey Creek Road**
Finishing Point:	**Bald Mountain**
Total Mileage:	**3.4 miles (one-way)**
Unpaved Mileage:	**3.4 miles**
Driving Time:	**1.5 hours (one-way)**
Elevation Range:	**6,800–7,826 feet**
Usually Open:	**July to November**
Best Time to Travel:	**July to November**
Difficulty Rating:	**5**
Scenic Rating:	**9**
Remoteness Rating:	**+0**

Special Attractions

- Moderately challenging trail for high-clearance 4WD vehicles.
- The old Bald Mountain Fire Lookout.
- Variety of backcountry campsites and panoramic views from along the trail.

History

The Bald Mountain Fire Lookout that gives its name to this route has been closed since 1979 because of lack of funding and the increased use of small planes to spot fires. Staffed lookouts are no longer necessary.

Looking west from Bald Mountain Fire Lookout, you can see Shaver Lake, the site of the Fresno Flume and Irrigation Company's sawmill and dam in the early 1890s. The lake is named for Charles B. Shaver, who became president of the lumber company in 1894. Shaver, born in Steuben County, New York, moved west to Michigan with his family. He entered the lumber industry in his teens and gained valuable experience in railroad construction.

The old Bald Mountain Fire Lookout offers panoramic views from 7,832 feet

By 1892, he had made his way to California, settling in Fresno. Shaver quickly realized the logging potential of the Sierra Nevada and invested in the recently formed Fresno Flume and Irrigation Company. Shaver's business enterprises expanded over the years, making him a notable contributor to Fresno's development. Charles Shaver passed away in 1907.

Shaver Lake covered the original sawmill and dam on Stevenson Creek when Shaver Dam was completed in the late 1920s.

Description

Bald Mountain OHV Route is a moderate trail that climbs to the fire lookout on Bald Mountain. It is a good trail for beginning off-road drivers to practice on before moving to harder trails. The route should be within the capabilities of most stock high-clearance 4WD vehicles. Navigation is difficult along the trail when it crosses over sections of bare granite; it is marked sporadically with jeep trail signs. Additional coordinates have been given in the route directions to aid navigation. The official forest service route describes a loop; however, the return portion of the loop is poorly marked. The route mapped out below is one way to the tower that has a fairly consistent level of difficulty and is marked by the official jeep route signs. You can either return the way you came or explore other marked routes in the vicinity.

This low-traction climb is deceptively steep, reaching angles of 25 degrees

The trail commences along a deteriorating paved road, but quickly turns into a formed dirt trail. One of the most difficult sections of the trail comes near the start. A steep, loose sandy climb with large embedded rocks will test your vehicle's traction. This slope reaches angles of 25 degrees; care is needed to pick a line that will avoid damaging your vehicle's underbody.

Once on the ridge, the trail turns right at an easily missed intersection. The turn appears to lead to campsites, and there is no jeep marker immediately visible. However, there is a marker a short distance after the turn. The trail undulates along smooth granite and scattered pine trees. There are views in all directions and a good variety of backcountry campsites.

The trail climbs continuously to the lookout. Some of the climbs are steep and have poor traction. Expect to encounter steep granite overlaid with fine sand (a combination that makes traction difficult for both hikers and vehicles), loose rock, and rock ledges up to 6 inches high in places.

The strenuous hiking trail to Bald Mountain joins the vehicle route, and the two run concurrently to the summit. An intersection, well marked with cairns, is the start of the final ascent to Bald Mountain Fire Lookout. The lookout is over a rise and not immediately visible.

Bald Mountain Fire Lookout (7,826 feet) stands on bare

rock and has a commanding 360-degree view. Shaver Lake is to the west, with Mount Stevenson behind it, and Musick Mountain is to the northwest. The Three Sisters are to the northeast and Nelson Mountain and Eagle Peak are to the east. Currently, it is possible to climb up the two flights of stairs to the walkway.

Current Road Information

Sierra National Forest
High Sierra Ranger District
PO Box 559
Prather, CA 93651
(559) 855-5360

Map References

BLM Shaver Lake
USFS Sierra National Forest
USGS 1:24,000 Dinkey Creek
1:100,000 Shaver Lake
Maptech CD-ROM: Central Coast/Fresno
Northern California Atlas & Gazetteer, p. 121
California Road & Recreation Atlas, p. 78
Other: Sierra National Forest OHV Guide

Route Directions

▼ 0.0		From Dinkey Creek, proceed 2.6 miles northwest on Dinkey Creek Road and turn right (north) onto Rock Creek Road at the sign for Dinkey Creek Trailhead. Proceed 3.3 miles to the start of the trail. Zero trip meter and turn southwest on dirt trail 9S43 at the sign for Mount Baldy OHV Route and pass through seasonal closure gate.
		GPS: N37°06.08′ W119°10.14′
▼ 0.3	BR	Information board on right; then unmarked, well-used track on left. Neither track is marked.
		GPS: N37°05.91′ W119°10.40′
▼ 0.4	SO	Track on left.
▼ 0.7	SO	Steep climb with loose surface and embedded rock.
▼ 0.9	BL	Track on right up granite boulders marked with jeep trail sign.
		GPS: N37°05.75′ W119°10.91′
▼ 1.1	TR	Track on left. Bear right past large granite boulders. There is a jeep marker shortly after the turn. Zero trip meter. This turn is easy to miss.
		GPS: N37°05.60′ W119°11.04′
▼ 0.0		Continue to the southwest.
▼ 0.2	BR	Track swings through trees and crosses wash line.
		GPS: N37°05.52′ W119°11.19′
▼ 0.3	SO	Small track on left.
▼ 0.6	SO	Cross over creek.
		GPS: N37°05.61′ W119°11.52′
▼ 0.9	BL	Small track on right.
		GPS: N37°05.83′ W119°11.54′
▼ 1.0	BR	Trail forks—to the right is the easier route. Trail starts to climb.
		GPS: N37°05.93′ W119°11.56′
▼ 1.1	SO	Trails rejoin.
		GPS: N37°05.93′ W119°11.62′
▼ 1.3	SO	Trail swings to the right around large pine.
		GPS: N37°05.89′ W119°11.80′
▼ 1.6	BR	Track on left.
		GPS: N37°06.07′ W119°11.96′
▼ 1.7	BL	Trail swings left.
		GPS: N37°06.18′ W119°11.98′
▼ 1.8	BR	Track on left marked by small cairns.
		GPS: N37°06.22′ W119°12.09′
▼ 2.1	BL	Two tracks on right are marked with an orange arrow. Bear left and continue up the hill. The intersection is marked all around with cairns. The cairns continue up the hill on either side of the trail.
		GPS: N37°06.34′ W119°12.21′
▼ 2.3		Bald Mountain Fire Lookout.
		GPS: N37°06.21′ W119°12.32′

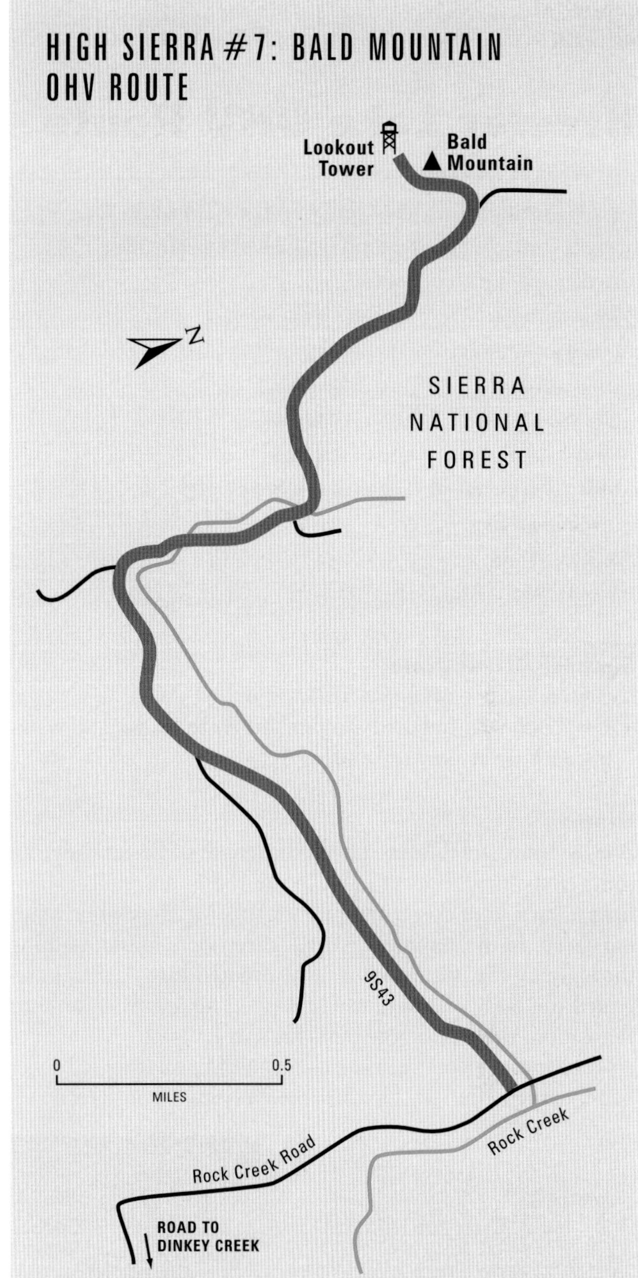

Brewer Lake OHV Route

Starting Point:	**Intersection of 9S69 and Foster Ridge Trail (9S10), east of Shaver Lake**
Finishing Point:	**Brewer Lake**
Total Mileage:	**4.3 miles (one-way)**
Unpaved Mileage:	**4.3 miles**
Driving Time:	**1 hour (one-way)**
Elevation Range:	**8,000–8,800 feet**
Usually Open:	**July to November**
Best Time to Travel:	**July to November**
Difficulty Rating:	**5**
Scenic Rating:	**9**
Remoteness Rating:	**+0**

Special Attractions

- Brewer Lake—a popular fishing spot.
- Dispersed vehicle-based camping on Foster Ridge and walk-in camping at Brewer Lake.

History

Brewer Lake OHV Route travels the length of Foster Ridge en route to the small Brewer Lake. In the 1880s, an English shepherd named John Foster camped at Cutts Meadow while tending sheep. In the summer of 1882, sheep were found roaming throughout the surrounding area unattended. A search revealed the body of John Foster propped up against a large fir tree on the ridge that now bears his name.

A mile east of Brewer Lake along an old pack trail is Tocher Lake, named after Dr. Lloyd Tocher, a doctor from Fresno.

A quiet reward at the end of Brewer Lake OHV Route

Description

Brewer Lake OHV Route is a moderate trail, suitable for all high-clearance 4WDs. Very wide vehicles will have to squeeze through the trees at the very beginning of the trail and also near the end. This popular route combines a scenic, moderately difficult trail with fishing and camping opportunities at Brewer Lake.

Most of the trail is rated less than a 5 for difficulty. The 5 rating comes from a short section of loose rock and large boulders and the final 0.3 miles of moderate to difficult rock crawling.

The trail initially climbs away from 9S69 along a formed dirt trail, meandering up to the ridge through red firs. Past the information board, the trail becomes harder, climbing along a moguled, sandy section to the top of Foster Ridge. The ridge divides waters draining north to the San Joaquin River or south to the Kings River. The trail travels through stands of red firs, which become less dense on the ridge tops. This section is mostly easygoing, following a sandy formed trail with some embedded rocks. There is one 5-rated section that climbs around a rocky ledge with large boulders and loose rock.

Few vehicles can pass between these boulders, 50 yards from the trail's end

The rocks become more abundant as the trail drops off the ridge, and the final 0.3 miles involve negotiating over and around large boulders. This section of the trail is also 5-rated and requires care to avoid damaging your vehicle's underbody. There are some awkwardly placed rocks that can catch a differential or side panel.

The final 50 yards are not accessible even to compact vehicles. Only the smallest vehicles will manage to squeeze between two boulders only 68 inches apart near the end of the trail. Find somewhere to pull off the trail and walk the final short distance to the lake. There is no vehicle-based camping at the lake because of the large boulders, but there are some walk-in campsites near the lakeshore that require a 200-yard hike. Anglers might like to make the short hike to Tocher and Beryl Lakes for additional fishing opportunities for rainbow and brook trout.

This trail is also popular with mountain bikers and is rated easy for them.

The trail is closed from December 1 to July 1 for resource protection, though exact dates vary.

Current Road Information

Sierra National Forest
High Sierra Ranger District
PO Box 559
Prather, CA 93651
(559) 855-5360

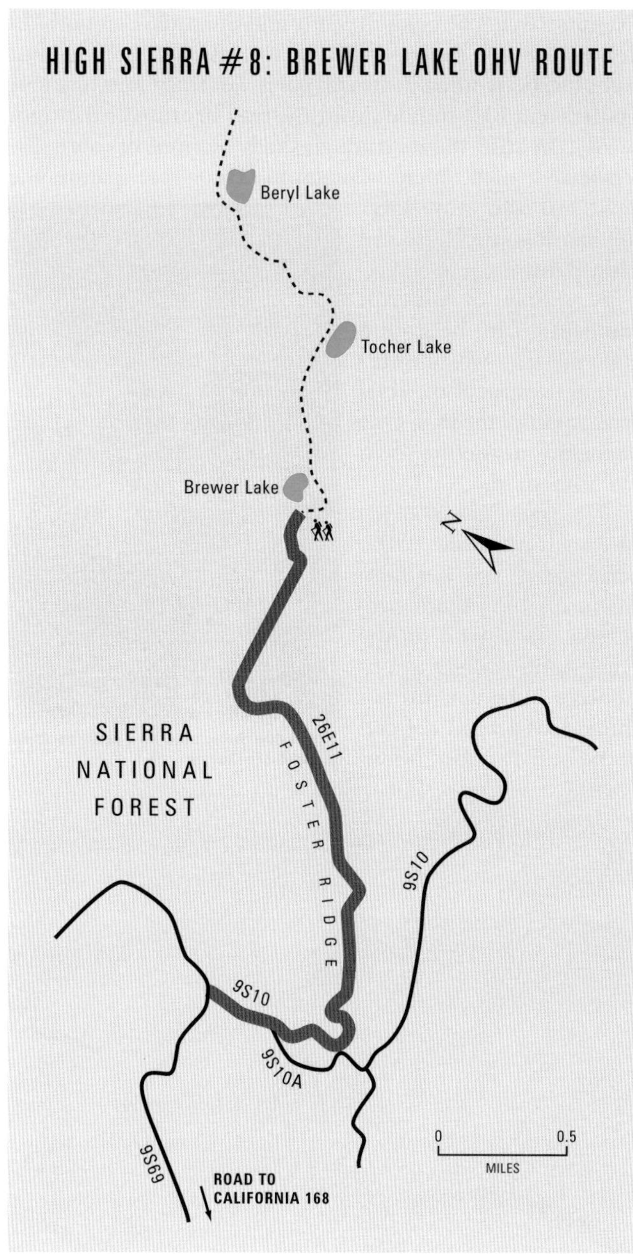

Map References

BLM Shaver Lake
USFS Sierra National Forest
USGS 1:24,000 Huntington Lake, Dogtooth Peak
1:100,000 Shaver Lake
Maptech CD-ROM: Central Coast/Fresno
Northern California Atlas & Gazetteer, pp. 121, 122
California Road & Recreation Atlas, p. 78
Other: Sierra National Forest OHV Guide, Tom Harrison Maps—Mono Divide High Country Trail Map

Route Directions

▼ 0.0		From Shaver Lake, take California 168 northeast to Tamarack Ridge Snowmobile Trailhead, 0.1 miles south of mile marker 56.5. Turn east on paved road 9S09, which leads out the back of the parking lot and is marked for Brewer Lake. Proceed 3.3 miles on 9S09; then turn left (northwest) onto 9S69, following the sign for Brewer Lake. Proceed 1.8 miles on 9S69 to the start of the trail, which begins at the intersection of 9S69 and Foster Ridge Trail (9S10). Zero trip meter and turn southeast on formed dirt trail, following the sign for Brewer Lake.
		GPS: N37°09.42' W119°09.35'
▼ 0.1	SO	Cross over creek.
▼ 0.3	SO	Track on left is 9S31.
▼ 0.9	SO	Track on right is 9S10A.
		GPS: N37°09.15' W119°09.36'
▼ 1.3	TL	4-way intersection. Follow the marker to Brewer Lake and zero trip meter.
		GPS: N37°08.89' W119°09.36'
▼ 0.0		Continue to the east.
▼ 0.1	SO	Seasonal closure gate and information board on right. Road is now marked 26E11. Trail starts to climb gradually.
▼ 1.0	SO	Top of climb on Foster Ridge.
▼ 2.3	SO	Short section of loose rock and large boulders.
		GPS: N37°09.86' W119°07.69'
▼ 2.4	SO	Trail starts to descend toward Brewer Lake.
▼ 2.7	SO	Tight squeeze between trees and boulders. From here to the end involves moderate to difficult rock crawling.
		GPS: N37°09.89' W119°07.51'
▼ 3.0		Brewer Lake. The final 50 yards of the trail are barely wide enough for the smallest 4WDs.
		GPS: N37°09.97' W119°07.45'

HIGH SIERRA #9

Big Creek Railroad Grade Trail

Starting Point:	**Huntington Lake Road, 0.8 miles south of the western entrance to Camp Sierra**
Finishing Point:	**Intersection of 9S07 and 8S08, 6.3 miles north of Pine Ridge and California 168**
Total Mileage:	**12.8 miles**
Unpaved Mileage:	**12.8 miles**
Driving Time:	**2 hours**
Elevation Range:	**3,200–5,000 feet**
Usually Open:	**May to November**
Best Time to Travel:	**May to November**
Difficulty Rating:	**1**
Scenic Rating:	**9**
Remoteness Rating:	**+0**

Special Attractions

- Trail follows the path of the Big Creek Railroad Grade.
- Views into the San Joaquin River Canyon.
- Winding trail well suited for mountain bikes.

Site of the old Chawanakee School on the San Joaquin River

Description

The old San Joaquin & Eastern Railroad grade that ran to Big Creek hasn't seen a train since the 1930s. However, a section of that grade is open to vehicle travel. The winding shelf road traverses the northern slopes of Musick Mountain, Flume Peak, and Mount Stevenson, traveling high above the San Joaquin River. The grade is gentle and the surface smooth. In dry weather it is generally suitable for passenger vehicles, but it should be avoided if the surface is wet from rain or snow. Trailers and RVs should avoid the trail because of the tight turns. The road travels through shady sections of forest, interspersed with open vegetation. There are panoramic views all the way—over the San Joaquin River and Lion Point.

The steep funicular and penstock climb to Kerkoff Dome

A couple of pleasant campsites can be found along the way, which is surprising because of the shelf road aspect of the trail. One of them is at the site of an old homestead.

The trail finishes at the intersection with 9S07, which takes you south to California 168. Alternatively, you can remain on the grade and continue to Auberry, although this becomes paved from the end of the trail described below.

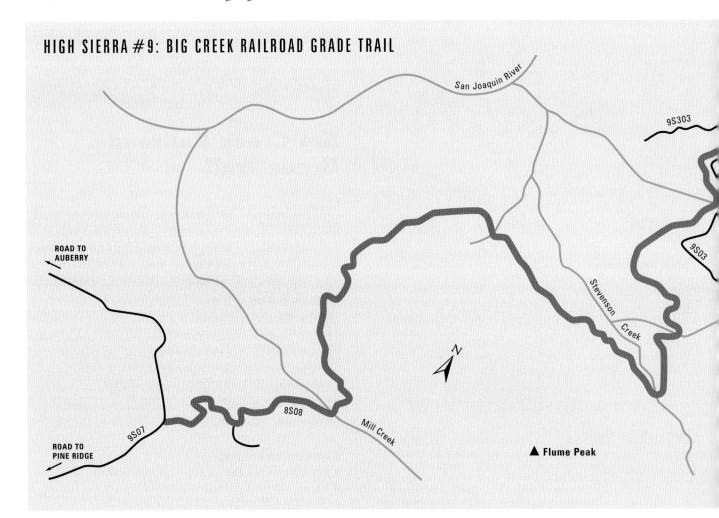

HIGH SIERRA #9: BIG CREEK RAILROAD GRADE TRAIL

San Joaquin River
9S303
ROAD TO AUBERRY
9S03
Stevenson Creek
N
8S08
Mill Creek
9S07
ROAD TO PINE RIDGE
▲ Flume Peak

Current Road Information
Sierra National Forest
High Sierra Ranger District
PO Box 559
Prather, CA 93651
(559) 855-5360

Map References
BLM Shaver Lake
USFS Sierra National Forest
USGS 1:24,000 Musick Mt.
1:100,000 Shaver Lake
Maptech CD-ROM: Central Coast/Fresno
Northern California Atlas & Gazetteer, p. 121
California Road & Recreation Atlas, p. 78

Route Directions

▼ 0.0			From Huntington Lake Road, 0.8 miles south of the western entrance to Camp Sierra, zero trip meter and turn west on graded dirt road 8S08. Railroad grade continues opposite, but is only open to hikers, equestrians, and mountain bikers.
	4.5 ▲		Trail ends at T-intersection with Huntington Lake Road. Turn right for Shaver Lake; turn left for Huntington Lake and Big Creek. Railroad grade continues opposite, but is only open to hikers, equestrians, and mountain bikers.
			GPS: N37°11.15' W119°16.46'
▼ 0.2		SO	Seasonal closure gate. Start of shelf road.
	4.3 ▲	SO	End of shelf road. Seasonal closure gate.
▼ 0.7		SO	Cross over Ely Creek.
	3.8 ▲	SO	Cross over Ely Creek.
			GPS: N37°10.95' W119°17.11'
▼ 1.0		SO	Cross over creek.
	3.5 ▲	SO	Cross over creek.
▼ 1.6		SO	Cross over creek.
	2.9 ▲	SO	Cross over creek.
▼ 1.9		SO	Cattle guard; then cross over penstock; then track on left and track on right.
	2.6 ▲	SO	Track on left and track on right; then cross over penstock; then cattle guard.
			GPS: N37°11.29' W119°18.00'
▼ 2.0		SO	Funicular on left with old cart.
	2.5 ▲	SO	Funicular on right with old cart.
			GPS: N37°11.21' W119°18.03'
▼ 2.6		SO	Track on right.
	1.9 ▲	SO	Track on left.
▼ 3.0		SO	Concrete remains of water tank on left.
	1.5 ▲	SO	Concrete remains of water tank on right.
			GPS: N37°10.90' W119°18.92'
▼ 3.2		SO	Track on right.
	1.3 ▲	SO	Track on left.

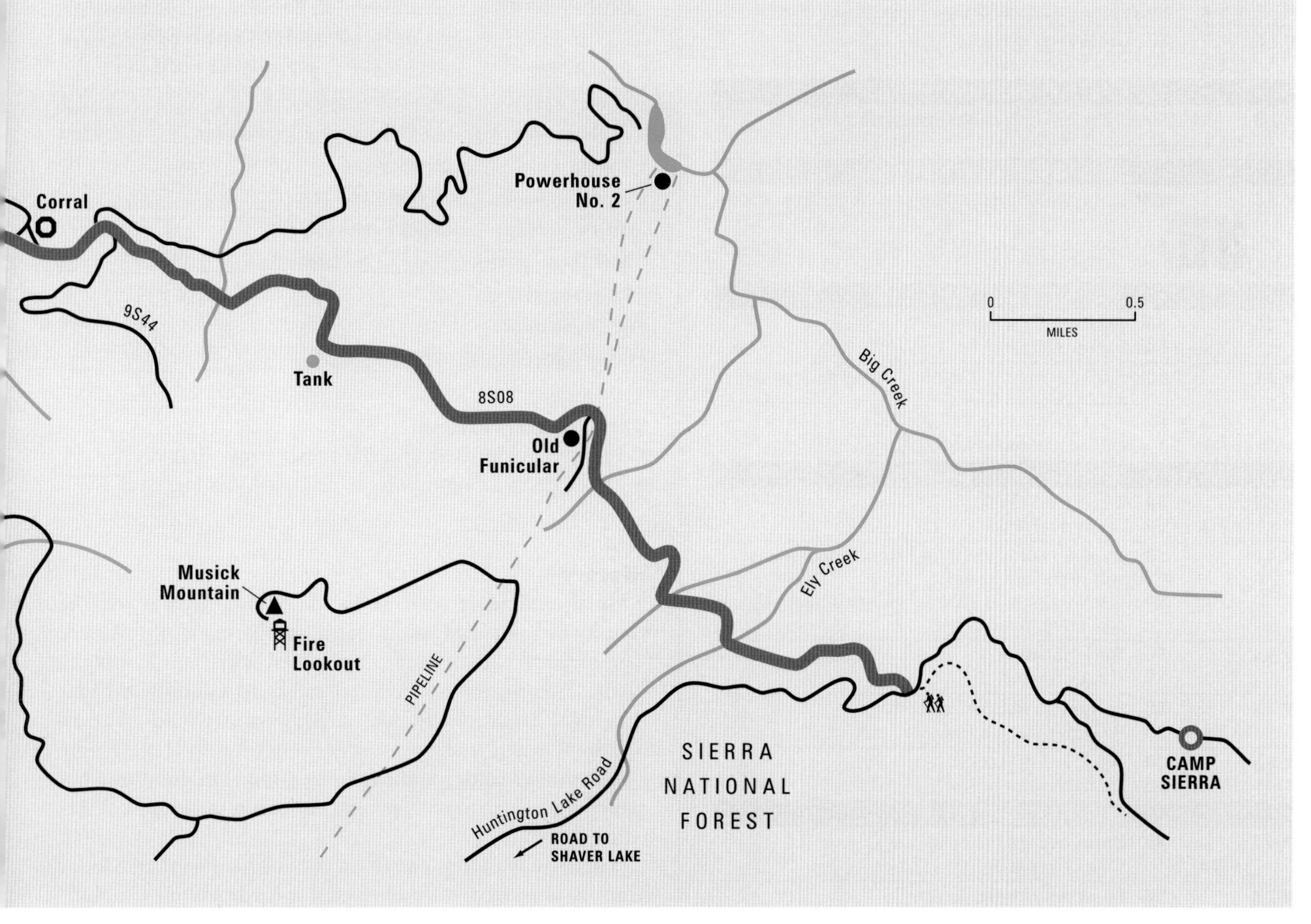

▼ 3.3		SO	Track on right.
	1.2 ▲	SO	Track on left.
▼ 3.6		SO	Cross over creek.
	0.9 ▲	SO	Cross over creek.
▼ 4.2		SO	Track on left is 9S44.
	0.3 ▲	BL	Track on right is 9S44.
			GPS: N37°10.78' W119°19.85'
▼ 4.3		SO	Track on right goes toward Powerhouse No. 2 on Big Creek but ends at a locked gate after 2 miles. End of shelf road.
	0.2 ▲	BR	Track on left goes to Powerhouse No. 2 on Big Creek but ends at a locked gate after 2 miles. Start of shelf road.
▼ 4.4		SO	Track on right.
	0.1 ▲	SO	Track on left.
▼ 4.5		SO	Track on right is 9S303 and corral on right; then track on left is 9S03 signposted to Musick Mountain Lookout and Shaver Lake. Zero trip meter.
	0.0 ▲		Continue to the northeast.
			GPS: N37°10.56' W119°20.10'
▼ 0.0			Continue to the southwest, following sign to Jose Basin and Auberry.
	8.3 ▲	SO	Track on right is 9S03 signposted to Musick Mountain Lookout and Shaver Lake; then track on left is 9S303 and corral on left. Zero trip meter.
▼ 0.5		SO	Cross over creek.
	7.8 ▲	SO	Cross over creek.
▼ 1.4		SO	Track on right is 9S15X.
	6.9 ▲	SO	Track on left is 9S15X.
▼ 2.0		SO	Cross over creek.
	6.3 ▲	SO	Cross over creek.
			GPS: N37°09.62' W119°19.65'
▼ 2.3		SO	Track on right to old homestead site.
	6.0 ▲	SO	Track on left to old homestead site.
			GPS: N37°09.43' W119°19.60'
▼ 2.5		SO	Campsite on right; then cross over Stevenson Creek.
	5.8 ▲	SO	Cross over Stevenson Creek; then campsite on left.
			GPS: N37°09.28' W119°19.54'
▼ 2.6		SO	Two tracks on right.
	5.7 ▲	SO	Two tracks on left.
▼ 3.1		SO	Track on right is 9S39 for hikers, equestrians, and mountain bikers.
	5.2 ▲	BL	Track on left is 9S39 for hikers, equestrians, and mountain bikers.
			GPS: N37°09.35' W119°20.12'
▼ 3.9		SO	Cross over creek.
	4.4 ▲	SO	Cross over creek.
▼ 4.2		SO	Track on left is 9S19 for hikers, equestrians, and mountain bikers.
	4.1 ▲	SO	Track on right is 9S19 for hikers, equestrians, and mountain bikers.
▼ 5.4		SO	Track on left.
	2.9 ▲	SO	Track on right.
▼ 5.8		SO	Power line access track on right.
	2.5 ▲	SO	Power line access track on left.
▼ 6.5		SO	Track on left is 9S21.
	1.8 ▲	SO	Track on right is 9S21.
			GPS: N37°08.28' W119°21.20'
▼ 6.7		SO	Cross over Mill Creek.
	1.6 ▲	SO	Cross over Mill Creek.
▼ 7.0		SO	Seasonal closure gate.
	1.3 ▲	SO	Seasonal closure gate.
▼ 7.5		SO	Track on left.
	0.8 ▲	SO	Track on right.
▼ 7.6		SO	Track on left under power lines.
	0.7 ▲	SO	Track on right under power lines.
▼ 8.3			Trail ends at intersection of 8S08 and 9S07. Bear left for Pine Ridge and Jose Basin; bear right over bridge for Auberry.
	0.0 ▲		Trail commences at intersection of 9S07 and 8S08, 6.3 miles north of Pine Ridge on California 168 and 10.5 miles east of Auberry. Zero trip meter and proceed north on graded dirt 8S08.
			GPS: N37°07.56' W119°22.21'

HIGH SIERRA #10

Balloon Dome Overlook Trail

Starting Point:	**Kaiser Pass Road (FR 80), 9.3 miles north of Lakeshore and California 168, 10 miles south of Mono Hot Springs**
Finishing Point:	**Stump Springs Road (FR 5), 1 mile north of West Kaiser USFS Campground**
Total Mileage:	**23.1 miles, plus 2-mile spur to Balloon Dome Overlook**
Unpaved Mileage:	**23.1 miles, plus 2-mile spur**
Driving Time:	**2 hours**
Elevation Range:	**5,400–8,600 feet**
Usually Open:	**June to November**
Best Time to Travel:	**June to November**
Difficulty Rating:	**2**
Scenic Rating:	**8**
Remoteness Rating:	**+0**

Special Attractions

- Views of Kaiser Peak and the Kaiser Creek drainage.
- Developed campgrounds at Sample Meadow and West Kaiser.

History

Early sheepherders such as D. C. Sample frequented the vicinity of Sample Meadow, at the southern end of this trail. The meadow's name is also associated with Sam Sample, a Native American who diverted creeks to establish broader meadows. Traditionally, Native Americans would camp in meadows where there was water, building lodgepole pine smoke houses to dry and smoke venison. The meadows became larger over time as people cut down trees and collected firewood.

Hoffman Meadow, passed on the northern flank of Mount Tom, is associated with another shepherd, Milton D. Huff-

Spur trail's view of Balloon Dome's southeast face, a challenging ascent even for experienced climbers

man. Huffman ranged his sheep throughout the mountains around the turn of the twentieth century.

The southern end of the trail crosses Kaiser Creek to finish just south of the old Kaiser Diggings Work Center. Downstream on Kaiser Creek, T. J. Dunlap struck it rich in 1853, shortly after arriving from the East. He and his cousin worked their mine successfully for several years before selling out at an enormous profit. Dunlap then operated a sawmill near today's Bass Lake and served on Fresno County's board of supervisors. Dunlap's fortune was long gone by the time he passed away at 89 years of age.

In 1879, John French began work on a wagon road based on an Indian trade route through the Sierra Nevada. The French Trail followed the San Joaquin River, passing below Dunlap's mine and around the base of Balloon Dome before climbing toward the east side of the Sierra Nevada. This route had the advantage of traveling at relatively low elevations, thereby avoiding the heavy snowfalls that plagued early travelers. French's ambitious undertaking was never completed; he lost financial support when the Mammoth Mining Company, on the eastern side of the Sierra, failed. The route is now being incorporated into the San Joaquin River Trail System, a planned 73-mile-long hiking and horse trail from Millerton Lake that will ultimately meet the Pacific Crest Trail.

Description

Balloon Dome Overlook Trail is a long, easy trail that follows various forest roads through Sierra National Forest. It commences by following Stump Springs Road, which connects Kaiser Pass Road and Lake Thomas A. Edison with Big Creek. As it winds through pines, red firs, and scattered aspens, the graded trail is paved in places to prevent erosion. It passes the Rattlesnake Hiking Trail, which travels 4 miles to the Rattlesnake Crossing of the San Joaquin River and continues farther into the Ansel Adams Wilderness to connect with other hiking trails.

There is a forest service campground just off the trail at Sample Meadow. Sites are dispersed among the trees and have picnic tables, fire rings, and pit toilets. Recent logging in the campground's vicinity has reduced the aesthetic value of the area.

As the trail continues, it heads out of the forest and descends high around the edge of the Kaiser Creek Valley. There are panoramic views of Kaiser Peak, Mount Tom, and the Kaiser Creek drainage. The shelf road is wide enough for two vehicles to easily pass each other. The route passes the start of High Sierra #11: Mount Tom Fire Lookout Trail—a short, moderate trail that climbs to the top of Mount Tom.

The spur trail, 150 yards before the Balloon Dome Overlook

Balloon Dome Overlook Trail meanders along narrower forest roads through the trees. The standard is still easygoing, single-vehicle width for much of the way and suitable for a high-clearance 2WD vehicle in dry weather.

A short spur trail leads down an old seldom-used logging trail to a clearing in the trees. A short 0.1-mile hike due north from the end of the vehicle trail leads to a viewpoint over Balloon Dome and magnificent views over the South Fork of the San Joaquin River. The granite Balloon Dome, located within the Ansel Adams Wilderness, is popular with rock climbers. The coordinates of the overlook are GPS: N37°26.33' W119°12.73'.

The main trail continues through the forest, past viewpoints over Squaw Dome, Balloon Dome, Triple Divide Peak, and the Minarets. It passes the forest service work station at Kaiser Diggings before finishing back on Stump Springs Road.

Kaiser Pass is usually open by Memorial Day each year, though exact dates vary.

Current Road Information

Sierra National Forest
High Sierra Ranger District
PO Box 559
Prather, CA 93651
(559) 855-5360

Map References

BLM Shaver Lake
USFS Sierra National Forest
USGS 1:24,000 Mt. Givens, Kaiser Peak, Balloon Dome
1:100,000 Shaver Lake
Maptech CD-ROM: Central Coast/Fresno
Northern California Atlas & Gazetteer, pp. 122, 121
California Road & Recreation Atlas, p. 78

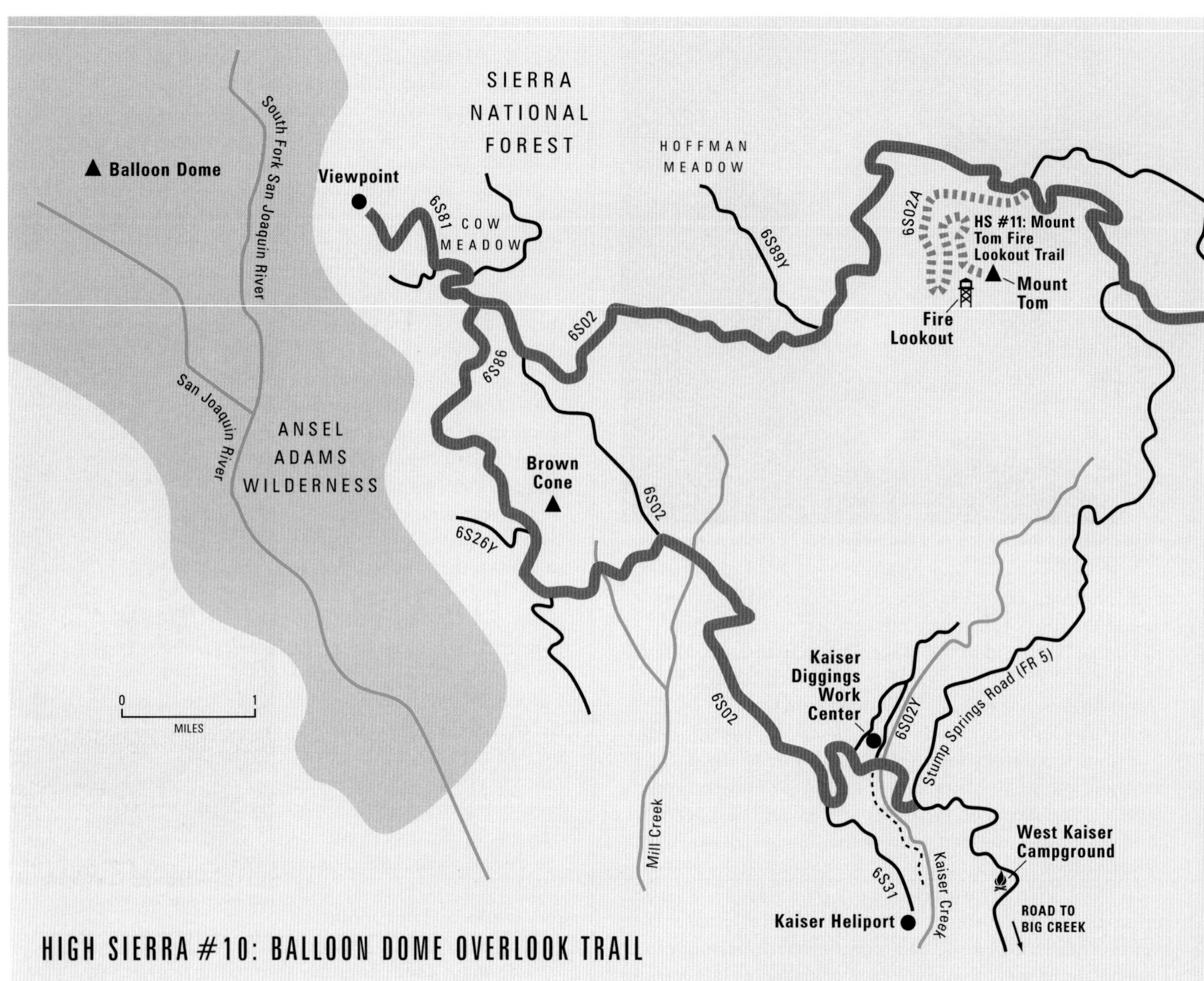

Route Directions

▼ 0.0		From Kaiser Pass Road (FR 80), 9.3 miles north of Lakeshore and 10 miles south of Mono Hot Springs, zero trip meter and turn west on graded dirt FR 5, marked for Sample Meadow Campground and Stump Springs Snowmobile Trail.
2.9 ▲		Trail ends at T-intersection with paved Kaiser Pass Road (FR 80). Turn right for Huntington Lake; turn left for Lake Thomas A. Edison.
		GPS: N37°18.71′ W119°06.85′
▼ 1.9	SO	Parking on right for Rattlesnake Trail (24E03.5)—riding and hiking trail to Rattlesnake Crossing. Hiking trail on left to Upper Twin Lake.
1.0 ▲	SO	Parking on left for Rattlesnake Trail (24E03.5)—riding and hiking trail to Rattlesnake Crossing. Hiking trail on right to Upper Twin Lake.
		GPS: N37°19.46′ W119°08.36′
▼ 2.6	SO	Seasonal closure gate.
0.3 ▲	SO	Seasonal closure gate.
▼ 2.7	SO	Track on left to small meadow.
0.2 ▲	SO	Track on right to small meadow.
▼ 2.9	SO	Track on left goes to Sample Meadow USFS Campground and Avalanche Hiking Trail. Zero trip meter and follow the sign to Mount Tom Lookout and Big Creek.
0.0 ▲		Continue to the south.
		GPS: N37°19.95′ W119°09.02′
▼ 0.0		Continue to the north.
2.5 ▲	SO	Track on right goes to Sample Meadow USFS Campground and Avalanche Hiking Trail. Zero trip meter and follow the sign to Kaiser Pass Road.
▼ 0.4	BL	Track on right is 6S70X.
2.1 ▲	SO	Track on left is 6S70X.
		GPS: N37°20.25′ W119°09.10′
▼ 0.6	SO	Old shingle cabins below trail on left.
1.9 ▲	SO	Old shingle cabins below trail on right.
▼ 0.7	SO	Track on left to cabins; then corral on left.
1.8 ▲	SO	Corral on right; then track on right to old shingle cabins below the trail.
		GPS: N37°20.42′ W119°09.37′
▼ 2.5	TR	Turn right onto 6S02, signposted to Mount Tom Lookout and also marked as Mount Tom Snowmobile Trail. Zero trip meter. FR 5 continues straight ahead to West Kaiser USFS Campground and Big Creek.

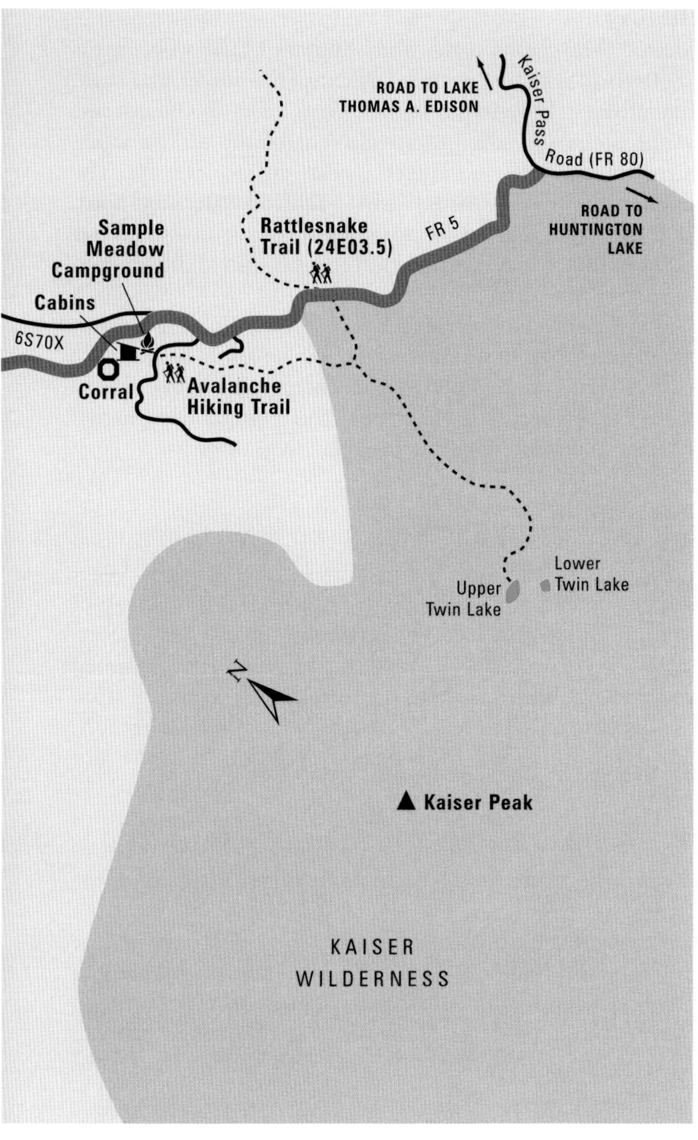

0.0 ▲ Continue to the southeast.

GPS: N37°21.66′ W119°10.14′

▼ 0.0 Continue to the northeast.
1.9 ▲ TL T-intersection with FR 5. Zero trip meter and follow the sign for Kaiser Pass Road. FR 5 goes to Big Creek to the right.

▼ 1.9 TL T-intersection. Turn left and immediately bear right. Track on left after the T-intersection is High Sierra #11: Mount Tom Fire Lookout Trail (6S02A), marked with a wooden sign. Zero trip meter.
0.0 ▲ Continue to the south.

GPS: N37°22.51′ W119°09.84′

▼ 0.0 Continue to the west.
6.2 ▲ TR Track on right is High Sierra #11: Mount Tom Fire Lookout Trail (6S02A), marked with a wooden sign. Turn right after this intersection onto unmarked well-used trail. Track continues straight ahead. Zero trip meter.

▼ 3.4 SO Track on right is 6S89Y to Hoffman Meadow.
2.8 ▲ SO Track on left is 6S89Y to Hoffman Meadow.

GPS: N37°23.19′ W119°11.71′

▼ 3.7 SO Track on right.
2.5 ▲ SO Track on left.

▼ 3.8 SO Track on left.
2.4 ▲ SO Track on right.

▼ 4.1 SO Track on left.
2.1 ▲ SO Track on right.

▼ 6.2 TR Turn right onto smaller dirt road 6S86 and zero trip meter. Track on left continues to Mill Creek.
0.0 ▲ Continue to the southeast.

GPS: N37°24.82′ W119°13.08′

▼ 0.0 Continue to the north.
0.5 ▲ TL Turn left onto larger dirt road 6S02, following the sign to Mount Tom Lookout. Zero trip meter.

▼ 0.3 SO Track on right is 6S86H.
0.2 ▲ SO Track on left is 6S86H.

▼ 0.5 SO Track on right is the spur to Balloon Dome Overlook (6S81). Zero trip meter.
0.0 ▲ Continue to the southeast.

GPS: N37°25.23′ W119°12.90′

Spur to Balloon Dome Overlook

▼ 0.0 Proceed north on 6S81.
▼ 0.6 TL Track continues ahead. Turn left on unmarked trail.

GPS: N37°25.38′ W119°12.75′

▼ 0.7 SO Seasonal closure gate. Closed to vehicles from May 15 to June 15 and from October 1 to November 30.
▼ 1.0 BR Track on left.

GPS: N37°25.64′ W119°12.83′

▼ 1.2 SO Track on right.

GPS: N37°25.84′ W119°12.52′

▼ 2.0 Trail ends at a small clearing. Hike north for 0.1 miles to view Balloon Dome.

GPS: N37°26.19′ W119°12.72′

Continuation of Main Trail

▼ 0.0 Continue to the northwest.
4.2 ▲ SO Track on left is the spur to Balloon Dome Overlook (6S81). Zero trip meter.

GPS: N37°25.23′ W119°12.90′

▼ 0.2 SO Track on right.
4.0 ▲ SO Track on left.

▼ 1.0 SO Views through the trees to the right of Balloon Dome.
3.2 ▲ SO Views through the trees to the left of Balloon Dome.

▼ 2.4 SO Track on right is 6S26Y through seasonal closure gate.
1.8 ▲ SO Track on left is 6S26Y through seasonal closure gate.

GPS: N37°24.20′ W119°14.26′

▼ 3.0 SO Small track on right.
1.2 ▲ SO Small track on left.

▼ 3.6 SO Cross over creek.
0.6 ▲ SO Cross over creek.

GPS: N37°23.75′ W119°14.25′

▼ 4.2 TR T-intersection with graded dirt 6S02, marked with small wooden sign. Zero trip meter.
0.0 ▲ Continue to the west.

GPS: N37°23.50′ W119°13.78′

▼ 0.0 Continue to the south.
4.9 ▲ TL Turn left onto well-used formed dirt trail 6S86 and zero trip meter.

▼ 0.3	SO	Cross over Mill Creek.
4.6 ▲	SO	Cross over Mill Creek.
▼ 0.5	SO	Track on left.
4.4 ▲	BL	Track on right.
▼ 2.0	SO	Track on right.
2.9 ▲	SO	Track on left.
▼ 3.2	BL	Track on right is 6S31 to Kaiser Heliport.
1.7 ▲	BR	Track on left is 6S31 to Kaiser Heliport.
		GPS: N37°21.65' W119°14.89'
▼ 3.8	SO	Cross over creek; then track on left.
1.1 ▲	SO	Track on right; then cross over creek.
▼ 3.9	SO	Kaiser Diggings Work Station on left.
1.0 ▲	SO	Kaiser Diggings Work Station on right.
		GPS: N37°21.78' W119°14.51'
▼ 4.0	SO	Track on left is 6S27.
0.9 ▲	SO	Track on right is 6S27.
▼ 4.3	SO	Track on left is 6S02Y, part of Kaiser Creek Trail (26E30) that also goes to the right. Cross over Kaiser Creek on bridge.
0.6 ▲	SO	Cross over Kaiser Creek on bridge. Track on right is 6S02Y, part of Kaiser Creek Trail (26E30) that also goes to the left.
		GPS: N37°21.53' W119°14.43'
▼ 4.9		Trail ends at T-intersection with paved Stump Springs Road (FR 5) opposite 7S27X. Turn left for Kaiser Pass Road; turn right for Big Creek.
0.0 ▲		Trail commences on Stump Springs Road (FR 5), 22 miles north of Big Creek and 1 mile north of West Kaiser USFS Campground. Zero trip meter and turn west on graded dirt road marked 6S02, signposted to Kaiser Diggings Station and Hoffman Meadow. Track opposite is 7S27X.
		GPS: N37°21.20' W119°14.58'

HIGH SIERRA #11

Mount Tom Fire Lookout Trail

Starting Point:	**High Sierra #10: Balloon Dome Overlook Trail, 7.3 miles northwest of Kaiser Pass Road**
Finishing Point:	**Mount Tom Fire Lookout**
Total Mileage:	**2.7 miles (one-way)**
Unpaved Mileage:	**2.7 miles**
Driving Time:	**30 minutes (one-way)**
Elevation Range:	**7,900–9,000 feet**
Usually Open:	**June to November**
Best Time to Travel:	**June to November**
Difficulty Rating:	**3**
Scenic Rating:	**10**
Remoteness Rating:	**+0**

Special Attractions

- Mount Tom Fire Lookout.
- 360-degree views from the lookout tower.

History

Mount Tom got its name from Thomas Clark, who, in the 1860s, made the first recorded ascent of this spectacular peak. Clark lived in Owensville, in the Owens Valley on the east side of the Sierra Nevada. Owensville, one of the earliest settlements in the valley, no longer appears on today's maps. The site was immediately east of Laws, a railroad water stop north of Bishop that can be found along High Sierra #44: Silver Canyon Trail. Clark credited local Indians with leading him to the top of the mountain.

The Civilian Conservation Corps (CCC) built the lookout on Mount Tom. It was one of the last lookouts built by the CCC. The 14- by 14-foot wooden cabin perched atop the K-braced steel tower is 43 feet above the ground. The external staircase is one long flight without landings or turns.

Description

This short, rewarding trail leaves High Sierra #10: Balloon Dome Overlook Trail and climbs steadily along a loose, roughly graded dirt road to the fire lookout tower on top of Mount Tom (9,018 feet). The tower is one of a few in Sierra National Forest still manned. If you visit during summer, you may be able to climb to the tower with permission from the lookout on duty. Visiting hours are Wednesday to Sunday 9 A.M. to 6 P.M.; it is generally closed on Mondays and Tuesdays.

The climb is steady and follows a shelf road for most of the way. There is a seasonal closure gate near the bottom; this is normally open when the tower is manned. Initially, the trail passes through shady pine and fir forest, but near the top the landscape opens out and is strewn with large granite outcrops and boulders. The views get better the higher you climb. The view from the tower includes Balloon Dome to the northwest and Lake Thomas A. Edison to the northeast. The Seven Gables, the Minarets, and the Ansel Adams Wilderness can also be seen.

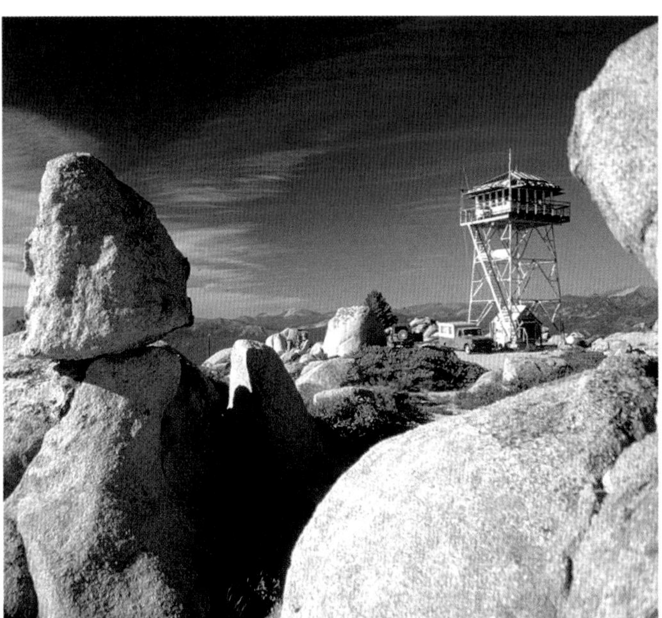

Mount Tom Fire Lookout provides 360-degree, 9,026-foot views of Ansel Adams Wilderness to the northeast and Kaiser Peak to the south

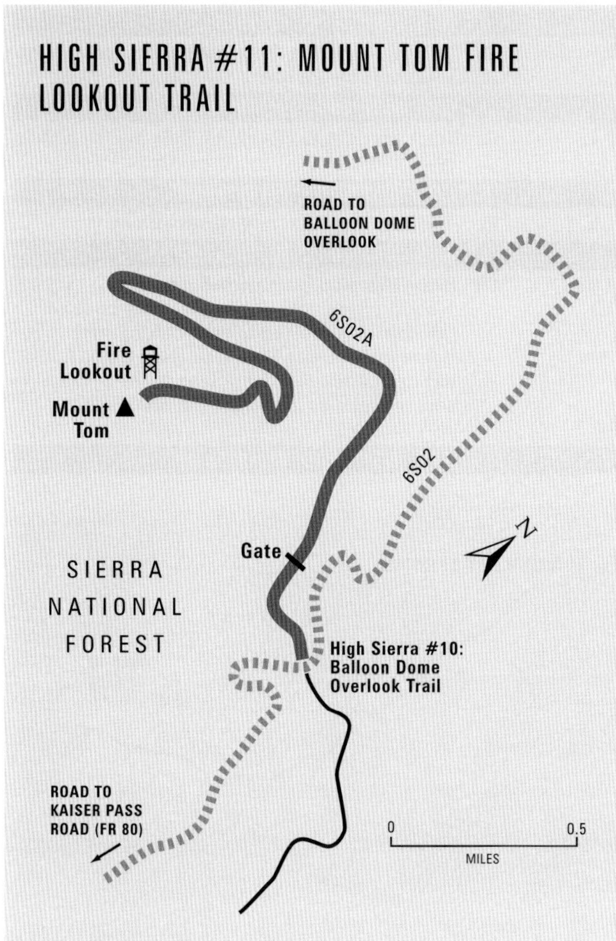

Current Road Information

Sierra National Forest
High Sierra Ranger District
PO Box 559
Prather, CA 93651
(559) 855-5360

Map References

BLM Shaver Lake
USFS Sierra National Forest
USGS 1:24,000 Balloon Dome
1:100,000 Shaver Lake
Maptech CD-ROM: Central Coast/Fresno
Northern California Atlas & Gazetteer, p. 121
California Road & Recreation Atlas, p. 78

Route Directions

▼ 0.0	BL	From High Sierra #10: Balloon Dome Overlook Trail (6S02) at the T-intersection at the foot of Mount Tom, 7.3 miles northwest of Kaiser Pass Road, zero trip meter and proceed west along the main trail. Immediately bear left, following the sign to Mount Tom Lookout.
		GPS: N37°22.51' W119°09.84'
▼ 0.3 ▼ 2.7	SO	Gate—usually open when tower is manned. Mount Tom Fire Lookout.
		GPS: N37°22.58' W119°10.69'

HIGH SIERRA #12

Bear Diversion Dam OHV Route

Starting Point:	Kaiser Pass Road (FR 80), 1.8 miles south of Mono Creek Campground and 1 mile northeast of Mono Hot Springs
Finishing Point:	Bear Diversion Dam
Total Mileage:	2.3 miles (one-way)
Unpaved Mileage:	2.3 miles
Driving Time:	30 minutes (one-way)
Elevation Range:	7,000–7,800 feet
Usually Open:	May to November
Best Time to Travel:	May to November
Difficulty Rating:	4
Scenic Rating:	10
Remoteness Rating:	+0

Special Attractions

- Bear Diversion Dam spillway—a popular spot for picnicking and fishing.
- Access to the John Muir Wilderness along Bear Creek for hikers and equestrians.

History

Bear Diversion Dam is part of the Big Creek Hydroelectric Power System. Under the control of H. E. Huntington, the Pacific Light and Power Corporation (PLPC), began construction of the initial Big Creek Powerhouse in 1911. A second powerhouse was added along Big Creek; Huntington Lake was developed; and various other dams and powerhouses were constructed in the following years.

Bear Diversion Dam

In 1917, PLPC merged with Southern California Edison and expansion of the Big Creek System continued into the 1920s. Shaver Lake was established in 1926, as was Florence Lake, located south of this trail. In 1927, the Bear Diversion Dam was added to the growing network of dams, all of which were connected by a series of tunnels, pipelines, and penstocks.

Bear Diversion Dam, along with many of the structures in the project, is now eligible for inclusion in the National Register of Historic Places.

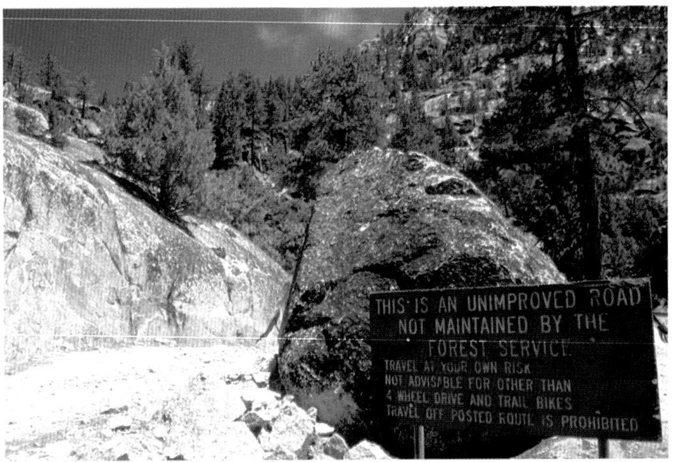

The trail is designated for 4WD vehicle and dirt bike use only

Description

This short trail is one of the most spectacular in the region. Southern California Edison maintains the trail to service its hydroelectric facilities at the Bear Diversion Dam, popular for fishing, picnicking, and camping. It is also the start of a hiking trail along Bear Creek. Anglers can fish for brook, brown, golden, and rainbow trout in the spillway.

The trail winds around spectacular granite domes and cliffs dotted with western junipers and Jeffrey pines; it is loose and scrabbly in places, with some moderately steep undulations and short sections of single-lane shelf road. It is suitable for most high-clearance 4WD vehicles.

The trail ends on a bare granite dome above the Bear Diversion Dam in the shadow of Bear Dome. You can camp here, but most of the campsites are on rock. One campsite near the end of the trail can be found along a track that leads to the dam.

Current Road Information

Sierra National Forest
High Sierra Ranger District
PO Box 559
Prather, CA 93651
(559) 855-5360

Map References

BLM Shaver Lake, Bishop
USFS Sierra National Forest
USGS 1:24,000 Mt. Givens, Florence Lake
1:100,000 Shaver Lake, Bishop
Maptech CD-ROM: Central Coast/Fresno; Kings Canyon/Death Valley
Northern California Atlas & Gazetteer, p. 122
California Road & Recreation Atlas, p. 78
Other: Sierra National Forest OHV Guide, Tom Harrison Maps—Mono Divide High Country Trail Map

Route Directions

▼ 0.0		From Kaiser Pass Road (FR 80), 1.8 miles south of Mono Creek Campground and 1 mile northeast of Mono Hot Springs, zero trip meter and turn east on formed dirt road marked Bear Route.
		GPS: N37°20.30′ W119°00.21′
▼ 0.1	BR	Two tracks on left. Bear right and pass through seasonal closure gate.
		GPS: N37°20.29′ W119°00.07′
▼ 0.4	BL	Track on right to viewpoint. This intersection is easy to miss.
		GPS: N37°20.12′ W118°59.91′
▼ 1.5	BL	Track on right to tunnel access point.
		GPS: N37°20.00′ W118°59.22′
▼ 2.2	SO	Bear Diversion Dam comes into view.
▼ 2.3		Track on right goes 0.1 miles to the base of the dam. The trail ends on a bare granite dome overlooking Bear Diversion Dam. A hiking trail continues along Bear Creek to intersect with the Pacific Crest National Scenic Trail.
		GPS: N37°20.19′ W118°58.49′

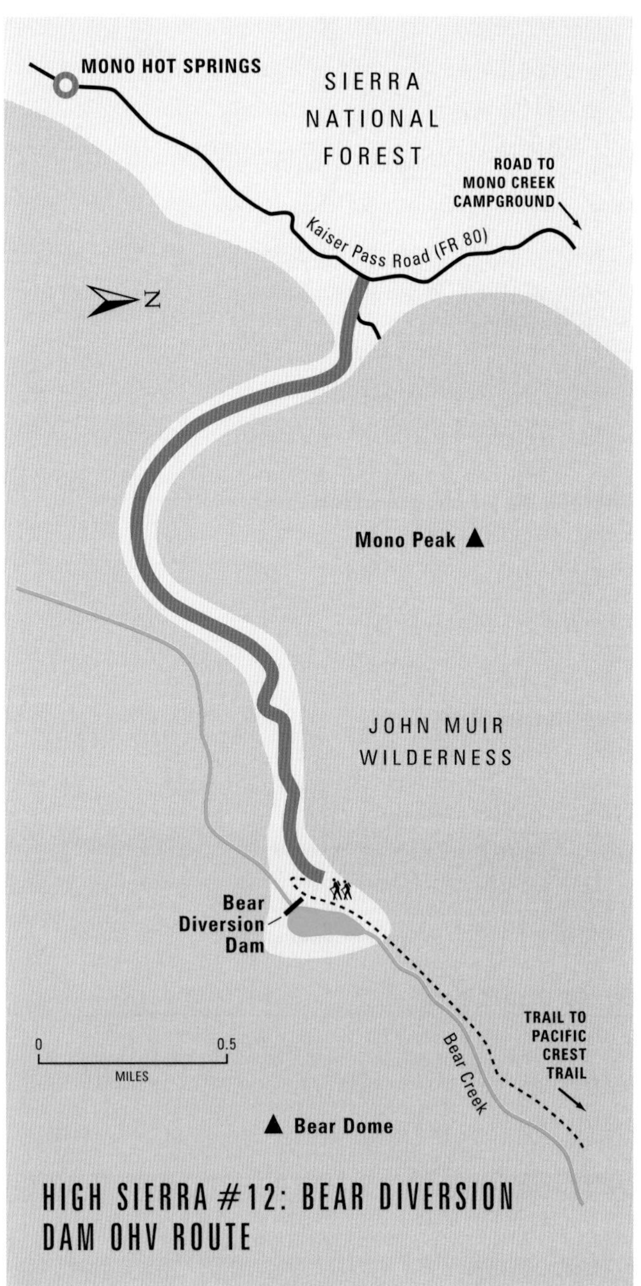

HIGH SIERRA #13

Onion Spring OHV Route

Starting Point:	**Entrance to Vermilion USFS Campground, 2 miles northwest of Lake Thomas A. Edison dam**
Finishing Point:	**Closure gate at Four Forks Creek before the Ansel Adams Wilderness**
Total Mileage:	**5.7 miles (one-way)**
Unpaved Mileage:	**5.7 miles**
Driving Time:	**1.25 hours (one-way)**
Elevation Range:	**7,600–8,200 feet**
Usually Open:	**June to November**
Best Time to Travel:	**June to November**
Difficulty Rating:	**4**
Scenic Rating:	**10**
Remoteness Rating:	**+1**

Special Attractions

- Trout fishing at Lake Thomas A. Edison.
- Views over the San Joaquin River Valley and the Ansel Adams Wilderness.
- Access to a network of hiking and equestrian trails leading into the Ansel Adams Wilderness.

Description

Onion Spring OHV Route is an easy to moderate spur trail that travels through a 300-foot-wide vehicle corridor into the Ansel Adams Wilderness. It commences on the western side of Lake Thomas A. Edison at the Vermilion USFS Campground. The lake is popular with anglers, who fish for German brown, rainbow, eastern brook, and golden trout. Boaters may take advantage of the free public boat ramp. The area is also the trailhead for many popular hiking and equestrian trails into the Ansel Adams Wilderness, including the Pacific Crest National Scenic Trail.

Lake Thomas A. Edison sits at the foot of the Mono Divide

In addition to Vermilion Campground, there are several undeveloped sites along the road from the dam to the start of this trail. Several of these sites have excellent views of the lake. Vermilion Campground has 31 sites for tents; some can accommodate camper trailers and small RVs; however, there are no hookups. Vermilion Valley Resort operates seasonally under a permit from the National Forest Service and has cabins, tents, boat rentals, and a small café; there is no gas. The resort operates a passenger ferry on Lake Thomas A. Edison, with two trips a day leaving the resort at 9 A.M. and 4 P.M. For a small fee, the ferry takes hikers to the Mono Creek Trail at the northeastern end of the lake.

Distant view of Lake Edison and Bear Dome from atop a granite ridge

Onion Spring OHV Route passes the trailhead parking for Devils Bathtub Trail and Goodale Pass Trail. Camping is permitted at the trailhead, and there are facilities for horses. Initially, the OHV trail runs along a ridge top past granite outcroppings and cliffs. There are great views south over the Ansel Adams Wilderness and the South Fork of the San Joaquin River Valley. Some lovely backcountry campsites with panoramic views are situated among red firs, Jeffrey pines, and manzanitas.

The trail surface is mainly sandy with some embedded rock. It is rated 4 for difficulty because of a couple of sections where care is needed with wheel placement to avoid catching the underbody; the majority of the trail is rated 3.

After 4 miles, the trail enters the forest and winds through denser vegetation, crossing through Onion Spring Meadow. An old campground, no longer maintained, at Onion Spring Meadow is still a pleasant place to stop for those wanting a more sheltered campsite than the sites along the ridge.

The trail ends at a closure gate and the start of a hiking trail into the Ansel Adams Wilderness. Onion Spring Trail leads off from the end of the OHV trail and intersects with other trails in the area. The very steep hiking trail has many switchbacks for the first 2.5 miles. A permit is not required for day use of the wilderness trail. However those planning to camp in the wilderness must get a permit from the Kings River–Pineridge Ranger District (fee charged). There are a limited number of permits issued between

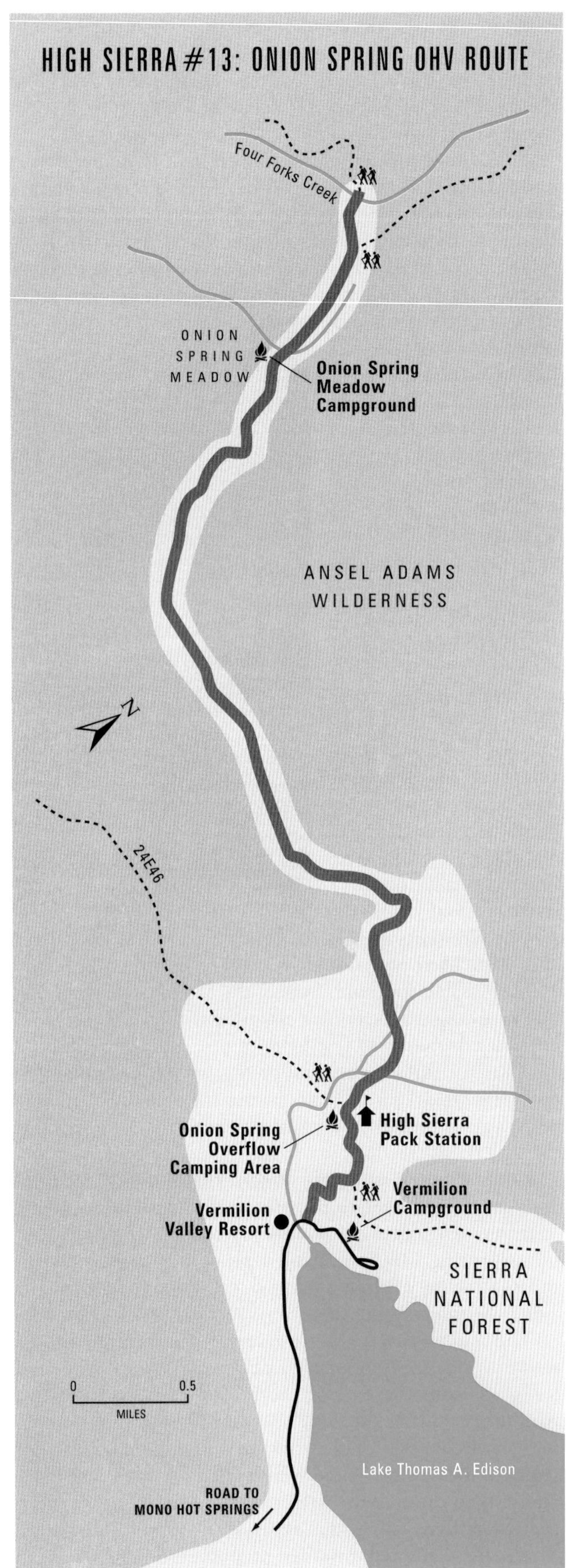

June and September and reservations are recommended.

The only access to the start of the trail is via Kaiser Pass Road, which is usually open by Memorial Day, though exact dates vary.

Current Road Information

Sierra National Forest
High Sierra Ranger District
PO Box 559
Prather, CA 93651
(559) 855-5360

Map References

BLM Shaver Lake
USFS Sierra National Forest
USGS 1:24,000 Sharktooth Peak
1:100,000 Shaver Lake
Maptech CD-ROM: Central Coast/Fresno
Northern California Atlas & Gazetteer, p. 122
California Road & Recreation Atlas, p. 78
Other: Sierra National Forest OHV Guide, Tom Harrison Maps—Mono Divide High Country Trail Map

Route Directions

▼ 0.0		From the entrance to the Vermilion USFS Campground at Lake Thomas A. Edison, 22 miles from Lakeshore and 2 miles northwest of the dam and FR 80, zero trip meter and continue to the northwest along graded dirt road, following the sign to Onion Spring.
		GPS: N37°22.66' W119°00.78'
▼ 0.2	BR	Track on left. Follow the sign for trailhead parking for Devils Bathtub Trail (27E03) and Goodale Pass Trail.
▼ 0.5	BL	Mono Creek Trailhead parking on right. Follow the sign to Onion Spring.
		GPS: N37°22.89' W119°00.80'
▼ 0.8	SO	Track on left.
▼ 0.9	SO	High Sierra Pack Station on right and Onion Spring Overflow Camping Area on left. Warm Springs Creek Hiking Trail (26E46) on left. Continue straight ahead past the sign for the unimproved road.
		GPS: N37°23.01' W119°01.12'
▼ 1.0	SO	Cross through creek.
		GPS: N37°23.16' W119°01.16'
▼ 1.2	BL	Track on right.
▼ 1.3	SO	Cross through creek.
▼ 1.6	SO	Cross over creek.
▼ 2.3	SO	Turnout on left with views over Lake Thomas A. Edison.
▼ 4.9	SO	Track on left to Onion Spring Meadow Campground; then cross through creek.
		GPS: N37°24.18' W119°04.25'
▼ 5.5	SO	Hiking trail on right enters the Ansel Adams Wilderness.
		GPS: N37°24.60' W119°04.43'
▼ 5.7		Trail ends at permanent closure gate at Four Forks Creek. Hikers and equestrians are permitted beyond the gate along the old vehicle trail into the Ansel Adams Wilderness to Rock Creek and Bear Meadow.
		GPS: N37°24.74' W119°04.64'

HIGH SIERRA #14

Peckinpah Road

Starting Point:	**CR 233, 3.3 miles northeast of North Fork**
Finishing Point:	**Minarets Road, 0.8 miles north of Rock Creek USFS Campground**
Total Mileage:	**20 miles**
Unpaved Mileage:	**18.5 miles**
Driving Time:	**2 hours**
Elevation Range:	**3,800–6,600 feet**
Usually Open:	**May to November**
Best Time to Travel:	**May to November**
Difficulty Rating:	**2**
Scenic Rating:	**8**
Remoteness Rating:	**+0**

Special Attractions

- Easy winding trail in Sierra National Forest.
- Access to a network of 4WD trails.
- Whisky Snowmobile Area.
- Wildflowers in late spring and early summer.

History

The Mono Indians of the Sierra Nevada and Great Basin summered in the North Fork of the San Joaquin River region for hundreds, if not thousands, of years. Gold prospector Joe Kinsman may have been the first settler in the region when he mistook the San Joaquin River for the Sacramento River. Joe settled among the Indians, took an Indian wife, and fathered a child. He lived in the region he learned to love until his death in 1917.

Miners and pioneers could buy last-minute supplies at the settlement of North Fork (originally known as Brown's) in Madera County, before heading deeper into the Sierra Nevada. When mining slowed, Brown's adapted. It became a major timber town and changed its name when the North Fork Lumber Company started up in 1892. A sawmill had existed as early as 1852. The logging era has passed, but North Fork survives as a gateway into the Sierra Nevada. Townsfolk are quick to point out the significance of North Fork's location. The community lies about 5 miles from what has been determined to be the exact center of California.

Peckinpah Road climbs high above the South Fork Bluffs and Browns Creek

Peckinpah Meadow, along the southwestern section of the trail, was the site of a sawmill operated by Charlie Peckinpah. He and his brothers started the mill in 1884 and worked it until 1905. Their enterprise gave the name to this old timber trail. Many members of the Peckinpah family homesteaded in the vicinity. Decades later, a member of the same family became a prominent movie director. Sam Peckinpah directed such classics as *The Wild Bunch* (1969), *Straw Dogs* (1971), *The Getaway* (1972), *Pat Garrett and Billy the Kid* (1973), and many more.

Description

Peckinpah Road travels from North Fork to Minarets Road through Sierra National Forest, passing Peckinpah Meadow, several backcountry campsites, and other 4WD, hiking, equestrian, and motorbike trails. Passenger vehicles can reach Whisky Falls USFS Campground easily. The section of road past the turnoff to the campground is better suited to high-clearance vehicles because of the uneven road surface.

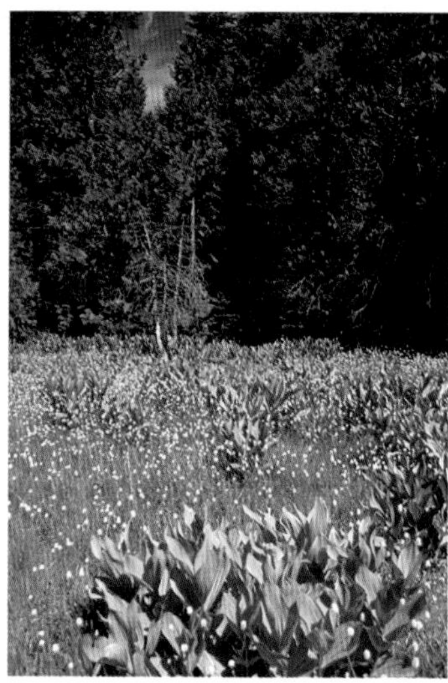

Meadows are studded with sunflowers, mule's ears, and other wildflowers along Peckinpah Road

There are a few backcountry campsites set in the pines on the edge of a ridge opposite Camp 5, where High Sierra #15: Whisky Ridge Trail leads off to the north. Although 4WD vehicles can travel this trail, it is primarily used by snowmobiles in winter and motorbikes in summer. It leads to excellent, but exposed, camping spots and panoramic viewpoints on the bare granite top of Whisky Ridge.

Peckinpah Road is a mixture of deteriorating paved and graded dirt roads. It is especially appealing in late spring and early summer when the meadows have a profusion of wildflowers in bloom.

The trail passes the southern end of High Sierra #16: Browns Meadow Trail, a moderate 4WD trail, and the northern end of High Sierra #15: Whisky Ridge Trail. It then descends gradually through the forest, below the bare granite Chiquito Ridge and Shuteye Peak, to join paved Minarets Road, a National Scenic Byway.

Current Road Information

Sierra National Forest
Bass Lake Ranger District
57003 CR 225
North Fork, CA 93643-9734
(559) 877-2218

Map References

BLM Shaver Lake
USFS Sierra National Forest
USGS 1:24,000 Cascadel Point, Shuteye Peak, Mammoth Pool Dam
1:100,000 Shaver Lake
Maptech CD-ROM: Central Coast/Fresno
Northern California Atlas & Gazetteer, p. 121
California Road & Recreation Atlas, p. 78

Route Directions

▼ 0.0		From North Fork, take CR 225 for 1.3 miles through South Fork; then turn left (east) onto CR 233, following the sign for Whisky Falls. Proceed 2 miles on CR 233; then zero trip meter and turn left (east) at 4-way intersection onto Peckinpah Road (8S09), following the sign for Whisky Falls. The road is initially paved and also marked as Autumn Ridge Way.
	5.0 ▲	Trail ends at 4-way intersection with CR 233.

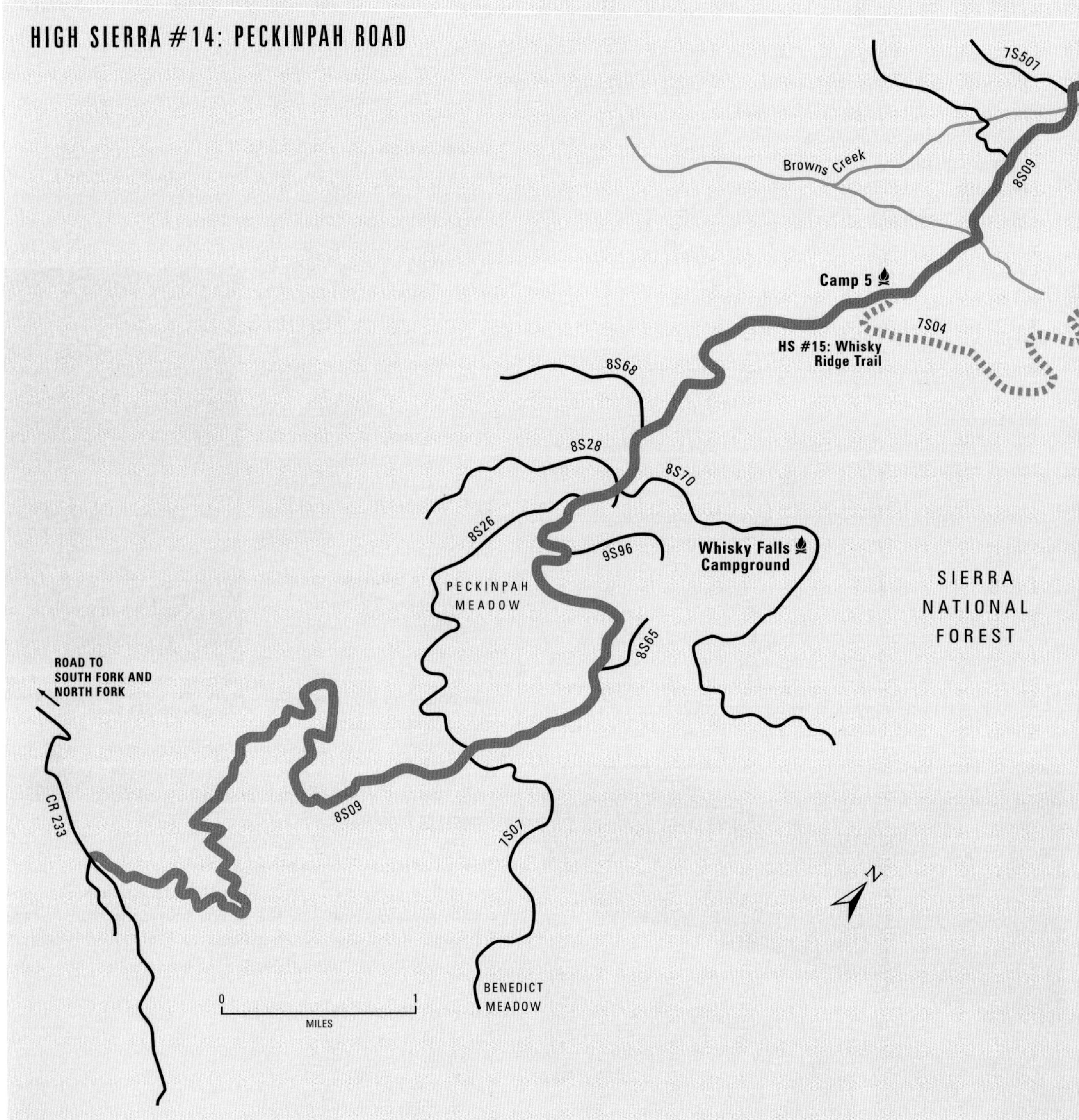

			Turn right and proceed 2 miles; then turn right again onto CR 225 for North Fork.
			GPS: N37°13.94' W119°28.10'
▼ 0.1		SO	Road turns to graded dirt.
	4.9 ▲	SO	Road becomes paved.
▼ 1.8		SO	Track on right is 8S09A.
	3.2 ▲	SO	Track on left is 8S09A.
			GPS: N37°14.36' W119°27.68'
▼ 2.8		SO	Track on left.

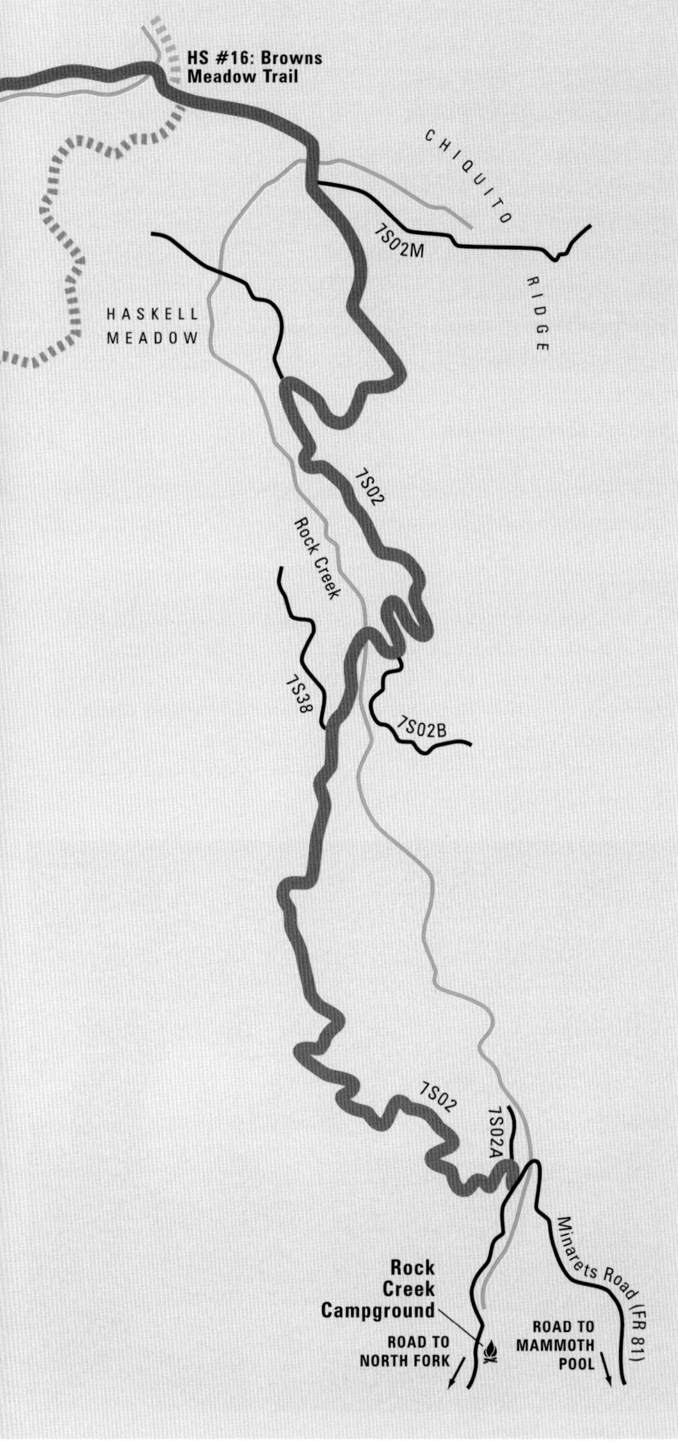

	2.2 ▲	SO	Track on right.
▼ 3.2		SO	Track on right.
	1.8 ▲	SO	Track on left.
▼ 3.6		SO	Road becomes paved.
	1.4 ▲	SO	Road turns to graded dirt.
▼ 4.4		SO	Track on left.
	0.6 ▲	SO	Track on right.
▼ 5.0		SO	Seasonal closure gate. Road turns to graded dirt; then graded road on right is 7S07 to Benedict Meadow. Zero trip meter. Entering Whisky Falls Snowmobile Area.
	0.0 ▲		Continue to the southeast and pass through seasonal closure gate. Leaving Whisky Falls Snowmobile Area.
			GPS: N37°15.44' W119°26.93'
▼ 0.0			Continue to the northwest on 8S09; then track on left is 8S26 to Peckinpah Meadow.
	2.6 ▲	SO	Track on right is 8S26 to Peckinpah Meadow; then graded road on left is 7S07 to Benedict Meadow. Zero trip meter.
▼ 0.1		SO	Track on left.
	2.5 ▲	SO	Track on right.
▼ 0.9		SO	Track on right is 8S65.
	1.7 ▲	SO	Track on left is 8S65.
			GPS: N37°16.12' W119°26.76'
▼ 1.5		SO	Track on left.
	1.1 ▲	SO	Track on right.
▼ 1.9		BL	Track on right is 9S96.
	0.7 ▲	BR	Track on left is 9S96.
			GPS: N37°16.38' W119°27.27'
▼ 2.4		SO	Track on left is 8S26.
	0.2 ▲	SO	Track on right is 8S26.
▼ 2.6		SO	5-way intersection. Track on left is 8S28 and small track on right; then graded road on right is 8S70, signposted to Whisky Falls Campground. Zero trip meter and remain on 8S09, following the sign to Browns Meadow and Camp 5.
	0.0 ▲		Continue to the south.
			GPS: N37°16.74' W119°27.32'
▼ 0.0			Continue to the north.
	2.0 ▲	SO	5-way intersection. Graded road on left is 8S70, signposted to Whisky Falls Campground; then track on right is 8S28 and small track on left. Zero trip meter and remain on 8S09, following the sign to North Fork.
▼ 0.3		SO	Track on left is 8S68.
	1.7 ▲	SO	Track on right is 8S68.
▼ 2.0		SO	Camp 5—backcountry campsites on left. Track on right is High Sierra #15: Whisky Ridge Trail. Zero trip meter.
	0.0 ▲		Continue to the southwest.
			GPS: N37°18.16' W119°26.99'
▼ 0.0			Continue to the northeast.
	2.6 ▲	SO	Camp 5—backcountry campsites on right. Track on left is High Sierra #15: Whisky Ridge Trail. Zero trip meter.
▼ 0.2		SO	Track on right is 8S09C.
	2.4 ▲	SO	Track on left is 8S09C.
▼ 0.6		SO	Cross over creek.
	2.0 ▲	SO	Cross over creek.
▼ 1.1		SO	Track on left.
	1.5 ▲	SO	Track on right.
▼ 1.5		SO	Cross over Browns Creek.
	1.1 ▲	SO	Cross over Browns Creek.
			GPS: N37°19.34' W119°26.93'

▼ 1.6		SO	Track on left is 7S507.
	1.0 ▲	SO	Track on right is 7S507.
▼ 2.5		SO	Cross over Browns Creek.
	0.1 ▲	SO	Cross over Browns Creek.
▼ 2.6		SO	Graded road on left is High Sierra #16: Browns Meadow Trail, signposted to Gaggs Camp. Zero trip meter and follow sign to Minarets Road.
	0.0 ▲		Continue to the west.
			GPS: N37°19.89' W119°26.32'
▼ 0.0			Continue to the east.
	7.8 ▲	SO	Graded road on right is High Sierra #16: Browns Meadow Trail, signposted to Gaggs Camp. Zero trip meter and continue on 8S09.
▼ 0.1		SO	Track on right is High Sierra #15: Whisky Ridge Trail.
	7.7 ▲	SO	Track on left is High Sierra #15: Whisky Ridge Trail.
			GPS: N37°19.92' W119°26.25'
▼ 0.7		SO	Cross over creek.
	7.1 ▲	SO	Cross over creek.
▼ 0.8		SO	Track on left is 7S02M.
	7.0 ▲	SO	Track on right is 7S02M.
▼ 1.0		SO	Track on right.
	6.8 ▲	SO	Track on left.
▼ 1.6		SO	Cross over creek.
	6.2 ▲	SO	Cross over creek.
▼ 1.7		SO	Track on left is 7S02H.
	6.1 ▲	SO	Track on right is 7S02H.
▼ 2.3		SO	Track on right goes to Haskell Meadow.
	5.5 ▲	SO	Track on left goes to Haskell Meadow.
			GPS: N37°19.43' W119°25.12'
▼ 2.5		SO	Track on right.
	5.3 ▲	SO	Track on left.
▼ 3.3		SO	Cross over creek.
	4.5 ▲	SO	Cross over creek.
▼ 4.0		BR	Track on left is 7S02B.
	3.8 ▲	BL	Track on right is 7S02B.
			GPS: N37°19.03' W119°24.00'
▼ 4.1		SO	Track on right is 7S02G and camping area; then cross over Rock Creek.
	3.7 ▲	SO	Cross over Rock Creek; then track on left is 7S02G and camping area.
▼ 4.7		SO	Track on right is 7S38.
	3.1 ▲	SO	Track on left is 7S38.
▼ 5.6		SO	Track on left is 7S02E.
	2.2 ▲	SO	Track on right is 7S02E.
▼ 6.8		SO	Track on left is 7S44.
	1.0 ▲	SO	Track on right is 7S44.
			GPS: N37°17.96' W119°22.68'
▼ 7.3		SO	Track on left.
	0.5 ▲	SO	Track on right.
▼ 7.7		SO	Track on left is 7S02A; then seasonal closure gate.
	0.1 ▲	SO	Seasonal closure gate; then track on right is 7S02A.
▼ 7.8			Trail ends at T-intersection with paved Minarets Road (FR 81). Turn left for Mammoth Pool; turn right for North Fork.
	0.0 ▲		Trail starts on Minarets Road (FR 81), 0.8 miles north of Rock Creek USFS Campground. Zero trip meter and turn north on graded dirt road 7S02, signposted to Whisky Falls USFS Campground and Browns Meadow.
			GPS: N37°18.03' W119°22.11'

HIGH SIERRA #15

Whisky Ridge Trail

Starting Point:	**High Sierra #14: Peckinpah Road at Camp 5, 2 miles north of the intersection with 8S70**
Finishing Point:	**High Sierra #14: Peckinpah Road, 0.1 miles east of the intersection with High Sierra #16: Browns Meadow Trail**
Total Mileage:	**4 miles**
Unpaved Mileage:	**4 miles**
Driving Time:	**45 minutes**
Elevation Range:	**6,200–6,900 feet**
Usually Open:	**November to May**
Best Time to Travel:	**November to May**
Difficulty Rating:	**4**
Scenic Rating:	**9**
Remoteness Rating:	**+0**

Special Attractions

- Camping on the open granite crest of Whisky Ridge.
- Trail is popular for motorbikes and ATVs.
- Snowmobile route in winter.

History

Whisky Falls and Peckinpah Meadow, to the south of the trail, were almost engulfed in the North Fork Fire of August 2001, which burned more than 4,132 acres in seven days. The old mill site in North Fork became the command post to direct 9 helicopters, 9 air tankers, 6 bulldozers, 68 engines, 13 water tankers, and 45 hand crews. The total estimated cost of containment was more than $3 million.

Scenic Chiquito Ridge

Haskell Meadow, below the northern end of the trail, was a popular camp for the Haskell brothers, Bill and John, who grazed sheep in this region in the summers. They would return to the San Joaquin Valley before the early winter freeze, which could mean death to men and stock.

The trail follows a 1920s logging route. The Sugar Pine Lumber Company had a network of grades for its timber trolleys throughout the Whisky Ridge region. Most of the gentle grades on this mountain make their way back to Camp 5, the starting point of this trail on High Sierra #14: Peckinpah Road. Some of the mature trees spared from logging help identify the camp's location. From Camp 5, trolleys made their way down the Browns Meadow trolley grade to the logging headquarters at Central Camp. There the logs were loaded onto standard gauge railroad cars for shipment to the company-run mill town of Pinedale, on the northern edge of Fresno.

Description

Whisky Ridge is a narrow trail suitable for motorbikes, mountain bikes, hikers, horses, and most 4WD vehicles as far as a bare granite top near Whisky Ridge. The descent from the ridge is a narrow and brushy path marked for motorbikes; it is open to 4WDs because it is a marked forest service road, but it is moderately brushy and many may not wish to make the descent. The entire trail is marked for snowmobile use.

The trail leaves High Sierra #14: Peckinpah Road opposite Camp 5 and climbs gradually around the ridge before reaching the top. The surface is loose and rocky, with some uneven, moguled stretches of dirt. At the top of the granite cap, keep a close eye on the trail to avoid missing the trail down. From the ridge top, there are some exposed campsites and open views to the east.

At the bottom of the descent, the trail wraps around the side of a hill, offering views of Chiquito Ridge and Shuteye Peak. It then rejoins High Sierra #14: Peckinpah Road opposite the start of High Sierra #16: Browns Meadow Trail. The trail is marked sporadically with orange snowmobile route markers.

Current Road Information

Sierra National Forest
Bass Lake Ranger District
57003 CR 225
North Fork, CA 93643-9734
(559) 877-2218

Map References

BLM Shaver Lake
USFS Sierra National Forest
USGS 1:24,000 Shuteye Peak
1:100,000 Shaver Lake
Maptech CD-ROM: Central Coast/Fresno
Northern California Atlas & Gazetteer, p. 121
California Road & Recreation Atlas, p. 78

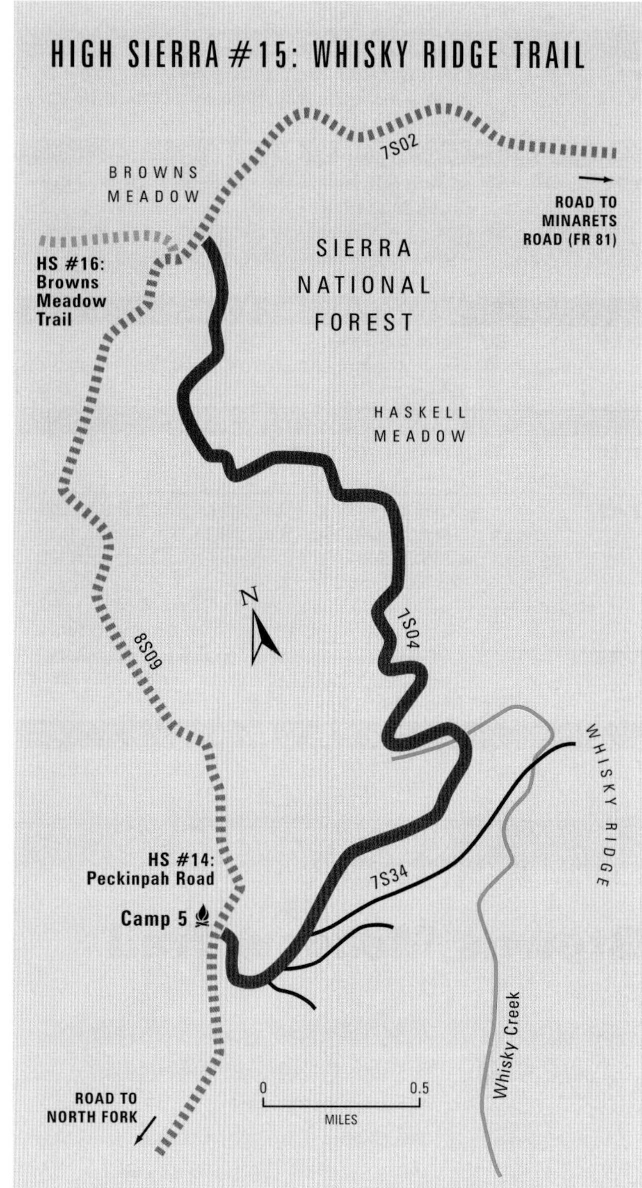

Route Directions

▼ 0.0			From High Sierra #14: Peckinpah Road at Camp 5, 2 miles north of the intersection with 8S70, zero trip meter and turn east on unmarked formed trail opposite the sign for Camp 5. Trail immediately starts to climb.
	4.0 ▲		Trail ends at T-intersection with High Sierra #14: Peckinpah Road at Camp 5. Turn left for North Fork; turn right to continue along Peckinpah Road.
			GPS: N37°18.16′ W119°26.99′
▼ 0.2		SO	Motorbike trail leaves to the right.
	3.8 ▲	SO	Motorbike trail leaves to the left.
▼ 0.3		BL	Track straight ahead goes toward Whisky Falls and Camp 14. Bear left onto 7S04.
	3.7 ▲	SO	Track on left goes toward Whisky Falls and Camp 14.
			GPS: N37°18.00′ W119°26.90′
▼ 0.4		BL	Track on right is 7S34.
	3.6 ▲	SO	Track on left is 7S34.
▼ 1.3		SO	Cross over creek.
	2.7 ▲	SO	Cross over creek.
			GPS: N37°18.41′ W119°26.00′
▼ 1.6		BR	Track on left is 7S508.

	2.4 ▲	BL	Track on right is 7S508.
			GPS: N37°18.46' W119°26.23'
▼ 1.7		SO	Start to cross open granite area—a couple of cairns mark the way. Proceed northeast.
	2.3 ▲	SO	Exit open area.
			GPS: N37°18.53' W119°26.16'
▼ 2.0		SO	Swing left, then right and head back into the trees to the north.
	2.0 ▲	SO	Swing left out of the trees and start to cross open granite area. Bear right and proceed southwest.
			GPS: N37°18.66' W119°26.06'
▼ 2.6		BL	Track on right.
	1.4 ▲	BR	Track straight ahead. Trail is marked for motorbikes at this point.
			GPS: N37°19.08' W119°25.96'
▼ 3.8		SO	Campsite on right.
	0.2 ▲	SO	Campsite on left.
▼ 4.0			Track on right is 7S04J; then trail ends at intersection with High Sierra #14: Peckinpah Road (7S02). Turn right for Minarets Road; turn left for North Fork.
	0.0 ▲		Trail commences on High Sierra #14: Peckinpah Road, 0.1 miles east of the intersection with High Sierra #16: Browns Meadow Trail. Zero trip meter and turn southeast on formed dirt trail marked 7S04.
			GPS: N37°19.92' W119°26.25'

HIGH SIERRA #16

Browns Meadow Trail

Starting Point:	**High Sierra #14: Peckinpah Road, 7.8 miles west of the intersection with Minarets Road**
Finishing Point:	**High Sierra #17: Central Camp Road, 9 miles southeast of Beasore Road**
Total Mileage:	**5.1 miles**
Unpaved Mileage:	**5.1 miles**
Driving Time:	**1.25 hours**
Elevation Range:	**5,700–6,700 feet**
Usually Open:	**May to November**
Best Time to Travel:	**May to November**
Difficulty Rating:	**4**
Scenic Rating:	**9**
Remoteness Rating:	**+1**

Special Attractions

- Moderate trail along a narrow shelf road.
- Developed campground at Gaggs Camp.

History

Browns Meadow Trail follows one of the many trolley grades built by the Sugar Pine Lumber Company. The company's headquarters was at Central Camp, immediately below this old grade, on the banks of Sand Creek. The logging community thrived during the 1920s, sending much of its wood back East. By 1931, the camp ceased operating because of massive financial losses. Only one grocery store and gas station remained open, and only a handful of families stayed. In 1932, the company's construction engineer bought up much of the camp's land and buildings.

The trail descends through massive granite outcroppings to the Central Camp railroad grade

Description

Browns Meadow Trail is a narrow, single-lane trail that descends steeply from High Sierra #14: Peckinpah Road to the forest service campground at Gaggs Camp. The start of the trail is wide and well graded, but it narrows almost immediately to a single lane. It passes close to Browns Meadow, then switchbacks its way down the side of the mountain along a shelf road. It is slightly brushy in places, especially for wider vehicles. The trail surface is uneven and rough in places, with a few off-camber sections and rocks to negotiate. It passes through the forest before running around the edges of a couple small meadows. In spring and early summer, these meadows are fragrant with honeysuckle and pink-flowered bushes.

Gaggs Camp is a fee area on the far side of a shallow cross-

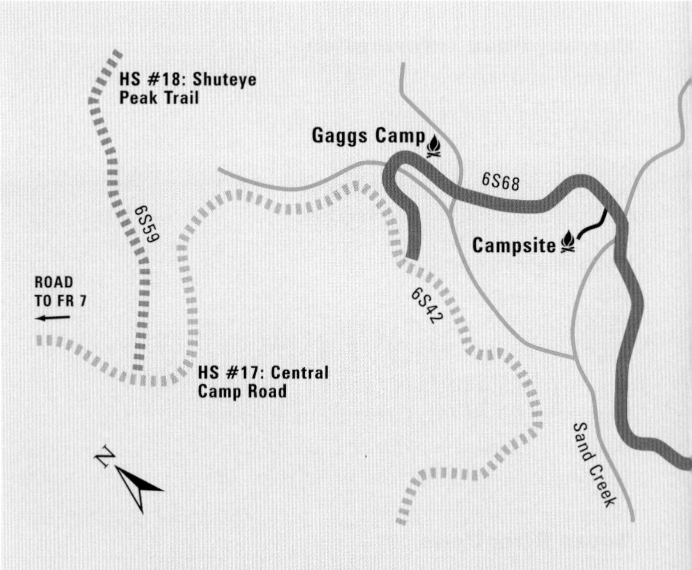

ing of Sand Creek. The campground is well shaded and has nine sites for tents or small self-contained vehicles. The road improves for the last mile past the campground before ending on High Sierra #17: Central Camp Road.

Current Road Information

Sierra National Forest
Bass Lake Ranger District
57003 CR 225
North Fork, CA 93643-9734
(559) 877-2218

Map References

BLM Shaver Lake
USFS Sierra National Forest
USGS 1:24,000 Shuteye Peak
1:100,000 Shaver Lake
Maptech CD-ROM: Central Coast/Fresno
Northern California Atlas & Gazetteer, p. 121
California Road & Recreation Atlas, p. 78

Route Directions

▼ 0.0			Trail commences on graded dirt High Sierra #14: Peckinpah Road (8S09), 12.2 miles north of CR 233. Zero trip meter and turn west on graded dirt road signposted to Gaggs Camp.
	3.7 ▲		Trail ends at T-intersection with High Sierra #14: Peckinpah Road. Turn left for North Fork via Minarets Road; turn right for North Fork via Peckinpah Road.
			GPS: N37°19.89' W119°26.32'
▼ 0.2		SO	Track on right is 7S02K.
	3.5 ▲	SO	Track on left is 7S02K.
▼ 0.4		SO	Cross over Browns Creek.
	3.3 ▲	SO	Cross over Browns Creek.
▼ 0.9		BR	Track on left is 7S02I. Bear right, remaining on 7S02, and start to descend shelf road.
	2.8 ▲	BL	Track on right is 7S02I. Bear left, remaining on 7S02. End of shelf road.
			GPS: N37°20.12' W119°27.16'
▼ 1.5		SO	Cross through creek; then track on right is a shortcut.
	2.2 ▲	SO	Track on left is shortcut; then cross through creek.
▼ 1.6		SO	Cross through creek.
	2.1 ▲	SO	Cross through creek.
▼ 2.3		SO	Cross through creek.
	1.4 ▲	SO	Cross through creek.
▼ 2.7		SO	Cross through creek.
	1.0 ▲	SO	Cross through creek.
			GPS: N37°20.60' W119°27.49'
▼ 2.8		SO	Cross through Timber Creek.
	0.9 ▲	SO	Cross through Timber Creek.
			GPS: N37°20.70' W119°27.49'
▼ 3.7		SO	Track on left goes toward Central Camp. Follow sign for Gaggs Camp. Zero trip meter.
	0.0 ▲		Continue to the southeast on FR 7S02.
			GPS: N37°21.00' W119°28.14'
▼ 0.0			Continue to the northwest.
	1.4 ▲	BL	Track on right goes toward Central Camp. Bear left, following sign to Browns Meadow. Zero trip meter.
▼ 0.5		SO	Pass around the edge of small meadow.
	0.9 ▲	SO	Pass around the edge of small meadow.
			GPS: N37°21.30' W119°27.98'
▼ 0.6		SO	Cross through Sand Creek; then track on left to campsite.
	0.8 ▲	BL	Track on right to campsite; then cross through Sand Creek.
			GPS: N37°21.37' W119°27.91'
▼ 0.9		BL	Track on right.
	0.5 ▲	SO	Track on left.
▼ 1.0		SO	Cross through Sand Creek; then enter Gaggs Camp USFS Campground.
	0.4 ▲	SO	Exit Gaggs Camp and cross through Sand Creek.
			GPS: N37°21.60' W119°28.10'

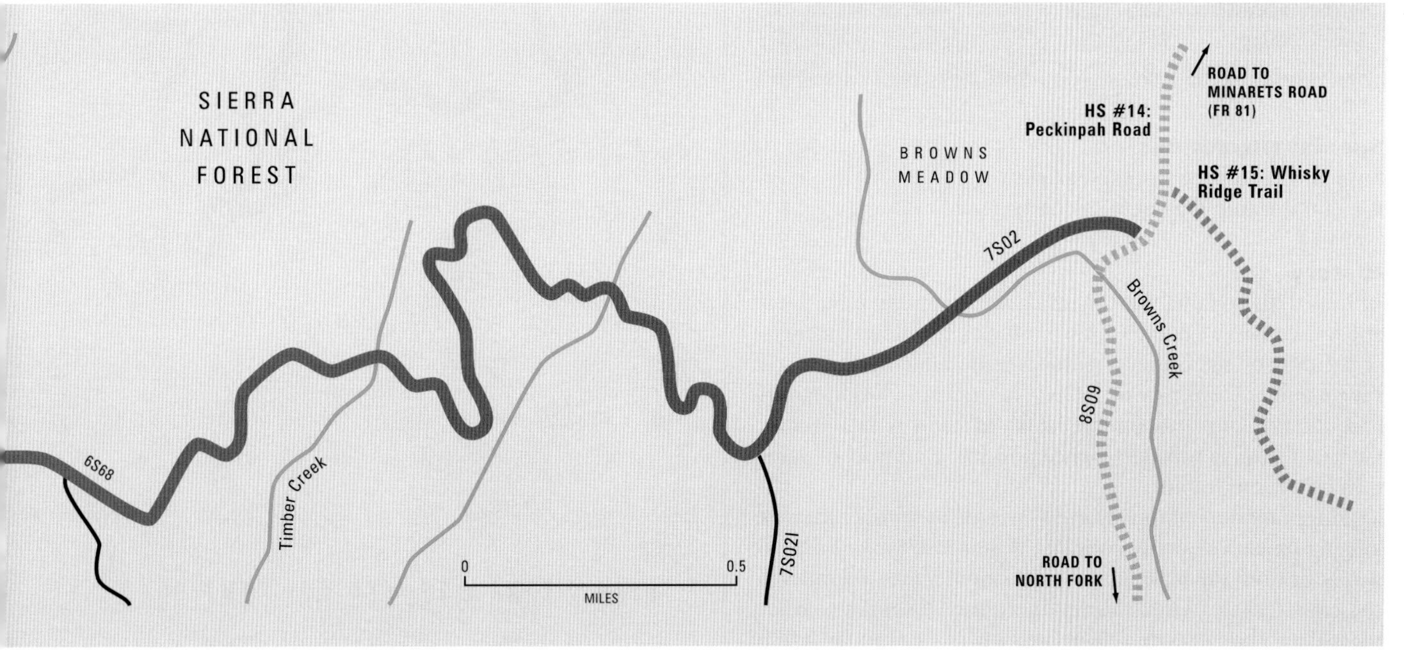

▼ 1.1	BL	Track on right into camp area at information board.
0.3 ▲	BR	Track on left into camp area at information board.
▼ 1.2	BL	Leave Gaggs Camp and cross over creek.
0.2 ▲	BR	Cross over creek. Bear right and enter Gaggs Camp USFS Campground.
		GPS: N37°21.72' W119°28.16'
▼ 1.4		Trail ends at T-intersection with High Sierra #17: Central Camp Road (6S42). Turn left for North Fork and Central Camp; turn right for Beasore Meadows and FR 7.
0.0 ▲		Trail commences on High Sierra #17: Central Camp Road (6S42), 11.7 miles north of North Fork and 9 miles southeast of Beasore Road. Zero trip meter and turn northeast on dirt road 6S68, signposted to Gaggs Camp.
		GPS: N37°21.60' W119°28.23'

HIGH SIERRA #17

Central Camp Road

Starting Point:	**Beasore Road (FR 7), 10 miles north of Bass Lake, 1.6 miles south of intersection of 6S10X at Cold Springs Meadow**
Finishing Point:	**North Fork to Bass Lake Road (CR 274) at the southern end of Bass Lake**
Total Mileage:	**17.8 miles**
Unpaved Mileage:	**17.8 miles**
Driving Time:	**1.5 hours**
Elevation Range:	**3,400–6,900 feet**
Usually Open:	**April to December**
Best Time to Travel:	**April to December**
Difficulty Rating:	**1**
Scenic Rating:	**8**
Remoteness Rating:	**+0**

Special Attractions

- Angling and boating on Bass Lake.
- Central Camp logging headquarters site.

History

In the 1920s, logging was the major activity in the mountains above Bass Lake. Central Camp Road closely follows the higher sections of the original railroad grade built by the Sugar Pine Lumber Company in 1923. The company headquarters at Central Camp was on the banks of Sand Creek. Today, Central Camp is privately owned and has a number of vacation homes and cabins.

Huge amounts of money were invested to set up a massive logging operation at this location. A standard gauge railroad was built from Pinedale, in the San Joaquin Valley, 39 miles as the crow flies to Central Camp. It required 64 miles of track to achieve the necessary elevation gain of just under 5,000 feet. Maintaining an even grade required constructing enormous trestles, some of which had five tiers. The entire project was completed in just one year. Special engines were designed to haul wood along the 4.5-degree grade from Bass Lake to Central Camp. The railroad was one of the most crooked lines in the world, making an average of two complete turns every mile.

The once bustling Central Camp mill site is deep in the forest

Central Camp was quite elaborate and cost nearly $600,000 to build. There were 70 timber structures; many were two stories high and had wide balconies and steeply pitched roofs to cope with heavy snows. The camp housed up to 700 workers and had a hospital and school. It was billed as one of the most expensive and lavish camps of the time.

The Sugar Pine Lumber Company built Pinedale, just north of Fresno, as its mill town. From Pinedale, lumber was shipped across the nation. Sugar pines (as the company name suggests) were the most sought-after trees of this region. The tall straight trees grow to 200 feet, with no branches until about a third of the way up the trunk. Cabinetmakers and homebuilders placed a high value on

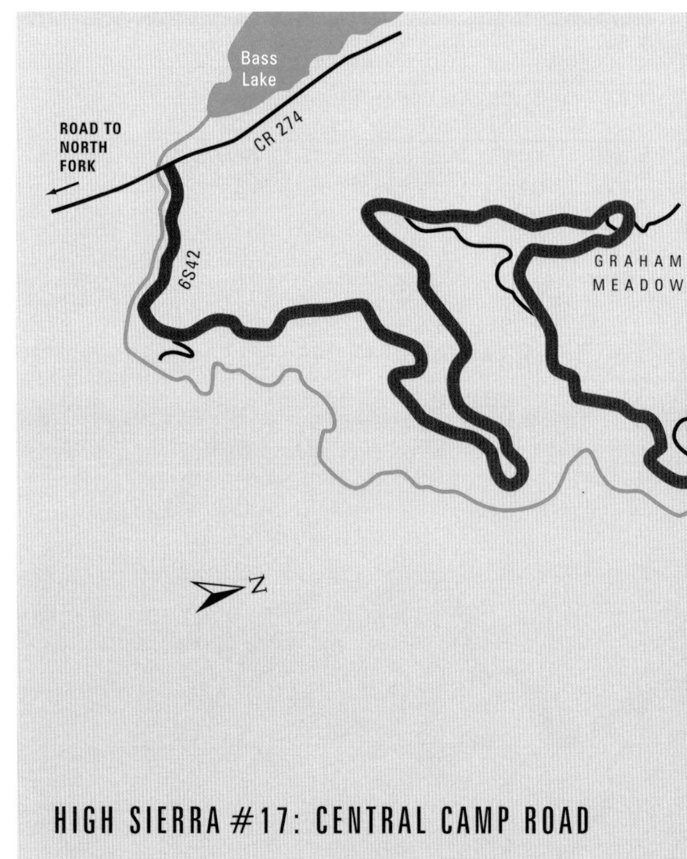

the fine wood of these beautiful trees.

Workers from the camp harvested enormous amounts of timber from the Sierra Nevada between 1923 and 1931. The overall logging operations cost an estimated $11 million. However, because initial investments were so great, the camp folded without ever breaking even.

Description

Central Camp Road is an easy graded dirt and deteriorated paved road that originally served Central Camp. The trail starts on paved Beasore Road (FR 7) north of Bass Lake. It travels through sugar pine and ponderosa forest, passing the start of High Sierra #18: Shuteye Peak Trail.

After 6.1 miles, it passes the turnoff to Gaggs Camp USFS Campground, which is also the southern end of the more difficult High Sierra #16: Browns Meadow Trail. Gaggs Camp is a pleasant campground set in the pines alongside Sand Creek. There are nine sites, mainly suitable for tents. A fee is charged.

The road passes through some private land around Central Camp before passing the turnoff to the Central Camp residential area. A second forest service campground—Whiskers—is passed on the North Fork of Sand Creek. It is set in a deep rocky gorge and is popular with anglers.

The road continues through the forest and drops down from Graham Mountain along a short section of shelf road. Bass Lake comes into view through the trees as the trail winds to a finish at the southeastern end of the lake. The lake is popular with anglers who fish for bass, kokanee salmon, catfish, crappie, as well as bluegill, rainbow, cutthroat, and golden trout. The man-made lake is 4 miles long and half a mile wide. Personal watercrafts are permitted on the lake, as is water skiing.

Current Road Information

Sierra National Forest
Bass Lake Ranger District
57003 CR 225
North Fork, CA 93643-9734
(559) 877-2218

Map References

BLM Shaver Lake
USFS Sierra National Forest
USGS 1:24,000 White Chief Mt., Little Shuteye Peak, Bass Lake, Shuteye Peak
1:100,000 Shaver Lake
Maptech CD-ROM: Central Coast/Fresno
Northern California Atlas & Gazetteer, p. 121
California Road & Recreation Atlas, p. 78

Route Directions

▼ 0.0	From Beasore Road (FR 7), 10 miles north of Bass Lake, zero trip meter and turn southeast on graded dirt road, following the sign to Central Camp. Road is marked 6S42. Immediately track on right; then pass through seasonal closure gate.
5.2 ▲	Seasonal closure gate; then track on left. Trail ends at T-intersection with paved Beasore

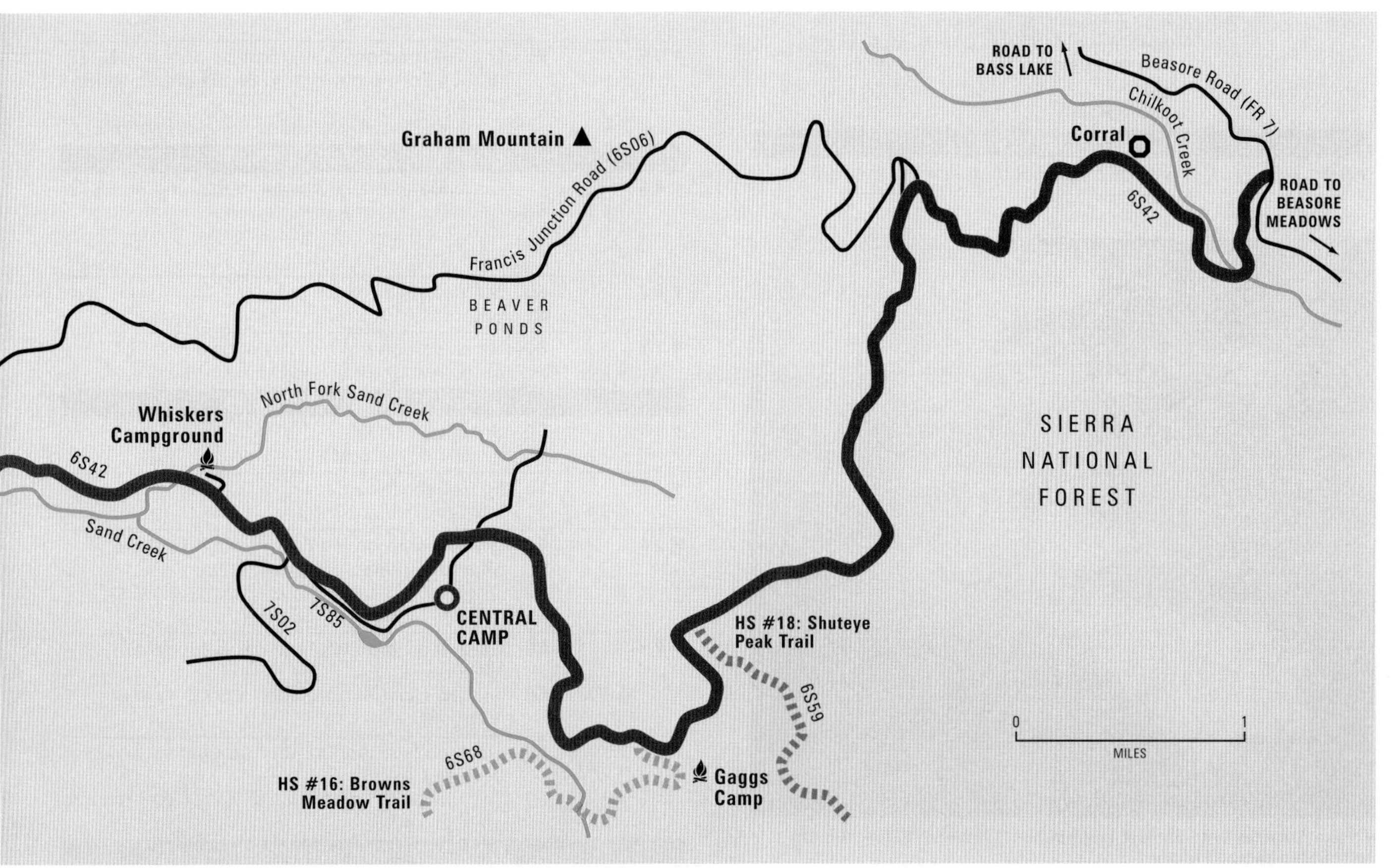

Road (FR 7). Turn left for Bass Lake; turn right for Beasore Meadows.

GPS: N37°24.01' W119°30.64'

▼ 0.5 SO Cross over Chilkoot Creek.
4.7 ▲ SO Cross over Chilkoot Creek.

▼ 0.7 SO Track on right.
4.5 ▲ SO Track on left.

▼ 1.2 SO Corral on right.
4.0 ▲ SO Corral on left.

▼ 2.6 SO Graded road on right is 6S06, signposted to Beaver Ponds. Follow sign to Central Camp.
2.6 ▲ SO Graded road on left is 6S06, signposted to Beaver Ponds. Follow sign to Beasore Meadows.

GPS: N37°22.71' W119°30.70'

▼ 2.7 SO Track on right to Beaver Ponds.
2.5 ▲ BR Track on left to Beaver Ponds.

▼ 3.6 SO Track on left.
1.6 ▲ SO Track on right.

▼ 4.9 SO Track on left.
0.3 ▲ SO Track on right.

▼ 5.2 SO Track on left is High Sierra #18: Shuteye Peak Trail. Zero trip meter.
0.0 ▲ Continue to the east.

GPS: N37°21.80' W119°28.79'

▼ 0.0 Continue to the southeast.
0.9 ▲ SO Track on right is High Sierra #18: Shuteye Peak Trail. Zero trip meter.

▼ 0.1 SO Track on right.
0.8 ▲ SO Track on left.

▼ 0.7 SO Track on right.
0.2 ▲ SO Track on left.

▼ 0.9 SO Track on left is High Sierra #16: Browns Meadow Trail (6S68), signposted to Gaggs Camp and Browns Meadow. Zero trip meter.
0.0 ▲ Continue to the north, following the sign for Beasore Road.

GPS: N37°21.60' W119°28.23'

▼ 0.0 Continue to the south, following the sign for North Fork.

Bass Lake, popular with anglers and boaters, glimmers below the old Central Camp railroad grade

3.9 ▲ SO Track on right is High Sierra #16: Browns Meadow Trail (6S68), signposted to Gaggs Camp and Browns Meadow. Zero trip meter.

▼ 0.2 SO Road passes through the private property of Central Camp.
3.7 ▲ SO Road leaves Central Camp.

▼ 1.5 SO 4-way intersection.
2.4 ▲ SO 4-way intersection.

GPS: N37°21.00' W119°29.21'

▼ 1.7 SO Track on right.
2.2 ▲ SO Track on left.

▼ 1.8 SO Track on right.
2.1 ▲ SO Track on left.

▼ 2.1 SO Track on left. Leaving the private property of Central Camp.
1.8 ▲ SO Entering the private property of Central Camp; then track on right.

▼ 2.4 SO Track on left is 7S85, which enters Central Camp.
1.5 ▲ BL Track on right is 7S85, which enters Central Camp.

GPS: N37°20.37' W119°29.07'

▼ 2.5 SO Track on left is 7S02.
1.4 ▲ BL Track on right is 7S02.

▼ 2.7 SO Track on left.
1.2 ▲ SO Track on right.

▼ 2.9 SO Track on right is 6S42A into Whiskers USFS Campground.
1.0 ▲ SO Track on left is 6S42A into Whiskers USFS Campground.

GPS: N37°20.09' W119°29.41'

▼ 3.1 SO Cross over the North Fork Sand Creek on bridge.
0.8 ▲ SO Cross over the North Fork Sand Creek on bridge.

▼ 3.9 BL Graded road on right is Francis Junction Road (6S06). Follow the sign to Bass Lake. Zero trip meter.
0.0 ▲ Continue to the northeast, remaining on 6S42.

GPS: N37°19.25' W119°29.63'

▼ 0.0 Continue to the southeast, remaining on 6S42.
7.8 ▲ BR Graded road on left is Francis Junction Road (6S06). Follow the sign to Central Camp. Zero trip meter.

▼ 0.2 SO Start of shelf road.
7.6 ▲ SO End of shelf road.

▼ 1.2 SO Small trail on right is part of bike trail 007.
6.6 ▲ SO Small trail on left is part of bike trail 007.

GPS: N37°18.65' W119°30.20'

▼ 1.3 SO Small trail on left.
6.5 ▲ SO Small trail on right.

▼ 1.9 SO End of shelf road.
5.9 ▲ SO Start of shelf road.

▼ 2.1 SO Graded road on left cuts through Graham Meadow; then track on right.
5.7 ▲ SO Track on left; then graded road on right cuts through Graham Meadow.

▼ 2.3 SO Graded road on left cuts through Graham Meadow.
5.5 ▲ SO Graded road on right cuts through Graham Meadow.

▼ 3.2 SO Track on left; then turnout on right with view of Bass Lake.
4.6 ▲ SO Turnout on left with view of Bass Lake; then track on right.

GPS: N37°18.06' W119°30.88'

▼ 3.4	SO	Small trail crosses road.
4.4 ▲	SO	Small trail crosses road.
▼ 5.3	SO	Track on right.
2.5 ▲	SO	Track on left.
▼ 6.9	SO	Track on left.
0.9 ▲	SO	Track on right.
▼ 7.7	SO	Seasonal closure gate; then bike trail 007 passes under road along the aqueduct.
0.1 ▲	SO	Bike trail 007 passes under road along the aqueduct; then seasonal closure gate.
▼ 7.8		Trail ends at T-intersection with North Fork to Bass Lake Road (CR 274). Turn right for Bass Lake; turn left for North Fork.
0.0 ▲		Trail commences on North Fork to Bass Lake Road (CR 274) at the southern end of Bass Lake. Zero trip meter and turn east on roughly paved road marked Central Camp Road (6S42), signposted to Central Camp.
		GPS: N37°17.29′ W119°31.11′

HIGH SIERRA #18

Shuteye Peak Trail

Starting Point:	**High Sierra #17: Central Camp Road, 5.2 miles southeast of Beasore Road (FR 7) and 0.9 miles northwest of the turn to Gaggs Camp**
Finishing Point:	**Shuteye Peak**
Total Mileage:	**6.6 miles (one-way)**
Unpaved Mileage:	**6.6 miles**
Driving Time:	**1.25 hours (one-way)**
Elevation Range:	**6,000–8,400**
Usually Open:	**May to November**
Best Time to Travel:	**May to November**
Difficulty Rating:	**5**
Scenic Rating:	**10**
Remoteness Rating:	**+0**

Special Attractions

- Rugged, moderately difficult trail suitable for most high-clearance 4WDs.
- Panoramic views from Shuteye Peak Fire Lookout.

History

Shuteye Peak was named for an Indian elder who was blind in one eye and called Shuteye by whites; his rancheria was along a well-used trail that traversed the Sierra Nevada.

Shuteye Peak was chosen as a lookout site in 1907. The initial structure was described as a compass lookout and was built at an elevation of 8,351 feet. A cabin was built on the peak in 1909, and a larger cabin was built the next year. By 1935, improvements included larger windows, which improved visibility over the San Joaquin Canyon, Bass Lake, North Fork, and to the crest of the Sierra Nevada. The present building dates from the late 1950s. Solar panels have been installed at the lookout—a first for any of the lookouts in the Sierra Nevada.

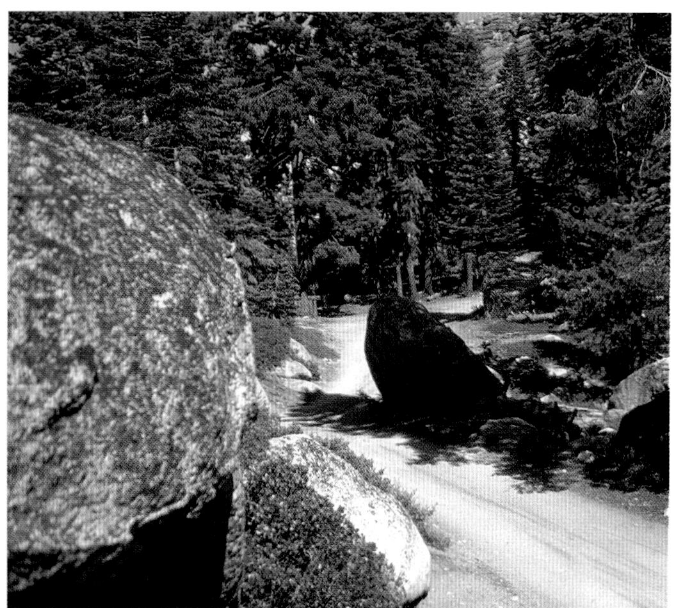

Winding past granite boulders at Little Shuteye Pass

Description

Shuteye Peak Trail is one of many designated OHV routes within Sierra National Forest. It is popular with mountain bikers as well as drivers of high-clearance 4WD vehicles.

The trail leaves High Sierra #17: Central Camp Road and travels along an easygoing graded dirt road that climbs toward Little Shuteye Pass and Chiquito Ridge. It fords through a creek that cascades over granite boulders before winding up to the pass through the pines.

After Little Shuteye Pass, the trail becomes rougher and climbs over loose granite rocks and broken rock slabs in a series of small rock steps. Views become wider as the vegetation thins out. On Chiquito Ridge, the trail passes areas of tilting granite slabs, which overlap to form spectacular shapes. The trail continues to climb somewhat steeply, winding toward the lookout across a mix of bare granite and formed trail. The trail is hard to spot in a couple of places, but it quickly becomes obvious which is the correct route—look for small cairns in a few spots and scout ahead to ascertain the correct route.

There are some good campsites along the way with excellent views. However, most of the sites are exposed and on rocky surfaces.

The trail ends at the Shuteye Peak Fire Lookout. The tower is usually manned during the summer. Visitors are welcome at the lookout and can enjoy the 360-degree views from the tower.

Current Road Information

Sierra National Forest
Bass Lake Ranger District
57003 CR 225
North Fork, CA 93643-9734
(559) 877-2218

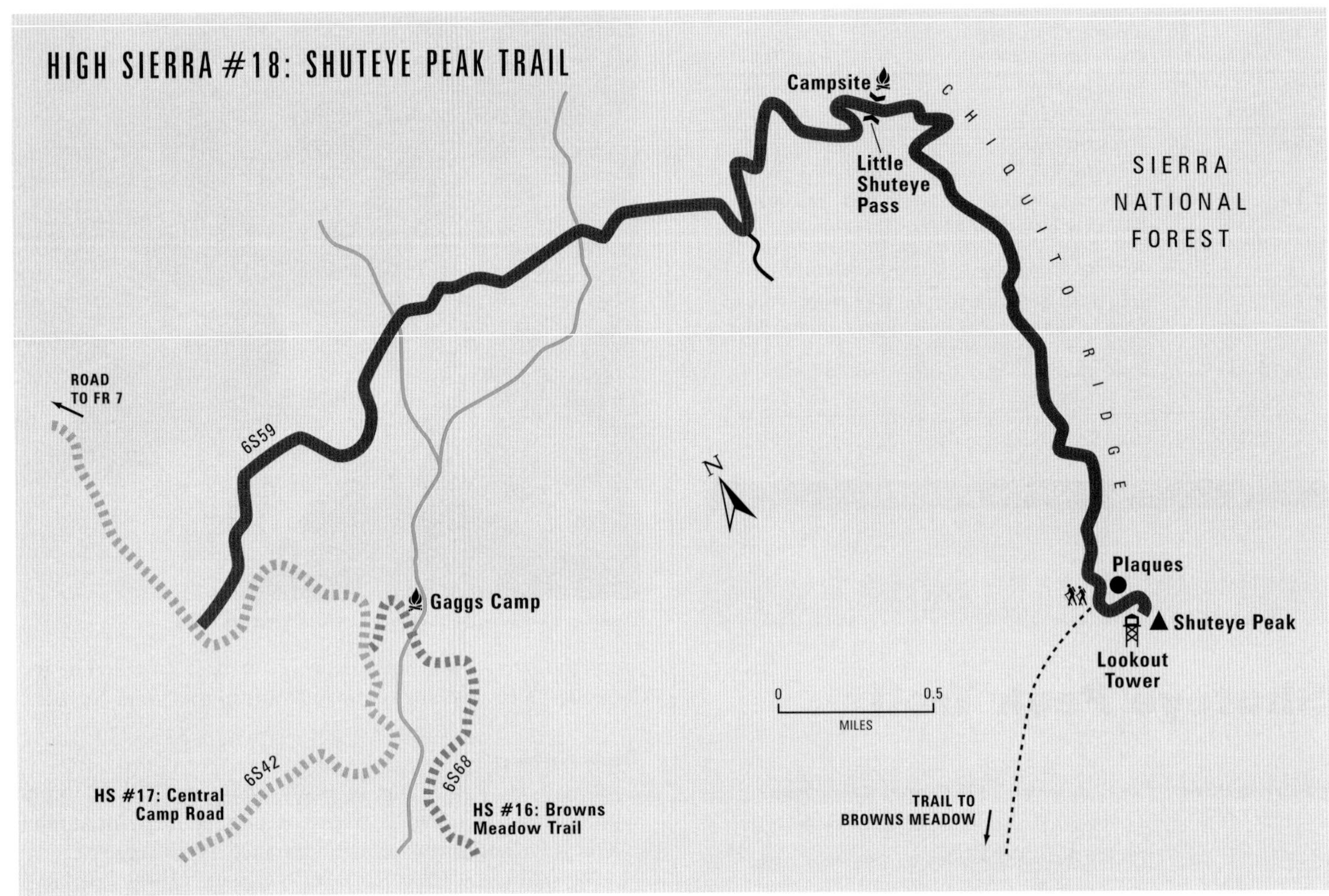

Map References

BLM Shaver Lake
USFS Sierra National Forest
USGS 1:24,000 Shuteye Peak, Little Shuteye Peak
1:100,000 Shaver Lake
Maptech CD-ROM: Central Coast/Fresno
Northern California Atlas & Gazetteer, p. 121
California Road & Recreation Atlas, p. 78

Route Directions

▼ 0.0		From High Sierra #17: Central Camp Road, 5.2 miles southeast of Beasore Road (FR 7), zero trip meter and turn northeast on 6S59, following the sign to Shuteye Pass and Shuteye Peak.
		GPS: N37°21.80' W119°28.79'
▼ 1.4	SO	Cross through creek.
		GPS: N37°22.43' W119°27.77'
▼ 2.2	SO	Cross through creek.
▼ 2.8	BL	Track on right.
		GPS: N37°22.31' W119°26.50'
▼ 3.3	SO	Small track on left.
		GPS: N37°22.56' W119°26.24'
▼ 4.0	SO	Little Shuteye Pass (6,960 feet). Campsite on left.
		GPS: N37°22.49' W119°25.82'
▼ 4.1	SO	Seasonal closure gate. Start of shelf road.
▼ 5.0	SO	End of shelf road.
▼ 6.3	SO	Hiking trail to Browns Meadow on right, marked by cairns.
		GPS: N37°21.05' W119°25.77'
▼ 6.4	SO	Plaques on the rock on left commemorate various forest rangers, supervisors, and forest service lookouts of the Sierra National Forest.
		GPS: N37°21.00' W119°25.71'
▼ 6.6		Shuteye Peak Fire Lookout.
		GPS: N37°20.97' W119°25.63'

HIGH SIERRA #19

Fresno Dome Road

Starting Point:	**6S10X, 1.5 miles from the intersection with Beasore Road**
Finishing Point:	**California 41, 0.4 miles south of Fish Camp**
Total Mileage:	**15.3 miles**
Unpaved Mileage:	**15.3 miles**
Driving Time:	**2.5 hours**
Elevation Range:	**5,000–7,600 feet**
Usually Open:	**May to November**
Best Time to Travel:	**May to November**
Difficulty Rating:	**2**
Scenic Rating:	**9**
Remoteness Rating:	**+0**

Special Attractions

- Access to Fresno Dome Hiking Trail.
- Choice of two developed USFS campgrounds and many backcountry sites.
- Mature forest.
- Swimming holes and waterfalls along Big Creek.

History

Fresno Dome Road begins at the headwaters of Beasore Creek, 1.5 miles upstream from the Jones Store in the heart of Beasore Meadows. An Indian named Tom Beasore was the first owner. Many ranchers drove cattle from the San Joaquin Valley up to greener mountain pastures in the spring and summer, and they bought supplies at the Jones Store. The store is named after Beasore's nephew Tom Jones.

When Beasore Road was built in 1936, a new store replaced the old one. It was then moved slightly to one side and expanded in the mid-1950s. The store has one of the few manual Globe gasoline pumps still in action. Ranchers, loggers, hunters, and tourists have come to expect warm hospitality at the old Jones Store, a tradition that has spanned the generations. The store hibernates under deep snow in winter, but each spring the big dig commences in time to have the store open by the time Beasore Road is clear of snow.

Locals refer to the initial section of Fresno Dome Road as Save the Rock Road. This name came about when realignment and improvement threatened a particular rock along the course of the old trail. The public's objection to proposed destruction of the rock resulted in a respectful diversion of the road. The location of the particular rock has been omitted; those genuinely interested may seek it out for themselves.

In the 1880s, Fish Camp, at the western end of the trail, was an important stop for tourists to Yosemite Valley who were going to the Wawona Hotel. Fish Camp blossomed in the 1920s when the Sugar Pine Lumber Company began logging in the area. Timber flumes and narrow-gauge railroads crisscrossed the landscape in the midst of great activity.

Description

Fresno Dome Road connects Beasore Road, north of Bass Lake, with California 41 at Fish Camp. Initially, the trail travels along graded road 5S39, known locally as Save the Rock Road, winding through a mature forest and passing its namesake boulder.

The trail passes the end of High Sierra #20: Quartz Mountain Trail and continues to wrap around the south face of White Chief Mountain. It passes a short hiking trail that leads to Fresno Dome—a large, granite monolith.

Campers will find plenty of spots to choose from along this trail. There are developed forest service campgrounds at Fresno Dome and Big Sandy. Both have large sites with a pleasing mixture of large trees and open areas, and both are situated beside Big Creek. A fee is charged at both. A number of quieter backcountry sites can also be found along the way. Some of the best are at Boggy Meadow, a short distance northwest of Fresno Dome Campground where the trail crosses Big Creek at a wide ford. Turning right out of the ford takes you to some lovely creekside campsites. Additional sites can be found west of the ford along Big Creek.

Past Fresno Dome Campground, the trail turns onto the smaller single-lane 6S07. The ford over Big Creek makes the trail unsuitable for passenger vehicles. Although it was once paved, there is a drop-off into the ford that will catch the underbodies of passenger vehicles. High-clearance vehicles will have little difficulty.

The trail continues along Big Creek, sometimes traveling along a shelf road high above the creek and other times traveling directly beside the creek. There are some wonderful spots to stop for a splash in the fast-flowing stream, and smooth granite boulders provide a great place to lay out and take in some sun. Just past Boggy Meadow, Big Creek cascades over a series of large granite boulders, with a set of falls near the top.

Cool sections along Fresno Dome Road are shaded from the hot summer sun

Big Sandy, the second campground along the trail, is set in a wide clearing alongside Big Creek. Past the campground, the trail winds through pines, oaks, and manzanitas, passing the southern end of High Sierra #22: Sugar Pine Road to finish at Fish Camp.

The entire trail is generally suitable for a high-clearance 2WD vehicle in dry weather. Sections of the trail follow along a narrow shelf road with adequate passing places.

Current Road Information

Sierra National Forest
Bass Lake Ranger District
57003 CR 225
North Fork, CA 93643-9734
(559) 877-2218

Map References

BLM Shaver Lake
USFS Sierra National Forest
USGS 1:24,000 Little Shuteye Peak, White Chief Mt., Fish Camp
1:100,000 Shaver Lake
Maptech CD-ROM: Central Coast/Fresno
Northern California Atlas & Gazetteer, pp. 121, 120
California Road & Recreation Atlas, p. 77

Route Directions

▼ 0.0	From 6S10X, 1.5 miles from the intersection with Beasore Road, zero trip meter and turn north on graded dirt 5S39, following the sign to Quartz Mountain and Iron Lakes. This section of road is known locally as Save the Rock Road.
3.0 ▲	Trail ends at T-intersection with graded dirt

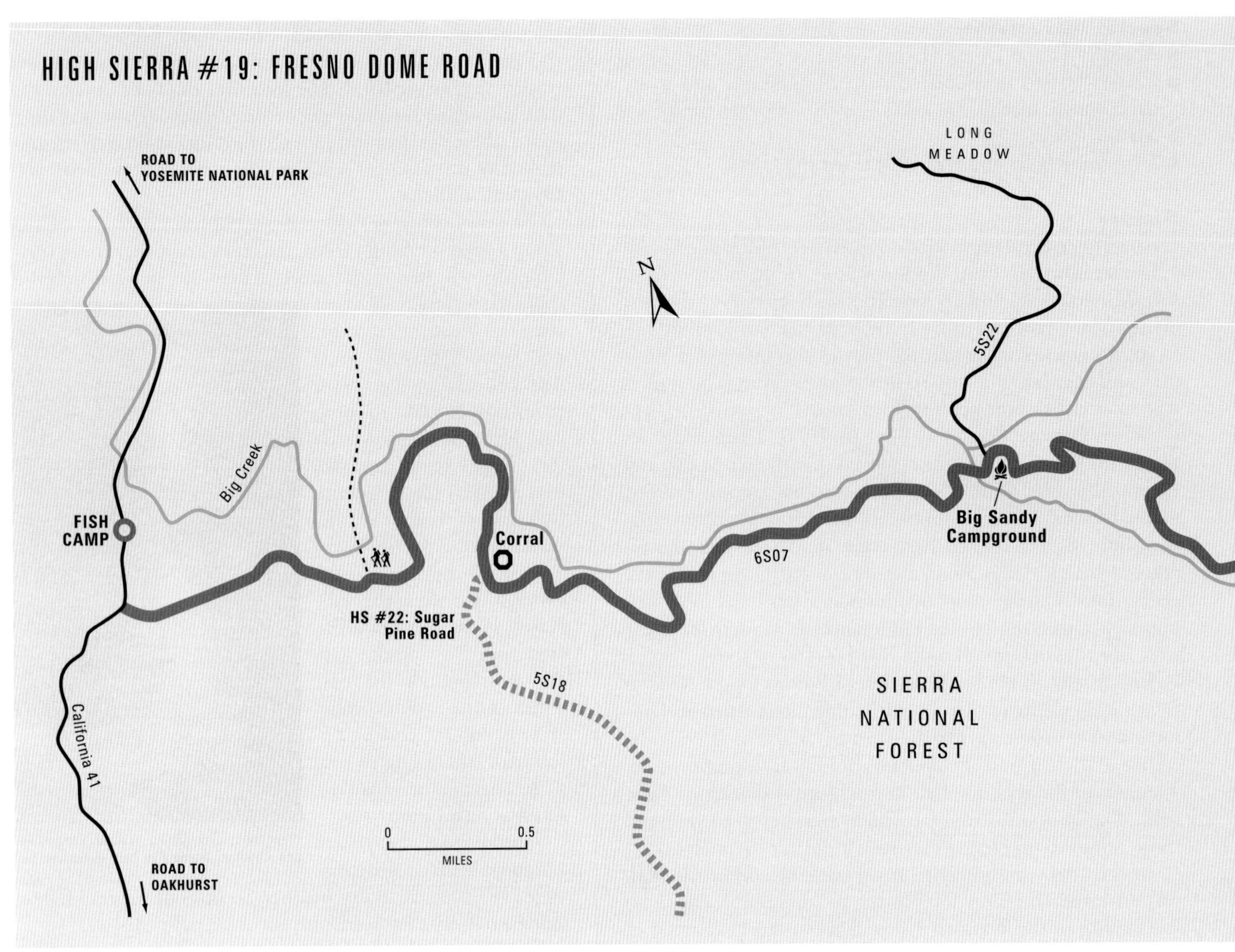

		6S10X. Turn right for Oakhurst; turn left to join Beasore Road (FR 7) to Bass Lake.
		GPS: N37°25.86′ W119°30.11′
▼ 0.8	SO	Track on right is 5S90 and track on left.
2.2 ▲	SO	Track on left is 5S90 and track on right.
▼ 1.2	SO	Track on right.
1.8 ▲	SO	Track on left.
▼ 2.5	SO	Track on right is 5S39A.
0.5 ▲	SO	Track on left is 5S39A.
▼ 3.0	BL	Bear left, following sign to Fresno Dome, and zero trip meter. Track on right is High Sierra #20: Quartz Mountain Trail.
0.0 ▲		Continue to the east. This section of road is known locally as Save The Rock Road.
		GPS: N37°27.79′ W119°30.01′
▼ 0.0		Continue to the southwest.
3.0 ▲	BR	Bear right, following sign to Bass Lake, and zero trip meter. Track on left is High Sierra #20: Quartz Mountain Trail.
▼ 0.5	SO	Track on left is 6S26.
2.5 ▲	SO	Track on right is 6S26.
		GPS: N37°27.66′ W119°30.43′
▼ 0.7	SO	Cross over creek.
2.3 ▲	SO	Cross over creek.
▼ 0.9	SO	Track on left.
2.1 ▲	SO	Track on right.
▼ 1.0	SO	Track on right is 5S02Y.
2.0 ▲	SO	Track on left is 5S02Y.
▼ 1.2	SO	Track on left.
1.8 ▲	SO	Track on right.
▼ 1.5	SO	Track on right.
1.5 ▲	SO	Track on left.
▼ 1.7	SO	Track on left is 6S10C, trailhead parking for Fresno Dome Trail (22E09). Cross over creek; then track on right is 6S10T.
1.3 ▲	SO	Track on left is 6S10T; then cross over creek. Track on right is 6S10C, trailhead parking for Fresno Dome Trail (22E09).
		GPS: N37°27.66′ W119°31.67′
▼ 2.4	SO	Track on right is 5S48.
0.6 ▲	SO	Track on left is 5S48.
▼ 3.0	BL	Graded road on right is 5S06 to Star Lakes. Zero trip meter and bear left, following sign to Fresno Dome USFS Campground and California 41.
0.0 ▲		Continue to the north.
		GPS: N37°27.72′ W119°32.41′
▼ 0.0		Continue to the southeast past track on right.
1.5 ▲	BR	Track on left; then graded road on left is 5S06 to Star Lakes. Zero trip meter and bear right, following the sign to Fresno Dome and Quartz Mountain Trailheads.

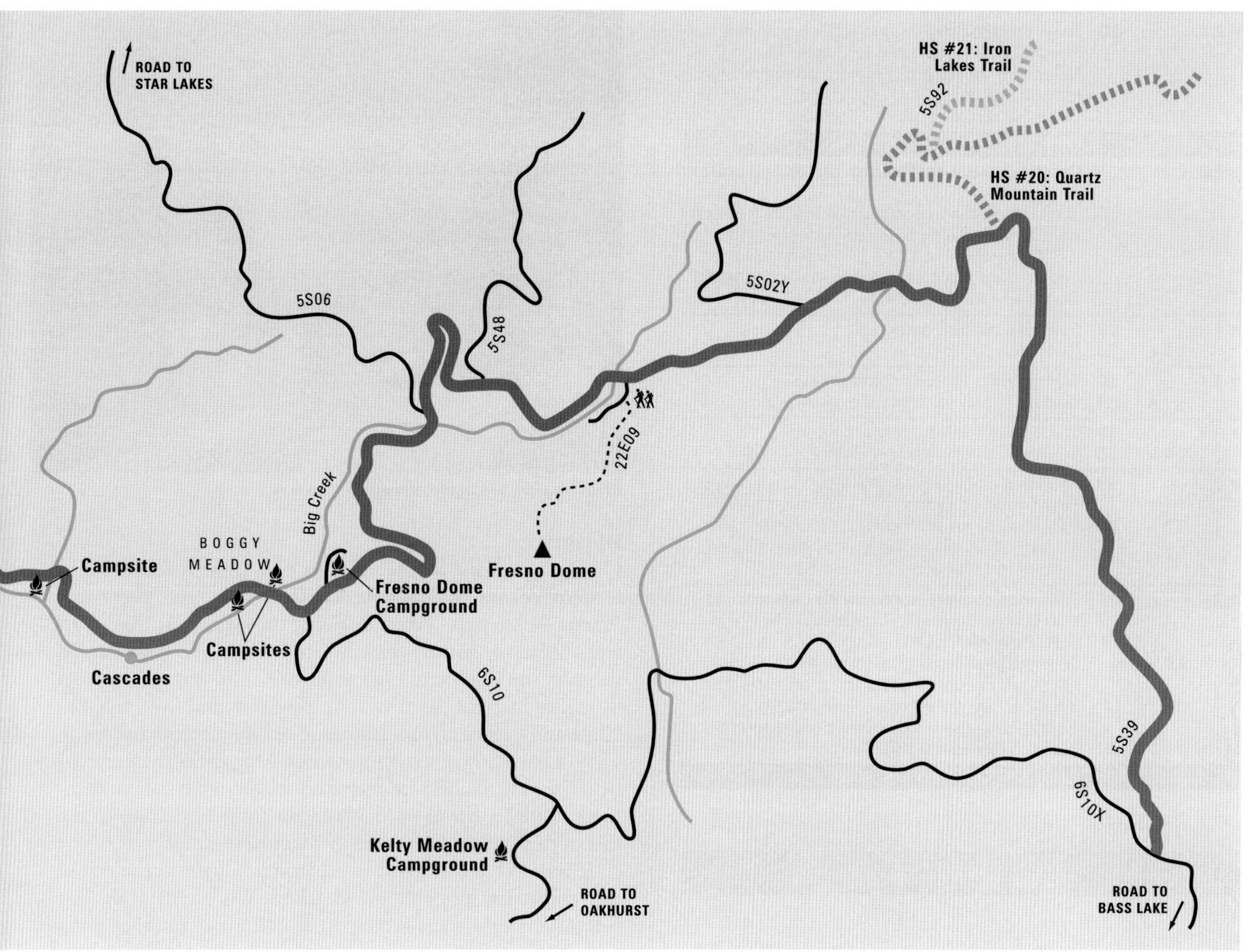

Mileage		Direction	Description
▼ 1.1		SO	Track on left.
	0.4 ▲	SO	Track on right.
▼ 1.4		SO	Track on right is 6S10D into Fresno Dome USFS Campground.
	0.1 ▲	SO	Track on left is 6S10D into Fresno Dome USFS Campground.
			GPS: N37°27.27′ W119°32.98′
▼ 1.5		TR	Graded road continues straight to Kelty Meadow USFS Campground and California 41. Zero trip meter and turn right onto 6S07, following sign to Big Sandy and Little Sandy USFS Campgrounds.
	0.0 ▲		Continue to the northeast.
			GPS: N37°27.23′ W119°33.02′
▼ 0.0			Continue to the west.
	2.7 ▲	TL	T-intersection with graded road 6S10. To the right goes to Kelty Meadow USFS Campground and California 41. Zero trip meter and turn left, following sign to Fresno Dome.
▼ 0.2		SO	Cross through Big Creek. Track on right in mid ford goes to camping area in Boggy Meadow.
	2.5 ▲	SO	Cross through Big Creek. Track on left in mid ford goes to camping area in Boggy Meadow.
			GPS: N37°27.33′ W119°33.18′
▼ 0.3		SO	Track on left to creekside campsite.
	2.4 ▲	SO	Track on right to creekside campsite.
▼ 0.7		SO	Cascades on left.
	2.0 ▲	SO	Cascades on right.
▼ 1.4		SO	Cross over creek; then track on left to campsite and track on right.
	1.3 ▲	SO	Track on right to campsite and track on left; then cross over creek.
			GPS: N37°27.55′ W119°33.97′
▼ 1.8		SO	Track on right.
	0.9 ▲	SO	Track on left.
▼ 2.7		TL	Big Sandy USFS Campground. Turn left into campground before the road ahead crosses over creek. Road 5S22 continues ahead to Long Meadow. Zero trip meter.
	0.0 ▲		Continue to the southeast.
			GPS: N37°28.10′ W119°34.85′
▼ 0.0			Continue to the southwest.
	2.7 ▲	TR	Turn right onto 6S07 and leave campground. Zero trip meter. Road 5S22 on left goes to Long Meadow.
▼ 0.1		SO	Ford through Big Creek; then track on left and track on right to camping areas. Leave campground.
	2.6 ▲	SO	Big Sandy USFS Campground. Track on left and track on right to camping areas. Ford through Big Sandy Creek.
▼ 0.8		SO	Cross over creek.
	1.9 ▲	SO	Cross over creek.

▼ 2.7		SO	Track on left is High Sierra #22: Sugar Pine Road (5S18), signposted to Sugar Pine and Nelder Grove. Zero trip meter and follow sign for Fish Camp.
	0.0 ▲		Continue to the south.
			GPS: N37°28.18' W119°36.89'
▼ 0.0			Continue to the north. Track on left and corral on right.
	2.4 ▲	SO	Track on right and corral on left; then track on right is High Sierra #22: Sugar Pine Road (5S18), signposted to Sugar Pine and Nelder Grove. Zero trip meter and follow sign for Big Sandy and Fresno Dome.
▼ 1.3		SO	Seasonal closure gate.
	1.1 ▲	SO	Seasonal closure gate.
▼ 1.4		SO	Trail on right for hikers and horses.
	1.0 ▲	SO	Trail on left for hikers and horses.
▼ 2.0		SO	Track on left and track on right.
	0.4 ▲	SO	Track on left and track on right.
▼ 2.2		SO	Seasonal closure gate. Road becomes paved. Paved road on right.
	0.2 ▲	BR	Paved road on left. Bear right and pass through seasonal closure gate. Road turns to formed dirt trail and is marked 6S07.
▼ 2.4			Trail ends at T-intersection with California 41 at Fish Camp. Turn right for Yosemite National Park; turn left for Oakhurst.
	0.0 ▲		Trail commences on California 41, 0.4 miles south of Fish Camp. Zero trip meter and turn southeast on paved road. Turn is at Mariposa County mile marker 3 and is signposted for Jackson/Big Sandy Road.
			GPS: N37°28.38' W119°38.25'

HIGH SIERRA #20

Quartz Mountain Trail

Starting Point:	**High Sierra #19: Fresno Dome Road, 3 miles north of Beasore Road**
Finishing Point:	**Viewpoint north of Quartz Mountain**
Total Mileage:	**9.2 miles (one-way)**
Unpaved Mileage:	**9.2 miles**
Driving Time:	**1 hour (one-way)**
Elevation Range:	**7,500–8,400 feet**
Usually Open:	**June to November**
Best Time to Travel:	**June to November**
Difficulty Rating:	**2**
Scenic Rating:	**9**
Remoteness Rating:	**+0**

Special Attractions

- Popular trail for snowmobilers and hunters during their respective seasons.
- Views into Yosemite National Park and hiking access to Chain Lakes and Ansel Adams Wilderness.
- Excellent backcountry campsites.

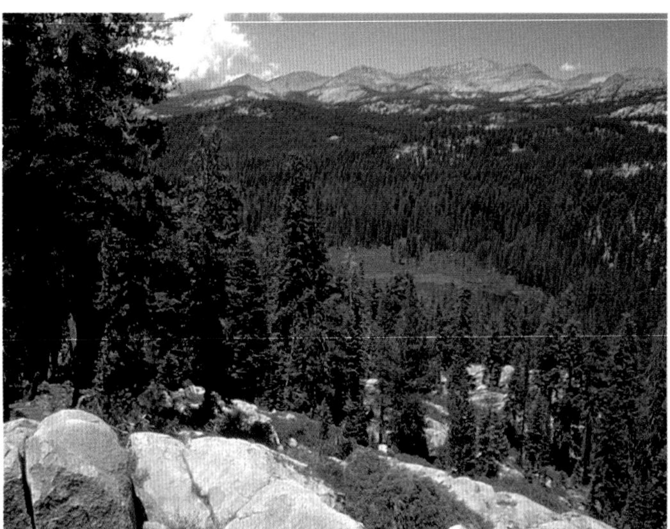

Chiquito Lake lies below the end of the trail

History

Quartz Mountain Trail is an access trail to the roadless southwestern corner of Yosemite National Park and the Ansel Adams Wilderness. The start of the trail is not far from Muglers Meadow, named for Christopher Mugler, who herded sheep in the vicinity of Quartz Mountain in the 1850s. Born in France in 1822, he arrived in New York and then sailed to Chile and eventually to California, reaching San Francisco in 1851. Like many of his compatriates, Mugler became a sheepherder and made his way deep into the Sierra Nevada in summers. Mulgers Meadow, downstream from Lost Lake to the east of this trail, was the sheepherder's base camp.

Chiquito Lake, reached by a pleasant hike from the end of the trail, is just inside the Ansel Adams Wilderness. It sits just below Chiquito Pass, which is in Yosemite National Park. *Chiquito* is Spanish for "little," an apt name for both features.

Description

This easygoing, roughly graded trail provides access to the Quartz Mountain Trailhead, which is a starting point for hiking access into Yosemite National Park. Along the way, the trail passes a pretty lake and offers views into Yosemite and over the South Fork of the Merced River. It winds along the southeast face of Iron Mountain, passing the end of the rougher High Sierra #21: Iron Lakes Trail, before passing several small meadows that are scattered with wildflowers in late spring and early summer. From the trail, excellent panoramic views open up to the east over the Sierra Nevada.

Small natural lake along Quartz Mountain Trail

After passing Iron Mountain, the trail goes by an unnamed reed-fringed lake set among the pines. There are a number of small side trails that lead to excellent campsites with wonderful views of the surrounding mountains. One of the best side trails goes a short distance to a viewpoint above the confluence of Grizzly Creek and the South Fork of the Merced River. A short hike along the ridge top offers stunning views into the gray granite canyon.

The trail forks near the end, with one fork accessing the Quartz Mountain Trailhead. This hiking trail leads 0.7 miles to Chiquito Lake and continues into Yosemite National Park to Chiquito Pass and the Chain Lakes. It is a 5-mile moderately strenuous hike to the Chain Lakes, with an elevation gain of 1,200 feet. A visitor permit is required for hiking in Yosemite. The other fork continues for a mile before finishing at a turnaround with views of Red Top to the northeast and Chiquito Pass to the north.

Current Road Information

Sierra National Forest
Bass Lake Ranger District
57003 CR 225
North Fork, CA 93643-9734
(559) 877-2218

Map References

BLM Shaver Lake, Yosemite Valley
USFS Sierra National Forest
USGS 1:24,000 Little Shuteye Peak, Sing Peak
1:100,000 Shaver Lake, Yosemite Valley
Maptech CD-ROM: Central Coast/Fresno; High Sierra/Yosemite
Northern California Atlas & Gazetteer, pp. 121, 111
California Road & Recreation Atlas, p. 77

Route Directions

▼ 0.0		From High Sierra #19: Fresno Dome Road, 3 miles north of Beasore Road, zero trip meter and turn west, following the sign to Quartz Mountain and Iron Lakes.
		GPS: N37°27.79' W119°30.01'
▼ 0.7	BR	Track on left is 6S10Z.
		GPS: N37°28.14' W119°30.33'
▼ 0.8	BR	Track on left is High Sierra #21: Iron Lakes Trail (5S92). Zero trip meter and follow the sign to Quartz Mountain.
		GPS: N37°28.05' W119°30.31'
▼ 0.0		Continue to the northeast.
▼ 0.3	BL	Track on right is 6S10F.
▼ 1.5	SO	Track on right to viewpoint and campsite.
▼ 2.9	SO	Track on right leads to campsites at Lost Lake.
▼ 3.1	SO	Small lake on right.
		GPS: N37°29.08' W119°28.18'
▼ 3.7	SO	Grizzly Lake Trail (23E03A) on left for hikers goes 1.25 miles to Grizzly Lake.
		GPS: N37°29.42' W119°28.06'
▼ 3.9	SO	Track on right is 5S40Z, which goes 0.3 miles to Lost Lake. Keep left at the small intersections and respect private property.
▼ 4.3	SO	Graded road on left is 5S49. Zero trip meter.
		GPS: N37°29.87' W119°28.03'
▼ 0.0		Continue to the north, following the sign for Quartz Mountain.

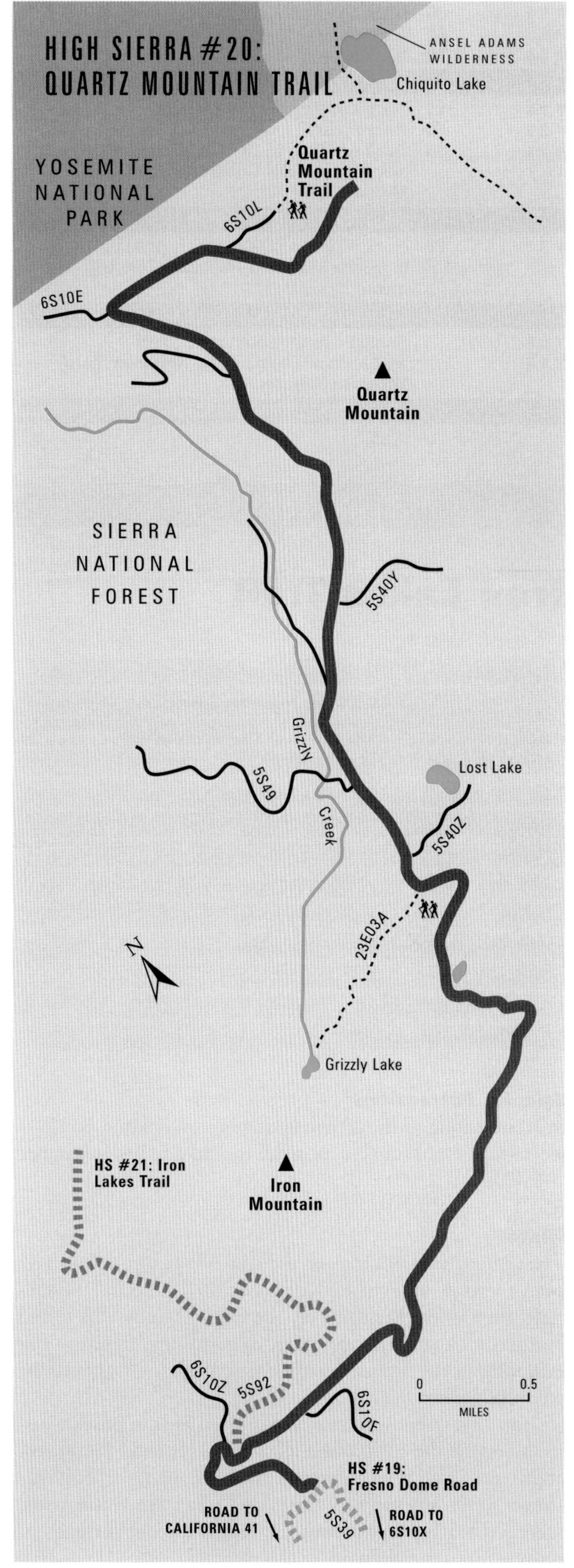

▼ 0.4	SO	Track on left.
▼ 0.5	SO	Track on left.
▼ 0.8	SO	Track on right is 5S40Y.
		GPS: N37°30.50' W119°27.65'
▼ 1.0	SO	Track on left and track on right.
▼ 2.0	SO	Track on left.
▼ 2.6	SO	Track on left is 6S10E to campsite and viewpoint over Grizzly Creek and South Fork Merced River.
		GPS: N37°31.88' W119°27.73'
▼ 3.1	BR	Track on left is 6S10L, which goes 0.4 miles to Quartz Mountain Trailhead. Zero trip meter.
		GPS: N37°31.86' W119°27.18'
▼ 0.0		Continue to the southeast.
▼ 1.0		Trail ends at a turnaround with views into Yosemite National Park.
		GPS: N37°31.76' W119°26.36'

HIGH SIERRA #21

Iron Lakes Trail

Starting Point:	**High Sierra #20: Quartz Mountain Trail, 0.8 miles from the intersection with High Sierra #19: Fresno Dome Road**
Finishing Point:	**Iron Lakes**
Total Mileage:	**3.1 miles (one-way)**
Unpaved Mileage:	**3.1 miles**
Driving Time:	**30 minutes (one-way)**
Elevation Range:	**7,700–8,600 feet**
Usually Open:	**June to November**
Best Time to Travel:	**June to November**
Difficulty Rating:	**5**
Scenic Rating:	**9**
Remoteness Rating:	**+0**

Special Attractions

- Trout fishing in the extremely scenic Iron Lakes.
- Moderate trail suitable for small to mid-size high-clearance 4WDs.

History

The remote, tranquil lakes in the Iron Mountain region have been a favorite of many for high elevation fishing and the solitude they offer. Residents of the San Joaquin Valley and foothills took summer pack trips to go fishing, hunting, and exploring in the Sierra Nevada. These pack trails can still be seen throughout the region.

Iron Lakes Trail was improved in the 1940s to provide easier access to the idyllic lakeside setting, situated 8,400 feet above sea level. The improved road through the boulder-strewn forest was still very twisty and rough. In recent years, increased logging in this area has brought about further improvement of the old road.

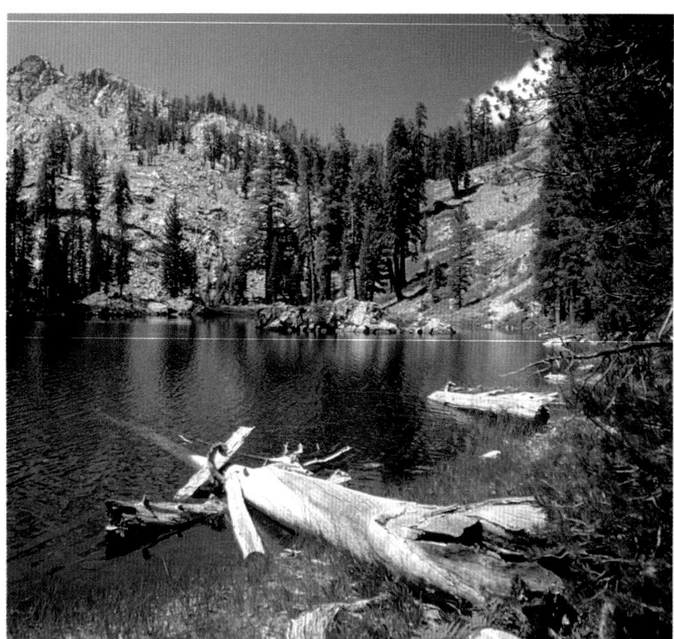

Iron Lakes, a short hike beyond the trail's end, feature spectacular gray and granite outcroppings

Description

Iron Lakes Trail is a short OHV trail that ends just before Iron Lakes, set in a depression in the red, rocky basin that gives the lakes their name. Initially, the formed trail travels through some old logging areas before turning onto the OHV trail proper at a stone route marker. This trail winds through the pines with some tight twists and turns through gaps in the trees, making the trail unsuitable for full-size or wide vehicles. Short wheelbase vehicles and compacts will be able to manage the turns.

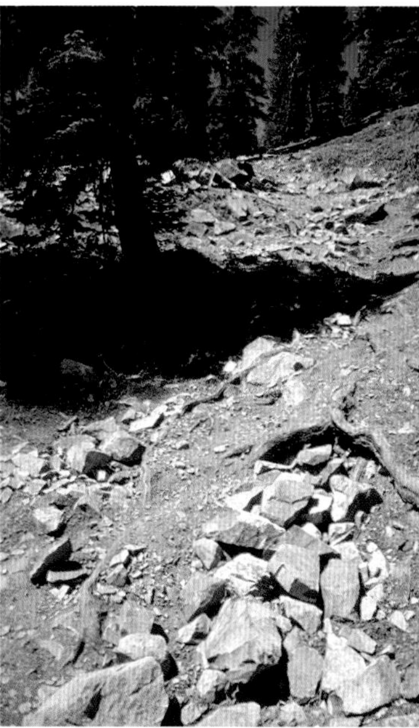

The trail's final 150-yard descent is rated 6 for difficulty

The trail gradually becomes rockier with some moguls and moderately steep grades before it begins the final descent to Iron Lakes. We suggest that you stop at a campsite and picnic table on the right of the trail. The vehicle trail continues past this point for 0.1 miles, but it is steep and rocky, rating a 6 for difficulty, and has little room to turn around at the end. It is a short hike past the end of the vehicle trail to the shores of Iron Lakes. The hiking trail zigzags down a steep path for about 250 yards to the shore of the crystal clear lake. There are a few walk-in campsites around the lakeshore that are popular with anglers. The second of the two lakes is a short distance farther along the hiking trail.

Current Road Information
Sierra National Forest
Bass Lake Ranger District
57003 CR 225
North Fork, CA 93643-9734
(559) 877-2218

Map References
BLM Shaver Lake
USFS Sierra National Forest
USGS 1:24,000 White Chief Mt., Little Shuteye Peak
1:100,000 Shaver Lake
Maptech CD-ROM: Central Coast/Fresno
Northern California Atlas & Gazetteer, p. 121
California Road & Recreation Atlas, p. 77

Route Directions

▼ 0.0		From High Sierra #20: Quartz Mountain Trail, 0.8 miles from the intersection with High Sierra #19: Fresno Dome Road, zero trip meter and turn north on small formed trail marked 5S92, following the sign to Iron Lakes.
		GPS: N37°28.05' W119°30.31'

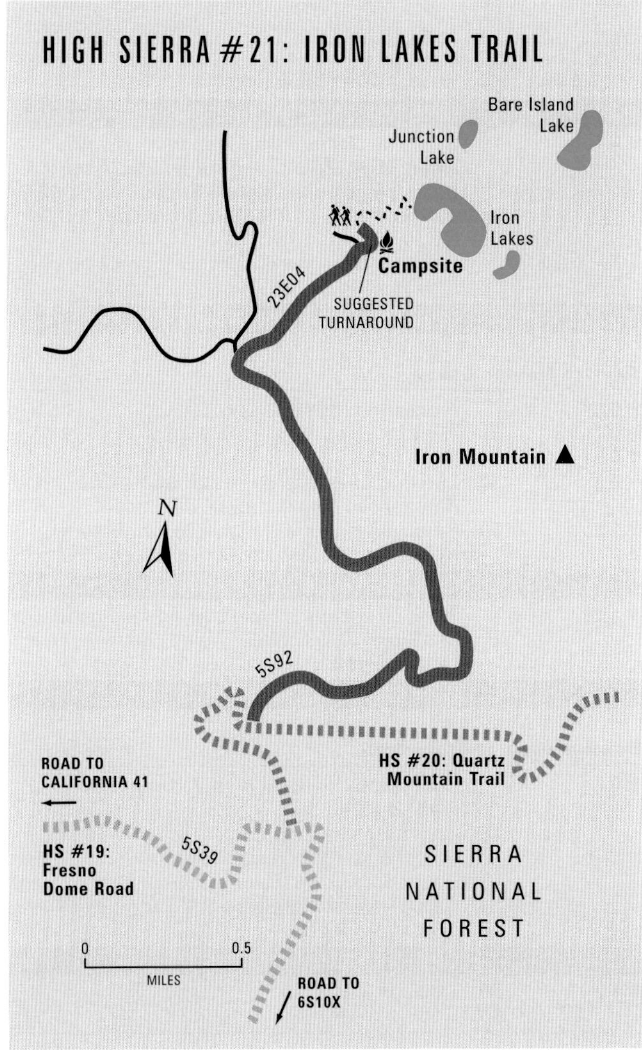

▼ 2.3	TR	Track on left and track straight ahead. Turn right onto 23E04 at the stone marker for Iron Lakes and zero trip meter.
		GPS: N37°29.02' W119°30.50'
▼ 0.0		Continue to the northeast.
▼ 0.6	BR	Track on left goes 0.1 miles to a water-filled depression. Hike past this point for a view of the Iron Lakes. Bear right (northeast) in slight depression and pass between two large trees.
		GPS: N37°29.38' W119°30.11'
▼ 0.7	SO	Campsite and picnic table on right. This is the suggested endpoint. The final 0.1 miles are rated 6 for difficulty.
		GPS: N37°29.38' W119°30.06'
▼ 0.8		Trail ends at a turnaround above Iron Lakes. Hiking trail ahead zigzags 250 yards to the shore of Iron Lakes.
		GPS: N37°29.42' W119°30.12'

HIGH SIERRA #22

Sugar Pine Road

Starting Point:	**High Sierra #19: Fresno Dome Road, 2.4 miles east of Fish Camp**
Finishing Point:	**California 41, 0.7 miles south of Merced County mile marker 45 and 5.2 miles south of Fish Camp**
Total Mileage:	**8 miles, plus 1.7-mile spur to Nelder Grove**
Unpaved Mileage:	**7.1 miles, plus 1.7-mile spur**
Driving Time:	**1.5 hours**
Elevation Range:	**4,300–5,700 feet**
Usually Open:	**May to November**
Best Time to Travel:	**May to November**
Difficulty Rating:	**3**
Scenic Rating:	**8**
Remoteness Rating:	**+0**

Special Attractions
- Trail travels part of the Sugar Pine Railroad grade.
- Easy trail for mountain bikers.
- Giant sequoias and interpretive trail at Nelder Grove.

Description
Sugar Pine Road follows part of the route of one of the old Sugar Pine Railroad grades. The small marked trail leaves High Sierra #19: Fresno Dome Road and immediately shows its colors as it climbs along a narrow, somewhat brushy trail. It follows along a shelf road for much of the way, winding through holly oaks, cedars, and pines around the western edge of Speckerman Mountain. The trail is single vehicle width, and passing places are extremely limited. The surface is uneven, typically composed of tree roots and lumpy ground. The trail is lightly used by vehicles. In April and May the forests display their annual show of wildflowers, especially along streams and seeps.

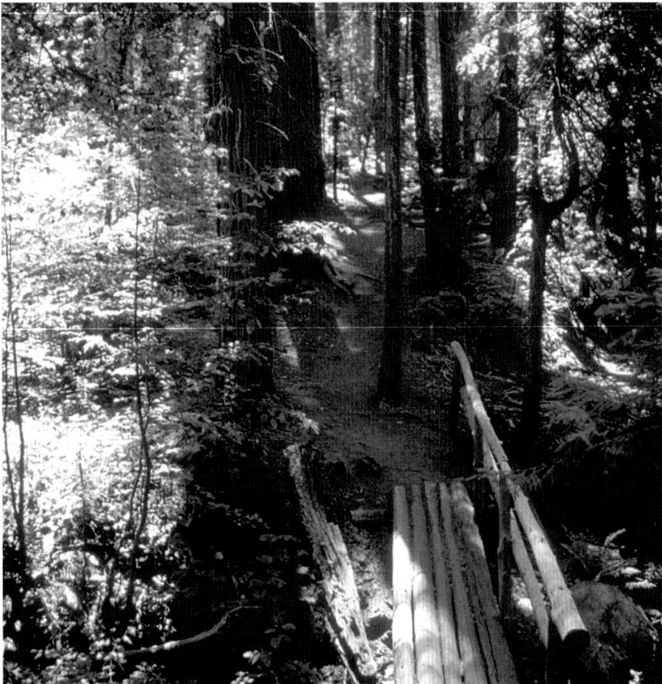

The Shadow of the Giants interpretive trail zigzags along Nelder Creek

The spur trail to Nelder Grove travels 1.7 miles to the start of an interpretive hiking trail called The Shadow of the Giants Trail. This 1-mile loop goes through the Nelder Grove of giant sequoias. There is a small picnic area on Nelder Creek. Nelder Grove is a 1,540-acre area in Sierra National Forest, which contains 101 mature giant sequoias among pines, firs, and incense cedars. Although they are not the oldest living trees on earth (that honor is held by bristlecone pines, which can be found along High Sierra #43: White Mountain Road), giant sequoias are the largest in total volume. The oldest sequoias are 2,500 to 3,000 years old, measuring up to 35 feet in diameter with heights of 250 to 300 feet.

The main trail continues through the settlement of Sugar Pine, once owned by the Sugar Pine Lumber Company and now private housing. The original paymaster's office still exists, but most of the buildings date from more modern times.

Current Road Information

Sierra National Forest
Bass Lake Ranger District
57003 CR 225
North Fork, CA 93643-9734
(559) 877-2218

Map References

BLM Shaver Lake
USFS Sierra National Forest
USGS 1:24,000 White Chief Mt., Fish Camp
1:100,000 Shaver Lake
Maptech CD-ROM: Central Coast/Fresno
Northern California Atlas & Gazetteer, p. 120
California Road & Recreation Atlas, p. 77

Route Directions

▼ 0.0			Trail begins on High Sierra #19: Fresno Dome Road, 2.4 miles east of Fish Camp. Zero trip meter and turn northwest on 5S18, following the sign to Sugar Pine and Nelder Grove.
	4.1 ▲		Trail ends at T-intersection with High Sierra #19: Fresno Dome Road. Turn left to exit to Fish Camp and California 41; turn right to travel Fresno Dome Road to Beasore Road.
			GPS: N37°28.18' W119°36.89'
▼ 0.1		SO	Start of shelf road.
	4.0 ▲	SO	End of shelf road.
▼ 0.7		SO	End of shelf road.
	3.4 ▲	SO	Start of shelf road.
▼ 1.3		SO	Campsite; then track on left.
	2.8 ▲	SO	Track on right; then campsite.
			GPS: N37°27.26' W119°36.57'
▼ 1.6		SO	Cross over creek.
	2.5 ▲	SO	Cross over creek.
▼ 2.0		SO	Cross through creek.
	2.1 ▲	SO	Cross through creek.
▼ 2.2		SO	Track on left.
	1.9 ▲	SO	Track on right.
			GPS: N37°26.59' W119°36.52'
▼ 2.4		SO	Track on left. Start of shelf road.
	1.7 ▲	SO	Track on right. End of shelf road.
▼ 3.4		SO	Track on left to campsite. End of shelf road.
	0.7 ▲	SO	Track on right to campsite. Start of shelf road.
▼ 3.5		SO	Track on right to campsite.
	0.6 ▲	SO	Track on left to campsite.
			GPS: N37°25.98' W119°36.79'
▼ 4.1		TR	Seasonal closure gate; then trail joins the larger 6S90. Zero trip meter and turn sharp right, following the sign to Sugar Pine. Track straight ahead at this point is the spur to Nelder Grove.
	0.0 ▲		Continue to the west-northwest on the upper road marked 5S18.
			GPS: N37°25.54' W119°36.77'

Spur to Nelder Grove

▼ 0.0		Proceed to the southeast.
▼ 0.2	BL	Track on right.
▼ 0.5	SO	Track on left.
▼ 0.9	SO	Entering private land. Private tracks on left and right for the next 0.7 miles.
▼ 1.6	SO	Re-entering Sierra National Forest. Entering Nelder Grove; then cross over creek.
		GPS: N37°25.56' W119°35.78'
▼ 1.7		Track on left is trailhead parking for Shadow of the Giants Trail (22E06), which continues over Nelder Creek.
		GPS: N37°25.57' W119°35.72'

Continuation of Main Trail

▼ 0.0			Continue to the west on the lower road marked 6S90.
	3.9 ▲	TL	Zero trip meter and turn sharp left onto small trail; then pass through seasonal closure gate. There is a sign at the intersection for the larger 6S90. Track straight ahead at this point is the spur to Nelder Grove.
			GPS: N37°25.54' W119°36.77'
▼ 1.2		SO	Track on left.
	2.7 ▲	SO	Track on right.

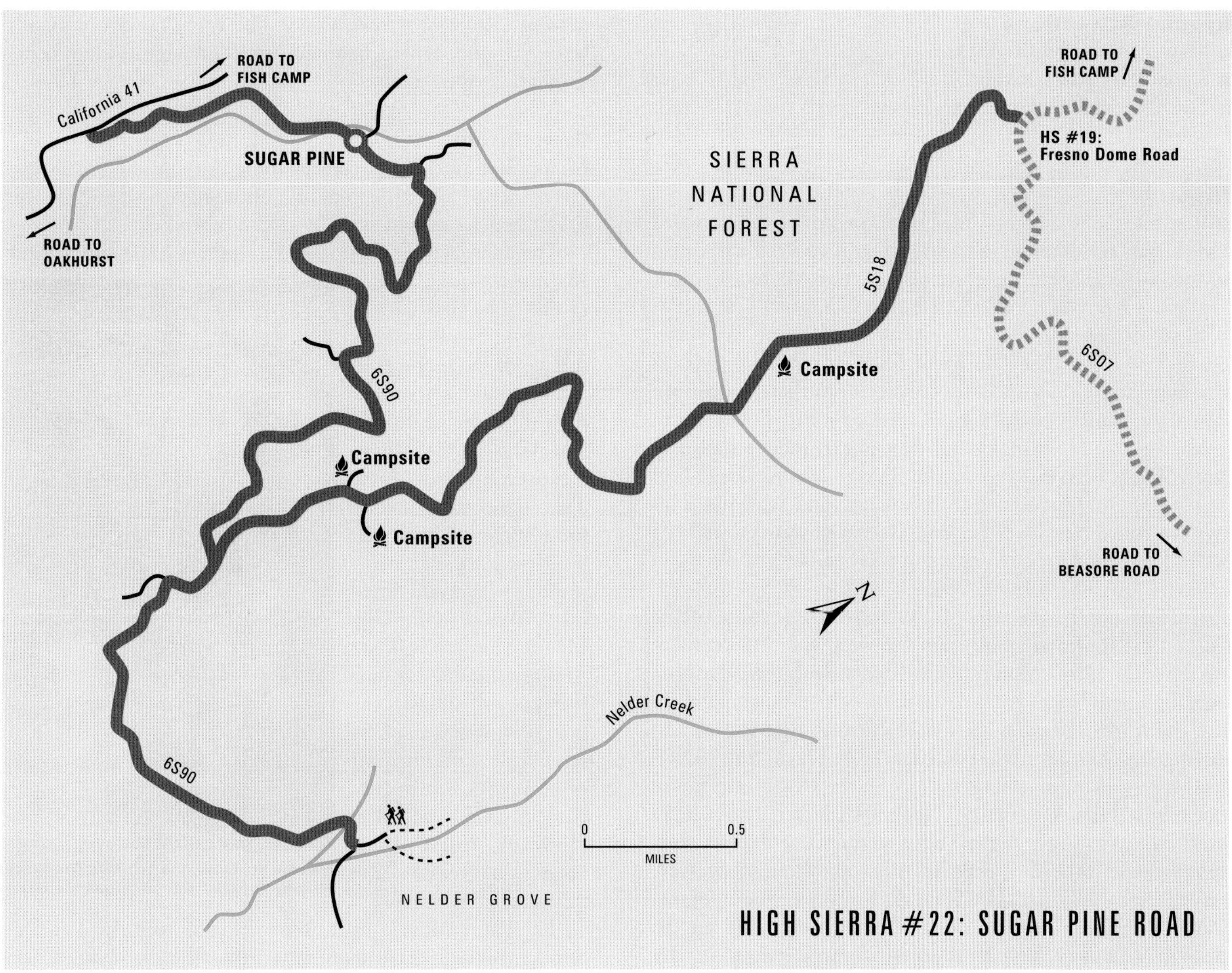

▼ 1.8		BR	Track on left is 6S91.
	2.1 ▲	SO	Track on right is 6S91.
			GPS: N37°26.19' W119°37.62'
▼ 2.3		SO	Cross over creek.
	1.6 ▲	SO	Cross over creek.
▼ 2.7		SO	Track on right.
	1.2 ▲	SO	Track on left.
▼ 2.9		SO	Pass through private property of Sugar Pine.
	1.0 ▲	SO	Leaving Sugar Pine. Track on left and track on right are private.
▼ 3.0		TL	Sugar Pine. Track on left and track on right are private. Turn left at T-intersection, following the sign for California 41; then cross over creek. Road becomes paved.
	0.9 ▲	TR	Cross over creek; then turn right, following the sign for Nelder Grove. Road turns to graded dirt.
			GPS: N37°26.48' W119°37.85'
▼ 3.9			Trail ends at T-intersection with California 41. Turn right for Fish Camp and Yosemite; turn left for Oakhurst.
	0.0 ▲		Trail commences on California 41, 5.2 miles south of Fish Camp. Zero trip meter and turn north on paved road, following the sign to Sugar Pine.
			GPS: N37°25.79' W119°38.29'

HIGH SIERRA #23

Miami Trail

Starting Point:	**California 41 at the Mariposa-Madera County line, 3.3 miles south of Fish Camp**
Finishing Point:	**Jerseydale Road, opposite Jerseydale USFS Campground**
Total Mileage:	**28.6 miles, plus 2-mile spur to Signal Peak Fire Lookout**
Unpaved Mileage:	**28.6 miles, plus 2-mile spur**
Driving Time:	**4 hours**
Elevation Range:	**3,500–6,900 feet**
Usually Open:	**April to December**
Best Time to Travel:	**Dry weather**
Difficulty Rating:	**3**
Scenic Rating:	**9**
Remoteness Rating:	**+1**

Special Attractions

- Miami Motorcycle Trails Area.
- Signal Peak Fire Lookout.
- Long easy trail with panoramic views over a variety of landscapes.

History

In the mid-1880s, Henry Washburn, owner of the Wawona Hotel, was instrumental in having a Southern Pacific Railroad spur constructed from Berenda, just north of Madera, to a station named Raymond after Walter Raymond of Raymond & Whitcomb Yosemite Tours. Raymond's company ran stagecoaches to Yosemite. The route followed Ahwahnee Road through the foothills to Grub Gulch. From there it dropped down the canyon to Ahwahnee, then climbed slowly up to Cedar Brook. Ahwahnee Road then joined today's trail near Silver Knob, bore east shortly after that to Miami Lodge near Timberloft, and proceeded to Fish Camp and Wawona. This was the route President Theodore Roosevelt traveled in 1903 when he spent four days camping with conservationist John Muir in Yosemite National Park.

Farther north, the Miami Trail travels a section of the Sugar Pine Railroad grade from the west face of Bald Rock to Battalion Pass. Major James Savage and the Mariposa Battalion may have crested the Chowchilla Mountains at this point in 1851 when they were skirmishing with Indians during the Mariposa War (see page 107). Devil Peak (6,989 feet) offers a commanding 360-degree view from the top of the Chowchilla Mountains. Henry Washburn had a road built to the summit in the 1880s so guests at the Wawona Hotel could take day trips to the top, where they were served a picnic lunch. The Standart brothers, who operated a mill at Miami, erected a board and batten cabin on the peak in the early 1900s. In 1906, the forest service took over the lookout and added a cupola to the cabin.

Miami Trail passes north of Kirby Peak as it starts the long descent into Snow Creek Valley. The Kirby family, originally from England, settled here and operated large cattle ranches throughout the region.

The 60 miles of trails within Miami Motorcycle Trails Area cover a variety of terrain

Description

Miami Trail travels a circuitous route through the northwestern corner of Sierra National Forest along a road suitable for 4WD vehicles as well as ATVs and motorbikes.

The trail starts on California 41, south of Fish Camp, at the Mariposa-Madera County line. The first part of the trail is an all-weather surface of loose gravel to facilitate access to more than 60 miles of motorbike trails in the Miami Motorcycle Trails Area. There are many small trails in this vicinity; only marked ones are mentioned in the route directions. All trails within the Miami Motorcycle Trails Area are suitable for motorbikes only unless signposted otherwise. These trails have a width limit of 40 inches, which precludes 4WD vehicles. However, forest roads open to all vehicles also run through the area.

Narrow in places, the Ten Mile Grade winds around the west side of Hogan Mountain

The entire route is open to all vehicles from April to December, though exact dates vary depending on weather, and much of the western portion of the route is open year-round. In addition, motorbikes and ATVs can bypass the closure gates and reach the Miami Motorcycle Trails year-round. The National Forest Service currently accepts this bypass, but it is always a good idea to check ahead and make sure this access is still legal. The area is part of the winter range for the Oakhurst deer herd.

The trail descends slowly through mixed forest to cross over Miami Creek. Campsites are scattered throughout the area, and there is a semi-developed camping area at the Kamook Staging Area. The climb away from Miami Creek is moderately steep, and the surface is lightly graveled. This section is closed to vehicles in winter.

As you continue past Pilot Peak along the ridge tops of the Chowchilla Mountains, the trail undulates, passing through dense forests and then into the more arid forests of the lower elevations. Bear clover covers the ground and the vegetation is a mix of oaks, manzanitas, and scattered pines. From March to May the area is dotted with wildflowers such as poppies, brodiaeas, and goldfields.

The trail turns onto unmarked forest road 5S62 and becomes a formed track that is difficult to travel in wet weather. It is a narrow single track, lightly brushy in spots, which continues along the ridge tops. It then joins the old railroad grade known locally as Ten Mile Grade, where it travels around Hogan Mountain along a single-lane shelf road, passing the prominent granite dome of Bald Rock. The rock, visible from the far side of the valley, stands out against the green forest.

The trail crosses a graded road immediately west of Summit USFS Campground. Continuing past the campground will return you to California 41 and Fish Camp. Continuing on the main trail takes you farther along the ridge tops, passing the unmarked turn to Signal Peak Fire Lookout. This tower is manned periodically during times of high fire danger. The final half-mile to the tower is closed to vehicles if the tower is unmanned, but you can still hike to the top.

The final section of the trail travels along Footman Ridge before descending gradually to finish on Jerseydale Road opposite the national forest campground. The final descent is often impassable in wet weather.

Current Road Information

Sierra National Forest
Bass Lake Ranger District
57003 CR 225
North Fork, CA 93643-9734
(559) 877-2218

Map References

BLM Shaver Lake, Yosemite Valley
USFS Sierra National Forest
USGS 1:24,000 Fish Camp, Wawona, Buckingham Mt.
1:100,000 Shaver Lake, Yosemite Valley
Maptech CD-ROM: Central Coast/Fresno; High Sierra/Yosemite
Northern California Atlas & Gazetteer, pp. 120, 110
California Road & Recreation Atlas, p. 77

Route Directions

▼ 0.0		From California 41 at the Mariposa-Madera County line, 3.3 miles south of Fish Camp, zero trip meter and turn southwest on 6S24, signposted for the Miami Motorcycle Trails Area. Immediately turn left (southeast) onto 6S15, following the sign for Kamook Staging Area. Track on left is 6S04C. Shady Trail for motorbikes and Powerline Trail for ATVs and motorbikes cross at the intersection.
2.2 ▲		Turn right at T-intersection with 6S24. Track on right is 6S04C. Shady Trail for motorbikes and Powerline Trail for ATVs and motorbikes cross at the intersection. Trail ends at T-intersection with California 41. Turn right for Oakhurst; turn left for Fish Camp.
		GPS: N37°26.51' W119°38.99'
▼ 0.3	SO	Powerline Trail crosses road.
1.9 ▲	SO	Powerline Trail crosses road.
▼ 0.6	SO	Powerline Trail crosses road.
1.6 ▲	SO	Powerline Trail crosses road.
▼ 0.9	SO	Shady Trail crosses road and track on left.
1.3 ▲	SO	Shady Trail crosses road and track on right.
▼ 1.2	SO	S Express Trail on right.
1.0 ▲	SO	S Express Trail on left.
▼ 1.3	SO	Trail on left.
0.9 ▲	SO	Trail on right.
▼ 1.6	SO	Track on left is 6S15X for 4WDs, ATVs, and motorbikes.
0.6 ▲	SO	Track on right is 6S15X for 4WDs, ATVs, and motorbikes.
		GPS: N37°25.37' W119°38.40'
▼ 2.2	SO	Kamook Staging and Camping Area. Graded road on left, graded road on right is 6S41, and trail on left. Zero trip meter.
0.0 ▲		Continue to the northwest on 6S15.
		GPS: N37°24.94' W119°38.15'
▼ 0.0		Continue to the southeast on 6S15.
4.8 ▲	SO	Kamook Staging and Camping Area. Graded road on right, graded road on left is 6S41, and trail on right. Zero trip meter.
▼ 0.1	BL	Track on right is 6S15B. Powerline Trail on right. Remain on main dirt road, leaving camping area.
4.7 ▲	BR	Powerline Trail on left. Track on left is 6S15B. Remain on main dirt road and pass through camping area.
▼ 0.2	SO	Simmons Trail on right.
4.6 ▲	SO	Simmons Trail on left.
▼ 0.3	SO	Powerline Trail crosses road.
4.5 ▲	SO	Powerline Trail crosses road.
▼ 0.7	SO	Martin Trail on right for ATVs and motorbikes.
4.1 ▲	SO	Martin Trail on left for ATVs and motorbikes.
▼ 1.9	SO	Track on right for 4WDs, ATVs, and motorbikes.
2.9 ▲	SO	Track on left for 4WDs, ATVs, and motorbikes.
		GPS: N37°23.68' W119°38.69'
▼ 2.3	SO	Cody Trail on left for ATVs and motorbikes; then track on left for 4WDs, ATVs, and motorbikes. Continue straight ahead on 6S17.
2.5 ▲	SO	Track on right for 4WDs, ATVs, and motorbikes; then Cody Trail on right for ATVs and motorbikes. Continue straight ahead on 6S15.
		GPS: N37°23.47 W119°38.86'
▼ 2.4	SO	Track on left is 6S17A for 4WDs, ATVs, and motorbikes; then seasonal closure gate.
2.4 ▲	SO	Seasonal closure gate; then track on right is 6S17A for 4WDs, ATVs, and motorbikes.
▼ 3.1	TL	MMTB Trail on right; then seasonal closure gate and campsite straight ahead. Turn left and cross over Miami Creek on bridge. Trail on right.
1.7 ▲	TR	Trail on left; then cross over Miami Creek on bridge. Campsite on left. Turn right and pass through seasonal closure gate. MMTB Trail on left.
		GPS: N37°23.60' W119°39.15'
▼ 3.3	SO	Track on right is 6S41.
1.5 ▲	SO	Track on left is 6S41.
		GPS: N37°23.75' W119°39.24'
▼ 3.4	SO	Seasonal closure gate.
1.4 ▲	SO	Seasonal closure gate.
▼ 4.8	SO	Seasonal closure gate; then Sunflower Trail for ATVs and motorbikes on left; then 4-way intersection. Track on left and right is 6S24 for 4WDs, ATVs, and motorbikes. Zero trip meter at intersection and continue up the hill.
0.0 ▲		Continue to the southeast on 6S17. Sunflower Trail on right for ATVs and motorbikes; then seasonal closure gate.
		GPS: N37°24.69' W119°40.01'
▼ 0.0		Continue to the northwest.

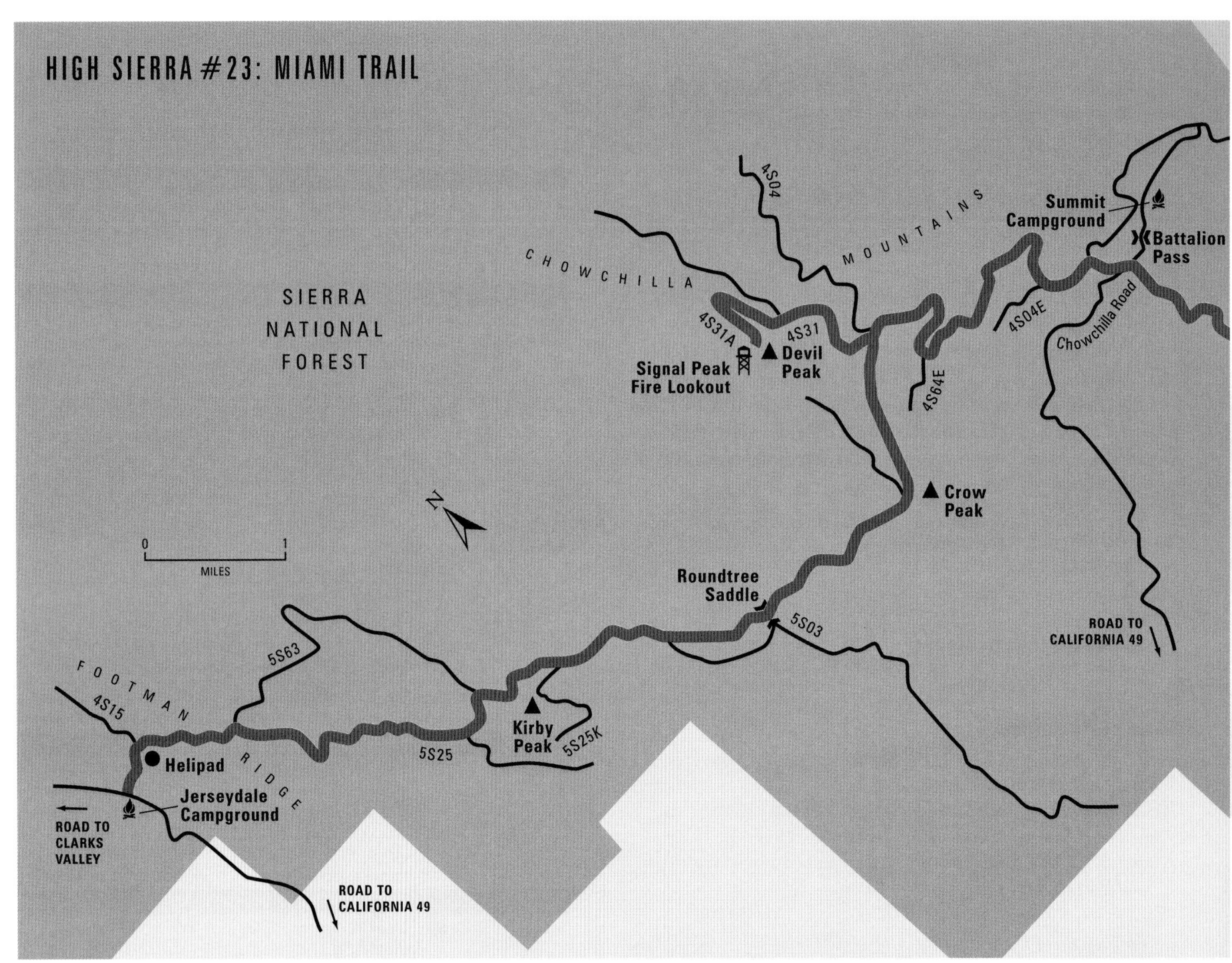

Mileage		Direction	Description
	1.6 ▲	SO	4-way intersection. Track on left and right is 6S24 for 4WDs, ATVs, and motorbikes. Zero trip meter.
▼ 0.3		BR	Track on left.
	1.3 ▲	BL	Track on right.
▼ 1.2		TR	4-way intersection with wide graded road 6S14. Turn right onto 6S14. Track straight ahead is 6S63 to Silver Knob. Leaving Miami Motorcycle Trails Area.
	0.4 ▲	TL	4-way intersection. Track on right is 6S63 to Silver Knob. Turn left onto smaller track 6S17, marked Ridge Track. Entering Miami Motorcycle Trails Area.
			GPS: N37°25.62' W119°40.30'
▼ 1.4		SO	Track on right into Miami Motorcycle Trails Area is 6S24X for 4WDs, ATVs, and motorbikes.
	0.2 ▲	SO	Track on left into Miami Motorcycle Trails Area is 6S24X for 4WDs, ATVs, and motorbikes.
▼ 1.5		SO	BLT Trail on right.
	0.1 ▲	SO	BLT Trail on left.
▼ 1.6		BL	Track continues straight ahead. Bear left up the hill onto gravel track 6S09 and zero trip meter.
	0.0 ▲		Continue to the south.
			GPS: N37°25.95' W119°40.51'
▼ 0.0			Continue to the west.
	7.2 ▲	SO	Track on left. Continue straight ahead joining 6S14 and zero trip meter.
▼ 1.0		SO	Track on right.
	6.2 ▲	SO	Track on left.
▼ 1.2		BL	Track on right.
	6.0 ▲	BR	Track on left.
			GPS: N37°26.55' W119°40.95'
▼ 1.5		SO	Track on left.
	5.7 ▲	SO	Track on right.
▼ 1.6		TR	Track continues straight ahead. Turn right onto unmarked trail 5S62 and climb hill.
	5.6 ▲	TL	Track on right. Turn left onto 6S09.
			GPS: N37°26.43' W119°41.31'
▼ 2.9		TL	T-intersection. Turn left onto 4S04. Start of shelf road.
	4.3 ▲	TR	Turn right onto 5S62. End of shelf road.
			GPS: N37°27.49' W119°41.31'
▼ 3.1		BL	Track on right.
	4.1 ▲	BR	Track on left.
▼ 3.3		SO	Cross over creek.
	3.9 ▲	SO	Cross over creek.
▼ 4.0		SO	Cross over creek.

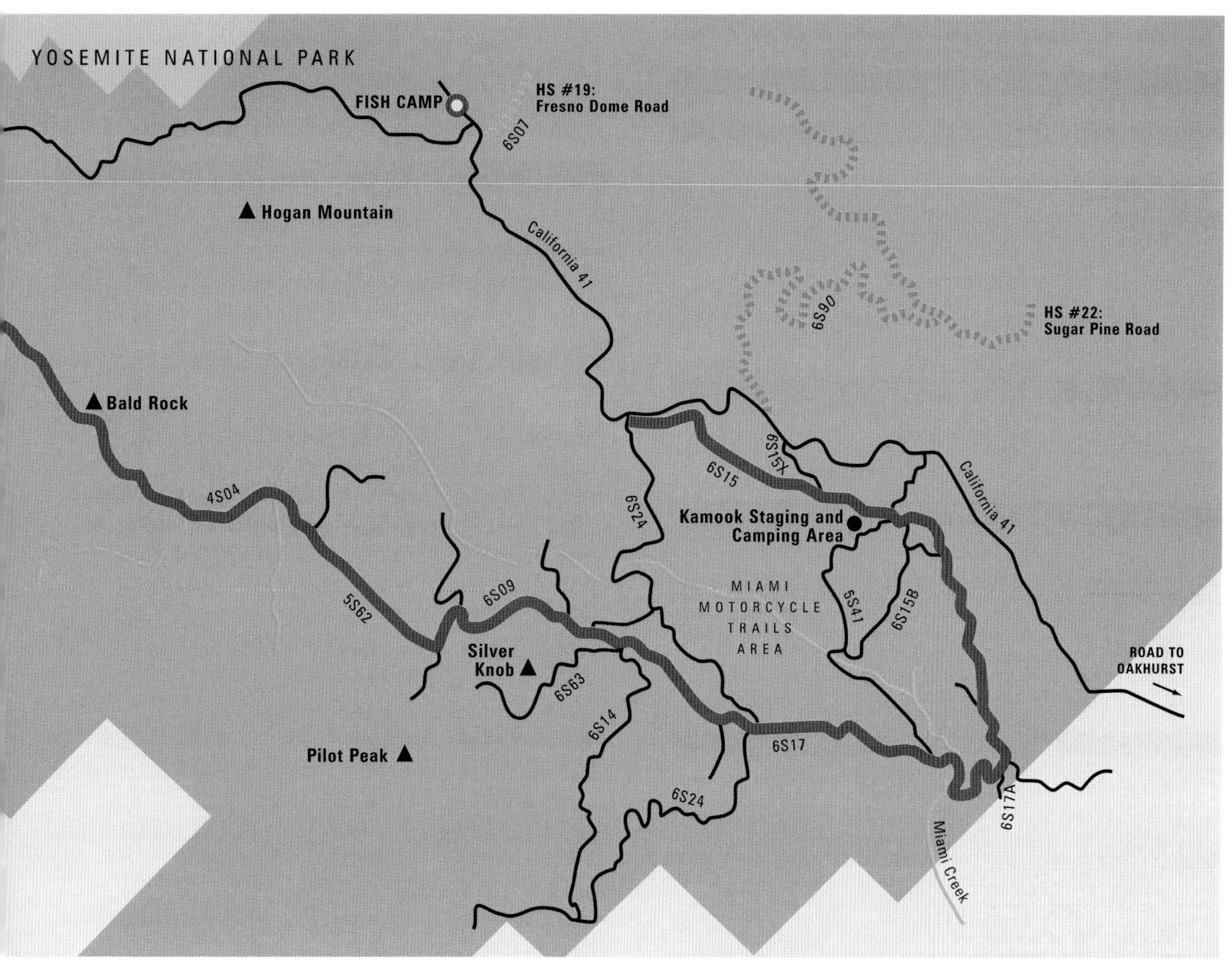

3.2 ▲	SO	Cross over creek.
▼ 4.4	SO	Cross over creek.
2.8 ▲	SO	Cross over creek.
▼ 4.5	SO	Bald Rock on right.
2.7 ▲	SO	Bald Rock on left.
▼ 6.3	SO	Track on right is 5S41; then track on left.
0.9 ▲	SO	Track on right; then track on left is 5S41.
		GPS: N37°29.87' W119°41.79'
▼ 7.2	SO	End of shelf road. 4-way intersection with graded Chowchilla Road. Summit Campground is 1 mile to the right over Battalion Pass. California 49 is to the left. Zero trip meter and follow sign to Crowsfoot.
0.0 ▲		Continue to the south on 4S04.
		GPS: N37°30.39' W119°42.00'
▼ 0.0		Continue to the north on 4S04.
3.5 ▲	SO	4-way intersection with graded Chowchilla Road. Summit Campground is 1 mile to the left over Battalion Pass. California 49 is to the right. Zero trip meter. Start of shelf road.
▼ 0.3	TL	T-intersection. Remain on 4S04 and follow sign to Crowsfoot and Jerseydale.
3.2 ▲	TR	Track continues straight ahead. Remain on 4S04.
▼ 0.6	SO	Track on left is 4S04E.
2.9 ▲	SO	Track on right is 4S04E.
▼ 0.9	SO	Track on right.
2.6 ▲	SO	Track on left.
▼ 1.1	SO	Track on left.
2.4 ▲	SO	Track on right.
▼ 2.3	SO	Track on left is 4S64E.
1.2 ▲	SO	Track on right is 4S64E.
		GPS: N37°30.95' W119°43.47'
▼ 2.5	SO	Small track on right.
1.0 ▲	SO	Small track on left.
▼ 2.6	SO	Track on right.
0.9 ▲	SO	Track on left.
▼ 3.5	BL	Track on right; then second track on right is 4S04 to Stove Pipe and Iron Mountain Saddle; then third track on right is 4S31, which climbs to Signal Peak Fire Lookout on Devil Peak. Zero trip meter and bear left onto 5S25.
0.0 ▲		Continue to the east.
		GPS: N37°31.24' W119°43.75'

Spur to Signal Peak Fire Lookout

▼ 0.0		Proceed to the west on unmarked road 4S31.
▼ 0.6	SO	Track on left is 4S31Y.
▼ 0.9	TL	Track continues straight ahead. Turn left on 4S31A.

			GPS: N37°31.74' W119°44.11'
▼ 1.5		SO	Closure gate. Closed if tower is not manned.
			GPS: N37°32.10' W119°44.35'
▼ 2.0			Signal Peak Fire Lookout.
			GPS: N37°31.75' W119°44.38'

Continuation of Main Trail

▼ 0.0			Continue to the south
	9.3 ▲	BR	Track on left is 4S31, which climbs to Signal Peak Fire Lookout on Devil Peak; then second track on left is 4S04 to Stove Pipe and Iron Mountain Saddle; then third track left. Zero trip meter. Bear right, joining 4S04, and follow the sign to Summit Campground and Chowchilla Road.
			GPS: N37°31.24' W119°43.75'
▼ 0.4		BR	Track on left is 5S25A.
	8.9 ▲	SO	Track on right is 5S25A.
▼ 1.3		SO	Track on right. Start of shelf road.
	8.0 ▲	SO	Track on left. End of shelf road.
			GPS: N37°30.43' W119°44.54'
▼ 2.5		SO	Track on left.
	6.8 ▲	SO	Track on right.
			GPS: N37°30.70' W119°45.67'
▼ 2.6		BR	Roundtree Saddle. Track on left is 5S03; then second track on left and small track on right. Remain on main trail.
	6.7 ▲	BL	Roundtree Saddle. Track on left and track on right; then second track on right is 5S03. Remain on main trail.
			GPS: N37°30.62' W119°45.78'
▼ 3.1		SO	Track on right.
	6.2 ▲	SO	Track on left.
▼ 3.5		SO	Track on left; then second small track on left.
	5.8 ▲	SO	Small track on right; then second track on right.
▼ 3.6		SO	Track on right.
	5.7 ▲	SO	Track on left.
▼ 4.4		SO	Track on left is 5S25K.
	4.9 ▲	SO	Track on right is 5S25K.
▼ 5.3		BL	Track on right.
	4.0 ▲	BR	Track on left.
			GPS: N37°31.59' W119°47.79'
▼ 5.7		SO	Small track on left climbs around Kirby Peak.
	3.6 ▲	SO	Small track on right climbs around Kirby Peak.
			GPS: N37°31.42' W119°48.06'
▼ 6.6		SO	Track on right.
	2.7 ▲	SO	Track on left.
▼ 6.8		SO	Track on left and two tracks on right.
	2.5 ▲	SO	Track on right and two tracks on left.
			GPS: N37°32.09' W119°48.85'
▼ 7.7		BL	Track on right is 5S63; then second track on right is 4S05; then third track on right is 4S06. Remain on main trail.
	1.6 ▲	BR	Track on left is 4S06; then second track on left is 4S05; then third track on left is 5S63. Remain on main trail.
			GPS: N37°32.57' W119°49.32'
▼ 8.7		SO	Helipad on left; then track on right is 4S15.
	0.6 ▲	SO	Track on left is 4S15; then helipad on right.
			GPS: N37°32.86' W119°49.97'
▼ 8.8		SO	Cattle guard.
	0.5 ▲	SO	Cattle guard.
▼ 9.3			End of shelf road. Trail ends at T-intersection with Jerseydale Road opposite Jerseydale USFS Campground, 2 miles north of Darrah. Turn left for California 49 and Mariposa; turn right for Sweetwater Mine and Clarks Valley.
	0.0 ▲		Trail starts on Jerseydale Road opposite Jerseydale USFS Campground, 8 miles north of California 49. Zero trip meter and turn east on graded dirt shelf road, following sign to Footman Ridge Road and Crowsfoot.
			GPS: N37°32.70' W119°50.22'

HIGH SIERRA #24

Ferguson Ridge Trail

Starting Point:	**Triangle Road, 2.5 miles east of California 140**
Finishing Point:	**High Sierra #25: Hite Cove Road, 4 miles north of Jerseydale USFS Campground**
Total Mileage:	**12.7 miles, plus 3.9-mile spur along Ferguson Ridge**
Unpaved Mileage:	**12.6 miles, plus 3.9-mile spur**
Driving Time:	**2.5 hours**
Elevation Range:	**2,800–4,300 feet**
Usually Open:	**Year-round**
Best Time to Travel:	**Year-round**
Difficulty Rating:	**2**
Scenic Rating:	**8**
Remoteness Rating:	**+0**

Special Attractions

- Long ridge-top trail with views of the Merced River and Yosemite National Park.
- Trail passes the site of the historic Sweetwater Mine.

History

Gold fever drove many miners to extreme measures. Such was the case at a mine at Sweetwater Point in 1865. A. J. Mann and his partner Clifton quarreled one day while returning from Buffalo Gulch. The quarrel became an all-out fight, with Mann the winner. Clifton, badly bruised and angry, returned to camp and borrowed a friend's six-shooter, claiming he wanted to shoot a squirrel. Instead he went after Mann. Mann dropped to his knees, begging for mercy, but Clifton killed him outright.

Mining had other hazards, too. In 1915, miners Meaki Phasr and John Rogers were placing dynamite in a round of holes to blast out a shaft at Sweetwater's Early Mine. Phasr, a 27-year-old native of Poland, failed to cut a long enough fuse for the two to reach safety. He died of severe injuries to his chest and face within hours and was buried at the Sweetwater Cemetery. Rogers was luckier; he escaped with minor bruises.

Description

Ferguson Ridge Trail travels through oaks and manzanitas on the extreme west side of Sierra National Forest. The trail is usually open year-round and is especially good in dry winter

Ferguson Ridge Trail meanders along the ridge top

weather. In summer, the open aspect of the lower elevations can make it uncomfortably hot.

The trail leaves Triangle Road at Carter Road, which leads through private property. When the private property ends, the road turns into a single-lane formed trail that travels into Sierra National Forest. It passes the old Sweetwater Mine, which is now private property. Please respect landowner's rights and do not trespass on the posted property. Some old mining trucks and remains of the stamp mill can be seen from the road.

Continuing on the main graded road will take you out to California 140, just north of Midpines. The route described here turns onto a formed trail that runs along Ferguson Ridge. The ridge is vegetated with manzanitas and oaks and can be moderately brushy in places. There are a few reasonable campsites and some good views to the west over Sweetwater Ridge. A spur takes you to a knoll with 360-degree views: California 140, which goes to Yosemite National Park, can be seen far below beside the Merced River to the north; Yosemite National Park is to the northeast; the South Fork of the Merced River is to the east; and Stanislaus National Forest is to the north.

The main trail continues for another couple of miles to finish at the start of High Sierra #25: Hite Cove Road, a continuation of Jerseydale Road.

Current Road Information

Sierra National Forest
Bass Lake Ranger District
57003 CR 225
North Fork, CA 93643-9734
(559) 877-2218

Map References

BLM Yosemite Valley
USFS Sierra National Forest
USGS 1:24,000 Kinsley, Feliciana Mt., Buckingham Mt.
1:100,000 Yosemite Valley
Maptech CD-ROM: High Sierra/Yosemite
Northern California Atlas & Gazetteer, p. 110
California Road & Recreation Atlas, p. 77
Trails Illustrated, Yosemite National Park (206)

Route Directions

▼ 0.0			From Mariposa, head north on California 140 for 4 miles; then turn east on Triangle Road and continue for 2.5 miles. Zero trip meter and turn north on small paved Carter Road.
	4.0 ▲		Trail ends at T-intersection with paved Triangle Road. Turn right for California 140 and Mariposa; turn left for Darrah
			GPS: N37°30.79' W119°53.60'
▼ 0.1		SO	Road turns to graded dirt.
	3.9 ▲	SO	Road is now paved.
▼ 0.3		SO	Deer Creek Road on right.
	3.7 ▲	SO	Deer Creek Road on left.
▼ 0.8		SO	Cattle guard.
	3.2 ▲	SO	Cattle guard.
▼ 1.1		SO	Cattle guard.
	2.9 ▲	SO	Cattle guard.
▼ 1.3		TL	Road on right is a dead end. Remain on Carter Road.
	2.7 ▲	TR	Road on left is a dead end. Remain on Carter Road.
			GPS: N37°31.71' W119°53.32'
▼ 1.8		BR	Track on left. Start of shelf road.
	2.2 ▲	BL	Track on right. End of shelf road.
▼ 2.6		SO	Entering Sierra National Forest at sign. Track on right and track on left. Road is now marked as 4S10.
	1.4 ▲	SO	Track on right and track on left. Leaving Sierra National Forest at sign.
			GPS: N37°32.15' W119°53.31'
▼ 2.9		SO	Track on left.
	1.1 ▲	SO	Track on right.
▼ 4.0		TL	Turn left onto 4S13. Track continues straight ahead to Buckingham Mountain. Zero trip meter.
	0.0 ▲		Continue to the west on 4S10.
			GPS: N37°32.33' W119°52.33'
▼ 0.0			Continue to the north on 4S13. Track on right.
	2.4 ▲	TR	Track on left; then T-intersection. Track on left goes to Buckingham Mountain. Zero trip meter and turn right, following the sign to Triangle Road.
▼ 0.5		SO	End of shelf road.
	1.9 ▲	SO	Start of shelf road.
▼ 0.9		SO	Cattle guard.
	1.5 ▲	SO	Cattle guard.

Early Dodge trucks at the Sweetwater Mine are a reminder of busier times; observe from the public road

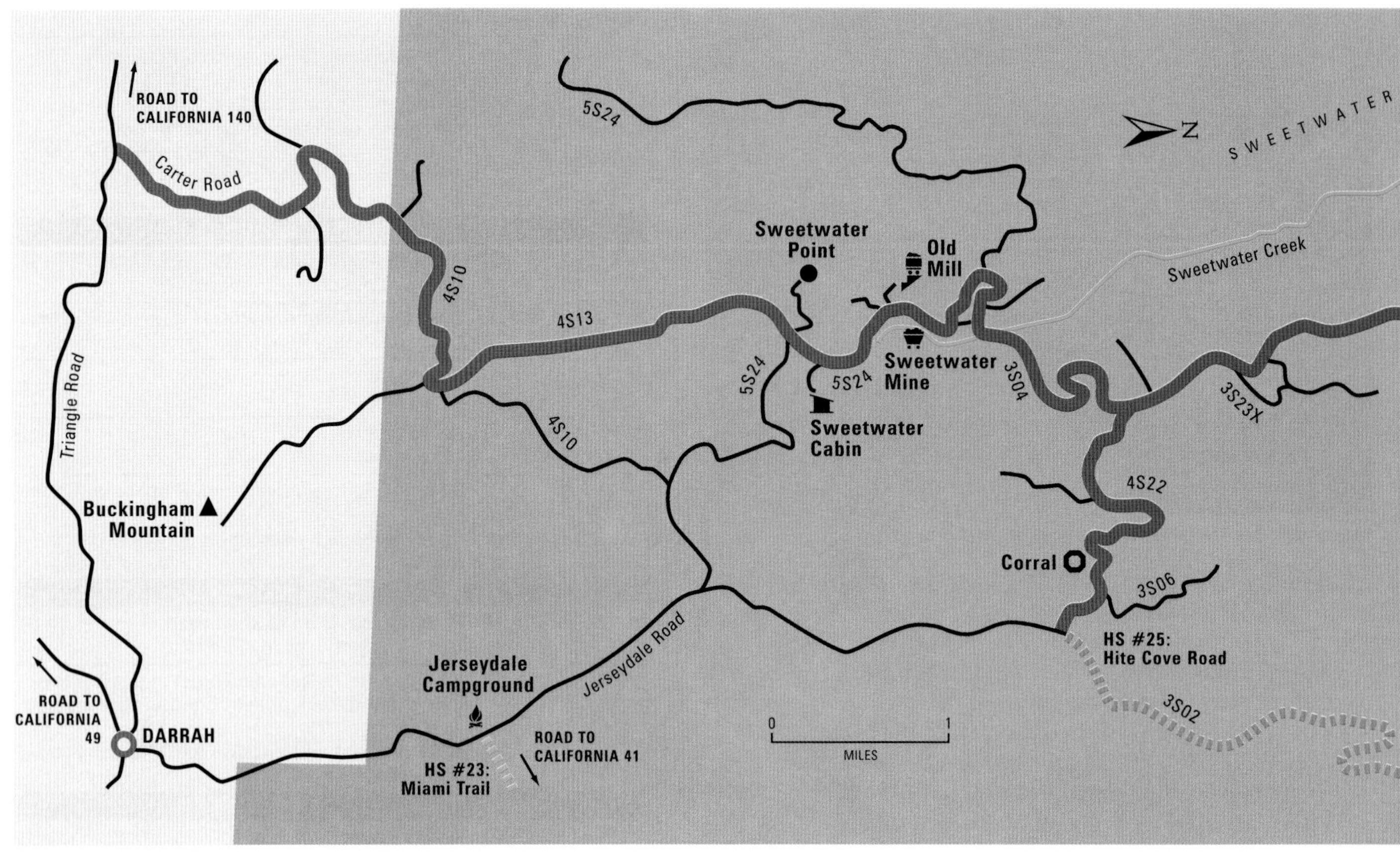

▼ 2.4 BL Track on right is 4S36. Small track on left. Graded road on right is 5S24. Bear left onto 5S24, following the sign to Sweetwater Mine and Feliciana Mountain. Zero trip meter.
0.0 ▲ Continue to the southeast on 4S13.

GPS: N37°34.14′ W119°52.74′

▼ 0.0 Continue to the northwest.
1.8 ▲ TR Graded road continues straight ahead. Turn right, following the sign to Buckingham Saddle. Track on left and track on right is 4S36. Zero trip meter.

▼ 0.3 BL Track on right is private road to Sweetwater Cabin.
1.5 ▲ SO Track on left is private road to Sweetwater Cabin.

GPS: N37°34.32′ W119°52.60′

▼ 0.9 SO Two tracks on left and track on right.
0.9 ▲ SO Two tracks on right and track on left.

▼ 1.0 SO Old stamp mill hidden in the trees on right; then pass through private property of the Sweetwater Mine.
0.8 ▲ SO Pass through private property of the Sweetwater Mine; then old stamp mill hidden in the trees on left.

GPS: N37°34.66′ W119°52.91′

▼ 1.2 SO Track on left.
0.6 ▲ SO Track on right.

▼ 1.3 BL Track on right. Follow the sign to Feliciana Mountain.
0.5 ▲ BR Track on left. Follow the sign to Jerseydale Station.

GPS: N37°34.90′ W119°52.86′

▼ 1.8 BR Road 5S24 on left continues to California 140. Zero trip meter and bear right onto 3S04, following the sign to Ferguson Dump.
0.0 ▲ Continue to the southeast.

GPS: N37°35.06′ W119°53.17′

▼ 0.0 Continue to the north.
2.2 ▲ BL T-intersection with 5S24. To the right goes to California 140. Bear left onto 5S24, following the sign to Jerseydale Station and zero trip meter.

▼ 0.5 BL Turning circle. Two tracks on right and track on left. Bear left and head north.
1.7 ▲ BR Turning circle. Track on right and two tracks on left. Bear right and head southeast.

GPS: N37°35.03′ W119°52.92′

▼ 0.6 SO Cross through Sweetwater Creek.
1.6 ▲ SO Cross through Sweetwater Creek.

▼ 1.0 SO Track on right.
1.2 ▲ SO Track on left.

▼ 1.2 SO Track on right.
1.0 ▲ SO Track on left.

▼ 1.3 SO Cross through creek.
0.9 ▲ SO Cross through creek.

▼ 1.7 SO Track on left.
0.5 ▲ SO Track on right.

▼ 2.2 TR Track straight ahead is 3S04, the spur along Ferguson Ridge. Zero trip meter.
0.0 ▲ Continue to the southeast on 3S04.

GPS: N37°35.89′ W119°52.49′

Spur along Ferguson Ridge

▼ 0.0 Proceed to the northwest. Track on left.
▼ 0.6 TL Turn left in clearing. Track straight ahead is 3S23X and small track on right.

GPS: N37°36.32′ W119°52.67′

▼ 0.9 SO Track on right.
▼ 2.1 BL Track on right is 3S07 to Gimasol Ridge; then track on left.

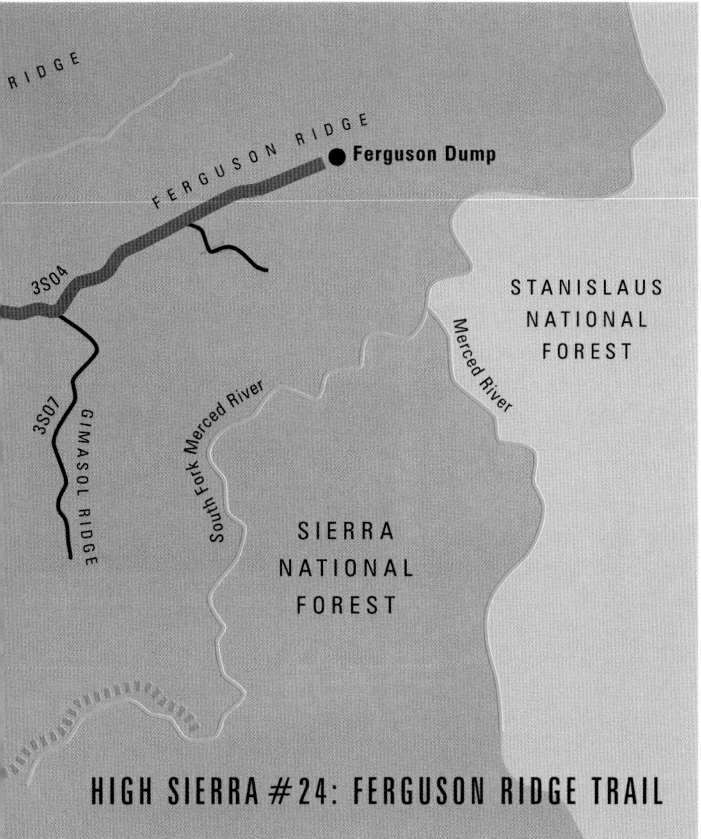

			GPS: N37°37.34' W119°53.14'
▼ 3.1		SO	Track on right.
			GPS: N37°38.03' W119°53.72'
▼ 3.9			Spur ends at viewpoint and turning circle at Ferguson Dump.
			GPS: N37°38.65' W119°54.10'

Continuation of Main Trail

▼ 0.0			Continue to the east on the upper road 4S22.
	2.3 ▲	TL	Track on right is 3S04, the spur along Ferguson Ridge. Zero trip meter.
			GPS: N37°35.89' W119°52.49'
▼ 0.2		SO	Track on right.
	2.1 ▲	SO	Track on left.
▼ 0.7		SO	Track on right.
	1.6 ▲	BR	Track on left.
▼ 1.1		BR	Track on left.
	1.2 ▲	BL	Track on right.
			GPS: N37°36.00' W119°51.72'
▼ 1.6		SO	Corral on right.
	0.7 ▲	SO	Corral on left.
▼ 1.9		SO	Track on left is 3S06.
	0.4 ▲	SO	Track on right is 3S06.
▼ 2.1		SO	Cattle guard.
	0.2 ▲	SO	Cattle guard.
▼ 2.2		SO	Track on left.
	0.1 ▲	SO	Track on right.
▼ 2.3			Trail ends at T-intersection with Jerseydale Road. To the left is the start of High Sierra #25: Hite Cove Road. Turn right for Jerseydale USFS Campground and California 49.
	0.0 ▲		Trail commences on High Sierra #25: Hite Cove Road (a continuation of the Jerseydale Road), 4 miles north of Jerseydale USFS Campground. Zero trip meter and turn northwest on graded dirt road following sign for Apperson Mine Road and Sweetwater Creek. Track straight ahead is the start of High Sierra #25: Hite Cove Road.
			GPS: N37°35.53' W119°51.08'

HIGH SIERRA #25

Hite Cove Road

Starting Point:	**Jerseydale Road, 4 miles north of the Jerseydale USFS Campground**
Finishing Point:	**Hite Cove**
Total Mileage:	**5.1 miles (one-way)**
Unpaved Mileage:	**5.1 miles**
Driving Time:	**1 hour (one-way)**
Elevation Range:	**1,600–3,900 feet**
Usually Open:	**Late April to late November**
Best Time to Travel:	**Dry weather**
Difficulty Rating:	**6**
Scenic Rating:	**10**
Remoteness Rating:	**+1**

Special Attractions

- Exciting and difficult 4WD trail for smaller high-clearance 4WDs.
- Fishing, gold panning, swimming, and wildflower viewing along the South Fork of the Merced River.
- Panoramic views from the shelf road above the South Fork of the Merced River.

History

The old mining settlement of Hite Cove on the South Fork of the Merced River was named for John R. Hite, who discovered a rich vein there in 1861. Tales of his discovery vary: One story was that an Indian woman led him to it; another says that Hite and his Indian wife both made the discovery. A third account says he was with an Indian woman who had saved his life. She rescued him from freezing to death when she found him unconscious in deep snow. The woman left camp one day without his approval to join a big Indian gathering at Indian Flat. Hite followed her and became tired from the chase. He stumbled and fell, discovering the gold-laden quartz vein.

Initially, the ore was processed in an arrastra, which was soon replaced by a water-driven 10-stamp mill constructed by John H. Singleton of Yellow Aster mining fame in Randsburg. Tunnels ran deep into the mountainside and a tramline took ore down to Hite's mill by the river. A small town grew up around the mine, including an impressive hotel and post office. Sadly, many buildings were lost in a fire in 1924.

Hite Cove produced more than $3 million worth of gold. John Hite accumulated enormous wealth, developing the Indian Peak Ranch and investing in San Francisco real estate. He also became the center of a bitter divorce wrangle in 1899, supposedly having left his Indian wife for another woman. The claimant sought his ranch and $600,000 in retribution. The suit received statewide coverage; it was settled out of court for an unknown amount. Speculations ranged from just a few thousand dollars to $20,000 and a house near Indian Ranch. Hite passed away in San Francisco on April 18, 1906, just hours before the powerful earthquake and fire destroyed the city.

Description

Hite Cove Road is an extremely narrow, steep shelf road that drops more than 2,000 feet from the ridge top to the South Fork of the Merced River at Hite Cove. The road is a tortuous route, best suited for small to mid-sized vehicles.

Initially, the road is graded because it is the main access to the Savage Lundy Trailhead. Past the turnoff to the trailhead, the standard quickly drops to a narrow, uneven formed trail. It starts to descend steeply down the shelf road. This trail should not be attempted in wet weather, when the off-camber shelf road becomes extremely greasy and dangerous.

The trail merits a 6 difficulty rating because the shelf road is extremely narrow and has only 10 places to pass in 3.8 miles. The passing places are not necessarily turning places, so once you commit yourself, there are few options for changing your mind. Remember you have to climb back up the steep grade to exit. Drivers should use caution because they may have to reverse up the steep grade for considerable distances to allow other vehicles to pass. Remember that vehicles traveling uphill have right of way, although common sense should always prevail. In addition, the surface is uneven, often tilting vehicles toward the drop. There are several rocky sections, with some rock steps that will require care with wheel placement. The worst rocky sections are around the trail's three switchbacks. In addition, the trail is moderately brushy and a few scratches may be inevitable.

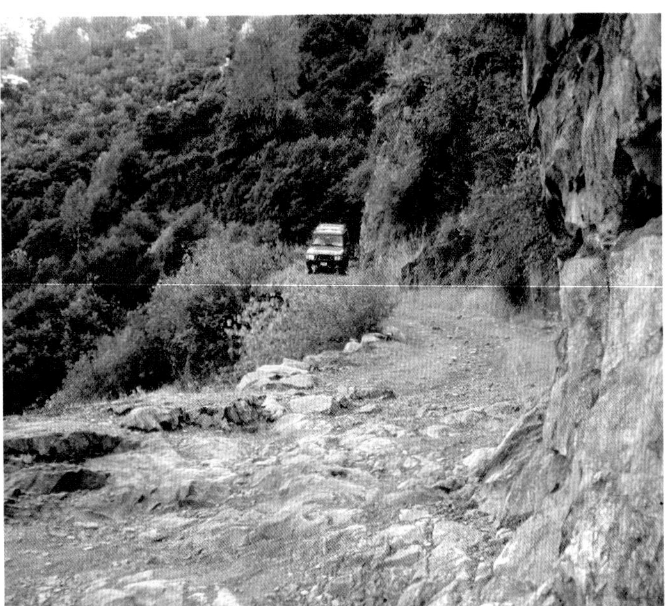

Most of Hite Cove Road is moderately steep and narrow, unlike this level section

The final 1.4 miles follow above or alongside the South Fork of the Merced River. Passing places are still limited. In places, you can see where miners built up the narrow trail. There are a few scattered campsites close to the river that are popular on weekends. The river is fast flowing and offers good trout fishing, swimming in some deep swimming holes, and gold panning where permitted. Remains of the Hoosier Mine can be seen on the far side of the river. There are two small buildings and the remains of some mining equipment.

Looking up the South Fork of the Merced River to Casa Diablo Peak

In spring, the Hite Cove area and the hiking trail out to California 140 are excellent places for wildflower viewing. More than 60 species of wildflowers can be found blooming as early as February through to April. Beware: Poison oak is also common.

Current Road Information

Sierra National Forest
Bass Lake Ranger District
57003 CR 225
North Fork, CA 93643-9734
(559) 877-2218

Map References

BLM Yosemite Valley
USFS Sierra National Forest
USGS 1:24,000 Buckingham Mt., El Portal
1:100,000 Yosemite Valley
Maptech CD-ROM: High Sierra/Yosemite
Northern California Atlas & Gazetteer, p. 110
California Road & Recreation Atlas, p. 77

Route Directions

▼ 0.0		From Hite Cove Road (a continuation of Jerseydale Road), 4 miles north of Jerseydale USFS Campground, zero trip meter and turn east on graded dirt road 3S02, following the sign for Hite Cove 4WD Road and Savage Lundy Trailhead. Track on left at the start of this trail is High Sierra #24: Ferguson Ridge Trail.
		GPS: N37°35.53' W119°51.08'
▼ 0.5	BL	Track on right to viewpoint.
▼ 1.0	SO	Track on left.

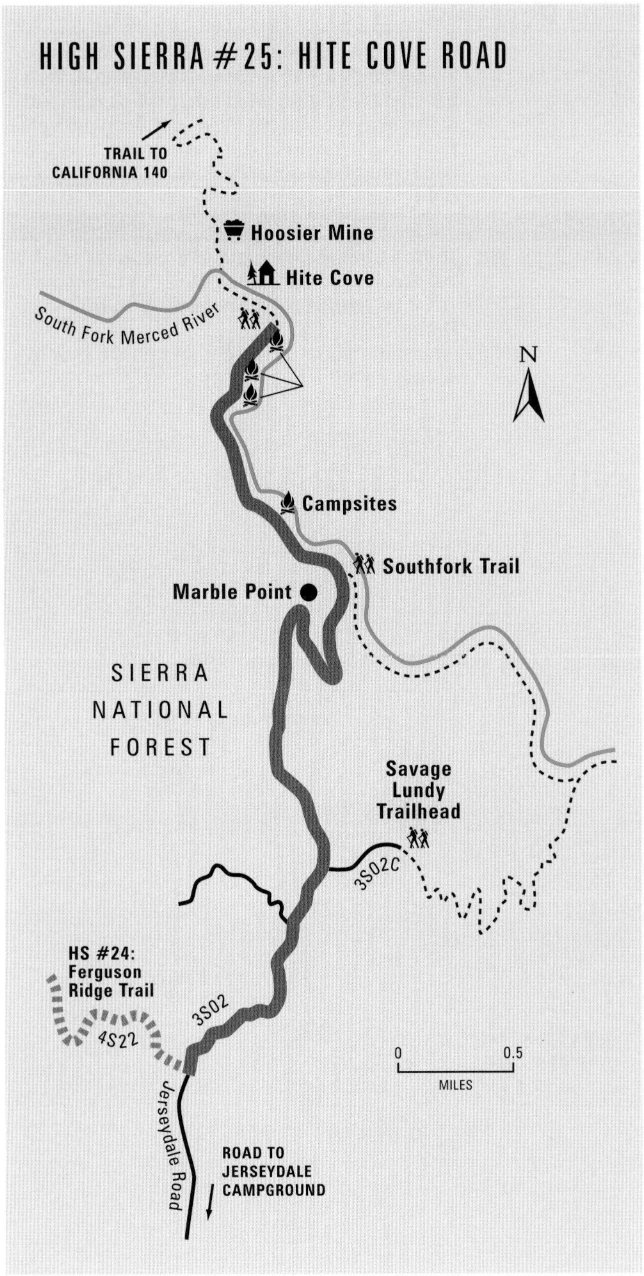

HIGH SIERRA #25: HITE COVE ROAD

TRAIL TO CALIFORNIA 140
Hoosier Mine
Hite Cove
South Fork Merced River
N
Campsites
Southfork Trail
Marble Point
SIERRA NATIONAL FOREST
Savage Lundy Trailhead
3S02C
HS #24: Ferguson Ridge Trail
4S22
3S02
0 0.5 MILES
Jerseydale Road
ROAD TO JERSEYDALE CAMPGROUND

▼ 1.3	BL	Track on right is 3S02C to Savage Lundy Trailhead. Bear left through gate onto formed dirt trail and zero trip meter.
		GPS: N37°36.29′ W119°50.42′
▼ 0.0		Continue to the north. Start of descent.
▼ 1.2	SO	Right-hand switchback at Marble Point.
		GPS: N37°37.22′ W119°50.50′
▼ 2.1	SO	Hiking trail on right is Southfork Trail to Devils Gulch.
		GPS: N37°37.36′ W119°50.37′
▼ 2.4	SO	End of descent. Campsites on right.
		GPS: N37°37.58′ W119°50.66′
▼ 2.5	SO	Cross through creek.
▼ 3.6	SO	Campsites on right alongside river.
▼ 3.8		Campsite on right; then trail ends at a campsite and turnaround beside the river.
		GPS: N37°38.22′ W119°50.61′

HIGH SIERRA #26

Merced River Road

Starting Point:	**California 140 in Briceburg**
Finishing Point:	**Gate before the Mountain King Mine**
Total Mileage:	**4.9 miles (one-way)**
Unpaved Mileage:	**4.9 miles**
Driving Time:	**30 minutes (one-way)**
Elevation Range:	**1,200–1,400 feet**
Usually Open:	**Year-round**
Best Time to Travel:	**Year-round**
Difficulty Rating:	**1**
Scenic Rating:	**10**
Remoteness Rating:	**+0**

Special Attractions

- Fishing, swimming, rafting, and gold panning (where permitted) on the Merced River.
- BLM campgrounds and backcountry campsites.
- A popular mountain bike trail that continues to California 49.

History

Merced River Road follows part of the Yosemite Valley Railroad grade that ran from the town of Merced along the Merced River to El Portal, an entrance to Yosemite National Park. Construction began in 1907 and was completed two years and more than $3 million later. Before the railroad, tourists had to take a two-day stagecoach ride to the park. Heavy dust and highway robberies were just some of the distractions from the spectacular scenery along the early wagon road. The "Shortcut to Paradise," as the line was called, reduced travel time to about four hours and greatly improved tourists' comfort. Few passengers complained about the $18.50 fare. In addition to passengers, the short line also carried sugar pines cut by the Yosemite Lumber Company to Merced. A steam-driven sawmill at Merced Falls processed more than 70 million board feet a year.

In 1921, the Merced Irrigation District proposed a major dam on the Merced River to feed its developing irrigation system. The proposed site, known as the Exchequer Dam, had one major drawback: The Yosemite Valley Railroad ran right through it. The railroad had to be rerouted at great expense, but until the route was worked out, trains ran right through the construction site. When the dam was nearly complete, a temporary arch was built through the base for trains, thus creating a most unusual tourist attraction. The dam was completed in June 1926.

In 1926, an all-weather road reached Yosemite Valley, enabling tourists to enter the park in the comfort of their own automobiles. Loss of the tourist trade was significant for the Yosemite Valley Railroad, although logging and limestone and barium mining continued to be the line's mainstay. Floods in 1937 and 1945 wiped out close to 30 miles of the grade, and the railroad ceased operating in August 1945.

Merced River's clear waters are popular for water recreation

Description

This short trail travels alongside the Merced River, designated a wild and scenic river and managed by the Bureau of Land Management. The trail is an easy one, suitable for passenger vehicles, and is open year-round. It leads to three BLM campgrounds (fee required), two permit-only public gold dredging sites, and a number of walk-in or boat-in campsites. The road is a popular in the summer because it provides easy access to many swimming holes along the river.

The 4.9-mile trail passes three sets of rapids that are part of a 28-mile stretch of river popular with rafters. This section of the river, from Red Bud to Bagby, is rated Class III to Class V with one mandatory portage. The river is also popular with anglers, who can fish for brown and rainbow trout.

The route for vehicles stops just short of the Halls Gulch Bridge. There is access to private property past this point as well as to the site of the Mountain King Mine, of which little remains. Hikers and intrepid mountain bikers can continue past the bridge to California 49.

Current Road Information

Bureau of Land Management
Folsom Field Office
63 Natoma Street
Folsom, CA 95630
(916) 985-4474

Map References

BLM Yosemite Valley, Oakdale
USFS Stanislaus National Forest
USGS 1:24,000 Feliciana Mt., Bear Valley
1:100,000 Yosemite Valley, Oakdale
Maptech CD-ROM: High Sierra/Yosemite
Northern California Atlas & Gazetteer, pp. 110, 109
California Road & Recreation Atlas, p. 77

Route Directions

▼ 0.0		At the BLM Information Center in Briceburg, immediately south of Bear Creek Bridge, zero trip meter and turn west on small paved road at the sign for Merced Wild and Scenic River, following the sign to the campgrounds. A day-use rafting take-out area is immediately on the right.
		GPS: N37°36.29′ W119°57.91′
▼ 0.1	BR	Track on left. Bear right and cross over steel suspension bridge to the site of old Briceburg. Track on right is High Sierra #27: Burma Grade Trail.
▼ 0.2	SO	Information board on right and public beach access on left.

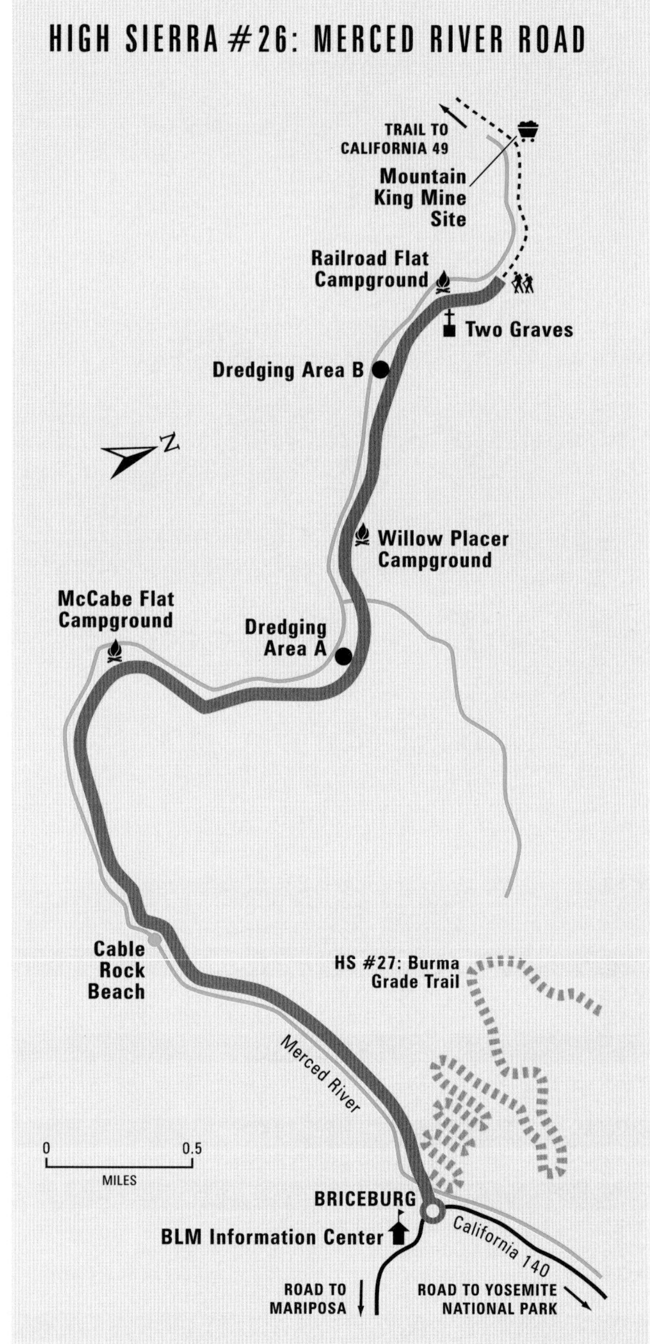

▼ 0.8	SO	Track on left to campsite.
		GPS: N37°36.05' W119°58.73'
▼ 1.4	SO	Rapids on left, pit toilet on right, and walk-in campsite on left at Cable Rock Beach.
		GPS: N37°35.70' W119°59.19'
▼ 2.2	SO	Split Rock rapids.
▼ 2.3	SO	Corner Pocket rapids.
▼ 2.4	BR	Entering McCabe Flat Campground. Track on left to walk-in campsites.
		GPS: N37°35.74' W120°00.12'
▼ 2.5	SO	Track on left rejoins.
▼ 3.3	SO	Dredging Area A on left.
		GPS: N37°36.46' W119°59.94'
▼ 3.6	SO	Cross over Good Gulch; then track on left to campsite.
▼ 3.8	SO	Entering Willow Placer Campground. Track on right to campsites.
		GPS: N37°36.54' W120°00.38'
▼ 4.3	SO	Track on left and parking on right; then gate. Leaving Willow Placer Campground. Start of Dredging Area B.
▼ 4.7	SO	Entering Railroad Flat Campground and rafting take-out. Track on left to campsite; then two graves behind white fences on right.
		GPS: N37°37.03' W120°01.14'
▼ 4.9		Trail ends for vehicles at gate. Mountain bikers and hikers can continue along the grade to California 49. The Mountain King Mine site is a short distance beyond the gate.
		GPS: N37°37.14' W120°01.13'

HIGH SIERRA #27

Burma Grade Trail

Starting Point:	**High Sierra #26: Merced River Road, 0.1 miles west of California 140 and Briceburg**
Finishing Point:	**Bull Creek Road (FR 20), 4.2 miles southeast of the intersection with High Sierra #28: Old Coulterville Road**
Total Mileage:	**15.4 miles**
Unpaved Mileage:	**15.4 miles**
Driving Time:	**2 hours**
Elevation Range:	**1,200–3,200 feet**
Usually Open:	**Year-round**
Best Time to Travel:	**Dry weather**
Difficulty Rating:	**3**
Scenic Rating:	**9**
Remoteness Rating:	**+1**

Special Attractions

- Long winding climb along the historic Burma Grade.
- Views of the Merced River.
- Pretty winding trail through the dry oak forests of Stanislaus National Forest.
- Popular mountain bike trail.

History

In 1892, William M. Brice, a native of Illinois, moved west and settled in Mariposa County. He worked the Schroeder Mine, situated high above the Merced River, 2 miles downstream from the settlement that would, in time, bear his name. Brice bought into the Colorado Store just south of the mine. He decided to move his store and young family to the confluence of Bear Creek and the Merced River when the Yosemite Valley Railroad was built through to El Portal in 1909. His store, on the north side of the river, also served as post office and railroad depot. Indians, prospectors, and ranchers all came to value the store. Just eight years later, in July 1917, William Brice passed away from complications related to diabetes.

His family continued to run the business, relocating to the south side of the river after the highway from Mariposa to Yosemite Valley was put through. Prisoners built the all-weather highway and a steel suspension bridge across the river to the temporary prison camp.

Suspension bridge over the Merced River at the foot of the Burma Grade

Brice's widow and her second husband, Frank Dovido, built the stone building on the south side of the old steel bridge now used by the BLM. They also built a much-needed restaurant and gas station to cater to visitors of Yosemite Valley.

The Texas Hill Mines can be found farther north along the trail. The cliff-hanging mines, high above the North Fork of the Merced River, were established in the mid-1860s and produced gold and small amounts of silver, copper, and lead. Mining was intermittent right up to 1943, the last recorded year of activity. Though a 10-stamp mill was constructed in 1919, only about $70,000 worth of ore was extracted from the mines.

Kinsley Guard Station, at the northern end of the trail, was named for James B. Kinsley, a native of Massachusetts who lived on Bull Creek, immediately north of the station. Kinsley was the postmaster of the self-named settlement. He died in November 1906 at age 77.

Description

Burma Grade Trail links the popular recreation sites along the Merced River near Briceburg with the higher elevations and trails in Stanislaus National Forest. The trail leaves Briceburg and immediately starts to climb along a steep shelf road that switchbacks up the ridge, ascending 1,500 feet in 5 miles. The trail is a narrow single-track for most of its length. There are

The Burma Grade snakes up the steep canyon of the Merced River

adequate passing places along the way, but you should be prepared to back up if you meet an oncoming vehicle. As you climb, sweeping views of the Merced River, Briceburg, the suspension bridge, and California 140 only get better. The area on top of the mountain is popular with mountain bikers, some of whom drive up the Burma Grade to the plateau before continuing by bike.

At the top of the grade, the vegetation is predominantly manzanita and oak. The route described here turns off the main trail at a 4-way intersection and follows smaller forest roads; these are no more difficult than the main trail. Continuing ahead at this point will take a more direct route to the end of the trail. The mapped route enters Stanislaus National Forest, skirting Black Mountain and passing close to Texas Hill. There is a great view of the North Fork of the Merced River from the track over Texas Hill, a 1-mile detour from the main route.

The trail drops down, passing the site of the Garibaldi Mine, where nothing remains, before crossing Skunk Gulch and rejoining Bull Creek Road near the Kinsley Fire Station. From here, it is 4.2 miles to the intersection with High Sierra #28: Old Coulterville Road.

Current Road Information

Bureau of Land Management
Folsom Field Office
63 Natoma Street
Folsom, CA 95630
(916) 985-4474

Stanislaus National Forest
Groveland Ranger District
24525 Highway 120
Groveland, CA 95321
(209) 962-7825

Map References

BLM Yosemite Valley, Oakdale
USFS Stanislaus National Forest
USGS 1:24,000 Feliciana Mt., Kinsley, Buckhorn Peak
1:100,000 Yosemite Valley, Oakdale
Maptech CD-ROM: High Sierra/Yosemite
Northern California Atlas & Gazetteer, pp. 110, 109
California Road & Recreation Atlas, pp. 77, 72

Route Directions

▼ 0.0			From High Sierra #26: Merced River Road, 0.1 miles west of California 140 and Briceburg and immediately north of the steel suspension bridge, zero trip meter and turn north on unmarked, well-used shelf road that climbs up the hill.
	6.7 ▲		Trail ends at T-intersection with High Sierra #26: Merced River Road. Turn left to exit to California 140; turn right to travel the Merced River Road.
			GPS: N37°36.27' W119°58.04'
▼ 2.9		SO	Track on left.
	3.8 ▲	SO	Track on right.
			GPS: N37°36.63' W119°58.74'
▼ 4.2		BL	Two tracks on right and track on left. First track

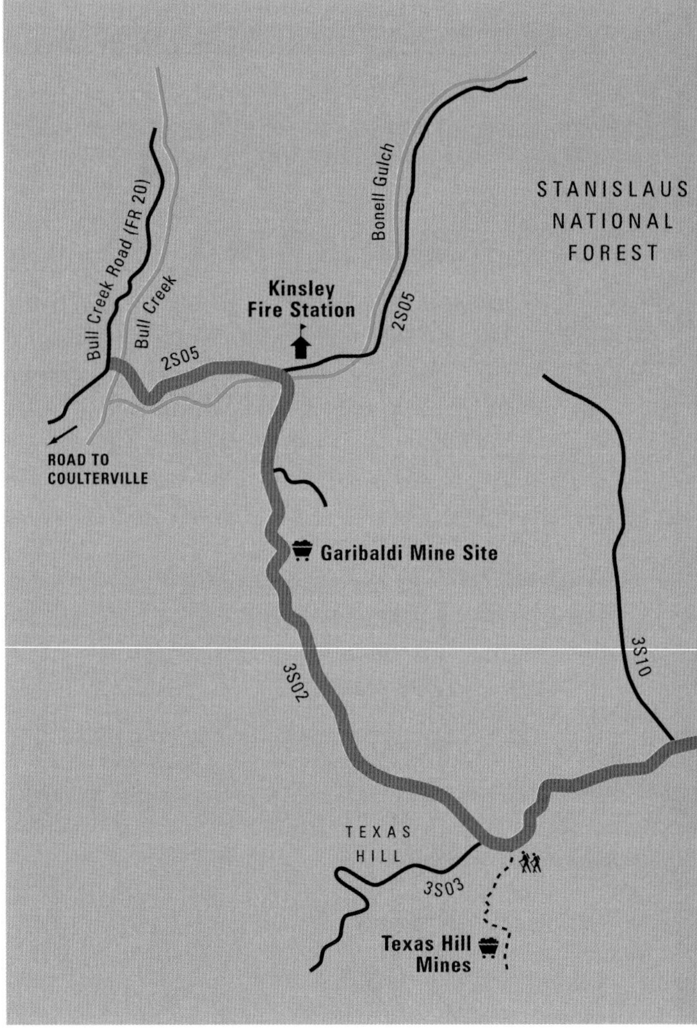

			on right, which climbs the hill, is 3S01. Bear left, remaining on the main trail. End of shelf road.
	2.5 ▲	BR	Start of shelf road. Two tracks on left and track on right. Second track on left, which climbs the hill, is 3S01. Bear right, remaining on the main trail.
			GPS: N37°37.51′ W119°58.65′
▼ 5.1		SO	Track on left.
	1.6 ▲	BL	Track on right.
			GPS: N37°37.85′ W119°59.35′
▼ 5.2		SO	Cross over creek; then track on left.
	1.5 ▲	SO	Track on right; then cross over creek.
▼ 5.7		SO	Spring on left; then cross over creek.
	1.0 ▲	SO	Cross over creek; then spring on right.
▼ 6.3		SO	Track on right.
	0.4 ▲	SO	Track on left.
▼ 6.6		SO	Track on left.
	0.1 ▲	SO	Track on right.
▼ 6.7		TL	Unmarked 4-way intersection on saddle. Zero trip meter.
	0.0 ▲		Continue to the southwest.
			GPS: N37°38.80′ W119°58.41′
▼ 0.0			Continue to the northwest.
	4.5 ▲	TR	Unmarked 4-way intersection on saddle. Zero trip meter.
▼ 2.0		BR	Track on left. Entering Stanislaus National Forest.
	2.5 ▲	SO	Track on right. Leaving Stanislaus National Forest.
			GPS: N37°39.06′ W119°59.83′
▼ 2.8		BL	Track on right.
	1.7 ▲	SO	Track on left.
			GPS: N37°39.42′ W119°59.48′
▼ 3.0		SO	Cross through Halls Gulch.
	1.5 ▲	SO	Cross through Halls Gulch.
▼ 3.8		BR	Track on left.
	0.7 ▲	SO	Track on right.
			GPS: N37°39.88′ W120°00.08′
▼ 4.5		SO	Small track on left is Black Mountain Fire Road; then second track on left is 3S15. Zero trip meter.
	0.0 ▲		Continue to the southeast.
			GPS: N37°40.28′ W120°00.27′
▼ 0.0			Continue to the northwest. Track on right.
	1.3 ▲	SO	Track on left; then track on right is 3S15; then second small track on right is Black Mountain Fire Road. Zero trip meter.
▼ 0.4		SO	Track on right; then second track on right is 3S10.
	0.9 ▲	SO	Track on left is 3S10; then second track on left.
▼ 1.2		SO	Hard to spot hiking trail to Texas Hill Mines on left.

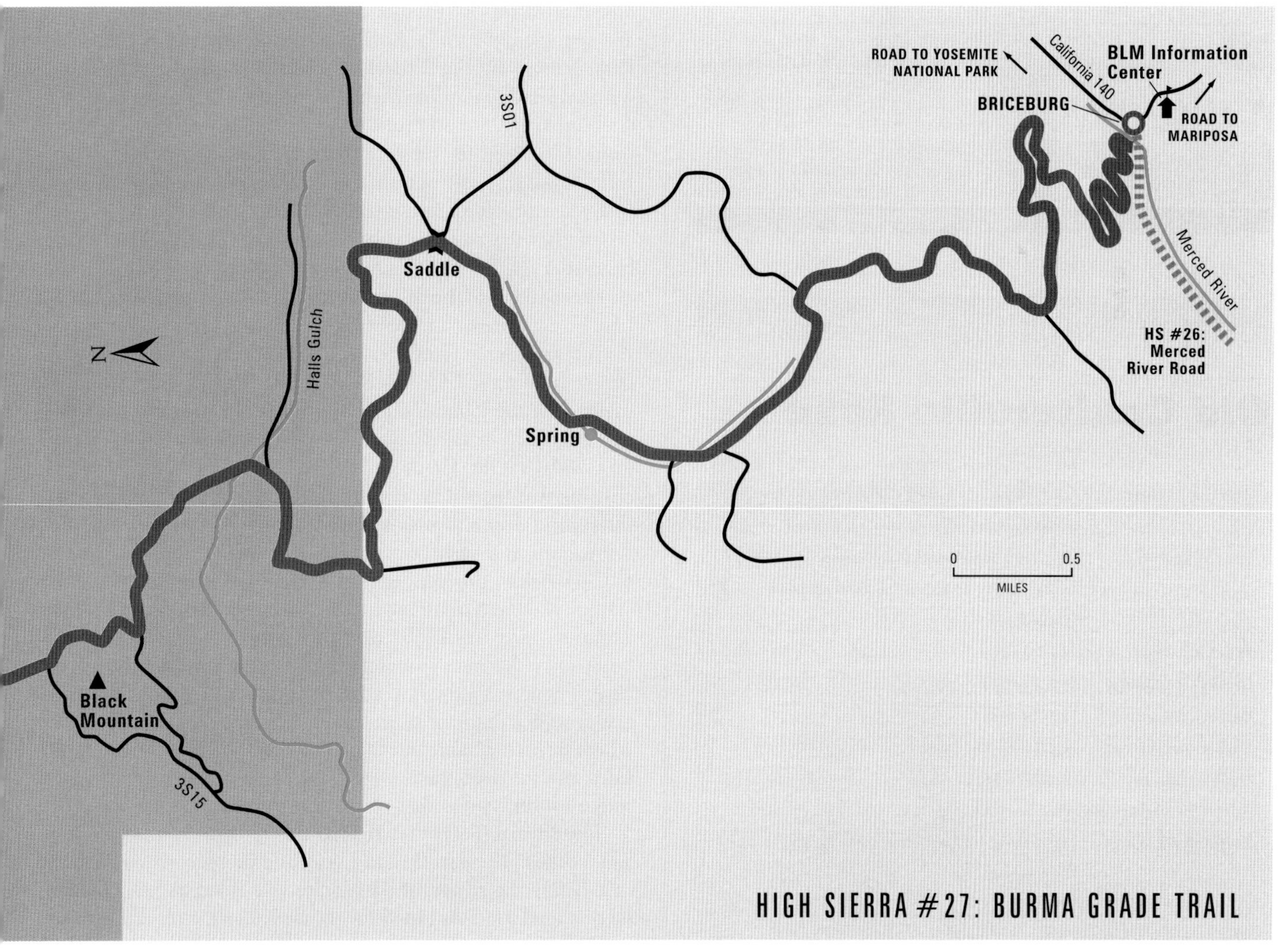

HIGH SIERRA #27: BURMA GRADE TRAIL

	0.1 ▲	SO	Hard to spot hiking trail to Texas Hill Mines on right.
			GPS: N37°41.17' W120°00.76'
▼ 1.3		BR	Track on left is 3S03, which goes 1 mile to Texas Hill and the viewpoint over North Fork Merced River. Zero trip meter at the sign.
	0.0 ▲		Continue to the south.
			GPS: N37°41.18' W120°00.75'
▼ 0.0			Continue to the northeast.
	2.9 ▲	BL	Track on right is 3S03, which goes 1 mile to Texas Hill and the viewpoint over North Fork Merced River. Zero trip meter at the sign to Black Mountain.
▼ 1.3		SO	Track on left.
	1.6 ▲	SO	Track on right.
▼ 1.4		SO	Site of Garibaldi Mine (nothing remains) on right.
	1.5 ▲	SO	Site of Garibaldi Mine (nothing remains) on left.
			GPS: N37°41.91' W119°59.63'
▼ 1.7		SO	Track on right.
	1.2 ▲	SO	Track on left.
▼ 2.2		TL	Cross through Bonell Gulch; then T-intersection with 2S05. Track on right returns to Briceburg via the Burma Grade. Kinsley Fire Station is 0.1 miles to the right.
	0.7 ▲	TR	Road continues straight ahead to Briceburg. Kinsley Fire Station is 0.1 miles straight ahead. Turn right onto 3S02 and cross through Bonell Gulch.
▼ 2.9			Cross over Bull Creek on bridge; then trail ends at T-intersection with gravel Bull Creek Road (FR 20). Turn left for Coulterville.
	0.0 ▲		Trail commences on Bull Creek Road (FR 20), 4.2 miles southeast of the intersection with High Sierra #28: Old Coulterville Road. Zero trip meter and turn south on graded road 2S05, following the sign to Kinsley Fire Station.
			GPS: N37°42.44' W119°58.82'

HIGH SIERRA #28

Old Coulterville Road

Starting Point:	**Old Yosemite Road (2S01) at the intersection with Bull Creek Road**
Finishing Point:	**Big Oak Flat Road (California 41), 3.3 miles west of the intersection with California 140**
Total Mileage:	**31.4 miles**
Unpaved Mileage:	**29.2 miles**
Driving Time:	**2.5 hours**
Elevation Range:	**2,500–5,400 feet**
Usually Open:	**April to December**
Best Time to Travel:	**Dry weather**
Difficulty Rating:	**1, 3 from Little Nellie Falls to Big Oak Flat Road**
Scenic Rating:	**10**
Remoteness Rating:	**+0**

Special Attractions

- Historic road to Yosemite National Park.
- Little Nellie Falls.
- Spectacular Bower Cave.

History

The Ahwahneeche, also known as Yosemite, a sub tribe of Miwok Indians, inhabited the Yosemite Valley prior to the arrival of Euro-Americans. Trappers and miners exploring the Sierra Nevada encountered members of the Miwok tribe and conflicts inevitably arose (see Mariposa War, page 107). In March 1851, James Savage led the Mariposa Battalion into Yosemite Valley to confront the Ahwahneechee. It wasn't long before firsthand accounts of the beautiful Yosemite Valley began attracting visitors to the region.

Getting to Yosemite Valley was not easy; pack trails provided the only routes in and out of the region. Many communities to the west of Yosemite started promoting the idea of a wagon road that would pass through their particular town. In the early 1870s, two roads were under construction, and the race to Yosemite was on. Rivalry developed between the Big Oak Flat Road, beginning west of Groveland and running through Tuolumne County, and the Coulterville-Yosemite Road, in Mariposa County. The Coulterville route had the added attraction of passing through the Merced Grove of giant sequoias, which is now included in Yosemite National Park. However, Big Oak Flat Road was progressing more quickly: that is, until it reached a cliff top at Gentrys Station. Carving a zigzag road into the rock face delayed the northerly route. Coulterville-Yosemite Road reached its destination in June 1874, just one month ahead of its rival, establishing the first wagon road to Yosemite Valley.

Of the two routes to the valley, the Big Oak Flat Road charged a toll but the Coulterville Road was free. Many drivers chose to evade the toll and travel east on Coulterville Road past Five Corners to Hazel Green Ranch. A connecting route from Hazel Green Ranch, called the Coulterville Trail, allowed people to join Big Oak Flat Road at Crane Flat. Those who remained on the Coulterville Road passed through the spectacular Merced Grove, descending alongside Moss Creek to rejoin today's Old Coulterville Road at Twin Bridges. This crossing was named for two bridges, the first over a creek and the second over a diversion ditch.

Wagons and stages traveling to Yosemite stopped at Bower Cave before proceeding to the stage station at today's McCauley Ranch. Sarah Haight, who was accompanying a honeymoon party in 1858, described Bower Cave as having boxwood elder trees growing out the top of the partially open cave. There was a small, cold clear lake to the right of the entrance and a flight of steps leading up to a "scapious shantie which bears the name of the ball room." The trees, rocks, and sides of the deep cave were covered with beautiful moss. Judge McRae, a member of the party, named it Bower Cave.

The Miwok people referred to this unusual feature as Oo-Tin, home of the First People. Locals and prospectors visited the cave before the advent of the Coulterville Road. A house nearby provided tours and food for travelers. Later, a service station was built here, but foundations are all that remain of it today.

Description

One of the main features of this trail is the unusual and dramatic series of blowholes that makes up Bower Cave. The sheer drops and ferns around the cave combine to make this a most impressive sight. To reach the cave from the Coulterville Toll Road historical marker, take the unmarked but well-used single-track hiking trail for about 0.1 miles. Be extremely careful in the area; there are unmarked drops and holes. Do not leave children or pets unattended. Guidelines for visiting the cave suggest doing so in daylight hours only and not attempting to enter the highly dangerous grotto. A permit is required to visit Bower Cave, now gated to prevent vandalism. Go to the Groveland Ranger Station to obtain a free permit and the combination number to enter the cave.

The main route starts at the end of the pavement on Old Yosemite Road, at the intersection of graded dirt Bull Creek Road, and winds around the south side of Pilot Ridge. The road passes through McCauley Ranch, the site of an old stage station, 2.8 miles from the start. Private ranch buildings mark the site nowadays.

A side trail goes a short distance to the fire lookout on Pilot Peak; the gate is locked when the lookout is not manned. The trail continues along an easy graded road that is generally suitable for passenger vehicles in dry weather. It travels through manzanita woodlands and pine forests before reaching the major intersection at Five Corners. Those not wanting to travel the full length of the trail have the option of an easy exit north to California 120 on paved FR 20. High Sierra #29: Crocker Ridge Trail also joins here. At the intersection, the main trail veers away from the original route of the Old Coulterville Road, which continues up Crocker Ridge Trail and then onto a hiking trail.

The main trail continues through low vegetation on Trumbull Ridge toward Trumbull Peak. It passes both ends of High Sierra #30: Trumbull Peak Trail, a loop that takes you south to the top of the peak. The trail then starts its descent toward Yosemite Valley, rejoining Old Coulterville Road at Twin Bridges, and passing into the wetter forests near Little Nellie Falls.

Little Nellie Falls

Passenger vehicles should stop at the point indicated and hike the final 0.2 miles to the falls. The descent to the falls is rough enough to warrant a high-clearance vehicle. The falls are small but very pretty, with the waters of Little Crane Creek tumbling down over granite boulders to a pool at the bottom. Ferns and other vegetation surround the creek. There is one picnic table at the falls, which makes a good place to stop or camp, although mosquitoes can be very prevalent at times.

Half Dome and El Capitan as seen from Old Coulterville Road

High-clearance 4WDs can continue past the falls to enter Yosemite National Park, although the gate may be closed at the park boundary. The trail exits through the community of Foresta. One point of interest along this route is the old Foresta Pioneer Cemetery, which has graves that date back to the 1880s. This exit is a good option in dry weather, but it is best avoided in wet weather. Keep in mind that you will be required to pay the park fee upon exiting the park.

The entire trail makes for a long and undulating mountain bike ride.

Current Road Information

Stanislaus National Forest
Groveland Ranger District
24525 Highway 120
Groveland, CA 95321
(209) 962-7825

Map References

BLM Oakdale, Yosemite Valley
USFS Stanislaus National Forest
USGS 1:24,000 Buckhorn Peak, Kinsley, Ascension Mt., Ackerson Mt., El Portal, El Capitan
1:100,000 Oakdale, Yosemite Valley
Maptech CD-ROM: High Sierra/Yosemite
Northern California Atlas & Gazetteer, pp. 109, 110
California Road & Recreation Atlas, p. 72
Trails Illustrated, Yosemite National Park (206) (incomplete)

Route Directions

▼ 0.0	Trail starts on Old Yosemite Road (2S01) at the intersection with Bull Creek Road at mile marker 23, 0.2 miles past the historical marker for

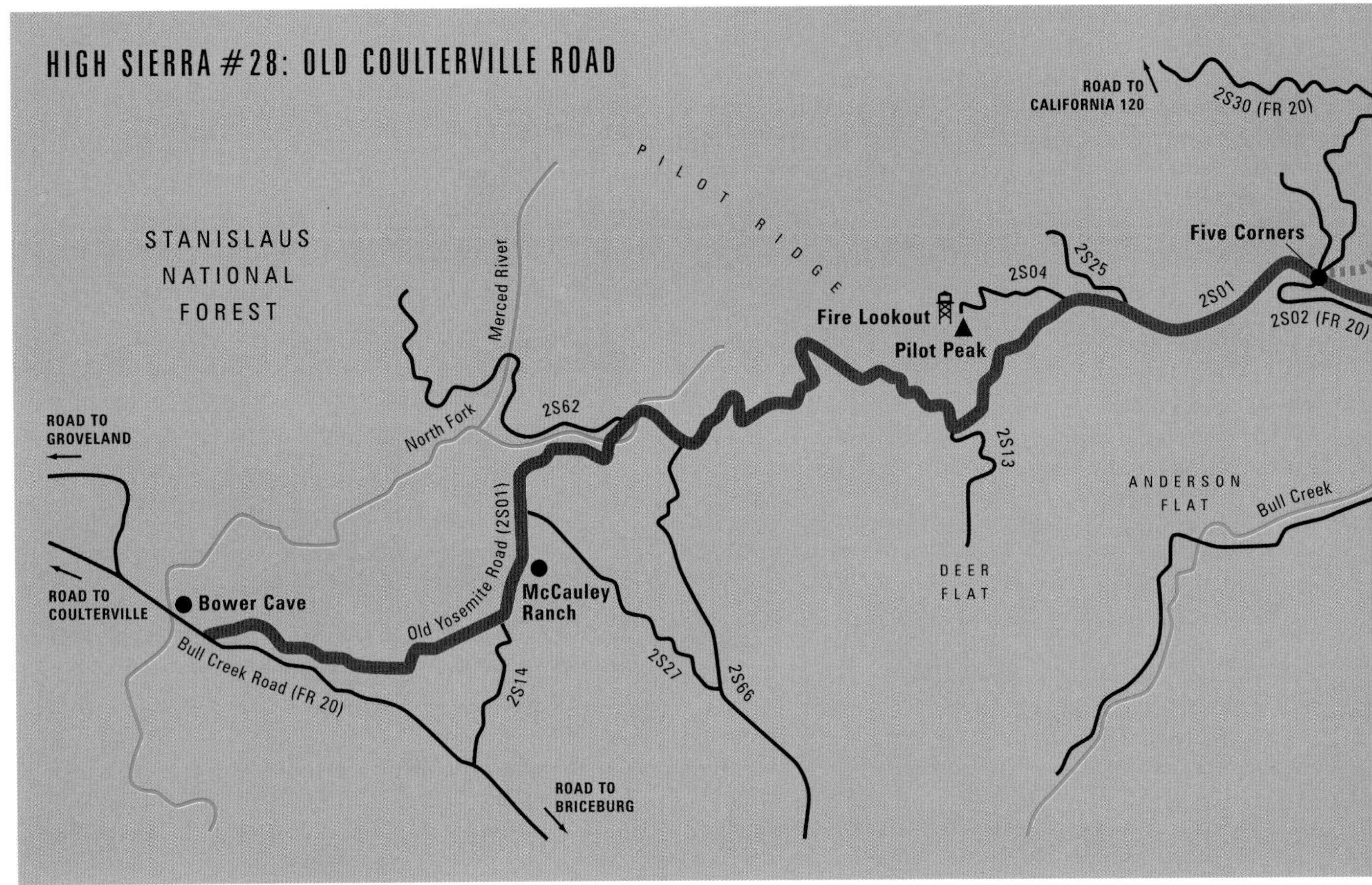

the Coulterville Toll Road, 4.6 miles east of CR J132 (east of Coulterville). Zero trip meter and proceed east, following the sign for Old Yosemite Road. Pavement ends at this point and the road turns to graded dirt.

4.4 ▲ Trail ends at the intersection with Bull Creek Road at the start of the pavement. Continue straight along Old Yosemite Road to exit to Coulterville or Groveland. Turn left to join High Sierra #27: Burma Grade Trail to Briceburg.

GPS: N37°44.68' W120°01.92'

▼ 0.1 SO Track on right.
4.3 ▲ SO Track on left.

▼ 2.3 SO Track on right is 2S14.
2.1 ▲ BR Track on left is 2S14.

GPS: N37°44.46' W119°59.71'

▼ 2.6 SO Track on right and track on left are private.
1.8 ▲ SO Track on right and track on left are private.

▼ 2.8 SO Passing through McCauley Ranch, site of an old stage station, now private property.
1.6 ▲ SO Passing through McCauley Ranch, site of an old stage station, now private property.

▼ 3.2 SO Track on right is 2S27.
1.2 ▲ SO Track on left is 2S27.

▼ 4.3 SO Cross over creek.
0.1 ▲ SO Cross over creek.

▼ 4.4 BR Track on left is 2S62 to North Fork Merced River and Scott Creek. Zero trip meter and cross over creek.
0.0 ▲ Continue to the south.

GPS: N37°45.48' W119°58.58'

▼ 0.0 Continue to the northeast.
3.7 ▲ BL Cross over creek; then track on right is 2S62 to North Fork Merced River and Scott Creek. Zero trip meter.

▼ 0.5 SO Track on right is 2S66.
3.2 ▲ SO Track on left is 2S66.

▼ 2.2 SO Cross over creek.
1.5 ▲ SO Cross over creek.

▼ 3.7 BL Track on right is 2S13 to Deer Flat. Remain on 2S01 and zero trip meter.
0.0 ▲ Continue to the north.

GPS: N37°45.21' W119°56.25'

▼ 0.0 Continue to the east.
1.3 ▲ BR Track on left is 2S13 to Deer Flat. Remain on 2S01 and zero trip meter.

▼ 1.3 SO Track on left is 2S04, which goes 1.2 miles to Pilot Peak Fire Lookout. Zero trip meter. The gate may be locked if the lookout is unmanned.
0.0 ▲ Continue to the southwest.

GPS: N37°45.79' W119°55.25'

▼ 0.0 Continue to the northeast.
2.0 ▲ SO Track on right is 2S04, which goes 1.2 miles to Pilot Peak Fire Lookout. Zero trip meter. The gate may be locked if the lookout is unmanned.

▼ 0.4 SO Track on left is 2S25.
1.6 ▲ SO Track on right is 2S25.

▼ 2.0 TL Track on left goes to Harden Flat Road; then 5-way intersection at Five Corners. Paved road on left is 2S30 (FR 20), which goes to California 120, second track on left is High Sierra #29: Crocker Ridge Trail (2S01), and

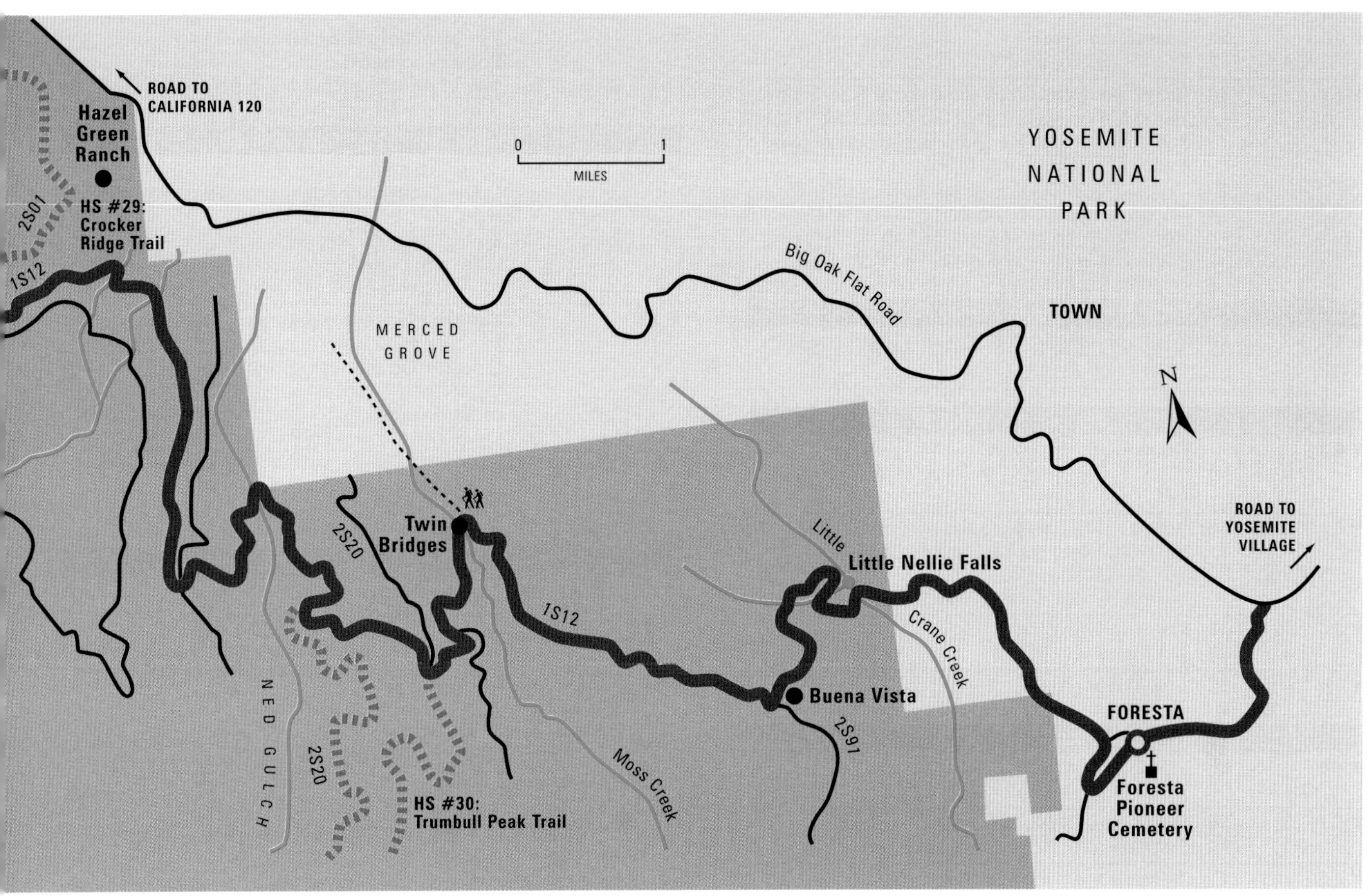

		paved road on right is 2S02 (FR 20) to Anderson Flat. Zero trip meter and continue straight ahead on 1S12, following the sign to Trumbull Peak.
0.0 ▲		Continue to the west. Track on right goes to Harden Flat Road.

GPS: N37°45.67′ W119°53.35′

▼ 0.0		Continue to the east.
4.0 ▲	TR	5-way intersection at Five Corners. Paved road on left is 2S02 (FR 20) to Anderson Flat, track on right is High Sierra #29: Crocker Ridge Trail (2S01), and paved road on right is 2S30 (FR 20), which goes to California 120. Zero trip meter and continue straight ahead, following the sign to Pilot Peak.
▼ 1.4	SO	Cross over Bull Creek.
2.6 ▲	SO	Cross over Bull Creek.
▼ 1.7	SO	Track on right.
2.3 ▲	SO	Track on left.

GPS: N37°45.55′ W119°51.94′

▼ 1.9	SO	Cross over creek.
2.1 ▲	SO	Cross over creek.
▼ 4.0	SO	Track on left and track on right on left-hand bend. Zero trip meter.
0.0 ▲		Continue to the northwest.

GPS: N37°43.83′ W119°51.86′

▼ 0.0		Continue to the east. Track on right.
2.7 ▲	SO	Track on left; then track on left and track on right on right-hand bend. Zero trip meter.
▼ 1.3	SO	Cross over Ned Gulch.
1.4 ▲	SO	Cross over Ned Gulch.
▼ 2.7	BL	Bear left, remaining on main graded road. Track on right is High Sierra #30: Trumbull Peak Trail (2S20). Zero trip meter.
0.0 ▲		Continue to the northeast.

GPS: N37°43.64′ W119°50.91′

▼ 0.0		Continue to the southwest.
1.3 ▲	SO	Track on left is High Sierra #30: Trumbull Peak Trail (2S20). Zero trip meter and remain on main trail.
▼ 1.0	SO	Track on left.
0.3 ▲	SO	Track on right.
▼ 1.3	BL/BR	Track on right is High Sierra #30: Trumbull Peak Trail. Zero trip meter and bear left, remaining on main graded road 1S12, following the sign to Little Nellie Falls. Then immediately bear right, remaining on 1S12. Track on left is 2S20, which goes 1.7 miles to a locked gate at Yosemite National Park boundary.
0.0 ▲		Continue to the north.

GPS: N37°43.16′ W119°50.11′

▼ 0.0		Continue to the east.
4.7 ▲	SO/BR	Track on right is 2S20, which goes 1.7 miles to a locked gate at Yosemite National Park boundary; then track on left at sign is High Sierra #30: Trumbull Peak Trail (2S20). Bear right, remaining on the main graded road 1S12 and zero trip meter.
▼ 0.1	SO	Seasonal closure gate.
4.6 ▲	SO	Seasonal closure gate.
▼ 0.6	SO	Gravel road on right.
4.1 ▲	SO	Gravel road on left.

GPS: N37°43.32′ W119°49.92′

▼ 0.9 SO Cross over creek.
3.8 ▲ SO Cross over creek.

▼ 1.7 SO Cross over Moss Creek at the site of Twin Bridges. Hiking trail on left is part of Old Coulterville Road and goes north to Merced Grove. Rejoin original route of Old Coulterville Road.
3.0 ▲ SO Cross over Moss Creek at the site of Twin Bridges. Hiking trail on right is part of Old Coulterville Road and goes north to Merced Grove. Road leaves original route of Old Coulterville Road.

GPS: N37°43.98′ W119°49.64′

▼ 4.7 SO Track on right is 2S91 to Eagle Peak. Zero trip meter.
0.0 ▲ Continue to the southwest.

GPS: N37°42.66′ W119°47.57′

▼ 0.0 Continue to the north.
2.0 ▲ SO Track on left is 2S91 to Eagle Peak. Zero trip meter.

▼ 0.1 SO Buena Vista—views to the east toward Yosemite National Park and El Capitan.
1.9 ▲ SO Buena Vista—views to the east toward Yosemite National Park and El Capitan.

▼ 0.4 SO Track on left.
1.6 ▲ SO Track on right.

▼ 1.0 SO Cross over creek.
1.0 ▲ SO Cross over creek.

GPS: N37°43.27′ W119°47.37′

▼ 1.4 SO Water tank on left.
0.6 ▲ SO Water tank on right.

▼ 1.7 SO Cross over creek; then track on right.
0.3 ▲ SO Track on left; then cross over creek.

▼ 2.0 TL Track straight ahead stops at a campsite in 0.2 miles. Turn sharp left and zero trip meter. Passenger vehicles should turn around here and not attempt to exit through Yosemite National Park.
0.0 ▲ Continue to the northwest.

GPS: N37°43.04′ W119°46.88′

▼ 0.0 Continue to the north.
5.3 ▲ TR Track straight ahead stops at a campsite in 0.2 miles. Turn sharp right and zero trip meter.

▼ 0.2 SO Picnic area and campsite on right and Little Nellie Falls on left. Cross through Little Crane Creek.
5.1 ▲ SO Cross through Little Crane Creek. Little Nellie Falls on right and picnic area and campsite on left.

GPS: N37°43.23′ W119°46.90′

▼ 0.5 SO Entering Yosemite National Park through gate.
4.8 ▲ SO Leaving Yosemite National Park through gate.

GPS: N37°43.20′ W119°46.64′

▼ 1.5 SO Closed track on left.
3.8 ▲ SO Closed track on right.

GPS: N37°43.09′ W119°45.89′

▼ 1.6 SO Seasonal closure gate.
3.7 ▲ SO Seasonal closure gate.

▼ 2.1 TL Turn left onto unmarked trail.
3.2 ▲ TR Turn right onto unmarked trail.

GPS: N37°42.54′ W119°45.70′

▼ 2.4 BR Trail forks.
2.9 ▲ SO Track on right.

▼ 3.0 TL T-intersection within area of private property. Turn left onto Dana Way.
2.3 ▲ TR Turn right onto First Street.

GPS: N37°41.91′ W119°45.47′

▼ 3.1 TL T-intersection. Turn left onto Foresta Road. Road becomes paved.
2.2 ▲ TR Turn right toward houses onto Dana Way. Road is now graded dirt.

GPS: N37°41.92′ W119°45.38′

▼ 3.2 SO Second Street on left; then cross over Crane Creek on bridge; then Third Street on right.
2.1 ▲ BR Third Street on left. Bear right, remaining on Foresta Road and cross over Crane Creek on bridge. Second Street on right.

▼ 3.5 SO Foresta Pioneer Cemetery on right; then parking area and information boards on left. Closed road on left is original route of Old Coulterville Road, which goes across the edge of Big Meadow.
1.8 ▲ BL Closed road ahead is original route of Old Coulterville Road, which goes across the edge of Big Meadow. Bear left onto Foresta Road. Parking area and information boards on right and Foresta Pioneer Cemetery on left.

GPS: N37°42.14′ W119°45.00′

▼ 4.1 SO Campground Road on right.
1.2 ▲ SO Campground Road on left.

▼ 5.3 Trail ends at T-intersection with Big Oak Flat Road (California 41). Turn left for Crane Flat and Big Oak Flat; turn right for Yosemite Village.
0.0 ▲ Trail starts on Big Oak Flat Road (California 41), 3.3 miles west of the intersection with California 140 and 6 miles south of Crane Flat. Zero trip meter and turn southwest on unmarked paved road at marker post B5 and the sign for Foresta.

GPS: N37°42.81′ W119°43.85′

HIGH SIERRA #29

Crocker Ridge Trail

Starting Point:	**FR 20 (2S30), 2.6 miles south of California 120**
Finishing Point:	**High Sierra #28: Old Coulterville Road at Five Corners**
Total Mileage:	**4.1 miles**
Unpaved Mileage:	**3.9 miles**
Driving Time:	**45 minutes**
Elevation Range:	**5,100–6,000 feet**
Usually Open:	**Year-round**
Best Time to Travel:	**May to November**
Difficulty Rating:	**3**
Scenic Rating:	**8**
Remoteness Rating:	**+0**

Special Attractions

- Scenic ridge-top trail with views over the Tuolumne River Valley and Yosemite National Park.
- Hiking access into Yosemite National Park.

Tuolumne River drainage and Harden Flat as seen from a side trail off Crocker Ridge

History

Crocker Ridge Trail joins the original Coulterville-Yosemite Road at the southern end of the trail at Five Corners. Immediately east of this intersection is the old Hazel Green Ranch, a stage station for visitors to Yosemite Valley traveling by stagecoach. The Mariposa Battalion named the location in 1851 for the abundant hazel bushes. James and Amanda Halstead ran the Hazel Green summer resort and stage station from 1874 until 1901. Amanda was born in Coulterville in 1855, just six years after George Coulter had opened a store there. After her husband died in 1901, Amanda continued to operate the business until 1903. She moved to Oakland in 1904, where she ran a lodging house until her death in November 1905.

The Yosemite Lumber Company constructed many railroad grades around Crocker Ridge and Hazel Green. Five Corners was a major railroad junction for timber transportation on the route down to the banks of the Merced River.

Crocker Ridge got its name from the Crocker Stage Station, located at the northern base of the ridge. Henry Robinson Crocker married Ellen Hall in 1873 and took over pastures that had previously been known as Bronson Meadows. The Crockers arrived while the Big Oak Flat Road to Yosemite Valley was being built, part of which ran through their pastures. This prompted a stage company superintendent to entice the Crockers to set up a stage stop. The Crockers constructed 15 buildings in 1880 and homesteaded the meadows that now bear their name in 1883. The family-run business, known as Crocker's Sierra Summer Resort, became a popular stop on the edge of the national park and developed into a destination point in its own right. Henry passed away in 1904. Ellen, 20 years his junior, and their family continued the business until moving to Lodi in 1910. By 1920, the resort was more or less out of business because of the improved road and facilities in Yosemite National Park.

Description

This short trail commences on paved FR 20 and travels a loop along Crocker Ridge to Five Corners. The trail is lightly used and is slightly brushy in short sections. It climbs steadily from FR 20 to the ridge. After 1.4 miles, a track heads off to the west, leading to a sweeping view over the Tuolumne River Valley and Yosemite National Park. The formed trail continues along an uneven surface. It can be extremely greasy and should be avoided in wet weather.

The trail finishes at Five Corners on High Sierra #28: Old Coulterville Road. From here you can return to California 120 or travel the Old Coulterville Road in either direction.

Current Road Information

Stanislaus National Forest
Groveland Ranger District
24525 Highway 120
Groveland, CA 95321
(209) 962-7825

Maps References

BLM Yosemite Valley
USFS Stanislaus National Forest
USGS 1:24,000 Ascension Mt., Ackerson Mt.
1:100,000 Yosemite Valley
Maptech CD-ROM: High Sierra/Yosemite
Northern California Atlas & Gazetteer, p. 110
California Road & Recreation Atlas, p. 72
Trails Illustrated, Yosemite National Park (206)

Route Directions

▼ 0.0		From FR 20 (2S30), 2.6 miles south of California 120 and Big Oak Flat, zero trip meter and turn southeast on small paved road marked 1S11.
1.4 ▲		Trail ends at T-intersection with paved road FR 20 (2S30). Turn right to exit to California 120 and Yosemite National Park; turn left to return to High Sierra #28: Old Coulterville Road.
		GPS: N37°47.69' W119°53.70'
▼ 0.1	SO	Track on left.
1.3 ▲	SO	Track on right.
▼ 0.2	SO	Road turns to dirt.
1.2 ▲	SO	Road is now paved.
▼ 0.3	BL	Turnout on right.
1.1 ▲	BR	Turnout on left.
▼ 1.4	BL	Track on right goes 0.8 miles to a viewpoint over the Tuolumne River Valley and Yosemite National Park. Zero trip meter.
0.0 ▲		Continue to the north.
		GPS: N37°46.95' W119°52.89'
▼ 0.0		Continue to the southeast.
1.6 ▲	BR	Track on left goes 0.8 miles to a viewpoint over the Tuolumne River Valley and Yosemite National Park. Zero trip meter.
▼ 0.9	SO	Track on left.
0.7 ▲	SO	Track on right.
		GPS: N37°46.48' W119°52.34'
▼ 1.3	BR	Well-used track on left is 1S11C, which goes 0.7 miles to the national park boundary.

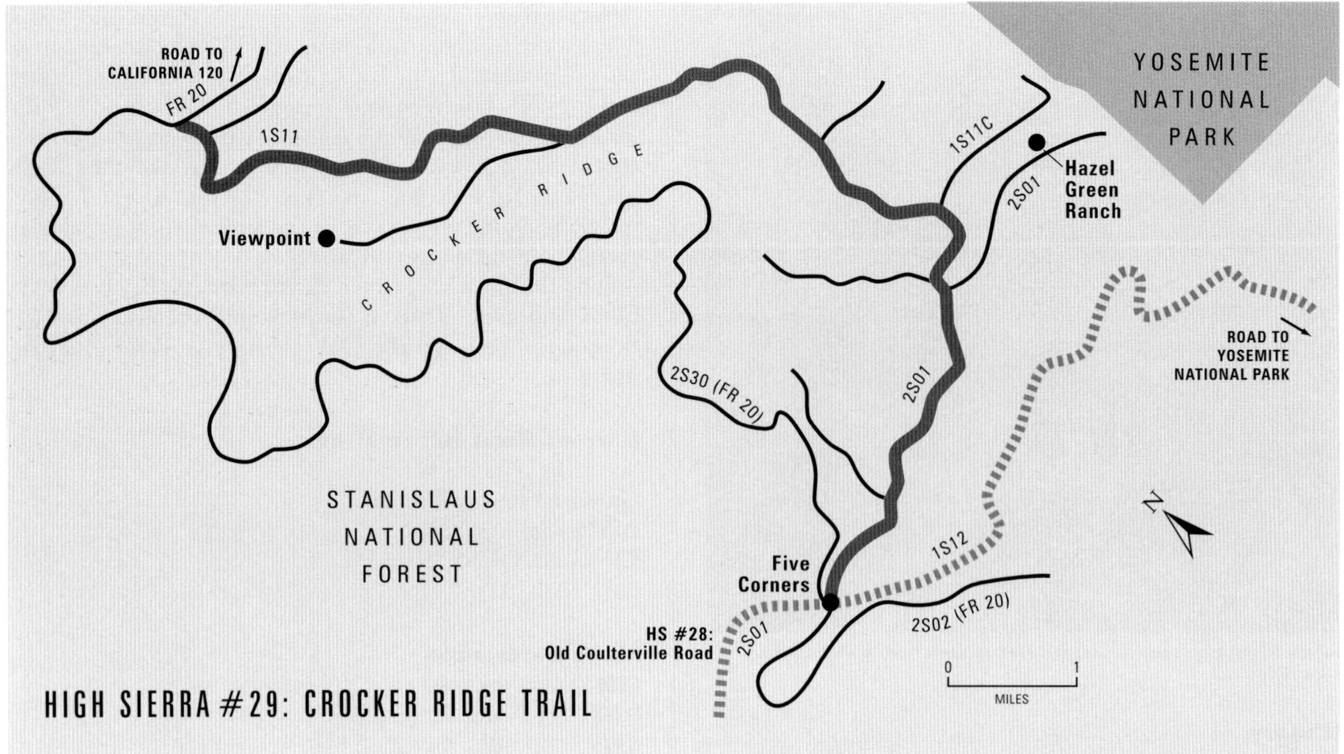

0.3 ▲ BL Well-used track on right is 1S11C, which goes 0.7 miles to the national park boundary.

GPS: N37°46.14' W119°52.23'

▼ 1.6 TL/TR T-intersection. To the right is a dead end logging road. Turn left and pass through seasonal closure gate and immediately come to a second T-intersection with 2S01. Zero trip meter and turn right, following the sign to Pilot Peak. To the left goes through private property of the Hazel Green Ranch to the national park boundary.

0.0 ▲ Continue to the north.

GPS: N37°46.00' W119°52.37'

▼ 0.0 Continue to the southwest.

1.1 ▲ TL/TR Road continues ahead through private property of the Hazel Green Ranch to the national park boundary. Zero trip meter. Turn left and pass through seasonal closure gate; then immediately turn right onto 1S11, following the sign to Crocker Ridge. Road straight ahead is a dead end logging road.

▼ 0.5 SO Track on right.

0.6 ▲ SO Track on left.

▼ 0.9 SO Track on right.

0.2 ▲ SO Track on left.

▼ 1.1 Trail ends at the intersection with High Sierra #28: Old Coulterville Road at Five Corners. Turn left onto 1S12 to travel this trail to Yosemite National Park. Paved road ahead is 2S02 (FR 20) to Anderson Flat; paved road on right is FR 20; and graded road on second right is High Sierra #28: Old Coulterville Road.

0.0 ▲ Trail commences on High Sierra #28: Old Coulterville Road at Five Corners, 2 miles east of the turn to Pilot Peak Fire Lookout. Zero trip meter and turn northeast onto 2S01.

GPS: N37°45.67' W119°53.35'

HIGH SIERRA #30

Trumbull Peak Trail

Starting Point:	**High Sierra #28: Old Coulterville Road, 6.7 miles southeast of Five Corners**
Finishing Point:	**High Sierra #28: Old Coulterville Road, 8 miles southeast of Five Corners**
Total Mileage:	**7.9 miles, plus 1-mile spur to Trumbull Peak**
Unpaved Mileage:	**7.9 miles, plus 1-mile spur**
Driving Time:	**1 hour**
Elevation Range:	**4,400–5,400 feet**
Usually Open:	**May to November**
Best Time to Travel:	**Dry weather**
Difficulty Rating:	**3**
Scenic Rating:	**10**
Remoteness Rating:	**+0**

Special Attractions

- Views from Trumbull Peak of El Capitan and Half Dome in Yosemite National Park.
- The old fire lookout and cabin on Trumbull Peak.

History

Trumbull Peak Trail travels a section of the logging railroad system used by the Yosemite Sugar Pine Lumber Company. Sugar pine was highly sought after by cabinetmakers and construction companies alike, running second only to ponderosa pine. However, transporting timber from these high mountains to the sawmill at Merced Falls, some 20 odd miles northeast of Merced, was a costly and difficult operation.

From 1923 to 1924, an incline railway was constructed to cover the nearly 1.4-mile distance and 2,400 feet of elevation loss from Trumbull Peak to the Merced River and Yosemite Valley Railroad. The incline railway was an engineering and financial feat for that era, carrying a price tag of nearly a million dollars. Logs were strapped onto cable cars, then lowered over the edge on a reciprocal style, dual incline railway, meaning that the weight of descending logs provided the energy to haul several empty cars to the top of the incline. A massive electric winch at the top kept things under control. All that remains today is the concrete base of the incline station. It sits on top of the ridge and is visible from the lookout tower. A few railway ties survived a fire in the 1980s and the A Rock Fire of 1990.

Trumbull Peak Fire Lookout and cabin are precariously perched on a rugged ridge above the Merced River Canyon

Initially, the Trumbull Peak Fire Lookout was the 19- by 30-foot, C-2 observation cabin, built by the Civilian Conservation Corps in 1935, which still sits precariously on stilts on the edge of the peak. The front porch, with its large windows on three sides, provided exceptional views up and down the Merced Canyon and distant views over the Yosemite Valley. Also excellent were the views south over Ferguson Ridge, the Merced River, California 140, and 12 miles to Devils Peak Fire Lookout. It's also possible to see the service centers of Incline and El Portal 3,000 feet below. The tall steel tower's tiny cabin was more than 40 feet higher than the original cabin and gave sentries better views in all directions. The lookout is no longer used, and the first flight of wooden steps up to the lookout has been removed for safety reasons.

Description

Trumbull Peak Trail is a short, moderately difficult loop that starts and finishes on High Sierra #28: Old Coulterville Road. The formed trail follows a shelf road along the west side of Trumbull Ridge, following the path of the old railroad grade. As it winds around the mountainside, there are views over Anderson Basin and across to Grizzly Mountain. The trail surface is easygoing in dry weather, but it can be greasy after rain. Some short sections of the trail are lightly brushy.

The real attraction of the trail comes after 4.1 miles. A 1-mile spur climbs gradually up a shelf road to the top of Trumbull Peak. As you climb, Yosemite National Park comes into view and you will see El Capitan and Half Dome. At the top, there is a campsite under the shade of a large pine tree. In mild weather, this campsite is unbeatable. A hiking trail leads 0.3 miles to the lookout on Trumbull Peak. This ridge top trail is narrow, but it has been well used over the years because it is the only way to the lookout.

El Capitan (left) and Half Dome (right) are just visible through the summer haze

The return portion of the loop continues along a rough shelf road to rejoin Old Coulterville Road. From here, you can exit via Little Nellie Falls and Yosemite National Park or retrace your steps to Five Corners.

Current Road Information

Stanislaus National Forest
Groveland Ranger District
24525 Highway 120
Groveland, CA 95321
(209) 962-7825

Map References

BLM Yosemite Valley
USFS Stanislaus National Forest
USGS 1:24,000 El Portal
1:100,000 Yosemite Valley
Maptech CD-ROM: High Sierra/Yosemite
Northern California Atlas & Gazetteer, p. 110
California Road & Recreation Atlas, p. 72
Trails Illustrated, Yosemite National Park (206)

Route Directions

▼ 0.0		From High Sierra #28: Old Coulterville Road (1S12), 6.7 miles southeast of Five Corners, zero trip meter and proceed west on formed dirt trail marked 2S20. Old Coulterville Road continues to the south at this point.
4.1 ▲		Trail ends at intersection back on High Sierra #28: Old Coulterville Road (1S12). Turn right to exit via Yosemite National Park; continue straight ahead to exit via Five Corners.
		GPS: N37°43.64' W119°50.91'
▼ 1.0	SO	Cross over creek.
3.1 ▲	SO	Cross over creek.
▼ 1.4	SO	Cross over creek.
2.7 ▲	SO	Cross over creek.
▼ 3.9	SO	Cross over creek.
0.2 ▲	SO	Cross over creek.

▼ 4.1	TL	Turn sharp left to continue the loop and zero trip meter. Track straight ahead is the spur to Trumbull Peak.
0.0 ▲		Continue to the north.
		GPS: N37°41.36' W119°51.35'

Spur to Trumbull Peak

▼ 0.0		Continue to the southwest past track on left.
▼ 1.0		Trail ends on Trumbull Peak at a viewpoint and campsite. The lookout tower is a short scramble over the rocks.
		GPS: N37°41.03' W119°51.59'

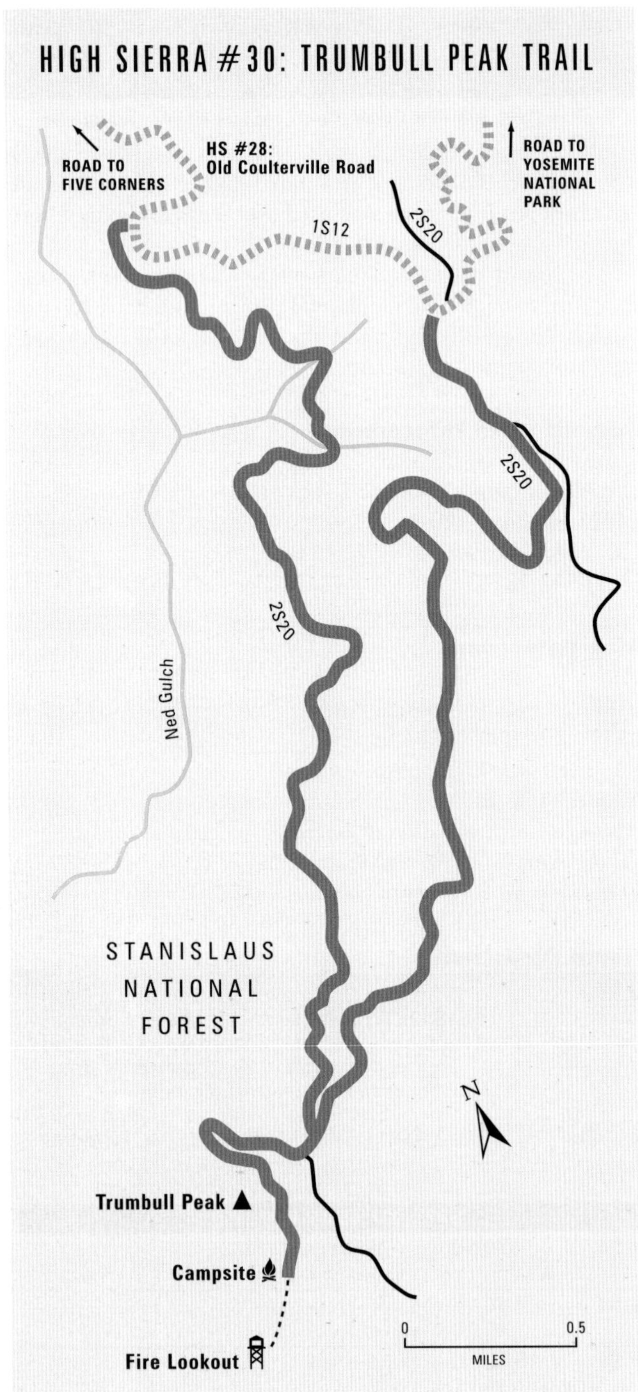

Continuation of Main Trail

▼ 0.0		Continue to the northeast.
3.8 ▲	TR	Turn sharp right to continue the loop on 2S20 and zero trip meter. Track straight ahead is the spur to Trumbull Peak.
		GPS: N37°41.36' W119°51.35'
▼ 1.1	SO	Track on left is 2S20C.
2.7 ▲	SO	Track on right is 2S20C.
▼ 2.7	SO	Track on left.
1.1 ▲	SO	Track on right.
▼ 3.3	SO	Track on right.
0.5 ▲	SO	Track on left.
		GPS: N37°42.84' W119°49.99'
▼ 3.8		Trail ends at T-intersection with High Sierra #28: Old Coulterville Road (1S12). Turn right to exit via Yosemite National Park; turn left to return to Five Corners.
0.0 ▲		Trail commences on High Sierra #28: Old Coulterville Road (1S12), 8 miles southeast of Five Corners. Zero trip meter and turn southwest on formed dirt trail 2S20, following the sign to Trumbull Peak.
		GPS: N37°43.16' W119°50.11'

HIGH SIERRA #31

Bodie Ghost Town Trail

Starting Point:	**California 182 at Bridgeport, 0.3 miles north of US 395**
Finishing Point:	**California 167, 7.1 miles east of US 395**
Total Mileage:	**26.6 miles, plus 1.5-mile spur to Travertine Hot Springs**
Unpaved Mileage:	**26 miles, plus 1.3 miles of the spur**
Driving Time:	**3 hours**
Elevation Range:	**6,400–9,200 feet**
Usually Open:	**April to November**
Best Time to Travel:	**April to November**
Difficulty Rating:	**2**
Scenic Rating:	**9**
Remoteness Rating:	**+0**

Special Attractions

- Extensive remains of Bodie ghost town.
- Travertine Hot Springs.
- Scenic Aurora and Cottonwood Canyons.
- Views of Mono Lake, Paoha Island, and Negit Island.

History

The ghost town of Bodie is on the arid east side of the Sierra Nevada, north of Mono Lake. Bodie is apparently a purposeful misspelling of Waterman S. Body's name, used to help pronounce the name correctly. In 1859, Body and his partner E. S. Taylor found gold and worked a claim north of Mono Lake. Body fell ill and died in a snowstorm in March 1860, too soon

One of the many remaining structures of Bodie ghost town, the red brick building was the last trading pub

to realize the wealth that would come from his discovery.

In their early days, mines around Bodie yielded only small quantities of ores, but by the late 1870s the Standard, Bodie, and Bulwar Mines were in full swing and the most productive in the region. By 1881, Bodie's population was more than 6,000. The town boasted such amenities as saloons, breweries, banks, newspapers, hotels, dance halls, and brothels. Such success quickly ushered in "The Bad Men of Bodie," a less desirable, lawless element. Claim jumping, fistfights, stage robberies, and gunfights were common, and the town resorted to all measures of punishment, including lynching.

Bodie's mining days declined in the late 1880s and '90s, and a fire in 1892 destroyed many of the original houses. The introduction of electricity brought a brief resurgence and the railroad and Mono Mills remained active until the mines significantly reduced their production in 1912. Bodie's heyday was over and workers headed for new mines. In 1932, a toddler gained notoriety as Bodie Bill. While playing with matches, he started a fire that nearly obliterated Bodie. Luckily, enough remained that it survived as a ghost town. The last bar closed in the early 1960s.

What remained of Bodie became a state historic park in 1962, and it earned a listing in the National Register of Historic Places. Hardy state park employees remain in the park in winter, when the town site attracts snowmobile enthusiasts.

Bridgeport became Mono County's seat by default. In 1860, the mining camp of Aurora northeast of Bodie, named for Aurora, goddess of the dawn, attracted 2,000 inhabitants within the year and was chosen to be the Mono County seat. However, a question arose as to whether it was in California or Nevada. After two years of haggling between the states, an independent survey showed Aurora to be just inside the Nevada border. Consequently, Mono County's seat moved to Bridgeport in 1864.

Mono County's elegant courthouse in Bridgeport owes a great debt to Bodie's Standard Mine. In 1881, county officials heard rumors that the mines around Bodie might close. They acted swiftly and levied a 6.5 percent property tax in order to acquire funds for a courthouse. Because of its extensive holdings in Mono County, the Standard Mine paid for most of the project. The courthouse is currently the second oldest county courthouse in California still in use.

Description

The well-preserved ghost town of Bodie, now a state park, attracts many visitors each year. Most visitors use the paved county road from Bridgeport. For those with a little more time and a high-clearance vehicle, there is an alternate route that passes Bodie at its midpoint.

The trail leaves California 182 along Aurora Canyon Road, which is marked with a street sign. For the first 0.6 miles, the trail travels through private property and passes a few houses. It swings left in front of the Bridgeport Cemetery and continues past the final few houses before entering BLM land. Once on public land, the trail becomes a roughly graded, narrow dirt road and winds along a rocky, sagebrush-covered landscape to enter Aurora Canyon. The rough-walled canyon is not deep, but it is very pretty.

The trail climbs gradually to the head of the canyon. The section near the intersection with High Sierra #32: Masonic Trail can be extremely boggy after heavy rain and is best avoided when wet. Bodie Ghost Town Trail continues over the open Bodie Hills, with great views west to the Sierra Nevada and Bridgeport Valley. The climbs are not steep, and high-clearance 2WDs can easily negotiate them in dry weather.

The trail meanders along hilltops and wraps across Rough Creek. Keep an eye out for pronghorn antelopes and coyotes along this stretch as well as pinyon jays. The trail from Rough Creek to Bodie descends along a shelf road known as the Geiger Grade. There is no fee for passing through Bodie. However, if you wish to stop and explore the ghost town, there is a small fee of $1 per person. Sage grouse occasionally stroll among the buildings in summer.

Once outside Bodie State Historical Park, the trail follows a wide, graded dirt road through Cottonwood Canyon to join California 167. This road is heavily used and can be very washboardy. The lower end of the canyon gives excellent views of Mono Lake and its two islands—Paoha and Negit. The lake is set against the backdrop of the snowcapped Sierra Nevada.

When enough snow is present, this trail is open to snowmobiles.

Bodie was a welcome sight to weary stagecoach travelers of yesteryear

Separate from the main trail, but included here because of its proximity is the road to Travertine Hot Springs. The rough graded dirt road leaves US 395 a short distance south of Bridgeport. The road to the springs is well used and rutted in places. A high-clearance vehicle is preferable, but a carefully driven passenger car can make the trip in dry weather. The springs are well known and very popular, so you are not likely to have them to yourself. Be aware that this is a clothing optional site and camping is not allowed.

The natural hot springs emerge from a ridge of travertine, a mineral of calcium carbonate. Channels cut through the ridge divert the water to small pools. A concrete pool at the parking lot is the most popular, but a short hike along the ridge top reveals a cluster of smaller, more natural pools. The pools at the lower end of the ridge are the most scenic and have views over the valley to the Sierra Nevada.

Current Road Information

Toiyabe National Forest
Bridgeport Ranger District
HCR 1 Box 1000
Bridgeport, CA 93517
(760) 932-7070

Bodie State Historical Park
PO Box 515
Bridgeport, CA 93517
(760) 647-6445

Map References

BLM Bridgeport
USFS Toiyabe National Forest: Bridgeport Ranger District
USGS 1:24,000 Bridgeport, Dome Hill, Bodie, Kirkwood, Negit Island
1:100,000 Bridgeport
Maptech CD-ROM: High Sierra/Yosemite
Northern California Atlas & Gazetteer, pp. 101, 102
California Road & Recreation Atlas, p. 73

Route Directions

Mileage		Directions
▼ 0.0		From the intersection of US 395 and California 182 in Bridgeport, proceed north on California 182 for 0.3 miles. Turn right (northeast) onto paved Aurora Canyon Road, which is marked with a street sign and initially travels past houses. Zero trip meter and remain on main road, ignoring turns to the left and right.
0.6 ▲		Trail ends at T-intersection with California 182 in Bridgeport. Turn left for Main Street and US 395.
		GPS: N38°15.56' W119°13.25'
▼ 0.3	TL	Bridgeport Cemetery is straight ahead. Remain on Aurora Canyon Road.
0.3 ▲	TR	T-intersection. Remain on Aurora Canyon Road. Bridgeport Cemetery is on the left.
▼ 0.6	SO	Sage Brush Drive on left. Zero trip meter.
0.0 ▲		Continue to the southwest on paved road.
		GPS: N38°15.89' W119°12.77'
▼ 0.0		Continue to the northeast on graded dirt road and cross over cattle guard. Road is now marked FR 168 and enters BLM land.
6.8 ▲	SO	Cross over cattle guard; then Sage Brush Drive on right. Zero trip meter. Road now passes through private property.
▼ 0.5	SO	Track on right; then track on left; then second track on right.
6.3 ▲	SO	Track on left; then track on right; then second track on left.
▼ 1.2	SO	Cattle guard.
5.6 ▲	SO	Cattle guard.
▼ 2.1	SO	Large tailings heap on right.
4.7 ▲	SO	Large tailings heap on left.
		GPS: N38°16.27' W119°10.49'
▼ 3.8	SO	Track on left through wire gate.
3.0 ▲	SO	Track on right through wire gate.
		GPS: N38°16.66' W119°08.84'
▼ 4.4	SO	Cattle guard.
2.4 ▲	SO	Cattle guard.
▼ 4.9	SO	Track on right.
1.9 ▲	SO	Track on left.
		GPS: N38°16.15' W119°07.87'
▼ 6.5	SO	Cattle guard.
0.3 ▲	SO	Cattle guard.
▼ 6.8	BR	Track on left is High Sierra #32: Masonic Trail (FR 169). Zero trip meter and join FR 169. Second track on left is continuation

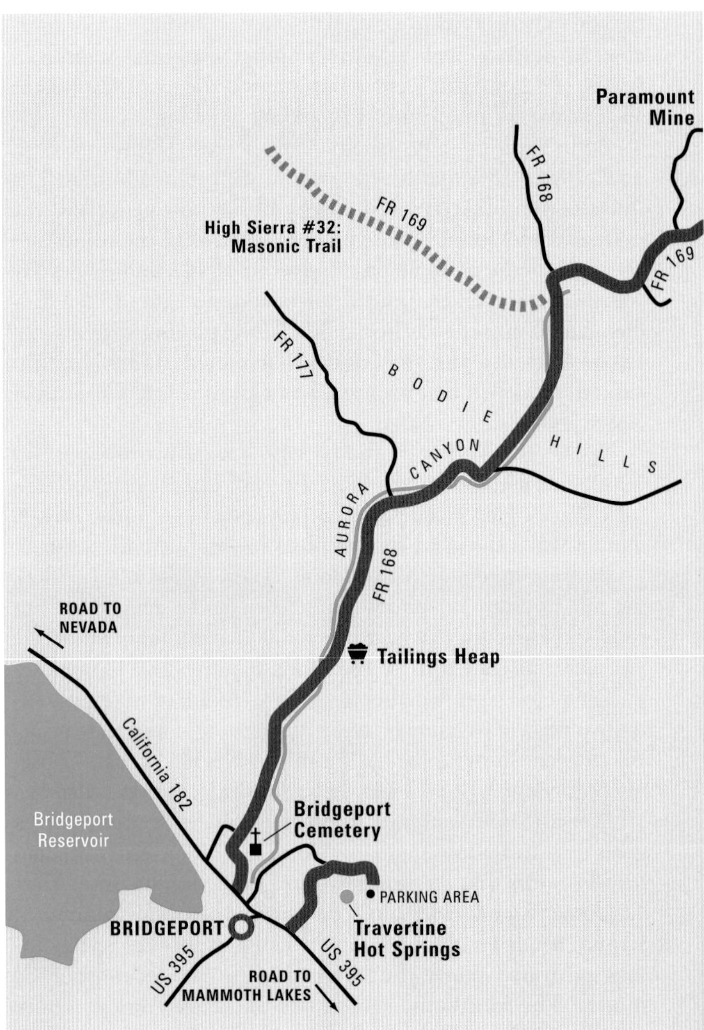

▼	▲		
			of FR 168 to China Camp.
	0.0 ▲		Continue to the southwest.
			GPS: N38°16.79' W119°05.91'
▼ 0.0			Continue to the northeast.
	8.4 ▲	BL	Track on right is FR 168 to China Camp; then second track on right is High Sierra #32: Masonic Trail, which is the continuation of FR 169. Join FR 168 and zero trip meter.
▼ 0.8		SO	Track on right.
	7.6 ▲	SO	Track on left.
▼ 1.0		SO	Track on right.
	7.4 ▲	SO	Track on left.
▼ 1.3		SO	Cattle guard.
	7.1 ▲	SO	Cattle guard.
▼ 1.6		SO	Track on left goes to Paramount Mine and Spring.
	6.8 ▲	SO	Track on right goes to Paramount Mine and Spring.
			GPS: N38°16.21' W119°04.72'
▼ 2.0		SO	Track on left.
	6.4 ▲	SO	Track on right.
▼ 2.7		SO	Track on right; then cross through creek. Potato Peak is on the right.
	5.7 ▲	SO	Cross through creek; then track on left. Potato Peak is on the left.
			GPS: N38°15.42' W119°04.52'
▼ 4.3		SO	Track on right; then cross over Rough Creek.
	4.1 ▲	SO	Cross over Rough Creek; then track on left.
			GPS: N38°14.30' W119°04.25'
▼ 4.8		SO	Track on left.
	3.6 ▲	SO	Track on right.
▼ 5.6		SO	Track on left.
	2.8 ▲	SO	Track on right.
▼ 6.2		SO	Track on left; then track on right.
	2.2 ▲	SO	Track on left; then track on right.
▼ 8.2		SO	Entering Bodie State Historical Park.
	0.2 ▲	SO	Exiting Bodie State Historical Park.
▼ 8.3		SO	Cattle guard.
	0.1 ▲	SO	Cattle guard.
▼ 8.4		TR	T-intersection with CR 270. Parking lot for Bodie is opposite. Zero trip meter.
	0.0 ▲		Continue to the west.
			GPS: N38°12.81' W119°00.86'
▼ 0.0			Continue to the south.
	0.4 ▲	TL	Parking area for Bodie on right. Turn left opposite the parking area onto an unmarked, well-used, graded dirt road that climbs alongside the creek. Zero trip meter.
▼ 0.4		BL	State park entrance booth (no charge if passing through without stopping). Bear left immediately after the entrance onto a wide, graded dirt road. There is a wooden sign for Lee Vining. Zero trip meter.

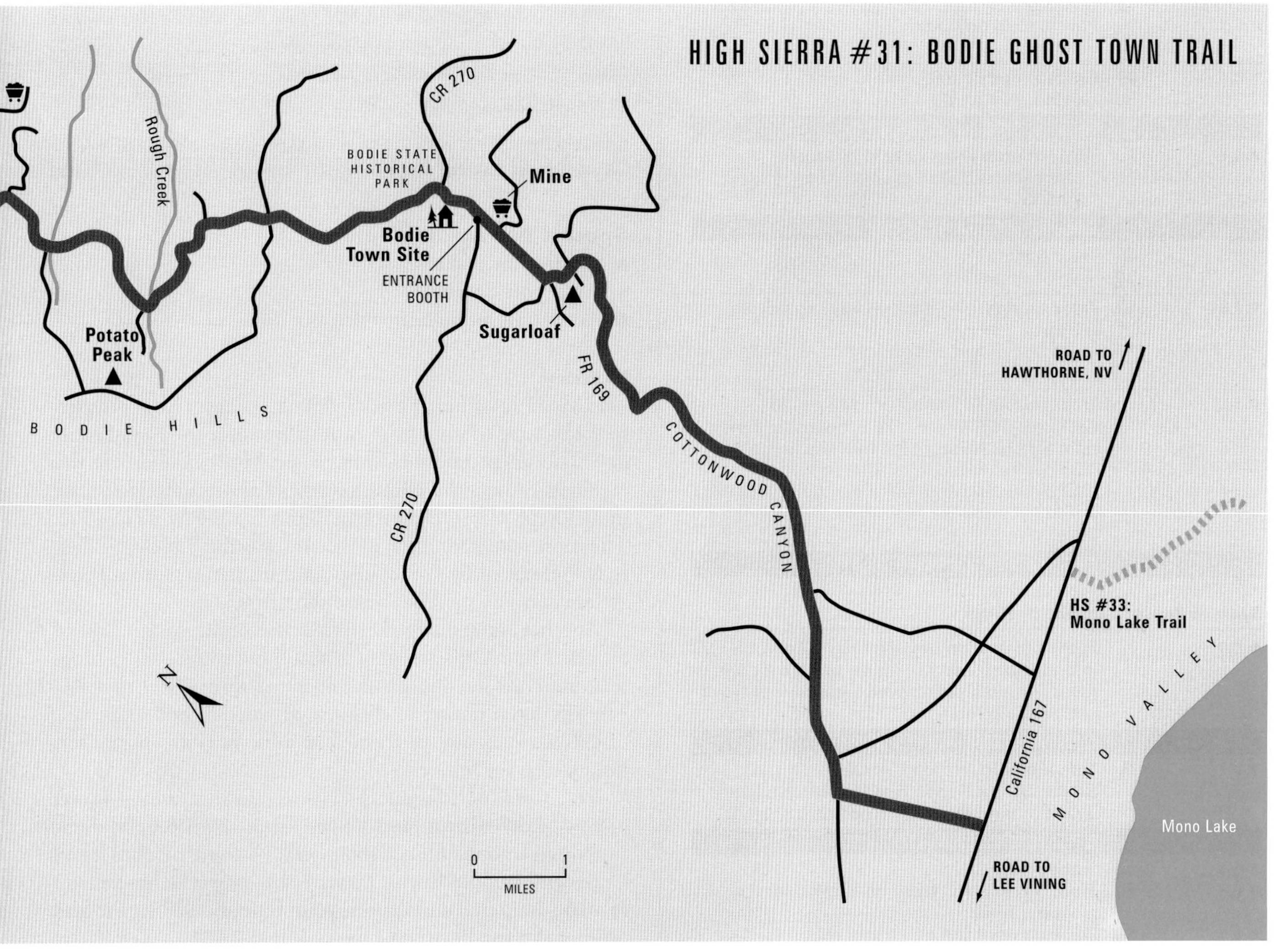

0.0 ▲		Continue to the north.
		GPS: N38°12.50' W119°00.81'
▼ 0.0		Continue to the south. Road is marked FR 169 after the turn.
10.4 ▲	BR	Bear right onto CR 270, which comes in on the left, and pass state park entrance booth (no charge if passing through without stopping). Zero trip meter.
▼ 0.3	SO	Track on left to diggings and mine remains.
10.1 ▲	SO	Track on right to diggings and mine remains.
▼ 0.7	SO	Cattle guard. Exiting Bodie State Historical Park.
9.7 ▲	SO	Cattle guard. Entering Bodie State Historical Park.
▼ 1.1	SO	Two tracks on right.
9.3 ▲	SO	Two tracks on left.
▼ 1.5	SO	Tracks on right and left under power lines.
8.9 ▲	SO	Tracks on right and left under power lines.
▼ 2.4	SO	Track on left to diggings and mine remains.
8.0 ▲	SO	Track on right to diggings and mine remains.
▼ 3.5	SO	Track on right.
6.9 ▲	SO	Track on left.
		GPS: N38°10.02' W119°01.36'
▼ 4.8	SO	Cattle guard.
5.6 ▲	SO	Cattle guard.
▼ 6.7	SO	Track on left; then cattle guard.
3.7 ▲	SO	Cattle guard; then track on right.
▼ 7.2	SO	Track on right.
3.2 ▲	SO	Track on left.
▼ 7.5	SO	Private road on right.
2.9 ▲	SO	Private road on left.
▼ 8.4	SO	Graded road on left.
2.0 ▲	SO	Graded road on right.
		GPS: N38°06.48' W119°03.02'
▼ 8.7	TL	Turn left onto wide, graded dirt road.
1.7 ▲	TR	T-intersection. Turn right onto wide, graded dirt road.
		GPS: N38°06.22' W119°03.23'
▼ 9.3	SO	Track on left.
1.1 ▲	SO	Track on right.
▼ 9.8	SO	Track on right and track on left into private property.
0.6 ▲	SO	Track on left and track on right into private property.
▼ 10.4		Trail ends at T-intersection with paved California 167. Mono Lake is opposite. Turn right for US 395; turn left for Hawthorne, NV.
0.0 ▲		Trail commences on California 167, 7.1 miles east of US 395. Zero trip meter and turn northwest onto wide graded dirt road at sign for Bodie ghost town.
		GPS: N38°04.93' W119°02.37'

Spur to Travertine Hot Springs

▼ 0.0		From intersection of California 182 and US 395 in Bridgeport, head south on US 395 for 0.4 miles. Turn left onto paved Jack Sawyer Road and zero trip meter.
		GPS: N38°15.01' W119°13.22'
▼ 0.2	TL	Turn left onto dirt road, immediately past County Works Depot. Road is well used and wraps around the ridge. Road on the left.
		GPS: N38°15.02' W119°12.95'
▼ 0.4	SO	Track on right.
▼ 0.5	SO	Track on right and track on left. Remain on main dirt road.
▼ 0.7	SO	Track on right and two tracks on left.
▼ 0.9	SO	Track on left.
▼ 1.1	SO	Track on right.
▼ 1.3	SO	Track on right leads to springs farther away.
		GPS: N38°14.84' W119°12.17'
▼ 1.5		Trail ends at parking area for Travertine Hot Springs. Small concrete pool at the parking area. Additional springs are farther down walking trail along the ridge.
		GPS: N38°14.75' W119°12.20'

HIGH SIERRA #32

Masonic Trail

Starting Point:	**California 182, 3.7 miles north of Bridgeport**
Finishing Point:	**High Sierra #31: Bodie Ghost Town Trail, 7.4 miles east of California 182**
Total Mileage:	**14.3 miles, plus 1-mile spur to Masonic's Lower Town**
Unpaved Mileage:	**14.3 miles, plus 1-mile spur**
Driving Time:	**1.75 hours**
Elevation Range:	**6,500–8,600 feet**
Usually Open:	**April to November**
Best Time to Travel:	**April to November**
Difficulty Rating:	**2**
Scenic Rating:	**8**
Remoteness Rating:	**+0**

Special Attractions

- Masonic town site.
- Bridgeport Reservoir.
- Scenic trail through the open Bodie Hills.

History

The Masonic Mining District was named after early prospectors who were Masons from Aurora, just over the Nevada state line. Though prospectors found some worthwhile ores in this region as early as the 1860s, no significant mining took place until Joseph Green claimed the Jump Up Joe Mine in 1902. The most successful mine in the area was the Pittsburg-Liberty Mine, staked by J. S. Phillips and his partners from Pennsylvania on July 4, 1902, hence the name.

Another mine along the trail is the optimistically named Success Mine. Only a couple of shafts and some tailings heaps remain. The Chemung Mine operated from 1909 to 1940. The site has a cluster of dilapidated wooden buildings; take care if you walk among them. The mine workings are a short distance up the hill.

The town of Masonic had three distinct areas—Lower Town, Middle Town, and Upper Town. By 1906, Masonic supported a population of about 500. Nothing much is left of Upper and Middle Towns. Lower Town, however, has remains of a 10-stamp mill and cyanide plant built in 1907 by the Stall brothers for the Pittsburg-Liberty Mine.

Description

The trail to Masonic follows a winding, graded dirt road into the Bodie Hills. It begins by climbing up a shelf road that is wide enough for two vehicles to pass. The trail becomes very greasy after heavy rains and should only be attempted by 4WD vehicles. At the top of the ridge the trail winds into the Bodie Hills, passing over open sagebrush hills and giving great views northwest toward the Sweetwater Mountains. The vegetation along the trail is mainly sagebrush interspersed with small pines and junipers. A scattering of aspens gives the area a golden color in fall.

The road is roughly graded, uneven in places, and slightly rutted. It crests New York Hill and descends toward Masonic town site, with views over the sharp ridges into Nevada. The remains at Masonic's Lower Town are a short distance from the main trail along the road to Sweetwater.

From Masonic, the trail climbs over open ridges covered with sagebrush. There is a good chance of seeing pronghorn antelopes and coyotes as the trail winds over the hills to join High Sierra #31: Bodie Ghost Town Trail. Part of the trail is a section of the Geiger Grade, the route used to transport lumber to Masonic by way of Bodie.

Current Road Information

Toiyabe National Forest
Bridgeport Ranger District
HCR 1 Box 1000
Bridgeport, CA 93517
(760) 932-7070

Map References

BLM Bridgeport
USFS Toiyabe National Forest: Bridgeport Ranger District
USGS 1:24,000 Bridgeport, Dome Hill
1:100,000 Bridgeport
Maptech CD-ROM: High Sierra/Yosemite
Northern California Atlas & Gazetteer, pp. 101, 102
California Road & Recreation Atlas, p. 73

Sharp eyes will spot antelope high in the Bodie Hills

Chemung Mine has slowly succumbed to nature and collectors

Route Directions

▼ 0.0		From Bridgeport, head north on California 182 for 3.7 miles. Zero trip meter and turn east onto graded dirt Masonic Road at marked intersection. The road is designated FR 046.
5.1 ▲		Trail ends at T-intersection with paved California 182. Turn left for Bridgeport; turn right for Wellington, NV.
		GPS: N38°18.56' W119°12.78'
▼ 0.3	SO	Cattle guard.
4.8 ▲	SO	Cattle guard.
▼ 0.8	SO	Track on left.
4.3 ▲	SO	Track on right.
▼ 0.9	SO	Track on right.
4.2 ▲	SO	Track on left.
▼ 1.6	SO	Cattle guard. Entering Toiyabe National Forest.
3.5 ▲	SO	Cattle guard. Leaving Toiyabe National Forest.
		GPS: N38°19.07' W119°11.40'
▼ 1.7	SO	Small track on left.
3.4 ▲	SO	Small track on right.
▼ 2.1	SO	Two tracks on left.
3.0 ▲	SO	Two tracks on right.
▼ 2.6	SO	Track on left.
2.5 ▲	SO	Track on right.
▼ 2.7	SO	Track on left.
2.4 ▲	SO	Track on right.
▼ 4.0	SO	Track on left.
1.1 ▲	SO	Track on right.
▼ 4.1	SO	Track on left and track on right.
1.0 ▲	SO	Track on left and track on right.
		GPS: N38°20.28' W119°09.25'
▼ 4.3	SO	Track on left to the Success Mine, which is visible on the left of the trail.
0.8 ▲	SO	Track on right to the Success Mine, which is visible on the right of the trail.
		GPS: N38°20.46' W119°09.33'
▼ 4.9	SO	Faint track on right.
0.2 ▲	SO	Faint track on left.
▼ 5.1	SO	Track on right goes a short distance to remains of the Chemung Mine. There are many wooden buildings. Zero trip meter.
0.0 ▲		Continue to the southwest.
		GPS: N38°20.99' W119°09.00'
▼ 0.0		Continue to the northeast.
2.8 ▲		Track on left goes a short distance to remains of the Chemung Mine. There are many wooden buildings. Zero trip meter.
▼ 0.1	SO	Track on left and two tracks on right to the Chemung Mine.

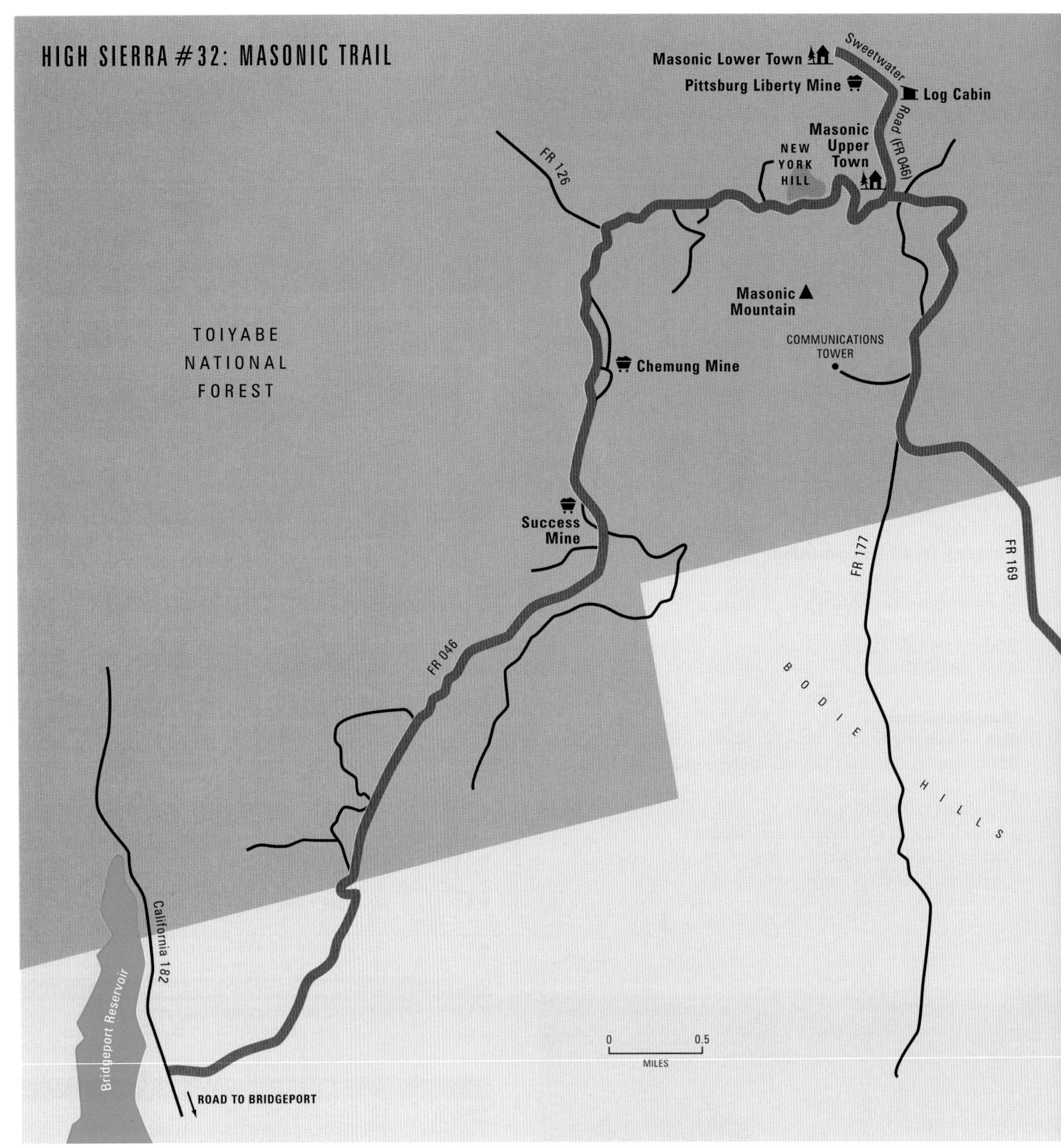

	2.7 ▲	SO	Track on right and two tracks on left to the Chemung Mine.
▼ 0.4		SO	Track on right.
	2.4 ▲	SO	Track on left.
▼ 0.8		BR	Track on left is FR 126.
	2.0 ▲	BL	Track on right is FR 126.
			GPS: N38°21.57′ W119°08.70′
▼ 0.9		SO	Track on right.
	1.9 ▲	SO	Track on left.
▼ 1.0		SO	Two tracks on right.
	1.8 ▲	SO	Two tracks on left.
▼ 1.2		SO	Track on right to mine diggings.
	1.6 ▲	SO	Track on left to mine diggings.
▼ 1.4		SO	Track on right to diggings.
	1.4 ▲	SO	Track on left to diggings.
▼ 1.5		SO	Cattle guard.
	1.3 ▲	SO	Cattle guard.
▼ 1.7		SO	Track on left.

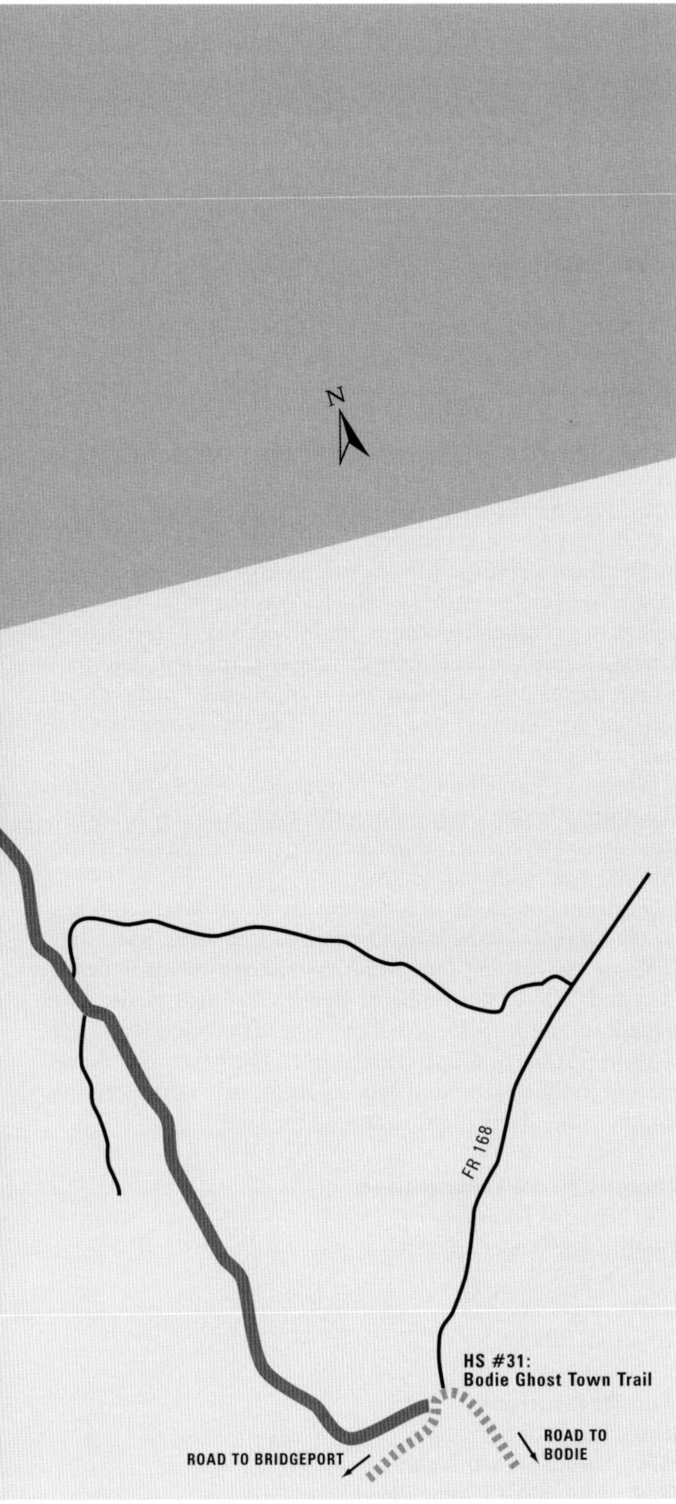

1.1 ▲ SO Track on right.

▼ 1.9 SO Track on right; then track on left.
0.9 ▲ SO Track on right; then track on left.

▼ 2.3 SO Two tracks on left.
0.5 ▲ SO Two tracks on right.

GPS: N38°21.44′ W119°07.24′

▼ 2.8 TR Turn right onto FR 169. Straight ahead, FR 046 is the spur to Masonic's Lower Town. There is a sign at the intersection for Bridgeport and Sweetwater. This intersection is the site of Masonic's Upper Town—only diggings remain. Zero trip meter.
0.0 ▲ Continue to the southwest.

GPS: N38°21.28′ W119°07.03′

Spur to Masonic's Lower Town

▼ 0.0 At the intersection of FR 046 and FR 169, proceed north, following sign to Sweetwater.

▼ 0.2 SO Tailings on right and wooden loading hopper on left.

GPS: N38°21.52′ W119°06.97′

▼ 0.6 SO Remains of log cabin on right.

GPS: N38°21.74′ W119°06.79′

▼ 1.0 Masonic's Lower Town.

GPS: N38°22.00′ W119°07.07′

Continuation of Main Trail

▼ 0.0 Continue to the east. Immediately track on right and track on left.
6.4 ▲ TL Track on right and track on left; then T-intersection. Turn left onto FR 046 following sign to Bridgeport. To the right, FR 046 is the spur to Masonic's Lower Town, signposted to Sweetwater. The intersection is the site of Masonic's Upper Town—only diggings remain. Zero trip meter.

GPS: N38°21.28′ W119°07.03′

▼ 0.1 SO Track on right; then track on left.
6.3 ▲ SO Track on right; then track on left.

▼ 0.6 SO Cattle guard.
5.8 ▲ SO Cattle guard.

▼ 1.1 SO Track on right through gate.
5.3 ▲ SO Track on left through gate.

▼ 1.4 SO Track on right to communications tower. Views ahead over the sage to the Sierra Nevada.
5.0 ▲ SO Second entrance to track on left.

GPS: N38°20.48′ W119°07.21′

▼ 1.6 SO Second entrance to track on right.
4.8 ▲ SO Track on left to communications tower.

▼ 1.7 BL Track on right is FR 177.
4.7 ▲ BR Track on left is FR 177.

GPS: N38°20.23′ W119°07.42′

▼ 2.3 SO Cattle guard.
4.1 ▲ SO Cattle guard.

▼ 2.5 SO Faint track on left.
3.9 ▲ SO Faint track on right.

▼ 3.8 SO Track on left.
2.6 ▲ SO Track on right.

▼ 4.0 SO Track on right.
2.4 ▲ SO Track on left.

▼ 5.6 SO Track on right along fence line.
0.8 ▲ SO Track on left along fence line.

GPS: N38°17.09′ W119°06.58′

▼ 6.4 Trail ends at intersection with High Sierra #31: Bodie Ghost Town Trail (FR 168). Continue straight ahead for Bodie ghost town; turn right to exit to California 182 via Aurora Canyon. Track on left goes toward Nevada.
0.0 ▲ Trail starts on High Sierra #31: Bodie Ghost Town Trail, 7.4 miles east of the intersection with California 182. Zero trip meter at the intersection and turn west onto a formed dirt trail marked FR 169.

GPS: N38°16.79′ W119°05.91′

HIGH SIERRA #33

Mono Lake Trail

Starting Point:	**California 167, 9.7 miles east of US 395**
Finishing Point:	**California 167, 12.9 miles east of US 395**
Total Mileage:	**12.5 miles**
Unpaved Mileage:	**12.5 miles**
Driving Time:	**1 hour**
Elevation Range:	**6,400–6,600 feet**
Usually Open:	**Year-round**
Best Time to Travel:	**Year-round**
Difficulty Rating:	**3**
Scenic Rating:	**8**
Remoteness Rating:	**+0**

Special Attractions

- Wide expanse of Mono Lake.
- Sandy trail along the shores of Mono Lake.
- Trail follows part of the historic route of the Bodie & Benton Railroad.

History

Mono Lake, a relic of a once larger glacial lake called Lake Russell, is best known for its tufa formations (see Mono Lake, page 112). Today's lake has no outlet and covers an area of about 60 square miles, though it is shrinking because of evaporation and irrigation projects that divert streams that naturally flow into it. The water is extremely salty, and the lake has blue-green algae, alkali flies, and small brine shrimp, which attract the thousands of California gulls that breed here. Many species of migratory birds stop here, including snowy plovers, phalaropes, and eared grebes. There are two volcanic islands in the center of the lake—the smaller is Negit, the larger is Paoha. The islands may be less than 500 years old. Geologist Israel C. Russell named Paoha for what he understood to be the local Indian's word *pauha*, meaning "water babies."

The Mono Basin National Forest Scenic Area, established in 1984, surrounds the lake. The visitor center is just south on US 395, in Lee Vining. The Mono Lake Tufa State Reserve is on the south shore.

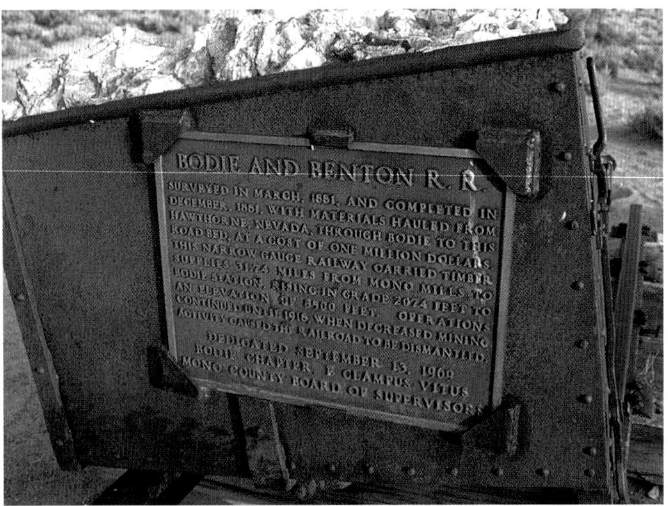

At the eastern end of the trail, this ore cart marks the Bodie & Benton Railroad, which was never completed

Description

This route follows single-track formed trails through sand dunes near the northeastern shore of Mono Lake. The sand is deep and soft, and the forest service warns drivers that it is easy to get bogged down. You will almost certainly need to lower tire pressures considerably in places.

The southern start of the trail leaves paved California 167 and almost immediately turns onto a small trail as it forks away from private property. This first section can be a little brushy for wide vehicles, but it is less than a mile long and with care your paintwork can emerge unscathed. Keep an eye out for fast-moving vehicles coming your way. The trail passes through the Mono Basin National Forest Scenic Area where no cross-country driving is permitted. The trail is faint in a couple of places, but it is generally well defined and easy to follow. If you are in any doubt, remain on the main trail.

There are limited views of Mono Lake. Instead, the sand dunes provide the scenery along this trail. You may see some mule deer as well as garter snakes and gopher snakes; in spring you may hear spadefoot toads.

The trail doubles back to California 167 at Warm Springs, the closest point to the lake. The springs seep warm water, but there are no bathing opportunities. The return leg is better used and follows the Bodie & Benton Railroad grade. The grade is on the western side of the vehicle trail, and the raised bed and occasional sleepers can be seen. The forest map shows the trail continuing around Mono Lake, which it does, but the sand becomes deeper farther around the lake.

Current Road Information

Inyo National Forest
Mono Lake Ranger District
PO Box 429
Lee Vining, CA 93541
(760) 647-3045

Map References

BLM Excelsior Mt.
USFS Inyo National Forest
USGS 1:24,000 Sulphur Pond
1:100,000 Excelsior Mt.
Maptech CD-ROM: High Sierra/Yosemite
Northern California Atlas & Gazetteer, p. 102
California Road & Recreation Atlas, p. 73 (route not shown)

Route Directions

▼ 0.0	From California 167, 9.7 miles east of US 395 and 2.9 miles east of the start of High Sierra #31: Bodie Ghost Town Trail, zero trip meter

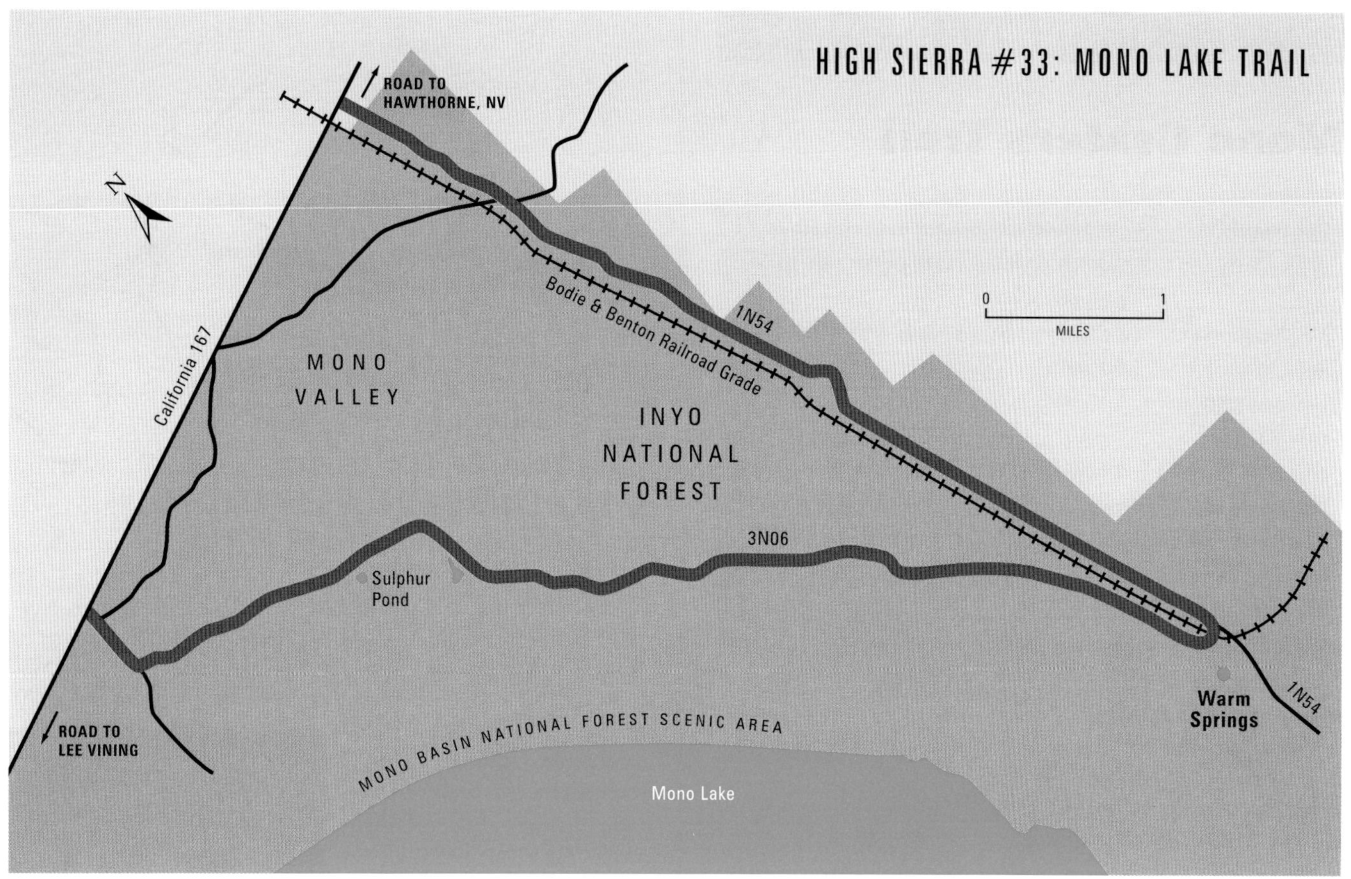

and turn south on formed dirt road, marked 3N06. Intersection is 3.2 miles west of the western end of the trail.

0.4 ▲ Trail ends back on California 167, 9.7 miles east of US 395. Turn left for Lee Vining; turn right for Hawthorne, NV.

GPS: N38°05.90′ W118°59.35′

▼ 0.1 SO Track on left. Entering Mono Basin National Forest Scenic Area.

0.3 ▲ SO Track on right. Leaving Mono Basin National Forest Scenic Area.

▼ 0.4 BL Track continues straight ahead. Bear left onto smaller formed trail and zero trip meter.

0.0 ▲ Continue to the north.

GPS: N38°05.55′ W118°59.34′

▼ 0.0 Continue to the southeast.

6.4 ▲ BR Join larger trail past track on left. Zero trip meter.

▼ 0.3 SO Track on right.

6.1 ▲ SO Track on left.

GPS: N38°05.45′ W118°59.02′

▼ 1.4 BL Track on right to spring; then second track on right. Sulphur Pond on right.

5.0 ▲ BR Track on left; then second track on left to spring. Sulphur Pond on left.

GPS: N38°05.21′ W118°57.89′

▼ 2.0 SO Pond on right.

4.4 ▲ SO Pond on left.

GPS: N38°04.93′ W118°57.35′

▼ 3.4 SO Very loose, deep, twisty ridge of sand.

3.0 ▲ SO Very loose, deep, twisty ridge of sand.

GPS: N38°04.08′ W118°56.28′

▼ 5.2 SO Track on right.

1.2 ▲ SO Track on left.

▼ 6.4 TL Well-used track on right is 1N54. Turn left, joining 1N54. There is a marker at the intersection. Zero trip meter.

0.0 ▲ Continue to the west.

GPS: N38°02.24′ W118°54.03′

▼ 0.0 Continue to the northwest.

5.7 ▲ TR Well-used track ahead is the continuation of 1N54. Turn right onto well-used unmarked trail, which is 3N06. Zero trip meter.

▼ 4.7 SO Track on right.

1.0 ▲ BR Track on left.

GPS: N38°06.05′ W118°55.77′

▼ 4.8 SO Track on left.

0.9 ▲ SO Track on right.

▼ 5.4 SO Track on right.

0.3 ▲ SO Track on left.

GPS: N38°06.68′ W118°56.05′

▼ 5.7 Trail ends at T-intersection back on California 167. Turn left for Lee Vining; turn right for Hawthorne, NV.

0.0 ▲ Trail commences on California 167, 12.9 miles east of US 395. Zero trip meter and turn southeast on formed sandy trail. There is a marker at the start for the Bodie & Benton Railroad and a small ore cart loaded with rocks. There is a sign on the highway for a point of historical interest that marks the intersection. Intersection is 3.2 miles east of the eastern end of the trail.

GPS: N38°06.94′ W118°56.16′

Mono Craters Trail

Starting Point:	US 395 at the turn for Bald Mountain Road, 11.1 miles north of the turn to Mammoth Lakes
Finishing Point:	California 120, 7.8 miles east of US 395
Total Mileage:	9.1 miles
Unpaved Mileage:	9.1 miles
Driving Time:	1 hour
Elevation Range:	7,000–8,000 feet
Usually Open:	Year-round
Best Time to Travel:	Year-round
Difficulty Rating:	3
Scenic Rating:	8
Remoteness Rating:	+0

Special Attractions

- Volcanic region of Mono Craters.
- Historic site of Mono Mills.
- Rockhounding for obsidian.
- Many backcountry campsites.

History

The Mono Craters are a 10-mile-long north-south chain of young volcanoes south of Mono Lake. The most recent eruption, according to radiocarbon dating of wood buried by it, was 640 years ago at Panum Crater in the Mono Basin National Forest Scenic Area. Mono Craters are plug-dome volcanoes like Lassen Peak (see page 111). Lava cooled to create a plug in the vent at the bottom of the original crater. It is likely that the volcanoes will erupt again some time in the future.

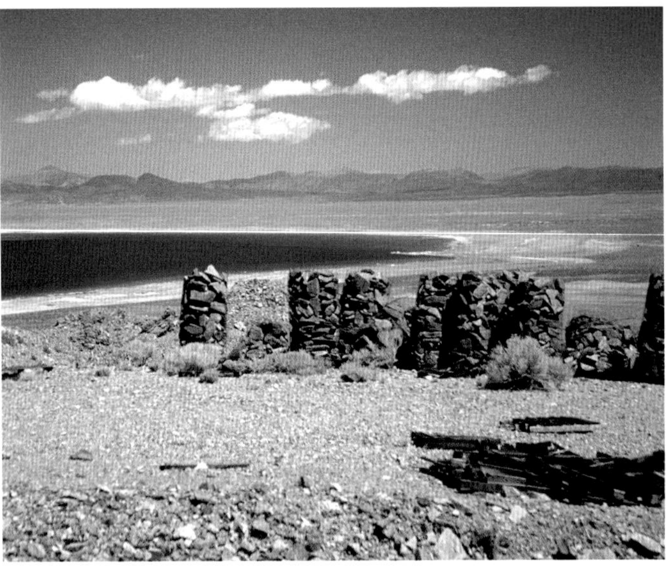

High above Mono Lake in the Mono Craters, pumice stone stacks guard an old mine

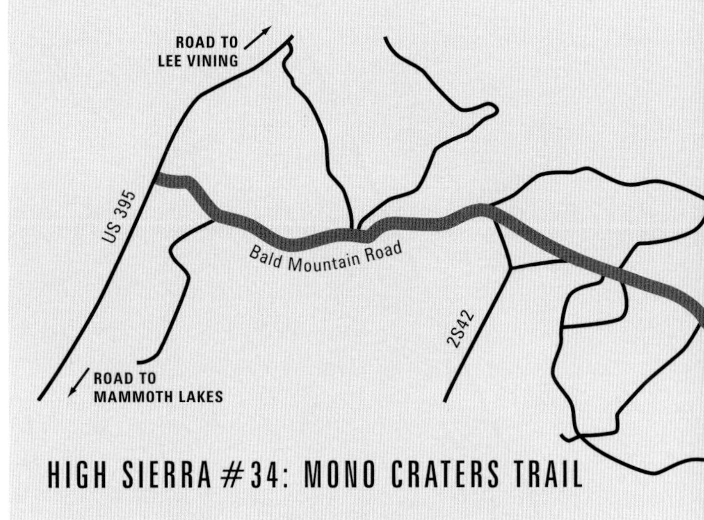

A lumber mill at Mono Mills, just east of the craters, supplied wood for mines and mining towns to the north, such as Bodie, Aurora, and Masonic. In its heyday, the two-story mill powered by a 16-inch steam engine could produce 80,000 board feet of lumber in a 10-hour shift. However, the mill rarely achieved peak production because the workforce was rarely sober. The mill was abandoned in 1917 when mining in the region slowed to a stop.

The Bodie & Benton Railroad was intended to facilitate shipping lumber from Mono Mills to Bodie and beyond. Residents of Bodie enthusiastically supported the idea as a link to the outside world and to show investors how vital their town was. Railroad investors wanted the route to go as far southeast as Benton where it would meet the narrow-gauge Carson & Colorado Railroad.

Mono Mills supplied firewood and lumber to Bodie mines via the supplies railroad, which followed the still shores of Mono Lake

Construction of the narrow-gauge railroad began in 1881, initially using Chinese labor, but a rowdy and inebriated bunch from Bodie drove the workers off. Eventually track was laid 30 miles between Bodie and the mill. The grade for the final haul from Lime Kiln to Bodie was the steepest, requiring one of the railroad's four engines to pull only three or four cars at a time.

Description

Mono Craters Trail heads north from US 395, passing the east side of the Mono Craters, en route to California 120. The historic site of Mono Mills is 1.4 miles east of the trail's northern

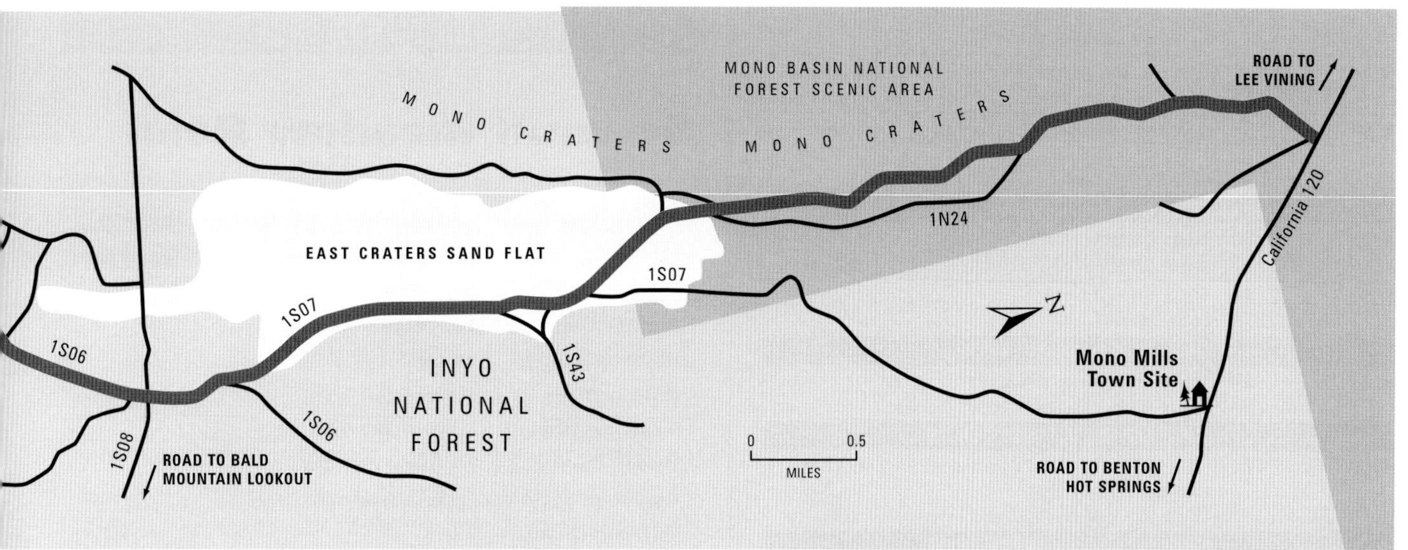

end on California 120. A plaque on the north side of the road marks the site. The coordinates are GPS: N37°53.29' W118°57.56'.

Initially, the trail follows Bald Mountain Road, a graded dirt road that travels through Jeffrey pine forest and meadows. Many tracks lead off to the left and right, and there are plenty of good seldom-used undeveloped campsites. The route then follows a smaller single-track vehicle trail alongside East Craters Sand Flat, an open area that provides good views southwest to the Sierra Nevada as well as toward the gray bulk of the Mono Craters on the far side of the flat. Many side trails lead to the base of the crater area as well as to other campsites. Obsidian, a black volcanic glass, is readily found.

Current Road Information

Inyo National Forest
Mono Lake Ranger District
PO Box 429
Lee Vining, CA 93541
(760) 647-3045

Map References

BLM Yosemite Valley, Benton Range
USFS Inyo National Forest
USGS 1:24,000 June Lake, Crestview, Mono Mills
1:100,000 Yosemite Valley, Benton Range
Maptech CD-ROM: High Sierra/Yosemite
Northern California Atlas & Gazetteer, p. 112
California Road & Recreation Atlas, p. 73
Other: Tom Harrison Maps—Mammoth High Country Trail Map

Route Directions

▼ 0.0			From US 395 at the sign for Bald Mountain Road, zero trip meter and turn northeast on the single-lane, graded dirt road. Immediately there is a track on right and track on left.
	3.3 ▲		Trail ends at T-intersection with US 395. Turn right for Lee Vining; turn left for Mammoth Lakes.
			GPS: N37°46.50' W119°00.78'
▼ 0.1		SO	Two tracks on left.
	3.2 ▲	SO	Two tracks on right.
▼ 0.4		SO	Track on right.
	2.9 ▲	SO	Track on left.
▼ 0.5		SO	Track on left.
	2.8 ▲	SO	Track on right.
▼ 0.6		SO	Track on right.
	2.7 ▲	SO	Track on left.
▼ 0.7		SO	Track on left; then track on right.
	2.6 ▲	SO	Track on left; then track on right.
▼ 0.9		SO	Three tracks on left.
	2.4 ▲	SO	Three tracks on right.
▼ 1.3		SO	Two tracks on left.
	2.0 ▲	SO	Two tracks on right.
▼ 1.6		SO	Track on left; then track on right.
	1.7 ▲	SO	Track on left; then track on right.
▼ 1.7		SO	Graded dirt road on right is 2S42.
	1.6 ▲	SO	Graded dirt road on left is 2S42.
			GPS: N37°47.82' W119°00.19'
▼ 2.0		SO	Track on right.
	1.3 ▲	SO	Track on left.
▼ 2.2		SO	Track on right.
	1.1 ▲	SO	Track on left.
▼ 2.3		SO	Track on left; then track on right.
	1.0 ▲	SO	Track on left; then track on right.
▼ 2.4		SO	Track on right.
	0.9 ▲	SO	Track on left.
▼ 2.6		SO	Track on right and track on left.
	0.7 ▲	SO	Track on right and track on left.
▼ 2.8		SO	Track on left.
	0.5 ▲	SO	Track on right.
▼ 3.3		BL	Track on right; then major fork in road. To the right, 1S08 goes to Bald Mountain Lookout. Follow the sign to Mono Mills and zero trip meter.
	0.0 ▲		Continue to the south. Track on left.
			GPS: N37°49.00' W118°59.00'
▼ 0.0			Continue to the north. Track on right and track on left are both 1S08. Remain on 1S06.
	2.1 ▲	SO	Track on left and track on right are both 1S08; then second entrance to 1S08 on left, which

		goes to Bald Mountain Lookout. Zero trip meter at second entrance.
▼ 0.2	SO	Two tracks on right and two tracks on left.
1.9 ▲	SO	Two tracks on right and two tracks on left.
▼ 0.4	BL	Bear left onto smaller formed trail marked 1S07.
1.7 ▲	SO	Join larger graded road 1S06.
		GPS: N37°49.33' W118°58.96'
▼ 0.8	SO	Track on left.
1.3 ▲	SO	Track on right.
▼ 1.6	SO	Track on right.
0.5 ▲	SO	Track on left.
		GPS: N37°50.38' W118°59.01'
▼ 2.0	SO	Track on right is 1S43.
0.1 ▲	BR	Track on left is 1S43.
		GPS: N37°50.76' W118°58.91'
▼ 2.1	BL	Bear left onto 1N24 (marker at intersection) and zero trip meter.
0.0 ▲		Continue to the south.
		GPS: N37°50.85' W118°58.91'
▼ 0.0		Continue to the northwest.
3.0 ▲	SO	Track on left is 1S07. Continue straight ahead on 1S07 and zero trip meter.
▼ 0.6	BR	Track on left goes to base of the craters. Entering Mono Basin National Forest Scenic Area.
2.4 ▲	BL	Track on right goes to base of the craters. Leaving Mono Basin National Forest Scenic Area.
		GPS: N37°51.30' W118°59.23'
▼ 0.7	BL	Track on right is 1N24; then small track on left.
2.3 ▲	SO	Small track on right; then track on left is 1N24.
		GPS: N37°51.41' W118°59.21'
▼ 1.3	SO	Track on left on rise.
1.7 ▲	SO	Track on right on rise.
		GPS: N37°51.99' W118°59.08'
▼ 2.3	TL	Crossroads in a small clearing. Turn left onto unmarked trail. Marked track on right is 1N24 rejoining main trail.
0.7 ▲	TR	Crossroads in a small clearing. Turn right onto unmarked trail and start to climb sandy hill. Marked track ahead is 1N24.
		GPS: N37°52.79' W118°59.10'
▼ 3.0	SO	Well-used track on left goes to base of the craters. Zero trip meter.
0.0 ▲		Continue to the southeast.
		GPS: N37°53.45' W118°59.12'
▼ 0.0		Continue to the northwest.
0.7 ▲	SO	Well-used track on right goes to base of the craters. Zero trip meter.
▼ 0.7		Track on right; then trail ends at T-intersection with paved California 120. Turn right for Benton Hot Springs; turn left for Lee Vining. Turn right and proceed 1.4 miles to visit Mono Mills site.
0.0 ▲		Trail commences on California 120, 7.8 miles east of the intersection with US 395. The turn is immediately after an Elevation 7,000 feet sign. Zero trip meter and turn southwest on unmarked, formed sandy trail. There is a large block of pumice marking the intersection. Immediately bear right, leaving a well-used track on your left.
		GPS: N37°53.97' W118°58.79'

HIGH SIERRA #35

Sawmill Meadow Road

Starting Point:	**California 120, 16 miles east of US 395, 3.5 miles east of Mono Mills Historical Site**
Finishing Point:	**Sawmill Meadow**
Total Mileage:	**29.4 miles (one-way)**
Unpaved Mileage:	**29.4 miles**
Driving Time:	**3 hours**
Elevation Range:	**7,200–9,200 feet**
Usually Open:	**April to November**
Best Time to Travel:	**April to November**
Difficulty Rating:	**2**
Scenic Rating:	**8**
Remoteness Rating:	**+0**

Special Attractions

- Camping and picnicking at Sawmill Meadow.
- Long easy trail through Inyo National Forest.
- Panoramic views from the shelf road.

History

Sawmill Meadow Road runs around the north side of Glass Mountain, a volcanic dome composed mostly of rhyolite and obsidian, formed several million years ago.

Taylor Canyon, midway along the trail, was named for E. S. Taylor, Waterman Body's partner in the 1859 strike near what became the town of Bodie. Bodie died in March 1860, but Taylor continued prospecting to the southeast and established a cabin in the vicinity of hot springs at nearby Benton. Angered at being displaced from their springs, Indians killed him.

McGee Canyon, just east of Taylor Canyon was named for the four McGee brothers, early pioneers who ran cattle in this part of Inyo County.

Description

The section of Inyo National Forest east of US 395, part of the Great Basin's Basin and Range province, is often neglected in favor of the more spectacular Sierra Nevada. However, the area is very beautiful in its own right. The long Sawmill Meadow Road describes an arc around the north and east sides of Glass Mountain, traveling on roughly graded, narrow dirt roads for most of its length. It passes through sagebrush-covered meadows, pine forests, and a long section of wide shelf road that offers views into the rugged canyons to the north. Deer, coyotes, and various raptors can often be seen along the trail.

The route travels along a series of numbered forest roads, making it easy to follow; there are directional signs at most of the major intersections. The trail is not officially closed in winter; rather, it closes naturally when the snow gets too deep. It may be open past the dates given above. Snowmobiles use it when there is enough snow. The trail finishes at Sawmill Meadow, an interconnecting series of small pine-fringed

Vistas of North Canyon through the pines

meadows. There are a couple of picnic tables and a pit toilet at the end of the trail, as well as several pleasant undeveloped campsites. From here you have the option of exiting via the narrower High Sierra #36: Kelty Meadows Trail, or retracing your route back to California 120.

Current Road Information

Inyo National Forest
Mono Lake Ranger District
PO Box 429
Lee Vining, CA 93541
(760) 647-3045

Map References

BLM Benton Range
USFS Inyo National Forest
USGS 1:24,000 Crestview, Dexter Canyon, Glass Mt.
1:100,000 Benton Range
Maptech CD-ROM: High Sierra/Yosemite
Northern California Atlas & Gazetteer, pp. 112, 113
California Road & Recreation Atlas, p. 73
Other: Tom Harrison Maps—Mammoth High Country Trail Map (incomplete)

Route Directions

▼	▲		
▼ 0.0			From California 120, 16 miles east of US 395, zero trip meter and turn southeast on graded gravel road at the sign for Crooked Meadows Road. Road is marked 1S17 and immediately crosses Big Sand Flat.
	1.3 ▲		Trail ends at T-intersection with California 120. Turn left for Lee Vining; turn right for Benton Hot Springs.
			GPS: N37°51.97′ W118°54.19′
▼ 0.4		SO	Track on left.
	0.9 ▲	SO	Track on right.
▼ 0.5		SO	Track on left.
	0.8 ▲	SO	Track on right.
▼ 0.6		SO	Track on left.
	0.7 ▲	SO	Track on right.
▼ 0.9		SO	Track on left.
	0.4 ▲	SO	Track on right.
▼ 1.1		SO	Track on left.
	0.2 ▲	SO	Track on right.
▼ 1.3		SO	Track on left; then 4-way intersection. Graded road on right is 1S12 to Mt. Baldy Lookout Road and graded road on left. Zero trip meter and follow the sign to Crooked Meadows Road.
	0.0 ▲		Continue to the northwest on 1S17 past track on right.
			GPS: N37°51.42′ W118°52.99′
▼ 0.0			Continue to the southeast.
	2.8 ▲	SO	4-way intersection. Graded road on left is 1S12 to Mt. Baldy Lookout Road and graded road on right. Zero trip meter and follow the sign to California 120.
▼ 0.8		SO	Track on right.
	2.0 ▲	SO	Track on left.
▼ 1.0		SO	Track on right and track on left are both Pilot Spring Road (1S04). Follow sign to Taylor Canyon.
	1.8 ▲	SO	Track on right and track on left are both Pilot Spring Road (1S04). Follow sign to California 120.
			GPS: N37°50.90′ W118°52.03′
▼ 1.1		SO	Track on left.
	1.7 ▲	SO	Track on right.
▼ 1.4		BR	Well-used track on left is 1S55 to Johnny Meadow. Remain on 1S17.
	1.4 ▲	SO	Well-used track on right is 1S55 to Johnny Meadow. Remain on 1S17.
			GPS: N37°50.67′ W118°51.74′
▼ 1.7		SO	Track on right.
	1.1 ▲	SO	Track on left.
▼ 1.9		SO	Track on right.
	0.9 ▲	SO	Track on left.
▼ 2.5		SO	Track on right.
	0.3 ▲	SO	Track on left.
▼ 2.8		SO	Graded road on left is 1S56 to Johnny Meadow. Continue into Crooked Meadows and zero trip meter. Track on right.
	0.0 ▲		Continue to the northwest on 1S17.
			GPS: N37°49.84′ W118°50.81′
▼ 0.0			Continue to the southeast on 1S17.
	2.5 ▲	BL	Graded road on right is 1S56 to Johnny Meadow. Bear left, remaining on 1S17 and following the sign to California 120. Zero trip meter. Track on left.
▼ 0.2		SO	Track on left.
	2.3 ▲	SO	Track on right.
▼ 0.4		SO	Track on left.
	2.1 ▲	SO	Track on right.
▼ 0.9		BL	Two tracks on right.
	1.6 ▲	BR	Two tracks on left.
▼ 1.1		SO	Campsite on left.
	1.4 ▲	SO	Campsite on right.
▼ 1.6		SO	Track on left.
	0.9 ▲	SO	Track on right.
▼ 1.7		SO	Track on left.
	0.8 ▲	SO	Track on right.
▼ 2.0		SO	Track on right.
	0.5 ▲	SO	Track on left.
▼ 2.2		SO	Track on right.
	0.3 ▲	SO	Track on left.
▼ 2.5		SO	Cattle guard; then track on right is Pilot Spring Road. Zero trip meter.
	0.0 ▲		Continue to the northwest.
			GPS: N37°47.98′ W118°49.97′

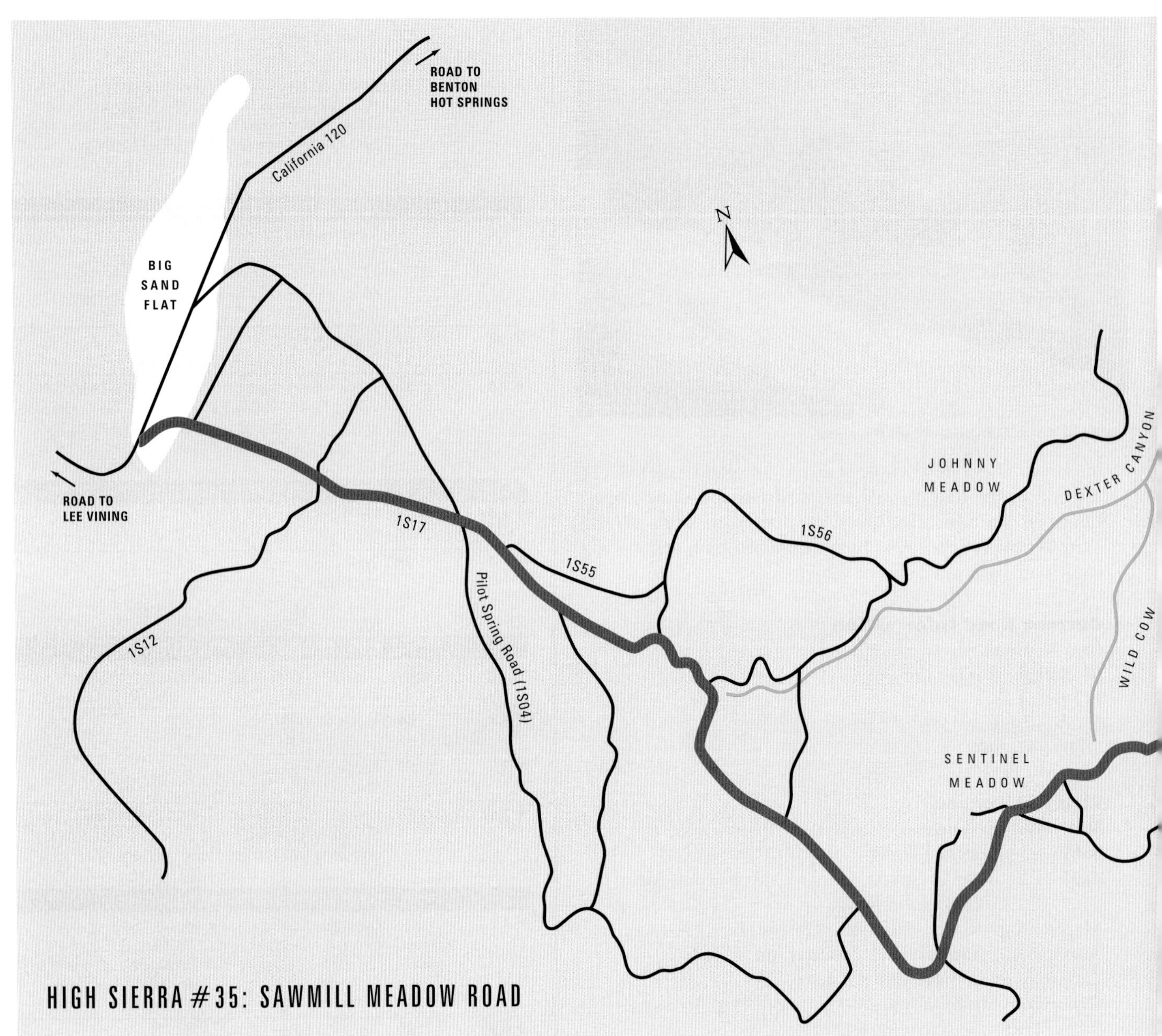

HIGH SIERRA #35: SAWMILL MEADOW ROAD

Mileage	Reverse	Dir	Description
▼ 0.0			Continue to the southeast.
	7.9 ▲	SO	Track on left is Pilot Spring Road; then cattle guard. Zero trip meter.
▼ 0.8		SO	Track on left and track on right.
	7.1 ▲	SO	Track on left and track on right.
			GPS: N37°47.51′ W118°49.53′
▼ 1.0		SO	Cattle guard.
	6.9 ▲	SO	Cattle guard.
▼ 2.0		SO	Track on left goes to Sentinel Meadow; then track on right.
	5.9 ▲	SO	Track on left; then track on right goes to Sentinel Meadow.
			GPS: N37°48.25′ W118°48.63′
▼ 2.3		SO	Track on right and track on left.
	5.6 ▲	SO	Track on right and track on left.
▼ 2.9		SO	Track on right.
	5.0 ▲	SO	Track on left.
▼ 3.1		SO	Track on right.
	4.8 ▲	SO	Track on left.
▼ 3.3		SO	Track on right.
	4.6 ▲	SO	Track on left.
▼ 4.2		SO	Track on left.
	3.7 ▲	SO	Track on right.
▼ 5.5		SO	Track on left.
	2.4 ▲	SO	Track on right.
▼ 6.2		SO	Turnout on left gives views over Dexter, Wild Cow, and Wet Canyons.
	1.7 ▲	SO	Turnout on right gives views over Dexter, Wild Cow, and Wet Canyons.
			GPS: N37°49.74′ W118°46.52′
▼ 6.9		SO	Track on left.
	1.0 ▲	SO	Track on right.
▼ 7.5		SO	Track on right.
	0.4 ▲	SO	Track on left.
			GPS: N37°50.01′ W118°45.63′
▼ 7.9		TR	Track ahead is Taylor Canyon Road (1S17).

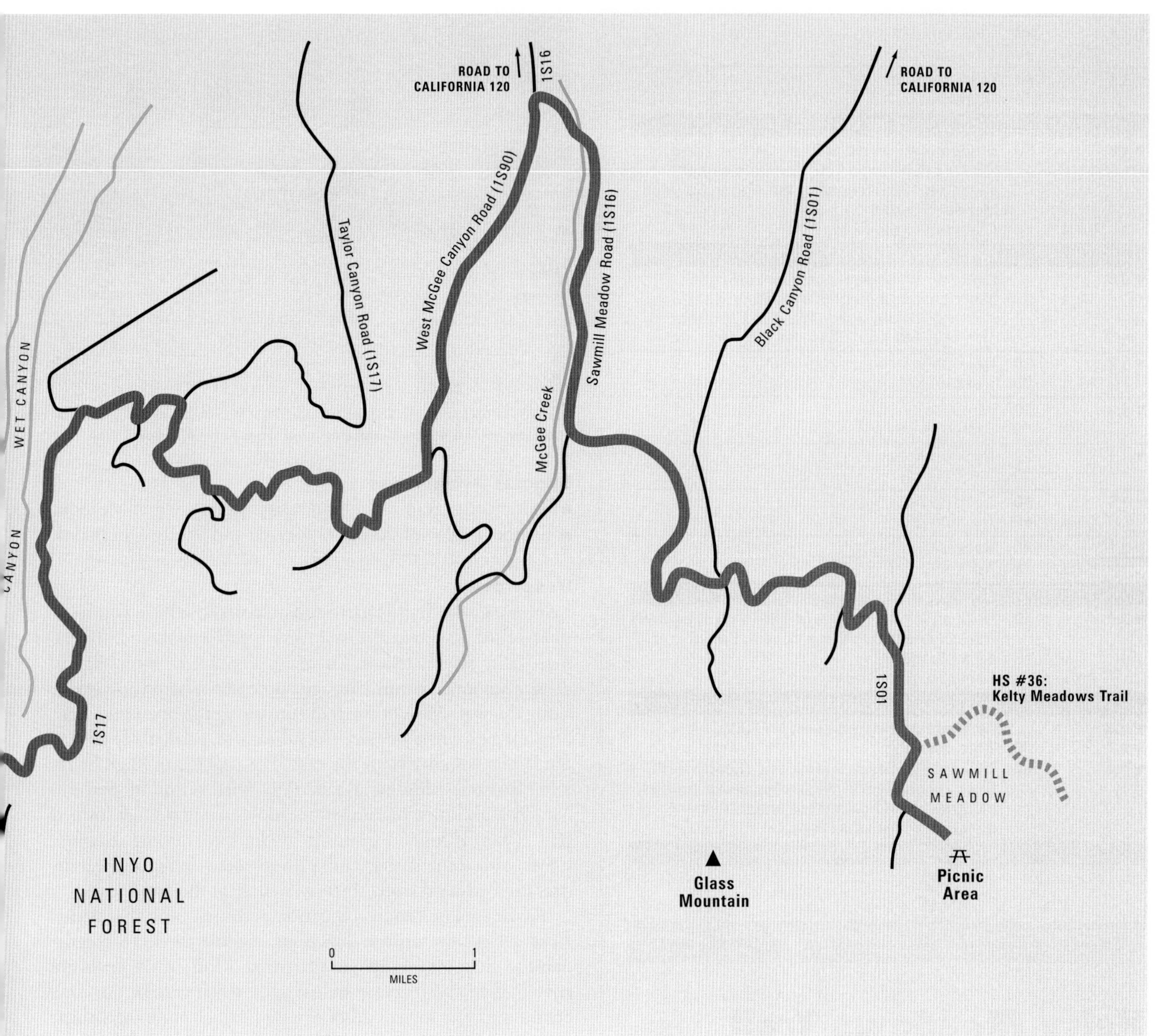

Mileage		Directions
		Turn right onto graded dirt West McGee Canyon Road (1S90) and zero trip meter.
0.0 ▲		Continue to the west.
		GPS: N37°50.02′ W118°45.26′
▼ 0.0		Continue to the south.
6.4 ▲	TL	Graded road on right is Taylor Canyon Road (1S17). Turn left onto graded dirt road, also 1S17, following sign to Crooked Meadows. Zero trip meter.
▼ 1.0	BL	Track on right. Remain on 1S90.
5.4 ▲	SO	Track on left.
		GPS: N37°49.54′ W118°45.25′
▼ 1.5	SO	Track on left.
4.9 ▲	SO	Track on right.
▼ 1.7	SO	Track on right.
4.7 ▲	SO	Track on left.
▼ 1.8	SO	Track on right.
4.6 ▲	SO	Track on left.
▼ 2.6	SO	Track on right.
3.8 ▲	SO	Track on left.
▼ 3.3	SO	Track on right.
3.1 ▲	SO	Track on left.
		GPS: N37°49.09′ W118°44.04′
▼ 3.5	SO	Track on left.
2.9 ▲	SO	Track on right.
▼ 3.8	SO	Track on right.
2.6 ▲	SO	Track on left.
▼ 6.4	TR	Turn sharp right onto Sawmill Meadow Road at sign and zero trip meter. Track ahead exits to California 120.
0.0 ▲		Continue to the south on 1S90.
		GPS: N37°51.07′ W118°42.01′
▼ 0.0		Continue to the east on 1S16
4.6 ▲	TL	Turn sharp left onto West McGee Canyon Road at sign and zero trip meter. Track on right exits to California 120.

▼ 2.3		SO	Track on right.
	2.3 ▲	SO	Track on left.
▼ 3.9		SO	Track on right.
	0.7 ▲	SO	Track on left.
			GPS: N37°48.12' W118°42.21'
▼ 4.6		SO	Graded road on left is Black Canyon Road (1S01) to California 120. Continue straight ahead on 1S01, following the sign to Sawmill Meadow. Zero trip meter.
	0.0 ▲		Continue to the west.
			GPS: N37°48.01' W118°41.77'
▼ 0.0			Continue to the east past track on right.
	3.0 ▲	BL	Track on left; then graded road on right is Black Canyon Road (1S01) to California 120. Bear left onto 1S16, and zero trip meter.
▼ 1.2		SO	Track on left and track on right.
	1.8 ▲	SO	Track on left and track on right.
▼ 1.3		SO	Campsite on left.
	1.7 ▲	SO	Campsite on right.
▼ 1.4		SO	Track on right.
	1.6 ▲	SO	Track on left.
▼ 1.6		SO	Track on right.
	1.4 ▲	SO	Track on left.
▼ 2.2		SO	Track on left.
	0.8 ▲	SO	Track on right.
			GPS: N37°47.35' W118°40.66'
▼ 3.0		SO	Track on left is High Sierra #36: Kelty Meadows Trail, signposted to Black Canyon Cow Camp. Zero trip meter.
	0.0 ▲		Continue to the north.
			GPS: N37°46.69' W118°40.67'
▼ 0.0			Continue to the southwest on 1S01.
▼ 0.4		SO	Track on right.
▼ 0.9		SO	Trail ends at Sawmill Meadow. There is a pit toilet, a couple of picnic tables, and a couple of undeveloped campsites under the pines on the edge of the small meadow.
			GPS: N37°46.08' W118°40.62'

HIGH SIERRA #36

Kelty Meadows Trail

Starting Point:	**High Sierra #35: Sawmill Meadow Road, 0.9 miles north of Sawmill Meadow**
Finishing Point:	**Benton Crossing Road (2S84), 4.5 miles east of the intersection with Owens Gorge Road**
Total Mileage:	**15.6 miles**
Unpaved Mileage:	**15.6 miles**
Driving Time:	**1.5 hours**
Elevation Range:	**7,100–9,500 feet**
Usually Open:	**April to November**
Best Time to Travel:	**Dry weather**
Difficulty Rating:	**3**
Scenic Rating:	**9**
Remoteness Rating:	**+1**

The steep-sided White Mountains seen from Kelty Meadows Trail

Special Attractions

- Seldom-used trail is an alternate exit from Sawmill Meadow.
- Excellent views of the Sierra Nevada and White Mountains.

Description

Kelty Meadows Trail is narrow, barely single-vehicle width for most of the way, but it is well used, well formed, and, for the most part, easy to follow. There are a couple of short slightly brushy sections, mainly through some of the stands of aspens along the way. Most of the trail runs along the open ridge top, providing excellent views in every direction, particularly toward the White Mountains to the east. The trail leaves High Sierra #35: Sawmill Meadow Road, 0.9 miles north of Sawmill Meadow, and runs onto open meadows along a small formed trail. There is a good campsite at the ford through Sawmill Creek with some shelter and a pretty view. Additional campsites can be found along the way, mainly at the upper end.

As the trail descends, navigation becomes somewhat tricky. Keep a close eye on the directions and use the GPS coordinates to help you locate correct turns. Most of the trails are equally used and it is easy to lose your way if you are not concentrating. The lower end of the trail exits from a sagebrush-covered valley onto a graded dirt road, which in turn leads to paved Benton Crossing Road.

Current Road Information

Inyo National Forest
Mono Lake Ranger District
PO Box 429
Lee Vining, CA 93541
(760) 647-3045

Map References

BLM Benton Range
USFS Inyo National Forest
USGS 1:24,000 Glass Mt., Watterson Canyon, Banner Ridge
1:100,000 Benton Range
Maptech CD-ROM: High Sierra/Yosemite
Northern California Atlas & Gazetteer, p. 113 (incomplete)
California Road & Recreation Atlas, p. 73 (route not shown)

Route Directions

Mileage		Directions
▼ 0.0		Trail commences on High Sierra #35: Sawmill Meadow Road, 0.9 miles north of its finishing point at Sawmill Meadow. Zero trip meter and turn northeast onto small formed trail, following sign to Black Canyon Cow Camp.
12.8 ▲		Trail finishes on High Sierra #35: Sawmill Meadow Road, 0.9 miles north of its finishing point at Sawmill Meadow. Turn right to exit to California 120.
		GPS: N37°46.69' W118°40.67'
▼ 0.2	SO	Cross through Sawmill Creek. Campsite on right.
12.6 ▲	SO	Cross through Sawmill Creek. Campsite on left.
▼ 0.6	SO	Track forks and rejoins almost immediately.
12.2 ▲	SO	Track forks and rejoins almost immediately.
▼ 0.8	SO	Track on left.
12.0 ▲	SO	Track on right.
▼ 1.1	BL	Track on right.
11.7 ▲	BR	Track on left.
		GPS: N37°46.45' W118°39.99'
▼ 1.9	SO	Track on left.
10.9 ▲	SO	Track on right.
▼ 2.0	SO	Track on left; then track on right.
10.8 ▲	SO	Track on left; then track on right.
		GPS: N37°45.97' W118°39.77'
▼ 2.8	SO	Track on right. Old cabin at the intersection on right.
10.0 ▲	SO	Track on left. Old cabin at the intersection on left.
		GPS: N37°45.48' W118°39.38'
▼ 3.0	BR	Swing right through fence line.
9.8 ▲	BL	Pass through fence line and bear left along fence line.
		GPS: N37°45.65' W118°39.24'
▼ 3.9	TR	Turn right, following most-used trail. Track on left.
8.9 ▲	TL	Turn left, following most-used trail. Track continues ahead.
		GPS: N37°46.05' W118°38.48'
▼ 4.2	SO	Cross through small creek.
8.6 ▲	SO	Cross through small creek.
▼ 4.9	SO	Cross through small creek.
7.9 ▲	SO	Cross through small creek.
		GPS: N37°45.27' W118°38.07'
▼ 5.2	SO	Pass through fence line.
7.6 ▲	SO	Pass through fence line.
▼ 5.8	TL	Turn left at unmarked T-intersection.
7.0 ▲	TR	Turn right at unmarked intersection.
		GPS: N37°44.92' W118°38.45'
▼ 5.9	SO	Gate.
6.9 ▲	SO	Gate.
▼ 6.5	TL	Turn left in front of hill at unmarked T-intersection.
6.3 ▲	TR	Turn right at unmarked intersection.
		GPS: N37°44.48' W118°38.86'
▼ 6.7	SO	Track on right climbs hill.
6.1 ▲	SO	Track on left climbs hill.
▼ 7.5	SO	Track on left.
5.3 ▲	SO	Track on right.
		GPS: N37°44.01' W118°38.01'
▼ 9.0	SO	Small track on left.
3.8 ▲	BL	Small track on right.
▼ 9.5	TR	Turn right onto equally used unmarked trail. Track continues ahead.
3.3 ▲	TL	T-intersection. Turn left onto equally used unmarked trail. Track on right.
		GPS: N37°42.93' W118°37.26'
▼ 9.7	SO	Pass through fence line.
3.1 ▲	SO	Pass through fence line.
▼ 10.1	SO	Track on right; then second track right.
2.7 ▲	BR	Track on left; then second track on left.
▼ 11.1	SO	Track on right.
1.7 ▲	BR	Track on left.
▼ 11.5	SO	Track on left.
1.3 ▲	BL	Track on right.
		GPS: N37°41.36' W118°37.49'
▼ 12.0	SO	Track on right.
0.8 ▲	SO	Track on left.
▼ 12.8	TL	T-intersection with 3S01 under power lines. Zero trip meter.
0.0 ▲		Continue to the north.
		GPS: N37°40.58' W118°38.22'
▼ 0.0		Continue to the southeast.
2.8 ▲	TR	Turn right onto smaller formed trail 3S49 and zero trip meter. Marker for 3S49 is on the right

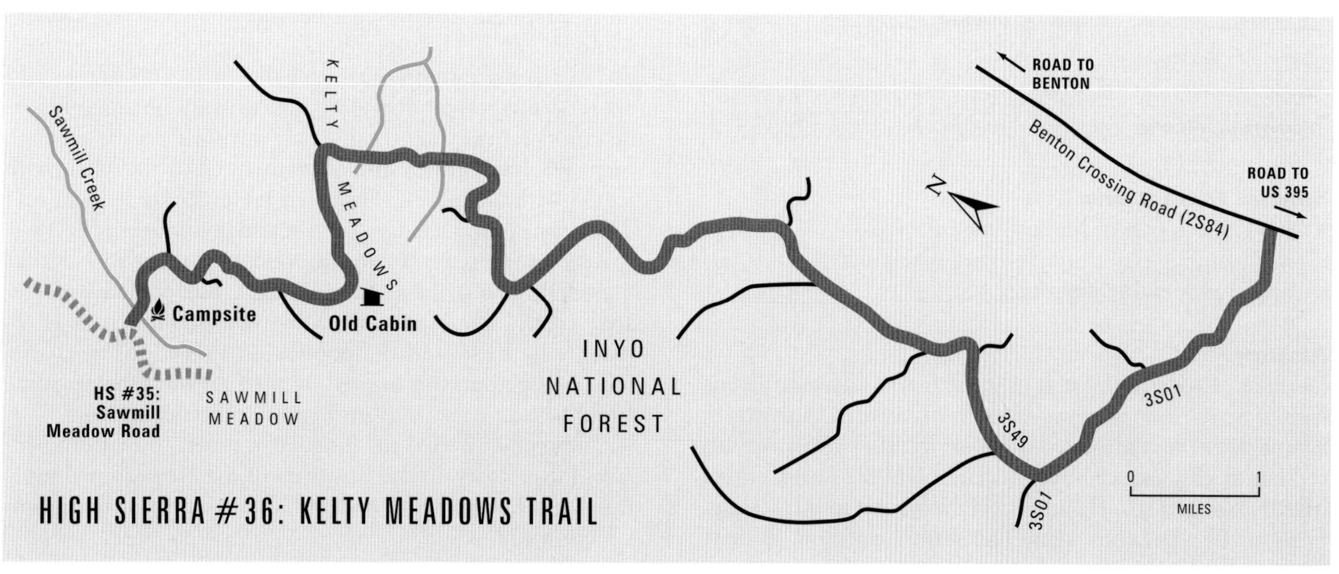

		of the trail and difficult to spot until you have made the turn.
▼ 0.5	SO	Enter wash.
2.3 ▲	SO	Exit wash.
▼ 0.6	SO	Exit wash.
2.2 ▲	SO	Enter wash.
▼ 1.0	SO	Cross through wash.
1.8 ▲	SO	Cross through wash.
▼ 1.2	SO	Track on left.
1.6 ▲	SO	Track on right.
		GPS: N37°40.20' W118°36.98'
▼ 1.5	SO	Cross through wash.
1.3 ▲	SO	Cross through wash.
▼ 2.7	SO	Track on left.
0.1 ▲	SO	Track on right.
▼ 2.8		Trail ends at intersection with paved Benton Crossing Road (2S84). Turn left for Benton; turn right for Toms Place and US 395.
0.0 ▲		Trail commences on paved Benton Crossing Road (2S84), 4.5 miles east of the intersection with Owens Gorge Road (4S02). Zero trip meter and turn west on graded dirt road. Turn is unmarked, but it is under a small set of power lines.
		GPS: N37°39.83' W118°35.43'

HIGH SIERRA #37

Deer Mountain Trail

Starting Point:	**US 395, 1 mile north of Owens River Road**
Finishing Point:	**California 203, 2.1 miles northwest of Mammoth Lakes**
Total Mileage:	**11.3 miles**
Unpaved Mileage:	**11.2 miles**
Driving Time:	**2 hours**
Elevation Range:	**7,600–8,200 feet**
Usually Open:	**April to November**
Best Time to Travel:	**April to November**
Difficulty Rating:	**3**
Scenic Rating:	**9**
Remoteness Rating:	**+0**

Special Attractions

- Inyo Craters, part of Mono Basin Lava Field.
- Small winding trail through Jeffrey pine forest.
- Popular mountain bike route.

History

Deadman Creek, at the start of this trail, may have earned its name when a prospector was killed by his partner. Farnsworth, a miner previously suspected of having killed a partner, arrived at Mammoth Lakes claiming he had found the Lost Cement Mine (see page 116). He wanted a new partner to finance diggings at the mine, but many miners shunned him. A newcomer, however, with $700 in his pocket and unaware of Farnsworth's reputation, decided to join him. Two days later Farnsworth reappeared in town riding his partner's horse and claiming that his partner had been killed by Indians. Given his track record, prospectors went to investigate. The search party found a decapitated body in a shallow grave and a head several yards away. Farnsworth had already skipped town by the time the search party returned, and the creek became known as Deadman Creek. Farnsworth got his comeuppance, however, when he fell to his death, kicked into a canyon and oblivion by one of his burros.

The undulating trail, also a mountain bike route, crosses open meadows on its way to Deer Mountain

Another explanation for Deadman Creek's name is that a mail carrier headed north from Mammoth Lakes to June Lake in bad weather never arrived. His body was found the following spring near the creek.

Two prospectors searching the Sierra northeast of Mammoth Mountain found what became known as the Cement Mine in 1857. They stumbled upon gold nuggets embedded in an odd outcrop of cement-like rock. One of the miners took nuggets to San Francisco to assay but died before he could return to the mine. He gave his doctor a rough map. Dr. Randall was one of many lured to the Mammoth region without success. However, James Parker led an expedition that found a ledge of silver and gold ore in June 1877 that he promoted as being the next best thing to Nevada's incredibly rich strike at Virginia City. The comparison created a rush. The Mammoth Mine was established in 1878, roads were built, and the population swelled. More than a thousand prospectors arrived by the following spring: some from Nevada via stage from Benton, others came from Bodie, and many traveled the long harsh desert route from Mojave. Prospectors on the west side of the Sierra joined mule trains at Oakhurst, in Madera County, and came across at Clover Meadow.

The vicinity of today's ski area and resort hummed with mining only briefly. It was too cold, and the rush that created Mammoth City, Mill City, and Pine City was over in just two years. The terrain and climate were inhospitable. Ore from the mine had to be transported down 3,000 feet to a mill. Winds blew down structures, and even mules, used to replace the tramway that hauled ore down the mountain, were blown off their feet. Returns were so low that shareholders and miners alike began to abandon the Mammoth region by 1880. Mining continued on a reduced scale into the 1890s with a few resurgences of activity in the 1930s and '50s. By then, mining was taking a backseat to recreational opportunities. Camping, hunting, and fishing drew many folks in the 1930s, and the snowfall that miners had found so daunting during long winters became an attraction. By the 1940s lodges catered to paying guests, who enjoyed the first rope tow on Mammoth Mountain. The *Inyo Register* reported on November 20, 1941, that more than 250 skiers visited Mammoth Mountain over the Thanksgiving weekend with the rope tow working overtime to accommodate the enthusiastic crowd. Mammoth Lakes has consolidated its position as a recreational mecca since then. A number of trails suitable for mountain bikes, snowmobiles, 4WDs, and ATVs surround the town.

Description

This formed trail winds through Jeffrey pine forests around Deer Mountain and the Inyo Craters. Initially, the trail leaves US 395 and follows graded dirt Deadman Creek Road alongside Deadman Creek. The road soon narrows to a single lane and passes the Deadman USFS Campground. It is an extremely pleasant drive along a single-track trail that sees heavy use by mountain bikes as well as vehicles, and it is marked frequently with bike trail markers. It can be heavily used, so be considerate of others. The trail passes through lava flows associated with the Inyo Craters, which erupted between 550 and 850 years ago. The trail surface is mainly smooth with a few lightly rutted sections; it is lumpy in some places with embedded rocks and exposed tree roots. There are some good undeveloped campsites and excellent views of the Sierra Nevada, particularly where the trail crosses an open meadow near Deer Mountain.

A short hiking trail leads to the ancient Inyo Craters

The Inyo Craters, 0.3 miles from the main trail, have small lakes, or explosion pits, on the crater floors. There is a large parking area and a short, gradually rising hiking trail to a viewpoint on the crater rim. The hike is an easy 0.5-mile round trip.

From Inyo Craters to Mammoth Lakes, the trail travels through more of the pine forest before exiting onto California 203 a couple of miles northwest of Mammoth Lakes. Mountain bikers have the choice of a more difficult single-track route as well as the main vehicle trail. The Inyo National Forest map does not show Deer Mountain Trail connecting through to California 203. However, the map is incorrect; the trail does run all the way out to the highway.

Jeffrey pines are the most predominate trees on the east side of the Sierra Nevada. One way to distinguish Jeffrey pines from the ponderosa pines of the west side is by their cones. The "gentle Jeffrey," as it is known, has smooth cones whereas the ponderosa has prickly cones.

Depending on snowfall, the trail may be open for longer than the times listed above. In years of light snowfall, it may be passable well into December. The road is not gated closed; rather it closes naturally as snow accumulates. The trail is a popular snowmobile route in winter.

Current Road Information

Inyo National Forest
Mammoth Ranger District
2500 Main Street
Mammoth Lakes, CA 93546
(760) 924-5500

Map References

BLM Benton Range
USFS Inyo National Forest
USGS 1:24,000 Old Mammoth, Mammoth Mt.
1:100,000 Benton Range
Maptech CD-ROM: High Sierra/Yosemite
Northern California Atlas & Gazetteer, p. 112
California Road & Recreation Atlas, p. 73
Other: Tom Harrison Maps—Mammoth High Country Trail Map

Route Directions

▼ 0.0		From US 395, zero trip meter and turn south on wide, graded dirt road at the sign for Deadman Creek Road. Turn is 1 mile north of Owens River Road, 8.3 miles north of the intersection with California 203.
3.8 ▲		Trail ends at intersection with US 395. Turn right for Mammoth Lakes; turn left for Lee Vining.
		GPS: N37°44.78' W118°58.77'
▼ 0.1	SO	Track on left and track on right along pipeline.
3.7 ▲	SO	Track on left and track on right along pipeline.
▼ 1.2	BL	Graded road on right is 2S49 to Crestview Guard Station.
2.6 ▲	BR	Graded road on left is 2S49 to Crestview Guard Station.
		GPS: N37°44.09' W118°59.77'
▼ 1.4	SO	Track on left and track on right; then second track on left.
2.4 ▲	SO	Track on right; then track on left and second track on right.
▼ 1.7	SO	Track on left.
2.1 ▲	SO	Track on right.

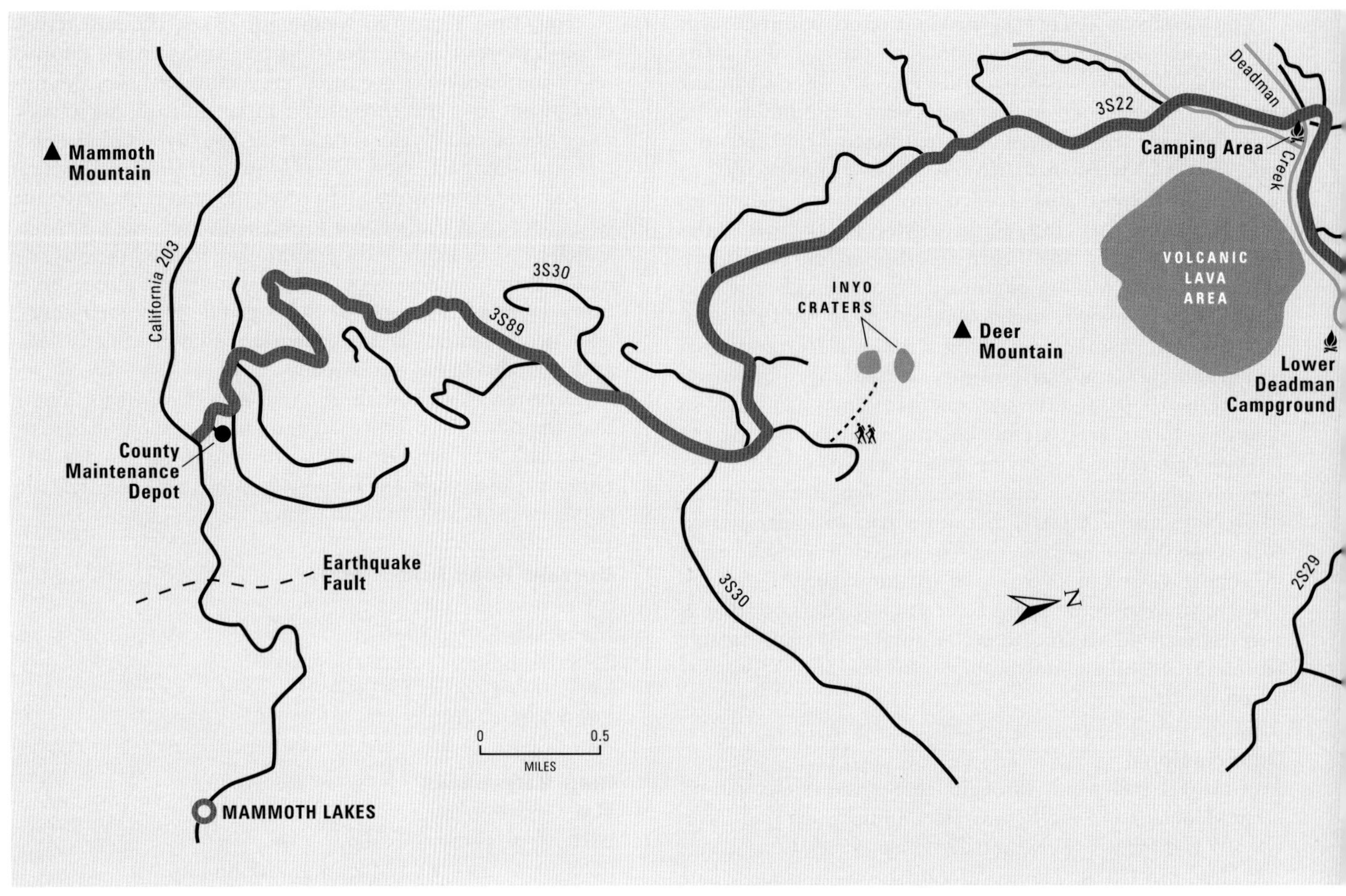

▼ 1.8	SO	Track on left; then track on right.
2.0 ▲	SO	Track on left; then track on right.
▼ 2.0	SO	Track on right.
1.8 ▲	SO	Track on left.
▼ 2.3	SO	Track on left is 2S29 to Mammoth Scenic Loop Road.
1.5 ▲	SO	Track on right is 2S29 to Mammoth Scenic Loop Road.
		GPS: N37°43.34′ W119°00.00′
▼ 2.4	SO	Track on right.
1.4 ▲	SO	Track on left.
▼ 2.5	SO	Track on right into Penny Pines Crestview Plantation.
1.3 ▲	SO	Track on left into Penny Pines Crestview Plantation.
▼ 2.7	SO	Track on right. Track on left goes into Lower Deadman USFS Campground.
1.1 ▲	SO	Track on left. Track on right goes into Lower Deadman USFS Campground.
		GPS: N37°43.33′ W119°00.42′
▼ 2.8	SO	Obsidian Flat Group Campground on right and Upper Deadman USFS Campground on left.
1.0 ▲	SO	Obsidian Flat Group Campground on left and Upper Deadman USFS Campground on right.
		GPS: N37°43.31′ W119°00.63′
▼ 3.2	SO	Two tracks on left.
0.6 ▲	SO	Two tracks on right.
▼ 3.3	SO	Track on right is 2S50 and track on right. Volcanic area is directly on the left.
0.5 ▲	SO	Track on left is 2S50 and track on left. Volcanic area is directly on the right.
▼ 3.7	SO	Track on right and track on left into camping area.
0.1 ▲	SO	Track on left and track on right into camping area.
		GPS: N37°43.18′ W119°01.48′
▼ 3.8	TL	Track on right. Turn left onto well-used formed trail. There is a mountain bike route marker at the intersection. Zero trip meter.
0.0 ▲		Continue to the east.
		GPS: N37°43.19′ W119°01.56′
▼ 0.0		Continue to the south.
3.6 ▲	TR	T-intersection with graded dirt Deadman Creek Road. Zero trip meter. There is a mountain bike route marker at the intersection and a small trail ahead.
▼ 0.1	BL	Campsite on right; then cross over Deadman Creek on bridge. Bear left after bridge following the mountain bike route marker. Track on right. Remain on main trail for the next 0.6 miles—small tracks on right and left mainly lead to undeveloped campsites.
3.5 ▲	BR	Bear right following the mountain bike route marker and cross over Deadman Creek on bridge. Track on left. Campsite on left after bridge.
▼ 0.7	SO	Track on right; then cross through a branch of Deadman Creek; then second track on right. Route is marked 3S22.
2.9 ▲	BR	Track on left; then cross through a branch of Deadman Creek; then second track on left. Remain on main trail for next 0.6 miles—small

tracks on right and left mainly lead to undeveloped campsites.

GPS: N37°42.65′ W119°01.67′

▼ 0.8 — SO — Track on left toward lava flow.
2.8 ▲ — SO — Track on right toward lava flow.

▼ 1.1 — BR — Track on left.
2.5 ▲ — SO — Track on right.

▼ 1.5 — SO — Small track on right.
2.1 ▲ — SO — Small track on left.

▼ 1.7 — SO — Track on left.
1.9 ▲ — SO — Track on right.

GPS: N37°41.92′ W119°01.55′

▼ 1.8 — SO — Track on right.
1.8 ▲ — SO — Track on left.

▼ 1.9 — SO — Track on right.
1.7 ▲ — SO — Track on left.

▼ 2.9 — SO — Track on right.
0.7 ▲ — BR — Track on left.

GPS: N37°40.95′ W119°01.05′

▼ 3.3 — TR — Turn right, following mountain bike route marker.
0.3 ▲ — TL — Turn left, remaining on 3S22.

GPS: N37°41.06′ W119°00.67′

▼ 3.6 — TR — Turn right onto larger trail marked 3S89 and zero trip meter. Track on left at sign goes 0.3 miles toward the Inyo Craters.
0.0 ▲ — Continue to the west.

GPS: N37°41.09′ W119°00.38′

▼ 0.0 — Continue to the south.
0.3 ▲ — TL — Turn left on smaller formed trail marked 3S22, following the mountain bike route marker. Zero trip meter. Track ahead at sign goes 0.3 miles toward the Inyo Craters.

▼ 0.1 — SO — Track on right.
0.2 ▲ — SO — Track on left.

▼ 0.3 — TR — Turn right onto well-used dirt road, following sign for Upper Dry Creek Road. It is also marked as a bike route. Zero trip meter.
0.0 ▲ — Continue to the west.

GPS: N37°40.91′ W119°00.28′

▼ 0.0 — Continue to the southwest.
3.6 ▲ — TL — Turn left onto dirt road, following sign for Inyo Craters. It is also marked as a bike route. Zero trip meter.

▼ 0.4 — BL — Track on right is 3S30 (shown on the forest map as 3S20). Bear left onto 3S89.
3.2 ▲ — SO — Track on left is 3S30 (shown on forest map as 3S20).

GPS: N37°40.59′ W119°00.57′

▼ 0.8 — BR — Track on left. Remain on 3S89.
2.8 ▲ — SO — Track on right. Remain on 3S89.

GPS: N37°40.34′ W119°00.76′

▼ 0.9 — SO — Track on right.
2.7 ▲ — SO — Track on left.

▼ 1.0 — SO — Track on right.
2.6 ▲ — SO — Track on left.

▼ 1.5 — SO — Track on right.
2.1 ▲ — SO — Track on left.

▼ 1.8 — SO — Track on right.
1.8 ▲ — SO — Track on left.

▼ 2.2 — SO — Mountain View Trail—difficult mountain bike route—on right. Main trail is marked Inyo Craters Mountain Bike Trail.
1.4 ▲ — SO — Mountain View Trail on left. Main trail is marked Inyo Craters Mountain Bike Trail.

GPS: N37°39.35′ W119°01.25′

▼ 2.6 — SO — Mountain View Trail leaves on the left.
1.0 ▲ — SO — Mountain View Trail—difficult mountain bike route—enters on right.

GPS: N37°39.50′ W119°00.96′

▼ 3.1 — SO — Track on right; then track on left. Remain on 3S89.
0.5 ▲ — BR — Track on right; then bear right at fork, remaining on 3S89.

GPS: N37°39.19′ W119°00.90′

▼ 3.3 — SO — Track on left.
0.3 ▲ — SO — Track on right.

▼ 3.4 — SO — Track on right and track on left.
0.2 ▲ — SO — Track on right and track on left.

▼ 3.5 — TR — Turn right onto small paved road. County maintenance depot is on the left.
0.1 ▲ — TL — Turn left immediately in front of the county maintenance depot onto small formed trail marked 3S89.

▼ 3.6 — Trail ends at T-intersection with California 203, 2.1 miles northwest of Mammoth Lakes. Turn left for Mammoth Lakes. There is a viewpoint over an earthquake fault 0.5 miles toward Mammoth Lakes on the left side of the highway.
0.0 ▲ — Trail commences on California 203, 2.1 miles northwest of Mammoth Lakes. Zero trip meter and turn northwest on small paved road that leads to the county maintenance depot. There is a faded sign at the turn for 3S89 Mountain Bike Trail.

GPS: N37°39.05′ W119°00.57′

HIGH SIERRA #38

Laurel Lakes Trail

Starting Point:	**Old Mammoth Road, 0.8 miles south of Mammoth Lakes**
Finishing Point:	**Laurel Lakes**
Total Mileage:	**8.7 miles (one-way)**
Unpaved Mileage:	**8.1 miles**
Driving Time:	**1.5 hours (one-way)**
Elevation Range:	**7,300–10,000 feet**
Usually Open:	**April to November**
Best Time to Travel:	**April to November**
Difficulty Rating:	**4**
Scenic Rating:	**10**
Remoteness Rating:	**+0**

Special Attractions

- Incredibly scenic trail that runs deep into the Sierra Nevada.
- Long sections of loose shelf road.
- Beautiful Laurel Lakes.

History

The Laurel Lakes, at the edge of the John Muir Wilderness, sit below Bloody Mountain. The mountain's name comes either from the blood-red color of its rocks or from a bloody fight that took place when Sheriff Robert Morrison of Benton and a posse caught up with escaped convicts from the Nevada State Penitentiary in September 1871. Morrison was killed at nearby Convict Lake (see High Sierra #39: Convict Lake Overlook Trail), but his posse eventually captured the convicts.

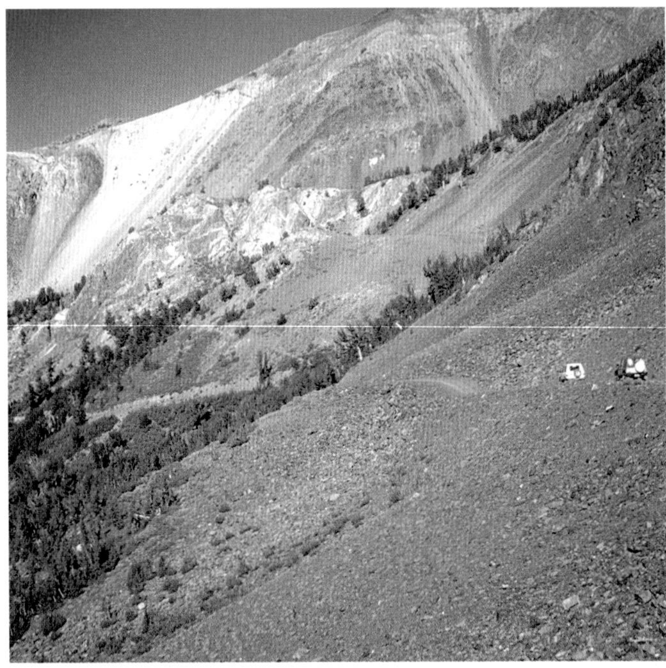

Vehicles crossing the single-lane shelf road on the talus slope of Laurel Mountain

Clear, cold Laurel Lakes attract fishermen and photographers alike

Description

Although the 4WD section of this trail is only 5 miles long, do not underestimate the time required to drive it. The rough and rocky trail is slow going, but the scenery is so outstanding that you will undoubtedly take extra time to admire and photograph the vistas.

The first few miles of the trail wind away from Mammoth Lakes along graded gravel Sherwin Creek Road. After 3.7 miles, the route turns onto a single-track formed trail that immediately starts to climb into the Sierra Nevada. A forest service sign designates the road as suitable for high-clearance vehicles, but because of the loose surface, 4WD is definitely recommended. The trail follows a series of easygoing switchbacks to a crest before running along Laurel Canyon. It runs high along the valley wall, traveling as a single-lane shelf road for most of its length. Passing places are limited, especially in the upper sections of the canyon, and you should be prepared to back up to allow oncoming vehicles to pass regardless of which way you are traveling. The surface is uneven and has embedded rocks and loose soil. It crosses a couple of rubbley talus slopes, but the entire trail should be within the capabilities of any high-clearance 4WD.

The final descent to Laurel Lakes includes a very tight switchback; most vehicles will need to back up to complete the turn. The trail ends on the banks of Laurel Lakes. You can fish for trout at the lakes between the last Saturday in April and October 31. The trail is likely to be blocked by snow between November and April.

Current Road Information

Inyo National Forest
Mammoth Ranger District
2500 Main Street
Mammoth Lakes, CA 93546
(760) 924-5500

Map References

BLM Benton Range
USFS Inyo National Forest
USGS 1:24,000 Old Mammoth, Bloody Mt.
1:100,000 Benton Range

Maptech CD-ROM: High Sierra/Yosemite
Northern California Atlas & Gazetteer, p. 112
California Road & Recreation Atlas, p. 78
Other: Tom Harrison Maps—Mammoth High Country Trail Map

Route Directions

▼ 0.0		From Mammoth Lakes, at the intersection of California 203 and Old Mammoth Road, proceed south on Old Mammoth Road for 0.8 miles. Immediately after crossing over Mammoth Creek, zero trip meter and turn east on paved Sherwin Creek Road.
3.7 ▲		Trail ends at T-intersection with Old Mammoth Road. Turn right for Mammoth Lakes; turn left for Old Mammoth.
		GPS: N37°38.09' W118°57.92'
▼ 0.2	SO	Road is now graded gravel and is designated 4S08.
3.5 ▲	SO	Road is now paved.
▼ 0.4	SO	Track on right and track on left.
3.3 ▲	SO	Track on right and track on left.
▼ 0.9	SO	Road is now paved.
2.8 ▲	SO	Road turns to graded gravel.
▼ 1.3	SO	Track on right goes to Sherwin Lakes Trailhead and motorcross area. Road is now graded gravel.
2.4 ▲	SO	Track on left goes to Sherwin Lakes Trailhead and motorcross area. Road is now paved.
		GPS: N37°37.73' W118°56.77'
▼ 1.7	SO	Cross over Sherwin Creek.
2.0 ▲	SO	Cross over Sherwin Creek.
▼ 1.8	SO	Sherwin Creek Picnic Area on right—day use only; then track on left into Sherwin Creek USFS Campground.
1.9 ▲	SO	Track on right into Sherwin Creek USFS Campground; then Sherwin Creek Picnic Area on left—day use only.
		GPS: N37°37.72' W118°56.22'
▼ 2.1	SO	Track on right.
1.6 ▲	SO	Track on left.
▼ 2.3	SO	Closure gate.
1.4 ▲	SO	Closure gate.
▼ 2.4	SO	Track on left.
1.3 ▲	SO	Track on right.
▼ 2.7	SO	Track on right; then track on left.
1.0 ▲	SO	Track on right; then track on left.
▼ 2.8	SO	Track on right.
0.9 ▲	SO	Track on left.
▼ 3.0	SO	Track on right is Summers Road.
0.7 ▲	SO	Track on left is Summers Road.
		GPS: N37°37.35' W118°55.13'
▼ 3.1	SO	Track on left.
0.6 ▲	SO	Track on right.
▼ 3.7	TR	Turn right onto Laurel Lakes Trail. There is a sign for Laurel Lakes and it is marked 4S86. Zero trip meter.
0.0 ▲		Continue to the northwest.
		GPS: N37°37.42' W118°54.35'
▼ 0.0		Continue to the south.
▼ 0.1	SO	Cattle guard.
▼ 1.5	SO	End of switchbacks. Trail levels out.
▼ 1.7	SO	Cattle guard.
		GPS: N37°36.37' W118°55.08'
▼ 2.0	SO	Track on right to campsite under large aspens by Laurel Creek.
		GPS: N37°36.13' W118°54.97'
▼ 3.1	BL	Track on right.
▼ 4.6	SO	Start of final descent to Laurel Lakes.
▼ 4.7	SO	Final tight switchback—most vehicles will need to back up to make the turn.
▼ 4.9	SO	Track on left.
▼ 5.0		Trail ends at the edge of Laurel Lakes. There is a turnaround area. The shore is very rocky and not suitable for camping.
		GPS: N37°34.57' W118°54.72'

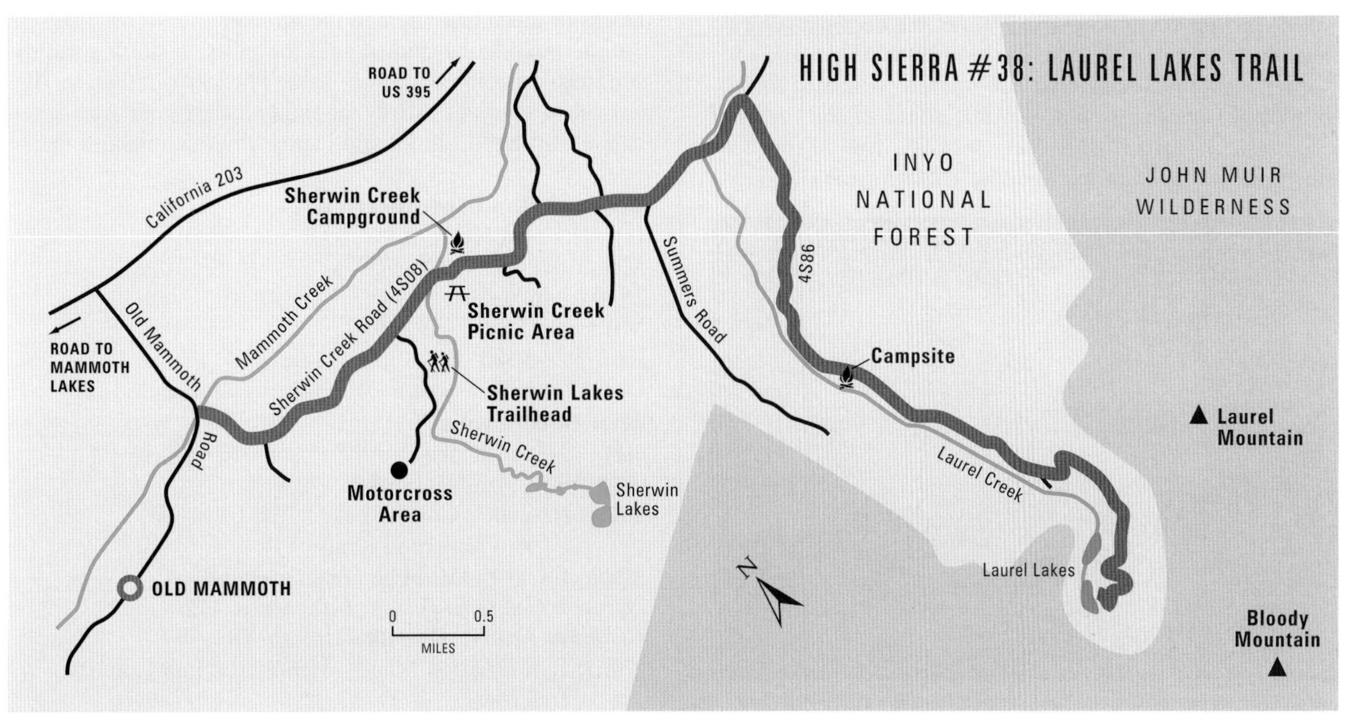

HIGH SIERRA #39

Convict Lake Overlook Trail

Starting Point:	**US 395, 5.6 miles south of the turn to Mammoth Lakes**
Finishing Point:	**Convict Lake Overlook**
Total Mileage:	**4 miles (one-way)**
Unpaved Mileage:	**3.7 miles**
Driving Time:	**30 minutes (one-way)**
Elevation Range:	**7,000–8,200 feet**
Usually Open:	**April to November**
Best Time to Travel:	**April to November**
Difficulty Rating:	**3**
Scenic Rating:	**9**
Remoteness Rating:	**+0**

Special Attractions

■ Viewpoint over beautiful Convict Lake.

History

Convict Lake was named for escapees from the Nevada State Penitentiary in 1871. Sheriff Robert Morrison of Benton and his posse caught up with them at the lake and a shootout ensued. Morrison was killed, and the convicts escaped temporarily. They were captured some 10 miles away. Morrison's name was given to Mount Morrison, immediately south of Convict Lake, high above the end of this trail. Bloody Mountain, about 3 miles southeast of Convict Lake, was the site of a skirmish between the escapees and posse. However, the deep red color of the mountain's rocks may also be the origin of the name.

McGee Mountain, southeast of the lake, is named for anthropologist, geologist, and one-time editor of the *National Geographic Magazine* WJ McGee. McGee surveyed much of this region of the Great Basin in the 1880s for the U.S. Geological Survey. In the 1930s, McGee Mountain was the place to ski. The McGee Ski School was instrumental in hosting ski races and other events in the 1930s and '40s. The base of the rope tow was located on the northeastern slope of the mountain, just off old highway 395, approximately a mile from the start this trail.

The deep blue waters of Convict Lake viewed from the end of the trail

Lake Crowley, the prominent body of water seen to the east when returning to US 395, is owned by the city of Los Angeles. The reservoir, fed by the Owens River and streams diverted from Mono Lake, formed behind the Long Valley Dam, which was built in 1941. It is part of the 238-mile-long Los Angeles Aqueduct, which supplies water to Los Angeles and helped transform the San Joaquin Valley into a rich agricultural region at the expense of the Owens Valley. Ironically, the lake was named for Father John Crowley, an advocate for Owens Valley farmers who lost homes, land, and water to the Owens Valley Project. Recently, Lake Crowley has become one of the most popular fishing spots of the eastern Sierra. As many as 30,000 anglers turn up for opening day each year to try to catch the lake's trout and perch.

Description

Convict Lake is one of the most popular day trips from Mammoth Lakes. The lake has parking and picnic areas and a small marina and café. It is set in a valley, between Sevehah Cliff on the west and Mount Morrison to the south.

If you just want to enjoy the beautiful Convict Lake from afar, take this dirt trail to the viewpoint. The only people you are likely to meet along this trail are shepherds with their sheep and dogs.

The trail heads off US 395 along Mount Morrison Road and almost immediately becomes a dirt road, just before the Mount Morrison Cemetery, established in 1989. It follows along small power lines for a mile or so before swinging alongside a small creek to enter the sage-covered Tobacco Flat. Flocks of sheep graze here in the summer.

The trail climbs gradually up the valley to finish abruptly at a steep drop above Convict Lake. The lake can be seen 700 feet below, framed by hardy mountain mahoganies, with Sevehah Cliff rising behind it and Laurel Mountain behind that.

Current Road Information

Inyo National Forest
Mammoth Ranger District
2500 Main Street
Mammoth Lakes, CA 93546
(760) 924-5500

Map References

BLM Benton Range
USFS Inyo National Forest
USGS 1:24,000 Convict Lake
1:100,000 Benton Range
Maptech CD-ROM: High Sierra/Yosemite
Northern California Atlas & Gazetteer, p. 112
California Road & Recreation Atlas, p. 78
Other: Tom Harrison Maps—Mammoth High Country Trail Map

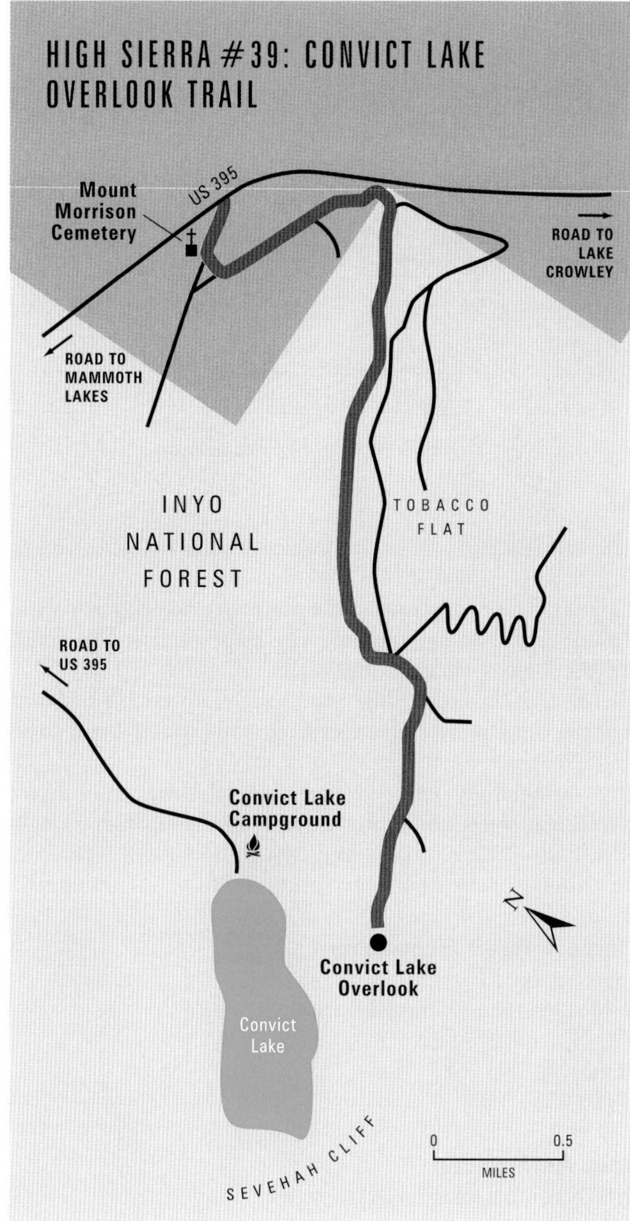

Route Directions

▼ 0.0		From US 395, 5.6 miles south of the turn to Mammoth Lakes, turn southwest on paved Mount Morrison Road and zero trip meter. There is a sign for the road on the highway.
		GPS: N37°36.96′ W118°48.84′
▼ 0.3	TL	Turn left onto graded dirt road immediately before the Mount Morrison Cemetery.
		GPS: N37°36.91′ W118°49.08′
▼ 0.4	TL	Turn left and follow alongside power lines.
▼ 0.7	SO	Track on right.
▼ 1.0	SO	Track on left through gate.
▼ 1.1	SO	Track on left.
		GPS: N37°36.48′ W118°48.47′
▼ 1.6	SO	Track on left.
▼ 1.7	SO	Pass through fence line.
▼ 2.7	SO	Faint track on right.
▼ 2.8	SO	Track on right.
		GPS: N37°35.70′ W118°49.98′
▼ 2.9	TR	4-way intersection. Zero trip meter.
		GPS: N37°35.68′ W118°49.92′
▼ 0.0		Continue to the south.
▼ 0.2	TR	Track straight ahead goes 0.4 miles to small diggings.
▼ 0.7	SO	Track on left and water trough on right.
▼ 1.1		Track on left; then trail ends at a viewpoint over Convict Lake. The trail continues for 0.2 miles before ending at a turnaround. This is a good place to park and hike farther up the valley. The track on left dead-ends a short distance up the hill (it has no good turnaround point).
		GPS: N37°35.23′ W118°50.83′

HIGH SIERRA #40

Casa Diablo Road

Starting Point:	**Owens Gorge Road, 9 miles north of Toms Place**
Finishing Point:	**US 6, 1 mile north of Bishop**
Total Mileage:	**23.5 miles, plus 4.4-mile spur to the swimming hole**
Unpaved Mileage:	**21.2 miles, plus 3.5 miles of the spur**
Driving Time:	**2 hours**
Elevation Range:	**4,200–7,600 feet**
Usually Open:	**April to December**
Best Time to Travel:	**April to December**
Difficulty Rating:	**1**
Scenic Rating:	**8**
Remoteness Rating:	**+0**

Special Attractions

- Casa Diablo Mine.
- Volcanic Tableland and views of the White Mountains.
- Secluded desert swimming hole.
- Climbing opportunities at the Happy and Sad Boulders.

History

Casa Diablo Mountain was named after the Casa Diablo Mine, established in 1895 to extract gold and silver. The route crosses a portion of the 325-square-mile Volcanic Tableland, composed of tuff, a volcanic rock of compacted pumice or ash, in this case, likely the result of numerous volcanic eruptions to the north.

Fish Slough, occasionally spelled Fish Slu, to the northeast of the road, is now included in an area of critical environmental concern. The slough was once called Sand Springs because of the number of sandy springs along its course. With its cool, bubbling springs, Fish Slough, between Benton, Adobe Meadows, and Bodie to the north and Bishop to the south, was an obvious spot for a stage station to change horses and refresh passengers. The road to Mammoth, which this route partially follows, intersected at the station, too.

The United Stage Company, a branch of the famed Wells, Fargo & Company, established a station at Fish Slough with Phillip Keough as superintendent in 1865. Travelers preferred the Fish Slough route in winter because mountain routes were often covered with snow. Generally the Fish Slough route was clear, but it could be blocked by snow for several weeks at a time, disrupting mail and passenger services. There was enormous pressure to get stagecoaches through at all costs—even if passengers had to get out and push, because when the mail wasn't delivered, contractors weren't paid.

Description

There are two main entrances to the Casa Diablo (Spanish for "House of the Devil") Road proper. This route takes the lesser-used entrance, which initially follows a small formed trail through open pine forests scattered with large red boulders. The surface is smooth and slightly sandy in places; a carefully driven passenger vehicle can negotiate it in dry weather. This dramatic landscape has many good undeveloped campsites among boulders beneath the pines.

The route then joins the main graded road that runs north-south along the western side of the boulder-strewn Casa Diablo Mountain. This is a wide, smooth graded road that runs across open landscape, offering excellent views west of the Sierra Nevada. Campers should consider finding a site along the first 6 miles of trail because the landscape is too exposed after that to provide good campsites.

Casa Diablo Mine is set in a tight valley on the northwest flank of Casa Diablo Mountain. Large tailings piles and the remains of old stone walls and adits can still be seen. Upon exiting Inyo National Forest, the route runs down onto the BLM-managed Volcanic Tableland with views of the White Mountains to the east and the Sierra Nevada to the west. Recently, the area has become a favorite place among rock

This welcoming, clear spring along Fish Slough in the Owens Valley is a relief on hot days

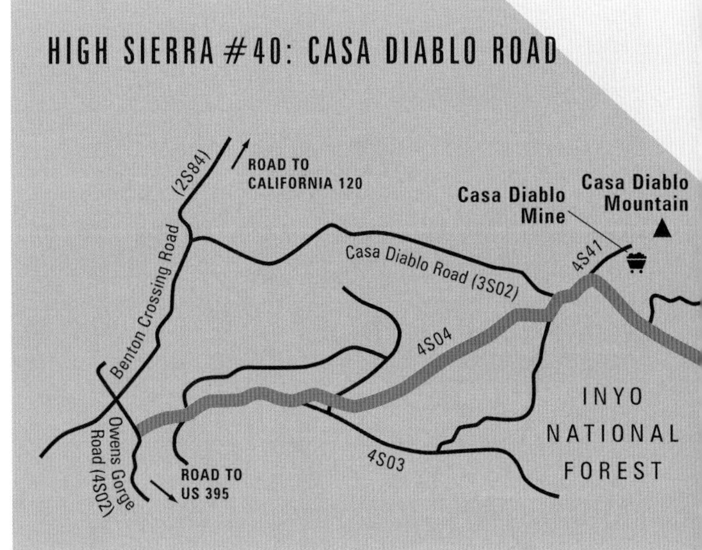

climbers. The rock shapes and surfaces provide climbers with a number of challenging routes. The Happy and Sad Boulders are just some of what the area offers.

The trail finishes 1 mile north of Bishop on US 6. Note that the route number changes from 4S04 to 3S02 and back to 4S04.

A wonderfully secluded, cool, crystal-clear, reed-fringed spring is 4 miles north of the main trail along Fish Slough Road. The water is usually deep enough for a swim. There are no camping places around the spring and fishing is prohibited.

Current Road Information

Inyo National Forest
White Mountain Ranger District
798 North Main Street
Bishop, CA 93514
(760) 873-2500

Map References

BLM Benton Range, Bishop
USFS Inyo National Forest
USGS 1:24,000 Watterson Canyon, Toms Place, Casa Diablo Mt., Rovana, Fish Slough
1:100,000 Benton Range, Bishop
Maptech CD-ROM: High Sierra/Yosemite; Kings Canyon/Death Valley
Northern California Atlas & Gazetteer, pp. 113, 123
California Road & Recreation Atlas, p. 79

Route Directions

▼ 0.0		From Owens Gorge Road, 9 miles north of intersection with US 395 at Toms Place, zero trip meter and turn east on formed trail, following sign for Casa Diablo. Trail is marked 4S04. Track on left.
2.1 ▲		Track on right; then trail ends at T-intersection with graded dirt Owens Gorge Road. Turn left to exit to US 395 at Toms Place.
		GPS: N37°37.91' W118°39.38'
▼ 0.1	SO	Track on right.

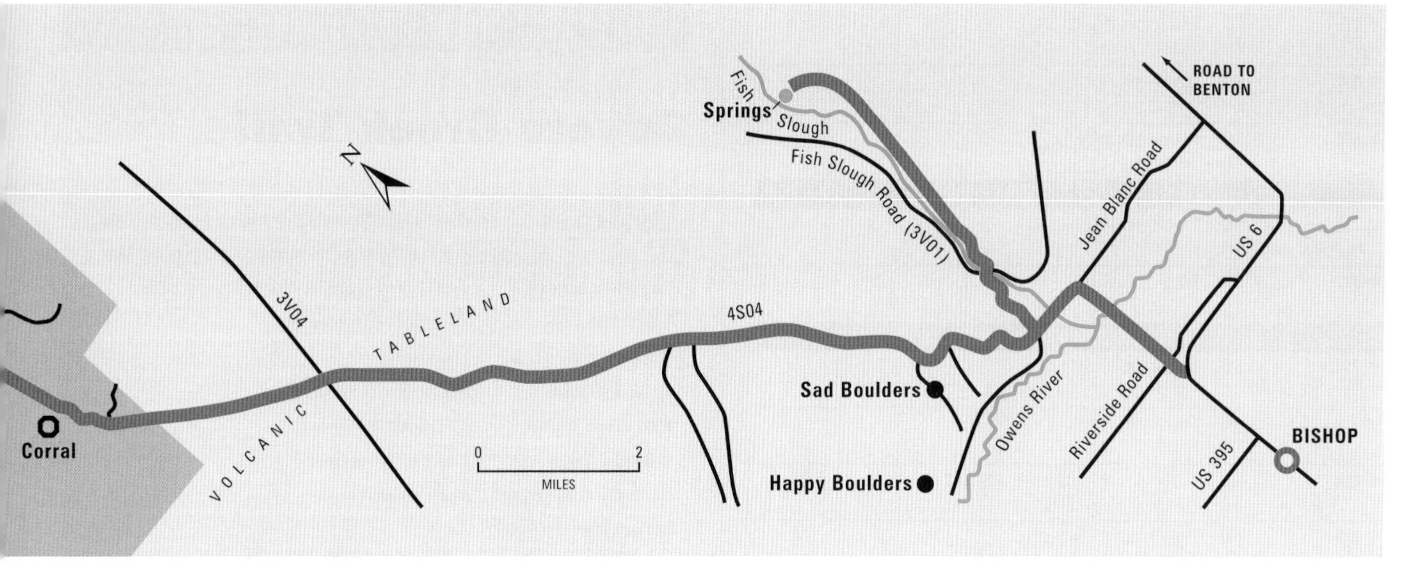

2.0 ▲ SO Track on left.

▼ 0.2 SO Track on right; then track on left.
1.9 ▲ SO Track on right; then track on left.

▼ 0.7 SO Track on left and track on right.
1.4 ▲ SO Track on left and track on right.

▼ 1.1 SO Track on left.
1.0 ▲ SO Track on right.

▼ 1.7 SO Track on left.
0.4 ▲ SO Track on right.

▼ 2.1 BL Track on right is 4S03. Follow sign for Casa Diablo Mountain. Zero trip meter.
0.0 ▲ Continue to the northwest on 4S04.

GPS: N37°36.74′ W118°37.66′

▼ 0.0 Continue to the east on 4S04.
3.7 ▲ BR Track on left is 4S03. Zero trip meter.

▼ 0.5 SO Track on right and track on left.
3.2 ▲ SO Track on right and track on left.

GPS: N37°36.43′ W118°37.39′

▼ 2.3 SO Track on left.
1.4 ▲ SO Track on right.

▼ 3.4 BL Track on right.
0.3 ▲ BR Track on left.

GPS: N37°35.18′ W118°34.64′

▼ 3.7 TR T-intersection with wide, graded Casa Diablo Road (3S02). Follow sign for Casa Diablo and zero trip meter.
0.0 ▲ Continue to the southwest.

GPS: N37°35.23′ W118°34.34′

▼ 0.0 Continue to the east. Casa Diablo Mountain is now directly ahead.
0.4 ▲ TL Turn left onto smaller trail marked 4S04. There is a directional sign at the intersection. Zero trip meter.

▼ 0.4 BR Track on left is 4S41, which goes 0.6 miles (keeping right at the intersections) to the remains of the Casa Diablo Mine. Zero trip meter.
0.0 ▲ Continue to the northwest on main graded road.

GPS: N37°35.14′ W118°33.92′

▼ 0.0 Continue to the southeast on main graded road.
6.0 ▲ BL Track on right is 4S41, which goes 0.6 miles (keeping right at the intersections) to the remains of the Casa Diablo Mine. Zero trip meter.

▼ 0.9 SO Track on left and track on right.
5.1 ▲ SO Track on left and track on right.

▼ 2.5 SO Corral on right.
3.5 ▲ SO Corral on left.

▼ 3.3 SO Track on right through pull-in area and small track on left.

Smooth going on Casa Diablo Road above the Owens Valley

2.7 ▲ SO Track on left through pull-in area and small track on right.

GPS: N37°32.32′ W118°33.33′

▼ 3.8 SO Leaving Inyo National Forest.
2.2 ▲ SO Entering Inyo National Forest.

GPS: N37°32.03′ W118°32.89′

▼ 6.0 SO Track on right and track on left under power lines is 3V04. Zero trip meter.
0.0 ▲ Continue to the northwest on 4S04.

GPS: N37°30.80′ W118°31.00′

▼ 0.0 Continue to the southeast.
9.0 ▲ SO Track on left and track on right under power lines is 3V04. Zero trip meter.

▼ 1.2 SO Track on right.
7.8 ▲ SO Track on left.

▼ 4.2	SO	Track on right.
4.8 ▲	SO	Track on left.
▼ 4.4	SO	Track on right.
4.6 ▲	SO	Track on left.
▼ 5.7	SO	Track on left.
3.3 ▲	SO	Track on right.
		GPS: N37°27.17' W118°26.51'
▼ 7.0	SO	Track on left.
2.0 ▲	SO	Track on right.
▼ 7.2	SO	Track on right.
1.8 ▲	SO	Track on left.
		GPS: N37°26.07' W118°25.71'
▼ 7.4	SO	Track on right.
1.6 ▲	SO	Track on left.
▼ 7.7	SO	Track on right.
1.3 ▲	SO	Track on left.
▼ 8.2	SO	Track on left; then track on right.
0.8 ▲	SO	Track on left; then track on right.
▼ 8.4	SO	Two tracks on right.
0.6 ▲	SO	Two tracks on left.
▼ 8.6	SO	Track on right.
0.4 ▲	SO	Track on left.
▼ 9.0	SO	4-way intersection. Zero trip meter. Paved Fish Slough Road (3V01) on left is the start of short spur to the swimming hole. Graded road on right. There is a BLM notice board at the intersection.
0.0 ▲		Continue to the west. Road is now graded dirt.
		GPS: N37°25.19' W118°24.53'

Spur to the Swimming Hole

▼ 0.0		Turn north at 4-way intersection and follow along paved Fish Slough Road.
▼ 0.9	TR	Turn right onto unmarked, formed dirt trail and cross over Fish Slough.
		GPS: N37°25.99' W118°24.37'
▼ 1.0	BL	Bear left and follow main formed trail.
▼ 4.4		Fenced springs on left make for a perfect swimming hole.
		GPS: N37°28.84' W118°24.13'

Continuation of Main Trail

▼ 0.0		Continue to the east. Road is now paved.
2.3 ▲	SO	4-way intersection. Zero trip meter and continue on graded dirt road 4S04. Paved Fish Slough Road (3V01) on right is the start of short spur to the swimming hole. Graded road on left. There is a BLM notice board at the intersection.
		GPS: N37°25.19' W118°24.53'
▼ 0.4	SO	Cattle guard.
1.9 ▲	SO	Cattle guard.
▼ 0.6	BR	Jean Blanc Road on left.
1.7 ▲	SO	Jean Blanc Road on right.
▼ 2.1	SO	Graded dirt road on left and right is Riverside Road.
0.2 ▲	SO	Graded dirt road on left and right is Riverside Road.
▼ 2.3	SO	Trail ends at T-intersection with US 6. Turn right for Bishop.
0.0 ▲		Trail commences on US 6, 1 mile north of Bishop. Zero trip meter and turn northwest on paved road, marked Five Bridges Road.
		GPS: N37°23.67' W118°23.62'

Coyote Creek Trail

Starting Point:	**West Line Street, 2.6 miles west of the intersection with Main Street in Bishop**
Finishing Point:	**Viewpoint over Rocky Bottom Lake**
Total Mileage:	**16.2 miles (one-way)**
Unpaved Mileage:	**16.2 miles**
Driving Time:	**2.5 hours (one-way)**
Elevation Range:	**4,400–10,800 feet**
Usually Open:	**April to November**
Best Time to Travel:	**April to November**
Difficulty Rating:	**3**
Scenic Rating:	**9**
Remoteness Rating:	**+1**

Special Attractions

- Steep trail that accesses the eastern slopes of the Sierra Nevada.
- Fishing at Rocky Bottom Lake.
- Salty Peterson Mine remains.

Description

A network of trails popular with ATVs and 4WDs traverses a beautiful area on the eastern flank of the Sierra Nevada, immediately west of Bishop. Coyote Creek Trail, the main trail into this area, leaves Bishop and crosses BLM land before entering Inyo National Forest.

The trail begins in the sagebrush-covered Owens Valley

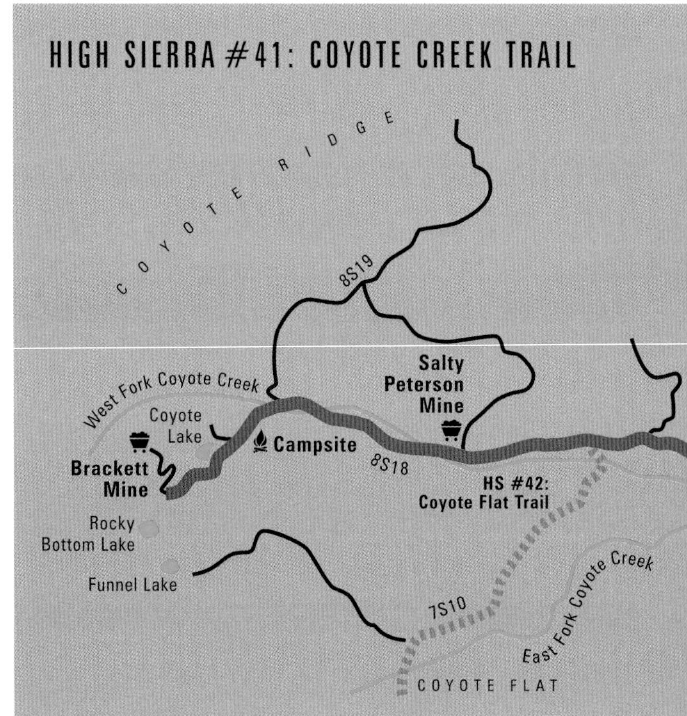

Granite boulders dot the landscape around the trail as it climbs out of the valley

and switchbacks steeply to gain more than 2,000 feet in only a couple of miles, passing pinyons and junipers at the higher elevations. The uneven surface is a mixture of rock and sand, which generally offers good traction. One short, steep section has had some rough tarmac added. The trail winds through a deep valley with large jumbled granite boulders before climbing out of the head of the valley toward the sagebrush-covered Coyote Flat, which, at over 10,000 feet, offers great views of the Sierra Nevada and Middle Palisade Glacier.

The trail passes the Peterson Mill site, where a couple of sheds and some wooden flooring remains are hidden in the vegetation, before intersecting with High Sierra #42: Coyote Flat Trail, a pretty trail that heads south to a remote camping area. The remains of the Salty Peterson Mine are a short distance farther along the main route.

Coyote Creek Trail continues alongside West Fork Coyote Creek in a narrow valley. It becomes rougher, but is still easily driven by most high-clearance 4WDs. The trail finishes at a viewpoint above small Rocky Bottom Lake. Scree slopes and the bare peaks of the Sierra rise above the lake.

Current Road Information

Inyo National Forest
White Mountain Ranger District
798 North Main Street
Bishop, CA 93514
(760) 873-2500

Map References

BLM Bishop
USFS Inyo National Forest
USGS 1:24,000 Bishop, Coyote Flat, Mt. Thompson
1:100,000 Bishop
Maptech CD-ROM: Kings Canyon/Death Valley
Northern California Atlas & Gazetteer, p. 123
California Road & Recreation Atlas, p. 79

Route Directions

▼ 0.0		In the center of Bishop, at the intersection of Main Street and West Line Street, proceed west on West Line Street for 2.6 miles. Turn south on Reata Road and zero trip meter. Remain on main paved road, ignoring turns to the right and left.
		GPS: N37°21.69' W118°26.54'
▼ 1.1	TR	Turn right onto graded dirt road at unmarked intersection. Zero trip meter.

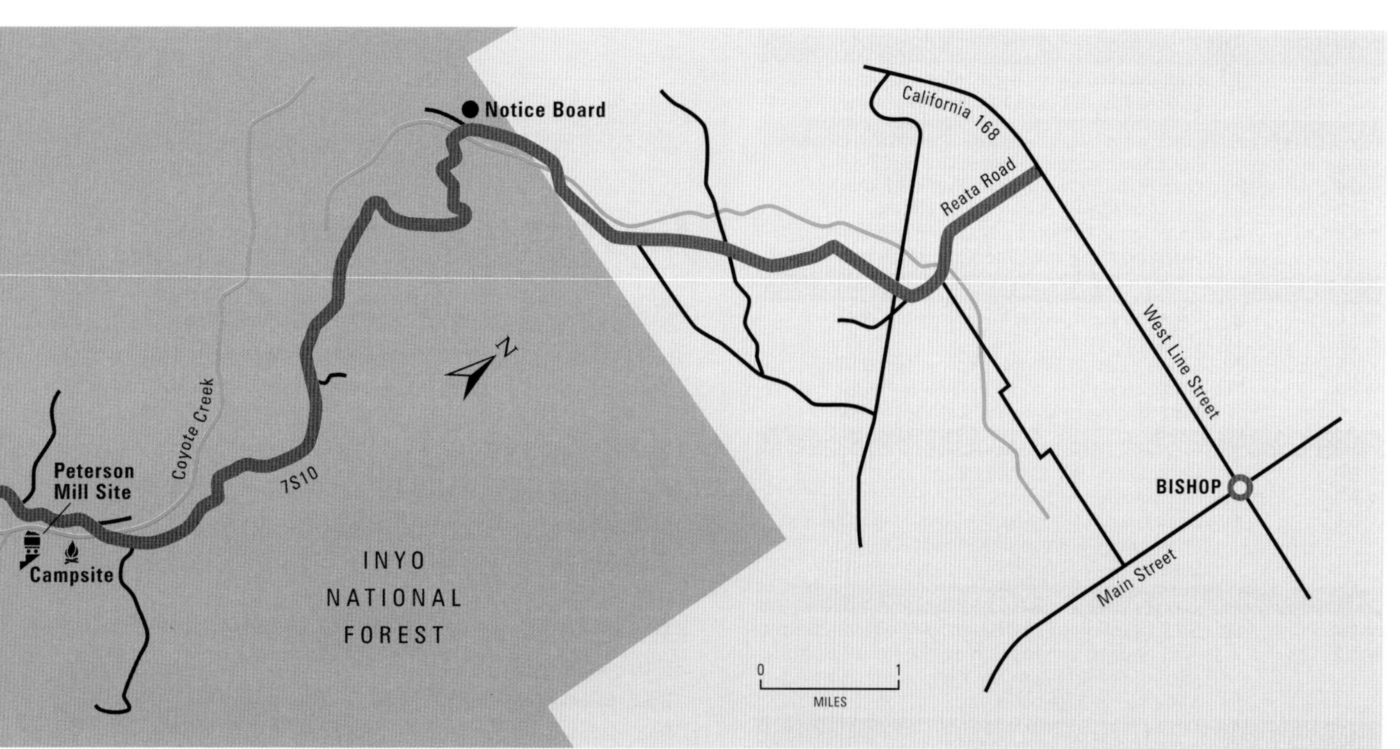

GPS: N37°20.80' W118°26.28'

- ▼ 0.0 — Continue to the south. Immediately track on right.
- ▼ 0.2 **BR** Track on left.
- ▼ 0.4 **SO** Pass under power lines. Track on right and track on left along power lines. Continue on small formed trail.
- ▼ 0.8 **SO** Track on right.
- ▼ 0.9 **SO** Track on right; then track on left.
- ▼ 1.4 **SO** Track on left.
- ▼ 1.7 **SO** Track on left and track on right.
- ▼ 2.4 **SO** Track on left.
- ▼ 3.2 **SO** Entering Inyo National Forest at sign. Zero trip meter.

GPS: N37°19.13' W118°28.76'

- ▼ 0.0 — Continue to the southwest.
- ▼ 0.5 **SO** Track on right.
- ▼ 0.6 **BL** Track on right at notice board.

GPS: N37°18.86' W118°29.28'

- ▼ 0.7 **SO** Cross through wash. Trail is now marked 7S10 for 4WDs, ATVs, and motorbikes.
- ▼ 0.8 **SO** Trail starts to climb shelf road.
- ▼ 1.8 **SO** End of climb and shelf road. Track on left.
- ▼ 4.1 **SO** Track on left.

GPS: N37°17.18' W118°28.36'

- ▼ 6.4 **SO** Two tracks on left.
- ▼ 6.6 **BL** Cross through Coyote Creek; then track on right. Zero trip meter.

GPS: N37°15.54' W118°28.39'

- ▼ 0.0 — Continue to the southwest.
- ▼ 0.1 **SO** Campsite beside creek on left.
- ▼ 0.4 **SO** Remains of the Peterson Mill on left.

GPS: N37°15.27' W118°28.69'

- ▼ 0.5 **SO** Two small sheds in bushes on the left are remains of the Peterson Mill.

GPS: N37°15.23' W118°28.72'

- ▼ 0.7 **SO** Track on right.
- ▼ 0.9 **SO** Track on right.

GPS: N37°15.15' W118°29.02'

- ▼ 1.3 **SO** Track on right.

GPS: N37°14.91' W118°29.34'

- ▼ 1.7 **SO** Well-used track on left is High Sierra #42: Coyote Flat Trail (7S10). Zero trip meter.

GPS: N37°14.64' W118°29.55'

- ▼ 0.0 — Continue to the southwest on 8S18.
- ▼ 0.9 **SO** Pass through fence line. Trail is following alongside West Fork Coyote Creek.
- ▼ 1.1 **SO** Cattle guard; then track on right. Salty Peterson Mine is on the right at the intersection.

GPS: N37°13.88' W118°30.08'

- ▼ 1.4 **SO** Cross through West Fork Coyote Creek.
- ▼ 1.6 **SO** Campsite on left.
- ▼ 2.1 **SO** Cross through West Fork Coyote Creek.
- ▼ 2.4 **BL** Track on right is 8S19 to Coyote Ridge. Follow sign to Coyote Lake and zero trip meter.

GPS: N37°13.09' W118°31.15'

- ▼ 0.0 — Continue to the southeast.
- ▼ 0.3 **SO** Campsite on left.
- ▼ 0.4 **BL** Bear left onto slightly less-used trail. Track ahead goes a short distance to Coyote Lake.

GPS: N37°12.76' W118°31.15'

- ▼ 0.7 **SO** Short section of shelf road with off-camber tilt.
- ▼ 1.2 — Trail ends at a viewpoint above Rocky Bottom Lake. It continues to the right to the Brackett Mine but is little used.

GPS: N37°12.19' W118°31.08'

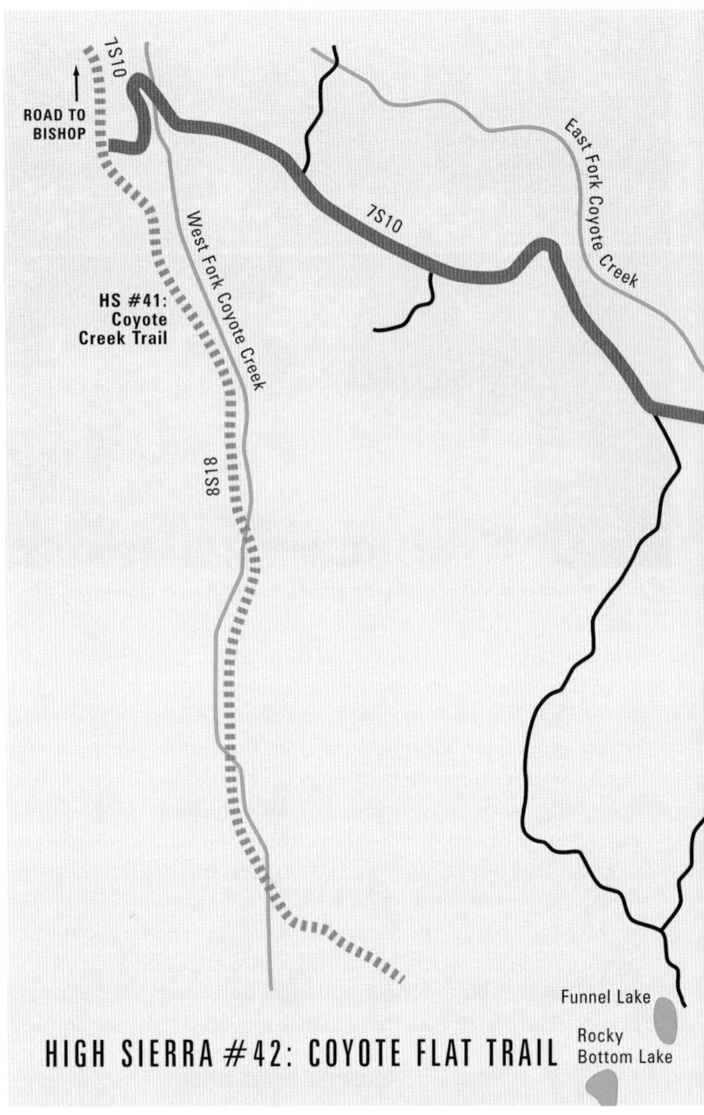

HIGH SIERRA #42

Coyote Flat Trail

Starting Point:	**High Sierra #41: Coyote Creek Trail, at the intersection of 7S10 and 8S18**
Finishing Point:	**Undeveloped campground beside Baker Creek**
Total Mileage:	**8.6 miles (one-way)**
Unpaved Mileage:	**8.6 miles**
Driving Time:	**1 hour (one-way)**
Elevation Range:	**9,500–10,400 feet**
Usually Open:	**April to November**
Best Time to Travel:	**April to November**
Difficulty Rating:	**4**
Scenic Rating:	**8**
Remoteness Rating:	**+1**

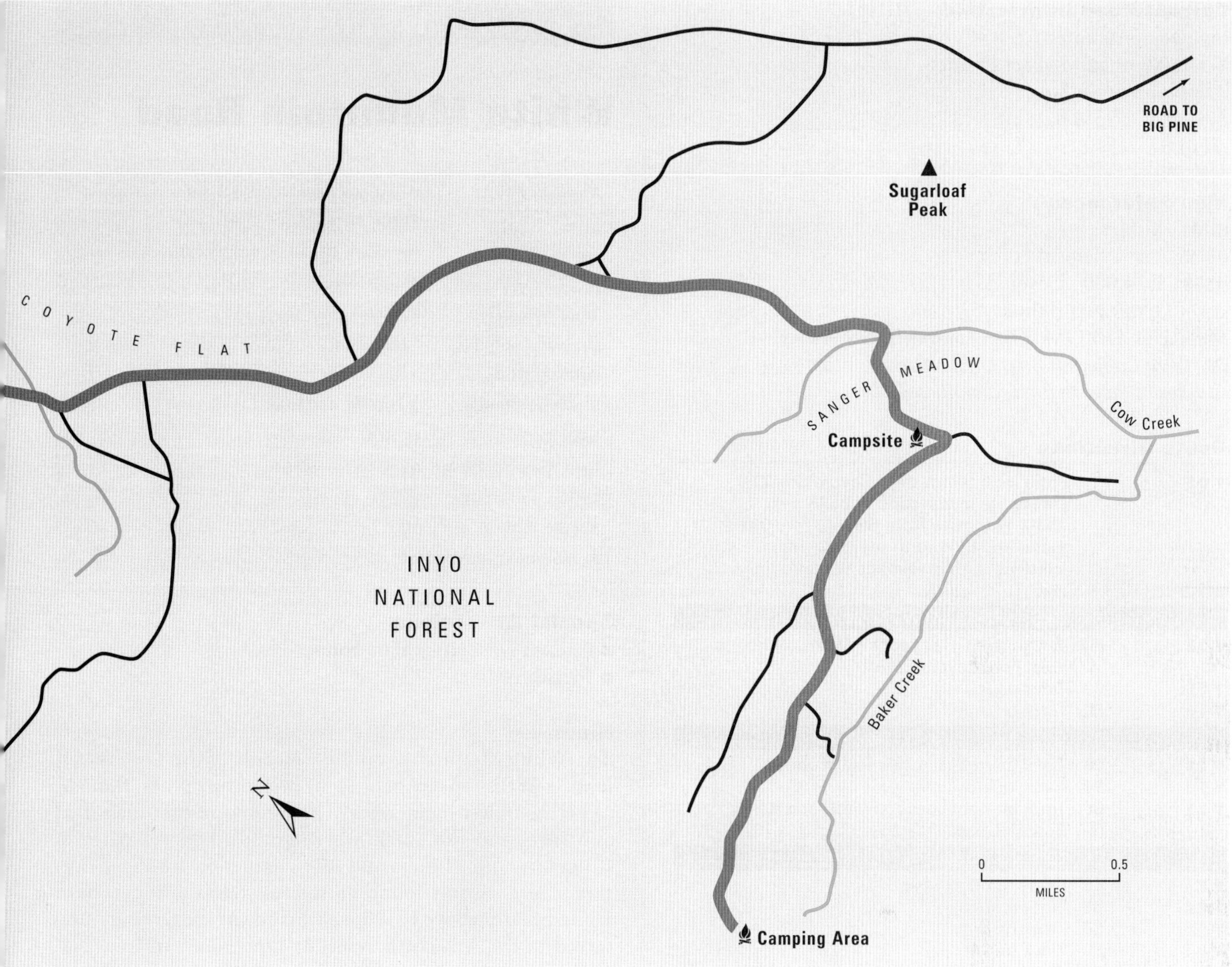

ROAD TO BIG PINE
Sugarloaf Peak
COYOTE FLAT
SANGER MEADOW
Campsite
Cow Creek
INYO NATIONAL FOREST
Baker Creek
N
0 0.5 MILES
Camping Area

Special Attractions

- Remote campsite on Baker Creek.
- Access to Rocky Bottom Lake and Funnel Lake.
- Long trail across Coyote Flat.

Description

This short trail is a pleasant spur off the longer High Sierra #41: Coyote Creek Trail. It heads south from Coyote Creek Trail, crossing through the West Fork of Coyote Creek before running along the open Coyote Flat. A well-used side trail goes toward the pretty Funnel Lake and Rocky Bottom Lake, but the main trail continues south along Coyote Flat, passing below Sugarloaf Peak. A small formed trail leads over a rise immediately before Sugarloaf Peak and eventually exits, via a number of twists and turns, to Big Pine. However, this trail is rocky, slow going, and can be difficult.

The main trail continues across Sanger Meadow, named after the family who raised horses in this vicinity, before heading toward Baker Creek past a couple of nice campsites. The trail ends at a rocky camping area beside Baker Creek, with a pit toilet but no other facilities. The best campsite is farther down the trail, past the toilet, under some large trees.

Autumn sunlight on the small meadow by Baker Creek at the end of Coyote Flat Trail

Current Road Information
Inyo National Forest
White Mountain Ranger District
798 North Main Street
Bishop, CA 93514
(760) 873-2500

Map References
BLM Bishop
USFS Inyo National Forest
USGS 1:24,000 Coyote Flat
1:100,000 Bishop
Maptech CD-ROM: Kings Canyon/Death Valley
Northern California Atlas & Gazetteer, p. 123
California Road & Recreation Atlas, p. 79

Route Directions

▼ 0.0		From High Sierra #41: Coyote Creek Trail at the intersection of 8S18 and 7S10, 12.6 miles from Bishop, zero trip meter and turn north on 7S10. Trail initially travels across the open Coyote Flat.
		GPS: N37°14.64' W118°29.55'
▼ 0.3	BR	Track on left. Bear right and cross through West Fork Coyote Creek.
▼ 0.8	SO	Track on left.
▼ 1.3	SO	Track on right.
		GPS: N37°13.73' W118°29.18'
▼ 1.6	SO	Track on right and two tracks on left.
▼ 1.9	SO	Cattle guard.
▼ 2.2	BL	Track on right goes to Funnel and Rocky Bottom Lakes.
		GPS: N37°13.04' W118°29.08'
▼ 2.5	SO	Cross through wash.
▼ 2.6	BL	Track on right.
▼ 2.9	SO	Track on right.
▼ 3.7	SO	Track on left.
▼ 4.6	SO	Track on left goes over rise and eventually exits to Big Pine. Zero trip meter.
		GPS: N37°11.76' W118°27.23'
▼ 0.0		Continue to the southeast.
▼ 0.2	SO	Second entrance to track on left.
▼ 1.2	SO	Cross through Cow Creek.
▼ 1.6	BL	Track on right; then cattle guard.
		GPS: N37°10.68' W118°26.90'
▼ 1.8	TR	Track on right and campsite under pines; then T-intersection. Turn right and zero trip meter.
		GPS: N37°10.54' W118°26.83'
▼ 0.0		Continue to the west.
▼ 0.7	SO	Track on right.
		GPS: N37°10.58' W118°27.61'
▼ 1.0	BR	Track on left.
		GPS: N37°10.40' W118°27.75'
▼ 1.2	SO	Track on left.
▼ 1.5	SO	Trail forks around lumpy section.
▼ 1.6	SO	Trail rejoins and forks again around lumpy section. It immediately rejoins.
▼ 2.2		Trail ends at an undeveloped camping area with a pit toilet but no other facilities.
		GPS: N37°10.12' W118°28.78'

HIGH SIERRA #43

White Mountain Road

Starting Point:	**Westgard Pass Road, 13 miles northeast of Big Pine**
Finishing Point:	**Patriarch Grove in Ancient Bristlecone Pine Forest**
Total Mileage:	**22 miles (one-way)**
Unpaved Mileage:	**12.3 miles**
Driving Time:	**2 hours**
Elevation Range:	**7,200–11,400 feet**
Usually Open:	**April to November**
Best Time to Travel:	**April to November**
Difficulty Rating:	**1**
Scenic Rating:	**10**
Remoteness Rating:	**+0**

Special Attractions

- Ancient Bristlecone Pine Forest.
- Mexican Mine.

History

The White Mountains, on the west side of the Owens Valley east of Bishop, are habitat for bristlecone pines, thought to be the oldest living trees. The trees were first identified as a species in the 1860s when a railroad survey party in Colorado noticed them and sent samples off for identification. They are only found in isolated stands in the western United States above 8,500 feet. Stands of the trees are preserved in the Ancient Bristlecone Pine Forest in Inyo National Forest.

In the 1950s, Dr. Edmund Schulman of the University of Arizona used bristlecones growing on White Mountain to study long-term climate changes. Bristlecones were ideal for the study because they live a long time, and their annual growth rings reflect how much water was available to the tree each year. The oldest known living tree in the world is the Methuselah Tree, which is estimated to be approximately 4,720 years old. It stands in a grove of trees, discovered by and named for Dr. Schulman, that are all more than 4,000 years old.

The Mexican Mine, just south of the Schulman Grove, operated sporadically from the mid-1800s to the early 1900s. Small quantities of silver, lead, and zinc were extracted. A few cabins built from a mix of bristlecone and limber pines still stand at the mine. No trees were cut down to build the cabins; tests have shown that only dead wood was used.

Wyman Creek flows through a canyon that cuts through the White Mountains to the east. It was named for Dan Wyman, who began prospecting for gold in the White Mountains in 1861. The first communications line to the Nevada goldfields from the west crossed the White Mountains up Silver Canyon and down Wyman Canyon.

Only bristlecones and sage survive on this rugged ridge of the White Mountains

Description

The Ancient Bristlecone Pine Forest is deservedly a highlight of any visit to the eastern Sierra Nevada. The trees, which include the oldest known living tree, are easily reached along a paved then graded dirt road that accesses the very beautiful and sparsely vegetated landscape of the White Mountains. The trail is very popular and you are unlikely to have the region to yourself. The Schulman Grove Visitor Center provides an excellent introduction to bristlecone pines. The visitor center, open daily from 10 A.M. to 5 P.M. when the road is open, is also the point at which the paved road turns to graded dirt. The center has picnic tables, a small gift shop, and a couple of self-guided hiking trails. A long hiking trail, the Methuselah Trail, takes visitors past the ancient Methuselah Tree. No camping is allowed within the bristlecone pines area.

Past the visitor center, the road winds along the windswept tops of the White Mountains. Winter temperatures have been recorded at 20 degrees below zero, with winds measuring 100 miles per hour.

Two worthwhile trails for high-clearance 4WDs lead off on either side of the main trail—High Sierra #44: Silver Canyon Trail and Wyman Canyon Trail. There are many parking areas along the way where you can stop and admire views west over the Owens Valley to the Sierra Nevada. The trail ends at the Patriarch Grove of bristlecone pines. Growing above 11,000 feet, these trees are as hardy and gnarled as they come. A second trail continues for an additional 4 miles before reaching a locked gate. The University of California's Barcroft Laboratory at the White Mountain Research Station is behind the gate; it is rarely open to the public.

Current Road Information

Inyo National Forest
White Mountain Ranger District
798 North Main Street
Bishop, CA 93514
(760) 873-2500

Map References

BLM Bishop, Benton Range
USFS Inyo National Forest
USGS 1:24,000 Westgard Pass, Blanco Mt., Mt. Barcroft
1:100,000 Bishop, Benton Range
Maptech CD-ROM: Kings Canyon/Death Valley; High Sierra/Yosemite
Northern California Atlas & Gazetteer, pp. 124, 114
California Road & Recreation Atlas, p. 79

Route Directions

▼ 0.0		From Westgard Pass Road (California 168), 13 miles northeast of Big Pine, zero trip meter and turn onto paved road marked for Bristlecone Pine Visitors Center. The intersection is well marked. Trail follows FR 01, a National Forest Scenic Byway.
3.1 ▲		Trail ends on Westgard Pass Road (California 168). Turn right for Big Pine.
		GPS: N37°16.95' W118°09.03'
▼ 0.4	SO	Control station.
2.7 ▲	SO	Control station.
▼ 0.7	SO	Track on left.
2.4 ▲	SO	Track on right.
▼ 1.1	SO	Track on left; then closure gate.
2.0 ▲	SO	Closure gate; then track on right.
▼ 1.7	SO	Track on right.
1.4 ▲	SO	Track on left.
▼ 1.9	SO	Track on right.
1.2 ▲	SO	Track on left.
▼ 2.2	SO	Track on right.
0.9 ▲	SO	Track on left.
▼ 2.5	SO	Track on left.
0.6 ▲	SO	Track on right.
▼ 2.8	SO	Track on left.
0.3 ▲	SO	Track on right.
▼ 3.1	SO	Pinon Picnic Area on right. Zero trip meter.
0.0 ▲		Continue to the south.
		GPS: N37°18.85' W118°10.83'
▼ 0.0		Continue to the north.
4.3 ▲	SO	Pinon Picnic Area on left. Zero trip meter.

Mexican Mine cabin made of brislecone pine and constructed into the mountainside for protection against the high elevation's harsh elements

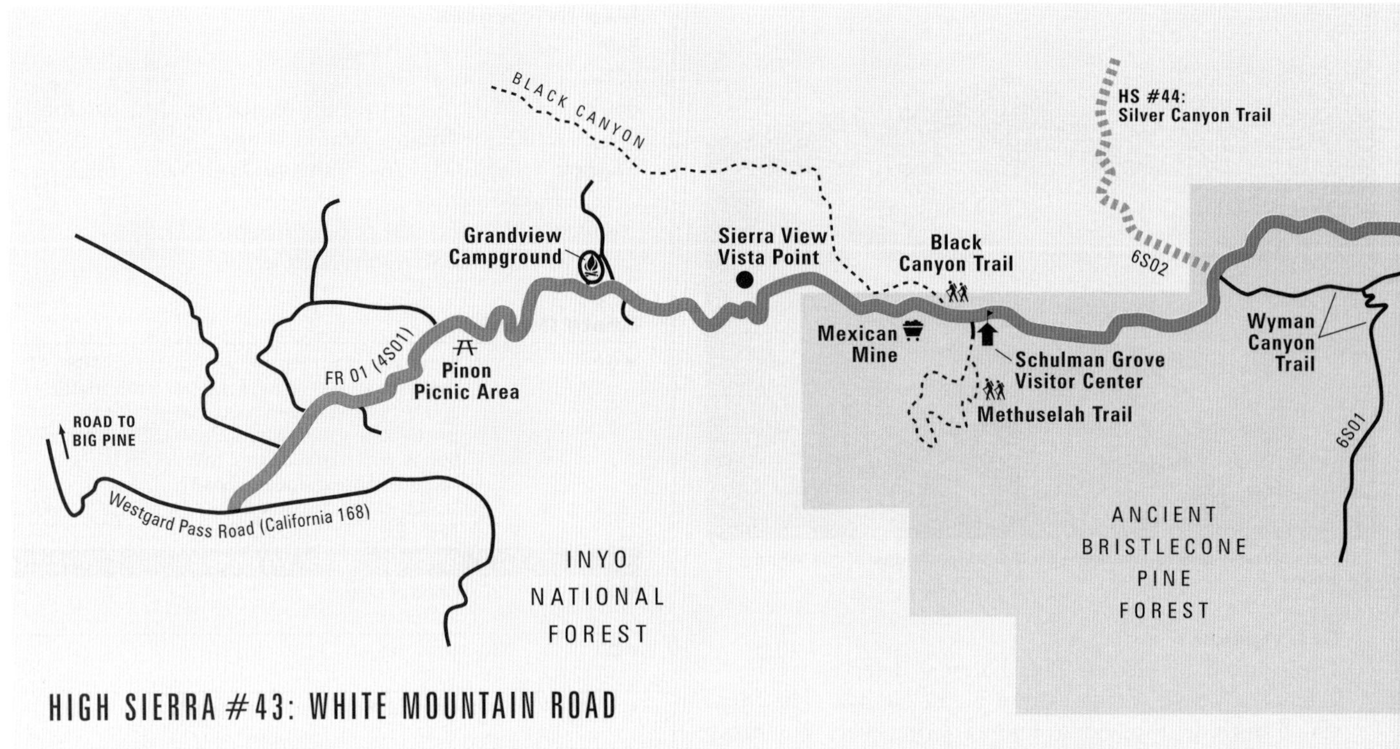

▼ 0.6 SO Track on left.
3.7 ▲ SO Track on right.

▼ 1.2 SO Track on left.
3.1 ▲ SO Track on right.

▼ 1.9 SO Track on left goes to Grandview USFS Campground.
2.4 ▲ SO Track on right goes to Grandview USFS Campground.

GPS: N37°20.04' W118°11.15'

▼ 2.1 SO Track on left.
2.2 ▲ SO Track on right.

▼ 2.3 SO Track on right.
2.0 ▲ SO Track on left.

▼ 2.9 SO Two tracks on left.
1.4 ▲ SO Two tracks on right.

▼ 3.5 SO Track on left.
0.8 ▲ SO Track on right.

▼ 4.3 SO Sierra View Vista Point on left. Zero trip meter.
0.0 ▲ Continue to the southeast.

GPS: N37°21.41' W118°11.14'

▼ 0.0 Continue to the northwest.
2.3 ▲ SO Sierra View Vista Point on right. Zero trip meter.

▼ 0.1 SO Closure gate.
2.2 ▲ SO Closure gate.

▼ 0.7 SO Entering Ancient Bristlecone Pine Forest.
1.6 ▲ SO Leaving Ancient Bristlecone Pine Forest.

▼ 1.8 SO Remains of Mexican Mine beside road on right. There is a tailings pile and the remains of two log cabins.
0.5 ▲ SO Remains of Mexican Mine beside road on left. There is a tailings pile and the remains of two log cabins.

GPS: N37°22.78' W118°10.95'

▼ 2.1 SO Black Canyon Trail (hiking) on left; parking area on right.
0.2 ▲ SO Black Canyon Trail (hiking) on right; parking area on left.

GPS: N37°22.97' W118°10.84'

▼ 2.3 SO Schulman Grove Visitor Center entrance on right (fee area). Zero trip meter.
0.0 ▲ Continue to the south; road is now paved.

GPS: N37°23.14' W118°10.82'

▼ 0.0 Continue to the north; road turns to graded dirt.
3.0 ▲ SO Schulman Grove Visitor Center entrance on left (fee area). Zero trip meter.

▼ 0.5 SO Closure gate.
2.5 ▲ SO Closure gate.

▼ 3.0 SO Track on left is High Sierra #44: Silver Canyon Trail (6S02) and track on right is Wyman Canyon Trail (6S01). Zero trip meter.
0.0 ▲ Continue to the southeast on 4S01.

GPS: N37°25.16' W118°11.29'

▼ 0.0 Continue to the northwest on 4S01.
▼ 3.6 BL Track on right goes to Wyman Canyon. Zero trip meter at sign.

GPS: N37°27.46' W118°11.55'

▼ 0.0 Continue to the north.
▼ 2.4 SO Graded road (5S01) on right goes to Cottonwood Creek. Zero trip meter.

GPS: N37°29.44' W118°11.18'

▼ 0.0 Continue to the northwest on 4S01.
▼ 1.5 SO Cross over Poison Creek. Road becomes paved.

GPS: N37°30.44' W118°12.15'

▼ 2.4 BR Bear right onto graded dirt road, following sign to Patriarch Grove. Graded road on left goes to Barcroft Research Station, but there is a locked gate after 4 miles.

GPS: N37°31.06' W118°12.09'

▼ 3.3 Trail ends at Patriarch Grove.

GPS: N37°31.66' W118°11.82'

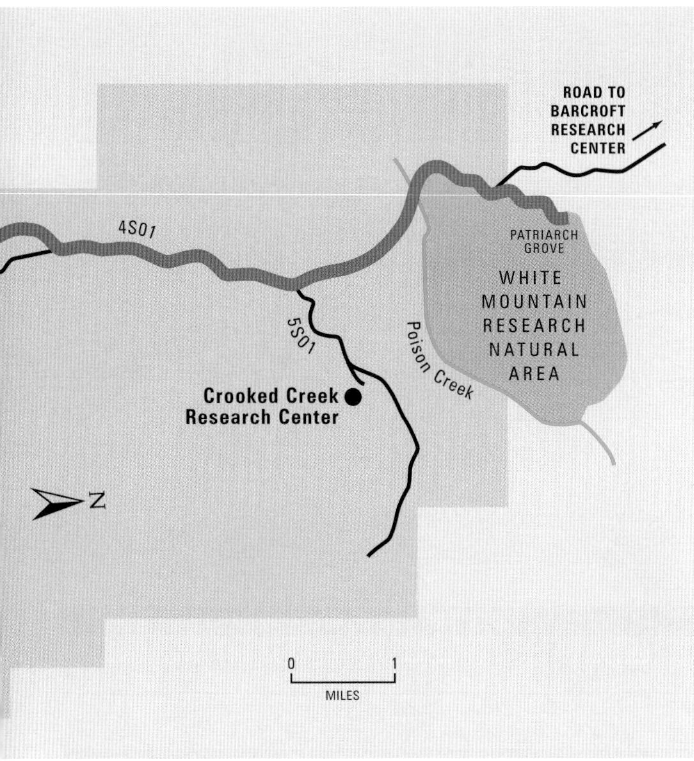

HIGH SIERRA #44

Silver Canyon Trail

Starting Point:	**High Sierra #43: White Mountain Road, 3 miles north of the Schulman Grove Visitor Center**
Finishing Point:	**US 6 at Laws**
Total Mileage:	**11.1 miles**
Unpaved Mileage:	**10.1 miles**
Driving Time:	**1.5 hours**
Elevation Range:	**4,100–10,500 feet**
Usually Open:	**April to November**
Best Time to Travel:	**April to November**
Difficulty Rating:	**3**
Scenic Rating:	**9**
Remoteness Rating:	**+0**

Special Attractions

- Steep twisty trail that winds down Silver Canyon.
- Can be used as an alternate route to or from High Sierra #43: White Mountain Road.
- Wildlife viewing—bighorn sheep.

History

Laws, at the western end of Silver Canyon Trail, was a station for the narrow-gauge Carson & Colorado Railroad that ran from Carson City to Keeler. The settlement was named for the railroad's assistant superintendent, R. J. Laws, and had a post office from 1887 until the early 1960s. Passenger service to Laws ended in 1932 and freight service to Nevada ended in 1943. After that, tracks were pulled up. Service continued between Laws and Keeler until April 1960, when Engine Number 9 made its last run to Laws. The Southern Pacific acquired the Carson & Colorado and Engine Number 9 is now in a railroad museum in Laws.

The site of the mining town of Owensville is a couple hundred yards west of Laws. Owensville had a post office from 1866 to 1869, and it was known as Glen Mary for a short time in 1868. The town's post office was moved to present-day Bishop, formerly Bishop Creek, in 1870. By 1871 Owensville had faded away.

Description

The extremely steep trail winds down Silver Canyon and makes for an exciting drive. It leaves High Sierra #43: White Mountain Road, 3 miles north of the Schulman Grove Visitor Center. The narrow trail is roughly graded as it descends into Silver Canyon. There are excellent views all the way, initially toward the Sierra Nevada and Bishop (6,000 feet below in the Owens Valley), and then into the rugged Silver Canyon.

The trail surface is slightly uneven and loose, but it should not cause any problems for most vehicles. Passing places are limited along the shelf road, so you will need to be prepared to back up for oncoming vehicles. Once down in the canyon, the trail crosses Silver Creek many times. The creek flows most of the year, and under normal conditions the crossings are fairly shallow.

A herd of about 30 bighorn sheep may be seen near the mouth of Silver Canyon. The best time to see them is in the early morning or late afternoon.

The trail descends from the White Mountains into Silver Canyon

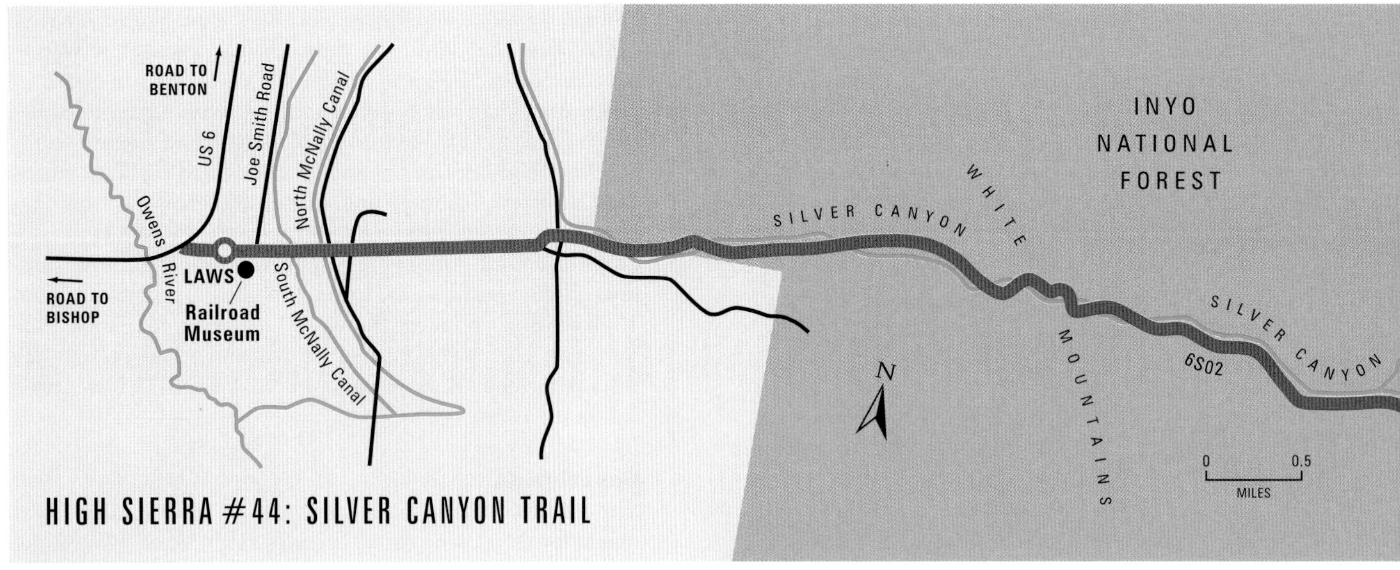

Current Road Information
Inyo National Forest
White Mountain Ranger District
798 North Main Street
Bishop, CA 93514
(760) 873-2500

Map References
BLM Bishop
USFS Inyo National Forest
USGS 1:24,000 Blanco Mt., Laws
1:100,000 Bishop
Maptech CD-ROM: Kings Canyon/Death Valley
Northern California Atlas & Gazetteer, pp. 124, 123
California Road & Recreation Atlas, p. 79

Route Directions

▼ 0.0		From High Sierra #43: White Mountain Road, 3 miles north of the Schulman Grove Visitor Center, zero trip meter and turn south on roughly graded trail following the sign to Bishop. The trail is marked 6S02. The start is opposite the turn for Wyman Canyon Trail.
8.8 ▲		Trail ends on High Sierra #43: White Mountain Road. Turn right to exit via the Schulman Grove Visitor Center; turn left to visit the Patriarch Grove at the northern end of White Mountain Road.
		GPS: N37°25.16′ W118°11.29′
▼ 0.2	BR	Leave Ancient Bristlecone Pine Forest Area; then track on left goes to a radio facility.
8.6 ▲	SO	Track on right goes to a radio facility; then enter Ancient Bristlecone Pine Forest Area.
▼ 0.3	SO	Viewpoint on right and track on left.
8.5 ▲	SO	Viewpoint on left and track on right.
		GPS: N37°24.96′ W118°11.44′
▼ 0.5	SO	Closure gate.
8.3 ▲	SO	Closure gate.
▼ 0.7	SO	Track on right.
8.1 ▲	SO	Track on left.
▼ 2.0	BL	Track on right.
6.8 ▲	BR	Track on left.
		GPS: N37°24.33′ W118°12.31′
▼ 2.7	SO	Track on right.
6.1 ▲	SO	Track on left.
▼ 3.8	SO	Closure gate.
5.0 ▲	SO	Closure gate.
		GPS: N37°24.07′ W118°13.24′
▼ 4.1	SO	Track on right.
4.7 ▲	SO	Track on left.
▼ 4.2	SO	Cross through creek; then closure gate.
4.6 ▲	SO	Closure gate; then cross through creek.
		GPS: N37°24.12′ W118°13.67′
▼ 4.9	SO	Track on right to mine adits.
3.9 ▲	SO	Track on left to mine adits.
		GPS: N37°24.13′ W118°14.50′
▼ 5.4	SO	Track on right.
3.4 ▲	SO	Track on left.
▼ 6.1	SO	Cross through creek; then track on right to mine.
2.7 ▲	SO	Track on left to mine; then cross through creek.
		GPS: N37°24.34′ W118°15.62′
▼ 6.3	SO	Cross through creek.
2.5 ▲	SO	Cross through creek.
▼ 6.4	SO	Cross through creek.
2.4 ▲	SO	Cross through creek.
▼ 6.7	SO	Cross through creek.
2.1 ▲	SO	Cross through creek.
▼ 6.9	SO	Cross through creek.
1.9 ▲	SO	Cross through creek.
▼ 7.5	SO	Track on left.
1.3 ▲	SO	Track on right rejoins.
▼ 7.6	SO	Track on left rejoins.
1.2 ▲	SO	Track on right.
▼ 7.7	SO	Cross through creek.
1.1 ▲	SO	Cross through creek.
▼ 8.2	SO	Cattle guard.
0.6 ▲	SO	Cattle guard.
▼ 8.4	SO	Cross through creek.
0.4 ▲	SO	Cross through creek.
		GPS: N37°24.34′ W118°18.07′
▼ 8.5	SO	Track on left.
0.3 ▲	SO	Track on right.

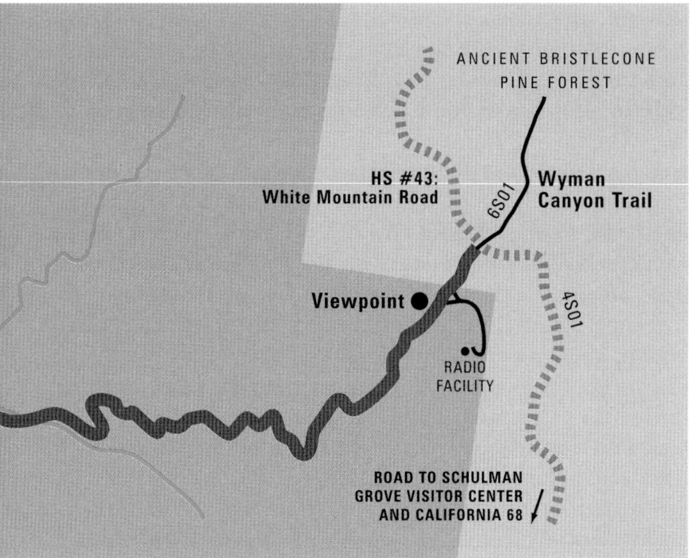

▼ 8.8	SO	Exiting Inyo National Forest at sign. Zero trip meter.
0.0 ▲		Continue to the east.
		GPS: N37°24.29' W118°18.55'
▼ 0.0		Continue to the west and cross through creek. Track on left.
2.3 ▲	SO	Track on right. Cross through Silver Creek. Entering Inyo National Forest at sign. Zero trip meter.
▼ 0.2	SO	Track on right.
2.1 ▲	SO	Track on left.
▼ 0.3	SO	Track on left; then track on right.
2.0 ▲	SO	Track on left; then track on right.
▼ 0.5	SO	Track on left.
1.8 ▲	SO	Track on right.
▼ 0.7	SO	Track on left.
1.6 ▲	SO	Track on right.
▼ 1.0	SO	Track on right.
1.3 ▲	SO	Track on left.
▼ 1.2	SO	Track on left.
1.1 ▲	SO	Track on right.
▼ 1.3	SO	Road is now paved.
1.0 ▲	SO	Road is now graded dirt.
▼ 1.4	SO	Paved road on left and track on right.
0.9 ▲	SO	Track on left and paved road on right.
		GPS: N37°24.12' W118°20.12'
▼ 1.5	SO	Track on left and track on right; then cross over North McNally Canal; then cattle guard.
0.8 ▲	SO	Cattle guard; then cross over North McNally Canal; then track on left and track on right.
▼ 1.7	SO	Cross over South McNally Canal.
0.6 ▲	SO	Cross over South McNally Canal.
▼ 1.9	SO	Joe Smith Road on right.
0.4 ▲	SO	Joe Smith Road on left.
▼ 2.3		Paved road on right; then trail ends at T-intersection with US 6. Turn left for Bishop.
0.0 ▲		Trail commences on US 6, 3.4 miles north of Bishop. Zero trip meter and turn east on paved road at the sign for Silver Canyon Road in the small settlement of Laws. There is also a sign for the Laws Railroad and Historic Museum.
		GPS: N37°24.00' W118°21.08'

HIGH SIERRA #45

Saline Valley Road

Starting Point:	**California 190, 9.5 miles east of the intersection with California 136**
Finishing Point:	**California 168, 2.5 miles east of Big Pine and the intersection with US 395**
Total Mileage:	**91.4 miles**
Unpaved Mileage:	**78.8 miles**
Driving Time:	**5.5 hours**
Elevation Range:	**1,000–7,600 feet**
Usually Open:	**Year-round, higher elevations may be closed in winter**
Best Time to Travel:	**October to May**
Difficulty Rating:	**2**
Scenic Rating:	**10**
Remoteness Rating:	**+2**

Special Attractions

- Old salt works and tramway.
- Saline Valley Dunes.
- Many old mining camps and remains in Saline Valley and Marble Canyon.
- Remote desert experience.

History

Saline Valley parallels the Owens Valley, on the east side of the Inyo Mountains and west side of the Saline Range, mostly in Death Valley National Park. The valley has a long history of mining. Borax was discovered in 1874, and the Conn and Trudo Borax Works operated in the valley from the late 1880s to the early 1900s. Saline Valley, along with Calico in San Bernardino County, was the principal producer of borax between 1888 and 1893. The valley also has salt deposits that were discovered about the same time, but they didn't become a large concern until 1903. The Saline Valley Salt Tramway was built between 1911 and 1913 to carry salt across the Inyo Mountains to Swansea, a site on Owens Lake that had a ferry and railroad connections. The tram is described as "the most scenic, historic, best preserved, oldest, and largest of its kind

Part of the aerial tramway that transported salt from Saline Valley into the Inyo Mountains

Ubehebe Peak reflected in the still water of Salt Marsh

remaining today," and it is listed on the National Register of Historic Places.

Gold mining in Marble Canyon, north of Saline Valley, began as limited placer mining in 1882, but operations were hindered because it was so remote and difficult to build roads. Large nuggets of gold were found in the canyon between gravel deposits and bedrock. Interest in the area revived in the 1930s and continued until 1960.

In October 1944, a B-24 bomber with a crew of seven was on a training mission when the plane developed engine trouble and crashed on a dry lake in Saline Valley. Only one crew member was seriously injured; his leg was almost completely severed from his body. The plane's radio was out, so the six uninjured crew members wrote the word "plasma" in 6-foot-high letters on the dry salt bed. Fortunately, a search plane spotted the crash and a rescue team was dispatched. It took hours and numerous flat tires before rescuers arrived. The injured man died on the way to Big Pine.

Description

Saline Valley Road is a long, mainly dirt road that takes the traveler from California 190 to California 168, finishing near Big Pine. The historic road is suitable for high-clearance 2WDs in dry weather, but it is not a journey to be taken lightly. The dusty road can be extremely corrugated, and there are no facilities or fuel anywhere along the way. Average daily high temperatures exceed 100 degrees Fahrenheit from June through September, and in winter, snow at the higher elevations may require the use of chains in order to pass through safely.

The trail commences along the original Saline Valley Road, which is now less used than the new route that begins farther east on California 190. The old and new routes merge 8.3 miles from the start of the trail. The first part of the route travels through the Talc City Hills, close to several old mine sites, before reaching the broad Santa Rosa Flat. The Santa Rosa Hills separate that area from Lee Flat, a broad valley with abundant Joshua trees.

From the intersection with Desert #49: Hidden Valley Road, the trail winds down the twisting Grapevine Canyon and crosses the creek several times. These crossings are likely to be dry in summer but may be icy in winter. The route spills out of Grapevine Canyon and heads into the wide, sage-covered Saline Valley. A well-used track to the right is the rougher, more difficult Desert #50: Lippincott Mine Road, which connects with Desert #51: Racetrack Road. These trails can all be found in the Desert section of *Backcountry Adventures: Southern California.*

Saline Valley Road is well defined, but dusty and washboardy, as it runs north the length of Saline Valley with the Nelson Range to the west. There are several small tracks that lead to the base of the range and to remains of mining camps. One noteworthy feature is the old salt works at Salt Marsh. A spur leads a short distance to the edge of the marsh, where you can see evaporation ponds and the remains of the tramway.

The Saline Valley Dunes, a low range of sand dunes that are lightly vegetated with creosote bush, are a great place for photographs. No vehicles are allowed on the dunes, which are a wilderness area. However, the road runs close enough that it is a very short, easy hike to reach them.

The start of the more difficult Steel Pass Trail is the next major intersection. Travelers may want to detour for the first few miles of this trail to check out the Palm Springs Hot Springs. Nudity is the norm at these popular springs, so if this offends you, you are probably better off staying on the main road.

The trail continues north along the broad Saline Valley, passing side tracks that lead to old mining camps. The trail climbs out of the valley into higher elevations, reaching 7,000 feet. There are several campsites tucked among the pinyons and junipers. No campfires are allowed at any time of year within Death Valley National Park.

The trail joins paved Eureka Canyon Road and passes the northern end of High Sierra #48: Harkless Flat Trail and High Sierra #46: Papoose Flat Trail, before finishing at the intersection with California 168, a short distance east of Big Pine. The trail is normally open year-round, but some sections may be impassable at times. Even light rainfall can make trails in this region impassable, and the National Park Service may temporarily close them when necessary.

Current Road Information

Death Valley National Park
PO Box 579
Death Valley, CA 92328-0579
(760) 786-2331

Maps References

BLM Saline Valley, Last Chance Range, Bishop, Darwin Hills
USFS Inyo National Forest (incomplete)
USGS 1:24,000 Talc City Hills, Santa Rosa Flat, Lee Wash, Jackass Canyon, Nelson Range, West of Ubehebe Peak, Craig Canyon, Lower Warm Springs, Pat Keyes Canyon, Waucoba Canyon, Waucoba Spring, Waucoba Mt., Cowhorn Valley, Uhlmeyer Spring, Big Pine
1:100,000 Saline Valley, Last Chance Range, Bishop, Darwin Hills

Maptech CD-ROM: Kings Canyon/Death Valley
Southern & Central California Atlas & Gazetteer, pp. 40, 28, 27
Northern California Atlas & Gazetteer, p. 124
California Road & Recreation Atlas, pp. 87, 80, 79
Trails Illustrated, Death Valley National Park (221)
Other: Free NPS Death Valley map, Tom Harrison Maps—Death Valley National Park Recreation Map

Route Directions

Mileage		Directions
▼ 0.0		Trail commences on California 190, 9.5 miles east of the intersection with California 136. Zero trip meter and turn north on small paved road. Intersection is unmarked.
1.9 ▲		Small paved road on left is Talc City Road; then trail ends at intersection with California 190. Turn right for Lone Pine; turn left for Death Valley.
		GPS: N36°19.84' W117°42.84'
▼ 0.1	SO	Track on left.
1.8 ▲	SO	Track on right.
▼ 0.7	SO	Track on left joins S9.
1.2 ▲	SO	Track on right joins S9.
▼ 1.2	SO	Track on left and track on right; then second track on left to Viking and White Swan Mines; then second track on right.
0.7 ▲	SO	Track on left; then track on right to Viking and White Swan Mines; then second track on left and second track on right.
		GPS: N36°20.65' W117°42.22'
▼ 1.4	SO	Cross through wash.
0.5 ▲	SO	Cross through wash.
▼ 1.8	SO	Track on right is S5, suitable for 4WDs, ATVs, and motorbikes, and goes toward the Sierra Mine.
0.1 ▲	SO	Track on left is S5, suitable for 4WDs, ATVs, and motorbikes, and goes toward the Sierra Mine.
▼ 1.9	SO	Track on left is S9, suitable for 4WDs, ATVs, and motorbikes, and goes to the Viking Mine, which is visible on the hillside to the left. Zero trip meter.
0.0 ▲		Continue to the south.
		GPS: N36°21.20' W117°41.74'
▼ 0.0		Continue to the north.
4.6 ▲	SO	Track on right is S9, suitable for 4WDs, ATVs, and motorbikes, and goes to the Viking Mine, which is visible on the hillside to the right. Zero trip meter.
▼ 0.5	SO	Track on left to mine.
4.1 ▲	SO	Track on right to mine.
		GPS: N36°21.56' W117°41.50'
▼ 1.6	SO	Track on left.
3.0 ▲	SO	Track on right.
▼ 1.7	SO	Cross through wash.
2.9 ▲	SO	Cross through wash.
▼ 2.1	SO	Track on right.
2.5 ▲	SO	Track on left.
▼ 3.1	SO	Many small wash crossings for the next 1.5 miles.
1.5 ▲	SO	End of wash crossings.
▼ 3.7	BR	Graded road on left is Santa Rosa Road.
0.9 ▲	SO	Graded road on right is Santa Rosa Road.
		GPS: N36°23.95' W117°40.25'
▼ 4.6	BR	Track on left is S5 for 4WDs, ATVs, and motorbikes. Zero trip meter.
0.0 ▲		Continue to the south. Trail is leaving Santa Rosa Flat. Many small wash crossings for the next 1.5 miles.
		GPS: N36°24.72' W117°39.91'
▼ 0.0		Continue to the northeast. End of wash crossings.
1.8 ▲	BL	Track on right is S5 for 4WDs, ATVs, and motorbikes. Zero trip meter.
▼ 0.4	SO	Cross through larger wash.
1.4 ▲	SO	Cross through larger wash.
		GPS: N36°24.86' W117°39.49'
▼ 1.1	SO	Faint track on right.
0.7 ▲	SO	Faint track on left.
▼ 1.5	SO	Cross through two channels of Santa Rosa Wash.
0.3 ▲	SO	Cross through two channels of Santa Rosa Wash.
▼ 1.8	SO	Join larger road that was once paved and zero trip meter. Alternate Saline Valley Road on right returns to California 190 in 4.7 miles. Intersection is unmarked.
0.0 ▲		Continue to the southwest across Santa Rosa Flat.
		GPS: N36°25.71' W117°38.39'
▼ 0.0		Continue to the northeast through the Santa Rosa Hills.
3.3 ▲	BR	Bear right onto smaller graded road, which is the original Saline Valley Road. Larger road ahead that was once paved is alternate Saline Valley Road, which joins California 190 in 4.7 miles. Intersection is unmarked. Zero trip meter.
▼ 0.5	SO	Track on left past cabin.
2.8 ▲	SO	Track on right past cabin.
▼ 1.1	SO	Track on right to Lee Mines.
2.2 ▲	SO	Track on left to Lee Mines.
		GPS: N36°26.10' W117°37.33'
▼ 1.3	SO	Track on left to mine.
2.0 ▲	SO	Track on right to mine.
▼ 2.5	SO	Entering Death Valley National Park at sign.
0.8 ▲	SO	Leaving Death Valley National Park at sign.
		GPS: N36°27.20' W117°37.38'
▼ 3.3	BR	Desert #47: Cerro Gordo Road on left. Intersection is large, but unmarked. Small track on right. Zero trip meter.
0.0 ▲		Continue to the southeast.
		GPS: N36°27.91' W117°37.55'
▼ 0.0		Continue to the north.
7.1 ▲	SO	Desert #47: Cerro Gordo Road on right. Intersection is large, but unmarked. Small track on left. Zero trip meter.
▼ 1.5	SO	Track on left. Track on right to site of Wilson Ranch.
5.6 ▲	SO	Track on left to site of Wilson Ranch. Track on right.
		GPS: N36°29.13' W117°36.97'
▼ 3.1	SO	Cross through wash.
4.0 ▲	SO	Cross through wash.
▼ 4.9	SO	Diggings on left.
2.2 ▲	SO	Diggings on right.
		GPS: N36°30.53' W117°34.44'
▼ 5.4	SO	Track on left past corral.
1.7 ▲	SO	Track on right past corral.
		GPS: N36°30.82' W117°34.04'
▼ 6.8	SO	Turnout on right gives views of the Panamint Dunes.

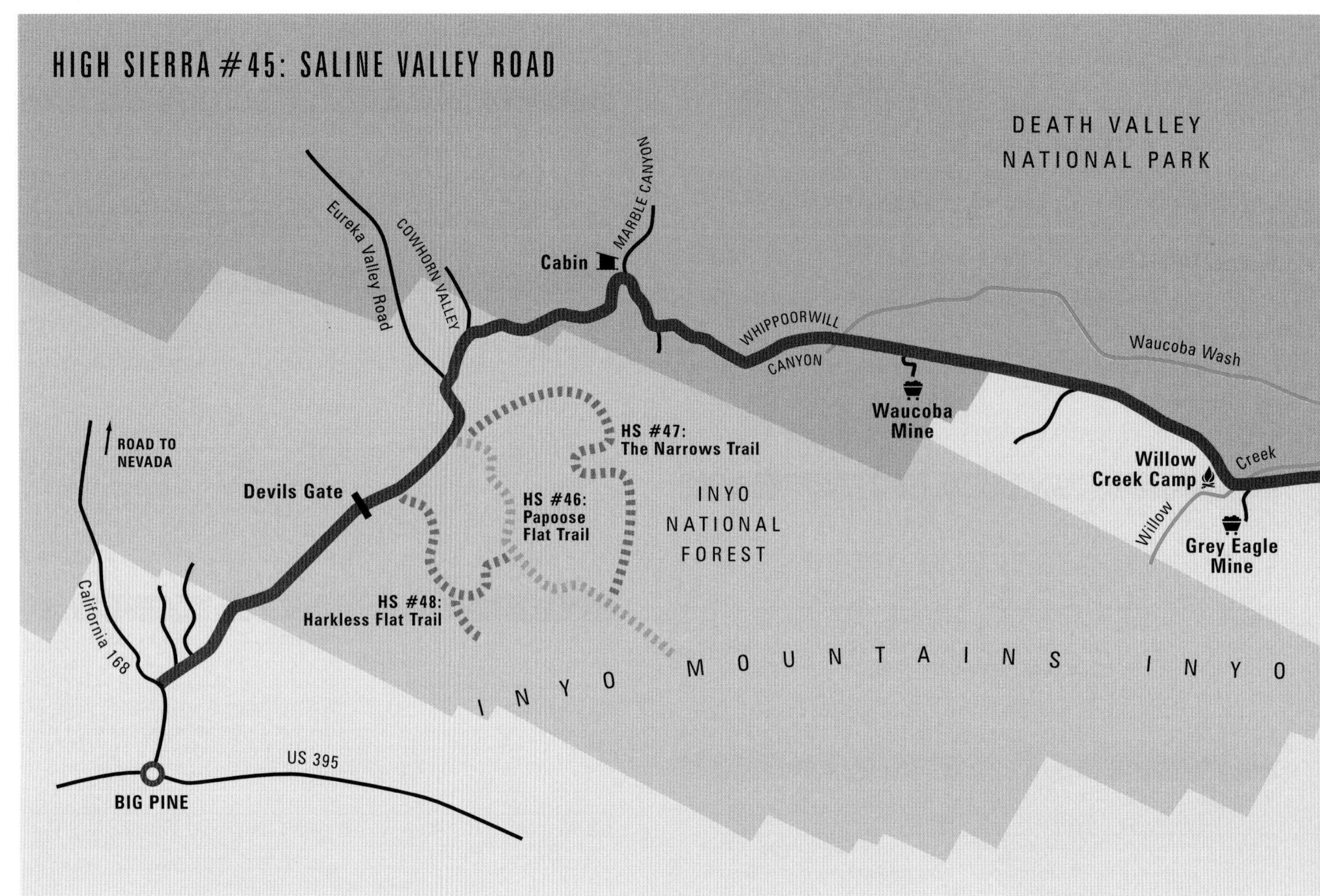

0.3 ▲ SO Turnout on left gives views of the Panamint Dunes.

▼ 7.1 SO Well-used track on right is Desert #49: Hidden Valley Road. Zero trip meter. Intersection is unmarked.
0.0 ▲ Continue to the south.

GPS: N36°31.62′ W117°32.75′

▼ 0.0 Continue to the northwest.
10.0 ▲ SO Well-used track on left is Desert #49: Hidden Valley Road. Zero trip meter. Intersection is unmarked.

▼ 2.6 SO Cross through Grapevine Creek many times in the next 1.6 miles.
7.4 ▲ SO Final crossing of Grapevine Creek.

GPS: N36°32.91′ WS117°34.37′

▼ 4.2 SO Final crossing of Grapevine Creek.
5.8 ▲ SO Cross through Grapevine Creek many times in the next 1.6 miles.

▼ 4.8 SO Track on right.
5.2 ▲ SO Track on left.

▼ 7.8 SO Cross through wash.
2.2 ▲ SO Cross through wash.

▼ 10.0 SO Graded track on right is Desert #50: Lippincott Mine Road. Intersection is unmarked apart from a large cairn. Zero trip meter.
0.0 ▲ Continue to the southeast.

GPS: N36°37.20′ W117°38.88′

▼ 0.0 Continue to the northwest.
10.6 ▲ SO Graded track on left is Desert #50: Lippincott Mine Road. Intersection is unmarked apart from a large cairn. Zero trip meter.

▼ 2.9 SO Track on right.
7.7 ▲ SO Track on left.

GPS: N36°39.38′ W117°40.58′

▼ 10.3 SO Track on left.
0.3 ▲ SO Track on right.

▼ 10.6 SO Track on left follows route of abandoned aerial tramway and heads toward Big Silver Mine. Track on right goes to the edge of Salt Lake with its old salt evaporator and some remains of the salt tramway. Zero trip meter.
0.0 ▲ Continue to the east.

GPS: N36°41.07′ W117°48.90′

▼ 0.0 Continue to the west.
8.1 ▲ SO Track on right follows the route of the abandoned aerial tramway and heads toward Big Silver Mine. Track on left goes to the edge of Salt Lake with its old salt evaporator and some remains of the salt tramway. Zero trip meter.

▼ 0.1 SO Track on left.
8.0 ▲ SO Track on right.

▼ 1.4 SO Track on right across cattle guard.
6.7 ▲ SO Track on left across cattle guard.

GPS: N36°41.91′ W117°49.86′

▼ 1.8 SO Track on left toward Vega Mine and the start of the steep pack route to Burgess Mine in the Inyo Mountains. Track on right.
6.3 ▲ SO Track on right toward Vega Mine and the start of the steep pack route to Burgess Mine in the Inyo Mountains. Track on left.

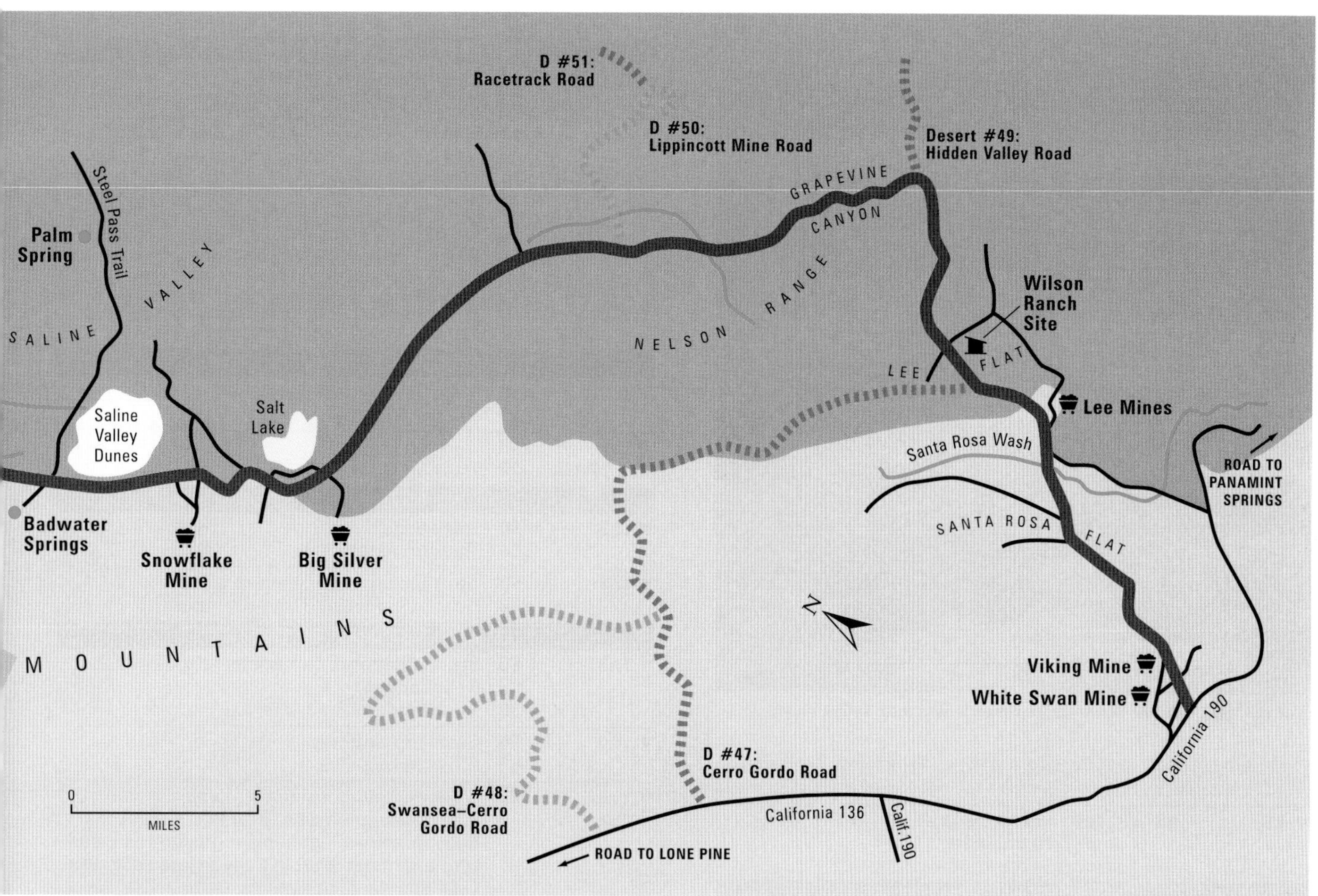

		GPS: N36°42.25' W117°49.67'
▼ 2.2	SO	Track on right.
5.9 ▲	SO	Track on left.
▼ 2.4	SO	Track on left goes to old works area.
5.7 ▲	SO	Track on right goes to old works area.
		GPS: N36°42.74' W117°49.90'
▼ 2.5	SO	Track on right.
5.6 ▲	SO	Track on left.
▼ 4.2	SO	Track on left to Snowflake Mine.
3.9 ▲	SO	Track on right to Snowflake Mine.
		GPS: N36°43.85' W117°50.51'
▼ 4.3	SO	Track on left to Snowflake Mine and track on right.
3.8 ▲	SO	Track on right to Snowflake Mine and track on left.
		GPS: N36°43.89' W117°50.52'
▼ 4.7	SO	Track on right.
3.4 ▲	SO	Track on left.
▼ 4.9	SO	Track on left to Snowflake Mine.
3.2 ▲	SO	Track on right to Snowflake Mine.
		GPS: N36°44.37' W117°50.96'
▼ 5.0	SO	Track on left and track on right.
3.1 ▲	SO	Track on right and track on left.
▼ 5.6	BR	Graded road on left.
2.5 ▲	SO	Graded road on right rejoins.
		GPS: N36°44.81' W117°51.41'
▼ 6.3	SO	Saline Valley Dunes are on the right.
1.8 ▲	SO	Saline Valley Dunes are on the left.
▼ 6.6	SO	Graded road on left rejoins.
1.5 ▲	BL	Graded road on right.
▼ 7.1	SO	Track on left.
1.0 ▲	SO	Track on right.
▼ 8.1	SO	Well-used track on right is Steel Pass Trail. Zero trip meter. Intersection is unmarked.
0.0 ▲		Continue to the southeast.
		GPS: N36°46.68' W117°52.74'
▼ 0.0		Continue to the northwest.
4.5 ▲	SO	Well-used track on left is Steel Pass Trail. Zero trip meter. Intersection is unmarked.
▼ 0.4	SO	Track on left to Badwater Springs.
4.1 ▲	SO	Track on right to Badwater Springs.
▼ 0.8	SO	Track on left.
3.7 ▲	SO	Track on right.
▼ 1.7	SO	Cross through wash.
2.8 ▲	SO	Cross through wash.
▼ 3.3	SO	Track on left.
1.2 ▲	SO	Second entrance to track on right.
		GPS: N36°49.30' W117°54.35'
▼ 3.4	SO	Second entrance to track on left.
1.1 ▲	SO	Track on right.
▼ 4.1	SO	Track on left to Grey Eagle Mine.
0.4 ▲	SO	Second track on right to Grey Eagle Mine.
		GPS: N36°49.89' W117°54.79'
▼ 4.2	SO	Second track on left to Grey Eagle Mine.
0.3 ▲	SO	Track on right to Grey Eagle Mine.
▼ 4.4	SO	Track on left; then cross through Willow Creek wash.

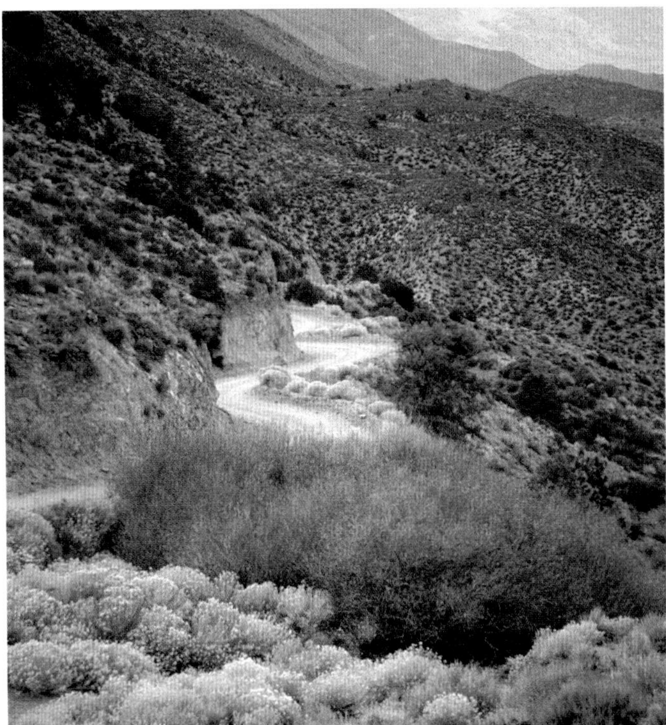

Part of the long descent down Grapevine Canyon into Saline Valley

0.1 ▲ SO Cross through Willow Creek wash; then track on right.

▼ 4.5 BR Graded road on left goes into Willow Creek Camp. Zero trip meter.
0.0 ▲ Continue to the southeast.

GPS: N36°50.16′ W117°54.97′

▼ 0.0 Continue to the north, following the sign for Big Pine, and cross through wash.
19.3 ▲ BL Cross through wash; then graded road on right goes into Willow Creek Camp. Zero trip meter.

▼ 0.1 SO Track on left.
19.2 ▲ SO Track on right.

▼ 0.6 SO Cross through many washes for the next 3.4 miles.
18.7 ▲ SO Cross through wash. End of wash crossings.

▼ 4.0 SO Cross through wash. End of wash crossings.
15.3 ▲ SO Cross through many washes for the next 3.4 miles.

▼ 5.4 SO Well-used track on left.
13.9 ▲ SO Well-used track on right.

GPS: N36°54.69′ W117°54.50′

▼ 7.8 SO Cross through wash.
11.5 ▲ SO Cross through wash.

▼ 8.6 SO Track on left.
10.7 ▲ SO Track on right.

▼ 8.7 SO Cross through wash.
10.6 ▲ SO Cross through wash.

▼ 9.8 SO Track on left goes to Waucoba Mine.
9.5 ▲ SO Track on right goes to Waucoba Mine.

GPS: N36°58.54′ W117°55.88′

▼ 10.7 SO Cross through wash.
8.6 ▲ SO Cross through wash.

▼ 11.5 SO Cross through Waucoba Wash.
7.8 ▲ SO Cross through Waucoba Wash.

▼ 12.0 SO Cross through wash.
7.3 ▲ SO Cross through wash.

GPS: N37°00.41′ W117°56.54′

▼ 12.3 SO Cross through wash.
7.0 ▲ SO Cross through wash.

▼ 12.6 SO Enter line of wash. Trail follows in or alongside wash, crossing it often for the next 2 miles.
6.7 ▲ SO Exit line of wash.

▼ 14.6 SO Exit line of wash and Whippoorwill Canyon.
4.7 ▲ SO Enter line of wash and Whippoorwill Canyon. Trail follows in or alongside wash, crossing it often for the next 2 miles.

▼ 15.0 SO Track on left. Entering Whippoorwill Flat.
4.3 ▲ SO Track on right. Exiting Whippoorwill Flat.

GPS: N37°02.06′ W117°58.41′

▼ 15.3 SO Track on left.
4.0 ▲ SO Track on right.

▼ 16.2 SO Track on left.
3.1 ▲ SO Track on right.

GPS: N37°03.06′ W117°58.47′

▼ 17.3 SO Track on left.
2.0 ▲ SO Track on right.

▼ 17.6 SO Track on left.
1.7 ▲ SO Second entrance to track on right.

GPS: N37°04.27′ W117°58.65′

▼ 17.8 SO Second entrance to track on left. Trail enters Opal Canyon.
1.5 ▲ SO Track on right. Trail enters Whippoorwill Flat.

▼ 18.0 SO Cross through wash.
1.3 ▲ SO Cross through wash.

▼ 19.3 BL Track on right goes down Marble Canyon to many mining remains. Bear left up Marble Canyon, remaining on main graded road, and zero trip meter. Marble Canyon intersects with Opal Canyon at this point.
0.0 ▲ Continue to the south.

GPS: N37°05.47′ W117°57.82′

▼ 0.0 Continue to the west.
7.6 ▲ BR Track straight ahead continues down Marble Canyon. Bear right up Opal Canyon, remaining on main graded road, and zero trip meter. Marble Canyon intersects with Opal Canyon at this point.

▼ 0.1 SO Old miner's cabin on right. There are many mining remains scattered along the floor of Marble Canyon.
7.5 ▲ SO Old miner's cabin on left. There are many mining remains scattered along the floor of Marble Canyon.

▼ 0.7 SO Track on right to mine.
6.9 ▲ SO Track on left to mine.

GPS: N37°05.35′ W117°58.53′

▼ 1.0 SO Entering Inyo National Forest.
6.6 ▲ SO Entering Death Valley National Park.

GPS: N37°05.29′ W117°58.88′

▼ 1.2 SO Track on left.
6.4 ▲ SO Track on right.

▼ 1.3 SO Track on left; then cross through wash; then second track on left.
6.3 ▲ SO Track on right; then cross through wash; then second track on right.

▼ 1.5 SO Track on right.
6.1 ▲ SO Track on left.

▼ 4.4 SO Track on left to game tank.
3.2 ▲ SO Track on right to game tank.

▼ 4.5 SO Track on left.

Mileage		Direction	Description
	3.1 ▲	SO	Track on right.
▼ 4.8		SO	Track on left.
	2.8 ▲	SO	Track on right.
▼ 4.9		SO	Track on right.
	2.7 ▲	SO	Track on left.
▼ 5.9		SO	Track on right enters Cowhorn Valley.
	1.7 ▲	SO	Track on left enters Cowhorn Valley.
			GPS: N37°08.15' W118°01.52'
▼ 6.0		BR	Trail forks. Take either trail.
	1.6 ▲	SO	Trail rejoins.
▼ 6.3		SO	Trail rejoins.
	1.3 ▲	SO	Trail forks. Take either trail.
▼ 6.5		SO	Old road cutting on left.
	1.1 ▲	SO	Old road rejoins.
▼ 6.6		SO	Old road rejoins.
	1.0 ▲	SO	Old road cutting on right.
▼ 7.6		TL	Track on left and track on right; then T-intersection with Eureka Valley Road (listed as Death Valley Road on some maps). Road on right is 9S18. Zero trip meter and turn left onto paved Eureka Valley Road.
	0.0 ▲		Continue to the east. Track on left and track on right.
			GPS: N37°08.24' W118°03.15'
▼ 0.0			Continue to the southwest.
	1.8 ▲	TR	Turn right onto graded dirt road, following the sign for Saline Valley Road, and zero trip meter. Paved road continues ahead and is marked 9S18.
▼ 1.2		SO	Track on left.
	0.6 ▲	SO	Track on right.
▼ 1.8		SO	Track on left is High Sierra #46: Papoose Flat Trail. Zero trip meter.
	0.0 ▲		Continue to the northeast.
			GPS: N37°07.38' W118°04.60'
▼ 0.0			Continue to the west.
	2.0 ▲	SO	Track on right is High Sierra #46: Papoose Flat Trail. Zero trip meter
▼ 0.6		SO	Track on right.
	1.4 ▲	SO	Track on left.
▼ 2.0		SO	Track on left is High Sierra #48: Harkless Flat Trail (9S13). Zero trip meter.
	0.0 ▲		Continue to the southeast.
			GPS: N37°08.04' W118°06.64'
▼ 0.0			Continue to the northwest.
	5.5 ▲	SO	Track on right is High Sierra #48: Harkless Flat Trail (9S13). Zero trip meter.
▼ 0.2		SO	Track on right.
	5.3 ▲	SO	Track on left.
▼ 1.1		SO	Pass through Devils Gate; then cross through wash.
	4.4 ▲	SO	Cross through wash; then pass through Devils Gate.
			GPS: N37°08.66' W118°07.47'
▼ 2.7		SO	Track on left.
	2.8 ▲	SO	Track on right.
▼ 4.9		SO	Track on left.
	0.6 ▲	SO	Track on right.
▼ 5.3		SO	Track on right.
	0.2 ▲	SO	Track on left.
▼ 5.5		SO	Exiting Inyo National Forest at sign. Zero trip meter.
	0.0 ▲		Continue to the east.
			GPS: N37°10.20' W118°11.81'
▼ 0.0			Continue to the west.
	3.3 ▲	SO	Entering Inyo National Forest at sign. Zero trip meter.
▼ 0.8		SO	Cross through wash.
	2.5 ▲	SO	Cross through wash.
▼ 1.1		SO	Track on right.
	2.2 ▲	SO	Track on left.
▼ 1.9		SO	Track on right.
	1.4 ▲	SO	Track on left.
▼ 2.5		SO	Track on right.
	0.8 ▲	SO	Track on left.
▼ 3.3			Trail ends at intersection with California 168. Turn left for Big Pine; turn right for Nevada.
	0.0 ▲		Trail commences on California 168, 2.5 miles east of US 395 and Big Pine. Zero trip meter and turn southeast on paved Saline Valley Road. It is signposted as Death Valley Road to Scotty's Castle.
			GPS: N37°11.10' W118°15.13'

HIGH SIERRA #46

Papoose Flat Trail

Starting Point:	**High Sierra #45: Saline Valley Road, 10.8 miles from the northern end**
Finishing Point:	**High Sierra #49: Mazourka Peak Trail, 18.4 miles from Independence**
Total Mileage:	**16.3 miles**
Unpaved Mileage:	**16.3 miles**
Driving Time:	**2.5 hours**
Elevation Range:	**7,000–9,500 feet**
Usually Open:	**April to November**
Best Time to Travel:	**April to November**
Difficulty Rating:	**4**
Scenic Rating:	**9**
Remoteness Rating:	**+1**

Special Attractions

- Rocky outcrops on Papoose Flat.
- Moderate rocky trail that traverses a variety of scenery within the Inyo Mountains.
- Backcountry camping and access to a network of other 4WD trails.
- Can be combined with High Sierra #47: The Narrows Trail to form a loop back to the starting point on High Sierra #45: Saline Valley Road.

Description

Before Euro-Americans came to the area, Paiute Indians spent the summer and fall in the Inyo Mountains gathering pinyon nuts and killing game for the winter, which they spent in the Owens Valley. This trail leaves High Sierra #45: Saline Valley Road and travels along a single vehicle width trail into the Inyo Mountains to Papoose and Badger Flats, areas used exten-

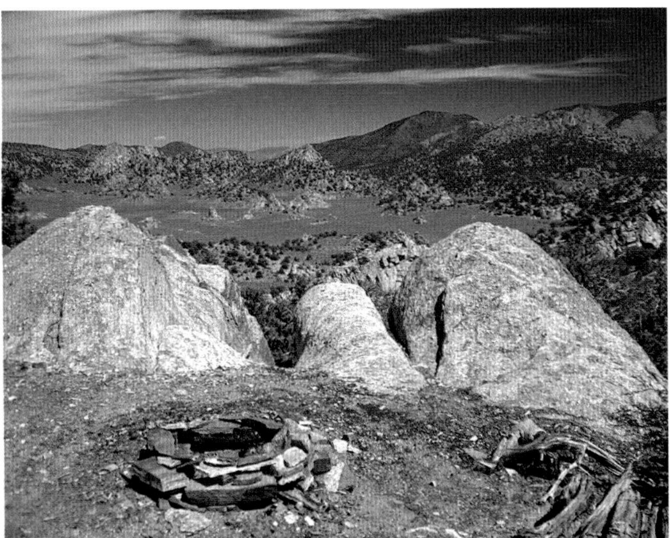

Granite outcroppings at Papoose Flat

sively by the Paiute. Watch out for occasional loose sand traps that turn to deep mud after rain.

Initially, the trail crosses sagebrush-covered flats and then heads into a wide valley before entering the line of a wash. The valley narrows to a tight canyon as you gradually climb. The grade increases as the trail switchbacks out of the valley, and views from the trail gradually improve as the Sierra Nevada comes into view on the western side of the Owens Valley. As the trail drops down onto Papoose Flat, views are some of the most striking along the trail. The wide flat is scattered with outcrops, or knobs, of granitic rock. To the west, the Sierra Nevada rises above the Owens Valley.

The section of trail from Papoose Flat to Badger Flat is the most challenging and requires a high-clearance 4WD. From Papoose Flat, the trail climbs steeply along a loose, ledgy, rutted surface, and some sections have poor traction. Some excellent campsites are tucked into the pinyons and junipers alongside the trail, with excellent views over Papoose Flat. The final mile of the trail descends to Badger Flat. Mazourka Peak is to the west, easily identified by the communications towers on its summit. The trail ends on the easier High Sierra #49: Mazourka Peak Trail.

High Sierra #47: The Narrows Trail begins and ends on Papoose Flat Trail. Anyone not wishing to tackle the 4-rated section of Papoose Flat Trail to Badger Flat can return along The Narrows to make a loop back to High Sierra #45: Saline Valley Road.

Current Road Information

Inyo National Forest
Mount Whitney Ranger District
640 South Main Street
Lone Pine, CA 93545
(760) 876-6200

Map References

BLM Bishop, Mt. Whitney
USFS Inyo National Forest
USGS 1:24,000 Waucoba Mt., Mazourka Peak
1:100,000 Bishop, Mt. Whitney
Maptech CD-ROM: Kings Canyon/Death Valley
Northern California Atlas & Gazetteer, p. 124
Southern & Central California Atlas & Gazetteer, p. 27
California Road & Recreation Atlas, p. 79

Route Directions

Mileage		Direction
▼ 0.0		From High Sierra #45: Saline Valley Road, 10.8 miles from the northern end, zero trip meter and turn south on Papoose Flat Road (9S15) at the sign.
4.9 ▲		Trail ends at intersection with High Sierra #45: Saline Valley Road. Turn left to exit to Lone Pine; turn right to travel Saline Valley Road to Death Valley.
		GPS: N37°07.37' W118°04.60'
▼ 0.2	BR	Bear right onto 9S15, following the sign to Papoose Flat. Track on left is High Sierra #47: The Narrows Trail (9S14).
4.7 ▲	SO	Track on right is High Sierra #47: The Narrows Trail (9S14).
		GPS: N37°07.26' W118°04.54'
▼ 0.7	SO	Track on left.
4.2 ▲	SO	Track on right.
▼ 1.2	SO	Track on right; then track on left.
3.7 ▲	SO	Track on right; then track on left.
▼ 1.6	SO	Track on right; then cross through wash.
3.3 ▲	BR	Cross through wash; then track straight ahead. Bear right leaving track on the left.
▼ 2.0	SO	Track on right.
2.9 ▲	SO	Track on left.
▼ 2.2	SO	Track on right.
2.7 ▲	SO	Track on left.
▼ 2.5	BL	Campsite on right. Trail enters line of wash.
2.4 ▲	BR	Trail leaves line of wash. Campsite on left.
		GPS: N37°05.76' W118°05.24'

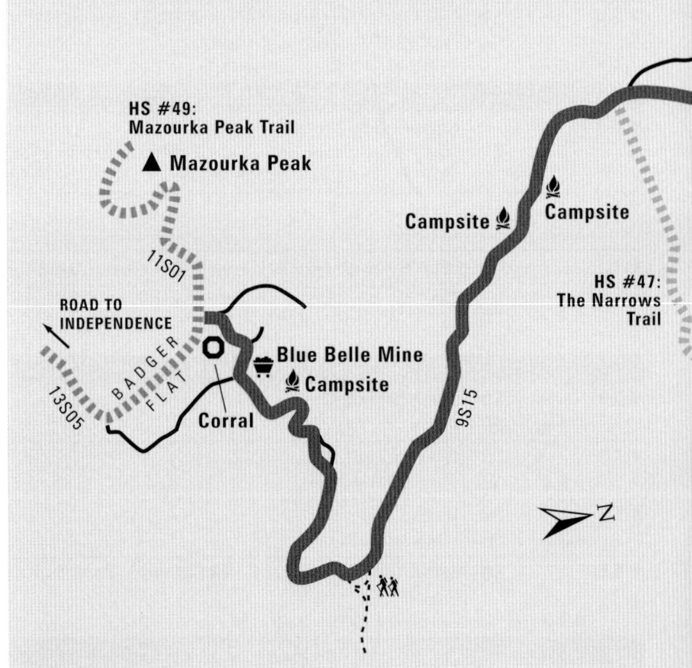

▼	▲		
▼ 3.1		SO	Track on left; then track on right. Leaving line of wash and exiting tight section of canyon.
	1.8 ▲	SO	Track on left; then track on right. Entering line of wash and heading into a tight canyon.
▼ 3.8		SO	Enter line of wash.
	1.1 ▲	SO	Exit line of wash.
▼ 4.0		TL	Trail swings sharp left. Track on right.
	0.9 ▲	TR	Track continues straight ahead. Turn sharp right.
			GPS: N37°05.19′ W118°06.42′
▼ 4.9		BL	Track on right is High Sierra #48: Harkless Flat Trail. Zero trip meter.
	0.0 ▲		Continue to the northeast.
			GPS: N37°04.85′ W118°06.78′
▼ 0.0			Continue to the south on 9S15 following sign to Papoose Flat.
	5.2 ▲	BR	Track on left is High Sierra #48: Harkless Flat Trail. Zero trip meter.
▼ 0.5		SO	Track on right.
	4.7 ▲	SO	Track on left.
▼ 1.7		BL	Well-used track on right. Remain on 9S15.
	3.5 ▲	BR	Well-used track on left. Remain on 9S15.
			GPS: N37°03.51′ W118°07.31′
▼ 3.0		SO	Track on left.
	2.2 ▲	SO	Track on right.
▼ 3.8		TL	Well-used track straight ahead. Start to drop down toward Papoose Flat.
	1.4 ▲	TR	T-intersection. Well-used track on left.
			GPS: N37°02.02′ W118°06.72′
▼ 4.0		SO	Track on right.
	1.2 ▲	BR	Track on left.
▼ 5.0		SO	Track on right.
	0.2 ▲	SO	Track on left.
▼ 5.1		SO	Track on right.
	0.1 ▲	BR	Track on left.
▼ 5.2		SO	Track on left is High Sierra #47: The Narrows Trail. Zero trip meter and follow sign to Badger Flat.
	0.0 ▲		Continue to the northwest along Papoose Flat.
			GPS: N37°00.93′ W118°07.22′
▼ 0.0			Continue to the southeast.
	5.6 ▲	SO	Track on right is High Sierra #47: The Narrows Trail. Zero trip meter at sign for Badger Flat, which is pointing back in the direction you have just come.
▼ 0.3		BL	Track on right.
	5.3 ▲	BR	Track on left.
			GPS: N37°00.71′ W118°07.21′
▼ 0.8		SO	Small campsite with view on left.
	4.8 ▲	SO	Small campsite with view on right.
▼ 1.0		BL	Campsite on right.
	4.6 ▲	BR	Campsite on left.
▼ 1.2		SO	Rise, with view of Mazourka Peak, the Sierra Nevada, and into the Inyo Mountains Wilderness.
	4.4 ▲	SO	Rise, with view of Mazourka Peak, the Sierra Nevada, and into the Inyo Mountains Wilderness.
▼ 1.5		SO	Cross through wash.
	4.1 ▲	SO	Cross through wash.
▼ 3.4		BR	Two tracks that lead into wilderness on left are for hikers and horses only.
	2.2 ▲	BL	Two tracks that lead into wilderness on right are for hikers and horses only.
			GPS: N36°59.40′ W118°04.61′
▼ 3.5		SO	Track on left that leads into wilderness is for hikers and horses only.
	2.1 ▲	SO	Track on right that leads into wilderness is for hikers and horses only.
▼ 4.5		BL	Track on right.
	1.1 ▲	SO	Track on left.
			GPS: N36°59.31′ W118°05.23′

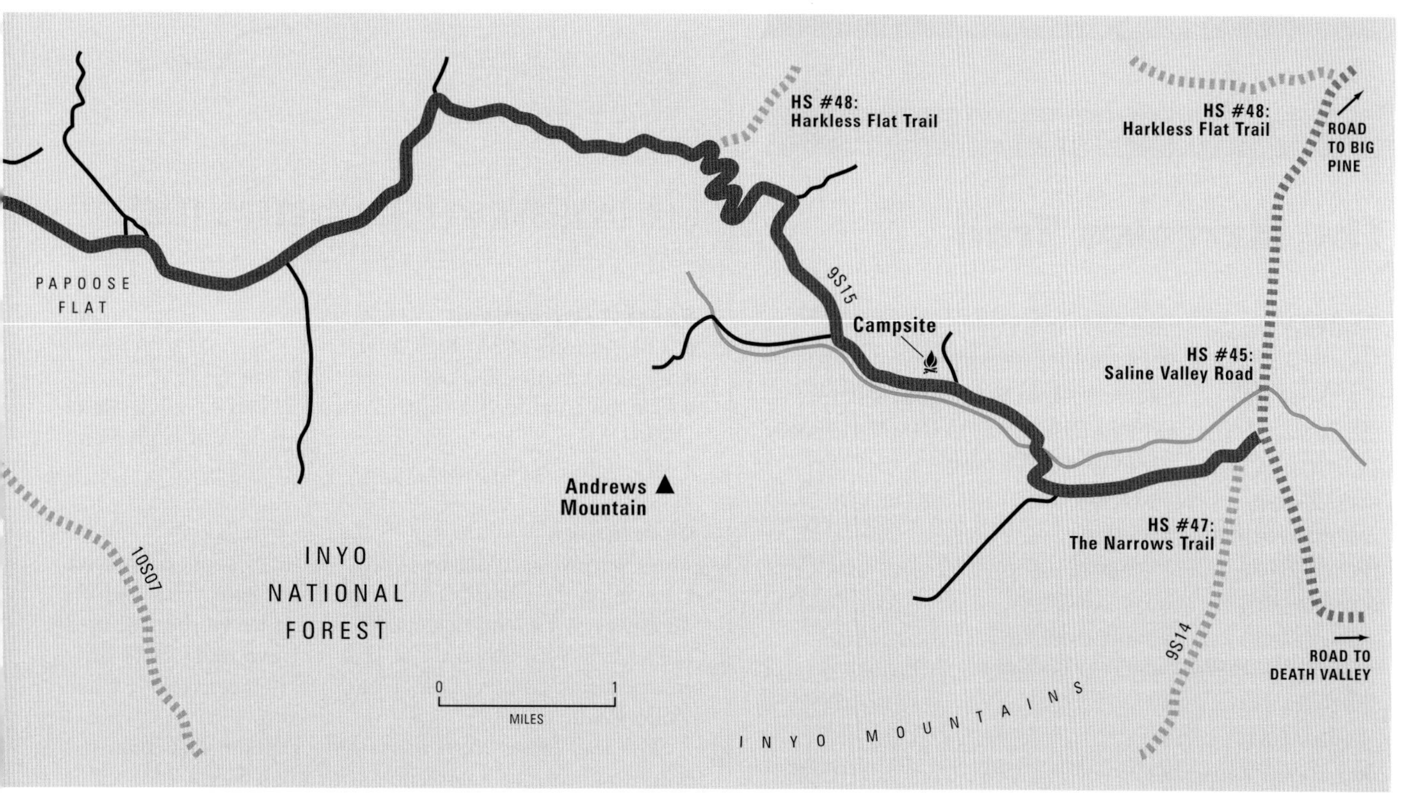

▼ 4.7	SO	Track on right.
0.9 ▲	SO	Track on left.
		GPS: N36°59.26' W118°05.49'
▼ 4.8	SO	Track on left and pull-in on right.
0.8 ▲	SO	Pull-in on left and track on right.
		GPS: N36°59.23' W118°05.53'
▼ 5.0	BL	Campsite on right.
0.6 ▲	BR	Campsite on left.
▼ 5.6	TR	T-intersection. Zero trip meter. There is a sign for Papoose Flat at the intersection pointing back the way you have come.
0.0 ▲		Continue to the north.
		GPS: N36°58.89' W118°05.89'
▼ 0.0		Continue to the northwest. Track on right to campsite.
0.6 ▲	TL	Track on left to campsite. Turn left following sign for Papoose Flat. Zero trip meter.
▼ 0.1	SO	Blue Bell Mine on right.
0.5 ▲	SO	Blue Bell Mine on left.
		GPS: N36°58.95' W118°05.95'
▼ 0.2	BL	Track on right.
0.4 ▲	BR	Track on left.
▼ 0.3	BL	Track on right.
0.3 ▲	BR	Track on left.
▼ 0.4	SO	Corral on left.
0.2 ▲	SO	Corral on right.
▼ 0.5	BL	Track on right.
0.1 ▲	BR	Track on left.
▼ 0.6		Trail ends at T-intersection with High Sierra #49: Mazourka Peak Trail. Turn right to ascend Mazourka Peak; turn left to exit to Independence.
0.0 ▲		Trail commences on High Sierra #49: Mazourka Peak Trail, 18.4 miles from Independence. Zero trip meter and turn northwest on small, well-used unmarked trail. There is a route marker on High Sierra #49: Mazourka Peak Trail for 11S01.
		GPS: N36°58.77' W118°06.22'

HIGH SIERRA #47

The Narrows Trail

Starting Point:	**High Sierra #46: Papoose Flat Trail, 0.2 miles from the northern end**
Finishing Point:	**High Sierra #46: Papoose Flat Trail at Papoose Flat, 10.1 miles from High Sierra #45: Saline Valley Road**
Total Mileage:	**14.1 miles**
Unpaved Mileage:	**14.1 miles**
Driving Time:	**2 hours**
Elevation Range:	**7,100–8,600 feet**
Usually Open:	**April to November**
Best Time to Travel:	**April to November**
Difficulty Rating:	**3**
Scenic Rating:	**9**
Remoteness Rating:	**+1**

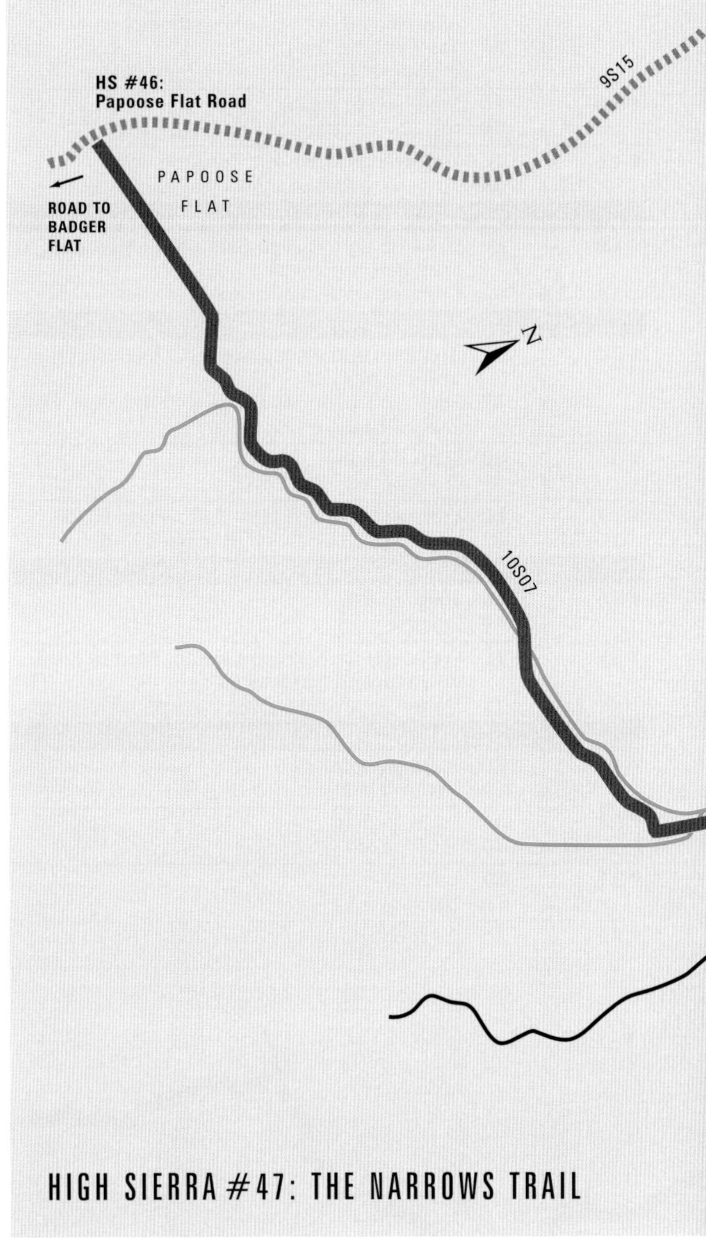

HIGH SIERRA #47: THE NARROWS TRAIL

Special Attractions

- The Narrows of Marble Canyon.
- Mining remains and old cabin at The Narrows.
- Can be combined with the northern end of High Sierra #46: Papoose Flat Trail to create a loop back to High Sierra #45: Saline Valley Road.

Description

The Narrows is a narrow, high-walled section of Marble Canyon on the east side of the Inyo Mountains. The Narrows Trail is part of a loop that starts and finishes on the well-used High Sierra #46: Papoose Flat Trail. The two trails can be driven together to complete a loop back to High Sierra #45: Saline Valley Road.

The trail leaves High Sierra #46: Papoose Flat Trail, 0.2 miles south of the intersection with High Sierra #45: Saline

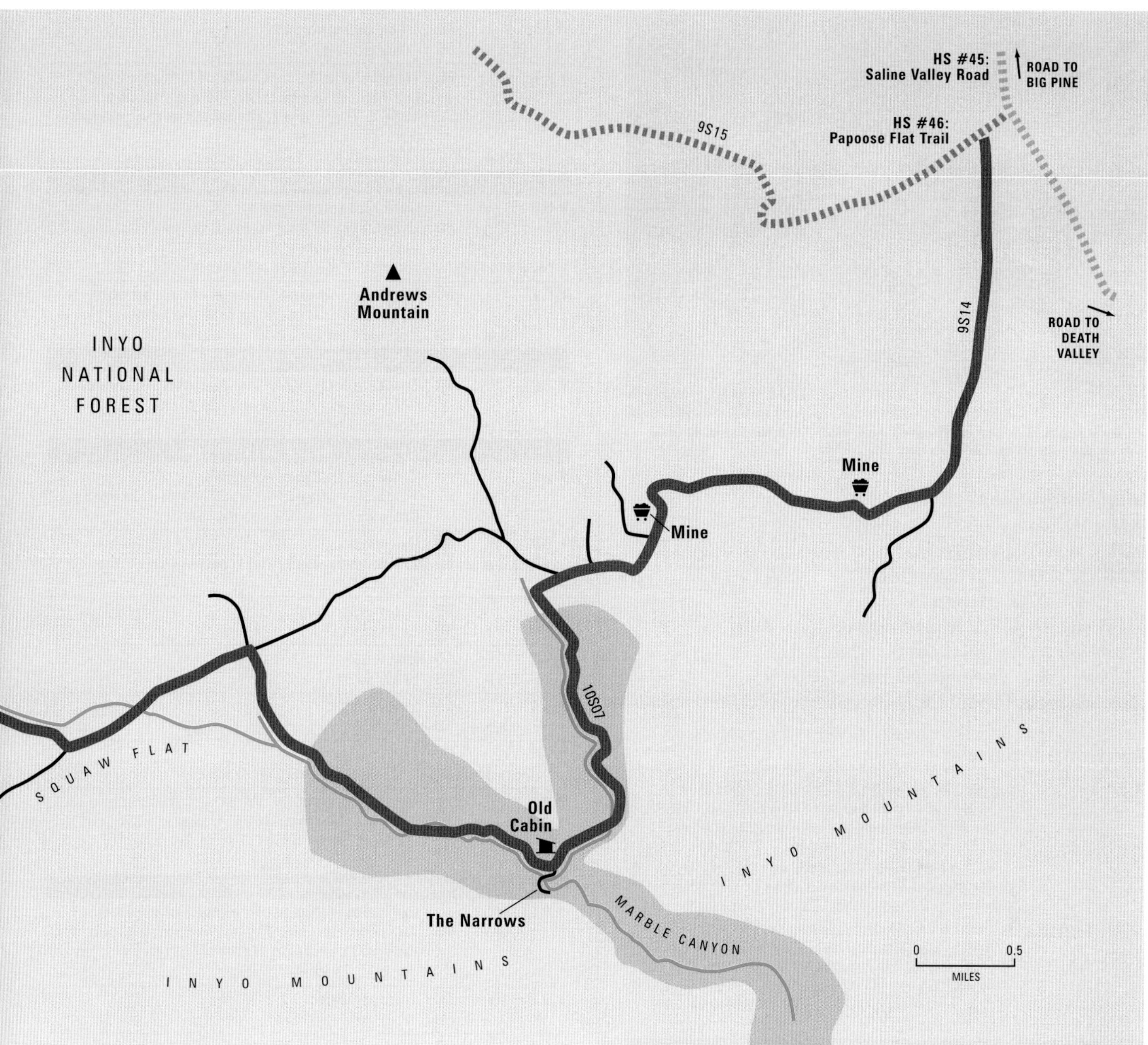

Valley Road. It heads up a canyon through pinyons and junipers and gradually climbs and narrows. The surface is slightly loose, and there are a few rough spots, but it should be well within the capabilities of any high-clearance 4WD.

After passing through a small open valley with abundant sagebrush, the trail doglegs and enters a side canyon. There are a few passing places in this section, and the trail is typically only wide enough for a single vehicle. The side canyon joins Marble Canyon at The Narrows; a remarkable gold nugget weighing nine ounces was found in the canyon. An old timber, stone, slate, and corrugated iron cabin stands opposite the entrance to The Narrows against the canyon wall. A side track leads through The Narrows to some mining remains a short distance away. Squaw Peak can be seen directly ahead from this intersection.

The trail stays mainly in Marble Canyon's wash line; this stretch is smoother than the side canyon. Sagebrush is abundant and is often roof high. The brush eases off as the trail leaves the wash, but there is a second slightly brushy section along Squaw Flat. The trail crosses the striking landscape of Papoose Flat, with its prominent rock outcrops, to meet High Sierra #46: Papoose Flat Trail. You have a choice: to go north back to High Sierra #45: Saline Valley Road, or go south along the 4-rated section to Badger Flat and High Sierra #49: Mazourka Peak Trail.

Current Road Information

Inyo National Forest
Mount Whitney Ranger District
640 South Main Street
Lone Pine, CA 93545
(760) 876-6200

Old miner's cabin made of corrugated iron, slate, and timber in Marble Canyon at the mouth of The Narrows

Map References

BLM Bishop
USFS Inyo National Forest
USGS 1:24,000 Waucoba Mt.
1:100,000 Bishop
Maptech CD-ROM: Kings Canyon/Death Valley
Northern California Atlas & Gazetteer, p. 124
California Road & Recreation Atlas, p. 79
Trails Illustrated, Death Valley National Park (221) (incomplete)

Route Directions

Mileage		Direction
▼ 0.0		From High Sierra #45: Saline Valley Road, 10.8 miles from the northern end, turn south on High Sierra #46: Papoose Flat Trail (9S15) at the sign and proceed for 0.2 miles to a fork in the trail. Bear left (east) onto 9S14, following the sign to The Narrows. Track on right is 9S15 to Papoose Flat. Zero trip meter.
4.1 ▲		The trail ends at intersection with High Sierra #46: Papoose Flat Trail, 0.2 miles from High Sierra #45: Saline Valley Road. Turn right to exit to Saline Valley Road. From there you can turn east to continue to Death Valley or west to Big Pine.
		GPS: N37°07.26' W118°04.54'
▼ 1.8	BR	Faint track on left.
2.3 ▲	SO	Faint track on right.
▼ 1.9	SO	Faint track on left.
2.2 ▲	BL	Faint track on right.
▼ 2.2	SO	Mine on right above trail. Adit on right.
1.9 ▲	SO	Mine on left above trail. Adit on left.
		GPS: N37°06.22' W118°02.90'
▼ 2.7	SO	Filled-in shaft on left; then track on right to campsite.
1.4 ▲	SO	Track on left to campsite; then filled-in shaft on right.
		GPS: N37°05.85' W118°03.22'
▼ 3.3	SO	Mine diggings with wood-lined adits on right.
0.8 ▲	SO	Mine diggings with wood-lined adits on left.
		GPS: N37°05.41' W118°03.31'
▼ 3.5	SO	Track on right on rise.
0.6 ▲	SO	Track on left on rise.
		GPS: N37°05.34' W118°03.13'
▼ 3.9	SO	Track on right.
0.2 ▲	SO	Track on left.
▼ 4.1	BL	Trail forks in a small valley. Unmarked well-used track on right. Bear left, remaining on 10S07. There is a trail marker at the intersection. Zero trip meter.
0.0 ▲		Continue to the north.
		GPS: N37°04.93' W118°03.08'
▼ 0.0		Continue to the south.
2.0 ▲	SO	Unmarked well-used track on left in a small valley. The trail you have just entered on is marked 10S07. Zero trip meter.
▼ 0.2	BL	Bear left and enter canyon. Track on right. Trail now travels in or alongside the wash.
1.8 ▲	BR	Exit canyon and bear right. Track on left.
		GPS: N37°04.77' W118°03.08'
▼ 2.0	BR	Track on left enters The Narrows. Remains of old cabin on right. Zero trip meter.
0.0 ▲		Continue to the north.
		GPS: N37°04.46' W118°01.64'
▼ 0.0		Continue to the southwest.
2.2 ▲	BL	Track on right enters The Narrows. Remains of old cabin on left. Zero trip meter.
▼ 0.6	SO	Exit wash.
1.6 ▲	SO	Enter wash. Trail now travels in or alongside the wash.
▼ 0.8	SO	Enter wash.
1.4 ▲	SO	Exit wash.
▼ 1.2	SO	Exit wash.
1.0 ▲	SO	Enter wash.
▼ 1.4	SO	Enter wash.
0.8 ▲	SO	Exit wash.
▼ 1.6	SO	Exit wash.
0.6 ▲	SO	Enter wash.
▼ 2.2	TL	4-way intersection. Well-used track ahead and on right. Trail marker on trail you have just come in on is 10S07. Zero trip meter.
0.0 ▲		Continue to the east.
		GPS: N37°03.52' W118°03.26'
▼ 0.0		Continue to the south along Squaw Flat.
5.8 ▲	TR	4-way intersection. Well-used track ahead and on left. Remain on 10S07. Trail marker at intersection. Zero trip meter.
▼ 0.1	SO	Track on right.
5.7 ▲	SO	Track on left.
▼ 1.1	BR	Well-used track continues along Squaw Flat on the left.
4.7 ▲	TL	Well-used track on right. Turn left and continue along Squaw Flat.
		GPS: N37°02.62' W118°03.08'
▼ 2.0	SO	Exiting Squaw Flat. Trail travels up canyon in wash.
3.8 ▲	SO	Entering Squaw Flat. Trail exits wash.
▼ 3.1	BL	Track on right.
2.7 ▲	BR	Track on left.
		GPS: N37°01.82' W118°04.73'
▼ 4.6	SO	Trail enters Papoose Flat.
1.2 ▲	SO	Trail leaves Papoose Flat.
▼ 5.4	SO	Track on right.
0.4 ▲	SO	Track on left.
▼ 5.8		Trail ends at T-intersection with High Sierra #46: Papoose Flat Trail. Turn left for Badger Flat; turn right to exit to High Sierra #45: Saline Valley Road.
0.0 ▲		Trail commences on High Sierra #46: Papoose

Flat Trail at Papoose Flat, 10.1 miles from High Sierra #45: Saline Valley Road. Zero trip meter and turn northeast on well-used trail that crosses Papoose Flat. There is a sign for "Badger Flat 4WD only" at this point that points along the continuation of Papoose Flat Trail.

GPS: N37°00.93' W118°07.22'

HIGH SIERRA #48

Harkless Flat Trail

Starting Point:	**High Sierra #46: Papoose Flat Trail, 4.9 miles south of High Sierra #45: Saline Valley Road**
Finishing Point:	**High Sierra #45: Saline Valley Road, 8.8 miles from the northern end**
Total Mileage:	**6.3 miles, plus 2.6-mile spur to viewpoint**
Unpaved Mileage:	**6.3 miles, plus 2.6-mile spur**
Driving Time:	**2 hours (including the spur)**
Elevation Range:	**6,600–9,000 feet**
Usually Open:	**April to November**
Best Time to Travel:	**April to November**
Difficulty Rating:	**5**
Scenic Rating:	**9**
Remoteness Rating:	**+0**

Special Attractions

- Challenging hill trail.
- Old cabin and viewpoint over Tinemaha Reservoir.

Description

The trail leaves High Sierra #46: Papoose Flat Trail and follows a single-track formed trail. After cresting a small rise, it starts to descend steeply toward Harkless Flat, named for a pioneer who gathered timber for sale here. The steep gradient means that the slightly loose surface is rutted and eroded from water runoff. Select a low gear and use the brakes sparingly to avoid slippage. It is this descent that gives the trail its difficulty rating of 5. There are great views over the Owens Valley, across to the Sierra Nevada, and north to the White Mountains.

A narrow hiking trail leads from the end of the spur trail toward the Blake Mine, high above the Tinemaha Reservoir

Harkless Flat is a wide sage-covered valley in the Inyo Mountains. A spur trail leads a short distance to the remains of an old cabin and a viewpoint and campsite on the edge of the range with a view directly over the Tinemaha Reservoir. A hiking trail continues a short way down to the site of the Blake Mine.

Back on the main route, the trail continues along the wide Harkless Flat, before exiting via a small canyon to join High Sierra #45: Saline Valley Road.

Current Road Information

Inyo National Forest
Mount Whitney Ranger District
640 South Main Street
Lone Pine, CA 93545
(760) 876-6200

Map References

BLM Bishop
USFS Inyo National Forest
USGS 1:24,000 Waucoba Mt., Tinemaha Reservoir, Cowhorn Valley
1:100,000 Bishop
Maptech CD-ROM: Kings Canyon/Death Valley
Northern California Atlas & Gazetteer, p. 124
California Road & Recreation Atlas, p. 79

Route Directions

▼ 0.0		From High Sierra #46: Papoose Flat Trail, 4.9 miles south of the intersection with High Sierra #45: Saline Valley Road, zero trip meter and turn northwest on well-used formed trail following the sign for Harkless Flat.
3.8 ▲		Trail ends at intersection with High Sierra #46: Papoose Flat Trail. Turn left to exit to High Sierra #45: Saline Valley Road; turn right to continue along the trail.
		GPS: N37°04.85' W118°06.78'
▼ 1.0	SO	Start of very steep descent.
2.8 ▲	SO	End of steep section.
		GPS: N37°05.23' W118°07.48'
▼ 1.5	SO	Track on left. End of very steep section.
2.3 ▲	BL	Track on right. Start of very steep climb.
		GPS: N37°05.03' W118°07.82'
▼ 2.5	SO	Well-used track on left.
1.3 ▲	SO	Well-used track on right.
		GPS: N37°05.62' W118°08.56'
▼ 2.8	SO	Track on left.
1.0 ▲	SO	Track on right.
▼ 3.0	SO	Trail enters Harkless Flat.
0.8 ▲	SO	Trail leaves Harkless Flat.
▼ 3.5	SO	Track on right on Harkless Flat.
0.3 ▲	BR	Track on left on Harkless Flat.
		GPS: N37°06.40' W118°08.31'
▼ 3.7	SO	Track on left.
0.1 ▲	BL	Track on right.

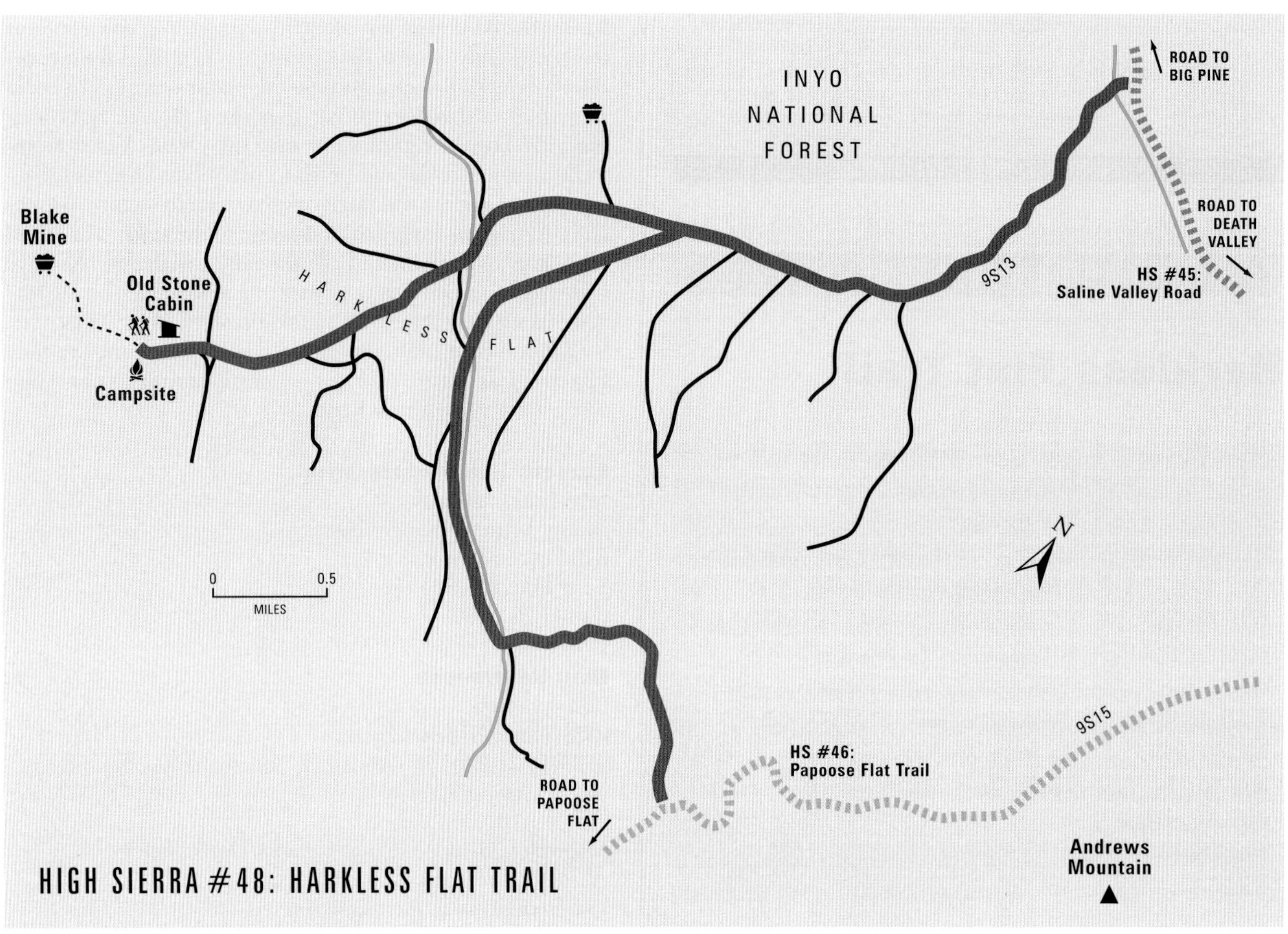

▼ 3.8		SO	Well-used unmarked track on left is start of spur to cabin and mine. Zero trip meter.
	0.0 ▲		Continue to the southwest.
			GPS: N37°06.65′ W118°08.11′

Spur to Overlook and Cabin

▼ 0.0		Continue to the west.
▼ 0.3	SO	Track on right to mine.
		GPS: N37°06.60′ W118°08.46′
▼ 0.9	BL	Track on right and track straight ahead. Bear left, heading up the valley.
		GPS: N37°06.29′ W118°08.94′
▼ 1.1	SO	Cross through wash. Track on left.
▼ 1.2	BL	Track on right.
▼ 1.7	SO	Track on left.
		GPS: N37°05.70′ W118°09.23′
▼ 2.0	SO	Track on left.
▼ 2.1	SO	Track on right; then track on left.
▼ 2.3	SP	Track on left; then immediately bear left past track on right. Keep heading toward the saddle visible ahead.
		GPS: N37°05.37′ W118°09.77′
▼ 2.4	SO	Track on left.
▼ 2.5	SO	Old stone cabin on right.
▼ 2.6	UT	Spur ends at viewpoint and campsite overlooking the Owens Valley immediately above Tinemaha Reservoir. A hiking trail continues down to the site of the Blake Mine—little remains.
		GPS: N37°05.23′ W118°10.00′

Continuation of Main Trail

▼ 0.0			Continue to the northeast.
	2.5 ▲	BL	Well-used unmarked track on right is start of spur to cabin and mine. Zero trip meter.
			GPS: N37°06.65′ W118°08.11′
▼ 0.3		SO	Track on right.
	2.2 ▲	BR	Track on left.
▼ 0.5		SO	Track on right.
	2.0 ▲	BR	Track on left.
▼ 0.7		BL	Track on right.
	1.8 ▲	SO	Track on left.
▼ 1.0		SO	Track on right.
	1.5 ▲	SO	Track on left.
▼ 1.1		SO	Well-used track on right. Trail enters line of wash.
	1.4 ▲	BR	Trail exits line of wash. Bear right past well-used track on left.
			GPS: N37°06.94′ W118°07.04′
▼ 2.4		SO	Cross through wash.
	0.1 ▲	SO	Cross through wash.
▼ 2.5			Trail ends at intersection with paved High Sierra #45: Saline Valley Road. Turn right for Death Valley; turn left for Big Pine.
	0.0 ▲		Trail commences on High Sierra #45: Saline Valley Road, 8.8 miles from the northern end. Zero trip meter and turn southwest on formed trail at sign for Harkless Flat. The trail is marked 9S13 immediately after the intersection.
			GPS: N37°08.04′ W118°06.64′

HIGH SIERRA #49

Mazourka Peak Trail

Starting Point:	**US 395, on the south edge of Independence**
Finishing Point:	**Communications towers on Mazourka Peak**
Total Mileage:	**20.4 miles (one-way)**
Unpaved Mileage:	**16.1 miles**
Driving Time:	**1.5 hours**
Elevation Range:	**3,800–9,400 feet**
Usually Open:	**April to November**
Best Time to Travel:	**April to November**
Difficulty Rating:	**2**
Scenic Rating:	**8**
Remoteness Rating:	**+0**

Special Attractions

- Panoramic views from Mazourka Peak over the Owens Valley toward the Sierra Nevada.
- Many mining remains.
- Backcountry camping opportunities on Badger Flat.

History

Mazourka Canyon, on the west side of the Inyo Mountains above Independence, was once the scene of placer and lode mining. A gold strike in 1863 led to the establishment of the Green Monster Mine, which had yields of up to $500 to the ton.

Independence, at the start of the trail, is the seat of government for Inyo County. Charles Putnam built a cabin here in 1861 and operated a trading post that catered to miners and settlers. Thomas Edwards bought him out in 1863 and laid out the settlement of Independence. He named the town for the cavalry post north of the site that had been established July 4, 1862, during a period of Indian unrest. Camp Independence, later Fort Independence, survived until 1877 when its buildings were sold at auction. The site has been Fort Independence Indian Reservation since 1915.

An impressive hopper still stands near the site of Kearsarge, near the juncture of Mazourka Canyon and the Owens River Valley

Kearsarge, on Mazourka Canyon Road east of Independence, was initially a mining district established in 1864. Gold and silver mines around Kearsarge flourished, and the town eventually had three mills, the largest being a 10-stamp mill. By 1888, mining declined and Kearsarge was almost deserted.

Independence lies near the Owens Valley Fault. An 1872 earthquake caused a 12-foot displacement, which is marked by a line of trees running north of Mazourka Canyon Road.

Description

The road to Mazourka Peak leaves the southern edge of Independence and crosses the Owens River Valley to enter Mazourka Canyon on the western side of the Inyo Mountains. It then travels up Al Rose Canyon to emerge on Badger Flat. The road passes many mines and a large wooden loading hopper can be seen at the entrance to the canyon. The trail is a smooth graded road until the turnoff for Santa Rita Flats, after that it becomes rougher and suitable for a high-clearance 2WD. It then enters the narrow, rugged Al Rose Canyon, which is prettier than Mazourka Canyon, and climbs to the wide Badger Flat. There are some good camping opportunities on the side trails around the edge of the flat with some sheltered sites among pinyons and junipers.

Mazourka Peak overlooks Tinemaha Reservoir in the Owens Valley

The trail passes the southern end of the rougher High Sierra #46: Papoose Flat Trail before it climbs up a wide shelf road to finish at the communications towers on Mazourka Peak. The views from various points of the summit are wonderful. To the west, the Sierra Nevada stretch from north to south. To the north and east are the Inyo Mountains with the White Mountains beyond them to the north. The wide Owens Valley separates the Inyo and White Mountains from the Sierra Nevada. High-clearance 4WDs can continue via High Sierra #46: Papoose Flat Trail to High Sierra #45: Saline Valley Road. Other vehicles should return the way they came.

Current Road Information

Inyo National Forest
Mount Whitney Ranger District
640 South Main Street
Lone Pine, CA 93545
(760) 876-6200

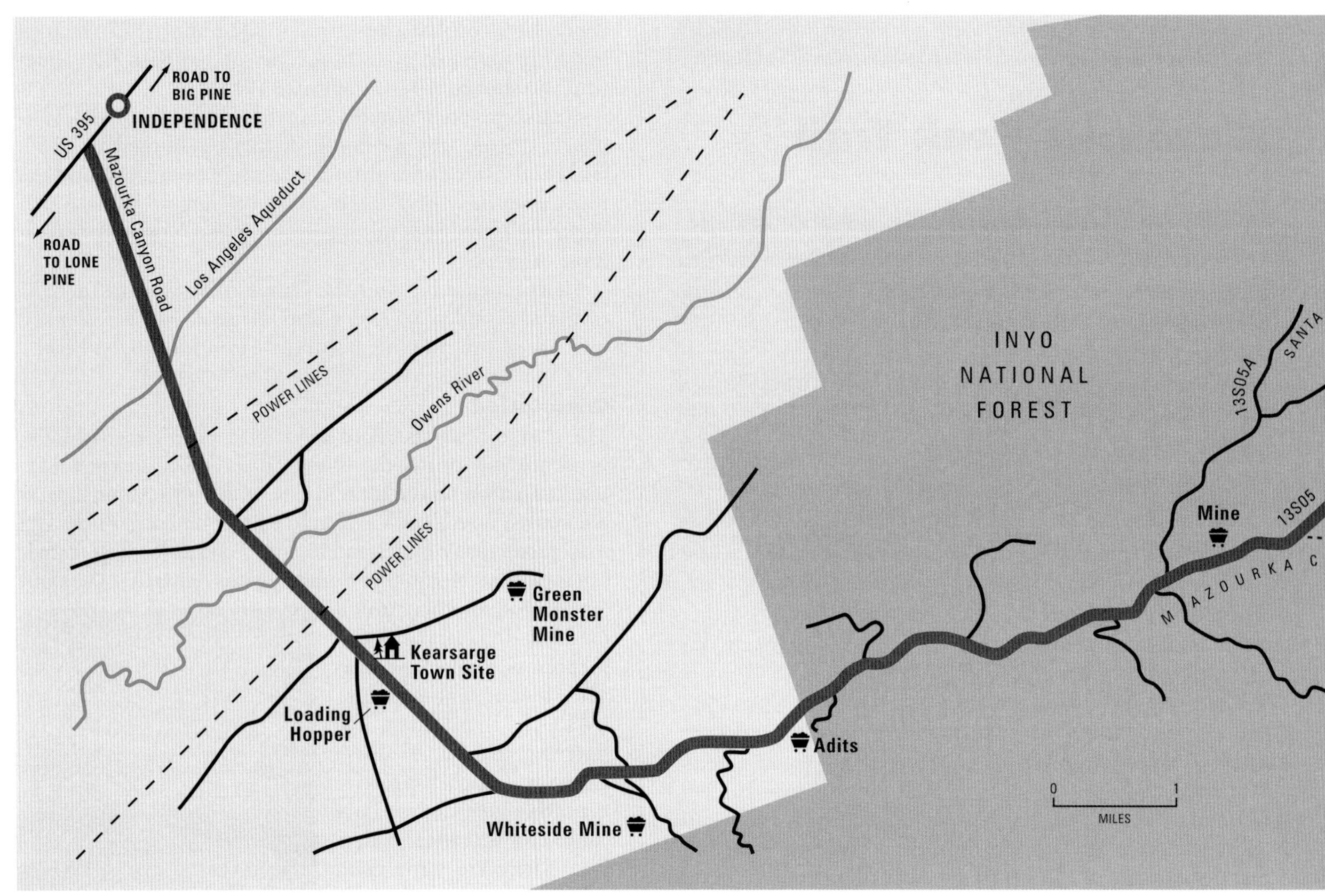

Map References

BLM Mt. Whitney
USFS Inyo National Forest
USGS 1:24,000 Independence, Bee Springs Canyon, Mazourka Peak
1:100,000 Mt. Whitney
Maptech CD-ROM: Kings Canyon/Death Valley
Southern & Central California Atlas & Gazetteer, p. 27
California Road & Recreation Atlas, p. 79

Route Directions

▼ 0.0 — Trail commences on US 395, on the south edge of Independence. Turn east on paved Mazourka Canyon Road and zero trip meter. Remain on paved road, ignoring turns to the right and left for the next 4.3 miles.
4.3 ▲ — Trail ends at intersection with US 395, on the south edge of Independence. Turn right for Independence; turn left for Lone Pine.

GPS: N36°47.84′ W118°11.72′

▼ 1.9 SO Cross over Los Angeles Aqueduct.
2.4 ▲ SO Cross over Los Angeles Aqueduct.

▼ 2.4 SO Track on left under power lines.
1.9 ▲ SO Track on right under power lines.

▼ 3.0 SO Track on right; then two tracks on left.
1.3 ▲ SO Two tracks on right; then track on left.

▼ 3.6 SO Track on left and track on right; then cross over Owens River.
0.7 ▲ SO Cross over Owens River; then track on left and track on right.

▼ 4.1 SO Graded road on left and right under power lines.
0.2 ▲ SO Graded road on left and right under power lines.

▼ 4.3 SO Track on left; then cattle guard and track on right. Road is now graded dirt. Zero trip meter.
0.0 ▲ Continue to the southwest. Remain on paved road, ignoring turns to the right and left for the next 4.3 miles.

GPS: N36°48.42′ W118°07.03′

▼ 0.0 Continue to the northeast.
7.5 ▲ SO Track on left and cattle guard; then track on right. Road is now paved. Zero trip meter.

▼ 0.1 SO Track on right.
7.4 ▲ SO Track on left.

▼ 0.2 SO Graded road on right.
7.3 ▲ SO Graded road on left.

▼ 0.5 SO Track on right; then large wooden loading hopper on right; then second track on right. This is close to the site of Kearsarge.
7.0 ▲ SO Track on left; then large wooden loading hopper on left; then second track on left. This is close to the site of Kearsarge.

GPS: N36°48.58′ W118°06.59′

▼ 0.8 SO Track on left.
6.7 ▲ SO Track on right.

▼ 1.2 SO Track on left.
6.3 ▲ SO Track on right.

▼ 1.5 SO Track on right.

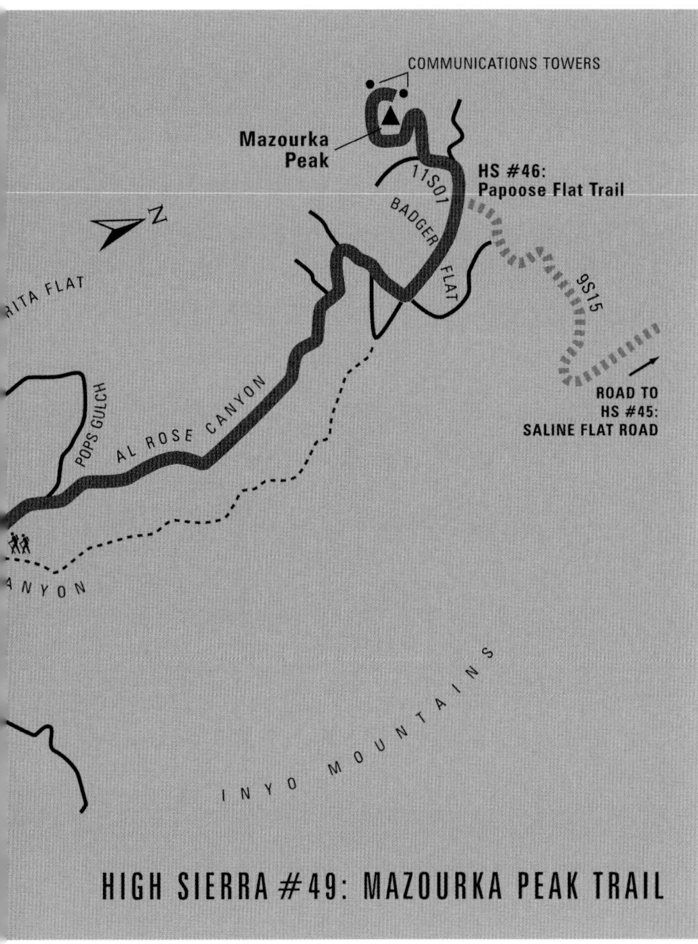

HIGH SIERRA #49: MAZOURKA PEAK TRAIL

	6.0 ▲	SO	Track on left.
▼ 1.6		SO	Track on left and track on right.
	5.9 ▲	SO	Track on left and track on right.
▼ 1.8		SO	Two tracks on right.
	5.7 ▲	SO	Two tracks on left.
▼ 1.9		SO	Track on right.
	5.6 ▲	SO	Track on left.
▼ 2.0		SO	Track on right.
	5.5 ▲	SO	Track on left.
▼ 2.1		SO	Track on right.
	5.4 ▲	SO	Track on left.
▼ 2.3		SO	Track on right.
	5.2 ▲	SO	Track on left.
▼ 2.4		SO	Enter wash.
	5.1 ▲	SO	Exit wash.
▼ 2.5		SO	Track on right to Whiteside Mine.
	5.0 ▲	SO	Track on left to Whiteside Mine.
			GPS: N36°49.85' W118°05.18'
▼ 2.7		SO	Track on left and track on right.
	4.8 ▲	SO	Track on right and track on left.
			GPS: N36°49.96' W118°05.14'
▼ 2.9		SO	Track on right.
	4.6 ▲	SO	Track on left.
▼ 3.3		SO	Track on right.
	4.2 ▲	SO	Track on left.
▼ 3.7		BL	Track on right climbs canyon wall.
	3.8 ▲	BR	Track on left climbs canyon wall.
			GPS: N36°50.88' W118°05.00'
▼ 4.0		SO	Track on right to mine.
	3.5 ▲	SO	Track on left to mine.
▼ 4.1		SO	Adits on right.
	3.4 ▲	SO	Adits on left.
▼ 4.3		SO	Entering Inyo National Forest; mine adit on right.
	3.2 ▲	SO	Mine adit on left; leaving Inyo National Forest.
			GPS: N36°51.33' W118°05.15'
▼ 4.5		SO	Track on right.
	3.0 ▲	SO	Track on left.
			GPS: N36°51.55' W118°05.17'
▼ 4.8		SO	Track on left.
	2.7 ▲	SO	Track on right.
▼ 5.4		SO	Track on left.
	2.1 ▲	SO	Track on right.
▼ 5.6		SO	Track on left.
	1.9 ▲	SO	Track on right.
▼ 6.9		SO	Track on right into mine.
	0.6 ▲	SO	Track on left into mine.
			GPS: N36°53.53' W118°04.90'
▼ 7.2		SO	Cattle guard.
	0.3 ▲	SO	Cattle guard.
▼ 7.3		SO	Track on right.
	0.2 ▲	SO	Track on left.
▼ 7.5		BR	Bear right onto 13S05 following the sign to Badger Flat. Graded road on left is 13S05A to Santa Rita Flat. Zero trip meter.
	0.0 ▲		Continue to the southeast.
			GPS: N36°54.03' W118°05.08'
▼ 0.0			Continue to the north.
	6.6 ▲	SO	Graded road on right is 13S05A to Santa Rita Flat. Zero trip meter.
▼ 0.5		SO	Track on left; then mine on left with a large adit partway up cliff face.
	6.1 ▲	SO	Mine on right with a large adit partway up cliff face; then track on right.
			GPS: N36°54.48' W118°05.05'
▼ 1.3		SO	Track on right up Mazourka Canyon is for hikers and horses only. Main trail now enters Al Rose Canyon.
	5.3 ▲	SO	Track on left up Mazourka Canyon is for hikers and horses only. Main trail now joins Mazourka Canyon.
▼ 1.8		SO	Adit on left.
	4.8 ▲	SO	Adit on right.
▼ 1.9		SO	Track on left up Pops Gulch.
	4.7 ▲	SO	Track on right up Pops Gulch.
			GPS: N36°55.57' W118°05.19'
▼ 2.5		SO	Diggings on right.
	4.1 ▲	SO	Diggings on left.
			GPS: N36°56.05' W118°05.18'
▼ 2.7		SO	Exit wash.
	3.9 ▲	SO	Enter wash.
▼ 4.0		SO	Track on left.
	2.6 ▲	SO	Track on right.
▼ 4.8		SO	Well-used track on left.
	1.8 ▲	SO	Well-used track on right.
			GPS: N36°57.80' W118°05.93'
▼ 5.2		BR	Track on left.
	1.4 ▲	BL	Track on right.
			GPS: N36°57.97' W118°06.22'
▼ 5.4		BR	Track on left.
	1.2 ▲	BL	Track on right.
▼ 5.5		BL	Track on right. Entering Badger Flat.

	1.1 ▲	SO	Track on left. Leaving Badger Flat.
▼ 5.8		TL	4-way intersection.
	0.8 ▲	TR	4-way intersection.
			GPS: N36°58.26' W118°05.70'
▼ 6.6		SO	Track on right is High Sierra #46: Papoose Flat Trail. Zero trip meter.
	0.0 ▲		Continue to the southeast.
			GPS: N36°58.77' W118°06.22'
▼ 0.0			Continue to the northwest. Trail is now marked 11S01.
▼ 0.4		TL	4-way intersection.
			GPS: N36°58.85' W118°06.57'
▼ 0.6		SO	Track on left.
▼ 1.0		SO	Gate.
▼ 1.5		SO	Track on right to communications towers.
▼ 1.7		SO	Track on left.
▼ 1.8		BR	Communications towers on left.
▼ 2.0			Trail ends at communications towers.
			GPS: N36°58.64' W118°07.22'

HIGH SIERRA #50

Sierra View Trail

Starting Point:	**US 395, 11 miles south of Big Pine**
Finishing Point:	**Campsite at the head of Armstrong Canyon**
Total Mileage:	**14.3 miles (one-way)**
Unpaved Mileage:	**8.6 miles**
Driving Time:	**1.75 hours (one-way)**
Elevation Range:	**3,800–8,300 feet**
Usually Open:	**April to November**
Best Time to Travel:	**April to November**
Difficulty Rating:	**5**
Scenic Rating:	**9**
Remoteness Rating:	**+0**

Special Attractions

- Very narrow, exciting shelf road.
- Views over the Sierra Nevada and White Mountains.

Description

This rugged trail to the few remains of the Sierra View and Valley View Mines is definitely not for the fainthearted. It is barely wide enough for a single vehicle in places and runs along a shelf road for much of its length. However, the views into the Owens Valley, across to the Inyo Mountains, and into deep, narrow glacial valleys of the Sierra Nevada make it a pleasure to drive.

The trail turns off US 395 and follows a graded dirt road that passes through a pleasant campground situated beneath trees on Taboose Creek. Taboose Creek Campground, run by Inyo County, spreads out along both sides of the narrow creek and is a lovely place to camp. A small fee is charged. The land around Taboose Creek is leased to Inyo County by the City of Los Angeles. There is a second campground, managed by the BLM, a slight distance away on Goodale Creek. This more open campground currently has no fee.

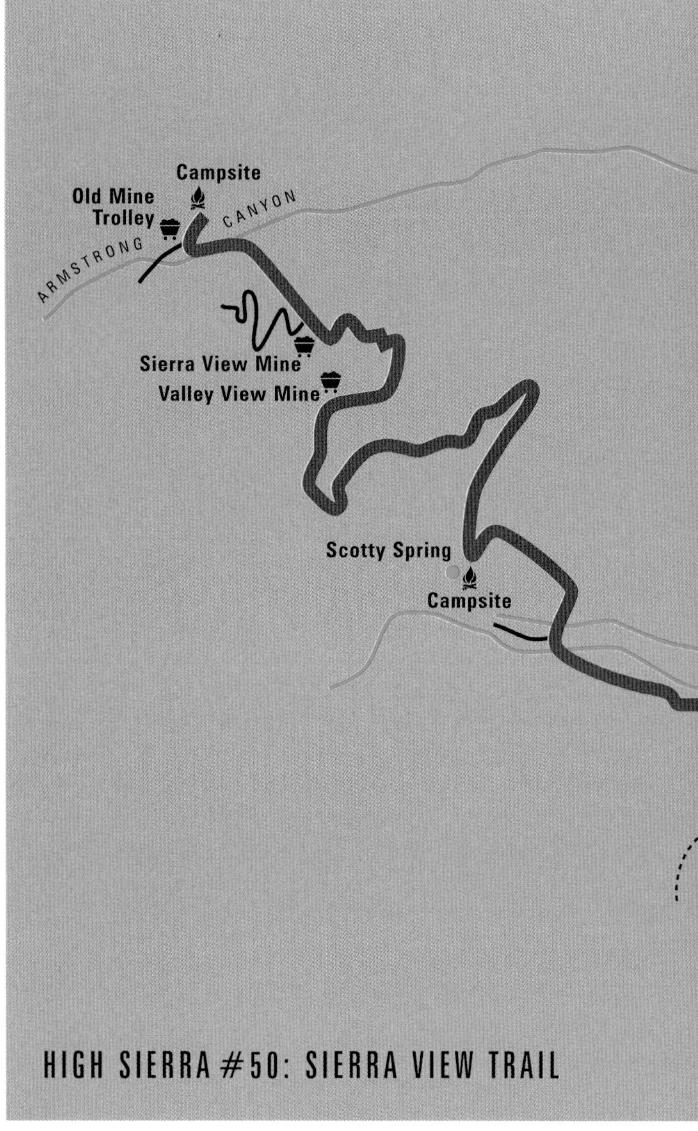

The trail proper begins at the turn up Division Creek Road, which passes the Division Creek Powerhouse and the Sawmill Pass Hiking Trailhead. The hiking trail leads into the John Muir Wilderness; a permit is needed for overnight stays but not for day hikes. Dogs are prohibited along the trail to protect bighorn sheep that frequent the area.

After passing a large campsite, the trail starts to climb along a shelf road that switchbacks up the eastern flank of the Sierra Nevada. Be aware of returning traffic. Passing places are few, and the surface is loose and off-camber in places, making it difficult to back up safely. Earthquakes are common and the trail may become blocked at any time, necessitating a long and tricky reverse. The trail continues along the shelf road, passing the sparse remains of the Valley View and Sierra View Mines, and forks near the second mine. The left-hand fork, which is the one shown on the map, becomes extremely narrow and is badly eroded after 0.7 miles. The right-hand fork continues 0.9 miles to the head of Armstrong

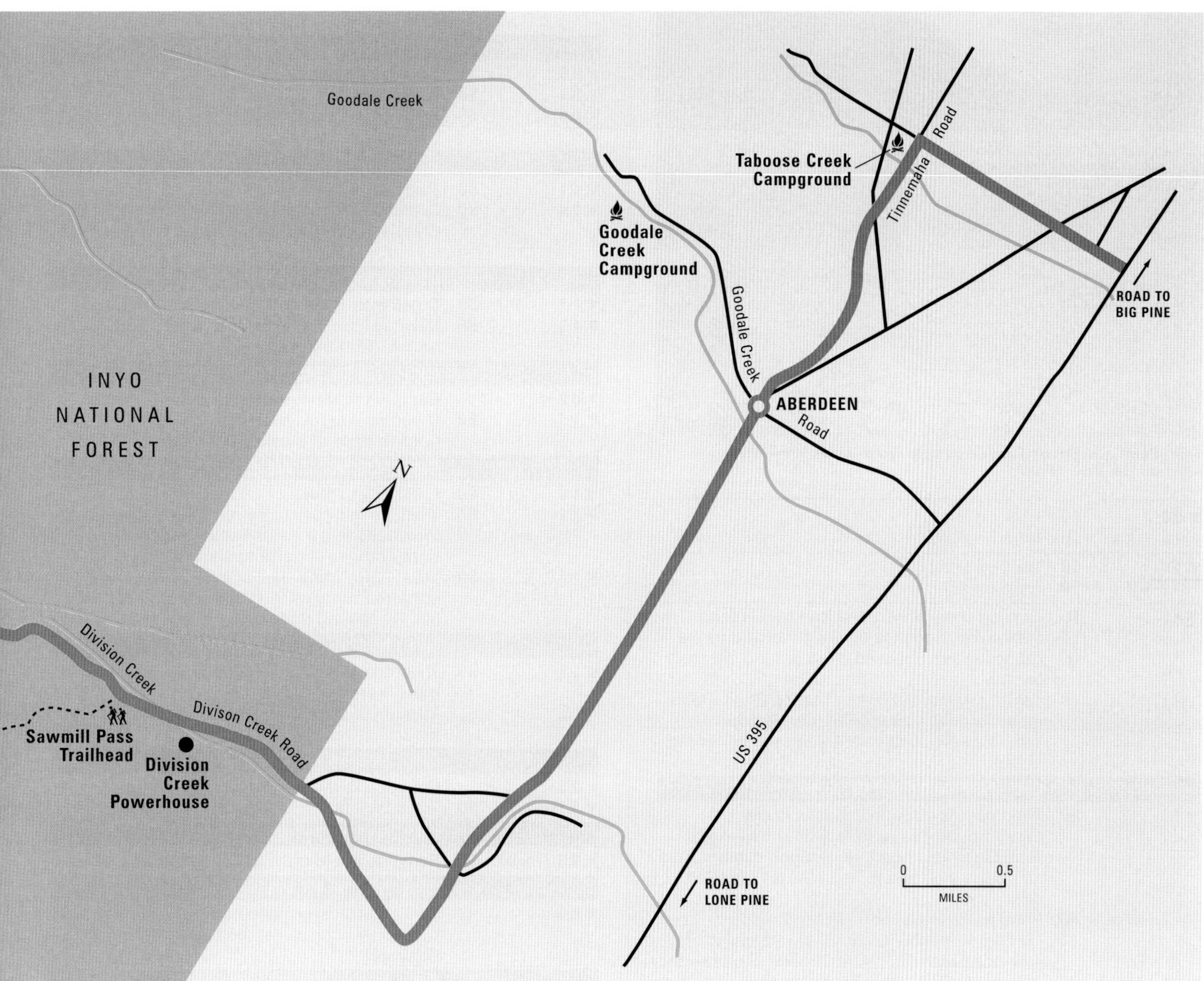

Canyon, where there is a sheltered campsite under large pine trees tucked between two rocky outcrops. This pretty little cove is a great spot for an overnight camp or picnic.

Current Road Information

Inyo National Forest
Mount Whitney Ranger District
640 South Main Street
Lone Pine, CA 93545
(760) 876-6200

Inyo National Forest
White Mountain Ranger District
798 North Main Street
Bishop, CA 93514
(760) 873-2500

Map References

BLM Mt. Whitney
USFS Inyo National Forest
USGS 1:24,000 Blackrock, Aberdeen
1:100,000 Mt. Whitney
Maptech CD-ROM: Kings Canyon/Death Valley
Southern & Central California Atlas & Gazetteer, pp. 27, 26
California Road & Recreation Atlas, p. 79 (incomplete)

Route Directions

▼ 0.0		From US 395, 11 miles south of Big Pine, zero trip meter and turn west on paved Taboose Creek Road. Road is also called Aberdeen Station Road.
5.6 ▲		Trail ends on US 395. Turn left for Big Pine; turn right for Lone Pine.
		GPS: N37°00.02' W118°13.92'
▼ 0.2	SO	Cattle guard; then track on right.
5.4 ▲	SO	Track on left; then cattle guard.
▼ 0.4	SO	Cattle guard; then road on left and track on right.
5.2 ▲	SO	Track on left and road on right; then cattle guard.
▼ 0.5	SO	Track on right.
5.1 ▲	SO	Track on left.

Sawmill Point and Spook Canyon as seen from Valley View Mine, halfway up the slow climb

▼ 0.6		SO	Track on left.
	5.0 ▲	SO	Track on right.
▼ 1.0		SO	Track on left.
	4.6 ▲	SO	Track on right.
▼ 1.1		TL	Turn left onto Tinnemaha Road. Aberdeen Station Road continues straight ahead to the Taboose Pass Trailhead. Also graded dirt road on right.
	4.5 ▲	TR	Turn right onto Aberdeen Station Road. Road on left is also Aberdeen Station Road to Taboose Pass Trailhead. Also graded dirt road ahead.
			GPS: N37°00.01' W118°15.19'
▼ 1.3		SO	Road passes through Taboose Creek Campground (fee required) on the banks of Taboose Creek. Continue through campground and cross over creek. Road turns to graded dirt.
	4.3 ▲	SO	Road passes through Taboose Creek Campground (fee required) on the banks of Taboose Creek. Continue through campground and cross over creek. Road is now paved.
			GPS: N37°59.89' W118°15.19'
▼ 1.6		SO	Track on left and track on right under power lines.
	4.0 ▲	SO	Track on left and track on right under power lines.
▼ 2.5		SO	Track on right; then track on left.
	3.1 ▲	SO	Track on right; then track on left.
▼ 2.6		SO	Road is now paved at the settlement of Aberdeen. 4-way intersection. Road on right and left is Goodale Creek Road. Right goes to Goodale Creek Campground.
	3.0 ▲	SO	Road turns to graded dirt at the settlement of Aberdeen. 4-way intersection. Road on right and left is Goodale Creek Road. Left goes to Goodale Creek Campground.
			GPS: N36°58.70' W118°15.19'
▼ 2.9		SO	Track on left.
	2.7 ▲	SO	Track on right.
▼ 4.8		SO	Track on right.
	0.8 ▲	SO	Track on left.
▼ 5.2		SO	Track on right and track on left.
	0.4 ▲	SO	Track on left and track on right.
▼ 5.6		TR	Turn right over cattle guard onto small paved Division Creek Road and zero trip meter.
	0.0 ▲		Continue to the north.
			GPS: N36°56.07' W118°15.37'
▼ 0.0			Continue to the west.
▼ 0.3		SO	Track on left.
▼ 0.9		SO	Track on right; then cattle guard. Entering Inyo National Forest.
			GPS: N36°56.40' W118°16.28'
▼ 1.1		SO	Track on right.
▼ 1.4		SO	Cattle guard; then track on left; then Division Creek Powerhouse on left. Road turns to graded dirt.
			GPS: N36°56.40' W118°16.89'
▼ 1.7		BR	Cross over Division Creek; then track on left.
▼ 1.9		BR	Sawmill Pass Trailhead and small parking area on left. Zero trip meter.
			GPS: N36°56.34' W118°17.37'
▼ 0.0			Continue to the northwest.
▼ 1.5		BR	Cross over creek; then bear right. Track on left goes to base of pipeline descent.
			GPS: N36°56.17' W118°18.83'
▼ 1.6		SO	Cross over creek.
▼ 2.1		BR	Track on left goes to campsite under large cottonwoods and oaks at Scotty Spring. Bear right onto small trail and start to climb.
▼ 4.9		SO	Valley View Mine—tailings and a few other scattered remains. Adit and shaft on left up hill. No turning point.
			GPS: N36°56.52' W118°20.24'
▼ 5.9		BR	Trail forks. Track on left continues up the hill to more workings but is very eroded. This is the location of the Sierra View Mine. Zero trip meter.
			GPS: N36°56.70' W118°20.49'
▼ 0.0			Continue to the northwest.
▼ 0.7		SO	Track on left.
			GPS: N36°56.71' W118°21.15'
▼ 0.8		SO	Remains of old mine trolley under tree on left.
			GPS: N36°56.77' W118°21.21'
▼ 0.9			Trail ends at large sheltered campsite between two rocky outcrops at the head of Armstrong Canyon.
			GPS: N36°56.84' W118°21.15'

The trail passes large granite boulders crumbled by extreme temperatures at high elevations

The Northern Sierra Region

Trails in the Northern Sierra Region

- NS1 Clavey Bridge Road *(DR: 3; 33.7 miles; page 296)*
- NS2 Lumsden Bridge Road *(DR: 2; 11.5 miles; page 300)*
- NS3 Bourland Trestle Trail *(DR: 2; 6.7 miles; page 303)*
- NS4 Dodge Ridge Trail *(DR: 3; 11.9 miles; page 305)*
- NS5 Crandall Peak Trail *(DR: 3; 36.6 miles; page 308)*
- NS6 Pinecrest Peak Trail *(DR: 4; 5.6 miles; page 314)*
- NS7 4,700-Foot Road *(DR: 2; 10 miles; page 316)*
- NS8 Black Springs Route *(DR: 4; 18.4 miles; page 318)*
- NS9 Calaveras Dome Trail *(DR: 2; 42 miles; page 320)*
- NS10 Corral Hollow OHV Route *(DR: 5; 12.5 miles; page 326)*
- NS11 Mattley Ridge Trail *(DR: 4; 5 miles; page 329)*
- NS12 Red and Blue Lakes Trail *(DR: 3; 10 miles; page 331)*
- NS13 Baltic Ridge Trail *(DR: 3/4; 15.6 miles; page 335)*
- NS14 Slate Mountain Road *(DR: 2; 18.5 miles; page 338)*
- NS15 Pony Express Trail *(DR: 2; 7.8 miles; page 342)*
- NS16 Angora Lakes Road *(DR: 1; 2.8 miles; page 344)*
- NS17 McKinney Creek Trail *(DR: 4; 11.5 miles; page 346)*
- NS18 Blackwood Canyon Trail *(DR: 5; 3.6 miles; page 350)*
- NS19 Mount Watson Trail *(DR: 3; 20.8 miles; page 351)*
- NS20 Soda Springs Road *(DR: 2/3; 26.4 miles; page 354)*
- NS21 Henness Pass Road *(DR: 2; 76 miles; page 359)*
- NS22 Boca Ridge and Verdi Peak Trail *(DR: 3/4; 16.9 miles; page 369)*
- NS23 Independence Lake Trail *(DR: 3; 21.5 miles; page 372)*
- NS24 Summit City Loop *(DR: 3; 17.1 miles; page 377)*
- NS25 North Bloomfield–Bowman Lake Trail *(DR: 2; 40.7 miles; page 381)*
- NS26 Alleghany Trail *(DR: 4; 31.1 miles; page 386)*

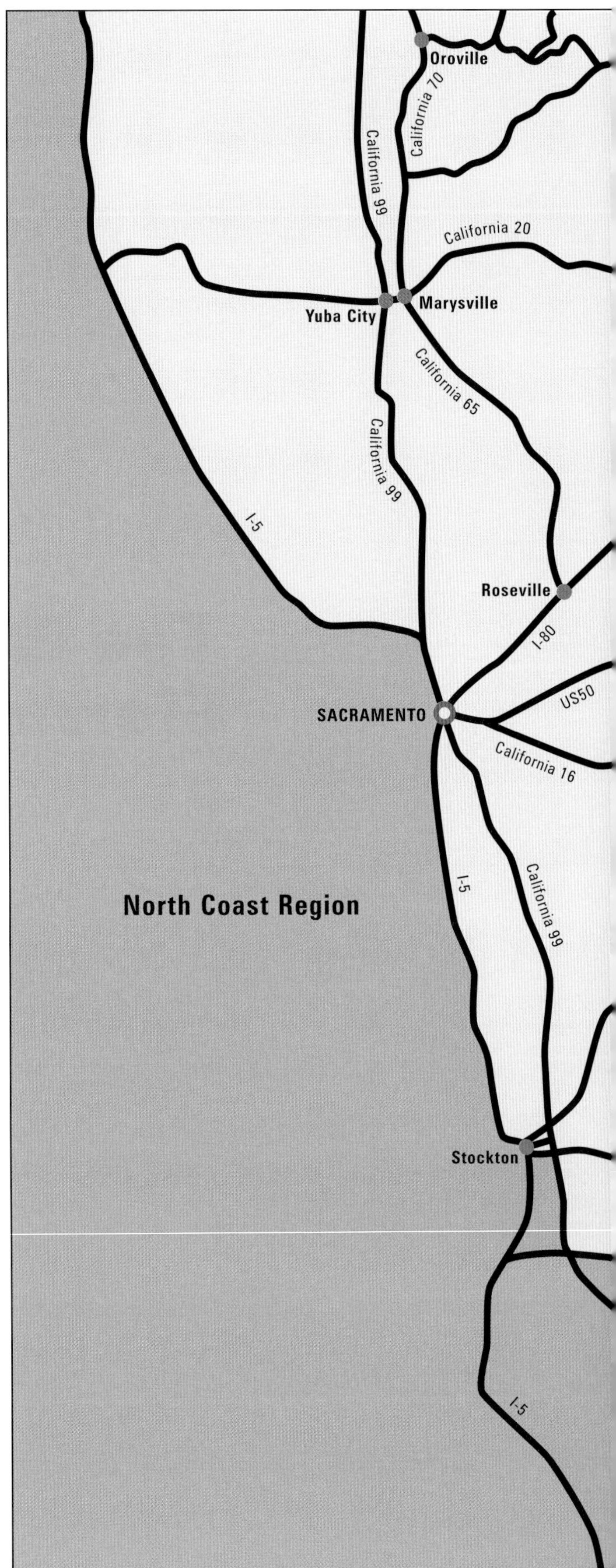

MAP CONTINUES ON PAGE 295

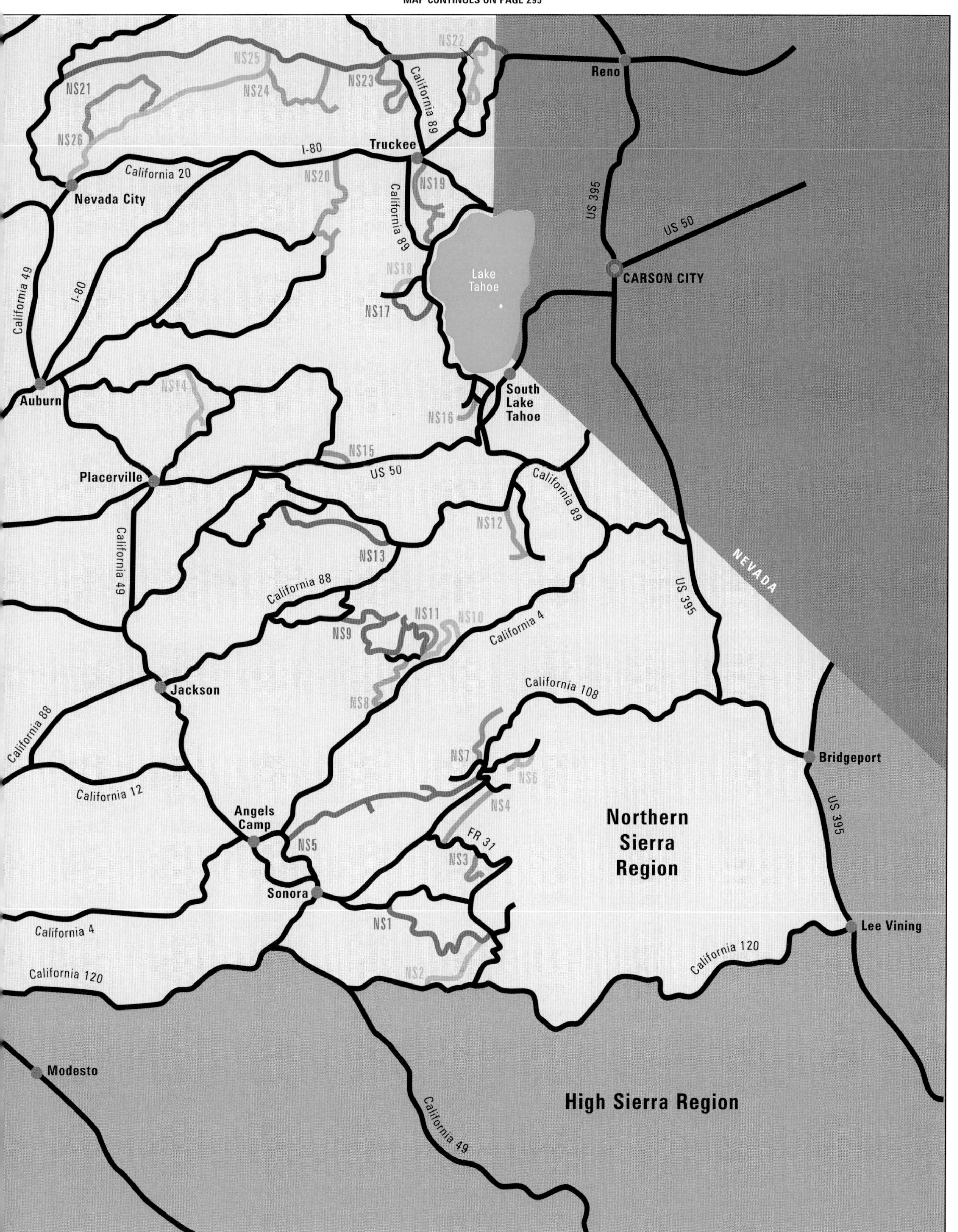

Reno
NS22
NS25
NS21
NS24
NS23
California 89
NS26
Truckee
I-80
California 20
NS20
NS19
Nevada City
US 395
California 89
US 50
Lake Tahoe
CARSON CITY
NS18
California 49
I-80
NS17
South Lake Tahoe
Auburn
NS14
NS16
NS15
Placerville
US 50
California 89
NS12
California 49
NS13
NEVADA
US 395
California 88
NS11
NS10
NS9
California 4
Jackson
California 108
NS8
California 88
NS7
Bridgeport
NS6
California 12
NS4
Angels Camp
FR 31
Northern Sierra Region
NS5
US 395
NS3
Sonora
NS1
Lee Vining
California 4
California 120
NS2
California 120
Modesto
High Sierra Region
California 49

Trails in the Northern Sierra Region

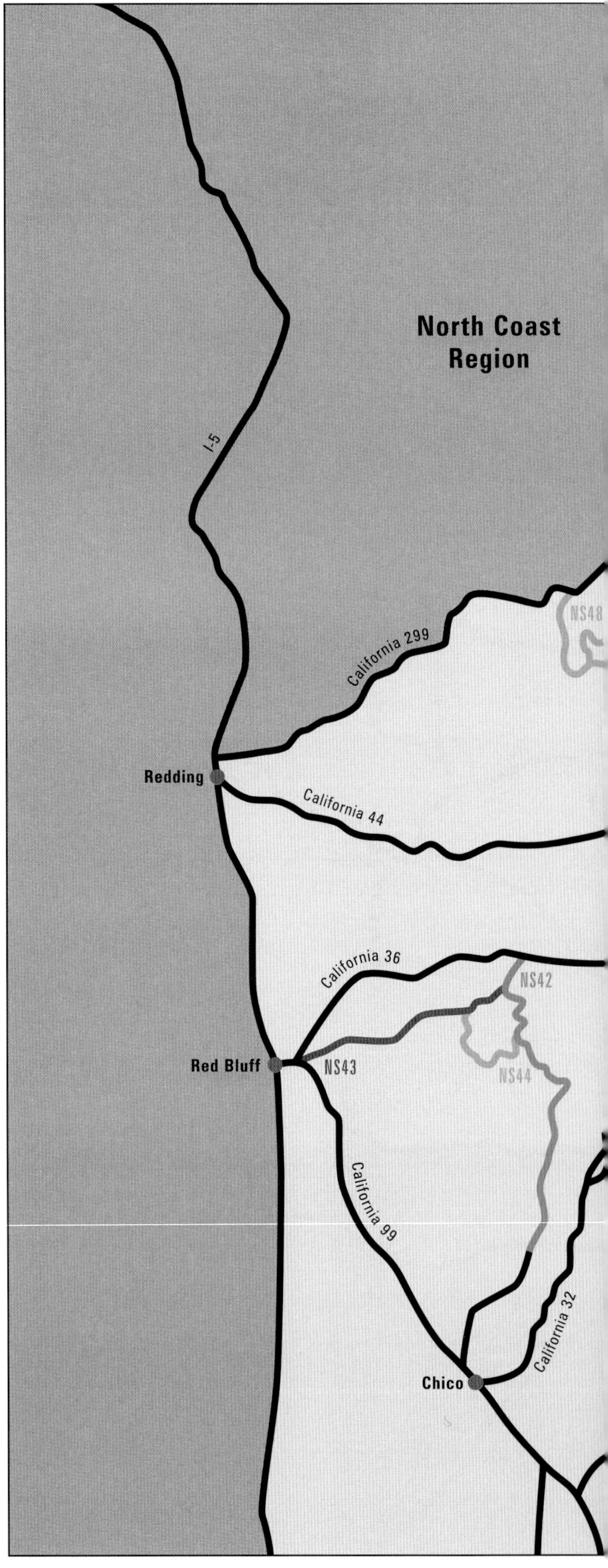

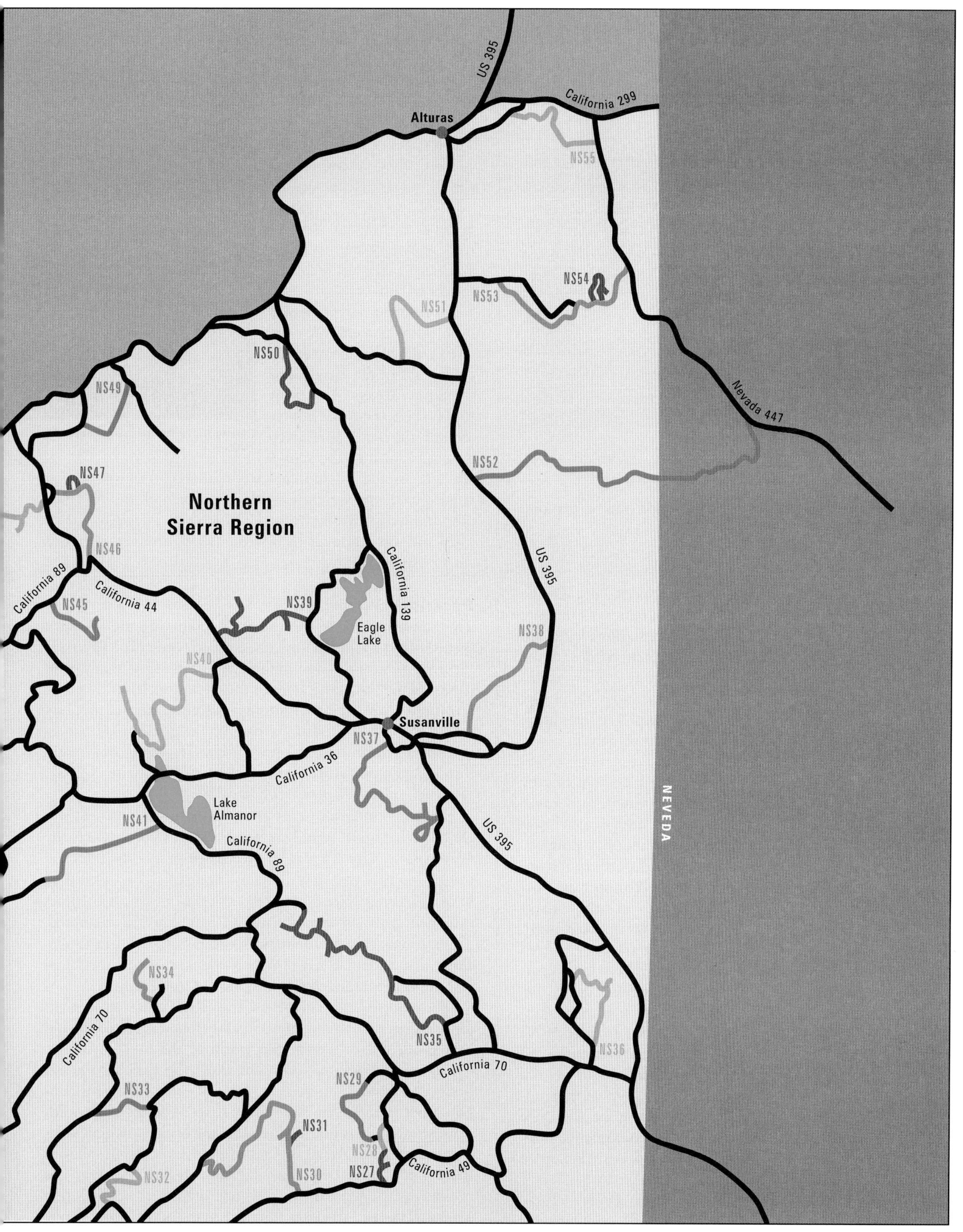

MAP CONTINUES ON PAGE 293

NORTHERN SIERRA #1

Clavey Bridge Road

Starting Point:	**Buchanan Road (FR 14), 2.3 miles northeast of Tuolumne**
Finishing Point:	**FR 31, 0.6 miles west of FR 17**
Total Mileage:	**33.7 miles**
Unpaved Mileage:	**33.7 miles**
Driving Time:	**3.5 hours**
Elevation Range:	**2,300–4,400 feet**
Usually Open:	**April to November**
Best Time to Travel:	**Dry weather**
Difficulty Rating:	**3**
Scenic Rating:	**9**
Remoteness Rating:	**+1**

Special Attractions

- Dramatic shelf road to the Clavey River.
- Long winding road with a network of side trails to explore.
- Angling for rainbow trout in the Clavey River.

History

Clavey Bridge Road begins along the North Fork of the Tuolumne River close to the Riverside Picnic Area, former site of the Riverside Guard Station. The ranger station's log cabin was built in July 1911 as the Basin Ranger Station house at the West Side Lumber Company's Camp 8, some 7 miles northeast of this location. The two-story log cabin and outbuildings were burned down in 1968 to eradicate a suspected infestation of kissing bugs. Less severe than their South American counterparts, the cone-nosed bugs are blood sucking by nature. They can cause varying degrees of irritation and illness to humans. Health departments continue to monitor any occurrence of the insect throughout the Southwest.

Clavey Bridge Road

William Clavey ranged cattle and sheep in this part of Tuolumne County before the turn of the twentieth century. In May 1897, Jane A. Clavey patented land just north of old Camp Clavey, farther upstream along the West Side Lumber Company Railroad. The camp was dismantled in 1968.

Clavey Bridge Road runs south of Duckwall Mountain and Duckwall Ridge. The Duckwall party of 1852 was among the many emigrant groups to endure the harsh conditions involved in crossing the Sierra Nevada. Their wagon was badly damaged as they attempted to climb out of Relief Valley, near the northern boundary of today's Emigrant Wilderness, quite some distance away and 6,000 feet higher in the mountains.

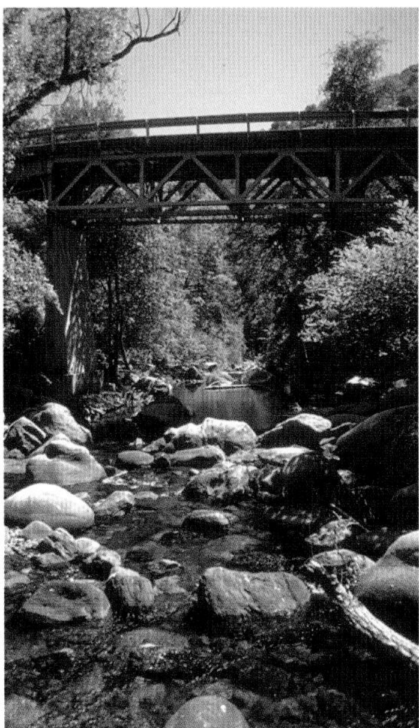

Clavey River Bridge, constructed in 1956

A hydroelectric plant was built downstream of the Clavey River Bridge near the confluence of the Clavey and Tuolumne Rivers. The plant supplied electricity for miners around the region. A steep road was cut into the southern face of the Tuolumne River Canyon to a bridge that crossed to the powerhouse on the north side of the river. The powerhouse was badly burned in the Cave Diggings Fire of 1928 and was destroyed by floods in 1937. Some foundations are all that remain.

Description

The trail leaves FR 14, northeast of Tuolumne, and follows a graded dirt road into Stanislaus National Forest. The Riverside Picnic Area, near the start of the trail, is a pleasant, shady place to stop along the North Fork of the Tuolumne River. The first few miles of the trail pass through parcels of private property within the national forest. Remain on the graded road, ignoring private tracks on the left and right. The long trail passes through an area burned in the Ackersop-Rogge Fire of 1997. However, the area is recovering quickly.

Past the turnoff for 1N46, the trail becomes a narrow, single-track that drops steadily down a series of switchbacks to the Clavey River. This is the most spectacular part of the trail, and the section that gives it a difficulty rating of 3. The shelf road has few passing places, and the surface is uneven. It becomes extremely greasy in wet weather and should not be attempted. The trail was closed for almost 10 years because of rockslides along this section. You will notice evidence of past rockslides and should be aware of the possibility of future slides.

The modern bridge over the Clavey River is the replacement for a bridge washed out in 1956. The foundations of the old bridge can still be seen to the north of the modern bridge. There are a couple of campsites along the river by the old bridge, but space is limited. Anglers will enjoy fishing for rainbow trout in the river. The Clavey River is designated a wild-trout stream and is not stocked. Past the bridge, the trail starts to climb steadily, zigzagging out of the Clavey River Valley to the top of a ridge, before passing through Bull Meadow. The meadow is the heart of the Jawbone mule deer herd's winter habitat. The herd migrates from the high country in Yosemite

National Park to spend winters at lower elevations. The National Park Service counts the migrating deer annually. Other roads in this region are closed in winter to protect deer habitat.

A worthwhile detour is to head south along 1N09, which takes you 3 miles down an easy road to the top of Jawbone Ridge. The ridge top provides excellent views over the grassy Jawbone lava field.

The trail passes the northern end of Northern Sierra #2: Lumsden Bridge Road at the old Jawbone Station. No longer in use, the buildings stand in the middle of a small meadow. From here it is a short distance to the end of the trail on paved FR 31. The final part of the trail passes through private property. FR 17, which heads northeast to Cherry Lake, is only a short distance to the east.

Current Road Information

Stanislaus National Forest
Mi-Wok Ranger District
24695 Highway 108
Mi-Wuk Village, CA 95346
(209) 586-3234

Map References

BLM Oakdale, Yosemite Valley
USFS Stanislaus National Forest
USGS 1:24,000 Tuolumne, Duckwall Mt., Cherry Lake South
1:100,000 Oakdale, Yosemite Valley
Maptech CD-ROM: High Sierra/Yosemite
Northern California Atlas & Gazetteer, pp. 109, 110
California Road & Recreation Atlas, p. 72

Route Directions

▼ 0.0		From Tuolumne, turn east on Buchanan Road (FR 14), following the sign for Cherry Lake. Travel 2.3 miles; then turn east on paved road immediately before the sign for Stanislaus National Forest. Zero trip meter and immediately cross over North Fork Tuolumne River on bridge. Road turns to graded dirt.
5.3 ▲		Trail ends at intersection with Buchanan Road (FR 14). Turn left for Tuolumne.
		GPS: N37°59.03′ W120°12.28′
▼ 0.1	SO	Riverside Picnic Area on right. Road is now marked 1N01.
5.2 ▲	SO	Riverside Picnic Area on left.
▼ 2.5	SO	Cattle guard.
2.8 ▲	SO	Cattle guard.
▼ 2.6	SO	Entering private property. Track on left through gate; then cross over Duckwall Creek.
2.7 ▲	SO	Cross over Duckwall Creek; then track on right through gate. Leaving private property.
		GPS: N37°57.64′ W120°11.84′
▼ 2.9	BL	Graded road on right is IN03. Alder Spring on right.
2.4 ▲	BR	Alder Spring on left. Graded road on left is IN03.
		GPS: N37°57.50′ W120°11.63′
▼ 4.9	SO	Cattle guard; then graded road on right is 1N20. Continue on IN01 and pass through seasonal closure gate.
0.4 ▲	SO	Seasonal closure gate; then graded road on left is 1N20; then cattle guard.
		GPS: N37°56.67′ W120°09.95′
▼ 5.3	BR	Track on left is 2N11. Remain on 1N01, following the sign to Hunter Creek, and zero trip meter.
0.0 ▲		Continue to the northwest.
		GPS: N37°56.52′ W120°09.57′
▼ 0.0		Continue to the southeast.
3.5 ▲	SO	Track on right is 2N11. Remain on 1N01, following the sign to Cottonwood Road, and zero trip meter.
▼ 0.8	SO	Track on left.
2.7 ▲	SO	Track on right.
▼ 1.3	SO	Cross Hunter Creek on bridge; then track on left.
2.2 ▲	SO	Track on right; then cross Hunter Creek on bridge.
▼ 1.8	SO	Spring on left.
1.7 ▲	SO	Spring on right.
		GPS: N37°55.67′ W120°08.87′
▼ 2.0	SO	Spring on left.
1.5 ▲	SO	Spring on right.
▼ 2.8	SO	Hiking trail on right is 17E38.
0.7 ▲	SO	Hiking trail on left is 17E38.
		GPS: N37°55.85′ W120°09.74′
▼ 3.2	BL	Track on right is 1N02 to Wet Meadow.
0.3 ▲	BR	Track on left is 1N02 to Wet Meadow.
		GPS: N37°55.60′ W120°09.68′
▼ 3.5	SO	Track on right on saddle is 1N17 to Sugarloaf Heliport. Zero trip meter and continue on 1N01.
0.0 ▲		Continue to the north.
		GPS: N37°55.66′ W120°09.44′
▼ 0.0		Continue to the south.
3.9 ▲	SO	Track on left on saddle is 1N17 to Sugarloaf Heliport. Zero trip meter and continue on 1N01.
▼ 0.3	SO	Track on right is 1N01H.
3.6 ▲	SO	Track on left is 1N01H.
▼ 0.4	SO	Spring on right.
3.5 ▲	SO	Spring on left.
▼ 2.5	SO	Track on left is 1N48B.
1.4 ▲	SO	Track on right is 1N48B.

Small creek cascades across the trail

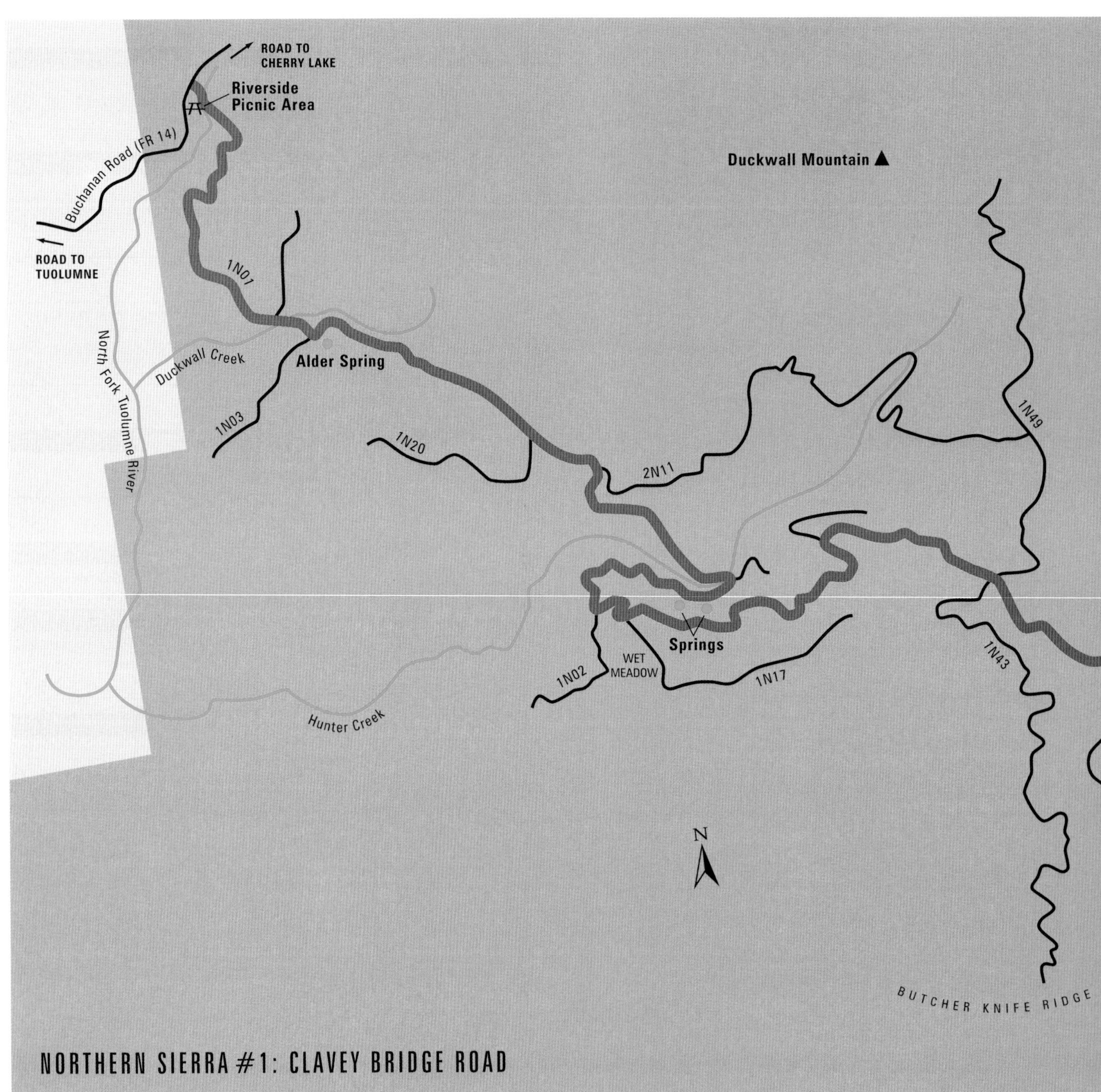

▼ 3.9 **SO** Track on right is 1N43 to Butcher Knife Ridge. Track on left is 1N49 to Duckwall Lookout and Cottonwood Road. Zero trip meter.

0.0 ▲ Continue to the northwest on 1N01. End of shelf road.

GPS: N37°55.52′ W120°06.74′

▼ 0.0 Continue to the east on 1N01. Road becomes a formed, single-track trail and descends along a shelf road to the Clavey River.

7.8 ▲ **SO** Track on left is 1N43 to Butcher Knife Ridge. Track on right is 1N49 to Duckwall Lookout and Cottonwood Road. Zero trip meter.

▼ 1.4 **SO** Track on left is 1N12 and track on right. Follow the sign to Clavey River.

6.4 ▲ **SO** Track on right is 1N12 and track on left. Follow the sign to Cottonwood Road.

GPS: N37°54.92′ W120°05.74′

▼ 2.3 **BL** Track on right is 1N46.

5.5 ▲ **BR** Track on left is 1N46.

▼ 2.9 **SO** Cross over creek.

4.9 ▲ **SO** Cross over creek.

▼ 5.0 **SO** Two mine adits in rock face on right.

2.8 ▲ **SO** Two mine adits in rock face on left.

GPS: N37°52.81′ W120°05.07′

▼ 6.8 **SO** Tank on left and campsite on right.

1.0 ▲ **SO** Tank on right and campsite on left.

▼ 7.1 **SO** Cross through creek. Waterfall on left and right.

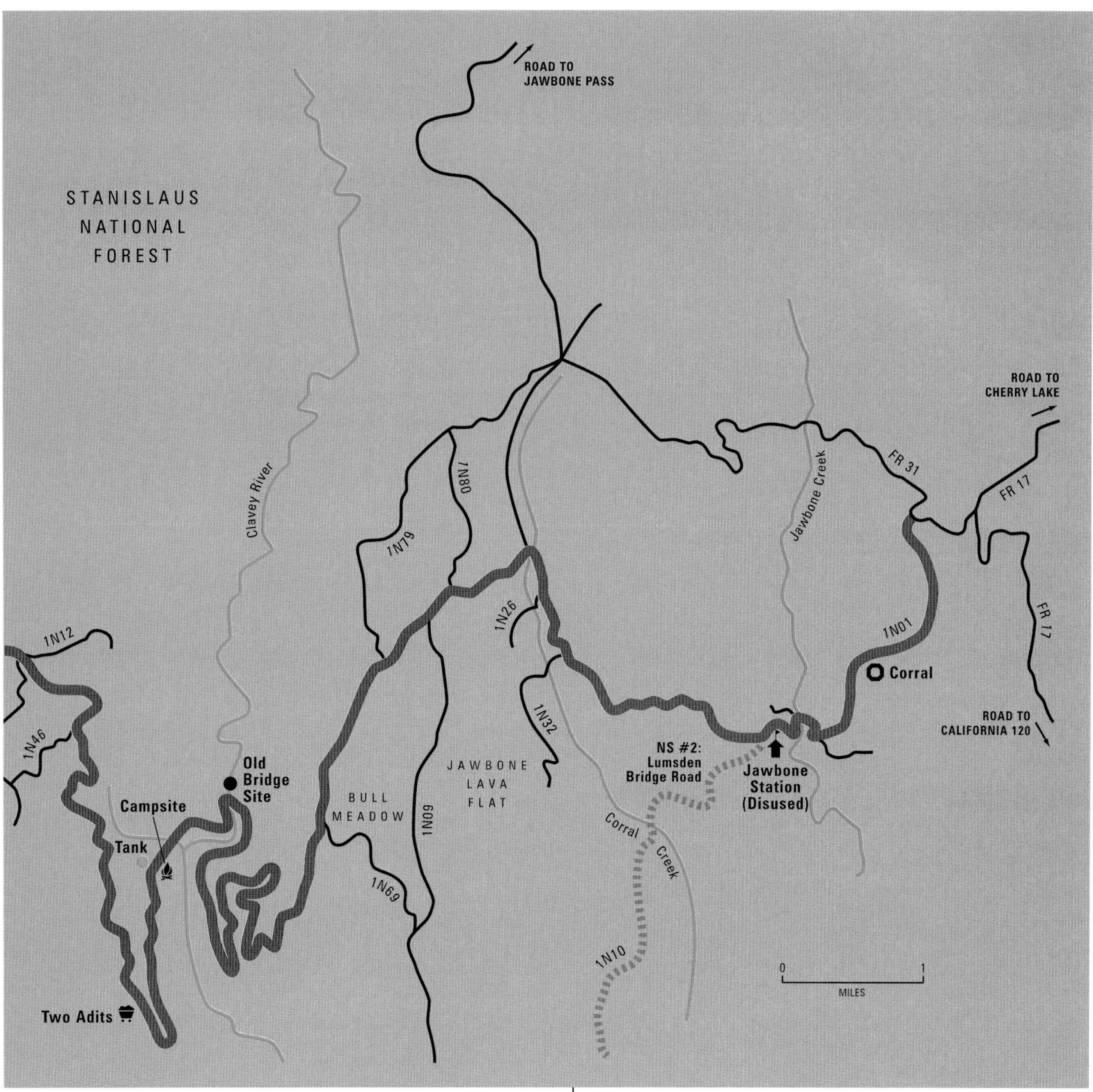

	0.7 ▲	SO	Cross through creek. Waterfall on left and right.
			GPS: N37°53.75′ W120°04.67′
▼ 7.8		BR	Track on left goes 0.1 miles to the old bridge site. Zero trip meter then cross over the Clavey River Bridge.
	0.0 ▲		Continue to the southwest.
			GPS: N37°53.94′ W120°04.28′
▼ 0.0			Continue to the east.
	6.8 ▲	BL	Cross over the Clavey River Bridge; then zero trip meter. Track on right goes 0.1 miles to the old bridge site.
▼ 0.1		BR	Track on left to old bridge site; then seasonal closure gate.
	6.7 ▲	BL	Seasonal closure gate; then track on right to old bridge site.
▼ 3.4		SO	Cross over creek.
	3.4 ▲	SO	Cross over creek.
▼ 4.1		SO	Top of climb. End of shelf road.
	2.7 ▲	SO	Start of shelf road. Road starts to descend.
▼ 5.0		SO	Track on right is 1N69.
	1.8 ▲	BR	Track on left is 1N69.
			GPS: N37°53.78′ W120°03.57′
▼ 5.6		SO	Track on right.
	1.2 ▲	SO	Track on left.
▼ 5.8		SO	Track on left is 1N28.
	1.0 ▲	BL	Track on right is 1N28.

▼ 6.2		SO	Cattle guard.
	0.6 ▲	SO	Cattle guard.
▼ 6.3		SO	Track on left is 1N79.
	0.5 ▲	SO	Track on right is 1N79.
			GPS: N37°54.65' W120°02.98'
▼ 6.8		SO	Track on right is 1N09, which goes through seasonal closure gate to Jawbone Ridge. Zero trip meter.
	0.0 ▲		Continue to the west.
			GPS: N37°54.87' W120°02.55'
▼ 0.0			Continue to the east.
	3.7 ▲	SO	Track on left is 1N09, which goes through seasonal closure gate to Jawbone Ridge. Zero trip meter.
▼ 0.1		BR	Track on left.
	3.6 ▲	BL	Track on right.
▼ 0.2		SO	Track on right.
	3.5 ▲	SO	Track on left.
▼ 0.4		SO	Track on left is 1N80.
	3.3 ▲	SO	Track on right is 1N80.
▼ 0.9		TR	Road continues ahead to Femmons Meadow. Turn sharp right onto small road.
	2.8 ▲	TL	Turn sharp left onto small road, following the sign to Clavey River.
			GPS: N37°55.17' W120°01.76'
▼ 1.6		SO	Track on right is 1N26.
	2.1 ▲	SO	Track on left is 1N26.
▼ 2.2		SO	Track on right is 1N32.
	1.5 ▲	SO	Track on left is 1N32.
▼ 2.6		SO	Track on left is 1N74.
	1.1 ▲	SO	Track on right is 1N74.
▼ 3.7		SO	Track on right is Northern Sierra #2: Lumsden Bridge Road (1N10), signposted to Groveland. Zero trip meter. Disused Jawbone USFS Station on right at the intersection.
	0.0 ▲		Continue to the south.
			GPS: N37°53.97' W120°00.05'
▼ 0.0			Continue to the north.
	2.7 ▲	BR	Disused Jawbone USFS station on left. Track on left is Northern Sierra #2: Lumsden Bridge Road (1N10), signposted to Groveland. Zero trip meter.
▼ 0.1		BR	Track on left.
	2.6 ▲	BL	Track on right.
▼ 0.4		SO	Cross over Jawbone Creek.
	2.3 ▲	SO	Cross over Jawbone Creek.
▼ 0.7		SO	Track on right.
	2.0 ▲	SO	Track on left.
▼ 1.2		SO	Cattle guard.
	1.5 ▲	SO	Cattle guard.
▼ 1.4		SO	Corral on right.
	1.3 ▲	SO	Corral on left.
▼ 1.9		SO	Cattle guard.
	0.8 ▲	SO	Cattle guard.
▼ 2.6		SO	Cross over creek.
	0.1 ▲	SO	Cross over creek.
▼ 2.7			Seasonal closure gate; then trail ends at T-intersection with paved FR 31. Turn left for Jawbone Pass; turn right for FR 17 and Cherry Lake.
	0.0 ▲		Trail commences on paved FR 31, 0.6 miles west of the intersection with FR 17, 13 miles south of Cherry Lake. Zero trip meter and turn northwest on graded dirt trail 1N01. Pass through seasonal closure gate.
			GPS: N37°55.13' W119°58.74'

NORTHERN SIERRA #2

Lumsden Bridge Road

Starting Point:	**Northern Sierra #1: Clavey Bridge Road at Jawbone Station, 2.7 miles west of FR 31**
Finishing Point:	**Ferretti Road, 1 mile northwest of California 120**
Total Mileage:	**11.5 miles**
Unpaved Mileage:	**11.5 miles**
Driving Time:	**1.5 hours**
Elevation Range:	**1,400–3,500 feet**
Usually Open:	**April to November**
Best Time to Travel:	**April to November**
Difficulty Rating:	**2**
Scenic Rating:	**9**
Remoteness Rating:	**+0**

Special Attractions

- Easy trail that follows the Tuolumne River, a designated Wild and Scenic River.
- Popular rafting and kayaking put-ins and many angling opportunities.
- Choice of three USFS campgrounds.

History

Jawbone Station sits along Jawbone Creek at the start of Lumsden Bridge Road. The original guard station was built in 1909. Forest ranger Jack Pestoni and his faithful mule Martha assisted in transporting construction materials to the site. The cabin that replaced the original was one of many backcountry structures built by the Civilian Conservation Corps (CCC) during the Depression.

Early forest rangers in the Groveland Ranger District oversaw grazing permits for cattle, swine, sheep, and horses. In 1910, 14,245 animals ranged throughout Stanislaus National Forest. That year, a mere 1,008 sheep and goats grazed within the district. Ten years later, 14,449 sheep and goats were roaming the region.

The original Lumsden Bridge was built by the Lumsden brothers, who were employed by the Big Oak Flat–Yosemite Road Company. The bridge was part of ongoing improvements to open the region for logging, mining, grazing, and tourism.

In 1920, steel girders were added to the bridge. Tuolumne County supplied the girders and the forest service carried them in on a World War I–era army truck. Transporting the girders from Sonora to Buck Meadows, south of this trail on California 120, was quite a trek for the slow-moving truck. Hauling girders down the narrow shelf road to the bridge site was even slower. Negotiating the series of tight, steep switchbacks to the bottom of the canyon took all day for the brave driver and his assistants. Many trees around the outside corners had to be cut down to make room for the overhanging girders. The large truck was forced to continuously back up and go forward to negotiate the tight curves.

The bridge was well used in the 1950s when the city and county of San Francisco were involved in building the dam on Cherry Creek to the northeast. The bridge was damaged when heavy machinery passed over the aging structure. Lumsden Bridge was rebuilt in 1997, following additional damage caused by flooding.

Buck Meadows was called Hamilton Station when originally homesteaded in 1892. The station was badly burned in the 1930s and a new lodge was built alongside what is now California 120, just east of Ferretti Road. Big Oak Lodge and Big Oak Flat Road were so named because of the presence of such fine examples of the tree. The trees have been removed over time, mostly because of their unfortunate proximity to this evolving tourist and construction route. The lodge and surrounding area enjoyed a boom time in the 1950s following construction of the Hetch Hetchy Reservoir, completed in 1934, and Cherry Lake. The lodge slowly fell into disrepair as travelers sped past it en route to Yosemite National Park. The structure was restored in 1978.

Description

This easygoing trail takes high-clearance vehicles down a gradual shelf road to the Tuolumne River. It follows the river for a while before climbing toward California 120. The trail commences on Northern Sierra #1: Clavey Bridge Road and almost immediately becomes a shelf road. The surface is rough enough that a passenger vehicle is not advised, but a high-clearance 2WD should have little trouble in dry weather. The shelf road has ample passing places.

The trail descends past oak and curl-leaf mahoganies in the shadow of Jawbone Ridge. As the views open up, you can see up and down the Tuolumne River Valley in both directions. After about 2.9 miles, a lightly used hiking trail of moderate difficulty heads down along the Tuolumne River to its confluence with the Clavey River. The start of the hiking trail can be difficult to find.

The Lumsden Bridge crosses the Tuolumne River

There are three forest service campgrounds around Lumsden Bridge. The first site, the Lumsden Bridge Campground, has nine shaded sites along the river. It is usually the quietest of the three because it is the farthest away from the raft put-ins. Past the bridge, the trail climbs a shelf road above the river again, before descending to the next two campgrounds—South Fork and Lumsden—and the raft put-in. Camping is permitted in campgrounds only. The trail continues along the wide shelf road to end on paved Ferretti Road, 1 mile north-

Lumsden Bridge Road

west of California 120 and the Groveland Ranger Station.

The Tuolumne River is designated a Wild and Scenic River, and fishing regulations and bag and size limits apply. These regulations are posted as you enter the area from either direction. Anglers can fish for brown and rainbow trout and salmon.

The road is heavily used in rafting season, which runs from April to October. During this time you are likely to encounter large tour buses ferrying customers to raft put-ins. A permit is required to float the river between May 1 and September 30. Permits are available at the Groveland Ranger Station, near the end of the trail. There is a fee for permit reservations, but walk-in permits are free (subject to availability). Rafters are encouraged to book ahead. The ranger station is open 7 days a week in rafting season. From the put-in point, it is an 18-mile, full-day float down to Wards Ferry Bridge. The route is one of the most challenging river runs in California, rated Class IV to V, and includes such rapids as Rock Garden, Nemesis, Gray Grindstone, Hell's Kitchen, and Evangelist.

Current Road Information

Stanislaus National Forest
Groveland Ranger District
24525 Highway 120
Groveland, CA 95321
(209) 962-7825

Map References

BLM Oakdale
USFS Stanislaus National Forest
USGS 1:24,000 Duckwall Mt., Jawbone Ridge
1:100,000 Oakdale
Maptech CD-ROM: High Sierra/Yosemite
Northern California Atlas & Gazetteer, p. 109
California Road & Recreation Atlas, p. 72

Route Directions

▼ 0.0	From Northern Sierra #1: Clavey Bridge Road, 2.7 miles west of the intersection with FR 31, zero trip meter and turn southwest onto 1N10 following the sign to Groveland. Jawbone USFS Station (closed) is at the intersection.

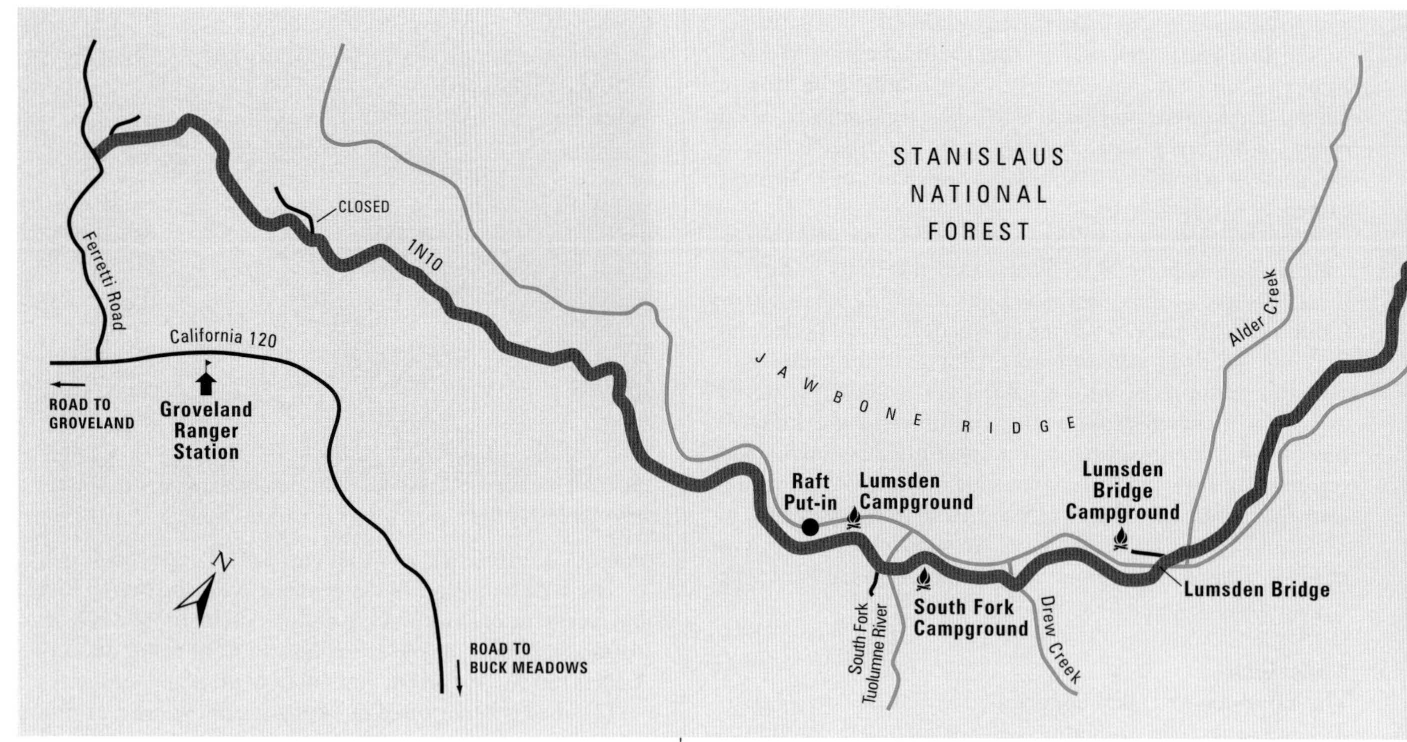

5.0 ▲ Trail ends at intersection with Northern Sierra #1: Clavey Bridge Road. Jawbone USFS Station (closed) is at the intersection. Turn left for Tuolumne; turn right to exit to FR 31 and FR 17.

GPS: N37°53.97′ W120°00.05′

▼ 0.3 SO Track on left.
4.7 ▲ SO Track on right.

▼ 0.5 SO Track on right.
4.5 ▲ SO Track on left.

▼ 1.4 SO Seasonal closure gate; then cattle guard; then cross over Corral Creek.
3.6 ▲ SO Cross over Corral Creek; then cattle guard; then seasonal closure gate.

GPS: N37°53.38′ W120°01.03′

▼ 1.8 SO Cross over creek.
3.2 ▲ SO Cross over creek.

▼ 2.0 SO Start of shelf road.
3.0 ▲ SO End of shelf road.

▼ 2.2 SO Entering Tuolumne Wild and Scenic River Area. Camping is allowed in designated sites only.
2.8 ▲ SO Leaving Tuolumne Wild and Scenic River Area.

GPS: N37°52.87′ W120.01.14′

▼ 2.9 SO Access to hiking trail along the Tuolumne River at pull-off on left by fishing regulation sign.
2.1 ▲ SO Access to hiking trail along the Tuolumne River at pull-off on right by fishing regulation sign.

▼ 4.8 SO Cross over Alder Creek.
0.2 ▲ SO Cross over Alder Creek.

GPS: N37°50.98′ W120°01.71′

▼ 5.0 TL End of descent. Track straight ahead goes 0.2 miles into Lumsden Bridge USFS Campground. Zero trip meter. Turn left and cross over the Tuolumne River on Lumsden Bridge.
0.0 ▲ Continue to the northeast.

GPS: N37°50.92′ W120°01.75′

▼ 0.0 Continue to the southeast.
6.5 ▲ TR Cross over the Tuolumne River on Lumsden Bridge; then track on left goes 0.2 miles into Lumsden Bridge USFS Campground. Zero trip meter.

▼ 0.8 SO Cross through Drew Creek.
5.7 ▲ SO Cross through Drew Creek.

▼ 1.3 SO Track on left into South Fork USFS Campground.
5.2 ▲ SO Track on right into South Fork USFS Campground.

GPS: N37°50.40′ W120°02.70′

▼ 1.5 TR Cross over South Fork Tuolumne River on bridge; then T-intersection.
5.0 ▲ TL Track straight ahead. Turn left and cross over South Fork Tuolumne River on bridge.

GPS: N37°50.28′ W120°02.83′

▼ 1.7 SO Lumsden USFS Campground on right.
4.8 ▲ SO Lumsden USFS Campground on left.

▼ 1.8 SO Parking area, river information, and raft put-in on right.
4.7 ▲ SO Parking area, river information, and raft put-in on left.

GPS: N37°50.20′ W120°03.14′

▼ 2.8 SO Cross over creek. Small waterfall on left.
3.7 ▲ SO Cross over creek. Small waterfall on right.

▼ 3.3 SO Leaving Tuolumne Wild and Scenic River Area.
3.2 ▲ SO Entering Tuolumne Wild and Scenic River Area. Camping in designated sites only.

GPS: N37°50.22′ W120°04.32′

▼ 4.2 SO Cross over creek.
2.3 ▲ SO Cross over creek.

▼ 5.1 SO Closed track on right.
1.4 ▲ SO Closed track on left.

▼ 6.4 SO Track on right. End of shelf road.
0.1 ▲ BR Track on left. Start of shelf road.

▼ 6.5 Track on right under power lines; then seasonal closure gate; then cattle guard. Trail ends at

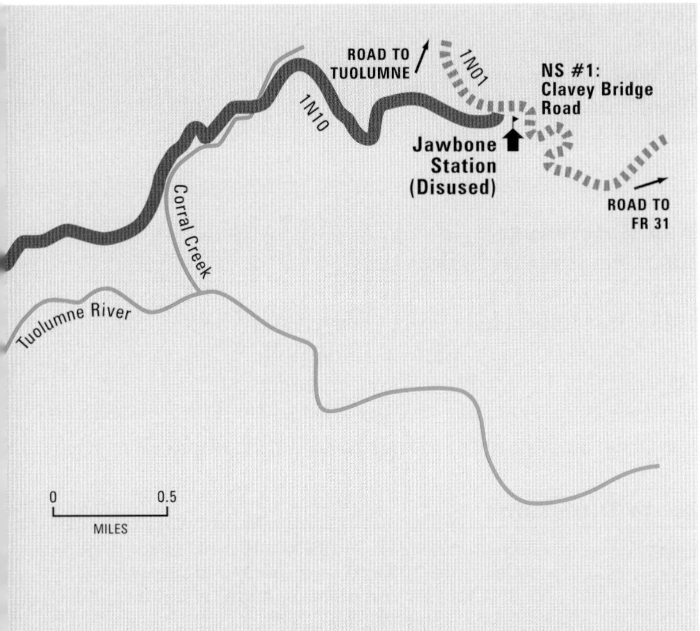

NORTHERN SIERRA #2: LUMSDEN BRIDGE ROAD

T-intersection with paved Ferretti Road. Turn left for California 120 and Groveland Ranger Station; turn right for alternate route to Groveland.

0.0 ▲ From Groveland Ranger Station, proceed southwest on California 120 for 0.3 miles; then turn northwest onto small paved Ferretti Road. Proceed northwest for 1 mile; then zero trip meter and turn north onto graded dirt road, following the sign for Tuolumne River. Cross cattle guard and pass through seasonal closure gate. Track on left under power lines.

GPS: N37°49.71' W120°07.02'

NORTHERN SIERRA #3

Bourland Trestle Trail

Starting Point:	**FR 31 (3N01), 16.5 miles south of California 108 and Long Barn**
Finishing Point:	**Bourland Trestle**
Total Mileage:	**6.7 miles (one-way)**
Unpaved Mileage:	**6.7 miles**
Driving Time:	**1 hour (one-way)**
Elevation Range:	**5,000–5,600 feet**
Usually Open:	**April to November**
Best Time to Travel:	**Dry weather**
Difficulty Rating:	**2**
Scenic Rating:	**8**
Remoteness Rating:	**+0**

Special Attractions

- Easy trail along the old West Side Lumber Company Railroad grade.
- Remains of the Bourland Trestle—until recently the last intact narrow-gauge logging railroad trestle in the western United States.
- Excellent mountain bike route.

History

In 1899, the West Side Flume and Lumber Company purchased a sawmill site in a small gold mining community called Summerville. Tuolumne, as it was later named, grew quickly as the company expanded to include 250 miles of temporary railroad spurs and 45 logging camps. Ponderosas and sugar pines were the company's mainstay. A narrow-gauge railroad system (36 inches wide) was chosen over standard gauge (56.5 inches wide) to cope with the mountainous terrain. This system reduced overall costs and required less grading.

Remains of the Bourland Trestle are the last of many high trestles that connected nearly 70 miles of railroad developed by the West Side Lumber Company. Built in 1923, the six-tiered trestle stood 75 feet high and spanned more than 315 feet across Bourland Creek. A railroad tender was stationed at the Bourland Trestle to walk and inspect the high structure for smoldering fires started by sparks from the trains heading to the sawmill.

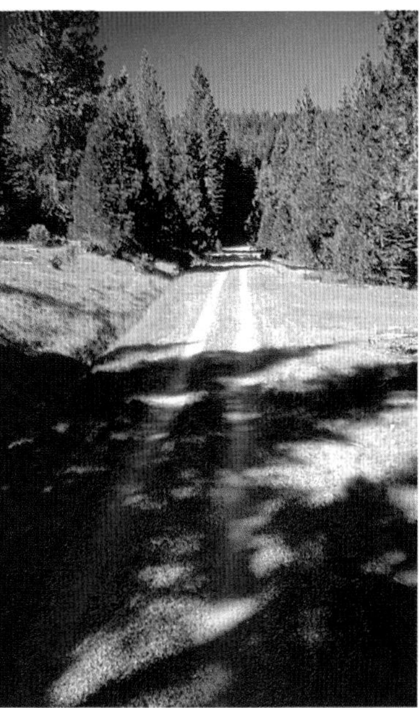
Bourland Trestle Trail

Enough logs went to the sawmill during warmer months to keep the mill operating throughout the winter. For the railroad, winter was a time of rebuilding and repairing locomotives and railcars. A series of Heisler and Shay locomotives were used on the logging railroads.

By the late 1940s, trucks were replacing trains on the old railroad grades. The Bourland Trestle remained in use until the 1950s. By the early 1960s, much of the railroad was falling into disuse because of labor and market demand issues. In 1967, the railroad tracks were removed and materials salvaged.

Bourland Creek, as with the trestle, was named after John L. Bourland, sheriff of Tuolumne County from 1865 to 1868.

Description

This short easy trail travels along graded dirt roads to the Bourland Trestle, following close to the original West Side Lumber Company Railroad grade. In places you can see the raised path of the grade.

The first part of the trail follows a shelf road high above the

Bourland Trestle, built in 1922, was part of the West Side Lumber Company's railroad system

Clavey River. The single-track shelf road has adequate passing places. The trail ends at the trestle itself, which spans Bourland Creek. Until recently the trestle was intact, but the middle section collapsed in the mid 1990s during heavy flooding of Bourland Creek. It is possible to walk down to the creek from the end of the vehicle trail along an old hiking trail. Do not attempt to walk onto the trestle; it is not stabilized and is considered unsafe.

Current Road Information

Stanislaus National Forest
Mi-Wok Ranger District
24695 Highway 108
Mi-Wuk Village, CA 95346
(209) 586-3234

Map References

BLM San Andreas, Bridgeport
USFS Stanislaus National Forest
USGS 1:24,000 Hull Creek, Cherry Lake North
1:100,000 San Andreas, Bridgeport
Maptech CD-ROM: High Sierra/Yosemite
Northern California Atlas & Gazetteer, pp. 99, 100
California Road & Recreation Atlas, p. 72 (incomplete)

Route Directions

▼ 0.0		From paved FR 31 (3N01), 16.5 miles south of California 108 and Long Barn, and opposite 3N10B, zero trip meter and turn south on graded dirt road, marked 2N29.
3.4 ▲		Trail ends at T-intersection with paved FR 31. Turn left for Long Barn and California 108; turn right for Cherry Lake.
		GPS: N38°03.94' W120°00.63'
▼ 0.4	BR	Track on left.
3.0 ▲	SO	Track on right.
▼ 0.7	SO	Trail joins the railroad grade.
2.7 ▲	SO	Trail leaves the railroad grade.
		GPS: N38°03.78' W120°01.07'
▼ 1.4	SO	Start of shelf road.
2.0 ▲	SO	End of shelf road.
▼ 2.6	SO	End of shelf road.
0.8 ▲	SO	Start of shelf road.

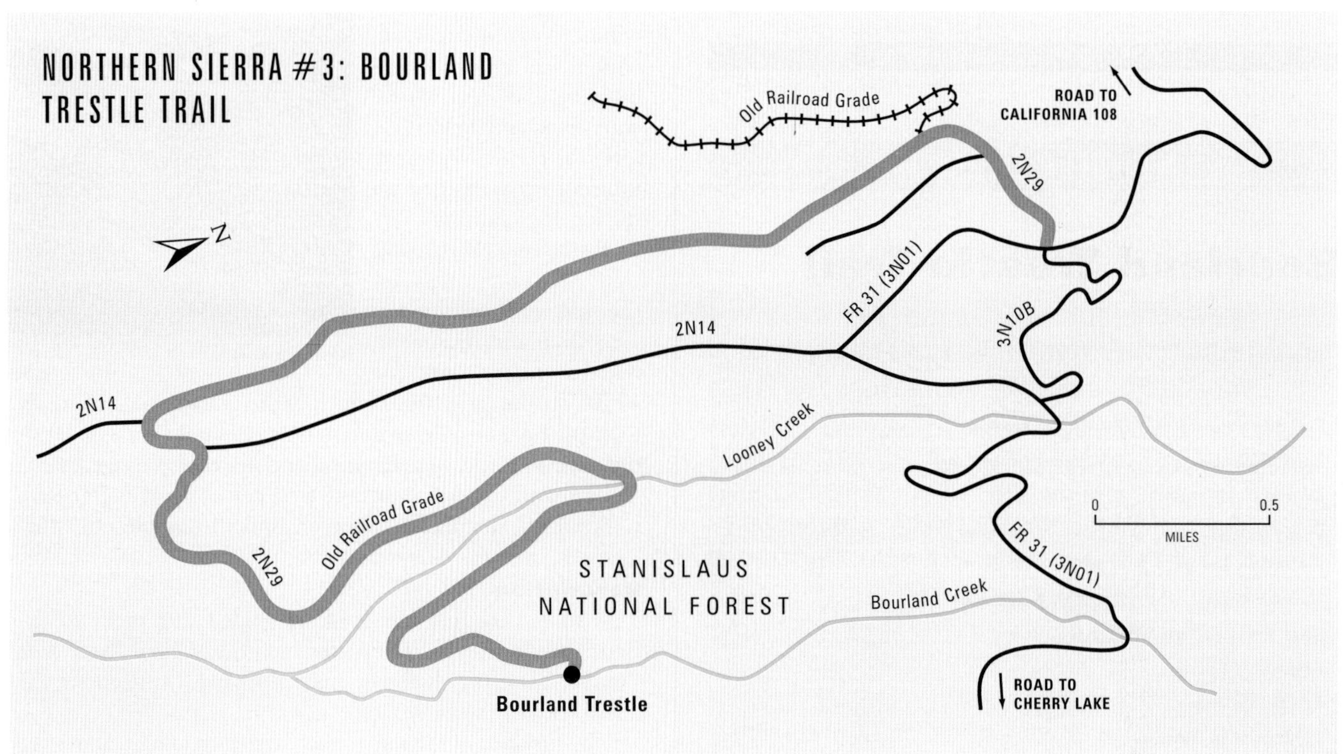

▼ 2.7		SO	Cross through creek.
	0.7 ▲	SO	Cross through creek.
▼ 3.1		SO	Seasonal closure gate; then track on right is 2N45.
	0.3 ▲	SO	Track on left is 2N45; then seasonal closure gate.
▼ 3.2		TL	T-intersection with 2N14.
	0.2 ▲	TR	2N14 continues straight ahead. Turn right onto 2N29.
			GPS: N38°01.74' W120°01.11'
▼ 3.4		TR	2N14 continues straight ahead and rejoins FR 31 in 2.6 miles. Turn right onto 2N29 and zero trip meter.
	0.0 ▲		Continue to the southwest.
			GPS: N38°01.86' W120°00.97'
▼ 0.0			Continue to the east on the old railroad grade.
▼ 1.9		SO	Cross over Looney Creek.
			GPS: N38°02.83' W120°00.40'
▼ 2.7		SO	Seasonal closure gate.
▼ 3.3			Trail ends at Bourland Trestle.
			GPS: N38°02.54' W119°59.93'

NORTHERN SIERRA #4

Dodge Ridge Trail

Starting Point:	**Merrill Springs Road (FR 31) opposite Fahey Cabin, 5.3 miles east of California 108**
Finishing Point:	**Crabtree Road (4N26), 4 miles east of Pinecrest**
Total Mileage:	**11.9 miles**
Unpaved Mileage:	**9.9 miles**
Driving Time:	**2.5 hours**
Elevation Range:	**5,400–7,000 feet**
Usually Open:	**May to November, exact dates vary**
Best Time to Travel:	**Dry weather**
Difficulty Rating:	**3**
Scenic Rating:	**8**
Remoteness Rating:	**+0**

Special Attractions

- Scenic drive along the forest service's marked auto tour.
- Sweeping views from Dodge Ridge that will appeal to landscape photographers and artists.

History

Dodge Ridge Trail commences at an old wooden cabin used by the Fahey family in the late 1800s. The Faheys, along with a number of other families, ran dairy cows in the region as far north as Bell Meadow, east of the northern end of Dodge Ridge. The Fahey family sailed to America from Ireland in the hope of new opportunities. Michael and John Fahey crossed the Atlantic in 1849 and settled in New Orleans, where their two brothers and sisters soon joined them. By the early 1850s, the entire Fahey family had relocated to the vicinity of Sonora, California. Though most immigrants of that era sought fortunes in the goldfields, the Faheys decided to raise cattle. Their land and cattle concerns grew considerably in the years that followed. Their cabin at Wrights Creek was in a summer range area where they developed a reputation for producing high-quality butter. The Fahey's cabin and holdings remained in the family until 1938, when the forest service purchased them. The cabin has been the subject of a recent stabilization project.

The historic Sierra crossing made by the Duckwall party in 1852 passed close to the Aspen Meadow Pack Station at the north end of the trail. The difficult wagon route took the emigrants past Burst Rock, high above Relief Valley, then dropped some 2,000 feet to Aspen Meadow. From there the group descended Dodge Ridge to Strawberry Meadow, near today's Pinecrest Lake, and continued southwest close to the route of today's California 108. Wagon trains stopped using this dangerous trail in 1853.

Description

Dodge Ridge Trail, also known as the Sierra Grandstand Tour, is a marked auto tour described on a leaflet put out by the forest service. It takes you through pine forests to the open top of Dodge Ridge, where several viewpoints overlook the Dardanelles, Bald Mountain, and Browns Meadow.

The route described below follows the forest service tour in reverse, giving it a 3 difficulty rating because of a couple of loose, scrabbly climbs onto the ridge. In reverse, the drive rates a 2.

Twisted conifer at the top of the ridge

The trail leaves road 3N96 east of Long Barn at the wooden Fahey Cabin, which stands in a meadow opposite the start of the trail. Initially, the road follows a graded, gravel road that climbs toward Dodge Ridge. An alternate route travels a smaller trail to Lightning Lookout, but this way can be slightly brushy. A short detour goes to Artists' Point and the famous view of the Dardanelles often captured by landscape artists and photographers. Additional viewpoints along the trail offer equally spectacular views of the steep volcanic cliffs that characterize the region.

The trail drops gradually from Dodge Ridge along progressively better maintained trails, finally joining small paved roads to finish at Aspen Meadow. The final viewpoint is just off the end of the trail. Large boulders called glacial erratics,

Sparse vegetation on Dodge Ridge

dropped by retreating glaciers thousands of years ago, are visible from here.

If traveling the trail in reverse, it is well marked by Sierra Grandstand Tour markers, with each point of interest indicated by a numbered post.

Current Road Information

Stanislaus National Forest
Mi-Wok Ranger District
24695 Highway 108
Mi-Wuk Village, CA 95346
(209) 586-3234

Map References

BLM San Andreas, Bridgeport
USFS Stanislaus National Forest
USGS 1:24,000 Hull Creek, Pinecrest, Strawberry
1:100,000 San Andreas, Bridgeport
Maptech CD-ROM: High Sierra/Yosemite
Northern California Atlas & Gazetteer, pp. 99, 100
California Road & Recreation Atlas, p. 72

Route Directions

Mileage		Direction
▼ 0.0		From California 108 at Long Barn, 3.8 miles northeast of Mi-Wok Ranger Station, zero trip meter and turn east at the sign for Long Barn (note that this is the second entrance to Long Barn if traveling north from Mi-Wuk Village) and zero trip meter. After 0.1 miles, turn left onto Merrill Springs Road (FR 31), following the sign for the North Fork of the Tuolumne River, and proceed 5.2 miles to the start of the trail. On a right-hand bend, zero trip meter and turn northeast on graded dirt road marked 3N96. Fahey Cabin, alongside Wrights Creek, is opposite the start of the trail.
3.3 ▲		Trail ends at T-intersection with paved Merrill Springs Road (FR 31). Turn right for Mi-Wuk Village. Fahey Cabin is opposite the end of the trail.
		GPS: N38°04.73′ W120°05.82′
▼ 0.9	SO	Track on right is 3N28Y.
2.4 ▲	SO	Track on left is 3N28Y.
▼ 1.5	SO	Two tracks on left at turnout.
1.8 ▲	SO	Two tracks on right at turnout.
		GPS: N38°05.66′ W120°04.77′
▼ 1.6	SO	Track on left is 3N20, marked for 4WDs, ATVs, and motorbikes, which goes 0.6 miles to Lightning Lookout and rejoins the main trail 0.6 miles after that. This alternate route is 3-rated and somewhat brushy.
1.7 ▲	SO	Alternate route 3N20 rejoins on right.
		GPS: N38°05.73′ W120°04.70′
▼ 2.0	SO	Track on left and track on right.
1.3 ▲	SO	Track on left and track on right.
▼ 2.4	BL	3N96 continues straight ahead. Bear left onto 3N55Y.
0.9 ▲	SO	3N96 joins from the left.
		GPS: N38°05.78′ W120°04.24′
▼ 3.0	SO	Track on left is Trail #26 for 4WDs, ATVs, and motorbikes.
0.3 ▲	SO	Track on right is Trail #26 for 4WDs, ATVs, and motorbikes.

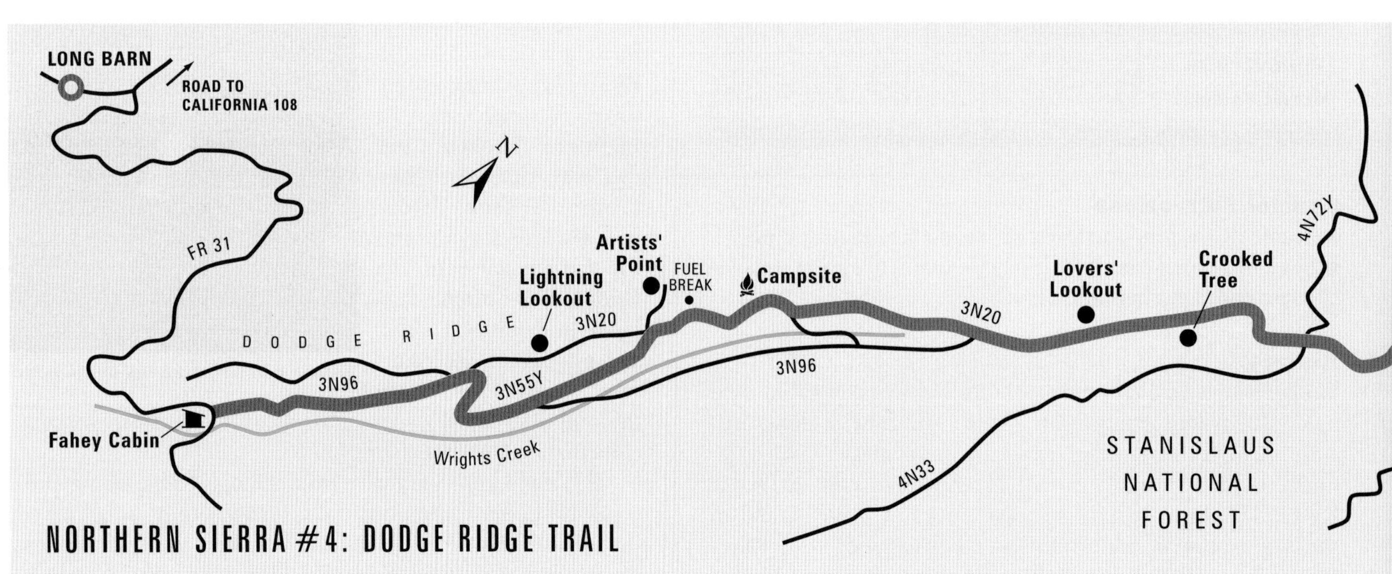

▼ 3.3 **TR** 4-way intersection. Track on left is 3N20, which is the end of alternate route via Lightning Lookout. Track straight ahead is 3N42, which goes 0.2 miles to Artists' Point. Zero trip meter and turn right onto 3N20.
0.0 ▲ Continue to the southeast.

GPS: N38°06.53′ W120°03.96′

▼ 0.0 Continue to the northeast.
4.2 ▲ **TL** 4-way intersection. Track on right is 3N42, which goes 0.2 miles to Artists' Point. Track straight ahead is 3N20, which goes 0.6 miles to Lightning Lookout and rejoins the main trail 0.6 miles after that. This alternate route is 3-rated and somewhat brushy. Zero trip meter and turn left onto 3N55Y.

▼ 0.3 **SO** Pass through fuel break (open area)—point 6 on Sierra Grandstand Tour.
3.9 ▲ **SO** Pass through fuel break (open area)—point 6 on Sierra Grandstand Tour.

▼ 0.7 **SO** Campsite and viewpoint on left.
3.5 ▲ **SO** Campsite and viewpoint on right.

▼ 0.8 **TR** Track on left is 3N49. Remain on 3N20.
3.4 ▲ **TL** Track straight ahead is 3N49. Remain on 3N20.

GPS: N38°07.05′ W120°03.42′

▼ 0.9 **BL** Track on right is 3N53Y. Remain on 3N20.
3.3 ▲ **SO** Track on left is 3N53Y. Remain on 3N20.

▼ 2.1 **SO** Track on right is 3N96. Follow sign to Pinecrest.
2.1 ▲ **SO** Track on left is 3N96. Follow sign to Fahey Cabin.

GPS: N38°07.56′ W120°02.29′

▼ 2.8 **SO** Lovers' Lookout on left—point 5 on Sierra Grandstand Tour.
1.4 ▲ **SO** Lovers' Lookout on right—point 5 on Sierra Grandstand Tour.

GPS: N38°07.95′ W120°01.74′

▼ 3.4 **SO** Crooked Tree on right—point 4 on Sierra Grandstand Tour.
0.8 ▲ **SO** Crooked Tree on left—point 4 on Sierra Grandstand Tour.

GPS: N38°08.37′ W120°01.32′

▼ 4.2 **SO** Track on left is 4N72Y and graded road on right is 4N33. Zero trip meter.
0.0 ▲ Continue to the southwest on 3N20.

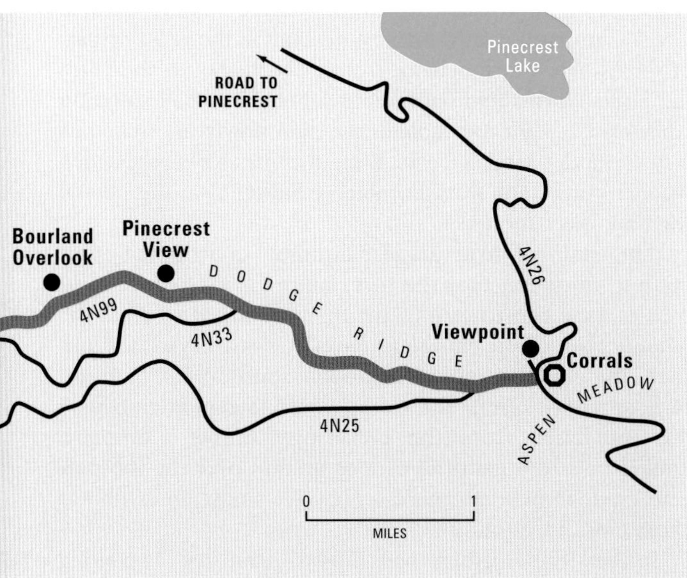

GPS: N38°08.64′ W120°00.61′

▼ 0.0 Continue to the east on 4N33.
4.4 ▲ **SO** Track on right is 4N72Y and graded road on left is 4N33. Zero trip meter.

▼ 0.1 **SO** Trail #24 on left for ATVs and motorbikes only—rated blue.
4.3 ▲ **SO** Trail #24 on right for ATVs and motorbikes only—rated blue.

▼ 0.6 **BL** Trail #12 on right for 4WDs, ATVs, and motorbikes—rated blue. 4N33 continues straight ahead. Bear left onto 4N99.
3.8 ▲ **BR** Track on left is 4N33. Trail #12 straight ahead for 4WDs, ATVs, and motorbikes—rated blue. Bear right onto 4N33.

GPS: N38°08.97′ W120°00.12′

▼ 1.3 **SO** Bourland Overlook, which looks east to Bourland Mountain and Bell Mountain—point 3 on Sierra Grandstand Tour.
3.1 ▲ **SO** Bourland Overlook, which looks east to Bourland Mountain and Bell Mountain—point 3 on Sierra Grandstand Tour.

GPS: N38°09.37′ W119°59.83′

▼ 1.9 **SO** View north of Pinecrest Lake and the effects of a 1997 wildfire—point 2 on Sierra Grandstand Tour.
2.5 ▲ **SO** View north of Pinecrest Lake and the effects of a 1997 wildfire—point 2 on Sierra Grandstand Tour.

GPS: N38°09.74′ W119°59.37′

▼ 2.4 **TL** T-intersection with 4N33. Road becomes paved.
2.0 ▲ **TR** 4N33 continues straight ahead. Turn right onto 4N99. Road turns to graded dirt.

GPS: N38°09.92′ W119°58.93′

▼ 2.5 **SO** Cattle guard; then track on right; then track on left is 4N71.
1.9 ▲ **SO** Track on right is 4N71; then track on left; then cattle guard.

▼ 2.7 **SO** Track on left is 4733B.
1.7 ▲ **SO** Track on right is 4733B.

▼ 4.1 **TL** T-intersection with paved 4N25.
0.3 ▲ **TR** 4N25 continues straight ahead. Turn right onto 4N33.

GPS: N38°10.41′ W119°57.39′

▼ 4.2 **SO** Track on right to Kerrick Corrals Horse Camp.
0.2 ▲ **SO** Track on left to Kerrick Corrals Horse Camp.

▼ 4.4 Trail ends at T-intersection with 4N26 opposite corrals. Turn left for Pinecrest; turn right for Gianelli Trailhead and Emigrant Wilderness. To reach Point 1 on the Sierra Grandstand Tour, turn left and head west past the sign marking the start of the Sierra Grandstand Scenic Drive. Proceed up the small dirt trail following the Sierra Grandstand Tour marker. The viewpoint is 0.1 miles up that trail.
0.0 ▲ From California 108, 2 miles southwest of the Summit Ranger Station at Strawberry, turn southeast on Crabtree Road (4N26) and proceed 6.3 miles to the start of trail. Trail commences on paved 4N26, 4 miles from Pinecrest. Zero trip meter opposite corrals and turn south on paved road 4N25, following the sign for Bell Meadow. There is a sign marking the start of the Sierra Grandstand Scenic Drive. To reach Point 1 of the tour, turn west up the small dirt trail, following the Sierra Grandstand Tour marker. The viewpoint is 0.1 miles up that trail.

GPS: N38°10.61′ W119°57.17′

NORTHERN SIERRA #5

Crandall Peak Trail

Starting Point:	**California 108, 2 miles north of Strawberry**
Finishing Point:	**Parrots Ferry Road (CR E18), 1 mile southeast of California 4**
Total Mileage:	**36.6 miles, plus 6.9-mile spur to Sand Bar Flat**
Unpaved Mileage:	**28.8 miles, plus 6.9-mile spur**
Driving Time:	**5 hours**
Elevation Range:	**1,000–6,000 feet**
Usually Open:	**April to November**
Best Time to Travel:	**Dry weather**
Difficulty Rating:	**3**
Scenic Rating:	**9**
Remoteness Rating:	**+1**

Special Attractions

- Access to the Middle Fork of the Stanislaus River at two points.
- Long winding ridge top trail with many excellent views.
- Access to the Crandall Peak OHV Area.

History

Laurence G. Crandall, for whom the peak and fire lookout were named, was a logging superintendent and camp boss at Camp Rath in the 1920s.

Crandall Peak Trail passes many examples of the development of California's natural resources, mainly timber and water. Strawberry Peak, at the eastern end of the trail, offers glimpses of Pinecrest Lake, a reservoir created to dam the South Fork of the Stanislaus River in 1916 by the predecessor of Pacific Gas & Electric (PG&E). Originally known as Strawberry Lake, it is part of a water storage system connecting the South and Middle Forks of the Stanislaus River. These waters combine to operate the Spring Gap Powerhouse on the south banks of the river's middle fork. The original Philadelphia Ditch was built in 1899 to provide water for mining operations near the western end of this trail. Modified since, the ditch diverts water to Spring Gap, which in turn drives the powerhouse. The Spring Gap Powerhouse, set 1,800 feet below the gap, was commissioned in 1921.

Manzanitas line the lower part of the ridge trail

The Stanislaus River at the far reaches of New Melones Lake

Schoettgen, pronounced Shotgun, Pass was a busy railroad junction on the Sugar Pine Railroad's network of tracks. The main railroad line operated out of Standard, just east of Sonora, and gradually made its way up the mountains to Long Barn, just southwest of Lyons Reservoir. From there it climbed to Schoettgen Junction at the northern end of the reservoir and began the long twisting route below Crandall Peak to Camp Strawberry. The busy railroad snaked past a logging camp called Crandall-in-the-Hole, carrying logs from the Strawberry region until 1929.

In 1927, a new railroad grade was constructed from Schoettgen Junction, up and over Schoettgen Pass, along what is today's 4N81. In 1929, a new logging camp was to be established below Spring Gap. The old buildings, including furniture, were loaded onto flatcars and moved nearly 50 miles from Camp Strawberry to Tunnell Creek Camp. Tunnell Creek Camp was named for a tunnel built in the 1850s as part of the Miners' Ditch Scheme to connect the South and Middle Forks of the Stanislaus River. Surely the small town on wheels was a sight to behold as the train slowly negotiated its way around Crandall Peak. Even the massive steel-banded wooden water tank from Bumblebee Siding, near the start of the trail, was relocated.

The main railroad grade continued to lengthen, proceeding northeast past the new camp. Many high, curved trestles were constructed as the line descended to cross the Middle Fork of the Stanislaus River at Beardsley Flat. From there the grade swung west through Sourdough Camp, on to Soap Creek Camp and Camp Grahl. Steam engine Shay #3, purchased from the Pickering Lumber Company, hauled massive quantities of logs up and over the 2.5-percent grade to Schoettgen Pass. Shay #3 is now on exhibit at the Sonora Fairgrounds.

In the 1950s, logging trains crossed Beardsley Dam along

the grade that is today's FR 15. The rail lines past Soap Creek Camp were becoming redundant by the late 1950s, and by 1961 more efficient and versatile logging trucks were introduced—the beginning of the end of a much-worked railroad system.

The last logging train to cross Beardsley Dam was in 1963. The train consisted of open-topped cars carrying employees bidding farewell to a major section of the Sugar Pine Railway. They had dinner at Soap Creek Camp to mark the closing of 32 miles of track. From then on, logging trucks were used to move felled trees to Schoettgen Pass, where they were loaded onto railcars.

Description

This long ridge top trail gets its difficulty rating of 3 from the section along Strawberry Ridge and the final descent to the Stanislaus River. Most of the trail is rated 2, and high-clearance 2WD vehicles can generally reach the middle sections by following one of the other graded dirt roads into the region.

The trail leaves California 108 north of Strawberry. Initially, it follows a well-used, formed trail to the radio towers on Strawberry Peak; past the peak, the trail is less used. It winds along Strawberry Ridge, through open woodlands carpeted with bear clover. The Stanislaus River Valley can be seen to the south, and Beardsley Lake and Whittakers Dardanelles can be seen to the north.

The trail joins a major graded road just east of the start of the spur to Sand Bar Flat. The 6.9-mile spur descends to a forest service campground beside the Stanislaus River. From the campground, you can take a dip in some great swimming holes or head out on 6 miles of hiking trails along the river. Note that the road shown as crossing the river from the campground is not open to the public. There is trailhead parking for the Crandall Peak OHV Area at the start of the spur, and a network of small trails, mostly suitable for motorbikes and ATVs only, crisscross the region.

Sand Bar Flat to Beardsley Lake hiking trail follows along the Stanislaus River

A couple of miles past the spur, a rough, loose-surfaced trail suitable for high-clearance 4WDs goes 2 miles to the site of an old fire lookout on Crandall Peak, built by the CCC in 1934. Continuing along the ridge top, the main trail crosses over Schoettgen Pass and skirts the north side of Mount Knight. It gradually descends the long ridge through oak and manzanita forest. The descent to the bridge over the Stanislaus River can be rough. It becomes extremely greasy in wet weather and is not recommended at those times. A keen eye will spot some old mining equipment half-hidden in the undergrowth in a gully near the bottom of the descent. The trail joins a paved road at the Stanislaus River and follows it around Bald Mountain to finish on Parrots Ferry Road near Vallecito.

Current Road Information

Stanislaus National Forest
Mi-Wok Ranger District
24695 Highway 108
Mi-Wuk Village, CA 95346
(209) 586-3234

Map References

BLM San Andreas
USFS Stanislaus National Forest
USGS 1:24,000 Strawberry, Crandall Peak, Stanislaus, Murphys, Columbia, Columbia SE
1:100,000 San Andreas
Maptech CD-ROM: High Sierra/Yosemite
Northern California Atlas & Gazetteer, pp. 98, 99
California Road & Recreation Atlas, pp. 72, 71

Route Directions

▼ 0.0			From California 108, 2 miles north of Strawberry, zero trip meter and turn southwest on graded dirt road 4N39. Pass through seasonal closure gate.
	5.5 ▲		Seasonal closure gate; then trail ends at T-intersection with California 108. Turn right for Strawberry; turn left for Sonora Pass.
			GPS: N38°12.37' W120°01.06'
▼ 0.1		SO	Track on right.
	5.4 ▲	SO	Track on left.
▼ 0.5		SO	Track on right.
	5.0 ▲	SO	Track on left.
▼ 0.9		BL	Track on right goes 0.3 miles to the radio towers on top of Strawberry Peak.
	4.6 ▲	SO	Track on left goes 0.3 miles to the radio towers on top of Strawberry Peak.
			GPS: N38°11.85' W120°01.72'
▼ 1.4		SO	Cattle guard.
	4.1 ▲	SO	Cattle guard.
▼ 4.9		SO	Track on left.
	0.6 ▲	SO	Track on right.
			GPS: N38°10.29' W120°05.40'
▼ 5.5		TL	T-intersection with 4N14. Road on right goes to Beardsley Lake. Zero trip meter.
	0.0 ▲		Continue to the east.
			GPS: N38°10.13' W120°06.06'
▼ 0.0			Continue to the southeast and cross cattle guard.
	2.0 ▲	TR	Cattle guard; then turn right following sign for Strawberry Ridge Road. Road continues straight ahead to Beardsley Lake. Zero trip meter.
▼ 0.1		TL	Cross over small aqueduct; then turn left in front of work station following sign for Fraser Flat. This does not appear on the map—it has

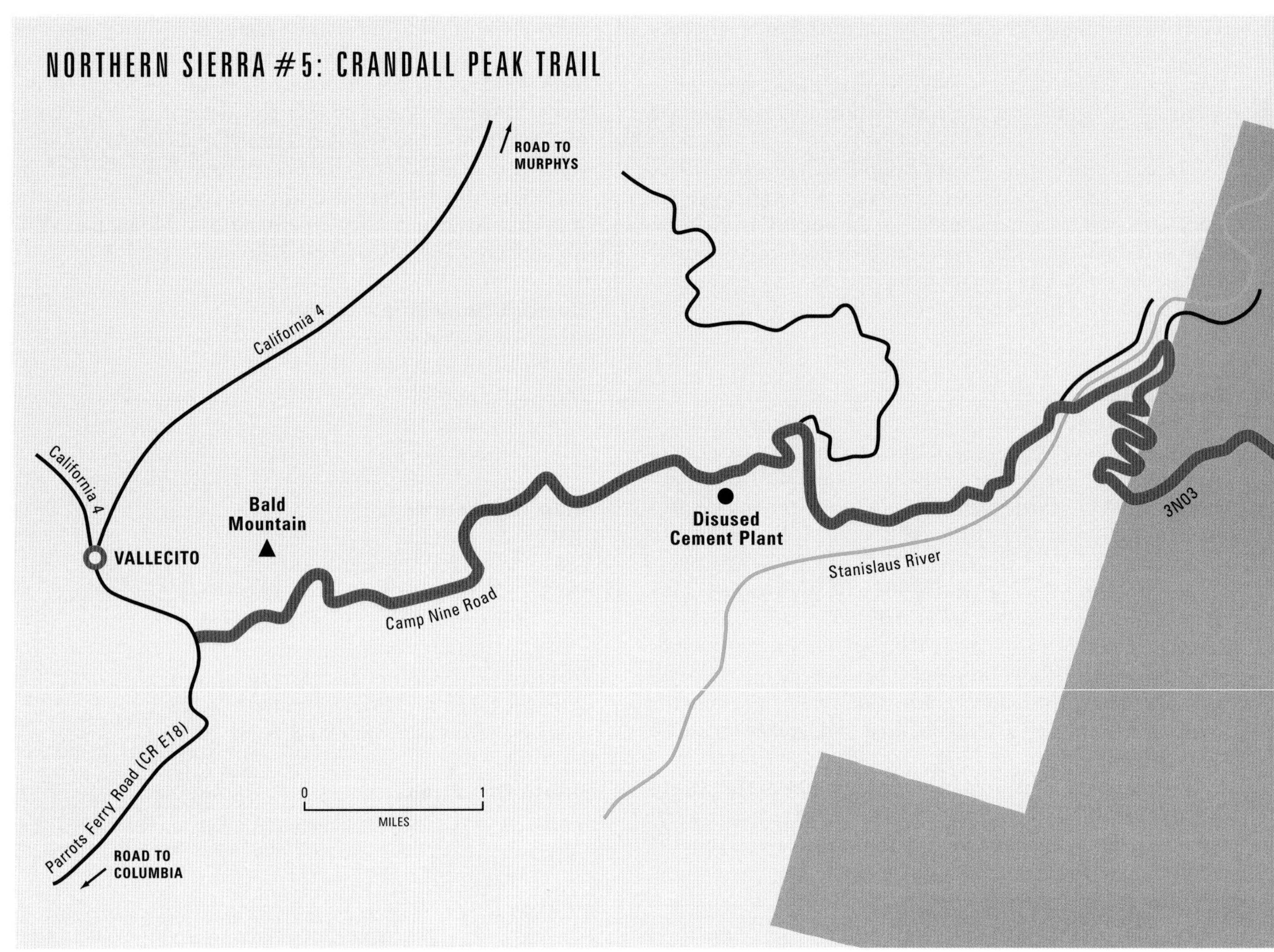

			been re-routed past the work station
	1.9 ▲	TR	Turn right in front of work station onto 4N14 following sign to Strawberry and cross over aqueduct.
			GPS: N38°10.09' W120°06.07'
▼ 0.3		TR	Turn sharp right onto graded road 4N01 following sign to Sand Bar Flat.
	1.7 ▲	TL	Turn sharp left onto 4N42 following sign for Spring Gap.
			GPS: N38°10.05' W120°05.89'
▼ 0.8		SO	Two tracks on right.
	1.2 ▲	SO	Two tracks on left.
▼ 1.3		SO	Track on right and track on left.
	0.7 ▲	SO	Track on right and track on left.
			GPS: N38°09.90' W120°06.78'
▼ 1.4		BR	Track on left. Remain on 4N01.
	0.6 ▲	SO	Track on right. Remain on 4N01.
▼ 1.6		SO	Track on right is 4N42.
	0.4 ▲	SO	Track on left is 4N42.
▼ 2.0		BR	Track on left is 4N88, which goes to Crandall Peak OHV Staging Area. Track on right is 4N88, which is the spur to Sand Bar Flat. Zero trip meter and bear right, remaining on 4N01 and following the sign to Mount Knight.
	0.0		Continue to the northeast on 4N01.
			GPS: N38°09.68' W120°07.39'

Spur to Sand Bar Flat

▼ 0.0			From the intersection of 4N01 and 4N88, zero trip meter and proceed northeast on 4N88—the lower of the two roads heading northeast—following the sign to Sand Bar Flat.
▼ 2.1		SO	Track on right is 4N86, which goes to a locked gate.
			GPS: N38°10.51' W120°06.45'
▼ 4.1		TL	4-way intersection. Turn left onto 4N85, following the sign for camping area; then turnout on left.
			GPS: N38°10.73' W120°07.26'
▼ 6.7		SO	Works buildings on left.
▼ 6.9			Spur ends at the Sand Bar Flat USFS Campground and day-use area—fee required. Road over the river is closed to the public. Excellent swimming holes at the campground. Hiking trail continues along river for 6 miles.
			GPS: N38°11.09' W120°09.24'

Continuation of Main Trail

▼ 0.0			Continue to the northwest on 4N01.
	2.8 ▲	SO	Track on right is 4N88, which goes to Crandall Peak OHV Staging Area. Track on left is 4N88, which is the spur to Sand Bar Flat. Zero trip meter and remain on 4N01—the upper of the two roads heading northeast.

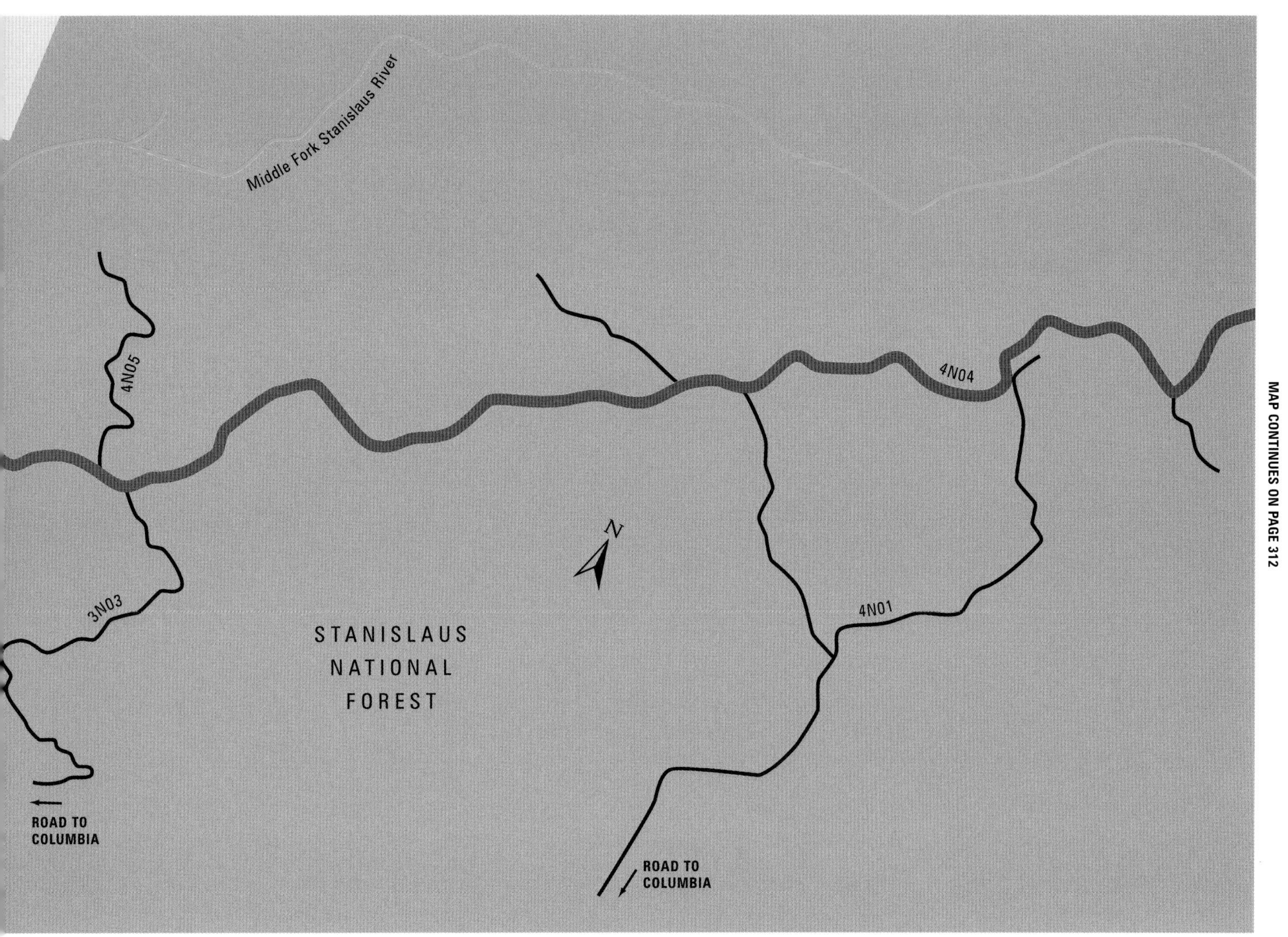

MAP CONTINUES ON PAGE 312

			GPS: N38°10.68′ W120°07.39′
▼ 0.1		SO	Track on left.
	2.7 ▲	SO	Track on right.
▼ 0.2		SO	Track on left.
	2.6 ▲	SO	Track on right.
▼ 2.8		SO	Track on left goes to the site of Crandall Peak Fire Lookout. Zero trip meter.
	0.0 ▲		Continue to the southeast.
			GPS: N38°10.20′ W120°09.25′
▼ 0.0			Continue to the northwest.
	8.2 ▲	SO	Track on right goes to the site of Crandall Peak Fire Lookout. Zero trip meter.
▼ 0.1		SO	Track on right.
	8.1 ▲	SO	Track on left.
▼ 0.8		BR	Well-used track on left is 4N02. Remain on 4N01.
	7.4 ▲	BL	Well-used track on right is 4N02. Remain on 4N01.
			GPS: N38°10.02′ W120°09.99′
▼ 1.2		TR	4-way intersection at Schoettgen Pass. Track on left is 4N81 and track straight ahead is 4N16. Turn right, remaining on 4N01; then track on right.
	7.0 ▲	TL	Track on left; then 4-way intersection at Schoettgen Pass. Track on right is 4N16 and track straight ahead is 4N81. Turn left, remaining on 4N01.
			GPS: N38°10.11′ W120°10.21′
▼ 1.3		BR	Track on left is 4N80.
	6.9 ▲	SO	Track on right is 4N80.
▼ 1.5		SO	Track on left.
	6.7 ▲	SO	Track on right.
▼ 2.6		SO	Track on left and track on right.
	5.6 ▲	SO	Track on left and track on right.
▼ 3.3		SO	Logging track on left.
	4.9 ▲	SO	Logging track on right.
▼ 3.4		SO	Track on right is 4N03Y.
	4.8 ▲	SO	Track on left is 4N03Y.
▼ 4.8		SO	Track on left is 4N18.
	3.4 ▲	SO	Track on right is 4N18.
			GPS: N38°10.16′ W120°13.30′
▼ 5.2		SO	Seasonal closure gate.
	3.0 ▲	SO	Seasonal closure gate.
			GPS: N38°10.14′ W120°13.70′
▼ 5.3		SO	Track on left.
	2.9 ▲	SO	Track on right.
▼ 5.4		SO	Track on left.
	2.8 ▲	SO	Track on right.
▼ 5.5		SO	Track on left.
	2.7 ▲	SO	Track on right.
▼ 6.7		SO	Track on right and track on left through gate are private property.

MAP CONTINUES ON PAGE 311

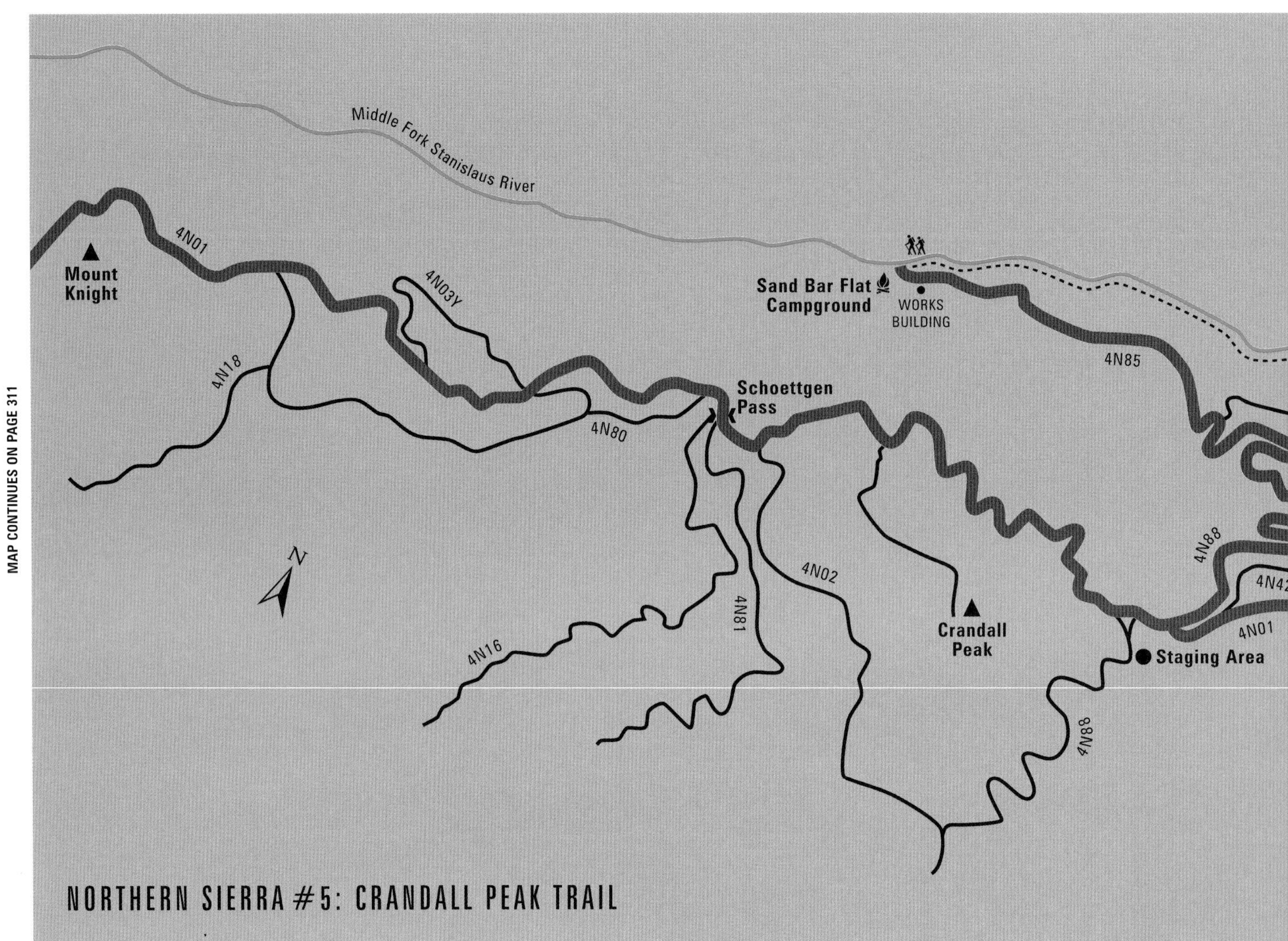

1.5 ▲	SO	Track on left and track on right through gate are private property.

GPS: N38°09.78′ W120°14.67′

▼ 7.4	SO	Track on left.
0.8 ▲	SO	Track on right.
▼ 7.5	SO	Track on left.
0.7 ▲	SO	Track on right.
▼ 7.6	SO	Track on right is 4N15Y.
0.6 ▲	SO	Track on left is 4N15Y.
▼ 7.9	SO	Track on right is 4N16Y.
0.3 ▲	SO	Track on left is 4N16Y.
▼ 8.2	TR	4-way intersection. 4N01 continues straight ahead and small track on left. Zero trip meter and turn right onto 4N04.
0.0 ▲		Continue to the east.

GPS: N38°09.61′ W120°15.64′

▼ 0.0		Continue to the north.
6.2 ▲	TL	4-way intersection. Small track straight ahead. Track on left and track on right are both 4N01. Zero trip meter and turn left onto 4N01.
▼ 0.3	SO	Track on left.
5.9 ▲	SO	Track on right.
▼ 0.9	SO	Track on left.
5.3 ▲	SO	Track on right.
▼ 1.5	BL	Two tracks on right.
4.7 ▲	BR	Two tracks on left.

GPS: N38°09.42′ W120°17.03′

▼ 1.9	BR	Track on left.
4.3 ▲	BL	Track on right.
▼ 2.4	SO	Two tracks on right into private property.
3.8 ▲	SO	Two tracks on left into private property.
▼ 5.3	SO	Trail starts to descend from ridge.
0.9 ▲	SO	Top of ridge.
▼ 5.6	SO	Track on left.
0.6 ▲	SO	Track on right.
▼ 6.0	SO	Private property on right.
0.2 ▲	SO	Private property on left.
▼ 6.2	BR	Graded road on left is 3N03 to Columbia and Twain Harte. Zero trip meter and follow sign to Stanislaus River and Vallecito.
0.0 ▲		Continue to the northeast.

GPS: N38°07.70′ W120°20.86′

▼ 0.0		Continue to the west.
4.1 ▲	BL	Graded road on right is 3N03 to Columbia and Twain Harte. Zero trip meter and bear left onto 4N04 following sign to Mount Knight.
▼ 0.2	SO	Track on right is 4N05. Remain on 3N03.
3.9 ▲	SO	Track on left is 4N05. Remain on 3N03.
▼ 0.4	SO	Cattle guard.
3.7 ▲	SO	Cattle guard.
▼ 0.9	SO	Cattle guard.
3.2 ▲	SO	Cattle guard.

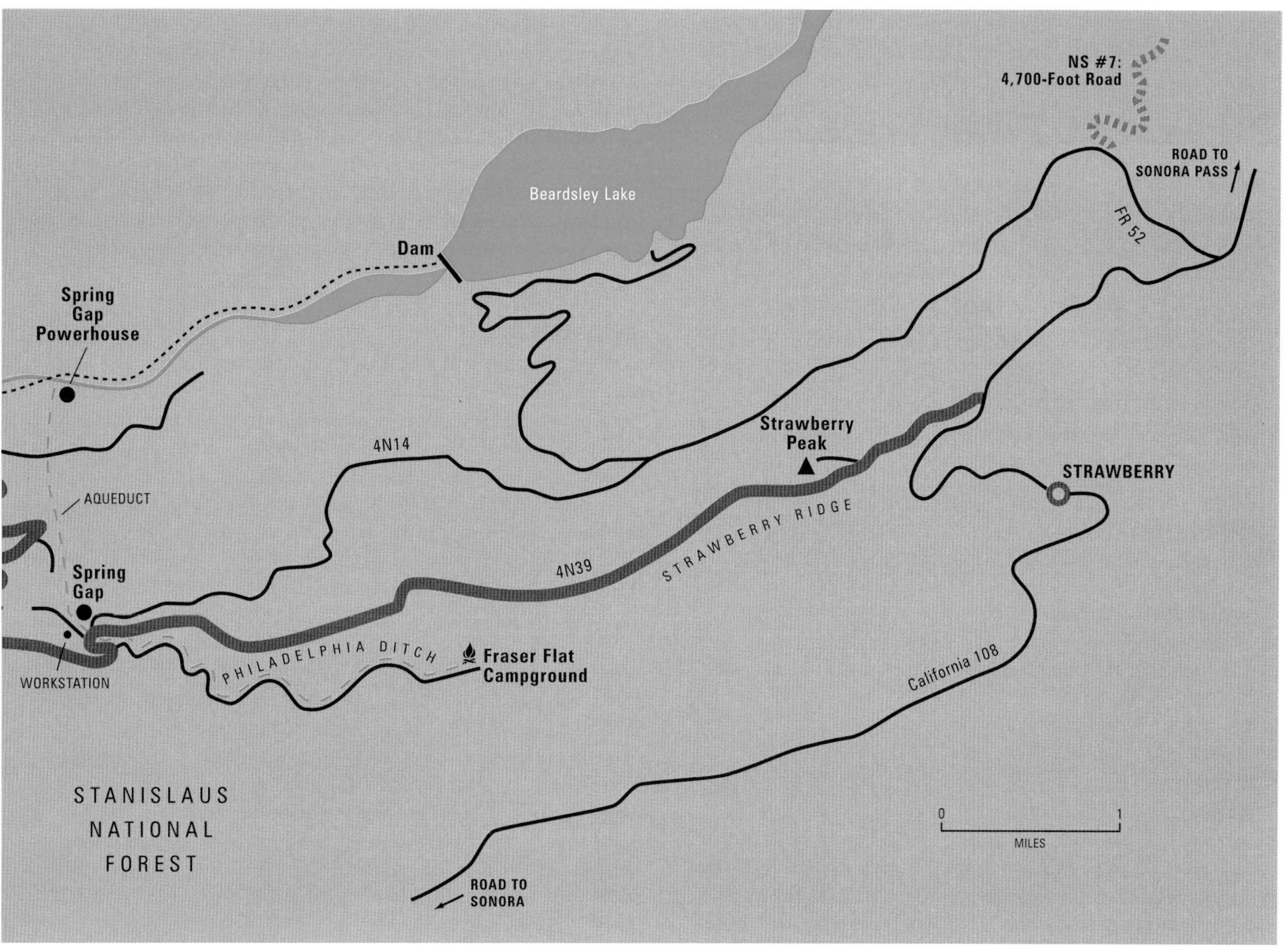

▼ 1.8		SO	Track on left.
	2.3 ▲	SO	Track on right.
			GPS: N38°07.23′ W120°22.44′
▼ 1.9		SO	Start of shelf road.
	2.2 ▲	SO	End of shelf road.
▼ 2.2		SO	View to the left of the Stanislaus River at the north end of New Melones Lake.
	1.9 ▲	SO	View to the right of the Stanislaus River at the north end of New Melones Lake.
▼ 3.3		SO	Exiting Stanislaus National Forest at sign.
	0.8 ▲	SO	Entering Stanislaus National Forest at sign.
			GPS: N38°07.58′ W120°22.76′
▼ 4.0		SO	Mine workings on left with machinery in gully, and shaft on right.
	0.1 ▲	SO	Mine workings on right with machinery in gully, and shaft on left.
			GPS: N38°07.91′ W120°22.49′
▼ 4.1		TL	T-intersection with paved road along the Stanislaus River. Zero trip meter.
	0.0 ▲		Continue to the east. Start of shelf road.
			GPS: N38°07.96′ W120°22.57′
▼ 0.0			Continue to the south. End of shelf road.
	7.8 ▲	TR	Turn right onto 3N03 and start to climb away from the river. Road is now graded dirt. Zero trip meter.
▼ 0.6		SO	Cross over Stanislaus River on bridge.
	7.2 ▲	SO	Exit bridge.
			GPS: N38°07.50′ W120°22.95′
▼ 0.7		SO	Exit bridge. Paved road on right. Trail now follows paved Camp Nine Road. Start of shelf road.
	7.1 ▲	SO	Paved road on left. End of shelf road. Cross over Stanislaus River on bridge.
			GPS: N38°07.50′ W120°23.05′
▼ 2.5		SO	Road veers away from river.
	5.3 ▲	SO	Road follows alongside the Stanislaus River.
▼ 3.1		SO	Track on right.
	4.7 ▲	SO	Track on left.
			GPS: N38°06.94′ W120°24.52′
▼ 3.9		SO	End of shelf road. Disused cement plant on left.
	3.9 ▲	SO	Disused cement plant on right. Start of shelf road.
▼ 7.4		SO	Paved road on right.
	0.4 ▲	SO	Paved road on left.
			GPS: N38°05.17′ W120°27.28′
▼ 7.8			T-intersection with paved Parrots Ferry Road (CR E18). Turn right for Vallecito; turn left for Columbia.
	0.0 ▲		Trail commences on Parrots Ferry Road (CR E18), 1 mile southeast of California 4 and Vallecito and 3.8 miles north of bridge over the Stanislaus River. Zero trip meter and turn east onto small paved Camp Nine Road following sign to Stanislaus Power House.
			GPS: N38°05.05′ W120°27.59′

Pinecrest Peak Trail

Starting Point:	4N12, 13.1 miles northeast of Strawberry
Finishing Point:	4N12, 11.4 miles northeast of Strawberry
Total Mileage:	5.6 miles, plus 1.1-mile spur to Pinecrest Fire Lookout site
Unpaved Mileage:	5.6 miles, plus 1.1-mile spur
Driving Time:	2 hours
Elevation Range:	7,900–8,700 feet
Usually Open:	May to November, exact dates vary
Best Time to Travel:	Dry weather
Difficulty Rating:	4
Scenic Rating:	10
Remoteness Rating:	+0

Special Attractions

- Moderate trail suitable for high-clearance 4WDs.
- Unparalleled views of the Dardanelles and the Emigrant Wilderness.
- Numerous backcountry campsites.
- Snowmobile trails in winter.

History

Pinecrest Peak Trail begins east of the old Bumblebee railroad siding, Cow Creek Camp, and Fiddlers Green. In the 1920s, the Sugar Pine Railroad ran through Strawberry to Bumblebee. This railroad spur was part of a massive network that grew to 70 miles of mainline railroad and more than 300 miles of spur lines. Large quantities of old growth trees were hauled out of Fiddlers Green to a sawmill at Standard, a few miles east of Sonora.

The toll wagon road over Sonora Pass, completed in 1868, was an important trade route from Sonora to Bodie and the Mono Lake region on the east side of the Sierra Nevada. A stage station catering to toll road traffic was established on Cow Creek, and in 1902, a forest service guard station was constructed at the same place at a cost of $65. Most of the lumber for the structure came from the Conlin Brothers sawmill at nearby Strawberry. In 1911, mule teams used the road to haul construction materials for the Relief Dam, high in the range at the present-day boundary of the Emigrant Wilderness.

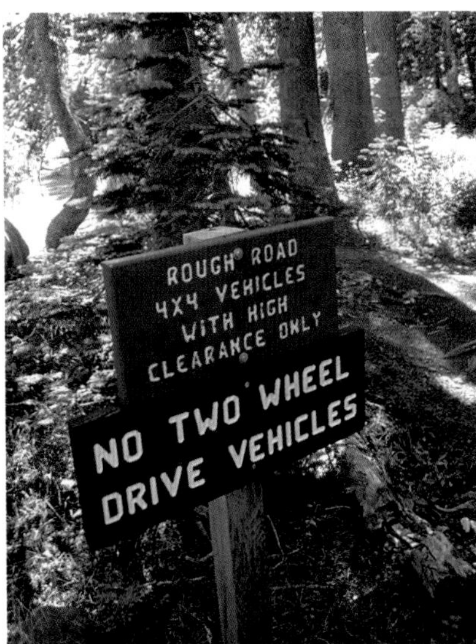

Signs along Pinecrest Peak Trail

An outbreak of hoof-and-mouth disease occurred in this region between 1923 and 1925. Cattle were rounded up, driven into an abandoned cutting along the old Sugar Pine Railroad, and slaughtered. The carcasses were heavily doused with quicklime and buried. During and after this outbreak, all railroad employees were under strict orders not to exit the railcars unnecessarily. Employees were sprayed with disinfectant on a regular basis in an effort to contain the disease. The main concern was that the railroad would spread the disease to the sawmill and thus release it to an even broader region.

Description

This short trail starts and finishes on the loop road 4N12 and can be driven in either direction. In itself, 4N12 is a highly scenic, easy drive that gives access not only to Pinecrest Peak Trail, but also to Eagle Peak Trail, campgrounds at Herring Creek Reservoir, and hiking trails into the Emigrant Wilderness. In winter, the 12.8-mile loop of 4N12 is use by snowmobilers and cross-country skiers, though it is not groomed.

The forest service only allows 4WD vehicles on the Pinecrest Peak Trail, also known as Madhatters Rim Trail, because the loose surface is easily disturbed by the spinning tires of 2WD vehicles. Initially, the graded dirt road heads southeast to the Cooper Meadow Trailhead. Past the trailhead, parking, and horse camping area, the small, formed trail becomes 4WD only. It climbs steeply up the ridge, passing volcanic slopes covered with yellow mule's ears in late spring and summer. This hardy plant thrives in the region's volcanic soils. The trail surface is smooth, but loose. You will see spots where other vehicles have lost traction and spun wheels. From the top of the ridge, there are unparalleled views east over the Emigrant Wilderness and Eagle Peak and north to the Dardanelles.

The trail drops from the ridge along a sloping off-camber section, before joining a roughly graded road to the Waterhouse Lake Trailhead. Waterhouse Lake Trail is a steep, moderately strenuous hike that goes to Waterhouse Lake in the Emigrant Wilderness. From the trailhead, the vehicle trail follows a small loop to Pinecrest Peak and the site of an old fire lookout. The lookout site is the best place to take in the scenery, with views over Pinecrest Lake, Double Dome, Herring Creek, Hammill Canyon, Eagle Peak, and the Dardanelles. From Pinecrest Peak itself, there are views over the ski runs at Pinecrest and the Emigrant Wilderness.

Campers will enjoy this region. In addition to campgrounds at Herring Creek Reservoir and Herring Creek (not marked on the forest map), there are many backcountry sites along the trail, most with shade and excellent views. The campgrounds do not have tables, but they do have fire rings and pit toilets. Anglers can fish for eastern brook, German brown, and rainbow trout in Herring Creek and Herring Creek Reservoir.

A short hiking trail called Trail of the Gargoyles begins near the campground at Herring Creek Reservoir. The 1.5-mile trail passes a variety of geologic features and viewpoints. An interpretative leaflet for the trail is available at the trailhead, which can be found on a small, unmarked vehicle trail that heads west from the start of the loop section of 4N12.

The trail offers unparalleled views north toward the Dardenelles

Current Road Information

Stanislaus National Forest
Summit Ranger District
1 Pinecrest Lake Road
Pinecrest, CA 96564
(209) 965-3434

Map References

BLM Bridgeport
USFS Stanislaus National Forest
USGS 1:24,000 Pinecrest
1:100,000 Bridgeport
Maptech CD-ROM: High Sierra/Yosemite
Northern California Atlas & Gazetteer, p. 100
California Road & Recreation Atlas, p. 72 (incomplete)

Route Directions

▼ 0.0 From Strawberry, proceed 2.3 miles north on California 108; then turn northeast on paved Herring Creek Road. Continue along this road for 6.5 miles; then bear right on 4N12, following the sign to Pinecrest Peak. After 2.6 miles, pass the western end of the trail (5N31). Continue on 4N12 for another 1.7 miles to the start of the trail. Zero trip meter and turn south on graded dirt road 5N67, following the sign for Cooper Meadows Trailhead.

3.1 ▲ Trail ends back on 4N12. Turn left to exit back to Strawberry.

GPS: N38°15.04' W119°53.09'

▼ 0.9 SO Cooper Meadows Trailhead on left at Coyote Meadows Horse Camp.

2.2 ▲ SO Cooper Meadows Trailhead on right at Coyote Meadows Horse Camp.

GPS: N38°14.45' W119°52.71'

▼ 1.0 BL Bear left out of camp and trailhead parking area. Trail drops in standard to become a narrow formed trail and starts to climb. 4WD-only past this point.

2.1 ▲ SO Pass through trailhead parking and camp area. Trail is now a roughly graded dirt road.

▼ 1.7 SO Top of climb. Walk to the north side of the trail for views over Eagle Peak and the Dardanelles.

1.4 ▲ SO Walk to the north side of the trail for views over Eagle Peak and the Dardanelles. Start of descent.

▼ 2.2 SO Trail starts to descend from ridge.

0.9 ▲ SO Top of ridge.

▼ 2.7 TR End of descent. Turn right at T-intersection.

0.4 ▲ TL Turn left on 5N67 and start to climb. 4WD-only past this point.

GPS: N38°14.03' W119°54.40'

▼ 3.1 SO Waterhouse Lake Trailhead on left; then 4-way intersection. Graded road on left is 5N55Y. Track straight ahead and to the right is 5N31. Zero trip meter.

0.0 ▲ Continue to the east on 5N67.

GPS: N38°14.12' W119°54.82'

▼ 0.0 Continue to the west on 5N31.

0.8 ▲ SO 4-way intersection. Graded road on right is 5N55Y and track on left is 5N31. Waterhouse Lake Trailhead on right. Zero trip meter.

▼ 0.8 BL Track straight ahead is spur to Pinecrest Lookout site. Zero trip meter and bear left onto 5N55Y.

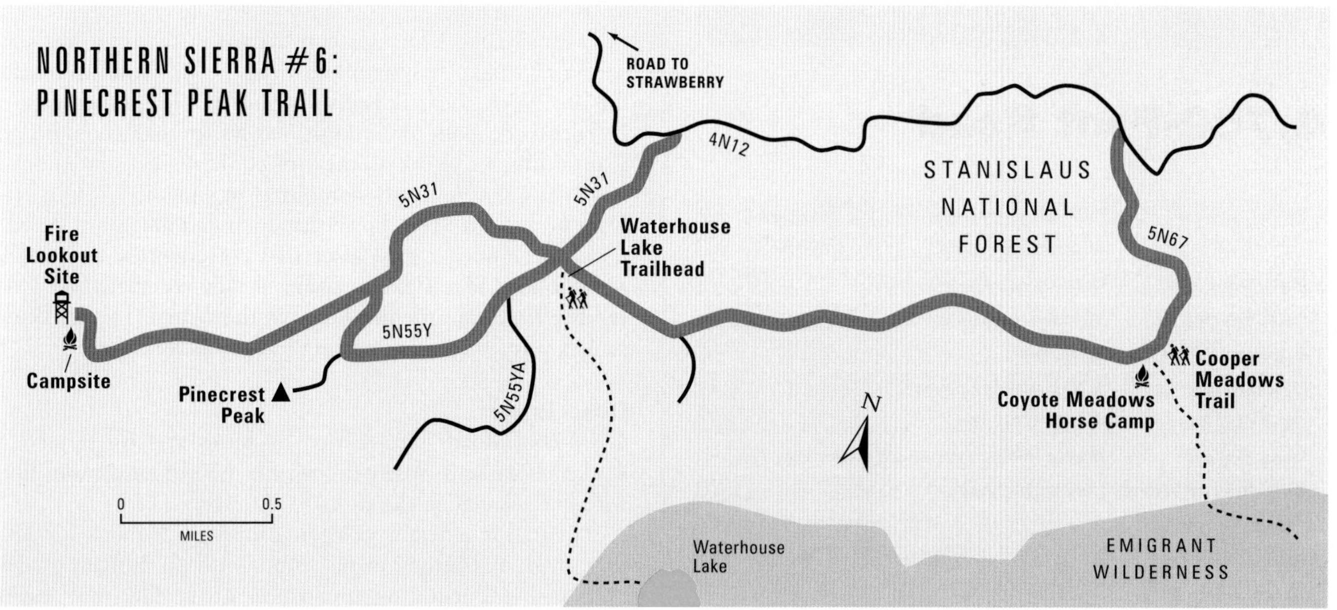

0.0 ▲		Continue to the north.
		GPS: N38°13.87' W119°55.41'

Spur to Pinecrest Lookout Site

▼ 0.0		Proceed to the southwest on 5N55Y.
▼ 0.9	SO	Viewpoint on left.
▼ 1.0	SO	Track on right.
▼ 1.1		Spur ends at viewpoint and campsite at Pinecrest Lookout site.
		GPS: N38°13.49' W119°56.44'

Continuation of Main Trail

▼ 0.0		Continue to the south.
1.1 ▲	SO	Track on left is spur to Pinecrest Lookout site. Zero trip meter and continue on 5N31.
		GPS: N38°13.87' W119°55.41'
▼ 0.3	TL	T-intersection. Track on right goes 0.2 miles to Pinecrest Peak.
0.8 ▲	TR	Track straight ahead goes 0.2 miles to Pinecrest Peak.
		GPS: N38°13.64' W119°55.44'
▼ 0.9	SO	Track on right is 5N55YA.
0.2 ▲	SO	Track on left is 5N55YA.
▼ 1.1	SO	4-way intersection at Waterhouse Lake Trailhead. Zero trip meter.
0.0 ▲		Continue to the south on graded road, 5N55Y.
		GPS: N38°14.12' W119°54.82'
▼ 0.0		Continue to the north on 5N31.
0.6 ▲	SO	4-way intersection at Waterhouse Lake Trailhead. Track on left is 5N67 and track on right is 5N31. Zero trip meter.
▼ 0.6		Trail ends at T-intersection with 4N12. Turn left to exit to Strawberry.
0.0 ▲		From Strawberry, proceed north for 2.3 miles on California 108; then turn northeast on paved Herring Creek Road. Continue along this road for 6.5 miles; then bear right on 4N12, following the sign to Pinecrest Peak. Proceed 2.6 miles to the start of the trail. Zero trip meter and turn east on graded dirt road, signposted to Pinecrest Peak.
		GPS: N38°14.56' W119°54.59'

NORTHERN SIERRA #7

4,700-Foot Road

Starting Point:	**Beardsley Road (FR 52), 0.9 miles west of California 108**
Finishing Point:	**Gate before Donnell Lake**
Total Mileage:	**10 miles (one-way)**
Unpaved Mileage:	**10 miles**
Driving Time:	**1.25 hours (one-way)**
Elevation Range:	**4,400–5,300 feet**
Usually Open:	**May to November, exact dates vary**
Best Time to Travel:	**May to November**
Difficulty Rating:	**2**
Scenic Rating:	**9**
Remoteness Rating:	**+0**

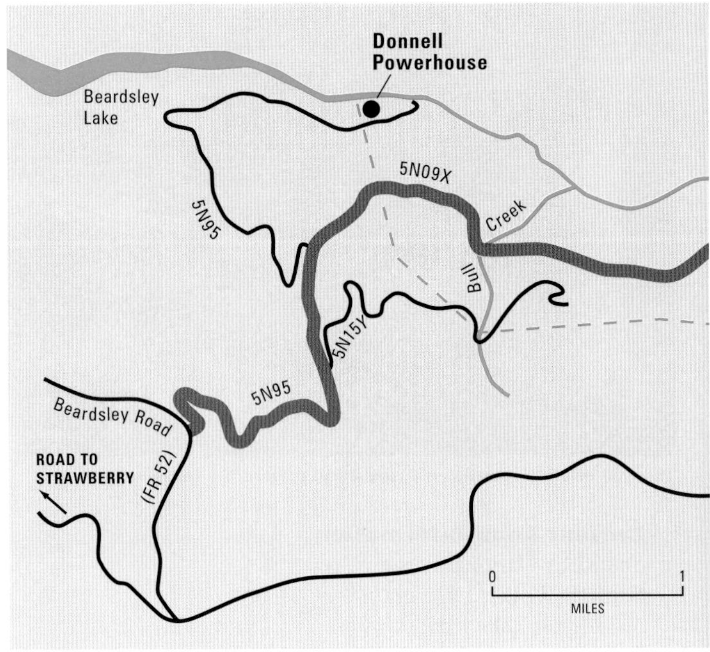

Special Attractions

- Waterfalls and wildflower viewing in spring.
- Panoramic views over Dome Rock and the Middle Fork of the Stanislaus River.

History

During the 1850s, the Middle Fork of the Stanislaus River near 4,700-Foot Road looked completely different. A wide riverside flat sat below the massive granite outcrops where Donnell Lake now occupies the full width of the canyon. A sawmill, constructed by an enterprising merchant from the nearby town of Columbia, operated on the flat. The mill supplied lumber for buildings in the booming gold rush town of Columbia as well as for aqueducts throughout the region. Wooden aqueducts and earthen ditches carried the water needed for the ecologically destructive practice of hydraulic mining.

Donnell Lake Dam was constructed in the mid-1950s as part of an irrigation system known as the Tri-Dam project. In the late 1930s, the Oakdale and South San Joaquin Irrigation District made plans for an improved system that would hedge against drought. Work on the project did not get started until 1948, and it was finally completed in June 1957. The Tri-Dam project involved the construction and linkage of Beardsley and Donnell Lakes, associated powerhouses, penstocks, and tunnels. The Melones Dam, already completed by November 1926, was the third dam in the system. The Tri-Dam project was a major engineering feat for its time.

Description

4,700-Foot Road is so-named by locals and forest service workers because it closely follows the 4,700-foot contour line with little change in elevation.

The trail is generally easygoing for high-clearance 2WDs. It is rough and lumpy in places but with no difficult grades or maneuvers requiring four-wheel drive. The trail leaves

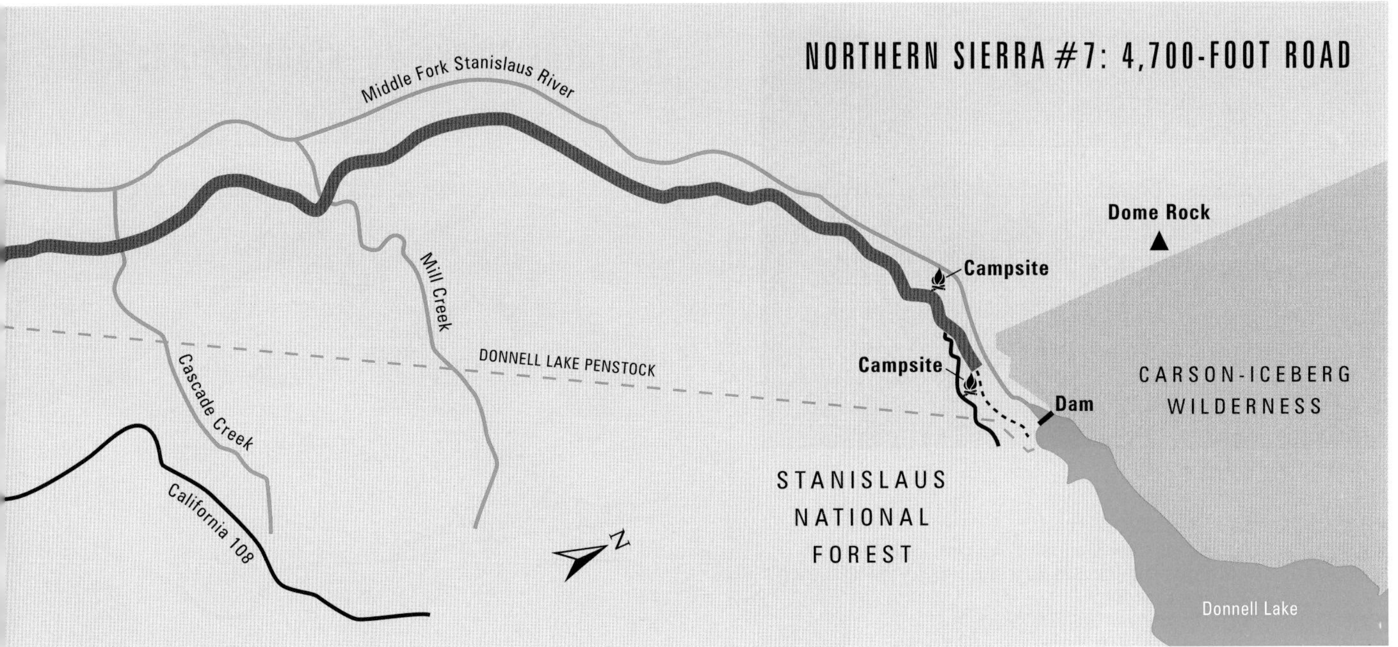

paved Beardsley Road and follows graded dirt 5N95 for 2 miles before turning onto the trail that runs north to Donnell Lake. The Stanislaus National Forest map shows this road as 5N06, but on the ground it is clearly marked 5N09X. The wide shelf road travels high above the Middle Fork of the Stanislaus River for most of its length. Two vehicles can pass easily along most of the road, but the sheer drop may make some nervous.

Along the way, the trail passes several small cascades and waterfalls. These are particularly spectacular in spring, when running full of snow melt. Wildflowers are abundant along the trail in April and early May.

Camping is limited because of the road's shelf aspect, but a good site can be found at the end of the trail. From the gate at the end of the trail, a half-mile, 20-minute hike takes you to the Donnell Lake Dam. There are no public recreation facilities at the reservoir. A short distance past the end of the vehicle trail is a good view north of Dome Rock, which towers above the dam.

4,700-Foot Road, carved into granite canyon walls during the construction of the Donnell Lake Dam

Current Road Information

Stanislaus National Forest
Summit Ranger District
1 Pinecrest Lake Road
Pinecrest, CA 96564
(209) 965-3434

Map References

BLM San Andreas, Bridgeport
USFS Stanislaus National Forest
USGS 1:24,000 Strawberry, Liberty Hill, Donnell Lake
1:100,000 San Andreas, Bridgeport
Maptech CD-ROM: High Sierra/Yosemite
Northern California Atlas & Gazetteer, pp. 99, 100
California Road & Recreation Atlas, p. 72

Route Directions

▼ 0.0		From California 108, 3.6 miles north of Strawberry, turn northwest on Beardsley Road (FR 52) and proceed 0.9 miles to the start of the trail. Zero trip meter and turn northwest on graded dirt road, marked 5N95. Pass through seasonal closure gate.
		GPS: N38°13.63' W120°00.72'
▼ 1.2	SO	Cross over Cow Creek.
▼ 1.3	SO	Track on right is 5N15Y.
▼ 1.9	SO	Track on right.
▼ 2.0	BR	Graded road on left is 5N95. Bear right onto 5N09X and zero trip meter.
		GPS: N38°14.38' W120°01.38'
▼ 0.0		Continue to the north past track on left.
▼ 0.1	SO	Seasonal closure gate. Track is marked as suitable for ATVs and motorbikes as well as larger vehicles.

Donnell Lake, dedicated in 1957

▼ 0.3	SO	Start of shelf road.
▼ 0.5	SO	Cross over Donnell Lake Penstock. Donnell Powerhouse is below the trail to the left; then track on left.
▼ 1.1	SO	Cross over Bull Creek.
▼ 2.1	SO	Track on left to tunnel works area.
▼ 2.9	SO	Three cascades on right are part of Cascade Creek.
		GPS: N38°16.43' W120°00.34'
▼ 3.9	SO	Track on left.
▼ 4.0	SO	Cross over Mill Creek on bridge.
		GPS: N38°17.32' W120°00.19'
▼ 5.3	SO	Pass beside bare granite rock face.
		GPS: N38°18.33' W120°00.01'
▼ 5.7	SO	Waterfall on right.
▼ 7.6	SO	Campsite on left.
		GPS: N38°19.56' W119°58.46'
▼ 7.9	SO	Track on right.
▼ 8.0		Trail ends at a campsite and gate before Donnell Lake. There is usually hiking access to the dam, which is 0.5 miles past the gate.
		GPS: N38°19.62' W119°58.16'

NORTHERN SIERRA #8

Black Springs Route

Starting Point:	**California 4, 3.5 miles north of Dorrington**
Finishing Point:	**7N09, 0.1 miles west of Northern Sierra #9: Calaveras Dome Trail**
Total Mileage:	**18.4 miles**
Unpaved Mileage:	**18.4 miles**
Driving Time:	**2 hours**
Elevation Range:	**5,300–7,400 feet**
Usually Open:	**May to November**
Best Time to Travel:	**Dry weather**
Difficulty Rating:	**4**
Scenic Rating:	**7**
Remoteness Rating:	**+0**

NORTHERN SIERRA #8: BLACK SPRINGS ROUTE

Route 1C (6N10)
SUMMIT LEVEL RIDGE
Route 1A
ROAD TO DORRINGTON

Special Attractions

- Access to a network of trails within the Black Springs OHV Area.
- Views from Summit Level Ridge and Bailey Ridge.

History

Black Springs Route starts north of Dorrington, formerly called Cold Spring Ranch. A stage stop at this location served travelers on the Big Trees–Carson Valley Road. Prospectors used this route to the southern mines of the Mother Lode as early as 1849. That same year, a Dr. Clark from Missouri was noted as being the first newcomer to see the nearby giant sequoia grove. In April 1851, Major John Ebbetts discovered an 8,731-foot pass over the Sierra Nevada (now called Ebbetts Pass) that had no snow on it in April. By 1855, a wagon road called Big Trees Route was established through Dorrington and over the Sierra Nevada via Ebbetts Pass. The route became a toll road in 1863 and fees were charged until 1910, two years after the first automobile crossed the Sierra Nevada via the Big Trees–Carson Valley Road.

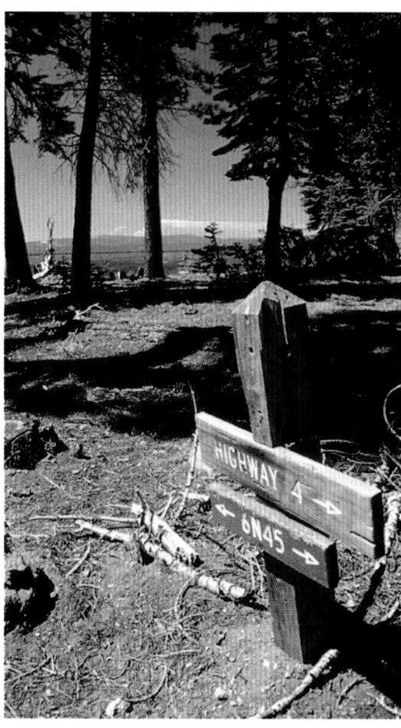

Some old forest signs remain on Bailey Ridge

Calaveras Big Trees State Park, established in 1931, lies just south of Dorrington. Research indicates that giant sequoias are related to a species that thrived in the region about 7 million years ago. Prior to the arrival of Euro-American settlers, the Northern Miwok lived on this rich land, making use

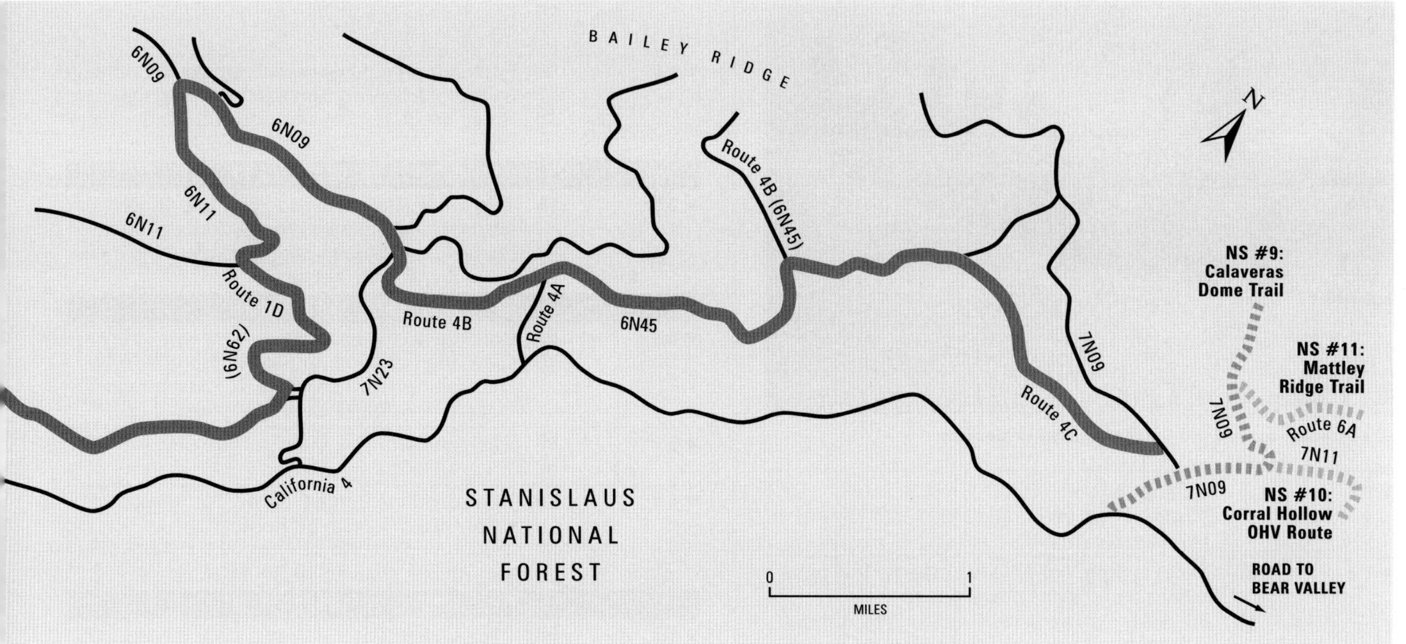

of abundant resources in the lower foothills. Mule deer, rabbit, tule elk, and pronghorn inhabited the region. Seed-producing grasses, forbs, and various trees provided additional diversity to their diets.

Description

This is one of the National Forest Service's listed OHV trails within the Black Springs OHV Area. The single-track trail, rated moderately difficult by the forest service, climbs onto the northern end of Summit Level Ridge. This first climb is the most difficult. Although the grade is only moderately steep, the loose fist-size rubble on top of soft earth provides very little in the way of traction. A few tree roots and moguls add to the difficulty.

The trail gets easier on top of Summit Level Ridge. Although it is single vehicle width and lined with manzanitas, the trail gets sufficient use that only the widest vehicles will find it lightly brushy.

The trail travels among sugar pines and scattered oaks. After crossing paved 7N23, it begins to climb onto Bailey Ridge. This climb is easier than the earlier climb onto Summit Level Ridge; the surface here is loose, but it lacks the rubble of the first ascent. The predominant vegetation along this section of trail is white fir.

The trail descends along a loose, moguled surface to finish on well-graded 7N09, just west of Northern Sierra #9: Calaveras Dome Trail, and a short distance north of California 4.

The opening and closing dates for this trail are approximate; most of the time it closes naturally with snowfall.

Current Road Information

Stanislaus National Forest
Calaveras Ranger District
5519 Highway 4
Hathaway Pines, CA 95233
(209) 795-1381

Map References

BLM San Andreas
USFS Stanislaus National Forest
USGS 1:24,000 Boards Crossing, Calaveras Dome, Dorrington
1:100,000 San Andreas
Maptech CD-ROM: High Sierra/Yosemite
Northern California Atlas & Gazetteer, p. 99
California Road & Recreation Atlas, p. 71 (incomplete)
Other: Calaveras Ranger District OHV Routes (forest service leaflet)

Route Directions

Mileage		Direction
▼ 0.0		From California 4, 3.5 miles north of Dorrington, zero trip meter and turn northwest on graded dirt road, marked 6N58. Immediately track on right and track on left.
5.5 ▲		Track on left and track on right. Trail ends at T-intersection with California 4. Turn left for Bear Valley; turn right for Dorrington.
		GPS: N38°19.86′ W120°14.16′
▼ 0.1	TL	Track on right. Trail is now marked Route 1A.
5.4 ▲	TR	Track on left.
▼ 0.3	SO	Track on left.
5.2 ▲	SO	Track on right.
▼ 1.5	SO	Campsite on left.
4.0 ▲	SO	Campsite on right.
▼ 2.0	SO	Track on left; then cattle guard.
3.5 ▲	SO	Cattle guard; then track on right.
		GPS: N38°19.97′ W120°15.48′
▼ 4.5	SO	Track on right.
1.0 ▲	SO	Track on left.
▼ 4.6	SO	Track on left.
0.9 ▲	SO	Track on right.
▼ 5.5	TR	Graded road continues ahead. Zero trip meter and turn right onto formed trail 6N10 (Route 1C) suitable for 4WDs, ATVs, and motorbikes.
0.0 ▲		Continue to the east.
		GPS: N38°20.97′ W120°15.02′

Views northeast toward the Carson-Iceberg Wilderness

▼ 0.0 Continue to the north.
4.2 ▲ TL T-intersection with graded road 6N58 (Route 1A). Zero trip meter.

▼ 3.6 SO Track on right into private property. Trail now follows along small power lines.
0.6 ▲ SO Trail leaves power lines. Track on left into private property.

▼ 4.1 TL Track on right. Then turn left, following marker for the OHV route. Trail leaves power lines.
0.1 ▲ TR T-intersection. Turn right onto Route 1C, suitable for 4WDs, ATVs, and motorbikes, following along small power lines. Immediately track on left.

GPS: N38°22.62' W120°11.74'

▼ 4.2 TL T-intersection with graded dirt road. Zero trip meter and turn left onto 6N62 (Route 1D), suitable for 4WDs, ATVs, and motorbikes.
0.0 ▲ Continue to the southeast.

GPS: N38°22.68' W120°11.74'

▼ 0.0 Continue to the west.
3.7 ▲ TR Graded road continues straight ahead. Zero trip meter and turn right onto small formed trail marked Route 1C.

▼ 1.1 BL Track on right.
2.6 ▲ SO Track on left.

▼ 1.2 BR Graded road 6N11 joins from left. Bear right onto 6N11.
2.5 ▲ BL Graded road 6N11 leaves to the right. Bear left onto 6N62.

GPS: N38°22.91' W120°12.45'

▼ 1.4 BR Track on left goes into private property. Follow marker for Route 1D.
2.3 ▲ BL Track on right goes into private property. Remain on Route 1D.

▼ 2.3 TR T-intersection with 6N09.
1.4 ▲ TL 6N09 continues ahead. Turn left onto 6N11.

GPS: N38°23.27' W120°13.33'

▼ 2.5 BR Graded road on left goes into private property. Remain on small formed trail.
1.2 ▲ BL Graded road on right goes into private property. Remain on small formed trail.

GPS: N38°23.32' W120°13.14'

▼ 3.5 SO Track on left. Remain on Route 1E.
0.2 ▲ SO Track on right. Remain on Route 1E.

▼ 3.7 SO 4-way intersection with paved 7N23. Zero trip meter.
0.0 ▲ Continue to the northwest on 6N09 (Route 1E).

GPS: N38°23.39' W120°11.85'

▼ 0.0 Continue to the east on Route 4B.
2.5 ▲ SO 4-way intersection with paved 7N23. Zero trip meter.

▼ 1.0 SO Route 4A on right goes to California 4. Continue on 6N45, following sign to Hermit Springs.
1.5 ▲ SO Route 4A on left goes to California 4. Continue on Route 4B, following sign to Buck Ranch.

GPS: N38°23.76' W120°11.17'

▼ 2.5 TR Track on left is continuation of Route 4B (6N45), which runs along Bailey Ridge. Turn right onto Route 4C and pass through gate. Zero trip meter.
0.0 ▲ Continue to the southeast.

GPS: N38°24.54' W120°10.28'

▼ 0.0 Continue to the east.
2.5 ▲ TL Gate; then turn left onto 6N45 (Route 4B). Track on right is also Route 4B, which runs along Bailey Ridge. Zero trip meter.

▼ 0.3 SO Track on right.
2.3 ▲ SO Track on left.

▼ 0.9 BR Track on left is Route F for 4WDs, ATVs, and motorbikes. Remain on Route 4C.
1.6 ▲ BL Track on right is Route F for 4WDs, ATVs, and motorbikes. Remain on Route 4C.

GPS: N38°25.11' W120°09.58'

▼ 1.3 BR Track on left.
1.2 ▲ SO Track on right.

▼ 2.5 Trail ends at T-intersection with graded dirt 7N09. Turn right for California 4 and Bear Valley.
0.0 ▲ Trail commences on graded dirt 7N09, 0.6 miles north of California 4. From the highway, 6.7 miles southwest of Bear Valley and 0.3 miles south of Cabbage Patch Station, proceed north on Northern Sierra #9: Calaveras Dome Trail (7N09). Bear left after 0.5 miles, following sign to Pumpkin Patch. After 0.1 miles, zero trip meter and turn south on formed dirt trail marked Route 4C, suitable for 4WDs, ATVs, and motorbikes—rated blue.

GPS: N38°25.14' W120°08.14'

NORTHERN SIERRA #9

Calaveras Dome Trail

Starting Point:	**California 4, 6.7 miles southwest of Bear Valley**
Finishing Point:	**FR 91 (8N05), southwest of Lower Bear River Reservoir**
Total Mileage:	**42 miles, plus 3.9-mile spur to Calaveras Dome and 4-mile spur to Salt Springs Reservoir**
Unpaved Mileage:	**40.4 miles, plus spurs**
Driving Time:	**5 hours**
Elevation Range:	**3,100–7,600 feet**
Usually Open:	**April to November**
Best Time to Travel:	**Dry weather**
Difficulty Rating:	**2**
Scenic Rating:	**9**
Remoteness Rating:	**+0**

Special Attractions

- Long trail through a wide variety of forest scenery.
- Angling, camping, and swimming at the North Fork of the Mokelumne River.
- Excellent rock climbing opportunities on Calaveras Dome.

History

The Mokelumne Wilderness, situated within Eldorado, Stanislaus, and Toiyabe National Forests, was established in 1964 and expanded in 1984. The wilderness encompasses 104,461 acres of remote mountainous terrain and the headwaters of the Mokelumne River, which flows about 140 miles west to join the San Joaquin River northwest of Stockton. Mokelumne Peak (9,334 feet) can be seen northeast of Salt Springs Reservoir.

Mokelumne is Miwok, meaning "the people of Mok." The suffix *-umne* means "people," and is also used in the Cosumnes River to the north and Tuolumne River to the south.

Salt Springs Reservoir, with a capacity of 141,817 acre-feet of water, was constructed in 1931 as part of a hydroelectric power system named Project 137. The Tiger Creek Regulatory Canal can be seen below the trail on the northern side of the Mokelumne River. The canal, made up of flumes, tunnels, trestles, and penstocks, flows southwest to Tiger Creek Reservoir. It was built in 1931 to attain greater elevation drop for power generation at the powerhouse on Tiger Creek Reservoir.

The trail commences near Cabbage Patch Station on the old Big Trees–Carson Valley Road. After the toll road was taken over by the state in 1910 it was renamed California 24 and later California 4. Will and Chas Gann ran stock near Cabbage Patch during summer. They purchased land from Dave Felipini, the original patent holder of this land. Their name lingers on in the settlement Gann, just over a mile west along the old toll road.

Description

Both ends of this long easy trail are generally suitable for passenger vehicles, but in its entirety the trail requires a high-clearance vehicle. It should be driven in dry weather only because some sections become very greasy and difficult when wet.

The trail leaves California 4 and initially follows the graded dirt and gravel forest road 7N09, which takes you past the western end of Northern Sierra #10: Corral Hollow OHV Route and both ends of Northern Sierra #11: Mattley Ridge Trail. It wraps around the small meadow at Hay Gulch, a good place to see wildflowers in late spring and early summer.

Calaveras Dome Trail winds down from Mattley Ridge

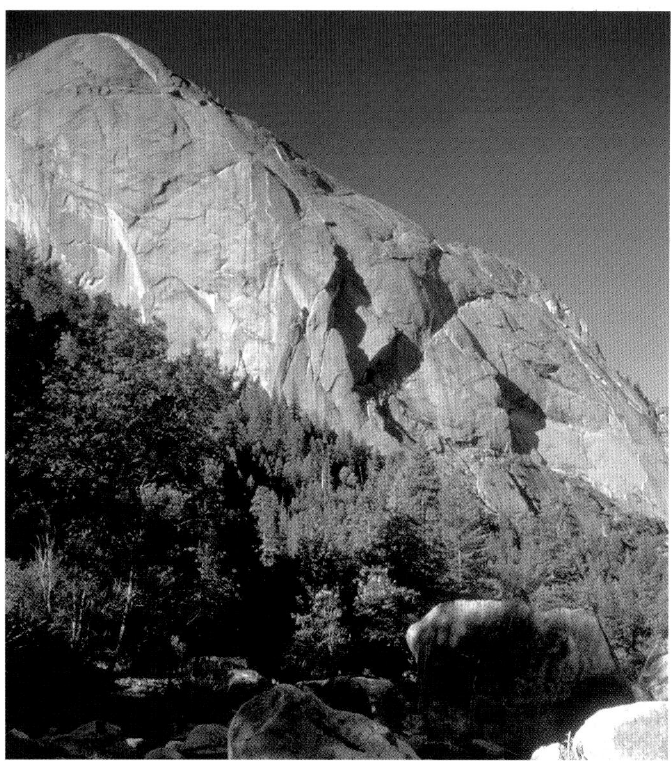

Calaveras Dome, nearly 1,500 feet above the Mokelumne River

The first spur goes to the top of Calaveras Dome, one of the main features of this trail. From the spur's end, you can walk a short distance to the top of the dome for a view over Salt Springs Reservoir. The dome itself is better seen from the lower road along the North Fork of the Mokelumne River. An excellent campsite and picnic spot can be found near the end of this spur.

The main trail continues on 7N09, traveling through the forest to join paved Winton Road. Passenger vehicles can return to California 4 along the continuation of 7N09 or continue along paved Winton Road to West Point, on California 26.

High-clearance vehicles can follow the main route, turning off Winton Road to head northeast on 7N08. This single-track trail descends through thick forest along a shelf road. It crosses Blue Creek, a pleasant place to cool off in summer, en route to the North Fork of the Mokelumne River. Once the trail reaches the river, campers will find many sites to choose from. Most have shade and many provide river access. Anglers can fish for rainbow trout—the river is stocked annually by the California Department of Fish and Game. Although the national forest map shows a number of campgrounds along the river, they are primarily undeveloped and have no picnic tables or trash collection.

The main trail crosses the North Fork of the Mokelumne River at Moore Creek Campground and turns southwest. A spur from this point heads northeast on a paved road and takes you 4 miles to Salt Springs Reservoir. There are plenty of camping, fishing, swimming, and picnicking opportunities, as

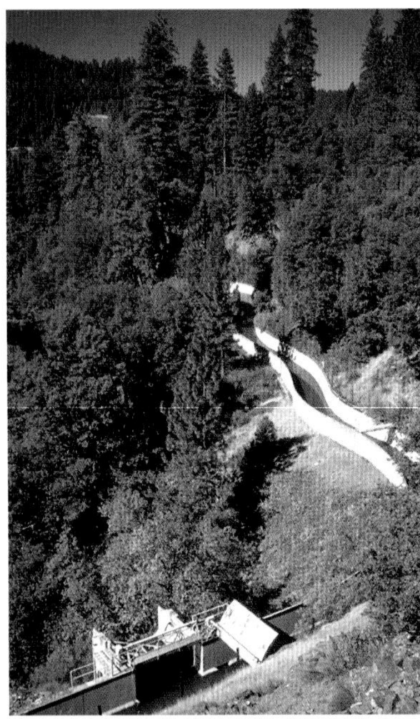
Tiger Creek Regulatory Canal runs below the trail along FR 9

well as views of the premier climbing destinations of Calaveras Dome and Hammer Dome. The granite monolith of Calaveras Dome, south of the trail, is the better known of the two. Climbing access to the dome's base is via very small, unmarked hiking trails. The dome has long routes for sport climbers as well as a number of bouldering opportunities. The dome's many different routes offer a challenge to climbers of all skill levels. Climbing the entire 1,200-foot vertical face often requires a night on the face.

The spur finishes at a picnic area at the base of the Salt Springs Dam. No overnight camping is allowed at the dam. From here, a hiking trail into the Mokelumne Wilderness snakes up the mountain to the left of the dam. A permit is required for overnight stays in the wilderness. The wilderness is a rugged area of volcanic ridges and peaks dominated by the Mokelumne River Canyon. Salt Springs Reservoir, at the southern edge of the wilderness, is at an elevation of about 3,900 feet.

The main trail continues along the Mokelumne River past a few more campsites and gradually climbs above the river. An aqueduct follows below this part of the trail. The trail ends at the intersection with FR 91 (8N05). From here you can exit north to California 88 or continue west along the small paved road to Tiger Creek Reservoir.

Current Road Information

Stanislaus National Forest
Calaveras Ranger District
5519 Highway 4
Hathaway Pines, CA 95233
(209) 795-1381

Map References

BLM San Andreas
USFS Stanislaus National Forest; El Dorado National Forest
USGS 1:24,000 Calaveras Dome, Garnet Hill
1:100,000 San Andreas
Maptech CD-ROM: High Sierra/Yosemite
Northern California Atlas & Gazetteer, p. 99
California Road & Recreation Atlas, p. 71

Route Directions

▼ 0.0		From California 4, 6.7 miles southwest of Bear Valley, zero trip meter and turn north on 7N09 at the marker. There is an information board immediately after the turn.
1.4 ▲		Trail ends at T-intersection with California 4. Turn left for Bear Valley; turn right for Dorrington.
		GPS: N38°24.79' W120°08.14'
▼ 0.1	SO	Track on right.
1.3 ▲	SO	Track on left.
▼ 0.5	SO	Graded road on left is 7N09 and small track on right. Continue straight ahead on 7N09 following the sign to Hay Gulch.
0.9 ▲	SO	Graded road on right is 7N09 and small track on left. Continue straight ahead on 7N09.
▼ 0.9	SO	Cattle guard; then track on right is Northern Sierra #10: Corral Hollow OHV Route.
0.5 ▲	SO	Track on left is Northern Sierra #10: Corral Hollow OHV Route; then cattle guard.
		GPS: N38°25.40' W120°07.66'
▼ 1.1	SO	Track on left.
0.3 ▲	SO	Track on right.
▼ 1.4	SO	Track on right is Northern Sierra #11: Mattley Ridge Trail. Zero trip meter.
0.0 ▲		Continue to the south.
		GPS: N38°25.54' W120°08.14'
▼ 0.0		Continue to the north.
6.6 ▲	SO	Track on left is Northern Sierra #11: Mattley Ridge Trail. Zero trip meter.
▼ 0.2	SO	Track on right is 7N09H.
6.4 ▲	SO	Track on left is 7N09H.
▼ 1.1	SO	Track on left is 7N09G.
5.5 ▲	SO	Track on right is 7N09G.
▼ 1.3	SO	Track on left.
5.3 ▲	SO	Track on right.
▼ 1.7	SO	Track on right; then cross over Middle Gulch.
4.9 ▲	SO	Cross over Middle Gulch; then track on left.
		GPS: N38°26.36' W120°08.26'
▼ 2.3	SO	Track on right is 7N69 (Route 6C) for 4WDs, ATVs, and motorbikes. Camping area on left.
4.3 ▲	SO	Track on left is 7N69 (Route 6C) for 4WDs, ATVs, and motorbikes. Camping area on right.
▼ 3.4	SO	Cross over Hay Gulch; then pass around the end of a meadow.
3.2 ▲	SO	Pass around the end of a meadow; then cross over Hay Gulch.
▼ 3.7	SO	Two tracks on right.
2.9 ▲	SO	Two tracks on left.
▼ 3.9	SO	Track on left to campsite.
2.7 ▲	SO	Track on right to campsite.
▼ 5.3	SO	Cross over Cottonwood Gulch; then track on right.
1.3 ▲	SO	Track on left; then cross over Cottonwood Gulch.
		GPS: N38°27.47' W120°09.56'
▼ 5.6	SO	Track on left.
1.0 ▲	SO	Track on right.
▼ 6.2	SO	Two tracks on left are 7N05.
0.4 ▲	SO	Two tracks on right are 7N05.
▼ 6.6	SO	4-way intersection. Track on right and track on left are both 7N59. Northern Sierra #11: Mattley Ridge Trail is to the right. Zero trip meter.
0.0 ▲		Continue to the southeast.
		GPS: N38°27.94' W120°10.10'
▼ 0.0		Continue to the northeast.
4.1 ▲	SO	4-way intersection. Track on right and track on left are both 7N59. Northern Sierra #11: Mattley Ridge Trail is to the left. Zero trip meter.

▼ 0.2 BL Track on right is Route 6E.
3.9 ▲ BR Track on left is Route 6E.

▼ 0.6 SO Track on left.
3.5 ▲ SO Track on right.

▼ 1.0 SO Cross over Moore Creek.
3.1 ▲ SO Cross over Moore Creek.

▼ 1.9 BL Graded road on right is 7N16 (Route 6H).
2.2 ▲ BR Graded road on left is 7N16 (Route 6H).

GPS: N38°28.59′ W120°10.43′

▼ 2.2 BL Graded road on right.
1.9 ▲ BR Graded road on left.

▼ 2.4 SO Track on right.
1.7 ▲ SO Track on left.

▼ 2.7 SO Cross over Moore Creek.
1.4 ▲ SO Cross over Moore Creek.

▼ 4.1 SO Track on right is 7N19, spur to the top of Calaveras Dome. Zero trip meter.
0.0 ▲ Continue to the northeast.

GPS: N38°28.15′ W120°11.61′

Spur to the top of Calaveras Dome

▼ 0.0 Continue to the north and pass through seasonal closure gate.
▼ 0.2 SO Track on left.
▼ 0.5 SO Cross over Moore Creek.
▼ 1.8 BL Track on right is 7N19. Bear left onto 7N76Y.

GPS: N38°28.33′ W120°12.45′

▼ 2.3 SO Track on right. Road turns from gravel to graded dirt.
▼ 2.8 SO Track on left ends after 0.2 miles.

GPS: N38°28.49′ W120°13.26′

▼ 3.2 SO Seasonal closure gate.
▼ 3.5 SO Track on left to campsite. This is the best access to the top of Calaveras Dome.
▼ 3.9 Trail is blocked by rockslide. Far below the trail to the north is Salt Springs Reservoir.

GPS: N38°29.00′ W120°13.02′

Continuation of Main Trail

▼ 0.0 Continue to the south.
6.2 ▲ SO Track on left is 7N19, spur to the top of Calaveras Dome. Zero trip meter.

GPS: N38°28.15′ W120°11.61′

▼ 0.4 SO Cross over creek.
5.8 ▲ SO Cross over creek.

▼ 0.5 BL Graded road on right is 7N28.
5.7 ▲ BR Graded road on left is 7N28.

▼ 1.5 SO Cattle guard; then track on right is 7N53.
4.7 ▲ SO Track on left is 7N53; then cattle guard.

GPS: N38°27.18′ W120°12.29′

▼ 2.1 SO Track on left; then track on right.
4.1 ▲ SO Track on left; then track on right.

▼ 3.1 SO Track on left.
3.1 ▲ SO Track on right.

▼ 3.3 BL Graded road on right is 7N24.
2.9 ▲ BR Graded road on left is 7N24.

▼ 3.5 SO Track on right to campsite; then cross over Blue Creek on bridge; then track on right.
2.7 ▲ SO Track on left; then cross over Blue Creek on bridge; then track on left to campsite.

GPS: N38°26.14′ W120°12.59′

▼ 3.8 SO Track on left.
2.4 ▲ SO Track on right.

▼ 3.9 SO Track on left.
2.3 ▲ SO Track on right.

▼ 4.2 SO Track on left.
2.0 ▲ SO Track on right.

▼ 4.5 SO Graded road 7N05 enters on left.
1.7 ▲ BL Graded road 7N05 continues to the right and joins California 4 in 14 miles. Follow the sign for Loop Road to Cabbage Patch Road.

GPS: N38°25.83′ W120°12.87′

▼ 5.0 SO Track on left.
1.2 ▲ SO Track on right.

▼ 5.9 SO Track on right.
0.3 ▲ SO Track on left.

▼ 6.2 SO Paved Winton Road (7N09) joins from the left. Zero trip meter and continue straight ahead on paved Winton Road, marked 7N03, following sign to West Point. Pass through seasonal closure gate.
0.0 ▲ Continue to the north.

GPS: N38°25.57′ W120°14.47′

▼ 0.0 Continue to the south.
5.6 ▲ SO Seasonal closure gate; then paved Winton Road swings right and becomes 7N09. Zero trip meter and continue straight ahead on graded dirt road, also 7N09, following the sign to Blue Creek.

▼ 0.7 SO Graded road on right is 7N60Y.
4.9 ▲ SO Graded road on left is 7N60Y.

▼ 3.5 SO Track on right is 7N49 (also called Spur 3).
2.1 ▲ SO Track on left is 7N49 (also called Spur 3).

▼ 3.7 SO Track on right.
1.9 ▲ SO Track on left.

▼ 3.8 SO Track on left is 7N45 (also called Spur 2).
1.8 ▲ SO Track on right is 7N45 (also called Spur 2).

▼ 5.6 TR Graded road on left is 7N26 to Forest Creek; then track on left and track on right are both 7N08. Zero trip meter and turn right onto formed trail 7N08.
0.0 ▲ Continue to the east.

GPS: N38°25.84′ W120°20.11′

▼ 0.0 Continue to the north.
6.6 ▲ TL T-intersection with paved Winton Road. Zero trip meter and turn left. Track opposite is also 7N08; then graded road on right is 7N26 to Forest Creek.

▼ 0.4 SO Track on right.
6.2 ▲ SO Track on left.

▼ 0.5 SO Track on left.
6.1 ▲ SO Track on right.

▼ 0.7 BR Track on right; then bear right at fork.
5.9 ▲ BL Bear left past track on right; then track on left.

GPS: N38°26.09′ W120°19.69′

▼ 0.9 SO Track on right is 7N07 and track on left.
5.7 ▲ SO Track on left is 7N07 and track on right.

▼ 1.2 BR Join graded road 7N28, which enters from the left. Cross over Blue Creek on bridge.
5.4 ▲ BL Cross over Blue Creek on bridge; then graded road 7N28 continues to the right.

▼ 1.3 TL Turn left immediately after bridge, remaining on 7N08. Track on right.
5.3 ▲ TR Graded road continues straight ahead. Turn right toward bridge.

GPS: N38°26.36′ W120°19.18′

▼ 1.4 SO Track on left.
5.2 ▲ SO Track on right.

▼ 1.9 SO Track on right is 7N63Y.
4.7 ▲ SO Track on left is 7N63Y.

▼ 2.2		SO	Track on left is 7N27.
	4.4 ▲	SO	Track on right is 7N27.
▼ 2.7		SO	Track on left is 7N80 and track on right.
	3.9 ▲	SO	Track on right is 7N80 and track on left.
▼ 2.9		SO	Track on right.
	3.7 ▲	SO	Track on left.
▼ 3.5		SO	Track on left.
	3.1 ▲	SO	Track on right.
▼ 4.2		SO	Track on right is 7N40.
	2.4 ▲	SO	Track on left is 7N40.
			GPS: N38°27.75′ W120°18.82′
▼ 4.4		SO	Seasonal closure gate.
	2.2 ▲	SO	Seasonal closure gate.
▼ 4.5		BR	Track on left is 7N33. Follow the sign for North Fork Mokelumne River and start to descend shelf road.
	2.1 ▲	BL	End of shelf road. Track on right is 7N33.
			GPS: N38°27.87′ W120°18.69′

▼ 5.4		SO	Cross over creek.
	1.2 ▲	SO	Cross over creek.
▼ 6.1		SO	Cross over creek.
	0.5 ▲	SO	Cross over creek.
▼ 6.6		SO	Unmarked track on left goes 0.1 miles to camping area alongside North Fork Mokelumne River. End of shelf road. Zero trip meter.
	0.0 ▲		Continue to the south.
			GPS: N38°28.35′ W120°18.11′
▼ 0.0			Continue to the northeast. Many campsites and tracks on left to campsites for next 0.6 miles.
	2.7 ▲	SO	Unmarked track on right goes 0.1 miles to camping area alongside North Fork Mokelumne River. Start of shelf road. Zero trip meter.
▼ 1.2		SO	Track on left to camping area.
	1.5 ▲	SO	Track on right to camping area.
▼ 2.1		SO	Start of Moore Creek Campground on left and right.

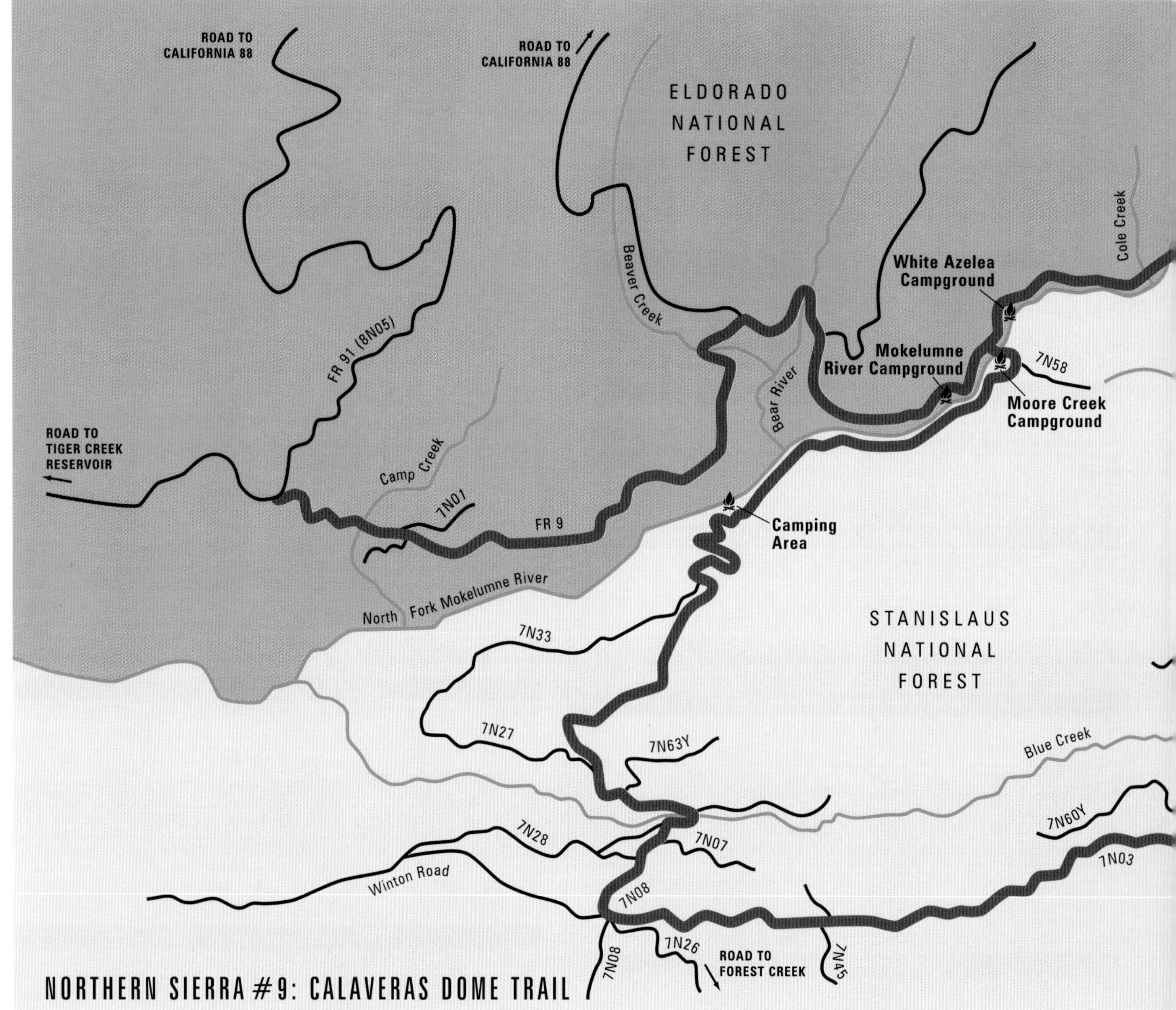

0.6 ▲	SO	Exit Moore Creek Campground.
▼ 2.3	SO	Track on left is 7N23; then cross over creek on concrete ford.
0.4 ▲	SO	Cross over creek on concrete ford; then track on right is 7N23.
		GPS: N38°28.81' W120°15.88'
▼ 2.5	BL	Track on right is 7N58.
0.2 ▲	BR	Track on left is 7N58.
▼ 2.7	TL	Cross over Mokelumne River on bridge; then T-intersection with paved road. Road on right is the spur to Calaveras Dome and Salt Springs Reservoir. Zero trip meter and exit Moore Creek Campground.
0.0 ▲		Continue to the southeast on dirt road.
		GPS: N38°28.95' W120°15.87'

Spur to Calaveras Dome and Salt Springs Reservoir

▼ 0.0		Proceed to the northeast on paved road. Many tracks on right and left to camping areas.
▼ 0.3	SO	White Azalea USFS Campground on right.
▼ 1.7	SO	Cross over Cole Creek on bridge.
▼ 1.9	SO	Cross over North Fork Mokelumne River on bridge. Faint hiking trails between here and the next bridge give climbing access to Calaveras Dome and Hidden Wall.
▼ 2.1	SO	Regulatory canal enters tunnel on far side of river and sometimes spills over at this point.
▼ 2.4	SO	Faint hiking trail on right gives climbing access to Calaveras Dome. Small cairn below pylon marks the spot.
		GPS: N38°29.33' W120°13.57'
▼ 2.8	TL	Turn left and cross North Fork Mokelumne River on bridge. Deadman Flat (private property) is straight ahead.
▼ 3.0	SO	Hiking trail on left gives climbing access to Hammer Dome; then cross over aqueduct. Power station on right.
		GPS: N38°29.75' W120°13.15'

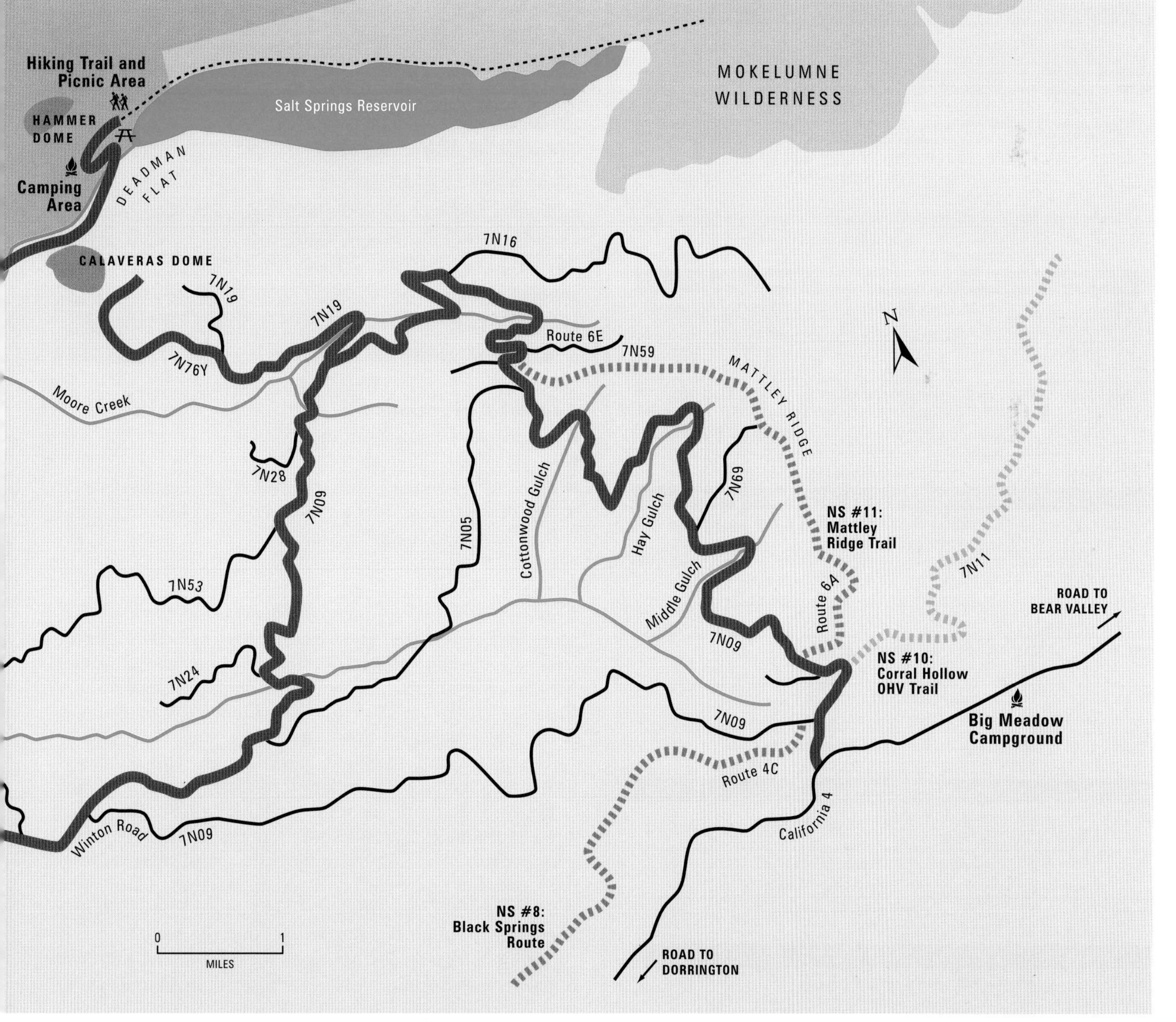

▼ 3.4	SO	Track on left under power lines.
▼ 3.6	SO	Hiking trail on left gives climbing access to Hammer Dome.
		GPS: N38°29.76' W120°13.32'
▼ 3.7	SO	Camping area on left.
▼ 4.0		Spur ends at Salt Springs Reservoir dam. Salt Springs Trail starts here and provides hiking access into the Mokelumne Wilderness. There is a small picnic area at the dam.
		GPS: N38°30.01' W120°12.94'

Continuation of Main Trail

▼ 0.0		Continue to the southwest.
2.8 ▲	TR	Paved road straight ahead is the spur to Calaveras Dome and Salt Springs Reservoir. Zero trip meter and turn right and cross over Mokelumne River on bridge and enter Moore Creek Campground.
		GPS: N38°28.95' W120°15.87'
▼ 0.5	SO	Mokelumne River USFS Campground on left.
2.3 ▲	SO	Mokelumne River USFS Campground on right.
		GPS: N38°28.73' W120°16.21'
▼ 1.6	SO	Cross over aqueduct.
1.2 ▲	SO	Cross over aqueduct.
▼ 1.8	SO	Track on right and track on left.
1.0 ▲	SO	Track on left and track on right.
		GPS: N38°28.95' W120°17.46'
▼ 2.3	SO	Paved road on right goes 10 miles to Bear River Reservoir. Follow the sign to California 88 (9 miles).
0.5 ▲	SO	Paved road on left goes 10 miles to Bear River Reservoir. Follow the sign to Salt Springs Reservoir.
		GPS: N38°29.38' W120°17.34'
▼ 2.5	SO	Cross over Bear River on bridge; then track on right.
0.3 ▲	SO	Track on left; then cross over Bear River on bridge.
▼ 2.8	TL	Paved road ahead goes 8 miles to California 88. Zero trip meter and turn left onto gravel FR 9, following the sign to Tiger Creek Reservoir. Start of wide shelf road.
0.0 ▲		Continue to the northeast.
		GPS: N38°29.43' W120°17.51'
▼ 0.0		Continue to the south and pass through seasonal closure gate.
6.0 ▲	TR	Seasonal closure gate; then T-intersection with paved FR 92 (8N25). Zero trip meter and turn right following the sign to Salt Springs Reservoir. End of shelf road.
▼ 0.9	SO	Cross over Beaver Creek.
5.1 ▲	SO	Cross over Beaver Creek.
▼ 1.6	SO	Track on left and track on right.
5.4 ▲	SO	Track on left and track on right.
▼ 3.1	SO	Track on left; then track on right.
2.9 ▲	SO	Track on left; then track on right.
		GPS: N38°28.33' W120°19.62'
▼ 3.7	SO	Track on right.
2.3 ▲	SO	Track on left.
▼ 4.7	SO	Gravel road on left. End of shelf road.
1.3 ▲	SO	Start of shelf road. Gravel road on right.
▼ 4.9	SO	Track on right is 7N01.
1.1 ▲	SO	Track on left is 7N01.
		GPS: N38°28.61' W120°21.32'
▼ 5.1	SO	Cross over Camp Creek.
0.9 ▲	SO	Cross over Camp Creek.
▼ 6.0		Trail ends at intersection with paved FR 91 (8N05). Turn right to exit to California 88 and Cooks Station; continue straight ahead to Tiger Creek Reservoir.
0.0 ▲		Trail commences at the intersection of FR 91 (8N05) and FR 9, 11 miles south of California 88. Zero trip meter and turn northeast on graded dirt FR 9, following the sign to Salt Springs Reservoir. Trail begins within State Game Refuge—no firearms allowed.
		GPS: N38°28.97' W120°22.15'

NORTHERN SIERRA #10

Corral Hollow OHV Route

Starting Point:	**California 4, 0.6 miles southwest of Bear Valley**
Finishing Point:	**Northern Sierra #9: Calaveras Dome Trail (7N09), 0.9 miles north of California 4**
Total Mileage:	**12.5 miles**
Unpaved Mileage:	**12.5 miles**
Driving Time:	**2 hours**
Elevation Range:	**6,800–8,100 feet**
Usually Open:	**May to November**
Best Time to Travel:	**Dry weather**
Difficulty Rating:	**5**
Scenic Rating:	**10**
Remoteness Rating:	**+0**

Special Attractions

- Wildflower viewing in spring.
- Historic Bear Trap Cabin.
- Extremely scenic ridge top trail with many beautiful views.
- Part of the trail forms a popular mountain bike trail called Bear Trap Basin Loop.

History

Corral Hollow OHV Route commences near Bloods Point, south of Bloods Ridge. These features were named for Harvey S. Blood, operator of a toll station and hotel at Bear Valley Meadow. The toll road, known as the Big Trees–Carson Valley Road, operated from 1863 to 1910. Mount Reba, to the north of the trail, was named after Harvey's daughter.

Before the toll road was put through, emigrants and prospectors used a basic pack trail to cross the Sierra Nevada at Ebbetts Pass, northeast of this trail. Major John Ebbetts led a group of miners over this newly found pass in 1850. Traffic increased greatly in 1859 with the discovery of silver at Nevada's Comstock Lode. Harvey Blood and Joethean Curtis were instrumental in getting the Big Trees–Carson Valley Turnpike Company to complete a wagon road over the pass.

Camp Tamarack, just south of the start of the trail, was originally called Onion Valley because of the abundance of onions in this summer pasturage. From the late 1860s to early '70s, C. Brown operated a sawmill at this location. A man known as Turkey Johnson later ran swine, chickens, sheep, and turkeys in the area. In the early 1920s, W. H. Hutchins constructed the first store, saloon, and dance hall here and named his resort Camp Tamarack. These buildings were relocated when California 4 was widened.

Thompson Meadow, just before the end of the trail, is a reminder of the legendary character John "Snowshoe" Thompson, who passed through the region regularly from 1856 to 1876. Thompson delivered mail along a 90-mile route across the snow-covered Sierra Nevada. Jon Torsteinsin-Rue hailed from Norway. At 24 years of age, he answered a call from Uncle Sam to deliver mail through the near impassable terrain between Placerville and Carson Valley, on the east side of the Sierra. Thompson hand-carved his own crude 25-pound oak skis, or snowshoes as he called them, and commenced bimonthly deliveries. All prior attempts by mail carriers using snowshoes had failed. The round-trip solo journey took Thompson five days to complete. He rubbed charcoal on his face to prevent sunburn and snow-blindness. He did not carry a rifle or blankets because his mail sack weighed anywhere from 60 to 120 pounds. Snowshoe, as he was affectionately known, passed away in 1876. Many attribute him as being the father of skiing in the West.

Description

Corral Hollow is a beautiful, moderately rated 4WD trail that passes a variety of scenery, from forest gullies to open ridge tops. Rated black, meaning most difficult, by the National Forest Service, only the eastern 4 miles rates a 5 for difficulty; the rest rates a 3.

The trail leaves California 4 on the Alpine-Calaveras County line, southwest of Bear Valley. The turn is not well signed on the highway; a small Jeep symbol is all that marks the turn. Once off the highway you will see an information board. Initially, the trail is lumpy as it heads toward Corral Hollow. Careful wheel placement will allow most vehicles to make it through unscathed. The trail as a whole is best suited for compact and subcompact vehicles because of a few tight turns through trees. Full-size vehicles should make it through with careful driving and maybe a bit of backing up to complete turns.

Bear Trap Cabin

As the trail leaves Corral Hollow, it starts to climb up to a ridge. Like many in the region, this climb has a dry, loose surface that means poor traction for vehicles. Some sections are moguled, and a few short off-camber sections will tilt vehicles to the side. The trail passes a few small meadows, which in spring and early summer are ablaze with wildflowers, predominantly yellow mule's ears. As you reach the top of the ridge, there are views to the north over Grouse Valley and Mokelumne Peak. Mount Reba Ski Area borders this point.

Southern face of Mokelumne Peak

The trail follows along the ridge for few miles, with great views on either side, before descending gradually toward Bear Trap Basin and the old two-story Bear Trap Cabin. Owned by the forest service, the cabin is maintained as an emergency refuge and is generally stocked with dry food and firewood in winter. It can be used at other times under a special use permit from the Calaveras Ranger District. The cabin is sparsely furnished and has a stove for heat. If you visit the cabin, please leave it in better condition than you found it; contributions of non-perishable foodstuffs and firewood are always welcome. There is a visitor book inside the cabin.

Past the cabin the trail becomes easier, crossing small meadows and passing a series of spurs before crossing Big Meadow Creek and coming to an end on 7N09, a short distance north of California 4.

A popular moderately difficult mountain bike route called Bear Trap Basin Loop follows this trail for part of the way, diverging near the end to return to the parking area on California 4.

Current Road Information

Stanislaus National Forest
Calaveras Ranger District
5519 Highway 4
Hathaway Pines, CA 95233
(209) 795-1381

Map References

BLM San Andreas
USFS Stanislaus National Forest
USGS 1:24,000 Tamarack, Calaveras Dome
1:100,000 San Andreas
Maptech CD-ROM: High Sierra/Yosemite
Northern California Atlas & Gazetteer, p. 99
California Road & Recreation Atlas, p. 72 (incomplete)
Other: Calaveras Ranger District OHV Routes (forest service leaflet)

Corral Hollow OHV Route

Route Directions

▼ 0.0		From California 4 on the Alpine-Calaveras County line, 0.6 miles southwest of Bear Valley, zero trip meter and turn west on small formed trail. There is a jeep marker on the highway and a Corral Hollow information board visible once you turn off the highway. The route is marked Route 7A, suitable for 4WDs, ATVs, motorbikes, and mountain bikes.
6.1 ▲		Trail ends at T-intersection with California 4. Turn left for Bear Valley; turn right for Dorrington.
		GPS: N38°27.42′ W120°03.11′
▼ 1.1	SO	Cross through creek.
5.0 ▲	SO	Cross through creek.
		GPS: N38°27.92′ W120°03.65′
▼ 1.4	SO	Cross through creek. Trail starts to climb.
4.7 ▲	SO	End of descent. Cross through creek.
▼ 2.3	BL	Turnout on right.
3.8 ▲	BR	Turnout on left.
		GPS: N38°28.77′ W120°03.78′
▼ 2.8	SO	Pass through wire gate.
3.3 ▲	SO	Pass through wire gate.
		GPS: N38°28.66′ W120°04.25′
▼ 3.0	SO	Turnout and viewpoint on right.
3.1 ▲	SO	Turnout and viewpoint on left.
▼ 3.3	SO	Cross through creek.
2.8 ▲	SO	Cross through creek.
		GPS: N38°28.82′ W120°04.66′
▼ 5.0	SO	Cross through creek.
1.1 ▲	SO	Cross through creek.
▼ 5.4	SO	Cross through creek.
0.7 ▲	SO	Cross through creek.
		GPS: N38°28.82′ W120°05.64′
▼ 6.1	SO	Cross through creek; then track on right goes short distance to Bear Trap Cabin. Zero trip meter.
0.0 ▲		Continue to the northeast and cross through creek.
		GPS: N38°28.30′ W120°05.43′
▼ 0.0		Continue to the southeast.
6.4 ▲	SO	Track on left goes short distance to Bear Trap Cabin. Zero trip meter.
▼ 0.2	SO	Cross through creek.
6.2 ▲	SO	Cross through creek.
▼ 0.8	SO	Cross through creek.
5.6 ▲	SO	Cross through creek.
▼ 1.1	SO	Track on left.
5.3 ▲	SO	Track on right.
▼ 1.7	SO	Track on right.

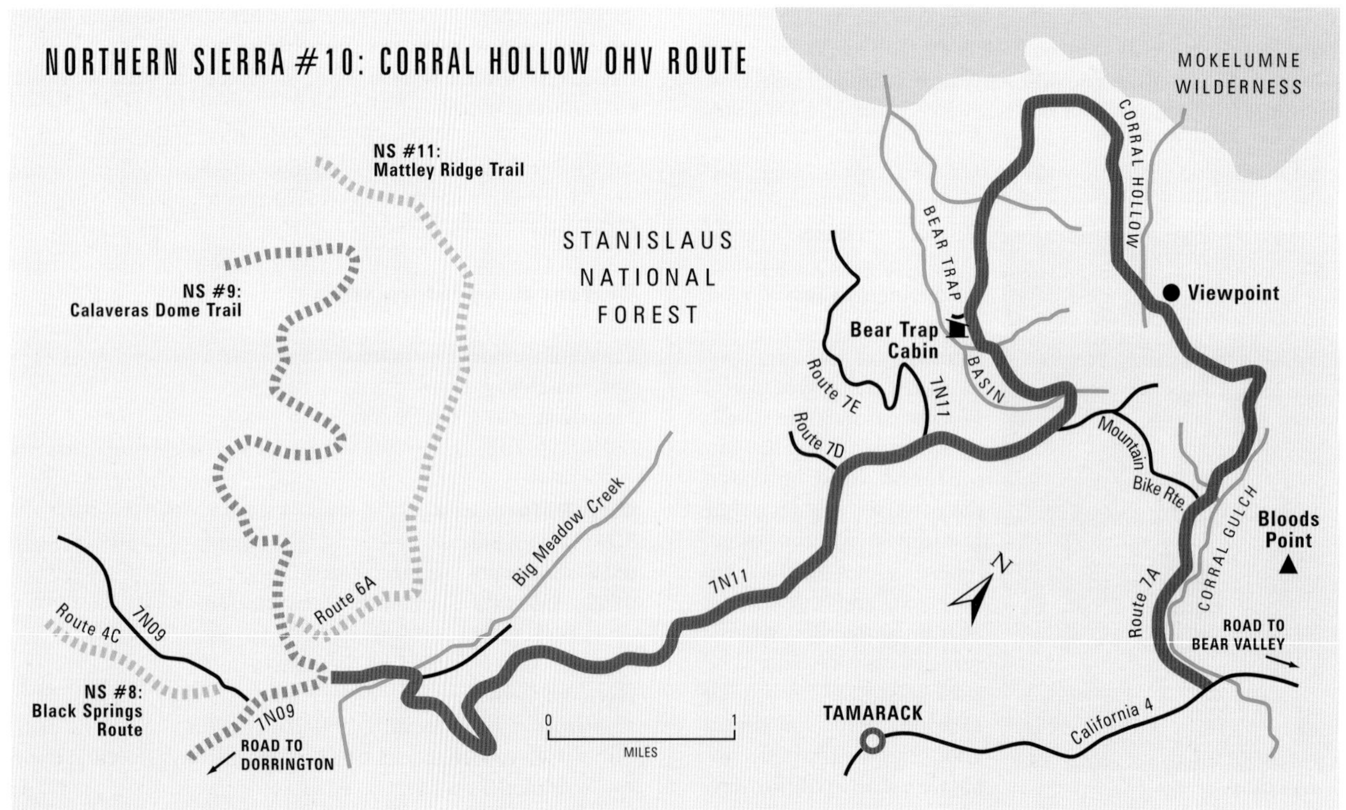

4.7 ▲	SO	Track on left.
▼ 1.8	SO	Track on right is 7N11 (Route 7E). Continue straight ahead and join 7N11.
4.6 ▲	BR	Track on left is 7N11 (Route 7E). Zero trip meter and bear right onto 7N11A.
		GPS: N38°27.67' W120°05.30'
▼ 2.2	SO	Track on right is Route 7D.
4.2 ▲	SO	Track on left is Route 7D.
		GPS: N38°27.39' W120°05.61'
▼ 4.0	SO	Track on right.
2.4 ▲	SO	Track on left.
		GPS: N38°26.11' W120°06.25'
▼ 4.4	SO	Track on right.
2.0 ▲	SO	Track on left.
▼ 5.1	SO	Turnout on left.
1.3 ▲	SO	Turnout on right.
▼ 5.7	SO	Cattle guard.
0.7 ▲	SO	Cattle guard.
▼ 5.8	BL	Track on right goes to private property.
0.6 ▲	BR	Track on left goes to private property.
		GPS: N38°25.63' W120°07.22'
▼ 5.9	SO	Cross over Big Meadow Creek on bridge.
0.5 ▲	SO	Cross over Big Meadow Creek on bridge.
▼ 6.3	SO	Track on left is Route 7B for ATVs and motorbikes.
0.1 ▲	SO	Track on right is Route 7B for ATVs and motorbikes.
▼ 6.4	SO	Trail ends at T-intersection with graded Northern Sierra #9: Calaveras Dome Trail (7N09). Turn left to exit to California 4; turn right to join Northern Sierra #11: Mattley Ridge Trail.
0.0 ▲		From California 4, 6.7 miles southwest of Bear Valley, zero trip meter and turn north on graded Northern Sierra #9: Calaveras Dome Trail (7N09) at the marker. Proceed 0.9 miles north; then zero trip meter and turn southeast on formed trail marked 7N11. There is an information board at the intersection.
		GPS: N38°25.40' W120°07.66'

NORTHERN SIERRA #11

Mattley Ridge Trail

Starting Point:	**Northern Sierra #9: Calaveras Dome Trail (7N09), 1.4 miles north of California 4**
Finishing Point:	**Northern Sierra #9: Calaveras Dome Trail (7N09), 8 miles north of California 4**
Total Mileage:	**5 miles**
Unpaved Mileage:	**5 miles**
Driving Time:	**1 hour**
Elevation Range:	**6,800–7,800 feet**
Usually Open:	**April to November**
Best Time to Travel:	**Dry weather**
Difficulty Rating:	**4**
Scenic Rating:	**8**
Remoteness Rating:	**+0**

Special Attractions

- Ridge top trail with views over Mokelumne Peak.
- Moderate trail suitable for most high-clearance 4WDs.

History

The Mokelumne Coast to Crest Trail (MCCT) is a nonmotorized, multi-use trail from the Pacific Ocean near San Francisco to the crest of the Sierra Nevada. Efforts to develop the trail commenced in 1990 and look promising to date. The ambitious trail will finish at Ebbetts Pass, an historic point on the old Big Trees–Carson Valley Toll Road. In 1993, Stanislaus National Forest completed an environmental analysis of constructing a section of the MCCT from Tiger Creek Reservoir to Mattley Creek and the Blue Hole Trailhead. In 2000, the forest service allocated $750,000 for the 15-mile section between Moore Creek Campground, downstream from Calaveras Dome, and Mattley Creek.

Mattley Creek begins below Flag Pole Point, east of the trail, and falls sharply more than 3.5 miles to join the North Fork of the Mokelumne River at Blue Hole. A pack trail follows close to the creek, zigzagging to the floor of the canyon—a drop of 3,600 feet.

Mule's ears along the trail as it climbs Mattley Ridge

Prospectors worked the North Fork of the Mokelumne River after the massive 1848 discovery of gold downstream at Mokelumne Hill. The Big Trees–Carson Valley Toll Road, near the start of the trail, was formerly a pack trail used by emigrants to the California goldfields. Prospectors and emigrants might turn in their shallow graves if they saw the funds available to develop recreational trails in the twenty-first century.

Description

This short, scenic trail leaves graded road 7N09 to climb along Mattley Ridge, passing open meadows carpeted with yellow mule's ears and interspersed with logged areas, be-

Luminous lichen on fir trees

fore descending to rejoin 7N09. The initial climb up the ridge is loose, with a gently moguled surface that can make traction difficult.

The trail undulates through stands of white firs on top of the ridge, passing recently logged-over areas. The very loose surface, particularly in the logged areas, can make getting adequate traction difficult, even on foot. This part of the trail can become difficult to impossible in wet weather and is best avoided.

Excellent views to the north over Mokelumne Peak and the Mokelumne Wilderness can be glimpsed from the ridge top.

Current Road Information

Stanislaus National Forest
Calaveras Ranger District
5519 Highway 4
Hathaway Pines, CA 95233
(209) 795-1381

Map References

BLM San Andreas
USFS Stanislaus National Forest
USGS 1:24,000 Calaveras Dome, Tamarack
1:100,000 San Andreas
Maptech CD-ROM: High Sierra/Yosemite
Northern California Atlas & Gazetteer, p. 99
California Road & Recreation Atlas, p. 72 (incomplete)
Other: Calaveras Ranger District OHV Routes (forest service leaflet)

Route Directions

Mileage		Directions
▼ 0.0		Trail commences on Northern Sierra #9: Calaveras Dome Trail (7N09), 1.4 miles north of California 4. Zero trip meter and turn northeast on Route 6A and 6B.
5.0 ▲		Trail ends at T-intersection with Northern Sierra #9: Calaveras Dome Trail (7N09). Turn left for California 4 and Bear Valley; turn right to follow Calaveras Dome Trail.
		GPS: N38°25.54' W120°08.14'
▼ 0.1	SO	Route 7B on right connects to Northern Sierra #10: Corral Hollow OHV Route for ATVs and motorbikes.
4.9 ▲	SO	Route 7B on left connects to Northern Sierra #10: Corral Hollow OHV Route for ATVs and motorbikes.
▼ 0.9	TL	Route 6B continues straight ahead. Turn left on formed trail Route 6A, which climbs up the side of a hill. Trail is unmarked except for a yellow OHV sign.
4.1 ▲	TR	T-intersection with the larger Route 6B.
		GPS: N38°25.94' W120°07.44'
▼ 2.1	BL	Track on right is Route 6F.
2.9 ▲	BR	Track on left is Route 6F.
		GPS: N38°26.92' W120°07.80'
▼ 2.2	SO	Start to cross meadow.
2.8 ▲	SO	Exit meadow.

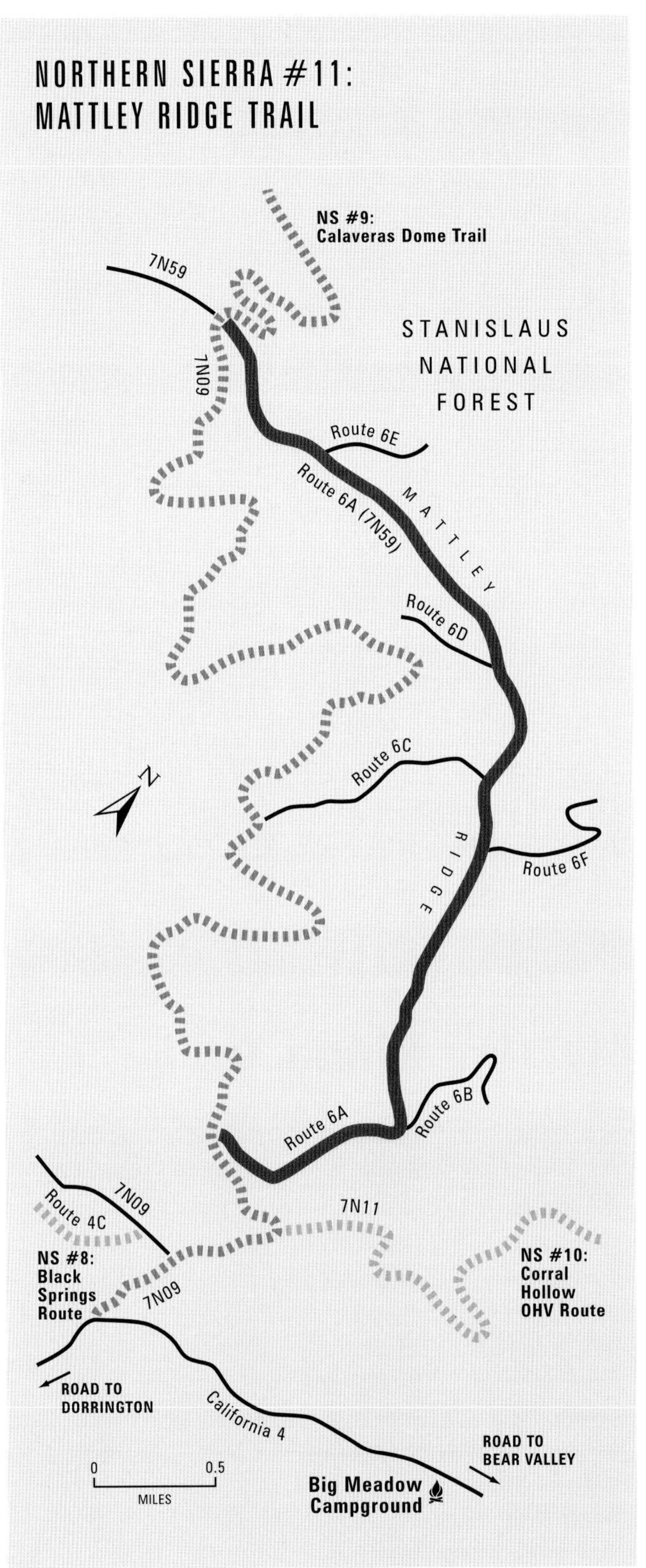

▼ 2.4	TR	Exit meadow. Track on left is Route 6C. Turn right, remaining on Route 6A, and follow the sign to Mattley Ridge.
2.6 ▲	TL	Track on right is Route 6C. Turn left, remaining on Route 6A, and start to cross meadow.
		GPS: N38°27.13′ W120°07.97′
▼ 2.8	SO	Track on right.
2.2 ▲	SO	Track on left.
▼ 2.9	BR	Track straight ahead is Route 6D. Bear right onto Route 6A.
2.1 ▲	SO	Track on right is Route 6D. Remain on Route 6A.
		GPS: N38°27.46′ W120°08.19′
▼ 3.1	SO	Track on right is Route 6G.
1.9 ▲	SO	Track on left is Route 6G.
		GPS: N38°27.58′ W120°08.33′
▼ 3.2	SO	Track on right.
1.8 ▲	BR	Track on left.
▼ 3.6	SO	Track on left.
1.4 ▲	SO	Track on right.
▼ 3.7	BL	Track on right.
1.3 ▲	SO	Track on left.
▼ 4.2	SO	Track on right is Route 6E.
0.8 ▲	SO	Track on left is Route 6E.
		GPS: N38°27.75′ W120°09.44′
▼ 4.5	SO	Small track on left.
0.5 ▲	SO	Small track on right.
▼ 5.0		Trail ends at 4-way intersection with graded dirt Northern Sierra #9: Calaveras Dome Trail (7N09). Turn left to return to California 4; turn right to travel Calaveras Dome Trail.
0.0 ▲		Trail commences at 4-way intersection on Northern Sierra #9: Calaveras Dome Trail (7N09), 8 miles northwest of California 4. Zero trip meter and turn southeast on small dirt road marked 7N59. The turn is on a sharp right-hand bend when approaching from the south. Track opposite the start is also 7N59.
		GPS: N38°27.94′ W120°10.10′

NORTHERN SIERRA #12

Red and Blue Lakes Trail

Starting Point:	**California 88, at the eastern end of Red Lake**
Finishing Point:	**Blue Lakes Road, 9.5 miles south of California 88**
Total Mileage:	**10 miles, plus 2.4-mile spur to Meadow Lake**
Unpaved Mileage:	**9.3 miles, plus 2.3 miles of the spur**
Driving Time:	**2 hours**
Elevation Range:	**7,700–8,900 feet**
Usually Open:	**June to November**
Best Time to Travel:	**June to November**
Difficulty Rating:	**3**
Scenic Rating:	**9**
Remoteness Rating:	**+0**

Special Attractions

- Fishing and camping at the many lakes along the trail.
- Spectacular open scenery above tree line.
- Basque carvings and the Alpine Sportsman Cabin.

History

Red and Blue Lakes Trail begins along an early emigrant trail over Carson Pass, which is above the western end of Red Lake. Kit Carson discovered the pass that retains his name. The renowned scout led Captain John C. Frémont and his group of explorers over the pass when traversing the Sierra Nevada in late June 1844. Emigrants had a choice of using this pass, or more northerly passes, one of which was named Donner Pass, after the unfortunate experiences of the Donner-Reed Party of 1846.

Upper and Lower Blue Lakes, Twin Lake, and Meadow Lake are all part of the Upper Mokelumne River Hydroelectric Project. The Alpine Sportsman Cabin was a grocery store built in 1938. The store, originally half its present size, catered to the many cabins scattered in this vicinity. Construction crews lived in the cabins while building dams for the hydroelectric project in the 1930s and '40s, and their needs kept the outpost busy. At other times campers and hunters were the store's main customers. The old log building below Lower Blue Lake Dam was an active stable in its heyday. The structure has been stabilized over the years and further restoration efforts are currently underway.

Old stables at Lower Blue Lake

Micky Green was the original storekeeper at the Alpine Sportsman Cabin. Her husband, Norm, was a caretaker for the surrounding dams. Sadly, Micky passed away at an early age, leaving Norm to care for their two children. Schooling was an obvious problem for a single parent in this remote region, so Norm sent the children off to boarding school. He remained at the old camp throughout the winter with his faithful dog. To stock up on supplies, Norm had to snowshoe approximately 15 miles into Markleeville, located east of the trail on present-day California 89. The journey had an elevation loss of 2,500 feet from his cabin. In the late 1940s, Norm's dog arrived in Markleeville without his master. Fearing the worst, a search party headed out and found Norm

Red and Blue Lakes Trail passes through a sparsely vegetated landscape

dead of a heart attack in his mountain cabin. The children were left orphans.

Current owners of the old Alpine Sportsman Cabin have managed to keep the heritage of the region alive. Efforts to pave the road to this little-changed region have resulted in the separation of the old store from its outhouse, an historic building in its own right.

A number of noteworthy Basque shepherd carvings can be found in the area, reminders of the many sheepherders who tended stock in the high alpine country. Sheepherding across the Sierra Nevada dates back to the late 1840s when Basques, like other emigrants, came to California to seek fortunes. Many became shepherds, a traditional occupation in their region of the Pyrenees. Tending sheep is a lonely profession, and carving tales and images on aspen trees was a form of storytelling that passed the time. Shepherds marked their favorite meadows and watering holes in this way. Some carvings give shepherds' names, where they came from, and the relevant date. Some are human images like one of the carvings near the Alpine Sportsman Cabin, which depicts a woman, seemingly representative of a prostitute. It was also a marker for her cabin in the meadow opposite.

These old, culturally rich inscriptions may be hard to decipher because they are written in Euskara, a native Basque language thought to be the earliest European language. As aspen trees die off, the carvings go too. Families of these Basque shepherds populated many towns and settlements in the Sierra Nevada, and their rich traditions remain in present-day Basque restaurants throughout the West.

Description

Red and Blue Lakes Trail is a pleasant, quiet road that accesses the Blue Lakes. The trail starts a short distance east of Carson Pass at Red Lake, a popular place to fish for rainbow trout. The Old Carson Pass Road, which runs along the south side of Red Lake to Carson Pass, is closed to motor vehicles, but it is popular with mountain bikers and hikers.

From Red Lake, the roughly graded dirt road climbs through stands of aspens onto an open ridge. The road is rough enough, with a loose uneven surface, to make 4WD preferable. From the ridge top there are views west to the humped peaks of Elephants Back (9,603 feet) and Round Top (10,381 feet) and north over the Carson Range. Photographers and landscape painters will especially enjoy the view. The trail continues along a narrow shelf road for some distance with the Pacific Crest National Scenic Trail running close to it. A side trail goes to campsites at Lost Lakes Dam and provides a good view of The Nipple, a prominent rock outcrop to the east.

From Lost Lakes, the trail descends to join a graded road at Upper Blue Lake. Four developed campgrounds owned and operated by the Pacific Gas & Electric Company are situated along the shores of Upper and Lower Blue Lakes. The campgrounds are normally open from May 1 to September 30; camping is limited to developed campgrounds on PG&E–owned land.

The Alpine Sportsman Cabin sits at the southern end of Lower Blue Lake. This historic cabin is privately owned and still uses its original outhouse, set back from the road a short distance away. The spur to Twin Lake and Meadow Lake leads off from the intersection in front of the cabin and heads past the stone-block dam of Lower Blue Lake. The old timber and shingle building you see here was a stable.

Anglers will enjoy the choice of lakes along the trail. Upper Blue Lake has excellent trout fishing. A particularly good spot is near the dam. Lost Lakes appear to have leaner pickings. All of the lakes along this trail are good for boating and boat-based fishing. Red Lake and Lower Blue Lake both have boat launches. Pacific Gas & Electric land along this spur is for day use only; no camping is allowed.

In addition to the developed campgrounds, campers will find many lovely backcountry sites along the trail. A large in-

Canadian geese on Lower Blue Lake

formal camping area can be found near the start, and other sites can be found tucked in the trees at Lost Lakes.

In winter, snowmobiles and cross-country skiers can reach the frozen lakes along ungroomed trails. The lakes have unstable ice and snow in winter and you should not attempt to venture onto them.

The section of graded road from the Alpine Sportsman Cabin north to the existing paved road is tentatively scheduled to be paved in 2002. Should this happen, the aligned road will no longer pass close to the Basque carving. Use the GPS coordinates to locate the tree and avoid rubbing or marking it in any way. The tree is marked by a plaque and the carving is about waist high.

Mountain bikers use this trail, and it is rated moderate for them, with some long climbs and a few difficult, technical sections.

Current Road Information

Eldorado National Forest
Amador Ranger District
26820 Silver Drive
Pioneer, CA 95666
(209) 295-4251

Map References

BLM Smith Valley
USFS Eldorado National Forest; Toiyabe National Forest: Carson Ranger District
USGS 1:24,000 Carson Pass, Pacific Valley
1:100,000 Smith Valley
Maptech CD-ROM: High Sierra/Tahoe
Northern California Atlas & Gazetteer, p. 90
California Road & Recreation Atlas, p. 67
Other: Fine Edge Productions—South Lake Tahoe Basin Recreation Topo Map

Route Directions

▼ 0.0		From California 88 at the eastern end of Red Lake, 6.5 miles west of the intersection with California 89 and 7.5 miles east of Kirkwood, zero trip meter and turn southeast on Forestdale Divide Road at the sign for Red Lake. Immediately paved road on right to Red Lake. Trail initially passes through private property.
5.4 ▲		Paved road on left to Red Lake; then trail ends on paved California 88. Turn left for Kirkwood; turn right for Lake Tahoe.
		GPS: N38°41.95' W119°57.91'
▼ 0.1	SO	Cattle guard.
5.3 ▲	SO	Cattle guard.
▼ 0.9	SO	Track on right.
4.5 ▲	SO	Track on left.
▼ 1.1	SO	Track on left.
4.3 ▲	SO	Track on right.
▼ 1.4	SO	Track on left is 013A for 4WDs, ATVs, and motorbikes.
4.0 ▲	SO	Track on right is 013A for 4WDs, ATVs, and motorbikes.
		GPS: N38°40.82' W119°57.61'
▼ 1.5	SO	Cross over Forestdale Creek on bridge; then track on right through large camping area.
3.9 ▲	SO	Track on left through large camping area; then cross over Forestdale Creek on bridge.
▼ 1.6	SO	Track on left is FR 146.
3.8 ▲	SO	Track on right is FR 146.
▼ 2.0	SO	Track on left.
3.4 ▲	SO	Track on right.
▼ 3.0	SO	Track on right goes 0.1 miles to the start of the Summit City Carson Trail (18E13).
2.4 ▲	SO	Track on left goes 0.1 miles to the start of the Summit City Carson Trail (18E13).
		GPS: N38°39.69' W119°57.96'
▼ 3.3	SO	Pacific Crest Trail crosses.
2.1 ▲	SO	Pacific Crest Trail crosses.
		GPS: N38°39.64' W119°57.70'
▼ 4.6	BR	Track on left is FR 018, which runs 0.3 miles around the side of Lost Lakes to the dam. Follow sign to Hope Valley. Pacific Crest Trail runs near this intersection.
0.8 ▲	BL	Track on right is FR 018, which runs 0.3 miles around the side of Lost Lakes to the dam. Follow sign to Red Lake. Pacific Crest Trail runs near this intersection.
		GPS: N38°38.87' W119°57.09'
▼ 5.4	TL	T-intersection at the north end of Upper Blue Lake. Track on right goes to Upper Blue Lake Campground. Zero trip meter. Evergreen Trailhead (18E21) on the right enters the Mokelumne Wilderness.
0.0 ▲		Continue to the northwest away from Upper Blue Lake.
		GPS: N38°38.46' W119°57.22'
▼ 0.0		Continue to the east and along the shore of Upper Blue Lake.
2.8 ▲	TR	Road continues straight ahead into Upper Blue Lake Campground. Evergreen Trailhead (18E21) on left enters the Mokelumne Wilderness. Zero trip meter and turn right onto roughly graded dirt road, marked suitable for 4WDs, ATVs, and motorbikes.
▼ 1.0	SO	Trail becomes paved as it passes through Upper Blue Lake Damsite Campground. Roads on right and left to campsites.
1.8 ▲	SO	Trail returns to graded dirt after the campground.
▼ 1.1	SO	Exit campground.
1.7 ▲	SO	Road passes through Upper Blue Lake Damsite Campground. Roads on right and left to campsites.
		GPS: N38°37.80' W119°56.27'
▼ 1.2	SO	Grouse Lake Trail (18E08) on right for hikers only.
1.6 ▲	SO	Grouse Lake Trail (18E08) on left for hikers only.
▼ 1.4	SO	Pass through Middle Creek Campground. Road turns back to graded dirt.
1.4 ▲	SO	Road turns to paved and passes through Middle Creek Campground. Start to follow along the shore of Upper Blue Lake.
▼ 2.0	SO	Trail passes the east side Lower Blue Lake.
0.8 ▲	SO	Trail leaves Lower Blue Lake.
▼ 2.5	SO	Road becomes paved as it enters Lower Blue Lake Campground. Roads on left and right to campsites.
0.3 ▲	SO	Road returns to graded dirt as it leaves Lower Blue Lake Campground.
▼ 2.8	BL	Exit campground. Paved road on right is

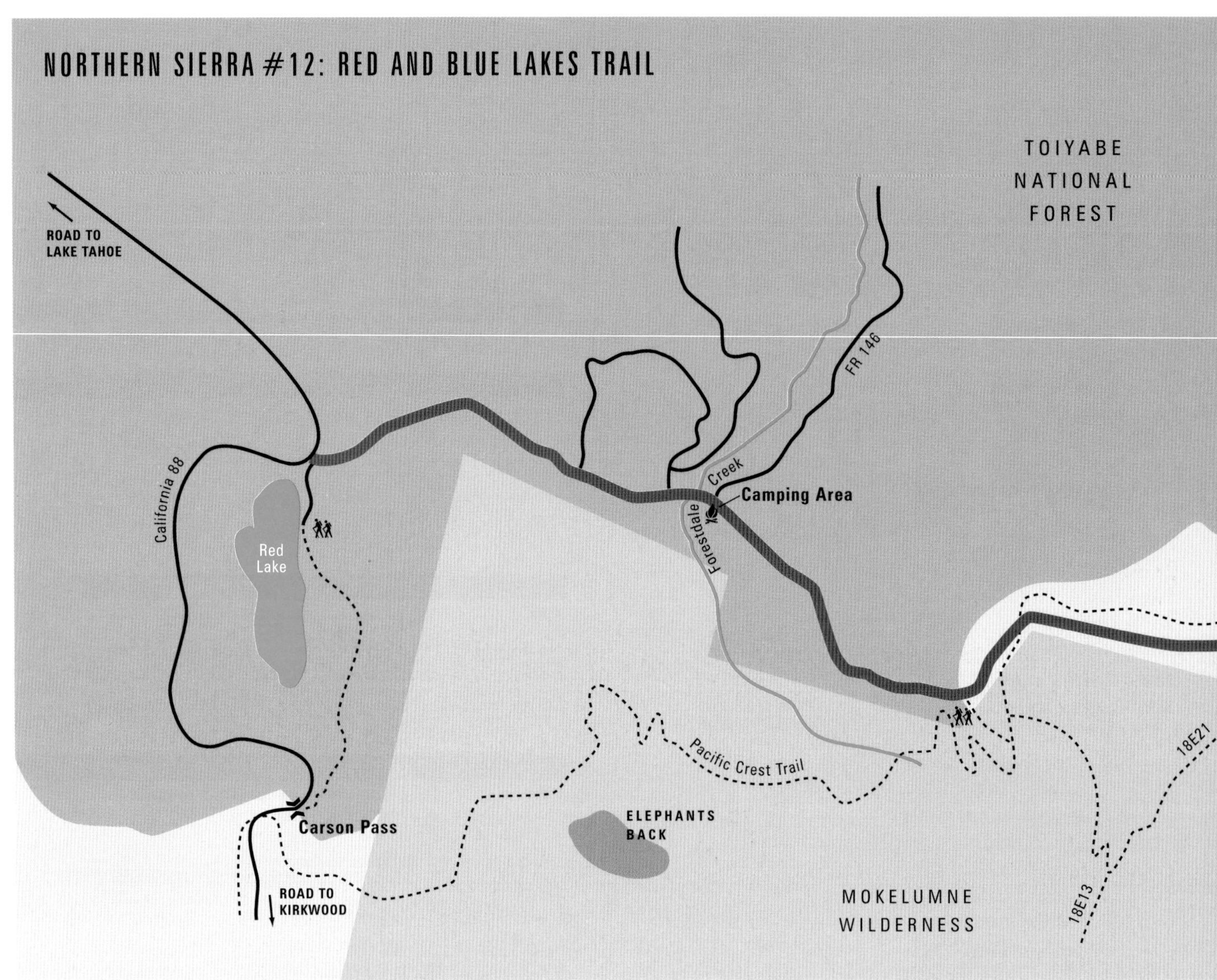

		the spur to Twin Lake and Meadow Lake. Zero trip meter and bear left away from Lower Blue Lake. Alpine Sportsman Cabin is at the intersection—private property.
0.0 ▲		Continue to the northwest. Road becomes paved.

GPS: N38°36.58′ W119°55.39′

Spur to Twin Lake and Meadow Lake

▼ 0.0		From the entrance to Lower Blue Lake Campground, proceed southwest on 9N01 and zero trip meter. Immediately road on left to campground supervisor and road on right to Lower Blue Lake Boat Launch. Follow sign to Meadow Lake.
▼ 0.1	BR	Road turns to dirt; then track on left is Deer Valley Trail (19E01) for 4WDs, ATVs, and motorbikes. Follow sign to Meadow Lake.
▼ 0.2	SO	Old cabin on left.
▼ 0.3	SO	Cross over Blue Creek below dam; then track on right to dam.
▼ 0.5	SO	Track on left.
▼ 0.8	SO	Track on left to Twin Lake.

GPS: N38°36.44′ W119°56.02′

▼ 1.9	SO	Track on right.
▼ 2.2	SO	Cross over Meadow Creek.
▼ 2.4		Trail ends at a viewpoint over Meadow Lake. It is a 0.3-mile hike to the lake.

GPS: N38°36.28′ W119°57.46′

Continuation of Main Trail

▼ 0.0		Continue to the northeast. Road returns to graded dirt.
1.8 ▲	BR	Enter Lower Blue Lake Campground. Paved road on left is the spur to Twin Lake and Meadow Lake. Zero trip meter and bear right, following the sign for campgrounds and start to pass along the eastern shore of Lower Blue Lake. Alpine Sportsman Cabin is at the intersection—private property.

GPS: N38°36.58′ W119°55.39′

▼ 0.2	SO	Basque carving on pine tree on right. The carving is about 3 feet up from the bottom with a wildlife tree marker directly above it. A second carving can be found slightly to the northeast on the opposite side of the road. The prostitute's cabin used to stand in the meadow opposite.
1.6 ▲	SO	Basque carving on pine tree on left. The carving is about 3 feet up from the bottom with a

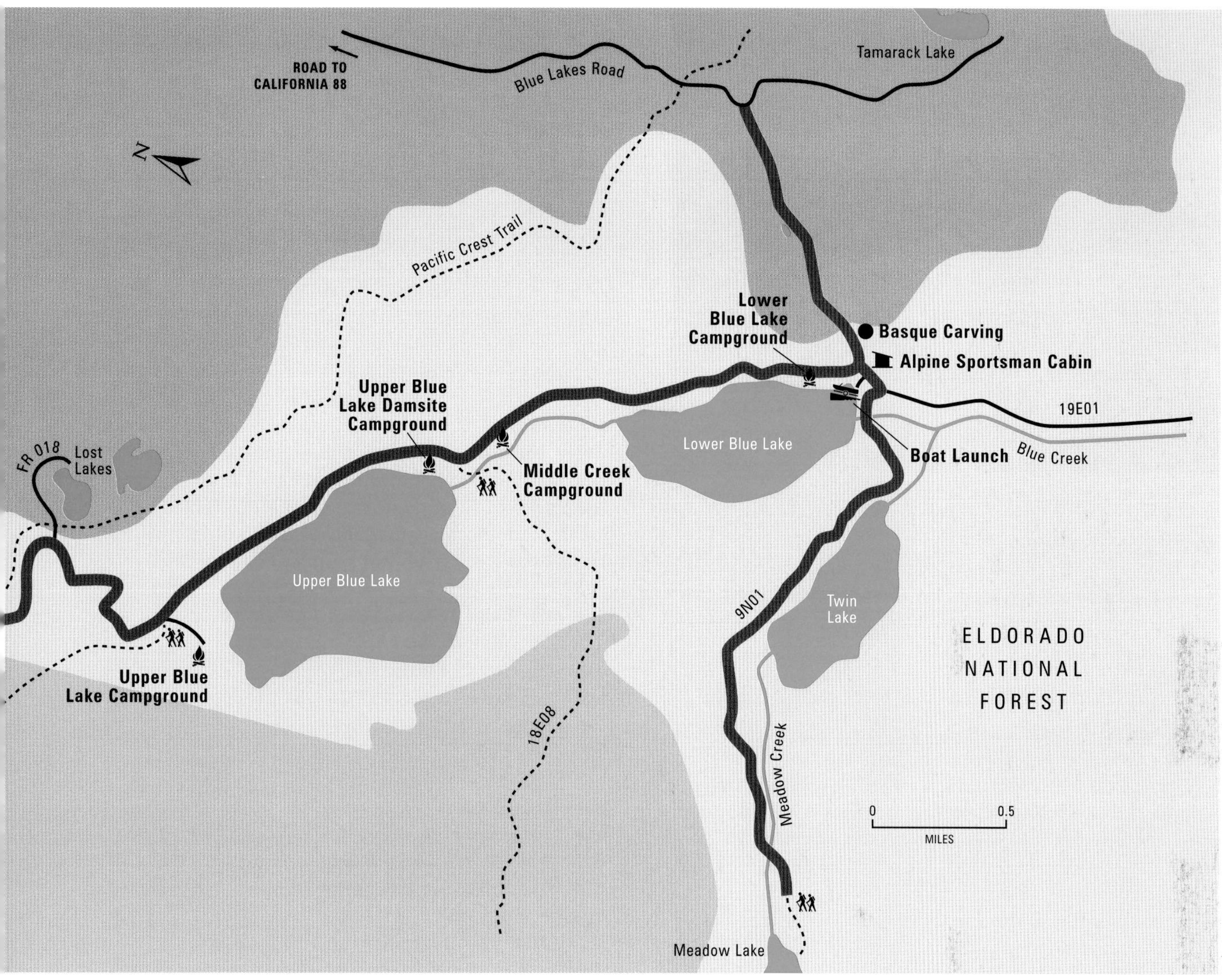

wildlife tree marker directly above it. A second carving can be found slightly to the northeast on the opposite side of the road. The prostitute's cabin used to stand in the meadow opposite.

GPS: N38°36.68′ W119°55.23′

▼ 0.3		SO	Entering Toiyabe National Forest.
	1.5 ▲	SO	Entering Eldorado National Forest.
▼ 0.7		SO	Small lake on left.
	1.1 ▲	SO	Small lake on right.

GPS: N38°36.92′ W119°54.91′

▼ 1.8		SO	Trail ends at intersection with Blue Lakes Road. Turn right for Tamarack Lake and Wet Meadows Trailhead; continue straight ahead on graded Blue Lakes Road, which becomes paved and joins California 88.
	0.0 ▲		Trail commences on Blue Lakes Road. The turn from California 88 is 2.4 miles west of the intersection of California 88 and California 89. Turn south, following the sign to Blue Lakes Road and proceed 9.5 miles to the start of the trail. At the intersection with Tamarack Lake Road, zero trip meter and continue southwest, following sign to Lower Blue Lake.

GPS: N38°37.17′ W119°54.61′

NORTHERN SIERRA #13

Baltic Ridge Trail

Starting Point:	**Mormon Emigrant Trail (FR 5), 2.7 miles west of California 88**
Finishing Point:	**Intersection of Cosumnes Mine Road and Bonetti Road, 6 miles south of CR 5**
Total Mileage:	**15.6 miles**
Unpaved Mileage:	**15.5 miles**
Driving Time:	**2 hours**
Elevation Range:	**4,600–7,400 feet**
Usually Open:	**June to October**
Best Time to Travel:	**June to October**
Difficulty Rating:	**3 (forward direction); 4 (reverse direction)**
Scenic Rating:	**7**
Remoteness Rating:	**+1**

Baltic Ridge Trail overlooks Camp Creek Valley

Special Attractions

- Trail follows part of the historic Mormon Emigrant Trail.
- Trail travels along a ridge top with views over Iron Mountain Ridge and Eldorado National Forest.

History

Baltic Ridge got its name from a mine of the same name on the western end of the ridge. Baltic Mine was a lode gold operation established in 1896 on the north face of Baltic Peak. To extract the ore, an adit was dug more than 500 feet into the mountainside with a 130-foot inclined shaft. A 10-stamp mill was constructed at the mine to process the ore. By 1907, operations were complete and all was quiet again at the mine site.

The trail starts at the junction of the Mormon Emigrant Trail and an early side trail that ran down Baltic Ridge. Kit Carson and John C. Frémont's expedition crossed the Sierra Nevada in the winter of 1844 en route to Sutter's Fort in the Sacramento Valley. Carson discovered a pass some 20-odd miles east of Baltic Ridge Trail. He carved his name on a tree at the pass that would come to bear his name and returned to camp. The Carson Trail, as it became known, followed close to today's Iron Mountain Road. From California 88, it traveled the length of Iron Mountain Ridge to Sly Park and Pleasant Valley.

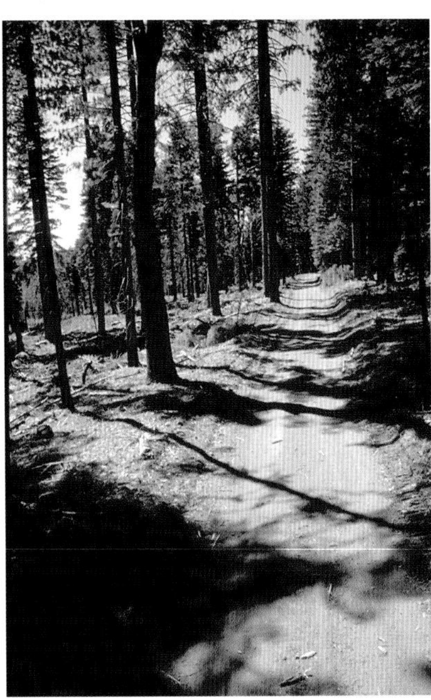

Western end of Baltic Ridge

Baltic Ridge Trail follows part of Grizzly Flat Road, a side trail developed by emigrants in 1848. The trail ran down Baltic Ridge roughly as far as North-South Road, bore south to cross the North Fork of the Cosumnes River, and continued toward Grizzly Flat.

Description

Baltic Ridge Trail follows a series of lightly-used forest roads within Eldorado National Forest, traveling through a mixture of revegetated forest and more recently logged areas. There are views north over the South Fork of the American River.

The trail is rated a 3 for difficulty in the forward direction, but in reverse it is rated a 4. The difference comes from one short section of shallow loose rock steps that is harder to climb than descend. Approximately 0.4 miles of the trail around this section is lightly brushy.

The trail is sporadically marked and can be a little hard to follow through areas that have seen recent logging activity. Newly constructed logging tracks often appear better used than the main trail and can make for confusing navigation. The final section of the trail travels through open forest and descends the northwestern end of Baltic Ridge to finish on small paved forest roads just south of Pollock Pines.

Current Road Information

Eldorado National Forest
Placerville Ranger District
4260 Eight Mile Road
Camino, CA 95709
(530) 644-2324

Map References

BLM Placerville
USFS Eldorado National Forest
USGS 1:24,000 Tragedy Spring, Leek Spring Hill, Stump Spring
1:100,000 Placerville
Maptech CD-ROM: High Sierra/Tahoe
Northern California Atlas & Gazetteer, pp. 89, 88
California Road & Recreation Atlas, p. 66 (incomplete)

Route Directions

▼ 0.0	From California 88, 7 miles northeast of the turn to Lower Bear River Reservoir and 0.7

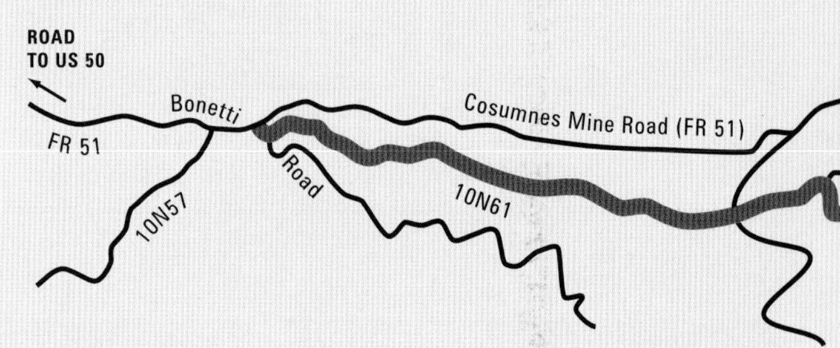

		miles southwest of Shot Rock Vista Point, turn northwest on paved road signposted for the Mormon Emigrant Trail (FR 5) and pass the closed Iron Mountain Ski Resort. Proceed 2.7 miles to the start of the trail and turn southwest on graded dirt road, marked 9N20. Zero trip meter. The turn is immediately south of a cattle guard. Immediately track on right.
3.4 ▲		Track on left; then trail finishes at T-intersection with the Mormon Emigrant Trail (FR 5). Turn left for Pollock Pines and US 50; turn right for California 88 and Lower Bear River Reservoir.
		GPS: N38°38.46' W120°14.87'
▼ 1.4	SO	Track on right; then cattle guard.
2.0 ▲	SO	Cattle guard; then track on left.
▼ 1.7	BR	Unmarked track on left.
1.7 ▲	SO	Unmarked track on right.
		GPS: N38°38.55' W120°16.24'
▼ 2.0	SO	Track on right.
1.4 ▲	SO	Track on left.
▼ 2.3	SO	Track on left.
1.1 ▲	SO	Track on right.
▼ 2.5	SO	Track on left is 9N20D.
0.9 ▲	SO	Track on right is 9N20D.
▼ 2.6	TL	T-intersection with graded dirt Meiss Road. To the right returns to the Mormon Emigrant Trail. Turn left, following sign for Capps Crossing.
0.8 ▲	TR	Meiss Road continues ahead to the Mormon Emigrant Trail. Turn right onto formed dirt trail, following small sign to California 88.
		GPS: N38°38.92' W120°17.00'
▼ 3.3	SO	Track on left.
0.1 ▲	SO	Track on right.
▼ 3.4	BR	Bear right onto unmarked, formed Baltic Ridge Road. Zero trip meter.
0.0 ▲		Continue to the southeast.
		GPS: N38°39.03' W120°17.82'
▼ 0.0		Continue to the north.
5.7 ▲	BL	Bear left onto unmarked, small, graded Meiss Road. Zero trip meter.
▼ 1.6	BR	Track on left. Bear right at marker for 9N20.
4.1 ▲	BL	Track on right. Bear left at marker for 9N20.
		GPS: N38°39.78' W120°19.14'
▼ 5.0	BL	Track on right. Trail forks and rejoins almost immediately.
0.7 ▲	BR	Track on left. Trail forks and rejoins almost immediately.
		GPS: N38°40.12' W120°22.52'
▼ 5.7	TR	Unmarked T-intersection with 10N46. Zero trip meter.
0.0 ▲		Continue to the east.
		GPS: N38°40.07' W120°23.25'
▼ 0.0		Continue to the north on wider trail.
3.6 ▲	TL	Wider trail 10N46 continues ahead. Zero trip meter and turn left onto small, formed trail marked 9N20.
▼ 0.6	TL	Turn sharp left onto small, formed trail, marked 9N20, that descends the hill.
3.0 ▲	TR	Turn sharp right onto wider unmarked trail.
		GPS: N38°40.45' W120°23.07'
▼ 0.8	BR	Track on left. Remain on 9N20.
2.8 ▲	SO	Track on right. Continue up the hill.
▼ 2.4	BR	Track on left. Remain on 9N20.
1.2 ▲	BL	Track on right. Remain on 9N20.
		GPS: N38°40.17' W120°24.89'
▼ 2.75	TL	T-intersection.
0.85 ▲	TR	Track continues straight ahead.
		GPS: N38°40.39' W120°25.17'
▼ 2.8	BR	Track on left. Follow marker for 9N20.
0.8 ▲	SO	Track on right.
▼ 3.6	SO	Cross over paved road, remaining on small trail, and zero trip meter. Trail is marked Baltic Ridge Road on paved road.
0.0 ▲		Continue to the southeast.
		GPS: N38°40.40' W120°26.11'
▼ 0.0		Continue to the northwest.
2.9 ▲	SO	Cross over paved road, remaining on small trail, and zero trip meter. Trail is marked Baltic Ridge Road on paved road.
▼ 2.4	SO	Track on left.
0.5 ▲	SO	Track on right.
		GPS: N38°41.43' W120°28.41'
▼ 2.8	TR	T-intersection with small paved Bonetti Road.
0.1 ▲	TL	Bonetti Road continues ahead. Turn left on small, unmarked trail 10N61.
		GPS: N38°41.55' W120°28.80'
▼ 2.9		Trail ends at T-intersection with paved Cosumnes Mine Road (FR 51). Turn left to exit to US 50.
0.0 ▲		Trail begins on paved Cosumnes Mine Road (FR 51), 6 miles south of CR 5. Zero trip meter at the intersection of FR 51 and Bonetti Road and turn southeast on Bonetti Road, following sign to Capps Crossing.
		GPS: N38°41.57' W120°28.84'

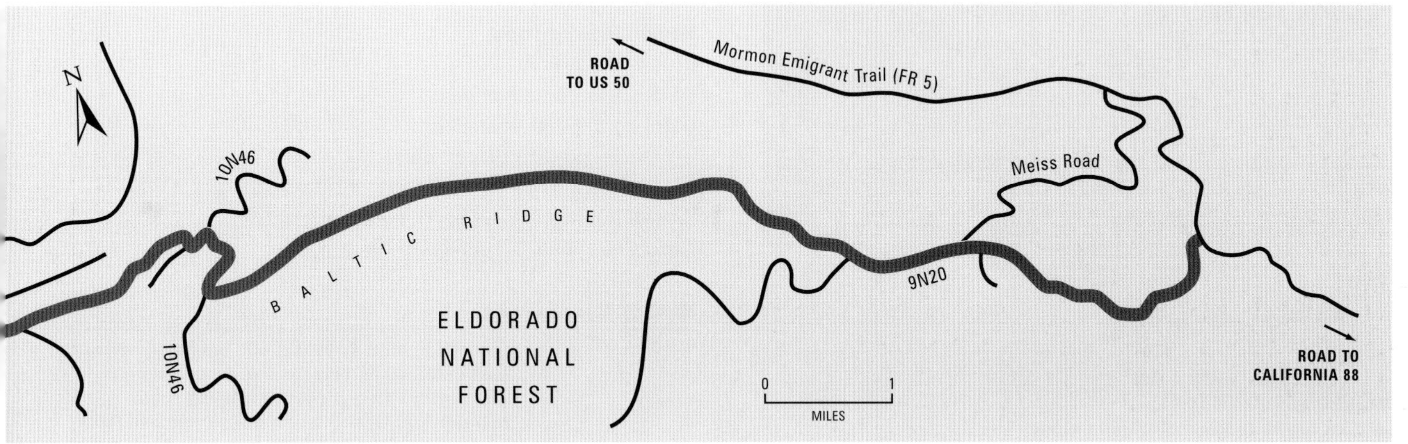

NORTHERN SIERRA #14

Slate Mountain Trail

Starting Point:	**Mosquito Road (CR 60), 9.5 miles northeast of US 50 and Placerville**
Finishing Point:	**CR 63 (FR 1), 6.4 miles east of Georgetown**
Total Mileage:	**18.5 miles, plus 2.8-mile spur to Slate Mountain Fire Lookout**
Unpaved Mileage:	**14.3 miles, plus 2.8-mile spur**
Driving Time:	**2 hours**
Elevation Range:	**2,600–3,700 feet**
Usually Open:	**May to November**
Best Time to Travel:	**Dry weather**
Difficulty Rating:	**2**
Scenic Rating:	**8**
Remoteness Rating:	**+0**

Special Attractions

- Slate Mountain Fire Lookout.
- Access to a network of 4WD, ATV, and motorbike trails.
- Cool shady, forest drive in Eldorado National Forest.

History

Slate Mountain Road commences just east of Mosquito Camp, originally a Civilian Conservation Corps camp that housed CCC workers while they completed projects in the region. The CCC boys, as they were called, received about $30 a month. Expenses were minimal: Lunch trucks accompanied road crews, and meals at the camp, which everyone helped prepare, cost about 13 cents. Movies were shown regularly at a cost of about 10 cents. Time off meant an opportunity to visit Motor City, south of the South Fork of the American River. Bed bugs were a major problem at the old camp and though regularly fumigated, the name "Camp Mosquito" seemed appropriate.

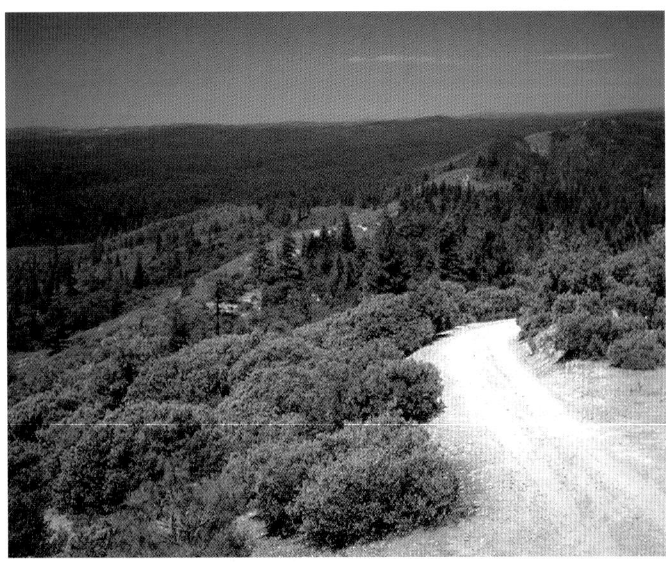

View from the Slate Mountain Fire Lookout

As early as 1849, gold miners were well rewarded around Mosquito and Little Mosquito Creeks. By 1854, the Mosquito Water Company had built a ditch to supply the growing number of miners, merchants, and fruit growers. The ditch drew water from Slab Creek, east of this trail near Cable Point on the old logging railroad.

Description

Slate Mountain Road begins north of Placerville near Finnon Reservoir. The graded dirt road is not suitable for passenger vehicles because of several rough, uneven sections interspersed with the smoother sections. To reach the start of the trail from Placerville, head northeast on Mosquito Road, ignoring turns to Finnon Reservoir. Once at the start of the trail, navigation is easy. Side roads and trails become quite numerous in the Rock Creek OHV Area, but the main trail is well marked. A spur from the main trail leads to the fire lookout on Slate Mountain; the reason for mountain's name becomes obvious along the spur because the shelf road cuts through layers of slate on its way to the top of the mountain. This route to the lookout is less used and slightly brushy. The tower is manned as needed during fire season, and the fire spotter travels to the tower from the other side, on CR 60. The gate to the lookout may be locked, but it is less than 0.1 miles to the tower.

The Slate Mountains, including Darling Ridge, is the winter habitat of the Pacific deer herd. Winter is the most stressful part of their year, with limited food, cold temperatures, and a concentration of their population. Adult does are typically in the later stages of pregnancy in April, with their bodies already weakened from winter hardships. The OHV area is closed from November 10 to May 1 to protect the herd.

Many trails lead off from Slate Mountain Road, and there is a network of trails in the Rock Creek OHV Area, mainly for motorbikes and ATVs although some trails are suitable for 4WDs.

Current Road Information

Eldorado National Forest
Georgetown Ranger District
7600 Wentworth Springs Road
Georgetown, CA 95634
(530) 333-4312

Map References

BLM Placerville
USFS Eldorado National Forest
USGS 1:24,000 Slate Mt., Tunnel Hill
1:100,000 Placerville
Maptech CD-ROM: High Sierra/Tahoe
Northern California Atlas & Gazetteer, p. 88
California Road & Recreation Atlas, p. 66

Route Directions

▼ 0.0	From Mosquito Road (CR 60), 9.5 miles northeast of US 50 and Placerville, zero trip meter and turn northwest on small paved road marked 12N70 (shown on forest map as FR 12).

4.8 ▲ Trail ends at T-intersection with paved Mosquito Road (CR 60). Turn right for Placerville and US 50, remaining on Mosquito Road and ignoring turns to Finnon Reservoir.

GPS: N38°48.24' W120°43.16'

▼ 0.2 SO Track on left; then cross over creek; then second track on left.
4.6 ▲ SO Track on right; then cross over creek; then second track on right.

▼ 0.3 SO Cattle guard. Entering Eldorado National Forest; then track on right is Crosier Run Loop 7 (11N81) for ATVs, motorbikes, hikers, horses, and mountain bikes—rated blue. This is closed to OHV travel November 10 to May 1.
4.5 ▲ SO Track on left is the return of Crosier Run Loop 7 (11N81).

GPS: N38°48.46' W120°43.21'

▼ 1.1 SO Track on left.
3.7 ▲ SO Track on right.

▼ 1.2 SO Track on left.
3.6 ▲ SO Track on right.

▼ 1.7 SO Track on right is the return of Crosier Run Loop 7 (11N81).
3.1 ▲ SO Track on left is Crosier Run Loop 7 (11N81) for ATVs, motorbikes, hikers, horses, and mountain bikes—rated blue. This is closed to OHV travel November 10 to May 1.

▼ 1.9 SO Track on right.
2.9 ▲ SO Track on left.

▼ 2.1 SO Corral on left and track on right. Road turns to graded dirt and is marked L7.
2.7 ▲ SO Corral on right and track on left. Road is now paved.

GPS: N38°49.59' W120°43.53'

▼ 3.8 SO Cross over creek.
1.0 ▲ SO Cross over creek.

▼ 4.0 BR Track on right; then track on left is Trail L6 (12N83). Bear right on Trail L6 and L7, following sign to Georgetown.
0.8 ▲ SO Track on right is Trail L6 (12N83). Follow sign to Mosquito; then track on left.

GPS: N38°50.30' W120°43.04'

▼ 4.8 BL Track on right is 12N76, the spur to Slate Mountain Fire Lookout. Zero trip meter and bear left, following Trail L6.
0.0 ▲ Continue to the southwest.

GPS: N38°50.37' W120°42.50'

Spur to Slate Mountain Fire Lookout

▼ 0.0 Proceed northeast on the upper road, marked Trail L7 (12N76) and zero trip meter. Trail starts to climb shelf road.
▼ 1.8 SO Small trail for motorbikes crosses road.
▼ 2.3 SO Small track on left is Trail 23-16 for motorbikes only—rated blue.

GPS: N38°49.68' W120°41.24'

▼ 2.6 SO Track on right on saddle.

GPS: N38°49.48' W120°41.14'

▼ 2.8 Track on right goes through gate. Slate Mountain Fire Lookout and radio towers are 0.1 miles past the gate. Trail L7 continues straight ahead and joins CR 60.

GPS: N38°49.44' W120°41.00'

Continuation of Main Trail

▼ 0.0 Continue to the north on the lower road.
5.9 ▲ SO Track on sharp left is 12N76, the spur to Slate Mountain Fire Lookout. Zero trip meter and continue on Trail L7.

Slate Mountain Fire Lookout

GPS: N38°50.37' W120°42.50'

▼ 1.4 SO Cross over creek in Slate Canyon.
4.5 ▲ SO Cross over creek in Slate Canyon.

▼ 2.4 SO Track on right is 12N75 for 4WDs, ATVs, and motorbikes; then two small tracks on left.
3.5 ▲ SO Two small tracks on right; then track on left is 12N75 for 4WDs, ATVs, and motorbikes.

GPS: N38°50.79' W120°41.93'

▼ 3.4 SO Cross over Sailor Ravine; then track on right is 12N74 for 4WDs, ATVs, and motorbikes.
2.5 ▲ SO Track on left is 12N74 for 4WDs, ATVs, and motorbikes; then cross over Sailor Ravine.

GPS: N38°51.09' W120°41.55'

▼ 4.1 SO Track on left; then track on right is 12N69.
1.8 ▲ BR Track on left is 12N69. Bear right, remaining on the main trail; then track on right.

▼ 4.5 SO Road becomes paved.
1.4 ▲ SO Road turns to graded dirt.

▼ 5.1 SO Cross over Whaler Creek; then track on right is 12N70H.
0.8 ▲ SO Track on left is 12N70H; then cross over Whaler Creek.

GPS: N38°52.15' W120°41.79'

▼ 5.7 SO Track on left is Trail L5 (12N70D).
0.2 ▲ SO Track on right is Trail L5 (12N70D).

▼ 5.9 SO Small track on left joins Ballarat Trail in 1 mile; then track on left is Ballarat Loop 5 (12N82) for 4WDs, ATVs, motorbikes, hikers, horses, and mountain bikes—rated blue. Paved road on right is 12N72 to Bald Mountain Lookout and Quintette. Immediately off that road is 12N38 for 4WDs, ATVs, and motorbikes. Zero trip meter and follow the sign to Georgetown.
0.0 ▲ Continue to the east. Road is now paved.

GPS: N38°52.51' W120°42.44'

▼ 0.0 Continue to the west. Road turns to gravel.
4.1 ▲ SO Track on right is Ballarat Loop 5 (12N82) for 4WDs, ATVs, motorbikes, hikers, horses, and mountain bikes—rated blue; then small track on right joins Ballarat Trail in 1 mile. Paved road on left is 12N72 to Bald Mountain Lookout and Quintette. Immediately off that road is 12N38 for 4WDs, ATVs, and motorbikes. Zero trip meter and follow the sign to Mosquito.

▼ 0.5 SO Cross over creek in Bald Mountain Canyon.

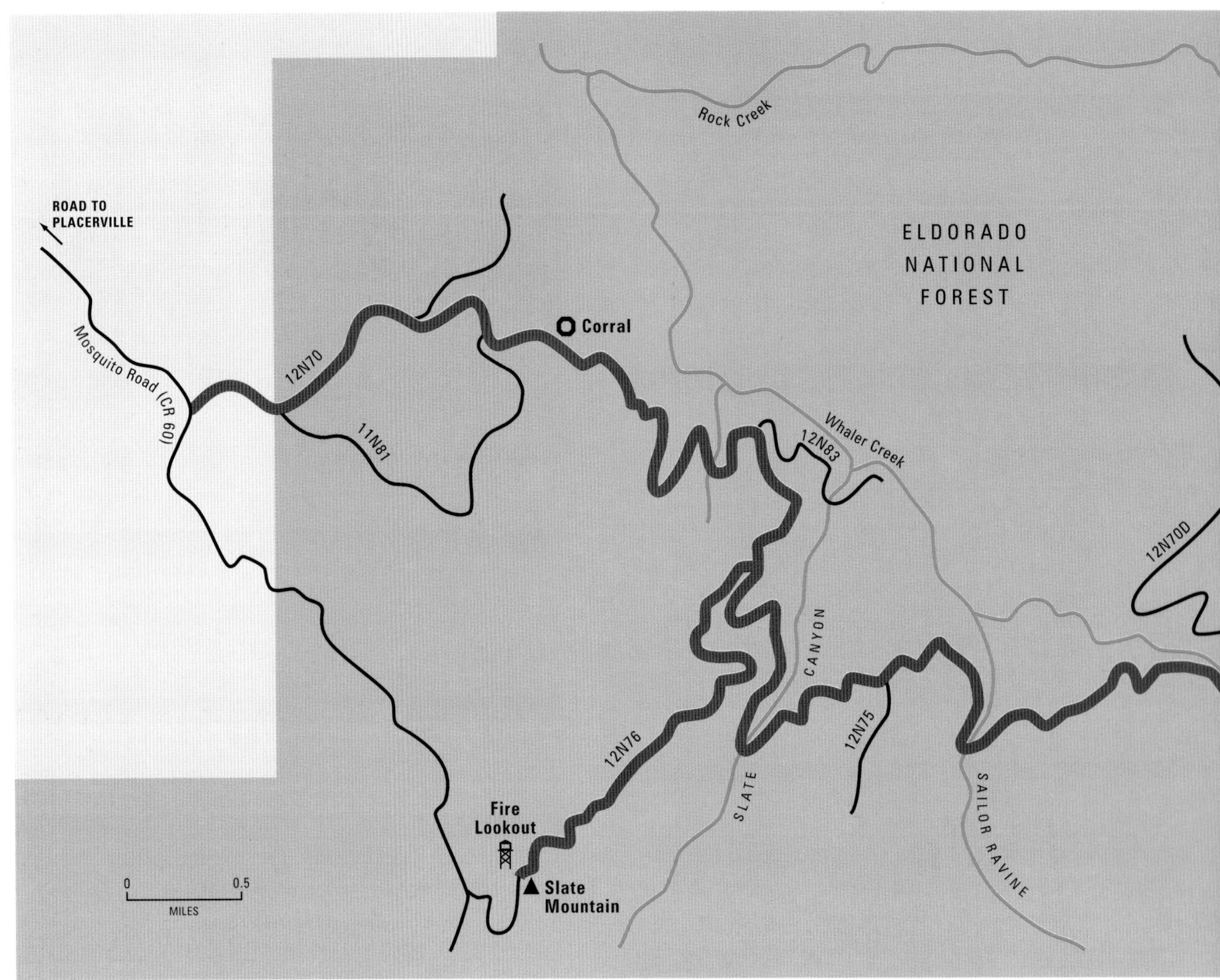

3.6 ▲	SO	Cross over creek in Bald Mountain Canyon.
▼ 0.8	SO	Track on right; then cross over creek in Bald Mountain Canyon.
3.3 ▲	SO	Cross over creek in Bald Mountain Canyon; then track on left.
▼ 1.5	SO	Small track on right is 9-12 for motorbikes only—rated blue.
2.6 ▲	SO	Small track on left is 9-12 for motorbikes only—rated blue.
▼ 1.6	BR	Two tracks on left. First is small trail 9-28 for motorbikes only—rated blue; then second track through seasonal closure gate is Trail L4 (12N21Y).
2.5 ▲	BL	Two tracks on right. First track through seasonal closure gate is Trail L4 (12N21Y); then second track is small trail 9-28 for motorbikes only—rated blue.
		GPS: N38°53.09′ W120°43.03′
▼ 2.2	SO	Track on right is Trail 9-12Y (12N20Y) for motorbikes only—rated blue. Track on left is 9-13 for motorbikes only—rated blue.
1.9 ▲	SO	Track on left is Trail 9-12Y (12N20Y) for motorbikes only—rated blue. Track on right is 9-13 for motorbikes only—rated blue.
▼ 2.4	SO	Small trail on left and right.
1.7 ▲	SO	Small trail on left and right.
▼ 3.1	SO	Cross over Al Brass Creek.
1.0 ▲	SO	Cross over Al Brass Creek.
		GPS: N38°53.86′ W120°43.11′
▼ 3.5	BR	Trail L4 on left and second small trail on left for motorbikes.
0.6 ▲	BL	Small trail on right and Trail L4 on right for motorbikes.
▼ 3.7	SO	Track on right is Trail 9-1 (12N18Y) for ATVs and motorbikes only—rated blue.
0.4 ▲	SO	Track on left is Trail 9-1 (12N18Y) for ATVs and motorbikes only—rated blue.
		GPS: N38°54.14′ W120°43.44′
▼ 3.8	SO	Cross over creek.
0.3 ▲	SO	Cross over creek.
▼ 4.1	BL	Track on right is 12N79, signposted to Quintette. Zero trip meter.
0.0 ▲		Continue to the south.
		GPS: N38°54.33′ W120°43.51′
▼ 0.0		Continue to the northwest.
3.7 ▲	BR	Track on left is 12N79, signposted to Quintette. Zero trip meter.

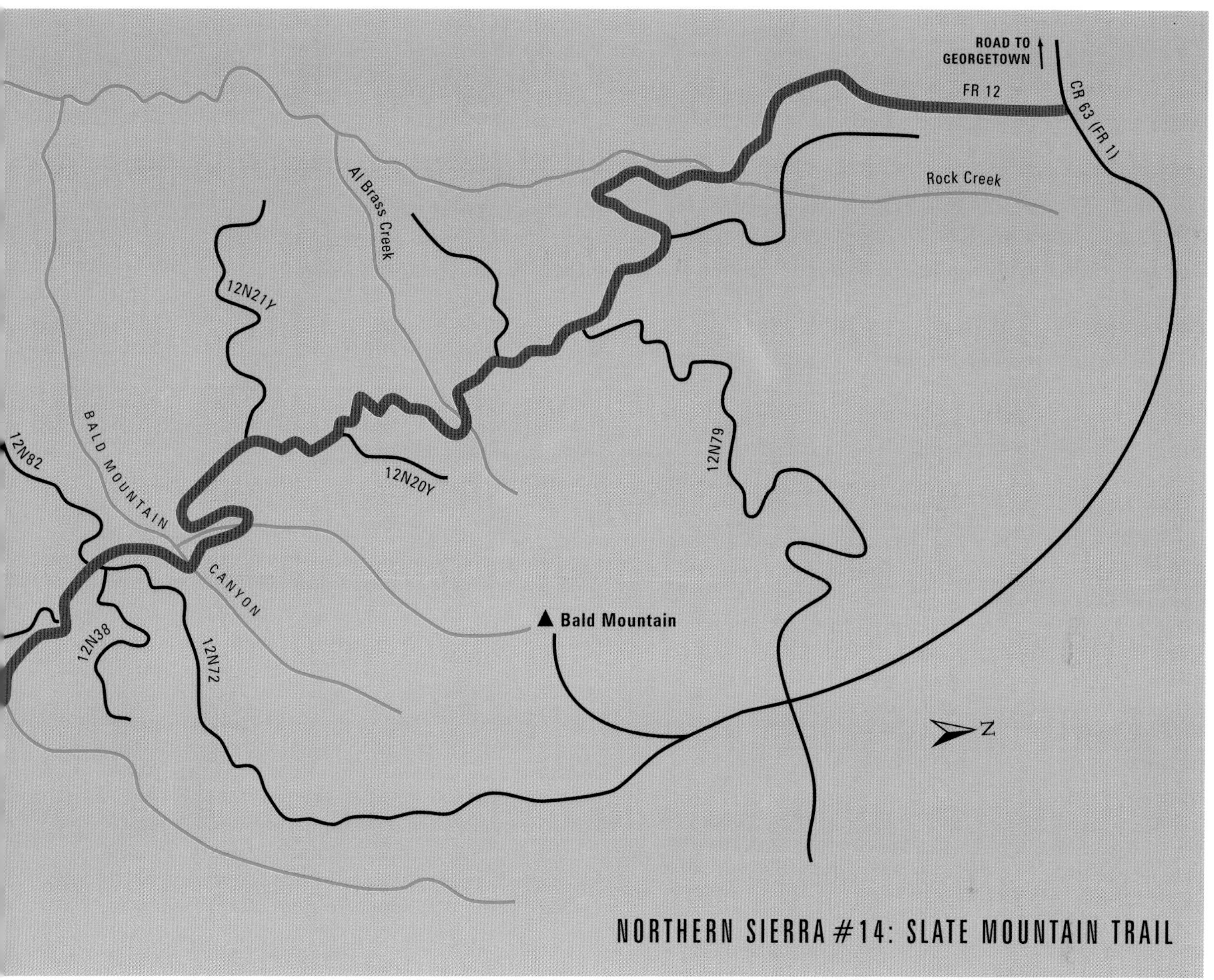

▼ 0.1		SO	Track on left is Trail 4 (also 9-15)—rated green. Track on right is Trail 9-16 for ATVs and motorbikes—rated green.
	3.6 ▲	SO	Track on right is Trail 4 (also 9-15)—rated green. Track on left is Trail 9-16 for ATVs and motorbikes—rated green.
▼ 0.3		SO	Track on left is Trail 9-15 for motorbikes—rated green; then second track on left is Trail 9-15 for motorbikes—rated black; then third track on left is 12N701 for ATVs and motorbikes. Track on right is 9-18-19 for motorbikes—rated blue.
	3.4 ▲	SO	Track on left is 9-18-19 for motorbikes—rated blue. Track on right is 12N701 for ATVs and motorbikes; then second track on right is Trail 9-15 for motorbikes—rated black; then third track on right is Trail 9-15 for motorbikes—rated green.
▼ 0.7		SO	Track on right through fence line is 9-18-19 for motorbikes—rated blue.
	3.0 ▲	SO	Track on left through fence line is 9-18-19 for motorbikes—rated blue.
▼ 1.8		SO	Cross over Rock Creek; then trail on left is Trail 9-21 for motorbikes and horses—rated blue.
	1.9 ▲	SO	Trail on right is Trail 9-21 for motorbikes and horses—rated blue; then cross over Rock Creek.
			GPS: N38°54.85' W120°44.26'
▼ 2.0		SO	Cross over Rock Creek; then track on right is 9-16 for motorbikes and horses—rated blue. Street-legal vehicles only past this point.
	1.7 ▲	SO	Track on left is 9-16 for motorbikes and horses—rated blue; then cross over Rock Creek. Green-sticker vehicles permitted past this point.
▼ 3.0		SO	Track on left is 12N70T and track on right. Exiting Eldorado National Forest on paved road. Remain on paved road, ignoring private roads and driveways to the left and right for the next 0.7 miles.
	0.7 ▲	SO	Entering Eldorado National Forest on paved road. Track on right is 12N70T and track on left.
▼ 3.7			Trail ends at T-intersection with paved CR 63 (FR 1). Turn left for Georgetown; turn right for Quintette.
	0.0 ▲		Trail commences at the intersection of paved CR 63 (FR 1) and FR 12, 6.4 miles east of Georgetown and 0.1 miles southwest of county mile marker 6.5. Zero trip meter and turn south on paved Rock Creek Road at the sign for FR 12 and marker 4 on the Georgetown District History Tour.
			GPS: N38°56.18' W120°44.55'

NORTHERN SIERRA #15

Pony Express Trail

Starting Point:	Ice House Road (FR 3), 3.5 miles north of US 50 and Riverton.
Finishing Point:	US 50, 0.3 miles west of Silver Fork
Total Mileage:	7.8 miles
Unpaved Mileage:	7.8 miles
Driving Time:	1 hour
Elevation Range:	4,000–4,800 feet
Usually Open:	April to November
Best Time to Travel:	Dry weather
Difficulty Rating:	2
Scenic Rating:	8
Remoteness Rating:	+0

Special Attractions

- Short easygoing trail that travels high above the South Fork of the American River.
- Pleasant detour to a trip along US 50.
- Trail travels part of the historic Pony Express route.

History

Traveling sections of the Pony Express Trail is a less hurried experience for today's traveler when compared with the speed of fearless Pony Express riders delivering mail. The Pony Express was an ambitious effort to develop communication between the East and West, an achievement that helped open up the West. The Pony Express (see page 69) operated between April 1860 and November 1861, and it successfully achieved its objective to deliver mail between St. Joseph, Missouri, and San Francisco. St. Joseph was linked to the telegraph system and could therefore easily communicate with Washington, D.C. Before the Pony Express, it could take as long as a month for mail to reach California by ship from New York.

Eastern end of the Pony Express Trail

Pony Express Trail is marked "XP"

What now seems like tame country along the American River was a wild mountain canyon in 1860. Riverton, just east of the start of this trail, was called Moore's Station in the mid nineteenth century. John M. Moore, a former member of the San Francisco Vigilance Committee, built and operated an outpost along a toll road here. The Pioneer Stage Company had a stage stop here in the 1850s and 1860s. Coming from the west, this was the first place to change weary horses after Sportsman Hall, or the Twelve-Mile House as it was known, in Pollock Pines. Moore's Station was also a remount station for Pony Express riders, their first stop after the Sportsman Hall as well.

In 1864, Wells Fargo expanded service to transport thousands of Comstock-bound Californians over the Sierra Nevada to Virginia City, Nevada. In doing so, the company bought out the Pioneer Stage Company and took over this vital stagecoach and freight route.

Another remount station for Pony Express riders was at Kyburz, at the eastern end of the trail. Webster's Station, as it was known, was located at Webster's Sugar Loaf House, so named because it was set at the base of a natural sugarloaf shaped mountain. The route of the Pony Express is now a National Historic Trail.

In the late 1850s, stage stations saw additional traffic from the construction of water ditches in the region. The very even grade of the Eldorado Water Ditch can still be seen on the far side of the deep canyon. The intake for this old ditch is on the South Fork of the American River, just below the eastern end of this trail where it rejoins US 50. Water was channeled through ditches, tunnels, flumes, and the Pollock Pines Forebay before dropping 1,900 feet through a penstock to drive the Pelton waterwheels of the El Dorado Powerhouse, northeast of Pollock Pines. In 1997, heavy rains caused a major landslide on the far side of the canyon, taking out a section of the Eldorado Water Ditch. A decision was made to abandon this section of the grade; a 1.8-mile-long tunnel now connects the ditch between Mill and Bull Creeks.

Description

This short trail makes for a pleasant detour from US 50 or is a lovely destination in its own right. Paved Ice House Road is well marked from US 50 at Riverton and swiftly climbs onto Peavine Ridge. A forest service information booth is passed after 2.8 miles, and the trail commences 0.7 miles after that. The graded road heads southeast from a turnout and travels slightly downhill, wrapping around the hillsides.

Initially the hills are open. The area was burned in the Cleveland Wildfire of 1992 and is still recovering. The trail provides excellent views over the South Fork of the American River, 1,200 feet below, as well as the small settlement of White Hall.

Little remains at the Weber Mill site; the most visible remnant is a loading ramp. The trail enters the forest before descending to finish on US 50. Shortly before finishing, it crosses the original route of the Pony Express Trail, which is now a hiking trail.

Current Road Information
Eldorado National Forest
Pacific Ranger District
7887 Highway 50
Pollock Pines, CA 95726
(530) 644-2349

Map References
BLM Placerville
USFS Eldorado National Forest
USGS 1:24,000 Riverton, Kyburz
1:100,000 Placerville
Maptech CD-ROM: High Sierra/Tahoe
Northern California Atlas & Gazetteer, p. 89
California Road & Recreation Atlas, p. 66 (incomplete)

Route Directions

▼ 0.0		Trail commences on Ice House Road, 3.5 miles north of US 50 and Riverton. Ice House Road intersects with US 50, 2.5 miles west of White Hall. Zero trip meter 0.7 miles north of Cleveland Corral USFS Information Center and turn southeast down graded dirt road signposted Weber Mill Road (11N38). Pass through seasonal closure gate. Start of shelf road.
4.6 ▲		Seasonal closure gate; then trail ends at T-intersection with paved Ice House Road. Turn left for US 50 and Pollock Pines; turn right for Ice House Reservoir.
		GPS: N38°47.11' W120°25.14'
▼ 0.4	SO	Turnout on right.
4.2 ▲	SO	Turnout on left.
▼ 1.7	SO	Cross over creek.
2.9 ▲	SO	Cross over creek.
▼ 1.8	BL	Track on right through seasonal closure gate.
2.8 ▲	SO	Track on left through seasonal closure gate.
		GPS: N38°47.05' W120°23.68'
▼ 2.0	SO	Track on right through seasonal closure gate is 11N.
2.6 ▲	SO	Track on left through seasonal closure gate is 11N.
▼ 2.6	SO	Track on right.
2.0 ▲	SO	Track on left.
▼ 3.1	SO	Track on left is 11N38E.
1.5 ▲	SO	Track on right is 11N38E.
		GPS: N38°46.90' W120°22.59'
▼ 3.3	SO	Cross over creek.
1.3 ▲	SO	Cross over creek.
▼ 3.6	SO	Cross over creek.
1.0 ▲	SO	Cross over creek.
		GPS: N38°47.07' W120°22.19'

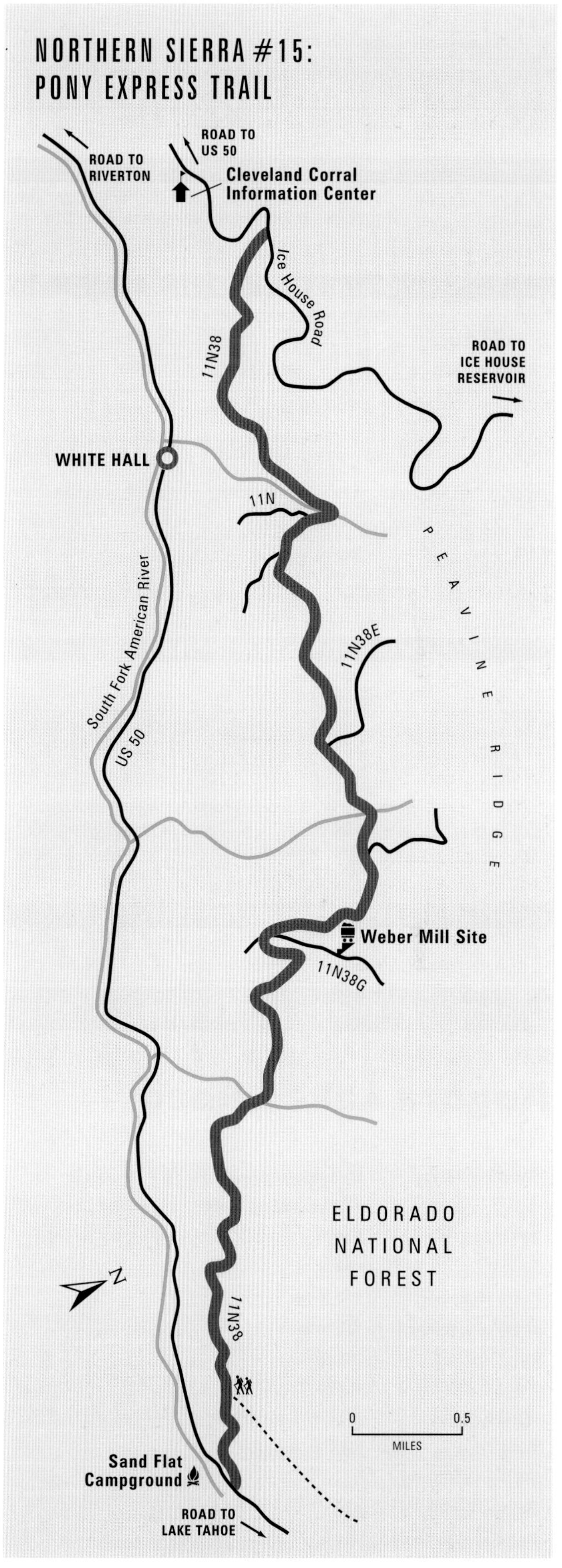

▼ 3.8		SO	Track on left.
	0.8 ▲	SO	Track on right.
▼ 4.2		SO	Track on right goes to loading ramp.
	0.4 ▲	SO	Track on left goes to loading ramp.
▼ 4.3		SO	Track on right is 11N38F.
	0.3 ▲	SO	Track on left is 11N38F.
			GPS: N38°46.74' W120°21.71'
▼ 4.6		SO	Track on left is 11N38G and unmarked track on right goes 0.1 miles to viewpoint. Zero trip meter.
	0.0 ▲		Continue to the northwest.
			GPS: N38°46.50' W120°21.71'
▼ 0.0			Continue to the northeast.
	3.2 ▲	SO	Track on right is 11N38G and unmarked track on left goes 0.1 miles to viewpoint. Zero trip meter.
▼ 0.5		SO	Track on right.
	2.7 ▲	SO	Track on left.
▼ 0.6		SO	Track on left is 11N38K.
	2.6 ▲	SO	Track on right is 11N38K.
▼ 1.0		SO	Cross over creek.
	2.2 ▲	SO	Cross over creek.
▼ 1.4		SO	Track on right.
	1.8 ▲	SO	Track on left.
▼ 2.7		SO	Pony Express Hiking Trail on left, marked XP.
	0.5 ▲	SO	Pony Express Hiking Trail on right, marked XP.
			GPS: N38°45.98' W120°19.62'
▼ 2.9		SO	Seasonal closure gate.
	0.3 ▲	SO	Seasonal closure gate.
▼ 3.2			Pass private property; then trail ends at intersection with US 50. Turn left for Lake Tahoe; turn right for Placerville.
	0.0 ▲		Trail commences on US 50, 0.2 miles east of Sand Flat USFS Campground and 0.3 miles west of Silver Fork. Zero trip meter and turn north on small formed trail marked 31 Milestone Tract (11N38) and zero trip meter. Pass through private property.
			GPS: N38°45.96' W120°19.13'

NORTHERN SIERRA #16

Angora Lakes Road

Starting Point:	**Unmarked paved road, 0.4 miles east of Fallen Leaf Road and Fallen Leaf Lake**
Finishing Point:	**Parking area, 0.7 miles north of Angora Lakes**
Total Mileage:	**2.8 miles**
Unpaved Mileage:	**1.3 miles**
Driving Time:	**30 minutes**
Elevation Range:	**6,700–7,200 feet**
Usually Open:	**May to September**
Best Time to Travel:	**May to September**
Difficulty Rating:	**1**
Scenic Rating:	**10**
Remoteness Rating:	**+0**

Special Attractions

- The historic complex of Angora Fire Lookout.
- Views of Fallen Leaf Lake and Lake Tahoe.
- Fishing, kayaking, and hiking at the scenic Angora Lakes.
- Fallen Leaf Lake and Tallac Historic Site near the start of the trail.

History

The narrow ridge top trail toward Angora Lakes and Peak offers excellent views over Fallen Leaf Lake and its lakeshore community, some 900 feet below yet only a third of a mile away as the crow flies. The panoramic views from the ridge made this a suitable spot to build a much needed fire lookout. The three small buildings along this trail provide a record of fire lookouts in the early half of the twentieth century.

The first lookout, which is still standing, was built in 1925. The Civilian Conservation Corps constructed the next lookout alongside the original 10 years later. The third structure is simply a garage. All three buildings are eligible for inclusion on the National Register of Historic Places.

The far-reaching views of Lake Tahoe can't help but make today's visitors wonder how idyllic and bountiful this mountain-ringed blue lake was for early inhabitants. Sadly, not many of these Washo people survived the influx of Euro-American settlers. The landscape the Washo knew was born out of turbulent geological times reaching back 10 million years (see Lake Tahoe, page 113). Waters once filled this massive basin to a depth several hundred feet deeper than we see today.

The Washo are possibly the oldest culture among the Sierran or Great Basin tribal groups. Their storytelling, a good indication of their background, goes no further than the region in which they lived. Their language has a somewhat distinct aspect, noticeably different from surrounding cultures. Like all native peoples, they lost out with the influx of newcomers to this magnificent region. Diseases, coupled with aggressive settlers brought about their demise. They knew Lake Tahoe as *dá'wa*, meaning "lake," which newcomers took on as Lake Tahoe. *Dá'wa* was a summer retreat for the Washo. They camped at the lakeshore, enjoying summer temperatures much more pleasant than the heat of Carson Valley, almost 2,000 feet lower. The remaining Washo still hope that one day they will once again hold the rights to their forefathers' land.

Mount Tallac rises above Fallen Leaf Lake

Description

This short easy trail is a popular trip for visitors staying near South Lake Tahoe. The graded dirt and paved road, known as Angora Ridge Road, is suitable for passenger vehicles and passes a variety of spectacular scenery. It begins near Fallen Leaf Lake and travels gradually onto Angora Ridge. The whole trail is a moderate ride for mountain bikers, who can continue along the trail to the lakes and resort.

Kayak on the lake at the foot of Angora Peak

The old Angora Fire Lookout sits on top of the ridge. The site is currently undergoing restoration. Spectacular views from the lookout include Fallen Leaf Lake, Lake Tahoe, Mount Tallac, and farther south toward Angora Peak.

The vehicle trail ends at a parking area after 2.8 miles. From here, it is a short, extremely rewarding 0.7-mile hike to Angora Lakes along the vehicle trail that serves an old resort. A full view of the first lake is reached 0.4 miles from the parking area, a view of the second at 0.7 miles.

The Angora Lakes Resort, operating since 1917, offers light refreshments and accommodations in shingle-roofed cabins. There can be a waiting list for the cabins of more than a year at times. The clear Angora Lakes are suitable for swimming and snorkeling and there is a small beach. Boat rentals are available at the lodge, which is normally open from June to September. Dogs must be kept on a leash on the entire trail and are not allowed in the lakes.

The trail borders the Desolation Wilderness, 63,960 acres of subalpine and alpine forest and glacially formed lakes. Permits are required year-round for both day and overnight use in the wilderness. Reservations are recommended.

In winter, the area around the northern end of Fallen Leaf Lake is marked for cross-country skiing. Advanced skiers can continue up Angora Lakes Road to the lookout and lakes. The road is also open to snowmobiles and snowshoers in winter. It is closed to motor vehicles until the surface dries.

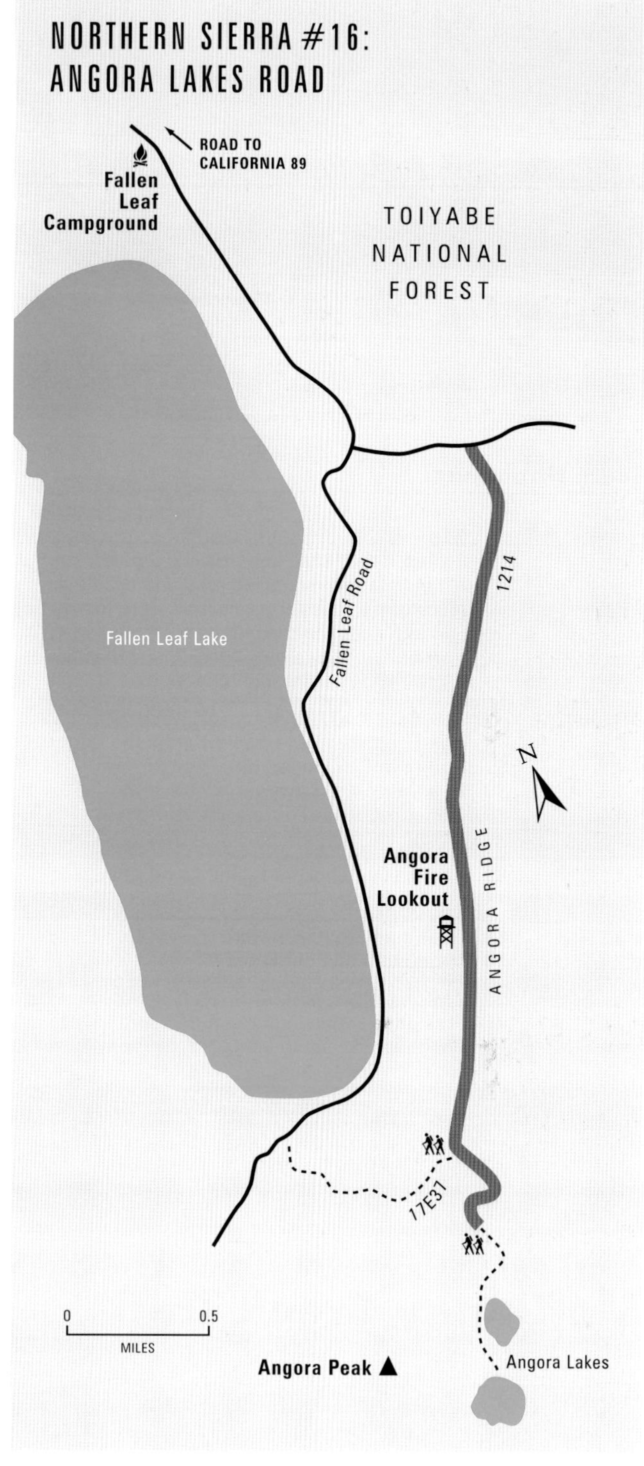

Current Road Information

Lake Tahoe Basin Management Unit
870 Emerald Bay Road, Suite #1
South Lake Tahoe, CA 96150
(530) 573-2600

Map References

BLM Placerville
USFS Toiyabe National Forest: Carson Ranger District; Eldorado National Forest
USGS 1:24,000 Emerald Bay, Echo Lake
1:100,000 Placerville

Maptech CD-ROM: High Sierra/Tahoe
Northern California Atlas & Gazetteer, p. 89
California Road & Recreation Atlas, p. 67
Trails Illustrated, Lake Tahoe, Marin County and Pt. Reyes National Seashore Bike Map (505)
Other: Fine Edge Productions—South Lake Tahoe Basin Recreation Topo Map, Tom Harrison Maps—Lake Tahoe Recreation Map, A Guide to the Desolation Wilderness

Angora Fire Lookout, constructed in 1925 and extended in 1935

Route Directions

▼ 0.0		From California 89, opposite the Tallac Historic Site and west of South Lake Tahoe, turn south on Fallen Leaf Road and proceed 2 miles. Turn left onto unmarked paved road and head 0.4 miles east to the start of the trail. Zero trip meter and turn south on graded dirt road marked 1214 (marked on Eldorado National Forest map as 12N14) and pass through closure gate.
		GPS: N38°54.21' W120°02.22'
▼ 0.6	SO	Road becomes paved as it climbs the ridge.
▼ 1.1	SO	Road turns to graded dirt.
▼ 1.3	SO	Road becomes paved.
▼ 1.4	SO	Non-motorized vehicle track on right.
		GPS: N38°53.25' W120°03.07'
▼ 1.8	SO	Angora Fire Lookout buildings on right.
		GPS: N38°52.93' W120°03.23'
▼ 2.3	SO	Road turns to graded dirt.
▼ 2.4	SO	Hiking trail on right is 17E37.
		GPS: N38°52.48' W120°03.67'
▼ 2.8		Trail ends at parking area for Angora Lakes. Park and hike south along the old vehicle trail for 0.7 miles to Angora Lakes.
		GPS: N38°52.26' W120°03.71'

NORTHERN SIERRA #17

McKinney Creek Trail

Starting Point:	California 89 in Tahoma
Finishing Point:	FR 03 at Barker Pass
Total Mileage:	11.5 miles
Unpaved Mileage:	9.1 miles
Driving Time:	3 hours
Elevation Range:	6,200–7,700 feet
Usually Open:	July to November
Best Time to Travel:	Dry weather only
Difficulty Rating:	4
Scenic Rating:	8
Remoteness Rating:	+0

Special Attractions

- Trail travels a short, easy section of the notorious Rubicon Trail.
- Access to the Pacific Crest National Scenic Trail, Tahoe Rim Trail, and Ellis Peak Trail for hikers.
- Can be combined with Northern Sierra #18: Blackwood Canyon Trail to make a loop back to California 89.

History

A wagon road called Burton Pass Road evolved from a fur trappers' and prospectors' route, bringing trade, livestock, and mining traffic through this picturesque region. Various creeks and springs near the Rubicon River, just inside El Dorado County, enhanced travel for Native Americans and settlers alike.

The eastern end of the trail follows McKinney Creek, named after John Washington McKinney, who arrived in this region in 1861 and established a hay pasture. Within two years, the cabin retreat on the shores of Lake Tahoe had already become popular with miners, hunters, and passing travelers. With time and popularity, McKinney's resort grew to include a saloon and pier, with fishing as the main attraction. John Muir was one of many who frequented McKinney's resort, relishing the majestic forests around the spectacular lake.

By the late 1860s, John and George Hunsucker, miners from the Kelsey region, had arrived on the scene and began improving the land around Rubicon Springs. They ran stock and bottled spring water for distribution to local mining communities. The quality of the water drew many travelers to its source. One such person, Mrs. S. P. Clark, bought land around the springs and turned it into a successful resort, which, by the late 1880s, was complete with a two-story hotel. Her fine furnishings, silverware, and high-quality food attracted many visitors, who traveled to the resort via the rough Burton Pass Road, which by that time had gained recognition as a public thoroughfare.

Sadly, the Rubicon Springs Hotel and outbuildings received a thorough lashing from the flash floods of 1908. The resort continued to operate, changing ownership and gaining and losing popularity with time. In the 1920s, the resort was having a tough time making ends meet. It was finally sold off to the Sierra Power Company in 1930. The hotel lasted until 1953, when the weight of winter snows destroyed what had been referred to as The Fountain of Youth Resort.

The lakeshore town of Tahoma, at the trail's start, was named after a hotel built by Joseph Bishop of San Francisco in 1916. Bishop seemingly played upon the combination of the words Tahoe and home, coming up with Tahoma. His well-appointed lakeside hotel enjoyed enormous popularity during the 1920s, boasting a swimming pool that stretched into the lake, a dance hall, and a dining room.

Description

McKinney Creek Trail follows a short section of the infamous Rubicon Trail (see page 67), a hardcore jeep trail for modified vehicles, before heading north to Barker Pass.

The trail leaves from the edge of Tahoma along a small paved road, following signs to the Rubicon OHV Trailhead. Past the trailhead, it becomes a rough dirt trail that has been stabilized with loose crushed rock to help minimize damage to the meadows and marshes. Please do not travel this trail in wet weather. Avoiding the trail when wet will minimize damage and help keep this historic route open.

Along McKinney Creek, the trail is loose in places with a few embedded rocks. The Sierra Nevada fault, a major California fault line, crosses the trail near Lake Tahoe.

The trail passes several lakes: The first two, McKinney Lake and Lily Lake, are covered with water lilies; the third, Miller Lake, is open water. The lakes were formed when eastbound glaciers dropped moraine, forming natural dams. A few campsites can be found near the lakes.

The trail forks after 5.8 miles. The Rubicon Trail continues to the left on its long journey to Georgetown. A short distance past the intersection, the Rubicon starts to show its colors and becomes 7-rated as it crawls over large boulders. The Rubicon Trail in its entirety is not suitable for stock vehicles. The main trail turns right at this intersection and follows a roughly graded road, climbing toward Barker Pass. The trail passes Bear Lake, which is set below the trail, and the rock bowl of Cothrin Cove. The final part of the route leaves the graded road and winds along the uneven Barker Meadow OHV Trail, passing beside Barker Meadow.

The trail comes to an end at a Pacific Crest National Scenic Trailhead at Barker Pass. The more difficult Northern Sierra #18: Blackwood Canyon Trail leaves from Barker Pass and can be combined with McKinney Creek Trail to make a loop back to California 89. For a more direct way back to the highway, turn right on Barker Pass Road (FR 03), which quickly becomes paved and drops swiftly to join California 89.

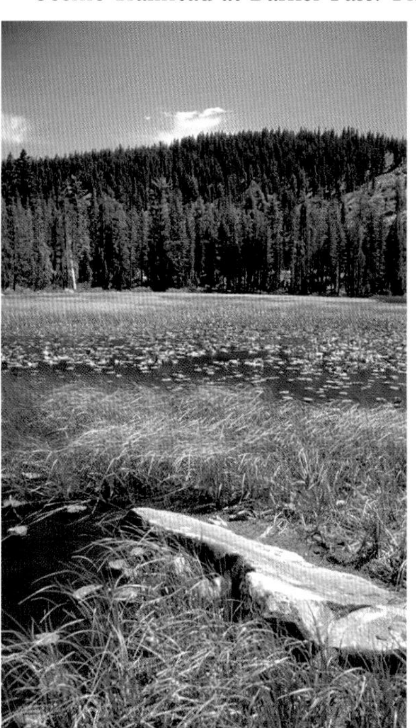

Lily Lake

At Barker Pass, a segment of the Tahoe Rim Trail and the Pacific Crest National Scenic Trail run concurrently. The TRT is a 150-mile loop around the Tahoe Basin open to hikers and equestrians and in some places to mountain bikers. In addition, the Ellis Peak Trail, a short moderate trail that climbs several switchbacks to Ellis Peak, leaves from the south side of the road, opposite the Pacific Crest National Scenic Trailhead.

In winter, most of this route is a cross-country ski trail. Snowmobilers also use some parts of it. A county ordinance closes the trail the last weekend in July and the first weekend in August each year for the annual Jeepers Jamboree. This organized trail run attracts hundreds of four-wheelers from all over the country.

Cothrin Cove sits below the trail to Barker Pass

Current Road Information

Lake Tahoe Basin Management Unit
870 Emerald Bay Road, Suite #1
South Lake Tahoe, CA 96150
(530) 573-2600

Tahoe National Forest
Truckee Ranger District
10342 Highway 89 North
Truckee, CA 96162
(530) 587-3558

Map References

BLM Truckee
USFS Eldorado National Forest; Tahoe National Forest
USGS 1:24,000 Homewood, Wentworth Springs
1:100,000 Truckee
Maptech CD-ROM: High Sierra/Tahoe
Northern California Atlas & Gazetteer, p. 81
California Road & Recreation Atlas, p. 66 (incomplete)
Trails Illustrated, Lake Tahoe, Marin County and Pt. Reyes National Seashore Bike Map (505)
Other: Fine Edge Productions—North Lake Tahoe Basin Recreation Topo Map, Fine Edge Productions—South Lake Tahoe Basin Recreation Topo Map (incomplete), Tom Harrison Maps—Lake Tahoe Recreation Map, A Guide to the Desolation Wilderness (incomplete)

Route Directions

▼ 0.0		From California 89, on the western shore of Lake Tahoe in Tahoma, zero trip meter and turn south on paved McKinney Rubicon Springs Road, following sign for OHV Access.
2.4 ▲		Trail ends at T-intersection with California 89 in Tahoma. Turn right for South Lake Tahoe; turn left for Tahoe City.
		GPS: N39°04.23′ W120°08.36′
▼ 0.3	TL	Turn left onto paved road following sign for Miller Lake Access and the Rubicon Trail.
2.1 ▲	TR	Turn right onto paved McKinney Rubicon

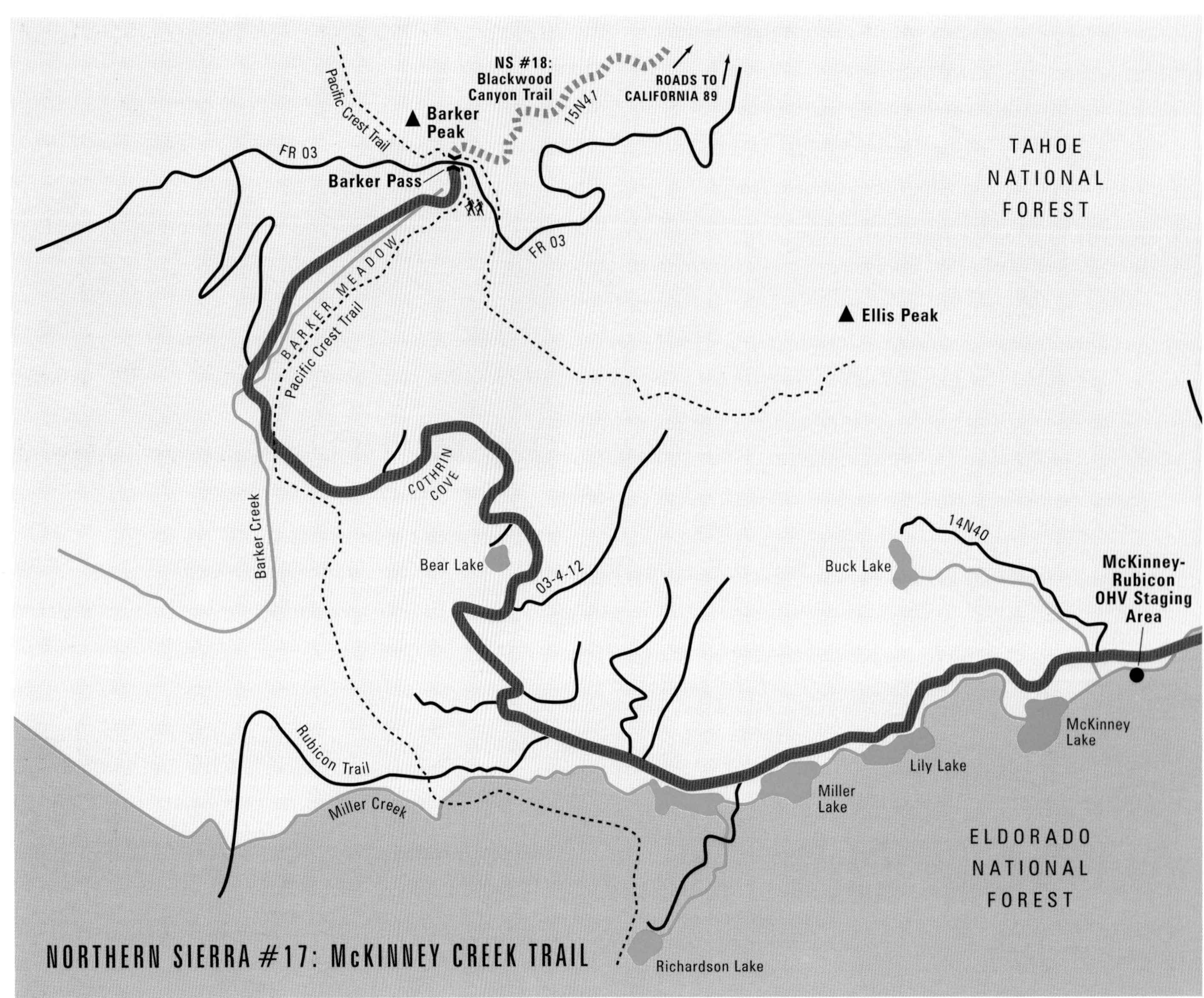

NORTHERN SIERRA #17: McKINNEY CREEK TRAIL

Mileage		Direction	Description
			Springs Road, following the sign for California 89.
▼ 0.5		TR	T-intersection. Turn right onto McKinney Road, following the sign for Miller Lake. Road becomes Springs Court.
	1.9 ▲	TL	Road becomes McKinney Road; then turn left onto Bellevue Avenue.
▼ 0.7		BL	Road on right. Bear left onto McKinney Rubicon Road, following sign for the Rubicon Trail
	1.7 ▲	BR	Road on left. Bear right onto Springs Court, following the sign for California 89.
▼ 0.8		SO	4-way intersection. Follow signs to the McKinney-Rubicon Staging Area.
	1.6 ▲	SO	4-way intersection.
			GPS: N39°03.74′ W120°08.75′
▼ 1.1		SO	Parking area on right.
	1.3 ▲	SO	Parking area on left.
▼ 1.5		SO	Track on right is 14N54.
	0.9 ▲	SO	Track on left is 14N54.
▼ 2.3		SO	Cross over McKinney Creek.
	0.1 ▲	SO	Cross over McKinney Creek.
▼ 2.4		SO	McKinney-Rubicon OHV Staging Area. Road is now a rough formed trail. Zero trip meter.
	0.0 ▲		Continue to the northeast.
			GPS: N39°02.76′ W120°10.03′
▼ 0.0			Continue to the southwest.
	3.4 ▲	SO	McKinney-Rubicon OHV Staging Area. Road is now paved. Zero trip meter.
▼ 0.2		SO	Track on right is 14N40, which goes to Buck Lake.
	3.2 ▲	SO	Track on left is 14N40, which goes to Buck Lake.
			GPS: N39°02.74′ W120°10.30′
▼ 0.4		SO	Cross through wash.
	3.0 ▲	SO	Cross through wash.
▼ 0.6		SO	McKinney Lake below road on the left.
	2.8 ▲	SO	McKinney Lake below road on the right.
			GPS: N39°02.60′ W120°10.62′
▼ 0.8		SO	Track on right.
	2.6 ▲	SO	Track on left.
▼ 1.5		SO	Lily Lake on left.
	1.9 ▲	SO	Lily Lake on right.
			GPS: N39°02.40′ W120°11.29′

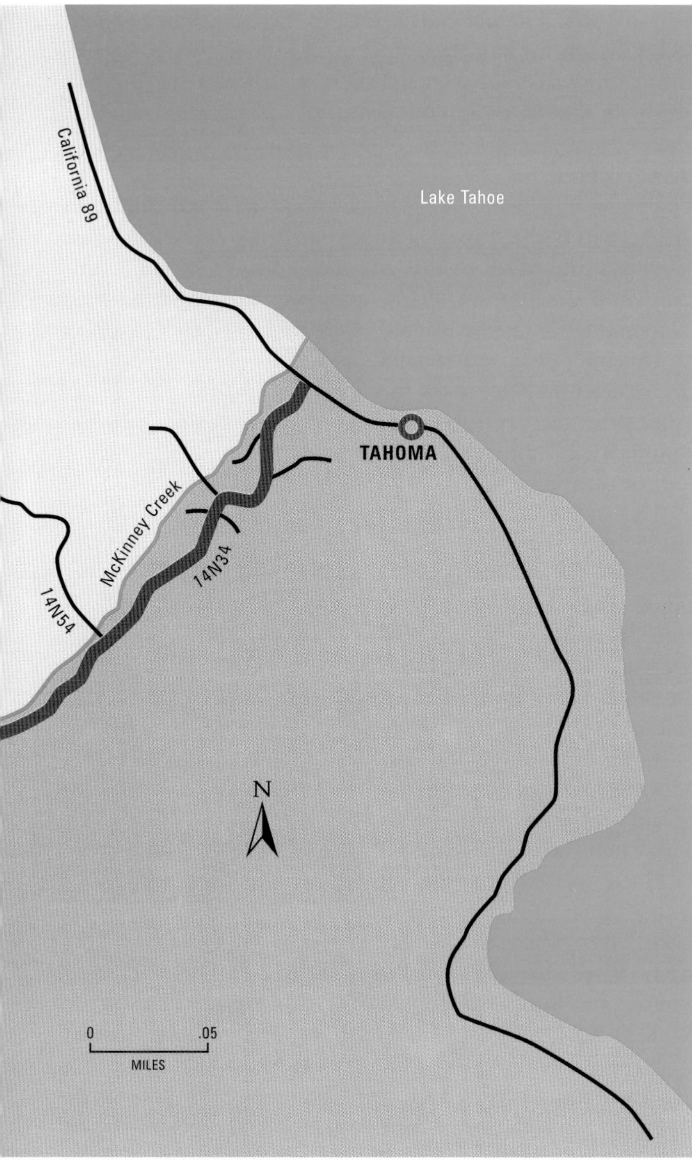

▼ 2.0		SO	Two tracks on left to campsites along Miller Lake.
	1.4 ▲	SO	Two tracks on right to campsites along Miller Lake.
▼ 2.1		SO	Miller Lake on left.
	1.3 ▲	SO	Miller Lake on right.
			GPS: N39°02.22' W120°11.94'
▼ 2.4		SO	Track on left to Richardson Lake.
	1.0 ▲	SO	Track on right to Richardson Lake.
▼ 2.6		SO	Lake on left.
	0.8 ▲	SO	Lake on right.
▼ 2.9		SO	Track on right; then cross through creek; then second track on right is OHV route for 4WDs, ATVs, and motorbikes.
	0.5 ▲	SO	Track on left is OHV route for 4WDs, ATVs, and motorbikes; then cross through creek; then second track on left.
			GPS: N39°02.18' W120°12.82'
▼ 3.0		SO	Cross over two concrete fords.
	0.4 ▲	SO	Cross over two concrete fords.
▼ 3.4		BR	Rubicon Trail continues to the left. Follow sign for Barker Pass. Zero trip meter.
	0.0 ▲		Continue to the east.
			GPS: N39°02.24' W120°13.29'
▼ 0.0			Continue to the west and pass through seasonal closure gate.
	4.0 ▲	SO	Seasonal closure gate; then track on right is the Rubicon Trail. Zero trip meter and join the Rubicon Trail, following sign for California 89 and Tahoe City.
▼ 0.3		SO	Track on left.
	3.7 ▲	SO	Track on right.
▼ 0.4		BL	Track on right.
	3.6 ▲	BR	Track on left.
▼ 1.2		BL	Track on right is 03-4-12 for 4WDs, ATVs, and motorbikes.
	2.8 ▲	BR	Track on left is 03-4-12 for 4WDs, ATVs, and motorbikes.
			GPS: N39°02.75' W120°13.56'
▼ 1.4		SO	Bear Lake below trail on the left.
	2.6 ▲	SO	Bear Lake below trail on the right.
			GPS: N39°02.87' W120°13.51'
▼ 1.8		SO	Track on left to Bear Lake and track on right.
	2.2 ▲	SO	Track on right to Bear Lake and track on left.
▼ 3.1		SO	Track on right.
	0.9 ▲	SO	Track on left.
▼ 3.6		SO	Track on left is OHV route.
	0.4 ▲	SO	Track on right is OHV route.
▼ 4.0		TR	Cross over Barker Creek; then track on left. Turn right onto small trail marked as an OHV Route and zero trip meter. This is the Barker Meadow OHV Trail.
	0.0 ▲		Continue to the east and cross over Barker Creek.
			GPS: N39°03.55' W120°15.07'
▼ 0.0			Continue to the north.
	1.7 ▲	TL	4-way intersection with roughly graded road. Track straight ahead. Zero trip meter.
▼ 0.7		SO	Cross through wash; then cross through creek; then track on right.
	1.0 ▲	SO	Track on left; then cross through creek; then cross through wash.
▼ 0.9		SO	Track on left; then cross through wash.
	0.8 ▲	SO	Cross through wash; then track on right.
▼ 1.1		SO	Cross through wash.
	0.6 ▲	SO	Cross through wash.
▼ 1.4		SO	Cross through wash.
	0.3 ▲	SO	Cross through wash.
▼ 1.5		SO	Track on right is a dead end.
	0.2 ▲	BR	Track on left is dead end. Bear right onto Barker Meadow OHV Trail.
▼ 1.7			Trail ends at 4-way intersection with graded Barker Pass Road (FR 03) at Barker Pass, opposite the Pacific Crest National Scenic Trailhead and the start of Northern Sierra #18: Blackwood Canyon Trail. Trailhead parking and picnic area at intersection. Turn right to exit to California 89. Continue straight ahead to exit to California 89 via the more difficult Blackwood Canyon Trail.
	0.0 ▲		Trail commences on graded Barker Pass Road (FR 03) at Barker Pass, 7.2 miles southwest of California 89. The Pacific Crest National Scenic Trailhead and the start of Northern Sierra #18: Blackwood Canyon Trail is opposite. Trailhead parking and picnic area at intersection. Zero trip meter and turn southeast on small formed trail, which is the start of the Barker Meadow OHV Trail.
			GPS: N39°04.60' W120°14.07'

NORTHERN SIERRA #18

Blackwood Canyon Trail

Starting Point:	**Barker Pass Road (FR 03), 2.2 miles west of California 89 and Idlewild**
Finishing Point:	**Barker Pass Road (FR 03), opposite Northern Sierra #17: McKinney Creek Trail**
Total Mileage:	**3.6 miles**
Unpaved Mileage:	**3.6 miles**
Driving Time:	**45 minutes**
Elevation Range:	**6,400–7,700 feet**
Usually Open:	**July to October**
Best Time to Travel:	**Dry weather**
Difficulty Rating:	**5**
Scenic Rating:	**8**
Remoteness Rating:	**+0**

Special Attractions

- Views of Blackwood Canyon and Lake Tahoe.
- Moderately challenging trail for compact and subcompact high-clearance 4WDs.
- Can be combined with Northern Sierra #17: McKinney Creek Trail to make a loop back to California 89.

History

Blackwood Canyon Trail reaches its highest point (7,610 feet) when it crests Barker Pass, just below a peak of the same name. In the nineteenth century, William A. Barker ran stock in the meadows south of the pass.

Looking back from the pass, the trail zigzags down a steep ridge to run alongside Blackwood Creek, 1,300 feet below. The creek is named for Hampton C. Blackwood, who settled here in 1866. Another early arrival to the Lake Tahoe region, Jock Ellis left his name attached to Ellis Peak, the tall mountain to the east. Ellis owned a dairy and later a sheep ranch nearby in the late nineteenth century.

Blackwood Canyon Trail at Barker Pass

Description

This short trail begins along Blackwood Creek and climbs up the ridge to Barker Pass. The route parallels paved Barker Pass Road, but the paved road is not visible from the trail. Compact and subcompact, high-clearance 4WDs are best suited for this trail; extra wide or full size vehicles may not make the squeeze between two trees encountered 2.6 miles from the start of the trail.

Distant view of Lake Tahoe

The trail gets its difficulty rating from the long, moderately steep, loose climb up a single vehicle width trail. A few embedded rocks must be negotiated along the trail. The hardest pinch is the final 50 yards before the top of the climb. However, a stock, high-clearance 4WD in low range should be able to negotiate the rocks with careful wheel placement.

Good views over Blackwood Canyon and a glimpse of Lake Tahoe make this a very scenic drive. The trail finishes at the Pacific Crest National Scenic Trailhead on Barker Pass. Northern Sierra #17: McKinney Creek Trail heads south from Barker Pass; the two trails can be combined for a longer loop back to California 89.

In winter, Blackwood Canyon Trail is used by cross-country skiers and snowmobilers. Avalanches are possible after snowstorms, and the trail is not marked for winter use.

Current Road Information

Lake Tahoe Basin Management Unit
870 Emerald Bay Road, Suite #1
South Lake Tahoe, CA 96150
(530) 573-2600

Map References

BLM Truckee
USFS Eldorado National Forest; Tahoe National Forest
USGS 1:24,000 Homewood
1:100,000 Truckee
Maptech CD-ROM: High Sierra/Tahoe
Northern California Atlas & Gazetteer, p. 81
California Road & Recreation Atlas, p. 66 (incomplete)
Trails Illustrated, Lake Tahoe, Marin County and Pt. Reyes National Seashore Bike Map (505)
Other: Fine Edge Productions—North Lake Tahoe Basin Recreation Topo Map, Tom Harrison Maps—Lake Tahoe Recreation Map

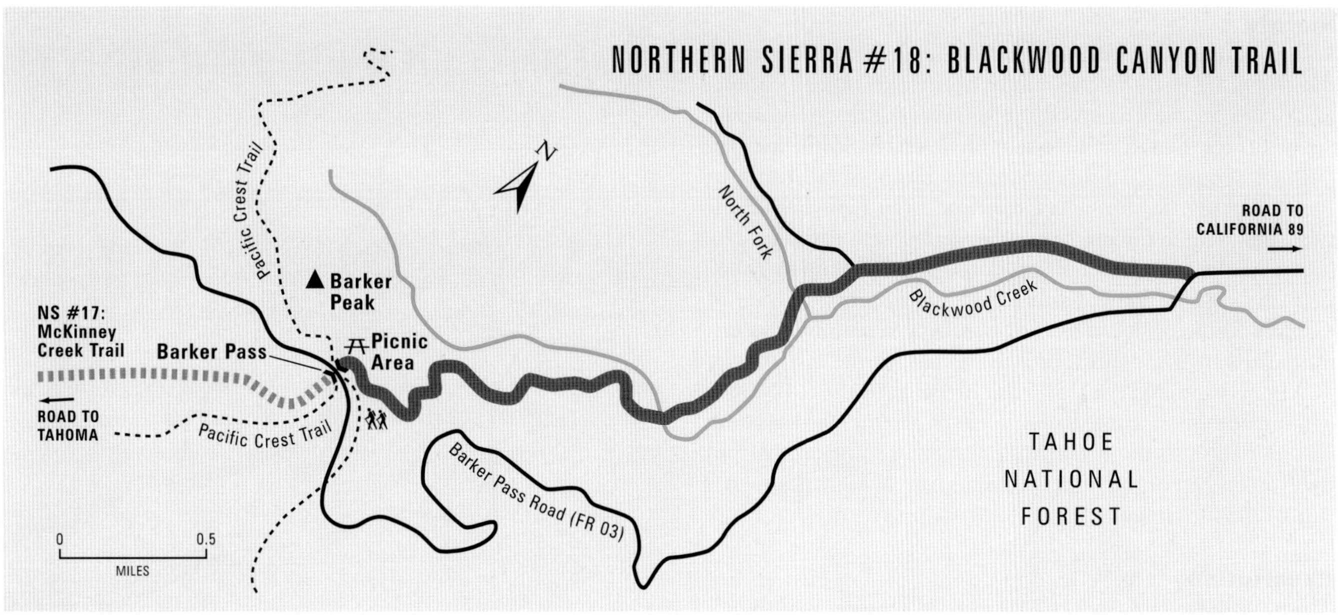

Route Directions

▼ 0.0		From Barker Pass Road (FR 03), immediately before it crosses over Blackwood Creek, 2.2 miles west of California 89 and Idlewild, zero trip meter and turn southwest on formed dirt trail, signposted to the OHV picnic and staging area.
3.6 ▲		Trail ends back on paved Barker Pass Road (FR 03). Turn left to return to California 89 and Lake Tahoe.
		GPS: N39°06.40' W120°11.74'
▼ 0.4	SO	Pass through OHV staging area. Track on right is 15N38A.
3.2 ▲	SO	Track on left is 15N38A. Pass through OHV staging area.
▼ 0.5	SO	Seasonal closure gate.
3.1 ▲	SO	Seasonal closure gate.
▼ 0.8	SO	Cross through wash.
2.8 ▲	SO	Cross through wash.
▼ 1.1	BL	Track on right.
2.5 ▲	BR	Track on left.
		GPS: N39°05.78' W120°12.74'
▼ 1.2	SO	Cross through wash.
2.4 ▲	SO	Cross through wash.
▼ 1.3	SO	Cross over North Fork Blackwood Creek.
2.3 ▲	SO	Cross over North Fork Blackwood Creek.
▼ 1.4	SO	Cross over creek.
2.2 ▲	SO	Cross over creek.
▼ 2.0	SO	Cross through creek. Trail starts to climb.
1.6 ▲	SO	End of descent. Cross through creek.
		GPS: N39°05.09' W120°12.97'
▼ 2.6	SO	Squeeze between two trees.
1.0 ▲	SO	Squeeze between two trees.
▼ 3.4	SO	Seasonal closure gate; then track on left. Trail is now graded dirt. End of climb.
0.2 ▲	SO	Trail is now a formed trail. Track on right; then seasonal closure gate. Trail starts to descend.
▼ 3.6	SO	Barker Pass. Picnic area on right and trailhead parking for the Pacific Crest and Tahoe Rim Trails. Trail ends at Barker Pass Road (FR 03). Turn left to return to California 89. Straight ahead is the start of Northern Sierra #17: McKinney Creek Trail.
0.0 ▲		Trail commences on Barker Pass Road (FR 03) at Barker Pass, 7.2 miles southwest of California 89 and Idlewild. Zero trip meter at the sign for Barker Pass and turn north on graded dirt road. Track opposite is the start of Northern Sierra #17: McKinney Creek Trail.
		GPS: N39°04.60' W120°14.07'

NORTHERN SIERRA #19

Mount Watson Trail

Starting Point:	**California 89 in Tahoe City, 0.2 miles southwest of the intersection with California 28**
Finishing Point:	**California 267, 0.4 miles south of Truckee**
Total Mileage:	**20.8 miles, plus 1.5-mile spur to Mount Watson and 0.9-mile spur to Watson Lake**
Unpaved Mileage:	**13.7 miles, plus spurs**
Driving Time:	**1.5 hours**
Elevation Range:	**5,900–8,200 feet**
Usually Open:	**July to October**
Best Time to Travel:	**Dry weather**
Difficulty Rating:	**3**
Scenic Rating:	**8**
Remoteness Rating:	**+0**

Special Attractions

- Watson Lake.
- Scenic route between Lake Tahoe and Truckee.
- The trail is popular with mountain bikers and intersects with many hiking trails.

History

Mount Watson Trail begins in Tahoe City at the headwaters of the Truckee River, the only outlet from Lake Tahoe. California 89 crosses the Truckee River at this point on the Virginia Street Bridge, a landmark of some renown. In 1906, the dissatisfied spouse of a leading national businessman came to Reno, Nevada, to annul her marriage. The high-profile divorce made Reno the place to get separated with panache. The final statement for such a dissolution was to travel up to Tahoe City and cast the now defunct wedding ring off the side of Virginia Street Bridge. This ring-throwing ceremony was immortalized by Marilyn Monroe in her last movie, *The Misfits.*

Mount Pluto Ski Area, 200 feet higher than the 8,424-foot Mount Watson, is immediately north of Mount Watson along this trail. The name, first mentioned in 1874, is taken from the Roman god of the underworld because of the volcanic nature of the mountain.

Description

This route, also known as the Fiberboard Freeway, mainly follows a series of developed logging roads. Most of the trail is rated a 2 for difficulty; the 3 rating comes from the section leading out of Tahoe City. This small, formed trail can be loose and steep enough to require four-wheel-drive; this section is seasonally closed to motor vehicles to protect the trail surface.

The trail winds through Tahoe National Forest, passing a mix of aspens and conifers and offering many opportunities for hiking or camping along the way. A short spur leads to a small clearing at the top of Mount Watson, which provides fantastic views of Lake Tahoe. A second short spur leads to Watson Lake, which is a good place to camp or picnic. The banks of the lake are fringed with wildflowers in spring. It is normally quiet and sees little of the crowds that visit Lake Tahoe. The Western States Trail, part of the American Discovery Trail, and the Tevis Cup Trail both follow part of the Mount Watson route along the ridge.

Past the spur to Watson Lake, the trail follows better graded roads below Sawtooth Ridge, descending gradually toward Truckee. To the west is Squaw Valley, one of the region's popular ski areas. The trail passes through subdivisions on the edge of Truckee, before ending on California 267, 0.4 miles east of the center of Truckee.

Watson Lake

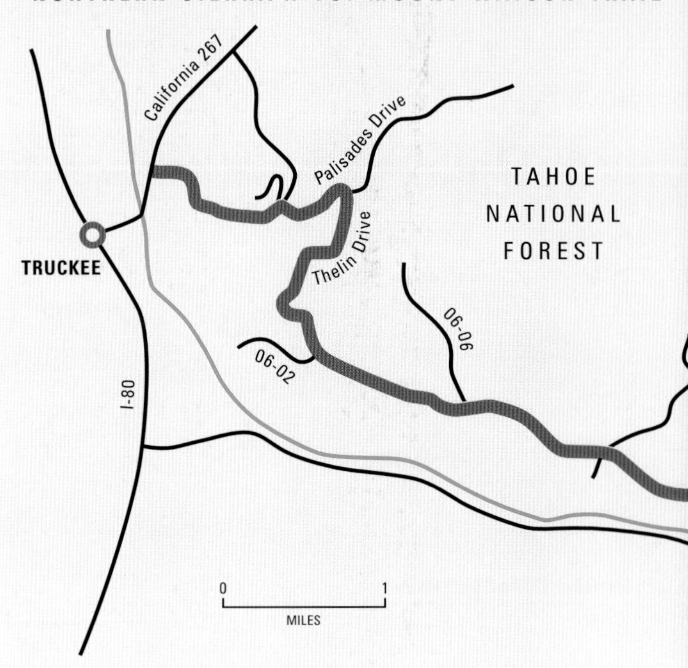

The trail is popular with mountain bikers, for whom it is a moderate ride with some long climbs. Other mountain bike trails intersect the main route. In winter, snowmobilers enjoy this region.

Current Road Information

Lake Tahoe Basin Management Unit
870 Emerald Bay Road, Suite #1
South Lake Tahoe, CA 96150
(530) 573-2600

Tahoe National Forest
Truckee Ranger District
10342 Highway 89 North
Truckee, CA 96162
(530) 587-3558

Map References

BLM Truckee
USFS Eldorado National Forest; Tahoe National Forest
USGS 1:24,000 Tahoe City, Truckee
1:100,000 Truckee
Maptech CD-ROM: High Sierra/Tahoe
Northern California Atlas & Gazetteer, p. 81
California Road & Recreation Atlas, p. 66
Trails Illustrated, Lake Tahoe, Marin County and Pt. Reyes National Seashore Bike Map (505)
Other: Fine Edge Productions—North Lake Tahoe Basin Recreation Topo Map, Tom Harrison Maps—Lake Tahoe Recreation Map (incomplete)

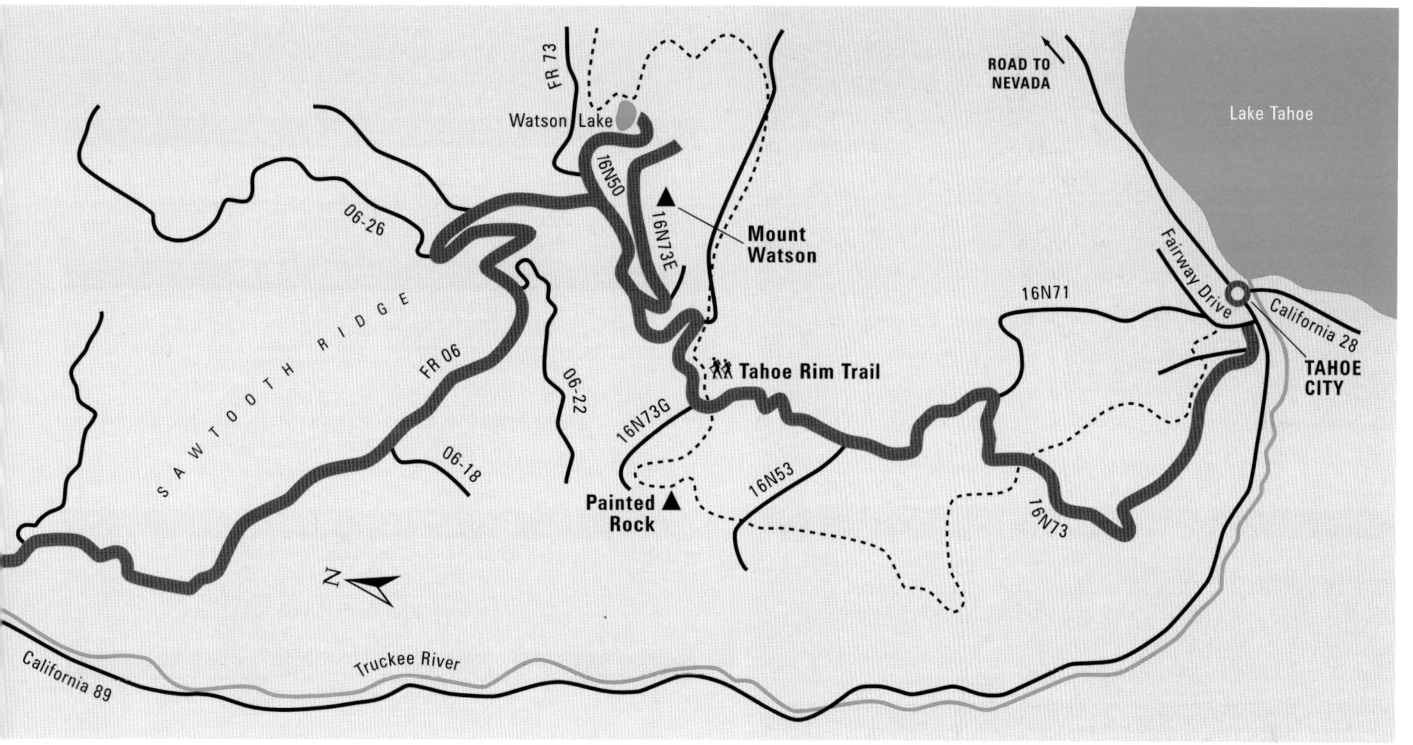

Route Directions

▼ 0.0		From California 89 in Tahoe City, 0.2 miles southwest of the intersection with California 28, zero trip meter and turn northwest on paved Fairway Drive. Proceed 0.1 miles to the start of the trail. Zero trip meter and turn west on formed dirt trail. Pass through seasonal closure gate.
4.2 ▲		Seasonal closure gate; then trail ends on paved Fairway Drive. Turn right and proceed 0.1 miles to reach California 89 in Tahoe City.
		GPS: N39°09.97' W120°08.78'
▼ 0.1	BL	Track on right is for 4WDs, ATVs, and motorbikes.
4.1 ▲	SO	Track on left is for 4WDs, ATVs, and motorbikes.
▼ 0.3	SO	Track on right.
3.9 ▲	SO	Track on left.
▼ 1.0	SO	Seasonal closure gate.
3.2 ▲	SO	Seasonal closure gate.
		GPS: N39°10.18' W120°09.70'
▼ 3.6	SO	Tahoe Rim Trail for hikers crosses.
0.6 ▲	SO	Tahoe Rim Trail for hikers crosses.
		GPS: N39°11.10' W120°09.98'
▼ 4.2	TL	Seasonal closure gate; then road becomes paved. Road on right is 16N71 for high-clearance vehicles. Zero trip meter.
0.0 ▲		Continue to the west.
		GPS: N39°11.27' W120°09.59'
▼ 0.0		Continue to the north.
3.9 ▲	TR	Road straight ahead is 16N71. Zero trip meter and turn right onto 16N73 and pass through seasonal closure gate. Road turns to graded dirt.
▼ 1.1	SO	Track on left is 16N53.
2.8 ▲	SO	Track on right is 16N53.
▼ 2.6	SO	Track on left is 16N73G.
1.3 ▲	SO	Track on right is 16N73G.
▼ 3.4	SO	Track on right is 16N73F.
0.5 ▲	SO	Track on left is 16N73F.
▼ 3.6	SO	Track on left.
0.3 ▲	SO	Track on right.
		GPS: N39°13.15' W120°09.67'
▼ 3.9	SO	Track on right is 16N73E, spur to Mount Watson. Zero trip meter.
0.0 ▲		Continue to the southwest.
		GPS: N39°13.34' W120°09.33'

Spur to Mount Watson

▼ 0.0		Proceed southeast on formed trail.
▼ 0.3	SO	Track on right.
▼ 0.4	SO	Start of shelf road.
▼ 1.2	SO	End of shelf road.
▼ 1.4	SO	Track on right.
▼ 1.5		Spur ends below Mount Watson with a view east of Lake Tahoe. A hiking trail continues to the northeast.
		GPS: N39°13.16' W120°08.25'

Continuation of Main Trail

▼ 0.0		Continue to the northeast.
0.6 ▲	BR	Track on left is 16N73E, spur to Mount Watson. Zero trip meter.
		GPS: N39°13.34' W120°09.33'
▼ 0.6	BL	Bear left onto FR 06. Road turns to graded dirt. Zero trip meter. Paved road ahead is the spur to Watson Lake.
0.0 ▲		Continue to the southwest. Road becomes paved.
		GPS: N39°13.51' W120°08.85'

Spur to Watson Lake

▼ 0.0		Proceed to the north.
▼ 0.3	TR	Turn right onto small paved road 16N50.
		GPS: N39°13.65' W120°08.67'
▼ 0.9		Road ends at Watson Lake. A spur of the Tahoe Rim Trail comes in from the southwest

The spur climbs Mount Watson

		at this point. In winter, a snowmobile route continues farther.
		GPS: N39°13.45' W120°08.21'

Continuation of Main Trail

Mileage		Directions
▼ 0.0		Continue to the northwest and pass through closure gate.
3.8 ▲	SO	Closure gate; then paved road on left is the spur to Watson Lake. Zero trip meter.
		GPS: N39°13.51' W120°08.85'
▼ 0.7	SO	Track on right is Spocket Mountain Bike Trail.
3.1 ▲	SO	Track on left is Spocket Mountain Bike Trail.
▼ 1.1	BL	Track on right is 06-26.
2.7 ▲	BR	Track on left is 06-26.
▼ 1.8	BR	Track on left is closed.
2.0 ▲	BL	Track on right is closed.
▼ 2.5	SO	Track on left is 06-22.
1.3 ▲	BL	Track on right is 06-22.
		GPS: N39°13.85' W120°09.51'
▼ 3.8	BR	Track on left is 06-18. Zero trip meter.
0.0 ▲		Continue to the southeast on FR 06.
		GPS: N39°14.39' W120°10.75'
▼ 0.0		Continue to the northwest on FR 06.
6.0 ▲	BL	Track on right is 06-18. Zero trip meter.
▼ 0.3	SO	Track on left.
5.7 ▲	SO	Track on right.
▼ 0.4	SO	Track on right.
5.6 ▲	SO	Track on left.
▼ 0.8	SO	Track on right; then track on left.
5.2 ▲	SO	Track on right; then track on left.
▼ 1.1	SO	Track on left and track on right.
4.9 ▲	SO	Track on left and track on right.
▼ 1.4	SO	Track on right.
4.6 ▲	SO	Track on left.
▼ 1.6	SO	Track on left.
4.4 ▲	SO	Track on right.
▼ 1.9	SO	Track on left.
4.1 ▲	SO	Track on right.
▼ 2.6	SO	Track on right.
3.4 ▲	SO	Track on left.
		GPS: N39°16.16' W120°11.83'
▼ 2.8	SO	Track on left; then second track on left.
3.2 ▲	SO	Track on right; then second track on right.
▼ 2.9	SO	Track on right.
3.1 ▲	SO	Track on left.
▼ 3.4	SO	Track on right.
2.6 ▲	SO	Track on left.
▼ 3.7	SO	4-way intersection. Track on left and graded road on right.
2.3 ▲	SO	4-way intersection. Track on right and graded road on left.
		GPS: N39°16.97' W120°11.86'
▼ 4.4	SO	Track on right.
1.6 ▲	SO	Track on left.
▼ 4.6	SO	Track on right is 06-06.
1.4 ▲	SO	Track on left is 06-06.
		GPS: N39°17.74' W120°11.76'
▼ 5.6	SO	Track on left is 06-02.
0.4 ▲	SO	Track on right is 06-02.
▼ 5.7	SO	Track on left. Road becomes paved.
0.3 ▲	SO	Road turns to graded dirt. Track on right.
▼ 6.0	TR	Seasonal closure gate; then turn right onto paved Thelin Drive. Zero trip meter.
0.0 ▲		Continue to the southwest and pass through seasonal closure gate.
		GPS: N39°18.81' W120°11.28'
▼ 0.0		Continue to the southeast on Thelin Drive.
2.3 ▲	TL	Turn left onto paved FR 06 and zero trip meter.
▼ 0.9	TL	T-intersection with Palisades Drive.
1.4 ▲	TR	Turn right onto Thelin Drive.
		GPS: N39°18.56' W120°10.44'
▼ 1.3	TL	4-way intersection. Turn left onto Ponderosa Drive.
1.0 ▲	TR	4-way intersection. Turn right onto Palisades Drive.
		GPS: N39°18.87' W120°10.61'
▼ 1.9	TR	Turn right onto Palisades Drive.
0.4 ▲	TL	Turn left onto Ponderosa Drive.
▼ 2.3		Trail ends on California 267. Turn left for the center of Truckee and I-80.
0.0 ▲		Trail starts on California 267, 0.4 miles south of the center of Truckee. Zero trip meter and turn south on Palisades Drive.
		GPS: N39°19.58' W120°10.58'

NORTHERN SIERRA #20

Soda Springs Road

Starting Point:	**Donner Pass Road, 0.8 miles south of I-80**
Finishing Point:	**FR 96 at the northeastern end of French Meadows Reservoir**
Total Mileage:	**26.4 miles, plus 2.1-mile spur to Snow Mountain Overlook and 1.8-mile spur to Talbot Campground**
Unpaved Mileage:	**24.3 miles, plus spurs**
Driving Time:	**4 hours**
Elevation Range:	**5,400–7,300 feet**
Usually Open:	**May to October**
Best Time to Travel:	**May to October**
Difficulty Rating:	**2 from Soda Springs to The Cedars; 3 from The Cedars to French Meadows Reservoir**
Scenic Rating:	**9**
Remoteness Rating:	**+0**

Special Attractions

- Remains of the Lost Emigrant Mine.
- Boating, angling, and camping at French Meadows Reservoir.
- Spectacular views of the Royal Gorge from several points along the trail.

History

Soda Springs, for which this trail is named, are located on the upper reaches of the North Fork of the American River, east of The Cedars community. Mark Hopkins and Leland Stanford established the summer resort in the early 1870s, calling it Hopkins Springs. Mark Hopkins and Leland Stanford were businessmen from Sacramento who, with Charles Crocker and Collis P. Huntington, made up the Big Four, financiers behind the construction of the Central Pacific Railroad. (For more on the Big Four see page 85.)

Early visitors to the springs traveled by train to what was then called Tinker's Station. From there it was a bumpy stage ride down Onion Creek to the resort. J. A. Tinker operated the freight service between Soda Springs and the various mines on Foresthill Divide. His name is also attached to a prominent landmark of Tinker Knob, set high above the old springs to the east of the trail.

The southern section of Soda Springs Road follows an early emigrant trail that developed from west to east. It roughly went up the Foresthill Divide through Robertson Flat, past the Lost Emigrant Mine to Soda Springs, before crossing sharply over the Sierra Crest to Squaw Valley.

In the 1860s, mining at the upper end of French Meadows was far from fruitful. The name Picayune Valley reflects the paltry sum extracted from the location. A picayune is a Spanish coin worth half a real, a rather small amount.

Description

The trail starts in the settlement of Soda Springs and initially travels along a paved road to Serene Lakes (shown as Ice Lakes on some maps), where it turns to graded dirt. It passes some of the groomed cross-country ski trails used by the Royal Gorge Cross Country Ski Resort in winter. The start of the trail is also near Donner Summit, a popular rock climbing area with approximately 400 routes of every skill level, including bouldering opportunities, sport routes, and multi-pitch crack climbing. Difficulties range from easy scrambles to expert routes rated as high as 5.13b.

Serena Creek cuts a deep gorge as it drops sharply to join the North Fork of the American River

The route briefly follows Serena Creek, which drops into a deep rocky gorge that feeds the North Fork of the American River. There are good views of the open forest, scattered firs, and rocky outcrops at the gorge.

Tinker Knob rises high above Soda Springs

The route passes through a lot of private property. Right of way is restricted to the county road and stopping is not encouraged, especially around The Cedars. Please respect the rights of the property owners as you pass through this vicinity and make sure you are within public lands before camping or diverging from the main trail.

After crossing the North Fork of the American River, a lumber company owns the forest, and access to side trails may be restricted at times. A worthwhile side trip is the 3-rated loop to a stunning viewpoint over Snow Peak and the North Fork of the American River through Royal Gorge.

The trail passes the southern end of the Palisade Creek Trail, which is for hikers only; equestrians are not permitted. The hiking route north from here to the North Fork of the American River is not maintained by the forest service. The northern portion of the Palisade Creek Trail is rated extremely difficult with many steep climbs. Another major hiking trail that intersects this route is the Tevis Cup Trail, which leads into the Granite Chief Wilderness.

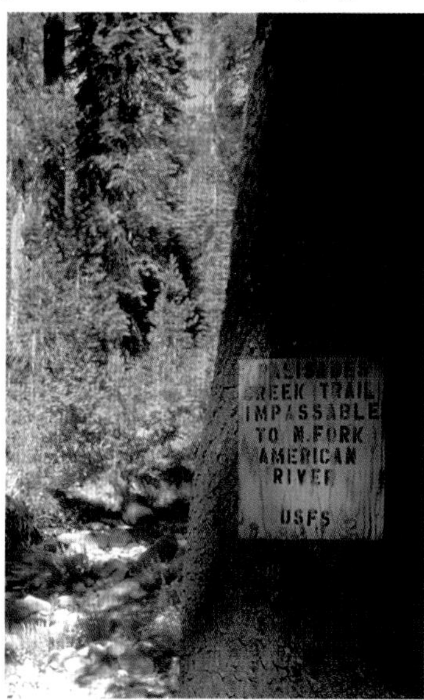

Sign at the southern end of the Palisades Creek Trail

A second worthwhile detour is a short side trail that leads to the Lost Emigrant Mine. The turn is unmarked and easy to miss. This rough 4-rated spur leads 0.4 miles down a loose, moguled hill to remains of the mine. Two old cabins, one predominately timber and the other predominantly tin, are all that remain.

The main trail, which becomes rougher than the northern section, turns off Soda Springs Road and descends to enter a state wildlife refuge. No hunting or firearms are allowed in the refuge. If you wish to transport firearms or bows through the refuge they must be unloaded, unstrung, and either dismantled or carried in a case. No camping is allowed except in designated areas.

The trail ends at the northeastern end of French Meadows Reservoir. There are three campgrounds around the lake, plus a walk-in site about a mile down the hiking trail around the north side of the lake. Because of the refuge, bears abound in the region so campers should take the necessary precautions.

The trail from the intersection of Soda Springs Road and Foresthill Road to French Meadows Reservoir is a marked snowmobile route in winter that continues to the dam at the western end of the lake, a total distance of 7.8 miles. The snowmobile trail is part of the Mosquito Ridge Trail. It intersects with the groomed Soda Springs Trail and continues toward Duncan Peak and Robinson Flat.

Current Road Information

Tahoe National Forest
Truckee Ranger District
10342 Highway 89 North
Truckee, CA 96162
(530) 587-3558

Tahoe National Forest
Foresthill Ranger District
22830 Foresthill Road
Foresthill, CA 95631
(530) 367-2226

Map References

BLM Truckee
USFS Tahoe National Forest
USGS 1:24,000 Soda Springs, Norden, Granite Chief, Royal Gorge
1:100,000 Truckee

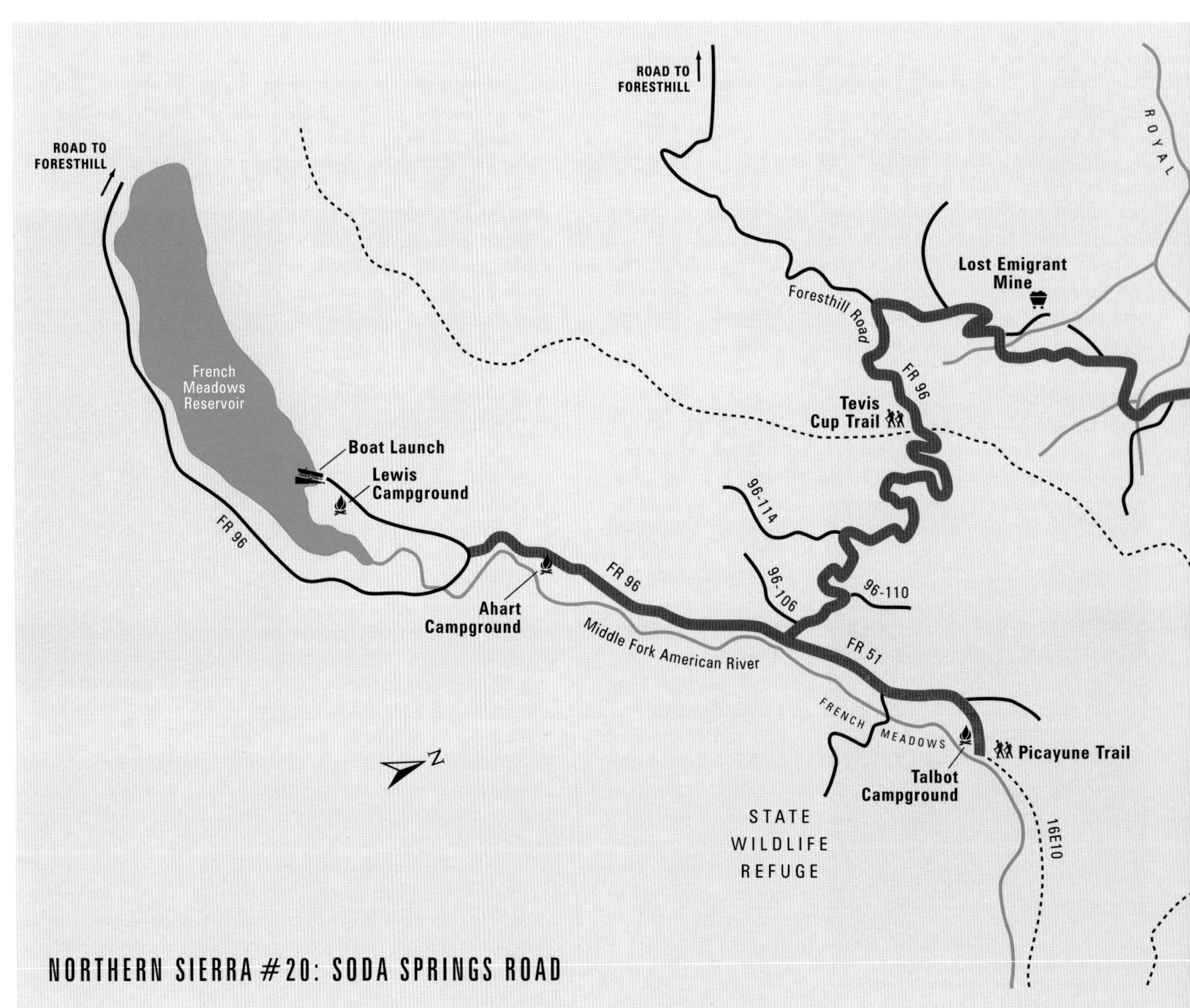

Maptech CD-ROM: High Sierra/Tahoe
Northern California Atlas & Gazetteer, p. 81
California Road & Recreation Atlas, p. 66

Route Directions

▼ 0.0		From the Soda Springs exit on I-80, zero trip meter on the south side of the freeway and proceed 0.8 miles east on Donner Pass Road. Zero trip meter and turn south on paved Soda Springs Road, following the signpost to Serene Lakes. Cross over railroad. Remain on paved road, ignoring turns to right and left for the next 2.1 miles.
6.3 ▲		Cross over railroad; then trail ends at Donner Pass Road in Soda Springs. Turn left for I-80; turn right for Norden.
		GPS: N39°19.41' W120°22.70'
▼ 0.1	SO	Soda Springs Alpine Resort on right.
6.2 ▲	SO	Soda Springs Alpine Resort on left.
▼ 0.8	SO	Royal Gorge Cross Country Ski Resort on right. Trails are privately owned and part of the resort.
5.5 ▲	SO	Royal Gorge Cross Country Ski Resort on left.
▼ 2.1	SO	Road turns to graded dirt. Serene Road and Serene Lakes on right.
4.2 ▲	SO	Road becomes paved. Serene Road and Serene Lakes on left.
		GPS: N39°17.67' W120°22.90'
▼ 2.4	SO	Three Nordic ski trails on right and one on the left.
3.9 ▲	SO	Three Nordic ski trails on left and one on the right.
▼ 2.5	SO	Leaving Royal Gorge Nordic ski track system.
3.8 ▲	SO	Entering Royal Gorge Nordic ski track system. Trails are privately owned and part of the resort.
▼ 3.3	SO	Two tracks on left. Views on right into the deep gorge of Serena Creek.
3.0 ▲	SO	Two tracks on right. Views on left into the deep gorge of Serena Creek.
▼ 4.2	SO	Track on right.
2.1 ▲	SO	Track on left.
▼ 5.9	SO	Cross over creek.

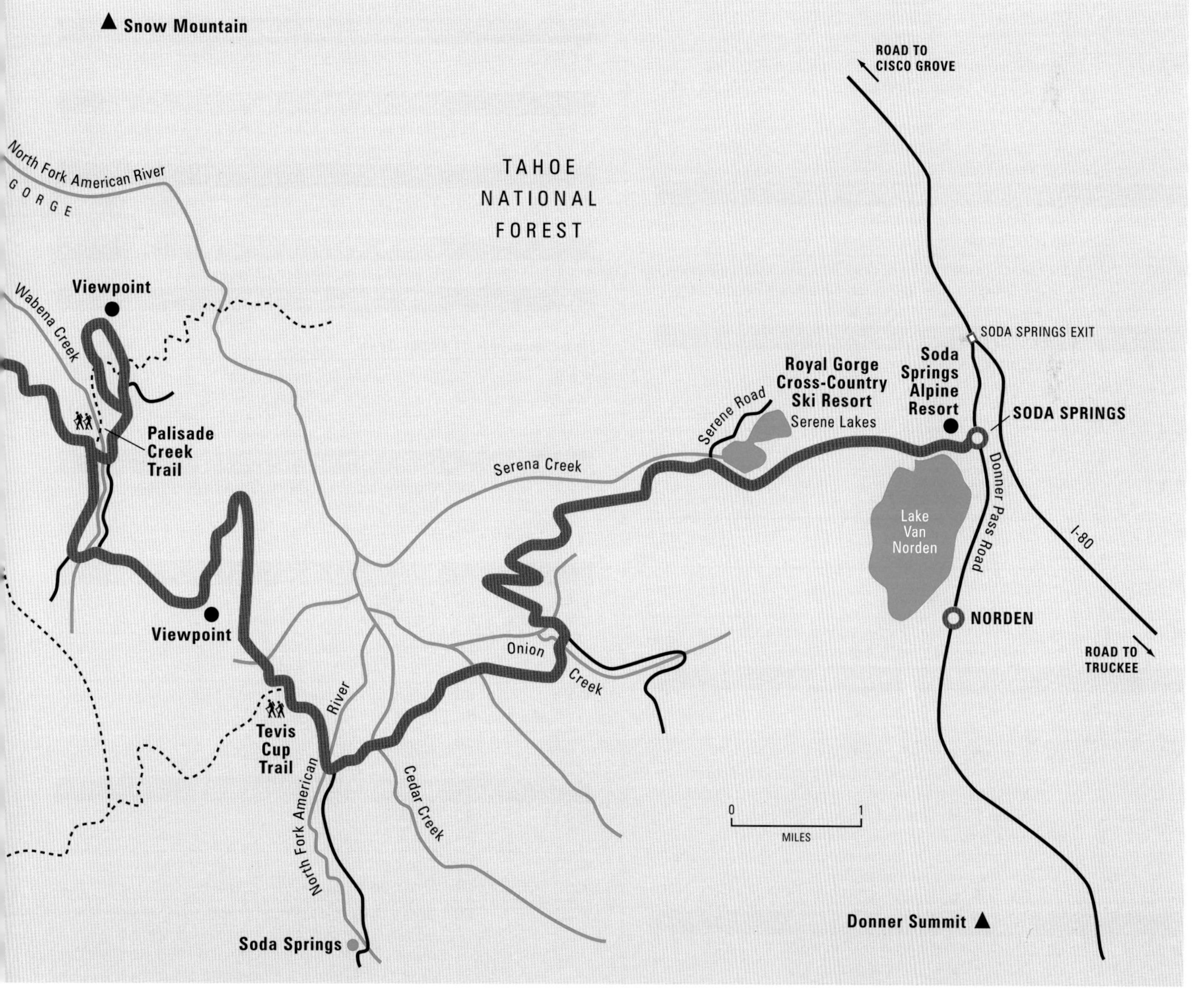

0.4 ▲	SO	Cross over creek.
▼ 6.1	SO	Well-used track on right.
0.2 ▲	SO	Well-used track on left.
▼ 6.3	SO	Track on left to Onion Creek Snow Survey Cabin and Onion Creek Experimental Forest; then track on right; then cross over Onion Creek on bridge. Zero trip meter at bridge.
0.0 ▲		Continue to the north. Track on left; then track on right to Onion Creek Snow Survey Cabin and Onion Creek Experimental Forest.
		GPS: N39°16.54' W120°21.70'
▼ 0.0		Continue to the south.
3.0 ▲	SO	Cross over Onion Creek on bridge and zero trip meter.
▼ 0.2	SO	Track on left.
2.8 ▲	SO	Track on right.
▼ 0.8	SO	Cross over creek.
2.2 ▲	SO	Cross over creek.
▼ 1.6	SO	Track on left under The Cedars archway.
1.4 ▲	SO	Track on right under The Cedars archway.
		GPS: N39°15.31' W120°21.17'
▼ 1.8	SO	Cross through Cedar Creek.
1.2 ▲	SO	Cross through Cedar Creek.
▼ 2.2	BR	Private road on left.
0.8 ▲	BL	Private road on right.
▼ 2.3	SO	Cross over North Fork American River on bridge. Soda Springs are upstream along the river.
0.7 ▲	SO	Cross over North Fork American River on bridge. Soda Springs are upstream along the river.
		GPS: N39°14.85' W120°21.08'
▼ 2.5	SO	Cross through wash.
0.5 ▲	SO	Cross through wash.
▼ 3.0	SO	Track on left is Tevis Cup Trail. Zero trip meter and follow the sign to French Meadows Reservoir.
0.0 ▲		Continue to the northeast.
		GPS: N39°14.66' W120°21.77'
▼ 0.0		Continue to the south.
4.3 ▲	SO	Track on right is Tevis Cup Trail. Zero trip meter.
▼ 0.2	SO	Track on left.
4.1 ▲	SO	Track on right.
▼ 0.3	SO	Track on right.
4.0 ▲	SO	Track on left.
▼ 0.4	SO	Cross over creek.
3.9 ▲	SO	Cross over creek.
▼ 0.5	SO	Track on left.
3.8 ▲	SO	Track on right.
▼ 1.5	BL	Track on right; then second track on right.
2.8 ▲	BR	Track on left; then second track on left.
		GPS: N39°14.58' W120°23.35'
▼ 2.1	SO	Track on right.
2.2 ▲	SO	Track on left.
▼ 2.4	SO	Viewpoint on left overlooks North Fork American River, Soda Springs, and behind them Mount Lincoln, Anderson Peak, Tinker Knob, Silver Peak, Granite Chief, and Needle Peak.
1.9 ▲	SO	Viewpoint on right overlooks North Fork American River, Soda Springs, and behind them Mount Lincoln, Anderson Peak, Tinker Knob, Silver Peak, Granite Chief, and Needle Peak.
		GPS: N39°14.23' W120°22.60'
▼ 2.6	SO	Track on left and track on right.
1.7 ▲	SO	Track on left and track on right.
▼ 2.8	SO	Track on right.
1.5 ▲	SO	Track on left.
▼ 3.4	SO	Track on left; then cross over Wabena Creek; then second track on left.
0.9 ▲	SO	Track on right; then cross over Wabena Creek; then second track on right.
		GPS: N39°13.51' W120°23.14'
▼ 3.8	SO	Track on left.
0.5 ▲	SO	Track on right.
▼ 4.3	SO	Track on right is the spur to Snow Mountain Overlook; then track on right is Palisade Creek Trail. Entering Tahoe National Forest. Zero trip meter at Palisade Creek Trail sign.
0.0 ▲		Continue to the east. Immediately track on left is the spur to Snow Mountain Overlook.
		GPS: N39°13.71' W120°23.99'

Spur to Snow Mountain Overlook

▼ 0.0		At the track a short distance east of the Palisade Creek Trail sign, zero trip meter and turn north on unmarked formed trail and cross through Wabena Creek; then track on left.
▼ 0.1	TL	Track on right.
▼ 0.25	SO	4-way intersection.
		GPS: N39°13.80' W120°23.94'
▼ 0.55	BR	Track on left is end of loop. Bear right and start loop.
		GPS: N39°13.98' W120°24.22'
▼ 0.8	TL	Track on right goes 0.5 miles to clearing and viewpoint. Palisade Creek Trail crosses.
		GPS: N39°14.00' W120°24.51'
▼ 1.4	SO	Viewpoint. To the west is Royal Gorge and Snow Mountain.
		GPS: N39°13.87' W120°25.03'
▼ 2.1		End of loop. Turn right to exit.
		GPS: N39°13.98' W120°24.22'

Continuation of Main Trail

▼ 0.0		Continue to the southwest
3.3 ▲	SO	Track on left is Palisade Creek Trail. Leaving Tahoe National Forest. Zero trip meter at Palisade Creek Trail sign.
		GPS: N39°13.71' W120°23.99'
▼ 0.7	SO	Viewpoint on right of Snow Mountain and Royal Gorge.
2.6 ▲	SO	Viewpoint on left of Snow Mountain and Royal Gorge.
		GPS: N39°13.46' W120°24.56'
▼ 1.3	SO	Track on left.
2.0 ▲	SO	Track on right.
▼ 1.6	SO	Cross through creek.
1.7 ▲	SO	Cross through creek.
▼ 1.8	SO	Cross through creek.
1.5 ▲	SO	Cross through creek.
▼ 2.4	SO	Track on right.
0.9 ▲	SO	Track on left.
		GPS: N39°12.57' W120°25.22'
▼ 3.1	SO	Track on left.
0.2 ▲	SO	Track on right.
▼ 3.2	SO	Track on left.
0.1 ▲	SO	Track on right.
▼ 3.3	SO	Cross over creek; then track on right and track on left. Intersection is unmarked. Zero trip meter. Track on right goes 0.4 miles to the Lost Emigrant Mine. It crosses the clearing,

descends the hill to the mine, and continues up to the diggings.

0.0 ▲ Continue to the east and cross over creek.

GPS: N39°11.93′ W120°25.48′

▼ 0.0 Continue to the west.

1.6 ▲ SO Track on right and track on left. Intersection is unmarked. Zero trip meter. Track on left goes 0.4 miles to the Lost Emigrant Mine. It crosses the clearing, descends the hill to the mine, and continues up to the diggings.

▼ 1.0 SO Track on left and track on right.

0.6 ▲ SO Track on left and track on right.

GPS: N39°11.64′ W120°25.82′

▼ 1.6 TL T-intersection with graded Foresthill Road. To the right goes to Foresthill, to the left goes to French Meadows. Zero trip meter and follow the sign to French Meadows.

0.0 ▲ Continue to the northwest.

GPS: N39°11.21′ W120°26.02′

▼ 0.0 Continue to the northeast on FR 96.

5.4 ▲ TR End of FR 96. Foresthill Road continues straight ahead to Foresthill. Zero trip meter and turn right onto graded Soda Springs Road, following the sign to Soda Springs.

▼ 1.1 SO Entering state wildlife refuge. Camping and campfires in designated sites only. Tevis Cup Trail crosses on left and right.

4.3 ▲ SO Tevis Cup Trail crosses on left and right. Leaving state wildlife refuge.

▼ 3.1 SO Cross over creek.

2.3 ▲ SO Cross over creek.

▼ 3.6 SO Cross over creek.

1.8 ▲ SO Cross over creek.

▼ 4.0 SO Track on right is 96-114.

1.4 ▲ SO Track on left is 96-114.

GPS: N39°10.70′ W120°24.23′

▼ 4.8 BR Track on left is 96-110.

0.6 ▲ BL Track on right is 96-110.

▼ 5.1 SO Cross over creek.

0.3 ▲ SO Cross over creek.

▼ 5.2 SO Cross over creek.

0.2 ▲ SO Cross over creek.

▼ 5.3 SO Track on right is 96-106.

0.1 ▲ SO Track on left is 96-106.

▼ 5.4 TR T-intersection. Graded road on left is FR 51, spur to Talbot USFS Campground. Zero trip meter and turn right following the sign to French Meadows Recreation Area.

0.0 ▲ Continue to the northwest.

GPS: N39°10.18′ W120°23.47′

Spur to Talbot Campground

▼ 0.0 Proceed north on FR 51, following sign to Talbot Campground.

▼ 0.1 SO Track on right.

▼ 0.2 SO Track on left.

▼ 0.7 SO Track on left.

▼ 0.8 SO Track on right.

▼ 1.4 BR Gravel road on left. Follow sign to Granite Chief Wilderness and Talbot Campground.

GPS: N39°11.23′ W120°22.76′

▼ 1.7 SO Picayune Hiking Trailhead and parking area on left. Trail heads into the Granite Chief Wilderness.

GPS: N39°11.37′ W120°22.42′

▼ 1.8 Spur ends at Talbot Campground. Trail 16E10, part of the Western States Trail, for hikers and horses, on left leads to Picayune Valley and the Granite Chief Wilderness.

GPS: N39°11.32′ W120°22.33′

Continuation of Main Trail

▼ 0.0 Continue to the south on FR 96.

2.5 ▲ TL Graded road FR 51 straight ahead is the spur to Talbot USFS Campground. Zero trip meter and turn left on FR 96, following the sign to Soda Springs.

GPS: N39°10.18′ W120°23.47′

▼ 1.1 SO Two tracks on left.

1.4 ▲ SO Two tracks on right.

▼ 1.3 SO Track on right is 96-96.

1.2 ▲ SO Track on left is 96-96.

▼ 1.5 SO Cross over creek.

1.0 ▲ SO Cross over creek.

▼ 1.8 SO Track on left is 96-91 into Ahart USFS Campground. Track continues past campground.

0.7 ▲ SO Track on right is 96-91 into Ahart USFS Campground. Track continues past campground.

GPS: N39°08.76′ W120°24.44′

▼ 2.0 SO Track on right is 96-90.

0.5 ▲ SO Track on left is 96-90.

▼ 2.1 SO Cross over creek.

0.4 ▲ SO Cross over creek.

▼ 2.5 Trail ends at the start of the paved road at the northeastern end of French Meadows Reservoir. Road on right goes 1.4 miles to Lewis Campground and boat ramp. Continue straight ahead on FR 96 following the sign to Foresthill, 38 miles, or retrace your steps to Soda Springs.

0.0 ▲ Trail commences on FR 96 at the northeastern end of French Meadows Reservoir, 38 miles east of Foresthill. Zero trip meter at the end of the paved road at the intersection with the road to Lewis Campground and boat ramp. Turn northwest on graded gravel FR 96.

GPS: N39°08.26′ W120°24.62′

NORTHERN SIERRA #21

Henness Pass Road

Starting Point:	**I-80 in Verdi, NV**
Finishing Point:	**California 49 in Camptonville**
Total Mileage:	**76 miles, plus 1-mile spur to Little Truckee River Bridge**
Unpaved Mileage:	**67.3 miles**
Driving Time:	**1 day minimum, 2 days preferable**
Elevation Range:	**2,700–7,000 feet**
Usually Open:	**May to November**
Best Time to Travel:	**May to November**
Difficulty Rating:	**2**
Scenic Rating:	**10**
Remoteness Rating:	**+0**

Sierra Buttes can be seen to the north of Henness Pass Road

Special Attractions

- Long easy road for high-clearance vehicles that follows much of the route of the historic Henness Pass Road.
- Trail passes many historic stage stop sites.
- Fishing and camping at Stampede Reservoir, Milton Reservoir, and Jackson Meadow Reservoir.

History

Henness Pass Road developed when transportation routes to the newfound wealth of the West were at a crucial stage. The few settlements along proposed corridors stood to catch the passing lucrative trade. Many vied, many invested, and many indulged in tall promotions, but few lasted. Henness Pass was one of the more notable east-west routes that drew heavy traffic over the northern reaches of the Sierra Nevada. The route was less challenging to stagecoaches and freight wagons than some proposed trails, yet in the long run, it lost out to a more favored route through El Dorado County to the south.

D. B. Scott surveyed this wagon road in 1855, in a bid by interested parties to attract overland emigrants to the Middle and North Yuba Rivers and the various towns in Yuba and Nevada Counties. Patrick Henness and his associate Jackson may have discovered the pass in 1850, or earlier in 1849. The promoted route would take travelers west from the Truckee River, on the California border, across the mountains to Camptonville. Construction of the wagon road took place in 1861.

From 1860 to 1868, Henness Pass Road was heavily used by stagecoaches and freighters because of the 1859 discovery of the Comstock lode at Virginia City, then in Utah Territory, and because it was before the completion of the Central Pacific Railroad. It became necessary to regulate traffic flow at times. Freight haulers could travel during the day, while stagecoaches were restricted to travel at night. Mountain House, 2,000 feet above Goodyears Bar and the present route of California 49, was a welcome sight to miners and travelers alike. Dan T. Cole built an inn on this spectacular ridge in 1860. By 1890, this popular stopping point had grown to a three-story guesthouse with a dance hall and dining room. Many such roadhouse establishments sprang up along this wagon road over the decades. Cornish House, Moore's Stage Station and hotel, Sleighville House, and Sardine Valley House are just some of the names that linger along this historic wagon road. (For more on this historic route, see page 66.)

Verdi, Nevada, at the eastern end of the road, was the site of the first train robbery in the West. In November 1870, school superintendent John Chapman led a band of six men to the town, where they boarded the Central Pacific, still in its first year of operation. They took over the train and uncoupled the cars, keeping just the engine and express car, which carried more than $40,000 in gold. They abandoned the train farther south, in the Truckee River Canyon and made off with the loot. The unhitched railcars coasted downhill to the abandoned engine. The train continued to Truckee to report the daring robbery. All members of the gang were caught within two days, before they had time to spend the money.

Description

Henness Pass Road is a long scenic trail that passes a number of historic sites through a variety of scenery. In its entirety, the trail is suitable for high-clearance vehicles. The forest service has a marked auto tour for the route, with numbered stops at points of interest. The trail described below follows part of this route, but it diverges onto smaller trails and spurs that more closely reflect the original wagon road.

The trail leaves Verdi, Nevada, and crosses the Truckee River and California state line before climbing along a graded dirt road to First Summit—the first point on the auto tour. The trail passes through the 7,310-acre area of the Crystal Burn Fire of August 1994. Currently, the area is being reforested. At First Summit passenger vehicles can follow a graded road around the side of the ridge, but high-clearance vehicles can descend into Dog Valley to pass one of the campsites used by emigrants. The trail rejoins the main graded road via a series of small, formed trails at Second Summit. Northern Sierra #22: Boca Ridge and Verdi Peak Trail touches here before veering off again.

A short hike off Henness Pass Road leads to waterfalls in the Middle Yuba River's Box Canyon

Immediately south of the trail, Stampede Reservoir is a good place to camp and fish for kokanee salmon and rainbow, brown, or Mackinaw trout. There is a boat launch 2 miles west of Stampede Dam on the south side of the lake. The route passes the small Davies Creek USFS Campground. Other campgrounds can be found to the south along CR 270, which travels down the eastern side of the reservoir. Dirt tracks lead to the water's edge at several points, but these are for day-use only; camping is restricted to developed campgrounds.

The auto tour marks a number of historic stage stop sites along the original route. Most of these are nothing more than sites, but they show how busy the road must have been in earlier times. The stop at Kyburz Flat, immediately east of California 89, is a great place to take a break. A short, handicap-accessible boardwalk leads around the site of Moore's Stage Station. The Kyburz Petroglyph is on the south side of the road. It is broken into three pieces—the picture in the brochure shows it in one piece. Take care not to inadvertently walk over it. The petroglyph consists of many small cupules in the rock and is best viewed late in the day when the angle of the sun makes the pockets stand out clearly. A short spur leads to Wheelers Sheep Camp, where an old Basque oven is now protected by a new wooden lean-to. The oven is functional, but those wishing to use it are asked to contact the forest service first. The camp has a couple picnic tables set in the shade and a spring at the south end of Kyburz Flat.

West of Kyburz Flat, the trail joins paved California 89 before turning off onto paved FR 07 and heading toward Jackson Meadow Reservoir. The original Henness Pass Road continues straight ahead at this point and crosses private property to travel down to the site of a bridge over the Little Truckee River. The old bridge, washed out in the 1980s, has not been rebuilt. A spur from the original trail accesses the bridge from the west side of the Little Truckee River along a county road. This spur passes through private property, but you can see an old line shack standing on the west side of the road. The timber building contains a cookhouse, covered verandah, and upstairs bunkhouse.

The main route crosses Little Truckee Summit, the nexus of a popular network of snowmobile trails. From the summit, you can access popular winter destinations such as Jackson Meadow Reservoir, Meadow Lake, Mount Lola, and Haypress Valley. There are three marked, groomed snowmobile routes that total approximately 90 miles. Overnight camping is permitted at Little Truckee Summit between November 16 and April 14.

The main route then turns off the paved road onto graded dirt roads that run slightly south of paved FR 07. The spur to the Little Truckee River bridge leads off from this point. The route passes through Perazzo Meadows and fords the shallow Perazzo Canyon Creek. Just south of the trail, some waterfalls on the Little Truckee River make for a pleasant stop.

Henness Pass (6,920 feet) is located on paved FR 07 east of Jackson Meadow Reservoir. Those taking two days to travel the trail may wish to take advantage of the forest service campgrounds west of the pass around Jackson Meadow Reservoir. The developed campgrounds are close to the lake and offer plenty of shade and lake views. Black bears are common in the area, and some of the campgrounds offer bear-proof boxes for food storage. (Be advised: Use them.) Jackson Meadow Reservoir is popular with anglers, who fish for rainbow and brown trout. The next reservoir along the trail, Milton Lake, is much smaller and has a few backcountry campsites along its shores. The lake has a two pan-size trout limit; larger trout must be released to provide natural control of non-game fish that otherwise threaten to overwhelm the trout.

The Middle Yuba River flows into Milton Reservoir

The graded road offers many spectacular vistas along its length. Possibly the most spectacular views, north over the Sierra Buttes, can be glimpsed along the next section of trail. These rugged buttes are prominently displayed on the far side of the North Yuba River. A worthwhile spur leads to the south from here to the Gates of the Antipodes and overlooks the deep Box Canyon No. 1 on the Middle Yuba River. The narrow, little-used spur leads partway down the side of the ridge and finishes at a collapsed two-story log cabin. The origins of the cabin are unknown, but it is likely that it was associated with mining since long-abandoned and collapsed shafts are nearby. The cabin may have been a halfway point for miners traveling the long route up from the river. The spur travels a narrow, rough shelf road that is rated a 4 for difficulty. The turnaround at the end is tight; longer vehicles may wish to turn on the switchback 0.1 miles before the end. The coordinates of the cabin are GPS: N39°31.51' W120°40.06'.

The Henness Pass route splits into two shortly after the spur. The lower, paved road takes travelers out to California 49 via Forest City. The upper road is still graded dirt, and travels past the site of Mountain House and continues along the ridge tops to finish on California 49 in Camptonville.

A final worthwhile stop near the end of the trail can be found 7 miles south on California 49. The 100-foot-long Oregon Creek Covered Bridge, located a short distance north of North San Juan, stands at the confluence of Oregon Creek and the Middle Yuba River. A day-use picnic area near the bridge makes for a wonderful stop.

Current Road Information

Tahoe National Forest
Sierraville Ranger District
317 South Lincoln
Sierraville, CA 96126
(530) 994-3401

Tahoe National Forest
Downieville Ranger District
15924 Highway 49
Camptonville, CA 95922
(530) 288-3231

Map References

BLM Reno (NV), Portola, Truckee, Yuba City
USFS Toiyabe National Forest, Tahoe National Forest
USGS 1:24,000 Verdi (NV), Dog Valley, Sardine Peak, Sierraville, Independence Lake, Webber Peak, Sattley, English Mt., Haypress Valley, Sierra City, Downieville, Alleghany, Pike, Camptonville
1:100,000 Reno (NV), Portola, Truckee, Yuba City

Maptech CD-ROM: High Sierra/Tahoe
Nevada Atlas & Gazetteer, p. 42
Northern California Atlas & Gazetteer, pp. 71, 81, 70, 80, 79
California Road & Recreation Atlas, pp. 61, 60

Route Directions

▼ 0.0		From the intersection of Third Street and Bridge Street in Verdi, just off I-80 in Nevada, zero trip meter and turn northwest onto Bridge Street, which is signposted to Dog Valley Road.
3.7 ▲		Trail ends in Verdi, NV in the center of town. Turn left for I-80 and Reno.
		GPS: N39°31.14' W119°59.28'
▼ 0.4	SO	Cross over Truckee River on bridge.
3.3 ▲	SO	Cross over Truckee River on bridge.
▼ 0.6	BR	Bear right onto Dog Valley Road.
3.1 ▲	BL	Bear left onto Bridge Street.
▼ 0.7	SO	Crystal Peak Cemetery on right.
3.0 ▲	SO	Crystal Peak Cemetery on left.
		GPS: N39°31.50' W119°59.86'
▼ 0.9	SO	California state line. Road is now Sierra Country Road 868. Remain on Dog Valley Road (Henness Pass Road).
2.8 ▲	SO	Nevada state Line.
		GPS: N39°31.49' W120°00.00'
▼ 1.5	SO	Road turns to graded dirt. Enter Toiyabe National Forest. Road is now marked as 002. Seasonal closure gate.
2.2 ▲	SO	Seasonal closure gate. Road is now paved. Leaving Toiyabe National Forest.
▼ 3.0	SO	Track on right; then track on left.
0.7 ▲	SO	Track on right; then track on left.
▼ 3.7	SO	Track on left is Northern Sierra #22: Boca Ridge and Verdi Peak Trail (FR 074). Information board on right and track on right. Zero trip meter.
0.0 ▲		Continue to the southeast.
		GPS: N39°32.91' W120°02.28'
▼ 0.0	BR	First Summit (auto tour stop 22). Bear right onto graded road 002 following signs to Dog Valley. Graded road on left is 027 to Stampede Dam via Second Summit. Proceed west on lower, graded road. Several tracks on right. Passenger vehicles should bear left via 027 at this point and rejoin the main trail in 2.5 miles at Second Summit.
3.0 ▲	SO	First Summit (auto tour stop 22). Several tracks on left; then graded road on right is 027 to Stampede Dam; then track on left at information board. Track on right is Northern Sierra #22: Boca Ridge and Verdi Peak Trail (FR 074). Zero trip meter.
▼ 0.7	BL	Bear left onto 012A. Track straight ahead is 002 and track on right is 010, which goes 0.4 miles into Dog Valley to a marker commemorating early travelers along this route. The marker post is located on the left of track 010, on the far side of the creek at GPS: N39°33.09' W120°02.63'. It can be hard to spot.
2.3 ▲	SO	Bear right onto 002 and head uphill. Track on left is 002 and track straight ahead is 010, which goes 0.4 miles into Dog Valley to a marker commemorating early travelers along this route. The marker post is located on the left of track 010, on the far side of the creek at GPS: N39°33.09' W120°02.63'. It can be hard to spot.
		GPS: N39°32.91' W120°02.99'
▼ 0.9	SO	Cross through Dog Creek; then track on left.
2.1 ▲	SO	Track on right; then cross through Dog Creek.
▼ 1.4	TL	T-intersection with trail 012. Camping area on left.
1.6 ▲	BR	Camping area on right. Turn right onto 012A.
		GPS: N39°32.64' W120°03.60'
▼ 1.5	BR	Track on left to campsite.
1.5 ▲	BL	Track on right to campsite.
▼ 1.9	TL	T-intersection with graded road 009. Turn left; then track on left.
1.1 ▲	TR	Track on right; then turn right onto unmarked formed trail 012. Graded road 009 continues straight ahead.
		GPS: N39°32.51' W120°04.06'
▼ 3.0	TR	Second Summit (auto tour stop 21). Turn right onto 027 and cross cattle guard. Two tracks ahead are both Northern Sierra #22: Boca Ridge and Verdi Peak Trail. Zero trip meter and bear right onto graded road 002, following sign to Boca Reservoir.
0.0 ▲		Continue to the northwest, entering Toiyabe National Forest.
		GPS: N39°31.57 W120°04.14'
▼ 0.0		Continue to the south, entering Tahoe National Forest. Track on left and track on right.
1.8 ▲	TL	Track on left and track on right. Second Summit (auto tour stop 21). Two tracks on right before and after cattle guard are both Northern Sierra #22: Boca Ridge and Verdi Peak Trail. Zero trip meter and turn left onto small, unmarked trail 009. Passenger vehicles should remain on main graded road 027 and rejoin the trail in 2.5 miles at First Summit.
▼ 0.6	SO	Track on right.
1.2 ▲	SO	Track on left.
▼ 1.6	SO	Track on right.
0.2 ▲	SO	Track on left.
▼ 1.7	SO	Track on left.
0.1 ▲	SO	Track on right.
▼ 1.8	SO	Paved road on left is CR 894 to Stampede Reservoir and I-80. Follow sign for Sardine Valley and zero trip meter. This is auto tour stop 20.
0.0 ▲		Continue to the northeast on CR 860.
		GPS: N39°30.41' W120°05.47'
▼ 0.0		Continue to the southwest on CR 860.
3.1 ▲	SO	Paved road on right is CR 894 to Stampede Reservoir and I-80. Follow sign for Verdi and zero trip meter. This is auto tour stop 20.
▼ 0.2	SO	Track on right through gate goes to Camp 21 site.
2.9 ▲	SO	Track on left through gate goes to Camp 21 site.
▼ 0.3	SO	Cross over Davies Creek twice. Camp in designated sites only.
2.8 ▲	SO	Cross over Davies Creek twice.

▼ 0.4	SO	Davies Creek USFS Campground on left; then track on left for day use only.
2.7 ▲	SO	Track on right for day use only; then Davies Creek USFS Campground on right.
		GPS: N39°30.39' W120°05.90'
▼ 0.6	BR	Graded road on left goes to Stampede Reservoir—day use only.
2.5 ▲	BL	Graded road on right goes to Stampede Reservoir—day use only.
▼ 1.5	SO	Track on right goes to Camp 21 site. The railroad camp site is at GPS: N39°30.86' W120°06.44'. Entering Sardine Valley.
1.6 ▲	SO	Track on left goes to Camp 21 site. The railroad camp site is at GPS: N39°30.86' W120°06.44'. Leaving Sardine Valley.
▼ 2.1	BR	Track on left.
1.0 ▲	SO	Track on right.
		GPS: N39°30.52' W120°07.65'
▼ 3.1	TL	Cross over Davies Creek; then graded road ahead goes to California 49. Turn left onto CR 450, following the sign for California 89, and zero trip meter. This is auto tour stop 19.
0.0 ▲		Continue to the south.
		GPS: N39°30.72' W120°08.54'
▼ 0.0		Continue to the west and cross cattle guard.
5.8 ▲	TR	Cattle guard; then T-intersection with CR 860. Graded road on left goes to California 49. Turn right onto CR 860, following the sign for Stampede Reservoir. Zero trip meter and cross over Davies Creek. This is auto tour stop 19.
▼ 1.3	SO	Track on left.
4.5 ▲	SO	Track on right.
▼ 1.8	SO	Graded road on right is CR 650 to Sardine Peak Lookout. Follow sign to California 89. Cross over creek; then track on right. This is auto tour stop 18.
4.0 ▲	SO	Track on left; then cross over creek; then graded road on left is CR 650 to Sardine Peak Lookout. This is auto tour stop 18. Follow sign to Stampede Reservoir.
		GPS: N39°30.69' W120°10.55'
▼ 2.5	SO	Track on right.
3.3 ▲	SO	Track on left.
▼ 2.7	SO	Track on left.
3.1 ▲	SO	Track on right.
▼ 3.6	SO	Track on right; then track on left is 450-20; then cattle guard; then track on right.
2.2 ▲	SO	Track on left; then cattle guard; then track on right is 450-20; then track on left.
		GPS: N39°30.45' W120°12.53'
▼ 4.1	SO	Cross over creek.
1.7 ▲	SO	Cross over creek.
▼ 4.7	SO	Entering Kyburz Flat.
1.1 ▲	SO	Leaving Kyburz Flat.
▼ 4.8	BR	Graded road on left is 450-10. Remain on CR 450.
1.0 ▲	BL	Graded road on right is 450-10. Remain on CR 450.
▼ 5.3	SO	Track on left.
0.5 ▲	SO	Track on right.
▼ 5.5	SO	Cross over creek.
0.3 ▲	SO	Cross over creek.
▼ 5.7	SO	Leaving Kyburz Flat. Start of interpretive trail around the old stage stop site on right.
0.1 ▲	SO	Entering Kyburz Flat. Start of interpretive trail around the old stage stop site on left.
		GPS: N39°30.37' W120°14.49'
▼ 5.8	SO	Kyburz Petroglyph on left, marked by a sign. This is auto tour stop 17. Track on right is 450-05, which goes 0.8 miles to Wheelers Sheep Camp (keep right at the only intersection along the spur). Zero trip meter.
0.0 ▲		Continue to the east.
		GPS: N39°30.40' W120°14.56'
▼ 0.0		Continue to the west.
2.2 ▲	SO	Kyburz Petroglyph on right, marked by a sign. This is auto tour stop 17. Track on left is 450-05, which goes 0.8 miles to Wheelers Sheep Camp (keep right at the only intersection along the spur). Zero trip meter.
▼ 1.0	TR	Turn right onto paved California 89. The original Henness Pass Road continues straight ahead at this point, but this is now private property.
1.2 ▲	TL	Turn left onto graded dirt CR 450, following sign to Kyburz Flat. The original Henness Pass Road went to the right at this point, but this is now private property.
		GPS: N39°30.29' W120°15.69'
▼ 2.2	TL	Little Truckee Summit. Turn left onto paved FR 07 following sign to Independence Lake. CR 451 on right. Zero trip meter.
0.0 ▲		Continue to the southeast.
		GPS: N39°30.35' W120°16.89'
▼ 0.0		Continue to the south. Treasure Mountain Road (FR 05), a groomed snowmobile trail, on right; then Little Truckee Summit snowmobile trailhead on right.
2.0 ▲	TR	Little Truckee Summit snowmobile trailhead on left; then Treasure Mountain Road (FR 05), a groomed snowmobile trail, on left; then 4-way intersection with California 89. Turn right onto paved California 89 following sign for Truckee. CR 451 is straight ahead. Zero trip meter.
▼ 1.4	TL	Turn left onto graded dirt road 07-10, following sign to Independence Lake, and cross over aqueduct. This is the start of Northern Sierra #23: Independence Lake Trail.
0.6 ▲	TR	Cross over aqueduct; then T-intersection with FR 07. Follow sign to California 89.
		GPS: N39°29.54' W120°17.83'
▼ 1.6	SO	Cross over Little Truckee River on bridge.
0.4 ▲	SO	Cross over Little Truckee River on bridge.
▼ 2.0	SO	Auto tour stop 16. Small track on left is a spur that follows the original route of Henness Pass Road to the Little Truckee River bridge. Old route also on right. Zero trip meter.
0.0 ▲		Continue to the west.
		GPS: N39°29.45' W120°17.24'

Spur to Little Truckee River Bridge

▼ 0.0		Turn onto small formed trail and head northeast, away from graded gravel road. The turn is opposite auto tour stop 16.
▼ 0.4	TL	Track on right; then turn left on graded gravel road. Track continues straight ahead.
		GPS: N39°29.69' W120°16.90'
▼ 0.7	SO	Track on left is private.
▼ 0.8	SO	Old timber building on left is a line shack (there is no access to it because it is on private property).
▼ 0.9	TL	Turn left past private property ahead.
▼ 1.0		Trail ends at washed out bridge over the Little Truckee River.
		GPS: N39°30.14' W120°16.62'

Continuation of Main Trail

▼ 0.0 — Continue to the east.
7.5 ▲ SO — Auto tour stop 16. Small track on right is a spur that follows the original route of Henness Pass Road to the Little Truckee River bridge. Old route also on left. Zero trip meter.

GPS: N39°29.45' W120°17.24'

▼ 0.2 TR — 4-way intersection. Turn right onto CR 301, which is a marked snowmobile route in winter. Northern Sierra #23: Independence Lake Trail, also a groomed snowmobile route in winter, continues straight ahead.
7.3 ▲ TL — 4-way intersection. Turn left onto graded road 07-10. Northern Sierra #23: Independence Lake Trail, a groomed snowmobile route in winter, on right.

GPS: N39°29.45' W120°17.06'

▼ 1.1 SO — Cross over creek.
6.4 ▲ SO — Cross over creek.

▼ 1.2 SO — Track on right.
6.3 ▲ SO — Track on left.

▼ 1.3 SO — Site of Davis Station (auto tour stop 15) on left.
6.2 ▲ SO — Site of Davis Station (auto tour stop 15) on right.

GPS: N39°29.39' W120°18.38'

▼ 1.5 SO — Cattle guard. Entering private property. Ignore tracks on left and right for next 1.4 miles.
6.0 ▲ SO — Cattle guard. Leaving private property.

▼ 2.9 SO — Cattle guard. Leaving private property.
4.6 ▲ SO — Cattle guard. Entering private property. Ignore tracks on left and right for next 1.4 miles.

▼ 3.0 SO — Graded road on left; then track on left.
4.5 ▲ SO — Track on right; then graded road on right.

▼ 3.3 SO — Track on left to Mount Lola Trailhead parking area. Mount Lola Trail, for hikers and equestrians, connects to the Pacific Crest National Scenic Trail.
4.2 ▲ SO — Track on right to Mount Lola Trailhead parking area. Mount Lola Trail, for hikers and equestrians, connects to the Pacific Crest National Scenic Trail.

GPS: N39°29.33' W120°20.32'

▼ 3.5 SO — Track on left.
4.0 ▲ SO — Track on right.

▼ 3.6 SO — Cross over Cold Stream on bridge.
3.9 ▲ SO — Cross over Cold Stream on bridge.

▼ 4.1 SO — Corral on right in Perazzo Meadows.
3.4 ▲ SO — Corral on left in Perazzo Meadows.

▼ 5.0 SO — Cross through Little Truckee River.
2.5 ▲ SO — Cross through Little Truckee River.

GPS: N39°29.18' W120°22.20'

▼ 5.5 SO — 4-way intersection. Track on left and track on right are both 07-30.
2.0 ▲ SO — 4-way intersection. Track on left and track on right are both 07-30.

GPS: N39°29.16' W120°22.76'

▼ 6.2 SO — Track on left goes 0.1 miles to waterfalls in Little Truckee River Canyon; then track on right.
1.3 ▲ SO — Track on left; then track on right goes 0.1 miles to waterfalls in Little Truckee River Canyon.

GPS: N39°29.14' W120°23.44'

▼ 7.5 TL — Turn left, remaining on dirt road, and zero trip meter. Paved FR 07 is immediately on the right. Marked snowmobile route ends here.

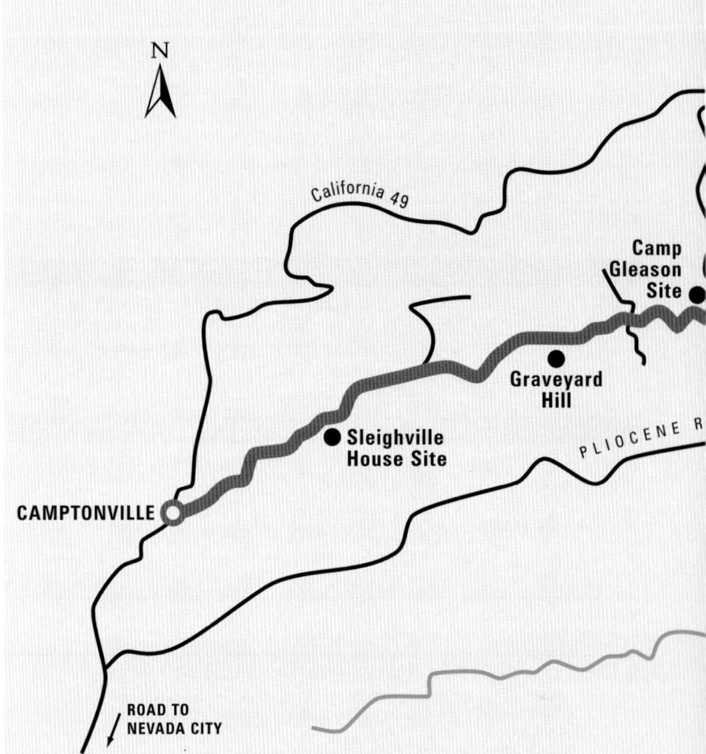

0.0 ▲ — Continue to the southeast.

GPS: N39°29.75' W120°24.58'

▼ 0.0 — Continue to the southwest.
1.2 ▲ TR — Turn right, remaining on dirt road, and zero trip meter. This is a marked snowmobile route in winter. Paved FR 07 is straight ahead.

▼ 0.2 BR — Cross over creek; then private property on left.
1.0 ▲ BL — Private property on right; then cross over creek.

▼ 1.2 SO — Track on left is Northern Sierra #24: Summit City Loop (FR 86). Zero trip meter.
0.0 ▲ — Continue to the southeast on CR 301.

GPS: N39°29.46' W120°25.66'

▼ 0.0 — Continue to the north, joining Summit City Loop.
2.9 ▲ BL — Northern Sierra #24: Summit City Loop (FR 86) leaves on right. Zero trip meter.

▼ 0.4 SO — Track on right.
2.5 ▲ BR — Track on left.

▼ 0.5 SO — California Cooperative Snow Survey Cabin on right.
2.4 ▲ SO — California Cooperative Snow Survey Cabin on left.

▼ 0.6 TL — T-intersection with paved FR 07. Follow sign to Jackson Meadows, remaining on paved road.
2.3 ▲ TR — Turn right onto graded dirt CR 301 following sign to Meadow Lake.

GPS: N39°29.95' W120°25.96'

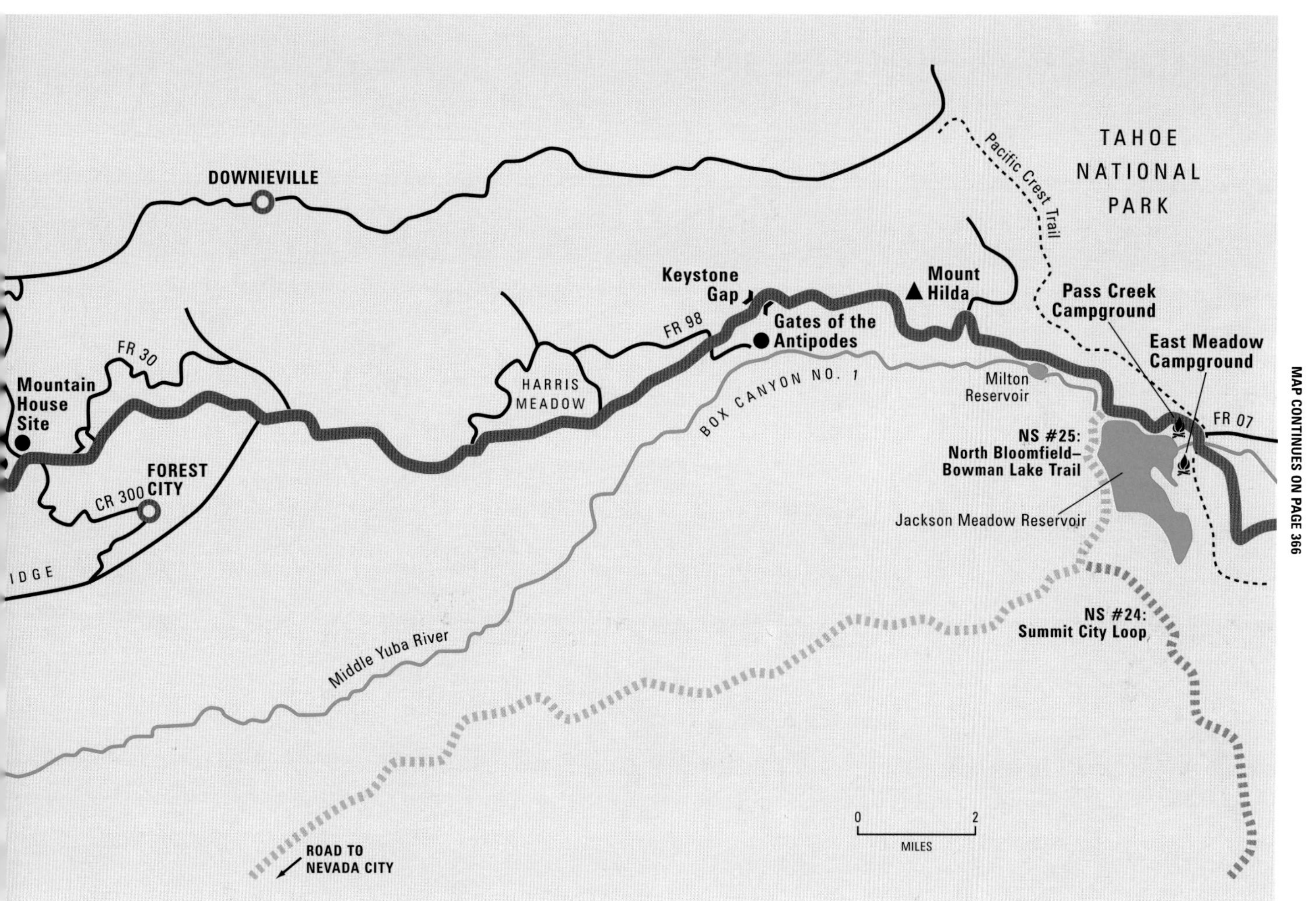

MAP CONTINUES ON PAGE 366

▼ 0.7	SO	Henness Pass (auto tour stop 14).
2.2 ▲	SO	Henness Pass (auto tour stop 14).
		GPS: N39°30.02′ W120°26.12′
▼ 0.8	SO	Graded road on left is 07-55 to Jones Valley. Graded road on right goes to Coppin Meadows.
2.1 ▲	SO	Graded road on right is 07-55 to Jones Valley. Graded road on left goes to Coppin Meadows.
▼ 1.1	TL	Turn left, back onto graded CR 301.
1.8 ▲	TR	T-intersection with paved FR 07.
		GPS: N39°30.10′ W120°26.55′
▼ 1.4	SO	Cross through creek.
1.5 ▲	SO	Cross through creek.
▼ 1.7	SO	Track on left.
1.2 ▲	SO	Track on right.
▼ 1.8	SO	Cross over creek.
1.1 ▲	SO	Cross over creek.
▼ 2.6	SO	Track on right.
0.3 ▲	SO	Track on left.
▼ 2.9	TL	Paved FR 07 is immediately to the right. Turn left onto Pass Creek Loop (FR 70) and zero trip meter.
0.0 ▲		Continue to the east. End of snowmobile route.
		GPS: N39°30.35′ W120°28.40′
▼ 0.0		Continue to the west. This is a groomed snowmobile route in winter.
7.3 ▲	TR	Turn right onto unmarked, graded CR 301, immediately before paved FR 70, and zero trip meter.
▼ 0.1	SO	Track on right.
7.2 ▲	SO	Track on left.
▼ 0.2	SO	Cross over Pass Creek.
7.1 ▲	SO	Cross over Pass Creek.
▼ 1.4	SO	Track on left is 70-20.
5.9 ▲	SO	Track on right is 70-20.
▼ 2.8	SO	Track on right is 70-30.
4.5 ▲	SO	Track on left is 70-30.
▼ 3.9	SO	Track on left is 70-40; then cross over creek.
3.4 ▲	SO	Cross over creek; then track on right is 70-40.
		GPS: N39°28.91′ W120°29.88′
▼ 4.1	SO	Track on right is 70-50.
3.2 ▲	SO	Track on left is 70-50.
▼ 4.6	SO	Track on left is 70-58.
2.7 ▲	SO	Track on right is 70-58.
▼ 4.8	SO	Track on right is 70-60; then cross over creek.
2.5 ▲	SO	Cross over creek; then track on left is 70-60.
▼ 4.9	SO	Track on left is 70-65.
2.4 ▲	SO	Track on right is 70-65.
▼ 5.6	SO	Little Lasier Meadow USFS Horse Camp on right; then hiking and equestrian trail on left joins Pacific Crest Trail in 0.75 miles.
1.7 ▲	SO	Hiking and equestrian trail on right joins Pacific Crest Trail in 0.75 miles; then second entrance to horse camp on left.
		GPS: N39°29.31′ W120°30.90′

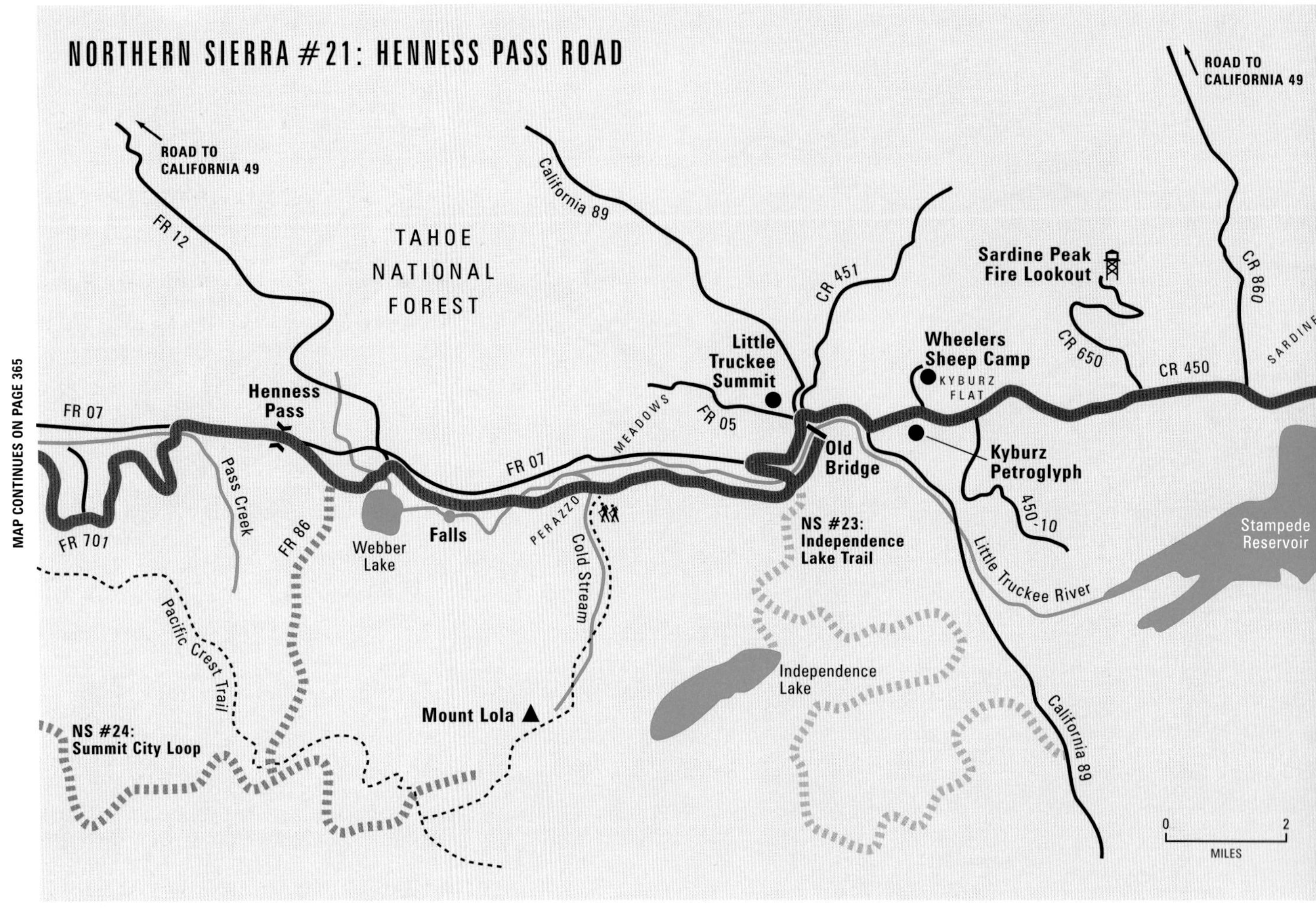

MAP CONTINUES ON PAGE 365

▼ 5.7	SO	Second entrance to horse camp on right; then cattle guard.
1.6 ▲	SO	Cattle guard; then Little Lasier Meadows USFS Horse Camp on left.
▼ 6.9	TR	T-intersection with paved road. Road on left is 70-80 to East Meadow USFS Campground. Turn right on paved road and cross over Pass Creek. Pacific Crest Trail joins road at this point.
0.4 ▲	TL	Cross over Pass Creek; then turn left on graded dirt FR 70. Paved road continues ahead to East Meadow USFS Campground. Pacific Crest Trail leaves road at this point.
		GPS: N39°30.14' W120°31.61'
▼ 7.0	SO	Track on right goes to sand pit; then Pacific Crest Trail leaves on right.
0.3 ▲	BR	Pacific Crest Trail joins road from the left at this point. Track on left goes to sand pit. Remain on paved road.
▼ 7.3	TL	T-intersection with paved FR 07. End of Pass Creek Loop. Zero trip meter and follow sign for Jackson Meadow.
0.0 ▲		Continue to the southeast. This is a groomed snowmobile route in winter.
		GPS: N39°30.36' W120°31.76'
▼ 0.0		Continue to the west. This is a groomed snowmobile route in winter.
1.4 ▲	TR	Turn right onto paved road following sign to East Meadow USFS Campground. Zero trip meter.
▼ 0.1	SO	Pass Creek USFS Campground and boat launch on left. Jackson Meadow Trailer Sanitary Station on right.
1.3 ▲	SO	Pass Creek USFS Campground and boat launch on right. Jackson Meadow Trailer Sanitary Station on left.
▼ 0.4	SO	Aspen Group Camps on right.
1.0 ▲	SO	Aspen Group Camps on left.
▼ 0.5	SO	Aspen Picnic Ground on left.
0.9 ▲	SO	Aspen Picnic Ground on right.
▼ 1.4	SO	Jackson Meadow Reservoir on left. Road on left is Northern Sierra #25: North Bloomfield–Bowman Lake Trail, which crosses the dam. This is auto tour stop 13. Zero trip meter.
0.0 ▲		Continue to the southeast. Road becomes paved.
		GPS: N39°30.59' W120°33.16'
▼ 0.0		Continue to the northwest. Road turns to graded dirt.
6.2 ▲	SO	Jackson Meadow Reservoir on right. Road on right is Northern Sierra #25: North Bloomfield–Bowman Lake Trail, which crosses the dam. This is auto tour stop 13. Zero trip meter.
▼ 0.2	SO	Look over edge on the left to see old bridge over the Middle Yuba River.
6.0 ▲	SO	Look over edge on the right to see old bridge over the Middle Yuba River.

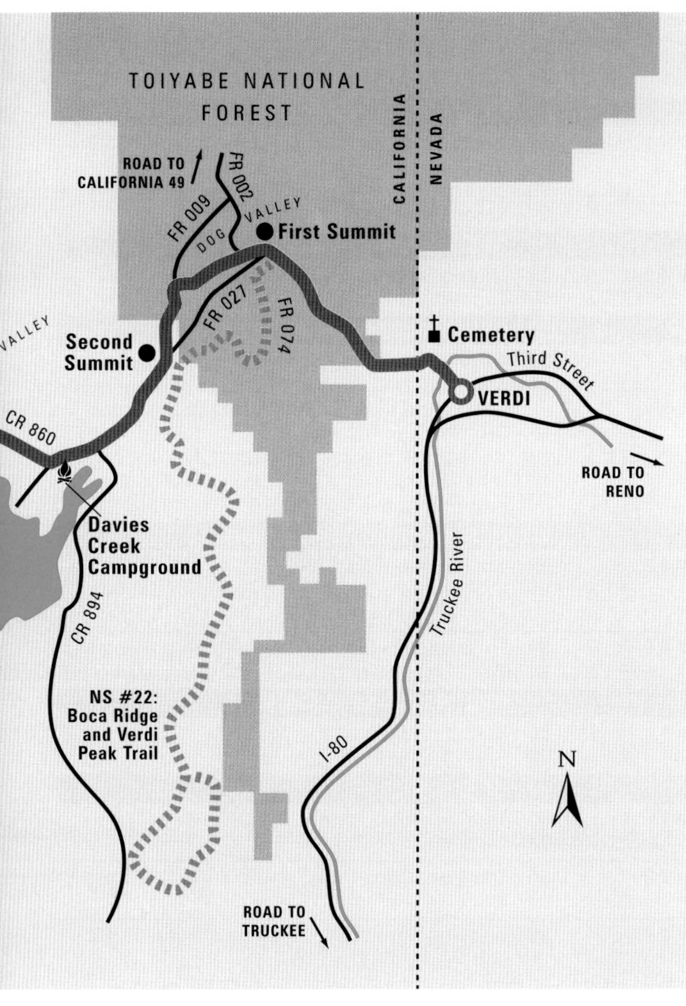

▼ 1.5		SO	Track on left.
	4.7 ▲	SO	Track on right.
			GPS: N39°31.27′ W120°34.17′
▼ 1.6		SO	Track on left.
	4.6 ▲	SO	Track on right.
▼ 1.7		SO	Milton Reservoir on left. This is auto tour stop 12.
	4.5 ▲	SO	Milton Reservoir on right. This is auto tour stop 12.
			GPS: N39°31.36′ W120°34.45′
▼ 2.2		SO	Track on left.
	4.0 ▲	SO	Track on right.
▼ 2.3		SO	Track on left.
	3.9 ▲	SO	Track on right.
▼ 2.4		SO	Track on left; then track on right.
	3.8 ▲	SO	Track on left; then track on right.
▼ 2.6		SO	Track on left goes 0.5 miles to the Milton-Bowman Tunnel. Follow sign to Alleghany.
	3.6 ▲	SO	Track on right goes 0.5 miles to the Milton-Bowman Tunnel.
			GPS: N39°31.49′ W120°35.32′
▼ 2.9		SO	Track on right.
	3.3 ▲	SO	Track on left.
▼ 3.4		SO	Track on right.
	2.8 ▲	SO	Track on left.
▼ 3.6		SO	Track on right.
	2.6 ▲	SO	Track on left.

▼ 3.8		BL	Graded road on right; then cross over wash; then track on right.
	2.4 ▲	BR	Track on left; then cross over creek; then graded road on left.
			GPS: N39°31.88′ W120°36.02′
▼ 5.4		SO	Track on right is 301-35.
	0.8 ▲	SO	Track on left is 301-35.
			GPS: N39°31.82′ W120°37.22′
▼ 6.0		SO	Cattle guard.
	0.2 ▲	SO	Cattle guard.
			GPS: N39°32.24′ W120°37.50′
▼ 6.2		SO	Track on left is 301-31 and track on right is 301-30. View on right over Sierra Buttes. Zero trip meter.
	0.0 ▲		Continue to the east.
			GPS: N39°32.23′ W120°37.78′
▼ 0.0			Continue to the west.
	3.4 ▲	SO	Track on right is 301-31 and track on left is 301-30. View on left over Sierra Buttes. Zero trip meter.
▼ 2.1		BL	Keystone Gap. Two tracks on right at viewpoint.
	1.3 ▲	BR	Keystone Gap. Two tracks on left at viewpoint.
			GPS: N39°32.25′ W120°39.85′
▼ 2.8		SO	Track on left.
	0.6 ▲	SO	Track on right.
▼ 3.4		SO	Graded road on right is FR 98. This is auto tour stop 11. Zero trip meter and follow sign to Alleghany.
	0.0 ▲		Continue to the northeast.
			GPS: N39°31.49′ W120°40.88′
▼ 0.0			Continue to the southwest.
	4.5 ▲	SO	Graded road on left is FR 98. This is auto tour stop 11. Zero trip meter and follow sign for Jackson Meadows.
▼ 0.1		SO	Track on right; then track on sharp left descends steeply along a little-used shelf road for 1 mile to a collapsed log cabin near the Gates of the Antipodes.
	4.4 ▲	BL	Track on right descends steeply along a little-used shelf road for 1 mile to a collapsed log cabin near the Gates of the Antipodes; then track on left.
			GPS: N39°31.41′ W120°40.98′
▼ 0.2		SO	Track on right and track on left.
	4.3 ▲	SO	Track on right and track on left.
▼ 0.9		SO	Track on right.
	3.6 ▲	SO	Track on left.
▼ 1.1		SO	Track and viewpoint on left.
	3.4 ▲	SO	Track and viewpoint on right.
▼ 1.7		SO	Track on right.
	2.8 ▲	SO	Track on left.
▼ 2.1		SO	Track on right to Harris Meadow and Negro Creek; then track on left.
	2.4 ▲	SO	Track on right; then track on left to Harris Meadow and Negro Creek.
			GPS: N39°30.50′ W120°42.81′
▼ 2.4		SO	Track on left and track on right.
	2.1 ▲	SO	Track on left and track on right.
▼ 2.6		SO	Track on left.
	1.9 ▲	SO	Track on right.
▼ 3.0		SO	Track on left to the Nixon Mine and track on right. Follow sign to Alleghany.
	1.5 ▲	SO	Track on right to the Nixon Mine and track on left. Follow sign to Jackson Meadows.
			GPS: N39°30.44′ W120°43.81′

▼ 3.5 SO Track on left and track on right.
1.0 ▲ SO Track on right and track on left.

▼ 4.5 SO Graded road on right is FR 98 to Harris Meadow. Join paved road following the sign to Alleghany. Zero trip meter.
0.0 ▲ Continue to the northeast.

GPS: N39°30.05′ W120°45.29′

▼ 0.0 Continue to the southwest.
4.0 ▲ BR Paved road ends. Graded road on left is FR 98 to Harris Meadow. Follow sign to Milton Reservoir. Zero trip meter.

▼ 0.3 SO Track on right.
3.7 ▲ SO Track on left.

▼ 0.5 SO Track on left is 301-14.
3.5 ▲ SO Track on right is 301-14.

▼ 0.8 SO Track on left is 301-12.
3.2 ▲ SO Track on right is 301-12.

▼ 1.3 SO Track on left.
2.7 ▲ SO Track on right.

▼ 1.7 SO Graded road on right is 301-8.
2.3 ▲ SO Graded road on left is 301-8.

GPS: N39°30.14′ W120°46.81′

▼ 1.8 SO Graded road on left is FR 84 to Lafayette Ridge Road.
2.2 ▲ SO Graded road on right is FR 84 to Lafayette Ridge Road.

GPS: N39°30.24′ W120°46.90′

▼ 1.9 SO Track on right.
2.1 ▲ SO Track on left.

▼ 2.0 SO Track on right is 301-6; then auto tour stop 10 on left. The site itself is set below the road on the left.
2.0 ▲ SO Auto tour stop 10 on right. The site itself is set below the road on the right. Track on left is 301-6.

GPS: N39°30.33′ W120°47.09′

▼ 2.5 SO Track on right.
1.5 ▲ SO Track on left.

▼ 3.0 SO Two tracks on left.
1.0 ▲ SO Two tracks on right.

▼ 3.5 SO Graded road on right and track on left is 301-2.
0.5 ▲ SO Graded road on left and track on right is 301-2.

GPS: N39°30.50′ W120°48.61′

▼ 4.0 TR Graded road on right is CR 302. Paved road straight ahead is the lower Henness Pass Road. Zero trip meter. This is auto tour stop 9.
0.0 ▲ Continue to the northeast.

GPS: N39°30.47′ W120°49.12′

▼ 0.0 Continue to the northwest.
4.7 ▲ TL T-intersection with paved CR 401. The lower Henness Pass Road joins from the right. This is auto tour stop 9. Zero trip meter.

▼ 0.4 SO Track on left.
4.3 ▲ SO Track on right.

▼ 1.0 SO Track on left and track on right.
3.7 ▲ SO Track on left and track on right.

▼ 1.1 SO Track on right goes into private property.
3.6 ▲ SO Track on left goes into private property.

▼ 1.7 SO Track on right.
3.0 ▲ SO Track on left.

▼ 2.4 SO Track on right.
2.3 ▲ SO Track on left.

▼ 2.9 SO Track on right.
1.8 ▲ SO Track on left.

▼ 3.1 SO Track on left.
1.6 ▲ SO Track on right.

▼ 3.6 SO Track on right; then two tracks on left.
1.1 ▲ SO Two tracks on right; then track on left.

GPS: N39°29.99′ W120°52.36′

▼ 4.1 SO Graded road on right is Alpha Colony Road (FR 30) to Ruby Mine; then track on right.
0.6 ▲ SO Track on left; then graded road on left is Alpha Colony Road (FR 30) to Ruby Mine.

GPS: N39°29.96′ W120°52.92′

▼ 4.4 TR T-intersection with CR 300.
0.3 ▲ TL Turn left on unmarked graded road CR 302.

GPS: N39°29.89′ W120°53.23′

▼ 4.7 BL Turnout on right at historical marker for Mountain House; then track on left; then graded road on right. Bear left onto graded road CR 293. Zero trip meter.
0.0 ▲ Continue to the east. Immediately track on right and turnout on left at the historical marker for Mountain House.

GPS: N39°30.01′ W120°53.41′

▼ 0.0 Continue to the south.
6.2 ▲ BR Graded road on left. Bear right onto CR 300 and zero trip meter.

▼ 0.9 SO Track on left is 293-20. Site of Camp Gleason.
5.3 ▲ SO Track on right is 293-20. Site of Camp Gleason.

GPS: N39°29.60′ W120°53.98′

▼ 1.3 SO Spring on right.
4.9 ▲ SO Spring on left.

GPS: N39°29.67′ W120°54.25′

▼ 1.6 SO Track on left.
4.6 ▲ SO Track on right.

▼ 2.0 SO Track on right.
4.2 ▲ SO Track on left.

▼ 2.6 SO Track on right is St. Catherine Road (293-18) and track on left is 390.
3.6 ▲ SO Track on right is 390 and track on left is St. Catherine Road (293-18).

GPS: N39°29.59′ W120°55.37′

▼ 3.0 SO Track on right is 34-15.
3.2 ▲ SO Track on left is 34-15.

▼ 3.7 SO Graveyard Hill on left; then track on left is 293-14. Site may be the final resting place of a power line worker who died in a snowstorm.
2.5 ▲ SO Track on right is 293-14; then Graveyard Hill on right. Site may be the final resting place of a power line worker who died in a snowstorm.

GPS: N39°29.38′ W120°56.37′

▼ 5.8 SO Track on right is Twin Quartz Road (34-13).
0.4 ▲ SO Track on left is Twin Quartz Road (34-13).

GPS: N39°28.97′ W120°58.53′

▼ 5.9 SO Track on left is 293-10.
0.3 ▲ SO Track on right is 293-10.

▼ 6.2 SO Track on right is Jouberts Road (34-7); then second track on right is Ditch Road (293-22). Track on left. Zero trip meter.
0.0 ▲ Continue to the northeast.

GPS: N39°28.90′ W120°58.91′

▼ 0.0 Continue to the southwest.
5.1 ▲ SO Track on right. Track on left is Ditch Road (293-22); then second track on left is Jouberts Road (34-7). Zero trip meter.

▼ 1.5 SO Road on left is 293-4.
3.6 ▲ SO Road on right is 293-4.

GPS: N39°28.28′ W121°00.19′

▼ 1.7 SO Track on right is 293-2.

	3.4 ▲	SO	Track on left is 293-2.
▼ 1.9		BR	Site of old stage stop Sleighville House (auto tour stop 3) on left; then bear right past tracks on left that go into private property.
	3.2 ▲	BL	Bear left past tracks on right that go into private property; then site of old stage stop Sleighville House (auto tour stop 3) on right.
			GPS: N39°28.28′ W121°00.52′
▼ 2.5		SO	Two tracks on right.
	2.6 ▲	SO	Two tracks on left.
▼ 2.9		SO	Track on left.
	2.2 ▲	SO	Track on right.
▼ 3.2		SO	Road becomes paved.
	1.9 ▲	SO	Road turns to graded dirt.
▼ 3.5		SO	Road on right.
	1.6 ▲	SO	Road on left.
▼ 4.6		BL	Mill Street on right. Bear left onto Cleveland Street.
	0.5 ▲	SO	Mill Street on left.
			GPS: N39°27.26′ W121°02.67′
▼ 4.9		SO	Auto tour stop 2 at historical marker for Camptonville and Lester Allen Pelton—inventor of the Pelton waterwheel.
	0.2 ▲	SO	Auto tour stop 2 at historical marker for Camptonville and Lester Allen Pelton—inventor of the Pelton waterwheel.
			GPS: N39°27.15′ W121°03.01′
▼ 5.1			Trail ends at T-intersection with California 49 in Camptonville. Turn left for Nevada City; turn right for Downieville.
	0.0 ▲		Trail starts on California 49 at Camptonville. Zero trip meter and turn east on Cleveland Avenue, following sign for Camptonville. The turn is 1.6 miles north of North Yuba USFS Ranger Station. Remain on Cleveland Street.
			GPS: N39°27.25′ W121°03.07′

NORTHERN SIERRA #22

Boca Ridge and Verdi Peak Trail

Starting Point:	**CR 894 at Boca Reservoir, 3.2 miles north of I-80**
Finishing Point:	**Northern Sierra #21: Henness Pass Road, 3.7 miles west of Verdi, NV**
Total Mileage:	**16.9 miles, plus optional 3.5-mile loop and 3-mile spur to Verdi Peak**
Unpaved Mileage:	**16.9 miles, plus optional 3.5-mile loop and 3-mile spur**
Driving Time:	**3 hours (20 minutes extra for 4-rated loop)**
Elevation Range:	**5,600–8,400 feet**
Usually Open:	**June to November**
Best Time to Travel:	**Dry weather**
Difficulty Rating:	**3 for the main trail; 4 for the optional loop**
Scenic Rating:	**8**
Remoteness Rating:	**+0**

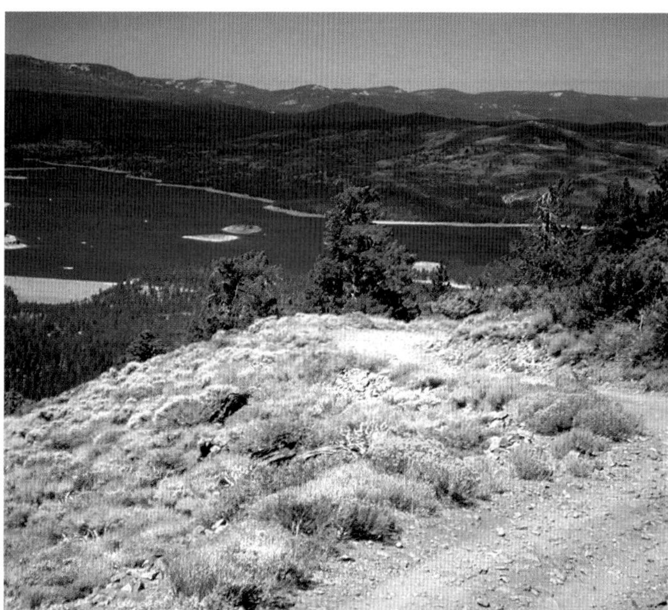

View of Stampede Reservoir from the spur trail to Verdi Peak

Special Attractions

- Fishing and camping at Boca Reservoir.
- Panoramic views from Verdi Peak Fire Lookout.
- Historic town site of Boca.

History

The southern approach to the Verdi Range begins on the eastern shore of Boca Reservoir and makes its way up the slopes of Boca Ridge. The original lake at Boca Reservoir was the scene of great activity during the late nineteenth and early twentieth centuries. Construction of the Central Pacific Railroad between 1866 and 1868 brought thousands of workers to the Sierra Nevada, and Boca was one of many base camps for workers on the grade. The railroad entered the spectacular Truckee Canyon at Boca, Spanish for "mouth." (For more on the Central Pacific Railroad, see page 70.)

A lumber mill at Boca supplied railroad ties for the new grade, and a dam ensured a plentiful water supply. The mill also provided timbers for mines and lumber for builders. Once the track was laid past Boca, the town became a stopping point for travelers who enjoyed the hospitality of its three-story hotel. In winter the lake froze, and the lumber company switched gears to harvest ice. Big blocks of ice were insulated in sawdust and shipped to various destinations via the railroad. Saloons did a roaring trade, and Boca gained a reputation for rowdiness and violence. In the late 1880s and early 1890s, the Boca Brewery supplied as many as 30,000 barrels of beer to towns throughout the West. Unfortunately, the brewery burned down just before the turn of the century. It seemed like the town would go on forever; however, the sawmill finally denuded the surrounding mountains and was forced to close in 1908. With no alternative employment, townspeople were forced to walk away from their homes. The final straw for Boca came when its last major employer, the ice foundry, closed in the 1920s.

All that remains of Boca is the small cemetery. The Boca Reservoir we see today was completed in 1940.

Verdi Peak Fire Lookout, perched above the Truckee River Canyon

Description

This interesting trail close to the Nevada state line travels north from Boca Reservoir to Northern Sierra #21: Henness Pass Road. Immediately after leaving I-80, take a few minutes to look at the old Boca town site and cemetery. There is a short interpretive trail, and although no buildings remain, the old cemetery is mute testimony to the hardships its citizens faced.

The trail starts at Boca Reservoir, opposite the Boca Rest USFS Campground. Set on the lakeshore, this campground has no shade but is popular because of its proximity to the lake. Anglers can fish for rainbow trout (which are stocked annually), brown trout, and kokanee salmon. There is a boat ramp on the southwest shore of Boca Reservoir.

An alternative to the main route begins 0.2 miles from the start of the trail and takes a slightly more circuitous route along a smaller, rougher trail. This alternate 3.5-mile route is rated 4 for difficulty because of loose uneven surfaces and a couple of short, moderately steep climbs. It travels closer to Boca Ridge along designated OHV routes before rejoining the main trail.

The main trail remains 2-rated at this stage, as it climbs around a shelf road, slowly winding toward Verdi Peak. The shelf road is predominantly single vehicle width, but it has plenty of passing places and offers views over low vegetation to Boca and Stampede Reservoirs.

A spur travels 3 miles through curl-leaf mahoganies, stands of aspens, and slopes covered in mule's ears to the Verdi Peak Fire Lookout. The lookout, perched on top of a rock outcrop at 8,445 feet, is in good condition; it has a narrow staircase to the top. The walkway provides 360-degree views: east into Nevada, north over Ladybug Peak and the Verdi Range, northwest over Sardine Valley, and west over Stampede and Boca Reservoirs. The lookout is manned during lightning storms.

Past the spur to Verdi Peak, the trail passes through part of the Crystal Burn Fire of August 1994, when a fire destroyed 7,310 acres. The trail touches Northern Sierra #21: Henness Pass Road before beginning the final 3-rated section that winds along a narrow shelf road around the south side of Beacon Point. This slightly brushy section offers great views into Nevada. Those not wishing to drive this final section can finish on Henness Pass Road.

The main trail is suitable for mountain bikes and forms part of a 28-mile loop from Henness Pass Road that is completed by continuing up the paved road from Boca Reservoir to Stampede Reservoir.

Note that this trail is not accurately shown on topographical maps. The forest service maps are the most accurate for the route described below.

Current Road Information

Tahoe National Forest
Truckee Ranger District
10342 Highway 89 North
Truckee, CA 96162
(530) 587-3558

Map References

BLM Truckee, Portola
USFS Tahoe National Forest, Toiyabe National Forest: Carson Ranger District
USGS 1:24,000 Boca, Dog Valley
1:100,000 Truckee, Portola
Maptech CD-ROM: High Sierra/Tahoe
Northern California Atlas & Gazetteer, pp. 81, 71
California Road & Recreation Atlas, p. 61

Route Directions

▼ 0.0	From CR 894 at Boca Reservoir, 3.2 miles north of the Hirschdale exit of I-80 at Boca, zero trip meter and turn east on FR 72, signposted to Boca Springs and Verdi Peak. The Boca Rest USFS Campground is opposite the turn. Road immediately turns to graded dirt.
0.2 ▲	Trail ends on CR 894 opposite the Boca Rest USFS Campground. Turn left for I-80 and Truckee; turn right for Stampede Reservoir.
	GPS: N39°25.14' W120°05.11'

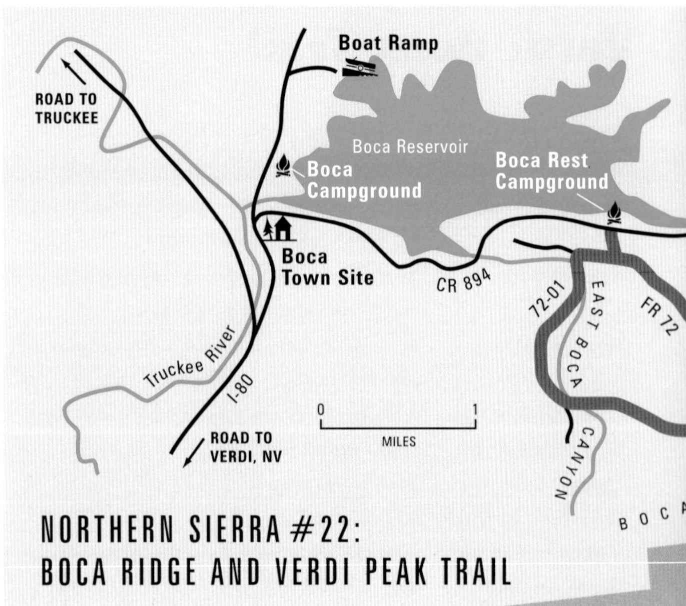

▼ 0.2	SO	Track on right is the start of the optional Boca Ridge Loop. Zero trip meter.
0.0 ▲		Continue to the west.
		GPS: N39°25.16′ W120°04.91′

Optional 4-rated Boca Ridge Loop

▼ 0.0	TR	Turn right (south) onto 72-01 and pass through seasonal closure gate.
3.5 ▲	TL	Seasonal closure gate; then end of optional loop. Turn left onto FR 72 to rejoin the final section of the main trail. Zero trip meter.
▼ 0.1	SO	Track on left.
3.4 ▲	SO	Track on right.
▼ 0.3	SO	Cross through wash; then track on right; then enter East Boca Canyon.
3.2 ▲	SO	Leave East Boca Canyon; then track on left; then cross through wash.
▼ 0.5	SO	Track on right.
3.0 ▲	SO	Track on left.
▼ 1.2	TL	Track on left is Verdi OHV Route for 4WDs, ATVs, and motorbikes. Turn left and cross through East Boca Canyon Creek.
2.3 ▲	TR	Cross through East Boca Canyon Creek; then T-intersection.
		GPS: N39°24.74′ W120°03.91′
▼ 1.6	TR	OHV route on left.
1.9 ▲	BL	OHV route on right.
		GPS: N39°25.10′ W120°03.85′
▼ 2.1	SO	Start of shelf road.
1.4 ▲	SO	End of shelf road.
▼ 2.8	SO	End of shelf road.
0.7 ▲	SO	Start of shelf road.
▼ 2.9	TL	Track ahead climbs hill and dead-ends. Turn left onto marked OHV route.
0.6 ▲	TR	T-intersection. Track on left climbs hill and dead-ends. Turn right and descend hill.
		GPS: N39°25.97′ W120°03.55′
▼ 3.5	TR	End of Boca Ridge Loop. Turn right onto FR 72 to continue along the main trail. Zero trip meter.
0.0 ▲		Continue to the northeast on alternate loop. Zero trip meter.
		GPS: N39°26.08′ W120°03.95′

Continuation of Main Trail

▼ 0.0	SO	Continue straight (northeast) on FR 72.
1.7 ▲	SO	Track on left is the southern end of the optional Boca Ridge Loop. Zero trip meter.
		GPS: N39°25.16′ W120°04.91′
▼ 0.1	SO	Cross through creek on ford.
1.6 ▲	SO	Cross through creek on ford.
▼ 0.4	TR	Track straight ahead is 72-02, which goes 0.3 miles to Boca Spring USFS Campground. Turn right and pass through seasonal closure gate.
1.3 ▲	TL	Seasonal closure gate; then track on right is 72-02, which goes 0.3 miles to Boca Spring USFS Campground.
		GPS: N39°25.46′ W120°04.58′
▼ 1.5	SO	Track on left.
0.2 ▲	SO	Track on right.
▼ 1.7	SO	Track on right is marked OHV route 72-6. This is the northern end of the alternate 4-rated Boca Ridge Loop. Zero trip meter.
0.0 ▲		Continue to the southwest.
		GPS: N39°26.08′ W120°03.95′
▼ 0.0		Continue to the north.
5.8 ▲	SO	Track on left is marked OHV route 72-6. This is the start of the alternate 4-rated Boca Ridge Loop. Zero trip meter and continue straight ahead to remain on the main trail; turn sharp left to drive the loop.
▼ 1.7	SO	Track on left.
4.1 ▲	SO	Track on right.
		GPS: N39°27.11′ W120°03.89′
▼ 2.3	SO	Track on left is 72-12.
3.5 ▲	SO	Track on right is 72-12.
		GPS: N39°27.38′ W120°03.81′
▼ 2.6	SO	Track on left is 72-16.
3.2 ▲	SO	Track on right is 72-16.
▼ 2.7	SO	Track on right.
3.1 ▲	SO	Track on left.
▼ 3.0	SO	Track on left is 72-22.
2.8 ▲	SO	Track on right 72-22.

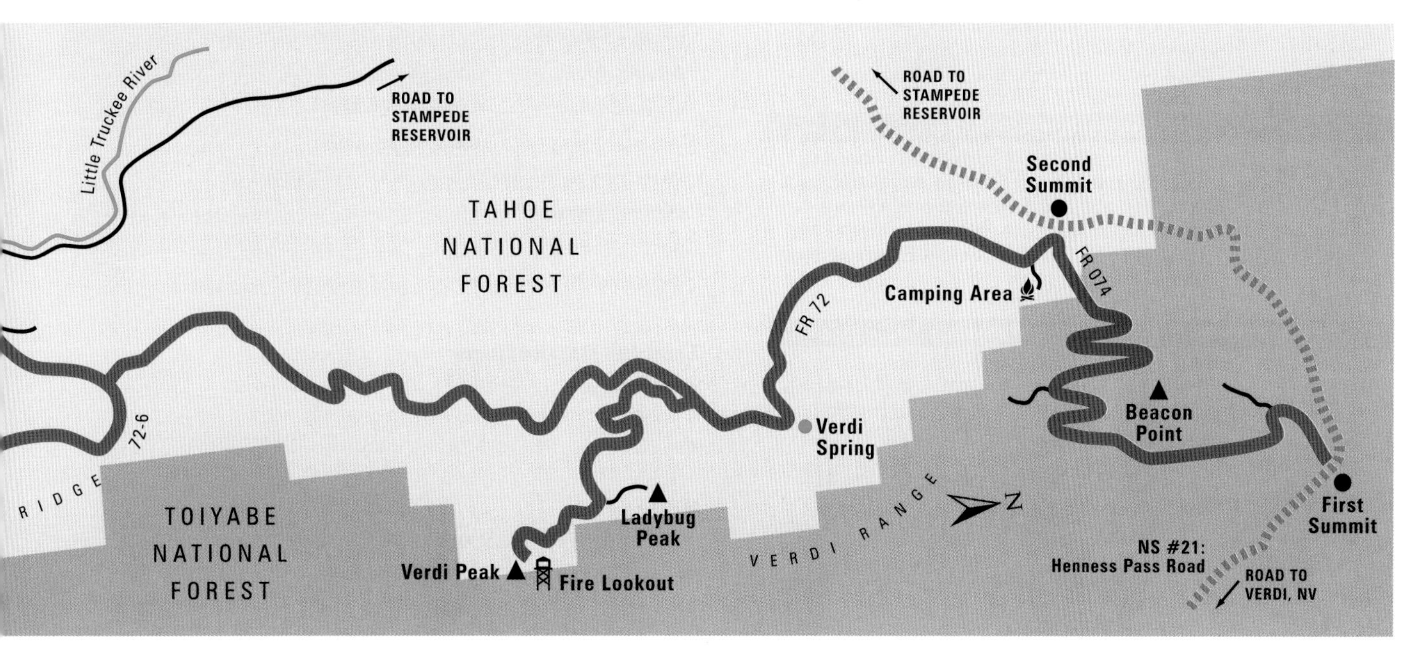

▼ 3.4		SO	Track on right goes 1.1 miles to the ridge top.
	2.4 ▲	SO	Track on left goes 1.1 miles to the ridge top.
			GPS: N39°28.15' W120°03.51'
▼ 4.3		SO	Track on left is 72-25.
	1.5 ▲	SO	Track on right is 72-25.
▼ 5.0		SO	Track on left.
	0.8 ▲	SO	Track on right.
▼ 5.7		SO	Track on left.
	0.1 ▲	SO	Track on right.
▼ 5.8		SO	Track on right is 72-28, spur to Verdi Peak. Zero trip meter and follow the sign to Henness Pass Road.
	0.0 ▲		Continue to the southwest on FR 72.
			GPS: N39°29.48' W120°03.14'

Spur to Verdi Peak Fire Lookout

▼ 0.0		Proceed to the south on 72-28, following sign to Verdi Peak.
▼ 0.1	SO	Seasonal closure gate.
▼ 0.8	SO	Track on right.
▼ 1.1	SO	Seasonal closure gate.
▼ 1.9	SO	Track on left goes 0.4 miles to Ladybug Peak. Continue straight ahead on designated route.
		GPS: N39°28.77' W120°02.72'
▼ 3.0		Spur ends at Verdi Peak Fire Lookout.
		GPS: N39°28.34' W120°02.34'

Continuation of Main Trail

▼ 0.0			Continue to the northeast on FR 72.
	3.6 ▲	BR	Track on left is 72-28, spur to Verdi Peak. Zero trip meter.
			GPS: N39°29.48' W120°03.14'
▼ 0.5		SO	Verdi Spring on right.
	3.1 ▲	SO	Verdi Spring on left.
			GPS: N39°29.92' W120°03.08'
▼ 0.8		SO	Track on left to camping area.
	2.8 ▲	SO	Track on right to camping area.
▼ 1.0		BL	Track on right.
	2.6 ▲	BR	Track on left.
▼ 2.1		SO	Track on right alongside power lines.
	1.5 ▲	SO	Track on left alongside power lines.
▼ 3.3		SO	Track on left to camping area; then track on right is 72-34.
	0.3 ▲	SO	Track on left is 72-34; then track on right to camping area.
			GPS: N39°31.35' W120°03.98'
▼ 3.6		TR	Trail touches Northern Sierra #21: Henness Pass Road at Second Summit and the boundary of Toiyabe and Tahoe National Forests. Turn right, immediately before Henness Pass Road, onto FR 074. Do not join Henness Pass Road. Zero trip meter.
	0.0 ▲		Continue to the southeast.
			GPS: N39°31.57 W120°04.14'
▼ 0.0			Continue to the east.
	5.6 ▲	TL	The trail meets Northern Sierra #21: Henness Pass Road at Second Summit and the boundary of Toiyabe and Tahoe National Forests. Turn left onto FR 72, following the sign for Boca Reservoir, and zero trip meter. Do not join Henness Pass Road.
▼ 0.8		SO	Start of shelf road.
	4.8 ▲	SO	End of shelf road.
▼ 2.0		SO	End of shelf road.
	3.6 ▲	SO	Start of shelf road.
▼ 2.5		TL	Turn left, remaining on FR 074.
	3.1 ▲	TR	Track straight ahead. Remain on FR 074.
			GPS: N39°31.39' W120°03°08'
▼ 3.0		SO	Start of shelf road.
	2.6 ▲	SO	End of shelf road.
▼ 5.1		TR	T-intersection. End of shelf road.
	0.5 ▲	TL	Track straight ahead. Remain on FR 074. Start of shelf road.
			GPS: N39°32.66' W120°02.72'
▼ 5.3		SO	Track on right.
	0.3 ▲	SO	Track on left.
▼ 5.4		SO	Track on right.
	0.2 ▲	SO	Track on left.
▼ 5.5		SO	Track on right.
	0.1 ▲	SO	Track on left.
▼ 5.6			Trails ends at T-intersection with Northern Sierra #21: Henness Pass Road at First Summit. Turn right for Verdi, NV and I-80; turn left to travel Henness Pass Road.
	0.0 ▲		Trail commences on Northern Sierra #21: Henness Pass Road at First Summit, 3.7 miles west of Verdi, NV. Zero trip meter and turn southwest on formed dirt trail FR 074. A USFS information board is opposite the turn.
			GPS: N39°32.91' W120°02.28'

NORTHERN SIERRA #23

Independence Lake Trail

Starting Point:	**Northern Sierra #21: Henness Pass Road (FR 07) at Little Truckee Summit, 1.4 miles west of California 89**
Finishing Point:	**California 89, 7 miles north of Truckee**
Total Mileage:	**21.5 miles, plus 0.9-miles spur to Independence Lake**
Unpaved Mileage:	**21.3 miles, plus 0.9-mile spur**
Driving Time:	**3 hours**
Elevation Range:	**6,200–7,600 feet**
Usually Open:	**April to November**
Best Time to Travel:	**Memorial Day to Labor Day**
Difficulty Rating:	**3**
Scenic Rating:	**8**
Remoteness Rating:	**+0**

Special Attractions

- Fishing and camping at Independence Lake.
- Lightly traveled trail with spectacular views.
- Access to a network of backcountry OHV trails.

History

Independence Lake is one of the major reservoirs of the Truckee River Storage Project. This project, from the early 1900s, provides irrigation and drinking water and flood control for the Truckee Meadows region. Independence Creek runs into the Little Truckee River, which flows into the Stampede and Boca Reservoirs, before joining the Truckee River at Truckee Canyon, and continuing to its end in Pyramid Lake, Nevada. The natural basin north of Carpenter Ridge where Independence Lake was established was important to Native Americans whose burial sites are reminders of their presence in this idyllic setting.

Accounts differ as to the year the lake received its name. One story attributes its naming to actress Lola Montez (see Grass Valley, page 37) in 1852, and another attributes it to Augustus Moore in 1862. Both accounts agree that the naming occurred on the Fourth of July.

This trail follows many of the late nineteenth century narrow-gauge railroad grades used by the Sierra Nevada Wood & Lumber Company. Most of the grades and spur lines ended at Hobart Mills, located to the southeast on California 89. Walter Scott Hobart, who founded the company in the 1860s, died in 1892 and the mill site was named for him. Hobart Mills was a liquor-free company town. The company favored hiring married men with families over single men, a policy not unusual for many early Western businesses. The Southern Pacific purchased the lumber company's railroad in 1932, renaming the line Hobart Southern. By 1935, logging activity was winding down as the company depleted timber on its lands. Hobart Mills survived until 1937, making it one of the last major logging companies in the region.

A bronze plaque at the site of Hobart Mills just north of Prosser Reservoir tells the tale of this once bustling community. One of the locomotives used at Hobart Mills, Shay #14, is still in action today. Built in 1916, Shay #14 now chugs along as part of the rolling stock of the Georgetown Loop Historic Railroad, just west of Denver, Colorado, off of I-70.

Description

The best time to travel this trail is between Memorial Day and Labor Day, when Independence Lake is open to the public. Sierra Pacific Industries, owners of the lake, allows fishing, boating, picnicking, and camping for a small fee.

Independence Lake was originally two lakes before dam construction

The trail leaves FR 07 along a graded gravel road, passing one of the original sections of the Henness Pass Road, before the standard drops to a roughly graded road. The spur to Independence Lake begins at an informally marked turn and travels to a fence around the lake. The gate is open when the lake is open to the public. A small fee is charged for driving to the lake area or camping at the informal campground. There is no charge for parking at the gate and walking down to the lake to fish. Visitors must stop and register at the office immediately past the gate. Past the office, an old two-story building on the right was once the hotel for the lumber settlement of Twin Lakes.

Independence Lake Trail above the Carpenter Valley

The lake has a boat launch, and is good for small sailboats, kayaks, as well as small fishing boats. Anglers will find good fishing for trout and salmon, particularly from a boat. Cutthroat trout must be immediately released. Be sure to read the fishing restrictions posted at the entrance. The lake hasn't been stocked since the 1970s.

The main loop continues through Tahoe National Forest along a rough trail that passes several logging areas. The trail turns south at a major intersection toward Sagehen Creek and the Sagehen USFS Campground. The campground has 10 undeveloped sites with vault toilets.

The Sagehen Watershed is the site of several cooperative long-term research projects sponsored by the University of California, the California Department of Forestry and Resource Management, and the National Forest Service. The primary goal of these projects is to determine the responses of plants and animals to timber management practices. Wetland areas around the creek, known as fens, are habitat to a small carnivorous plant.

Some aspens around Sagehen Creek have carvings made by Basque sheepherders, who tended flocks in these regions. The creek has small rainbow, brook, and brown trout, and fishing regulations apply.

Past Sagehen Creek, the trail turns onto a smaller, formed shelf road that is lightly brushy and climbs around the Sagehen Hills. Some of the best views along the trail can be glimpsed south from here over the open meadows of Carpenter Valley and the North Fork of Prosser Creek. The trail rounds a hill and enters into a network of OHV trails that descend through the forest to travel near the south side of Sagehen Creek. In summer, vehicle travel must be limited to existing roads or trails posted as ORV routes. Certain roads are closed all year and others are closed seasonally to protect deer fawning habitat.

The trail finishes on California 89, a short distance north of the Hobart Mills site.

In winter the area is used by snowmobilers; oversnow travel is permitted when there is 12 inches of snowpack. The Prosser Hill Snowmobile Staging Area is south of the trail's end and 3.7 miles north of Truckee. The southern end of the trail along Sagehen Creek is also used by cross-country skiers, although the route is unmarked and ungroomed.

Current Road Information

Tahoe National Forest
Truckee Ranger District
10342 Highway 89 North
Truckee, CA 96162
(530) 587-3558

Map References

BLM Truckee
USFS Tahoe National Forest
USGS 1:24,000 Independence Lake, Hobart Mills
1:100,000 Truckee
Maptech CD-ROM: High Sierra/Tahoe
Northern California Atlas & Gazetteer, p. 81
California Road & Recreation Atlas, p. 61

Route Directions

Mileage		Direction
▼ 0.0		Trail starts on Northern Sierra #21: Henness Pass Road (FR 07) at Little Truckee Summit, 1.4 miles west of the intersection with California 89. Zero trip meter and turn southeast on graded dirt road 07-10, signposted to Independence Lake. Immediately cross over aqueduct on bridge. Trail follows Henness Pass Road for the first 0.7 miles.
3.5 ▲		Cross over aqueduct on bridge; then trail ends at T-intersection with FR 07. Turn right for California 89 and Truckee; turn left for Jackson Meadow Reservoir.
		GPS: N39°29.54' W120°17.83'
▼ 0.2	SO	Cross over Little Truckee River on bridge.
3.3 ▲	SO	Cross over Little Truckee River on bridge.
▼ 0.5	SO	Henness Pass auto tour stop 16 on right marks a section of the original road bed. Small track on left is a spur along Northern Sierra #21: Henness Pass Road.
3.0 ▲	SO	Henness Pass auto tour stop 16 on left marks a section of the original road bed. Small track on right is a spur along Northern Sierra #21: Henness Pass Road.
		GPS: N39°29.45' W120°17.24'
▼ 0.7	SO	Graded road on left and right. Track on right is Northern Sierra #21: Henness Pass Road (CR 301).
2.8 ▲	SO	Graded road on left and right. Track on left is Northern Sierra #21: Henness Pass Road (CR 301). Trail follows Henness Pass Road for final 0.7 miles.
		GPS: N39°29.45' W120°17.06
▼ 1.1	BR	Track on left; then graded road on left is 07-10. Bear right onto graded road.
2.4 ▲	SO	Graded road on right is 07-10; then track on right.
		GPS: N39°29.16' W120°16.98'

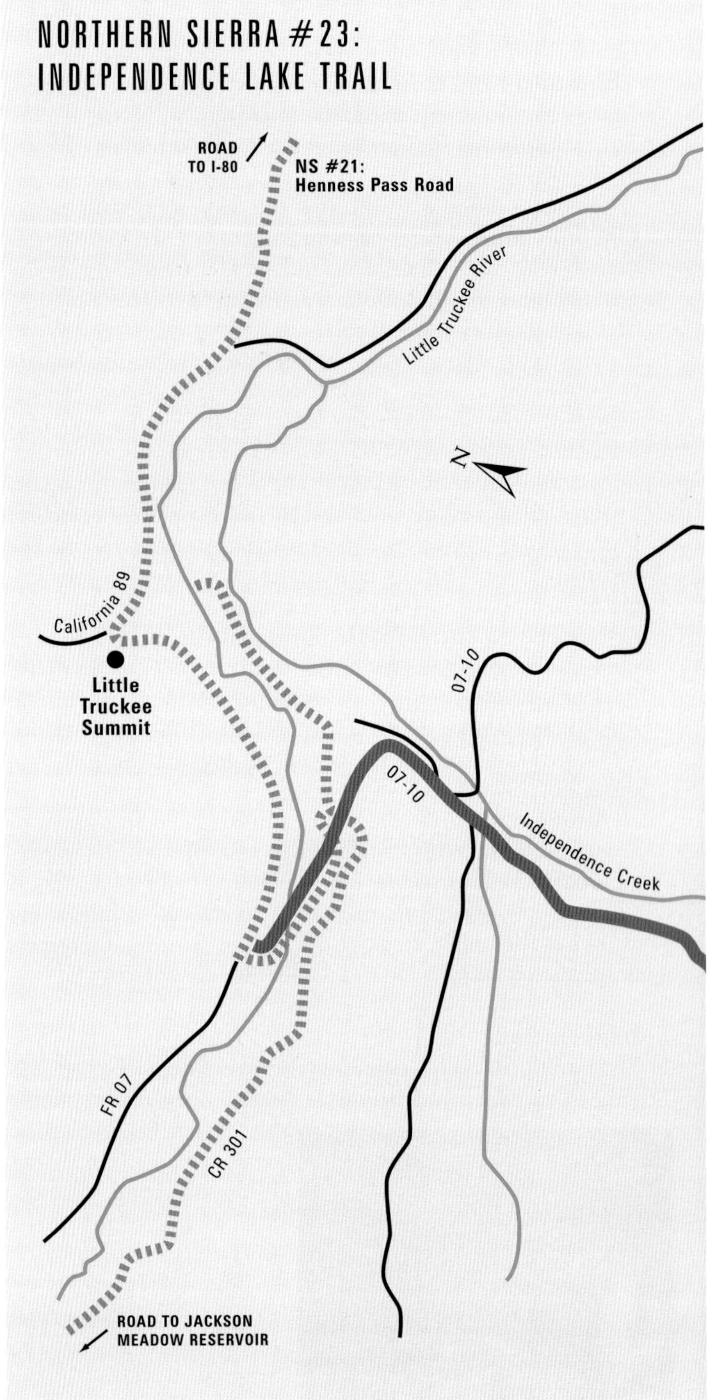

Mileage		Direction
▼ 1.3	SO	Well-used track on right; then cross through creek.
2.2 ▲	SO	Cross through creek; then well-used track on left.
▼ 1.4	SO	Track on left to campsite.
2.1 ▲	SO	Track on right to campsite.
▼ 1.9	BR	Track on left.
1.6 ▲	SO	Track on right.
▼ 3.5	TL	Track straight ahead is the spur to Independence Lake. Zero trip meter.
0.0 ▲		Continue to the north.
		GPS: N39°27.68' W120°17.48'

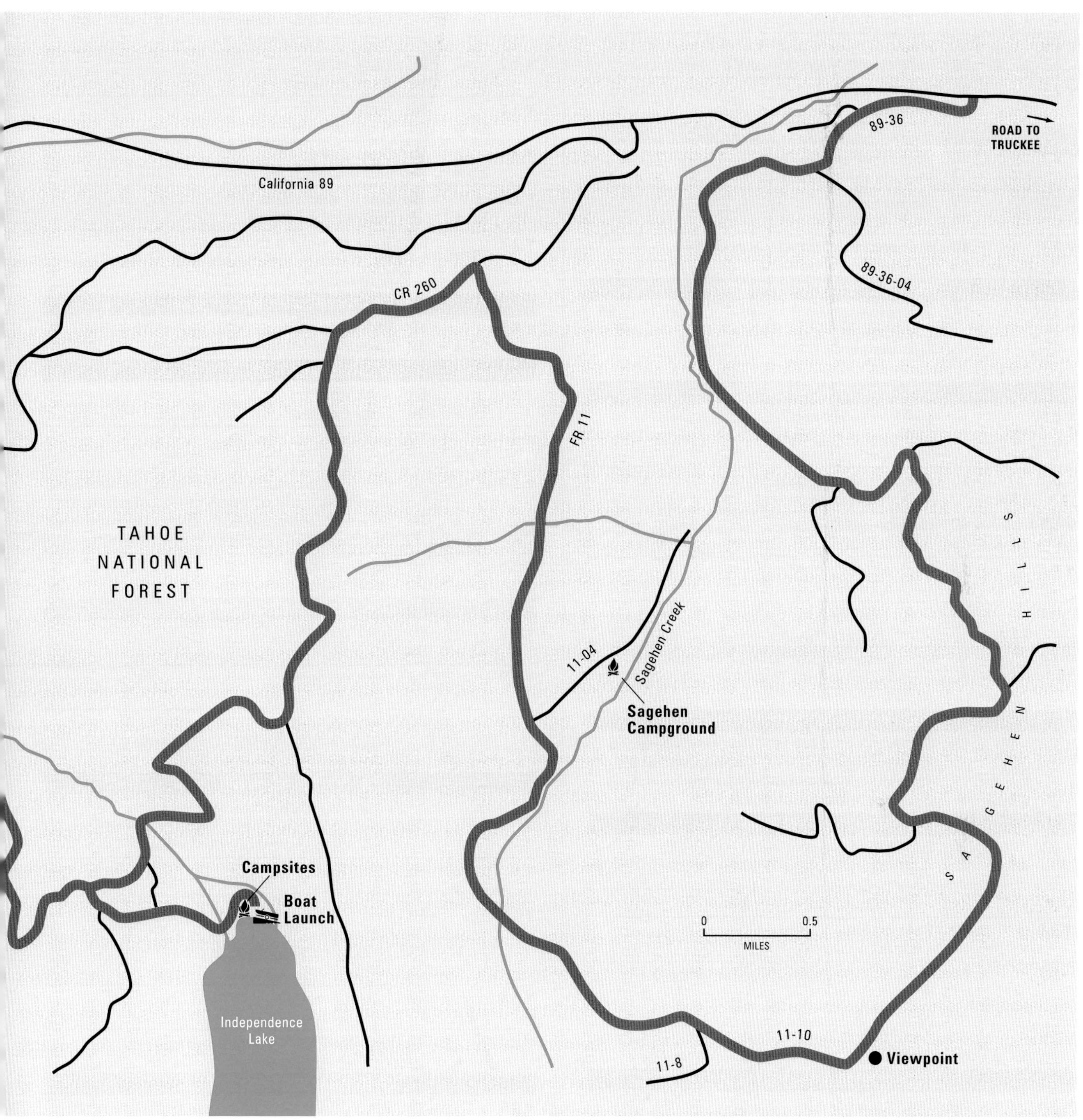

Spur to Independence Lake

▼ 0.0		Continue to the south.
▼ 0.1	BL	Track on right.
▼ 0.4	SO	Track on left.
▼ 0.6	SO	Entering Independence Lake fee area. Fee required for driving and camping past this point. Free parking here for day use.
▼ 0.7	SO	Cross over lake outlet.
▼ 0.8	SO	Track on left and track on right to camping areas.
▼ 0.9		End of trail at Independence Lake.
		GPS: N39°27.07′ W120°17.25′

Continuation of Main Trail

▼ 0.0			Continue to the east.
	4.6 ▲	TR	T-intersection. To the left is the spur to Independence Lake. Zero trip meter.
			GPS: N39°27.68′ W120°17.48′
▼ 0.3		SO	Track on right; then second track on right for non-motorized use only.
	4.3 ▲	SO	Track on left for non-motorized use only; then second track on left.
▼ 0.4		SO	Track on right; then cross over Independence Creek on bridge; then gate.
	4.2 ▲	SO	Gate; then cross over Independence Creek

on bridge; then track on left.

▼ 1.9	BL	Seasonal closure gate; then track on right.
2.7 ▲	BR	Track on left; then seasonal closure gate.
▼ 2.1	SO	Track on left.
2.5 ▲	SO	Track on right.
		GPS: N39°27.24' W120°16.11'
▼ 3.2	SO	Track on left is 351-10.
1.4 ▲	SO	Track on right is 351-10.
▼ 3.8	SO	Track on left.
0.8 ▲	SO	Track on right.
▼ 3.9	SO	Well-used track on left. Join CR 260.
0.7 ▲	BL	Well-used track on right.
		GPS: N39°27.57' W120°14.35'
▼ 4.6	TR	Gravel road straight ahead. Turn right onto FR 11, following sign to Sagehen Campground. Zero trip meter.
0.0 ▲		Continue to the west.
		GPS: N39°27.16' W120°13.80'
▼ 0.0		Continue to the south.
2.6 ▲	TL	T-intersection. Turn left onto gravel road. Zero trip meter.
▼ 0.1	SO	Seasonal closure gate.
2.5 ▲	SO	Seasonal closure gate.
▼ 0.5	SO	Track on left.
2.1 ▲	SO	Track on right.
▼ 0.8	SO	Track on left.
1.8 ▲	SO	Track on right.
▼ 1.4	SO	Cross over creek.
1.2 ▲	SO	Cross over creek.
▼ 2.4	SO	Road becomes paved. Track on right is 11-2.
0.2 ▲	SO	Track on left is 11-2. Road turns back to graded dirt.
		GPS: N39°26.38' W120°15.74'
▼ 2.6	BR	Graded road on left is 11-04, which goes 0.5 miles to Sagehen USFS Campground. Zero trip meter. Road turns back to graded dirt.
0.0 ▲		Continue to the north on FR 11.
		GPS: N39°26.28' W120°15.81'
▼ 0.0		Continue to the southwest on FR 11.
2.3 ▲	BL	Graded road on right is 11-04, which goes 0.5 miles to Sagehen USFS Campground. Zero trip meter. Road is now paved.
▼ 0.5	SO	Track on left.
1.8 ▲	SO	Track on right.
▼ 0.9	SO	Track on right. Follow sign for Carpenter Ridge.
1.4 ▲	SO	Track on left.
▼ 1.2	SO	Cross over Sagehen Creek on bridge.
1.1 ▲	SO	Cross over Sagehen Creek on bridge.
		GPS: N39°26.05' W120°16.83'
▼ 1.6	SO	Track on left is 11-6.
0.7 ▲	SO	Track on right is 11-6.
▼ 2.3	BL	Track on right is 11-8, which goes to Carpenter Ridge. In winter it is a cross-country ski route. Follow sign to the Sagehen Hills. Zero trip meter.
0.0 ▲		Continue to the northeast on FR 11.
		GPS: N39°25.23' W120°16.88'
▼ 0.0		Continue to the south on 11-10.
5.3 ▲	BR	Track on left is 11-8, which goes to Carpenter Ridge. In winter it is a cross-country ski route. Zero trip meter.
▼ 0.9	SO	Hike up ridge on right for panoramic views of Carpenter Valley, Red Mountain, and North Fork Prosser Creek.
4.4 ▲	SO	Hike up ridge on left for panoramic views of Carpenter Valley, Red Mountain, and North Fork Prosser Creek.
▼ 1.2	BR	Track on left.
4.1 ▲	SO	Track on right.
▼ 1.3	SO	Track on left.
4.0 ▲	SO	Track on right.
▼ 1.4	SO	Start of shelf road.
3.9 ▲	SO	End of shelf road.
▼ 2.1	SO	End of shelf road.
3.2 ▲	SO	Start of shelf road.
▼ 2.2	BL	Track on right is marked as a dead end.
3.1 ▲	BR	Track on left is marked as a dead end. Bear right onto 11-10.
		GPS: N39°24.33' W120°15.44'
▼ 2.5	SO	Well-used track on right; then track on left.
2.8 ▲	SO	Track on right; then well-used track on left.
		GPS N39°24.57' W120°15.44'
▼ 2.7	BR	Track on left.
2.6 ▲	BL	Track on right.
▼ 3.0	SO	Well-used track on left.
2.3 ▲	BL	Well-used track on right.
▼ 3.1	SO	Views of Stampede Reservoir to the northeast and Prosser Creek Reservoir to the southeast.
2.2 ▲	SO	Views of Stampede Reservoir to the northeast and Prosser Creek Reservoir to the southeast.
▼ 3.6	SO	Track on right.
1.7 ▲	SO	Track on left.
		GPS: N39°24.52' W120°14.68'
▼ 4.0	SO	Track on right.
1.3 ▲	SO	Track on left.
▼ 4.9	BL	Track on right.
0.4 ▲	BR	Track on left.
▼ 5.3	BL	Track on right is OHV route. Zero trip meter and pass through seasonal closure gate.
0.0 ▲		Continue to the southwest.
		GPS: N39°25.41' W120°14.08'
▼ 0.0		Continue to the northwest.
3.2 ▲	BR	Seasonal closure gate; then track on left is OHV route. Zero trip meter.
▼ 0.1	SO	Track on left.
3.1 ▲	SO	Track on right.
▼ 1.2	SO	Seasonal closure gate to protect deer fawning habitat.
2.0 ▲	SO	Seasonal closure gate to protect deer fawning habitat.
▼ 1.3	SO	Track on right.
2.9 ▲	SO	Track on left.
▼ 2.2	SO	Well-used track on right is 89-36-04.
1.0 ▲	SO	Well-used track on left is 89-36-04.
		GPS: N39°26.03' W120°12.67'
▼ 2.6	SO	Track on left through seasonal closure gate.
0.6 ▲	BL	Track on right through seasonal closure gate.
		GPS: N39°25.91' W120°12.25'
▼ 3.1	TL	Track straight ahead continues 1.6 miles to closure gate. Information board at intersection.
0.1 ▲	TR	T-intersection in front of information board.
▼ 3.2		Seasonal closure gate; then trail ends at T-intersection with California 89. Turn left for Sierraville; turn right for Truckee.
0.0 ▲		Trail commences on California 89, 1.7 miles north of Hobart USFS Work Center and 7 miles north of Truckee. Zero trip meter and turn west on graded trail 89-36 and pass through seasonal closure gate. There is a Penny Pines sign at the intersection.
		GPS: N39°25.53' W120°12.01'

NORTHERN SIERRA #24

Summit City Loop

Starting Point:	**Northern Sierra #25: North Bloomfield–Bowman Lake Trail, 3 miles south of Northern Sierra #21: Henness Pass Road**
Finishing Point:	**Northern Sierra #21: Henness Pass Road (FR 07), 2 miles west of Webber Lake**
Total Mileage:	**17.1 miles, plus 2.2-mile spur to Baltimore Lake and 5.9-mile spur to White Rock Lake**
Unpaved Mileage:	**17.1 miles, plus spurs**
Driving Time:	**5 hours (including both spurs)**
Elevation Range:	**6,200–7,900 feet**
Usually Open:	**April to November**
Best Time to Travel:	**April to November**
Difficulty Rating:	**3 (spurs are rated 5 and 4 respectively)**
Scenic Rating:	**9**
Remoteness Rating:	**+0**

Special Attractions

- Trail passes five lakes and reservoirs that offer excellent backcountry camping and fishing.
- Historic site of Summit City and its cemetery.
- Trail is a groomed snowmobile route in winter.

History

The site of Summit City, a busy mining town of the 1860s, is on the western shore of Meadow Lake. Henry Hartley staked the Excelsior mining claim here in June 1863, and a settlement, originally called Excelsior, had a population of 600 by 1864. Word of the find leaked out and as news traveled, the strike became richer and richer. Concerns about a production drop in Nevada's Comstock Lode quickly drew thousands of miners to what many were calling Little Comstock. In 1866, postal authorities approved the name Meadow Lake for the town's post office. Living conditions at 7,400 feet were far from easy in the winter. Residents often scrambled out of their houses through upstairs windows, and snow depths reached levels that required digging tunnels between houses.

Miners staked claims by the thousands, stamp mills were built, and the population climbed to more than 4,000. Schools, breweries, saloons, and stores flourished in this boom town from the mid to late 1860s. The settlement of Hudsonville, on the far side of Meadow Lake, attracted miners to its entertainment houses.

The winter of 1867–68 brought record levels of snow, trapping thousands. Communication with the outside world was restricted, but the legendary Snowshoe Thompson, a Norwegian emigrant who made his own oak skis, kept up mail delivery to the community.

Though gold-bearing ore kept prospectors interested, extracting it was the real battle. Most gave up as the years went on, leaving only 60 residents in Summit City by 1869. Henry Hartley never gave up. He stayed on into the 1870s, living a hermit's life at the ghost town he truly believed in. Hartley's tombstone in Summit City Cemetery recounts his dream: that he, like his town, would be resurrected to live another day.

Setting up camp at Meadow Lake

Description

Summit City Loop is an easy to moderate trail that passes five very different lakes as well as the historic site of Summit City.

The trail begins on Northern Sierra #25: North Bloomfield–Bowman Lake Trail, 3 miles south of Jackson Meadow Reservoir. The uneven formed trail travels through a mix of forest and small meadows. The first two lakes—Catfish and Tollhouse—are small lakes set in granite basins and surrounded by firs. Some excellent backcountry campsites can be found on the shores of both lakes. Anglers will enjoy fishing in the small lakes as well as in Jackson Meadow Reservoir. French Lake is a short distance off the trail. Vehicle travel is permitted for the first 0.3 miles, but you must hike the remaining distance to the lake. Mountain bikes are permitted to travel the entire way to the lake.

The historic Summit City Cemetery is a short distance off the main trail. Graves are marked by steel crosses and there is a large monument to Summit City's founder Henry Hartley. Opposite the graveyard on the other side of the trail, foundations of the town's brickworks can be seen in a clearing. Be careful and tread lightly in this area—the old bricks are very fragile. Summit City's

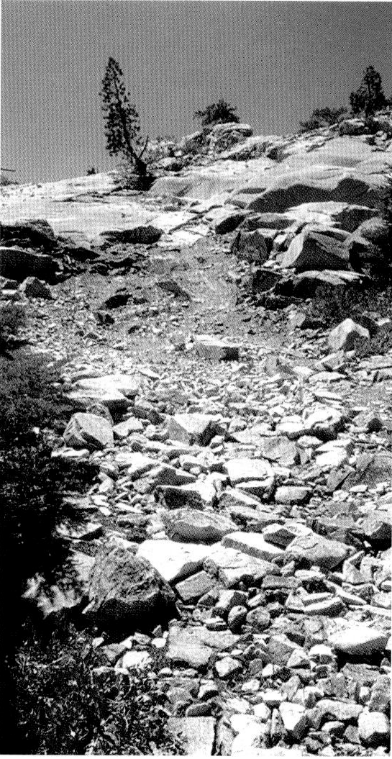

A short section of slickrock on the Baltimore spur trail

site is on the shores of Meadow Lake and is indicated by a historical marker.

The old town site is the starting point for the very difficult Fordyce Jeep Trail (an extreme hardcore trail for modified, short wheel-base vehicles only) and also the start of the 5-rated spur toward Baltimore Lake. The spur travels 2.2 miles southwest along loose uneven rock before finishing on a saddle a short distance from Baltimore Lake. French Lake can be seen to the north from here. The lakes themselves are in an area that prohibits motorized vehicles. Mountain bikers, hikers, and equestrians can descend to the thickly forested basin of Baltimore Lake. The hiking trail continues over a saddle to a group of four lakes known as Beyer Lakes.

Past Summit City, the trail becomes graded and the standard improves slightly, passing a number of designated campsites on the shores of Meadow Lake. From the ridge above Meadow Lake, excellent views open up over the granite dome landscape, with Fordyce Lake in the distance.

The second spur, to White Rock Lake, is rated a 4 for difficulty. This rating is due to the final section that winds down to campsites along the lake's edge. This lake, surrounded by high pale-colored granite and ringed by firs, is among the prettiest in the area. The campsites at the lake have no facilities.

Past the spur to White Rock Lake, the trail is a graded gravel road maintained by the forest service that finishes on paved FR 07, 2 miles west of Webber Lake.

The main loop is a groomed snowmobile route in winter and is marked with orange arrows high on the trees.

Current Road Information

Tahoe National Forest
Sierraville Ranger District
317 South Lincoln
Sierraville, CA 96126
(530) 994-3401

Map References

BLM Truckee
USFS Tahoe National Forest
USGS 1:24,000 English Mt., Webber Peak
1:100,000 Truckee
Maptech CD-ROM: High Sierra/Tahoe
Northern California Atlas & Gazetteer, pp. 80, 81
California Road & Recreation Atlas, pp. 60, 61

Route Directions

▼ 0.0		Trail begins on Northern Sierra #25: North Bloomfield–Bowman Lake Trail, 3 miles south of Northern Sierra #21: Henness Pass Road. Zero trip meter and turn southeast on graded road (called Meadow Lake Road on some maps), following sign to Catfish Lake and Meadow Lake. Cross over creek.
6.6 ▲		Cross over creek; then trail ends at T-intersection with Northern Sierra #25: North Bloomfield–Bowman Lake Trail. Turn right for Jackson Meadow Resevoir; turn left for Nevada City.
		GPS: N39°28.44′ W120°33.73′
▼ 0.3	SO	Track on left.
6.3 ▲	SO	Track on right.
▼ 0.5	SO	Track on right goes 0.5 miles to Catfish Lake.
6.1 ▲	SO	Track on left goes 0.5 miles to Catfish Lake.
		GPS: N39°28.34′ W120°33.16′
▼ 1.1	SO	Cross over creek.
5.5 ▲	SO	Cross over creek.
▼ 1.3	SO	Track on left.

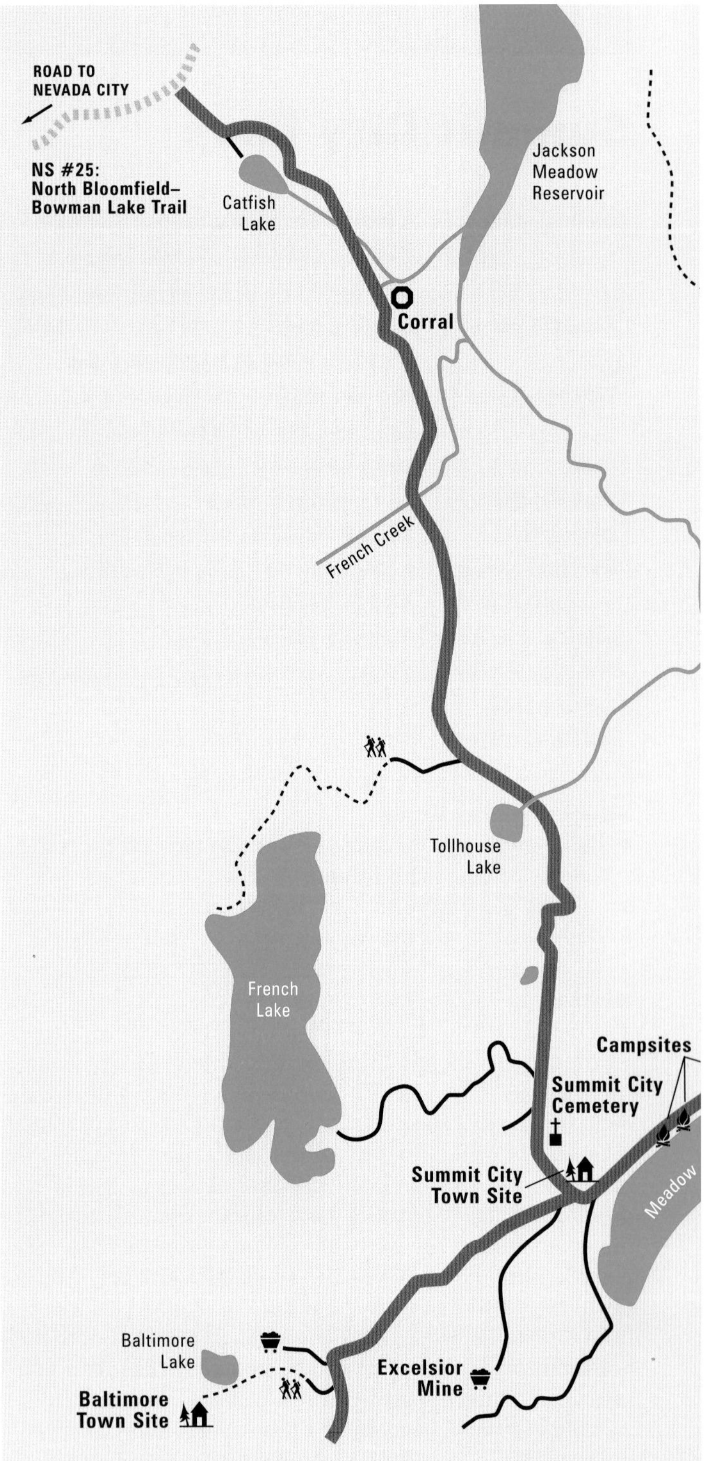

NORTHERN SIERRA #24: SUMMIT CITY LOOP

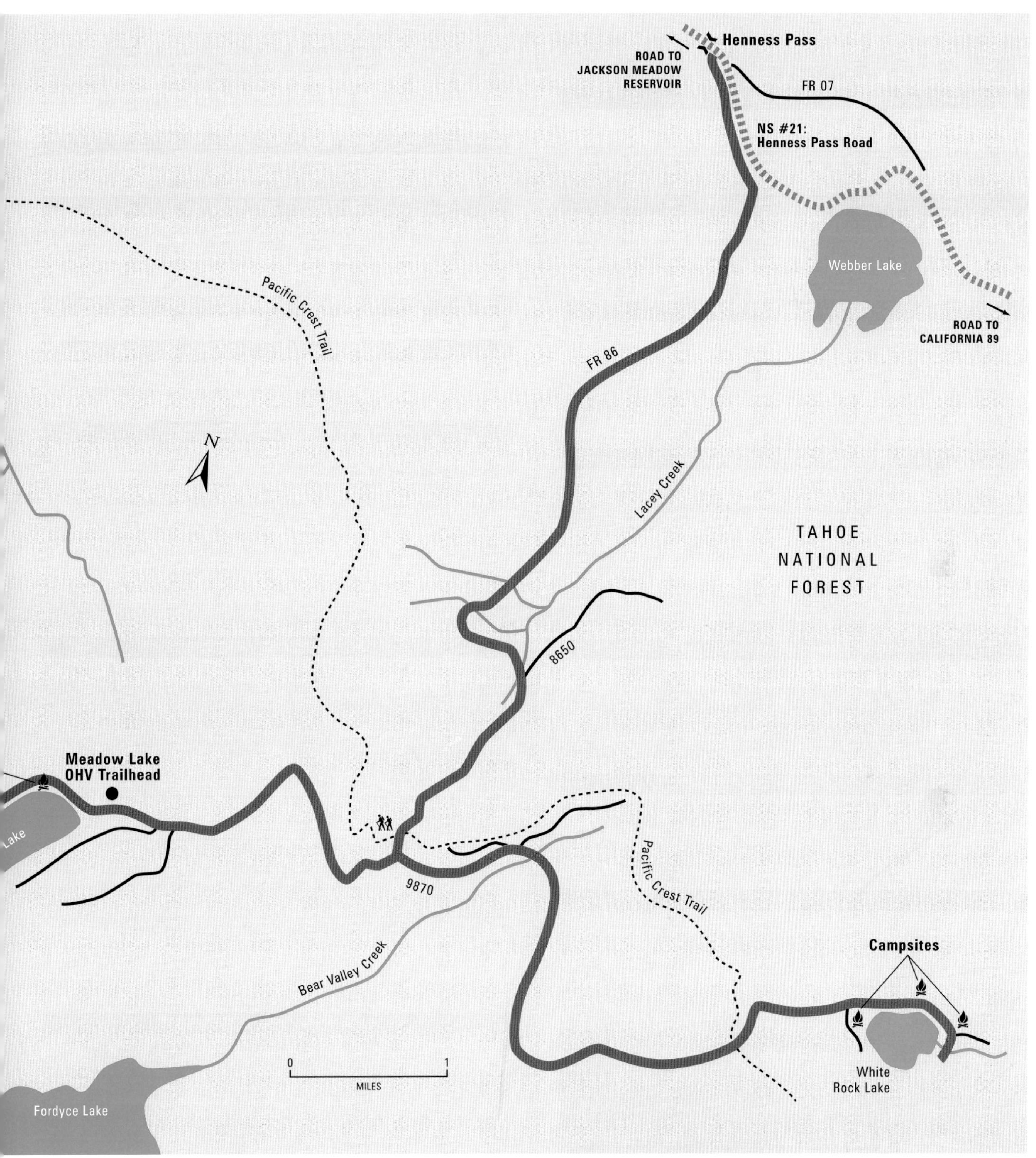

	5.3 ▲	SO	Track on right.
▼ 1.4		SO	Corral on left.
	5.2 ▲	SO	Corral on right.
▼ 1.6		SO	Track on right; then cross over creek.
	5.0 ▲	SO	Cross over creek; then track on left.
▼ 2.3		SO	Track on right.
	4.3 ▲	SO	Track on left.
▼ 2.5		SO	Cross through French Creek.
	4.1 ▲	SO	Cross through French Creek.
			GPS: N39°27.10' W120°31.98'
▼ 3.7		SO	Cross through meadow.
	2.9 ▲	SO	Cross through meadow.
▼ 3.8		SO	Well-used but unmarked track on right goes 1.6 miles to French Lake. Motorized vehicle

use prohibited after 0.3 miles.

2.8 ▲ SO Well-used but unmarked track on left goes 1.6 miles to French Lake. Motorized vehicle use prohibited after 0.3 miles.

GPS: N39°26.15′ W120°31.40′

▼ 4.0 SO Track on right.
2.6 ▲ SO Track on left.

▼ 4.1 SO Track on left. Tollhouse Lake on right.
2.5 ▲ SO Track on right. Tollhouse Lake on left.

GPS: N39°26.07′ W120°31.02′

▼ 4.2 SO Cross through creek.
2.4 ▲ SO Cross through creek.

▼ 4.6 BR Track on left. Follow sign to Meadow Lake.
2.0 ▲ BL Track on right.

GPS: N39°25.68′ W120°30.65′

▼ 5.1 BR Track on left.
1.5 ▲ BL Track on right.

▼ 5.2 SO Track on right; then track on left.
1.4 ▲ SO Track on right; then track on left.

▼ 5.4 SO Small lake on right.
1.2 ▲ SO Small lake on left.

GPS: N39°25.41′ W120°30.66′

▼ 5.5 SO Track on left.
1.1 ▲ SO Track on right.

▼ 5.7 SO Turnout on right.
0.9 ▲ SO Turnout on left.

▼ 5.8 SO Track on right.
0.8 ▲ SO Track on left.

▼ 6.0 SO Track on right.
0.6 ▲ SO Track on left.

GPS: N39°24.84′ W120°30.52′

▼ 6.1 SO Unmarked track on left to Summit City Cemetery. Remains of the brickworks are in the small clearing opposite.
0.5 ▲ SO Unmarked track on right to Summit City Cemetery. Remains of the brickworks are in the small clearing opposite.

GPS: N39°24.78′ W120°30.50′

▼ 6.6 TL Track on right is the spur to Baltimore Lake and also leads toward Excelsior Mine and Fordyce Lake. Site of Summit City is marked by a sign. Zero trip meter.
0.0 ▲ Continue to the west-southwest.

GPS: N39°24.58′ W120°30.13′

View of Fordyce Dam at the end of the Baltimore spur trail

Spur to Baltimore Lake

▼ 0.0 At the sign for Summit City, turn south-southwest. Immediately bear right at fork in trail. Track on left is the start of the Fordyce Jeep Trail. Tracks on right to campsites.

▼ 0.2 BR Track on left goes to Excelsior Mine.

GPS: N39°24.51′ W120°30.30′

▼ 1.4 SO Hard-to-spot track on right goes 0.3 miles to mine and is rated 6 for difficulty.

GPS: N39°23.68′ W120°31.18′

▼ 1.6 BL Track on right goes 0.1 miles to saddle. No motorized vehicles allowed past the saddle. Hikers and mountain bikers can climb along the old trail to Baltimore Lake.

GPS: N39°23.58′ W120°31.21′

▼ 2.1 SO Trail climbs slickrock.

GPS: N39°23.27′ W120°31.23′

▼ 2.2 Trail ends just east of Baltimore town site at an overlook of Fordyce Lake. Trail is little used by vehicles past this point.

GPS: N39°23.25′ W120°31.23′

Continuation of Main Trail

▼ 0.0 Continue to the north. Immediately track on right and track on left.
4.1 ▲ TR Track on right and track on left. Track straight ahead is the spur to Baltimore Lake and also leads toward Excelsior Mine and Fordyce Lake. Turn right in front of the Summit City sign, following the sign to Tollhouse Lake. Zero trip meter.

GPS: N39°24.58′ W120°30.13′

▼ 0.1 SO Track on right to designated campsite. Many tracks on right to campsites for the next 1.2 miles.
4.0 ▲ SO Track on left to designated campsite. End of designated campsites.

▼ 0.8 SO Track on left.
3.3 ▲ SO Track on right.

▼ 0.9 SO Track on left.
3.2 ▲ SO Track on right.

▼ 1.3 SO End of designated camping area.
2.8 ▲ SO Start of designated camping area. Many tracks on left to designated campsites for the next 1.2 miles.

▼ 1.5 BR Graded road on left is parking area for Meadow Lake OHV Trail; then track on left.
2.6 ▲ BL Track on right; then graded road on right is parking area for Meadow Lake OHV Trail.

GPS: N39°25.20′ W120°28.87′

▼ 1.7 SO Track on left; then track on right.
2.4 ▲ SO Track on left; then track on right.

▼ 1.8 SO Track on right.
2.3 ▲ SO Track on left.

▼ 2.1 BL Track on right is 84305.
2.0 ▲ BR Track on left is 84305.

GPS: N39°25.21′ W120°28.18′

▼ 3.6 SO Track on left.
0.5 ▲ SO Track on right.

▼ 4.1 SO Start of FR 86. Graded road on right is spur to White Rock Lake. Zero trip meter.
0.0 ▲ Continue to the northwest. Road becomes rougher.

GPS: N39°25.35′ W120°26.86′

Spur to White Rock Lake

▼ 0.0			Turn southeast on graded road 9870, following sign to White Rock Lake. Immediately track on right.
▼ 0.8		BR	Well-used track on left; then small track on left. Cross over Bear Valley Creek.
			GPS: N39°25.52' W120°26.12'
▼ 1.2		BL	Well-used track on right at sign for Deer Zone D-3.
▼ 3.5		SO	Cross through wash.
▼ 3.6		SO	Track on right.
			GPS: N39°24.71' W120°24.51'
▼ 4.2		BL	Track on right; then Pacific Crest Trail crosses.
			GPS: N39°25.04' W120°24.13'
▼ 4.9		BL	Trail forks. Left goes to campsites (for high-clearance vehicles only) and right goes 0.3 miles to campsites.
			GPS: N39°25.24' W120°23.43'
▼ 5.2		SO	Many campsites along the edge of White Rock Lake.
			GPS: N39°25.30' W120°23.09'
▼ 5.7		SO	Track on left; then cross through creek.
			GPS: N39°25.23' W120°22.67'
▼ 5.9			Trail ends at lakeshore.
			GPS: N39°25.12' W120°22.68'

Continuation of Main Trail

▼ 0.0			Continue to the northeast, following sign to Webber Lake. Road improves.
	6.4 ▲	SO	End of FR 86. Graded road on left is spur to White Rock Lake. Follow sign to Meadow Lake and zero trip meter.
			GPS: N39°25.35' W120°26.86'
▼ 0.2		SO	Pacific Crest Trail crosses.
	6.2 ▲	SO	Pacific Crest Trail crosses.
▼ 0.4		SO	Track on right.
	6.0 ▲	SO	Track on left.
▼ 1.4		SO	Track on right is 8650; then cross over Lacey Creek.
	5.0 ▲	SO	Cross over Lacey Creek; then track on left is 8650.
▼ 2.2		SO	Cross over creek.
	4.2 ▲	SO	Cross over creek.
▼ 2.5		SO	Cross over creek.
	3.9 ▲	SO	Cross over creek.
▼ 2.8		SO	Formed road on right is 9840; then track on right.
	3.6 ▲	SO	Track on left; then formed road on left is 9840.
			GPS: N39°27.14' W120°26.44'
▼ 3.8		SO	Track on left.
	2.6 ▲	SO	Track on right.
▼ 5.0		SO	Seasonal closure gates.
	1.4 ▲	SO	Seasonal closure gates.
▼ 5.8		SO	Graded road on right is Northern Sierra #21: Henness Pass Road (CR 301). Trail follows Henness Pass Road for final 0.6 miles.
	0.6 ▲	BR	Graded road on left is eastern continuation of Northern Sierra #21: Henness Pass Road (CR 301).
			GPS: N39°29.41' W120°25.70'
▼ 6.2		SO	Track on right.
	0.2 ▲	SO	Track on left.
▼ 6.4			Trail ends at T-intersection with paved FR 07, part of Northern Sierra #21: Henness Pass Road, at Henness Pass. Turn right for California 89; turn left for Jackson Meadow Reservoir.
	0.0 ▲		Trail commences on paved Northern Sierra #21: Henness Pass Road (FR 07) at Henness Pass, 2 miles west of Webber Lake. Zero trip meter and turn southwest on graded dirt road CR 301, following the sign to White Rock Lake and Meadow Lake. Turn is immediately west of county mile marker 9.47. Trail follows Henness Pass Road for first 0.6 miles.
			GPS: N39°29.90' W120°26.00'

NORTHERN SIERRA #25

North Bloomfield–Bowman Lake Trail

Starting Point:	**California 49 in Nevada City, 0.3 miles west of California 20**
Finishing Point:	**Northern Sierra #21: Henness Pass Road at Jackson Meadow Reservoir**
Total Mileage:	**40.7 miles**
Unpaved Mileage:	**30.7 miles**
Driving Time:	**5 hours**
Elevation Range:	**2,000–6,600 feet**
Usually Open:	**Year-round**
Best Time to Travel:	**Dry weather**
Difficulty Rating:	**2**
Scenic Rating:	**9**
Remoteness Rating:	**+0**

Special Attractions

- Bowman Lake and Jackson Meadow Reservoir.
- Malakoff Diggins State Park.
- Historic town of Graniteville and Graniteville Cemetery.

History

Traveling the North Bloomfield–Bowman Lake Trail offers an opportunity to follow in the footsteps of miners from a time long gone, but not quite forgotten. Nevada City, at the start of the trail, may seem busy nowadays, but try to imagine the scene in 1850, when 10,000 gold-hungry men and boys tried to make this newly discovered camp their home. On the northwest side of Sugarloaf Mountain is the site of Allan's Foundry, the first manufacturing site of the renowned Pelton waterwheel. Lester Allan Pelton's wheel revolutionized hydraulic mining by harnessing nearly all the energy of water. The first wheel was used in the highly productive North Star Mine in Grass Valley, which produced $33 million in gold by 1928. The invention opened the door for the hydroelectric power industry.

Establishing wagon roads to the mines was of utmost importance, but it was quite a challenge in country cut by steep canyons. The first bridge to the Malakoff Diggins was built in the 1850s at Edwards Crossing over the South Yuba River. Today's high arched steel bridge, built in 1904, is the fourth

Graniteville's historic buildings

bridge at this location.

The settlement of Lake City, also known as Painesville, was settled in 1853, east of the Malakoff Diggins. By 1857, more than 300 people lived at the site. No buildings survive, but a sign marks the location of Bridget Waldron's livery stable.

The drive downhill to Malakoff Diggins is an eye-opener on how hydraulic mining changed the landscape. Between the 1850s and 1880s gold miners channeled creeks high in the mountains to create enough pressure for hydraulic operations at lower elevations. High-powered water jets directed by giant monitor nozzles collapsed hillsides so that dirt and rocks could be washed for gold. An estimated $3.5 million worth of gold was extracted from this vicinity. By 1884, farmers had managed to lobby a ban on hydraulic mining because silt and mud buried fields and changed the flow of downstream rivers and waterways. The site of North Bloomfield (see page 47), on the edge of Malakoff Diggins, has an excellent selection of miners' dwellings, stores, and a museum.

Farther to the northeast the trail passes the site of Quinn Ranch, a former stage stop called Shand that was no doubt a welcome sight to travelers. From here they went to Graniteville, formerly known as Eureka. Today, the site is a far cry from its gold mining days of the 1860s. Surface mines were worked as early as 1850, though these played out by the end of the decade. A return to lode mining rekindled the town in the mid 1860s. Hotels, stores, a blacksmith shop, and several saloons operated until the 1870s.

Picturesque Bowman Lake, set below Quartz Hill, was an important water source for some of the mining communities at lower elevations. The dam was built on the old Bowman Ranch. Bowman House, just below the dam, was at the junction of two important wagon roads. The early route up through Eureka (Graniteville), on past Marsh Mill (operated by Charles Marsh), to Bowman House was an alternative to the Henness Pass Road. The Pacific Turnpike Road, also known as Culbertson's Road, joined in from the south at this point. From here these separate routes headed northeast to Jackson's Meadow, nowadays Jackson Meadow Reservoir.

Description

This easy, graded road travels from Nevada City past the northern shore of Bowman Lake to finish on Northern Sierra #21: Henness Pass Road at Jackson Meadow Reservoir.

From Nevada City, the trail drops steeply along a small paved road to cross over the South Yuba River at Edwards Crossing. The South Yuba Trail, an enjoyable hike along the South Yuba River, crosses the road at this point. This moderate trail is 15 miles long and takes hikers east to Washington. The river is stocked yearly with rainbow trout. The road turns to graded dirt after the bridge, and it climbs to the top of the ridge, where Northern Sierra #26: Alleghany Trail heads off to the north. The main trail bears east and passes the developed South Yuba BLM Campground, which has 16 campsites in a shaded gully at the site of some old mine workings. A small fee is charged.

The trail enters Malakoff Diggins State Park, once the site of some of the most prosperous and active hydraulic mining ventures in California. You can view the mine face and see the massive changes in the landscape caused by hydraulic mining. Many of the original buildings from the settlement of North Bloomfield can also be seen in the park. The park has a campground and a few cabins in the main part of town. There is plenty to see and do in the park, and many people choose to make it an overnight stop along the trail. There are several short and interesting hiking trails, including the 3-mile Rim Trail around the perimeter of the Malakoff Diggins, and the 3-mile Diggins Trail through the works.

Continuing east through Tahoe National Forest, the trail passes Snowtent Spring, a flowing cold-water spring with an informal camping area behind it. Northern Sierra #26: Alleghany Trail rejoins shortly before Graniteville and the historic Graniteville Cemetery, which is a short distance west of the settlement. There are no services in Graniteville, but the settlement has some wonderful old, historic houses that are used as summer homes.

Past Graniteville, the trail drops in standard to become a roughly graded dirt road. It winds past oaks, manzanitas, and firs to Bowman Lake, a popular destination for outdoor enthusiasts. The trail drops in standard again—this section of road is not maintained by the forest service. A wonderful se-

Edwards Crossing bridges the South Yuba River

lection of backcountry campsites is scattered along the lakeshore among large granite boulders and firs. There is an informal boat launch, and both boat and shore anglers will enjoy fishing for brown and rainbow trout. The lake is stocked annually with fingerlings.

As the trail leaves the lakeshore, additional camping areas can be found, including the Bowman Lake Campground, where there are a couple of scattered tables, and the more maintained Jackson Creek USFS Campground. Note that the Bowman Lake Campground does not appear on the Tahoe National Forest map.

The trail ends at the intersection with Northern Sierra #21: Henness Pass Road at Jackson Meadow Reservoir.

Current Road Information

Tahoe National Forest
Nevada City Ranger District
631 Coyote Street
Nevada City, CA 95959
(530) 265-4531

Map References

BLM Yuba City, Truckee, Portola
USFS Tahoe National Forest
USGS 1:24,000 Nevada City, North Bloomfield, Pike, Alleghany, Graniteville, English Mt., Haypress Valley
1:100,000 Yuba City, Truckee, Portola
Maptech CD-ROM: High Sierra/Tahoe
Northern California Atlas & Gazetteer, pp. 79, 80, 70
California Road & Recreation Atlas, pp. 65, 60

Route Directions

▼ 0.0		From the intersection of California 49 and California 20 at Nevada City, exit the divided road onto California 49, following sign for Downieville. Proceed 0.3 miles west; then zero trip meter and turn north on paved North Bloomfield Road (CR 522). Remain on paved North Bloomfield Road, ignoring turns to the left and right.
8.5 ▲		Trail ends at T-intersection with California 49 in Nevada City.
		GPS: N39°16.16' W121°01.19'
▼ 0.5	TR	T-intersection. Remain on North Bloomfield Road, following sign for South Yuba Campground. Lake Vera Road is on the left.
8.0 ▲	TL	Lake Vera Road is straight ahead. Turn left, remaining on North Bloomfield Road.
▼ 7.1	SO	South Yuba Trail (hiking) to Round Mountain on left; then cross over South Yuba River on bridge. Road turns to graded dirt.
1.4 ▲	SO	Road becomes paved. Cross over South Yuba River on bridge; then South Yuba Trail (hiking) to Round Mountain on right.
		GPS: N39°19.78' W120°59.04'
▼ 7.2	SO	Hiking access on right to river and continuation of the South Yuba Trail.
1.3 ▲	SO	Hiking access on left to river and continuation of the South Yuba Trail.
▼ 8.0	SO	Track on left.
0.5 ▲	SO	Track on right.
▼ 8.5	BR	Graded road on left is Northern Sierra #26: Alleghany Trail (Grizzly Hill Road). Zero trip meter and remain on North Bloomfield Road, following sign to Malakoff Diggins State Park.
0.0 ▲		Continue to the south.
		GPS: N39°20.48' W120°58.50'
▼ 0.0		Continue to the northeast.
5.3 ▲	BL	Graded road on right is Northern Sierra #26: Alleghany Trail (Grizzly Hill Road). Zero trip meter.
▼ 0.2	SO	Track on right into South Yuba BLM Campground and access to South Yuba Trail.
5.1 ▲	SO	Track on left into South Yuba BLM Campground and access to the South Yuba Trail.
▼ 0.6	SO	Track on left.
4.7 ▲	SO	Track on right.
▼ 0.9	SO	Track on left and track on right.
4.4 ▲	SO	Track on left and track on right.
▼ 1.4	SO	Track on right.
3.9 ▲	SO	Track on left.
▼ 1.6	SO	Track on right.
3.7 ▲	SO	Track on left.
▼ 2.1	SO	Track on right.
3.2 ▲	SO	Track on left.
▼ 2.3	SO	Site of Lake City on both sides of the road; then track on left.
3.0 ▲	SO	Track on right; then site of Lake City on both sides of the road.
		GPS: N39°21.49' W120°56.52'
▼ 2.4	BR	Lake City Road on left; then Back Bone Road on left. Remain on North Bloomfield Road, following sign for Malakoff Diggins. Enter Malakoff Diggins State Park.
2.9 ▲	TL	Back Bone Road on right; then Lake City Road on right. Remain on North Bloomfield Road and exit state park.
		GPS: N39°21.54' W120°56.47'
▼ 3.2	SO	Rim Trail (hiking) to campground on left.
2.1 ▲	SO	Rim Trail (hiking) to campground on right.
		GPS: N39°21.92' W120°55.87'
▼ 3.7	SO	Diggins Loop Trail access on left.
1.6 ▲	SO	Diggins Loop Trail access on right.
▼ 3.9	SO	Humbug Trail (hiking) on right.
1.4 ▲	SO	Humbug Trail (hiking) on left.
		GPS: N39°21.92' W120°55.35'
▼ 4.0	SO	Cross over North Bloomfield Drain Tunnel.
1.3 ▲	SO	Cross over North Bloomfield Drain Tunnel.
▼ 4.5	SO	Road becomes paved. Two cabins on right; then Diggins overlook and historical marker on left.
0.8 ▲	SO	Diggins overlook and historical marker on right; then two cabins on left. Road turns to graded dirt.
▼ 5.0	SO	Track on left to cemetery. Then St. Columncille's Catholic Church on left and Le Du Mine overlook on right.
0.3 ▲	SO	Le Du Mine overlook on left and St. Columncille's Catholic Church on right. Then track on right to cemetery.
		GPS: N39°22.00' W120°54.26'
▼ 5.1	SO	Track on left; then China Garden on right.
0.2 ▲	SO	China Garden on left; then track on right.
▼ 5.3	SO	North Bloomfield. Zero trip meter at the intersection of North Bloomfield Road and Relief Hill Road.
0.0 ▲		Continue to the southwest, following sign for Nevada City.

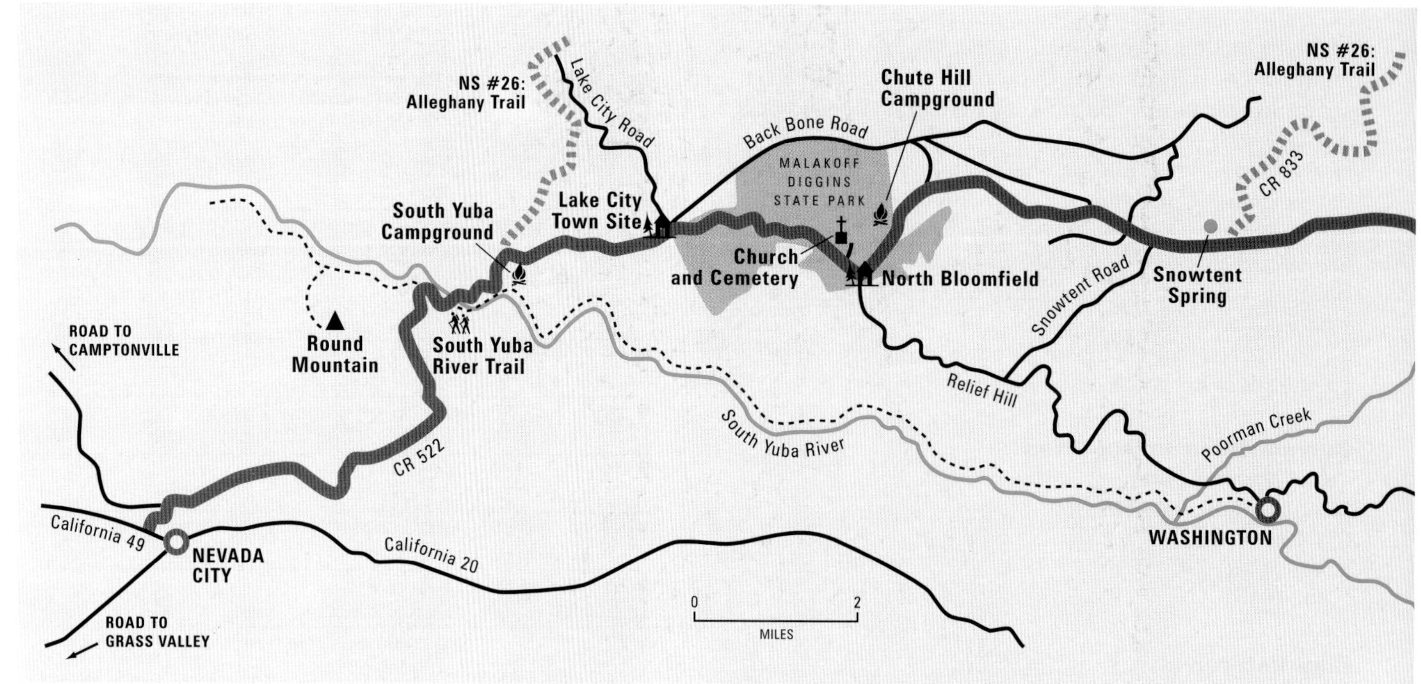

Mileage		Directions
		GPS: N39°22.08' W120°53.95'
▼ 0.0		Continue to the northeast, following sign for Graniteville.
5.4 ▲	SO	North Bloomfield. Zero trip meter at the intersection of North Bloomfield Road and Relief Hill Road.
▼ 0.2	SO	Picnic area at Blair Lake on right.
5.2 ▲	SO	Picnic area at Blair Lake on left.
▼ 0.6	SO	Blair Trail (hiking) crosses road. Paved road on left goes to Chute Hill Campground—run by the Malakoff Diggins State Historic Park.
4.8 ▲	SO	Paved road on right goes to Chute Hill Campground—run by the Malakoff Diggins State Historic Park. Blair Trail (hiking) crosses road.
▼ 1.3	SO	Paved road continues to the left. Continue straight ahead onto graded dirt road.
4.1 ▲	SO	Paved road enters from right. Continue straight ahead and join paved road.
		GPS: N39°23.17' W120°53.68'
▼ 3.6	BR	Track on right; then bear right and join graded road, following sign for Graniteville.
1.8 ▲	BL	Graded road continues straight ahead. Bear left onto graded road; then track on left.
		GPS: N39°23.75' W120°51.40'
▼ 4.1	SO	Track on right and graded road on left.
1.3 ▲	SO	Track on left and graded road on right.
▼ 4.5	SO	Track on right is Snowtent Road to Relief Hill.
0.9 ▲	SO	Track on left is Snowtent Road to Relief Hill.
		GPS: N39°23.73' W120°50.43'
▼ 4.6	SO	Track on left is 522-2.
0.8 ▲	SO	Track on right is 522-2.
▼ 5.1	SO	Track on right and track on left; then second track on left.
0.3 ▲	SO	Track on right; then second track on right and track on left.
▼ 5.2	SO	Snowtent Spring and camping area on left.
0.2 ▲	SO	Snowtent Spring and camping area on right.
		GPS: N39°23.98' W120°49.71'
▼ 5.4	SO	Road on right is Robbins Ranch Road. Track on left is Northern Sierra #26: Alleghany Trail (CR 833) signposted to Moores Flat and Bucks Ranch. Zero trip meter.
0.0 ▲		Continue to the southwest.
		GPS: N39°24.09' W120°49.52'
▼ 0.0		Continue to the northeast.
6.0 ▲	SO	Road on left is Robbins Ranch Road. Track on right is Northern Sierra #26: Alleghany Trail (CR 833) signposted to Moores Flat and Bucks Ranch. Zero trip meter.
▼ 0.3	SO	Track on right.
5.7 ▲	SO	Track on left.
▼ 0.4	SO	Track on right.
5.6 ▲	SO	Track on left.
▼ 1.7	SO	Track on left and track on right.
4.3 ▲	SO	Track on left and track on right.
▼ 2.7	SO	Track on left; then track on right.
3.3 ▲	SO	Track on left; then track on right.
▼ 3.1	SO	Graded road on right.
2.9 ▲	SO	Graded road on left.
▼ 3.2	SO	Track on left.
2.8 ▲	SO	Track on right.
▼ 3.6	SO	Track on left.
2.4 ▲	SO	Track on right.
▼ 3.7	SO	Track on right.
2.3 ▲	SO	Track on left.
▼ 4.1	SO	Track on left and track on right.
1.9 ▲	SO	Track on right and track on left.
▼ 4.4	SO	Track on left.
1.6 ▲	SO	Track on right.
▼ 4.8	SO	Track on left.
1.2 ▲	SO	Track on right.
▼ 4.9	SO	Track on right.
1.1 ▲	SO	Track on left.
▼ 5.1	SO	Graded road on left is S2248.
0.9 ▲	SO	Graded road on right is S2248.

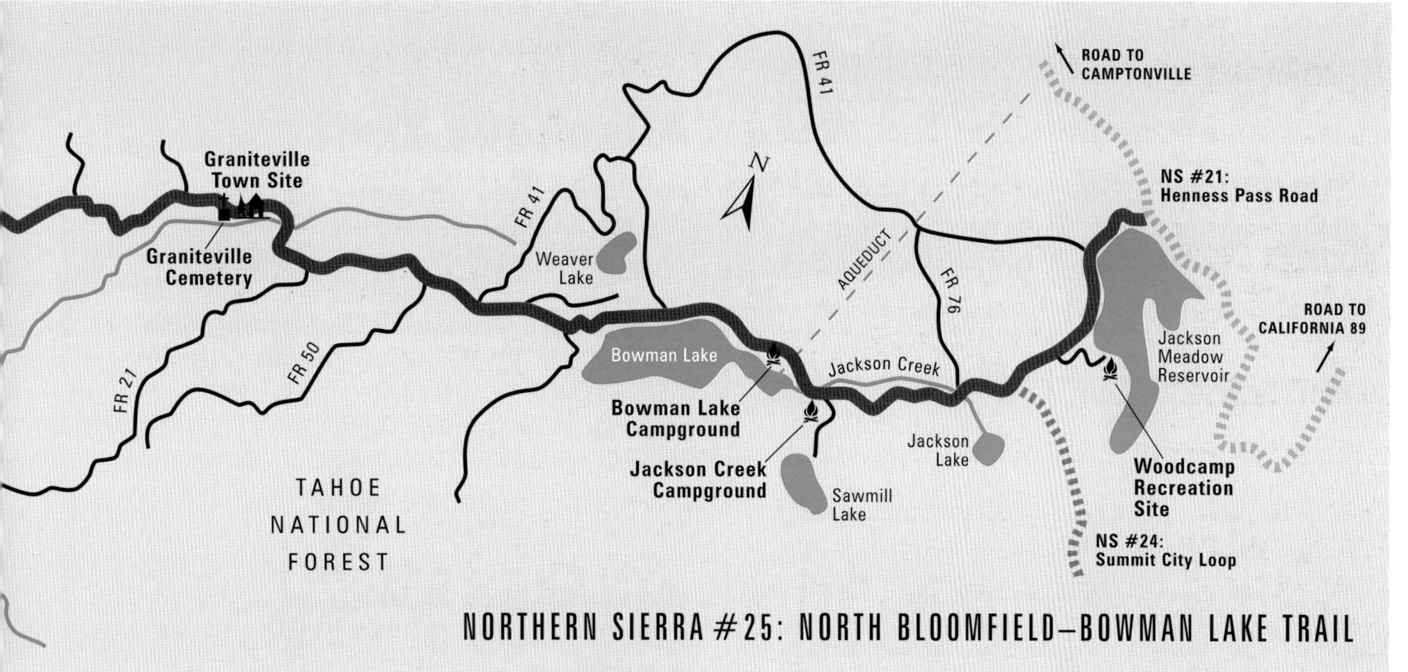

NORTHERN SIERRA #25: NORTH BLOOMFIELD–BOWMAN LAKE TRAIL

GPS: N39°26.29' W120°45.31'

▼ 5.8 SO Graniteville Cemetery on right. Track on left.
0.2 ▲ SO Graniteville Cemetery on left. Track on right.

GPS: N39°26.38' W120°44.71'

▼ 6.0 SO Entering Graniteville. Historical marker and public telephone on left. Zero trip meter.
0.0 ▲ Continue to the southwest.

GPS: N39°26.35' W120°44.49'

▼ 0.0 Continue to the northeast.
7.0 ▲ SO Leaving Graniteville. Historical marker and public telephone on right. Zero trip meter.

▼ 0.5 SO Track on left. Leaving Graniteville.
6.5 ▲ SO Track on right. Entering Graniteville.

▼ 0.8 SO Track on left; then cross over Poorman Creek on bridge.
6.2 ▲ BL Cross over Poorman Creek on bridge; then bear left past track ahead.

▼ 1.0 SO Track on left.
6.0 ▲ SO Track on right.

▼ 1.6 SO Track on left.
5.4 ▲ SO Track on right.

▼ 1.8 TL Graded road on right is FR 21 to Washington. Bear left onto graded road. Immediately track on left.
5.2 ▲ TR Track on right; then turn right onto unmarked graded road. Track ahead goes to Washington.

GPS: N39°26.24' W120°43.17'

▼ 2.8 SO Track on left and track on right.
4.2 ▲ SO Track on left and track on right.

▼ 3.4 SO Graded road on right is FR 50.
3.6 ▲ SO Graded road on left is FR 50.

GPS: N39°26.64' W120°41.69'

▼ 3.9 SO Graded road on left is Pinoli Ridge Road (FR 41) to Jackson Meadow Reservoir.
3.1 ▲ SO Graded road on right is Pinoli Ridge Road (FR 41) to Jackson Meadow Reservoir.

GPS: N39°26.62' W120°41.07'

▼ 4.3 BR Graded road on left; then seasonal closure gate.
2.7 ▲ SO Seasonal closure gate; then graded road on right.

GPS: N39°26.65' W120°40.63'

▼ 5.3 SO Track on right.
1.7 ▲ SO Track on left.

▼ 5.4 TL Seasonal closure gate; then T-intersection. Track on right goes to base of the dam wall.
1.6 ▲ TR Track ahead goes to base of the dam wall. Turn right and pass through seasonal closure gate.

GPS: N39°26.80' W120°39.54'

▼ 6.0 SO Track on right.
1.0 ▲ SO Track on left.

▼ 6.2 SO Track on left. Bowman Lake on right.
0.8 ▲ SO Track on right. Road is now marked as FR 18.

▼ 6.3 SO Two tracks on right give access to Bowman Lake.
0.7 ▲ SO Two tracks on left give access to Bowman Lake.

▼ 7.0 SO Well-used, unmaintained track on left and track on right to campsite. Zero trip meter.
0.0 ▲ Continue to the southwest.

GPS: N39°27.32' W120°38.60'

▼ 0.0 SO Continue to the northeast.
5.5 ▲ SO Well-used, unmaintained track on right and track on left to campsite. Zero trip meter.

▼ 1.4 SO Campsites on right.
4.1 ▲ SO Campsites on left.

▼ 1.5 SO Leaving shore of Bowman Lake.
4.0 ▲ SO Trail starts to follow alongside Bowman Lake.

▼ 1.7 SO Track on right to campsites.
3.8 ▲ SO Track on left to campsites.

▼ 1.9 SO Track on right to Bowman Lake Campground; then cross over Milton Reservoir to Bowman Lake Tunnel Aqueduct. Many tracks on right to camping areas for the next 0.6 miles.
3.6 ▲ SO Cross over the Milton Reservoir to Bowman

		Lake Tunnel Aqueduct. Track on left to Bowman Lake Campground.
		GPS: N39°27.64' W120°36.62'
▼ 2.2	SO	Track on right. Last access point to Bowman Lake.
3.3 ▲	SO	Track on left. First access point to Bowman Lake.
▼ 2.5	SO	Cross over Jackson Creek.
3.0 ▲	SO	Cross over Jackson Creek. Many tracks on left to camping areas for the next 0.6 miles.
▼ 2.6	SO	Cross over Jackson Creek; then Jackson Creek USFS Campground on right. Track on right goes to Sawmill Lake.
2.9 ▲	SO	Track on left goes to Sawmill Lake. Jackson Creek USFS Campground on left; then cross over Jackson Creek.
		GPS: N39°27.47' W120°36.04'
▼ 2.9	SO	Track on right.
2.6 ▲	SO	Track on left.
▼ 3.5	SO	Track on right.
2.0 ▲	SO	Track on left.
▼ 3.8	SO	Track on right.
1.7 ▲	SO	Track on left.
▼ 4.0	SO	Track on right.
1.5 ▲	SO	Track on left.
▼ 4.9	SO	Graded road on left is Austin Meadows Road (FR 76).
0.6 ▲	SO	Graded road on right is Austin Meadows Road (FR 76).
		GPS: N39°28.15' W120°34.34'
▼ 5.5	SO	Graded road on right is Northern Sierra #24: Summit City Loop. Zero trip meter.
0.0 ▲		Continue to the southwest.
		GPS: N39°28.44' W120°33.73'
▼ 0.0		Continue to the north.
3.0 ▲	BR	Graded road on left is Northern Sierra #24: Summit City Loop. Zero trip meter.
▼ 0.4	SO	Entering Jackson Meadow Recreation Area; then track on left.
2.6 ▲	SO	Track on right; then leaving Jackson Meadow Recreation Area.
▼ 0.6	SO	Road becomes paved.
2.4 ▲	SO	Road turns to graded dirt.
▼ 0.7	SO	Paved road on right goes to Woodcamp Recreation Sites—camping, picnicking, and boat launch. Road turns back to graded dirt.
2.3 ▲	SO	Road is now paved. Paved road on left goes to Woodcamp Recreation Sites—camping, picnicking, and boat launch.
		GPS: N39°28.96' W120°33.33'
▼ 2.1	SO	Graded road on left is FR 41 to Round Valley. Follow sign to Jackson Meadow Dam. Road is now paved.
0.9 ▲	SO	Graded road on right is FR 41 to Round Valley. Follow sign to Bowman Lake. Road turns to graded dirt.
		GPS: N39°30.11' W120°33.62'
▼ 2.7	SO	Start to cross Jackson Meadow Dam.
0.3 ▲	SO	Leave dam.
▼ 3.0		Trail ends at T-intersection with Northern Sierra #21: Henness Pass Road. Turn right for California 89; turn left for Milton Reservoir.
0.0 ▲		Trail commences on Northern Sierra #21: Henness Pass Road at Jackson Meadow Reservoir. Zero trip meter and turn southwest on unmarked paved road and start to cross the dam.
		GPS: N39°30.59' W120°33.16'

NORTHERN SIERRA #26

Alleghany Trail

Starting Point:	**Northern Sierra #25: North Bloomfield–Bowman Lake Trail, 8.5 miles north of Nevada City**
Finishing Point:	**Northern Sierra #25: North Bloomfield–Bowman Lake Trail, 6 miles west of Graniteville**
Total Mileage:	**31.1 miles**
Unpaved Mileage:	**28.8 miles**
Driving Time:	**5 hours**
Elevation Range:	**2,200–4,800 feet**
Usually Open:	**April to November**
Best Time to Travel:	**Dry weather**
Difficulty Rating:	**4**
Scenic Rating:	**10**
Remoteness Rating:	**+1**

Special Attractions

- Historic town of Alleghany.
- Two long shelf road descents to the Middle Yuba River.
- Trout fishing in the Middle Yuba River.

History

Traveling the Alleghany Trail gives an insight into how impenetrable this deep canyon country would have been to Indians and prospectors alike. The influx of gold-hungry miners opened up this region in the early 1850s. Smiths Flat, founded in 1851, was the first mining camp in this locale. Kanaka Flat, Wet Ravine, Cumberland, and Kanaka City all followed within a few months. In 1853, J. McCormick and Perry Bonham, from Allegheny, Pennsylvania, started the Alleghany Mine. By 1856, the town of Alleghany was laid out. A post office was established the following year, having moved from Chips Flat on the south side of Kanaka Creek. Mines were popping up all over; many had colorful names such as Brush Creek, Gold Canyon, Ireland, and the Kate Hardy Mine, which had a covered bridge over the Oregon Creek. Other mines along this trail are the

Old Ophir Mine five stamp mill north of Kanaka Creek bridge

Italian stonemasons constructed this shelf road to Alleghany

Oriental Mine, Yellow Jacket Mine, and of course the Sixteen-to-One Mine.

In 1855, John Thomas Bradbury was digging in his backyard in Alleghany when he hit a quartz outcrop. He started a tunnel and discovered what would become one of the richest and longest lasting mines in the West, the Sixteen-to-One Mine. H. L. Johnson, a schoolteacher from Ohio, took over the Tightner Mine, just northeast of the Sixteen-to-One and immediately struck it rich. In 1916, it became evident that these two mines were tapping into the same vein. Johnson built one of the finest houses in town, sold his mine for $550,000, and moved to Berkeley. The Tightner Mine stayed in business for nearly 60 years.

Hotels, saloons, stores, schools, churches, boardwalks, and brass bands all had their day in Alleghany. Sadly, fires were a constant enemy for this community, perched on the side of Kanaka Creek Canyon. Two-story hotels were destroyed and rebuilt even before the turn of the twentieth century. In 1933, a fire burned many of the remaining wooden buildings in town. (For more on Alleghany, see page 23.)

Alleghany Trail follows a memorable section of the Tyler Foote Grade, a narrow wagon road from Nevada City to Alleghany. Completed over a period of six months in 1913, the road was financed by Mr. Foote, a mine owner in Grass Valley, to the tune of $85,000. Italian stonemasons were employed by the contractor to construct the high stone embankment walls needed to get around the tight curves of the cliff above the Middle Yuba River. These painstakingly hand-built retaining walls are still in place today and are clearly visible as you drive along the canyon walls. The hair-raising stagecoach trip from Nevada City to Alleghany could take as long as two days. Some newcomers refused to invest in the town after they traveled this frightening single-lane route.

If this old road seems manageable today, imagine how it was when it was even narrower, and then try to imagine delivering six tons of winter supplies in an early truck and trailer through several feet of snow. Sam Bidwell delivered mail using a canvas-covered Dodge Power Wagon pickup, fitted with chains during winter. At times Sam was forced to use a diesel Caterpillar bulldozer to get the groceries and mail through deep snow on Tyler Foote Road.

Description

This trail starts and finishes on Northern Sierra #25: North Bloomfield–Bowman Lake Trail, crossing the Middle Yuba River twice and traveling through the historic settlement of Alleghany, site of one of the oldest operating gold mines in California.

The trail leaves North Bloomfield–Bowman Lake Trail 8.5 miles north of Nevada City along a well-graded road. It heads north through Tahoe National Forest, passing through the settlement of Columbia Hill before making a steep descent along a roughly graded, single-lane shelf road to Foote Crossing. The road widens in enough places so that passing is not a problem. The Middle Yuba River flows through the deep canyon; this descent and the subsequent climb up the far side offer incredible views over the river. There are some good swimming holes at Foote Crossing but no camping spots. Anglers can fish for brown and rainbow trout. The road becomes slightly wider as it climbs away from Foote Crossing on the north side of the river. Stunning views over jagged granite ridges continue on this side of the river.

The trail follows a graded dirt road through the forest, winding above Kanaka Creek to Alleghany. Some of the area is privately owned, and a number of mining claims are scattered along the trail. If you plan to pan or prospect in this potentially rich area, be sure you are not inadvertently trespassing on somebody else's claim. Check with the national forest office in Nevada City for current regulations.

The old Kanaka Creek bridge in Allegany is now overgrown

The trail joins paved Main Street to travel through Alleghany. Many old structures remain: both residential and commercial buildings connected with the local mining industry. The original office of the Sixteen-to-One Mine stands on Miners Street, a short distance past the mine itself, which continues to turn a profit to this day. There is no gas in Alleghany, but there is a bar and a small café.

The route leaves town along Kanaka Creek Road and crosses over Kanaka Creek on a new bridge. The original bridge is below the road to the right. An old stamp mill can be seen beside the bridge, covered in vegetation.

Past the creek, the trail takes on more of a 4WD character. It climbs steeply up loose, scrabbly soil away from the creek and passes through Chips Flat, the site of the region's original post office, onto Lafayette Ridge. Dropping once again to the Middle Yuba River, the trail passes close to Plumbago and the Plumbago Mine, both still operational and currently owned by the Sixteen-to-One Mining Company. This part of the trail should not be attempted in wet weather; steep grades, a narrow shelf road, and a surface that turns extremely greasy make this section very dangerous when wet. The shelf road here is narrow with few passing places as it descends to Gold Canyon.

There are some pleasant campsites tucked alongside the river on either side of the bridge over the Middle Yuba. There is also a great swimming hole 0.1 miles northwest of the bridge. Once over the bridge, the trail becomes lumpy with embedded and loose boulders—this section is often rearranged when the river floods. Drivers should exercise care and watch their vehicle's underbody in a couple of spots. However, it should be well within the capabilities of most stock SUVs or 4WD pickups.

The trail climbs steeply from the river to rejoin Northern Sierra #25: North Bloomfield–Bowman Lake Trail. The road becomes graded and travels through some private property and logging areas.

This trail is suitable for mountain bikers, although it is a punishing ride even for the fittest.

Current Road Information

Tahoe National Forest
Nevada City Ranger District
631 Coyote Street
Nevada City, CA 95959
(530) 265-4531

Tahoe National Forest
Downieville Ranger District
15924 Highway 49
Camptonville, CA 95922
(530) 288-3231

Map References

BLM Truckee
USFS Tahoe National Forest
USGS 1:24,000 North Bloomfield, Pike, Alleghany
1:100,000 Truckee
Maptech CD-ROM: High Sierra/Tahoe
Northern California Atlas & Gazetteer, pp. 79, 80
California Road & Recreation Atlas, pp. 65, 60

Route Directions

▼ 0.0		From Northern Sierra #25: North Bloomfield–Bowman Lake Trail, 8.5 miles north of Nevada City, zero trip meter and turn left (northwest) onto Grizzly Hill Road, following the sign for North Columbia. North Bloomfield–Bowman Lake Trail bears northeast at this point along North Bloomfield Road and heads toward Malakoff Diggins.
3.1 ▲		Trail ends back on Northern Sierra #25: North Bloomfield–Bowman Lake Trail. Turn left to visit Malakoff Diggins and Bowman Lake; continue straight ahead for Nevada City.
		GPS: N39°20.48' W120°58.50'
▼ 0.1	SO	Graded road on left is Mountain Springs Road.
3.0 ▲	SO	Graded road on right is Mountain Springs Road.

NORTHERN SIERRA #26: ALLEGHANY TRAIL

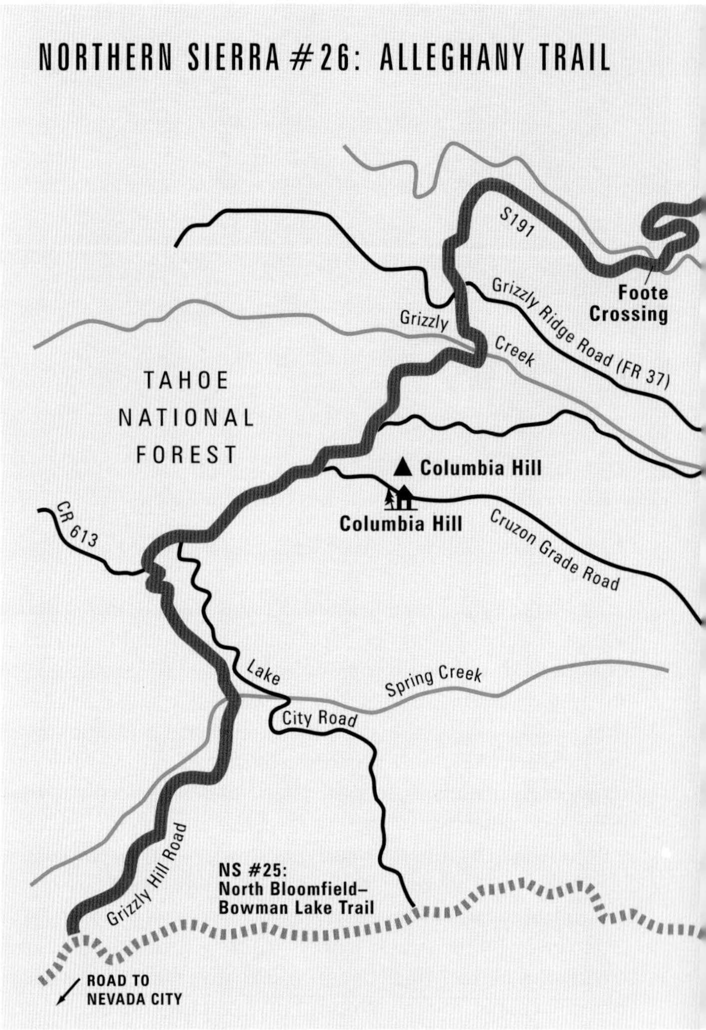

▼ 0.8	SO	Road on right is Jennet Trail.
2.3 ▲	SO	Road on left is Jennet Trail.
▼ 1.5	SO	Track on left and track on right.
1.6 ▲	SO	Track on left and track on right.
▼ 2.1	SO	Cross over Spring Creek.
1.0 ▲	SO	Cross over Spring Creek.
▼ 2.3	BL	Graded road on right; then track on left.
0.8 ▲	BR	Track on right; then graded road on left. Bear right, following sign to South Yuba Campground and Trail.
		GPS: N39°22.12' W120°58.45'
▼ 2.9	SO	Road becomes paved.
0.2 ▲	SO	Road turns to graded dirt.
▼ 3.1	TR	T-intersection with paved Tyler Foote Crossing Road (CR 613). Zero trip meter.
0.0 ▲		Continue to the east.
		GPS: N39°22.37' W120°59.18'
▼ 0.0		Continue to the north.
3.1 ▲	TL	Turn left onto paved Grizzly Hill Road and zero trip meter.
▼ 0.2	SO	Graded road on right is Lake City Road.
2.9 ▲	SO	Graded road on left is Lake City Road.
▼ 1.2	TL	Turn left onto graded dirt Tyler Foote Crossing Road at Columbia Hill. Cruzon Grade Road continues straight ahead.
1.9 ▲	TR	T-intersection with paved road at Columbia

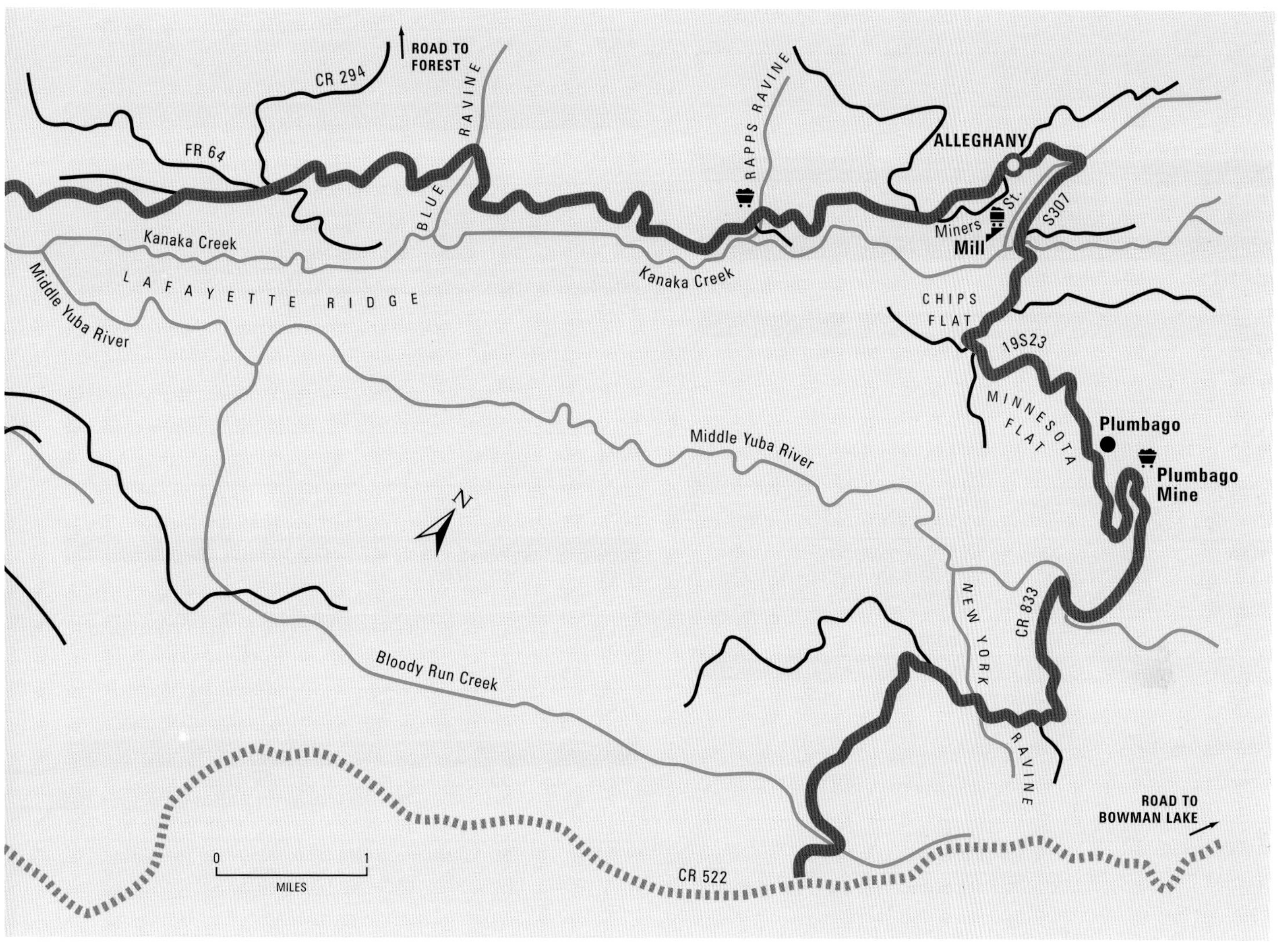

		Hill. Cruzon Grade Road on left. Remain on Tyler Foote Crossing Road. Road is now paved.
		GPS: N39°23.23′ W120°58.50′
▼ 1.6	SO	Track on right.
1.5 ▲	SO	Track on left.
▼ 1.9	SO	Track on right.
1.2 ▲	SO	Track on left.
▼ 2.0	SO	Track on left.
1.1 ▲	SO	Track on right.
▼ 2.6	SO	Track on left; then cross over Grizzly Creek. Private road on right and track on left.
0.5 ▲	SO	Private road on left and track on right. Cross over Grizzly Creek; then track on right.
		GPS: N39°24.16′ W120°57.85′
▼ 3.1	BL	Two tracks on left; then graded road on right is Grizzly Ridge Road (FR 37). Zero trip meter and bear left onto S191, following sign to Foote Crossing.
0.0 ▲		Continue to the southeast past two tracks on right. End of shelf road.
		GPS: N39°24.38′ W120°58.17′
▼ 0.0		Continue to the west. Start to descend shelf road to Foote Crossing.
5.8 ▲	BR	Graded road on left is Grizzly Ridge Road (FR 37). Zero trip meter and bear right, following sign for Graniteville Road.

▼ 0.9	SO	Track on left.
4.9 ▲	BL	Track on right.
▼ 2.2	SO	Hiking trail on left goes down to river.
3.6 ▲	SO	Hiking trail on right goes down to river.
		GPS: N39°25.00′ W120°57.25′
▼ 2.3	SO	Cross over the Middle Yuba River on bridge at Foote Crossing. Track on left after bridge is a hiking trail that goes past mining claim and adit.
3.5 ▲	SO	Track on right is a hiking trail that goes past mining claim and adit. Cross over the Middle Yuba River on bridge at Foote Crossing.
		GPS: N39°25.00′ W120°57.07′
▼ 2.6	SO	Hiking trail on right to river on left-hand bend.
3.2 ▲	SO	Hiking trail on left to river on right-hand bend.
▼ 5.3	SO	Track on left. End of shelf road.
0.5 ▲	SO	Start of shelf road. Track on right.
		GPS: N39°25.88′ W120°55.85′
▼ 5.8	SO	Graded road on left is FR 64 to Squirrel Creek; then second graded road on left is CR 294 to the town of Forest. Zero trip meter and follow sign to Alleghany. Track on right.
0.0 ▲		Continue to the southwest.
		GPS: N39°26.11′ W120°55.31′
▼ 0.0		Continue to the northeast.
6.8 ▲	SO	Track on left. Graded road on right is CR 294 to the town of Forest; then second graded

road on right is FR 64 to Squirrel Creek. Zero trip meter and follow sign to Foote Crossing.

▼ 0.8 SO Track on right.
6.0 ▲ SO Track on left.

▼ 1.1 SO Track on right and track on left.
5.7 ▲ SO Track on left and track on right.

GPS: N39°26.59' W120°54.58'

▼ 1.9 SO Cross over Blue Ravine.
4.9 ▲ SO Cross over Blue Ravine.

GPS: N39°26.88' W120°54.09'

▼ 4.9 SO Mine on left.
1.9 ▲ SO Mine on right.

GPS: N39°27.25' W120°52.09'

▼ 5.0 BL Cross over Rapps Ravine; then two tracks on right.
1.8 ▲ BR Two tracks on left; then cross over Rapps Ravine.

▼ 5.2 SO Track on left. Start of shelf road.
1.6 ▲ SO End of shelf road. Track on right.

▼ 6.2 SO Cross over creek.
0.6 ▲ SO Cross over creek.

▼ 6.8 SO 4-way intersection with paved roads on the edge of Alleghany. Zero trip meter and cross Miners Street; then bear right to join Main Street.
0.0 ▲ Continue to the south.

GPS: N39°27.84' W120°50.84'

▼ 0.0 Continue to the north. Remain on Main Street through town.
3.2 ▲ SO Bear left off Main Street; then 4-way intersection with Miners Street. Zero trip meter and continue straight ahead to join Foote Crossing Road. Road is now graded dirt.

▼ 0.5 SO Road on right is Miners Street.
2.7 ▲ BR Road on left is Miners Street.

▼ 0.7 SO Volunteer fire department on right down Plaza Street.
2.5 ▲ SO Volunteer fire department on left down Plaza Street.

▼ 0.8 TR Turn right on Kanaka Creek Road (S307), immediately after the post office.
2.4 ▲ TL T-intersection with Main Street. Enter Alleghany past post office on left.

GPS: N39°28.38' W120°50.53'

▼ 0.9 SO Road turns to graded dirt.
2.3 ▲ SO Road is now paved.

▼ 1.4 SO Cross over creek.
1.8 ▲ SO Cross over creek.

▼ 2.0 SO Old mill remains on right on far side of canyon.
1.2 ▲ SO Old mill remains on left on far side of canyon.

▼ 2.1 TR Graded road on left.
1.1 ▲ TL Graded road on right.

GPS: N39°27.98' W120°50.23'

▼ 2.2 SO Cross over Kanaka Creek on bridge. Start of shelf road.
1.0 ▲ SO End of shelf road. Cross over Kanaka Creek on bridge.

▼ 2.4 SO Track on left.
0.8 ▲ SO Track on right.

▼ 2.8 SO Track on right; then track on left. End of shelf road.
0.4 ▲ SO Track on right; then track on left. Start of shelf road.

▼ 2.9 SO Track on left.
0.3 ▲ SO Track on right.

▼ 3.0 BL Chips Flat. Track on right. Follow sign for OHV trail.
0.2 ▲ SO Chips Flat. Track on left.

GPS: N39°27.40' W120°50.16'

▼ 3.2 TR Track on right; then second track on right signposted to Minnesota Flat; then immediately turn right onto third track on right (19S23, CR S200) signposted to German Bar. Zero trip meter.
0.0 ▲ Continue to the southwest.

GPS: N39°27.30' W120°50.16'

▼ 0.0 Continue to the east.
6.8 ▲ TL T-intersection. Zero trip meter. Turn left; then immediately track on left signposted to Minnesota Flat. Continue straight ahead following sign for Malone Orchard; then immediately track on left.

▼ 0.7 SO Track on right.
6.1 ▲ SO Track on left.

▼ 1.7 SO Plumbago on left—private property.
5.1 ▲ SO Plumbago on right—private property.

GPS: N39°27.10' W120°48.96'

▼ 1.8 SO Track on left.
5.0 ▲ SO Track on right.

▼ 1.9 SO Start of shelf road descending to the Middle Yuba River.
4.9 ▲ SO End of shelf road.

▼ 2.8 BR Track on left to Plumbago Mine.
4.0 ▲ BL Track on right to Plumbago Mine.

GPS: N39°27.07' W120°48.73'

▼ 4.0 SO Track on left. End of shelf road.
2.8 ▲ BL Bear left, following sign to Alleghany. Start of shelf road.

▼ 4.1 SO Turnout on left; then cross over the Middle Yuba River on bridge. Road is now CR 833.
2.7 ▲ SO Cross over the Middle Yuba River on bridge; then turnout on right.

GPS: N39°26.22' W120°48.73'

▼ 4.3 SO Campsite on right. There are mining claims around the river. Start of shelf road.
2.5 ▲ SO End of shelf road. Campsite on left. There are mining claims around the river.

▼ 5.3 SO Cross over creek.
1.5 ▲ SO Cross over creek.

▼ 5.5 BR Track on left. End of shelf road.
1.3 ▲ BL Track on right. Start of shelf road.

▼ 5.8 SO Track on left.
1.0 ▲ SO Track on right.

GPS: N39°25.64' W120°48.53'

▼ 6.2 SO Track on left; then track on right.
0.6 ▲ SO Track on left; then track on right.

▼ 6.4 SO Cross over creek in New York Ravine.
0.4 ▲ SO Cross over creek in New York Ravine.

▼ 6.8 SO Unmarked graded road on right. Zero trip meter.
0.0 ▲ Continue to the east.

GPS: N39°25.60' W120°49.33'

▼ 0.0 Continue to the west past track on left.
2.3 ▲ BR Track on right; then unmarked graded road on left. Bear right onto unmaintained road CR 833. Zero trip meter.

▼ 0.3 SO Track on right.
2.0 ▲ SO Track on left.

▼ 0.5 SO Track on right.

	1.8 ▲	SO	Track on left.
▼ 1.8		SO	Cross over Bloody Run Creek.
	0.5 ▲	SO	Cross over Bloody Run Creek.
			GPS: N39°24.44' W120°49.41'
▼ 2.1		SO	Track on left.
	0.2 ▲	SO	Track on right.
▼ 2.3			Trail ends at 4-way intersection with Northern Sierra #25: North Bloomfield–Bowman Lake Trail (CR 522). Robbins Ranch Road is straight ahead. Turn left for Bowman Lake; turn right to return to Nevada City.
	0.0 ▲		Trail commences on Northern Sierra #25: North Bloomfield–Bowman Lake Trail (CR 522), 6 miles west of Graniteville. Zero trip meter and turn north onto CR 833 at the sign for Moores Flat and Bucks Ranch. Robbins Ranch Road is opposite the start of the trail.
			GPS: N39°24.09' W120°49.52'

NORTHERN SIERRA #27

Sierra Buttes Trail

Starting Point:	**FR 93, 0.3 miles south of Packer Lake Saddle**
Finishing Point:	**Sierra Buttes Road, 1 mile west of Sierra City**
Total Mileage:	**6.6 miles, plus 1.2-mile spur to Sierra Buttes Fire Lookout**
Unpaved Mileage:	**6.6 miles, plus 1.2-mile spur**
Driving Time:	**1.75 hours, plus 1 hour round-trip for hike to the lookout**
Elevation Range:	**4,200–7,700 feet**
Usually Open:	**July to November**
Best Time to Travel:	**Dry weather**
Difficulty Rating:	**5**
Scenic Rating:	**10**
Remoteness Rating:	**+0**

Special Attractions

- Long section of narrow shelf road with views of Sierra Buttes and the North Yuba River Valley.
- Moderately strenuous hike to the Sierra Buttes Fire Lookout.
- Access to a network of 4WD trails and many lakes for fishing and camping.

History

The volcanic Sierra Buttes rise about 4,500 feet above the old mining town of Sierra City. Sierra Buttes Mine, on the south face of the buttes, was one of the earliest mines in this vicinity. Starting operations in the early 1850s, it was a big employer in the area and produced more than $17 million in gold by the time it closed in 1937. Stamp mills, flumes, and boarding houses came and went over the decades.

Lower Sardine Lake, visible to the northeast from the Sierra Buttes Fire Lookout, was the headwater dam for the flume and ditch that delivered water around the steep slope of the buttes to the Sierra Buttes Mine. The lake was also the site of the Young America Mine, which operated from 1884 to 1893, producing an average of $20,000 to $30,000 in gold a month. Watt Hughes, part owner of the mine, built a sizable house in nearby Sierra City, which is now the Holly House Bed & Breakfast.

The long shelf road to Sierra City is narrow with limited passing places

By 1858, Sierra City had evolved from a number of dispersed mining camps into a lively town on the banks of the North Yuba River, where miners had their choice of several bars and saloons. Thompson's Saloon, Capital Hotel, Phelan's Saloon, Socarracco Hotel, Rose's Hotel, and Carrollo Saloon were just a few of the establishments that catered to thirsty miners.

Description

The prominent volcanic peaks of Sierra Buttes, visible for miles around, are one of the most distinctive geological features in the northern Sierra Nevada. As you approach the buttes, the forest service's small lookout can be seen perched precariously on the uppermost peak (8,587 feet). Although no longer used for spotting fires, the lookout is now one of the most popular hiking destinations in the region. On warm summer weekends, it is not unusual to see 30 or more hikers admiring the views from the lookout platform.

Most hikers reach the lookout from the Sierra Buttes Trailhead near the start of this trail. For those with a high-clearance 4WD, there is a second option. The Sierra Buttes OHV Trail travels along a well-used, roughly graded trail for 2.6 miles to a spur to the lookout. The spur immediately starts to climb to the northeast, averaging a consistent slope of about 20 degrees. The surface is uneven, but apart from a few patches of rock and embedded

Permanent snow on the northern face of the Sierra Buttes above Upper Sardine Lake

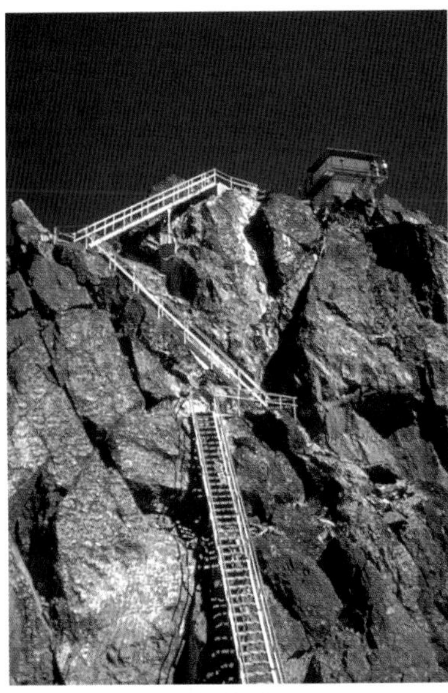
Steep ascent to the lookout tower

boulders, it is smooth though loose in places. Most of the spur travels through the forest, but a few areas open up and provide views over low vegetation. A spectacular campsite 0.4 miles along the spur offers breathtaking, panoramic views. The spur ends for vehicles after 1.2 miles. Park your vehicle and hike the remaining distance to the lookout. The trail is easy to follow, and it ascends a series of switchbacks, first as a foot trail, then joining the old road to the peak. Allow an hour round-trip for the hike, not including time spent at the top. The final ascent to the lookout climbs three flights of metal grating stairs that were affixed to the rock in 1964 by five forest service employees.

The lookout platform provides 360-degree views. To the north are the Sardine Lakes and Sand Pond, with Volcano Lake to the northeast and Packer Lake and Gold Valley to the northwest. On a clear day, you can see as far north as Lassen Peak and Mount Shasta. To the east is the Sierra Valley, an important summer range for foothill ranchers. To the south you can see Jackson Meadow Reservoir and the deep cut of the North Yuba River, about 3,000 feet below. The small burned area to the west is the result of the August 1978 Cap Fire above Downieville.

The main trail continues toward Sierra City, passing the turn to the Monumental Mine before making the long shelf road descent to the valley floor. Passing places are extremely limited along the narrow road, especially near the northern end. The final 1.3 miles are maintained by Sierra County and are wide enough for two vehicles to pass with care.

Current Road Information

Tahoe National Forest
Downieville Ranger District
15924 Highway 49
Camptonville, CA 95922
(530) 288-3231

Map References

BLM Portola
USFS Tahoe National Forest; Plumas National Forest
USGS 1:24,000 Sierra City
1:100,000 Portola
Maptech CD-ROM: High Sierra/Tahoe
Northern California Atlas & Gazetteer, p. 70
California Road & Recreation Atlas, p. 60
Other: Lakes Basin, Sierra Buttes and Plumas Eureka State Park Recreation Guide, Plumas National Forest OHV Map—Summer Use

Route Directions

▼ 0.0 From the intersection of FR 93-03 and FR 93, 11 miles north of California 49, continue 0.4 miles east. Zero trip meter and turn southeast on small graded road 93-02, following sign to Sierra Buttes Lookout. Coming from the east, the trail starts 0.3 miles south of Packer Lake Saddle.
2.6 ▲ Trail ends at intersection with paved FR 93. Continue straight ahead for Packer Lake and Northern Sierra #28: Gold Lake Trail; turn left for California 49.

GPS: N39°36.86' W120°39.94'

▼ 0.2 SO Sierra Buttes Trailhead. Sierra Buttes Trail (12E06) on left for hikers to fire lookout and Pacific Crest Trail. Continue straight ahead, following sign for Sierra Buttes OHV Trail.
2.4 ▲ SO Sierra Buttes Trailhead. Sierra Buttes Trail (12E06) on right for hikers to fire lookout and Pacific Crest Trail.

GPS: N39°36.70' W120°39.86'

▼ 0.7 SO Track on right.
1.9 ▲ SO Track on left.

▼ 0.9 SO Track on left.
1.7 ▲ SO Track on right.

▼ 1.4 SO Remains of Holmes Cabin on right. Track on right; then track on left is 93-21.
1.2 ▲ SO Track on right is 93-21; then track on left. Remains of Holmes Cabin on left.

GPS: N39°36.10' W120°40.52'

▼ 1.8 SO Track on right is 93-22. Trail is now a formed dirt trail.
0.8 ▲ SO Track on left is 93-22. Trail is now a graded dirt road.

GPS: N39°35.81' W120°40.23'

▼ 2.3 SO Spring on left.

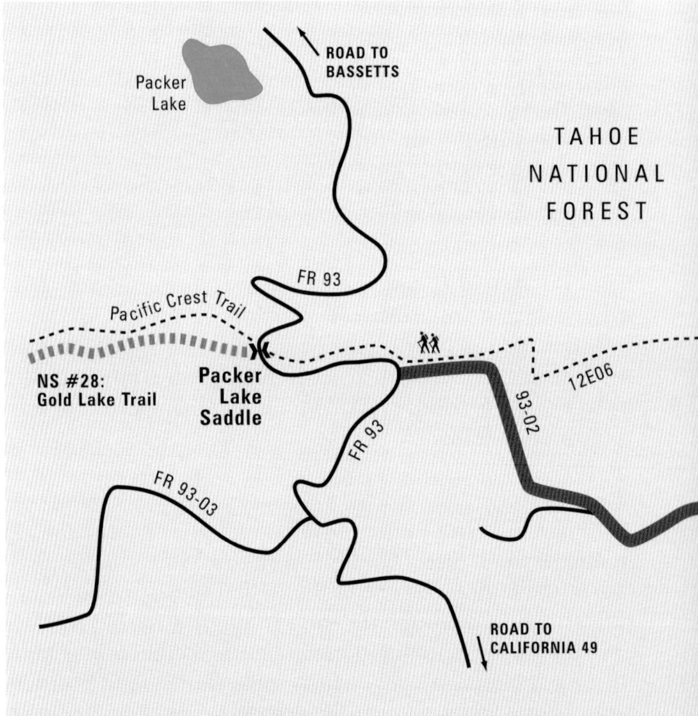

	0.3 ▲	SO	Spring on right.
			GPS: N39°35.52' W120°40.04'
▼ 2.6		BR	Track on left is 93-23, spur to Sierra Buttes Fire Lookout. Track straight ahead is a dead end. Follow sign to Sierra City. Zero trip meter.
	0.0 ▲		Continue to the northwest.
			GPS: N39°35.26' W120°40.01'

Spur to Sierra Buttes Fire Lookout

▼ 0.0		Head northeast on 93-23.
▼ 0.2	BR	Track on left.
▼ 0.4	SO	Campsite with spectacular view on right; then track on left rejoins. Pacific Crest Trail crosses.
		GPS: N39°35.32' W120°39.67'
▼ 1.2		End of vehicle trail. Hiking trail from the Sierra Buttes Trailhead comes in from the northwest and continues east along a steep 0.8-mile trail to the lookout.
		GPS: N39°35.73' W120°39.18'

Continuation of Main Trail

▼ 0.0			Continue to the south.
	4.0 ▲	BL	Track on right is a dead end; then second track on right is 93-23, spur to the Sierra Buttes Lookout. Zero trip meter.
			GPS: N39°35.26' W120°40.01'
▼ 0.5		SO	Track on left; then track on right.
	3.5 ▲	BR	Bear right, following the sign to Sierra Buttes; then track on right.
			GPS: N39°35.06' W120°40.39'
▼ 0.6		SO	Track on left. Track on right goes 0.3 miles to viewpoint. Trail starts to descend single-lane shelf road.
	3.4 ▲	SO	End of shelf road. Track on left goes 0.3 miles to viewpoint. Track on right.
▼ 1.5		SO	Cross over creek.
	2.5 ▲	SO	Cross over creek.
▼ 1.6		SO	Track on right.
	2.4 ▲	SO	Track on left.
▼ 1.8		SO	Cross over creek.
	2.2 ▲	SO	Cross over creek.
▼ 2.3		SO	Cross over creek.
	1.7 ▲	SO	Cross over creek.
▼ 2.4		SO	Spring on right.
	1.6 ▲	SO	Spring on left.
			GPS: N39°34.65' W120°39.39'
▼ 2.6		BL	Track on right rejoins in 0.1 miles.
	1.4 ▲	BR	Track on left rejoins.
▼ 2.7		BL	Track on right rejoins; then well-used track on right goes to Columbo Mine. Start of county-maintained road.
	1.3 ▲	BR	Well-used track on left goes to Columbo Mine; then track on left rejoins in 0.1 miles. Follow sign to Sierra Buttes. End of county-maintained road.
			GPS: N39°34.59' W120°39.63'
▼ 3.0		SO	Cross over creek.
	1.0 ▲	SO	Cross over creek.
			GPS: N39°34.56' W120°39.30'
▼ 4.0			Trail ends at the Sierra City Transfer Station. Turn left for California 49 and Sierra City.
	0.0 ▲		From Main Street in Sierra City, zero trip meter and turn northwest onto Butte Street. Proceed 0.1 miles and turn left onto Sierra Buttes Road, following sign for Buttes Lookout. Proceed 1 mile to the Sierra City Transfer Station and the start of the trail. Zero trip meter and turn east on graded dirt Sierra Buttes Road (SR 520). Start of shelf road.
			GPS: N39°34.03' W120°39.10'

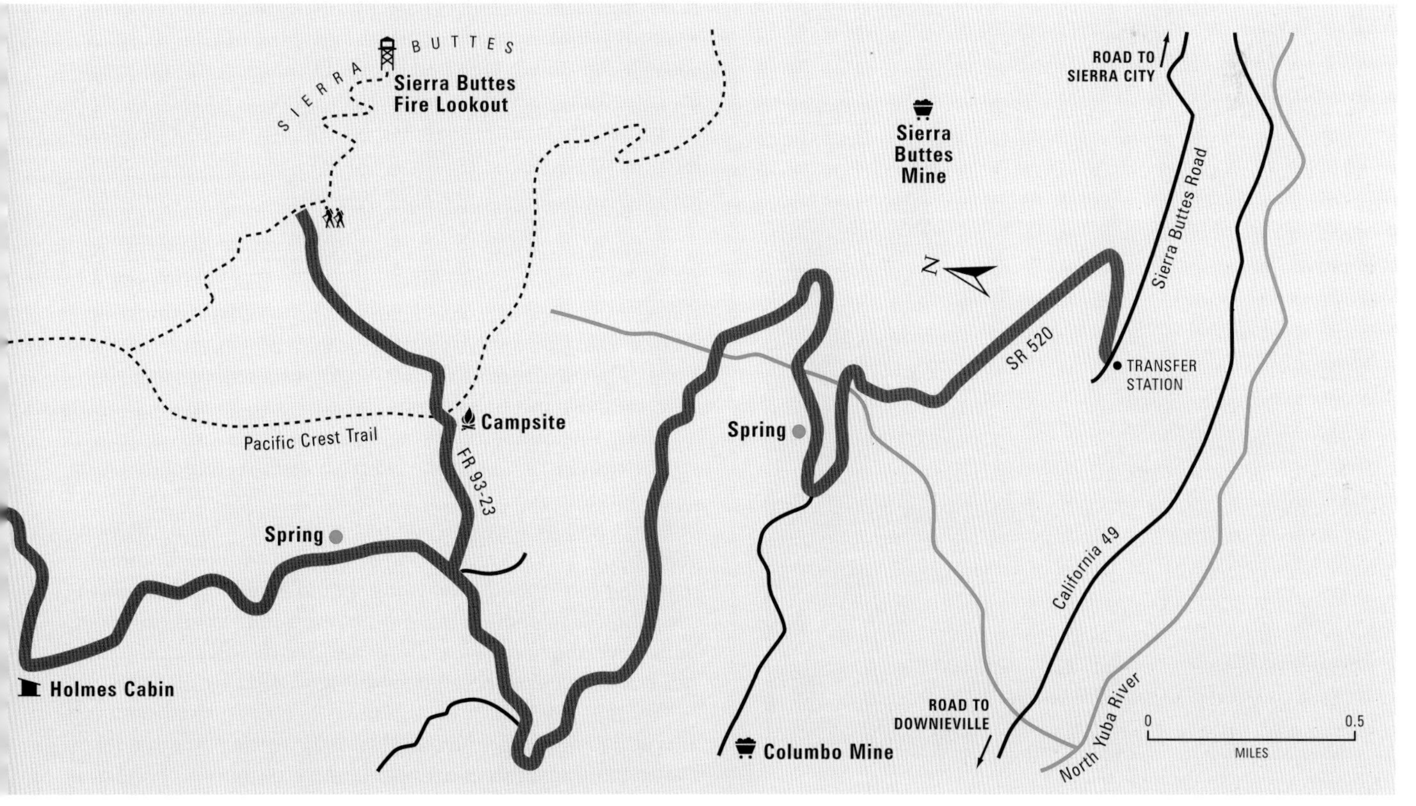

Gold Lake Trail

Starting Point:	**FR 93 at Packer Lake Saddle, 1.5 miles west of Packer Lake**
Finishing Point:	**Gold Lake Road at Gold Lake, 9 miles south of Graeagle**
Total Mileage:	**6.4 miles**
Unpaved Mileage:	**5.9 miles**
Driving Time:	**1.5 hours**
Elevation Range:	**6,400–7,200 feet**
Usually Open:	**July to November**
Best Time to Travel:	**Dry weather**
Difficulty Rating:	**5**
Scenic Rating:	**9**
Remoteness Rating:	**+0**

Special Attractions

- Lakes Basin Petroglyphs and Lakes Basin Campground near the northern end of the trail.
- Fantastic camping along the shores of Gold Lake.
- Moderately challenging trail that passes by or near a number of lakes.

History

Maidu Indians used this area for about a thousand years, and Paleo-Indians may have frequented the area as much as 8,000 to 10,000 years earlier. Petroglyphs north of Gold Lake offer a link to these early people; however, the meaning of these carvings is still very much open to debate.

In the late 1850s a lodge catered to tourists at Gold Lake. In 1913, the road to Gold Lake was put through, providing much easier access to the scenic lake.

Sierra Buttes, seen from the ridge top trail

Packer Lake, near the southern end of the trail, was a resting point along a pack trail. By 1926, a lakeside lodge was attracting a growing number of visitors. Several cabins and a number of platforms for seasonal tents were added as demand grew. Activities such as fishing, boating, horseback riding, and hiking drew people seeking to escape the heat of the Central Valley in summer.

Description

This short, moderately rated trail takes drivers with high-clearance 4WDs directly past two lakes, with another three less than 0.5 miles from the main trail and accessible by vehicle. The trail, initially marked as Deer Lake Road, leaves from Packer Lake Saddle. It quickly becomes a 4WD trail as it travels onto the ridge top. The Pacific Crest National Scenic Trail runs close to the vehicle trail on top of the ridge. Spectacular views from the ridge include Gold Valley and Craycroft Ridge to the west. The deep blue Deer Lake, nestled in a rocky basin and surrounded by firs, can be seen some 350 feet below to the east. Deer Lake is one of the few bodies of water where it is possible to catch eastern brook trout. It can be reached by a steep 0.3-mile descent.

From Deer Lake, the single-lane trail is marked as Summit OHV Trail and travels through loose, deep soils. Some steep downhill sections are interspersed with loose off-camber slopes and tight maneuvers through the trees. At the shadier, more enclosed Summit Lake, the trail swings east toward Gold Lake. Other OHV trails lead off from here—west to Gold Valley and north to Oakland Pond. The main route enters Plumas National Forest and the Lakes Basin Recreation Area and descends to the edge of Gold Lake. Camping within the recreation area is limited to designated sites only, but campers need not worry. One of the prettiest forest service campgrounds is located on the southeastern shore of Gold Lake. Because it can only be reached by 4WD vehicles, it is often quiet, providing campers with their choice of 16 lakeside campsites, most with picnic tables and fire rings. The campground has a pit toilet but no other facilities. Backcountry campsites can also be found at Summit Lake and on the ridge above Deer Lake.

Lakes Basin is one of the prime fishing areas in Plumas National Forest, with nearly 50 small glacial lakes and many cold-water trout streams. Gold Lake is a prime destination where anglers can fish for Mackinaw, brook, brown, and rainbow trout. The area is stocked every two years with several thousand rainbow and brook trout.

From the campground, the main trail follows along the southern shore of Gold Lake, where it earns its difficulty rating of 5. You will have to crawl over some embedded rocks and boulders and along loose sections of rubble. This is the most challenging and slowest section of the trail. Although slow and requiring care, the rock crawling should be within the capabilities of most high-clearance 4WDs, even full size or extra long ones. Several day-use areas along this stretch will appeal to picnickers, anglers, or those just wanting to relax by the lake.

Another side trail leads 0.5 miles to a designated camping area at Squaw Lake. The trail then follows the paved road past busier camping areas and a boat launch to finish on Gold Val-

Gold Lake in the Lakes Basin Recreation Area

ley Road. A point of interest near the Lakes Basin Campground, a short distance from the end of the trail, is a group of large boulders covered with petroglyphs, weathered and faint with age but still discernible. To reach the petroglyphs from the end of the trail, proceed north on Gold Lake Road for 2.3 miles; then turn southwest, following the sign to Lakes Basin Campground. Pass the campground and follow the sign for Elwell Lodge. The petroglyphs are 0.4 miles from Gold Lake Road on the right, at coordinates GPS: N39°41.95' W120°39.61'.

Current Road Information

Tahoe National Forest
Downieville Ranger District
15924 Highway 49
Camptonville, CA 95922
(530) 288-3231

Plumas National Forest
Beckwourth Ranger District
23 Mohawk Road
Blairsden, CA 96103
(530) 836-2575

Map References

BLM Portola
USFS Plumas National Forest; Tahoe National Forest
USGS 1:24,000 Sierra City, Gold Lake
1:100,000 Portola
Maptech CD-ROM: High Sierra/Tahoe
Northern California Atlas & Gazetteer, p. 70
California Road & Recreation Atlas, p. 60 (incomplete)
Other: Lakes Basin, Sierra Buttes and Plumas Eureka State Park Recreation Guide, Plumas National Forest OHV Map—Summer Use

Route Directions

▼ 0.0			From paved FR 93 at Packer Lake Saddle, 5.7 miles west of Gold Lake Road and Bassetts and 1.5 miles west of Packer Lake, zero trip meter at 4-way intersection and turn north on unmaintained road, signposted Deer Lake Road (93-01). Northern Sierra #27: Sierra Buttes Trail commences 0.3 miles south of the saddle.
	2.0 ▲		Trail ends on paved FR 93 at Packer Lake Saddle. Turn left for Packer Lake, Gold Lake Road, and Bassetts; continue straight ahead 0.3 miles south to travel Northern Sierra #27: Sierra Buttes Trail.
			GPS: N39°37.17' W120°39.98'
▼ 0.8		SO	Track on right. Follow the OHV trail sign.
	1.2 ▲	SO	Track on left.
			GPS: N39°37.88' W120°40.20'
▼ 1.7		SO	Track on right to campsite; then Deer Lake vis-

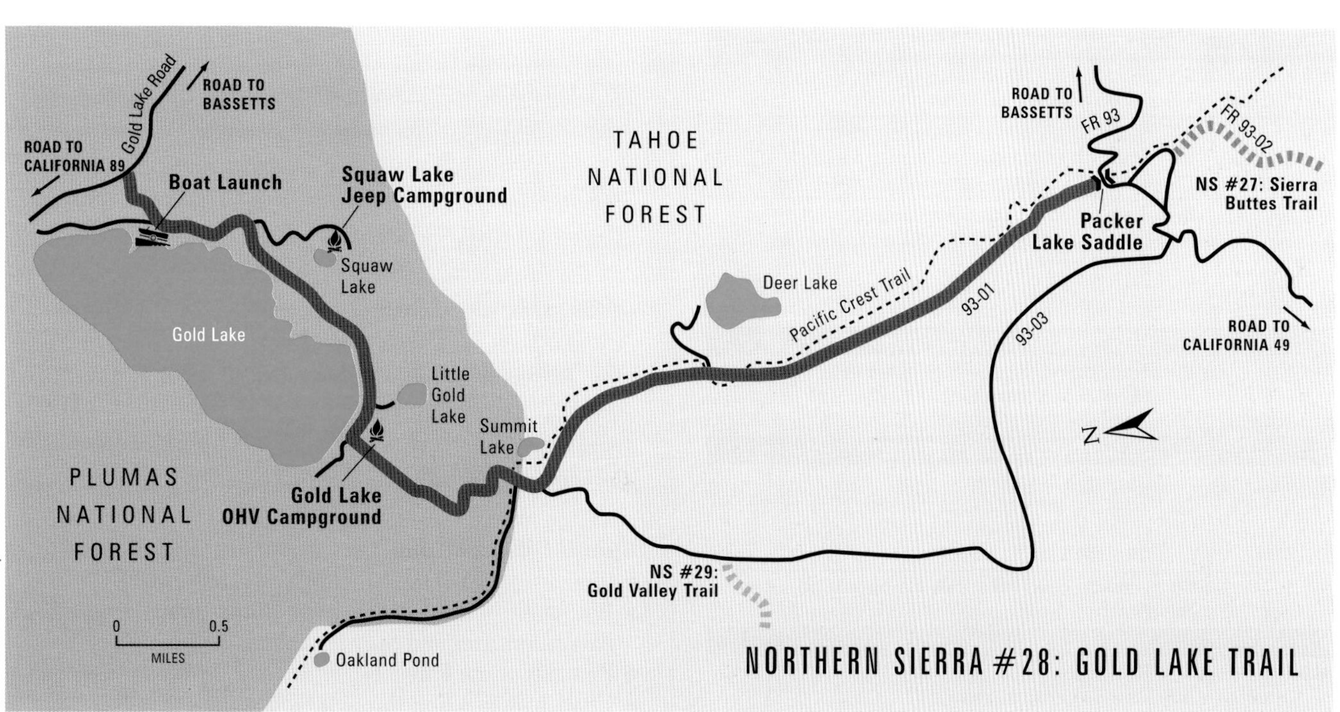

			ible below trail on the right. Pacific Crest Trail runs parallel with the route at this point.
	0.3 ▲	SO	Deer Lake is visible below trail on the left. Pacific Crest Trail runs parallel with the route at this point. Track on left to campsite.
			GPS: N39°38.63′ W120°40.33′
▼ 1.9		SO	Pacific Crest Trail crosses.
	0.1 ▲	SO	Pacific Crest Trail crosses.
▼ 2.0		SO	Track on right is Deer Lake OHV Trail, which descends 0.3 miles to Deer Lake. Zero trip meter and follow the sign for Summit OHV Trail. Pacific Crest Trail crosses at the intersection.
	0.0 ▲		Continue to the southwest.
			GPS: N39°38.85′ W120°40.24′
▼ 0.0			Continue to the north.
	1.1 ▲	SO	Track on left is Deer Lake OHV Trail, which descends 0.3 miles to Deer Lake. Zero trip meter. Pacific Crest Trail crosses at the intersection.
▼ 1.1		SO	Track on left goes 1.2 miles to the southern end of Northern Sierra #29: Gold Valley Trail. Zero trip meter. Summit Lake is on the right.
	0.0 ▲		Continue to the south.
			GPS: N39°39.66′ W120°40.52′
▼ 0.0			Continue to the northeast.
	1.3 ▲	BL	Track on right goes 1.2 miles to the southern end of Northern Sierra #29: Gold Valley Trail. Zero trip meter and follow the sign to Deer Lake OHV Trail. Summit Lake is on the left.
▼ 0.1		SO	Track on left is a marked OHV trail that goes to Oakland Pond. Follow sign to Little Gold Lake and enter Plumas National Forest and Lakes Basin Recreation Area. Camping is allowed in designated sites only.
	1.2 ▲	SO	Track on right is a marked OHV trail to Oakland Pond. Leaving Plumas National Forest and Lakes Basin Recreation Area. Dispersed camping is permitted past this point.
▼ 0.2		SO	Pacific Crest Trail crosses.
	1.1 ▲	SO	Pacific Crest Trail crosses.
▼ 0.3		BL	Track on right.
	1.0 ▲	BR	Track on left.
			GPS: N39°39.81′ W120°40.38′
▼ 0.7		SO	Track on left; then cattle guard.
	0.6 ▲	SO	Cattle guard; then track on right.
▼ 0.8		SO	Track on right to private property.
	0.5 ▲	BR	Track on left to private property. Follow sign to Summit Lake.
▼ 1.2		BR	Start of Gold Lake OHV Campground. Private property on left. Bear right and follow around the lakeshore.
	0.1 ▲	BL	End of designated camping area. Private property on right. Bear left away from the lake.
			GPS: N39°40.27′ W120°39.98′
▼ 1.3		SO	Track on right goes 0.25 miles to Little Gold Lake. Zero trip meter.
	0.0 ▲		Continue to the west.
			GPS: N39°40.18′ W120°39.87′
▼ 0.0			Continue to the east.
	2.0 ▲	SO	Track on left goes 0.25 miles to Little Gold Lake. Zero trip meter and follow sign to Summit Lake.
▼ 0.3		SO	Leaving Gold Lake OHV Campground.
	1.7 ▲	SO	Entering Gold Lake OHV Campground.
			GPS: N39°40.16′ W120°39.62′
▼ 0.4		SO	Day-use area on left.
	1.6 ▲	SO	Day-use area on right.
▼ 0.5		SO	Track on left to lakeshore is for day use only.
	1.5 ▲	SO	Track on right to lakeshore is for day use only.
▼ 0.7		SO	Track on left to lakeshore is for day use only.
	1.3 ▲	SO	Track on right to lakeshore is for day use only.
			GPS: N39°40.31′ W120°39.19′
▼ 1.0		SO	Turnout on left provides foot access to beach.
	1.0 ▲	SO	Turnout on right provides foot access to beach.
▼ 1.1		BL	Track on right to Squaw Lake and Squaw Lake Jeep Campground.
	0.9 ▲	SO	Track on left to Squaw Lake and Squaw Lake Jeep Campground.
			GPS: N39°40.39′ W120°38.86′
▼ 1.5		TR	Parking area straight ahead provides foot access to the lake. Turn right onto paved road.
	0.5 ▲	TL	Parking area on right provides foot access to lake. Turn left, following the sign for Little Gold Lake and Summit Lake. Trail is now designated OHV Route 60 (21N93) for 4WDs, ATVs, and motorbikes—rated black. Trail is now a rough, formed trail.
▼ 1.6		SO	Track on left to boat launch and undeveloped campground.
	0.4 ▲	SO	Track on right to boat launch and undeveloped campground.
▼ 2.0			Trail finishes on Gold Lake Road. Turn left for the Lakes Basin Petroglyphs and Graeagle; turn right for Bassetts and California 49.
	0.0 ▲		From Gold Lake Road, 6 miles north of Bassetts and California 49, zero trip meter and turn southwest onto paved road, following sign for Gold Lake Boat Launch Facility. Trail runs along the southern shore of Gold Lake.
			GPS: N39°40.78′ W120°38.42′

NORTHERN SIERRA #29

Gold Valley Trail

Starting Point:	**CR A14, immediately south of Johnsville**
Finishing Point:	**FR 93-03, 6.2 miles north of the intersection with FR 93**
Total Mileage:	**15.4 miles**
Unpaved Mileage:	**14.2 miles**
Driving Time:	**4 hours**
Elevation Range:	**5,200–7,200 feet**
Usually Open:	**July to November**
Best Time to Travel:	**July to November**
Difficulty Rating:	**6**
Scenic Rating:	**9**
Remoteness Rating:	**+1**

Special Attractions

- Plumas Eureka State Park and historic Johnsville.
- Panoramic ridge top trail with views of the Lakes Basin Recreation Area and Spencer Lake.
- Remains of the Four Hills Mine.
- Challenging section through Gold Valley.

History

Gold Valley Trail begins just south of Johnsville at the Plumas Eureka State Park Museum. The open-air museum, established in 1959, offers insight on life in a gold mining community during the latter half of the nineteenth century.

Mohawk Mill is at the base of Eureka Peak, called Gold Mountain during the early mining days. This gigantic mill cost nearly $50,000 to construct in 1876 and contained a whopping 60 stamps, capable of processing 5,000 pounds of ore in a single day. A museum is housed in what was formerly a miners' bunkhouse.

This trail makes its way up a hand-built wagon road that led to many mining camps farther up Jamison Creek. Grass Lake, southeast of the trail past the Jamison Mine, was the site of a fish camp for an outfit based in Johnsville. Because of the difficult terrain, everything that went to the camp had to be taken in by pack mules. All that remains today at the site are foundations.

The Four Hills, Willoughby, and Empire are prominent mines passed as you proceed up and over the range toward Pauley Creek. People packed in supplies to these mines from Downieville. In those days it was a day's trip with a fully laden mule; today it is an afternoon's mountain bike ride through what was called Devils Den.

An Englishman named Hunt operated the Four Hills Mine. He would make his way over the mountains into Sierra City for supplies and a rewarding whiskey and soda. On one of his infrequent visits to the Upper Hotel, the bartender accidentally gave him whiskey and something from a cream soda bottle. Hunt went mad after taking his first gulp, screaming that he'd been poisoned. He was almost right. It seems someone had accidentally left the local remedy for bed bugs, a common problem in those days, in a soda bottle behind the counter. Hunt survived, but he was not as amused as the hotel staff and clientele. Hunt's Four Hills Mine went on to produce almost half a million dollars worth of gold. The mine buildings remained well into the twentieth century, until a local youth blasted them to bits. The kid was spotted by a cowboy tending cattle in Gold Valley and ended up in jail.

The Mohawk Stamp Mill, constructed in 1877

Description

The trail starts in Johnsville at the Plumas Eureka State Park office and museum. Before starting the trail, the Johnsville Cemetery, a short distance north just off the main street in Johnsville, is well worth a visit. The state park has an open-air display of mining artifacts and the Mohawk Mill can be seen on the slope below Eureka Peak from the south side of the museum parking lot.

By 1888, the Eureka Mine had tunneled a mile into the mountain

The first mile of the trail is paved because it leads to the park's developed campground. The trail runs around the southeastern side of Eureka Peak along Jamison Creek, with Mount Washington to the south. Sections of hand-stacked rock wall that support this section of shelf road were built by miners. Irene Falls, a series of small falls on Jamison Creek, are immediately west of the undeveloped Ross Camp.

The trail briefly joins a graded gravel road on its way to the site of A-Tree Camp, passing the head of the deep Florentine Canyon before turning onto a small formed trail that climbs steeply to the ridge top. This ridge offers some of the most scenic vistas along the trail, which winds through a landscape of bare broken granite, scattered fir trees, and slopes covered with mule's ears. To the north is the Lakes Basin Recreation Area, with the glacial Wades, Rock, and Jamison Lakes 600 feet below. Spencer Lakes and the Sierra Buttes are visible to the south. The trail follows the southern boundary of the recreation area, which is also the boundary separating Tahoe and Plumas National Forests. It passes the remains of the Four Hills Mine. Deep shafts and surface workings are scattered about on several levels; concrete footings of what might have been a mill can also be seen.

The trail is rated a 4 for difficulty as far as the mine because of some moderately loose and rocky climbs and because the deep, dusty surface makes traction difficult. The section from Four Hills Mine to Hawley Lake is rated a 5 for difficulty. It winds down to the lake along a steep, loose, and moguled slope. If you intend to retrace your route to Johnsville, be sure you can climb back up the hill before beginning the descent. The trail only gets more difficult from here.

Near Hawley Lake the trail passes through Camp Nejedly, private property deeded to the Boy Scouts of America in 1964. In addition to use by the scouts, the camp regularly hosts mentally and physically impaired children. Local four-wheel-drive clubs help transport campers into the area. The Boy Scouts of America require a permit to camp at the lake.

Past the camp, the trail quickly earns its difficulty rating of 6. Those without high-clearance and sturdy tires, or those driving full-size vehicles should consider turning back. The

Wades, Rock, and Jamison Lakes

difficulty comes from steep loose descents and a rocky surface. Watch your vehicle's underbody on some of the tight maneuvers. You will have to ride large boulders to avoid underbody damage. Full-size vehicles are likely to find some of the turns through trees and rocks too tight for comfort; this section is best suited for compact and sub-compact vehicles.

As the trail enters Gold Valley, it becomes lightly brushy, crossing and re-crossing Pauley Creek. However, the bushes here are softer and more forgiving on paintwork or clothing than the brittle manzanitas found throughout much of Northern California. This brushy section goes for approximately 0.6 miles. Rock hounds may enjoy hunting for pyrite around the creek.

The trail re-enters the forest and continues to wind past the OHV trailheads to Pauley Creek and Smiths Lake. There are a few more loose and rocky climbs, but none as difficult to negotiate as the ones at the north end of Gold Valley. This section is heavily used by mountain bikers, who are shuttled up from Downieville to take advantage of the exhilarating downhill runs back to the town via Pauley Creek Trail, Butcher Ranch Trail, 3rd Divide Trail, or 2nd Divide Trail. Butcher Ranch Trail is excellent for spring wildflower viewing. In winter the section south of Hawley Lake is an ungroomed snowmobile trail.

The trail finishes at the intersection with 93-03, 6.2 miles north of paved FR 93. The intersection is not well marked, but it is well used and has an OHV sign past the turn.

Current Road Information

Plumas National Forest
Beckwourth Ranger District
23 Mohawk Road
Blairsden, CA 96103
(530) 836-2575

Map References

BLM Portola
USFS Plumas National Forest; Tahoe National Forest
USGS 1:24,000 Johnsville, Gold Lake, Mt. Fillmore
1:100,000 Portola
Maptech CD-ROM: High Sierra/Tahoe
Northern California Atlas & Gazetteer, p. 70
California Road & Recreation Atlas, p. 60
Other: Plumas National Forest OHV Map—Summer Use, Lakes Basin, Sierra Buttes and Plumas Eureka State Park Recreation Guide

Route Directions

▼ 0.0		From CR A14 immediately south of Johnsville, zero trip meter and turn southwest on small paved road at the Plumas Eureka State Park office and museum. Trail begins through the parking lot.
4.5 ▲		Trail ends at the Plumas Eureka State Park office and museum immediately south of Johnsville. Turn right for California 70 and Portola.
		GPS: N39°45.42' W120°41.82'
▼ 0.1	SO	Campground and Museum Trail for hikers on left.
4.4 ▲	SO	Campground and Museum Trail for hikers on right.
▼ 0.3	SO	Emigrant Trail marker on right.
4.2 ▲	SO	Emigrant Trail marker on left.
▼ 1.1	SO	Upper Jamison Creek Campground on left.
3.4 ▲	SO	Upper Jamison Creek Campground on right.
		GPS: N39°44.55' W120°42.38'
▼ 1.2	SO	Road turns to graded dirt. Sections of shelf

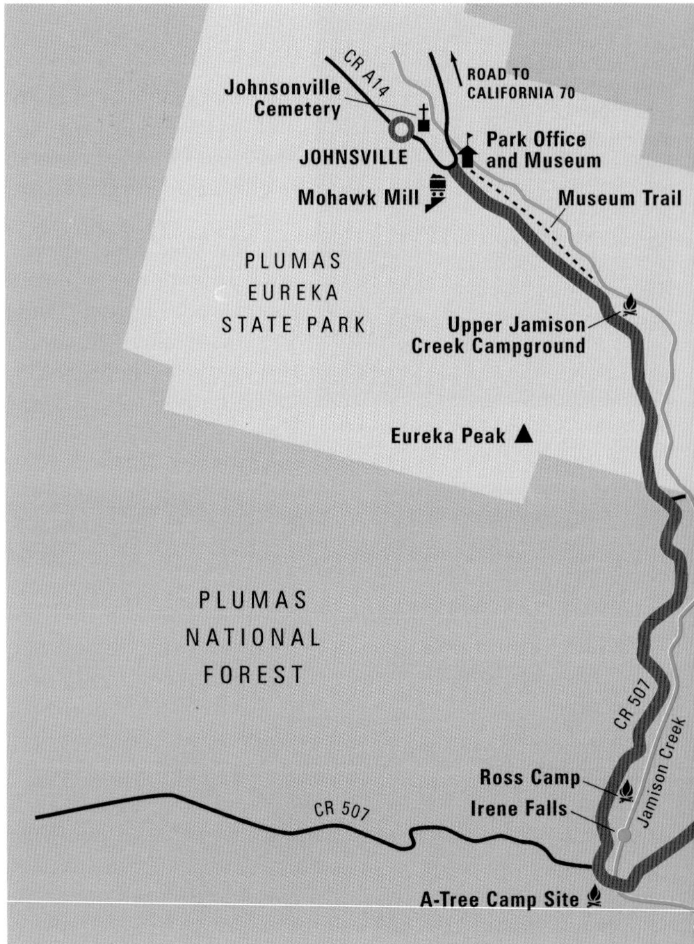

			road for the next 2.6 miles.
	3.3 ▲	SO	Road is now paved. End of shelf road.
▼ 2.0		SO	Turnout on left. Exiting Plumas Eureka State Park into Plumas National Forest.
	2.5 ▲	SO	Exiting Plumas National Forest into Plumas Eureka State Park. Turnout on right.
			GPS: N39°44.25′ W120°43.21′
▼ 2.1		SO	Track on left. Road is now designated OHV Route 36B for 4WDs, ATVs and motorbikes—rated green.
	2.4 ▲	SO	Track on right.
▼ 2.3		SO	Track on left.
	2.2 ▲	SO	Track on right.
▼ 2.6		SO	Track on left to campsite.
	1.9 ▲	SO	Track on right to campsite.
▼ 3.8		SO	End of shelf road.
	0.7 ▲	SO	Sections of shelf road for the next 2.6 miles.
▼ 3.9		SO	Track on left.
	0.6 ▲	SO	Track on right.
▼ 4.0		SO	Track on left.
	0.5 ▲	SO	Track on right.
▼ 4.1		SO	Ross Camp—unimproved USFS camping area—on left.
	0.4 ▲	SO	Ross Camp—unimproved USFS camping area—on right.
			GPS: N39°44.08′ W120°45.03′
▼ 4.2		SO	Track on left to Irene Falls on Jamison Creek.
	0.3 ▲	SO	Track on right to Irene Falls on Jamison Creek.
▼ 4.5		TL	T-intersection. CR 507 (OHV Route 36) continues to the right. Turn left, following sign to A-Tree and Four Hills Mine, and zero trip meter. Trail is now designated OHV Route 62 for 4WDs, ATVs, and motorbikes—rated green.
	0.0 ▲		Continue to the east.
			GPS: N39°44.10′ W120°45.35′
▼ 0.0			Continue to the south.
	2.0 ▲	TR	Graded road continues ahead. Turn right and join CR 507 (OHV Route 36) for 4WDs, ATVs, and motorbikes—rated green. Zero trip meter.
▼ 0.1		SO	A-Tree Road Camp—unimproved USFS camping area—on right; then cross over Jamison Creek on bridge; then track on right.
	1.9 ▲	SO	Track on left; then cross over Jamison Creek on bridge; then A-Tree Road Camp—unimproved USFS camping area—on left.
▼ 2.0		TL	Graded road bears right toward A-Tree. Stay on the upper road. Turn left onto OHV Route 62 for 4WDs, ATVs, and motorbikes—rated blue. Zero trip meter. Pacific Crest Trail crosses at this intersection.
	0.0 ▲		Continue to the north.
			GPS: N39°42.92′ W120°44.64′
▼ 0.0			Continue to the southeast.
	3.1 ▲	TR	T-intersection with graded road. To the left goes toward A-Tree. Turn right and zero trip meter. Pacific Crest Trail crosses at this intersection.

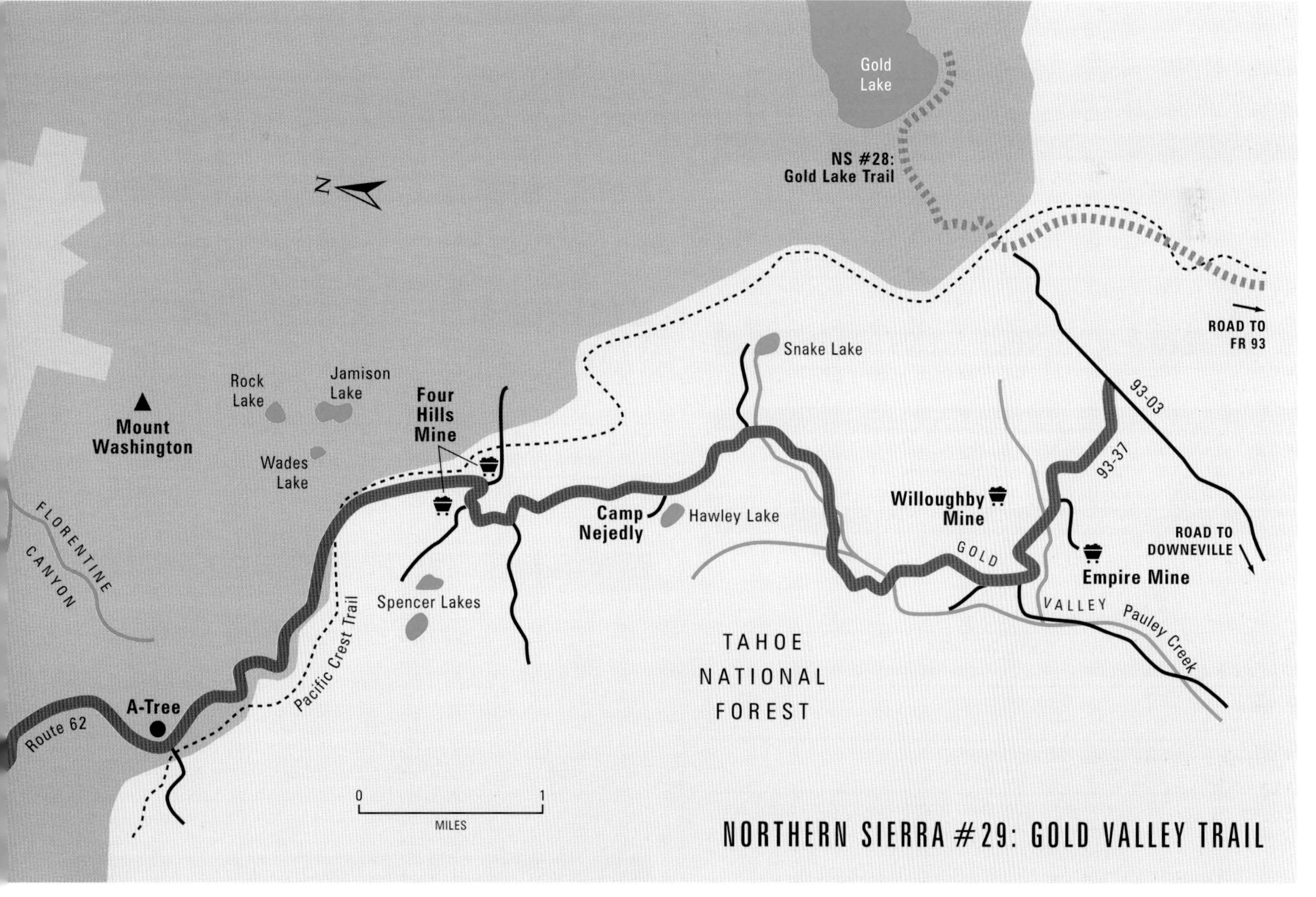

NORTHERN SIERRA #29: GOLD VALLEY TRAIL

▼ 1.5 SO Turnout on right.
1.6 ▲ SO Turnout on left.

GPS: N39°42.44′ W120°43.52′

▼ 1.8 SO Pacific Crest Trail crosses. To the left goes into the Lakes Basin Recreation Area to Wades Lake, Mount Washington, and Grass Lake.
1.3 ▲ SO Pacific Crest Trail crosses. To the right goes into the Lakes Basin Recreation Area to Wades Lake, Mount Washington, and Grass Lake.

GPS: N39°42.49′ W120°43.19′

▼ 2.0 TL Spencer Lakes to the right. Turn left for a spectacular viewpoint over Wades Lake, Rock Lake, and Jamison Lake.
1.1 ▲ TR Rejoin main trail. Spencer Lakes to the left.

GPS: N39°42.43′ W120°43.07′

▼ 2.2 TL Rejoin main trail; then Pacific Crest Trail leaves to the left.
0.9 ▲ TR Pacific Crest Trail joins on the right; then turn right for a spectacular viewpoint over Wades Lake, Rock Lake, and Jamison Lake.

GPS: N39°42.34′ W120°42.94′

▼ 2.8 SO Remains of Four Hills Mine on left and right. Track on left.
0.3 ▲ SO Track on right. Remains of Four Hills Mine on left and right.

GPS: N39°41.90′ W120°42.66′

▼ 2.9 BR Track on left toward Mud Lake.
0.2 ▲ BL Track on right toward Mud Lake.

GPS: N39°41.79′ W120°42.66′

▼ 3.1 TL Track on right to the bottom of the Four Hills Mine; then well-used trail continues straight ahead to Spencer Lakes. There is a jeep and motorbike sign on a tree, but no other markings. The Four Hills Mine mill site is at the intersection. Zero trip meter.
0.0 ▲ Continue to the west. Track on left to the bottom of the Four Hills Mine.

GPS: N39°41.86′ W120°42.75′

▼ 0.0 Continue to the south.
1.2 ▲ TR T-intersection. Well-used track on left goes to Spencer Lakes. Zero trip meter and turn right up hill. The intersection is unmarked. The Four Hills Mine mill site is at the intersection.

▼ 0.3 SO Track on right.
0.9 ▲ SO Track on left.

GPS: N39°41.66′ W120°42.81′

▼ 0.8 SO Entering Camp Nejedly—private property.
0.4 ▲ SO Leaving Camp Nejedly.

GPS: N39°41.33′ W120°42.56′

▼ 1.2 SO Hawley Lake on right. Track on right to lakeshore. Zero trip meter.
0.0 ▲ Continue to the north.

GPS: N39°41.04′ W120°42.47′

▼ 0.0 Continue to the south, following sign to Gold Valley.
3.1 ▲ SO Hawley Lake on left. Track on left to lakeshore. Zero trip meter.

▼ 0.2 SO Leaving Camp Nejedly.
2.9 ▲ SO Entering Camp Nejedly—private property.

▼ 0.6 SO Cross through creek.
2.5 ▲ SO Cross through creek.

▼ 0.7 SO Cross through creek.
2.4 ▲ SO Cross through creek.

▼ 0.8 TR Track on right; then immediately turn right and cross over Pauley Creek. Track on left goes to Snake Lake.
2.3 ▲ TL Cross over Pauley Creek; then track on right goes to Snake Lake. Turn left and immediately pass track on left.

GPS: N39°40.64′ W120°41.94′

▼ 0.9 TL Track on right. Trail can be slightly brushy for the next 0.6 miles.
2.2 ▲ TR Track on left.

▼ 1.1 SO Cross through creek twice.
2.0 ▲ SO Cross through creek twice.

▼ 1.2 SO Cross over creek twice.
1.9 ▲ SO Cross over creek twice.

▼ 1.3 SO Entering Gold Valley.
1.8 ▲ SO Leaving Gold Valley.

GPS: N39°40.28′ W120°42.12′

▼ 1.4 SO Cross through creek twice.
1.7 ▲ SO Cross through creek twice.

▼ 1.5 SO Cross through Pauley Creek.
1.6 ▲ SO Cross through Pauley Creek. Trail can be slightly brushy for the next 0.6 miles.

GPS: N39°40.19′ W120°42.28′

▼ 1.6 SO Track on right.
1.5 ▲ SO Track on left.

GPS: N39°40.17′ W120°42.34′

▼ 1.7 SO Track on left to campsite by small cascades. Trail standard has improved to a 4.
1.4 ▲ SO Track on right to campsite by small cascades. Trail enters the 6-rated section.

▼ 1.8 SO Cross through creek.
1.3 ▲ SO Cross through creek.

▼ 2.2 SO Cross through Pauley Creek.
0.9 ▲ SO Cross through Pauley Creek.

GPS: N39°39.84′ W120°42.61′

▼ 2.3 SO Track on right.
0.8 ▲ SO Track on left.

▼ 2.9 TL T-intersection with small formed trail. There is an OHV trail sign after the turn.
0.2 ▲ TR Track continues straight ahead. Follow OHV marker on the tree.

GPS: N39°39.34′ W120°42.45′

▼ 3.1 SO Track on right is Pauley Creek Trail to Smith Lake. (Sign is high on the tree and hard to spot.) Zero trip meter and continue up the hill.
0.0 ▲ Continue to the north.

GPS: N39°39.19′ W120°42.42′

▼ 0.0 Continue to the south.
1.5 ▲ SO Track on left is Pauley Creek Trail to Smith Lake. (Sign is high on the tree and hard to spot.) Zero trip meter.

▼ 0.6 SO Cross through creek.
0.9 ▲ SO Cross through creek.

▼ 0.8 SO Track on right to Empire Mine—private property.
0.7 ▲ BR Track on left to Empire Mine—private property.

GPS: N39°39.12′ W120°41.85′

▼ 1.5 Trail ends at T-intersection with 93-03. Turn left to intersect with Northern Sierra #28: Gold Lake Trail; turn right to exit to Downieville.
0.0 ▲ Trail commences on 93-03, 6.2 miles north of the intersection with FR 93, which in turn is 11 miles north of California 49. Zero trip meter and turn southwest on formed trail 93-37, marked with a mountain bike sign "Downieville Downhill," and also marked to Gold Valley. After the turn, the route is marked to OHV trails: Gold Valley, Pauley Creek, and Smith Lake.

GPS: N39°39.02′ W120°41.13′

NORTHERN SIERRA #30

Poker Flat OHV Trail

Starting Point:	**California 49, on the western edge of Downieville**
Finishing Point:	**La Porte Road at North Star Junction, 2.5 miles north of Strawberry Valley**
Total Mileage:	**41.5 miles**
Unpaved Mileage:	**41.5 miles**
Driving Time:	**8 hours**
Elevation Range:	**3,000–6,400 feet**
Usually Open:	**May to October**
Best Time to Travel:	**Dry weather**
Difficulty Rating:	**5**
Scenic Rating:	**10**
Remoteness Rating:	**+1**

Special Attractions

- Long trail that passes many pioneer mining settlements and cemeteries.
- Site of Poker Flat.
- Steep, challenging grades to and from Poker Flat.
- Panoramic views from Saddleback Fire Lookout.

History

Poker Flat OHV Trail follows a well-used miners' trail that has been in use from the 1850s to the present. Fortune seekers established Downieville, on the banks of the turbulent North Yuba River, in 1849. Among the eager arrivals was a Scot named William Downie. His leadership qualities in the town's formative years may have been the reason why his name was adopted for the camp known previously as The Forks. The far-flung outpost flourished in no time, gaining a somewhat boisterous reputation (see page 33).

Old wooden building on Poker Flat

The steep trail that leads out of Downieville passes a site known as Red Ant. The forest service had a station at the top of the thousand-foot climb from the North Yuba River. Every morning during fire season, a ranger would climb to the lookout on top of Red Ant Mountain and return in the evening to a cabin at Red Ant. The lookout on Saddleback Mountain had not yet been built. Just north of Red Ant are the remains of the Monte Cristo Mine. The Monte Cristo Hotel was just below the road at a small intersection.

The town of Fir Cap, also called Fir Cap Diggings, was situated on the flat northwest of the Telegraph Mine. A post office established there in 1869 was discontinued in 1886.

Miners from Sicily, England, and Russia rest in St. Louis Cemetery

The site of Poker Flat, established in the early 1850s, has always been a difficult place to reach. The steep grades on both sides of Canyon Creek were as dangerous for pack mules then as they are for vehicles today. A packer hauling a dead man out of town on one of his mules commented, "They're not bad to pack out, you know. You've got to be gruesome...If the relatives see the guy draped over the saddle, tied down and gurgling, they holler, you know."

The steep trail out of Poker Flat on the north side of Canyon Creek was built in the 1890s. A fallen tree was often tied to the back of wagons descending the trail to act as a brake. Come winter, this part of the Sierra Nevada saw its fair share of snow, which was often too deep and dangerous for laden mules, forcing packers to carry goods in and out on their backs. They tied rope around wooden skis to provide grip on the steep trails.

At one time Poker Flat supported several stores, a Masonic Hall, numerous saloons, a blacksmith, a jeweler, butcher shops, and three hotels, and the town's population approached 2,000. A fire in 1859 destroyed much of the town, but most residents stayed and rebuilt. A school was established in 1863 for children from town and the surrounding mining camps.

Howland Flat, also referred to as Table Rock, is one of a series of mining camps that developed along the northern side of Port Wine Ridge. Queen City, St. Louis, Pine Grove, and Scales are just a few others. Howland Flat's post office was established in 1857 and was discontinued in 1922. The town had numerous stores, a theater, a bakery, a brewery, and several busy saloons. The mining town reached a peak of 1,500 residents, and most worked at nearby hydraulic, placer, and drift mines. An estimated $14 million worth of ore was extracted during the life of the mines.

Another mining camp along the trail, Port Wine, allegedly was named for a cask of port wine discovered near the settlement. Ironically, the town was described as sober and religious. Large-scale hydraulic mining washed away most of the original town.

Description

Poker Flat OHV Trail leaves California 49 from the western edge of Downieville. The well-marked, formed CR 509 immediately starts to climb away from the North Yuba River along a shelf road. The trail, initially suited for high-clearance 2WD vehicles, climbs into Tahoe National Forest and travels below the flat-topped Fir Cap. An OHV trail rated more difficult by the forest service runs over the top of Fir

View of Fir Cap from Saddleback Lookout

Cap, providing excellent views from the summit. This trail can be very brushy.

The short trail to Saddleback Fire Lookout is a worthwhile detour from the main route. Rated 3 for difficulty, this narrow shelf road offers views east to the Sierra Buttes and beyond. It ends at a fire lookout, built in 1933, that is still manned during the summer. You can usually climb up to the tower, perched on an outcrop of rock, with permission from the lookout. Panoramic views from the tower include Tahoe and Plumas National Forests and great views of the Sierra Buttes. On a clear day you can just make out the shape of the lookout on Sierra Buttes (See Northern Sierra #27: Sierra Buttes Trail, page 391). Table Rock and Pilot Peak are visible to the north.

Back on the main trail, you will pass the start of Northern Sierra #31: Chimney Rock OHV Trail before reaching the spur to the volcanic Devils Postpile. The main trail then descends steeply along Grizzly Ridge to the historic settlement of Poker Flat. The 2-mile descent is steep and loose, narrow at times, with an uneven surface and poor traction. Two-wheel-drive vehicles should not attempt this part of the trail. Much of the land at Poker Flat is privately owned, and there are active mining claims all along Canyon Creek. If you want to try your hand at gold panning, be sure to get permission from the mining claimant. The BLM's Folsom field office is the best place to find this information; the phone number is (916)-985-4474. The BLM's website can also tell you what you need to know.

The lumpy crossing over Canyon Creek is rearranged almost every year by spring runoff, but it is normally passable with a high-clearance 4WD. The open area of Poker Flat OHV Campground on the north side of Canyon Creek has a few tables and fire rings.

The historical marker for Poker Flat is next to one of the few surviving timber buildings; wildfires have burned the area on two separate occasions. A track continues farther east along Canyon Creek to various mining claims. The main trail swings north and starts to climb the steep, loose Wild Steer Surveys Route. The grade is more or less constant, averaging 20 degrees. At times it travels through cuttings, where runoff and years of traffic, both wagon and vehicle, have eroded the roadbed 10 to 15 feet into the surrounding hillside. The surface is loose and scrabbly with patches of fist-size rubble interspersed with a fine loose surface. Low range 4WD and a slow, steady pace will carry most vehicles safely to the top. Vehicles traveling downhill may need to reverse at times because passing places are scarce.

Watch out for piles of rocks at the intersection at the top of the climb, where 22N43 leads away in a small clearing. Miners working at Poker Flat would weigh their pickups down with rocks from the creek to give them traction for the climb up the steep grade. At the top of the climb, they would dump the rocks, creating the piles you see today. The steep descent and ascent on either side of Poker Flat gives the trail its difficulty rating of 5.

From the top of the northern climb, the trail becomes easier and is rated between a 2 and 3 for the remainder of the route. This section passes through one historic mining settlement after another. The first settlement is Howland Flat, where little remains. Only a few old buildings and a cemetery with graves dating from the late nineteenth century remain at Potosi. Please respect the gravesites. Note that most of the area is held under mining lease and that the cabins and structures along the way are privately owned. The cabins of the Wink Eye Mine are not in use, but they are still private property.

A popular 19-mile mountain bike trail, the Howland Flat Loop, joins this trail at Howland Flat and leaves it at Queen City. The full loop travels through La Porte and Lake Delahunty and is rated most difficult by the forest service.

The trail passes north of Sugarloaf Hill and starts to run along Port Wine Ridge. A side trail, 21N69, just north of Queen City travels east above Canyon Creek past the site of Wahoo, the Monumental Mine, and on to the Pacific Mine. Hydraulic mining eroded the hillsides here, and flumes and aqueducts along the trail are reminders of the area's long history of mining.

After crossing over Cedar Grove Ravine, the sites of Queen City and Port Wine are reached. Foundations and the ruins of a few old buildings are all that remain of these mining towns. Port Wine's cemetery is a short distance from the main trail, with many old graves lying in secluded spots.

Scales is now a privately owned site. The Scales Cemetery, just east of the settlement, has many headstones that reflect the hardships of early mining life; many of the deceased were victims of accidents and women who died during childbirth.

The final section of the trail is narrow and runs around the edge of a hillside; it is lightly brushy in places and can be avoided by taking paved FR 30, which intersects the trail in several places. The paved road takes a more circuitous route to exit to Strawberry Valley. The trail finishes north of Strawberry Valley on La Porte Road, 0.7 miles north of the turnoff to Strawberry USFS Campground, which is on the edge of the now silted up Sly Creek Reservoir.

Current Road Information
Tahoe National Forest
Downieville Ranger District
15924 Highway 49
Camptonville, CA 95922
(530) 288-3231

Plumas National Forest
Beckwourth Ranger District
23 Mohawk Road
Blairsden, CA 96103
(530) 836-2575

Map References
BLM Portola, Chico
USFS Tahoe National Forest; Plumas National Forest
USGS 1:24,000 Downieville, Mt. Fillmore, La Porte, Goodyears Bar, Strawberry Valley
1:100,000 Portola, Chico
Maptech CD-ROM: High Sierra/Tahoe
Northern California Atlas & Gazetteer, pp. 70, 69
California Road & Recreation Atlas, p. 60
Other: Plumas National Forest OHV Map—Summer Use

Route Directions

▼ 0.0		From California 49, on the western edge of Downieville, zero trip meter and turn northwest on dirt road. Climb up the hillside, following sign to Chimney Rock Trail and Poker Flat OHV Trail. Road is a single-lane shelf road.
7.6 ▲		Trail finishes on California 49 on the western edge of Downieville.
		GPS: N39°33.49' W120°49.99'
▼ 0.8	SO	Cross over creek in Coyote Ravine.
6.8 ▲	SO	Cross over creek in Coyote Ravine.
▼ 1.9	BR	Cross over creek; then track on left.
5.7 ▲	SO	Track on right; then cross over creek.
▼ 2.0	SO	Track on left; then track on right.
5.6 ▲	SO	Track on left; then track on right.
▼ 2.3	SO	Track on right.
5.3 ▲	SO	Track on left.
▼ 2.8	BR	Track on left; then road forks. The lower road is Oak Ranch Road. Take the upper of the two roads, which is unmarked. Track on right.
4.8 ▲	SO	Track on left; then track on right is Oak Ranch Road; then track on right.
		GPS: N39°34.48' W120°51.53'
▼ 3.5	SO	Track on right.
4.1 ▲	SO	Track on left.
▼ 3.7	SO	Slightly cleared area is the site of Red Ant.
3.9 ▲	SO	Slightly cleared area is the site of Red Ant.
		GPS: N39°35.18' W120°51.50'
▼ 4.4	SO	Track on right is the start of Fir Cap OHV Trail, which goes 0.3 miles to an unmarked graveyard on the right of the trail. Coordinates of the graves are N39°35.66' W120°51.31'.
3.2 ▲	SO	Track on the left is the start of Fir Cap OHV Trail, which goes 0.3 miles to an unmarked graveyard on the right of the trail. Coordinates of the graves are N39°35.66' W120°51.31'.
		GPS: N39°35.70' W120°51.44'
▼ 4.7	SO	Cabin on left and track on left at the Monte Cristo Mine.
2.9 ▲	SO	Cabin on right and track on right at the Monte Cristo Mine.
		GPS: N39°35.87' W120°51.53'
▼ 5.3	SO	Track on left into the White Bear Mine.
2.3 ▲	SO	Track on right into the White Bear Mine.
		GPS: N39°36.27' W120°51.48'
▼ 5.8	SO	Track on left.
1.8 ▲	SO	Track on right.
▼ 6.3	SO	Track on left to Telegraph Diggings.
1.3 ▲	BL	Track on right to Telegraph Diggings.
		GPS: N39°36.85' W120°51.91'
▼ 6.5	SO	Track on left.
1.1 ▲	SO	Track on right.
▼ 7.6	BR	Track on right is Fir Cap OHV Trail (25-23-2); then track on left is 25-19 and second track on left is FR 25 to Devils Postpile. Bear right onto 25-23 following sign to Saddleback Lookout and Poker Flat. Zero trip meter.
0.0 ▲		Continue to the east.
		GPS: N39°37.82' W120°51.74'
▼ 0.0		Continue to the northwest.
2.3 ▲	BL	Track on right is FR 25 to Devils Postpile and second track on right is 25-19; then track on left is Fir Cap OHV Trail (25-23-2). Bear left and follow the sign to Downieville. Zero trip meter.
▼ 0.4	SO	Track on right goes 0.7 miles up a 3-rated track to Saddleback Lookout.
1.9 ▲	SO	Track on left goes 0.7 miles up a 3-rated track to Saddleback Lookout.
		GPS: N39°38.02' W120°52.00'
▼ 1.2	SO	Track on left. Follow sign to Chimney Rock Trail.
1.1 ▲	SO	Track on right.
		GPS: N39°38.57' W120°51.84'
▼ 1.8	SO	Track on left.
0.5 ▲	SO	Track on right.
▼ 2.3	BL	Track on right is Northern Sierra #31:Chimney Rock OHV Trail. Track on left. Zero trip meter and bear left, following sign to Poker Flat OHV Trail.
0.0 ▲		Continue to the southeast.
		GPS: N39°39.33' W120°51.76'
▼ 0.0		Continue to the northwest.
1.8 ▲	SO	Track on left is Northern Sierra #31: Chimney Rock OHV Trail. Track on right. Zero trip meter.
▼ 0.7	TR	T-intersection with roughly graded road. Follow sign to Poker Flat OHV Trail.
1.1 ▲	TL	Graded road continues ahead. Turn sharp left and climb up hill on smaller unmarked trail. There is a sign for Poker Flat OHV Trail at the intersection.
		GPS: N39°39.82' W120°51.60'
▼ 0.8	SO	Turnout on left.
1.0 ▲	SO	Turnout on right.
▼ 1.2	SO	Track on right.
0.6 ▲	SO	Track on left.
▼ 1.4	SO	Track on left.
0.4 ▲	SO	Track on right.
▼ 1.7	SO	Track on left.
0.1 ▲	SO	Track on right.
▼ 1.8	SO	Track on left is the spur to the Devils Postpile. Zero trip meter and follow the sign to Poker Flat OHV Trail. Track on right is Tamarack OHV Trail.
0.0 ▲		Continue to the south. End of climb.
		GPS: N39°40.47' W120°51.37'

Spur to Devils Postpile

▼ 0.0			Proceed west at the start of the OHV part of the trail.
▼ 0.1		SO	Track on right.
▼ 0.2		SO	Track on right.
▼ 0.4		BL	Track on right goes 0.6 miles north of Deadwood Peak.
			GPS: N39°40.40' W120°51.83'
▼ 1.7			Hiking trail on right is Devils Postpile Trail (10E26); then track on left.
			GPS: N39°40.09' W120°52.89'

Continuation of Main Trail

▼ 0.0			Continue to the north and start descent to Poker Flat.
	2.1 ▲	SO	Track on right is the spur to the Devils Postpile. Zero trip meter. Track on left is Tamarack OHV Trail.
			GPS: N39°40.47' W120°51.37'
▼ 0.4		SO	Cross through creek; then track on left to Deadwood Mine.
	1.7 ▲	SO	Track on right to Deadwood Mine; then cross through creek.
			GPS: N39°40.65' W120°51.15'
▼ 0.5		SO	Track on right.
	1.6 ▲	SO	Track on left.
▼ 0.8		SO	Start of shelf road.
	1.3 ▲	SO	End of shelf road.
▼ 1.2		SO	End of shelf road.
	0.9 ▲	SO	Start of shelf road.
▼ 1.7		SO	Track on right.
	0.4 ▲	BR	Track on left.
			GPS: N39°41.46' W120°50.62'
▼ 1.8		BL	Trail forks coming into Poker Flat. Track on right goes to mining claims and Blind Street.
	0.3 ▲	BR	Leaving Poker Flat. Track on left goes to mining claims and Blind Street.
			GPS: N39°41.51' W120°50.60'
▼ 1.9		BR	Track on left and track on right to private property. End of descent. Cross through Canyon Creek; then track on left. Entering Plumas National Forest on north side of creek.
	0.2 ▲	BL	Track straight ahead. Bear left and cross through Canyon Creek; then track on right and track on left to private property. Entering Tahoe National Forest on south side of creek. Start to climb away from Poker Flat.
			GPS: N39°41.57' W120°50.69'
▼ 2.0		SO	Poker Flat OHV Campground on right at the confluence of Grizzly Creek and Canyon Creek.
	0.1 ▲	SO	Poker Flat OHV Campground on left at the confluence of Grizzly Creek and Canyon Creek.
			GPS: N39°41.65' W120°50.62'
▼ 2.1		TL	Old building on right; then turn left up the hill. Track continues ahead along Canyon Creek. Zero trip meter.
	0.0 ▲		Continue to the southwest.
			GPS: N39°41.67' W120°50.55'
▼ 0.0			Continue to the northwest and start to climb away from Poker Flat.
	1.9 ▲	TR	T-intersection in front of old building in Poker Flat. Track on left goes along Canyon Creek. Zero trip meter.
▼ 0.5		SO	Cross over creek.
	1.4 ▲	SO	Cross over creek.

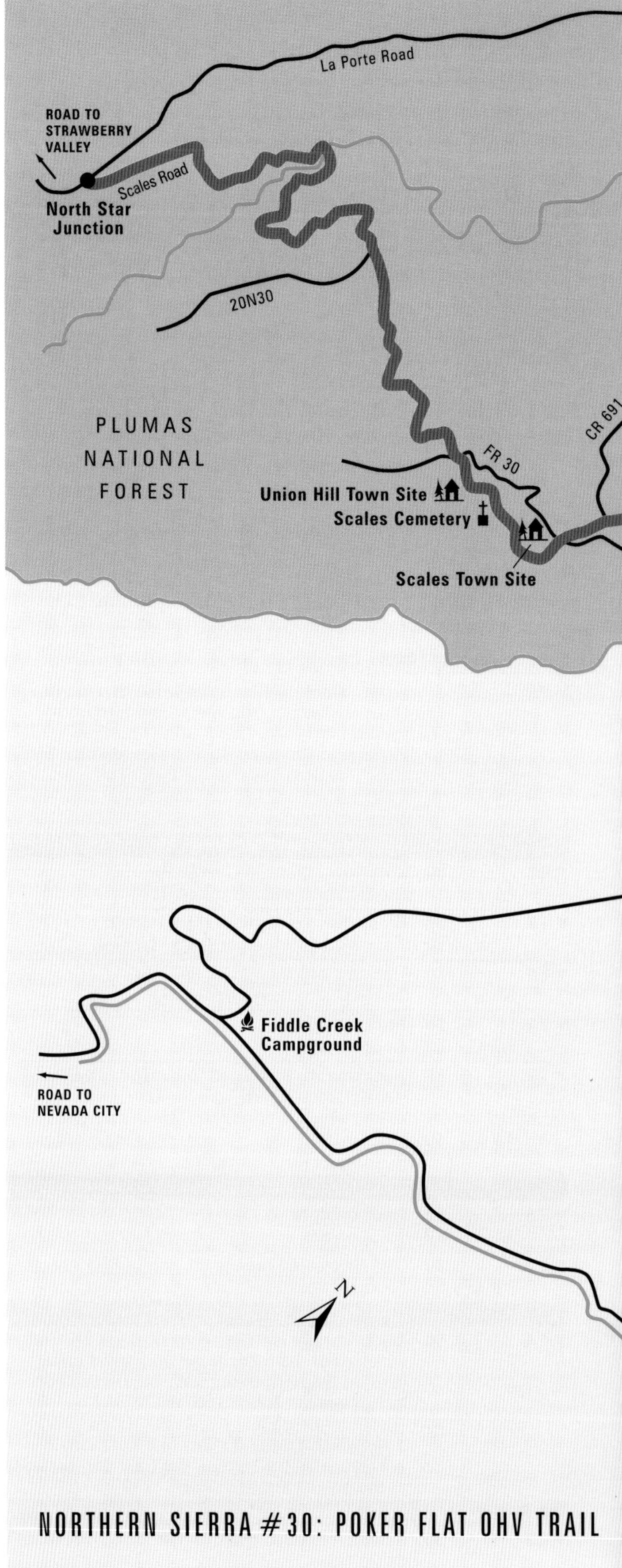

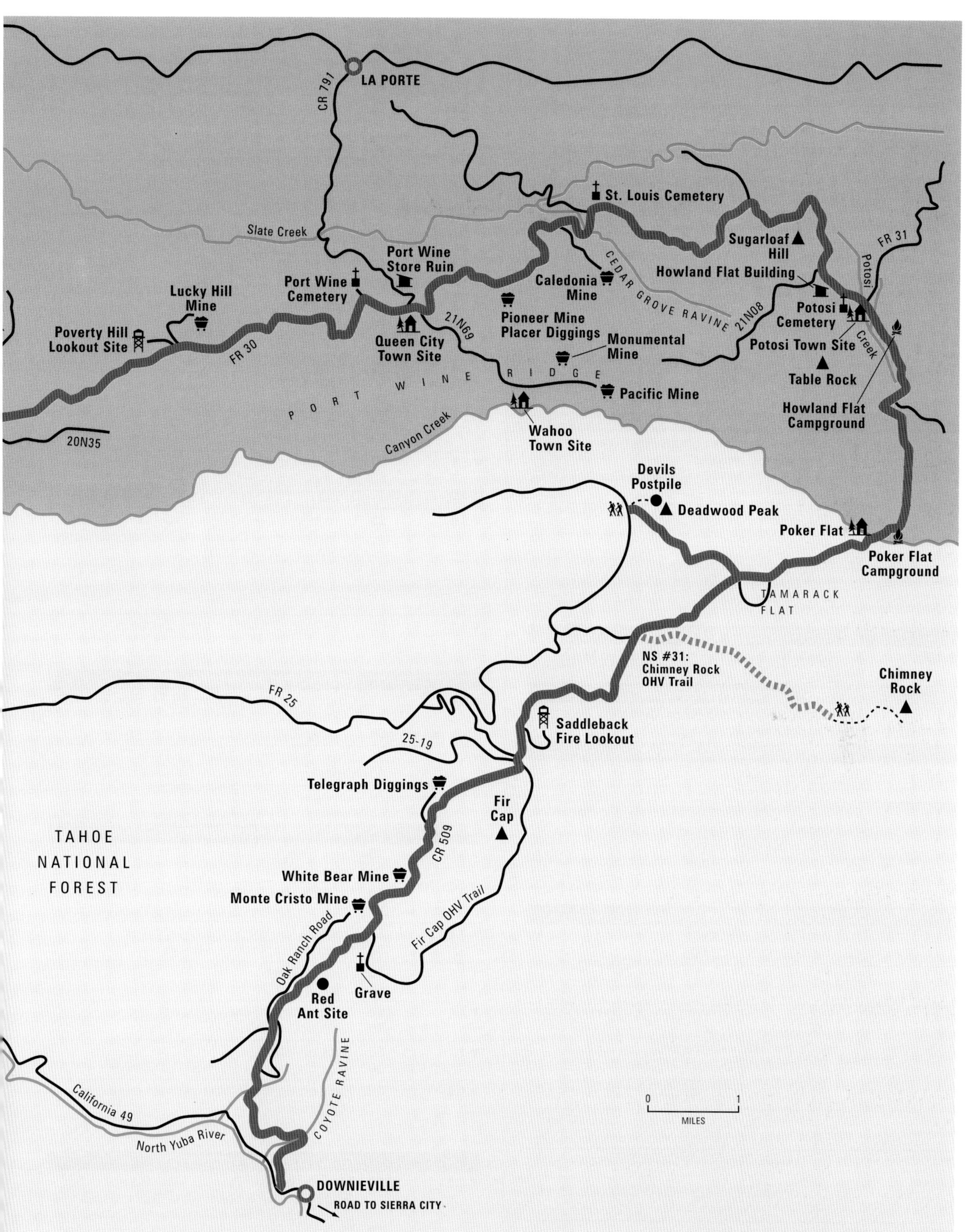
LA PORTE
CR 791
St. Louis Cemetery
Slate Creek
Sugarloaf Hill
FR 31
Potosi
Port Wine Store Ruin
Caledonia Mine
Howland Flat Building
Port Wine Cemetery
Lucky Hill Mine
CEDAR GROVE RAVINE
21N08
Potosi Cemetery
Poverty Hill Lookout Site
Queen City Town Site
21N69
Pioneer Mine Placer Diggings
Monumental Mine
Potosi Town Site
Creek
FR 30
Table Rock
PORT WINE RIDGE
Pacific Mine
Howland Flat Campground
20N35
Canyon Creek
Wahoo Town Site
Devils Postpile
Deadwood Peak
Poker Flat
Poker Flat Campground
TAMARACK FLAT
NS #31: Chimney Rock OHV Trail
Chimney Rock
FR 25
Saddleback Fire Lookout
25-19
Telegraph Diggings
Fir Cap
TAHOE NATIONAL FOREST
CR 509
White Bear Mine
Monte Cristo Mine
Fir Cap OHV Trail
Oak Ranch Road
Grave
Red Ant Site
COYOTE RAVINE
0
1
MILES
California 49
North Yuba River
DOWNIEVILLE
ROAD TO SIERRA CITY

▼ 1.6	SO	Track on right.
0.3 ▲	SO	Track on left.
▼ 1.8	BR	Track on left.
0.1 ▲	BL	Track on right.
▼ 1.9	SO	Well-used track on right. Zero trip meter. End of climb from Poker Flat. Note the piles of rocks at the intersection used by miners coming up the hill.
0.0 ▲		Continue to the south on FR 32 and start to descend to Poker Flat.
		GPS: N39°42.58' W120°51.60'
▼ 0.0		Continue to the north.
6.1 ▲	SO	Well-used track on left. Continue onto FR 32 following the sign for Poker Flat OHV Campground. Zero trip meter. Note the piles of rocks at this intersection used by miners coming up the hill.
▼ 0.2	SO	Cross over creek.
5.9 ▲	SO	Cross over creek.
▼ 0.7	SO	Howland Flat USFS Campground on right.
5.4 ▲	SO	Howland Flat USFS Campground on left.
		GPS: N39°42.93' W120°52.16'
▼ 1.0	SO	Cross over creek on bridge; then track on left to old mining remains.
5.1 ▲	SO	Track on right to old mining remains; then cross over creek on bridge.
▼ 1.2	BL	Track on right is FR 31—rated black. Bear left and cross over Potosi Creek. This is the site of Potosi.
4.9 ▲	BR	Potosi town site. Cross over Potosi Creek; then track on left is FR 31—rated black. Bear right onto FR 32 for 4WDs, ATVs, and motorbikes—rated blue.
		GPS: N39°43.02' W120°52.67'
▼ 1.3	SO	Two old cabins on right at Wink Eye Mine.
4.8 ▲	SO	Two old cabins on left at Wink Eye Mine.
		GPS: N39°43.01' W120°52.80'
▼ 1.4	SO	Track on right; then Potosi Cemetery on left.
4.7 ▲	SO	Potosi Cemetery on right; then track on left.
		GPS: N39°42.94' W120°52.88'
▼ 1.7	SO	Track on right.
4.4 ▲	SO	Track on left.
▼ 1.8	SO	Track on left. Remains of a Howland Flat stone building with circular well out back on left; then cross over creek.
4.3 ▲	SO	Cross over creek; then remains of a Howland Flat stone building with circular well out back on right; then track on right.
		GPS: N39°42.87' W120°53.28'
▼ 1.9	SO	Track on left is 21N08.
4.2 ▲	SO	Track on right is 21N08.
▼ 2.1	SO	Track on right.
4.0 ▲	SO	Track on left.
▼ 2.2	SO	Cross over creek. Trail is passing through an area where hydraulic mining took place. Sugarloaf Hill is on the left.
3.9 ▲	SO	Trail is passing through an area where hydraulic mining took place. Cross over creek. Sugarloaf Hill is on the right.
▼ 2.3	SO	Track on left.
3.8 ▲	SO	Track on right.
▼ 2.5	SO	Cross over creek. Slate Creek Ravine is on the right.
3.6 ▲	SO	Cross over creek. Slate Creek Ravine is on the left.
▼ 2.9	SO	Two tracks on right.
3.2 ▲	SO	Two tracks on left.
▼ 3.0	SO	Track on left to Debi D Mine.
3.1 ▲	SO	Track on right to Debi D Mine.
		GPS: N39°43.15' W120°53.99'
▼ 3.8	SO	Two tracks on right.
2.3 ▲	SO	Two tracks on left.
▼ 4.0	SO	Track on left and track on right.
2.1 ▲	SO	Track on left and track on right.
▼ 4.8	SO	Track on left.
1.3 ▲	SO	Track on right.
▼ 5.1	SO	Track on left and track on right.
1.0 ▲	SO	Track on left and track on right.
▼ 5.4	SO	Track on left.
0.7 ▲	SO	Track on right.
▼ 5.5	SO	Track on right.
0.6 ▲	SO	Track on left.
▼ 5.6	SO	Track on right.
0.5 ▲	SO	Track on left.
▼ 5.7	SO	Track on left.
0.4 ▲	SO	Track on right.
▼ 5.8	SO	Track on right.
0.3 ▲	SO	Track on left.
▼ 5.9	SO	Track on right is 21N96.
0.2 ▲	SO	Track on left is 21N96.
		GPS: N39°41.86' W120°55.70'
▼ 6.0	SO	Unmarked track on right goes 0.1 miles to St. Louis Cemetery. Coordinates of cemetery are N39°41.86' W120°55.82'.
0.1 ▲	SO	Unmarked track on left goes 0.1 miles to St. Louis Cemetery. Coordinates of cemetery are N39°41.86' W120°55.82'.
▼ 6.1	BL	Wide graded track on right. Zero trip meter.
0.0 ▲		Continue to the north. End of shelf road.
		GPS: N39°41.70' W120°55.79'
▼ 0.0		Continue to the south on FR 31. Start of shelf road.
3.4 ▲	BR	Wide graded track on left. Zero trip meter.
▼ 0.3	SO	Cross over Cedar Grove Ravine on bridge.
3.1 ▲	SO	Cross over Cedar Grove Ravine on bridge.
▼ 0.4	SO	Spring on left.
3.0 ▲	SO	Spring on right.
		GPS: N39°41.51' W120°55.66'
▼ 0.6	SO	Track on left.
2.8 ▲	SO	Track on right.
▼ 0.7	SO	Track on left is 21N55 to Caledonia Mine.
2.7 ▲	SO	Track on right is 21N55 to Caledonia Mine.
▼ 1.4	SO	Track on left; then cross over creek.
2.0 ▲	SO	Cross over creek; then track on right.
▼ 1.5	SO	Track on right.
1.9 ▲	SO	Track on left.
▼ 1.6	SO	Two tracks on right.
1.8 ▲	SO	Two tracks on left.
▼ 1.7	SO	Track on left.
1.7 ▲	SO	Track on right.
▼ 1.9	SO	Track on right into old hydraulic mining area is now private.
1.5 ▲	SO	Track on left into old hydraulic mining area is now private.
		GPS: N39°40.75' W120°55.85'
▼ 2.0	SO	Track on left into Pioneer Mine Placer Diggings; then Pioneer Mine Trail crosses over Deacon Long Ravine.
1.4 ▲	SO	Pioneer Mine Trail crosses over Deacon Long

Ravine; then track on right into Pioneer Mine Placer Diggings.

GPS: N39°40.63' W120°55.93'

▼ 2.4	SO	Track on left; then track on right is 21N58.
1.0 ▲	SO	Track on left is 21N58; then track on right.

GPS: N39°40.47' W120°56.27'

▼ 2.5	SO	Track on left is 21N69, which goes 2.4 miles to the Pacific Mine site. Access varies.
0.9 ▲	SO	Track on right is 21N69, which goes 2.4 miles to the Pacific Mine site. Access varies.

GPS: N39°40.39' W120°56.33'

▼ 2.9	SO	Track on right.
0.5 ▲	SO	Track on left.
▼ 3.2	SO	Cross over Pats Gulch. Spring on left.
0.2 ▲	SO	Spring on right. Cross over Pats Gulch.
▼ 3.3	SO	Track on left is 21N12.
0.1 ▲	SO	Track on right is 21N12.
▼ 3.4	SO	Well-used track on right is CR 791. Zero trip meter.
0.0 ▲		Continue to the north on FR 31 for 4WDs and motorbikes.

GPS: N39°39.90' W120°56.41'

▼ 0.0		Continue to the south on FR 30 for 4WDs and motorbikes—rated green.
6.4 ▲	SO	Well-used track on left is CR 791. Zero trip meter.
▼ 0.2	SO	Cross over creek.
6.2 ▲	SO	Cross over creek.
▼ 0.3	SO	Track on left. Part of Queen City site on right and up the track on left.
6.1 ▲	SO	Track on right. Part of Queen City site on left and up the track on right.
▼ 0.5	SO	Track on left; then second track on left and track on right. Port Wine store ruin is on the left.
5.9 ▲	SO	Track on left and track on right; then second track on right. Port Wine store ruin is on the right.

GPS: N39°39.65' W120°56.80'

▼ 0.7	BL	Track on right is 21N59, which goes 0.1 miles to Port Wine Cemetery. A historical board marks the intersection.
5.7 ▲	BR	Track on left is 21N59, which goes 0.1 miles to Port Wine Cemetery. A historical board marks the intersection.

GPS: N39°39.65' W120°56.93'

▼ 0.8	SO	Dam on left.
5.6 ▲	SO	Dam on right.
▼ 1.9	SO	Track on right is 21N48Y.
4.5 ▲	SO	Track on left is 21N48Y.
▼ 2.4	SO	Cross over creek.
4.0 ▲	SO	Cross over creek.
▼ 3.4	SO	Track on right is 21N48Y to Lucky Hill Mine site. Remain on FR 30.
3.0 ▲	SO	Track on left is 21N48Y to Lucky Hill Mine site. Remain on FR 30.

GPS: N39°38.17' W120°57.94'

▼ 3.5	SO	Track on right goes to Poverty Hill lookout site.
2.9 ▲	SO	Track on left goes to Poverty Hill lookout site.
▼ 4.8	SO	Track on left.
1.6 ▲	SO	Track on right.
▼ 5.4	BR	Three tracks on left and old cabin on left; then track on left.
1.0 ▲	BL	Track on right; then old cabin on right and three tracks on right.

GPS: N39°36.76' W120°58.63'

▼ 5.5	SO	Track on left.
0.9 ▲	SO	Track on right.
▼ 5.9	SO	Track on right.
0.5 ▲	SO	Track on left.
▼ 6.0	BL	Well-used track on right is CR 691. Remain on FR 30.
0.4 ▲	BR	Well-used track on left is CR 691. Remain on FR 30.

GPS: N39°36.35' W120°58.97'

▼ 6.4	SO	4-way intersection. Track on left is 20N35 and paved road on right is FR 30 (CR 690). Zero trip meter.
0.0 ▲		Continue to the north, joining FR 30 (CR 690).

GPS: N39°36.03' W120°59.12'

▼ 0.0		Continue to the south on unmarked CR 590.
7.2 ▲	SO	4-way intersection. Track on right is 20N35 and paved road on left is FR 30 (CR 690). Zero trip meter.
▼ 0.1	SO	Cross over Rock Creek on bridge.
7.1 ▲	SO	Cross over Rock Creek on bridge.
▼ 0.2	SO	Track on left and track on right.
7.0 ▲	SO	Track on left and track on right.
▼ 0.4	SO	Track on left.
6.8 ▲	SO	Track on right.
▼ 0.7	SO	Scales town buildings on right are now private property.
6.5 ▲	SO	Scales town buildings on left are now private property.

GPS: N39°35.89' W120°59.53'

▼ 0.9	SO	Scales Cemetery on left. Hydraulic mining pit is behind it.
6.3 ▲	SO	Scales Cemetery on right. Hydraulic mining pit is behind it.

GPS: N39°35.89' W120°59.74'

▼ 1.0	TR	Track straight ahead goes to mine diggings.
6.2 ▲	TL	T-intersection. Track on right goes to mine diggings.

GPS: N39°35.84' W120°59.84'

▼ 1.2	SO	Track on right; then cross over Rock Creek twice on bridge; then track on right.
6.0 ▲	SO	Track on left; then cross over Rock Creek twice on bridge; then track on left.
▼ 1.5	SO	Track on left. Site of Union Hill.
5.7 ▲	SO	Track on right. Site of Union Hill.
▼ 1.7	SO	Cross over paved FR 30 (CR 690).
5.5 ▲	SO	Cross over paved FR 30 (CR 690).

GPS: N39°35.92' W121°00.30'

▼ 2.3	SO	Track on left.
4.9 ▲	SO	Track on right.

GPS: N39°35.80' W121°00.69

▼ 2.9	BR	Track on left.
4.3 ▲	BL	Track on right.

GPS: N39°35.97' W121°01.06'

▼ 3.2	SO	Track on left.
4.0 ▲	SO	Track on right.
▼ 3.7	BR	Track on left.
3.5 ▲	BL	Track on right.

GPS: N39°36.11' W121°01.61'

▼ 3.8	SO	Cross over gravel FR 30. Track on right is 21N11F. Continue straight across and swing around to the southwest.
3.4 ▲	SO	Cross over gravel FR 30. Track on left is 21N11F.

GPS: N39°36.18' W121°01.56'

▼ 4.6		SO	Track on left is 20N30 and track on right is 20N63A.
	2.6 ▲	SO	Track on right is 20N30 and track on left is 20N63A.
			GPS: N39°36.49' W121°02.31'
▼ 5.1		SO	Track on left and track on right are both 20N28.
	2.1 ▲	SO	Track on left and track on right are both 20N28.
▼ 6.1		SO	Track on left and track on right are both 20N28.
	1.1 ▲	SO	Track on left and track on right are both 20N28.
			GPS: N39°36.01' W121°03.07'
▼ 7.2		BL	Bear left and cross over Slate Creek on two bridges. Track on right after bridges goes to Slate Creek Reservoir. Zero trip meter.
	0.0 ▲		Continue to the north.
			GPS: N39°36.74' W121°03.29'
▼ 0.0			Continue to the southeast. Start of shelf road.
	2.7 ▲	BR	Track on left. Zero trip meter and cross over Slate Creek on two bridges.
▼ 0.6		SO	Cross over creek.
	2.1 ▲	SO	Cross over creek.
▼ 1.0		SO	End of shelf road.
	1.7 ▲	SO	Start of shelf road.
▼ 2.0		SO	Track on right and track on left.
	0.7 ▲	SO	Track on right and track on left.
▼ 2.1		SO	Track on right; then track on left.
	0.6 ▲	SO	Track on right; then track on left.
▼ 2.4		BR	Track on left.
	0.3 ▲	BL	Track on right.
▼ 2.5		SO	Track on left.
	0.2 ▲	SO	Track on right.
▼ 2.7			North Star Junction. Trail finishes at T-intersection with paved La Porte Road. Turn left for Strawberry Valley; turn right for La Porte.
	0.0 ▲		Trail begins at North Star Junction on paved La Porte Road, 0.7 miles north of Strawberry USFS Campground. Zero trip meter and turn northeast onto graded dirt Scales Road. There is a street sign at the intersection.
			GPS: N39°35.27' W121°04.59'

NORTHERN SIERRA #31

Chimney Rock OHV Trail

Starting Point:	**Northern Sierra #30: Poker Flat OHV Trail, 9.9 miles north of Downieville**
Finishing Point:	**Chimney Rock Trailhead**
Total Mileage:	**2.4 miles (one-way)**
Unpaved Mileage:	**2.4 miles**
Driving Time:	**20 minutes (one-way)**
Elevation Range:	**6,000–6,600 feet**
Usually Open:	**April to October**
Best Time to Travel:	**Dry weather**
Difficulty Rating:	**4**
Scenic Rating:	**9**
Remoteness Rating:	**+0**

Special Attractions

- Short challenging spur from the longer Northern Sierra #30: Poker Flat OHV Trail.
- Very popular mountain bike route.
- Easy hiking trail to Chimney Rock.

History

Chimney Rock (6,698 feet) is one of a series of striking peaks that rises sharply from the northern end of Craycroft Ridge. Needle Point, Rattlesnake Peak, Gibraltar, Tennessee Mountain, Saddleback Mountain, and the aptly named Cloud Splitter form a ring of peaks around Chimney Rock. Deep ravines, canyons, and valleys separate these cone-like spires. Present-day visitors enjoy this striking landscape, but it was a navigation nightmare for miners of the late nineteenth and early twentieth centuries.

A string of pack trails ran through the canyons and up the ridges to reach various mining camps across the mountains. Craycroft Ridge Trail was one of the major pack trails running north from Downieville. It ran from the Gold Bluff Mine, one of the earliest lode mines, all the way up the ridge past Needle Point and Rattlesnake Peak, and on to Sunnyside Meadow. Sheepherders drove their flocks up this trail to reach the pastures and spring at Sunnyside, then known as Sheep Ranch. The narrow trail also passed the Craycroft Mine and the Garibaldi Cabin, named for its first occupant.

Getting supplies and mail to these camps proved to be quite a challenge for packers, who were quite often a miner's only contact with the outside world. It was important for packers to stop a while and have a meal with the camp residents. An observant packer knew if he was welcome or if he should move on; some lone miners could hardly afford to feed themselves, never mind a hungry visitor.

Other pack trails went to mining camps north of Chimney

View from the hiking trail to Chimney Rock

The off-camber approach to Chimney Rock can be loose

Rock. A trail leading out of Poker Flat wound up Tennessee Ravine to the Tennessee Mine, where small-scale hydraulic mining continued into the 1910s (even though it was outlawed in 1884). The trail continued up the East Fork of Canyon Creek to the Gibraltar Mine. From there it zigzagged up the side of Rattlesnake Peak to the old Craycroft Ridge Trail. The trail continued north toward Gibraltar by way of the Cowell Mine, where it connected with a trail at the head of Nelson Creek. A fork to the northeast took pack trains down to McRae Meadow and additional mining camps.

Many of the surrounding pack trails are overgrown nowadays. However, with a keen eye, experienced hikers or horseback riders can follow these old supply routes, once the sole domain of packers and their trusted mules.

Description

Chimney Rock OHV Trail is a short detour from Northern Sierra #30: Poker Flat OHV Trail that leads to the Chimney Rock Trailhead.

The first 1.5 miles of Chimney Rock OHV Trail are suitable for any high-clearance vehicle; the final 0.9 miles give the trail its difficulty rating of 4. This part is best suited for compact and mid-size SUVs. Full-size SUVs and pickups may find the shelf road a little too narrow for safety. Steep grades and a very loose, friable surface make it very easy for vehicles to loose traction and grind to a stop on the return trip. Two-wheel-drive vehicles should not attempt the deceptively difficult final mile.

The OHV trail ends at the Chimney Rock Trailhead. From here, a well-defined, narrow trail for hikers and mountain bikers runs around the side of the mountain and zigzags up to Chimney Rock. The huge volcanic rock, a little more than 1 mile from the trailhead, measures approximately 12 feet in diameter and 25 feet in height. The trail eventually connects to the Empire Creek Trail. Hikers or bikers who can arrange a pickup can continue via Empire Creek Canyon on the long trip to Downieville.

Current Road Information

Tahoe National Forest
Downieville Ranger District
15924 Highway 49
Camptonville, CA 95922
(530) 288-3231

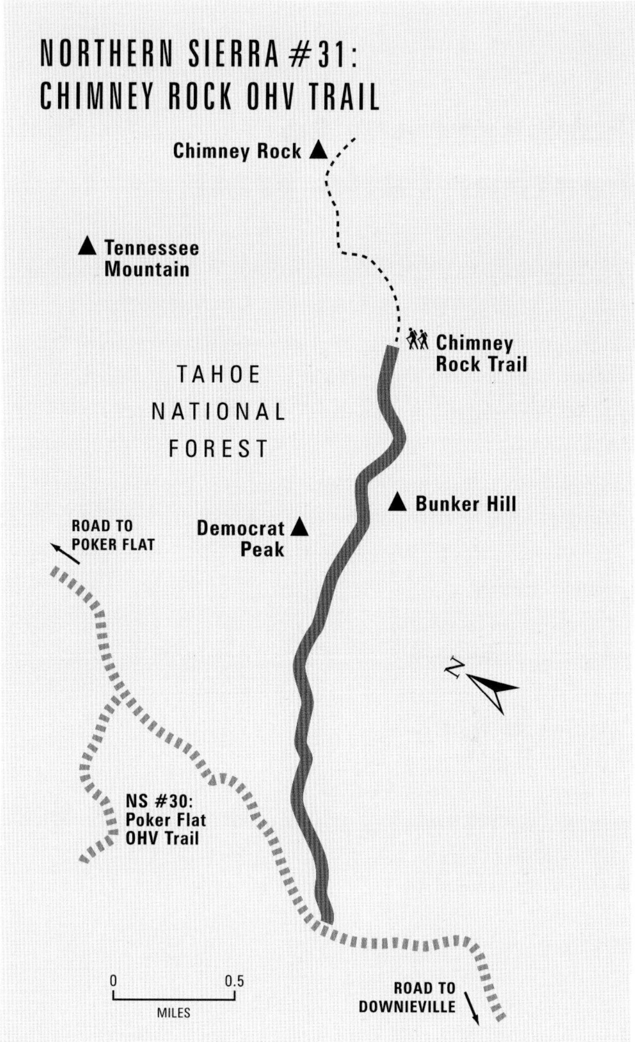

Map References

BLM Portola
USFS Tahoe National Forest; Plumas National Forest
USGS 1:24,000 Mt. Fillmore
1:100,000 Portola
Maptech CD-ROM: High Sierra/Tahoe
Northern California Atlas & Gazetteer, p. 70
California Road & Recreation Atlas, p. 60 (incomplete)
Other: Plumas National Forest OHV Map—Summer Use

Route Directions

▼ 0.0		From Northern Sierra #30: Poker Flat OHV Trail, 9.9 miles north of Downieville, zero trip meter and proceed north on formed trail following sign to Chimney Rock Trail.
		GPS: N39°39.33' W120°51.76'
▼ 0.5	SO	Track on left.
▼ 0.6	SO	Track on right; then two tracks on left.
▼ 1.5	SO	Bunker Hill. Bunker Democrat Channel Mine sign on tree. High-clearance 4WDs only past this point.
		GPS: N39°40.00' W120°50.45'
▼ 2.4		Trail ends at the Chimney Rock Trailhead.
		GPS: N39°40.24' W120°49.49'

Forbestown to Feather Falls Trail

Starting Point:	**Forbestown Road, 1.1 miles northwest of Forbestown**
Finishing Point:	**FR 27, on the eastern edge of Feather Falls**
Total Mileage:	**18.1 miles**
Unpaved Mileage:	**17.3 miles**
Driving Time:	**2 hours**
Elevation Range:	**900–3,400 feet**
Usually Open:	**April to November**
Best Time to Travel:	**Dry weather only**
Difficulty Rating:	**4**
Scenic Rating:	**7**
Remoteness Rating:	**+1**

Special Attractions

- Sunset Hill Fire Lookout.
- Fishing at Ponderosa Reservoir.
- Long winding forest trail with a moderately difficult, 4-rated section.
- Forbestown Cemetery.

History

Old Forbestown dates back to the early days of California's gold rush. Ben F. Forbes and James D. Forbes, emigrants from Wisconsin, were among the first to prospect and invest at this location. Ben prospected in Forbes Ravine (now called Forbestown Ravine), opened a trading post, and later opened a post office to cater to the influx of miners. James built the United States Hotel and began the first stagecoach service from Oroville to the boomtown of Forbestown (see page 34).

Ponderosa Reservoir

Forbestown was a supply center for the surrounding communities of New York Flat and Ohio. By the late 1850s, more than 2,000 people had moved to the town, which by that time boasted a number of hotels and saloons, a blacksmith, a library, and a Masonic Hall. A fire in 1861 burned down most of the town, but the settlers rebuilt.

Concrete vault in Feather Falls

In 1885, the appropriately named Gold Bank Mine was established at the junction of Mosquito Gulch and Forbestown Ravine, northeast of town. Harry P. Stow owned the mine, and his mansion reflected his wealth. For the next two decades, the mine brought prosperity to Forbestown. After ores played out in 1904, many employees left town.

Forbestown went through a series of revivals into the late 1930s, most revolving around the re-worked Gold Bank Mine. Sadly, the town center was unable to survive and has faded with time. All that remains today is the Masonic Hall established in 1854, one of the oldest in California, and the cemetery. Several hundred headstones tell tales of times long since forgotten. The headstone of young Elish belongs to a boy killed in a cave-in on the banks of the nearby Feather River.

Feather Falls was predominantly a company town—bare spaces indicate the sites where buildings once stood. A concrete vault on the main street is all that is left of the old company headquarters.

Description

Two worthwhile features of this trail are just off the main route near the southern end. The Sunset Hill Fire Lookout, 0.5 miles west of the start of the trail, is still manned during summer. The gate is normally open when there is a lookout on duty, and you can often climb up the tower with the lookout's permission. Constructed in the 1960s, the tower is not one of the most important in the region. Its view is perpendicular to the surrounding ridges with only one face visible, which makes it of limited use in spotting fires. However it does offer great views of Lake Oroville, Bloomer Mountain, and Mooretown Ridge.

Historic Forbestown Cemetery, 0.6 miles east of the start down Old Forbestown Road, has graves dating to the late 1880s. The Forbestown Lodge was built in 1854 and stands near the cemetery. Coordinates of the lodge are GPS: N39°31.57' W121°16.66'.

The main trail descends well-graded forest roads to the small Ponderosa Reservoir, which is surrounded by firs and formed by a dam on the South Fork of the Feather River. No gas-powered boats are allowed on the reservoir. There are a couple of pleasant picnic spots with limited shade. This section follows the old Ponderosa Way, a firebreak road put in by the Civilian Conservation Corps. (For more on the Ponderosa

Way, see Northern Sierra #42: Ponderosa Way, page 448.)

Once on the north side of the river, the trail swiftly turns to 4WD only, climbing formed trail 20N94X toward the ridge. This section should only be attempted in dry weather; deep ruts attest to the greasy and friable nature of the trail's surface. 4WD will be needed to negotiate the ruts, which account for the 4 rating of this trail.

On top of the ridge, the trail enters forest owned by Sierra Pacific Industries. Logging may restrict access at times, but the route primarily follows county and forest roads to finish on A Line Road, 0.3 miles east of Feather Falls. No camping or campfires are permitted on Sierra Pacific Industries land.

This route is not shown in its entirety on topographical or forest maps.

Current Road Information

Plumas National Forest
Beckwourth Ranger District
23 Mohawk Road
Blairsden, CA 96103
(530) 836-2575

Map References

BLM Chico
USFS Plumas National Forest (incomplete)
USGS 1:24,000 Forbestown, Clipper Mills
1:100,000 Chico
Maptech CD-ROM: High Sierra/Tahoe
Northern California Atlas & Gazetteer, pp. 69, 68
California Road & Recreation Atlas, p. 60 (incomplete)
Other: Plumas National Forest OHV Map—Summer Use

Route Directions

Mileage		Direction	Description
▼ 0.0			From Forbestown Road, 1.1 miles northwest of Forbestown, 0.5 miles northeast of Sunset Hill Fire Lookout, zero trip meter and turn southwest on graded dirt Lower Forbestown Road. Immediately track on right.
	6.5 ▲		Track on left; then trail ends on paved Forbestown Road. Turn right for Sunset Hill Fire Lookout and Oroville; turn left for Forbestown Cemetery and Challenge.
			GPS: N39°31.73' W121°17.23'
▼ 0.8		SO	Track on left.
	5.7 ▲	SO	Track on right.
▼ 1.4		TR	Graded road continues straight ahead. Road is now paved.
	5.1 ▲	TL	Graded road continues straight ahead. Road is now graded dirt.
			GPS: N39°31.26' W121°18.45'
▼ 1.7		SO	Track on left.
	4.8 ▲	SO	Track on right.
▼ 1.8		SO	Track on right.
	4.7 ▲	SO	Track on left.
▼ 2.1		SO	Track on right; then track on left.
	4.4 ▲	SO	Track on right; then track on left.
			GPS: N39°31.62' W121°18.92'
▼ 2.2		SO	Track on left. Road is now graded dirt. Start of shelf road.
	4.3 ▲	SO	End of shelf road. Road is now paved. Track on right.
▼ 4.6		SO	Track on left and turnout on right.
	1.9 ▲	SO	Track on right and turnout on left.
▼ 5.0		SO	Two tracks on left.
	1.5 ▲	SO	Two tracks on right.
			GPS: N39°32.49' W121°18.79'
▼ 6.0		SO	Track on right.
	0.5 ▲	SO	Track on left.
▼ 6.4		BL	Turnout on right. Cross over Ponderosa Reservoir Dam. End of shelf road.
	0.1 ▲	BR	Cross over Ponderosa Reservoir Dam. Turnout on left. Start of shelf road.
▼ 6.5		TL	T-intersection on north side of dam. Track on right goes to campsite. Zero trip meter.
	0.0 ▲		Continue to the southwest.
			GPS: N39°32.99' W121°18.14'
▼ 0.0			Continue to the west.
	3.8 ▲	TR	Track continues straight ahead to campsite. Zero trip meter and turn right toward Ponderosa Reservoir Dam.
▼ 0.2		TR	Two tracks on left, track straight ahead, and small track on sharp right. Turn right onto larger graded road and start to climb up the hill.
	3.6 ▲	TL	Two tracks straight ahead, track on right, and small track on left. Turn left onto larger graded road.
			GPS: N39°33.15' W121°18.16'
▼ 1.1		BL	Track on right.
	2.7 ▲	SO	Track on left.
▼ 2.1		SO	Two gated tracks on left and two tracks straight ahead, second of which is 20N94X. Major track on right also. Continue straight ahead onto 20N94X, which heads up the hill.
	1.7 ▲	SO	Major track on left, track on right, and two gated tracks straight ahead. Continue straight ahead on major ungated trail, heading downhill.
			GPS: N39°33.56' W121°16.82'
▼ 2.9		SO	Two tracks on right.
	0.9 ▲	SO	Two tracks on left.
▼ 3.1		BL	Track on right.
	0.7 ▲	SO	Track on left.
			GPS: N39°33.41' W121°15.83'
▼ 3.8		BR	End of climb. Well-used track on left. Zero trip meter.
	0.0 ▲		Continue downhill to the south.
			GPS: N39°33.57' W121°15.24'
▼ 0.0			Continue to the east.
	7.8 ▲	BL	Track continues to the right. Zero trip meter.
▼ 0.3		SO	Track on left under power lines.
	7.5 ▲	SO	Track on right under power lines.
▼ 0.6		BL	Track on right.
	7.2 ▲	BR	Track on left.
			GPS: N39°33.31' W121°14.85'
▼ 0.9		SO	Track on right under power lines.
	6.9 ▲	SO	Track on left under power lines.
▼ 1.0		SO	Track on right in cleared area.
	6.8 ▲	SO	Track on left in cleared area.
▼ 1.1		SO	Track on right.
	6.7 ▲	SO	Track on left.
▼ 1.3		SO	Gate.
	6.5 ▲	SO	Gate.
			GPS: N39°33.78' W121°14.34'
▼ 1.5		SO	Track on left and track on right.
	6.3 ▲	SO	Track on left and track on right.
▼ 1.7		BR	Well-used track on left.
	6.1 ▲	BL	Well-used track on right.

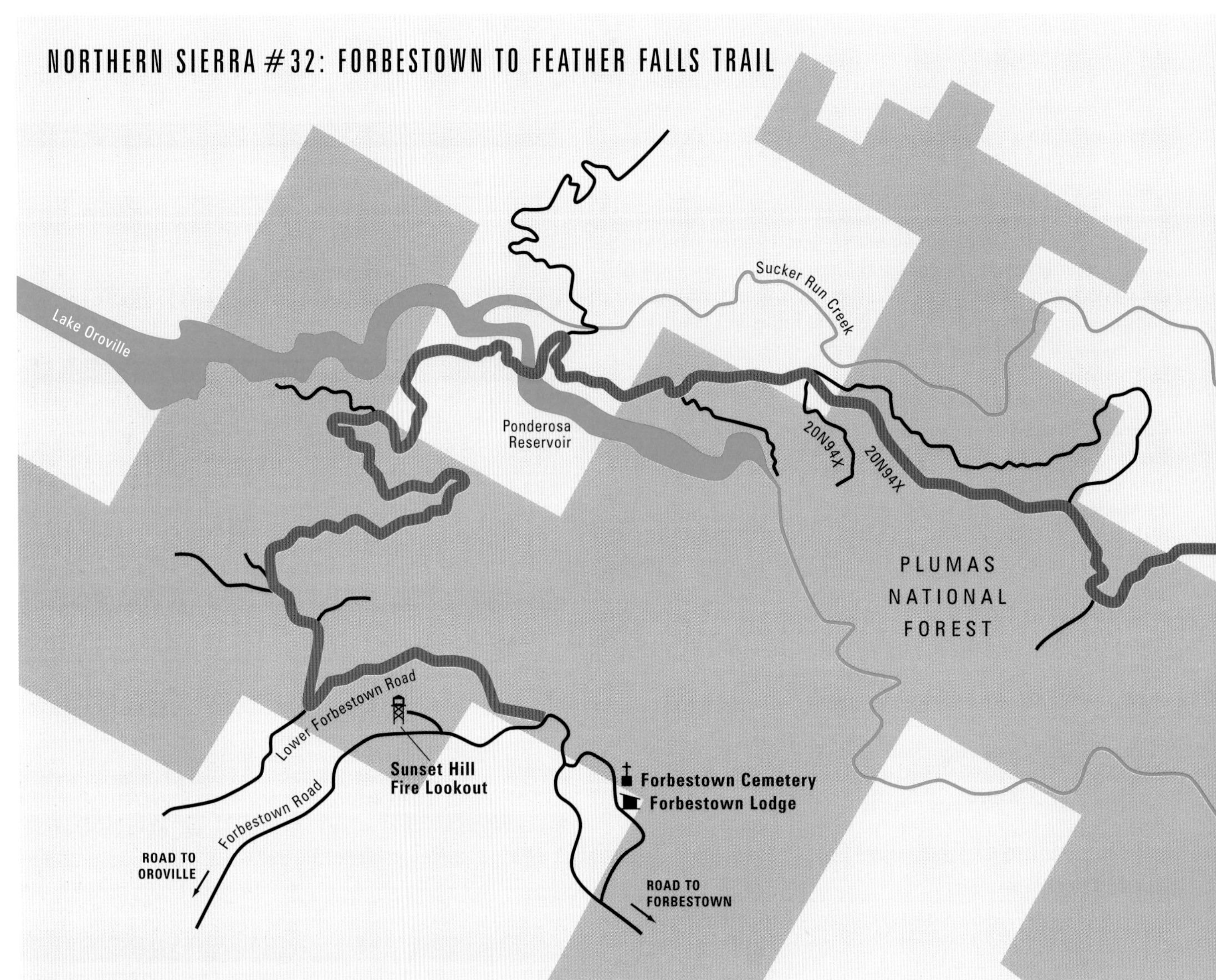

		GPS: N39°33.88' W121°14.00'
▼ 1.9	SO	Track on left and track on right.
5.9 ▲	SO	Track on left and track on right.
▼ 2.5	SO	Track on left; then gate.
5.3 ▲	SO	Gate; then track on right.
		GPS: N39°33.86' W121°13.22'
▼ 2.8	BL	Track on right.
5.0 ▲	BR	Track on left.
		GPS: N39°33.94' W121°13.01'
▼ 3.1	SO	Track on left and track on right.
4.7 ▲	SO	Track on left and track on right.
▼ 3.3	SO	Track on left.
4.5 ▲	SO	Track on right.
▼ 3.4	SO	Cross over Owl Creek; then track on right.
4.4 ▲	SO	Track on left; then cross over Owl Creek.
▼ 4.0	SO	Track on right.
3.8 ▲	BR	Track on left.
		GPS: N39°34.56' W121°13.50'
▼ 4.5	SO	Track on left.
3.3 ▲	SO	Track on right.
▼ 4.8	BR	Track on left.
3.0 ▲	BL	Track on right.
▼ 5.1	SO	Cross over Sucker Run Creek on bridge.
2.7 ▲	SO	Cross over Sucker Run Creek on bridge.
		GPS: N39°35.11' W121°13.88'
▼ 5.5	SO	Cross over Little Buckeye Creek.
2.3 ▲	SO	Cross over Little Buckeye Creek.
		GPS: N39°35.10' W121°14.28'
▼ 6.4	SO	Gate.
1.4 ▲	SO	Gate.
		GPS: N39°34.57' W121°14.39'
▼ 7.1	BR	Track on right.
0.7 ▲	BR	Track on left.
▼ 7.6	SO	Gate; then track on right under power lines.
0.2 ▲	SO	Track on left under power lines; then gate.
▼ 7.8		Trail ends at T-intersection with paved A Line Road (FR 27). Turn left for Feather Falls; turn right for Cascade.
0.0 ▲		Trail begins on paved FR 27, 0.2 miles north of the intersection of A Line Road (FR 27) and B Line Road on the eastern edge of Feather Falls. Zero trip meter and turn southeast on formed dirt road marked 20N41.
		GPS: N39°35.58' W121°14.86'

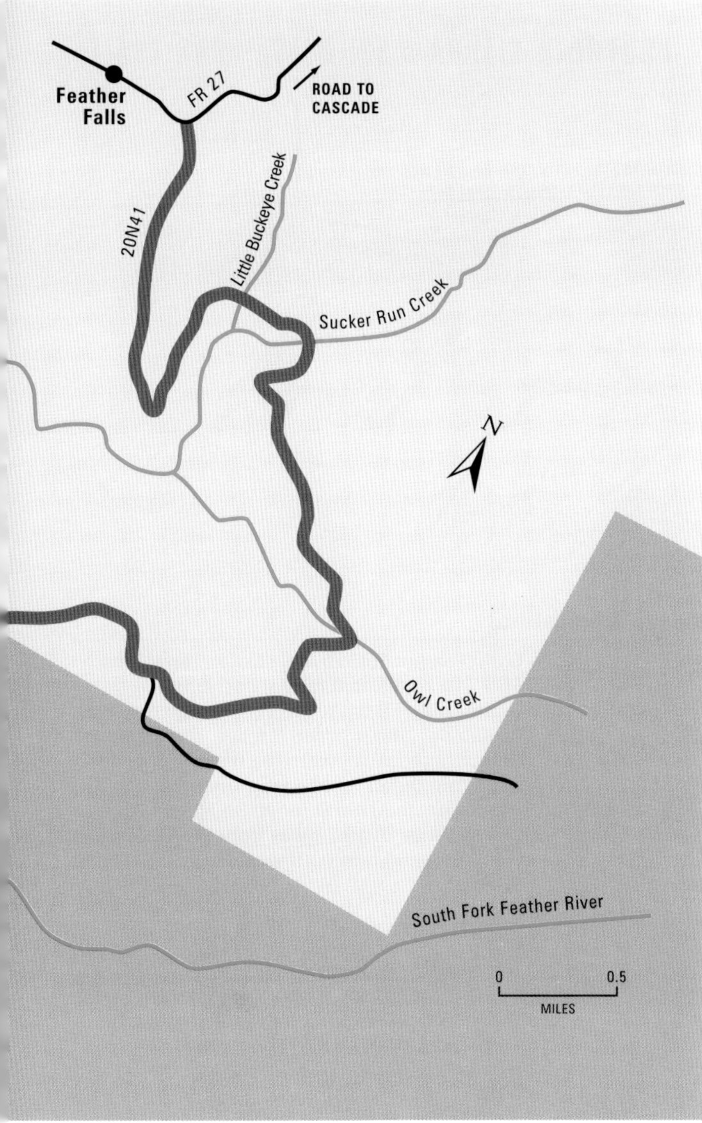

NORTHERN SIERRA #33

Milsap Bar Trail

Starting Point:	**FR 94, 10.7 miles northeast of FR 27**
Finishing Point:	**Oroville-Quincy Highway at the Brush Creek USFS Work Center**
Total Mileage:	**15.5 miles**
Unpaved Mileage:	**15.1 miles**
Driving Time:	**1.5 hours**
Elevation Range:	**1,800–4,200 feet**
Usually Open:	**April to November**
Best Time to Travel:	**Dry weather**
Difficulty Rating:	**2**
Scenic Rating:	**9**
Remoteness Rating:	**+0**

Special Attractions

- Excellent fishing at Milsap Bar.
- Riverside camping and swimming in the Middle Fork of the Feather River.
- Access to Big Bald Rock Trailhead for hikers.
- Historic Cascade Bar near the start of the trail.

History

Milsap Bar Trail commences deep within Plumas National Forest on the edge of Mountain Spring House Ridge, some 2,300 feet above the Middle Fork of the Feather River. The site of old Mountain Spring House, 700 feet above the trail's starting point, has panoramic views of the forest. From the ridge top house, one old pack trail ran west down Mountain Spring House Ridge and another, called Hansons Bar Trail, ran to the north; both dropped steeply to the river. You can still hike the Hansons Bar Trail to the sites of Graves Cabin and Kennedy Cabin, 1.7 miles upstream on the Middle Fork. All of these old pack trails are now within the Middle Fork Feather Wild & Scenic River Reserve. The reserve, established in October 1968, stretches a total of 77 miles along this river canyon. Feather Falls is in the Feather Falls Scenic Area, some 8 miles downstream from Milsap Bar Bridge. With a 640-foot-drop, Feather Falls is the third tallest in the United States.

Cascade Bar has the oldest liquor license in California

The entire region surrounding the trail on the south side of the river was the scene of extensive logging in the first half of the twentieth century. The Feather River Pine Mills, known as Hutchinson Lumber Company prior to 1927, had a far-reaching network of logging roads, and the company built a new sawmill at the town of Feather Falls in 1939.

Construction of the Oroville Dam to the west spelled doom for the industry here. Rising lake waters submerged the outgoing railroad to Oroville known as the Feather Falls Railway. The old Hutchinson Lumber Company locomotive #3 pulled its last trainload out of Feather Falls on March 19, 1965.

Cascade is east along Cascade Creek, a short distance from the start. The settlement is now the Cascade Resort, a collection of summer cabins and home of the Cascade Bar. This small log cabin at the edge of a meadow on Cascade Creek boasts the oldest continually operating liquor license in California and has been trading since 1876. The bar is open from April to December; if a bartender is not on hand, ring the triangle on the front verandah and someone will open the bar for you. You will not only get a beverage at the Cascade Bar, but a slice of California history as well. The two-story dwelling next to the Cascade Bar was once a popular lodging house. An

Indian named Williams opened a trading post here in 1876, a business he operated until he was hanged in Feather River for allegedly cheating in a game of chance.

Description

The trail leaves FR 94, 10.7 miles northeast of Feather Falls. It is unsigned at first, but marked FR 62 a short distance past the start. The trail immediately starts to descend a shelf road through a mix of forest, winding down the side of the valley toward the Middle Fork of the Feather River. The trail surface is uneven enough to require a high-clearance vehicle.

A small forest service campground sits alongside the Middle Fork of the Feather River at Milsap Bar. There is currently no fee for camping there. The campground is popular with anglers because Milsap Bar offers some of the best rainbow trout fishing in the region.

On the north side of the river, the trail climbs a moderate grade to join Oroville-Quincy Highway, passing some private property at the upper end.

Near the end of the trail a spur leads to the Big Bald Rock Trailhead, a hiking trail that goes up to the open granite dome. The trail ends on Oroville-Quincy Highway at the Brush Creek Work Center.

Current Road Information

Plumas National Forest
Beckwourth Ranger District
23 Mohawk Road
Blairsden, CA 96103
(530) 836-2575

Map References

BLM Chico
USFS Plumas National Forest
USGS 1:24,000 Cascade, Brush Creek
1:100,000 Chico
Maptech CD-ROM: High Sierra/Tahoe
Northern California Atlas & Gazetteer, pp. 68, 69
California Road & Recreation Atlas, p. 59
Other: Plumas National Forest OHV Map—Summer Use

Milsap Bar Trail

NORTHERN SIERRA #33: MILSAP BAR TRAIL

ROAD TO BUCKS LAKE
ROAD TO OROVILLE
Brush Creek Work Center
Oroville-Quincy Highway
PUMAS NATIONAL FOREST
FR 62
21N49
21N49
Bald Rock Road
ROAD TO BIG BALD ROCK TRAILHEAD

Route Directions

▼ 0.0		From Feather Falls, travel east on paved road FR 27 (A Line Road) for 7 miles. Turn left (north) onto FR 94, following the sign for Milsap Bar, and proceed 8 miles. A signposted detour here takes you to the historic Cascade Bar. From there, retrace your route back to FR 94 and proceed north for an additional 2.7 miles (a total of 10.7 miles from FR 27). Zero trip meter and turn northwest on graded dirt FR 62.
7.9 ▲		Trail ends at FR 94. Turn right and follow above directions, in reverse, to Cascade Bar and Feather Falls.
		GPS: N39°42.38′ W121°12.93′
▼ 0.4	SO	Track on right goes 1.7 miles to Hansons Bar Trailhead. Corral on left. Main trail is now marked FR 35 for 4WDs, ATVs, and motorbikes.
7.5 ▲	SO	Track on left goes 1.7 miles to Hansons Bar Trailhead. Corral on right.
		GPS: N39°42.66′ W121°13.08′
▼ 2.3	SO	Start of shelf road.
5.6 ▲	SO	End of shelf road.
▼ 5.8	SO	Cross over creek.
2.1 ▲	SO	Cross over creek.
		GPS: N39°43.11′ W121°14.79′
▼ 7.2	SO	Crooked Bar visible below—identified by a bend in the river.
0.7 ▲	SO	Crooked Bar visible below—identified by a bend in the river.
▼ 7.4	SO	Track on right goes out toward Crooked Bar.
0.5 ▲	SO	Track on left goes out toward Crooked Bar.
		GPS: N39°42.85′ W121°16.08′
▼ 7.9	SO	Road becomes paved. Track on sharp left goes into Milsap Bar USFS Campground. Zero trip meter.
0.0 ▲		Continue to the southeast.
		GPS: N39°42.53′ W121°16.14′
▼ 0.0		Continue to the northwest.
7.6 ▲	BL	Road returns to graded dirt. Track on right goes into Milsap Bar USFS Campground. Zero trip meter.
▼ 0.1	SO	Cross over Middle Fork Feather River on bridge

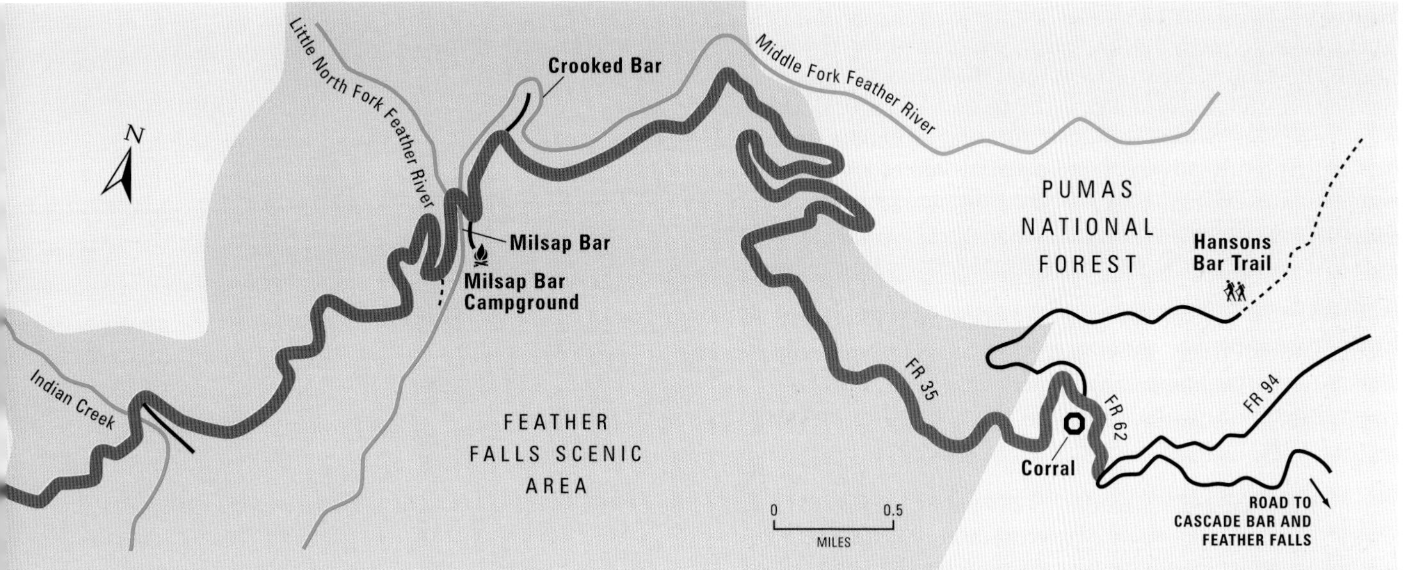

		at confluence of Little North Fork Feather River.
7.5 ▲	SO	Cross over Middle Fork Feather River on bridge at the confluence of Little North Fork Feather River.
		GPS: N39°42.58′ W121°16.19′
▼ 0.2	SO	Road turns to graded dirt.
7.4 ▲	SO	Road is now paved.
▼ 0.4	SO	Hiking trail to river on left.
7.2 ▲	SO	Hiking trail to river on right.
▼ 3.0	SO	Cross over creek; then track on left.
4.6 ▲	SO	Track on right; then cross over creek.
		GPS: N39°41.53′ W121°17.37′
▼ 3.1	SO	Cross over Indian Creek.
4.5 ▲	SO	Cross over Indian Creek.
▼ 4.0	SO	End of shelf road.
3.6 ▲	SO	Start of shelf road.
▼ 4.6	SO	Track on left.
3.0 ▲	SO	Track on right.
		GPS: N39°40.84′ W121°18.45′
▼ 5.0	SO	Track on left; then second track on left and track on right.
2.6 ▲	SO	Track on left and track on right; then second track on right.
▼ 5.2	SO	Track on right.
2.4 ▲	SO	Track on left.
▼ 5.4	SO	Track on left.
2.2 ▲	SO	Track on right.
▼ 5.6	SO	Track on left is 21N49; then track on right.
2.0 ▲	SO	Track on left; then track on right is 21N49.
		GPS: N39°41.02′ W121°19.17′
▼ 6.2	SO	Kaelin Road on left.
1.4 ▲	BL	Kaelin Road on right.
▼ 6.3	SO	Two tracks on right.
1.3 ▲	SO	Two tracks on left.
▼ 7.2	TR	T-intersection with paved Bald Rock Road. Track on left goes 3.3 miles to Big Bald Rock Trailhead.
0.4 ▲	TL	Paved road ahead goes 3.3 miles to Big Bald Rock Trailhead. Turn left onto graded dirt FR 62 (22N62, OHV Route 1) for 4WDs, ATVs, and motorbikes—rated green. Follow the sign to Milsap Bar Campground.
		GPS: N39°41.08′ W121°20.55′
▼ 7.6		Trail ends at T-intersection with Oroville-Quincy Highway at the Brush Creek USFS Work Center. Turn right for Bucks Lake; turn left for Oroville.
0.0 ▲		Trail commences on the Oroville-Quincy Highway, 24 miles south of Bucks Lake at the Brush Creek USFS Work Center. Zero trip meter and turn south on paved Bald Rock Road.
		GPS: N39°41.41′ W121°20.29′

NORTHERN SIERRA #34

Three Lakes Trail

Starting Point:	**FR 33 at Lower Bucks Lake, 2.8 miles north of Oroville-Quincy Highway**
Finishing Point:	**Three Lakes**
Total Mileage:	**10 miles (one-way)**
Unpaved Mileage:	**10 miles**
Driving Time:	**1 hour (one-way)**
Elevation Range:	**5,000–6,200 feet**
Usually Open:	**May to November**
Best Time to Travel:	**May to November**
Difficulty Rating:	**3**
Scenic Rating:	**9**
Remoteness Rating:	**+0**

Special Attractions

- Excellent fishing in Lower Bucks Lake and Three Lakes.
- Hiking access to the Pacific Crest National Scenic Trail and the Bucks Lake Wilderness.
- A hundred miles of groomed snowmobile trails in the Bucks Lake region.

History

Bucks Lake, formerly Buck's Ranch, was named for Horace "Buck" Bucklin. Natives of New York, Bucklin and his partner Francis Walker settled here in the autumn of 1850. Buck's Ranch lay along what became the Oroville to Quincy stage and express route and served as the supply center for outlying mining camps. The property changed hands several times and eventually had a hotel.

The Feather River Power Company established Bucks Lake in the late 1920s as part of the Bucks Creek Hydroelectric Power Project. The project involved constructing Bucks Lake Dam, Lower Bucks Lake Dam, Three Lakes Dam, Milk Ranch Creek Conduit, Grizzly Creek Forebay Dam, aqueducts, lengthy penstocks, an incline railway, and finally the Bucks Creek Powerhouse on the Feather River.

A narrow-gauge railroad was built to move the huge amounts of material across this mountainous terrain. Contractor H. H. Boomer used a Bucyrus steam-driven shovel to load rock onto railcars. The massive steam shovel, built by the Bucyrus Erie firm of South Milwaukee, took nine men to operate. It was a forerunner of today's gigantic Ruston Bucyrus earthmoving machinery. Upon reaching the construction site, rock was offloaded by tipping the railcars sideways. It took approximately 326,000 cubic yards of rock to complete Bucks Lake Dam. Little of the narrow-gauge railroad is visible today.

The shelf road to Three Lakes sits on top of the Milk Ranch Creek Conduit. This lengthy underground pipe boosts Lower Bucks Lake with waters from Three Lakes.

Description

The trail to Three Lakes travels a long shelf road built to service the aqueduct connecting Three Lakes to Lower Bucks Lake, part of the Pacific Gas & Electric's hydroelectric power scheme. For the most part, the 2-rated trail is suitable for high-clearance 2WDs. However, the final couple of miles where the trail leaves the level grade of the aqueduct and climbs to Three Lakes is loose, rough, and requires 4WD.

Lower Bucks Lake, excellent for catching silver salmon

The trail leaves from the western side of Bucks Lake, which has excellent fishing for kokanee salmon and Mackinaw and rainbow trout. Lower Bucks Lake is renowned for its silver salmon. There are developed campgrounds around Bucks Lake and Lower Bucks Lake; these pleasant shaded, lakeside sites are the best places to camp along the trail. The campsites along Lower Bucks Lake are limited to self-contained RVs; tent camping is restricted to sites on Bucks Lake.

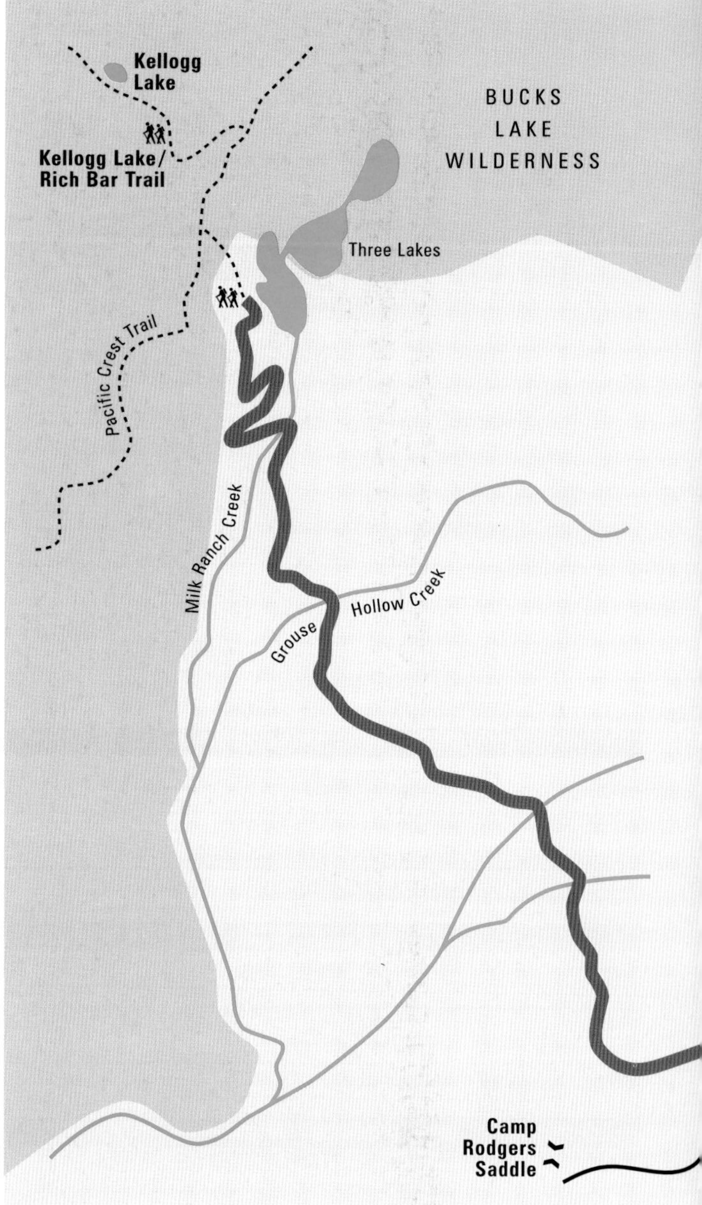

The graded trail traverses a level grade on the side of Bald Eagle Mountain. Many small creeks spill over the trail; for the most part they have concrete fords to prevent the trail from washing away. The vehicle trail ends at the Pacific Crest National Scenic Trail, where it enters the Bucks Lake Wilderness. The hiking trail to Kellogg Lake and Rich Bar leaves the Pacific Crest National Scenic Trail a short distance east of the trailhead. Three Lakes are visible from the trailhead. Water levels fluctuate because of hydroelectric use. A couple of small, rocky campsites can be found at the end of the trail, but these are not as pleasant as the campgrounds at Bucks Lake. Anglers will enjoy fishing for brook and golden trout at Three Lakes.

In winter, snowmobilers and cross-country skiers use the trail system around Bucks Lake and Little Bucks Lake. The area, with 100 miles of groomed trails and an annual snowfall of 75 inches, is one of the most popular snowmobile trail systems in the state.

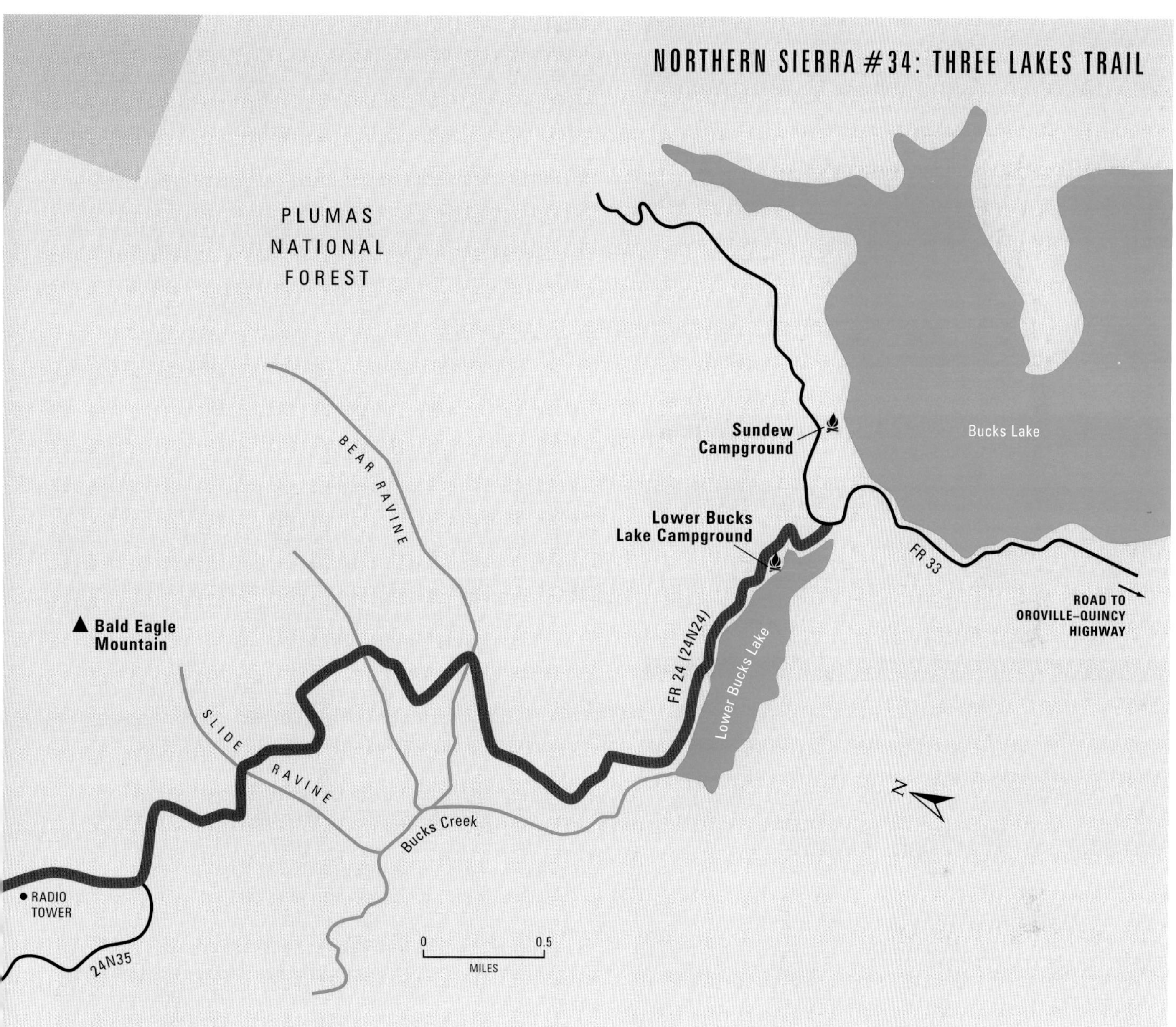

Current Road Information

Plumas National Forest
Mt. Hough Ranger District
39696 Highway 70
Quincy, CA 95971
(530) 283-0555

Map References

BLM Chico
USFS Plumas National Forest
USGS 1:24,000 Bucks Lake, Storrie
1:100,000 Chico
Maptech CD-ROM: High Sierra/Tahoe
Northern California Atlas & Gazetteer, p. 69
California Road & Recreation Atlas, p. 60
Other: Plumas National Forest OHV Map—Summer Use

Route Directions

▼ 0.0		From Oroville-Quincy Highway on the western edge of Bucks Lake, zero trip meter and turn north on FR 33 following the sign to Lower Bucks Lake. Proceed 2.8 miles north; then zero trip meter and turn northwest on the graded dirt FR 24 (24N24, OHV Route 10) for 4WDs, ATVs, and motorbikes—rated blue. The route is signed to Lower Bucks and Three Lakes. The trail immediately passes along the north shore of Lower Bucks Lake, passing through Lower Bucks USFS Campground.
		GPS: N39°53.89' W121°12.30'
▼ 0.3	SO	Cross over creek. Hiking trail on right.
▼ 1.0	BR	Track on left to final lakeside campsite. Bear right, through seasonal closure gate, remaining on OHV Route 10.
		GPS: N39°54.17' W121°13.17'
▼ 1.4	SO	Dam on left. Start of shelf road.
▼ 2.7	SO	Cross over Bear Ravine.

		GPS: N39°54.98' W121°13.55'
▼ 3.5	SO	Cross through creek.
		GPS: N39°55.53' W11°13.90'
▼ 3.6	SO	Cross through creek.
▼ 4.2	SO	Cross through Slide Ravine.
▼ 5.0	BR	Track on left is 24N35. Remain on marked OHV Route 10 and zero trip meter.
		GPS: N39°55.73' W121°15.03'
▼ 0.0		Continue to the west.
▼ 0.5	SO	Radio tower on left. Views to the west look down Bucks Creek to North Fork Feather River.
▼ 1.0	SO	Camp Rodgers Saddle on left. Views on left to North Fork Feather River and Rock Creek Dam, set below Ben Lomond.
▼ 1.6	SO	Cross through creek.
▼ 1.9	SO	Cross through creek.
▼ 3.2	SO	Cross through Grouse Hollow Creek.
		GPS: N39°57.72' W121°14.25'
▼ 3.9	SO	Cross through Milk Ranch Creek. Trail starts to climb.
		GPS: N39°58.05' W121°13.72'
▼ 4.9	BL	Pull-in on right.
▼ 5.0		Trail ends at Three Lakes and the Pacific Crest Trailhead on the edge of the Bucks Lake Wilderness. The Kellogg Lake/Rich Bar Trail leads off of the Pacific Crest Trail just east of the trailhead. Three Lakes are a short distance through the trees to the east.
		GPS: N39°58.28' W121°13.34'

NORTHERN SIERRA #35

Grizzly Ridge Trail

Starting Point:	**CR 207 at Taylorsville, 4.6 miles east of California 89**
Finishing Point:	**Lake Davis Road (CR 112), 5 miles north of Portola**
Total Mileage:	**43.8 miles, plus 3.1-mile spur to Crystal Lake, 1.5-mile spur to Grizzly Peak, and 1.1-mile spur to Argentine Rock**
Unpaved Mileage:	**43.6 miles, plus spurs**
Driving Time:	**6 hours**
Elevation Range:	**3,600–7,400 feet**
Usually Open:	**July to late November**
Best Time to Travel:	**June to November**
Difficulty Rating:	**2, spurs are rated 3 and 4**
Scenic Rating:	**9**
Remoteness Rating:	**+0**

Special Attractions

- Fossil shell impressions near Taylorsville.
- Mount Hough Fire Lookout, Smith Peak Fire Lookout, and the site of the Argentine Rock Fire Lookout.
- Crystal Lake and Lake Davis.

History

Taylorsville, at the start of the trail, honors Jobe Terrill Taylor, identified as the town's founder. Taylor passed through the vicinity in 1850 and returned in 1852 to settle. The Maidu who lived here were apparently peaceful, thus making the area attractive to settlers. There are two points of interest near Taylorsville. The first, a site for fossil shell casts, is near the Taylorsville Campground. From the start of the trail, continue east through Taylorsville for 0.7 miles to a T-intersection at the Taylorsville Campground and Rodeo Grounds. Turn left (north) and travel 0.1 miles. The reddish and greenish shale on the east side of the road has imprints of shells left behind by receding waters of an ancient lake. The second site, the Taylorsville Cemetery, is on the east side of town. Turn south on Cemetery Street, and the cemetery will be on the left. It contains graves of many pioneers, including that of founder Jobe Terrill Taylor.

Maidu Indians continue to live in what is now called Indian Valley. The Worldmaker, as Maidu elders tell the story, made the country safe by clearing it of man-killers. Monster Snake Pool and Canoe Hammering Point feature in Maidu stories. Monster Snake Pool was supposedly formed by a giant snake, and some Maidu refused to swim in the lake because they did not wish to disturb the sleeping snake. Canoe Hammering Point, off to the north, was home to a man-eating monster who hammered all day long on a wooden canoe until Worldmaker tricked the monster into showing him his weapons. Worldmaker grabbed one of the weapons and cut off the monster's head, ridding the valley of the threat to the Maidu.

Mount Hough commands excellent views over Indian Valley and beyond, making it an obvious choice for a fire lookout. The first lookout was built around 1916, and the present lookout was built in the late 1980s.

Walker Mine, at an elevation of 6,000 feet on the northern side of Grizzly Ridge, was a major copper mining operation established after the turn of the twentieth century. J. R. Walker and two associates staked claims here based on a mining engineer's report. The mine employed nearly 600 men at its peak, and the settlement at the mine had more than 60 private houses, 4 bunkhouses, and more than 100 company houses as well as a motion picture hall, hospital, schools, service station, and more. The mine had 13 levels and yielded an estimated 167 million tons of copper during its working life. The extremely large tailings pond and concrete mill site have been declared a toxic site, and the mine has long been involved in pollution issues.

Winter was a force to be dealt with by residents at the Walker Mine settlement. There was literally no escape once cold weather set in. Snow depths made travel via horse, carriage, or foot impossible. The truly desperate tried to use the 9-mile aerial tramway that had buckets loaded with ore. Tension towers spanning great distances across canyons had no clearance for passengers on top of outward-bound ore, winds could blow them off of their perch, and they could freeze before reaching the end. Tram riders, men familiar with the workings of the tramway, would search for and try to rescue those who tried to flee. They endured hours of

Walker Mine mill

freezing conditions and would typically find victims in the deep snow below the tramway.

Description

Grizzly Ridge Trail is a long, scenic road in Plumas National Forest that winds past three fire lookouts and a small, pretty lake before finishing at Lake Davis. Part of the route is included in the national forest's network of OHV trails, so ATVs and motorbikes also use the trail. In winter, cross-country skiers and snowmobilers enjoy the trail, especially around Lake Davis and up to the Smith Peak Fire Lookout.

The trail leaves Taylorsville up the China Grade, an easy climb that leads swiftly to the top of Grizzly Ridge. The shelf road has sporadic views of Indian Valley and Mount Jura. The trail follows the eastern boundary of the Mount Hough State Game Reserve. A very worthwhile 4-rated spur leads to the Mount Hough Fire Lookout and continues to Crystal Lake. The lookout is manned during fire season, and you may climb up to the tower with permission from the lookout on duty. The view encompasses Indian Valley, Lake Almanor, Round Lake, Mount Jura, Grizzly Peak, and the town of Quincy. Hang-gliders use Mount Hough as a launch site. There is no platform, and the launch site is considered moderately difficult. The spur continues to Crystal Lake, a small lake set in a natural rock bowl. The final, steep descent to the lake is what gives the spur its 4 difficulty rating. One campsite can be found among the trees on the lakeshore.

Back on the main trail, the route continues through the forest along Grizzly Ridge. A second spur leads toward the top of Grizzly Peak, stopping below the summit on the east side. Most of this spur is rated a 4 for difficulty. The recommended turnaround point is given in the route directions. Although the trail continues 0.2 miles past this point, the difficulty rating increases to 5 because of the steep, loose slope and off-camber side slope. In addition, there is no safe place to turn around. There are only narrow turning points that put a vehicle crossways on a steep slope, thus risking rolling over.

The third spur is 5 miles farther along the ridge. This one goes a short distance to the closed Argentine Rock Fire Lookout. Rated a 3 for difficulty, the spur finishes below the lookout, which is perched high on the outcropping of Argentine Rock. From here, Grizzly Ridge can be seen to the north and south, and the Middle Fork of the Feather River and Sierra Buttes can be seen to the south. The small USFS campground of Bradys Camp is near Argentine Rock. The camp is near a stream at the edge of a small meadow renowned for the pitcher plants growing in marshy areas. The campground currently has no fee and limited facilities, but it makes a pleasant overnight stop.

From Argentine Rock, the trail continues through the forests on the north side of Grizzly Ridge. The standard of the road varies between small, formed trails and wider graded dirt roads. The trail detours slightly to pass the Walker Mine; work is currently underway to restore the area. The mill remains can be seen from the road below the site.

Past the Walker Mine, the route briefly intersects the Beckwourth Trail near Emigrant Creek. From here the trail stays below Grizzly Ridge and passes beside Summit Marsh. The wide meadows with Little Grizzly Creek running through them are a particularly pretty part of the trail. These meadows and Grizzly Ridge are both deer fawning habitat.

Smith Peak Fire Lookout, perched high above Lake Davis, offers a panoramic view that includes much of the route just traveled. Visitors are welcome between 9:30 A.M. and 6:00 P.M. when the lookout is manned during fire season. You will need to hike the final 0.2 miles up to the lookout, but the view is well worth the climb.

The trail finishes on the edge of the Lake Davis Recreation Area. The reservoir was developed for recreation rather than hydroelectric use, and it is stocked annually with rainbow, German brown, and lake trout. Bullhead are also regularly caught. Hunting in season for mule deer, waterfowl, and quail is permitted in the recreation area. Camping is limited to developed campgrounds only, normally open from late April to late October. The lake is also used for picnicking, jet skiing, swimming, and boating. There are four boat launches on the lake, and an 18.4-mile mountain bike loop runs around the lake. In winter it is used for ice fishing,

Argentine Rock Fire Lookout above the Middle Fork of the Feather River

snowmobiling, and cross-country skiing.

With the exception of the spurs, the trail is suitable for high-clearance 2WDs in dry weather. In wet weather, it is best avoided because of easily damaged, greasy sections. The trail closes naturally with snowfall; it is normally open from July to November, but exact dates vary each year.

Current Road Information

Plumas National Forest
Beckwourth Ranger District
23 Mohawk Road
Blairsden, CA 96103
(530) 836-2575

Plumas National Forest
Feather River Ranger District
875 Mitchell Avenue
Oroville, CA 95965
(530) 534-6500

Map References

BLM Susanville, Portola
USFS Plumas National Forest
USGS 1:24,000 Taylorsville, Crescent Mills, Spring Garden, Mt. Ingalls, Grizzly Valley, Blairsden, Portola
1:100,000 Susanville, Portola

Maptech CD-ROM: Shasta Lake/Redding; High Sierra/Tahoe
Northern California Atlas & Gazetteer, pp. 60, 59, 70
California Road & Recreation Atlas, p. 60
Other: Plumas National Forest OHV Map—Summer Use

Route Directions

▼ 0.0		From California 89, turn east on paved road to Taylorsville (CR 207) and proceed 4.6 miles. On the western edge of Taylorsville, zero trip meter and turn south on graded dirt road marked China Grade. Trail immediately follows along the Mount Hough State Game Refuge boundary (on the right) along CR 208.
5.1 ▲		Trail ends on CR 207, immediately west of Taylorsville. Turn left to exit to California 89.
		GPS: N40°04.53' W120°50.50'
▼ 0.4	BL	Track on right.
4.7 ▲	SO	Track on left.
▼ 0.9	SO	Two tracks on right and track on left.
4.2 ▲	SO	Two tracks on left and track on right.
▼ 1.1	SO	Track on right.
4.0 ▲	SO	Track on left.
▼ 2.5	SO	Track on left; then graded road on right to California 89. Continue straight past two more tracks on left.
2.6 ▲	BR	Two tracks on right; then graded road on left to California 89. Bear right following sign to Taylorsville; then track on right.
		GPS: N40°03.03' W120°51.09'
▼ 5.1	SO	Track on sharp right is FR 403 (OHV Route 51)

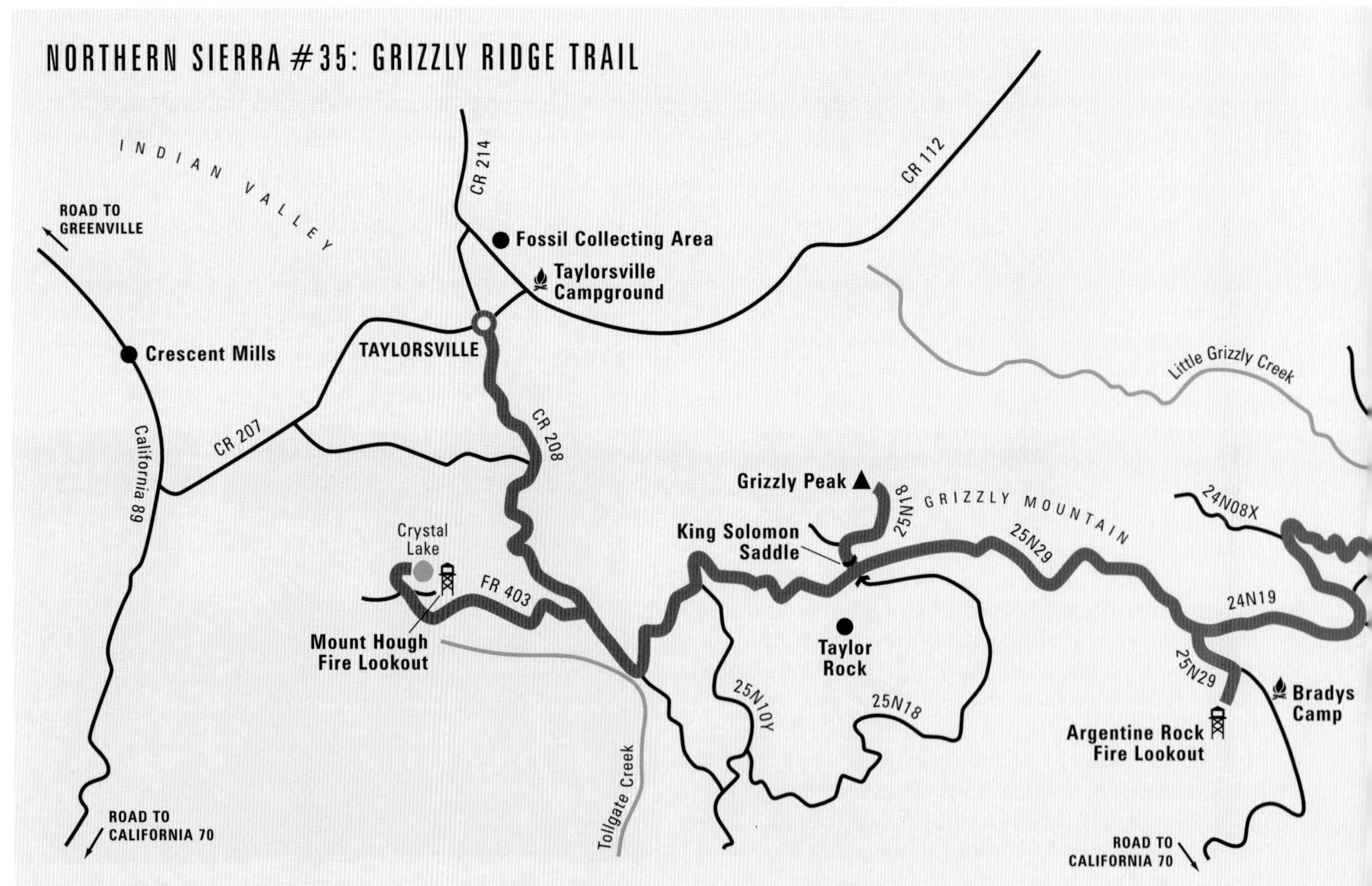

for 4WDs, ATVs, and motorbikes—rated green. This is the spur to Mount Hough Fire Lookout and Crystal Lake. Zero trip meter.
0.0 ▲ Continue to the north on CR 208.

GPS: N40°01.57′ W120°51.63′

Spur to Mount Hough Fire Lookout and Crystal Lake

▼ 0.0 Proceed northwest on FR 403 (OHV Route 51).
▼ 0.5 SO Track on right.
▼ 0.6 SO Track on right.
▼ 1.6 SO Track on right.
▼ 2.3 SO Track on right.
▼ 2.4 BL Track on right goes 0.3 miles to Mount Hough Fire Lookout. Track is now marked 403N11; then track on right.

GPS: N40°02.80′ W120°53.29′

▼ 2.5 SO Track on left; then track on right.
▼ 2.7 TR Track continues straight ahead. Turn sharp right and start the 4-rated descent.

GPS: N40°03.05′ W120°53.36′

▼ 3.1 Spur ends at Crystal Lake. There is one campsite in the trees by the lake's edge.

GPS: N40°02.95′ W120°53.07′

Continuation of Main Trail

▼ 0.0 Continue to the south, joining FR 403.
5.3 ▲ BR Track on left is FR 403 (OHV Route 51) for 4WDs, ATVs, and motorbikes—rated green. This is the spur to Mount Hough Fire Lookout and Crystal Lake. Zero trip meter.

GPS: N40°01.57′ W120°51.63′

▼ 0.9 TL Turn left onto unmarked track in a clearing before Tollgate Creek. This is Rhinehart Meadow. Leaving boundary of the Mount Hough State Game Reserve.
4.4 ▲ TR T-intersection with larger trail. Trail now follows along boundary of the Mount Hough State Game Reserve on the left. This clearing is Rhinehart Meadow.

GPS: N40°00.82′ W120°51.54′

▼ 2.6 TL T-intersection with 25N10Y.
2.7 ▲ TR Turn right onto unmarked track. There is a marker opposite the intersection for 25N10Y.

GPS: N40°01.14′ W120°50.22′

▼ 3.1 SO Track on left is 25N29K.
2.2 ▲ SO Track on right is 25N29K.

▼ 4.7 SO Track on right.
0.6 ▲ SO Track on left.

▼ 5.1 SO Track on left. Taylor Rock on right.
0.2 ▲ SO Track on right. Taylor Rock on left.

GPS: N40°00.33′ W120°48.79′

▼ 5.3 SO King Solomon Saddle. Track on right is 25N18. Then track on left, also 25N18, is the spur to Grizzly Peak (OHV Route 52) for 4WDs, ATVs, and motorbikes—rated blue. Zero trip meter.
0.0 ▲ Continue to the west on 25N29 (OHV Route 52)—rated green.

GPS: N40°00.28′ W120°48.63′

Spur to Grizzly Peak

▼ 0.0 Turn north on 25N18.

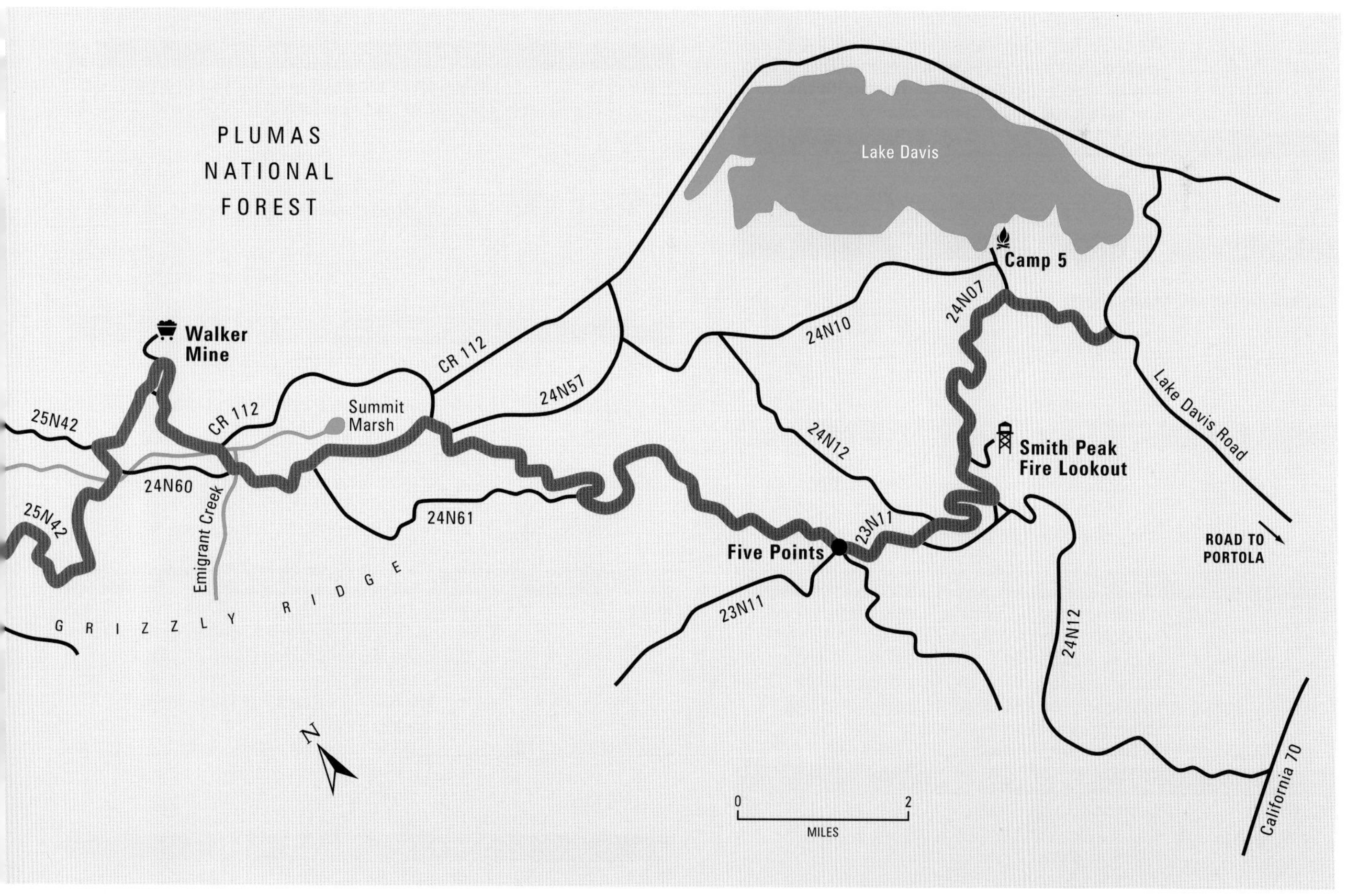

▼ 0.3 BR Track on left. Remain on OHV Route 52.
▼ 0.7 SO Track on right.

GPS: N40°00.53′ W120°48.11′

▼ 1.0 SO Track on left.
▼ 1.5 Spur ends below Grizzly Peak. Trail continues for 0.2 miles, but it becomes 5-rated with dangerous turning places. This is the last safe turning point. Views south overlook Grizzly Mountain.

GPS: N40°00.85′ W120°47.70′

Continuation of Main Trail

▼ 0.0 Continue to the east on 25N29 (OHV Route 52)—rated green.
4.6 ▲ SO King Solomon Saddle. Track on right is 25N18, the spur to Grizzly Peak (OHV Route 52) for 4WDs, ATVs, and motorbikes—rated blue. Track on left is also 25N18. Zero trip meter.

GPS: N40°00.28′ W120°48.63′

▼ 3.0 SO Track on left.
1.6 ▲ SO Track on right.

▼ 4.2 SO Track on right.
0.4 ▲ SO Track on left.

▼ 4.6 BL Track on right is 25N29, spur to Argentine Rock. Zero trip meter.
0.0 ▲ Continue to the northwest on 25N29 (OHV Route 52).

GPS: N39°57.83′ W120°45.50′

Spur to Argentine Rock

▼ 0.0 Turn south on 25N29, following the sign to Squirrel Creek and California 70.
▼ 0.6 BR Track on left goes 0.1 miles to Bradys Camp USFS Campground and continues to California 70. (Turn left again immediately after the intersection, following sign to the campground.) To continue to Argentine Rock, bear right up unmarked road that climbs the hill.

GPS: N39°57.37′ W120°45.35′

▼ 0.8 SO Track on right.
▼ 1.1 Trail ends immediately below the closed Argentine Rock Fire Lookout.

GPS: N39°57.10′ W120°45.69′

Continuation of Main Trail

▼ 0.0 Continue to the east on 24N19 (OHV Route 52).
2.0 ▲ BR Track on left is 25N29, spur to Argentine Rock. Zero trip meter.

GPS: N39°57.83′ W120°45.50′

▼ 2.0 TR T-intersection with 25N42A.
0.0 ▲ TL Immediately after last intersection, 25N42A continues straight ahead. Turn left onto 24N19 (OHV Route 52) for 4WDs, ATVs, and motorbikes—rated blue.

GPS: N39°56.91′ W120°43.76′

▼ 2.0 TL 4-way intersection immediately after last intersection. Straight ahead is 24N19. To the right is OHV Route 52 for 4WDs, ATVs, and motorbikes—rated green. Turn left onto 25N42 (OHV Route 61) for 4WDs, ATVs, and motorbikes—rated green. Zero trip meter.
0.0 ▲ Continue to the west.

GPS: N39°56.89′ W120°43.75′

▼ 0.0 Continue to the north.
8.1 ▲ TR 4-way intersection. Track on left is 24N19. Straight ahead is OHV Route 52 for 4WDs, ATVs, and motorbikes—rated green. Turn right onto 25N42A and zero trip meter.

▼ 0.8 SO Track on right.
7.3 ▲ BR Track on left.

▼ 1.4 BR Track on left is 24N08X.
6.7 ▲ BL Track on right is 24N08X.

▼ 2.0 SO Track on left.
6.1 ▲ SO Track on right.

▼ 2.3 SO Track on right is 24N94Y and track on left is 25N42F.
5.8 ▲ SO Track on left is 24N94Y and track on right is 25N42F.

▼ 3.4 SO Track on left is 24N42J.
4.7 ▲ SO Track on right is 24N42J.

GPS: N39°57.39′ W120°42.65′

▼ 4.2 SO Track on right is 25N42D.
3.9 ▲ SO Track on left is 25N42D.

▼ 6.2 BL Track on right is 24N60, signposted to Emigrant Creek. Bear left onto 25N42.
1.9 ▲ BR Track on left is 24N60, signposted to Emigrant Creek. Bear right and join 25N42 (OHV Route 61).

GPS: N39°57.26′ W120°41.29′

▼ 6.8 TR T-intersection. To the left is 25N42 (CR 112). Turn right and join CR 112.
1.3 ▲ TL Track straight ahead is 25N42 (CR 112).

GPS: N39°57.64′ W120°41.39

▼ 8.0 SO Track on right.
0.1 ▲ SO Track on left.

▼ 8.1 TR Track on left goes 0.2 miles to remains of the Walker Mine mill—concrete buildings and tailings. Turn sharp right, following sign to Lake Davis, and zero trip meter.
0.0 ▲ Continue to the southwest on the lower track.

GPS: N39°57.80′ W120°39.97′

▼ 0.0 Continue to the south on the upper track.
4.3 ▲ TL Track straight ahead goes 0.2 miles to remains of the Walker Mine mill—concrete buildings and tailings. Turn sharp left, following sign to Genesee, and zero trip meter.

▼ 0.2 SO Track on right to Genesee. Continue straight ahead on CR 112.
4.1 ▲ BR Track on left to Genesee. Bear right on 24N09, following sign to Nye Meadows and Mount Ingalls.

GPS: N39°57.70′ W120°40.14′

▼ 1.3 SO Track on right to Walker Mine tailings; then cattle guard.
3.0 ▲ BR Cattle guard; then track on left to Walker Mine tailings.

▼ 1.4 TR CR 112 continues straight ahead. Turn right onto 24N60 and cross over Little Grizzly Creek, following sign to Emigrant Creek.
2.9 ▲ TL Cross over Little Grizzly Creek; then T-intersection with CR 112.

GPS: N39°56.85′ W120°40.00′

▼ 1.7 TL T-intersection. To the right is OHV Route 61 to Cascade Creek. Emigrant Creek is immediately to the right. Turn left onto 24N57, following sign to Paradise Creek. The northwest corner of the intersection has a Beckwourth Trail marker in the trees.
2.6 ▲ TR OHV Route 61 goes straight ahead to Cascade Creek. Emigrant Creek is straight ahead. The northwest corner of the intersection has a Beckwourth Trail marker in the trees.

GPS: N39°56.60′ W120°40.04′

▼ 2.4 SO Track on right.

	1.9 ▲	SO	Track on left.
			GPS: N39°56.17' W120°39.57'
▼ 2.7		BL	Track on right is 24N58, which goes 2 miles to Grizzly Ridge. Bear left on 24N57.
	1.6 ▲	SO	Track on left, also 24N58, goes 2 miles to Grizzly Ridge.
			GPS: N39°56.18' W120°39.21'
▼ 2.8		SO	Track on right is also 24N58.
	1.5 ▲	SO	Track on left is 24N58.
▼ 3.8		SO	Cattle guard.
	0.5 ▲	SO	Cattle guard.
▼ 4.1		SO	Track on left is 24N57B.
	0.2 ▲	SO	Track on right is 24N57B. Continue on OHV Route 61.
			GPS: N39°55.79' W120°37.79'
▼ 4.2		SO	Track on right is 24N11X; then track on left.
	0.1 ▲	SO	Track on right; then track on left is 24N11X.
▼ 4.3		TR	Well-used track on left is 24N85Y. Summit Marsh on left. Zero trip meter.
	0.0 ▲		Continue to the southwest, remaining on OHV Route 61.
			GPS: N39°55.79' W120°35.56'
▼ 0.0			Continue to the south, remaining on OHV Route 61.
	3.4 ▲	TL	Track straight ahead is 24N85Y. Summit Marsh is straight ahead. Zero trip meter.
▼ 0.3		SO	Track on left is 24N57.
	3.1 ▲	SO	Track on right is 24N57.
▼ 2.4		SO	Track on left is 24N85YB.
	1.0 ▲	SO	Track on right is 24N85YB.
			GPS: N39°54.39' W120°36.58'
▼ 3.1		SO	Track on right is 24N61. Continue straight ahead on 25N85Y (OHV Route 61).
	0.3 ▲	SO	Track on left is 24N61. Continue straight ahead on 25N85Y (OHV Route 61).
			GPS: N39°54.20' W120°36.58'
▼ 3.4		TL	Turn left, remaining on 24N85Y, following the sign to Smith Peak. OHV Route 61 continues straight ahead and becomes 24N97 to Happy Valley. Zero trip meter.
	0.0 ▲		Continue to the west.
			GPS: N39°54.03' W120°36.29'
▼ 0.0			Continue to the northeast.
	6.6 ▲	TR	T-intersection with OHV Route 61. OHV Route 61 continues to the left and becomes 24N97 to Happy Valley. Turn right following sign to Grizzly Creek, remaining on 24N85Y and joining OHV Route 61 for 4WDs, ATVs, and motorbikes—rated green. Zero trip meter.
▼ 0.1		SO	Track on left is 24N89Y.
	6.5 ▲	SO	Track on right is 24N89Y rejoining.
▼ 1.9		SO	Track on left is 24N89Y rejoining.
	4.7 ▲	BL	Track on right is 24N89Y.
▼ 3.9		TL	4-way intersection with 23N11 at Five Points. To the right goes to Happy Valley. Note that the track signed to Smith Peak no longer goes there and should be ignored.
	2.7 ▲	TR	4-way intersection at Five Points. Straight ahead is the continuation of 23N11 to Happy Valley. Turn right on 23N26X, following sign to Grizzly Ridge. Note that the track signed to Smith Peak (on left) no longer goes there and should be ignored.
			GPS: N39°52.25' W120°34.33'
▼ 4.8		SO	Track on right is 23N26X.
	1.8 ▲	SO	Track on left is 23N26X.
▼ 5.1		TR	Track on left is 24N12. Turn right onto 24N12.
	1.5 ▲	TL	Turn left on 23N11. 24N12 continues straight ahead.
			GPS: N39°51.85' W120°33.45'
▼ 6.6		TL	4-way intersection. 24N12 continues straight ahead. Track on right is 23N82. Track on left is 24N07. Turn left, following sign to Smith Peak Fire Lookout, and zero trip meter.
	0.0 ▲		Continue to the northwest.
			GPS: N39°51.61' W120°32.37'
▼ 0.0			Continue to the northeast. Trail now runs along the edge of the Smith Peak State Game Refuge.
	4.4 ▲	TR	4-way intersection. Straight ahead is 23N82. Track on left is 24N12. Zero trip meter and turn right onto 24N12, following sign to Lake Davis.
▼ 0.8		SO	Track on right is 24N07A, which goes 1.1 miles to Smith Peak Fire Lookout.
	3.6 ▲	SO	Track on left is 24N07A, which goes 1.1 miles to Smith Peak Fire Lookout.
			GPS: N39°52.13' W120°32.33'
▼ 1.4		SO	Track on left.
	3.0 ▲	SO	Track on right.
▼ 1.9		BR	Track on left is 23N88.
	3.5 ▲	BL	Track on right is 23N88.
▼ 2.1		BL	Track on right.
	2.3 ▲	BR	Track on left.
▼ 2.6		SO	Track on right is 24N07C and track on left is 24N07B.
	1.8 ▲	SO	Track on left is 24N07C and track on right is 24N07B.
			GPS: N39°52.81' W120°31.40'
▼ 2.8		SO	Entering Lake Davis Recreation Area.
	1.6 ▲	SO	Leaving Lake Davis Recreation Area.
▼ 2.9		TR	T-intersection with gravel road 24N10. Follow sign to Portola. Exiting Smith Peak State Game Refuge. Lake Davis is opposite.
	1.5 ▲	TL	Turn left onto graded dirt road 24N07. Trail follows along boundary of the Smith Peak State Game Refuge.
			GPS: N39°53.20' W120°30.61'
▼ 3.2		SO	Two tracks on right.
	1.2 ▲	SO	Two tracks on left.
▼ 3.5		SO	Track on right; then gravel road on left to Eagle Point Fishing Access.
	0.9 ▲	SO	Gravel road on right to Eagle Point Fishing Access; then track on left.
			GPS: N39°52.71' W120°30.29'
▼ 4.2		SO	Track on right is 23N15Y. Road becomes paved.
	0.2 ▲	SO	Track on left is 23N15Y. Road turns to graded dirt.
▼ 4.3		BR	Track on left joins main road. Follow sign to Portola.
	0.1 ▲	BL	Track on right rejoins main road. Follow sign to Smith Peak.
▼ 4.4			Trail ends at T-intersection with Lake Davis Road (CR 112, 23N06). Turn right for Portola.
	0.0 ▲		Trail begins on Lake Davis Road (CR 112, 23N06), 5 miles north of Portola. Zero trip meter and turn northwest on paved road, following sign for Camp 5 and boat ramp. To reach the start of the trail from California 70, follow the sign for Lake Davis and turn north up West Street, which turns into Joy Street, and finally into Lake Davis Road. From California 70, it is 5 miles to the start of the trail.
			GPS: N39°52.24' W120°29.89'

NORTHERN SIERRA #36

Diamond Mountains Trail

Starting Point:	**Frenchman Lake Road (FR 176), 1.2 miles north of California 70 and Chilcoot**
Finishing Point:	**Forest Road 24N01 at the north end of Frenchman Lake**
Total Mileage:	**22 miles, plus 0.6-mile spur to Crystal Peak**
Unpaved Mileage:	**22 miles, plus 0.6-mile spur**
Driving Time:	**3 hours**
Elevation Range:	**5,200–7,600 feet**
Usually Open:	**April to November**
Best Time to Travel:	**Dry weather**
Difficulty Rating:	**4**
Scenic Rating:	**9**
Remoteness Rating:	**+1**

Special Attractions

- Boating, fishing, and camping at Frenchman Lake.
- Spectacular Diamond Mountains.
- Access to other OHV routes in the area.

History

Diamond Mountains Trail begins just north of the settlement of Chilcoot and the historic Beckwourth Pass, both of which are along the Beckwourth Emigrant Trail. Chilcoot, established in about 1900, was likely named for Alaska's Chilkoot Pass on the overland trail from Skagway to the headwaters of the Yukon River in the Yukon Territory. The Chilkoot Trail was used in 1897 during the Klondike gold rush.

Chilcoot, California, is just west of the pass discovered by African-American mountain man James Pierson Beckwourth in the spring of 1850. Like many prospectors of that era, Beckwourth was taken with tales of a gold lake, reportedly somewhere in the northern part of the state. Though he never found his gold lake, he did discover a pass that was an alternative to passes farther south. The route needed little improvement, and at 5,228 feet, it was the lowest to cross the Sierra Nevada. Beckwourth promoted the route from Truckee Meadows (now Reno, Nevada), up and over his gentle pass, on to the American Valley (now Quincy), and then to Bidwell's Bar. Bidwell's Bar is now submerged under the waters of Lake Oroville. Beckwourth's route was open by late 1851, and he led the first group of settlers along his trail to Marysville, south of Bidwell's Bar.

As more emigrant trains came his way in 1852, Beckwourth set up a trading post and hotel at his War Horse Ranch, just west of the present-day town of Beckwourth. Beckwourth's trading post was a welcome sight for westbound emigrants, who could stock up on basic supplies and see a friendly face. A restored cabin at the northern end of Sierra Valley is representative of the original trading post and is now open to visitors. Beckwourth's trail received considerably less use by the mid-1850s, as other trails to the south were becoming more popular.

Frenchman Lake

Description

Diamond Mountains Trail, on the northeastern edge of the Sierra Nevada, offers interesting contrast to the many trails that travel through the range's pine and fir forests. The granitic Diamond Mountains are just south of the Honey Lake fault.

The trail leaves the eastern edge of the wide Sierra Valley—an old lakebed caught between volcanic and granitic mountain ranges now used extensively by ranchers as a summer pasture. The sandy trail travels north toward the southern end of the Diamond Mountains. The predominant vegetation is sagebrush and junipers, with small pines becoming more prevalent as the trail climbs through spectacular scenery.

The first part of the trail is a single track with patches of loose, deep sand. This section partly accounts for the difficulty rating of 4. As the trail meanders through the range, it joins larger roads, some of which form the OHV trail shown on the Plumas National Forest OHV Map—Summer Use.

After passing a small open valley, the seldom-used trail leaves the OHV route behind and starts to climb toward Crystal Peak and Adams Peak. This section can be lightly brushy because it is not used much. It also has loose surfaces and some short rocky sections to contend with.

Near Crystal Peak, a bunch of trails wind around the mountain at different levels, making navigation confusing; GPS coordinates will help you follow the correct route. There are some forest markers, but many intersections are unsigned. The trail joins OHV Route 76, which leads to within 0.6 miles of Crystal Peak. From there, a short rough 4-rated spur leads to the top of the peak and excellent views of Long Valley, Honey Lake, and Adams Peak.

The main trail remains on OHV Route 76 and starts to descend to Frenchman Lake. The main trail appears little used at first, but it soon turns into a well-defined, formed trail. The descent twists past granite boulders to cross Galeppi Creek before continuing to Frenchman Lake, a short distance south of the Salmon Egg Shoal Fishing Access point.

Frenchman Lake, at the headwaters of the Feather River, was created in 1962 for recreation and offers many outdoor activities in summer and winter. Summer fun includes camping, hiking, picnicking, hunting, fishing, water skiing, and boating (there are two boat launches at the lake). Anglers can catch rainbow and German brown trout, and hunters can find mule deer and waterfowl. Camping is permitted in developed campgrounds only, which are normally open from late April to October. In winter, the lake is used for ice fishing, cross-country skiing, and snowmobiling. A mountain bike trail coincides with this route from Chilcoot to Crystal Peak. The 10.5-mile bike trail is rated more difficult and takes approximately two hours each way.

Current Road Information

Plumas National Forest
Feather River Ranger District
875 Mitchell Avenue
Oroville, CA 95965
(530) 534-6500

Map References

BLM Portola
USFS Plumas National Forest
USGS 1:24,000 Chilcoot, Beckwourth Pass, Constantia, Frenchman Lake
1:100,000 Portola
Maptech CD-ROM: High Sierra/Tahoe
Northern California Atlas & Gazetteer, p. 71
California Road & Recreation Atlas, p. 61 (incomplete)
Other: Plumas National Forest OHV Map—Summer Use

Route Directions

Mileage		Description
▼ 0.0		From California 70 at Chilcoot, 5.6 miles west of US 395 and Hallelujah Junction, zero trip meter and turn north on paved Frenchman Lake Road (FR 176, CR 284), following the sign to Frenchman Lake. Proceed 1.2 miles to the start of the trail. Zero trip meter and turn east (right) on the formed sandy trail marked 24N88 (OHV Route 74) for 4WDs, ATVs, and motorbikes—rated green. The trail crosses private property for the first 0.3 miles.
5.0 ▲		Trail ends on paved Frenchman Lake Road (FR 176, CR 284). Turn right for Frenchman Lake; turn left for California 70 and Chilcoot.
		GPS: N39°48.92' W120°08.23'
▼ 0.3	SO	Fence line. Entering BLM land.
4.7 ▲	SO	Fence line. The trail crosses private property from here to the finish.
▼ 0.4	BL	Track on right.
4.6 ▲	SO	Track on left.
▼ 0.7	SO	Track on right; then gate; then track on left and track on right along fence line.
4.3 ▲	SO	Track on left and track on right along fence line; then gate; then track on left.
▼ 1.0	SO	Track on right is 23N62. Entering Plumas National Forest.
4.0 ▲	SO	Leaving Plumas National Forest. Track on left is 23N62.
		GPS: N39°49.46' W120°07.47'
▼ 1.2	BR	Track continues ahead. Bear right onto 23N67 (OHV Route 74).
3.8 ▲	TL	Track on right. Turn left onto 24N88.
		GPS: N39°49.68' W120°07.48'

View of Adams Peak from the trail

Mileage		Description
▼ 1.9	BL	Track on right.
3.1 ▲	BR	Track on left.
▼ 2.2	BR	Track on left goes 0.4 miles to a spring.
2.8 ▲	SO	Track on right goes 0.4 miles to a spring.
		GPS: N39°50.02' W120°07.05'
▼ 3.2	SO	Track on left.
1.8 ▲	SO	Track on right.
▼ 3.4	SO	Track on right is 23N62.
1.6 ▲	SO	Track on left is 23N62.
		GPS: N39°50.79' W120°06.81'
▼ 4.4	SO	Track on left.
0.6 ▲	SO	Track on right.
▼ 4.7	BL	Track on right. Follow marker for OHV Route 74.
0.3 ▲	BR	Track on left. Follow marker of OHV Route 74.
		GPS: N39°51.79' W120°06.94'
▼ 5.0	TR	T-intersection with formed trail 24N44. OHV Route 74 goes left at this point. Ahead is a small valley. Zero trip meter.
0.0 ▲		Continue to the east.
		GPS: N39°52.02' W120°07.06'
▼ 0.0		Continue to the northwest.
6.6 ▲	TL	Trail continues to the right around a small valley. Turn left, following marker for OHV Route 74. Zero trip meter.
▼ 0.3	SO	Track on left to the edge of Snow Lake, which is often dry in summer.
6.3 ▲	SO	Track on right to the edge of Snow Lake, which is often dry in summer.
▼ 0.7	SO	Track on right.
5.9 ▲	SO	Track on left.
▼ 1.1	SO	Wire gate.
5.5 ▲	SO	Wire gate.
		GPS: N39°52.77' W120°07.00'
▼ 2.6	SO	Cross through creek; then track on left.
4.0 ▲	SO	Track on right; then cross through creek.
		GPS: N39°53.77' W120°06.68'
▼ 3.2	SO	Saddle. Adams Peak is to the northeast.
3.4 ▲	SO	Saddle. Adams Peak is to the northeast.
		GPS: N39°54.13' W120°06.67'
▼ 3.9	SO	Trail passes through private property.
2.7 ▲	SO	Exit private property.
▼ 4.2	SO	Exit private property.
2.4 ▲	SO	Trail passes through private property.
▼ 4.3	SO	Cross through creek; then track on right.
2.3 ▲	SO	Track on left; then cross through creek.
▼ 4.4	TR	Track continues straight ahead. Turn right up well-used track.
2.2 ▲	TL	T-intersection with 24N44.

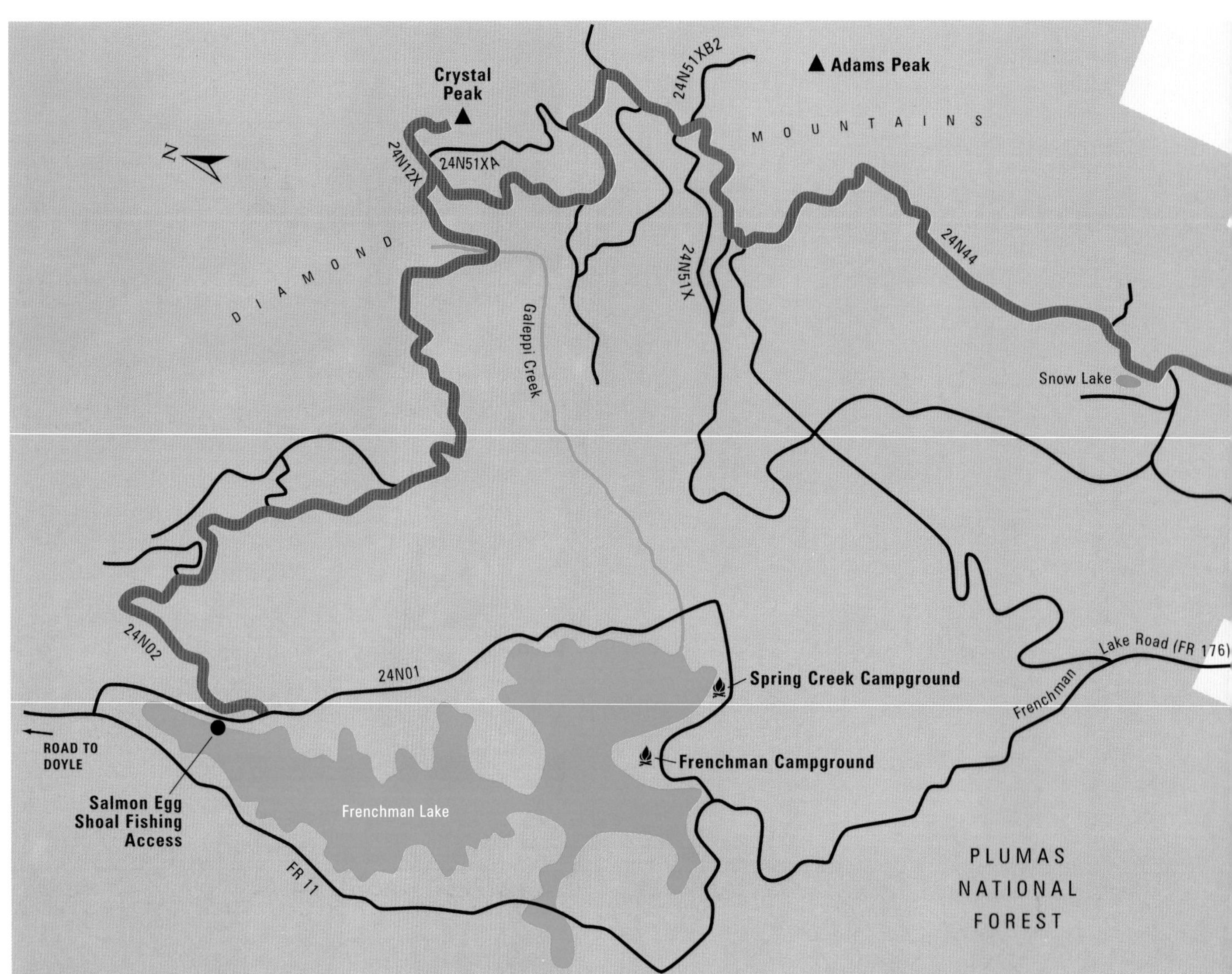

		GPS: N39°54.60′ W120°07.42′
▼ 4.5	SO	Track on left and track on right. Continue straight ahead, bearing right then left. Proceed north past second track on left.
2.1 ▲	SO	Track on right; then track on left and track on right. Continue straight ahead to the south.
▼ 4.6	SO	Track on left and track on right.
2.0 ▲	SO	Track on left and track on right.
		GPS: N39°54.70′ W120°07.36′
▼ 5.7	SO	Track on right is 24N51XB2 toward Adams Peak.
0.9 ▲	BR	Track on left is 24N51XB2 toward Adams Peak. Remain on 24N51XB.
		GPS: N39°55.19′ W120°06.74′
▼ 5.8	TR	T-intersection with 24N51X.
0.8 ▲	TL	24N51X continues straight ahead. Turn sharp left onto 24N51XB.
		GPS: N39°55.23′ W120°06.83′
▼ 6.1	BL	Track on right. Bear left onto 24N55X.
0.5 ▲	SO	Track on left. Continue straight ahead onto 24N51X.
		GPS: N39°55.41′ W120°06.70′
▼ 6.2	TR	Track continues ahead. Turn right onto unmarked track.
0.4 ▲	TL	T-intersection with unmarked, well-used track.
		GPS: N39°55.49′ W120°06.73′
▼ 6.3	SO	Track on right. Rejoining 24N51X.
0.3 ▲	BR	Track on left.
▼ 6.6	TL	Track continues straight ahead. Turn left onto well-used, unmarked track and zero trip meter.
0.0 ▲		Continue to the southeast.
		GPS: N39°55.78′ W120°06.63′
▼ 0.0		Continue to the southwest.
2.8 ▲	TR	Track on left. Zero trip meter.
▼ 0.5	SO	Track on right is 24N51XA (OHV Route 75) for 4WDs, ATVs, and motorbikes—rated green.
2.3 ▲	SO	Track on left is 24N51XA (OHV Route 75) for 4WDs, ATVs, and motorbikes—rated green.
		GPS: N39°55.82′ W120°07.10′
▼ 1.1	SO	Two tracks on right; then collapsed wooden building on left.
1.7 ▲	SO	Collapsed wooden building on right; then two tracks on left.
▼ 1.2	TR	Track continues straight ahead. Turn right and continue north on 24N12X (OHV Route 75).
1.6 ▲	TL	T-intersection. Proceed east on 24N51X (OHV Route 75).
		GPS: N39°55.59′ W120°07.58′
▼ 2.0	SO	Track on left.
0.8 ▲	SO	Track on right.

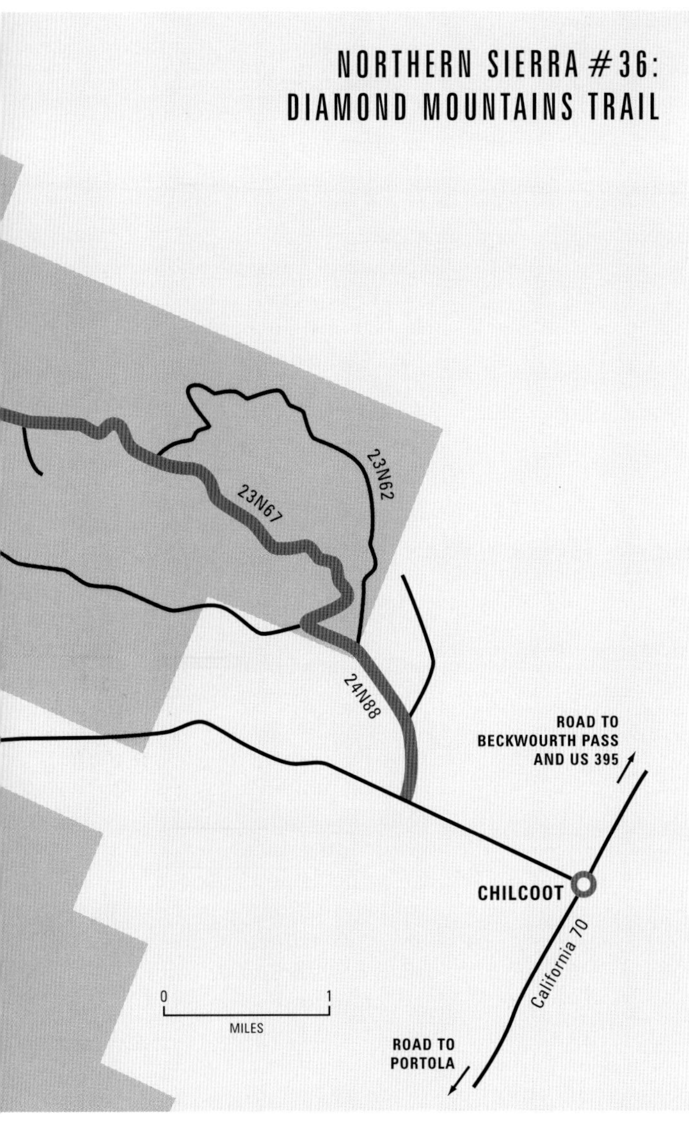

▼ 2.8	TL	Track on right is 24N12X (OHV Route 76), spur to Crystal Peak—rated blue. Zero trip meter and turn left, also onto OHV Route 76—rated green.
0.0 ▲		Continue to the southeast.
		GPS: N39°56.51′ W120°07.82′

Spur to Crystal Peak

▼ 0.0		Proceed east on 24N12X (OHV Route 76).
▼ 0.1	SO	Track on right is OHV Route 75—rated green.
▼ 0.6		Track on left to diggings and views over Doyle, Long Valley, and north to Honey Lake. Then trail ends at small loop around Crystal Peak.
		GPS: N39°56.54′ W120°07.45′

Continuation of Main Trail

▼ 0.0		Continue to the west and immediately bear left, following marker for 24N02 (OHV Route 76). Track on right goes 0.2 miles to cabin.
7.6 ▲	TR	Track on left goes 0.2 miles to cabin; then track straight ahead is 24N12X (OHV Route 76), spur to Crystal Peak—rated blue. Zero trip meter and turn right onto 24N02 (OHV Route 75).
		GPS: N39°56.51′ W120°07.82′
▼ 0.7	TR	Track continues ahead. Turn right and cross over Galeppi Creek; then track on left. Bear right, remaining on OHV Route 76.
6.9 ▲	TL	Track straight ahead. Turn left and cross over Galeppi Creek; then track on right. Turn left again, remaining on OHV Route 76.
		GPS: N39°56.14′ W120°08.28′
▼ 1.6	SO	Track on right.
6.0 ▲	SO	Track on left.
▼ 3.5	SO	Track on right.
4.1 ▲	SO	Track on left.
		GPS: N39°56.02′ W120°10.14′
▼ 4.5	SO	Track on right.
3.1 ▲	BR	Track on left.
▼ 5.6	SO	Track on right. Remain on OHV Route 76.
2.0 ▲	BR	Track on left. Remain on OHV Route 76.
		GPS: N39°57.08′ W120°11.44′
▼ 5.9	SO	Cattle guard.
1.7 ▲	SO	Cattle guard.
▼ 6.1	BL	Track on right.
1.5 ▲	BR	Track on left.
▼ 7.2	SO	Track on right.
0.4 ▲	BR	Track on left.
▼ 7.5	SO	Track on left is 24N07X. Remain on OHV Route 76.
0.1 ▲	BL	Track on right is 24N07X. Remain on OHV Route 76.
▼ 7.6		Cattle guard; then trail ends at T-intersection with graded 24N01 at the north end of Frenchman Lake. Turn left for Chilcoot; turn right for Doyle.
0.0 ▲		Trail begins on graded road 24N01 at the north end of Frenchman Lake, 0.2 miles south of Salmon Egg Shoal Fishing Access and 1.5 miles south of the intersection with FR 11. Zero trip meter and turn northeast on formed dirt trail 24N02 (OHV Route 76) for 4WDs, ATVs, and motorbikes—rated blue.
		GPS: N39°56.24′ W120°12.10′

NORTHERN SIERRA #37

Thompson Peak Trail

Starting Point:	**CR 208, 4.6 miles south of US 395 and Janesville**
Finishing Point:	**Richmond Road (CR 203), 3 miles south of Susanville**
Total Mileage:	**28.9 miles, plus 9.1-mile loop past Wemple Cabin and 2.5-mile spur to Thompson Peak**
Unpaved Mileage:	**25.3 miles, plus spurs**
Driving Time:	**5 hours**
Elevation Range:	**4,200–7,700 feet**
Usually Open:	**May to November**
Best Time to Travel:	**Dry weather**
Difficulty Rating:	**2**
Scenic Rating:	**9**
Remoteness Rating:	**+0**

Red Rock Spring

Special Attractions

- Excellent views from two fire lookouts along the northwestern end of the Diamond Mountains.
- Raptor viewing in spring and fall from Thompson Peak.

History

Thompson Peak Trail offers excellent views east over the Honey Lake Valley as it climbs through the Diamond Mountains. Honey Lake Valley was an important corridor to settlers making their way west. The Lassen Trail, just to the west, had such a bad reputation that it was nicknamed the Horn Route because it was so difficult, dangerous, and slow that emigrants might as well have taken the sea route around Cape Horn. A number of parties had to be rescued from Peter Lassen's torturous route (see page 66). Many chose to bear south on the Beckwourth Trail and others went north to Oregon. This meant that much of northeastern California missed out on emigrant trade, a valuable asset to developing communities.

William B. Nobles sought to correct this in 1851. The following year, with $2,000 from businessmen in Shasta, he set out to find an alternate route to Lassen's. His trail left the Lassen Trail at what is now Black Rock, Nevada, bearing southwest to the northern reaches of Honey Lake. From there, Noble's trail followed the Susan River through present-day Susanville and continued northwest, through Nobles Pass in what is now Lassen National Forest, to rejoin the Lassen Trail near Bogard Station on present-day California 44. Noble's trail was faster and much easier, and it succeeded in drawing most wagon trains bound for California north of the Mother Lode.

Isaac Roop built a log cabin close to the Susan River in the summer of 1854 and developed a trading post known as Roop's House. At the trading post, emigrants along the Nobles Trail could rest up, water their stock, and take on provisions for the rest of their journey. After a gunfight in 1863 known as the Sagebrush War, the cabin became known as Roop's Fort. Roop's establishment, located in central Susanville (see page 59), is now open to visitors. In time, the Nobles Trail became an important freight route through the mountains.

Description

Thompson Peak Trail is generally suitable for high-clearance 2WDs in dry weather. Drivers of passenger vehicles can usually make it to the Wemple Cabin, but they will find the remainder of the trail too rough, especially the final climb to Thompson Peak. The trail is a snowmobile route in winter. The main snowmobile route is rated easy, with the spur to Thompson Peak rated moderate.

The trail leaves CR 208 south of Janesville and is initially well signed to Thompson Peak. The graded, lightly graveled road travels through Plumas National Forest. A loop near the start of the trail leads to the Wemple Cabin, set in a small meadow. The wooden two-story cabin and adjacent corral are in good order.

A second spur leads to the Thompson Peak Fire Lookout. The road to the lookout is rough enough to require a high-clearance vehicle. The lookout is perched atop the rocky spine of the Diamond Mountains; the steep slopes drop dizzyingly to Long Valley and Honey Lake. The lookout is manned during fire season, and you are normally welcome to climb up to the tower with permission from the lookout on duty. The square concrete building next to the lookout is a former radar site. From the lookout, there are views over Susanville to the north, Shaffer Mountain to the northeast, and Honey Lake to the east. The fire lookout on Red Rock can be seen to the northwest and the fire lookout on Smith Peak is visible to the south. On a clear day, the distinctive shape of the Sierra Buttes can just be seen on the horizon to the south.

In addition to serving as a fire lookout, the peak is noted as an observation point for spring and fall raptor migrations. Warm air rising from Honey Lake creates thermals that the birds use to gain the altitude necessary to carry them over mountains and the Modoc Plateau to the north. Commonly seen raptors include prairie falcons, Swainson's hawks, peregrine falcons, bald eagles, golden eagles, red-tailed hawks, northern goshawks, and ospreys. White pelicans and sandhill cranes also migrate past this area. In fall, large flocks of sandhill cranes can often be seen on their way to the Central Valley. Hang-gliders also use the thermal lift of the scarp slope; a hang-glider launch site is on the northern face of the cliff.

The Sierra Army Depot borders Honey Lake to the east of Thompson Peak. The army detonates outdated ordnance in the Honey Lake region. Detonations often happen twice a day at a black area visible from the Thompson Peak Fire Lookout.

Thompson Peak Fire Lookout on the ridge of the Diamond Mountains

The main trail continues through the northern

Wemple Cabin sits beside Antelope Creek

end of the Diamond Mountains, skirting the northern end of Wildcat Ridge. The volcanic cap of the ridge can be seen to the right; bare, jagged peaks form the very edge of the escarpment that drops down to Honey Lake Valley. Many small meadows, usually ringed by aspens, can be seen along the trail. One such meadow is the site of Wheeler Sheep Camp, a Basque sheepherders' regional base.

Approaching the Red Rock Fire Lookout, the trail enters a more open landscape composed of loose volcanic slopes. The lookout, built in the 1940s, stands on the northern end of the Diamond Mountains. Like the one on Thompson Peak, the lookout is manned during fire season, and you can normally climb to the tower with permission from the lookout on duty. From the tower, you can see Smith Peak and the fire lookout on Mount Hough to the south, with Taylorsville and the Indian Valley to the southwest. To the north is Lassen Peak, and on a clear day, you can see as far as Mount Shasta. Antelope Lake is to the southeast, and Diamond Mountain is immediately to the northeast.

Past the lookout, the road gradually descends toward Susanville, following Gold Run Creek for much of the way and joining CR 204. The trail ends 3 miles south of Susanville at the intersection with CR 203. Much of this trail is impassable in wet weather and should not be attempted then.

Current Road Information

Plumas National Forest
Mt. Hough Ranger District
39696 Highway 70
Quincy, CA 95971
(530) 283-0555

Bureau of Land Management
Eagle Lake Field Office
2950 Riverside Drive
Susanville, CA 96130
(530) 257-0456

Map References

BLM Susanville
USFS Plumas National Forest; Lassen National Forest
USGS 1:24,000 Antelope Lake, Janesville, Diamond Mt., Susanville
1:100,000 Susanville
Maptech CD-ROM: Shasta Lake/Redding
Northern California Atlas & Gazetteer, p. 60
California Road & Recreation Atlas, pp. 60, 54

Route Directions

Mileage		Direction	Description
▼ 0.0			From US 395 at Janesville, proceed south on CR 208 for 4.6 miles to the start of the trail. Zero trip meter and turn southeast on wide graded road 28N02, following the sign to Thompson Lookout.
	1.3 ▲		Trail ends at T-intersection with paved CR 208. Turn right for Antelope Lake; turn left for Janesville and US 395.
			GPS: N40°14.65' W120°31.02'
▼ 0.5		BR	Track on left; then graded road on left is 28N26. Remain on 28N02.
	0.8 ▲	BL	Graded road on right is 28N26; then track on right. Remain on 28N02.
▼ 0.7		SO	Track on left is 28N02E.
	0.6 ▲	SO	Track on right is 28N02E.
▼ 0.9		SO	Track on right is 28N02B.
	0.4 ▲	SO	Track on left is 28N02B.
▼ 1.0		SO	Track on right.
	0.3 ▲	SO	Track on left.
▼ 1.1		SO	Track on left is 28N02G.
	0.2 ▲	SO	Track on right is 28N02G.
▼ 1.3		SO	Track on left is 27N04, the loop past Wemple Cabin. Zero trip meter and follow sign to Thompson Lookout.
	0.0 ▲		Continue to the northeast.
			GPS: N40°14.25' W120°31.70'

Loop past Wemple Cabin

Mileage	Direction	Description
▼ 0.0		Turn southeast on 27N04.
▼ 0.4	TR	Track on left is 27N04 to Murdock Crossing. Turn right onto 27N46, following sign to Wemple Cabin.
		GPS: N40°13.95' W120°31.90'
▼ 0.9	SO	Track on left is 27N60, which is the end of the loop.
		GPS: N40°13.82' W120°32.32'
▼ 1.8	SO	Track on left.
▼ 2.0	SO	Track on right; then cross over Antelope Creek.
▼ 2.9	SO	Track on left is 27N46A.
		GPS: N40°13.39' W120°33.68'
▼ 4.4	BL	Track on right is 27N46. Bear left onto 27N61.
		GPS: N40°12.58' W120°34.13'
▼ 4.6	SO	Track on left.
▼ 5.1	SO	Two tracks on right.
▼ 5.3	SO	Track on left; then cross over Antelope Creek; then track on right.
▼ 5.4	TL	Track straight ahead is 27N60. Zero trip meter and turn left onto unmarked trail 27N60.
		GPS: N40°12.00' W120°33.39'
▼ 0.0		Continue to the northeast. Wemple Cabin can be seen in the meadow on the left.
▼ 0.1	SO	Track on left.
▼ 0.8	SO	Track on right. Follow sign to US 395.
▼ 1.8	SO	Track on right.
▼ 2.1	SO	Track on right.
▼ 2.3	SO	Track on left.
▼ 2.4	SO	Track on right is 27N37.
		GPS: N40°13.53' W120°32.47'
▼ 2.8		End of loop. Turn right and travel 0.9 miles back to the main trail.
		GPS: N40°13.82' W120°32.32'

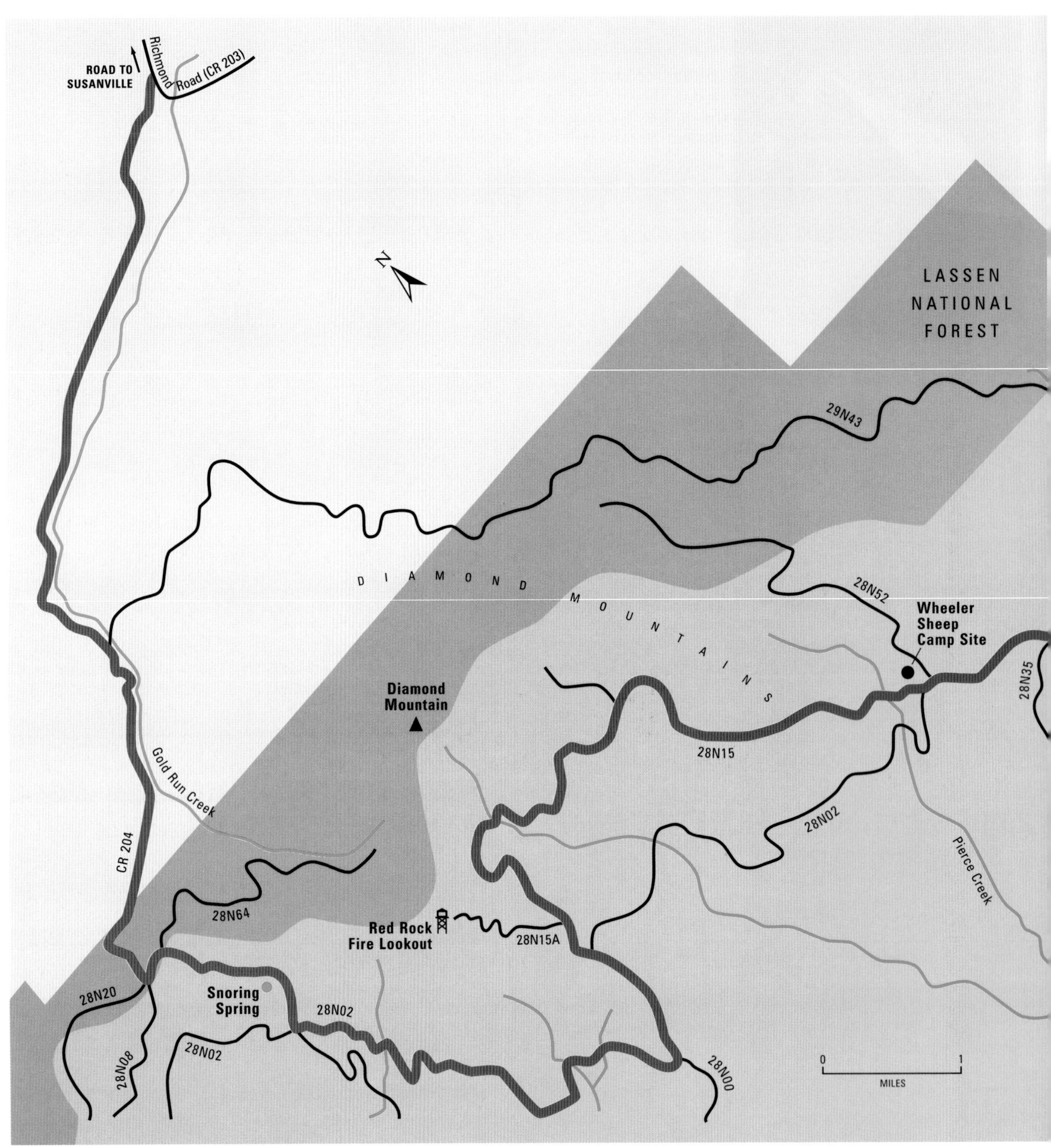

Continuation of Main Trail

▼ 0.0			Continue to the southwest.
	1.2 ▲	SO	Track on right is 27N04, the loop past Wemple Cabin. Zero trip meter and follow sign to Janesville.
			GPS: N40°14.25' W120°31.70'
▼ 0.8		SO	Track on right is 28N02F.
	0.4 ▲	SO	Track on left is 28N02F.
▼ 1.2		BL	Track on right is 28N02A, spur to Thompson Peak Fire Lookout. Zero trip meter.
	0.0 ▲		Continue to the southeast on 28N02.
			GPS: N40°14.31' 120°32.89'

Spur to Thompson Peak Fire Lookout

▼ 0.0		Proceed northwest on 28N02A.
▼ 0.3	SO	Track on left is 28N14. Remain on 28N02A. Trail is marked as a snowmobile route—rated blue.
▼ 2.5		Spur ends at Thompson Peak Fire Lookout.

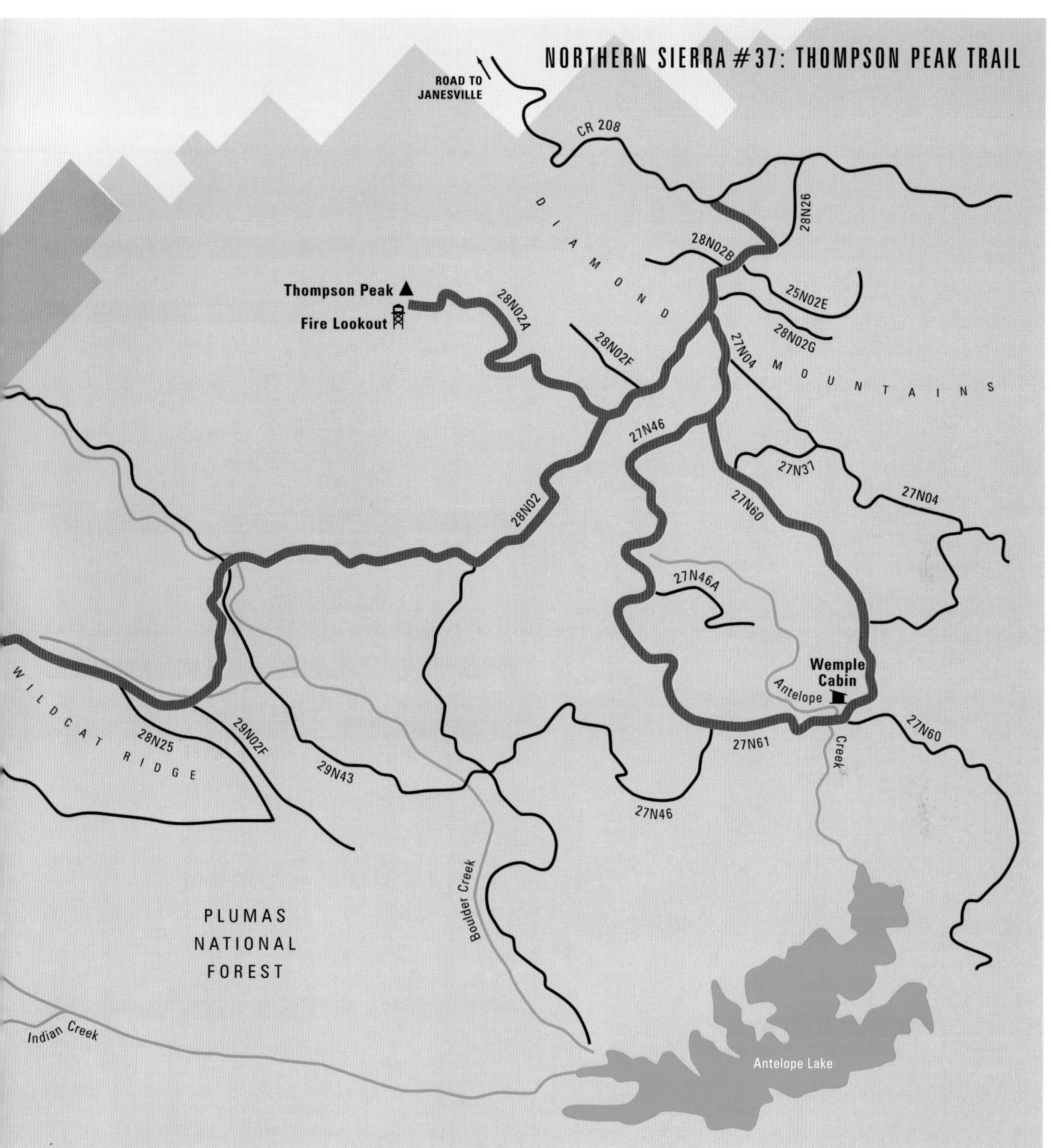

GPS: N40°15.66′ 120°33.37′		

Continuation of Main Trail

▼ 0.0		Continue to the west on 28N02.
3.5 ▲	BR	Track on left is 28N02A, spur to Thompson Peak Fire Lookout. Zero trip meter.
		GPS: N40°14.31′ 120°32.89′
▼ 0.3	SO	Cattle guard.
3.2 ▲	SO	Cattle guard.
▼ 0.7	SO	Track on right is 28N02H.
2.8 ▲	SO	Track on left is 28N02H.
▼ 1.7	SO	Track on left.
1.8 ▲	SO	Track on right.
▼ 2.4	SO	Track on left.
1.1 ▲	SO	Track on right.
		GPS: N40°14.78′ W120°35.02′

▼ 3.5	BL	Cross over Boulder Creek; then track on left to Lowe Flat; then graded road on right is the continuation of 29N43 to Susanville. Zero trip meter and bear left onto 29N43, following sign to Antelope Lake. Also small track on left.
0.0 ▲		Continue to the southeast. Track on right to Lowe Flat; then cross over Boulder Creek.
		GPS: N40°15.41′ W120°35.85′
▼ 0.0		Continue to the west.
3.6 ▲	BR	Small track on right; then graded road on left is continuation of 29N43 to Susanville. Zero trip meter and bear right onto 28N02, following sign to Janesville.
▼ 0.5	BR	Graded road on left is 29N43 to Antelope Lake. Bear right onto 28N02, following the sign to Red Rock.
3.1 ▲	SO	Graded road on right is 29N43. Follow the sign to Janesville.
		GPS: N40°15.20′ W120°36.22′
▼ 0.9	SO	Track on left.
2.7 ▲	SO	Track on right.
▼ 1.0	SO	Track on right is 28N02C.
2.6 ▲	SO	Track on left is 28N02C.
▼ 1.2	SO	Track on right; then cross over creek; then track on left is 29N02F.
2.4 ▲	SO	Track on right is 29N02F; then cross over creek; then track on left.
▼ 1.7	SO	Track on left is 28N25.
1.9 ▲	SO	Track on right is 28N25.
		GPS: N40°15.49′ W120°37.12′
▼ 2.5	SO	Cattle guard.
1.1 ▲	SO	Cattle guard.
▼ 2.6	SO	Track on left is 28N35.
1.0 ▲	SO	Track on right is 28N35.
▼ 3.0	SO	Track on right is 28N02P.
0.6 ▲	SO	Track on left is 28N02P.
▼ 3.1	SO	Cross over creek.
0.5 ▲	SO	Cross over creek.
▼ 3.3	SO	Track on left is 28N26X.
0.3 ▲	SO	Track on right is 28N26X.
▼ 3.5	BL	Track on right is 28N52. Follow sign to Red Rock Lookout.
0.1 ▲	BR	Track on left is 28N52. Follow sign to Lowe Flat.
		GPS: N40°16.49′ W120°38.37′
▼ 3.6	BR	Track on left is 28N02. Follow the sign to Red Rock Lookout and zero trip meter. The flat on the right is the site of Wheeler Sheep Camp.
0.0 ▲		Continue to the southeast on 28N02.
		GPS: N40°16.55′ W120°38.54′
▼ 0.0		Continue to the north on 28N15.
5.1 ▲	BL	Track on right is 28N02. Follow the sign to Lowe Flat. The flat on the left is the site of Wheeler Sheep Camp. Zero trip meter.
▼ 0.2	SO	Track on right.
4.9 ▲	SO	Track on left.
▼ 0.3	SO	Cross over Pierce Creek.
4.8 ▲	SO	Cross over Pierce Creek.
▼ 0.4	BL	Track on right; then cross over creek.
4.7 ▲	BR	Cross over creek; then track on left.
		GPS: N40°16.75′ W120°38.90′
▼ 0.7	SO	Track on left.
4.4 ▲	SO	Track on right.
▼ 0.8	SO	Track on right.
4.3 ▲	SO	Track on left.
▼ 2.1	SO	Track on right.
3.0 ▲	SO	Track on left.
▼ 2.7	SO	Track on right.
2.4 ▲	SO	Track on left.
▼ 3.1	SO	Track on left.
2.0 ▲	SO	Track on right.
▼ 3.3	SO	Cross over creek.
1.8 ▲	SO	Cross over creek.
▼ 3.4	SO	Cross over creek.
1.7 ▲	SO	Cross over creek.
		GPS: N40°17.95′ W120°41.02′
▼ 3.6	SO	Track on left; then spring on left.
1.5 ▲	SO	Spring on right; then track on right.
		GPS: N40°17.81′ W120°41.19′
▼ 3.8	TR	Track on left.
1.3 ▲	TL	Track on right.
▼ 4.1	SO	Track on right; then cross over Indian Creek.
1.0 ▲	SO	Cross over Indian Creek; then track on left.
▼ 4.9	SO	Track on right.
0.2 ▲	SO	Track on left.
▼ 5.1	SO	Track on right is 28N15A, which goes 1.4 miles to Red Rock Fire Lookout. Zero trip meter.
0.0 ▲		Continue to the north.
		GPS: N40°17.28′ W120°41.90′
▼ 0.0		Continue to the south.
5.2 ▲	SO	Track on left is 28N15A, which goes 1.4 miles to Red Rock Fire Lookout. Zero trip meter.
▼ 0.4	SO	Graded road on left is 28N02.
4.8 ▲	BL	Graded road on right is 28N02. Bear left onto 28N15.
		GPS: N40°16.97′ W120°41.89′
▼ 1.2	BR	Graded road on left is 28N00.
4.0 ▲	BL	Graded road on right is 28N00.
		GPS: N40°16.23′ W120°42.00′
▼ 1.9	SO	Cross over creek.
3.3 ▲	SO	Cross over creek.
▼ 2.5	SO	Cross over creek.
2.7 ▲	SO	Cross over creek.
▼ 4.1	SO	Track on left.
1.1 ▲	SO	Track on right.
▼ 4.5	SO	Cross over creek.
0.7 ▲	SO	Cross over creek.
▼ 5.2	TR	4-way intersection. Straight ahead goes to Moonlight Valley. Track on left goes to Greensville. Follow sign to Susanville and zero trip meter.
0.0 ▲		Continue to the east on 28N02.
		GPS: N40°18.12′ W120°44.06′
▼ 0.0		Continue to the north.
9.0 ▲	TL	4-way intersection. Straight ahead goes to Greensville. Track on right goes to Moonlight Valley. Zero trip meter and follow sign to Red Rock Lookout.
▼ 0.5	SO	Track on right and Snoring Spring on left; then track on left.
8.5 ▲	SO	Track on right; then Snoring Spring on right and track on left.
		GPS: N40°18.49′ W120°43.85′
▼ 1.3	BL	Track on right is 28N64.
7.7 ▲	BR	Track on left is 28N64.
▼ 1.6	TR	4-way intersection. To the left is 28N08 and straight ahead is 28N20.Turn right onto unmarked CR 204.
7.4 ▲	TL	4-way intersection. Straight ahead is 28N08 and track on right is 28N20. Turn

		left onto the major road.
		GPS: N40°19.05' W120°44.55'
▼ 1.7	SO	Track on left.
7.3 ▲	SO	Track on right.
▼ 2.0	SO	Track on left.
7.0 ▲	SO	Track on right.
▼ 3.0	SO	Track on left. Trail is now following along Gold Run Creek.
6.0 ▲	SO	Track on right.
▼ 4.0	SO	Track on right.
5.0 ▲	SO	Track on left.
▼ 4.3	SO	Road on right.
4.7 ▲	BR	Road on left.
		GPS: N40°20.51' W120°42.80'
▼ 4.8	SO	Two tracks on left.
4.2 ▲	SO	Two tracks on right.
▼ 5.4	SO	Road becomes paved. Remain on Gold Run Road, ignoring turns to the left and right.
3.6 ▲	SO	Road turns to graded dirt.
▼ 9.0		Trail ends at T-intersection with Richmond Road (CR 203). Turn left for Susanville.
0.0 ▲		Trail commences on Richmond Road (CR 203), 3 miles south of Susanville. Richmond Road is initially called Weatherlow Street as it leaves Main Street at the stoplight. Zero trip meter and turn southwest on the paved Gold Run Road (CR 204). Remain on the paved road, ignoring turns to the left and right for 3.6 miles.
		GPS: N40°22.65' W120°39.20'

NORTHERN SIERRA #38

Belfast Petroglyphs Trail

Starting Point:	**CR A27, 10 miles east of Susanville**
Finishing Point:	**US 395, 18 miles south of Ravendale**
Total Mileage:	**19.7 miles**
Unpaved Mileage:	**19.7 miles**
Driving Time:	**3 hours**
Elevation Range:	**4,100–4,600 feet**
Usually Open:	**April to December**
Best Time to Travel:	**Spring and fall, in dry weather**
Difficulty Rating:	**3**
Scenic Rating:	**8**
Remoteness Rating:	**+1**

Special Attractions

- Belfast Petroglyphs and other petroglyphs near Balls Canyon.
- Wildlife watching at Biscar National Cooperative Wildlife Management Area.
- Remote, lightly traveled trail.

History

Belfast Petroglyphs Trail leads off from the historic Nobles Trail (see page 66) on the northern edge of the Honey Lake Valley. This old trail, founded by William H. Nobles in 1852,

Belfast Petroglyphs on the dark boulders above Willow Creek

was developed to draw westbound emigrants to Shasta City, far off to the northwest. This alternative to the Lassen Trail made its way southwest via Honey Lake, up the Susan River, through present-day Susanville, and continued northwest past Lassen Peak along the route of present-day California 44.

The Belfast Petroglyphs are in a region shared among the Maidu, generally from the Sierra Nevada; the Paiute, from the Great Basin to the east; and the Modoc, from the north. Petroglyphs in this area may depict visions seen by shamans; however, the true meaining of these images remains a mystery. We can only marvel at such indecipherable work left behind by those who came before us.

Description

Belfast Petrolglyphs Trail is a remote, lightly used trail that travels through an arid volcanic landscape with rough lava boulders and sagebrush. The trail leaves CR A27 along a maintained, graded dirt county road initially marked Belfast Road. Past Belfast, the trail narrows and crosses private ranchland before entering BLM land. A short distance from the trail, the Belfast Petroglyphs can be found along basalt boulders overlooking Willow Creek. The site is not marked, but it is easy to find; a turnout marks the spot. Follow the trail approximately 100 yards to a drop-off above Willow Creek. Many of the carvings have been badly eroded by the elements. The more sheltered ones or those on dark rocks are easier to see.

The main trail swings east at this point and joins a formed single track that travels across the wide sagebrush-covered valley on the western side of Shaffer Mountain. The rough trail surface is littered with sharp volcanic rocks. It is not difficult, just very slow going. Taking the trail at high speeds might cause tire damage and will certainly shake passengers about. Hikers may find additional petroglyphs at various points along or slightly away from the trail.

The trail drops steeply from a rise, down a rocky pinch that will require some care. In the valley, the trail has a smooth sandy surface with some deep sand traps. It passes beside Shaffer Well before briefly entering the Biscar National Cooperative Wildlife Management Area. A track leads 0.1 miles to the

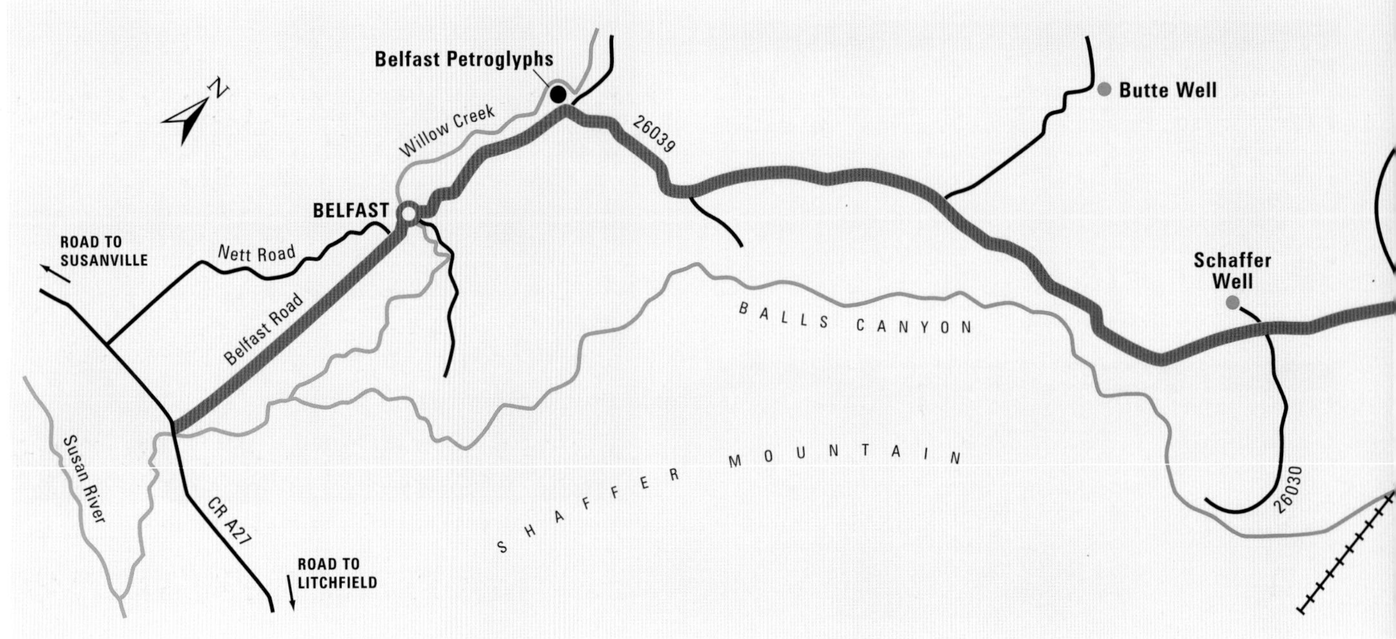

dam of Biscar Reservoir, a good spot for viewing waterfowl. This area, and the trail in general, offers excellent opportunities to view golden eagles, prairie falcons, red-tailed hawks, chukars, and pronghorn antelope.

The trail becomes a graded dirt road and crosses the Southern Pacific Railroad at the old Karlo Siding, before swinging east to cross Secret Creek and finish on US 395. In wet weather the trail becomes impassable because the dry, friable soils quickly turn to deep, gooey mud.

Current Road Information

Bureau of Land Management
Eagle Lake Field Office
2950 Riverside Drive
Susanville, CA 96130
(530) 257-0456

The trail along Balls Canyon, northwest of Schaffer Mountain

Map References

BLM Susanville, Eagle Lake
USGS 1:24,000 Litchfield, Petes Valley, Karlo, Five Springs
1:100,000 Susanville, Eagle Lake
Maptech CD-ROM: Shasta Lake/Redding
Northern California Atlas & Gazetteer, pp. 60, 61, 51
California Road & Recreation Atlas, p. 55
Other: BLM Recreation Guide for Northeastern California and Northwestern Nevada

Route Directions

▼ 0.0		From Susanville, proceed south on US 395 to the edge of town and turn east onto CR A27. Proceed 10 miles to the start of the trail. Zero trip meter and turn north on graded dirt Belfast Road (CR 246).
4.5 ▲		Trail ends at T-intersection with paved Center Road (CR A27). Turn right for Susanville; turn left for Litchfield.
		GPS: N40°24.07' W120°27.03'
▼ 2.6	SO	Track on left is Nett Road.
1.9 ▲	SO	Track on right is Nett Road.
▼ 2.8	SO	Belfast. Cross over Willow Creek on bridge.
1.7 ▲	SO	Belfast. Cross over Willow Creek on bridge.
▼ 2.9	BL	Road on right. Bear left past the "End of County Maintenance" sign and pass through gate.
1.6 ▲	SO	Gate; then road on left.
		GPS: N40°26.65' W120°27.03'
▼ 3.1	BR	Track on left; then track on right.
1.4 ▲	BL	Track on left; then track on right.
▼ 3.7	SO	Pass through fence line. Road is marked 26032.
0.8 ▲	SO	Pass through fence line.
▼ 4.5	BR	Cattle guard; then bear right onto small, formed trail marked 26039 and zero trip meter. From the turnout on left, the Belfast Petroglyphs are 100 yards along a track to the left. Park at the turnout and walk the short distance west to where the gorge drops down to the creek.

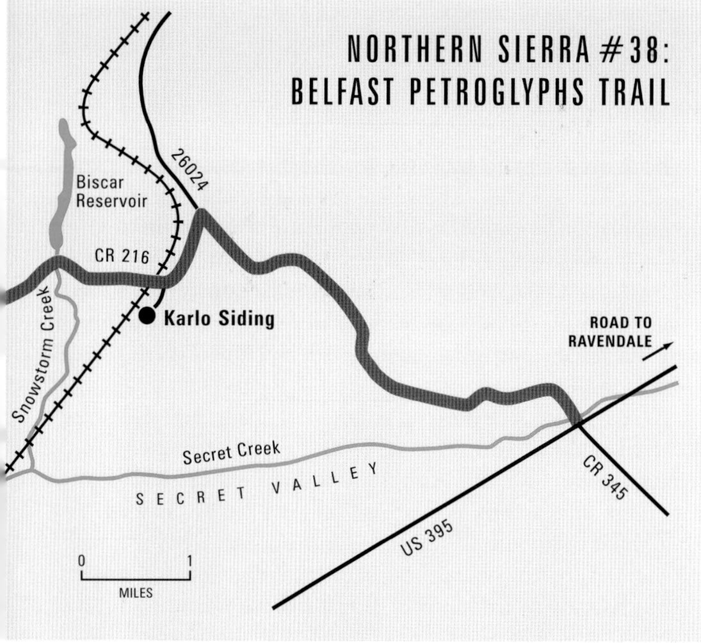

0.0 ▲ Continue to the south and cross cattle guard.

GPS: N40°28.06' W120°26.83'

▼ 0.0 Continue to the northeast.
7.2 ▲ TL T-intersection. From the turnout on right, the Belfast Petroglyphs are 100 yards along the track to the right. Park at the turnout and walk the short distance west to where the gorge drops down to the creek. Zero trip meter.

▼ 1.5 BL Track on right toward Balls Canyon.
5.7 ▲ BR Track on left toward Balls Canyon.

GPS: N40°28.39' W120°25.31'

▼ 3.8 SO Well-used track on left goes to Butte Well.
3.4 ▲ SO Well-used track on right goes to Butte Well.

GPS: N40°29.86' W120°23.57'

▼ 4.9 SO Pass through wire gate.
2.3 ▲ SO Pass through wire gate.

GPS: N40°30.12' W120°22.33'

▼ 5.4 SO Trail passes close to the edge of Balls Canyon.
1.8 ▲ SO Trail passes close to the edge of Balls Canyon.

▼ 6.0 SO Pass through wire gate.
1.2 ▲ SO Pass through wire gate.

▼ 6.2 SO Short rough drop off of rise.
1.0 ▲ SO Short rough climb up rise.

GPS: N40°30.43' W120°20.91'

▼ 7.2 SO 4-way intersection. Track on left goes to Shaffer Well. Track on right is 26030. Zero trip meter and follow sign to Karlo.
0.0 ▲ Continue to the south on 26039.

GPS: N40°31.20' W120°20.55'

▼ 0.0 Continue to the northeast on 26039.
1.8 ▲ SO 4-way intersection. Track on right goes to Shaffer Well. Track on left is 26030. Zero trip meter and follow sign to Belfast.

▼ 1.3 SO Track on left.
0.5 ▲ SO Track on right.

▼ 1.7 SO Cattle guard.
0.1 ▲ SO Cattle guard.

GPS: N40°32.52' W120°19.70'

▼ 1.8 TR Track on left enters the Biscar National Cooperative Wildlife Management Area and goes 0.1 miles to a dam. Zero trip meter and cross through Snowstorm Creek wash.
0.0 ▲ Continue to the southeast. Road is now a formed trail.

GPS: N40°32.65' W120°19.72'

▼ 0.0 Continue to the northeast on CR 216. Road is now graded dirt.
6.2 ▲ TL Cross through Snowstorm Creek wash; then track straight ahead enters the Biscar National Cooperative Wildlife Management Area and goes 0.1 miles to a dam. Zero trip meter.

▼ 0.2 SO Track on right to cabin.
6.0 ▲ SO Track on left to cabin.

▼ 0.9 BL Cross over railroad; then track on right to Karlo Siding.
5.3 ▲ BR Track on left to Karlo Siding; then cross over railroad.

GPS: N40°33.18' W120°18.88'

▼ 1.7 BR Track on left is 26024; then cross cattle guard over creek.
4.5 ▲ BL Cross cattle guard over creek; then track on right is 26024.

GPS: N40°33.77' W120°19.13'

▼ 6.1 SO Cross over Secret Creek.
0.1 ▲ SO Cross over Secret Creek.

▼ 6.2 Cattle guard; then trail ends at intersection with US 395. Turn left for Ravendale; turn right for Susanville. Track opposite is Shinn Ranch Road (CR 345).
0.0 ▲ Trail commences on US 395 at mile marker 92, 18 miles south of Ravendale. Zero trip meter and turn west on graded dirt road. Cross cattle guard and follow the sign to Karlo Road and wildlife viewing area. Shinn Ranch Road (CR 345) is opposite.

GPS: N40°35.04' W120°14.98'

NORTHERN SIERRA #39

Antelope Mountain and Crater Lake Trail

Starting Point:	**CR A-1, 2.2 miles north of Christie USFS Campground**
Finishing Point:	**California 44, 0.1 miles southeast of Bogard USFS Work Station**
Total Mileage:	**15.6 miles, plus 3.8-mile spur to Antelope Mountain Fire Lookout and 4.8-mile spur to Crater Lake**
Unpaved Mileage:	**15.6 miles, plus spurs**
Driving Time:	**3 hours**
Elevation Range:	**5,300–7,600**
Usually Open:	**May to December**
Best Time to Travel:	**May to December**
Difficulty Rating:	**1**
Scenic Rating:	**9**
Remoteness Rating:	**+0**

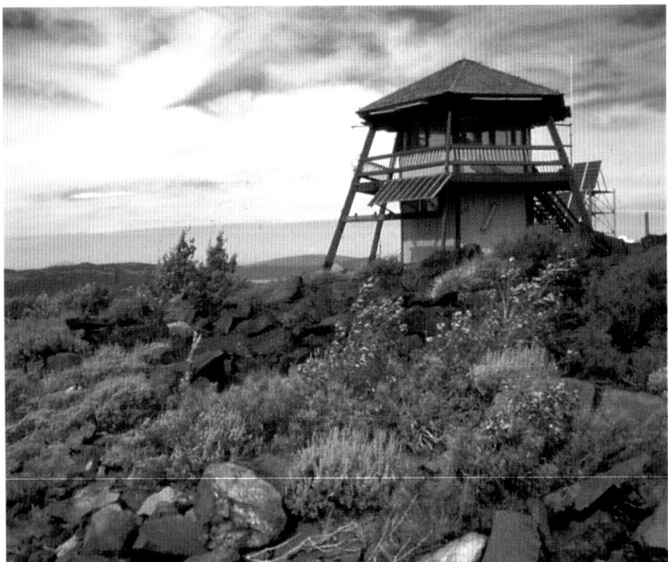

Antelope Mountain Fire Lookout

Special Attractions

- Panoramic views from Antelope Mountain Fire Lookout
- Fishing and camping at Crater and Eagle Lakes.
- Trail intersects with the historic Nobles and Lassen Trails.

Description

Eagle Lake and Honey Lake are part of the Basin and Range province of the Great Basin. Both Eagle and Honey Lakes are remnants of an ancient glacial lake called Lake Lahontan. Eagle Lake, the second largest natural lake in the state, has no outlet, and it is well known for having excellent angling opportunities, mainly for Eagle Lake trout. Most closely related to rainbow trout, these fish have adapted to Eagle Lake's alkaline water and thrive where introduced species do not. One reason for their survival is that the fish are extremely long lived; some have been estimated to be 11 years old. They spawn in Pine Creek, but dry conditions often mean that they cannot do so annually. Evolution has favored the long-lived fish that are able to spawn later in life. Eagle Lake trout are extremely fast growing, and a 4-year-old can be more than 22 inches long and weigh 4 pounds. Attempts to introduce game fish have repeatedly failed. Since 1956, the California Department of Fish and Game has successfully stocked Eagle Lake trout in other lakes across the state. As many as 200,000 are planted in various lakes each year, primarily for sport fishing.

Bird-watchers at Eagle Lake may see some of the 95 species known to be in the lake's vicinity, including bald eagles, golden eagles, pelicans, and ospreys. Hunting for mule deer and waterfowl (in season) are also popular activities around the lake.

The trail begins just west of Eagle Lake and travels through Lassen National Forest along a graded road toward Antelope Mountain Fire Lookout. A spur heads south to the modern lookout, which is manned during fire season; visitors are normally welcome to climb up to the tower with permission from the lookout on duty. Views from the top include Eagle Lake to the northeast, volcanic Lassen Peak (see page 111) to the west, and the open area of Pine Creek Valley to the southwest. Whaleback Mountain and Logan Mountain are to the north, with Antelope Valley beyond them. On a clear day, the snow-covered peak of Mount Shasta can be seen way off to the northwest.

Back on the main trail, the road swiftly descends to cross the Pine Creek Valley. The valley previously had a large Indian population, with many villages and campsites in this fertile hunting and fishing ground. Today, the trail winds around the edge of the valley and passes many backcountry campsites tucked into the trees. Part of the trail follows an old lumber railroad grade, long since abandoned, put in to carry felled trees to mill.

A second spur from the main trail leads 4.8 miles to Crater Lake, which is set in a volcanic crater. The lake has a pretty, developed USFS campground by the shore with scattered firs and aspens providing shade; a fee is charged. A small boat ramp allows you to get out onto the lake in small motorboats or rowboats. The main trail ends on California 44, a short distance south of Bogard Work Station and 28 miles northeast of Susanville. Bogard was an important rest stop for travelers along the Lassen and Nobles Trails, which crossed this route a short distance from the national scenic byway of California 44.

The entire trail, including the spurs to Antelope Mountain and Crater Lake, is a groomed snowmobile route in winter, classed as easiest. The Bogard snowmobile area at the end of the trail has 80 miles of groomed, designated snowmobile trails along forest roads, all rated easy.

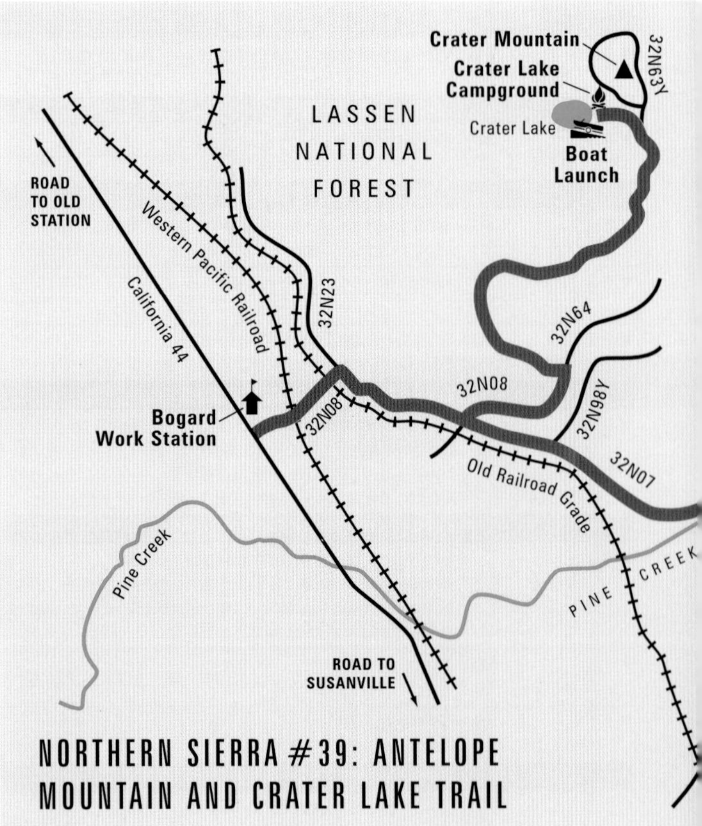

Current Road Information
Lassen National Forest
Eagle Lake Ranger District
477-050 Eagle Lake Road
Susanville, CA 96130
(530) 257-4188

Map References
BLM Eagle Lake, Burney
USFS Lassen National Forest
USGS 1:24,000 Pikes Point, Antelope Mt., Pine Creek Valley, Harvey Mt.
1:100,000 Eagle Lake, Burney
Maptech CD-ROM: Shasta Lake/Redding
Northern California Atlas & Gazetteer, pp. 50, 49
California Road & Recreation Atlas, p. 54
Other: BLM Recreation Guide for Northeastern California and Northwestern Nevada (incomplete)

Route Directions

▼ 0.0		From CR A-1 just west of Eagle Lake, 7.3 miles south of the intersection with Spalding Tract Road and 2.2 miles north of Christie USFS Campground, zero trip meter and turn west on graded dirt FR 21, following sign for Antelope Lookout. Immediately track on left.
4.4 ▲		Track on right; then trail ends on paved CR A-1 on the western side of Eagle Lake. Turn left for Adin and California 139; turn right for Susanville.
		GPS: N40°36.08' W120°50.89'
▼ 0.9	SO	Track on left is 32N75.
4.5 ▲	SO	Track on right is 32N75.
▼ 1.7	SO	Track on left.
2.7 ▲	SO	Track on right.
▼ 1.8	SO	Track on right is 33N38; then cattle guard.
2.6 ▲	SO	Cattle guard; then track on left is 33N38.
		GPS: N40°36.98' W120°52.40'
▼ 2.1	SO	Track on left is 32N69 and track on right is 32N90Y.
2.3 ▲	SO	Track on right is 32N69 and track on left is 32N90Y.
		GPS: N40°37.15' W120°52.65'
▼ 2.4	SO	Track on right is 33N31 to Prison Springs. Remain on FR 21, following the sign to Antelope Lookout.
2.0 ▲	SO	Track on left is 33N31 to Prison Springs. Remain on FR 21.
		GPS: N40°37.20' W120°52.92'
▼ 2.5	SO	Track on left.
1.9 ▲	SO	Track on right.
▼ 3.3	SO	Track on right.
1.1 ▲	SO	Track on left.
▼ 3.7	SO	Track on right is 32N70.
0.7 ▲	SO	Track on left is 32N70.
▼ 3.9	SO	Track on left is 32N02C.
0.5 ▲	SO	Track on right is 32N02C.
▼ 4.0	SO	Summit Camp on right—undeveloped USFS camping area.
0.4 ▲	SO	Summit Camp on left—undeveloped USFS camping area.
		GPS: N40°37.18' W120°54.71'
▼ 4.4	SO	Track on left is 32N73, spur to Antelope

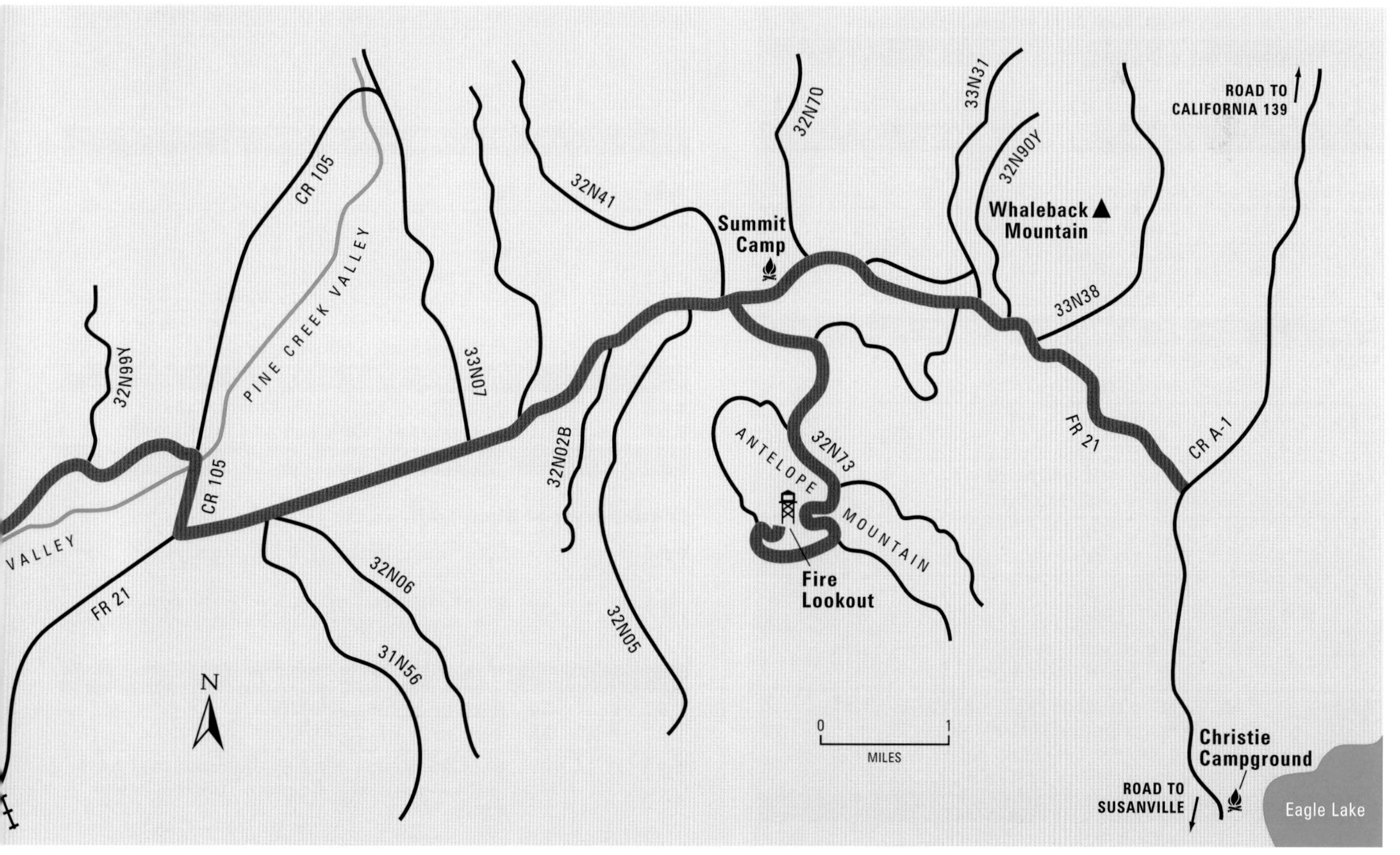

Aspens and firs ring Crater Lake

		Mountain Fire Lookout. Track on right is 32N41. Zero trip meter.
0.0 ▲		Continue to the northeast.
		GPS: N40°37.07' W120°55.12'

Spur To Antelope Mountain Fire Lookout

▼ 0.0		Proceed southeast on 32N73, following sign to Antelope Lookout.
▼ 0.7	SO	Track on left.
▼ 1.5	SO	Track on right.
▼ 2.1	BR	Two tracks on left.
		GPS: N40°35.85' W120°53.99'
▼ 2.9	TR	Track on left; then track continues straight ahead. Turn right onto well-used track.
		GPS: N40°35.52' W120°53.92'
▼ 3.7	SO	Track on left.
▼ 3.8		Spur ends at Antelope Mountain Fire Lookout.
		GPS: N40°35.56' W120°54.57'

Continuation of Main Trail

▼ 0.0		Continue to the southwest.
4.9 ▲	SO	Track on right is 32N73, spur to Antelope Mountain Fire Lookout. Track on left is 32N41. Zero trip meter.
		GPS: N40°37.07' W120°55.12'
▼ 0.2	SO	Track on left is 32N05.
4.7 ▲	SO	Track on right is 32N05.
▼ 0.5	SO	Track on right.
4.4 ▲	SO	Track on left.
▼ 0.9	SO	Track on left is 32N02B.
4.0 ▲	SO	Track on right is 32N02B.
▼ 1.4	SO	Track on left and track on right.
3.5 ▲	SO	Track on left and track on right.
▼ 2.2	SO	Track on right.
2.7 ▲	SO	Track on left.
▼ 2.4	SO	Cattle guard. Entering Pine Creek Valley.
2.5 ▲	SO	Cattle guard. Leaving Pine Creek Valley.
▼ 2.5	SO	Graded road on right is 33N07 to Champs Flat. Follow sign to California 44.
2.4 ▲	SO	Graded road on left is 33N07 to Champs Flat. Follow sign to Eagle Lake.
		GPS: N40°35.88' W120°57.31'
▼ 3.5	SO	Track on left.
1.4 ▲	SO	Track on right.
▼ 3.9	SO	Track on left.
1.0 ▲	SO	Track on right.
▼ 4.2	SO	Two tracks on left—first is 32N06, second is 31N56.
0.7 ▲	SO	Two tracks on right—first is 31N56, second is 32N06.
▼ 4.9	TR	FR 21 continues straight ahead. Zero trip meter and turn sharp right onto CR 105.
0.0 ▲		Continue to the northeast.
		GPS: N40°35.09' W120°59.74'
▼ 0.0		Continue to the north.
4.5 ▲	TL	T-intersection with FR 21. Zero trip meter and turn sharp left, following sign to Eagle Lake.
▼ 0.6	TL	Cross over Pine Creek; then cattle guard; then turn left on 32N07, following sign for Bogard Station.
3.9 ▲	TR	T-intersection with CR 105. Turn right and cross over cattle guard; then cross over Pine Creek.
		GPS: N40°35.64' W120°59.63'
▼ 1.5	SO	Track on right is 32N99Y.
3.0 ▲	SO	Track on left is 32N99Y.
▼ 1.8	SO	Cattle guard.
2.7 ▲	SO	Cattle guard.
▼ 1.9	SO	Track on right. Many tracks on right to backcountry campsites along the edge of the valley.
2.6 ▲	SO	Track on left.
▼ 3.2	SO	Track on left.
1.3 ▲	SO	Track on right.
▼ 3.7	SO	Track on right is 32N98Y.
0.8 ▲	SO	Track on left is 32N98Y.
▼ 3.8	SO	Track on left.
0.7 ▲	SO	Track on right.
▼ 4.5	SO	4-way intersection. Track on left. Graded road on right is 32N08, spur to Crater Lake. Zero trip meter and join the graded road.
0.0 ▲		Continue to the east on 32N07, following the sign to CR 105. Many tracks on left to backcountry campsites along the edge of the valley.
		GPS: N40°35.43' W121°03.52'

Spur to Crater Lake

▼ 0.0		Proceed northeast on 32N08, following sign to Crater Lake.
▼ 1.0	BL	Track on right is 32N64.
▼ 4.3	SO	Track on right is 32N63Y, which travels a small loop around Crater Mountain and gives a view of the lake from above.
		GPS: N40°37.53' W121°02.21'
▼ 4.6	SO	Enter Crater Lake USFS Campground.
▼ 4.8		Spur ends at boat ramp on Crater Lake.
		GPS: N40°37.54' W121°02.63'

Continuation of Main Trail

▼ 0.0		Continue to the west, following sign to California 44.
1.8 ▲	SO	4-way intersection. Track on right. Graded road on left is 32N08, spur to Crater Lake. Zero trip meter.
		GPS: N40°35.43' W121°03.52'
▼ 0.7	SO	Track on right is 32N07E.
1.1 ▲	SO	Track on left is 32N07E.
▼ 1.0	BL	Track on right is 32N23; then cross over hard-to-distinguish railroad grade. Road is now 32N08.
0.8 ▲	BR	Cross over hard-to-distinguish railroad grade;

		then track on left is 32N23. Road is now 32N07.
▼ 1.3	SO	Bogard Well on left.
0.5 ▲	SO	Bogard Well on right.
▼ 1.5	SO	Cattle guard; then cross over Western Pacific Railroad.
0.3 ▲	SO	Cross over Western Pacific Railroad; then cattle guard.
▼ 1.6	SO	Lassen and Nobles Trails cross road.
0.2 ▲	SO	Lassen and Nobles Trails cross road.
		GPS: N40°35.29' W121°05.04'
▼ 1.8		Track on right; then trail ends at T-intersection with California 44. Turn left for Susanville; turn right for Old Station.
0.0 ▲		Trail commences on California 44, 0.1 miles southeast of the Bogard USFS Work Station, rest area, and snowmobile trailhead, 28 miles northwest of Susanville. Zero trip meter and turn north on graded road 32N08 at the sign for Crater Lake Campground. Immediately track on left.
		GPS: N40°35.19' W121°05.26'

NORTHERN SIERRA #40

Susan River to Juniper Lake Trail

Starting Point:	**Mooney Road (CR A-21), 4.1 miles south of California 44**
Finishing Point:	**Juniper Lake Road (CR 318), 6.2 miles north of Chester**
Total Mileage:	**35.7 miles, plus 5.6-mile spur to Juniper Lake**
Unpaved Mileage:	**35.7 miles, plus 5.6-mile spur**
Driving Time:	**5 hours**
Elevation Range:	**5,000–7,000 feet**
Usually Open:	**May to December**
Best Time to Travel:	**May to December**
Difficulty Rating:	**2**
Scenic Rating:	**9**
Remoteness Rating:	**+0**

Special Attractions

- Fishing and camping at Silver, Echo, and Juniper Lakes.
- Lassen Volcanic National Park.
- Hiking access to the Caribou Wilderness and trails within Lassen Volcanic National Park.
- Long, meandering forest trail for vehicles, mountain bikes, and horses in summer and snowmobiles in winter.

History

This route passes Mount Harkness (8,045 feet) in Lassen Volcanic National Park near the end of the trail. The summit is approximately 1,300 feet above picturesque Juniper Lake, and the climb to it is an enjoyable hike, with the added attraction of visiting an historic lookout. This cone-shaped mountain was chosen as a fire lookout site back in 1930.

The task of getting materials and food up the mountain was left to the capable operator of a Fordson Tractor, who used a sled to transport the goods in winter. Obtaining sufficient water during fire season was an ongoing problem. The lookouts shoveled spring snow into a 1,000-gallon tank and let it melt. This offered a very basic water supply for the coming season. In time, attempts to drop water by air also proved to be rather laborious. Like many others, this lookout tower dropped out of regular service in the late 1970s when aerial surveillance compensated for the reduced number of lookouts, though many forestry officials were unhappy with such coverage. The National Forest Service and the National Park Service reintroduced fire spotters at the aging tower for a period in the late 1980s.

Description

Susan River to Juniper Lake Trail is a pleasant drive through Lassen National Forest. Along the way, it passes small lakes, shady campgrounds, and beautiful forest scenery to finish in the southeast corner of Lassen Volcanic National Park. Although much of the trail is suitable for passenger vehicles, some rough spots require high-clearance.

Last Chance Creek

The trail leaves CR A-21 south of California 44 and follows the good graded road to Silver Lake. Two developed campgrounds are set among the trees, back from the lake's edge; the Silver Beach Picnic Area and a small boat launch are set directly on the water's edge. Much of Silver Lake's shoreline is taken up by vacation homes.

Past Silver Lake, the trail passes above small Betty Lake, visible below the trail, and then alongside Shotoverin Lake. Later, Echo Lake and the small, but heavily used campground beside it can be found a short distance north of the main trail.

Past Echo Lake, the trail turns off FR 10 and travels to Hay Meadow and a hiking trailhead into the Caribou Wilderness. From here, hikers and equestrians can reach many of the small mountain lakes within the wilderness, including Evelyn, Long, and Triangle Lakes. Some pleasant, walk-in backcountry campsites are near the trailhead around the edge of Hay Meadow.

The vehicle trail travels along roads established primarily for logging, following a loop out of Lassen National Forest into Pacific Gas & Electric–owned forest and then back into

Juniper Lake, at the end of the spur in Lassen Volcanic National Park

Lassen National Forest. Camping is prohibited in PG&E forest except at designated campgrounds. Back in the national forest, the trail travels along Last Chance Creek, which drains south to Lake Almanor—visible from several points along the trail. Last Chance Creek is fed by four springs, so it has good flow throughout the summer.

A worthwhile spur leads 4.8 miles north to Juniper Lake in Lassen Volcanic National Park. From here, several hiking trails penetrate farther into the park, taking hikers to destinations such as Cameron Meadows, Snag Lake, Cinder Cone, and Horseshoe Lake. A very pleasant developed campground can be found on the south side of the lake, with views across the water to Lassen Peak. The hiking trail to Mount Harkness starts at the campground and climbs 1.9 miles to the old fire lookout at the peak. The lookout's cabin is currently being restored by the National Park Service. Allow three hours for the round-trip hike.

From Silver Lake to Last Chance Creek, the trail is a groomed snowmobile route in winter. It is part of the system of groomed trails accessed from the Bogard Staging Area.

Current Road Information

Lassen National Forest
Almanor Ranger District
PO Box 767
Chester, CA 96020
(530) 258-2141

Lassen Volcanic National Park
PO Box 100
Mineral, CA 96063
(530) 595-4444

Map References

BLM Lake Almanor, Burney
USFS Lassen National Forest
USGS 1:24,000 Swain Mt., Bogard Buttes, Red Cinder, Chester, Mt. Harkness
1:100,000 Lake Almanor, Burney
Maptech CD-ROM: Shasta Lake/Redding
Northern California Atlas & Gazetteer, pp. 59, 49
California Road & Recreation Atlas, p. 54 (incomplete)
Other: A Guide to the Ishi, Thousand Lakes, & Caribou Wilderness (incomplete)

Route Directions

Mileage		Directions
▼ 0.0		From California 44, 24 miles northeast of Susanville, zero trip meter and turn south on paved Mooney Road (CR A-21), following the sign to Silver Lake and Westwood. Proceed 4.1 miles to the start of the trail. Zero trip meter and turn west on Silver Lake Road.
4.7 ▲		Trail ends at intersection with paved Mooney Road (CR A-21). Turn left for California 44 and Susanville; turn right for Westwood.
		GPS: N40°29.43' W121°04.49'
▼ 0.6	SO	Track on right. Many campsites on the Susan River on left.
4.1 ▲	SO	Track on left.
▼ 1.2	SO	Track on right.
3.5 ▲	SO	Track on left.
▼ 2.2	SO	Track on right.
2.5 ▲	SO	Track on left.
▼ 2.6	SO	Track on right.
2.1 ▲	SO	Track on left.
▼ 3.5	SO	Track on right.
1.2 ▲	SO	Track on left.
▼ 3.6	SO	Cross over the Susan River; then track on left.
1.1 ▲	SO	Track on right; then cross over the Susan River. Many campsites on the Susan River on right.
		GPS: N40°29.98' W121°08.08'
▼ 4.7	BL	FR 10 goes to the right and left. Entering Silver Lake Recreation Area. To the right goes to North Shore, Caribou Wilderness, and Silver Bowl USFS Campground. Zero trip meter and bear left, following the sign to East Shore and Rocky Knoll Campground.
0.0 ▲		Continue to the southeast on Silver Lake Road.
		GPS: N40°29.96' W121°09.15'
▼ 0.0		Continue to the southwest.
3.1 ▲	BR	FR 10 continues to the left and goes to North Shore, Caribou Wilderness, and Silver Bowl USFS Campground. Leaving Silver Lake Recreation Area. Zero trip meter.
▼ 0.1	TL	4-way intersection. Silver Beach Picnic Area is straight ahead and Rocky Knoll USFS Campground is on the right. Turn left, remaining on FR 10 and following the sign to California 36.
3.0 ▲	TR	4-way intersection. Road on left goes 0.1 miles to Silver Beach Picnic Area. Rocky Knoll USFS Campground is straight ahead. Turn right, following the sign for CR A-21.
		GPS: N40°29.92' W121°09.28'
▼ 0.3	TL	4-way intersection. Track straight ahead goes to East Shore and track on right goes into picnic area. Turn left following the sign to Echo Lake, remaining on FR 10.
2.8 ▲	TR	4-way intersection. Track on left goes to East Shore and track straight ahead goes into picnic area. Turn right, following sign to the campground.
		GPS: N40°29.80' W121°09.33'
▼ 0.8	SO	Trail on right goes to Trail Lake, Echo Lake, and Heckles Ranch for hikers, equestrians, and mountain bikers.

2.3 ▲ SO Trail on left goes to Trail Lake, Echo Lake, and Heckles Ranch for hikers, equestrians, and mountain bikers.

GPS: N40°29.40′ W121°09.19′

▼ 1.2 SO Betty Lake is a short distance below the road to the left.
1.9 ▲ SO Betty Lake is a short distance below the road to the right.

▼ 1.6 SO Two tracks on right go to the edge of Shotoverin Lake.
1.5 ▲ SO Two tracks on left go to the edge of Shotoverin Lake.

GPS: N40°28.95′ W121°08.65′

▼ 2.0 SO Track on right.
1.1 ▲ SO Track on left.

▼ 2.5 SO Track on right.
0.6 ▲ SO Track on left.

▼ 3.0 SO Track on left.
0.1 ▲ SO Track on right.

▼ 3.1 TR Major graded road on left is 30N21. Zero trip meter.
0.0 ▲ Continue to the northwest on FR 10.

GPS: N40°28.86′ W121°07.32′

▼ 0.0 Continue to the southwest on FR 10.
6.2 ▲ TL Major graded road ahead is 30N21. Zero trip meter.

▼ 0.6 SO Track on left is 32N10M.
5.6 ▲ SO Track on right is 32N10M.

▼ 1.3 SO Track on right is 32N10L; then track on left is 32N10H.
4.9 ▲ SO Track on right is 32N10H; then track on left is 32N10L.

▼ 1.5 SO Track on right.
4.7 ▲ SO Track on left.

▼ 1.8 SO Cross over creek.
4.4 ▲ SO Cross over creek.

▼ 1.9 SO Track on right is 32N10G.
4.3 ▲ SO Track on left is 32N10G.

▼ 2.4 SO Major graded road on left is 30N81 to CR A-21.
3.8 ▲ SO Major graded road on right is 30N81 to CR A-21.

GPS: N40°27.09′ W121°08.29′

▼ 3.0 SO Graded road on left is 30N07, which goes to Swain Mountain Staging Area on CR A-21, also marked as a mountain bike and snowmobile route. Track on right is 30N57. Continue on FR 10, following the sign to the Caribou Wilderness.
3.2 ▲ SO Graded road on right is 30N07, which goes to Swain Mountain Staging Area on CR A-21, also marked as a mountain bike and snowmobile route. Track on left is 30N57. Continue on FR 10, following the sign to Silver Lake.

GPS: N40°26.66′ W121°08.52′

▼ 4.5 SO Track on right.
1.7 ▲ SO Track on left.

▼ 4.7 SO Track on right is 32N10T.
1.5 ▲ SO Track on left is 32N10T.

▼ 5.6 TL 4-way intersection. Track on right is 30N64, which goes 0.6 miles to Echo Lake and Echo Lake USFS Campground. Track straight ahead is 30N65. Remain on FR 10 (32N10), following the sign to Caribou Wilderness.
0.6 ▲ TR 4-way intersection. Track on left is 30N65. Track straight ahead is 30N64, which goes 0.6 miles to Echo Lake and Echo Lake USFS Campground. Remain on FR 10 (32N10), following the sign to Silver Lake.

GPS: N40°25.52′ W121°10.02′

▼ 6.2 TR Track on left; then paved road ahead goes to California 36. Zero trip meter and turn right onto graded road 30N25, following sign to the Caribou Wilderness.
0.0 ▲ Continue to the northeast past track on right.

GPS: N40°25.08′ W121°10.14′

▼ 0.0 Continue to the northwest.
1.4 ▲ TL T-intersection with FR 10. Paved road on right goes to California 36. Zero trip meter and turn left, following the sign to Silver Lake.

▼ 0.1 SO Track on right; then cross over creek; then track on left.
1.3 ▲ SO Track on right; then cross over creek; then track on left.

▼ 0.7 SO Track on left.
0.7 ▲ SO Track on right.

▼ 0.9 SO Track on left.
0.5 ▲ SO Track on right.

▼ 1.1 SO Track on right.
0.3 ▲ SO Track on left.

▼ 1.4 TL Track continues 0.2 miles straight ahead to Hay Meadow Trailhead. Zero trip meter.
0.0 ▲ Continue to the east.

GPS: N40°25.91′ W121°11.06′

▼ 0.0 Continue to the south on well-used unmarked trail.
9.2 ▲ TR T-intersection. To the left goes 0.2 miles to Hay Meadow Trailhead. Zero trip meter.

▼ 0.3 SO Track on right to Hay Meadow; then cross through Bailey Creek; then track on left.
8.9 ▲ SO Track on right; then cross through Bailey Creek; then track on left to Hay Meadow.

▼ 0.4 SO Track on right.
8.8 ▲ SO Track on left.

▼ 1.2 SO Track on left.
8.0 ▲ SO Track on right.

GPS: N40°25.90′ W121°12.24′

▼ 1.5 TR Turn right at T-intersection with graded road; then track on left.
7.7 ▲ TL Track on right; then graded road continues straight ahead.

GPS: N40°26.05′ W121°12.54′

▼ 1.9 SO Track on left.
7.3 ▲ SO Track on right.

▼ 2.3 SO Track on left.
6.9 ▲ SO Track on right.

▼ 2.5 SO Track on left.
6.7 ▲ SO Track on right.

▼ 2.9 SO Track on left.
6.3 ▲ SO Track on right.

▼ 3.4 SO Track on left.
5.8 ▲ SO Track on right.

GPS: N40°25.55′ W121°14.01′

▼ 4.2 SO Track on right.
5.0 ▲ SO Track on left.

▼ 4.4 SO Track on left.
4.8 ▲ SO Track on right.

▼ 5.3 SO Track on left and track on right.
3.9 ▲ SO Track on left and track on right.

▼ 6.8 BL Track on right.
2.4 ▲ BR Track on left.

▼ 6.9 SO Track on right; then track on left.
2.3 ▲ SO Track on right; then track on left.

▼ 7.9	SO	Well-used graded road on left.
1.3 ▲	SO	Well-used graded road on right.
		GPS: N40°23.44' W121°12.31'
▼ 8.0	SO	Cross over Mud Creek; then track on left.
1.2 ▲	SO	Track on right; then cross over Mud Creek.
		GPS: N40°23.57' W121°12.22'
▼ 8.6	SO	Well-used track on right.
0.6 ▲	BR	Well-used track on left.
▼ 8.9	SO	Track on left.
0.3 ▲	SO	Track on right.
▼ 9.2	TR	4-way intersection. Track straight ahead is the continuation of 30N72 to California 36. Zero trip meter.
0.0 ▲		Continue to the northwest.
		GPS: N40°22.67' W121°11.34'
▼ 0.0		Continue to the south.
4.7 ▲	TL	4-way intersection. Track on right and left is 30N72. To the right goes to California 36. Zero trip meter and follow the sign to Mud Creek Rim.
▼ 0.3	SO	Track on right.
4.4 ▲	SO	Track on left.
▼ 0.7	SO	Cross over Mud Creek.
4.0 ▲	SO	Cross over Mud Creek.
		GPS: N40°22.67' W121°12.06'
▼ 0.8	SO	Track on right.
3.9 ▲	BR	Track on left.
▼ 0.9	SO	Track on right.
3.8 ▲	SO	Track on left.
▼ 1.6	SO	Track on right.
3.1 ▲	SO	Track on left.
▼ 1.7	SO	Track on right.
3.0 ▲	SO	Track on left.
▼ 1.8	SO	Track on right.
2.9 ▲	SO	Track on left.
▼ 1.9	SO	Track on left and corral on left.
2.8 ▲	SO	Track on right and corral on right.
▼ 2.2	TR	Graded road on left.
2.5 ▲	TL	Road swings right. Turn left onto graded road.
		GPS: N40°21.42' W121°11.99'
▼ 2.6	SO	Track on right.
2.1 ▲	SO	Track on left.
▼ 3.5	SO	Track on left and track on right.
1.2 ▲	SO	Track on left and track on right.
▼ 3.6	SO	Track on right.
1.1 ▲	SO	Track on left.
▼ 4.6	SO	Track on right.
0.1 ▲	SO	Track on left.
▼ 4.7	TR	4-way intersection. Track on left on left-hand bend is 90L; also road continues straight ahead. Zero trip meter
0.0 ▲		Continue to the east.
		GPS: N40°21.81' W121°13.82'
▼ 0.0		Continue to the northwest up hill on trail marked with logging marker 140K.
5.1 ▲	TL	4-way intersection. Track straight ahead is 90L. Zero trip meter.
▼ 0.2	SO	Track on right.
4.9 ▲	SO	Track on left.
▼ 0.8	BR	Track on left.
4.3 ▲	SO	Track on right.
▼ 1.7	TL	T-intersection. Turn left onto 29N36Y and cross over Last Chance Creek.
3.4 ▲	TR	Cross over Last Chance Creek; then track continues straight ahead.

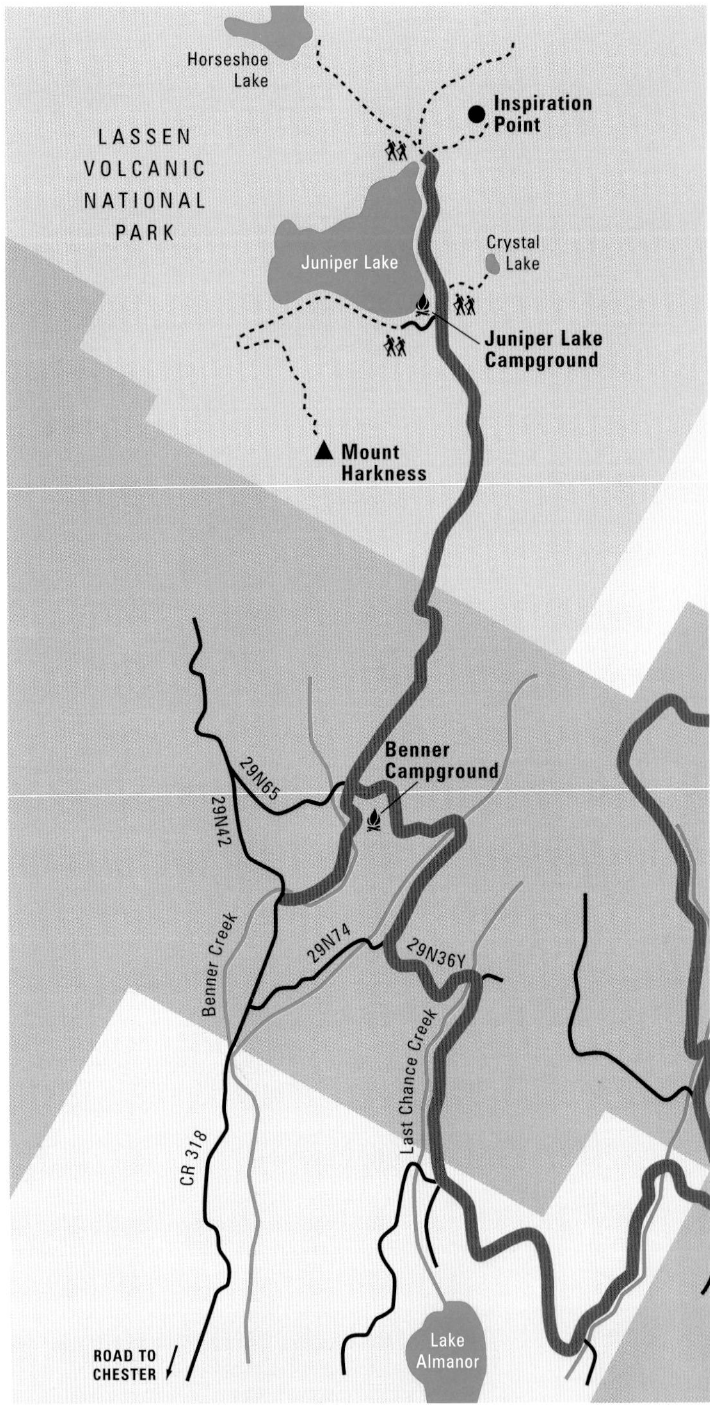

		GPS: N40°23.19' W121°14.37'
▼ 2.8	TR	T-intersection with 29N74. To the left joins Juniper Lake Road in 1 mile. Turn right, also signed to Juniper Lake Road.
2.3 ▲	TL	Road continues ahead to rejoin Juniper Lake Road. Turn left onto unmarked road at the signpost for Juniper Lake Road.
		GPS: N40°23.15' W121°15.29'
▼ 3.8	SO	Cross over a tributary of Benner Creek; then track on right.
1.3 ▲	SO	Track on left; then cross over a tributary of Benner Creek.
▼ 3.9	BL	Two tracks on right.

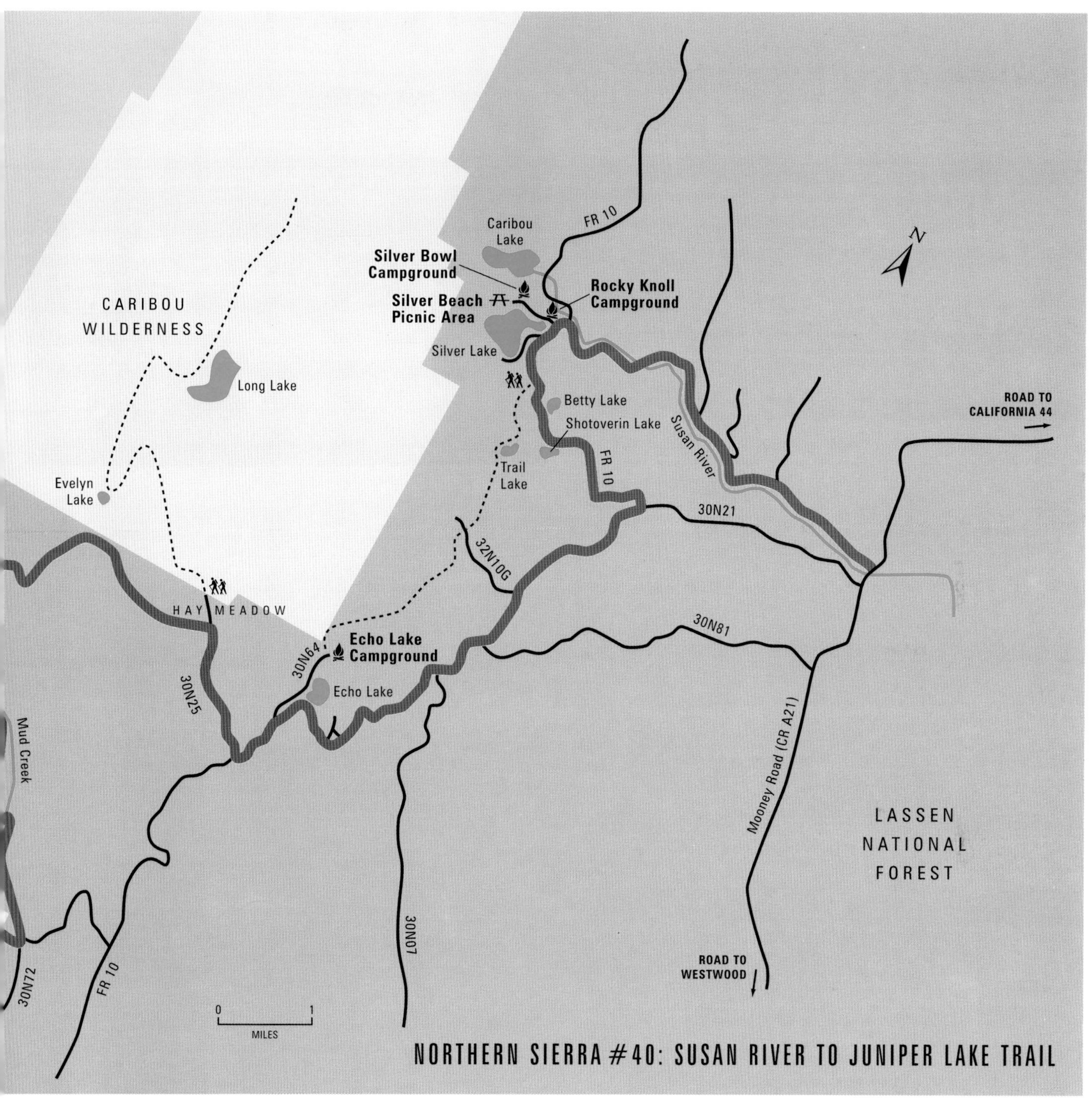

1.2 ▲	BR	Two tracks on left.
▼ 4.8	SO	Track on left.
0.3 ▲	SO	Track on right.
▼ 5.1	TL	4-way intersection. Juniper Lake Road is to the left and right. Straight ahead is 29N65. Zero trip meter. Spur to Juniper Lake is to the right.
0.0 ▲		Continue to the northeast on graded road.
		GPS: N40°23.91′ W121°16.27′

Spur to Juniper Lake

▼ 0.0		Turn northwest on graded Juniper Lake Road.
▼ 0.2	SO	Track on left.
▼ 0.5	SO	Track on left.
▼ 1.9	SO	Cattle guard. Entering Lassen Volcanic National Park—no firearms or hunting camps permitted in the park.
		GPS: N40°25.41′ W121°16.54′
▼ 4.2	SO	Park fee station; then track on left goes 0.4 miles to Juniper Lake Campground and Mount Harkness Hiking Trail. Follow sign to Snag Lake and Horseshoe Lake.
		GPS: N40°27.07′ W121°17.57′
▼ 4.5	SO	Hiking trail on right goes 0.4 miles to Crystal Lake.
		GPS: N40°27.27′ W121°17.72′
▼ 5.6	SO	Hiking trail on right goes 0.6 miles to

Inspiration Point; then trail ends at picnic area on the shore of Juniper Lake. Other hiking trails go to Cameron Meadows (1.6 miles), Snag Lake (2.9 miles), Cinder Cone (7.6 miles), Horseshoe Lake (1.4 miles), Lower Twin Lake (5.3 miles), Summit Lake (9 miles), and Warner Valley (9.1 miles). Private cabins are immediately past the end of the road.

GPS: N40°28.00' W121°18.47'

Continuation of Main Trail

▼ 0.0			Continue to the southeast on graveled Juniper Lake Road.
	1.3 ▲	TR	4-way intersection. Juniper Lake Road continues straight ahead and is the spur to Juniper Lake. Track on left is 29N65. Zero trip meter.
			GPS: N40°23.91' W121°16.27'
▼ 0.3		SO	Benner USFS Campground on left.
	1.0 ▲	SO	Benner USFS Campground on right.
			GPS: N40°23.71' W121°16.06'
▼ 0.4		SO	Cross over Benner Creek.
	0.9 ▲	SO	Cross over Benner Creek.
▼ 0.8		SO	Track on left.
	0.5 ▲	SO	Track on right.
▼ 1.3			Trail ends at intersection with graded road 29N42 on right. Bear left on paved road CR 318 to exit to Chester.
	0.0 ▲		Trail commences on CR 318, 6.2 miles north of Chester. To reach the start of the trail from California 36, zero trip meter at the northeastern edge of Chester and turn northwest on Feather River Drive. Proceed 0.7 miles and turn right onto Chester–Juniper Lake Road (CR 318), following the sign for Juniper Lake. Proceed 5.5 miles on the paved road to the start of the trail. At the intersection with graded dirt 29N42 on the left, zero trip meter and bear right (northeast) onto graded dirt 28N42, following the sign for Juniper Lake.
			GPS: N40°23.03' W121°16.35'

NORTHERN SIERRA #41

Humboldt Trail

Starting Point:	**California 89, 4 miles south of the intersection with California 36**
Finishing Point:	**CR 91422 at Jonesville Snowmobile Park, 4.2 miles east of Butte Meadows**
Total Mileage:	**20.4 miles**
Unpaved Mileage:	**19.1 miles**
Driving Time:	**2 hours**
Elevation Range:	**4,600–6,600 feet**
Usually Open:	**May to November**
Best Time to Travel:	**May to November**
Difficulty Rating:	**2**
Scenic Rating:	**8**
Remoteness Rating:	**+0**

Meadows around Butt Creek

Special Attractions

- Historic route of the Humboldt Trail.
- Jonesville Snowmobile Park and a network of groomed snowmobile trails in winter.
- Humboldt Peak and Robbers Roost.

History

The Humboldt Trail travels a section of a longer trail known as the Chico and Humboldt Wagon Road. This route was developed in the early 1860s as a mine supply route that began in Chico and headed northeast across the Sierra Nevada. John Bidwell (see page 82) and associated businessmen vied with others for the contract to build this valuable passage from the Sacramento Valley. Their route was established with the help of the Maidu, a people who knew the footpaths across the Sierra Nevada. The road joined the Nobles Trail in Susanville and was intended for prospectors and supply wagons heading to the diggings of what were the territories of Utah and Washington, today's Nevada and Idaho.

Stage drivers stopped off at the Ruffa Ranch, beside Butt Creek and below Eagle Rocks on the eastern approach to Humboldt Summit, where they could refresh their horses or change teams before making the rough climb to the 6,610-foot summit, more than a thousand feet higher. The basic wagon road was described as having many small summits before the main one. The tiring, dusty route had several switchbacks on either side of the summit and caused a number of high-centers. This was more a reflection of the typical road conditions of the day as opposed to a complaint.

The winding climb passed Robbers Roost near the summit, which was the scene of several stagecoach robberies. Once past the Roost, drivers could breathe a sigh of relief and begin the slow twisting route down the western side of the mountain. Starting in 1866, this road was used as a mail route between Chico and Boise City, Idaho Territory. It also opened new regions for development. Logging increased greatly and settlers took up land in the Jonesville and Butte Meadows areas in the late 1860s and '70s. Large wagons pulled by six or eight oxen hauled lumber to the newly built Woodsum Brothers sawmill below Lomo, north of present-day Yuba City. Come springtime, cattlemen found this a good road on which to drive their herds into the mountain meadows.

Jonesville Stage Stop, beside Jones Creek, grew large enough to support a fine two-story hotel, a welcome sight to weary travelers. People wishing to escape the Central Valley's summer heat also came to cabins and resorts along this mountain road. The historic Jonesville Hotel still stands near the end of the described trail, though it does not operate as a hotel anymore.

Description

Humboldt Trail leaves California 89 on the western shore of Lake Almanor opposite the start of the Lake Almanor Recreation Trail, a 9.7-mile loop for hikers, mountain bikers, and cross-country skiers. The paved loop follows an easy grade and is barrier free. Lake Almanor is a great spot for trout fishing and wildlife viewing for black-tail deer, ospreys, eagles, and waterfowl.

Humboldt Trail is graded dirt all the way, but there are some spots, particularly on the west side of Humboldt Peak, that make it better suited for high-clearance 2WDs. Initially, the trail travels through private forest owned by the Pacific Gas & Electric Company. No camping or fires are allowed along this section. The trail then enters Lassen National Forest at a meadow on Butt Creek, a pretty place with a zigzag pole fence bisecting the meadow.

Ruffa Ranch buildings

The trail continues through the forest and passes two parts of the privately owned Ruffa Ranch. The ranch has some old buildings still standing and a collapsed log cabin. In fall, groves of mature aspens provide splashes of gold against a backdrop of the Eagle Peaks to the south and Butt Mountain to the north. The trail climbs to Humboldt Summit, below Humboldt Peak, passing the rocky outcrops of Robbers Roost along the way. A short section of shelf road is only wide enough for a single vehicle. The Pacific Crest National Scenic Trail crosses the summit, traveling 1.5 miles south up a moderately steep grade to Humboldt Peak (7,087 feet), before continuing to the southeast. There is trailhead parking at the summit.

Crossing into Tehama County, the trail descends a wide road toward Jonesville. Those wanting a longer drive can loop back to Lake Almanor along the Humbug Summit Road, another historic route that will return you via a selection of forest roads. The main trail ends at the Jonesville Snowmobile Park, a staging area for a network of groomed winter trails. A gate at the snowmobile park closes the road to vehicles from January 1 to March 15.

Current Road Information

Lassen National Forest
Almanor Ranger District
PO Box 767
Chester, CA 96020
(530) 258-2141

Map References

BLM Lake Almanor
USFS Lassen National Forest
USGS 1:24,000 Almanor, Humbug Valley, Humboldt Peak, Jonesville
1:100,000 Lake Almanor
Maptech CD-ROM: Shasta Lake/Redding
Northern California Atlas & Gazetteer, pp. 58, 59
California Road & Recreation Atlas, pp. 60, 59

Route Directions

▼ 0.0		From California 89, 4 miles south of the intersection with California 36 at Chester, zero trip meter and turn southwest at the sign for Humboldt Trail and Humbug Trail. Road opposite goes 0.1 miles to one of the Lake Almanor Recreation Trailheads and 0.3 miles to an archery area in the national forest. Immediately track on right and track on left are both 400A. Trail initially passes through PG&E-owned forest
4.8 ▲		Track on right and track on left are both 400A; then trail ends at T-intersection with the scenic byway California 89. Turn left for Chester; turn right for Quincy. Road opposite goes 0.1 miles to one of the Lake Almanor Recreation Trailheads and 0.3 miles to an archery area.
		GPS: N40°13.64' W121°12.45'
▼ 0.4	SO	Track on right is 461 and track on left.
4.4 ▲	SO	Track on left is 461 and track on right.
▼ 0.6	BR	Graded road on left is Humbug Trail.
4.2 ▲	BL	Graded road on right is Humbug Trail.
		GPS: N40°13.13' W121°12.48'
▼ 0.9	SO	Track on left and track on right.
3.9 ▲	SO	Track on left and track on right.
▼ 1.0	SO	Track on left is 460 and track on right.
3.8 ▲	SO	Track on right is 460 and track on left.
▼ 1.5	SO	Track on right and track on left are both 450.
3.3 ▲	SO	Track on right and track on left are both 450.
▼ 1.8	SO	Track on left and track on right.
3.0 ▲	SO	Track on left and track on right.
▼ 1.9	SO	Track on left is 600 and track on right.
2.9 ▲	SO	Track on right is 600 and track on left.
▼ 2.2	SO	Track on right.
2.6 ▲	SO	Track on left.
▼ 2.5	SO	Track on right.
2.3 ▲	SO	Track on left.
▼ 2.6	SO	Track on right is 145 and track on left.
2.2 ▲	SO	Track on left is 145 and track on right.
		GPS: N40°12.60' W121°14.49'

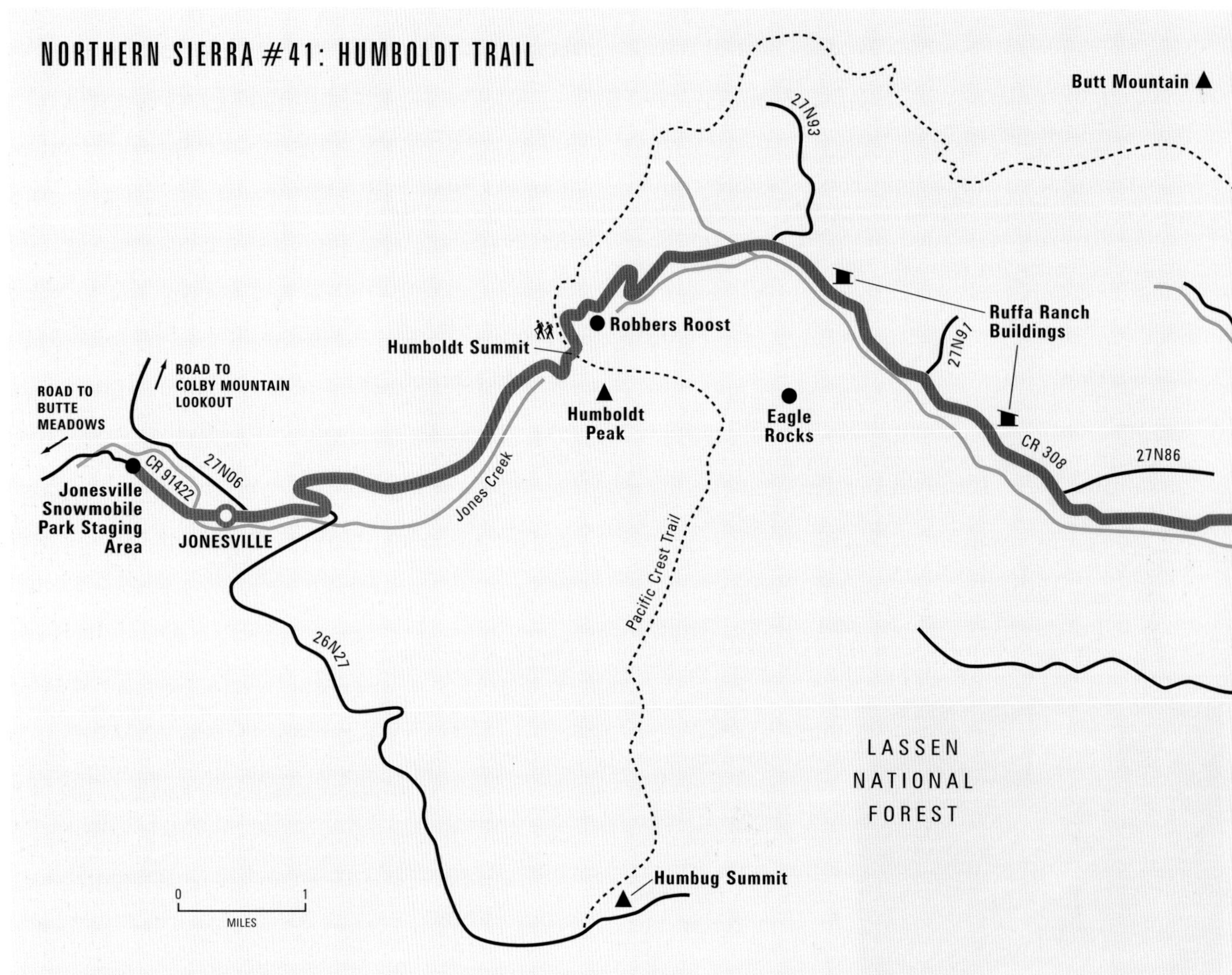

▼ 3.2 SO Track on left and track on right are both 660.
1.6 ▲ SO Track on left and track on right are both 660.

▼ 3.6 SO Track on left and track on right are both 600.
1.2 ▲ SO Track on left and track on right are both 600.

▼ 3.9 SO Track on left is 652 and track on right.
0.9 ▲ SO Track on right is 652 and track on left.

▼ 4.0 SO Track on right goes to Soldier Meadows USFS Campground and track on left.
0.8 ▲ SO Track on left goes to Soldier Meadows USFS Campground and track on right.

GPS: N40°12.13′ W121°15.68′

▼ 4.3 SO Track on right is 654.
0.5 ▲ SO Track on left is 654.

▼ 4.8 SO Cross over Soldier Creek on bridge; then 4-way intersection. Graded road on left is 27N65 to Humbug Valley and Yellow Creek. Graded road on right is 28N36. Zero trip meter and follow sign for Humboldt Summit. Entering Lassen National Forest.
0.0 ▲ Continue to the east on CR 308 and cross over Soldier Creek on bridge.

GPS: N40°12.05′ W121°16.50′

▼ 0.0 Continue to the west on CR 308.
5.6 ▲ SO 4-way intersection. Graded road on right is 27N65 to Humbug Valley and Yellow Creek. Graded road on left is 28N36. Zero trip meter and follow sign to California 89 and Chester.

▼ 0.4 SO Two tracks on left; then track on right is 27N15.
5.2 ▲ SO Track on left is 27N15; then two tracks on right.

▼ 1.5 SO Track on left.
4.1 ▲ SO Track on right.

▼ 2.1 SO Cattle guard.
3.5 ▲ SO Cattle guard.

▼ 2.3 SO Track on right.
3.3 ▲ SO Track on left.

▼ 2.5 BL Track on right is Shanghai Road (27N16); then track on left.
3.1 ▲ SO Track on right; then track on left is Shanghai Road (27N16).

GPS: N40°11.45′ W121°19.14′

▼ 2.8 BR Graded road on left to corrals.
2.8 ▲ SO Graded road on right to corrals.

▼ 3.0 SO Cross over creek; then tank on left and track on right.
2.6 ▲ SO Track on left and tank on right; then cross over creek.

GPS: N40°11.39′ W121°19.77′

▼ 3.1 SO Cross over Shanghai Creek.
2.5 ▲ SO Cross over Shanghai Creek.

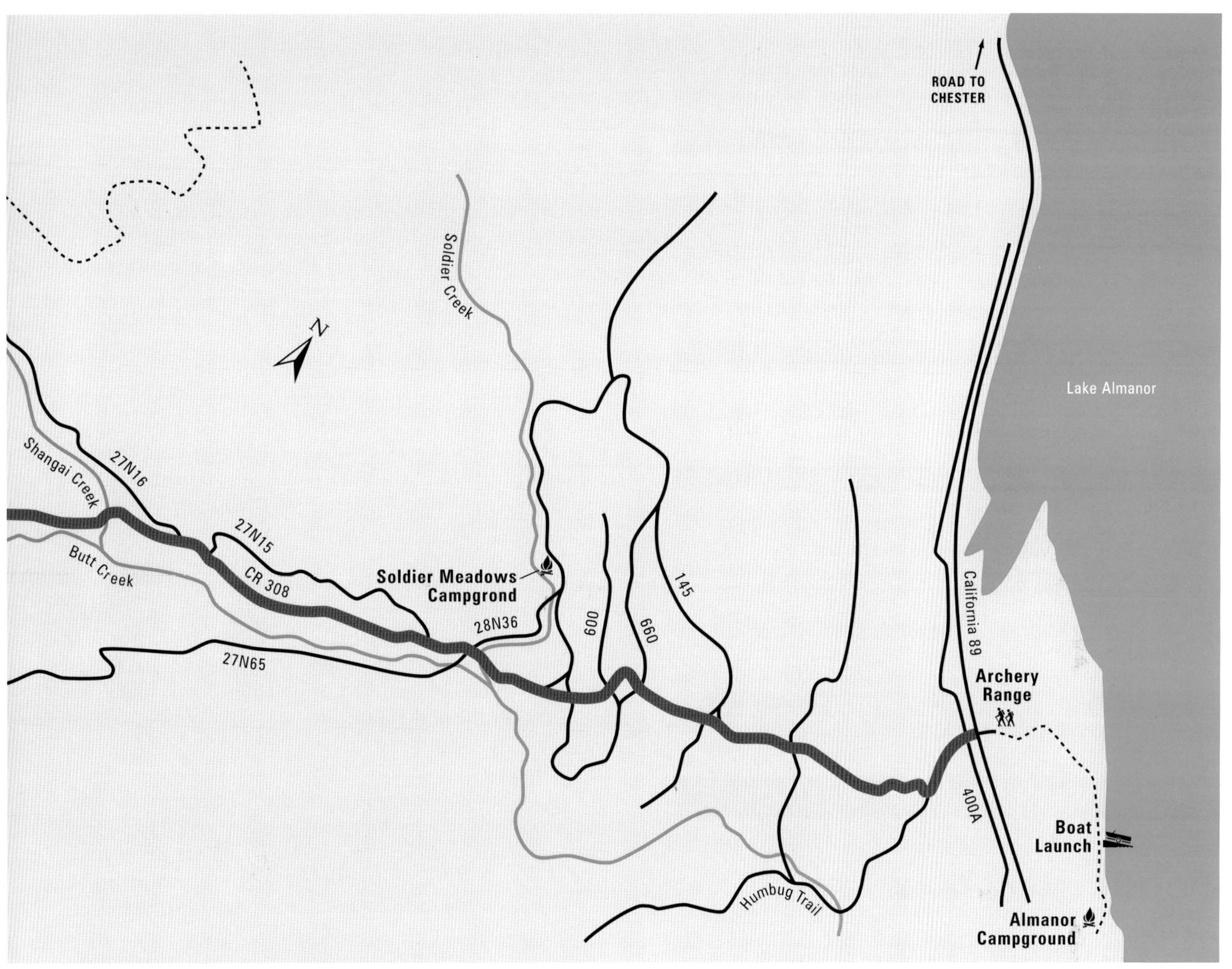

			GPS: N40°11.31' W121°19.88'
▼ 4.7		SO	Track on right.
	0.9 ▲	SO	Track on left.
▼ 5.6		SO	Graded road on right is 27N86. Zero trip meter.
	0.0 ▲		Continue to the southeast.
			GPS: N40°10.31' W121°22.06'
▼ 0.0			Continue to the northwest.
	5.4 ▲	SO	Graded road on left is 27N86. Zero trip meter.
▼ 0.3		SO	Track on right.
	5.1 ▲	SO	Track on left.
▼ 0.7		SO	Ruffa Ranch buildings on right.
	4.7 ▲	SO	Second group of Ruffa Ranch buildings on left.
			GPS: N40°10.37' W121°22.82'
▼ 1.3		SO	Track on right is 27N91.
	4.1 ▲	SO	Track on left is 27N91.
▼ 2.3		SO	Second section of Ruffa Ranch. Butt Mountain is on the right and Eagle Rocks are on the left.
	3.1 ▲	SO	Ruffa Ranch. Butt Mountain is on the left and Eagle Rocks are on the right.
			GPS: N40°10.49' W121°24.55'
▼ 2.4		SO	Cabins on left and right and collapsed log cabin on right—part of the Ruffa Ranch.
	3.0 ▲	SO	Cabins on left and right and collapsed log cabin on left—part of the Ruffa Ranch.
▼ 2.6		SO	Cross over a tributary of Butt Creek.
	2.8 ▲	SO	Cross over a tributary of Butt Creek.
▼ 3.0		SO	Graded road on right is 27N93.
	2.4 ▲	SO	Graded road on left is 27N93.
▼ 3.1		SO	Cross over creek.
	2.3 ▲	SO	Cross over creek.
▼ 3.2		SO	Track on left.
	2.2 ▲	SO	Track on right.
▼ 4.1		BR	Track on left.
	1.3 ▲	BL	Track on right.
▼ 4.9		SO	Start of shelf road to Humboldt Summit.
	0.5 ▲	SO	End of shelf road.
▼ 5.4		SO	Entering Tehama County at Humboldt Summit; then Pacific Crest Trail crosses. To the left it climbs toward Humboldt Peak and continues to Cold Spring. Parking area on right. Zero trip meter at summit. End of shelf road.
	0.0 ▲		Continue to the north on CR 308.
			GPS: N40°09.13' W121°26.11'
▼ 0.0			Continue to the southeast on CR 91422.
	3.2 ▲	SO	Pacific Crest Trail crosses. To the right it climbs toward Humboldt Peak and continues to Cold Spring. Parking area on left; then entering

			Plumas County at Humboldt Summit. Zero trip meter. Start of shelf road.
▼ 3.2		SO	Track on left is 26N27 to Humbug Summit and CR 307. Zero trip meter. Road becomes paved.
	0.0 ▲		Continue to the north.
			GPS: N40°07.20' W121°27.30'
▼ 0.0			Continue to the southwest.
	1.4 ▲	BL	Track on right is 26N27 to Humbug Summit and CR 307. Zero trip meter and follow sign to Humboldt Summit.
▼ 0.4		SO	Graded road on right is 27N06 to Colby Mountain Lookout. This is Jonesville—private property.
	1.0 ▲	SO	Graded road on left is 27N06 to Colby Mountain Lookout. This is Jonesville —private property.
			GPS: N40°06.95' W121°27.62'
▼ 0.5		SO	Leaving Lassen National Forest.
	0.9 ▲	SO	Entering Lassen National Forest.
▼ 0.8		SO	Cross over Jones Creek.
	0.6 ▲	SO	Cross over Jones Creek.
			GPS: N40°06.75' W121°28.05'
▼ 1.4			Trail ends at Jonesville Snowmobile Park Staging Area. This is the road closure point in winter. Continue straight ahead for Butte Meadows.
	0.0 ▲		Trail commences at the Jonesville Snowmobile Park Staging Area, 4.2 miles east of Butte Meadows along CR 91422. This is the road closure point in winter. Zero trip meter at the seasonal closure gate and proceed east along paved CR 91422.
			GS: N40°06.81' W121°28.66'

NORTHERN SIERRA #42

Ponderosa Way

Starting Point:	**California 36, 9 miles west of Mineral**
Finishing Point:	**Cohasset Road in Cohasset, 16 miles north of Chico**
Total Mileage:	**59 miles, plus 2.4-mile spur to McCarthy Point Lookout**
Unpaved Mileage:	**57 miles, plus 2.4-mile spur**
Driving Time:	**7 hours**
Elevation Range:	**1,800–4,300 feet**
Usually Open:	**May to November**
Best Time to Travel:	**Dry weather**
Difficulty Rating:	**3**
Scenic Rating:	**10**
Remoteness Rating:	**+1**

Special Attractions

- Long trail along part of historic firebreak put in by the Civilian Conservation Corps.
- Dizzying ascents and descents into the deep canyons of Antelope Creek, Mill Creek, and Deer Creek.
- Lookout tower at McCarthy Point can be rented for overnight stays.

History

The official Ponderosa Way Firebreak and Truck Trail was developed during World War II in response to the threat of Japanese incendiary bombs. This ambitious trail promoted by Stuart B. Show was designed to stretch some 700 miles along the west side of the Sierra Nevada, from the Kern River in the south to the Pit River at the northern end of the range. The intention was to cut a wide path between the lower level oak vegetation and the mixed conifer forests of the higher elevations. This would safeguard the forests from fires that might rage up the mountainsides from the Central Valley.

Although the firebreak and trail were never completed, the Civilian Conservation Corps (CCC) did install several hundred miles of the intended route. A total of 24 CCC camps were involved in the enormous project. Thousands of hours of labor were required to clear steep slopes and move massive amounts of soil and rock by blasting and digging. The CCC also constructed the McCarthy Point Fire Lookout in 1936, reached by a spur from Ponderosa Way. With the outbreak of World War II, fire spotters were given the added duty of looking for enemy aircraft. This precaution was part of the Aircraft Warning Service (AWS), which had observation points that stretched the length of the West Coast. See North Coast #15: Redwood National Park Coastal Drive (page 533) for a more elaborate enemy detection station that was also a vital part of the early warning system. McCarthy Point Fire Lookout was manned until the mid 1960s.

Description

Nowadays, it is impossible to travel the full length of the Ponderosa Way, but this one long section offers a good glimpse of the hand-built road. The trail leaves California 36, 9 miles west of the hamlet of Mineral, which sits on the edge of Battle Creek Meadows, a volcanic caldera formed by the collapse of Mount Maidu.

The trail passes through private subdivisions before descending steeply to cross Paynes Creek. It passes the eastern end of Northern Sierra #43: Hogsback Road, which descends west to Red Bluff. Ponderosa Way continues through the forest and passes undeveloped camping areas before starting to descend into Antelope Canyon, the first of the major east-west running canyons. The volcanic plug of Black Butte is immediately south of the trail at the start of the descent.

Rock shapes along Ponderosa Way

The undeveloped South Antelope Campground, along Antelope Creek, has a few sites in a shady gully beside the creek. Farther south, Northern Sierra #44: Peligreen-Grapevine

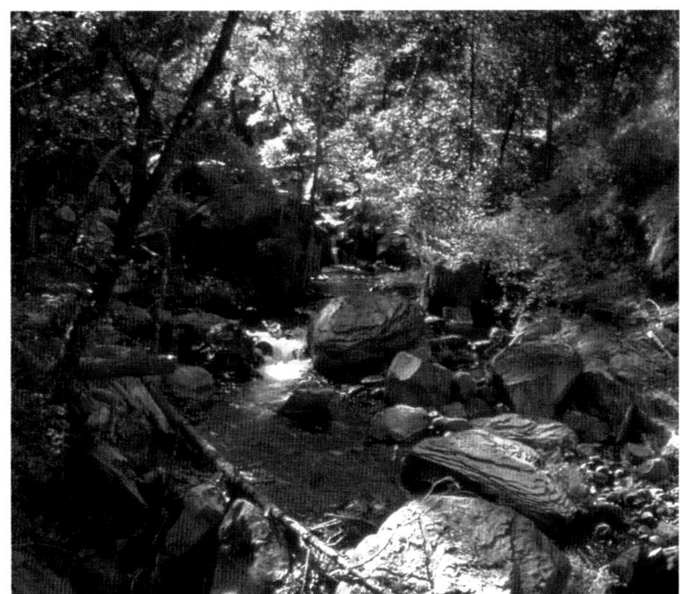
The South Fork of Antelope Creek

Jeepway leads off to the west. The main trail continues through Lassen National Forest and privately owned forest maintained by PG&E for timber harvesting. The slow descent along a winding, narrow shelf road follows Mill Creek Rim down to Mill Creek. This is one of the most scenic sections of the drive.

Black Rock, an unusual basalt plug several hundred feet tall, is in Mill Creek; it diverts water around it to form a waterfall and a swimming hole at the bottom. A developed forest service campground at Black Rock has several sites beside Mill Creek among oaks, camphor laurels, and walnut trees.

Past Mill Creek, the trail climbs steeply out of the canyon to a spur that leads 2.4 miles to McCarthy Point Fire Lookout. At The Narrows, the trail drops steeply on either side into separate drainages. This point was well known to early travelers on the Lassen Trail; a historical marker at the spot records some of their thoughts. The lookout is perched at 3,600 feet on the very edge of Mill Creek Canyon's southern rim. It was once used to spot fires in the Mill Creek drainage. In 1994, forest service workers and volunteers restored the lookout. It has a two-room cabin that can sleep eight, a kitchen, and a bathroom. For a small fee, it can be rented for a two-night minimum stay. Contact the Almanor Ranger District for information and reservations. A short walk along a paved trail takes you to the lookout. If the lookout is occupied, please be considerate and leave the occupants alone.

Much of this section of the Ponderosa Way skirts the eastern edge of the Ishi Wilderness. Several hiking trails start along Ponderosa Way and go into the wilderness. One of the most popular is the Deer Creek Trail, a moderate 7-mile hike that offers spectacular views of Deer Creek Canyon and the region's basalt cliffs and spires. Other trails, such as Devils Den, are better suited for more experienced hikers because of steep grades and difficult navigation. Devils Den Trail parallels Deer Creek for 4.5 miles before climbing up to the ridge top. The Moak Trail is an easy 7-mile hike that is excellent for springtime wildflower viewing, but it has little shade and is often uncomfortably hot in summer. Navigation is difficult along this trail because sections of it are poorly defined.

South of the turnoff to McCarthy Point, much of Ponderosa Way passes through PG&E owned forests. Many logging trails branch off to the left and the right. The Lassen Trail follows the main route for a short section and passes the site of Bruff Camp, a stopping point for early emigrants.

The final deep east-west canyon is the one cut by Deer Creek; like the others, it is a fast flowing creek in a rugged canyon. The final section of the trail travels through more privately owned forest, passing the site of the Campbell Fire Lookout, to join gravel Cohasset Road. It ends 16 miles north of Chico in the small settlement of Cohasset.

Current Road Information

Bureau of Land Management
Redding Field Office
355 Hemsted Drive
Redding, CA 96002
(530) 224-2100

Lassen National Forest
Almanor Ranger District
PO Box 767
Chester, CA 96020
(530) 258-2141

Map References

BLM Lake Almanor, Chico
USFS Lassen National Forest
USGS 1:24,000 Finley Butte, Panther Spring, Barkley Mt., Devils Parade Ground, Cohasset
1:100,000 Lake Almanor, Chico
Maptech CD-ROM: Shasta Lake/Redding; High Sierra/Tahoe
Northern California Atlas & Gazetteer, pp. 57, 58, 68
California Road & Recreation Atlas, pp. 53, 59
Other: A Guide to the Ishi, Thousand Lakes, & Caribou Wilderness

Route Directions

▼ 0.0			From California 36, 9 miles west of Mineral, zero trip meter and turn south on paved CR 707A at the sign for Ponderosa Way. Canyon View Road is opposite the turn. Cross cattle guard and immediately track on left.
	8.2 ▲	BL	Track on right; then cattle guard. Trail ends at intersection with California 36. Turn right for Mineral; turn left for Red Bluff.
			GPS: N40°20.82' W121°45.77'
▼ 0.1		BL	Road on right.
	8.1 ▲	BR	Road on left.
▼ 0.2		SO	Track on left. Remain on paved road, passing through private property.
	8.0 ▲	SO	Track on right.
▼ 1.0		BL	Navion Road on right.
	7.2 ▲	BR	Navion Road on left.
▼ 1.1		SO	Road turns to graded dirt.
	7.1 ▲	SO	Road becomes paved.
▼ 1.7		SO	Cross through Paynes Creek; then track on left.

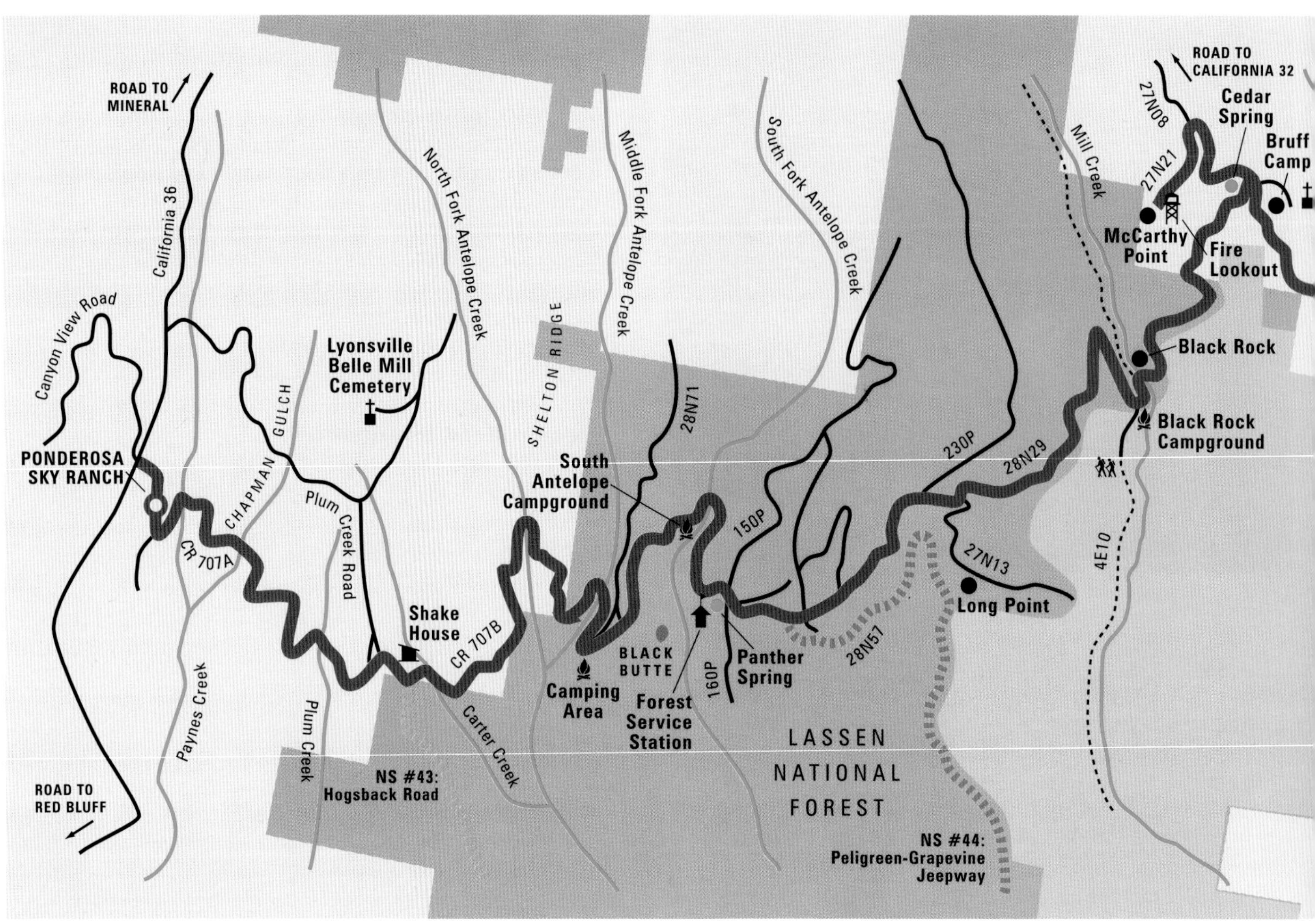

	6.5 ▲	SO	Track on right; then cross through Paynes Creek.
			GPS: N40°20.35' W121°46.09'
▼ 1.9		BL	Track on right.
	6.3 ▲	SO	Track on left.
▼ 2.3		SO	Cross over creek.
	5.9 ▲	SO	Cross over creek.
▼ 2.9		SO	Track on left.
	5.3 ▲	SO	Track on right.
▼ 3.6		SO	Cross through Chapman Gulch.
	4.6 ▲	SO	Cross through Chapman Gulch.
			GPS: N40°19.65' W121°46.53'
▼ 4.4		SO	Track on right.
	3.8 ▲	SO	Track on left.
▼ 4.6		SO	Track on right.
	3.6 ▲	SO	Track on left.
▼ 4.8		SO	Two tracks on left.
	3.4 ▲	SO	Two tracks on right.
▼ 5.5		SO	Track on right.
	2.7 ▲	SO	Track on left.
▼ 6.2		SO	Cross over Plum Creek.
	2.0 ▲	SO	Cross over Plum Creek.
▼ 7.7		BR	Track on left.
	0.5 ▲	BL	Track on right.
▼ 7.8		BR	Bear right and join paved Plum Creek Road.
	0.4 ▲	BL	Bear left onto graded dirt Ponderosa Way.
			GPS: N40°18.10' W121°47.70'
▼ 8.2		TL	Shake House on left (private property). Paved road ahead is Northern Sierra #43: Hogsback Road. Zero trip meter and turn left onto paved CR 707B (28N29), following the sign for Black Rock.
	0.0 ▲		Continue to the northeast on Plum Creek Road. Shake House on right (private property).
			GPS: N40°17.87' W121°48.04'
▼ 0.0			Continue to the east. Immediately track on right.
	9.0 ▲	TR	Track on left; then T-intersection with paved Plum Creek Road. To the left is Northern Sierra #43: Hogsback Road. Zero trip meter.
▼ 0.1		SO	Road turns to graded dirt.
	8.9 ▲	SO	Road becomes paved.
▼ 0.5		SO	Cross over Carter Creek on bridge.
	8.5 ▲	SO	Cross over Carter Creek on bridge.
▼ 0.9		SO	Track on right; then track on left.
	8.1 ▲	SO	Track on right; then track on left.
▼ 1.0		SO	Track on left.
	8.0 ▲	SO	Track on right.
▼ 1.2		SO	Track on left.
	7.8 ▲	SO	Track on right.
▼ 1.8		SO	Track on left.
	7.2 ▲	SO	Track on right.
▼ 2.9		BR	Track on left.
	6.1 ▲	BL	Track on right.
▼ 3.1		BL	Track on right.
	5.9 ▲	BR	Track on left.
▼ 3.6		SO	Cross through North Fork Antelope Creek.

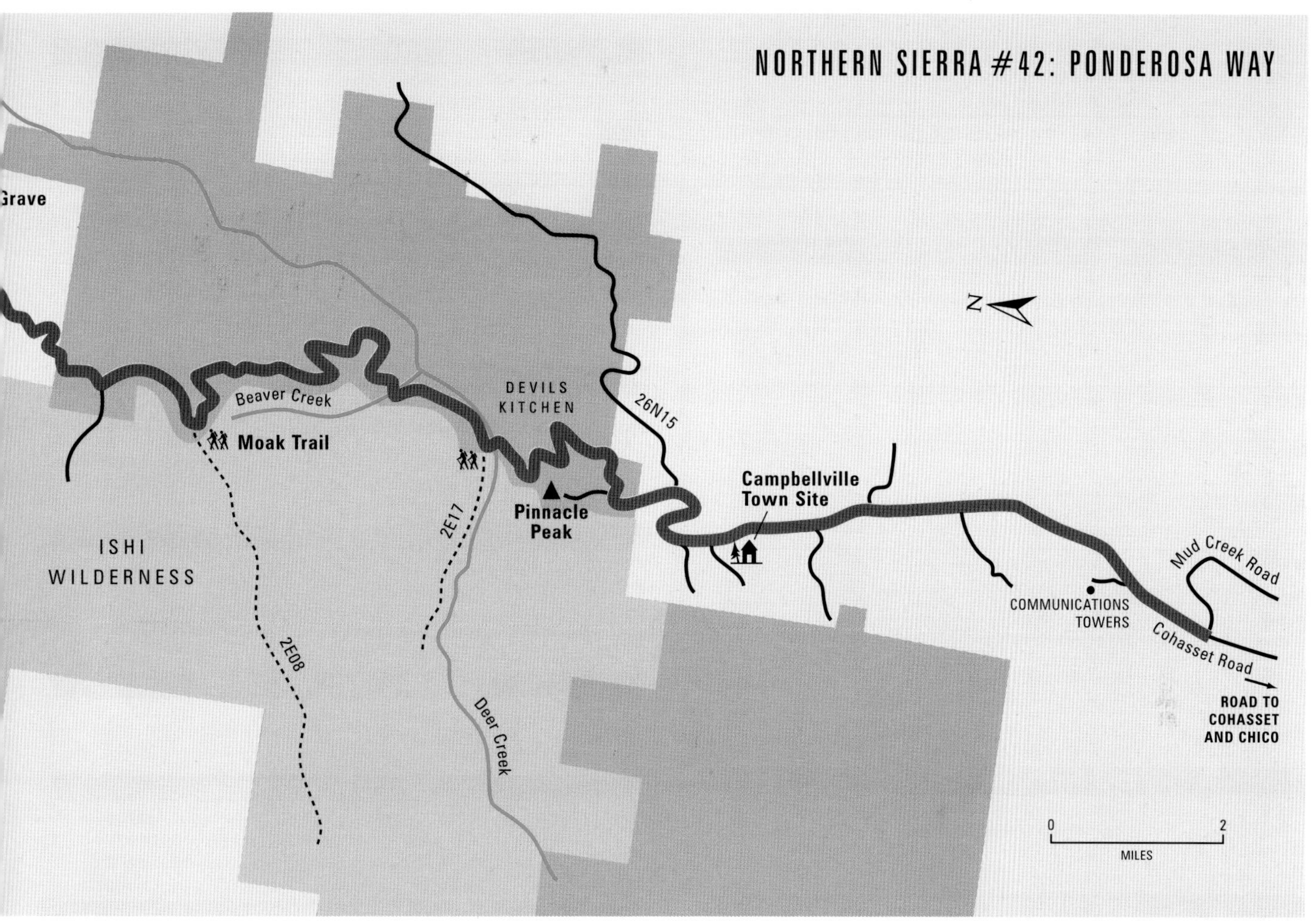

5.4 ▲	SO	Cross through North Fork Antelope Creek.
		GPS: N40°16.86′ W121°45.81′
▼ 4.1	SO	Track on right along Shelton Ridge; then track on left.
4.9 ▲	SO	Track on right; then track on left along Shelton Ridge.
▼ 4.3	SO	Track on left.
4.7 ▲	SO	Track on right.
▼ 4.9	SO	Track on left.
4.1 ▲	SO	Track on right.
▼ 5.2	SO	Track on left.
3.8 ▲	SO	Track on right.
▼ 5.3	SO	Entering Lassen National Forest.
3.7 ▲	SO	Exiting Lassen National Forest.
		GPS: N40°16.34′ W121°46.92′
▼ 5.8	SO	Cross over Middle Fork Antelope Creek on bridge.
2.2 ▲	SO	Cross over Middle Fork Antelope Creek on bridge.
▼ 6.8	SO	Camping area on right (no sign) and track on left.
2.2 ▲	SO	Camping area on left (no sign) and track on right.
		GPS: N40°16.07′ W121°47.32′
▼ 6.9	SO	Track on right.
2.1 ▲	SO	Track on left.
▼ 7.2	SO	Graded road on left is Upper Middle Ridge Road (28N71).
1.8 ▲	SO	Graded road on right is Upper Middle Ridge Road (28N71).
		GPS: N40°15.79′ W121°46.93′
▼ 7.4	SO	Track on right.
1.6 ▲	SO	Track on left.
▼ 7.5	SO	Black Butte on right, high above South Fork Antelope Creek.
1.5 ▲	SO	Black Butte on left, high above South Fork Antelope Creek.
▼ 8.5	SO	Track on left.
0.5 ▲	SO	Track on right.
▼ 9.0	SO	Track on right into South Antelope USFS Campground. Zero trip meter.
0.0 ▲		Continue to the west.
		GPS: N40°15.25′ W121°45.42′
▼ 0.0		Continue to the southeast.
3.0 ▲	SO	Track on left into South Antelope USFS Campground. Zero trip meter.
▼ 0.1	SO	Cross over South Fork Antelope Creek on bridge.
2.9 ▲	SO	Cross over South Fork Antelope Creek on bridge.
▼ 1.7	SO	Panther Spring Forest Service Station on right.
1.3 ▲	SO	Panther Spring Forest Service Station on left.
		GPS: N40°14.90′ W121°46.26′
▼ 2.0	SO	Track on right.
1.0 ▲	SO	Track on left.
▼ 2.1	SO	Track on right is 160P; track on left is 150P; then second track on left is 28N29F.

	0.9 ▲	SO	Track on right is 28N29F; then track on left is 160P; second track on right is 150P.
▼ 2.2		SO	Two tracks on right.
	0.8 ▲	SO	Two tracks on left.
▼ 3.0		SO	Graded road on right is Northern Sierra #44: Peligreen-Grapevine Jeepway (28N57). Zero trip meter at the turn and follow the sign to Mill Creek.
	0.0 ▲		Continue to the northwest.
			GPS: N40°14.07' W121°46.50'
▼ 0.0			Continue to the southeast.
	2.8 ▲	SO	Graded road on left is Northern Sierra #44: Peligreen-Grapevine Jeepway (28N57). Zero trip meter at the turn and follow the sign to Panther Springs.
▼ 0.1		SO	Track on right.
	2.7 ▲	SO	Track on left.
▼ 0.2		SO	Track on left is 28N29G.
	2.6 ▲	SO	Track on right is 28N29G.
▼ 0.3		SO	Track on right.
	2.5 ▲	SO	Track on left.
▼ 0.9		SO	Track on left is N Line.
	1.9 ▲	SO	Track on right is N Line.
▼ 1.6		SO	Track on left.
	1.2 ▲	SO	Track on right.
▼ 1.8		SO	Track on right is 220P.
	1.0 ▲	SO	Track on left is 220P.
▼ 2.4		SO	Track on left is 230P.
	0.4 ▲	SO	Track on right is 230P.
			GPS: N40°12.94' W121°44.58'
▼ 2.8		SO	Track on right is 27N13, which goes 1 mile to Long Point. Zero trip meter and follow the sign to Black Rock.
	0.0 ▲		Continue to the northwest.
			GPS: N40°12.60' W121°44.58'
▼ 0.0			Continue to the east.
	4.7 ▲	SO	Track on left is 27N13, which goes 1 mile to Long Point. Zero trip meter and follow the sign to Panther Springs.
▼ 0.7		SO	Start of shelf road.
	4.0 ▲	SO	End of shelf road.
▼ 4.4		SO	Well-used track on right.
	0.3 ▲	BR	Well-used track on left.
			GPS: N40°11.07' W121°42.87'
▼ 4.5		SO	Cross over creek on bridge.
	0.2 ▲	SO	Cross over creek on bridge.
▼ 4.7		SO	Track on right goes into Black Rock USFS Campground and Mill Creek Trail (4E10), which travels up and down the creek. Zero trip meter.
	0.0 ▲		Continue to the west.
			GPS: N40°11.03' W121°42.65'
▼ 0.0			Continue to the east.
	4.9 ▲	BR	Track on left goes into Black Rock USFS Campground and Mill Creek Trail (4E10), which travels up and down the creek. Zero trip meter.
▼ 0.1		SO	Cross over Mill Creek on curved wooden bridge. Black Rock is on the left. Entering state game refuge.
	4.8 ▲	SO	Cross over Mill Creek on curved wooden bridge. Black Rock is on the right. Leaving state game refuge.
▼ 0.4		SO	Cross over creek on bridge.
	4.5 ▲	SO	Cross over creek on bridge.
▼ 0.5		SO	Mill Creek Trailhead on right.
	4.4 ▲	SO	Mill Creek Trailhead on left.
			GPS: N40°10.88' W121°42.77'
▼ 0.7		SO	Cross over creek on bridge.
	4.2 ▲	SO	Cross over creek on bridge.
▼ 2.5		SO	Cross over creek.
	2.4 ▲	SO	Cross over creek.
▼ 4.9		BR	End of shelf road. Cedar Spring on left. Graded road on left is 27N08, spur to McCarthy Point Fire Lookout. Zero trip meter and bear right, remaining on 28N29 and following the sign to Deer Creek. Join the Lassen Trail.
	0.0 ▲		Continue to the southwest. Entering Lassen National Forest. Cedar Spring on right. Start of shelf road.
			GPS: N40°10.21' W121°39.93'

Spur to McCarthy Point Fire Lookout

▼ 0.0		Turn north on 27N08, following the sign to The Narrows.
▼ 0.3	SO	The Narrows.
		GPS: N40°10.45' W121°39.95'
▼ 0.4	SO	Track on right.
▼ 0.7	SO	Track on right.
▼ 1.2	TL	Graded road continues straight ahead to California 32. Turn left onto 27N21, following marker for the lookout.
		GPS: N40°10.82' W121°39.38'
▼ 1.4	SO	Track on left.
▼ 1.8	SO	Track on right.
▼ 2.1	TL	Turn left onto 740L3.
		GPS: N40°10.98' W121°40.27'
▼ 2.4		Locked gate. To reach the lookout, walk past the gate for a short distance to the sheds and parking area; then turn right and follow the narrow paved trail for 0.1 miles to the lookout.
		GPS: N40°11.05' W121°40.43'

Continuation of Main Trail

▼ 0.0			Continue to the south. Entering PG&E forest.
	4.4 ▲	BL	Graded road on right is 27N08, spur to McCarthy Point Fire Lookout. Zero trip meter and bear left, remaining on 28N29 and following the sign to Black Rock.
			GPS: N40°10.21' W121°39.93'
▼ 0.1		SO	Track on left is 770L.
	4.3 ▲	SO	Track on right is 770L.
▼ 0.4		SO	Track on right is 778L; then second track on right is 780L.
	4.0 ▲	SO	Track on left is 780L; then second track on left is 778L.
▼ 0.8		SO	Bruff Camp on left at sign.
	3.6 ▲	SO	Bruff Camp on right at sign.
			GPS: N40°09.93' W121°40.51'
▼ 0.9		SO	Track on left is 800L.
	3.5 ▲	SO	Track on right is 800L.
▼ 1.2		SO	Track on right is 810L.
	3.2 ▲	SO	Track on left is 810L.
▼ 1.4		SO	Track on right is 820L.
	3.0 ▲	SO	Track on left is 820L.
▼ 2.0		SO	Track on right; then two tracks on left.
	2.4 ▲	SO	Two tracks on right; then track on left.
▼ 2.3		SO	Track on right.
	2.1 ▲	SO	Track on left.
▼ 2.7		BL	Two tracks on right and track straight ahead; then track on right.

Mileage			Directions
	1.7 ▲	BR	Track on left; then two tracks on left and track straight ahead.
			GPS: N40°08.82' W121°41.73'
▼ 3.2		SO	Track on right and track on left.
	1.2 ▲	SO	Track on right and track on left.
▼ 3.4		SO	Track on left; then second track on left.
	1.0 ▲	SO	Track on right; then second track on right.
▼ 3.5		SO	Track on right is 4500.
	0.9 ▲	SO	Track on left is 4500.
▼ 4.4		BL	Three tracks on right at information boards. Zero trip meter. There is a Lassen Trail marker at this point. The Lassen Trail leaves the main route to the right.
	0.0 ▲		Continue to the north.
			GPS: N40°08.10' W121°42.32'
▼ 0.0			Continue to the east.
	8.8 ▲	BR	Three tracks on left at information boards. Zero trip meter. There is a Lassen Trail marker at this point. The Lassen Trail now follows the main route.
▼ 0.7		SO	Re-entering Lassen National Forest. No sign.
	8.1 ▲	SO	Entering PG&E-owned forest.
▼ 1.6		BL	Hiking trailhead on right for the Moak Trail (2E08), which enters the Ishi Wilderness. Start to descend shelf road.
	7.2 ▲	BR	Hiking trailhead on left for the Moak Trail (2E08), which enters the Ishi Wilderness. End of shelf road.
			GPS: N40°07.10' W121°42.59'
▼ 3.5		SO	Viewpoint on right.
	5.3 ▲	SO	Viewpoint on left.
▼ 7.3		SO	Cross through Beaver Creek.
	1.5 ▲	SO	Cross through Beaver Creek.
			GPS: N40°05.20' W121°41.78'
▼ 7.7		SO	Track on left. End of shelf road.
	1.1 ▲	SO	Track on right. Start of shelf road.
▼ 8.0		SO	Track on left.
	0.8 ▲	SO	Track on right.
▼ 8.1		SO	Track on left.
	0.7 ▲	SO	Track on right.
▼ 8.2		SO	Track on left.
	0.6 ▲	SO	Track on right.
▼ 8.6		SO	Hiking trailhead on right is 2E17.
	0.2 ▲	SO	Hiking trailhead on left is 2E17.
			GPS: N40°04.27' W121°42.15'
▼ 8.8		SO	Cross over Deer Creek on bridge. Zero trip meter at far end; then track on left.
	0.0 ▲		Continue to the northeast and cross over Deer Creek on bridge. Entering state game refuge.
			GPS: N40°04.23' W121°42.21'
▼ 0.0			Continue to the southwest. Exiting state game refuge.
	5.4 ▲	SO	Track on right; then zero trip meter at the bridge over Deer Creek.
▼ 0.1		SO	Track on right goes 0.1 miles to Devils Den Trail (2E09). Forest service information boards on right.
	5.3 ▲	SO	Track on left goes 0.1 miles to Devils Den Trail (2E09). Forest service information boards on left.
▼ 0.8		SO	Cross over creek. Start of shelf road.
	4.6 ▲	SO	Cross over creek. End of shelf road.
▼ 1.1		SO	Cross over creek.
	4.3 ▲	SO	Cross over creek.
▼ 1.5		SO	Cross over creek.
	3.9 ▲	SO	Cross over creek.
▼ 1.7		SO	Viewpoint on left over Devils Kitchen.
	3.7 ▲	SO	Viewpoint on right over Devils Kitchen.
			GPS: N40°03.79' W121°42.37'
▼ 2.4		SO	Cross over creek.
	3.0 ▲	SO	Cross over creek.
▼ 4.3		SO	Track on right to Pinnacle Peak. End of shelf road.
	1.1 ▲	SO	Track on left to Pinnacle Peak. Start of shelf road.
			GPS: N40°02.96' W121°42.66'
▼ 4.8		SO	Exiting Lassen National Forest at sign.
	0.6 ▲	SO	Entering Lassen National Forest at sign.
			GPS: N40°02.60' W121°42.67'
▼ 5.4		SO	Major 4-way intersection. Track on right is 260H, graded road on left is N Line (26N15). Zero trip meter.
	0.0 ▲		Continue to the northeast.
			GPS: N40°02.17' W121°42.53'
▼ 0.0			Continue to the southwest on unmarked graded road 28N29. Two tracks on left are both 250H.
	7.8 ▲	SO	Two tracks on right are both 250H; then 4-way intersection. Track on left is 260H, graded road on right is N Line (26N15). Zero trip meter.
▼ 0.3		SO	Track on left.
	7.5 ▲	SO	Track on right.
▼ 0.8		BL	Track on right is 230H.
	7.0 ▲	BR	Track on left is 230H.
▼ 1.2		SO	Track on right is 220H; then cleared area on left is the site of the Campbellville Fire Lookout.
	6.6 ▲	SO	Cleared area on right is the site of the Campbellville Fire Lookout; then track on left is 220H.
			GPS: N40°02.09' W121°43.07'
▼ 1.5		SO	Track on right; then graded road on right at Campbellville—nothing remains.
	6.3 ▲	SO	Graded road on left at Campbellville—nothing remains; then track on left.
▼ 1.6		SO	Track on right.
	6.2 ▲	SO	Track on left.
▼ 1.8		SO	Track on left.
	6.0 ▲	SO	Track on right.
▼ 2.8		SO	Two tracks on right.
	5.0 ▲	SO	Two tracks on left.
▼ 3.4		SO	Track on right is 180H.
	4.4 ▲	SO	Track on left is 180H.
▼ 3.5		SO	Track on left is 170H.
	4.3 ▲	SO	Track on right is 170H.
▼ 3.7		SO	Track on right is 160H.
	4.1 ▲	SO	Track on left is 160H.
▼ 4.0		SO	Track on left is 150H.
	3.8 ▲	SO	Track on right is 150H.
▼ 4.1		SO	Track on left is 140H.
	3.7 ▲	SO	Track on right is 140H.
▼ 4.4		SO	Track on left is 130H and track on right is 120H.
	3.4 ▲	SO	Track on right is 130H and track on left is 120H.
			GPS: N39°59.37' W121°42.10'
▼ 5.4		SO	Track on right is 90H; then track on left is 80H.
	2.4 ▲	SO	Track on right is 80H; then track on left is 90H.
▼ 5.8		SO	Track on right is 60H.
	2.0 ▲	SO	Track on left is 60H.
▼ 6.6		SO	Track on right to communications towers.
	1.2 ▲	SO	Track on left to communications towers.

▼ 7.4	SO	Road becomes paved. Entering Cohasset.
0.4 ▲	SO	Road turns to graded dirt.
▼ 7.8		Trail ends in Cohasset at the intersection with Mud Creek Road on the left. Continue straight ahead on paved Cohasset Road to exit to Chico and California 99.
0.0 ▲		To reach the start of the trail, take Cohasset Road north from California 99 in Chico for 16 miles. Trail commences on Cohasset Road in Cohasset, at the intersection of Mud Creek Road. Zero trip meter and proceed north on paved Cohasset Road.
		GPS: N39°56.73' W121°43.28'

NORTHERN SIERRA #43

Hogsback Road

Starting Point:	**California 99, 0.5 miles east of the intersection with California 36**
Finishing Point:	**Northern Sierra #42: Ponderosa Way, 8.2 miles south of California 36**
Total Mileage:	**22.9 miles**
Unpaved Mileage:	**22.4 miles**
Driving Time:	**2.5 hours**
Elevation Range:	**300–3,200 feet**
Usually Open:	**April to November**
Best Time to Travel:	**Spring and fall**
Difficulty Rating:	**2**
Scenic Rating:	**9**
Remoteness Rating:	**+0**

Special Attractions

- Views into rugged Antelope Canyon.
- Many pioneer sites along the way.
- Can be combined with Northern Sierra #42: Ponderosa Way and Northern Sierra #44: Peligreen-Grapevine Jeepway to make a loop.
- William B. Ide State Historic Park near the start of the trail.

History

The historic Hogsback Road commences in the old nut grove plantations outside Red Bluff (see page 50), some 2.5 miles east of William and Susan Ide's property. Their picturesque adobe dwelling, dating back to the mid-1840s, sits on the western bank of the Sacramento River in the shade an enormous oak tree.

The Hogback, for which this wagon road was named, was a challenge to cross before the introduction of basic horse-drawn graders. Before ascending the hogback, try to imagine a stagecoach making its way to the Tuscan Springs Resort, approximately 4 miles north of today's route along the original stock trail.

A series of establishments, each more lavish than its predecessor, drew crowds seeking health and relaxation at the idyllic retreat. Settlers began taking over Tuscan Springs in 1854, when Dr. John Veach saw Indians enjoying the waters in a simple hut built above the springs. By the turn of the century, not an Indian was to be seen. Instead, an elaborate four-story hotel with all the attractions of a country club stood at the site. In the 1910s, the first automobile in Tehama County operated a shuttle service between Red Bluff and Tuscan Springs. In 1916, fire destroyed the resort, and efforts to rebuild continued into the late 1940s. Today, little remains of the resort.

Hogsback Road was formerly known as Belle Mill Road. In its time, loggers traveled the route to take advantage of the abundant timber in what is now Lassen National Forest.

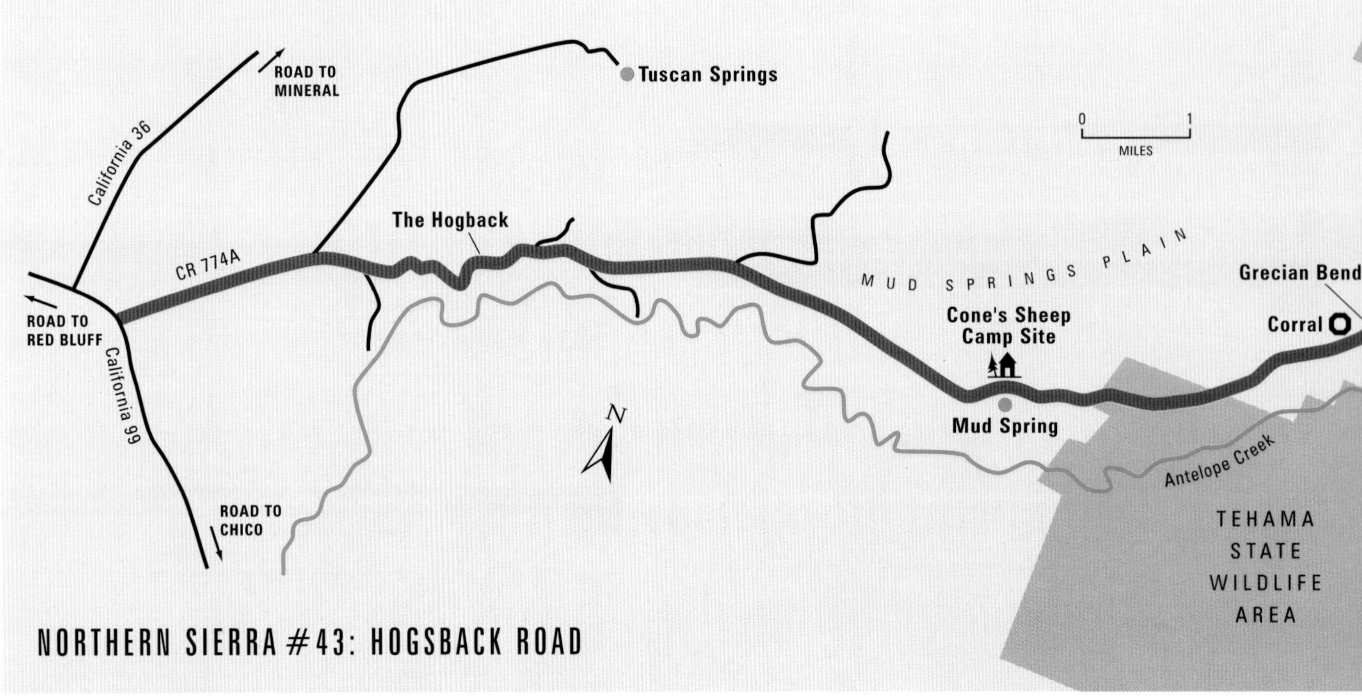

Description

Hogsback Road begins just east of Red Bluff and climbs along the spine of Hogback Ridge to join Northern Sierra #42: Ponderosa Way in Lassen National Forest. The historic route once led to the large, productive Belle Mill at Lyonsville. A flume once paralleled much of this route, but no traces of it remain.

Initially, the paved road serves as access to homes in the valley near Red Bluff. It quickly turns into a washboardy dirt road that climbs through private property to cross the Hogback. Past the Hogback, the trail crosses Mud Springs Plain through private, BLM, and Tehama State Wildlife Area lands. Most of the trail is clearly signed, but you should always make sure that you are on public lands before stopping or camping. The sparsely vegetated ridge top has fantastic views into the deep Antelope Creek Canyon, the wild and remote canyon region that enabled the Yahi called Ishi (see page 87) to remain undetected for so many years. The canyon is volcanic in origin, lined with rough, dark lava rock.

At Grecian Bend, the trail leaves Mud Springs Plain to travel across what locals once called Jack Rabbit Ridge. The whole area is marked on today's maps as Hogback Ridge.

The trail passes the north end of Northern Sierra #44: Peligreen-Grapevine Jeepway as it enters Lassen National Forest. Some excellent campsites tucked among large oaks have brilliant views over Antelope Creek. The trail briefly joins paved Plum Creek Road to finish at the intersection with Northern Sierra #42: Ponderosa Way. Turning right here allows you to loop back to Hogsback Road by following part of Ponderosa Way and then taking Northern Sierra #44: Peligreen-Grapevine Jeepway. A minimum of one full day should be allowed for the entire loop.

A point of interest close to the end of the trail is the Lyonsville–Belle Mill Cemetery, which can be found at GPS: N40°18.26' W121°44.59'. Many early settlers are buried in the Lyonsville–Belle Mill Cemetery, a quiet graveyard near the end of the trail.

The trail is 2-rated all the way, except for one 3-rated spot that requires high-clearance.

Current Road Information

Bureau of Land Management
Redding Field Office
355 Hemsted Drive
Redding, CA 96002
(530) 224-2100

Lassen National Forest
Almanor Ranger District
PO Box 767
Chester, CA 96020
(530) 258-2141

Map References

BLM Red Bluff, Lake Almanor
USFS Lassen National Forest
USGS 1:24,000 Red Bluff East, Tuscan Springs, Dewitt Peak, Inskip Hill, Finley Butte
1:100,000 Red Bluff, Lake Almanor
Maptech CD-ROM: Shasta Lake/Redding
Northern California Atlas & Gazetteer, p. 57
California Road & Recreation Atlas, pp. 58, 59

Route Directions

▼ 0.0 From California 99, on the east side of Red Bluff, 0.5 miles east of the intersection with California 36, zero trip meter and turn northwest on paved road at the sign for Hogsback Road (CR 774A). Remain on paved road for 1.5 miles.

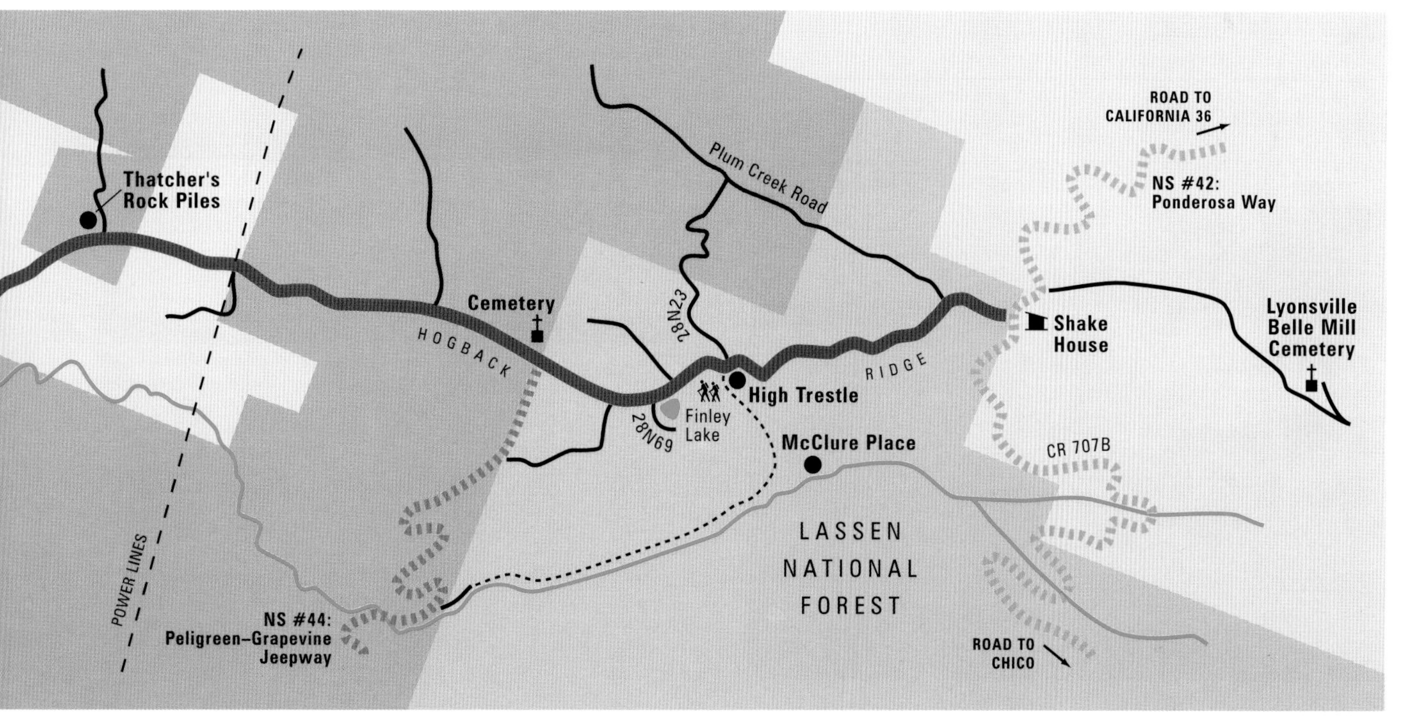

4.1 ▲		Trail ends at T-intersection with California 99. Turn right for Red Bluff.
		GPS: N40°11.06' W122°10.51'
▼ 1.5	SO	Road turns to graded dirt.
2.6 ▲	SO	Road becomes paved.
▼ 1.7	SO	Graded road on left to Tuscan Springs.
2.4 ▲	SO	Graded road on right to Tuscan Springs.
▼ 2.2	SO	Road on right through gate.
1.9 ▲	SO	Road on left through gate.
▼ 3.7	SO	Trail crosses the Hogback.
0.4 ▲	SO	Trail crosses the Hogback.
▼ 4.1	SO	Cattle guard. Zero trip meter.
0.0 ▲		Continue to the southwest.
		GPS: N40°12.79' W122°06.88'
▼ 0.0		Continue to the east. Track on right and track on left.
5.3 ▲	SO	Track on right and track on left; then cattle guard. Zero trip meter.
▼ 0.3	SO	Track on left to building.
5.0 ▲	SO	Track on right to building.
▼ 0.5	SO	Track on left and track on right.
4.8 ▲	SO	Track on left and track on right.
▼ 1.8	SO	Track on left through gate.
3.5 ▲	SO	Track on right through gate.
▼ 2.1	SO	Track on right.
3.2 ▲	SO	Track on left.
▼ 2.3	SO	Cattle guard.
3.0 ▲	SO	Cattle guard.
		GPS: N40°13.25' W122°04.35'
▼ 4.6	SO	Mud Spring on right. Stone remains on left and right were the site of Cone's Sheep Camp.
0.7 ▲	SO	Mud Spring on left. Stone remains on left and right were the site of Cone's Sheep Camp.
		GPS: N40°13.19' W122°01.74'
▼ 5.3	SO	Cattle guard. Zero trip meter.
0.0 ▲		Continue to the southwest.
		GPS: N40°13.31' W122°00.94'
▼ 0.0		Continue to the northeast.
5.9 ▲	SO	Cattle guard. Zero trip meter.
▼ 0.6	SO	Track on right.
5.3 ▲	SO	Track on left.
▼ 1.2	SO	Track on right; then track on left; then cattle guard.
4.7 ▲	SO	Cattle guard; then track on right; then track on left.
		GPS: N40°13.74' W121°59.70'
▼ 2.3	SO	Corral on left.
3.6 ▲	SO	Corral on right.
▼ 2.8	BL	Grecian Bend. Track on right over cattle guard.
3.1 ▲	BR	Grecian Bend. Track on left over cattle guard.
		GPS: N40°14.64' W121°58.32'
▼ 4.1	SO	Cattle guard.
1.8 ▲	SO	Cattle guard.
		GPS: N40°15.52' W121°57.82'
▼ 4.4	SO	Track on left.
1.5 ▲	SO	Track on right.
		GPS: N40°15.73' W121°57.57'
▼ 4.6	SO	Track on left at Thatcher's Rock Piles.
1.3 ▲	SO	Track on right at Thatcher's Rock Piles.
		GPS: N40°15.83' W121°57.36'
▼ 4.9	SO	Cattle guard.
1.0 ▲	SO	Cattle guard.
▼ 5.9	SO	Cattle guard under major power line; then track on right. Zero trip meter.
0.0 ▲		Continue to the west.
		GPS: N40°16.00' W121°55.87'
▼ 0.0		Continue to the east. Dam on left.
2.9 ▲	SO	Dam on right; then track on left; then cattle guard under major power line. Zero trip meter.
▼ 0.7	SO	Track on left.
2.2 ▲	SO	Track on right.
		GPS: N40°16.04' W121°55.15'
▼ 1.0	SO	Track on right.
1.9 ▲	SO	Track on left.
▼ 1.1	SO	Cattle guard.
1.8 ▲	SO	Cattle guard.
▼ 1.9	SO	Track on left.
1.0 ▲	SO	Track on right.
▼ 2.0	SO	Cattle guard; then well-used track on left.
0.9 ▲	SO	Well-used track on right; then cattle guard.
		GPS: N40°16.25' W121°53.60'
▼ 2.8	SO	Track on left at small cemetery enclosed by wire fence.
0.1 ▲	SO	Track on right at small cemetery enclosed by wire fence.
		GPS: N40°16.23' W121°52.61'
▼ 2.9	SO	Well-used track on right is Northern Sierra #44: Peligreen-Grapevine Jeepway; then cattle guard. Entering Lassen National Forest at sign. Zero trip meter.
0.0 ▲		Continue to the southwest. Road is now designated CR 774A.
		GPS: N40°16.20' W121°52.49'
▼ 0.0		Continue to the east. Track on left.
4.7 ▲	SO	Track on right; then cattle guard. Leaving Lassen National Forest. Well-used track on left is Northern Sierra #44: Peligreen-Grapevine Jeepway. Zero trip meter.
▼ 0.1	SO	Track on right.
4.6 ▲	SO	Track on left.
▼ 0.4	SO	Track on left.
4.3 ▲	SO	Track on right.
▼ 0.8	SO	Track on right.
3.9 ▲	SO	Track on left.
▼ 1.0	SO	Track on left.
3.7 ▲	SO	Track on right.

Rough sections of the Hogsback Road require 4WD

▼ 1.1		SO	Track on right is 28N69 around Finley Lake.
	3.6 ▲	SO	Track on left is 28N69 around Finley Lake.
			GPS: N40°16.22' W121°51.24'
▼ 1.3		SO	Track on left.
	3.4 ▲	SO	Track on right.
▼ 1.9		SO	Graded road on left is 28N23 and track on right. This is High Trestle. Parking area for hiking trail to McClure Place and North Fork Antelope Creek.
	2.8 ▲	SO	Graded road on right is 28N23 and track on left. This is High Trestle. Parking area for hiking trail to McClure Place and North Fork Antelope Creek.
			GPS: N40°16.63' W121°50.66'
▼ 2.2		SO	Track on right. Many tracks on right and left to campsites for the next 2 miles.
	2.5 ▲	SO	Track on left.
▼ 3.4		SO	Cattle guard.
	1.3 ▲	SO	Cattle guard.
▼ 4.2		TR	T-intersection with paved Plum Creek Road.
	0.5 ▲	TL	Paved Plum Creek Road continues straight ahead. Turn left onto graded dirt Hogsback Road. Many tracks on right and left to campsites for the next 2 miles.
			GPS: N40°17.79' W121°48.64'
▼ 4.7			Trail finishes at intersection with Northern Sierra #42: Ponderosa Way. Turn right to travel this trail to Chico; turn left to exit to California 36 and Mineral. Shake House (private property) is at the intersection.
	0.0 ▲		Trail commences on Northern Sierra #42: Ponderosa Way, 8.2 miles south of California 36. Zero trip meter and turn southwest onto paved Plum Creek Road. Ponderosa Way heads southeast to Black Rock. Shake House (private property) is at the intersection.
			GPS: N40°17.87' W121°48.04'

NORTHERN SIERRA #44

Peligreen-Grapevine Jeepway

Starting Point:	**Northern Sierra #42: Ponderosa Way, 1.3 miles south of Panther Spring Forest Service Station**
Finishing Point:	**Northern Sierra #43: Hogsback Road, 4.7 miles west of Northern Sierra #42: Ponderosa Way**
Total Mileage:	**19.8 miles**
Unpaved Mileage:	**19.8 miles**
Driving Time:	**5 hours**
Elevation Range:	**1,400–3,900 feet**
Usually Open:	**April to November**
Best Time to Travel:	**Spring and fall**
Difficulty Rating:	**6**
Scenic Rating:	**10**
Remote Rating:	**+1**

Looking down toward Mill Creek from atop the ridge

Special Attractions

- Moderate to difficult trail that can be driven in conjunction with Northern Sierra #43: Hogsback Road and Northern Sierra #42: Ponderosa Way.
- Trail wraps around the Ishi Wilderness with many hiking access points.
- Panoramic views of the volcanic region around Antelope Creek.

History

The harsh yet beautiful landscape through which this trail passes was home to the last members of the Yahi, a subgroup of the Yana tribe (see page 96). The Yahi occupied the eastern side of the Sacramento Valley and like the Nomlaki on the western side of the valley, they were losing land to settlers by the mid-1800s.

In the 1860s, territorial conflicts resulted in bloodshed on both sides. The Three Knolls Massacre of 1866 was one attempt by settlers to rid the valley of Indians. Dozens were killed; a few, including a mother and her six-year-old son, escaped. Like hunted animals, the remaining Yahi took shelter in nearby mountains, where they led a dangerous life on the run. They couldn't even have a fire because it would alert settlers who were determined to kill any survivors.

The Peligreen-Grapevine Jeepway passes north of Kingsley Cove, the scene of one of the last bloody massacres. In 1871, 30 members of the Yahi tribe were killed in a single day. Intermittent Indian sightings occurred over the next few years, though none were substantiated. Both settlers and army troops seemed satisfied they had killed the last of the Yahi.

In August 1911, a frail man was discovered in a slaughterhouse corral in Oroville, quite some distance to the south. After questioning through sign language, it was determined that he was the six-year-old boy who survived the Three Knolls Massacre of 1866. Given the name Ishi, meaning man in the Yahi language, he was called the last wild Indian. He and three members of his family had managed to survive for 40 years in hiding.

Description

Peligreen-Grapevine Jeepway follows sections of two OHV trails—the Peligreen Jeep Trail, which takes its name from Peligreen Place midway along the route, and the Grapevine Jeepway, which follows above Grapevine Canyon. The trail's 6 difficulty rating comes from several steep, loose-surface ascents and descents, which will test your tires' grip. Fist-size, rubbly volcanic rocks combined with smaller stones provide little traction.

The trail leaves Northern Sierra #42: Ponderosa Way through mixed conifer forest along a graded dirt road that quickly becomes a well-used formed trail. An alternate route to the one described below follows the sign for the Peligreen Jeep Trail at its first point of divergence, 1.4 miles from the start. This route travels down into the gully and climbs back up to rejoin the main trail near Peligreen Place; it is rougher than the main route, which travels around the hillside.

Much of this trail skirts the northern edge of the Ishi Wilderness, providing many wilderness access points for hikers. The Rancheria Trailhead is the first access point. From here, the Rancheria Trail drops swiftly, more than 1,000 feet in 2 miles, to join the Mill Creek Trail. Because it is so steep and strenuous, the Rancheria Trail is for experienced hikers only. The Mill Creek Trail is gentler and follows the creek west to Papes Place and east to other trails within the wilderness. Many swimming holes and fishing spots can be found along Mill Creek, as can small fossil shells.

The Ishi Wilderness in the southern Cascade foothills encompasses 41,000 acres of low-elevation wilderness. It has basalt outcroppings, caves, and pillar lava formations. Most of the ridges in the wilderness run east to west. The vegetation is a mixture. Chaparral covers the lower southern slopes, and white pines and oaks grow in the moister, higher areas. More than 90 percent of the wilderness was burned in the Campbell Fire of 1990; it is still recovering.

The Tehama deer herd, the largest migratory herd in California, winters in this area, much of which is a state wildlife refuge where hunting is prohibited. Other animals in the refuge include wild hogs, mountain lions, black bears, coyotes, and bobcats. The area provides nesting sites for raptors, turkeys, quails, and a number of songbirds. The region is also habitat for a large number of western diamondback rattlesnakes. Ticks and poison oak are also common.

The trail becomes rougher after it passes the site of Peligreen Place and starts to follow the Peligreen Jeep Trail. This section is slow going as it is littered with rough volcanic rocks and boulders. The trail runs along the ridge top and offers views south over Mill Creek, and west over the Sacramento Valley. The low scrub vegetation provides little shade, and it can get blisteringly hot in summer; spring and fall are the ideal times to travel this trail. You are likely to see other travelers in fall because the region is popular with deer hunters. It is very lightly used at other times of year.

A second wilderness access point for hikers is at Black Oak Grove, a large grove of mature black oaks on top of the ridge. The USFS map shows an undeveloped camping area here; there are no facilities, but it is possible to find a pleasant shady campsite. Other camping areas along the trail often have fabulous views but are very exposed. Past Black Oak Grove, the trail is used less, but still well defined. Several steep loose slopes make traction a challenge. However, a carefully driven stock, high-clearance 4WD with good tires should be able to handle it.

At Wild Horse Corral, the trail turns right and follows the Grapevine Jeepway above Grapevine Canyon. Initially, the trail appears lightly used and narrower than the previous section of the Peligreen Jeep Trail. Moguls and uneven off-camber sections will tilt vehicles sideways and test wheel articulation. Once the trail enters the Tehama State Wildlife Area, the surface improves somewhat and the trail becomes easier. It drops down to join the graded road, which in turn drops down to cross through the North Fork of Antelope Creek. A second USFS camping area is north of the creek. This one has picnic tables, fire rings, a pit toilet, and several shady sites. It is located near Payne Place, another early homestead site where nothing remains. A

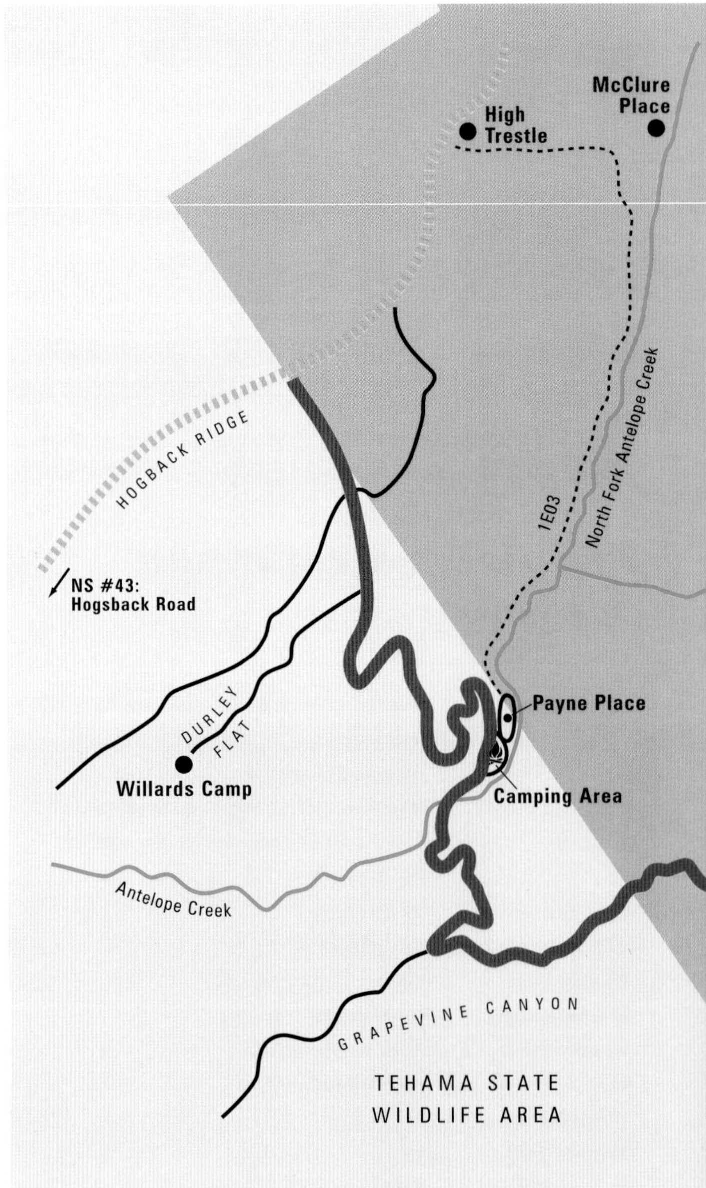

hiking trail leads out from Payne Place to McClure Point and High Trestle.

The graded road finishes at the intersection with Northern Sierra #43: Hogsback Road. The trail should not be attempted in wet weather.

Current Road Information

Lassen National Forest
Almanor Ranger District
PO Box 767
Chester, CA 96020
(530) 258-2141

Map References

BLM Lake Almanor
USFS Lassen National Forest
USGS 1:24,000 Panther Spring, Dewitt Peak, Inskip Hill
1:100,000 Lake Almanor
Maptech CD-ROM: Shasta Lake/Redding
Northern California Atlas & Gazetteer, p. 57
California Road & Recreation Atlas, p. 59 (incomplete)
Other: Off Highway Vehicle Trails of the Almanor Ranger District, A Guide to the Ishi, Thousand Lakes, & Caribou Wilderness

Route Directions

▼ 0.0		From Northern Sierra #42: Ponderosa Way, 20.2 miles south of California 36 and 1.3 miles south of Panther Spring Forest Service Station, zero trip meter and turn southwest on graded dirt road 28N57, following the sign for Peligreen Jeep Trail.
1.4 ▲		Trail ends at T-intersection with Northern Sierra #42: Ponderosa Way. Turn left for California 36 and Mineral; turn right for Chico.
		GPS: N40°14.07'W121°46.50'
▼ 0.1	SO	Track on right is 180P.

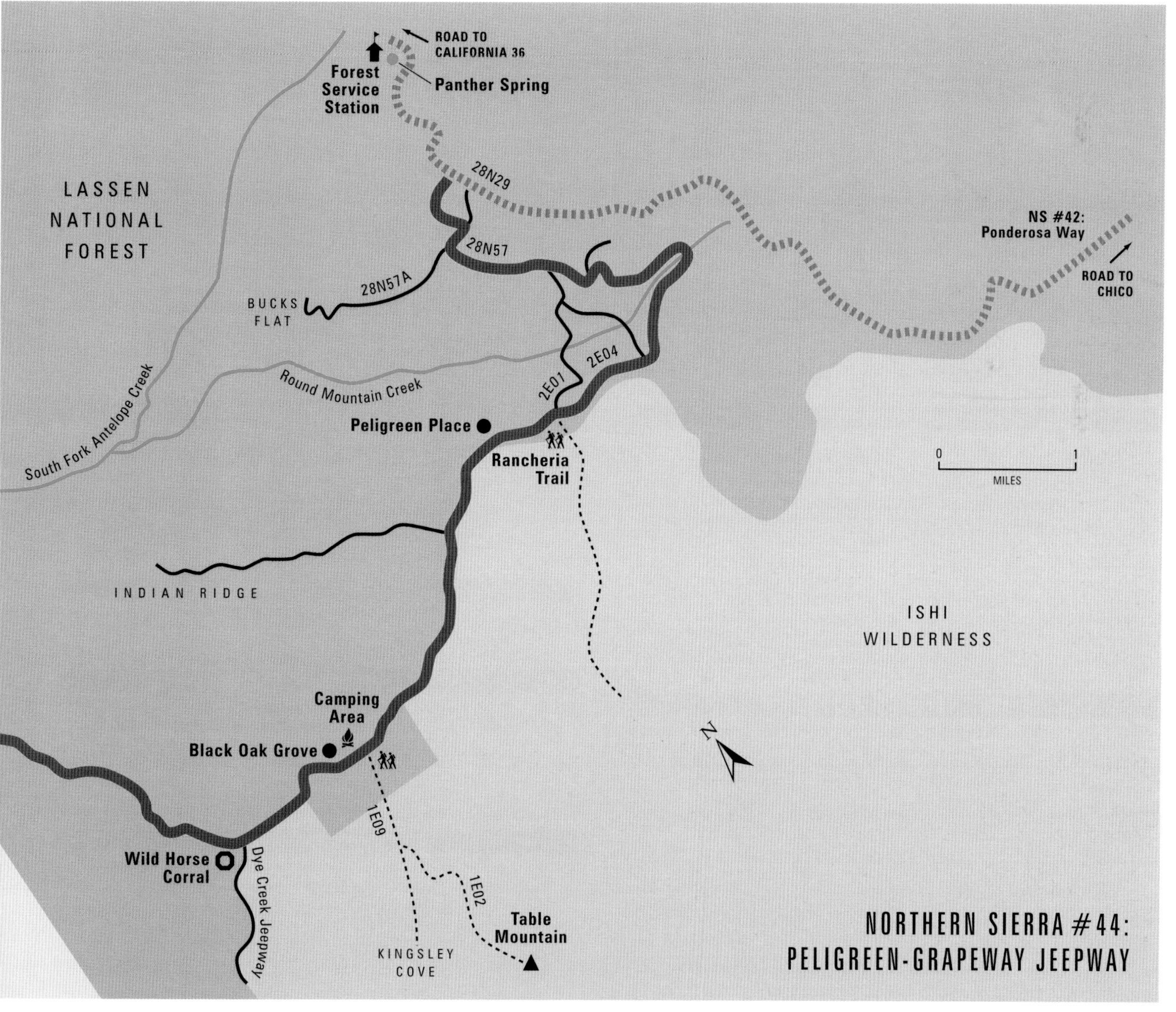

The ford through the fast-flowing North Fork Antelope Creek has metal grating for traction

1.3 ▲ SO Track on left is 180P.

▼ 0.5 SO Track on left.
0.9 ▲ SO Track on right.

▼ 0.7 BL Track on right is 28N57A to Bucks Flat. Bear left; then track on left.
0.7 ▲ BR Track on right; then track on left is 28N57A to Bucks Flat. Follow the sign for Panther Spring.

GPS: N40°13.73' W121°46.80'

▼ 0.9 SO Track on left.
0.5 ▲ SO Track on right.

▼ 1.2 SO Track on right.
0.2 ▲ SO Track on left.

▼ 1.4 SO Track on right is Peligreen Jeep Trail, which goes 2 miles to the Rancheria Trailhead. Camping area on left. Zero trip meter.
0.0 ▲ Continue to the west.

GPS: N40°13.31' W121°46.23'

▼ 0.0 Continue to the east.
3.1 ▲ SO Track on left is Peligreen Jeep Trail, which goes 2 miles to the Rancheria Trailhead. Camping area on right. Zero trip meter.

▼ 0.4 SO Track on left.
2.7 ▲ SO Track on right.

▼ 1.3 SO Cross over Round Mountain Creek. Trail drops in standard and is now designated OHV Route 2E04.
1.8 ▲ SO Cross over Round Mountain Creek. Trail improves in standard and is now designated 28N57.

GPS: N40°12.89' W121°45.16'

▼ 1.9 SO Track on right.
1.2 ▲ SO Track on left.

▼ 2.1 SO Track on right.
1.0 ▲ SO Track on left.

▼ 2.3 SO Track on right.
0.8 ▲ SO Track on left.

▼ 2.4 SO Track on left.
0.7 ▲ SO Track on right.

▼ 2.7 SO Track on right.
0.4 ▲ SO Track on left.

▼ 3.1 TL Rancheria Trailhead on left provides hiking access to the Ishi Wilderness; then track on right is the Peligreen Jeep Trail (OHV Route 2E01) rejoining. Follow sign to Black Oak Grove and zero trip meter.
0.0 ▲ Continue to the south onto 2E04. Rancheria Trailhead on right provides hiking access to the Ishi Wilderness.

GPS: N40°12.53' W121°46.77'

▼ 0.0 Continue to the west, joining Peligreen Jeep Trail (OHV Route 2E01).
4.5 ▲ TR Peligreen Jeep Trail (OHV Route 2E01) leaves main route to the left at this point. Zero trip meter.

▼ 0.5 SO Site of Peligreen Place.
4.0 ▲ SO Site of Peligreen Place.

GPS: N40°12.58' W121°47.34'

▼ 1.2 BL Track on right leads onto Indian Ridge.
3.3 ▲ BR Track on left leads onto Indian Ridge.

GPS: N40°12.30' W121°48.02'

▼ 1.4 SO Pass through fence line.
3.1 ▲ SO Pass through fence line.

▼ 2.1 SO Pass through fence line.
2.4 ▲ SO Pass through fence line.

▼ 3.1 SO Kingsley Cove Trail (1E09) and Table Mountain Trail (1E02) on left provide hiking access to the Ishi Wilderness. Undeveloped USFS camping area at Black Oak Grove on right.
1.4 ▲ SO Kingsley Cove Trail (1E09) and Table Mountain Trail (1E02) on right provide hiking access to the Ishi Wilderness. Undeveloped USFS camping area at Black Oak Grove on left.

GPS: N40°11.48' W121°49.49'

▼ 3.5 SO Pass through fence line.
1.0 ▲ SO Pass through fence line.

▼ 3.8 SO Pass through fence line.
0.7 ▲ SO Pass through fence line.

▼ 4.5 TR Wild Horse Corral. Track straight ahead is Dye Creek Jeepway. Zero trip meter and follow the sign for Grapevine Jeepway.
0.0 ▲ Continue to the northeast on Peligreen Jeep Trail.

GPS: N40°11.42' W121°50.79'

▼ 0.0 Continue to the northwest.
4.2 ▲ TL T-intersection at Wild Horse Corral. Track on right is Dye Creek Jeepway. Zero trip meter.

▼ 2.8 SO Cattle guard. Entering Tehama State Wildlife Area.
1.4 ▲ SO Cattle guard. Leaving Tehama State Wildlife Area.

GPS: N40°13.02' W121°52.47'

▼ 4.2 TR Intersection with graded road. Turn sharp right and zero trip meter.
0.0 ▲ Continue to the southeast.

GPS: N40°13.35' W121°53.82'

▼ 0.0 Continue to the east.
6.6 ▲ TL Zero trip meter and turn sharp left onto rough formed trail at unmarked intersection. Start to climb up the ridge.

▼ 2.0 SO Cross through Antelope Creek.
4.6 ▲ SO Cross through Antelope Creek.

GPS: N40°13.91' W121°53.08'

▼ 2.3 SO Track on right over cattle guard to undeveloped USFS camping area. Main trail starts to climb.
4.3 ▲ SO Second entrance to camping area on left. End of descent.

▼ 2.5 SO Second entrance to camping area. Track on right loops around the site of Payne Place.

			Hiking trail 1E03 to McClure Place and High Trestle leaves from the loop.
	4.1 ▲	SO	Track on left loops around the site of Payne Place. Hiking trail 1E03 to McClure Place and High Trestle leaves from the loop. Track on left to undeveloped USFS camping area.
			GPS: N40°14.07' W121°52.66'
▼ 4.6		SO	End of climb from river. Start to cross Durley Flat.
	2.0 ▲	SO	Leave Durley Flat and start to descend to river.
▼ 5.3		SO	Track on left goes to the site of Willards Camp.
	1.3 ▲	SO	Track on right goes to the site of Willards Camp.
			GPS: N40°15.07' W121°52.81'
▼ 5.7		SO	Track on right.
	0.9 ▲	SO	Track on left.
▼ 5.8		SO	Track on left and track on right; then cattle guard.
	0.8 ▲	SO	Cattle guard; then track on right and track on left.
▼ 6.6			Seasonal closure gate; then trail ends at T-intersection with Northern Sierra #43: Hogsback Road. Turn left to travel the trail to Red Bluff; turn right to exit to Northern Sierra #42: Ponderosa Way and California 36.
	0.0 ▲		Trail commences on Northern Sierra #43: Hogsback Road, 4.7 miles west of Northern Sierra #42: Ponderosa Way. Zero trip meter and turn south on graded dirt road and pass through seasonal closure gate. Trail initially crosses Durley Flat.
			GPS: N40°16.20' W121°52.49'

NORTHERN SIERRA #45

West Prospect Peak Trail

Starting Point:	**California 44/89, 8.5 miles northeast of the northern entrance to Lassen Volcanic National Park**
Finishing Point:	**West Prospect Peak**
Total Mileage:	**11.1 miles (one-way)**
Unpaved Mileage:	**11.1miles**
Driving Time:	**1 hour (one-way)**
Elevation Range:	**4,800–8,000 feet**
Usually Open:	**May to November**
Best Time to Travel:	**May to November**
Difficulty Rating:	**1**
Scenic Rating:	**9**
Remoteness Rating:	**+0**

Special Attractions

- Views of Lassen Peak and Chaos Crags.
- West Prospect Peak Fire Lookout.

History

The final climb to West Prospect Peak provides an excellent opportunity to observe a volcanic landscape. Between 1914 and 1921, Lassen Peak (see page 111) exploded in a series of

Approaching the base of West Prospect Peak

eruptions. In 1915, locals witnessed a massive eruption that sent a 7-mile-high cloud of steam and ash into the stratosphere. A national park was established in 1916 to preserve the landscape resulting from this dramatic activity. Lassen Peak was then the most recently active volcano in the contiguous United States, a title it held until Washington's Mount St. Helens erupted in 1980. Varying degrees of recovery can be seen across this explosive landscape of lava beds, cinder cones, and steaming hot springs. Conifers are returning to some areas, and in some regions different kinds of trees have established themselves than were there prior to the eruptions. The cinder cones southeast of West Prospect Peak have seen little re-growth since the eruptions.

West Prospect Peak Fire Lookout, active since 1935

Prospect Peak, a conical and slightly higher peak immediately southeast of West Prospect Peak, was the site of a fire lookout from 1912 to 1935. In 1935, the Civilian Conservation Corps constructed a 10-foot-tall enclosed structure just outside the national park boundary on West Prospect Peak. Today's tower, at an elevation of 8,172 feet, is still in service. The fire spotter can watch over an area of more than 200,000 acres, including Lassen National Forest to the north and Lassen Volcanic National Park to the south.

Description

This graded gravel road travels through Lassen National Forest and climbs to West Prospect Peak Fire Lookout. The trail leaves California 44/89 and travels past the site of Twin Bridges, a stop-

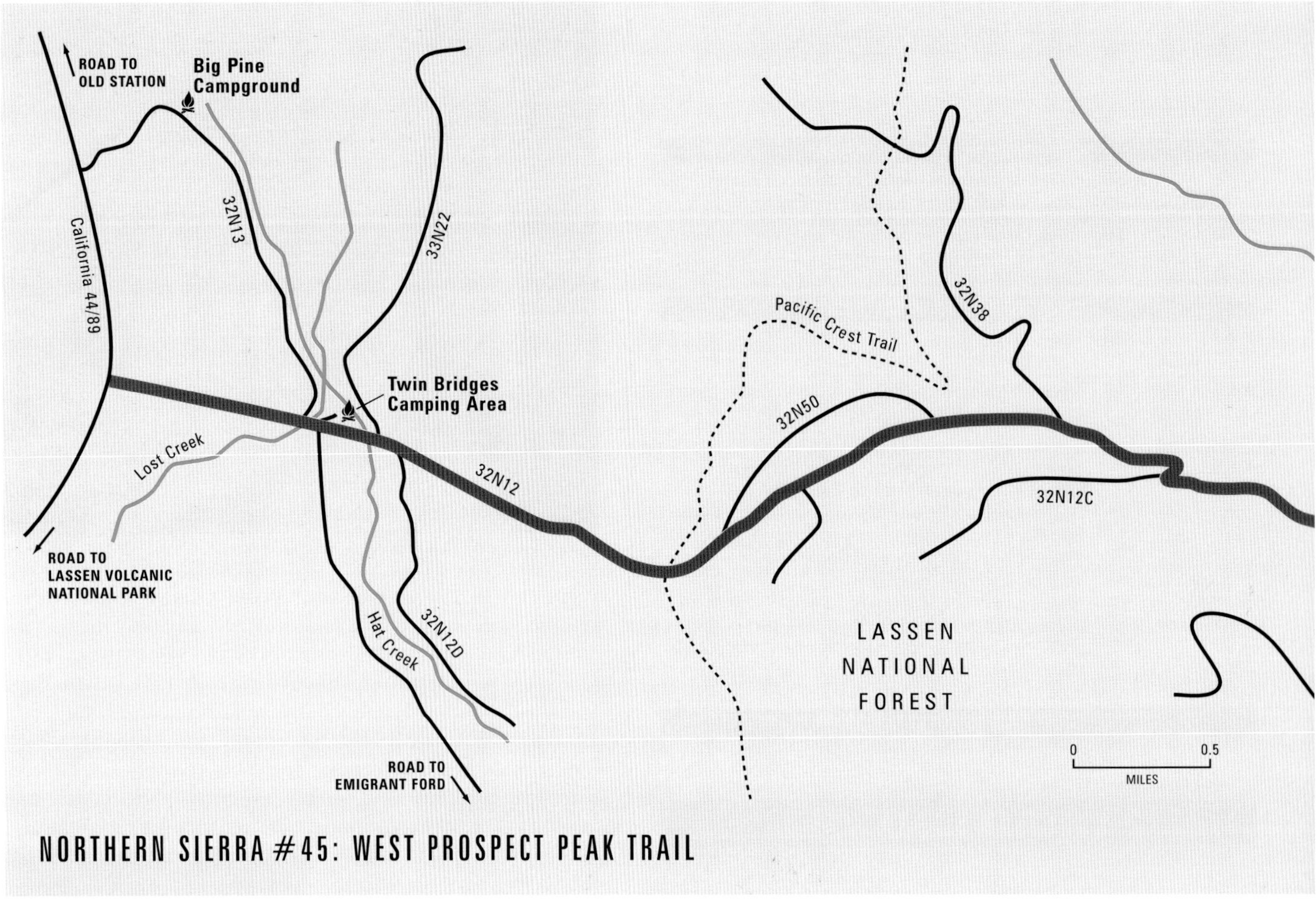

ping point on the Nobles Trail. An undeveloped USFS camping area is at Twin Bridges, and there are some excellent backcountry campsites along Hat Creek on 32N13.

The main trail runs close to the northern boundary of Lassen Volcanic National Park. The park can be reached via the Pacific Crest National Scenic Trail, which crosses the vehicle trail and connects with hiking trails in the park, or via a couple of vehicle trails that stop at the park's boundary.

The trail climbs a shelf road toward the lookout; views over the surrounding area open up the higher you get. The lookout tower is manned during fire season and can be reached by climbing up a short flight of stairs. Visitors are welcome to admire the sweeping 360-degree view between 8:30 A.M. and 5:30 P.M. Mount Sugarloaf is a prominent symmetrical cone to the northwest, with the open area of Old Station at its base. Lassen Peak, Mount Loomis, and the Chaos Crags, among others, stand out to the southwest. The lookout has pointers to the main peaks around its interior walls. Hat Creek Rim is a prominent feature to the north.

Current Road Information

Lassen National Forest
Hat Creek Ranger District
43225 East Highway 299
Fall River Mills, CA 96028
(530) 336-5521

Map References

BLM Burney
USFS Lassen National Forest
USGS 1:24,000 West Prospect Peak, Prospect Peak
1:100,000 Burney
Maptech CD-ROM: Shasta Lake/Redding
Northern California Atlas & Gazetteer, p. 48
California Road & Recreation Atlas, p. 53

Route Directions

▼ 0.0		From California 44/89, 8.5 miles northeast of the junction of California 89 and California 44 and the northern entrance to Lassen Volcanic National Park, zero trip meter and turn east onto graded dirt road 32N12, following the sign to West Prospect Lookout.
		GPS: N40°37.38' W121°28.80'
▼ 0.2	SO	Cattle guard.
▼ 0.3	SO	Track on right.
▼ 0.4	SO	Track on right.
▼ 0.7	SO	Track on left is 32N13; then cross over Lost Creek. Graded road on right goes to Emigrant Ford; then track on left goes into Twin Bridges undeveloped USFS camping area. Nobles Trail on left and right at this point.
		GPS: N40°36.94' W121°28.12'
▼ 0.9	SO	Cross over Hat Creek on bridge; then track on left is 33N22. Camping area at intersection.
▼ 1.0	SO	Track on right is 32N12D.

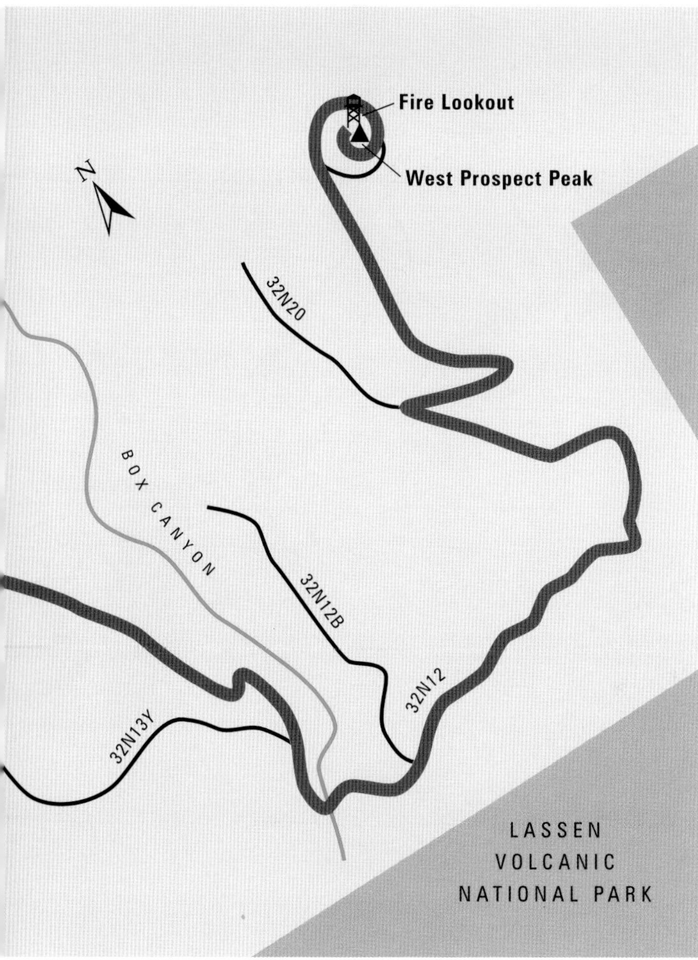

▼ 1.2	SO	Cattle guard.
▼ 1.6	SO	Track on left.
▼ 1.8	SO	Track on left.
▼ 2.1	SO	Pacific Crest Trail crosses main route; then track on right.
		GPS: N40°35.99' W121°27.22'
▼ 2.3	SO	Track on left is 32N50.
		GPS: N40°35.99' W121°26.91'
▼ 2.6	SO	Track on right.
▼ 3.1	SO	Track on left is 32N50.
▼ 3.5	SO	Track on left is 32N38. Zero trip meter.
		GPS: N40°35.76' W121°25.51'
▼ 0.0		Continue to the southeast, following sign to the lookout.
▼ 0.6	TL	Track straight ahead is 32N12C.
▼ 2.5	SO	Track on right is 32N13Y.
		GPS: N40°34.24' W121°24.10'
▼ 2.7	SO	Track on right; then cross over creek.
▼ 3.1	SO	Track on left is 32N12B.
▼ 4.0	SO	Track on left.
▼ 4.6	SO	View on left over a boulder field to Lassen Peak.
▼ 5.2	SO	Track on left.
▼ 5.4	BR	Track on left on right-hand bend is 32N20.
		GPS: N40°34.89' W121°23.10'
▼ 6.5	SO	Start of shelf road.
▼ 6.8	SO	Track on right.
▼ 7.3	SO	Track on left.
▼ 7.6		Trail ends at West Prospect Peak Fire Lookout.
		GPS: N40°35.65' W121°22.71'

NORTHERN SIERRA #46

Hat Creek Rim Trail

Starting Point:	**California 44, 2.7 miles east of California 89 and Old Station**
Finishing Point:	**Doty Road, 1.3 miles east of California 89**
Total Mileage:	**18.9 miles, plus 1.6-mile spur to the lookout site**
Unpaved Mileage:	**16.5 miles, plus 1.6-mile spur**
Driving Time:	**3 hours**
Elevation Range:	**3,300–5,000 feet**
Usually Open:	**April to October**
Best Time to Travel:	**Dry weather**
Difficulty Rating:	**1**
Scenic Rating:	**8**
Remoteness Rating:	**+0**

Special Attractions

- Subway Cave.
- Hat Creek Rim scenic overlook at the southern end of the trail.
- Hang gliding launch pad at the northern end of the trail.
- University of California Hat Creek Radio Observatory.

History

The name Hat Creek dates back to the mid-1850s. The name may come from the Achomawi word *hatiwiwi*, their name for Hat Creek. Another origin may be that a member of William H. Nobles' emigrant party dropped his hat in the stream.

The route runs close to a cutoff along the Nobles Trail, which ran below present-day California 44. Called the Yreka and Fort Crook Road, it branched due north from the main trail to Lockhart's Ferry via Government Well and was used by stagecoaches traveling between California and Oregon in 1856.

The Hat Creek Rim Fire Lookout, along the upper reach-

Subway Cave

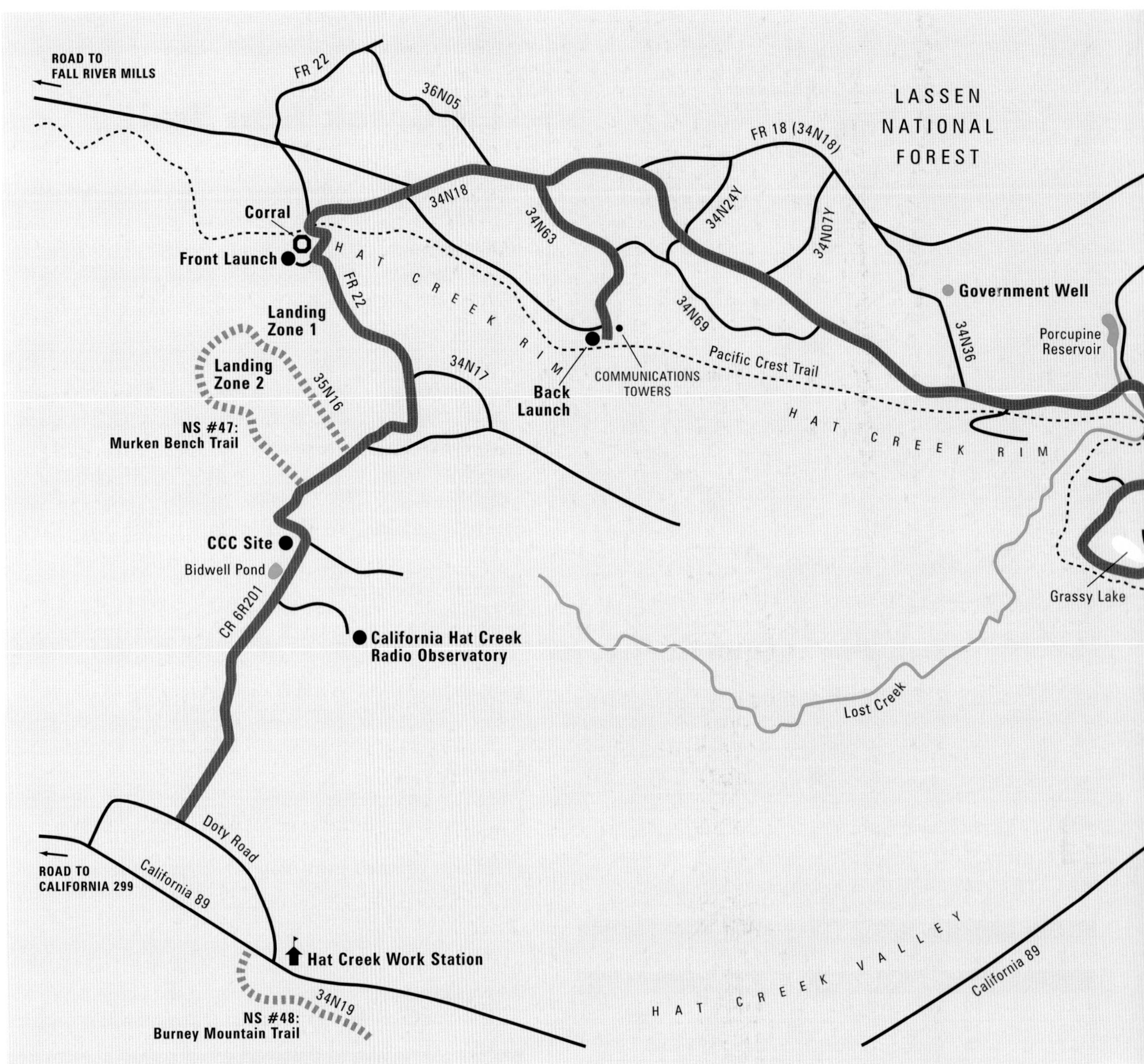

es of the rim, was destroyed in the 1987 Lost Fire. Lightning caused the fire and ultimately burned nearly 23,000 acres. All that remains of the old tower is the steel frame base.

One not-to-be-missed feature of this area is a short distance from the start of the trail. Subway Cave, a lava tube, formed less than 20,000 years ago when molten lava flowed out of a series of north-south fissures in the earth. Surface lava cooled and hardened, but lava below the surface continued to flow, eventually draining away to leave the tube. A marked trail runs through the cave and returns to the parking area aboveground. A reliable flashlight is essential because there is zero visibility inside the cave, and the floor is very rough. The temperature in the cave remains a constant 46 degrees Fahrenheit year-round, so you might want to bring along a jacket. Inside the cave, you can see hardened lava formations, chambers, and burst lava bubbles. Subway Cave is just off California 89, 0.5 miles north of the intersection of California 44 and California 89 at Old Station.

Description

The trail proper leaves California 44, 2.7 miles east of Old Station. The Hat Creek Rim scenic overlook, at the start of the trail, is an interpretive site that provides a panoramic view of the Hat Creek Valley and surrounding volcanic peaks. On a clear day, Mount Shasta is clearly visible to the northwest. Mud flows from the 1915 eruption of Lassen Peak poured into the Hat Creek drainage. Snowmelt from Lassen Peak, Big Spring, and Rising River feed the stream, and it is regularly stocked with brook, brown, and rainbow trout in summer. Good fishing can be found near the southern end of the trail

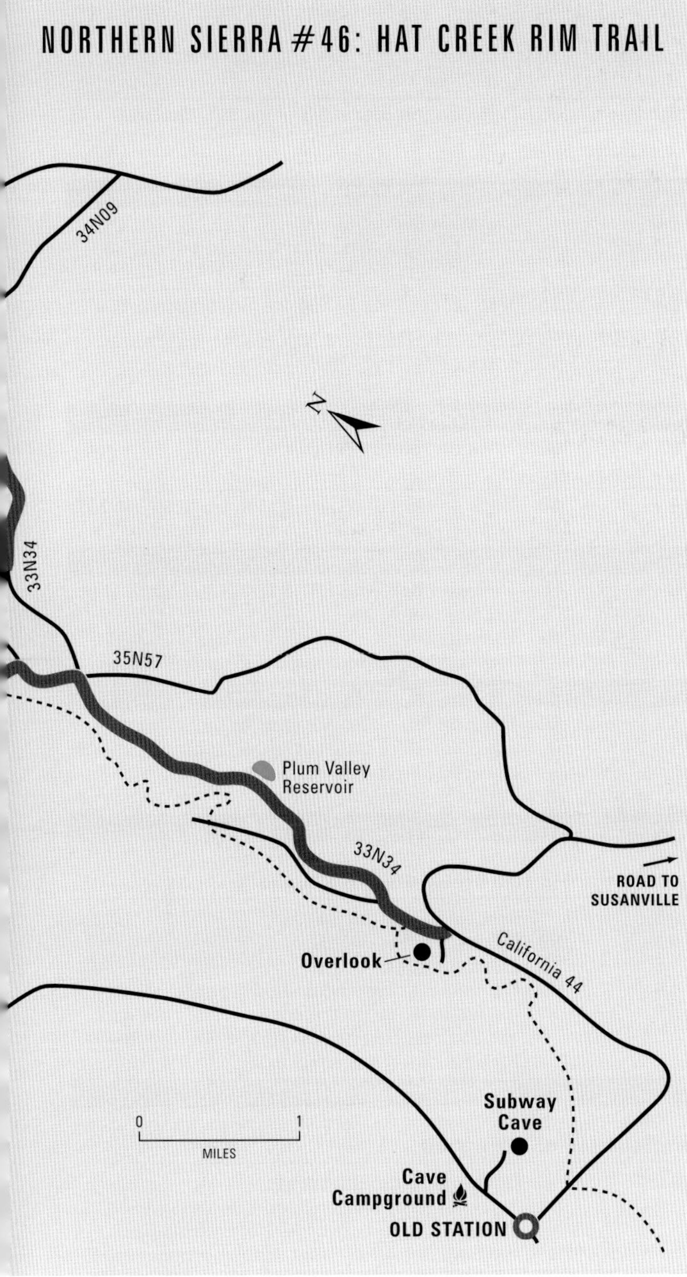

at Hat Creek Campground, Old Station Day-Use Area, and Cave Campground. The graded road heads north from the scenic overlook, following close to the geological fault of Hat Creek Rim. Nearly a million years ago, a block of the Earth's crust dropped 1,000 feet below the rim (Hat Creek Valley), leaving behind the fault scarp known as Hat Creek Rim.

The easy trail is generally suitable for passenger vehicles. One small loop near the start leaves the main graded road to travel closer to the rim; this section is rated 2 and is more suitable for high-clearance vehicles. If you do not wish to drive the loop, remain on graded road 34N34—the loop rejoins in 0.8 miles.

The trail stays back from the rim most of the way, but a spur leads to the site of the old fire lookout tower, now used for communications equipment and as an alternative launch site for hang gliders. This Back Launch was constructed in 1993 and is considered more difficult than the more popular Front Launch farther north along the trail. Back Launch should only be used by experienced pilots. The Pacific Crest National Scenic Trail runs past this launch site very close to the rim.

The Front Launch for hang gliders and paragliders is marked partway along the descent to Hat Creek Valley. For non-flyers, this is a wonderful viewpoint and picnic area, with the added bonus that you may be lucky enough to see hang gliders launching from the pad. The site has a reliable updraft in summer and is used from spring through to October. Northern Sierra #47: Murken Bench Trail loops off from the main trail and passes beside two landing sites at the base of the rim.

The road then becomes paved and passes the University of California Hat Creek Radio Observatory. Visitors are welcome on weekdays between 9:00 A.M. and 4:00 P.M. The facility houses the University of California at Berkeley's Radio Astronomy Laboratory.

The trail ends at a T-intersection with Doty Road, which you can take either way back to California 89.

Current Road Information

Lassen National Forest
Hat Creek Ranger District
43225 East Highway 299
Fall River Mills, CA 96028
(530) 336-5521

Map References

BLM Burney
USFS Lassen National Forest
USGS 1:24,000 Old Station, Murken Bench, Burney Mt. East
1:100,000 Burney
Maptech CD-ROM: Shasta Lake/Redding
Northern California Atlas & Gazetteer, p. 48
California Road & Recreation Atlas, p. 53

Route Directions

Mileage		Direction
▼ 0.0		From California 44, 2.7 miles east of the intersection with California 89 at Old Station, zero trip meter and turn southwest, following the sign for the Hat Creek Rim scenic overlook. Immediately turn right onto graded road 34N34, following the sign for Plum Valley Reservoir. Paved road continues ahead for another 0.2 miles to the Hat Creek Rim scenic overlook.
3.1 ▲		T-intersection with paved road. To the right goes 0.2 miles to the Hat Creek Rim scenic overlook. Turn left; then trail immediately ends at the T-intersection with California 44. Turn left for Susanville; turn right for Old Station and California 89.
		GPS: N40°41.91' W121°23.97'
▼ 0.2	SO	Trails West marker for the Nobles Trail on right.
2.9 ▲	SO	Trails West marker for the Nobles Trail on left.
▼ 0.3	SO	Track on left.
2.8 ▲	SO	Track on right.

University of California Hat Creek Radio Observatory

▼ 0.4	SO	Track on left to Pacific Crest Trailhead.
2.7 ▲	SO	Track on right to Pacific Crest Trailhead.
▼ 0.6	SO	Track on left; then second track on left is 34N34G.
2.5 ▲	SO	Track on right is 34N34G; then second track on right.
▼ 0.8	SO	Track on right is 33N15Y.
2.3 ▲	SO	Track on left is 33N15Y.
▼ 1.6	SO	Track on left is 34N34D.
1.5 ▲	SO	Track on right is 34N34D.
▼ 1.7	SO	Plum Valley Reservoir on right; then track on right; then second track on right is 34N34E; then cattle guard.
1.4 ▲	SO	Cattle guard; then track on left is 34N34E; then second track on left; then Plum Valley Reservoir on left.
		GPS: N40°43.30' W121°23.78'
▼ 1.9	SO	Track on right.
1.2 ▲	SO	Track on left.
▼ 2.3	SO	Track on left.
0.8 ▲	SO	Track on right.
▼ 3.1	TL	4-way intersection. Graded road on right is 33N57. Graded road straight ahead is 34N34. Zero trip meter.
0.0 ▲		Continue to the southwest on 34N34.
		GPS: N40°44.39' W121°23.81'
▼ 0.0		Continue to the northwest on 34N34C.
3.7 ▲	TR	4-way intersection. Graded road straight ahead is 33N57. Graded road on right and left is 34N34. Zero trip meter.
▼ 0.4	BL	Track on right. Grassy Lake (dry) on right.
3.3 ▲	BR	Track on left. Grassy Lake (dry) on left.
▼ 1.2	SO	Track on left.
2.5 ▲	BL	Track on right.
		GPS: N40°45.19' W121°24.12'
▼ 1.7	BR	Track on left.
2.0 ▲	BL	Track on right.
▼ 1.9	TL	T-intersection with 34N34. Rejoin 34N34.
1.8 ▲	TR	Turn right onto unmarked formed trail 34N34B.
		GPS: N40°45.02' W121°23.46'
▼ 2.7	SO	Graded road on right is 34N09 to Porcupine Reservoir.
1.0 ▲	SO	Graded road on left is 34N09 to Porcupine Reservoir.
		GPS: N40°45.48' W121°22.80'
▼ 2.9	SO	Cross over Lost Creek; then cattle guard; then track on left.
0.8 ▲	SO	Track on right; then cattle guard; then cross over Lost Creek.
▼ 3.7	SO	Track on left drops 0.8 miles to Little Lake. Zero trip meter.
0.0 ▲		Continue to the southeast.
		GPS: N40°46.10' W121°23.53'
▼ 0.0		Continue to the north.
4.2 ▲	SO	Track on right drops 0.8 miles to Little Lake. Zero trip meter.
▼ 0.4	SO	Track on right is 34N36 via Government Well.
3.8 ▲	SO	Track on left is 34N36 via Government Well.
▼ 1.5	SO	Track on left is 34N69.
2.7 ▲	SO	Track on right is 34N69.
		GPS: N40°47.39' W121°23.75'
▼ 2.1	SO	Track on right is 34N07Y.
2.1 ▲	SO	Track on left is 34N07Y.
▼ 2.7	SO	Track on right and track on left are both 34N24Y.
1.5 ▲	SO	Track on left and track on right are both 34N24Y.
		GPS: N40°48.48' W121°23.79'
▼ 3.3	TL	T-intersection with FR 18 (34N18). Follow sign to Fall River Mills.
0.9 ▲	TR	Turn right onto small graded road 34N34, following sign to Government Well.
		GPS: N40°48.94' W121°23.48'
▼ 4.2	SO	Track on left is 34N63, spur to the old Hat Creek Rim Fire Lookout (now communications towers). Zero trip meter.
0.0 ▲		Continue to the southeast.
		GPS: N40°49.52' W121°24.01'

Spur to the old Hat Creek Rim Fire Lookout

▼ 0.0		Proceed south on 34N63.
▼ 0.8	BR	Track on left is 34N69.
▼ 1.5	SO	Track on right.
▼ 1.6		Spur ends at communications towers (site of the old fire lookout) on the edge of Hat Creek Rim. Pacific Crest Trail runs along the rim, with the Back Launch a few steps along it to the north.
		GPS: N40°48.53' W121°24.83'

Continuation of Main Trail

▼ 0.0		Continue to the northwest.
2.2 ▲	SO	Track on right is 34N63, spur to the old Hat Creek Rim Fire Lookout (now communications towers). Zero trip meter.
		GPS: N40°49.52' W121°24.01'
▼ 0.2	SO	Track on left goes to Murken Bench Plantation; then cattle guard; then second track on left.
2.0 ▲	SO	Track on right; then cattle guard; then track on right goes to Murken Bench Plantation.
▼ 0.3	SO	Track on right is 36N05.
1.9 ▲	SO	Track on left is 36N05.
▼ 0.8	SO	Track on left.
1.4 ▲	SO	Track on right.
▼ 0.9	BL	Graded road on right goes to Sixmile Hill and Fall River Mills. Bear left on 34N18, following sign for California 89.
1.3 ▲	SO	Graded road on left goes to Sixmile Hill and Fall River Mills. Remain on 34N18.
		GPS: N40°50.17' W121°24.60'
▼ 1.8	BL	Graded road on right goes to Bald Mountain Reservoir. Bear left, joining FR 22; then track on right.
0.4 ▲	BR	Track on left; then graded road on left goes to

Mileage		Direction	Description
			Bald Mountain Reservoir. Bear right onto 34N18, following sign to Bainbridge Reservoir.
			GPS: N40°50.68' W121°25.35'
▼ 1.9		SO	Pacific Crest Trail crosses.
	0.3 ▲	SO	Pacific Crest Trail crosses.
▼ 2.0		SO	Corral on right; then cattle guard. Start of shelf road descending from the rim.
	0.2 ▲	SO	End of shelf road. Cattle guard; then corral on left.
▼ 2.2		SO	Track on right goes 0.1 miles to Front Launch and viewpoint. Zero trip meter.
	0.0 ▲		Continue to the northeast.
			GPS: N40°50.52' W121°25.55'
▼ 0.0			Continue to the southeast.
	2.2 ▲	SO	Track on left goes 0.1 miles to Front Launch and viewpoint. Zero trip meter.
▼ 1.3		SO	Track on left is 34N17.
	0.9 ▲	SO	Track on right is 34N17.
▼ 2.1		SO	Track on left.
	0.1 ▲	SO	Track on right.
▼ 2.2		SO	Track on right over cattle guard is the start of Northern Sierra #47: Murken Bench Trail (35N16), also marked LZ-1 (Landing Zone 1). Zero trip meter.
	0.0 ▲		Continue to the east.
			GPS: N40°49.66' W121°26.80'
▼ 0.0			Continue to the west.
	3.5 ▲	SO	Track on left over cattle guard is the end of Northern Sierra #47: Murken Bench Trail (35N16), also marked LZ-1 (Landing Zone 1). Zero trip meter.
▼ 0.4		SO	Track on right over cattle guard is the end of Northern Sierra #47: Murken Bench Trail, also marked LZ-2 (Landing Zone 2).
	3.1 ▲	SO	Track on left over cattle guard is Northern Sierra #47: Murken Bench Trail, also marked LZ-2 (Landing Zone 2).
▼ 0.8		SO	Exposed basalt pillars on left.
	2.7 ▲	SO	Exposed basalt pillars on right.
			GPS: N40°49.85' W121°27.58'
▼ 1.1		TR	Road ahead into private property. Turn right onto paved road. Remain on paved CR 6R201 for the next 2.4 miles.
	2.4 ▲	TL	T-intersection. Track on right goes into private property. Turn left onto FR 22 following the sign for Bainbridge Reservoir and hang glider launch. Road is now graded dirt.
			GPS: N40°49.61' W121°27.58'
▼ 1.4		SO	Parking area on right at site of old Civilian Conservation Corps camp.
	2.1 ▲	SO	Parking area on left at site of old Civilian Conservation Corps camp.
			GPS: N40°49.62' W121°27.80'
▼ 1.5		SO	Bidwell Pond on right was put in by the Bidwell Ranch to provide water seepage to the valley.
	2.0 ▲	SO	Bidwell Pond on left was put in by the Bidwell Ranch to provide water seepage to the valley.
▼ 1.7		SO	University of California Hat Creek Radio Observatory on left.
	1.8 ▲	SO	University of California Hat Creek Radio Observatory on right.
▼ 3.5			Trail ends at T-intersection with Doty Road. Turn either right or left to exit to California 89.
	0.0 ▲		Trail commences on Doty Road (6R200), 1.3 miles east of California 89. Zero trip meter and turn east on paved Bidwell Road, following sign to the Hat Creek Radio Observatory.
			GPS: N40°49.41' W121°30.17'

NORTHERN SIERRA #47

Murken Bench Trail

Starting Point:	**Northern Sierra #46: Hat Creek Rim Trail, 3.5 miles from the northern end**
Finishing Point:	**Northern Sierra #46: Hat Creek Rim Trail, 3.1 miles from the northern end**
Total Mileage:	**3 miles**
Unpaved Mileage:	**3 miles**
Driving Time:	**30 minutes**
Elevation Range:	**3,500–3,600 feet**
Usually Open:	**Year-round**
Best Time to Travel:	**Dry weather**
Difficulty Rating:	**2**
Scenic Rating:	**8**
Remoteness Rating:	**+0**

Special Attractions

- Views along the face of Hat Creek Rim.
- Chance to see hang gliders and paragliders soaring above the rim.
- Backcountry campsites in the open forest below Hat Creek Rim.

History

The Atsugewi occupied the Murken Bench and Hat Creek region prior to the arrival of explorers and settlers. They lived in nearby villages at Burney and Cassel, and along Hat Creek in winter and moved to higher ground around Lassen Peak in summer. Hat Creek had salmon, pike, and trout; deer were abundant; and there were berries, seeds, and basketry materials. Atsugewi shamans visited the nearby high mountains in search of spiritual guidance.

Ponderosas at the foot of Hat Creek Rim

John Work and a band of trappers crossed Hat Creek just west of Murken Bench on two occasions in the 1830s.The first was in November 1832 en route to the Sacramento Valley from the British outpost at Fort Nez Perce in what was then called Oregon Country. The second was on the return trip in August 1833. A substantial number of the trappers became ill while traveling in the Sacramento and San Joaquin Valleys. Southbound trappers may have unknowingly started an epidemic, which killed thousands of Indians in the Sacramento Valley. Those still alive were too weak to dispose of the dead and a foul stench permeated the villages. These Native Americans had no resistance to the introduced disease thought to be malaria. The Atsugewi people, however, fared better than their neighbors. They continue to live in the Hat Creek Valley.

Description

This short loop starts and finishes on Northern Sierra #46: Hat Creek Rim Trail and provides excellent views of the rim's escarpment from below. It is a formed trail, well used by hang gliders and paragliders who land their crafts at one of the two landing sites along the loop. The launch site can be spotted on the rim by looking for the wind cones.

The trail winds its way through pines, junipers, and open grassland. In wet weather, the packed dirt trail is very muddy and may be impassable. The first landing site is a short distance off the main trail to the right. This is the smaller of the two sites and is recommended for experienced pilots only. The second, more popular landing zone is at the apex of the loop along an open grassland area on Murken Bench. Note that the northernmost part of this area is unmarked private property. If camping, keep to the trees at the southern end of the landing zone, away from the open area. This area offers excellent backcountry camping with views of Hat Creek Rim. Late afternoon and sunset are good times to see hang gliders.

Current Road Information

Lassen National Forest
Hat Creek Ranger District
43225 East Highway 299
Fall River Mills, CA 96028
(530) 336-5521

Map References

BLM Burney
USFS Lassen National Forest
USGS 1:24,000 Murken Bench
1:100,000 Burney
Maptech CD-ROM: Shasta Lake/Redding
Northern California Atlas & Gazetteer, p. 48
California Road & Recreation Atlas, p. 53

Landing Zone 2 at the foot of Hat Creek Rim

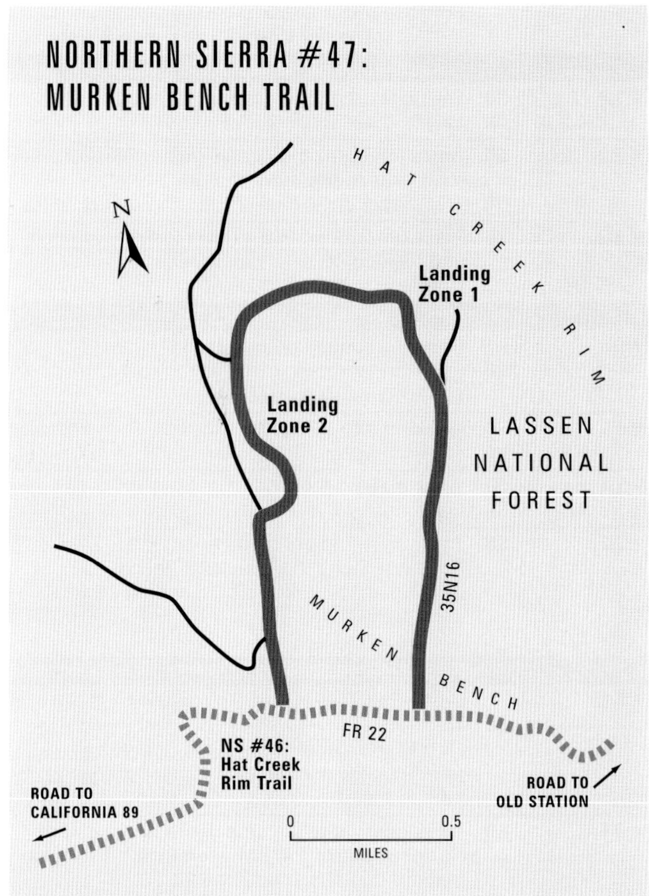

Route Directions

▼ 0.0		From Northern Sierra #46: Hat Creek Rim Trail, 3.5 miles from the northern end, zero trip meter and turn north over cattle guard on 35N16, also marked LZ-1 (Landing Zone 1).
1.9 ▲		Trail ends at T-intersection with Northern Sierra #46: Hat Creek Rim Trail. Turn right for California 89; turn left to travel this trail to Old Station.
		GPS: N40°49.66' W121°26.80'
▼ 0.9	SO	Track on right to Landing Zone 1.
1.0 ▲	SO	Track on left to Landing Zone 1.
		GPS: N40°50.36' W121°26.37'
▼ 1.6	SO	Track on right.
0.3 ▲	SO	Track on left.
▼ 1.9	SO	Well-used, unmarked track on right. Zero trip meter.
0.0 ▲		Continue to the north toward the rim.
		GPS: N40°50.69' W121°26.97'
▼ 0.0		Continue to the south toward the hang gliding landing site.
1.1 ▲	BR	Well-used, unmarked track on left. Zero trip meter.
▼ 0.3	SO	Hang gliding landing site on left in open area of Murken Bench.
0.8 ▲	SO	Hang gliding landing site on right in open area of Murken Bench.
		GPS: N40°50.43' W121°26.95'
▼ 0.5	SO	Track on right.
0.6 ▲	SO	Track on left.
▼ 0.6	SO	Track on right.

	0.5 ▲	SO	Track on left.
▼ 0.9		SO	Track on right.
	0.2 ▲	SO	Track on left.
▼ 1.1			Trail ends at T-intersection with Northern Sierra #46: Hat Creek Rim Trail. Turn right to return to California 89; turn left to travel the trail to Old Station.
	0.0 ▲		Trail commences on Northern Sierra #46: Hat Creek Rim Trail, 3.1 miles from the northern end on California 89. Zero trip meter and turn north over cattle guard on formed dirt trail. There is a sign for LZ-2 (Landing Zone 2) on the gatepost.
			GPS: N40°49.78' W121°27.21'

NORTHERN SIERRA #48

Burney Mountain Trail

Starting Point:	**California 89, 0.3 miles north of Hat Creek USFS Work Center**
Finishing Point:	**California 299, 0.9 miles west of Burney**
Total Mileage:	**22.2 miles, plus 2.5-mile spur to Cypress Trailhead and 8.5-mile spur to Burney Mountain Fire Lookout**
Unpaved Mileage:	**21.9 miles, plus spurs**
Driving Time:	**4 hours**
Elevation Range:	**3,200–7,700 feet**
Usually Open:	**May to November**
Best Time to Travel:	**Dry weather**
Difficulty Rating:	**2**
Scenic Rating:	**9**
Remoteness Rating:	**+0**

Special Attractions

- Panoramic views from Burney Mountain Fire Lookout.
- Upper Burney Creek Baker Cypress Grove.
- Hiking access to the Thousand Lakes Wilderness.

History

The last half of Burney Mountain Trail travels a section of the Tamarack Road, established in 1874. David B. "Kentuck" Branstetter pushed the trail through to connect the upper reaches of the Sacramento Valley with Burney (see page 28). In time, the trail became a popular wagon route because it was not a toll road. The route left Redding via the Millville Plains and climbed northeast along Old Cow Creek to an overnight camp at Whitmore, a place once used as summer grazing pasture. In the 1890s, James Burton built a store at Whitmore, halfway between Redding and Burney, and offered accommodations at his nearby two-story house. By the early 1900s, a hotel and post office operated by the Sheridans were catching both passing and local trade, and an 80-foot-deep, hand-dug well provided a reliable supply of cool water.

The Tamarack Grade northeast of Whitmore was a long twisting climb and one of the worst sections of the trail. Quite often, drivers would hitch teams together to pull wagons up the steep grade. Going down the hill could be dangerous as well. Too much momentum and a teamster could lose his load and his life. Teamsters sometimes dragged a log behind their wagons to help control their downhill speed. On the far side of the Tamarack Grade, the trail was somewhat easier because it made a gentle descent all the way to Burney.

Burney Mountain (7,863 feet) can be seen clearly to the east as the trail descends toward Haynes Flat. The Burney Mountain Fire Lookout was built in 1934 and the present steel cabin was constructed in 1965.

Description

Burney Mountain rises west of the Hat Creek Valley, opposite the Hat Creek Rim. Like all the peaks in the region, it is a cinder cone. Burney Mountain, and other volcanic peaks in the vicinity, marks the southern extent of the Cascade Range.

The trail begins along a well-marked, graded forest road, heading west from California 89. It travels through Lassen National Forest and sections of privately owned forest managed for timber harvesting. If you plan to camp along the trail, make sure that you are in the national forest.

The first spur leads to the Cypress Trailhead, a hiking trail into the Thousand Lakes Wilderness. The wilderness has many small lakes and volcanic and glacial features traversed by 22 miles of backcountry trails. The best time to hike here is from mid-June to mid-October. High peaks include Crater Peak (8,677 feet), Magee Peak (8,550), and Fredonyer Peak (8,054 feet).

The second spur winds up a long shelf road to the fire lookout on top of Burney Mountain. The shelf road is generally wide enough for two vehicles to pass each other, but it travels above a dizzyingly sheer drop of several hundred feet, so use care when passing. The trail crosses several boulder-strewn slopes before reaching the lookout tower, which is normally manned from late spring until October. Visitors are welcome to climb to the tower with permission from the lookout on duty. The climb is well worth it. Mount Shasta dominates the

View of Mount Shasta and the town of Burney from the lookout

skyline, rising to an elevation of 14,162 feet to the north. The town of Burney can be seen below in the valley. Lassen Peak (10,457 feet) is to the south and the Hat Creek Valley and Hat Creek Rim can be seen to the east. The gate below the tower is locked daily at 6 P.M. when the tower is manned. In addition, the trail is closed after hunting season. Hang gliders sometimes launch from Burney Mountain, but the winds are erratic, and the site is not as popular as the nearby Hat Creek Rim sites.

Another interesting feature along the trail is the grove of rare Baker cypresses. The trees grow up to 70 feet tall and are only found in 11 isolated groves in Northern California and Southern Oregon. They grow on volcanic and serpentine soils at elevations between 3,500 and 7,000 feet. These trees can be recognized by their gray-green needles and small cones about an inch in diameter.

The trail ends on California 299 on the outskirts of Burney.

Current Road Information

Lassen National Forest
Hat Creek Ranger District
43225 East Highway 299
Fall River Mills, CA 96028
(530) 336-5521

Map References

BLM Burney
USFS Lassen National Forest
USGS 1:24,000 Burney Mt. East, Thousand Lakes Valley, Burney Mt. West
1:100,000 Burney
Maptech CD-ROM: Shasta Lake/Redding
Northern California Atlas & Gazetteer, pp. 47, 48
California Road & Recreation Atlas, p. 53
Other: Modoc Country USFS/BLM Map (incomplete), A Guide to the Ishi, Thousand Lakes, & Caribou Wilderness (incomplete)

Route Directions

▼ 0.0		From California 89, 0.3 miles north of Hat Creek USFS Work Station at Hat Creek, zero trip meter and turn west on graded dirt FR 26 (34N19), following the sign for Burney Springs and Burney Mountain Lookout.
4.8 ▲		Trail finishes at T-intersection with California 89 at Hat Creek USFS Work Station. Turn left for California 299; turn right for Old Station.
		GPS: N40°48.57' W121°30.77'
▼ 0.2	SO	Track on right; then second track on right is 34N19D.
4.6 ▲	SO	Track on left is 34N19D; then second track on left.
▼ 0.5	SO	Track on left is 34N44 for official vehicles only.
4.3 ▲	SO	Track on right is 34N44 for official vehicles only.
▼ 1.1	SO	Track on right.
3.7 ▲	SO	Track on left.
▼ 1.5	SO	Track on right.
3.3 ▲	SO	Track on left.
▼ 1.7	SO	Track on left and track on right.
3.1 ▲	SO	Track on left and track on right.
▼ 1.9	SO	Track on right.
2.9 ▲	SO	Track on left.
▼ 2.3	SO	Track on right.
2.5 ▲	SO	Track on left.
▼ 2.8	SO	Track on left; then track on right.
2.0 ▲	SO	Track on left; then track on right.
▼ 3.4	TR	Track on right is 34N19G; then 4-way intersection. Track straight ahead is 34N78A. Graded road on left goes to Tamarack Trailhead. Remain on FR 26, following the sign to Burney Spring; then track on left.
1.4 ▲	TL	Track on right; then 4-way intersection. Track on right is 34N78A. Graded road continues

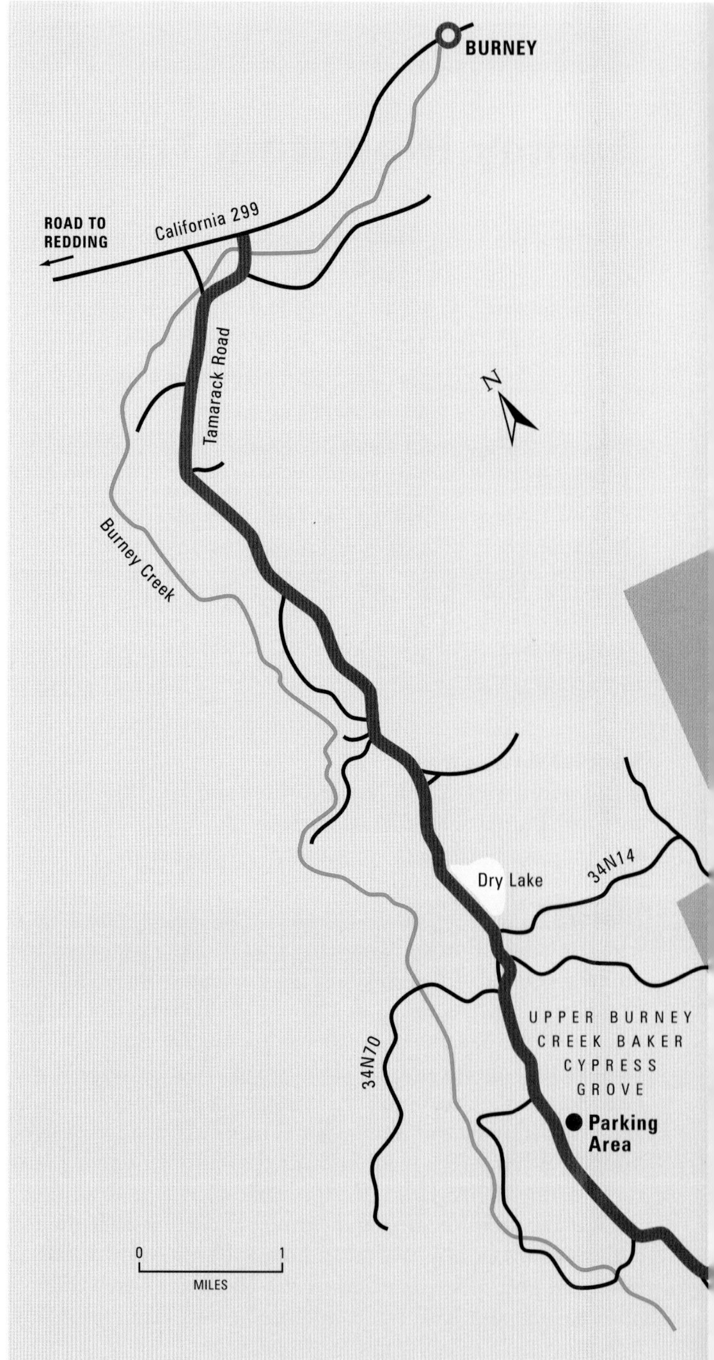

			straight ahead to Tamarack Trailhead. Remain on FR 26, following the sign to California 89. Immediately track on left is 34N19G.
			GPS: N40°46.75′ W121°32.16′
▼ 3.7		SO	Track on left.
	1.1 ▲	SO	Track on right.
▼ 3.9		SO	Track on right.
	0.9 ▲	SO	Track on left.
▼ 4.0		SO	Track on left.
	0.8 ▲	SO	Track on right.
▼ 4.1		SO	Track on left.
	0.7 ▲	SO	Track on right.
▼ 4.2		SO	Track on left.
	0.6 ▲	SO	Track on right.
▼ 4.6		SO	Two tracks on left.
	0.2 ▲	SO	Two tracks on right.
▼ 4.8		TL	4-way intersection. Track straight ahead is 35N35. Track on right is 34N77, which goes 1 mile to seasonal Cornaz Lake. Zero trip meter and follow sign to Burney Mountain Lookout.
	0.0 ▲		Continue to the southeast on FR 26.
			GPS: N40°47.55′ W121°33.38′
▼ 0.0			Continue to the west on FR 26.
	2.8 ▲	TR	4-way intersection. Track on left is 35N35. Track straight ahead is 34N77, which goes 1 mile to the seasonal Cornaz Lake. Zero trip meter and follow the sign to California 89.

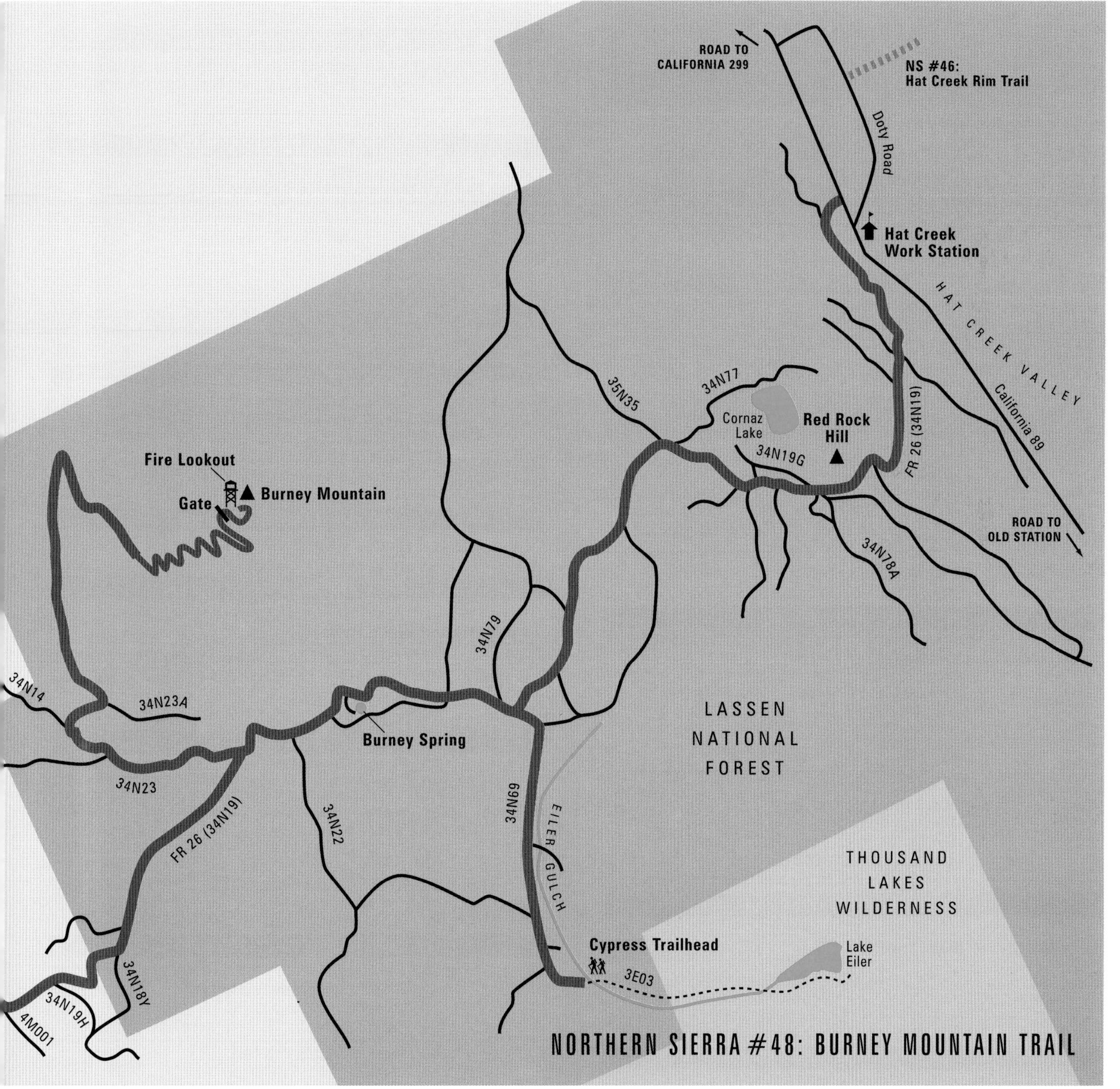

Burney Mountain Fire Lookout

Mileage		Directions
▼ 0.6	SO	Track on left; then track on right is 34N19A; then track on left.
2.2 ▲	SO	Track on right; then track on left is 34N19A; then track on right.
▼ 0.8	BR	Track on left.
2.0 ▲	SO	Track on right.
		GPS: N40°47.16′ W121°34.08′
▼ 1.4	SO	Track on left.
1.4 ▲	SO	Track on right.
▼ 1.6	SO	Track on left.
1.2 ▲	SO	Track on right.
▼ 1.7	SO	Track on left.
1.1 ▲	SO	Track on right.
▼ 1.8	SO	Track on right.
1.0 ▲	SO	Track on left.
▼ 2.2	SO	Track on left.
0.6 ▲	SO	Track on right.
▼ 2.8	TR	T-intersection. To the left is 34N69, spur to Cypress Trailhead. Zero trip meter and follow the sign to Burney Mountain Lookout.
0.0 ▲		Continue to the east on FR 26.
		GPS: N40°46.24′ W121°35.88′

Spur to Cypress Trailhead

Mileage		Directions
▼ 0.0		Proceed southeast on 34N69, following the sign to Cypress Trailhead.
▼ 0.2	SO	Track on left.
▼ 1.2	SO	Track on left.
▼ 1.7	SO	Track on right.
▼ 2.0	SO	Track on left.
▼ 2.2	SO	Track on right.
▼ 2.3	SO	Track on right.
▼ 2.5		Spur ends at the Cypress Trailhead parking area. Hiking trail 3E03 goes up Eiler Gulch to Lake Eiler in the Thousand Lakes Wilderness.
		GPS: N40°44.30′ W121°36.41′

Continuation of Main Trail

Mileage		Directions
▼ 0.0		Continue to the northwest on FR 26.
2.9 ▲	TL	Graded road straight ahead is 34N69, spur to Cypress Trailhead. Zero trip meter and follow the sign to California 89.
		GPS: N40°46.24′ W121°35.88′
▼ 0.1	SO	Track on right is 34N79.
2.8 ▲	SO	Track on left is 34N79.
▼ 0.6	SO	Track on left and track on right.
2.3 ▲	SO	Track on left and track on right.
▼ 1.1	SO	Track on right.
1.8 ▲	SO	Track on left.
▼ 1.5	SO	Burney Spring. Small track on left; then well-used track on left.
1.4 ▲	SO	Burney Spring. Well-used track on right; then small track on right.
		GPS: N40°46.85′ W121°37.28′
▼ 1.9	SO	Cattle guard.
1.0 ▲	SO	Cattle guard.
▼ 2.1	SO	Track on left.
0.8 ▲	SO	Track on right.
▼ 2.3	SO	Graded road on left is 34N22.
0.6 ▲	SO	Graded road on right is 34N22.
		GPS: N40°46.79′ W121°38.02′
▼ 2.9	BL	Graded road on right is 34N23, spur to Burney Mountain Fire Lookout. Zero trip meter and follow the sign to California 44.
0.0 ▲		Continue to the east on FR 26.
		GPS: N40°46.82′ W121°38.53′

Spur to Burney Mountain Fire Lookout

Mileage		Directions
▼ 0.0		Proceed west on 34N23, following the sign to Burney Mountain Lookout.
▼ 0.5	SO	Track on right.
▼ 1.0	SO	Track on left.
▼ 1.2	SO	Track on left.
▼ 1.7	TR	Track straight ahead is 34N14. Zero trip meter and follow the sign to Burney Mountain Lookout.
		GPS: N40°47.49′ W121°40.06′
▼ 0.0		Continue to the northwest, remaining on 34N23.
▼ 0.4	BL	Track on right is 34N23A; then pass through seasonal closure gate.
▼ 2.0	SO	Start of shelf road.
▼ 4.5	SO	Game tank on right.
▼ 6.2	SO	Gate. Closed at 6 P.M.
		GPS: N40°48.48′ W121°37.77′
▼ 6.8		Spur ends at Burney Mountain Fire Lookout (7,863 feet).
		GPS: N40°48.42′ W121°37.61′

Continuation of Main Trail

Mileage		Directions
▼ 0.0		Continue to the southwest on FR 26.
3.3 ▲	BR	Graded road on left is 34N23, spur to Burney Mountain Fire Lookout. Zero trip meter and follow the sign to Cypress Trailhead.
		GPS: N40°46.82′ W121°38.53′
▼ 0.4	SO	Track on right.
2.9 ▲	SO	Track on left.
▼ 0.5	SO	Track on left.
2.8 ▲	SO	Track on right.
▼ 1.9	SO	Track on right.
1.4 ▲	SO	Track on left.
▼ 2.0	BR	Track on left is 34N18Y.
1.3 ▲	SO	Track on right is 34N18Y.
		GPS: N40°45.89′ W121°40.46′
▼ 2.2	SO	Leaving Lassen National Forest and entering Sierra Pacific Industries forest. No fires or camping past this point.
1.1 ▲	SO	Entering Lassen National Forest.
▼ 2.9	SO	Track on left is 34N19H.
0.4 ▲	SO	Track on right is 34N19H.

▼ 3.0		SO	Track on left.
	0.3 ▲	SO	Track on right.
▼ 3.3		TR	T-intersection with graded road. Zero trip meter and follow the sign to Burney.
	0.0 ▲		Continue to the northeast on FR 26 (34N19).
			GPS: N40°45.84' W121°41.79'
▼ 0.0			Continue to the northwest on CR 4M001.
	8.4 ▲	TL	CR 4M001 continues straight ahead. Zero trip meter and follow the sign to Burney Mountain Lookout.
▼ 0.5		SO	Track on left.
	7.9 ▲	SO	Track on right.
▼ 0.8		SO	Track on right.
	7.6 ▲	SO	Track on left.
▼ 1.2		SO	Track on left.
	7.2 ▲	SO	Track on right.
▼ 1.4		SO	Upper Burney Creek Baker Cypress Grove parking area on right, with a trail around a grove of rare Baker cypresses.
	7.0 ▲	SO	Upper Burney Creek Baker Cypress Grove parking area on left, with a trail around a grove of rare Baker cypresses.
			GPS: N40°46.95' 121°42.35'
▼ 1.7		SO	Track on left.
	6.7 ▲	SO	Track on right.
▼ 1.9		SO	Track on left.
	6.5 ▲	SO	Track on right.
▼ 2.1		SO	Track on left; then track on right.
	6.3 ▲	SO	Track on left; then track on right.
▼ 2.4		SO	Track on left is 34N70; then track on left to corral.
	6.0 ▲	SO	Track on right to corral; then track on right is 34N70.
			GPS: N40°47.82' W121°42.30'
▼ 2.7		SO	Track on right; then track on left.
	5.7 ▲	BR	Track on right; then track on left.
▼ 2.9		BL	Track on right.
	5.5 ▲	SO	Track on left.
▼ 3.0		SO	Track on right is 34N14.
	5.4 ▲	BR	Track on left is 34N14.
			GPS: N40°48.19' W121°42.23'
▼ 3.4		SO	Track on left; then Dry Lake on right.
	5.0 ▲	SO	Dry Lake on left; then track on right.
▼ 3.6		SO	Track on right.
	4.8 ▲	SO	Track on left.
▼ 4.0		SO	Track on right.
	4.4 ▲	SO	Track on left.
▼ 4.1		SO	Track on right.
	4.3 ▲	SO	Track on left.
▼ 4.5		SO	Three tracks on left.
	3.9 ▲	SO	Three tracks on right.
			GPS: N40°49.48' W121°42.46'
▼ 4.9		SO	Track on right.
	3.5 ▲	SO	Track on left.
▼ 5.3		SO	Track on left.
	3.1 ▲	SO	Track on right.
▼ 5.4		SO	Track on right.
	3.0 ▲	SO	Track on left.
▼ 5.5		SO	Track on right.
	2.9 ▲	SO	Track on left.
▼ 5.7		SO	Track on left.
	2.7 ▲	SO	Track on right.
▼ 6.4		SO	Track on left and track on right.
	2.0 ▲	SO	Track on left and track on right.
▼ 6.7		SO	Track on left under power line.
	1.7 ▲	SO	Track on right under power line.
▼ 6.8		SO	Track on right.
	1.6 ▲	SO	Track on left.
▼ 7.2		SO	Track on left.
	1.2 ▲	SO	Track on right.
▼ 7.3		SO	Track on left.
	1.1 ▲	SO	Track on right.
▼ 7.5		SO	Track on right.
	0.9 ▲	SO	Track on left.
▼ 7.8		BR	Graded road continues straight ahead. Bear right onto graded road.
	0.6 ▲	SO	Graded road joins on right.
			GPS: N40°52.12' W121°42.31'
▼ 8.0		SO	Track on right.
	0.4 ▲	SO	Track on left.
▼ 8.1		SO	Track on right. Road is now paved. Remain on paved road until the end of the trail.
	0.3 ▲	SO	Track on left. Road turns to graded dirt.
▼ 8.3		SO	Cross over Burney Creek on bridge.
	0.1 ▲	SO	Cross over Burney Creek on bridge.
▼ 8.4			Trail ends at T-intersection with California 299. Turn left for Redding; turn right for Burney.
	0.0 ▲		Trail commences on California 299, 0.9 miles west of Burney. Zero trip meter and turn south on paved Tamarack Road. Note that there is also a Tamarack Avenue on the edge of town, which is a different road.
			GPS: N40°52.38' W121°41.79'

NORTHERN SIERRA #49

Popcorn Cave Trail

Starting Point:	**Cassel Fall River Road (CR 7R02), 3.7 miles south of Fall River Mills**
Finishing Point:	**Little Valley Road (CR 404), 2.1 miles south of Pittville**
Total Mileage:	**11.1 miles**
Unpaved Mileage:	**9.1 miles**
Driving Time:	**1 hour**
Elevation Range:	**3,300–4,000 feet**
Usually Open:	**April to November**
Best Time to Travel:	**April to November**
Difficulty Rating:	**1**
Scenic Rating:	**8**
Remoteness Rating:	**+0**

Special Attractions

- Easy trail through a volcanic region.
- Volcanic landscape around Popcorn Cave and Big Cave.

History

Pittville, near the eastern end of this trail was established in 1873. The settlement's primary activity was agriculture. A post office was added in 1878, and the town was officially named

Popcorn Cave Trail

Pittville (at a time when the river was still spelled Pitt). In 1871, William Henry Winter established a flourmill at the site that became Fall River Mills (see page 34). A hamlet grew around the mill, and by 1886, the population was about 300. Businesses included two hotels, a blacksmith shop, three stores, two saloons, Winter's flourmill, and a door and sash factory.

The Lockhart Ferry was established at the junction of the Pit and Fall Rivers in 1856 and later relocated below the Fall River Falls, named when John C. Frémont passed through the vicinity in the 1840s.

Description

This graded cinder loop starts and finishes just off California 299 and travels through an arid volcanic region that is part of the Modoc Plateau. The trail passes stands of ponderosa pines, oaks, and manzanitas. It is a short, pleasant drive suitable for passenger vehicles in dry weather.

Midway around the loop, a short spur leads to a parking area alongside a volcanic boulder field. The large rocks are the site of Popcorn Cave and Big Cave. Although very hard to spot, it is fun to scramble over the rough boulders and explore the depressions and ridges of hardened lava.

The trail continues north of Bald Mountain to join CR 111, which wraps around to the north, joining CR 404 south of the small settlement of Pittville.

Current Road Information

Bureau of Land Management
Redding Field Office
355 Hemsted Drive
Redding, CA 96002
(530) 224-2100

Map References

BLM Burney, McArthur
USFS Lassen National Forest
USGS 1:24,000 Hogback Ridge, Coble Mt., Pittville
1:100,000 Burney, McArthur
Maptech CD-ROM: Shasta Lake/Redding; Shasta-Trinity/Modoc
Northern California Atlas & Gazetteer, pp. 38, 48
California Road & Recreation Atlas, p. 53
Other: Modoc Country USFS/BLM Map

Route Directions

Mileage		Description
▼ 0.0		From California 299 in Fall River Mills, proceed south on CR 7R02, marked Main Street, and cross over the Pit River. Continue 3.7 miles south, remaining on Cassel Fall River Road. Zero trip meter and turn east on unmarked graded dirt road and cross over cattle guard.
3.6 ▲		The trail is 0.1 miles south of Chaffey Court. Trail ends on Cassel Fall River Road (CR 7R02). Turn right for Fall River Mills; turn left for Old Station.
		GPS: N40°57.38' W121°26.31'
▼ 0.2	SO	Track on right.
3.4 ▲	SO	Track on left.
▼ 0.3	SO	Track on left.
3.3 ▲	SO	Track on right.
▼ 0.5	SO	Track on left.
3.1 ▲	SO	Track on right.
▼ 0.6	SO	Track on right; then cattle guard; then track on left.
3.0 ▲	SO	Track on right; then cattle guard; then track on left.
▼ 0.9	SO	Track on left.
2.7 ▲	SO	Track on right.
▼ 1.1	SO	Track on right.
2.5 ▲	SO	Track on left.
▼ 1.4	SO	Track on left and track on right.
2.2 ▲	SO	Track on left and track on right.
▼ 2.6	SO	Cattle guard.
1.0 ▲	SO	Cattle guard.
		GPS: N40°56.89' W121°23.55'
▼ 3.6	SO	Unmarked cinder track on left goes 0.3 miles to Popcorn Cave. Zero trip meter.
0.0 ▲		Continue to the west.
		GPS: N40°56.87' W121°22.45'
▼ 0.0		Continue to the east.
3.1 ▲	SO	Unmarked cinder track on right goes 0.3 miles to Popcorn Cave. Zero trip meter.
▼ 1.3	BL	Track on right.
1.8 ▲	SO	Track on left.
▼ 1.4	SO	Cinder pit on right.
1.7 ▲	SO	Cinder pit on left.
▼ 1.6	SO	Graded road on right.
1.5 ▲	BR	Graded road on left.
		GPS: N40°56.53' W121°20.81'
▼ 1.7	SO	Track on right.
1.4 ▲	SO	Track on left.
▼ 1.8	SO	Track on right.

Ponderosas, oaks, and rabbitbrush along the trail

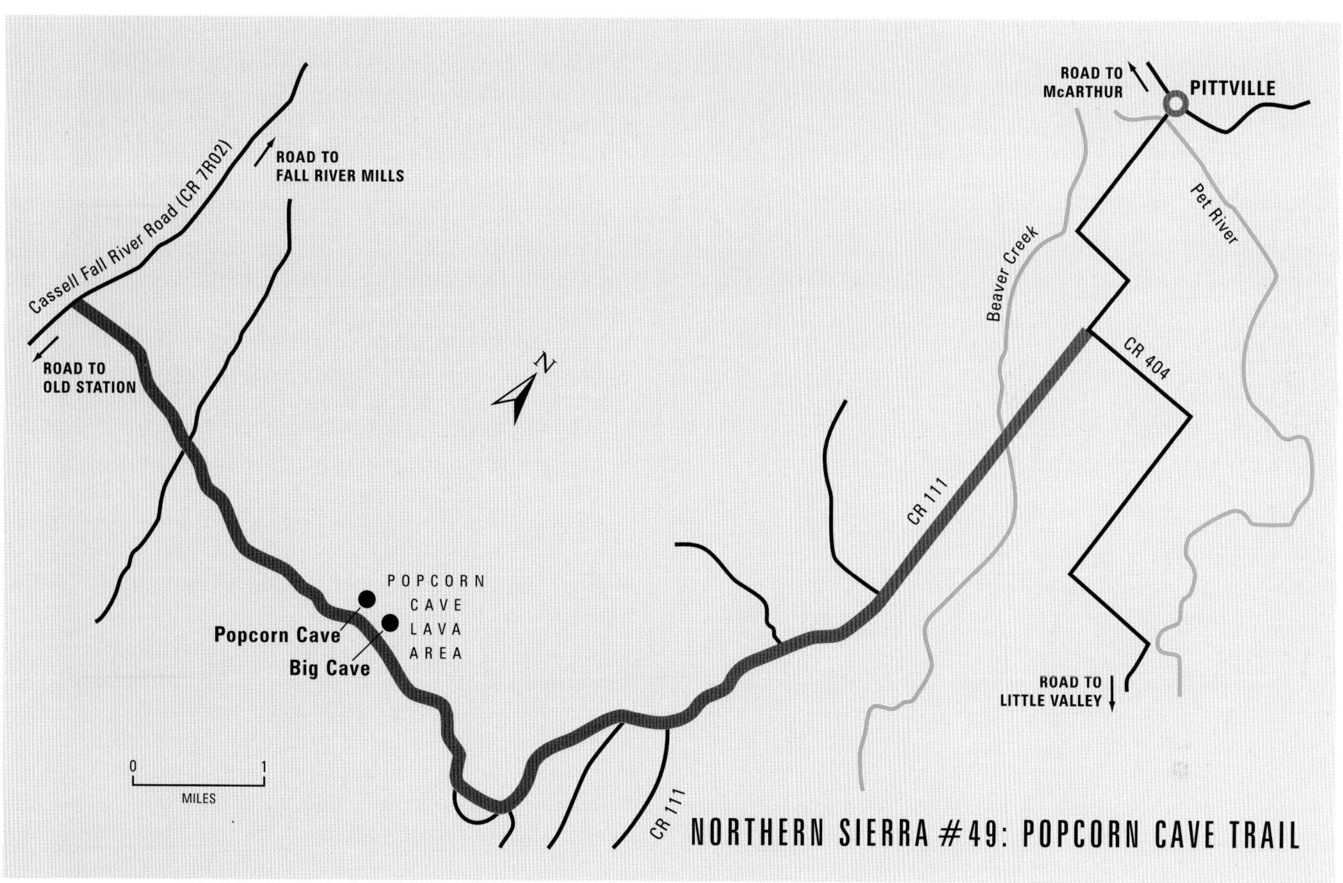

	1.3 ▲	SO	Track on left.
▼ 1.9		SO	Track on left.
	1.2 ▲	SO	Track on right.
▼ 2.1		SO	Cattle guard.
	1.0 ▲	SO	Cattle guard.
▼ 2.3		SO	Track on right.
	0.8 ▲	SO	Track on left.
▼ 2.8		SO	Track on right.
	0.3 ▲	SO	Track on left.
▼ 3.0		SO	Track on left.
	0.1 ▲	SO	Track on right.
▼ 3.1		TL	Cattle guard; then T-intersection with CR 111. Zero trip meter.
	0.1 ▲		Continue to the southwest.
			GPS: N40°57.65′ W121°20.07′
▼ 0.0			Continue to the northwest.
	4.4 ▲	TR	CR 111 continues straight ahead. Zero trip meter and turn right on unmarked graded road and cross cattle guard.
▼ 1.1		SO	Track on left.
	3.3 ▲	SO	Track on right.
▼ 1.9		SO	Track on left; then cattle guard.
	2.5 ▲	SO	Cattle guard; then track on right.
▼ 2.4		SO	Road becomes paved. Remain on paved road for next 2 miles, ignoring turns to the left and right.
	2.0 ▲	SO	Road turns to graded dirt.
▼ 3.4		SO	Cross over Beaver Creek on bridge.
	1.0 ▲	SO	Cross over Beaver Creek on bridge.
▼ 4.4		SO	Road on right; then trail ends at intersection with Little Valley Road (CR 404). Continue straight ahead for McArthur; turn right for Little Valley.
	0.0 ▲		Trail starts on Little Valley Road (CR 404) at the intersection with CR 111, 2.1 miles south of Pittville. Zero trip meter and turn south on CR 111. Remain on paved road for next 2 miles, ignoring turns to the left and right.
			GPS: N41°01.37′ W121°19.24′

NORTHERN SIERRA #50

Hayden Hill Trail

Starting Point:	**Susanville Road (CR A2), 0.4 miles west of the intersection with California 139**
Finishing Point:	**California 139, 1.3 miles north of Willow Creek Campground**
Total Mileage:	**16.6 miles**
Unpaved Mileage:	**16.5 miles**
Driving Time:	**1.5 hours**
Elevation Range:	**4,400–5,800 feet**
Usually Open:	**April to November**
Best Time to Travel:	**Dry weather**
Difficulty Rating:	**1**
Scenic Rating:	**7**
Remoteness Rating:	**+0**

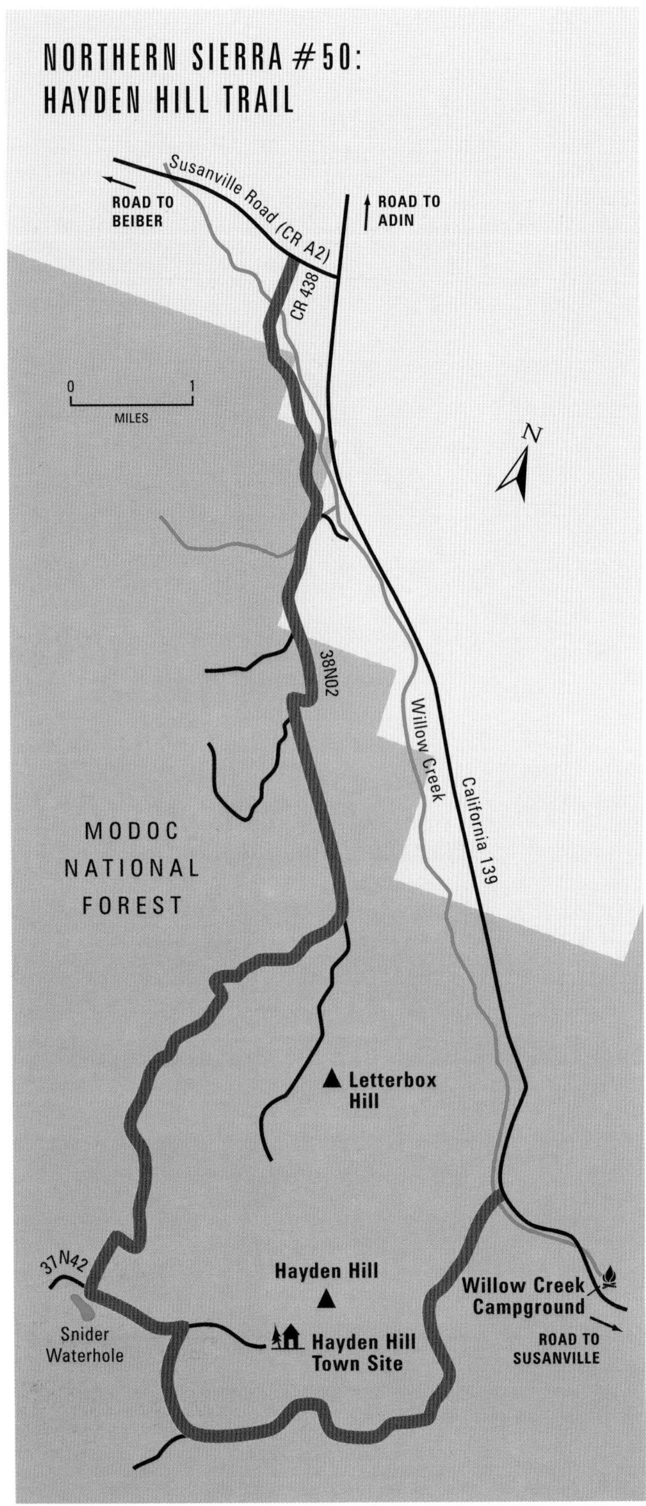

Special Attractions

- Easy winding trail through Modoc National Forest.
- Trail passes close to the historic site of Hayden Hill.

History

The Providence Mine, the first mine established at Hayden Hill, may have been accidentally discovered by prospectors from Yreka in search of the fabled Lost Cabin Mine in the fall of 1869. Another story is that clergymen staked the claim in 1870 while traveling north from Susanville to Adin. Regardless of which tale is true, the mines were well established by the end of 1870.

After J. W. Hayden and Seneca Lewis established the Providence Mine, a horde of prospectors followed. A mill was hauled to Hayden Hill from a failed mining operation at Hardin City, Nevada.

By April 1871, the Hayden post office opened; its name was later changed to Haydenhill. During the late 1870s a mini gold rush brought several hundred people to the area. Businesses, including a butcher shop, hotel, blacksmith, and saloon opened. The White Swan, Brush Hill, Golden Eagle, Juniper, Blue Bells, Idaho, Evening Star, and Vicuna Mines supported the town. The Lassen Mining Company owned many of the mines and operated a mill. More than $2 million worth of gold was extracted from the area around Hayden Hill between 1880 and 1911. The Hayden Hill Consolidated Mining Company continued small-scale mining for a few years after 1911.

Description

Hayden Hill Trail loops into Modoc National Forest, passing near the former gold mining settlement. The uneven, narrow road winds through semi-open forest and meadows, and passes some private property. The trail swings west to join the good, graded road that serves as access to mines around Hayden Hill. As you approach, the re-vegetated terraces of Hayden Hill stand out clearly to the south. There is no public access to the privately owned mines. In the past, rock hounds have found rhyolite around the old site of Hayden Hill.

The trail passes through a state game refuge—no firearms allowed—to finish on California 139, 13 miles south of Adin.

Current Road Information

Modoc National Forest
Big Valley Ranger District
508 South Main
Adin, CA 96006
(530) 299-3215

Map References

BLM Alturas, Eagle Lake
USFS Modoc National Forest
USGS 1:24,000 Letterbox Hill, Silva Flat Reservoir, Said Valley, Lane Reservoir
1:100,000 Alturas, Eagle Lake
Maptech CD-ROM: Shasta-Trinity/Modoc; Shasta Lake/Redding
Northern California Atlas & Gazetteer, pp. 39, 40, 49, 50
California Road & Recreation Atlas, p. 54
Other: BLM Recreation Guide for Northeastern California and Northwestern Nevada

Route Directions

▼ 0.0	From Susanville Road (CR A2), 0.4 miles west of California 139 and 11 miles east of Beiber, zero trip meter and turn south on graded cin-

Heavily mined Hayden Hill

			der Armstrong Road (CR 438, 38N02).
	5.5 ▲		Trail ends on Susanville Road (CR A2). Turn left for Beiber; turn right for California 139 and Adin.
			GPS: N41°06.83′ W120°55.65′
▼ 0.4		SO	Cross over Willow Creek.
	5.1 ▲	SO	Cross over Willow Creek.
▼ 0.8		SO	Cattle guard.
	4.7 ▲	SO	Cattle guard.
▼ 1.7		SO	Track on right.
	3.8 ▲	SO	Track on left.
▼ 2.1		BR	Track on left.
	3.4 ▲	BL	Track on right.
▼ 2.2		SO	Cross through creek.
	3.3 ▲	SO	Cross through creek.
▼ 2.5		SO	Cattle guard. Entering Modoc National Forest. Road is now designated 38N02. Follow sign to Hayden Hill.
	3.0 ▲	SO	Leaving Modoc National Forest. Cattle guard.
			GPS: N41°04.91′ W120°54.73′
▼ 3.2		SO	Track on right.
	2.3 ▲	SO	Track on left.
▼ 3.9		SO	Track on right.
	1.6 ▲	SO	Track on left.
▼ 5.5		BR	Track on left. Zero trip meter.
	0.0 ▲		Continue to the northwest on 38N02.
			GPS: N41°02.64′ W120°53.33′
▼ 0.0			Continue to the south on 38N02.
	4.5 ▲	BL	Track on right. Zero trip meter.
▼ 0.5		SO	Track on left.
	4.0 ▲	SO	Track on right.
▼ 0.8		SO	Track on right.
	3.7 ▲	SO	Track on left.
▼ 3.7		SO	Cattle guard.
	0.8 ▲	SO	Cattle guard.
			GPS: N41°00.04′ W120°54.15′
▼ 4.5		TL	T-intersection with graded road 37N42. Zero trip meter and follow the sign to Hayden Hill. Snider Waterhole is straight ahead.
	0.0 ▲		Continue to the north.
			GPS: N40°59.63′ W120°54.43′
▼ 0.0			Continue to the east.
	6.6 ▲	TR	Track straight ahead is 37N42 to Summit Spring. Zero trip meter and turn right onto 38N02, following the sign to Adin. Snider

			Waterhole is to the left.
▼ 0.8		TR	Cattle guard; then turn right on major graded road and enter state game refuge. Track on left goes to Hayden Hill.
	5.8 ▲	TL	Graded road continues straight ahead to Hayden Hill. Turn left over cattle guard onto unmarked graded road and enter Modoc National Forest.
			GPS: N40°59.67′ W120°53.52′
▼ 1.9		SO	Track on right.
	4.7 ▲	SO	Track on left.
▼ 2.6		SO	Track on right.
	4.0 ▲	SO	Track on left.
▼ 6.5		SO	Cattle guard. Road is now paved. Track on left.
	0.1 ▲	SO	Track on right. Road turns to graded dirt. Cattle guard.
▼ 6.6			Cross over Willow Creek; then trail ends at T-intersection with California 139. Turn right for Eagle Lake and Susanville; turn left for Adin.
	0.0 ▲		Trail commences on California 139, 1.3 miles north of Willow Creek USFS Campground, 13 miles south of Adin. Zero trip meter and turn south on paved road at the sign for Hayden Hill.
			GPS: N41°01.23′ W120°51.08′

NORTHERN SIERRA #51

Likely Mountain Trail

Starting Point:	**Ash Valley Road (CR 527), 9 miles west of Madeline**
Finishing Point:	**US 395, 4.5 miles south of Likely**
Total Mileage:	**23.2 miles**
Unpaved Mileage:	**23.2 miles**
Driving Time:	**4 hours**
Elevation Range:	**5,200–6,700 feet**
Usually Open:	**May to November**
Best Time to Travel:	**Dry weather**
Difficulty Rating:	**3**
Scenic Rating:	**8**
Remoteness Rating:	**+0**

Special Attractions

- Trail passes the sites of Portuguese and Fleming Sheep Camps.
- Panoramic views from Likely Fire Lookout.
- Mountain bike trail from US 395 to Likely Fire Lookout.
- Lightly traveled trail through a variety of forest and open landscapes.

History

Likely Mountain Trail follows a well-beaten path made by shepherds and their flocks in the vicinity of Sears Flat and Knox Mountain. The Fleming and Portuguese Sheep Camps were regular stops when flocks were moved. Sheep were intro-

A well and cattle trough remain at Portuguese Sheep Camp

duced to the northeastern corner of California in the late 1860s. The animals could be herded for hundreds of miles across open range. By the end of the nineteenth century and into the next, large-scale sheep ranches came into conflict with cattle operations. Cattlemen thought sheep overgrazed the range. Intensive lobbying by cattlemen reduced the wide-ranging movement of sheep. Some herds came from Idaho to Madeline, the northernmost terminus on the Nevada-California-Oregon Railway.

National forest lands were established around the Warner Mountains in order to put a stop to sheep grazing. Some sheep owners bought small plots of land and moved their flocks from patch to patch, grazing as they went.

Description

Likely Mountain Trail leaves Ash Valley Road (CR 527) and travels a long arc through a mixture of vegetation to finish on US 395. The well-used formed trail leaves from the west side of Holbrook Reservoir near the site of Fleming Sheep Camp; little remains of the camp. It travels up the eastern side of Knox Mountain through a wide rabbitbrush-covered valley and passes the site of Portuguese Sheep Camp, where only a collapsed wooden building remains. Wildlife that can typically be seen along this trail includes blue grouse, golden mantle ground squirrels, chipmunks, black-tail deer, and occasionally mountain lions. After entering Modoc National Forest, the trail swings east around the top of the loop to pass Big John Spring, set among ponderosa pines. The many tracks in the area can make navigation a bit confusing, but generally the most-used trail is the correct one. The route leaves the forest to cross through sagebrush and junipers on Sears Flat.

Likely Fire Lookout

The lumpy trail surface is formed all the way with embedded rocks. Although it makes for slow travel, it is not a difficult trail. After passing through Water Canyon, the trail climbs up to join the graded county road to the Likely Fire Lookout, an active fire lookout perched amid communications towers on Likely Mountain. The tower is manned from May to mid-October (depending on weather), and visitors are usually welcome to climb the steep stairway to the tower. Panoramic views include Tule Mountain directly to the east, Moon Lake to the southeast, and Nelson Corral Reservoir to the south. The trail across Sears Flat is visible to the northwest and the settlement of Likely is visible in the valley to the north. From the lookout tower, the trail follows the graded county road to finish on US 395.

Current Road Information

Bureau of Land Management
Eagle Lake Field Office
2950 Riverside Drive
Susanville, CA 96130
(530) 257-0456

Modoc National Forest
Big Valley Ranger District
508 South Main
Adin, CA 96006
(530) 299-3215

Map References

BLM Alturas
USFS Modoc National Forest
USGS 1:24,000 Ash Valley, Knox Mt., Likely
1:100,000 Alturas
Maptech CD-ROM: Shasta-Trinity/Modoc
Northern California Atlas & Gazetteer, p. 40
California Road & Recreation Atlas, pp. 54, 48 (incomplete)
Other: BLM Recreation Guide for Northeastern California and Northwestern Nevada (incomplete), Modoc Country USFS/BLM Map

Route Directions

▼ 0.0		From Ash Valley Road (CR 527), 9 miles west of Madeline and 23 miles east of Adin and California 139, 0.1 miles west of Holbrook Reservoir, zero trip meter and turn northwest on unmarked graded dirt road. There is no directional sign pointing up the road, but there is a BLM sign giving directions for Adin and Madeline.
6.1 ▲		Trail ends at T-intersection with Ash Valley Road (CR 527). Turn left for US 395 and Madeline; turn right for California 139 and Adin.
		GPS: N41°04.62' W120°37.98'
▼ 0.5	SO	Track on right.
5.6 ▲	SO	Track on left.
▼ 2.1	SO	Dam on left.
4.0 ▲	SO	Dam on right.
▼ 2.2	SO	Track on left.
3.9 ▲	SO	Track on right.
▼ 3.0	SO	Track on right.

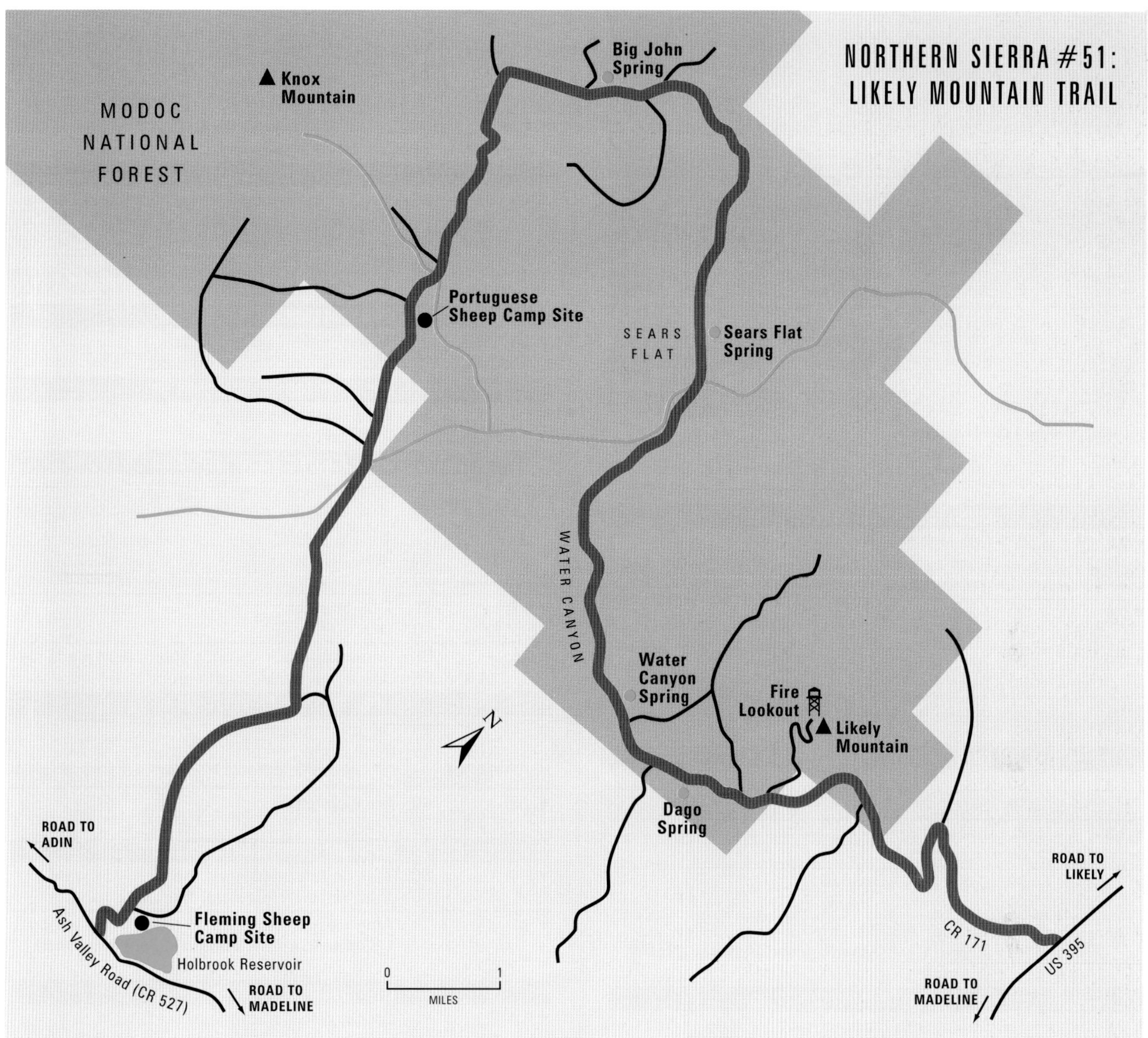

3.1 ▲	SO	Track on left.
		GPS: N41°06.88' W120°37.88'
▼ 3.5	SO	Track on left.
2.6 ▲	SO	Track on right.
▼ 4.9	SO	Track on left.
1.2 ▲	SO	Track on right.
▼ 5.1	SO	Cross over creek.
1.0 ▲	SO	Cross over creek.
▼ 5.3	SO	Track on left.
0.8 ▲	SO	Track on right.
		GPS: N41°08.74' W120°38.98'
▼ 5.6	SO	Track on left.
0.5 ▲	SO	Track on right.
▼ 6.0	SO	Track on left.
0.1 ▲	SO	Track on right.
▼ 6.1	SO	Pass through fence line. Leaving National Resource Lands. Zero trip meter at sign.
0.0 ▲		Continue to the southeast.
		GPS: N41°09.35' W120°39.35'
▼ 0.0		Continue to the northwest.
2.7 ▲	SO	Pass through fence line. Entering National Resource Lands. Zero trip meter and follow sign for Ash Valley Road.
▼ 0.4	SO	Site of Portuguese Sheep Camp.
2.3 ▲	SO	Site of Portuguese Sheep Camp.
		GPS: N41°09.67' W120°39.49'
▼ 0.5	SO	Track on left opposite well.
2.2 ▲	SO	Track on right opposite well.
▼ 0.9	SO	Cross through wash; then track on left.
1.8 ▲	SO	Track on right; then cross through wash.
▼ 1.1	SO	Gate. Entering Modoc National Forest.
1.6 ▲	SO	Gate. Leaving Modoc National Forest.
		GPS: N41°10.22' W120°39.61'
▼ 2.1	SO	Gate.
0.6 ▲	SO	Gate.
▼ 2.2	SO	Track on left.
0.5 ▲	SO	Track on right.
▼ 2.7	BR	Trail continues straight ahead. Bear right onto

Trail heading toward Likely Mountain

			unmarked, formed trail and zero trip meter.
	0.0 ▲		Continue to the southwest.
			GPS: N41°11.43′ W120°40.30′
▼ 0.0			Continue to the north.
	2.6 ▲	SO	Track on right. Continue on unmarked formed trail and zero trip meter.
▼ 0.6		SO	Track on right.
	2.0 ▲	SO	Track on left.
▼ 0.8		SO	Track on left.
	1.8 ▲	SO	Track on right.
▼ 1.1		SO	Big John Spring on left.
	1.5 ▲	SO	Big John Spring on right.
			GPS: N41°12.00′ W120°39.32′
▼ 1.2		SO	Gate.
	1.4 ▲	SO	Gate.
▼ 1.3		BL	Track on right.
	1.3 ▲	BR	Track on left.
▼ 2.5		SO	Cross through wash.
	0.1 ▲	SO	Cross through wash.
▼ 2.6		BR	Track on left. Zero trip meter and follow old sign to Likely Mountain and Highway 395.
	0.0 ▲		Continue to the west.
			GPS: N41°12.25′ W120°37.90′
▼ 0.0			Continue to the southeast.
	7.7 ▲	BL	Track on right. There is a directional sign for Likely Mountain at the intersection pointing back the way you have come. Zero trip meter.
▼ 0.1		SO	Cross through wash.
	7.6 ▲	SO	Cross through wash.
▼ 1.4		SO	Gate.
	6.3 ▲	SO	Gate.
▼ 1.6		SO	Cross through wash.
	6.1 ▲	SO	Cross through wash.
▼ 1.7		SO	Water tank on left at Sears Flat Spring.
	6.0 ▲	SO	Water tank on right at Sears Flat Spring.
			GPS: N41°11.03′ W120°37.10′
▼ 2.2		SO	Cross through wash.
	5.5 ▲	SO	Cross through wash.
▼ 2.7		SO	Cross through wash.
	5.0 ▲	SO	Cross through wash.
▼ 3.3		SO	Gate; then cross through wash.
	4.4 ▲	SO	Cross through wash; then gate.
			GPS: N41°09.84′ W120°36.90′
▼ 3.5		SO	Cross through wash. Leaving Sears Flat.
	4.2 ▲	SO	Entering Sears Flat. Cross through wash.
▼ 3.6		SO	Cross through wash.
	4.1 ▲	SO	Cross through wash.
▼ 3.9		SO	Cross through wash.
	3.8 ▲	SO	Cross through wash.
▼ 4.1		SO	Well-used track on right.
	3.6 ▲	SO	Well-used track on left.
			GPS: N41°09.25′ W120°36.69′
▼ 4.5		SO	Cross through wash. Trail enters Water Canyon. Many wash crossings for the next 1.5 miles.
	3.2 ▲	SO	Cross through wash. Trail leaves Water Canyon.
▼ 5.4		SO	Tank on left is supplied by Water Canyon Spring.
	2.3 ▲	SO	Tank on right is supplied by Water Canyon Spring.
			GPS: N41°08.53′ W120°35.65′
▼ 5.5		SO	Water Canyon Spring on left.
	2.2 ▲	SO	Water Canyon Spring on right.
			GPS: N41°08.52′ W120°35.56′
▼ 5.7		SO	Track on left across wash.
	2.0 ▲	SO	Track on right across wash.
			GPS: N41°08.40′ W120°35.29′
▼ 6.0		SO	Cross through wash.
	1.7 ▲	SO	Cross through wash. Many wash crossings for the next 1.5 miles.
▼ 6.1		SO	Tank on left.
	1.6 ▲	SO	Tank on right.
▼ 6.2		SO	Tank on right.
	1.5 ▲	SO	Tank on left.
▼ 6.3		BL	Unmarked track on right enters BLM land.
	1.4 ▲	BR	Unmarked track on left enters BLM land.
			GPS: N41°08.30′ W120°34.81′
▼ 6.6		SO	Dago Spring on right.
	1.1 ▲	SO	Dago Spring on left.
			GPS: N41°08.39′ W120°34.49′
▼ 7.3		SO	Track on left.
	0.4 ▲	BL	Track on right.
			GPS: N41°08.57′ W120°33.87′
▼ 7.4		SO	Tank on left; then gate; then track on right.
	0.3 ▲	SO	Track on left; then gate; then tank on right.
▼ 7.7		TR	T-intersection with graded road. To the left goes 1.3 miles to Likely Mountain. Zero trip meter.
	0.0 ▲		Continue to the southwest.
			GPS: N41°08.75′ W120°33.55′
▼ 0.0			Continue to the northeast on CR 171.
	4.1 ▲	TL	Graded road continues straight ahead for 1.3 miles to Likely Mountain. Zero trip meter and follow the sign to Sears Flat.
▼ 1.0		SO	Track on right.
	3.1 ▲	SO	Track on left.
▼ 2.5		SO	Track on left.
	1.6 ▲	SO	Track on right.
▼ 2.7		SO	Track on right under power lines.
	1.4 ▲	SO	Track on left under power lines.
▼ 3.7		SO	Track on right.
	0.4 ▲	SO	Track on left.
▼ 3.9		SO	Cattle guard.
	0.2 ▲	SO	Cattle guard.
▼ 4.0		SO	Track on left and track on right.
	0.1 ▲	SO	Track on left and track on right.
▼ 4.1			Trail ends at T-intersection with US 395. Turn left for Likely and Alturas; turn right for Susanville.
	0.0 ▲		Trail commences on US 395, 4.5 miles south of Likely and 0.3 miles south of Lassen County mile marker 137. Zero trip meter and turn southwest on unmarked graded dirt road.
			GPS: N41°09.33′ W120°30.45′

Buckhorn Backcountry Byway

Starting Point:	**US 395 at Termo**
Finishing Point:	**Nevada 447, 30.5 miles southeast of Eagleville, CA**
Total Mileage:	**49.1 miles**
Unpaved Mileage:	**48.4 miles**
Driving Time:	**3 hours**
Elevation Range:	**4,800–6,500 feet**
Usually Open:	**Year-round**
Best Time to Travel:	**Spring and fall**
Difficulty Rating:	**1**
Scenic Rating:	**8**
Remoteness Rating:	**+1**

Special Attractions

- Fishing and backcountry camping at small reservoirs along the trail.
- Chance to see wild horses.
- Remote byway suitable for passenger vehicles.

Description

The Buckhorn Backcountry Byway is one of a number of backcountry roads nationwide that have been designated for their remote and scenic qualities. The Buckhorn route travels past low hills, dry lakes, and country covered in sagebrush and rabbitbrush. The trail is well-graded, often graveled, for its entire length, and it is generally suitable for passenger vehicles. However, access to Buckhorn Reservoir and the Round Corral Wetlands requires a high-clearance vehicle. The trail is remote, and you are unlikely to see other travelers. There are many pleasant backcountry campsites along ridge tops, among junipers, and around the dry lakes. There are no developed campgrounds along the trail.

Mustangs near Cedar Canyon

Initially, the trail passes through private land as it leaves US 395 and Termo, crosses Juniper Ridge, and descends to Coyote Flat. After joining the road from Ravendale, the route travels toward Buckhorn Canyon. Buckhorn Reservoir is a short distance from the main trail, and although listed on the BLM map as an angling spot, it is often dry in summer and fall. A second reservoir—Round Corral—is marked as wetlands but is also usually dry. Some good campsites at the reservoir are accessible by high-clearance 2WDs in dry weather only.

Continuing along the main route, the trail crosses into Nevada at dry Pilgrim Lake, before crossing a ridge and descending to the large, open dry area of Burnt Lake. This is a good place to spot the herds of wild horse that roam these ranges. Small bands of horses are often found around the lakes along the trail. Do not approach them! They are wild and easily spooked.

Basalt blocks

The trail drops down off the ridge to Cedar Canyon, passing beside some of the basalt pillars characteristic of this volcanic region. It finishes on Nevada 447, 37.5 miles northwest of Gerlach, Nevada, and 30.5 miles southeast of Eagleville, California.

Current Road Information

Bureau of Land Management
Eagle Lake Field Office
2950 Riverside Drive
Susanville, CA 96130
(530) 257-0456

Map References

BLM Eagle Lake, Gerlach
USGS 1:24,000 Termo, Ravendale, Juniper Ridge, Dodge Reservoir, Observation Peak, Buckhorn Canyon, Buckhorn Lake, Hole in the Ground, Burnt Lake, Rye Patch Canyon
1:100,000 Eagle Lake, Gerlach
Maptech CD-ROM: Shasta Lake/Redding
Northern California Atlas & Gazetteer, p. 51
Nevada Atlas & Gazetteer, p. 26
California Road & Recreation Atlas, p. 55
Other: BLM Recreation Guide for Northeastern California and Northwestern Nevada, Modoc Country USFS/BLM Map

Route Directions

▼ 0.0		From US 395 at Termo, zero trip meter and turn east on graveled Juniper Ridge Road (CR 508) and cross over railroad tracks.
10.9 ▲		Cross over railroad tracks; then trail ends on US 395 at Termo. Turn right for Alturas; turn left for Susanville.
		GPS: N40°51.99' W120°27.57'
▼ 0.1	SO	Cattle guard.
10.8 ▲	SO	Cattle guard.
▼ 1.0	BR	Road on left is Jones Road (CR 522).

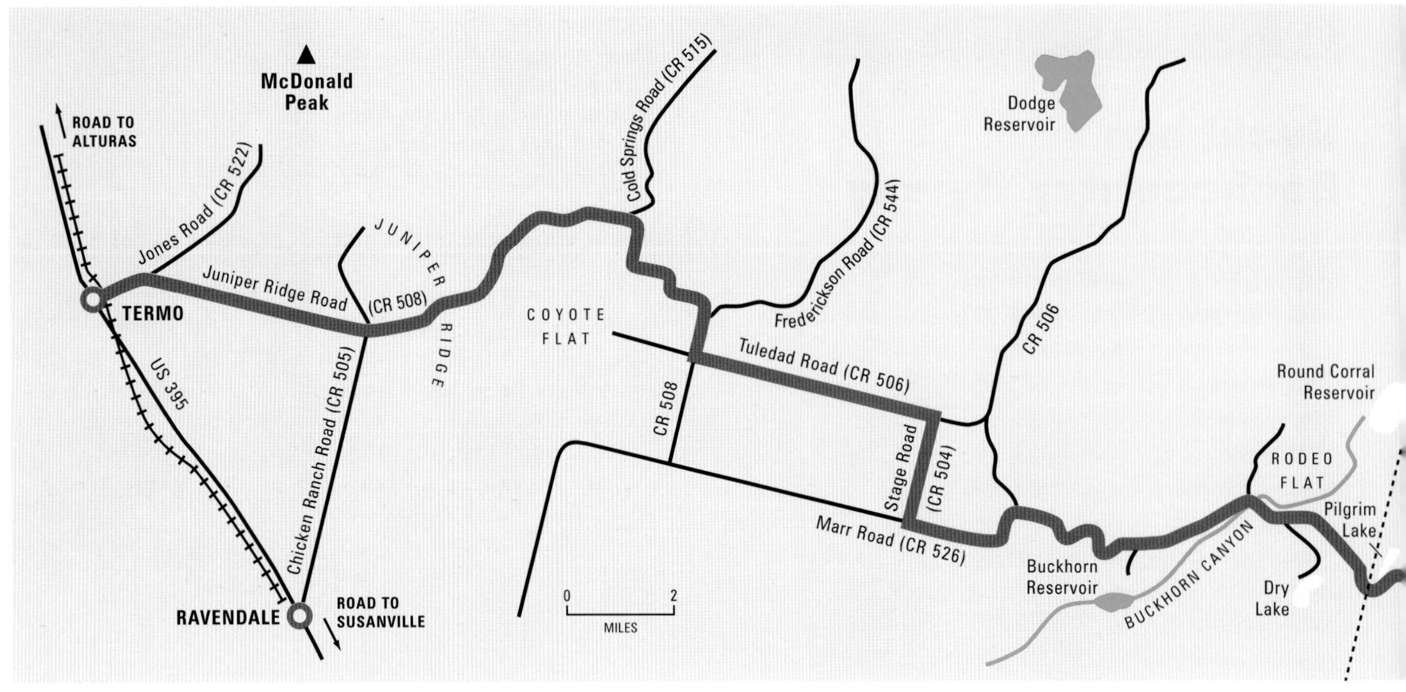

9.9 ▲	BL	Road on right is Jones Road (CR 522).
▼ 3.4	SO	Graded road on right.
7.5 ▲	SO	Graded road on left.
▼ 4.9	SO	Graded road on right is Chicken Ranch Road (CR 505, but marked CR 502 on BLM map). Track on left. Continue straight ahead on CR 508. McDonald Peak is to the left.
6.0 ▲	SO	Graded road on left is Chicken Ranch Road (CR 505, but marked CR 502 on BLM map). Track on right. Continue straight ahead on CR 508. McDonald Peak is to the right.
		GPS: N40°52.45' W120°21.86'
▼ 5.8	SO	Cresting Juniper Ridge—views east to Coyote Flat.
5.1 ▲	SO	Cresting Juniper Ridge—views west to Madeline Plains.

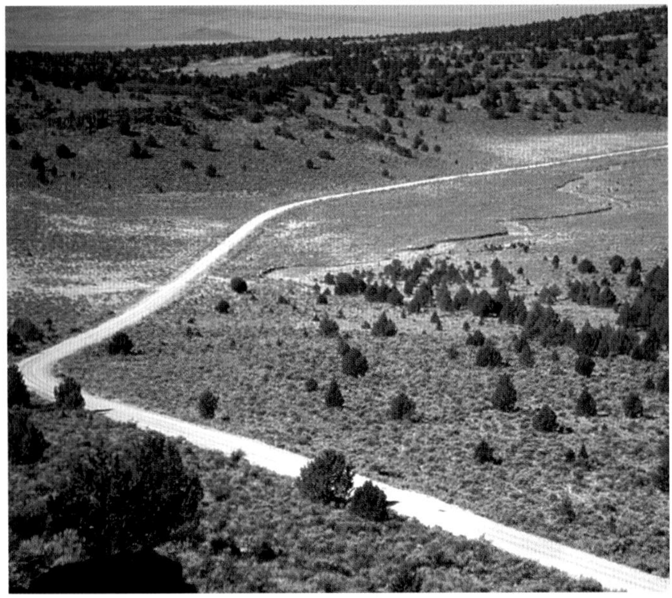

The trail over Rodeo Flat near Buckhorn Canyon

▼ 10.9	BR	Graded road on left is Cold Springs Road (CR 515). Zero trip meter.
0.0 ▲		Continue to the west.
		GPS: N40°55.08' W120°16.73'
▼ 0.0		Continue to the southeast.
7.6 ▲	BL	Graded road on right is Cold Springs Road (CR 515). Zero trip meter.
▼ 2.5	SO	Graded road on left is Frederickson Road (CR 544). Road becomes paved.
7.1 ▲	SO	Graded road on right is Frederickson Road (CR 544). Road turns to graded dirt.
		GPS: N40°53.99' W120°14.96'
▼ 3.2	TL	4-way intersection. Paved Mail Route (CR 508) continues straight ahead. Track on right. Turn left onto graded dirt Tuledad Road (CR 506).
4.4 ▲	TR	4-way intersection. Track straight ahead. Paved road on left and right is Mail Route (CR 508). Turn right onto paved road.
		GPS: N40°53.33' W120°14.97'
▼ 5.2	SO	Cattle guard.
2.4 ▲	SO	Cattle guard.
▼ 7.6	TR	Cattle guard; then road ahead is the continuation of CR 506 to Dodge Reservoir. Zero trip meter.
0.0 ▲		Continue to the west and cross cattle guard.
		GPS: N40°53.37' W120°09.78'
▼ 0.0		Continue to the south on Stage Road (CR 504).
6.9 ▲	TL	T-intersection with Tuledad Road (CR 506). To the right goes to Dodge Reservoir. Zero trip meter.
▼ 1.9	TL	T-intersection with Marr Road (CR 526).
5.0 ▲	TR	Road continues ahead to Ravendale. Turn right onto Stage Road (CR 504).
		GPS: N40°51.62' W120°09.77'
▼ 4.1	BR	Track on left. Entering BLM land. Road is now marked as the Buckhorn Back Country Byway. Leaving Coyote Flat.
2.8 ▲	BL	Track on right. Leaving BLM land.
▼ 5.4	SO	Cattle guard.

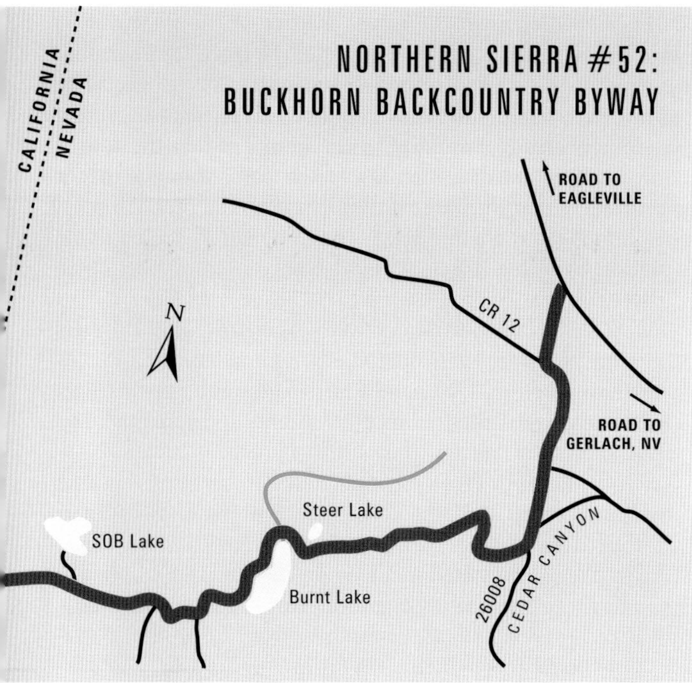

1.5 ▲	SO	Cattle guard.
▼ 5.9	SO	Track on right.
1.0 ▲	SO	Track on left.
▼ 6.7	SO	Track on right.
0.2 ▲	SO	Track on left.
▼ 6.9	SO	Cross over creek; then small, unmarked sandy track on right goes 0.8 miles to Buckhorn Reservoir, which is visible down in the valley. Zero trip meter.
0.0 ▲		Continue to the west and cross over creek.
		GPS: N40°52.12' W120°05.02'
▼ 0.0		Continue to the northeast.
3.6 ▲	SO	Small, unmarked sandy track on left goes 0.8 miles to Buckhorn Reservoir, which is visible down in the valley. Zero trip meter.
▼ 0.9	SO	Two tracks on right to campsite.
2.7 ▲	SO	Two tracks on left to campsite.
▼ 1.1	SO	Track on left and track on right.
2.5 ▲	SO	Track on left and track on right.
▼ 2.3	SO	Track on left across Rodeo Flat. Buckhorn Canyon is to the right.
1.3 ▲	SO	Track on right across Rodeo Flat. Buckhorn Canyon is to the left.
		GPS: N40°53.20' W120°02.87'
▼ 3.0	SO	Track on right to Dry Lake.
0.6 ▲	SO	Track on left to Dry Lake.
▼ 3.6	SO	Unmarked formed track on left goes 0.5 miles to Round Corral Reservoir. Zero trip meter.
0.0 ▲		Continue to the northwest.
		GPS: N40°53.18' W120°01.46'
▼ 0.0		Continue to the southeast.
15.3 ▲	SO	Unmarked formed track on right goes 0.5 miles to Round Corral Reservoir. Zero trip meter.
▼ 1.7	SO	Track on right is 26029 and track on left. Entering Washoe County, Nevada, at sign. Pilgrim Lake on left; then track on right.
13.6 ▲	SO	Track on left; then Pilgrim Lake on right. Entering Lassen County, California, at sign. Track on left is 26029 and track on right.
		GPS: N40°52.30' W119°59.89'
▼ 2.2	SO	Cattle guard; then track on left to lake's edge.
13.1 ▲	SO	Track on right to lake's edge; then cattle guard.
▼ 2.9	SO	Cattle guard.
12.4 ▲	SO	Cattle guard.
▼ 4.3	SO	Track on left toward SOB Lake.
11.0 ▲	SO	Track on right toward SOB Lake.
		GPS: N40°52.89' W119°57.10'
▼ 5.8	SO	Track on right.
9.5 ▲	SO	Track on left.
▼ 6.8	SO	Track on right.
8.5 ▲	SO	Track on left.
▼ 7.8	SO	Two tracks on right at the southern end of Burnt Lake.
7.5 ▲	SO	Two tracks on left at the southern end of Burnt Lake.
		GPS: N40°53.38' W119°53.71'
▼ 9.2	SO	Cross over outlet from Burnt Lake.
6.1 ▲	SO	Cross over outlet from Burnt Lake.
▼ 9.5	SO	Track on left to dry Steer Lake.
5.8 ▲	SO	Track on right to dry Steer Lake.
▼ 12.0	SO	Track on right.
3.3 ▲	SO	Track on left.
▼ 13.5	SO	Start of drop toward Cedar Canyon.
1.8 ▲	SO	End of climb away from Cedar Canyon.
▼ 14.4	SO	Track on right.
0.9 ▲	SO	Track on left.
▼ 15.3	SO	Well-used track on right is 26008. Zero trip meter.
0.0 ▲		Continue to the southwest, remaining on Buckhorn Road.
		GPS: N40°55.15' W119°48.09'
▼ 0.0		Continue to the north, remaining on Buckhorn Road.
4.8 ▲	BR	Well-used track on left is 26008. Zero trip meter.
▼ 0.2	SO	Track on right.
4.6 ▲	SO	Track on left.
▼ 1.4	SO	Track on right; then cattle guard.
3.4 ▲	SO	Cattle guard; then track on left.
▼ 1.9	SO	Track on right into private property; then cattle guard; then track on left.
2.9 ▲	SO	Track on right; then cattle guard; then track on left into private property.
		GPS: N40°56.84' W119°48.10'
▼ 2.9	SO	Two tracks on left.
1.9 ▲	SO	Two tracks on right.
▼ 3.1	SO	Track on left.
1.7 ▲	SO	Track on right.
▼ 3.4	BR	Graded road on left is CR 12. Small track on right.
1.4 ▲	BL	Graded road on right is CR 12. Small track on left.
		GPS: N40°58.02' W119°48.66'
▼ 4.8		Trail ends at T-intersection with Nevada 447. Turn left for Eagleville, CA; turn right for Gerlach, NV
0.0 ▲		Trail commences on Nevada 447, 37.5 miles northwest of Gerlach, NV, and 30.5 miles southeast of Eagleville, CA. Zero trip meter and turn south onto graded dirt road, following the sign for Buckhorn Road and US 395. Round Mountain is opposite.
		GPS: N40°59.23' W119°48.65'

NORTHERN SIERRA #53

South Warner Mountains Trail

Starting Point:	**Jess Valley Road (CR 64), 5.9 miles east of Likely and US 395**
Finishing Point:	**Surprise Valley Road (CR 1), 3 miles south of Eagleville**
Total Mileage:	**31.8 miles**
Unpaved Mileage:	**31.6 miles**
Driving Time:	**4 hours**
Elevation Range:	**4,500–7,600 feet**
Usually Open:	**June to December**
Best Time to Travel:	**Dry weather**
Difficulty Rating:	**3**
Scenic Rating:	**9**
Remoteness Rating:	**+0**

Special Attractions

- Aspen viewing in the fall.
- Fishing and camping at Blue Lake and West Valley Reservoir.
- Hiking and equestrian trails into the South Warner Wilderness.

History

The Warner Mountains were named for Captain William H. Warner, who was killed along with his guide in a surprise Indian attack on September 26, 1849. The attack occurred just north of Surprise Valley, beyond the northern end of the mountains that now bear his name. With the help of a few scouts, the captain was trying to find a safe route for emigrants to travel through the mountains.

Wheelchair fishing access point on Blue Lake

The trail begins in the upper reaches of the Pit River in West Valley, just east of the town of Likely. In 1878, townsfolk from South Fork tried to establish a post office there. They submitted several names, but each one was rejected because a post office already existed with the name. When the fourth name was suggested, a member of the party thought that it was unlikely that this one would be accepted either. All present jumped on the name Likely, thinking surely such a name would be available. Likely was indeed accepted by post office authorities.

West Valley and Jess Valley were easier to name. Brothers Rollin and Herbert West purchased and amalgamated ranches in the valley in 1878, naming the region after themselves. Three years earlier, the Jess brothers, Archie and Jonathan, settled in the valley that now bears their name.

Settling lands in Pit River country was a dangerous venture for all concerned. Indians considered emigrants as invaders and their oxen as food. Newcomers discovered that their lives were in danger. Scattered incidents in the late 1840s and '50s brought about the establishment of Camp Hollenbush on the Fall River in 1857. A large cattle drive from Oregon to Nevada City passed through this region in August 1861, and Pit River Indians attacked it. A number of cowboys managed to escape, but the owners of the 800 head of cattle, Joseph and Samuel Evans, were killed in the fight. Two patrols of dragoons were dispatched from Camp Hollenbush, later renamed Fort Crook, to retrieve the cattle and punish the Indians. Fewer than 200 head of cattle were retrieved and several Pit River warriors were killed. One of the many skirmishes with the Indians occurred during a second patrol in West Valley, near the start of this trail.

Description

South Warner Mountains Trail runs south of the South Warner Wilderness, which covers much of the southern Warner Mountains. The trail crosses the range from west to east, past two very different lakes and a mixture of forests. It leaves Jess Valley Road east of Likely and immediately starts to climb into the range along a rough and lumpy formed trail. Side trails lead down to the edge of West Valley Reservoir, where there are campsites and fishing opportunities when water levels permit.

The trail travels around the north side of Parsnip Peak before passing along Parsnip Creek, which flows through lush green, aspen-fringed meadows. The creek crossing comes about a mile before the trail briefly intersects with paved Blue Lake Road. Blue Lake, a short distance farther down the paved road, has a USFS campground, a boat launch, and wheelchair fishing access. You can fish for rainbow and brown trout at the lake. A national recreation trail—the Blue Lake Trail—circles the 160-acre lake. Much of this area was burned by the Blue Fire of August 2001, which was caused by lightning strikes. Measures have been taken to prevent ash and eroded material from silting up the lake.

The trail leaves the paved road and rejoins a smaller, formed trail that travels through mixed conifer forest to the open Long Valley. Several aspens in the meadows southeast of Long Valley around Jenkins Spring have carvings made by

Fording through Parsnip Creek

Basque shepherds. A few flocks of sheep graze in the wilderness under a permit system. This section of the trail is particularly pretty in fall, when the many stands of aspens are resplendent in golden foliage.

At the north end of Long Valley, the trail passes near the Patterson USFS Guard Station, a small campground, and the Summit Trailhead. The Summit Trail begins here and runs the 27-mile length of the South Warner Wilderness, ending at the Pepperdine USFS Campground. It also connects with other trails within the wilderness area. The small campground near the guard station has a handful of sites tucked among the trees. Patterson is also an equestrian trailhead, with a corral for as many as 10 horses and a parking lot for trailers.

The standard of the road increases from here, becoming a graded, lightly graveled road. It passes both ends of Northern Sierra #54: Bearcamp Flat Trail, a more difficult loop to the north. Some good backcountry campsites can be found around Homestead Flat near the start of the loop. The trail drops abruptly to Surprise Valley, descending more than 1,700 feet in the final few miles. It finishes on Surprise Valley Road on the edge of Lower Lake.

Current Road Information

Modoc National Forest
Warner Mountain Ranger District
385 Wallace Street
Cedarville, CA 96104
(530) 279-6116

Map References

BLM Alturas
USFS Modoc National Forest
USGS 1:24,000 Tule Mt., Jess Valley, Emerson Peak, Snake Lake, Eagleville
1:100,000 Alturas
Maptech CD-ROM: Shasta-Trinity/Modoc
Northern California Atlas & Gazetteer, p. 41
California Road & Recreation Atlas, p. 49
Other: Modoc Country USFS/BLM Map

Route Directions

Mileage		Directions
▼ 0.0		From Jess Valley Road (CR 64), 5.9 miles east of Likely and US 395, zero trip meter and turn southeast on graded dirt road 39N19, following the sign to West Valley Reservoir and Blue Lake Campground.
2.4 ▲		Trail ends at T-intersection with Jess Valley Road (CR 64). Turn left for US 395 and Likely; turn right for Jess Valley.
		GPS: N41°14.05' W120°23.80'
▼ 0.1	SO	Track on left; then cross over South Fork Pit River on bridge. Seasonal closure gate; then track on right and track on left.
2.3 ▲	SO	Track on left and track on right; then seasonal closure gate. Cross over South Fork Pit River on bridge; then track on right.
▼ 0.2	SO	Track on left and track on right.
2.2 ▲	SO	Track on left and track on right.
▼ 0.3	SO	Track on left.
2.1 ▲	SO	Track on right.
▼ 0.4	SO	Gate.
2.0 ▲	SO	Gate.
▼ 0.7	SO	Track on right and track on left. Cross over ditch.
1.7 ▲	SO	Cross over ditch. Track on right and track on left.
▼ 0.9	SO	Track on left.
1.5 ▲	SO	Track on right.
▼ 1.1	SO	Unmarked track on right goes to West Valley Reservoir.
1.3 ▲	SO	Unmarked track on left goes to West Valley Reservoir.
		GPS: N41°13.15' 120°23.64'
▼ 1.6	SO	Track on right.
0.8 ▲	SO	Track on left.
▼ 1.8	SO	Cross through wash.
0.6 ▲	SO	Cross through wash.
▼ 2.0	SO	Track on left; then cattle guard.
0.4 ▲	SO	Cattle guard; then track on right.
▼ 2.4	BL	Unmarked track on right goes 0.4 miles to West Valley Reservoir. Zero trip meter.
0.0 ▲		Continue to the north.
		GPS: N41°12.19' W120°22.96'
▼ 0.0		Continue to the east.
5.8 ▲	BR	Unmarked track on left goes 0.4 miles to West Valley Reservoir. Zero trip meter.
▼ 0.7	SO	Cross through wash.
5.1 ▲	SO	Cross through wash.
▼ 0.8	SO	Cross through wash.
5.0 ▲	SO	Cross through wash.
▼ 1.4	SO	Track on left. West Valley Spring on left.
4.4 ▲	SO	Track on right. West Valley Spring on right.
		GPS: N41°12.03' W120°21.44'
▼ 1.6	SO	Cross through wash.
4.2 ▲	SO	Cross through wash.
▼ 2.2	SO	Pass through fence line.
3.6 ▲	SO	Pass through fence line.
▼ 3.2	SO	Tank on left.
2.6 ▲	SO	Tank on right.
▼ 3.4	SO	Track on right.
2.4 ▲	BR	Track on left.
		GPS: N41°11.04' W120°20.12'
▼ 3.5	SO	Track on right toward Parsnip Mountain.
2.3 ▲	SO	Track on left toward Parsnip Mountain.
▼ 3.6	SO	Gate.
2.2 ▲	SO	Gate.

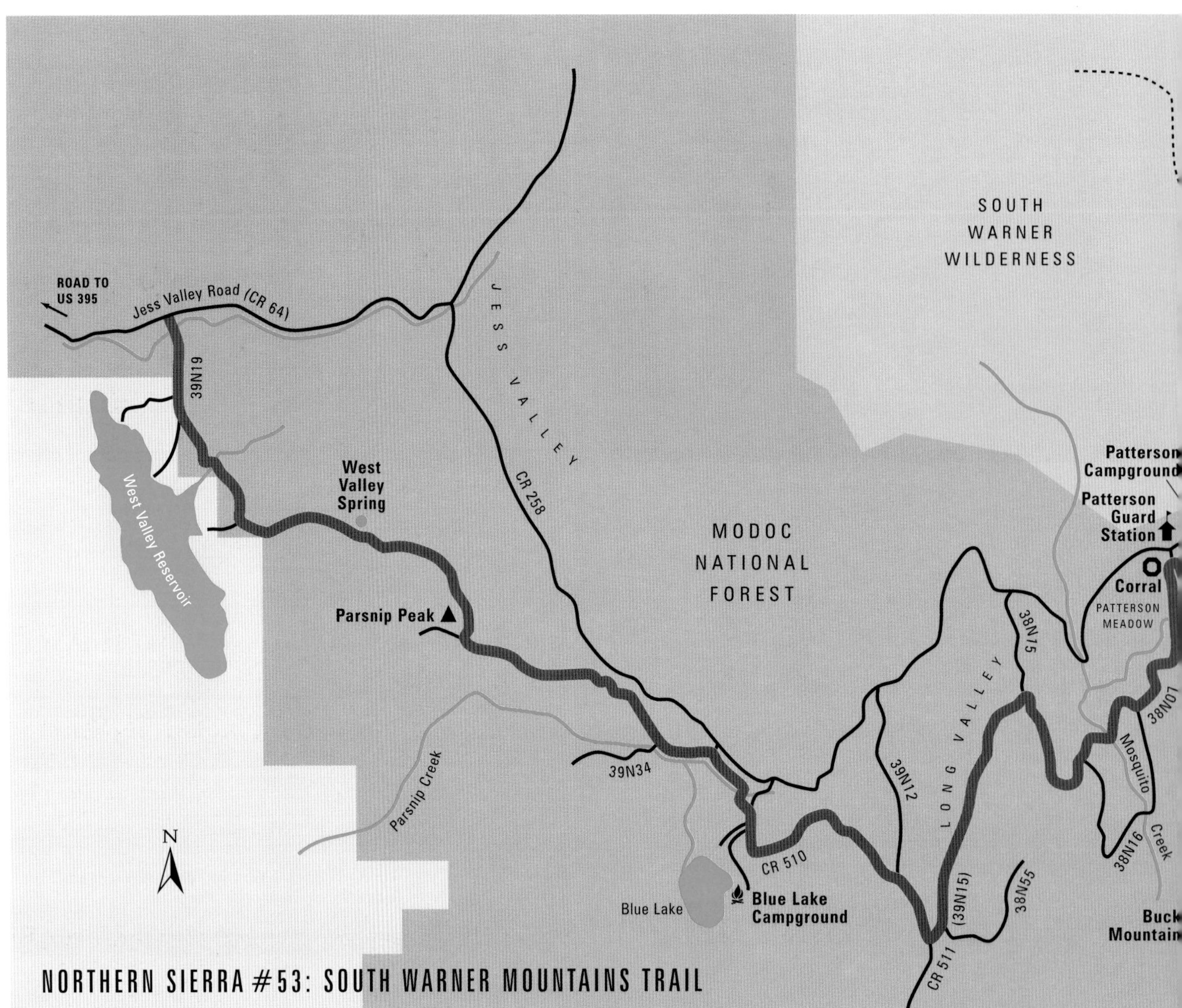

▼ 5.4	SO	Gate.
0.4 ▲	SO	Gate.
▼ 5.8	TL	T-intersection with 39N34. Parsnip Creek is straight ahead. Zero trip meter.
0.0 ▲		Continue to the north on unmarked formed trail.
		GPS: N41°10.07' W120°17.74'
▼ 0.0		Continue to the east on graded road.
1.7 ▲	TR	Graded road continues straight ahead. Zero trip meter. Parsnip Creek is on the left.
▼ 0.3	SO	Track on right to meadows surrounding Parsnip Creek.
1.4 ▲	SO	Track on left to meadows surrounding Parsnip Creek.
▼ 0.6	TR	Cattle guard and seasonal closure gate; then small track on right; then T-intersection with paved CR 258. Turn right onto small formed track immediately before paved road.
1.1 ▲	TL	T-intersection with graded road immediately in front of paved CR 258, which is on the right. Turn left onto graded dirt 39N34; then small track on left. Cross cattle guard and seasonal closure gate.
		GPS: N41°10.03' W120°17.06'
▼ 1.2	SO	Cross through creek.
0.5 ▲	SO	Cross through creek.
		GPS: N41°09.60' W120°16.69'
▼ 1.4	SO	Track on left joins paved road.
0.3 ▲	SO	Track on right joins paved road.
▼ 1.5	TR	Join paved road 39N30 to Blue Lake.
0.2 ▲	TL	Turn off paved road onto small formed trail, which runs parallel to paved road along the fence line. This turn is hard to spot.
		GPS: N41°09.44' W120°16.62'
▼ 1.7	TL	Small track on right. Turn left onto unmarked, graded CR 510. The turn is immediately before a cattle guard. The paved road continues straight ahead for 0.6 miles to Blue Lake. Zero trip meter.
0.0 ▲		Continue to the north.
		GPS: N41°09.29' W120°16.60'
▼ 0.0		Continue to the southeast.

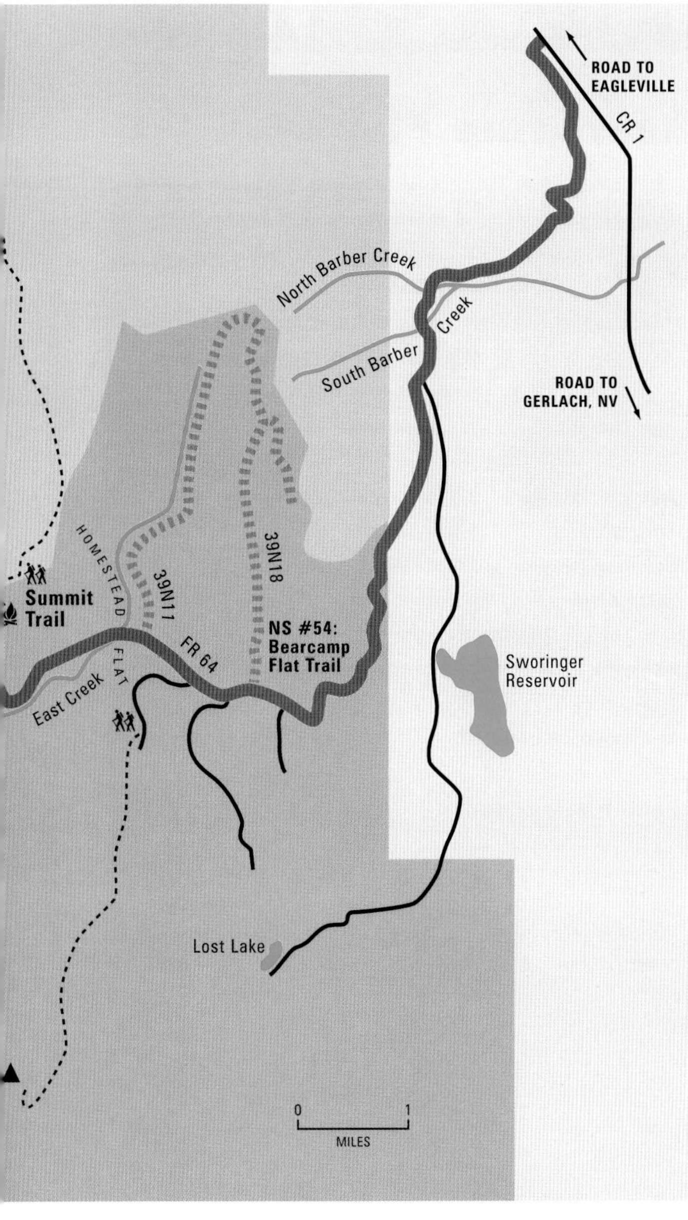

3.0 ▲	TR	T-intersection with paved Blue Lake Road (39N30). To the left goes 0.6 miles to Blue Lake. Small track straight ahead. Zero trip meter and turn right alongside paved road.
▼ 1.0	BR	Track on left to Parsnip Creek.
2.0 ▲	SO	Track on right to Parsnip Creek.
▼ 1.2	SO	Track on left to Parsnip Creek.
1.8 ▲	SO	Track on right to Parsnip Creek.
▼ 1.6	SO	Tank on left.
1.4 ▲	SO	Tank on right.
▼ 2.1	SO	Track on right.
0.9 ▲	SO	Track on left.
		GPS: N41°08.88' W120°14.99'
▼ 2.3	TR	T-intersection with graded dirt road 39N12.
0.7 ▲	TL	Graded road continues ahead. Turn left onto unmarked formed trail CR 510, which leads downhill.
		GPS: N41°08.79' W120°14.73'
▼ 2.4	SO	Cattle guard.
0.6 ▲	SO	Cattle guard.
▼ 3.0	TL	T-intersection with CR 511 (39N15). Corral on right. Zero trip meter.
0.0 ▲		Continue to the northwest on unmarked graded road 39N12.
		GPS: N41°08.19' W120°14.38'
▼ 0.0		Continue to the north.
2.9 ▲	TR	Graded road continues straight ahead past corral. Zero trip meter.
▼ 0.3	SO	Track on right is 38N55.
2.6 ▲	SO	Track on left is 38N55.
▼ 1.2	SO	Track on right.
1.7 ▲	SO	Track on left.
▼ 2.9	TR	Corporation Meadow. Graded road straight ahead is 38N15. Zero trip meter and follow the sign to Patterson Guard Station.
0.0 ▲		Continue to the south on 39N15.
		GPS: N41°10.45' W120°13.17'
▼ 0.0		Continue to the southeast.
4.4 ▲	TL	Graded road straight ahead is 38N15. Zero trip meter and follow the sign for Madeline.
▼ 0.2	SO	Two tracks on right and two tracks on left.
4.2 ▲	SO	Two tracks on left and two tracks on right.
▼ 1.5	SO	Track on right is 38N16.
2.9 ▲	SO	Track on left is 38N16.
▼ 2.0	SO	Cross over Mosquito Creek.
2.4 ▲	SO	Cross over Mosquito Creek.
▼ 2.1	SO	Track on left goes to East Creek Bridge. Follow the sign to Patterson Guard Station.
2.3 ▲	SO	Track on right goes to East Creek Bridge. Follow the sign to Long Valley Road.
		GPS: N41°10.08' W120°12.08'
▼ 2.7	SO	Track on right is Mosquito Creek Loop Road (38N16).
1.7 ▲	SO	Track on left is Mosquito Creek Loop Road (38N16).
▼ 3.2	SO	Track on right.
1.2 ▲	SO	Track on left.
▼ 4.0	SO	Cross over creek.
0.4 ▲	SO	Cross over creek.
		GPS: N41°11.21' W120°11.31'
▼ 4.4	TR	Corral on left at Patterson Meadow. FR 64 goes 0.3 miles ahead to Patterson USFS Campground, Patterson Guard Station, and Summit Trailhead. Zero trip meter and turn right onto FR 64, following the sign to CR 1.
0.0 ▲		Continue to the south.
		GPS: N41°11.62' W120°11.37'
▼ 0.0		Continue to the east.
2.1 ▲	TL	Patterson Meadow. FR 64 continues 0.3 miles to the right to Patterson USFS Campground, Patterson Guard Station, and Summit Trail. Zero trip meter and turn left onto 38N07, following sign to Corporation Meadow.
▼ 1.8	SO	Track on left to campsite; then cross over East Creek.
0.3 ▲	SO	Cross over East Creek; then track on right to campsite.
▼ 2.0	SO	Cattle guard.
0.1 ▲	SO	Cattle guard.
▼ 2.1	SO	Track on left is the western end of Northern Sierra #54: Bearcamp Flat Trail (39N11). Zero trip meter.
0.0 ▲		Continue to the west.
		GPS: N41°11.78' W120°09.52'
▼ 0.0		Continue to the southeast.
1.2 ▲	SO	Track on right is the western end of Northern

		Sierra #54: Bearcamp Flat Trail (39N11). Zero trip meter.
▼ 0.6	SO	Track on right goes to Buck Mountain Trail.
0.6 ▲	SO	Track on left goes to Buck Mountain Trail.
▼ 1.1	SO	Track on right goes to Camp One.
0.1 ▲	SO	Track on left goes to Camp One.
▼ 1.2	SO	Track on left is the eastern end of Northern Sierra #54: Bearcamp Flat Trail. Zero trip meter.
0.0 ▲		Continue to the west.
		GPS: N41°11.37' W120°08.47'
▼ 0.0		Continue to the east.
4.1 ▲	SO	Track on right is the eastern end of Northern Sierra #54: Bearcamp Flat Trail. Zero trip meter.
▼ 0.3	SO	Track on right.
3.8 ▲	SO	Track on left.
▼ 0.6	SO	Track on right; then start to descend to Surprise Valley. Sworinger Reservoir is visible below.
3.5 ▲	SO	End of climb from Surprise Valley. Sworinger Reservoir is visible below. Track on left.
▼ 0.9	SO	Track on left.
3.2 ▲	SO	Track on right.
▼ 2.8	SO	Cattle guard. Leaving Modoc National Forest.
1.3 ▲	SO	Cattle guard. Entering Modoc National Forest.
		GPS: N41°12.60' W120°06.88'
▼ 3.7	SO	Unmarked track on right.
0.4 ▲	SO	Unmarked track on left.
		GPS: N41°13.39' W120°06.58'
▼ 4.1	SO	Graded road on right goes to Lost Lake. Zero trip meter and follow the sign to Eagleville.
0.0 ▲		Continue to the south, remaining on FR 64.
		GPS: N41°13.69' W120°06.65'
▼ 0.0		Continue to the north, remaining on FR 64.
4.2 ▲	BL	Graded road on left goes to Lost Lake. Zero trip meter and follow the sign to Patterson Campground.
▼ 0.1	SO	Cattle guard.
4.1 ▲	SO	Cattle guard.
▼ 0.5	SO	Cross over South Barber Creek.
3.7 ▲	SO	Cross over South Barber Creek.
▼ 0.6	SO	Track on left to private property.
3.6 ▲	SO	Track on right to private property.
▼ 0.8	SO	Cross over North Barber Creek; then track on left.
3.4 ▲	SO	Track on right; then cross over North Barber Creek.
▼ 2.1	SO	Track on left.
2.1 ▲	SO	Track on right.
▼ 2.3	SO	Track on right to viewpoint.
1.9 ▲	SO	Track on left to viewpoint.
▼ 3.0	SO	Track on left.
1.2 ▲	SO	Track on right.
▼ 4.2		Track on left; then cattle guard; then trail ends at T-intersection with paved Surprise Valley Road (CR 1). Turn left for Eagleville; turn right for Gerlach, NV.
0.0 ▲		Trail commences on Surprise Valley Road (CR 1), 3 miles south of Eagleville. Zero trip meter and turn southwest on graded dirt road, marked CR 42. Cattle guard; then immediately track on right.
		GPS: N41°16.32' W120°05.33'

NORTHERN SIERRA #54

Bearcamp Flat Trail

Starting Point:	**Northern Sierra #53: South Warner Mountains Trail, 2.4 miles east of Patterson Guard Station**
Finishing Point:	**Northern Sierra #53: South Warner Mountains Trail, 3.6 miles east of Patterson Guard Station**
Total Mileage:	**7.1 miles, plus 1.2-mile spur to Horse Mountain**
Unpaved Mileage:	**7.1 miles, plus 1.2-mile spur**
Driving Time:	**1.5 hours**
Elevation Range:	**7,300–8,500 feet**
Usually Open:	**May to October**
Best Time to Travel:	**Dry weather**
Difficulty Rating:	**5**
Scenic Rating:	**10**
Remoteness Rating:	**+0**

Special Attractions

- Aspen viewing in fall.
- Panoramic views over Surprise Valley and the South Warner Wilderness.
- Hiking access to the South Warner Wilderness via the Bear Camp Trail.

History

In the 1800s, Pit River Indians were living near the Pit River drainage when fur trappers and explorers first met them. Their tribal area spanned from Mount Shasta to the Warner Mountains, and Goose Lake to Lassen Peak. Several small bands with different dialects lived within this area. An eastern band upriver known as the Hammawi occupied a large area in the natural bowl of Bearcamp Flat, flanked by Emerson Peak and Horse Mountain. A rancheria was located to the south of the flat.

A flat such as Bearcamp was an important source of edible roots, sunflower seeds, grass seeds, and insects. The roots would be dug up during early summer and dried for use in winter. After drying, the sunflower and grass seeds were combined and often mashed into a cake-like form for cooking in an earthen oven. The Hammawi hunted deer, elk, mountain goats, antelope, and smaller animals. In general these people enjoyed a bountiful environment.

Settlers also reaped the benefits of this country. Cattle ranching and sheep herding were major activities in the northeastern corner of California, and Bearcamp Flat was ideal for summer grazing.

Basque sheepherders, like other emigrants, made their way to California during the gold rush. Instead of being miners, many turned to feeding miners and tended sheep in summer.

Cold Spring

Bearcamp Flat was a favorite Basque camp location, where the sheep could graze in somewhat of a natural corral. The sheepherders built a Basque style oven that can be seen near the start of this trail.

Description

This short loop trail starts and finishes on the longer Northern Sierra #53: South Warner Mountains Trail, which crosses the range from west to east. Bearcamp Flat Trail is rated a 5 for difficulty because of one loose moguled slope, and a long section of side slope that will tilt vehicles toward the drop. Most of the trail is rated a 3 or 4 for difficulty because of the uneven formed surface and embedded rocks that can catch a vehicle's underbody.

The trail starts by traveling up the eastern side of Homestead Flat, where many pleasant campsites are situated among the trees. On the right-hand side of the trail, a short distance from the start, a keen eye will spot the old Basque oven at the edge of the woods. The trail gradually climbs through sagebrush and stands of aspens to the Bear Camp Trailhead. This hiking trail leads through the wilderness and connects to the Emerson Trail and the network of trails within the South Warner Wilderness.

The return portion of the loop travels high on Horse Mountain. A spur leads to a campsite and a breathtaking vista, with views north over the wilderness and east over Surprise Valley, Lower Lake, and into Nevada. It continues to a second viewpoint high on the mountain above Waterbox Canyon. The main route travels down the west side of the mountain, through more stands of aspens, to finish back on Northern Sierra #53: South Warner Mountains Trail.

This trail is particularly pretty in fall, when the turning leaves look like bright splashes of gold against the gray-green sagebrush.

Current Road Information

Modoc National Forest
Warner Mountain Ranger District
385 Wallace Street
Cedarville, CA 96104
(530) 279-6116

Map References

BLM Alturas
USFS Modoc National Forest
USGS 1:24,000 Emerson Peak
1:100,000 Alturas
Maptech CD-ROM: Shasta-Trinity/Modoc
Northern California Atlas & Gazetteer, p. 41
California Road & Recreation Atlas, p. 49 (incomplete)
Other: Modoc Country USFS/BLM Map

Route Directions

▼ 0.0		From Northern Sierra #53: South Warner Mountains Trail, 2.4 miles east of Patterson Guard Station, zero trip meter and turn northwest on formed trail 39N11, following the sign to Bearcamp Flat.
	3.3 ▲	Trail ends back on Northern Sierra #53: South Warner Mountains Trail. Turn right for

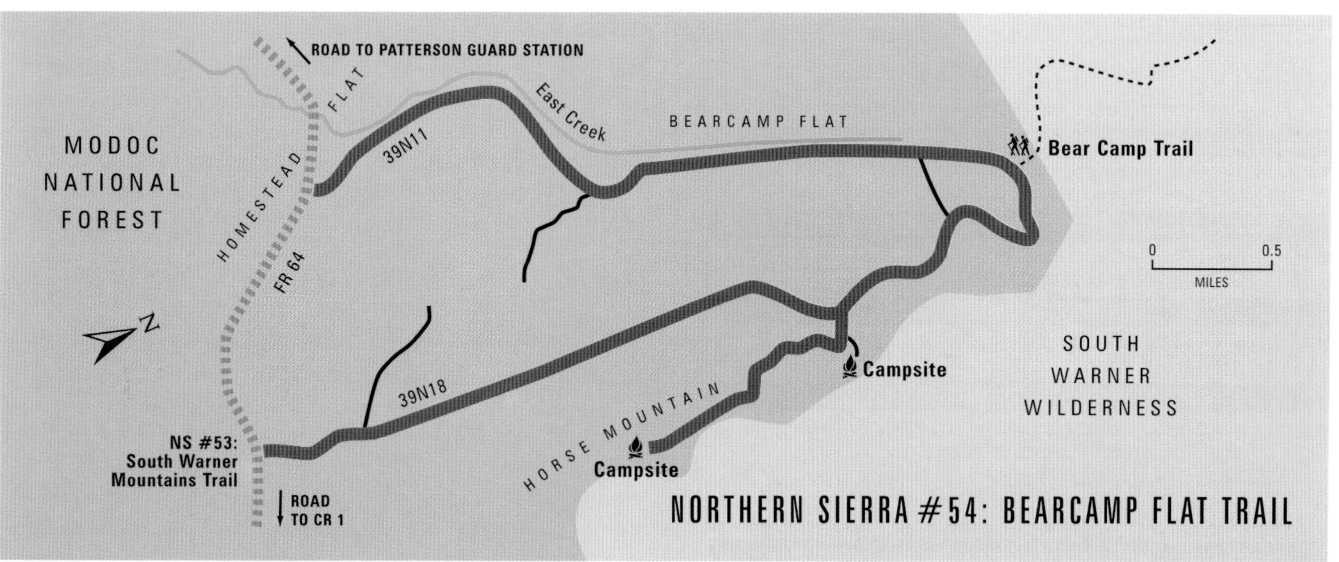

NORTHERN SIERRA #54: BEARCAMP FLAT TRAIL

Patterson Guard Station; turn left for CR 1.

GPS: N41°11.78' W120°09.52'

▼ 0.2		BR	Track on left through fence line.
	3.1 ▲	SO	Track on right through fence line.
▼ 0.5		SO	Track on right; then cross through wash.
	2.8 ▲	SO	Cross through wash; then track on left.
▼ 1.2		SO	Spring on left.
	2.1 ▲	SO	Spring on right.
			GPS: N41°12.60' W120°09.50'
▼ 1.5		SO	Track on right; then cross through wash.
	1.8 ▲	SO	Cross through wash; then track on left.
▼ 1.6		SO	Cross through wash.
	1.7 ▲	SO	Cross through wash.
▼ 2.7		BR	Track on left.
	0.6 ▲	SO	Track on right.
			GPS: N41°13.75' W120°08.92'
▼ 2.8		BL	Track on right. Follow sign to Bear Camp Trail.
	0.5 ▲	SO	Track on left.
▼ 3.3		BR	Bear Camp Trailhead at information board. The hiking trail leads to the north. Zero trip meter.
	0.0 ▲		Continue to the southwest.
			GPS: N41°14.19' W120°08.66'
▼ 0.0			Continue to the east.
	1.3 ▲	BL	Bear Camp Trailhead at information board. The hiking trail leads to the north. Zero trip meter.
▼ 0.3		TR	T-intersection.
	1.0 ▲	TL	Track continues straight ahead.
▼ 0.5		TL	T-intersection.
	0.8 ▲	TR	Track continues straight ahead.
			GPS: N41°13.92' W120°08.55'
▼ 1.3		TR	Track straight ahead is the spur to the top of Horse Mountain. Zero trip meter.
	0.0 ▲		Continue to the northwest.
			GPS: N41°13.43' W120°08.24'

Spur to Horse Mountain

▼ 0.0		Continue to the east.
▼ 0.2	TR	Track on left goes 0.1 miles to viewpoint and campsite overlooking Surprise Valley.
		GPS: N41°13.39' W120°08.16'
▼ 1.2		Spur ends at a viewpoint and campsite.
		GPS: N41°12.66' W120°07.96'

Continuation of Main Trail

▼ 0.0			Continue to the southwest.
	2.5 ▲	TL	T-intersection. Track on right is the spur to the top of Horse Mountain. Zero trip meter.
			GPS: N41°13.43' W120°08.24'
▼ 0.7		SO	Spring on left.
	1.8 ▲	SO	Spring on right.
			GPS: N41°12.89' W120°08.49'
▼ 1.3		SO	Spring on left.
	1.2 ▲	SO	Spring on right.
			GPS: N41°12.37' W120°08.42'
▼ 1.5		SO	Track on right.
	1.0 ▲	SO	Track on left.
			GPS: N41°12.15' W120°08.42'
▼ 2.1		TL	T-intersection with graded road. To the right goes 0.7 miles to quarry.
	0.4 ▲	TR	Graded road continues straight ahead for 0.7 miles to quarry. Turn right onto unmarked formed trail.
			GPS: N41°11.64' W120°08.41'
▼ 2.5			Trail ends back on Northern Sierra #53: South Warner Mountains Trail. Turn right for Patterson Guard Station; turn left for CR 1.
	0.0 ▲		Trail commences on Northern Sierra #53: South Warner Mountains Trail, 3.6 miles east of Patterson Guard Station. Zero trip meter and turn north on graded road 39N18.
			GPS: N41°11.37' W120°08.47'

NORTHERN SIERRA #55

Payne Peak Trail

Starting Point:	**Alpine Road (CR 58), 9.2 miles east of Alturas**
Finishing Point:	**Surprise Valley Road (CR 1), 3.5 miles south of Cedarville**
Total Mileage:	**22.1 miles, plus 1.3-mile spur to Payne Peak and 0.6-mile spur to Pepperdine Camp**
Unpaved Mileage:	**22.1 miles, plus spurs**
Driving Time:	**3 hours**
Elevation Range:	**4,600–7,600 feet**
Usually Open:	**June to November**
Best Time to Travel:	**Dry weather**
Difficulty Rating:	**3**
Scenic Rating:	**9**
Remoteness Rating:	**+0**

Special Attractions

- Aspen viewing in fall.
- Rockhounding for petrified wood in Granger Canyon.
- Old hunting cabins at Pepperdine Camp.
- Panoramic views from Payne Peak.

History

This trail provides a good opportunity to view the early wagon road through Cedar Pass (present-day California 299). From an elevation of 7,618 feet on Payne Peak, you can look down on the lower Cedar Pass (6,305 feet) and imagine how delighted settlers must have been to discover it. The route ran from Dorris Bridge (present-day Alturas) through the high Warner Mountains to Surprise Valley. Access to arable lands on the west side of Surprise Valley was highly sought after by early settlers. However, attacks by the Northern Paiute discouraged settlers moving into the valley.

Henry Talbert settled in the Cedarville area in 1864 when he built a log cabin at Deep Creek, just north of the exit point of this trail. Talbert sold out to James Townsend, who ran a store out of the cabin and catered to wagon trains. Indians killed Townsend in 1867. Two men from Red Bluff, J. H. Bonner and W. T. Cressler, saw an opportunity in this developing valley and relocated the cabin to Cedar Creek at the site of present-day Cedarville (see page 29). Like Townsend, they catered to wagon trains and people camping by the creek before and after crossing Cedar Pass. The old trading post cabin has been preserved in Cedarville Park.

A road ran north from Cedar Creek up the valley to Fort Bidwell and south toward what would become Reno, Nevada. Early descriptions of life in the valley describe the foothills as being a "Utopia to stockraisers." Fattened cattle were driven from here, south to Reno, bound for markets in Nevada and San Francisco. As agriculture brought wealth to the region, Bonner and Cressler's business flourished. A daily stage ran from Reno to Cedarville, and up through Cedar Pass to Alturas. Stages also traveled north over Fandango Pass to Goose Lake. The fate of two cabins at Pepperdine Camp, reached by a spur on the Payne Peak Trail, is in doubt. Leases on the Hunting Cabin, built in 1930, and the Reid Cabin, built in 1948, were held through the forest service, but they expired in 2000.

Description

Payne Peak rises directly south of Cedar Pass in the Warner Mountains. Although it is usually accessed along a graded road from Cedarville, there is a lesser known trail that links the towns of Alturas and Cedarville and avoids the traffic of California 299.

The trail leaves the paved county road east of Alturas and follows a graded dirt county road through private property before entering Modoc National Forest. Once in the forest, the formed winding trail gradually climbs into the Warner Mountains. A side trail branches south to the Dry Creek Trailhead, and the main trail continues to travel west beneath the looming bulk of the rugged Sheep Rock, which rises immediately to the north.

The trail joins major graded FR 31 and travels north around the southern slope of Payne Peak. A worthwhile spur leads through stands of curl-leaf mahoganies to 360-degree views from the top of the peak. The 3-rated climb is not difficult, but the surface is loose enough that 4-wheel-drive is preferred. There is a communications tower on top of the peak. The Warner Mountains extend to the north and south, with Bear Mountain immediately to the north. Warren Peak is the highest point visible to the south. To the east are Cedarville and the Surprise Valley. The edge of Goose Lake can be seen to the northwest and Mount Shasta and Alturas are prominent features to the west. Cedar Pass and California 299 are below the peak to the north.

Petrified wood chips on the exposed slopes of Granger Canyon

A second short spur leads to Pepperdine Camp, Reid Cabin, and the start of the Summit Trail into the South Warner Wilderness. Pepperdine Trailhead, like the Pepperdine cabins, has corrals for horses and pack animals, as well as a five-site campground. From here, it is possible to hike through the wilderness and connect to the many hiking and equestrian trails leading to the Patterson Guard Station on Northern Sierra #53: South Warner Mountains Trail.

Granger Canyon's fall colors

The main trail swings east and descends toward Granger Canyon, becoming smaller and traveling on an uneven formed surface that requires high-clearance 4WD. Gardner Canyon is one of the prettiest parts of the trail. Its creek flows year round and is edged with aspens and cottonwoods. A highlight for rock hounds is the petrified wood that can easily be found on exposed slopes of the canyon. The wood fragments are easy to spot because they are light bone-colored chips that stand out against the dark background material. You will need to climb up the slopes to see some of the finer specimens, but take care; the slope is very steep and the surface is very loose. It is extremely easy to lose your footing and risk an undignified swift descent or worse. Check with the forest office for current regulations before collecting.

The trail within the canyon is small. A flood in 1997 washed out much of it, and although it is passable, small landslides have deposited material across the trail, which has now become part of the surface. As you descend through the deep canyon, the surface gradually improves until the trail spills out onto the county road on the western side of Surprise Valley. The trail finishes at the intersection with CR 1, south of Cedarville.

In fall, aspens and cottonwoods give the trail a golden color. Aspens are normally at their peak color between mid-September and mid-October.

Current Road Information

Modoc National Forest
Warner Mountain Ranger District
385 Wallace Street
Cedarville, CA 96104
(530) 279-6116

Map References

BLM Cedarville, Alturas
USFS Modoc National Forest
USGS 1:24,000 Surprise Station, Payne Peak, Shields Creek, Warren Peak
1:100,000 Cedarville, Alturas
Maptech CD-ROM: Shasta-Trinity/Modoc
Northern California Atlas & Gazetteer, pp. 30, 31, 41
California Road & Recreation Atlas, p. 49
Other: Modoc Countery USFS/BLM Map

Route Directions

▼ 0.0		From US 395 in Alturas, take CR 56 for 6.5 miles east; then turn left on Alpine Road (CR 58), following the sign for Cedar Pass. Proceed 2.7 miles and zero trip meter. Turn southeast on graded dirt CR 58B at the sign and cross cattle guard.
2.9 ▲		Cattle guard; then the trail ends at T-intersection with Alpine Road (CR 58). Turn left and travel 2.7 miles to CR 56. Turn right on CR 56 and travel an additional 6.5 miles to reach US 395 in Alturas.
		GPS: N41°31.43' W120°23.49'
▼ 0.5	SO	CR 58C on left.
2.4 ▲	SO	CR 58C on right.
▼ 0.9	SO	Cattle guard.
2.0 ▲	SO	Cattle guard.
▼ 1.4	TL	Turn left, following the sign to Dry Creek Basin.
1.5 ▲	TR	Track on left.
▼ 2.6	SO	Entering Modoc National Forest at gate.
0.3 ▲	SO	Leaving Modoc National Forest at gate.
		GPS: N41°31.08' W120°20.97'
▼ 2.9	SO	Track on right goes 2 miles to the start of Dry Creek Trail and Lower Dry Creek. Zero trip meter and follow the sign to Upper Dry Creek Basin and Deep Creek.
0.0 ▲		Continue to the northwest.
		GPS: N41°30.93' W120°20.81'
▼ 0.0		Continue to the southeast.
4.0 ▲	SO	Track on left goes 2 miles to the start of Dry Creek Trail and Lower Dry Creek. Zero trip meter.
▼ 0.6	SO	Cross through creek.
3.4 ▲	SO	Cross through creek.
▼ 1.1	SO	Cross over creek.
2.9 ▲	SO	Cross over creek.
▼ 1.3	SO	Track on left.
2.7 ▲	SO	Track on right.
		GPS: N41°30.81' W120°19.40'
▼ 1.5	SO	Cross through Dry Creek; then gate—private property on left and right.
2.5 ▲	SO	Gate—private property on left and right; then cross through Dry Creek.
▼ 1.6	SO	Track on right is private.
2.4 ▲	SO	Track on left is private.
▼ 1.8	SO	Pass through fence line.
2.2 ▲	SO	Pass through fence line.
▼ 1.9	SO	Track on right.
2.1 ▲	SO	Track on left.
▼ 2.2	SO	Track on right.
1.8 ▲	SO	Track on left.
▼ 2.5	SO	Spring on left.
1.5 ▲	SO	Spring on right.
		GPS: N41°30.48' W120°18.26'
▼ 2.6	SO	Cross over creek.
1.4 ▲	SO	Cross over creek.
▼ 2.8	SO	Track on right.
1.2 ▲	BR	Track on left.
		GPS: N41°30.40' W120°18.04'
▼ 4.0	TL	T-intersection with graded dirt road. Zero trip meter.
0.0 ▲		Continue to the west on 42N30.
		GPS: N41°30.30' W120°16.73'
▼ 0.0		Continue to the northwest on FR 31.
2.0 ▲	TR	FR 31 continues straight ahead. Zero trip meter and follow the sign to Dry Creek Basin.
▼ 0.6	SO	Track on right.
1.4 ▲	SO	Track on left.
▼ 0.9	SO	Cattle guard.
1.1 ▲	SO	Cattle guard.
▼ 1.1	SO	Track on left; then track on right.
0.9 ▲	SO	Track on left; then track on right.
▼ 1.2	SO	Track on right.
0.8 ▲	SO	Track on left.
▼ 1.3	SO	Track on right.
0.7 ▲	SO	Track on left.
▼ 1.6	SO	Track on right.
0.4 ▲	SO	Track on left.
▼ 2.0	TR	Track on left is 42N43, spur to Payne Peak. Zero trip meter.
0.0 ▲		Continue to the southeast on FR 31.
		GPS: N41°31.68' W120°16.89'

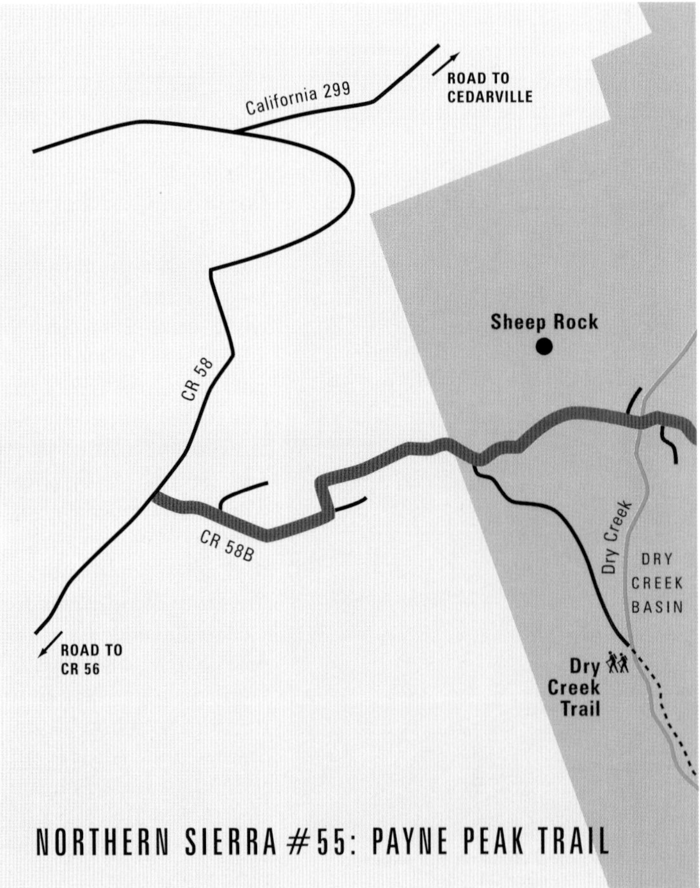

NORTHERN SIERRA #55: PAYNE PEAK TRAIL

Spur to Payne Peak

▼ 0.0			Proceed northwest on 42N43.
▼ 0.2		SO	Track on left.
▼ 0.4		SO	Track on left and track on right.
▼ 0.5		TR	Track continues straight ahead through gate. Turn right before gate.
			GPS: N41°32.02′ W120°16.86′
▼ 1.3			Spur ends at the communications towers on Payne Peak.
			GPS: N41°32.49′ W120°16.57′

Continuation of Main Trail

▼ 0.0			Continue to the east on FR 31.
	1.5 ▲	TL	Track on right is 42N43, spur to Payne Peak. Zero trip meter.
			GPS: N41°31.68′ W120°16.89′
▼ 0.5		SO	Track on left.
	1.0 ▲	SO	Track on right.
▼ 1.5		TR	Track on left is 42N31 to Cedarville. Zero trip meter.
	0.0 ▲		Continue to the west, joining 42N31.
			GPS: N41°31.06′ W120°15.55′
▼ 0.0			Continue to the southeast on 42N49.
	5.4 ▲	TL	Track straight ahead is 42N31 to Cedarville. Zero trip meter and follow the sign to Deep Creek.
▼ 0.6		SO	Turnout on right.
	4.8 ▲	SO	Turnout on left.
▼ 1.0		SO	Cross over South Deep Creek.
	4.4 ▲	SO	Cross over South Deep Creek.
▼ 2.4		SO	Track on left.
	3.0 ▲	SO	Track on right.
▼ 4.0		SO	Track on left is 42N02.
	1.4 ▲	SO	Track on right is 42N02.
			GPS: N41°28.64′ W120°14.79′
▼ 4.3		TL	Cattle guard; then turn left at T-intersection with FR 31.
	1.1 ▲	TR	Turn right on unmarked, well-used trail and cross cattle guard.
			GPS: N41°28.41′ W120°14.88′
▼ 5.4		TL	FR 31 continues to the right and is the spur to Pepperdine Camp. Zero trip meter and turn left onto 42N79 following the sign to Granger Canyon. Small track straight ahead.
	0.0 ▲		Continue to the north.
			GPS: N41°27.59′ W120°14.43′

Spur To Pepperdine Camp

▼ 0.0			Proceed west on FR 31, following the sign to Pepperdine Camp.
▼ 0.2		TL	Turn left at the sign for Pepperdine Camp and Trailhead.
			GPS: N41°27.55′ W120°14.64′
▼ 0.3		BR	Track on left goes 0.4 miles to Pepperdine Trailhead and USFS Campground.
▼ 0.6			Cross through creek; then spur ends at Pepperdine Camp and Reid Cabin.
			GPS: N41°27.20′ W120°14.75′

Continuation of Main Trail

▼ 0.0			Continue to the east.
	6.3 ▲	TR	Small track on left. Road ahead is FR 31 and is

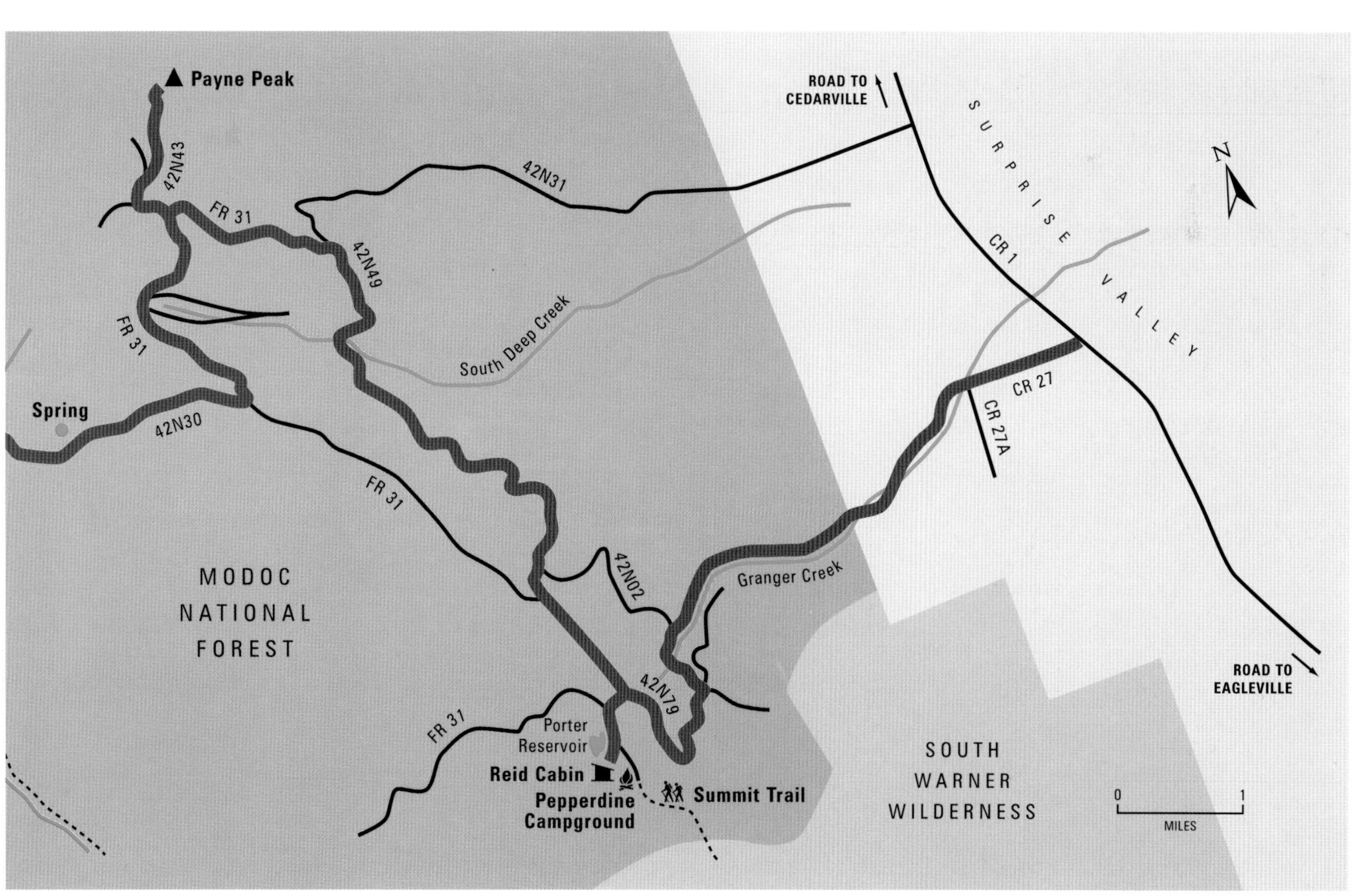

the spur to Pepperdine Camp. Zero trip meter and join FR 31, following the sign to Deep Creek Summit.

GPS: N41°27.59' W120°14.43'

▼ 1.3 **TL** Track on right. Bear left, remaining on main trail; then 4-way intersection. Track on right goes to Tom Lee Meadows—privately owned and closed to the public. Track straight ahead. Turn left, remaining on main trail.

5.0 ▲ **TR** 4-way intersection. Track on left. Track straight head goes to Tom Lee Meadows—privately owned and closed to the public. Turn right, remaining on main trail; then track on left.

GPS: N41°27.42' W120°13.78'

▼ 1.6 **SO** Cross over Granger Creek; then track on left.

4.7 ▲ **SO** Track on right; then cross over Granger Creek.

▼ 1.7 **SO** Track on left; then track on right.

4.6 ▲ **SO** Track on left; then track on right.

▼ 2.2 **SO** Cross through creek.

4.1 ▲ **SO** Cross through creek.

▼ 2.3 **SO** Cross over creek. Petrified wood can be found on the bare slopes on the left.

4.0 ▲ **SO** Cross over creek. Petrified wood can be found on the bare slopes on the right.

▼ 3.0 **SO** Cross through wash.

3.3 ▲ **SO** Cross through wash.

▼ 3.4 **SO** Cross through Granger Creek twice.

2.9 ▲ **SO** Cross through Granger Creek twice.

GPS: N41°28.02' W120°12.47'

▼ 4.0 **SO** Cattle guard.

2.3 ▲ **SO** Cattle guard.

GPS: N41°28.21' W120°11.89'

▼ 4.1 **SO** Track on left; then cross through wash.

2.2 ▲ **SO** Cross through wash; then track on right.

▼ 4.4 **SO** Cross through wash.

1.9 ▲ **SO** Cross through wash.

▼ 5.3 **SO** Track on right into private property.

1.0 ▲ **BR** Track on left into private property.

▼ 5.4 **SO** Cross through Granger Creek; then paved road on right is CR 27A. Continue on CR 27. Road becomes paved.

0.9 ▲ **SO** Road turns to graded dirt; then paved road on left is CR 27A. Cross through Granger Creek.

GPS: N41°28.73' W120°10.56'

▼ 6.3 Trail ends at T-intersection with paved Surprise Valley Road (CR 1). Turn left for Cedarville; turn right for Eagleville.

0.0 ▲ Trail commences on paved Surprise Valley Road (CR 1), 3.5 miles south of the center of Cedarville, 0.6 miles south of Modoc County mile marker 26. Zero trip meter and turn west on paved road marked CR 27.

GPS: N41°28.72' W120°09.48'

The North Coast Region

Trails in the North Coast Region

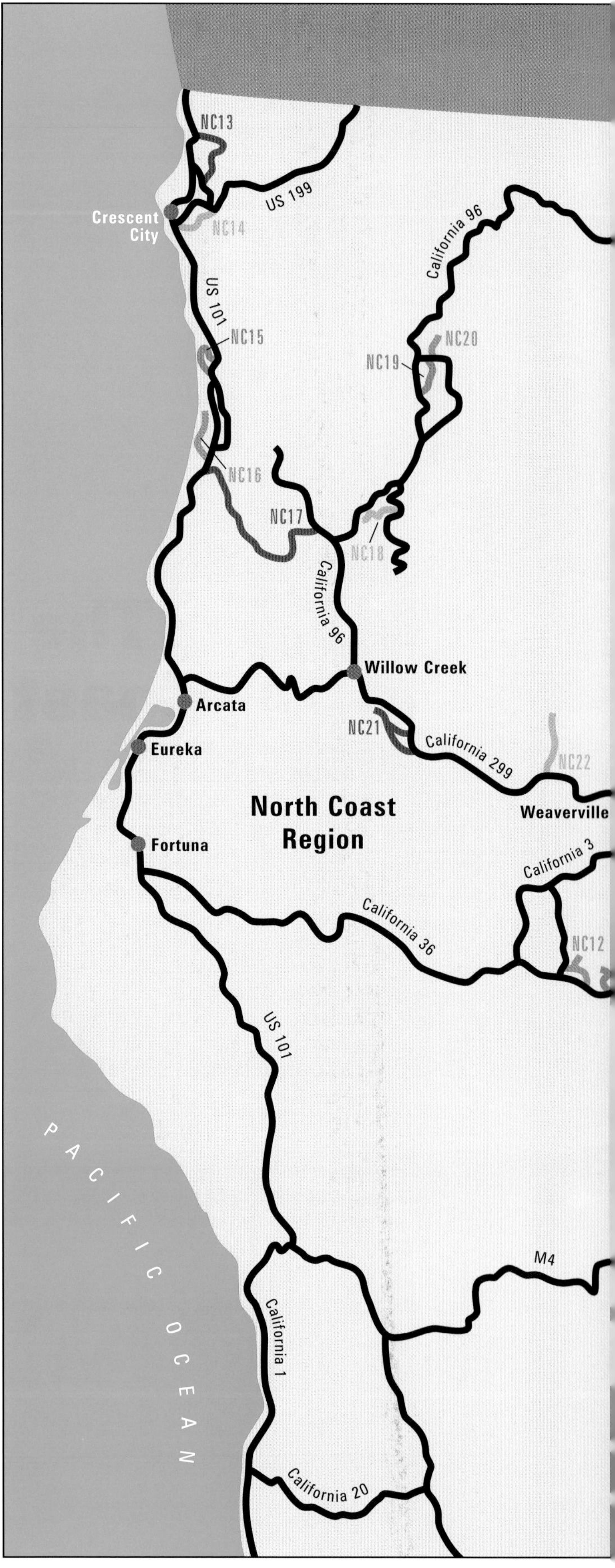

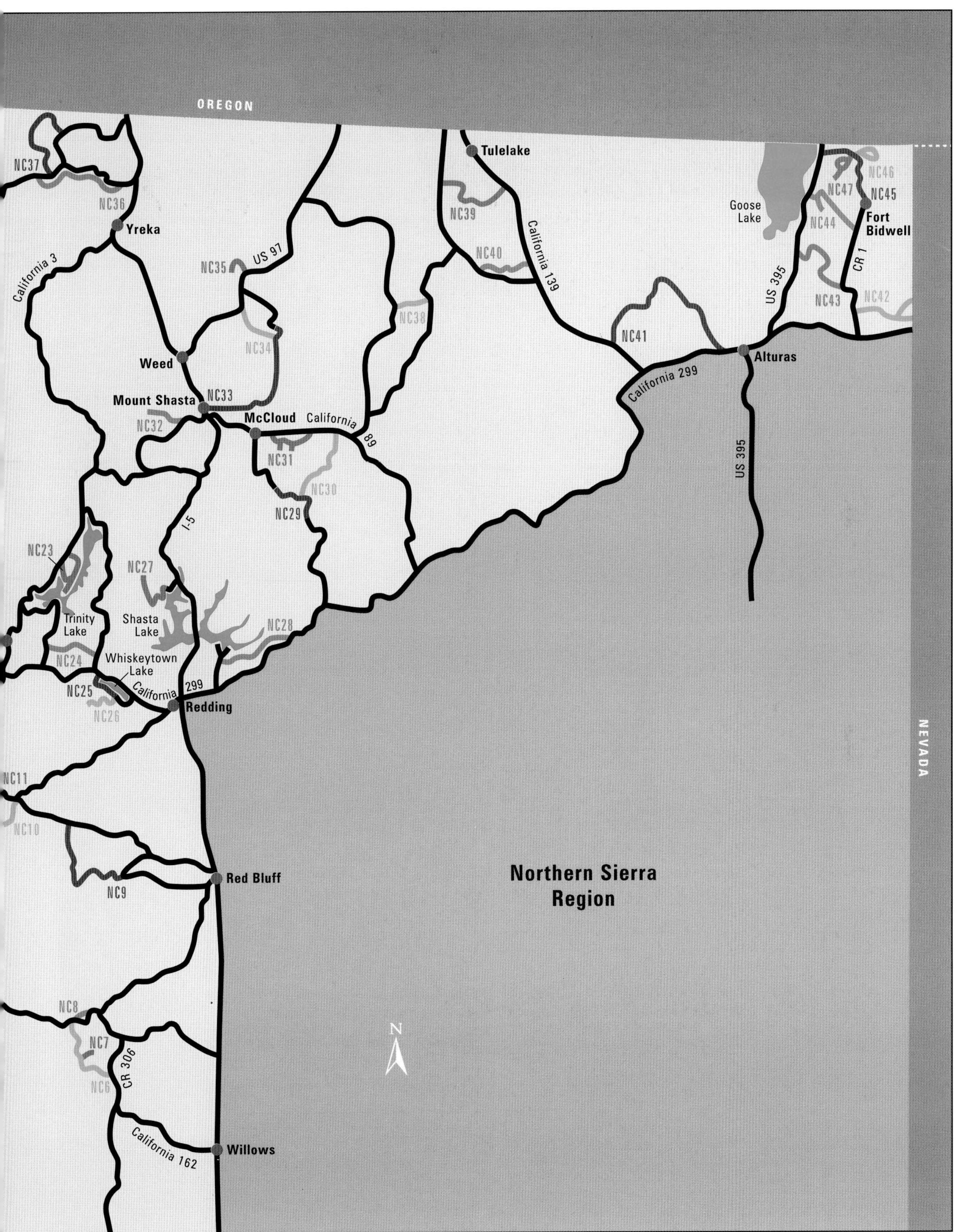
OREGON
NEVADA
NC37
NC36
Yreka
California 3
NC35
US 97
Weed
NC34
Mount Shasta
NC33
NC32
McCloud
California 89
NC31
NC30
NC29
NC38
Tulelake
NC39
NC40
California 139
NC41
California 299
Alturas
US 395
Goose Lake
NC46
NC47
NC45
Fort Bidwell
NC44
CR 1
NC43
NC42
I-5
NC23
NC27
Trinity Lake
Shasta Lake
NC28
NC24
Whiskeytown Lake
NC25
California 299
NC26
Redding
NC11
NC10
Red Bluff
NC9
Northern Sierra Region
NC8
NC7
CR 306
NC6
California 162
Willows
N

MAP CONTINUES ON PAGE 499

Trails in the North Coast Region

MAP CONTINUES ON PAGE 497

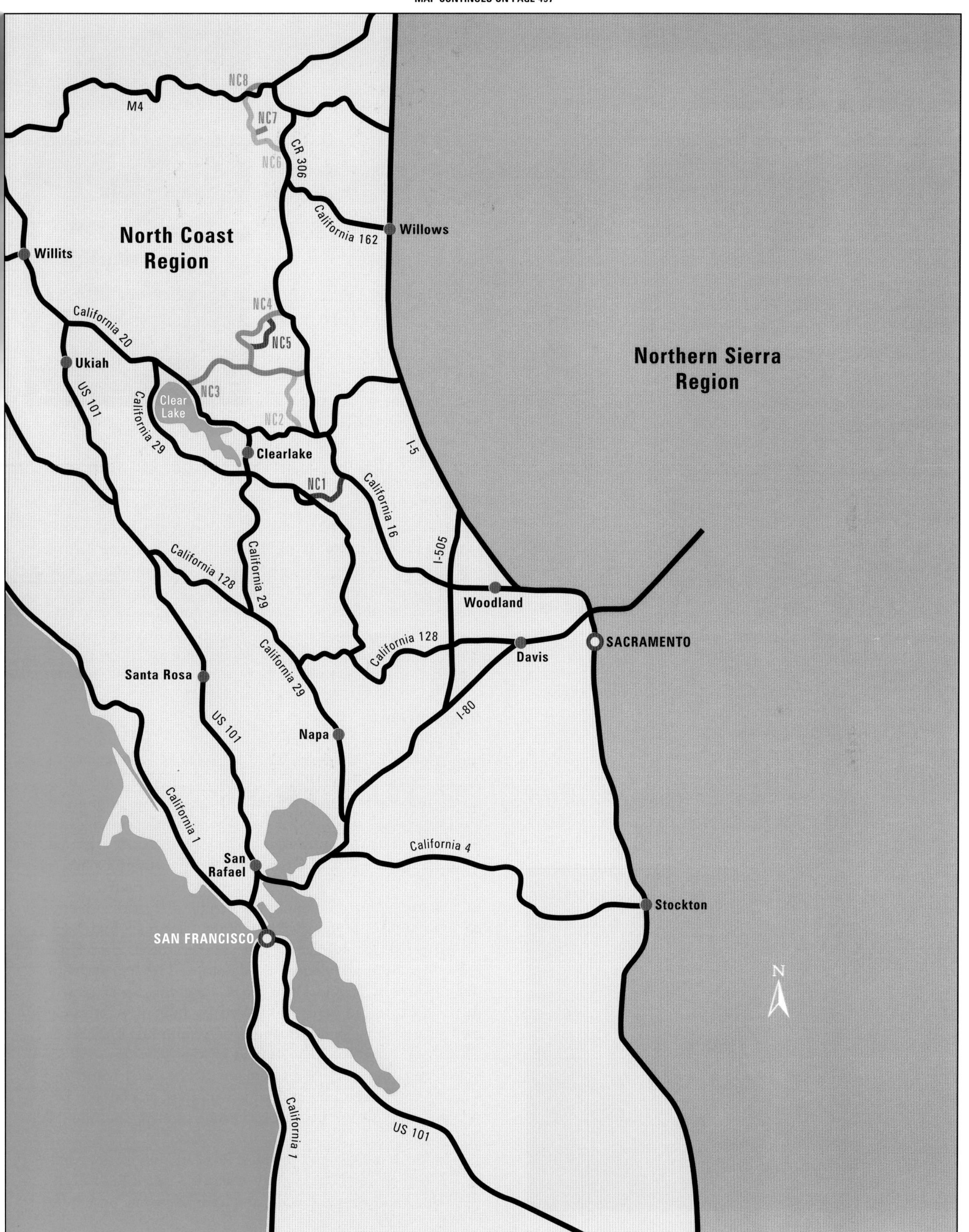

NORTH COAST #1

Rayhouse Road

Starting Point:	California 16, 9 miles south of the intersection with California 20
Finishing Point:	Morgan Valley Road, 12.5 miles southeast of the intersection of California 53 and California 29
Total Mileage:	13.1 miles
Unpaved Mileage:	13.1 miles
Driving Time:	1.5 hours
Elevation Range:	600–2,500 feet
Usually Open:	Year-round
Best Time to Travel:	Dry weather
Difficulty Rating:	3
Scenic Rating:	8
Remoteness Rating:	+0

Special Attractions

- Picnic area beside Cache Creek in Cache Creek Canyon Regional Park.
- Varied scenery, from ridge tops to canyons.
- Canoe put-in on Cache Creek and access to hiking and mountain bike trails.

History

Cache Creek, at the start of this trail, was named by explorer and fur trapper Ewing Young. In 1832, Young camped just downstream in Cañada de Capay, also know as the Capay Valley, and cached goods nearby, remembering the river as Cache Creek. *Kaipai,* as local Patwin Indians knew the cañada or valley, means "stream." The confluence of Cache and Bear Creeks, 2 miles upstream from the start of the described trail, was once the location of a Patwin village named Tebti, meaning "confluence." The picnic area at the start of the trail was once the site of Lopa, another Patwin village.

The trail from Blue Ridge toward Davis Creek Reservoir

The settlement of Rumsey, in the upper reaches of Cañada de Capay, was named for Captain D. C. Rumsey, who settled here in 1892. The town was the end of the line for a railroad that was intended to connect Vacaville and Clear Lake. The ambitious railroad up the spectacular steep-sided Cache Creek Canyon never progressed north of Rumsey.

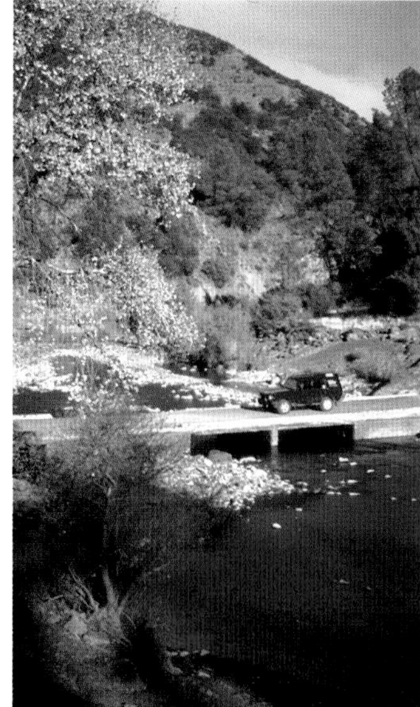
High water in Cache Creek can close the trail

Rumsey had an earthquake of unknown magnitude sometime after the quake that devasted San Francisco in 1906. The earthquake caused a landslide that blocked the confluence of Crack and Cache Creeks, some 10 miles upstream from the start of this trail. Water backed up beginning at the lower end of Kennedy Flats, where the river narrows at the foot of Baldy Mountain. It didn't take long for people in Rumsey to notice that Cache Creek had all but dried up. Fearing the worst, most of the community took to the surrounding hills, while a daring party headed up the canyon to determine the cause. They found that the landslide was impounding Cache Creek's water up to 4 miles behind the dam. When the water finally broke through, the flood caused immense damage to Rumsey, but the hardy townsfolk rebuilt.

Description

This trail crosses the southern end of Blue Ridge and travels through BLM and private lands. It begins at a picnic area in Cache Creek Canyon Regional Park and immediately dips down to ford through wide Cache Creek. Do not attempt to cross if the creek is in flood. A pleasant creekside camping area is a short distance north along California 16. As the trail climbs onto Blue Ridge, a couple of different trails for hikers and mountain bikers branch off from the main route.

The easy going trail climbs up a wide shelf road with ample passing places. On top of Blue Ridge, one track leads back down toward California 16 and another travels past Fiske Lake and continues along the ridge tops. The trail starts to descend steeply toward Davis Creek Reservoir, an extremely pretty reed-fringed lake surrounded by hills; it is privately owned, and no fishing, boating, or swimming is allowed. This narrow and rough shelf road is what gives the trail its difficulty rating of 3. Some remains of the Reed Mine, including some old cabins and mine workings, can be seen beside the road. Again, these are on private property and should not be disturbed.

The road, designated Rayhouse Road in Yolo County, improves as you enter Lake County, where it is called Reiff Road. Reiff Road is graded and wide, and leads to private properties off Morgan Valley Road.

Current Road Information
Bureau of Land Management
Ukiah Field Office
2550 North State Street
Ukiah, CA 95482
(707) 468-4000

Map References
BLM Healdsburg
USGS 1:24,000 Glascock Mt., Knoxville, Jericho Valley, Wilson Valley
1:100,000 Healdsburg
Maptech CD-ROM: North Coast/Mendocino
Northern California Atlas & Gazetteer, p. 84
California Road & Recreation Atlas, p. 64

Route Directions

Mileage		Direction
▼ 0.0		From California 16, 9 miles south of the intersection with California 20, zero trip meter and turn southwest onto CR 40. The road leads off through the Cache Creek Canyon Regional Park picnic area—lower site. The picnic area is on the right. The trail immediately swings around and descends toward Cache Creek.
4.6 ▲		Trail ends at T-intersection with California 16 at the Cache Creek Canyon Regional Park picnic area—lower site. Turn right for Woodland; turn left for California 20.
		GPS: N38°54.52′ W122°18.64′
▼ 0.1	SO	Seasonal closure gate; then cattle guard.
4.5 ▲	SO	Cattle guard; then seasonal closure gate.
▼ 0.2	SO	Cross over Cache Creek on concrete ford.
4.4 ▲	SO	Cross over Cache Creek on concrete ford.
▼ 0.3	SO	Blue Ridge Trail for hikers through gate on left; then cattle guard.
4.3 ▲	SO	Cattle guard; then Blue Ridge Trail for hikers through gate on right.
▼ 0.5	SO	Cross over Fiske Creek on bridge. Start of shelf road.
4.1 ▲	SO	End of shelf road. Cross over Fiske Creek on bridge.
▼ 0.7	SO	Frogpond Trail, a 5-mile loop for hikers, equestrians, and mountain bikers, on right.
3.9 ▲	SO	Frogpond Trail, a 5-mile loop for hikers, equestrians, and mountain bikers, on left.
		GPS: N38°54.22′ W122°18.58′
▼ 2.5	SO	Fish Creek Trail for hikers, equestrians, and mountain bikers on left.
2.1 ▲	SO	Fish Creek Trail for hikers, equestrians, and mountain bikers on right.
		GPS: N38°53.53′ W122°19.03′
▼ 2.6	SO	Track on right.
2.0 ▲	SO	Track on left.
▼ 2.9	SO	Alternative Fish Creek Trail for hikers, equestrians, and mountain bikers on left goes to Fiske Creek Road; then track on right.
1.7 ▲	SO	Track on left; then alternative Fish Creek Trail for hikers, equestrians, and mountain bikers on right goes to Fiske Creek Road.
		GPS: N38°53.42′ W122°19.19′
▼ 3.1	BL	Track on right.
1.5 ▲	BR	Track on left.
▼ 4.6	SO	4-way intersection on saddle. Track on right goes to Buck Island. Track on left goes to Fiske Lake and Blue Ridge Trail. Zero trip meter.
0.0 ▲		Continue to the north.
		GPS: N38°52.68′ W122°19.60′
▼ 0.0		Continue to the south.
8.5 ▲	SO	4-way intersection on saddle. Track on left goes to Buck Island. Track on right goes to Fiske Lake and Blue Ridge Trail. Zero trip meter.
▼ 0.3	SO	Cross through wash.
8.2 ▲	SO	Cross through wash.
▼ 2.7	SO	End of shelf road. Davis Creek Reservoir on left.
5.8 ▲	SO	Leave Davis Creek Reservoir. Start of shelf road.
▼ 3.1	SO	Cross over spillway; then pass along dam.
5.4 ▲	SO	Pass along dam; then cross over spillway.
		GPS: N38°51.84′ W122°21.15′
▼ 4.2	SO	Cross over Davis Creek. Remains of the Reed Mine on left and right.
4.3 ▲	SO	Remains of the Reed Mine on left and right. Cross over Davis Creek; then Davis Creek Reservoir on right.
		GPS: N38°51.80′ W122°22.14′
▼ 5.2	SO	Cross over creek.
3.3 ▲	SO	Cross over creek.

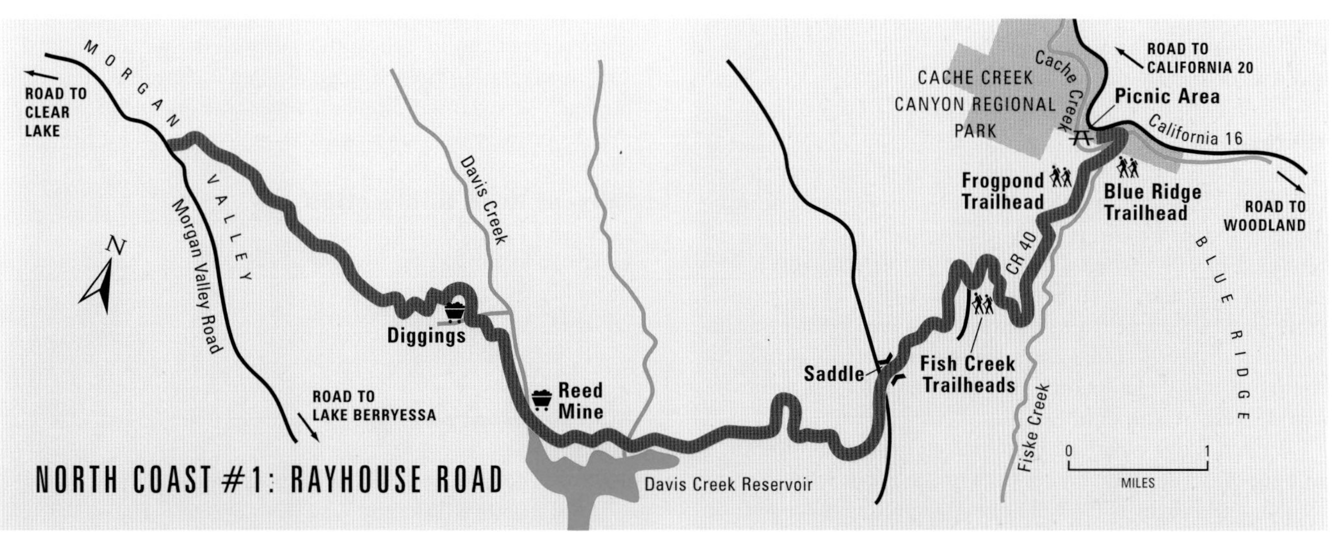

NORTH COAST #1: RAYHOUSE ROAD

▼ 5.4	SO	Track on left into diggings.
3.1 ▲	SO	Track on right into diggings.
		GPS: N38°52.31' W122°22.92'
▼ 6.2	SO	Closure gate; then track on left.
2.3 ▲	SO	Track on right; then closure gate.
▼ 6.3	SO	Track on right and track on left.
2.2 ▲	SO	Track on right and track on left.
▼ 6.4	SO	Track on left.
2.1 ▲	SO	Track on right.
▼ 8.5		Trail ends at T-intersection with paved Morgan Valley Road. Turn right for Clear Lake; turn left for Lake Berryessa.
0.0 ▲		Trail commences on Morgan Valley Road, 12.5 miles southeast of the intersection of California 53 and California 29 at Lower Lake. Zero trip meter and turn northeast on graded dirt Reiff Road.
		GPS: N38°52.55' W122°25.40'

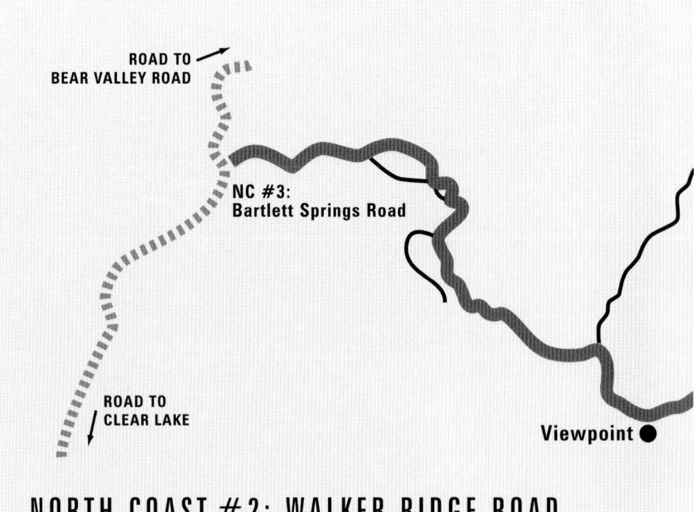

NORTH COAST #2

Walker Ridge Road

Starting Point:	**North Coast #3: Bartlett Springs Road, 2.8 miles from the eastern end**
Finishing Point:	**California 20, 5.9 miles west of the intersection with California 16**
Total Mileage:	**14 miles**
Unpaved Mileage:	**14 miles**
Driving Time:	**1.5 hours**
Elevation Range:	**1,900–3,400 feet**
Usually Open:	**Year-round**
Best Time to Travel:	**Dry weather**
Difficulty Rating:	**1**
Scenic Rating:	**8**
Remoteness Rating:	**+0**

Special Attractions

- Winding ridge top trail.
- Views of Indian Valley Reservoir.

History

Walker Ridge Road overlooks Indian Valley Reservoir in Little Indian Valley, formerly a favorite camping and hunting grounds for the Patwin tribe. The $9 million reservoir was established in 1975 when a dam was constructed across a narrow section of the North Fork of Cache Creek. The reservoir's convoluted shoreline stretches nearly 40 miles, creating a surface area of nearly 4,000 acres when the reservoir is full. Although it is in Lake County, the reservoir provides water for Yolo County to the southeast.

Walker Ridge Road ends immediately west of Wilbur, a mining community that dates back to the 1860s when Ezekial Wilbur and Edwin T. Howell began prospecting for copper on the banks of the West Fork of Sulphur Creek. Their mining venture failed, but the hot springs in the creek paid off. Howell opted out of the failed mine, while Wilbur turned his attention to the springs and established the Wilbur Springs Hotel in 1865. The resort immediately became a favorite stage stop. A Victorian-style hotel was added in 1915, and it continues to be a popular retreat.

The Manzanita Gold Mine, just upstream from the hot springs, was established in the late 1880s and became one of the most productive gold mines in Colusa County. Eventually the Manzanita produced mercury. Many other mines appeared along the West Fork of Sulphur Creek. The Empire, Wide Awake, Central, and Elgin Mines all had their day in this picturesque canyon.

Description

Walker Ridge Road connects North Coast #3: Bartlett Springs Road with California 20. It runs across an open ridge top and offers excellent views in all directions. The trail is an easy, graded road, and passenger vehicles should generally be able to reach the start of the trail by traveling the first 2.8 miles of the 2-rated Bartlett Springs Road. From the ridge top, Indian Valley Reservoir can be seen in the valley to the west.

The vegetation on the ridge is mainly chaparral. The road originally served mines along the way, some of which are still active. Its primary use nowadays is as an access road for hunters.

Current Road Information

Bureau of Land Management
Ukiah Field Office
2550 North State Street
Ukiah, CA 95482
(707) 468-4000

Map References

BLM Lakeport
USGS 1:24,000 Leesville, Wilbur Springs
1:100,000 Lakeport

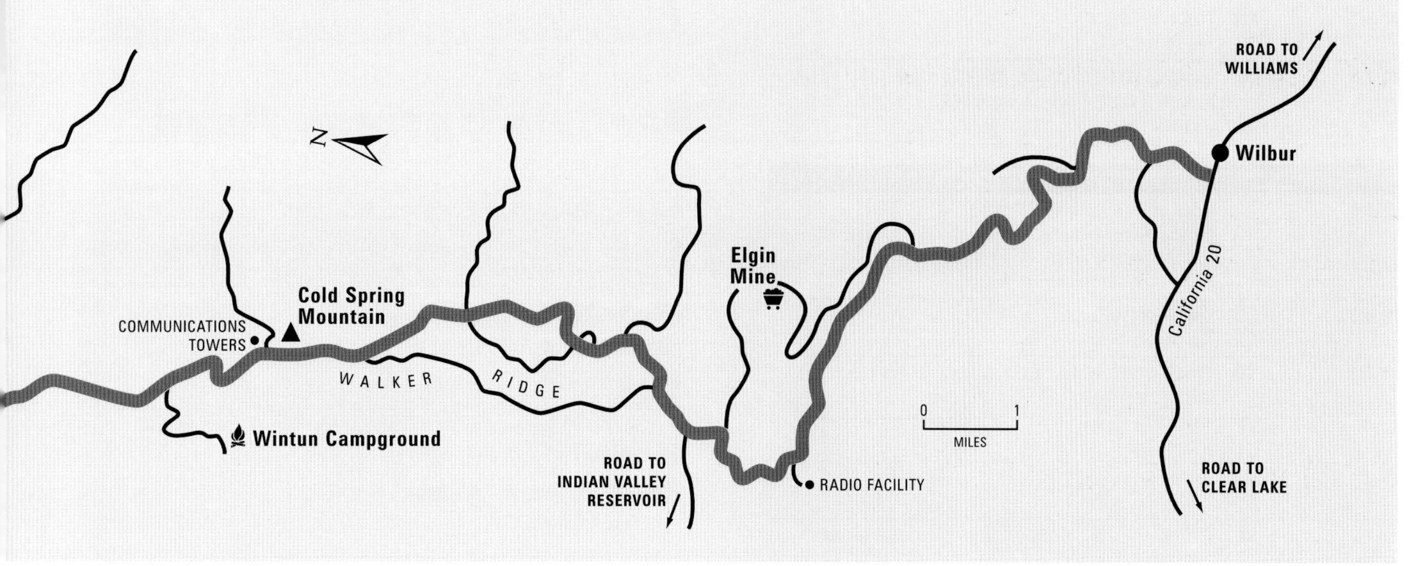

Maptech CD-ROM: North Coast/Mendocino
Northern California Atlas & Gazetteer, p. 76

Route Directions

▼ 0.0		From a 4-way intersection on North Coast #3: Bartlett Springs Road, 2.8 miles from the eastern end, zero trip meter and turn southeast on graded dirt road, following the BLM sign for Indian Valley Dam.
4.9 ▲		Trail ends at a 4-way intersection with North Coast #3: Bartlett Springs Road. Turn left to follow this trail to Nice and Clear Lake; turn right to exit to Leesville and Williams.
		GPS: N39°09.51′ W122°28.73′
▼ 0.8	SO	Track on right.
4.1 ▲	SO	Track on left.
▼ 0.9	SO	Track on left.
4.0 ▲	SO	Track on right.
▼ 1.4	BL	Two tracks on right.
3.5 ▲	BR	Two tracks on left.
▼ 1.5	SO	Track on right.
3.4 ▲	SO	Track on left.
▼ 1.9	SO	Track on right.
3.0 ▲	SO	Track on left.
▼ 2.8	SO	Track on left.
2.1 ▲	SO	Track on right.
▼ 3.2	SO	Track on left.
1.7 ▲	SO	Track on right.
▼ 3.8	SO	Turnout on right with views of Indian Valley Reservoir.
1.1 ▲	SO	Turnout on left with views of Indian Valley Reservoir.
		GPS: N39°07.19′ W122°29.93′
▼ 4.0	SO	Track on left.
0.9 ▲	SO	Track on right.
▼ 4.9	SO	Graded road on right goes to Wintun Campground. Zero trip meter.
0.0 ▲		Continue to the northwest.
		GPS: N39°06.36′ W122°29.59′
▼ 0.0		Continue to the southeast.
4.0 ▲	SO	Graded road on left goes to Wintun Campground. Zero trip meter.
▼ 0.8	SO	Cold Spring Mountain. Track on left goes past communications towers.
3.2 ▲	SO	Cold Spring Mountain. Track on right goes past communications towers.
		GPS: N39°05.90′ W122°29.27′
▼ 1.3	SO	Track on right.
2.7 ▲	SO	Track on left.
▼ 2.1	SO	Track on left and track on right.
1.9 ▲	SO	Track on right and track on left.
▼ 2.6	SO	Track on right.
1.4 ▲	SO	Track on left.
▼ 3.0	SO	Two tracks on right and track on left.
1.0 ▲	SO	Two tracks on left and track on right.
▼ 3.1	SO	Track on left.
0.9 ▲	SO	Track on right.
▼ 3.3	SO	Track on left.
0.7 ▲	SO	Track on right.

Cold Spring Mountain, the highest point along the ridge

▼ 3.7		SO	Track on right.
	0.3 ▲	SO	Track on left.
▼ 4.0		BL	Graded road on right goes to Blue Oak and Indian Valley Dam. Also track on right. Zero trip meter.
	0.0 ▲		Continue to the northeast.
			GPS: N39°03.78′ W122°29.36′
▼ 0.0			Continue to the southeast.
	5.1 ▲	BR	Graded road on left goes to Blue Oak and Indian Valley Dam. Also second track on left. Zero trip meter.
▼ 0.3		SO	Track on left.
	4.8 ▲	SO	Track on right.
▼ 1.1		SO	Track on right to radio facility; then track on left.
	4.0 ▲	SO	Track on right; then track on left to radio facility.
▼ 2.2		SO	Track on left.
	2.9 ▲	SO	Track on right.
▼ 2.6		SO	Graded road on left to Elgin Mine—private property.
	2.5 ▲	SO	Graded road on right to Elgin Mine—private property.
			GPS: N39°02.75′ W122°27.95′
▼ 3.1		SO	Track on left.
	2.0 ▲	SO	Track on right.
▼ 3.3		SO	Track on right.
	1.8 ▲	SO	Track on left.
▼ 4.1		SO	Track on left.
	1.0 ▲	SO	Track on right.
▼ 4.7		SO	Track on right.
	0.4 ▲	SO	Track on left.
▼ 5.1			Track on left; then trail ends at T-intersection with California 20 near Wilbur. Turn right for Clear Lake; turn left for Williams.
	0.0 ▲		Trail commences on California 20, 5.9 miles west of the intersection with California 16. Zero trip meter and turn north on graded dirt road, following sign for Walker Ridge Road.
			GPS: N39°01.39′ W122°27.15′

Indian Valley Reservoir

NORTH COAST #3

Bartlett Springs Road

Starting Point:	**Bear Valley Road, 11 miles south of Lodoga**
Finishing Point:	**California 20, at the southern end of Nice on the northern shores of Clear Lake**
Total Mileage:	**33.7 miles**
Unpaved Mileage:	**33.5 miles**
Driving Time:	**2.5 hours**
Elevation Range:	**1,400–3,900 feet**
Usually Open:	**April to December**
Best Time to Travel:	**April to December**
Difficulty Rating:	**2**
Scenic Rating:	**9**
Remoteness Rating:	**+1**

Special Attractions

- Clear Lake—California's largest natural lake entirely within the state.
- Fishing at Indian Valley Reservoir.
- Long winding trail that travels through canyons and ridge tops in Mendocino National Forest.

History

Bartlett Springs Road follows a stagecoach route that connected Leesville, a settlement now abandoned in Bear Valley, with a number of mountain resorts to the west. The road crosses Bartlett Mountain to end at an old mineral water bottling plant beside Clear Lake.

Kentuckian Greene Bartlett drove cattle to California in the 1850s and eventually settled in Napa County in the early 1860s. Bartlett's health was poor, so he took his doctor's advice and moved to higher elevations in the vicinity of the North Fork of Cache Creek; he discovered Bartlett Springs in 1870 and established a resort. Word spread about its healthful waters and within three years, the resort boasted a large hotel and some 40 cabins. In its fourth year, Bartlett Springs had nearly 80 cabins, and a steady stream of stagecoaches plied the bumpy wagon road to its doors. The springs' mineral waters were bottled at a plant on Clear Lake.

A community developed at the resort to cater to the ever-increasing numbers of guests. By the turn of the twentieth century, stores, a post office, and other business were well established. Unfortunately, a disastrous fire in 1934 brought an end to the resort. By 1935, the post office had closed and only a few people remained in the valley.

Stages passed through the community of Barkerville before stopping at the well-known Hough Springs Resort. Built in the early 1880s, the resort's hotel and cabins were a welcome sight to the passengers after the rough and dusty wagon ride. From here, stages proceeded up the North Fork of the Cache Creek Valley, past Allen Springs, to the more developed Bartlett Springs Resort.

Description

Bartlett Springs Road is a pleasant drive through a variety of scenery in Mendocino National Forest. The trail begins in the wide Bear Valley and travels west past Indian Valley Reservoir. Many side trails lead down to the shore of the reservoir, but there are no developed facilities at its north end. After crossing the North Fork of Cache Creek, the trail enters BLM land and passes a large, well-used informal camping area. The route follows the North Fork of Cache Creek in its narrow canyon for some distance, and the road is narrow and rough enough that a high-clearance vehicle is recommended.

North Coast #4: Pacific Ridge Trail joins this trail at Hough Springs. Bartlett Springs Road continues along a wider graded dirt road toward Clear Lake. There is some private property along this county-maintained road, and there are few camping opportunities. Be sure to remain on marked trails to avoid straying onto private property. Watch out for coyotes, deer, and bobcats on the open ridge top, and raptors soaring in the air currents above. The trail descends toward Clear Lake to finish on California 20 at the southern edge of Nice. The final part of the trail provides views over Clear Lake to the distant Mayacmas Mountains.

Current Road Information

Bureau of Land Management
Ukiah Field Office
2550 North State Street
Ukiah, CA 95482
(707) 468-4000

Mendocino National Forest
Upper Lake Ranger District
10025 Elk Mountain Road
Upper Lake, CA 95485
(707) 275-2361

Map References

BLM Lakeport
USFS Mendocino National Forest
USGS 1:24,000 Leesville, Hough Springs, Bartlett Springs, Bartlett Mt., Lucerne
1:100,000 Lakeport
Maptech CD-ROM: North Coast/Mendocino
Northern California Atlas & Gazetteer, pp. 76, 75
California Road & Recreation Atlas, p. 63

Route Directions

▼ 0.0			From Bear Valley Road, 11 miles south of Lodoga, zero trip meter and turn southwest on paved road, following the sign to Indian Valley Reservoir and Bartlett Springs.
	2.8 ▲		Trail ends at T-intersection with paved Bear Valley Road. Turn left for Lodoga and Williams; turn right for California 20.
			GPS: N39°09.87′ W122°26.38′
▼ 0.1		SO	Cross over Bear Creek. Road turns to graded dirt.
	2.7 ▲	SO	Cross over Bear Creek. Road is now paved.
▼ 0.3		SO	Cross over Mill Creek on bridge.
	2.5 ▲	SO	Cross over Mill Creek on bridge.

Bartlett Mineral Springs, established in 1867, is now abandoned

▼ 0.5		SO	Cross over creek.
	2.3 ▲	SO	Cross over creek.
▼ 1.7		SO	Cross over creek.
	1.1 ▲	SO	Cross over creek.
▼ 2.8		SO	4-way intersection. Graded road on left is North Coast #2: Walker Ridge Road. Graded road on right. Zero trip meter.
	0.0 ▲		Continue to the northeast.
			GPS: N39°09.51′ W122°28.73′
▼ 0.0			Continue to the west.
	7.3 ▲	SO	4-way intersection. Graded road on right is North Coast #2: Walker Ridge Road. Graded road on left. Zero trip meter.
▼ 1.9		SO	Cross through Kilpepper Creek.
	5.4 ▲	SO	Cross through Kilpepper Creek.
			GPS: N39°10.01′ W122°30.41′
▼ 2.1		SO	Cross over creek on bridge.
	5.2 ▲	SO	Cross over creek on bridge.
▼ 2.9		SO	Hiking trail on left; then cross over creek on bridge.
	4.4 ▲	SO	Cross over creek on bridge; then hiking trail on right.
▼ 3.0		SO	Track on right; then track on left. Indian Valley Reservoir on left.
	4.3 ▲	SO	Track on right; then track on left. Leaving Indian Valley Reservoir.
▼ 3.3		SO	Start to cross dam.
	4.0 ▲	SO	Leave dam.
			GPS: N39°10.05′ W122°32.03′
▼ 3.5		SO	Leave dam.
	3.8 ▲	SO	Start to cross dam.
▼ 4.0		SO	Track on left. Many tracks on left lead down to the lakeshore for the next 3.3 miles.
	3.3 ▲	SO	Track on right.
▼ 4.3		SO	Two tracks on right.
	3.0 ▲	SO	Two tracks on left.
▼ 4.6		SO	Cross over creek.
	2.7 ▲	SO	Cross over creek.
▼ 4.7		SO	Track on right.
	2.6 ▲	SO	Track on left.
			GPS: N39°09.52′ W122°32.89′
▼ 5.0		SO	Track on right; then cross over creek.
	2.3 ▲	SO	Cross over creek; then track on left.

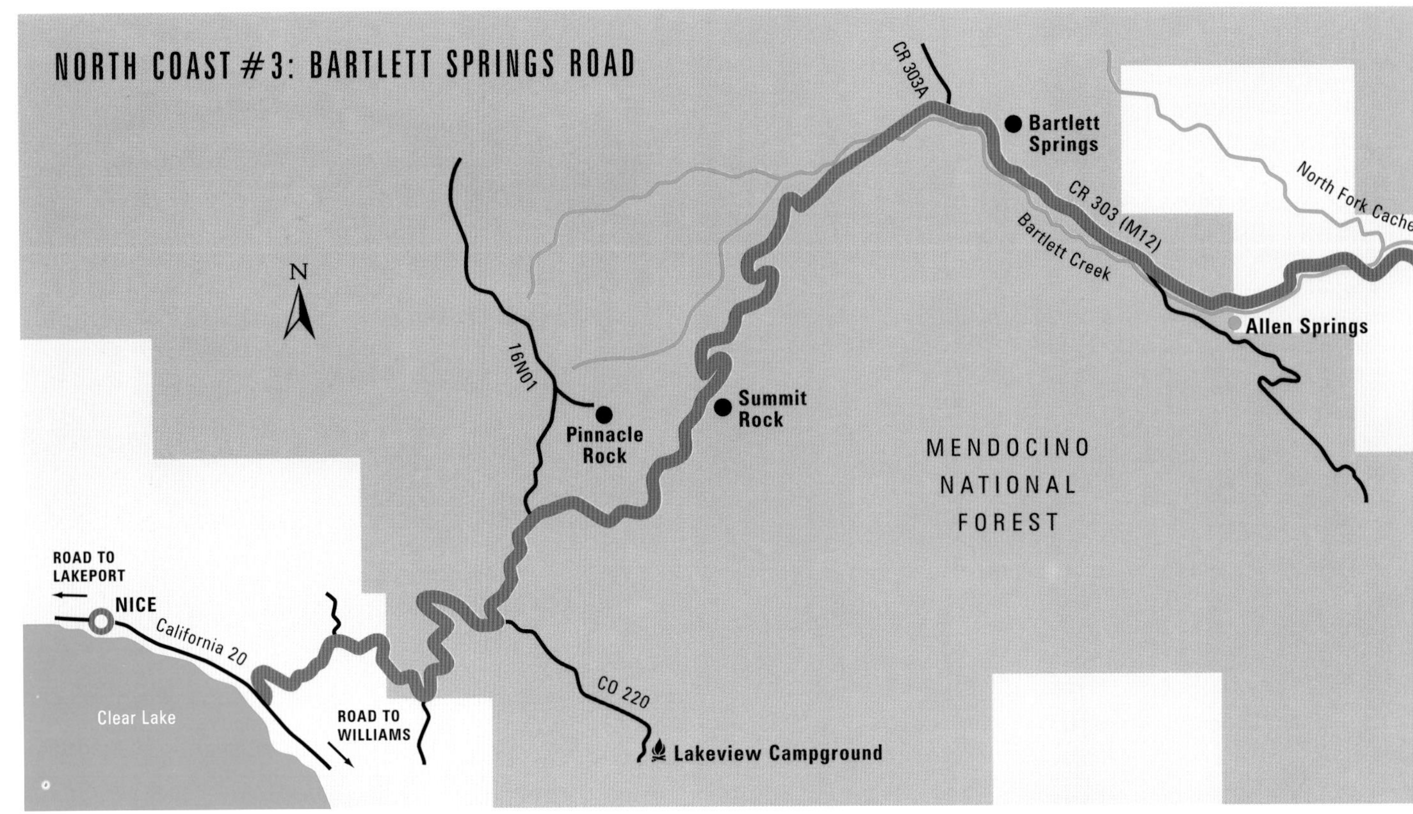

▼ 5.6	SO	Track on right.
1.7 ▲	SO	Track on left.
▼ 6.7	SO	Track on right.
0.6 ▲	SO	Track on left.
▼ 7.3	SO	Track on right; then cross over North Fork Cache Creek on bridge. Camping areas on the right and left after bridge. End of tracks on left. Zero trip meter on far side of bridge.
0.0 ▲		Continue to the northeast. Track on left at far end of bridge. Many tracks on right lead down to lakeshore for next 3.3 miles.
		GPS: N39°09.40′ W122°35.12′
▼ 0.0		Continue to the southwest.
1.7 ▲	SO	Camping areas on the left and right. Zero trip meter and cross over North Fork Cache Creek on bridge.
▼ 0.1	SO	Track on left into camping area and track on right.
1.6 ▲	BL	Track on right into camping area and track on left.
▼ 0.5	SO	Track on right.
1.2 ▲	SO	Track on left.
▼ 0.8	SO	Track on right.
0.9 ▲	SO	Track on left.
▼ 0.9	SO	Track on right.
0.8 ▲	SO	Track on left.
▼ 0.9	SO	Track on right.
0.7 ▲	SO	Track on left.
▼ 1.6	SO	Hough Springs on left—little remains.
0.1 ▲	SO	Hough Springs on right—little remains.
▼ 1.7	SO	Track on left. Track on right is North Coast #4: Pacific Ridge Trail, which drops down to cross through North Fork Cache Creek. Intersection is unmarked. Zero trip meter.
0.0 ▲		Continue to the southeast.
		GPS: N39°09.92′ W122°36.75′
▼ 0.0		Continue to the northwest.
7.2 ▲	SO	Track on right. Track on left is North Coast #4: Pacific Ridge Trail, which immediately drops down to cross through North Fork Cache Creek. Intersection is unmarked. Zero trip meter.
▼ 0.1	SO	Track on left.
7.1 ▲	SO	Track on right.
▼ 0.8	SO	Track on right.
6.4 ▲	SO	Track on left.
▼ 0.9	SO	Track on right.
6.3 ▲	SO	Track on left.
▼ 2.7	SO	Cross over Bartlett Creek on bridge.
4.5 ▲	SO	Cross over Bartlett Creek on bridge.
		GPS: N39°09.92′ W122°38.67′
▼ 4.0	SO	Track on left.
3.2 ▲	SO	Track on right.
▼ 4.8	SO	Track on left.
2.4 ▲	SO	Track on right.
▼ 6.8	SO	Passing through Bartlett Mineral Springs property.
0.4 ▲	SO	Passing through Bartlett Mineral Springs property.
		GPS: N39°11.01′ W122°42.17′
▼ 7.2	SO	Track on right is CR 303A (17N04) to Twin Valley. Zero trip meter and follow the sign to Bartlett Flat.
0.0 ▲		Continue to the east.
		GPS: N39°11.07′ W122°42.48′
▼ 0.0		Continue to the west on CR 303 (M12).
7.9 ▲	SO	Track on left is CR 303A (17N04) to Twin Valley. Zero trip meter and follow the sign to Bartlett Springs.
▼ 0.6	SO	Cross over creek on bridge.

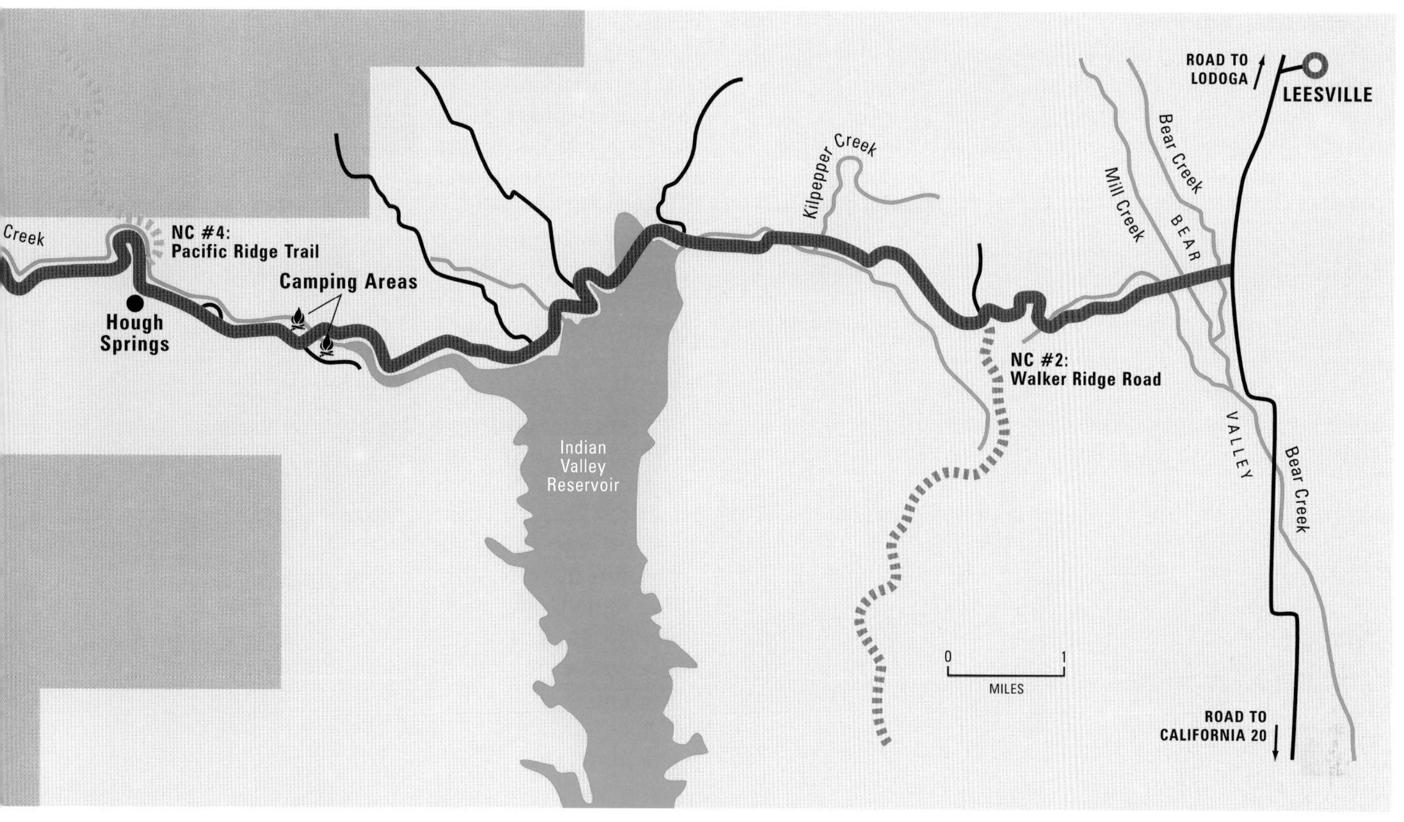

	7.3 ▲	SO	Cross over creek on bridge.
▼ 4.7		BR	Two tracks on left.
	3.2 ▲	BL	Two tracks on right.
▼ 5.1		SO	Pinnacle Rock on right and Summit Rock on left.
	2.8 ▲	SO	Pinnacle Rock on left and Summit Rock on right.
			GPS: N39°09.01' W122°44.74'
▼ 6.2		SO	Track on left.
	1.7 ▲	SO	Track on right.
▼ 7.3		SO	Track on right.
	0.6 ▲	SO	Track on left.
▼ 7.9		SO	Track on right is16N01 to Pinnacle Rock . Zero trip meter and follow the sign to California 20.
	0.0 ▲		Continue to the north.
			GPS: N39°08.08' W122°46.54'
▼ 0.0			Continue to the south.
	5.8 ▲	SO	Track on left is 16N01 to Pinnacle Rock. Zero trip meter and follow the sign to Bartlett Springs.
▼ 0.8		SO	Track on left.
	5.0 ▲	SO	Track on right.
▼ 1.1		BR	Track on left is CO 220 to Lakeview USFS Campground. Remain on CO 303.
	4.7 ▲	BL	Track on right is CO 220 to Lakeview USFS Campground. Remain on CO 303.
			GPS: N39°07.33' W122°46.81'
▼ 3.2		SO	Track on left.
	2.6 ▲	SO	Track on right.
▼ 3.7		SO	Leaving Mendocino National Forest.
	2.1 ▲	SO	Entering Mendocino National Forest.
▼ 4.7		BL	Track on right and Fife Road on right.
	1.1 ▲	BR	Fife Road on left and track on left.
▼ 5.7		SO	Road becomes paved.
	0.1 ▲	SO	Road turns to graded dirt.
▼ 5.8			Trail ends at T-intersection with California 20 on the northern shore of Clear Lake. Turn left for Williams; turn right for Lakeport.
	0.0 ▲		Trail commences on California 20 on the north shore of Clear Lake at the southern end of Nice. Zero trip meter and turn north on paved road, following the sign for Bartlett Springs and Hough Springs. There is a sign for Bartlett Mineral Springs at the intersection
			GPS: N39°06.75' W122°49.14'

NORTH COAST #4

Pacific Ridge Trail

Starting Point:	**Lodoga-Stonyford Road, 2 miles west of Lodoga and 6 miles south of Stonyford**
Finishing Point:	**North Coast #3: Bartlett Springs Road at Hough Springs**
Total Mileage:	**20.4 miles**
Unpaved Mileage:	**20.4 miles**
Driving Time:	**2 hours**
Elevation Range:	**1,300–3,600 feet**
Usually Open:	**Year-round**
Best Time to Travel:	**Dry weather**
Difficulty Rating:	**2**
Scenic Rating:	**9**
Remoteness Rating:	**+0**

Special Attractions

- Access to a network of 4WD trails in the Stonyford OHV Area.
- Exceptional views from long sections of shelf road.
- Can be combined with North Coast #5: Lovelady Ridge Trail to make a challenging loop.

History

This trail begins at the settlement of Lodoga in Indian Valley, and makes its way across Pacific Ridge before dropping down to the North Fork of Cache Creek. The Patwin Indians, a subtribe of the Wintun, occupied this region prior to the arrival of settlers in the mid-nineteenth century. The Patwin, whose name means a single person or man in their language, lived on the western side of the lower Sacramento Valley. Their diet consisted mainly of acorns, pine nuts, wild grapes, and venison as well as salmon and steelhead, which spawned in the Sacramento River across the flat of Colusa Basin. The Patwin caught fish in weirs and then dried and pulverized them to make an easy to carry meal for later consumption.

Bahka, a group of Patwin villages, was located in Indian Valley near the site of Lodoga. Another village called Tsuhelmem was also located in the aptly named valley.

Hough Springs, on the banks of the North Fork of Cache Creek, was a popular mountain resort in the early 1880s. The resort had an attractive hotel, separate cottages, and camping areas to entice visitors to its tranquil setting and cool summer temperatures.

Description

This trail follows Little Stony Creek before climbing up and over Pacific Ridge. It is rated a 2 for difficulty, mainly due to rough sections of shelf road along Pacific Ridge and a couple of shallow creek crossings that should not be difficult for high-clearance 2WD vehicles but will be impassable for low-slung vehicles. Like all creek crossings, high waters change conditions, and even those with high-clearance 4WDs should think twice before crossing in those conditions.

Hillside above Wyley Glade

The first part of the trail, along pretty Little Stony Creek, passes through the Stonyford OHV Area, which has a USFS campground and a day-use staging area. Many small trails lead off into the OHV area; some are only suitable for ATVs and motorbikes, but there are plenty of challenging and interesting runs for high-clearance 4WDs. Many of them are steep and climb high onto the ridge tops above Little Stony Creek. One of these trails, the 7-rated North Coast #5: Lovelady Ridge Trail, can be combined with the first part of this trail to make a more challenging loop.

Little Stony Creek's fall color

Much of the middle part of the trail is a shelf road that winds above the creek. The trail then joins the better-graded forest road M5 and travels over Pacific Ridge. A long descent

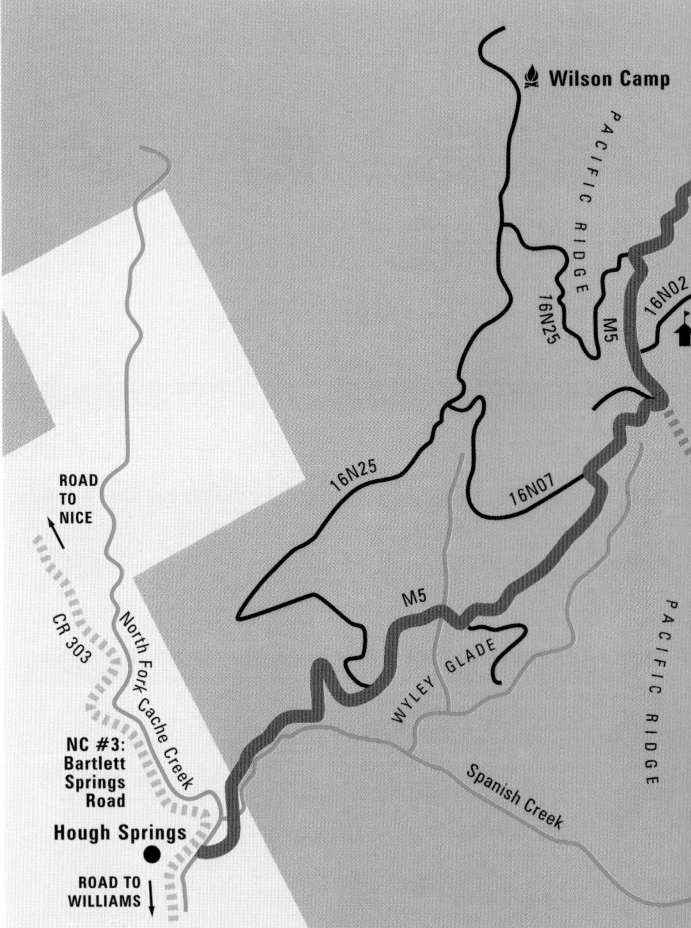

takes you to the final part of the trail and the rough crossing over the North Fork of Cache Creek at Hough Springs. The trail ends at the intersection with North Coast #3: Bartlett Springs Road.

Current Road Information

Bureau of Land Management
Ukiah Field Office
2550 North State Street
Ukiah, CA 95482
(707) 468-4000

Mendocino National Forest
Grindstone Ranger District
825 North Humboldt Avenue
Willows, CA 95988
(530) 934-3316

Map References

BLM Lakeport
USFS Mendocino National Forest
USGS 1:24,000 Gilmore Peak, Fouts Springs, Hough Springs, Bartlett Springs
1:100,000 Lakeport
Maptech CD-ROM: North Coast/Mendocino
Northern California Atlas & Gazetteer, pp. 76, 75
California Road & Recreation Atlas, p. 63
Other: Stonyford OHV Area Guide (incomplete)

Route Directions

▼ 0.0		From Lodoga-Stonyford Road, 2 miles west of Lodoga and 6 miles south of Stonyford, zero trip meter and turn south on graded dirt Goat Mountain Road, following the sign for Goat Mountain.
4.3 ▲		Trail ends at T-intersection with Lodoga-Stonyford Road. Turn right for Lodoga; turn left for Stonyford.
		GPS: N39°18.30′ W122°31.55′
▼ 1.2	SO	Entering Mendocino National Forest.
3.1 ▲	SO	Leaving Mendocino National Forest.
▼ 3.2	SO	Cattle guard.
1.1 ▲	SO	Cattle guard.
▼ 3.5	SO	Little Stony USFS Campground on left. Track on right is #26 for 4WDs, ATVs, and motorbikes—rated blue.
0.8 ▲	SO	Track on left is #26 for 4WDs, ATVs, and motorbikes—rated blue. Little Stony USFS Campground on right.
		GPS: N39°17.23′ W122°34.58′
▼ 3.7	SO	Day-use staging area on left. Track on right is #24 for ATVs and motorbikes only—rated green.
0.6 ▲	SO	Day-use staging area on right. Track on left is #24 for ATVs and motorbikes only—rated green.
▼ 4.3	SO	Track on left is North Coast #5: Lovelady Ridge Trail (#01) for 4WDs, ATVs, and motorbikes—rated blue. Track on right is also #01, but is for

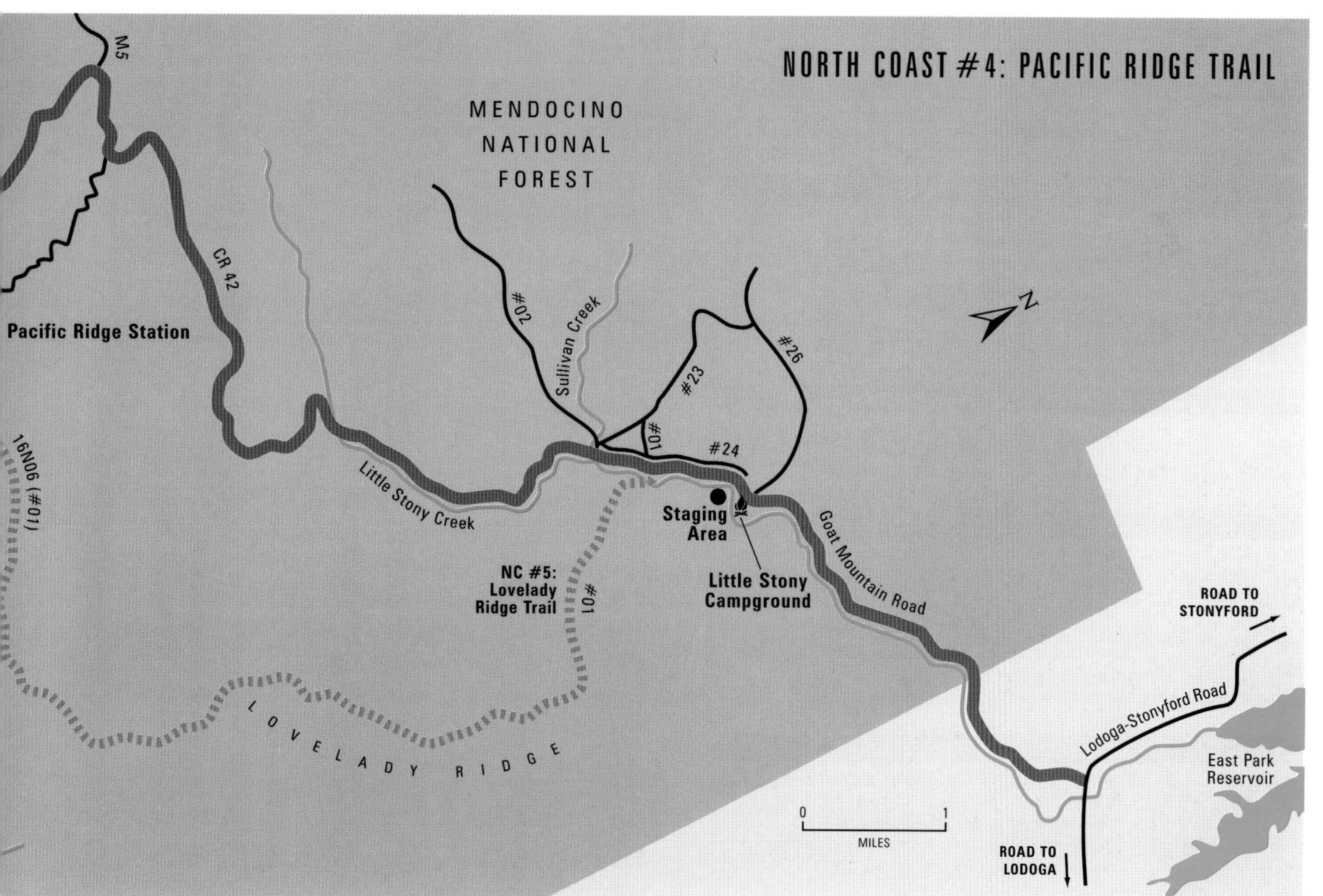

		ATVs and motorbikes only—rated black. Zero trip meter. Start of shelf road along creek.
0.0 ▲		Continue to the north. End of shelf road.

GPS: N39°16.77' W122°35.13'

▼ 0.0		Continue to the south.
7.4 ▲	SO	Track on right is North Coast #5: Lovelady Ridge Trail (#01) for 4WDs, ATVs, and motorbikes—rated blue. Track on left is also #01, but is for ATVs and motorbikes only—rated black. Zero trip meter.
▼ 0.4	SO	Track on right is #24 for ATVs and motorbikes only—rated green; second track on right is #02 for motorbikes only—rated black. Cross over Sullivan Creek on bridge.
7.0 ▲	SO	Cross over Sullivan Creek on bridge; then track on left is #02 for motorbikes only—rated black. Second track on left is #24 for ATVs and motorbikes only—rated green.

GPS: N39°16.56' W122°35.43'

▼ 0.5	SO	Track on right is #02 for motorbikes only—rated black.
6.9 ▲	SO	Track on left is #02 for motorbikes only—rated black.
▼ 2.8	SO	Cross over Little Stony Creek on bridge; then track on right.
4.7 ▲	SO	Track on left; then cross over Little Stony Creek on bridge.

GPS: N39°15.21' W122°36.50'

▼ 4.9	SO	Track on left. End of shelf road.
2.5 ▲	SO	Track on right. Start of shelf road.
▼ 5.4	SO	Track on right.
2.0 ▲	SO	Track on left.
▼ 6.8	BR	Track on left. Follow sign for Goat Mountain.
0.6 ▲	BL	Track on right.

GPS: N39°14.76' W122°39.09'

▼ 7.4	TL	T-intersection with M5. Zero trip meter and follow the sign for Pacific Ridge.
0.0 ▲		Continue to the northeast on CR 42.

GPS: N39°14.89' W122°39.67'

▼ 0.0		Continue to the south.
2.8 ▲	TR	M5 continues straight ahead. Zero trip meter and follow the sign for Stonyford.
▼ 0.2	SO	Track on left; then track on right.
2.6 ▲	SO	Track on left; then track on right.
▼ 1.7	SO	Track on right is 16N25 to Wilson Camp.
1.1 ▲	SO	Track on left is 16N25 to Wilson Camp.

GPS: N39°13.62' W122°38.99'

▼ 2.4	SO	Track on left is 16N02 to Pacific Ridge Station. Follow the sign to Hough Springs.
0.4 ▲	SO	Track on right is 16N02 to Pacific Ridge Station. Follow the sign to Cedar Camp.

GPS: N39°13.35' W122°38.38'

▼ 2.7	SO	Track on right.
0.1 ▲	SO	Track on left.
▼ 2.8	TR	Track straight ahead is North Coast #5: Lovelady Ridge Trail (16N06), signposted to Kanaka Glade. Zero trip meter and follow the sign for Hough Springs.
0.0 ▲		Continue to the northwest, remaining on M5.

GPS: N39°13.40' W122°37.99'

▼ 0.0		Continue to the west, heading downhill and remaining on M5.
5.9 ▲	TL	Track straight ahead is North Coast #5: Lovelady Ridge Trail (16N06), signposted to Kanaka Glade. Zero trip meter and follow the sign for Goat Mountain.
▼ 0.9	TL	Track ahead is 16N07 to Wilson Camp. Follow the sign to Hough Springs. Road is now marked 16N44 as well as M5.
5.0 ▲	TR	T-intersection. Track on left is 16N07 to Wilson Camp. Remain on M5

GPS: N39°12.80' W122°37.80'

▼ 2.5	SO	Track on left to Wyley Glade.
3.4 ▲	BL	Track on right to Wyley Glade.

GPS: N39°11.80' W122°37.27'

▼ 2.6	SO	Cattle guard; then cross over creek.
3.3 ▲	SO	Cross over creek; then cattle guard.
▼ 3.4	SO	Track on right is 16N25. Continue straight ahead, joining 16N25 and following the sign for Hough Springs.
2.5 ▲	SO	Track on left is 16N25. Continue straight ahead on 16N44, following the sign to Pacific Ridge.

GPS: N39°11.28' W122°37.19'

▼ 3.5	SO	Track on left.
2.4 ▲	SO	Track on right.
▼ 5.2	SO	Exiting Mendocino National Forest.
0.7 ▲	SO	Entering Mendocino National Forest.

GPS: N39°10.25' W122°37.03'

▼ 5.3	SO	Track on right; then cross through Spanish Creek.
0.6 ▲	BR	Cross through Spanish Creek; then track on left.
▼ 5.7	SO	Start to cross through North Fork Cache Creek.
0.2 ▲	SO	Exit North Fork Cache Creek.
▼ 5.8	BR	Bear right and exit creek.
0.1 ▲	BL	Bear left and start to cross through North Fork Cache Creek.
▼ 5.9		Trail ends at T-intersection with North Coast #3: Bartlett Springs Road (CR 303) at Hough Springs. Turn right to follow this trail to Nice; turn left to follow this trail to Leesville and on to Williams.
0.0 ▲		Trail begins on North Coast #3: Bartlett Springs Road (CR 303) at Hough Springs, 11.8 miles west of the eastern end in Bear Valley and 20.9 miles east of Nice. Zero trip meter and turn east onto unmarked trail that descends toward North Fork Cache Creek. The formed trail is well used and rough.

GPS: N39°09.92' W122°36.75'

NORTH COAST #5

Lovelady Ridge Trail

Starting Point:	**North Coast #4: Pacific Ridge Trail, 5.9 miles from the southern end**
Finishing Point:	**North Coast #4: Pacific Ridge Trail, 4.3 miles from the northern end**
Total Mileage:	**8.8 miles**
Unpaved Mileage:	**8.8 miles**
Driving Time:	**1 hour**
Elevation Range:	**1,600–3,800 feet**
Usually Open:	**Year-round**
Best Time to Travel:	**Dry weather**
Difficulty Rating:	**7**
Scenic Rating:	**9**
Remoteness Rating:	**+0**

Special Attractions

- Very steep, challenging trail for stock high-clearance 4WDs.
- Excellent views from the open ridge top.
- Access to a network of trails within the Stonyford OHV Area.

History

Lovelady Ridge is named for a pioneer family who settled at the base of the hill in the late 1860s. Joshua West Lovelady, an Alabama native, married Nancy McGaha of Tennessee in February 1851. Together, they made their way west as members of the ill-fated Fancher party in the spring of 1857. The couple's seven-month overland wagon trip almost ended in tragedy before reaching California. Captain Alexander Fancher, a Tennesseean, organized a 40-wagon emigrant train in northwestern Arkansas. The group followed a southern route to California, and their trip across the Plains and over the Rockies into what was then Utah Territory was relatively uneventful. However, this all changed on September 11, 1857, when the party was attacked by Mormons and Indians at Mountain Meadows, in present-day southwestern Utah. More than 100 members of the party lost their lives in the massacre; the only survivors were a few children. Fortunately, the Lovelady family had left the wagon train two days before the bloody massacre.

Joshua and Nancy Lovelady lived in Nevada County for 10 years before moving to Colusa County. The 11-member Lovelady family eventually acquired a ranch of more than 300 acres at the southern end of Indian Valley. Joshua died 1886 and Nancy died in 1910.

Description

This challenging and extremely steep trail is an enjoyable run for experienced drivers of stock, high-clearance 4WDs. The trail, one of many within the Stonyford OHV Area, travels along Pacific Ridge, then Lovelady Ridge, and finally drops sharply to Little Stony Creek and North Coast #4: Pacific Ridge Trail. The trail's difficulty comes from the steepness of some sections that reach an angle of 30 degrees in places. The surface is mainly smooth, but some loose, low-traction sections combined with the steep grade make for a challenging run. Low-range 4WD is definitely required.

Ascending the Pacific Ridge

The trail leaves North Coast #4: Pacific Ridge Trail and travels a short distance along Pacific Ridge to Pacific Point. The trail is easygoing at this point —high-clearance 2WDs can generally reach Pacific Point. However, they should go no farther. Views from Pacific Point are spectacular, with Indian Valley Reservoir to the east and the ridges of the Coast Ranges to the north and south.

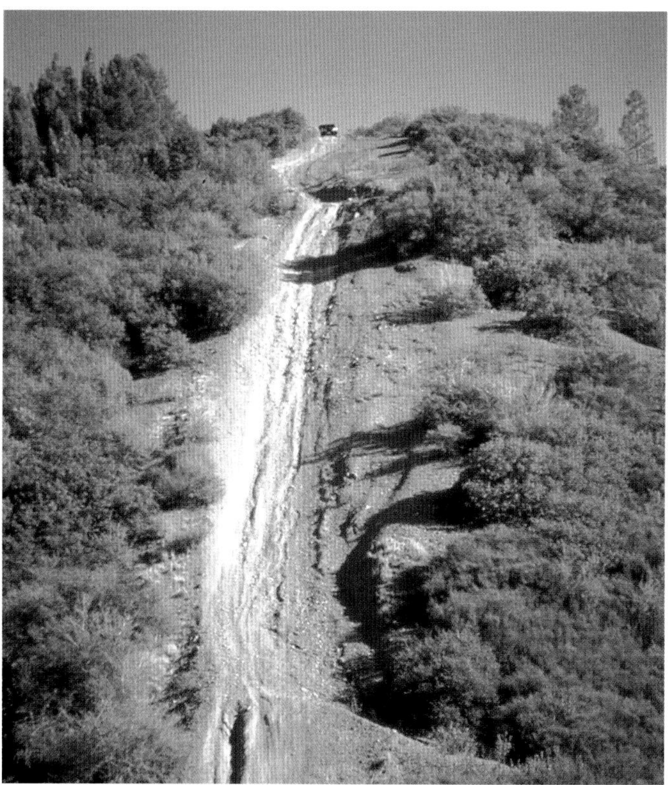

Challenging descent along Lovelady Ridge

For the next few miles the trail undulates along Lovelady Ridge. You are mainly heading downhill in the forward direction, but there are a few steep climbs in either direction. One particularly steep section (downhill in the forward direction) has an alternate route rated 8 because of the uneven and extremely low-traction surface. Avoiding the alternate route keeps the trail's difficulty to a 7. The final mile drops steeply off the end of the ridge to cross through Little Stony Creek, finally finishing back on North Coast #4: Pacific Ridge Trail.

Trails in the OHV area are closed if there is 2 inches of moisture in a 24-hour period. This trail is definitely one to avoid in wet weather because the surface becomes greasy and extremely dangerous. Note that the Stonyford OHV Area map shows the northern end of this trail as suitable for ATVs and motorbikes only. This is incorrect—the trail is clearly marked on the ground as suitable for vehicles, and it is more than ample width.

Current Road Information

Mendocino National Forest
Grindstone Ranger District
825 North Humboldt Avenue
Willows, CA 95988
(530) 934-3316

Map References

BLM Lakeport
USFS Mendocino National Forest

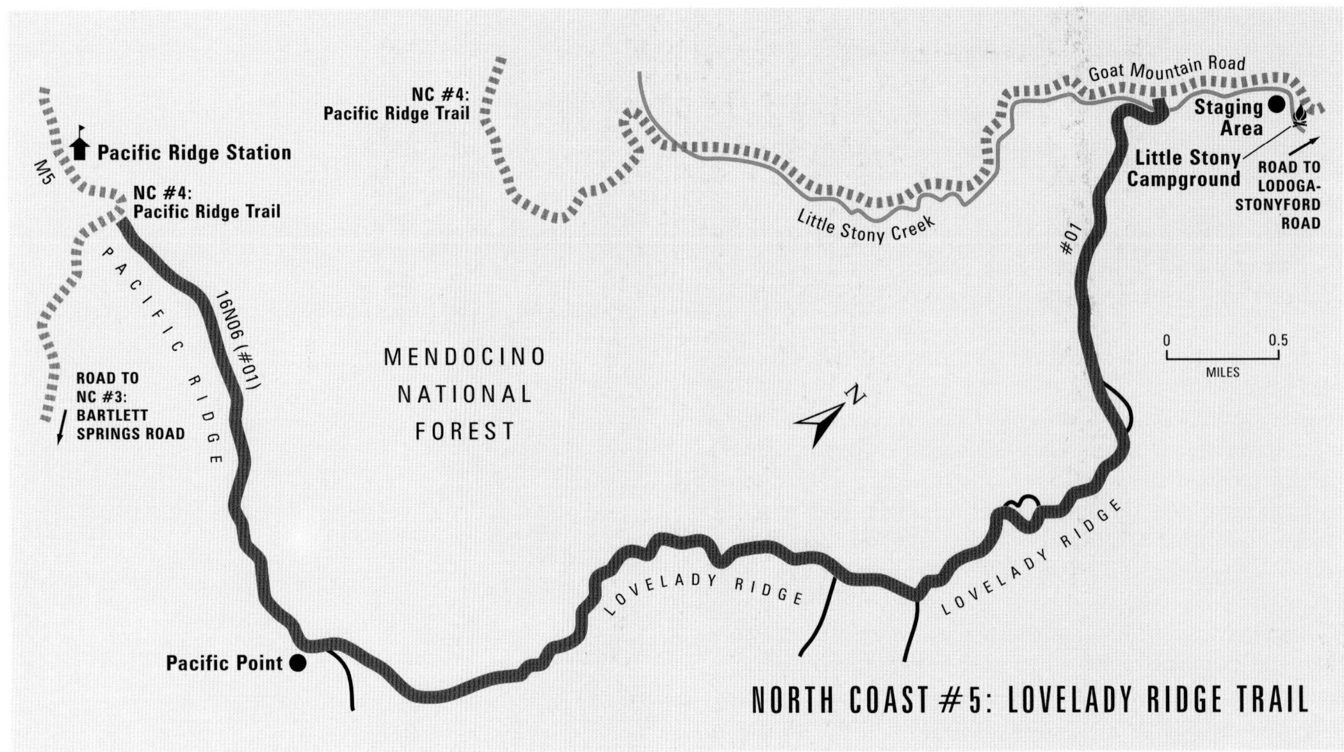

USGS 1:24,000 Bartlett Springs, Hough Springs, Gilmore Peak
1:100,000 Lakeport
Maptech CD-ROM: North Coast/Mendocino
Northern California Atlas & Gazetteer, p. 76
California Road & Recreation Atlas, p. 63 (route not shown)
Other: Stonyford OHV Area Guide

Route Directions

▼ 0.0		From North Coast #4: Pacific Ridge Trail, 5.9 miles from the southern end, zero trip meter and proceed southeast on 16N06, following the sign to Kanaka Ridge and Pacific Point. Road is also marked as #01 for 4WDs, ATVs, and motorbikes—rated blue.
2.4 ▲		Trail ends back on North Coast #4: Pacific Ridge Trail. Turn right to return to Lodoga-Stonyford Road; turn left to follow Pacific Ridge Trail to North Coast #3: Bartlett Springs Road.
		GPS: N39°13.40' W122°37.99'
▼ 2.4	BL	Trail forks at unmarked intersection. Zero trip meter. Pacific Point is the rise on the right.
0.0 ▲		Continue to the south.
		GPS: N39°12.93' W122°35.78'
▼ 0.0		Continue to the north.
4.6 ▲	SO	Track on left at unmarked intersection. Zero trip meter. Pacific Point is the rise on the left.
▼ 0.6	SO	Track on left.
4.0 ▲	SO	Track on right.
▼ 2.2	SO	Track on right.
2.4 ▲	SO	Track on left.
▼ 2.3	SO	Track on right.
2.3 ▲	SO	Track on left.
		GPS: N39°14.39' W122°34.81'
▼ 2.4	SO	Track on right.
2.2 ▲	SO	Track on left.
▼ 2.6	SO	Track on right.
2.0 ▲	SO	Track on left.
▼ 2.8	BL	Track on right.
1.8 ▲	BR	Track on left.
		GPS: N39°14.66' W122°34.37'
▼ 3.0	SO	Two tracks on right.
1.6 ▲	SO	Two tracks on left.
▼ 3.2	SO	Track on right.
1.4 ▲	SO	Track on left.
▼ 3.9	SO	Track on left is a cut-across. Remain on main trail.
0.7 ▲	SO	Cut-across rejoins.
▼ 4.0	SO	Cut-across rejoins.
0.6 ▲	BL	Track on right is a cut-across. Remain on main trail.
		GPS: N39°15.39' W122°33.97'
▼ 4.4	SO	Track on right.
0.2 ▲	SO	Track on left.
▼ 4.6	TR	Track straight ahead is a steeper, alternate 8-rated route. Zero trip meter and turn right onto well-used track.
0.0 ▲		Continue to the southeast.
		GPS: N39°15.85' W122°33.99'
▼ 0.0		Continue to the north.
1.8 ▲	TL	Alternate route rejoins.
▼ 0.2	SO	Alternate route rejoins.
1.6 ▲	BL	Track on right is a steeper, alternate 8-rated route.
▼ 1.7	SO	Cross through Little Stony Creek.
0.1 ▲	SO	Cross through Little Stony Creek.
▼ 1.8		Trail ends at T-intersection with North Coast #4: Pacific Ridge Trail. Turn right to exit to Lodoga-Stonyford Road; turn left to travel this trail to North Coast #3: Bartlett Springs Road.
0.0 ▲		From North Coast #4: Pacific Ridge Trail, 4.3

miles from the northeastern end, zero trip meter and turn east on formed dirt trail marked Lovelady Ridge Trail (#01) for 4WDs, ATVs, and motorbikes—rated blue. Trail #01 continues on the far side of the road, but is for ATVs and motorbikes only—rated black.

GPS: N39°16.77' W122°35.13'

NORTH COAST #6

Log Spring Ridge Trail

Starting Point:	**Round Valley Road (M4), 13.5 miles southwest of Paskenta**
Finishing Point:	**CR 306, 8 miles north of Elk Creek**
Total Mileage:	**19.3 miles**
Unpaved Mileage:	**18.6 miles**
Driving Time:	**2 hours**
Elevation Range:	**800–4,500 feet**
Usually Open:	**April to December**
Best Time to Travel:	**Dry weather**
Difficulty Rating:	**1**
Scenic Rating:	**9**
Remoteness Rating:	**+0**

Special Attractions

- Optional 3-rated side trail to Buck Point overlook.
- Panoramic views of Rocky Ridge and the Coast Ranges.
- Access to a network of back roads and 4WD trails.

Description

Log Spring Ridge Trail, called Hull Road on some maps, follows a chaparral-covered ridge along the west side of the Sacramento Valley and overlooks Mendocino National Forest in the Coast Ranges and Rocky Ridge. The trail is an easy one; generally suitable for passenger vehicles in dry weather, but suitable only for high-clearance 4WDs in wet weather. It accesses a network of backcountry roads and 4WD trails.

Most of the trail travels through an area where motorized travel is restricted to numbered roads and trails. However, there are plenty to choose from. One spur leads to Buck Point, which overlooks Grindstone and Grindstone Creek, as well as Rocky Ridge and the Sacramento Valley. A more difficult trail, 21N80, parallels much of the road and offers an alternate route for high-clearance 4WDs that travels more along the actual ridge top. The main trail ends by descending to the valley toward Elk Creek.

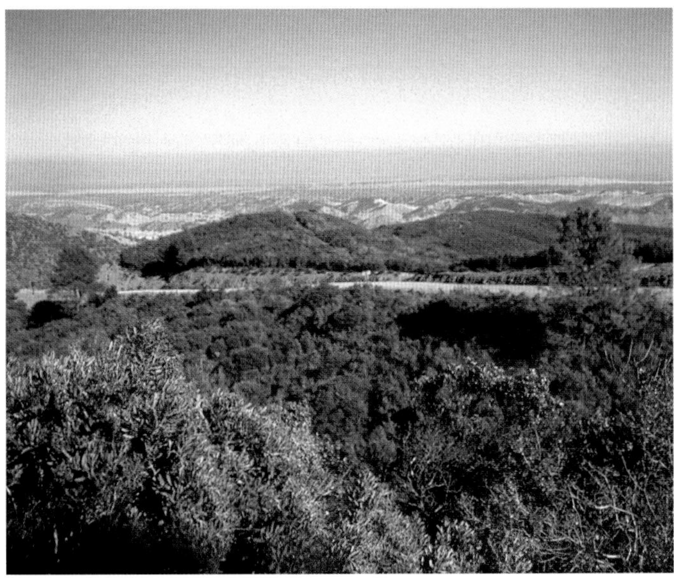

Log Spring Ridge above the Sacramento Valley

Current Road Information

Mendocino National Forest
Grindstone Ranger District
825 North Humboldt Avenue
Willows, CA 95988
(530) 934-3316

Map References

BLM Willows
USFS Mendocino National Forest
USGS 1:24,000 Hall Ridge, Alder Springs, Chrome
1:100,000 Willows
Maptech CD-ROM: North Coast/Mendocino
Northern California Atlas & Gazetteer, pp. 65, 66
California Road & Recreation Atlas, p. 58

Route Directions

▼ 0.0			From Round Valley Road (M4), at mile marker 14, 13.5 miles southwest of Paskenta, and 0.5 miles west of the west end of North Coast #8: Nome Cult Mountain House Trail, 12 miles east of Log Springs USFS Work Station zero trip meter and turn east on graded dirt road 23N05. Intersection is unmarked.
	4.0 ▲		Trail ends at T-intersection with Round Valley Road (M4). Turn right for Paskenta.
			GPS: N39°49.62' W122°40.56'
▼ 0.3		BL	Paved road on right goes to Black Bear USFS Campground and Conklin Orchard.
	3.7 ▲	BR	Paved road on left goes to Black Bear USFS Campground and Conklin Orchard. Follow sign to Paskenta.
			GPS: N39°49.46' W122°40.50'
▼ 1.2		SO	Track on right and track on left.
	2.8 ▲	SO	Track on right and track on left.
▼ 1.6		SO	Closed road on left is 23N05E to Houghton Place.
	2.4 ▲	SO	Closed road on right is 23N05E to Houghton Place.
			GPS: N39°48.48' W122°40.51'
▼ 2.7		SO	Track on right.
	1.3 ▲	SO	Track on left.
▼ 3.4		SO	Entering Glenn County. Track on right.
	0.6 ▲	SO	Track on left. Entering Tehama County.
▼ 4.0		SO	Track on left to Freshwater Heliport. Zero trip meter.
	0.0 ▲		Continue to the northwest.
			GPS: N39°47.29' W122°39.81'

NC #8: Nome Cult Mountain House Trail
ROAD TO PASKENTA
Black Bear Camp
Round Valley Road (M4)
23N05
Houghton Place
DIGGER RIDGE
Deer Mountain
HEIFER RIDGE
Red Mountain
22N75
CONKLIN ORCHARD
ROAD TO COVELO
LOG SPRING RIDGE
Way's Road
M9
NC #7: Red Mountain Trail
Buck Point
22N01
21N80
Hardin Hole Springs

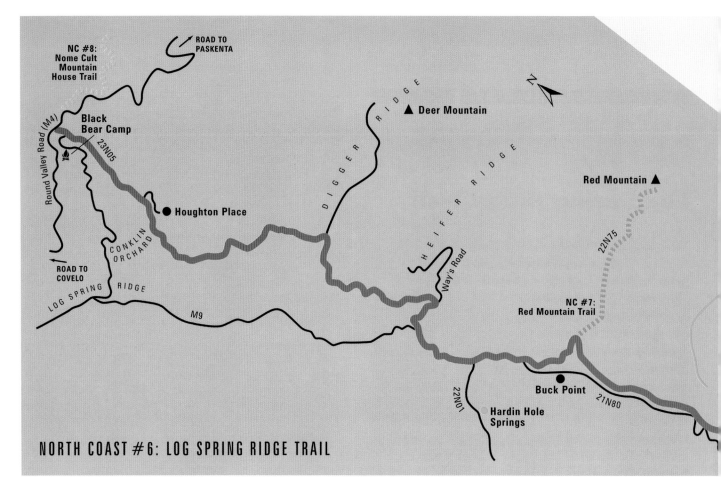

NORTH COAST #6: LOG SPRING RIDGE TRAIL

▼ 0.0		Continue to the south.
3.6 ▲	SO	Track on right to Freshwater Heliport. Zero trip meter.
▼ 0.5	SO	Track on left to water point.
3.1 ▲	SO	Track on right to water point.
▼ 0.7	SO	Track on left through gate.
2.9 ▲	SO	Track on right through gate.
▼ 3.0	SO	Road on left is Way's Road.
0.6 ▲	BL	Road on right is Way's Road.
		GPS: N39°45.64' W122°39.36'

View from Buck Point

▼ 3.6	TL	T-intersection with graded road M9. Zero trip meter and follow the sign to Doe Peak and Elk Creek.
0.0 ▲		Continue to the northeast.
		GPS: N39°45.54' W122°39.76'
▼ 0.0		Continue to the south.
2.4 ▲	TR	M9 continues straight ahead. Zero trip meter and turn right onto 23N05, following sign to Paskenta.
▼ 0.6	SO	Entering motor vehicle restricted travel area.
1.8 ▲	SO	Leaving motor vehicle restricted travel area.
▼ 0.9	BL	Graded road on right is 22N01 to Hardin Hole Springs.
1.5 ▲	SO	Graded road on left is 22N01 to Hardin Hole Springs.
		GPS: N39°44.96' W122°39.58'
▼ 1.6	SO	Track on right is 21N80; then cattle guard; then track on right is also 21N80, which goes 0.5 miles to Buck Point—rated 3.
0.8 ▲	SO	Track on left is 21N80, which goes 0.5 miles to Buck Point—rated 3; then cattle guard; then track on left is also 21N80.
		GPS: N39°44.54' W122°39.17'
▼ 2.4	TR	Track on left; then track straight ahead is North Coast #7: Red Mountain Trail (22N75, shown on map as 22N04). Zero trip meter.
0.0 ▲		Continue to the west, remaining on M9. Immediately second track on right.
		GPS: N39°44.29' W122°38.55'
▼ 0.0		Continue to the south, remaining on M9.
2.0 ▲	TL	Track on right is North Coast #7: Red

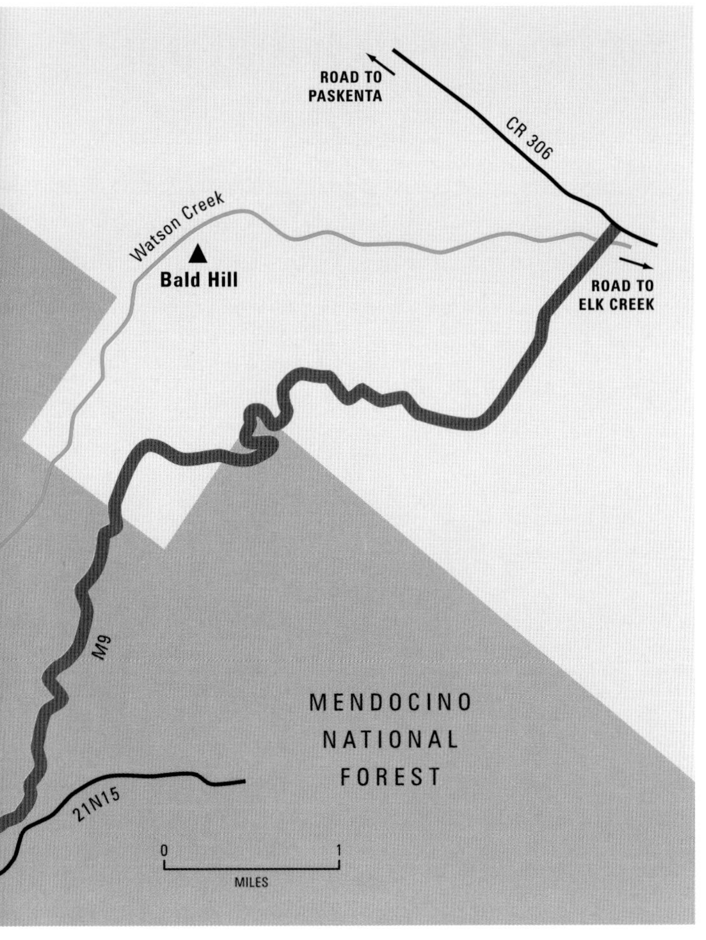

Mountain Trail (22N75, shown on map as 22N04). Zero trip meter.

▼ 0.6		SO	Track on right. Ridge top trail crosses numerous times on left and right for the next 3.6 miles.
	1.4 ▲	SO	Track on left.
▼ 1.9		SO	Track on right is 21N80. Tank on right.
	0.1 ▲	SO	Track on left is 21N80. Tank on left.
			GPS: N39°42.87′ W122°38.45′
▼ 2.0		SO	Cattle guard; then track on right is 21N80. Second track on right at same intersection is 21N15 to Doe Peak and Manzanita Springs. Zero trip meter and follow the sign to Elk Creek.
	0.0 ▲		Continue to the north, remaining on M9.
			GPS: N39°42.75′ W122°38.50′
▼ 0.0			Continue to the southeast, remaining on M9.
	7.3 ▲	SO	Track on left is 21N15 to Doe Peak and Manzanita Springs. Second track on left at same intersection is 21N80. Zero trip meter and follow the sign to Log Springs.
▼ 1.2		SO	Track on right is 21N75.
	6.1 ▲	SO	Track on left is 21N75.
▼ 2.2		SO	End of tracks crossing ridge tops.
	5.1 ▲	SO	Ridge top trail crosses numerous times on left and right for the next 3.6 miles.
▼ 2.4		SO	Cattle guard.
	4.9 ▲	SO	Cattle guard.
▼ 2.6		SO	Leaving Mendocino National Forest.
	4.7 ▲	SO	Entering Mendocino National Forest.
			GPS: N39°43.10′ W122°36.25′
▼ 6.1		SO	Cattle guard.
	1.2 ▲	SO	Cattle guard.
▼ 6.3		SO	Cattle guard. Leaving motor vehicle restricted travel area.
	1.0 ▲	SO	Cattle guard. Entering motor vehicle restricted travel area.
▼ 6.5		SO	Track on right into private property.
	0.8 ▲	BR	Track on left into private property.
			GPS: N39°41.90′ W122°33.91′
▼ 6.6		SO	Track on right into private property. Road becomes paved.
	0.7 ▲	SO	Track on left into private property. Road turns to graded dirt.
▼ 6.7		SO	Cattle guard; then track on left.
	0.6 ▲	BL	Track on right; then cattle guard.
▼ 7.2		SO	Cross over Watson Creek on bridge.
	0.1 ▲	SO	Cross over Watson Creek on bridge.
▼ 7.3			Cross over creek on bridge; then trail ends at T-intersection with CR 306. Turn left for Paskenta; turn right for Elk Creek.
	0.0 ▲		Trail begins on CR 306, 3 miles north of intersection with California 162, 8 miles north of Elk Creek. Zero trip meter and turn west on paved road M9 (CR 313).
			GPS: N39°41.94′ W122°32.94′

NORTH COAST #7

Red Mountain Trail

Starting Point:	**North Coast #6: Log Spring Ridge Trail, 10 miles south of the northern end**
Finishing Point:	**Red Mountain**
Total Mileage:	**2.4 miles (one-way)**
Unpaved Mileage:	**2.4 miles**
Driving Time:	**30 minutes (one-way)**
Elevation Range:	**3,000–3,600 feet**
Usually Open:	**April to December**
Best Time to Travel:	**Dry weather**
Difficulty Rating:	**3**
Scenic Rating:	**9**
Remoteness Rating:	**+0**

Special Attractions

- Beautiful addition to North Coast #6: Log Spring Ridge Trail.
- Panoramic views from Red Mountain.

History

The summit of Red Mountain rises 2,700 feet above the settlement of Chrome, named for chrome mines on the slopes below the peak. The mines, run by the Burrow family, operated until the middle of the twentieth century. Burrows Gap is one of the few passes in the 10-mile-long, north-south Rocky Ridge; it is clearly visible from the viewpoint on Red Mountain.

Red Mountain Trail

The striking lowlands below Red Mountain attracted many settlers, who typically raised sheep. William and Harriet Cushman set up ranch here in 1872. Harriet, from Connecticut, welcomed the move to warmer climes because her doctor feared her frail health would lead to tuberculosis. When she arrived after a long and dusty wagon ride from Sacramento she commented on the few shacks in the vicinity saying, "I could never live in a place like that." Much to her dismay, it was exactly where she was to live. Harriet and William planted orchards and raised sheep and goats. Harriet Cushman died in Orland in 1934 at age 95.

Description

This short spur branches off North Coast #6: Log Spring Ridge Trail near its midpoint and travels along a narrow shelf road to the old fire lookout site on Red Mountain. Communications equipment now stands on the mountain. The trail rates a 3 for difficulty because of the narrow shelf road and loose climb to the summit. From the top, 360-degree views include Black Butte Lake, Lassen Peak, and Rocky Ridge to the east; Mount Shasta to the north; and Stony Gorge Reservoir to the southeast. A small hiking trail leads off the ridge toward some mining remains.

Current Road Information

Mendocino National Forest
Grindstone Ranger District
825 North Humboldt Avenue
Willows, CA 95988
(530) 934-3316

Map References

BLM Willows
USFS Mendocino National Forest
USGS 1:24,000 Alder Springs, Chrome
1:100,000 Willows
Maptech CD-ROM: North Coast/Mendocino
Northern California Atlas & Gazetteer, pp. 65, 66
California Road & Recreation Atlas, p. 58

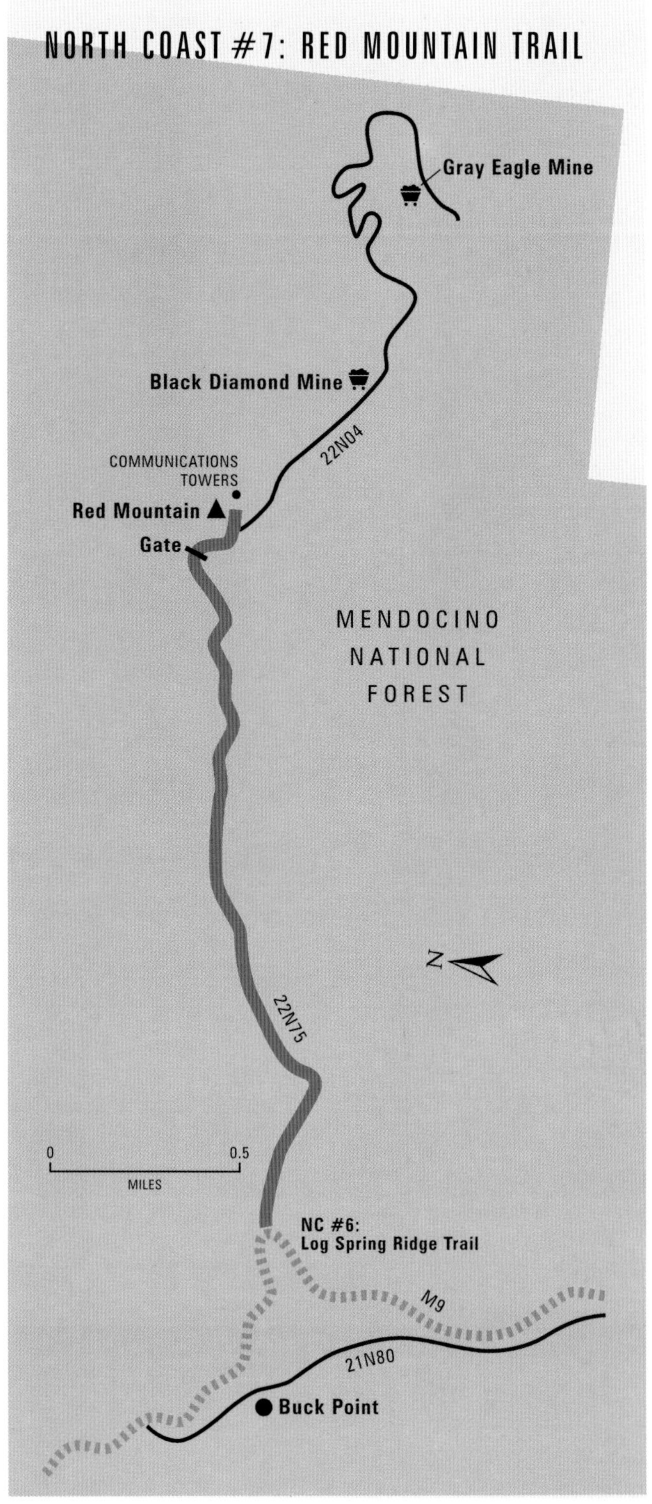

Route Directions

▼ 0.0		From North Coast #6: Log Spring Ridge Trail, 10 miles south of the northern end at Round Valley Road (M4), zero trip meter and turn east on dirt trail 22N75. Note that this road is shown on the forest service map as 22N04. Start of shelf road.
		GPS: N39°44.29' W122°38.55'
▼ 0.4	SO	Small track on right.

▼ 1.7	SO	End of shelf road.
		GPS: N39°44.53′ W122°36.93′
▼ 2.1	SO	Gate. Start of shelf road.
		GPS: N39°44.61′ W122°36.63′
▼ 2.2	SO	Small track on right is 22N04 to the Black Diamond and Gray Eagle Mines. End of shelf road.
▼ 2.3		Trail ends at communications towers on Red Mountain.
		GPS: N39°44.56′ W122°36.52′

NORTH COAST #8

Nome Cult Mountain House Trail

Starting Point:	**Round Valley Road (M4), 6.9 miles southwest of Paskenta**
Finishing Point:	**Round Valley Road (M4), 13.3 miles southwest of Paskenta**
Total Mileage:	**4 miles**
Unpaved Mileage:	**4 miles**
Driving Time:	**30 minutes**
Elevation Range:	**1,000–3,000 feet**
Usually Open:	**April to December**
Best Time to Travel:	**Dry weather**
Difficulty Rating:	**4**
Scenic Rating:	**9**
Remoteness Rating:	**+0**

Special Attractions

- Trail travels a section of the historic Nome Cult Trail.
- Excellent views of Rocky Ridge and the Sacramento Valley.
- Access to the hiking trail to Thomes Gorge.

History

After the arrival of settlers to this part of California, Indians were rounded up in 1854 and placed on the Nome Lackee Indian Reservation near Paskenta. Relocating the Nomlaki was as much a means to control them as it was to protect them from new settlers.

Another group of Indians, mainly Maidu, had been rounded up in Chico after five settlers' children were killed in Butte County. The settlers banded together to rid the northern Sacramento Valley of every Indian, and on September 4, 1863, 461 Indians left Chico under a cavalry escort to walk to the newly established Nome Cult Reservation in Round Valley. This 4WD trail follows part of their horrific 100-mile journey.

The ascent from the Sacramento Valley into the Coast Ranges marked the end for some of the Indians who had already walked more than 50 miles. They arrived at Mountain House on September 12, 1863, and camped for two days. About 150 Indians who were too old or sick to go on were left at Mountain House with four weeks provisions. The rest continued, forced to climb more than 6,000 feet before descending to Round Valley. Some mothers tried to kill their babies, fearing the children would be abandoned should the mothers die. Only 277 Indians completed the difficult journey to Round Valley.

Beginning of Nome Cult Mountain House Trail

Description

This short trail climbs the ridge and serves as a shortcut from the main forest road. Rated for 4WD vehicles only by the forest service, the trail is an easy to moderate run with a few rough spots for most high-clearance 4WDs. It switchbacks its way from oak-studded grasslands to chapparal-covered hillsides.

The Thomes Gorge Nomlaki Hiking Trail crosses the vehicle trail and heads north to the river gorge. There is limited parking at the trailhead. The hiking trail is rated difficult to very difficult, because of elevation changes along its 4.2-mile route.

Current Road Information

Bureau of Land Management
Redding Field Office
355 Hemsted Drive
Redding, CA 96002
(530) 224-2100

Mendocino National Forest
Grindstone Ranger District
825 North Humboldt Avenue
Willows, CA 95988
(530) 934-3316

Map References

BLM Willows
USFS Mendocino National Forest
USGS 1:24,000 Hall Ridge
1:100,000 Willows
Maptech CD-ROM: North Coast/Mendocino
Northern California Atlas & Gazetteer, p. 65
California Road & Recreation Atlas, p. 58

Route Directions

▼ 0.0	From Paskenta, zero trip meter and turn south on Round Valley Road (M4). The road enters Mendocino National Forest after 6.3 miles.

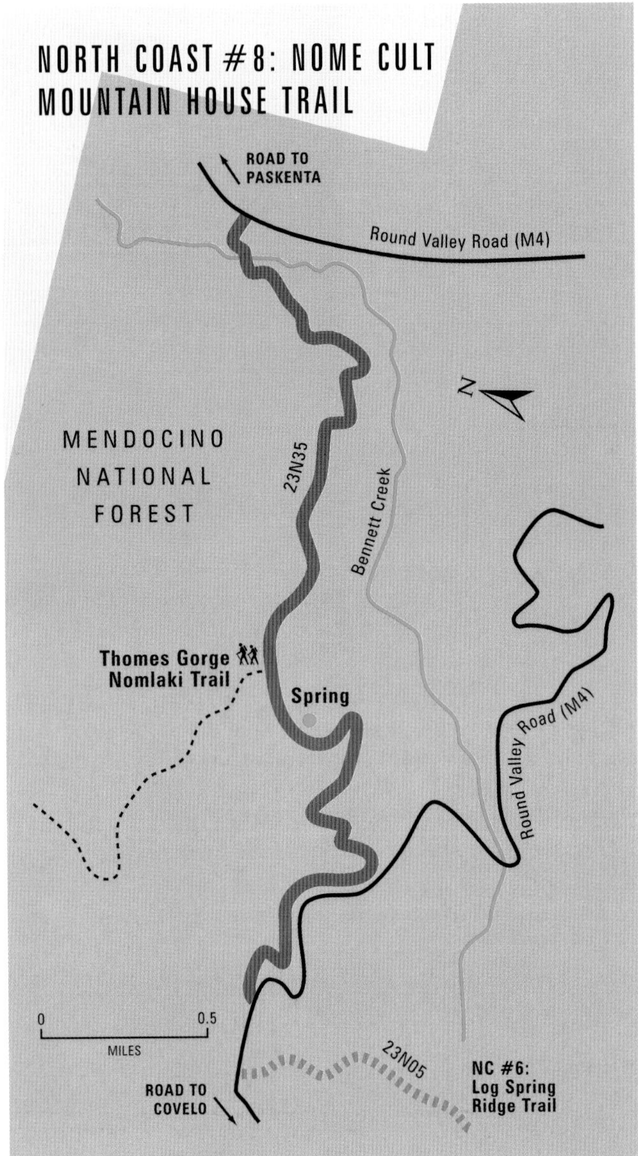

There is a marker for the original Nome Cult Trail at the national forest boundary. Mountain House, a site along the original Nome Cult Trail, was just north of the boundary. Continue 0.6 miles past the boundary to the start of the trail. Zero trip meter and turn west onto graded dirt road marked 23N35 (shown on the forest service map as 23N69). Road is marked for 4WDs only.

4.0 ▲ Trail ends back on Round Valley Road (M4). Turn left for Paskenta; turn right for Covelo.

GPS: N39°50.14' W122°37.84'

▼ 0.2 SO Cross over Bennett Creek on bridge.
3.8 ▲ SO Cross over Bennett Creek on bridge.

▼ 1.8 SO Track on right.
2.2 ▲ SO Track on left.

▼ 1.9 SO Turnout on right; then Thomes Gorge Nomlaki Trail on right for hikers; then track on left through gate.
2.1 ▲ SO Track on right through gate; then Thomes Gorge Nomlaki Trail on left for hikers; then turnout on left.

GPS: N39°49.81' W122°39.20'

▼ 2.2 SO Track on left to spring at Mud Flat Camp.
1.8 ▲ SO Track on right to spring at Mud Flat Camp.

GPS: N39°49.67' W122°39.44'

▼ 2.8 SO Track on right.
1.2 ▲ SO Track on left.

▼ 4.0 Trail ends at T-intersection with paved Round Valley Road (M4). Turn left for Paskenta; turn right for Covelo.
0.0 ▲ Trail commences on paved Round Valley Road (M4), 12.5 miles east of Log Springs USFS Work Station and 0.2 miles east of North Coast #6: Log Spring Ridge Trail. Zero trip meter and turn northeast on dirt road 23N35, marked for 4WDs only.

GPS: N39°49.63' W122°40.34'

NORTH COAST #9

Vestal and Pettyjohn Roads

Starting Point:	**California 36, 12.5 miles east of Platina**
Finishing Point:	**Reeds Creek Road on Table Mountain, 17.5 miles west of Red Bluff**
Total Mileage:	**22.1 miles**
Unpaved Mileage:	**20.2 miles**
Driving Time:	**2 hours**
Elevation Range:	**800–1,600 feet**
Usually Open:	**March to January**
Best Time to Travel:	**March to January**
Difficulty Rating:	**1**
Scenic Rating:	**8**
Remoteness Rating:	**+1**

Special Attractions

- Wildlife viewing—deer, quail, and bobcat.
- Pretty winding road through the low rangeland east of Shasta-Trinity National Forests.

History

This trail begins about 30 miles east of Red Bluff on California 36 on the banks of Dry Creek, just east of Budden Canyon. Early ranchers like William Budden, a native of England, raised stock in the undulating foothills of the Coast Ranges. Budden emigrated to California at 20 years of age and lived at Beegum, just west of Budden Canyon, for most of 40 years. During his lifetime, he farmed at Dry Creek and also worked at Rosewood Ranch, to the east of Vestal Road. Vestal Road recalls the Vestals, a prominent family in Red Bluff's butcher industry.

Henry Wescott, from Oroville, operated a store along the old wagon road east of Red Bluff (now the route of California 36). In 1890, Joe Durrer, a Swiss, and his wife Elizabeth Schanick, a German, purchased the store and added an im-

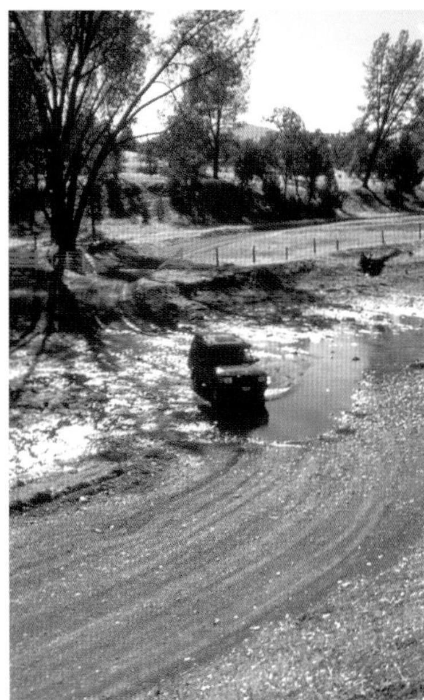

Fording through Wells Creek near the beginning of the trail

pressive cabin to house their young family. The site gained a post office, called Rosewood because of the wild roses that grew along Salt Creek. The 1894 gold strike at Harrison Gulch, west of Beegum, brought a surge of miners and merchants past the Rosewood trading post. A stage stop was established to provide food and accommodations for teamsters and a barn for their horses. Teamsters always carried rifles because breakdowns were inevitable on this lonely wagon road, and wildcats were prevalent in the region.

The Midas Mine at Harrison Gulch produced several million dollars worth of gold over a 20-year period, beginning in 1894. The mine superintendent delivered gold bars to Red Bluff weekly; he drove a distinctive four-wheel, two-seater carriage pulled by especially fast and capable horses. Speed was essential because of the constant threat of bandits in this remote region. The superintendent would stop off at the Durrer's stage stop to change horses. He supposedly carried fake gold bars to hand over in case of a holdup.

Description

This backcountry drive passes through some quiet, pretty scenery between the Sacramento Valley and the eastern side of the Coast Ranges. The route passes through ranchlands along county roads, first Vestal Road and then Pettyjohn Road. Because it is entirely on private lands, there are no camping, hunting, or other recreational opportunities. However, you can expect to see deer, quail, and other wildlife along the way, even a bobcat if you are lucky.

Weemasoul Spring and Creek

The first half of the route is a narrow formed trail that winds through grasslands with occasional stands of oaks. The crossings of Wells Creek near the start of the trail normally have water. Drivers of low-clearance vehicles should assess the crossing before proceeding—the first is normally the deepest. Of course, if the creek is in flood or excessively deep, all vehicles should avoid the crossing.

The trail standard improves at the settlement of Cold Fork, and it follows a well-graded road to the end.

Current Road Information

Bureau of Land Management
Redding Field Office
355 Hemsted Drive
Redding, CA 96002
(530) 224-2100

Map References

BLM Red Bluff
USFS Shasta-Trinity National Forests (incomplete)
USGS 1:24,000 Chickabally Mt., Cold Fork, Oxbow Bridge
1:100,000 Red Bluff
Maptech CD-ROM: Shasta Lake/Redding
Northern California Atlas & Gazetteer, pp. 55, 56
California Road & Recreation Atlas, p. 58

Route Directions

▼ 0.0			From California 36, 0.2 miles west of Tehama County mile marker 9.5, 33 miles west of Red Bluff and 12.5 miles east of Platina, zero trip meter and turn south on Vestal Road (CR 107) and cross cattle guard.
	7.6 ▲		Cattle guard; then trail ends at T-intersection with California 36. Turn right for Red Bluff; turn left for Platina.
			GPS: N40°18.26′ W122°42.98′
▼ 0.9		SO	Ford through Wells Creek; then cattle guard.
	6.7 ▲	SO	Cattle guard; then ford through Wells Creek.
▼ 1.2		SO	Ford through Wells Creek.
	6.4 ▲	SO	Ford through Wells Creek.
▼ 1.5		SO	Ford through Wells Creek.
	6.1 ▲	SO	Ford through Wells Creek.
▼ 2.7		SO	Cattle guard.
	4.9 ▲	SO	Cattle guard.
			GPS: N40°16.31′ W122°42.48′
▼ 3.2		SO	Cattle guard.
	4.4 ▲	SO	Cattle guard.
▼ 3.7		SO	Corral on right at Wilson Flat.
	3.9 ▲	SO	Corral on left at Wilson Flat.
▼ 3.9		SO	Cattle guard.
	3.7 ▲	SO	Cattle guard.
▼ 4.2		SO	Unmarked graded road on right.
	3.4 ▲	SO	Unmarked graded road on left.
			GPS: N40°15.14′ W122°42.67′
▼ 5.0		SO	Track on right; then cattle guard.
	2.6 ▲	SO	Cattle guard; then track on left.
▼ 5.1		SO	Cross through Salt Creek.
	2.5 ▲	SO	Cross through Salt Creek.
▼ 5.3		SO	Cross through creek.

Trail along Wilson Field

Mileage		Direction	Instruction
	2.3 ▲	SO	Cross through creek.
▼ 5.4		SO	Cross through creek.
	2.2 ▲	SO	Cross through creek.
▼ 5.5		SO	Cross through creek.
	2.1 ▲	SO	Cross through creek.
▼ 6.2		SO	Cattle guard.
	1.4 ▲	SO	Cattle guard.
▼ 6.8		SO	Cross through creek.
	0.8 ▲	SO	Cross through creek.
▼ 7.6		TR	T-intersection. Vestal Road continues to the left. Zero trip meter.
	0.0 ▲		Continue to the west on Vestal Road.
			GPS: N40°12.93′ W122°41.11′
▼ 0.0			Continue to the south.
	3.6 ▲	TL	Graded road continues ahead. Zero trip meter.
▼ 0.4		SO	Cross through Weemasoul Creek; then cattle guard.
	3.2 ▲	SO	Cattle guard; then cross through Weemasoul Creek.
▼ 0.5		SO	Cross through creek.
	3.1 ▲	SO	Cross through creek.
▼ 0.6		SO	Cross through creek.
	3.0 ▲	SO	Cross through creek.
▼ 0.9		SO	Weemasoul Spring on left.
	2.7 ▲	SO	Weemasoul Spring on right.
			GPS: N40°12.29′ W122°41.48′
▼ 1.1		SO	Cross through creek.
	2.5 ▲	SO	Cross through creek.
▼ 1.2		BL	Track on right.
	2.4 ▲	SO	Track on left.
▼ 1.8		SO	Cross through creek twice.
	1.8 ▲	SO	Cross through creek twice.
▼ 2.3		SO	Cattle guard.
	1.3 ▲	SO	Cattle guard.
▼ 3.3		SO	Cattle guard.
	0.3 ▲	SO	Cattle guard.
▼ 3.6		TL	Gate; then T-intersection with small paved road at Cold Fork. Zero trip meter and join the paved road.
	0.0 ▲		Continue to the north. Road is now graded dirt.
			GPS: N40°10.38′ W122°40.48′
▼ 0.0			Continue to the east. Road is now paved Pettyjohn Road.
	5.9 ▲	TR	On a left-hand bend, zero trip meter and turn right onto a small dirt road and pass through a gate. Note that this intersection is unmarked, and appears to lead into private property.
▼ 0.1		SO	Cross over Cold Fork River on bridge; then cattle guard.
	5.8 ▲	SO	Cattle guard; then cross over Cold Fork River on bridge.
▼ 0.2		SO	Road turns back to graded dirt.
	5.7 ▲	SO	Road is now paved.
▼ 2.7		SO	Guyre Creek Spring on right.
	3.2 ▲	SO	Guyre Creek Spring on left.
			GPS: N40°10.66′ W122°38.30′
▼ 2.9		SO	Cattle guard.
	3.0 ▲	SO	Cattle guard.
▼ 3.1		SO	Track on right to Van Horn Corral.
	2.8 ▲	SO	Track on left to Van Horn Corral.
▼ 4.4		SO	Cattle guard; then cross through creek.
	1.5 ▲	SO	Cross through creek; then cattle guard.
▼ 5.6		SO	Road becomes paved.
	0.3 ▲	SO	Road turns to graded dirt.

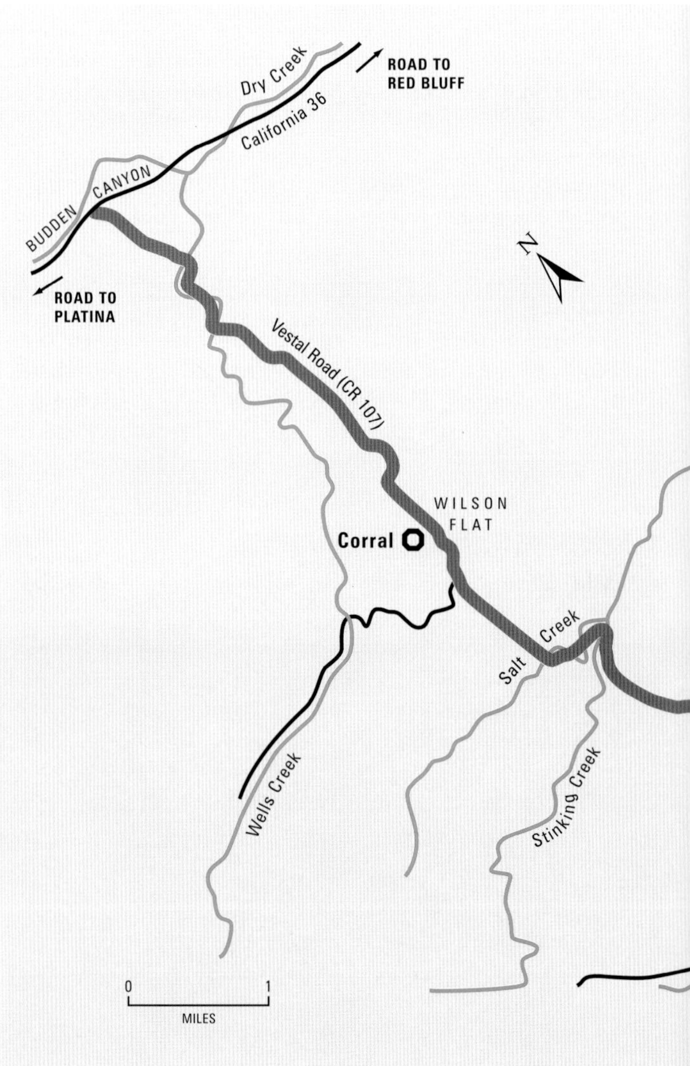

▼ 5.8	SO	Cattle guard.
0.1 ▲	SO	Cattle guard.
▼ 5.9	SO	Cross over creek; then road on right through entrance way. Zero trip meter.
0.0 ▲		Continue to the west and cross over creek. Road is now paved.
		GPS: N40°11.20′ W122°35.50′
▼ 0.0		Continue to the east. Road is now graded dirt.
5.0 ▲	SO	Road on left through entrance way. Zero trip meter.
▼ 1.3	SO	Cattle guard.
3.7 ▲	SO	Cattle guard.
▼ 1.7	SO	Cross through creek.
3.3 ▲	SO	Cross through creek.
▼ 2.1	SO	Road becomes paved.
2.9 ▲	SO	Road turns to graded dirt.
▼ 2.9	SO	Cross over South Fork Cottonwood Creek on Oxbow Bridge.
2.1 ▲	SO	Cross over South Fork Cottonwood Creek on Oxbow Bridge.
		GPS: N40°11.16′ W122°33.00′
▼ 3.5	SO	Road turns to graded dirt.
1.5 ▲	SO	Road is now paved.
▼ 4.0	SO	Track on right.
1.0 ▲	SO	Track on left.
▼ 4.1	SO	Cattle guard.
0.9 ▲	SO	Cattle guard.
▼ 5.0		Trail ends at 4-way intersection at Table Mountain. Turn right onto Reeds Creek Road for I-5 and Red Bluff. To reach Red Bluff, proceed east on Reeds Creek Road for 15 miles to Wilder Road (CR A7); then turn left at the T-intersection, remaining on CR A7, which turns into Walnut Street. Walnut Street intersects with Main Street in Red Bluff. It is 17.5 miles to Red Bluff from the end of the trail.
0.0 ▲		To reach the start of the trail from Main Street in Red Bluff, turn southwest on Walnut Street, which leads off from the center of town. Remain on Walnut Street for 2.5 miles, which swings south and joins Wilder Road (CR A7). Turn right onto Reeds Creek Road and proceed 15 miles to the start of the trail. Trail begins at the 4-way intersection at Table Mountain. To the north is Canyon Road and to the west is Vestal Road. Zero trip meter and turn south on graded dirt Pettyjohn Road.
		GPS: N40°11.13′ W122°31.55′

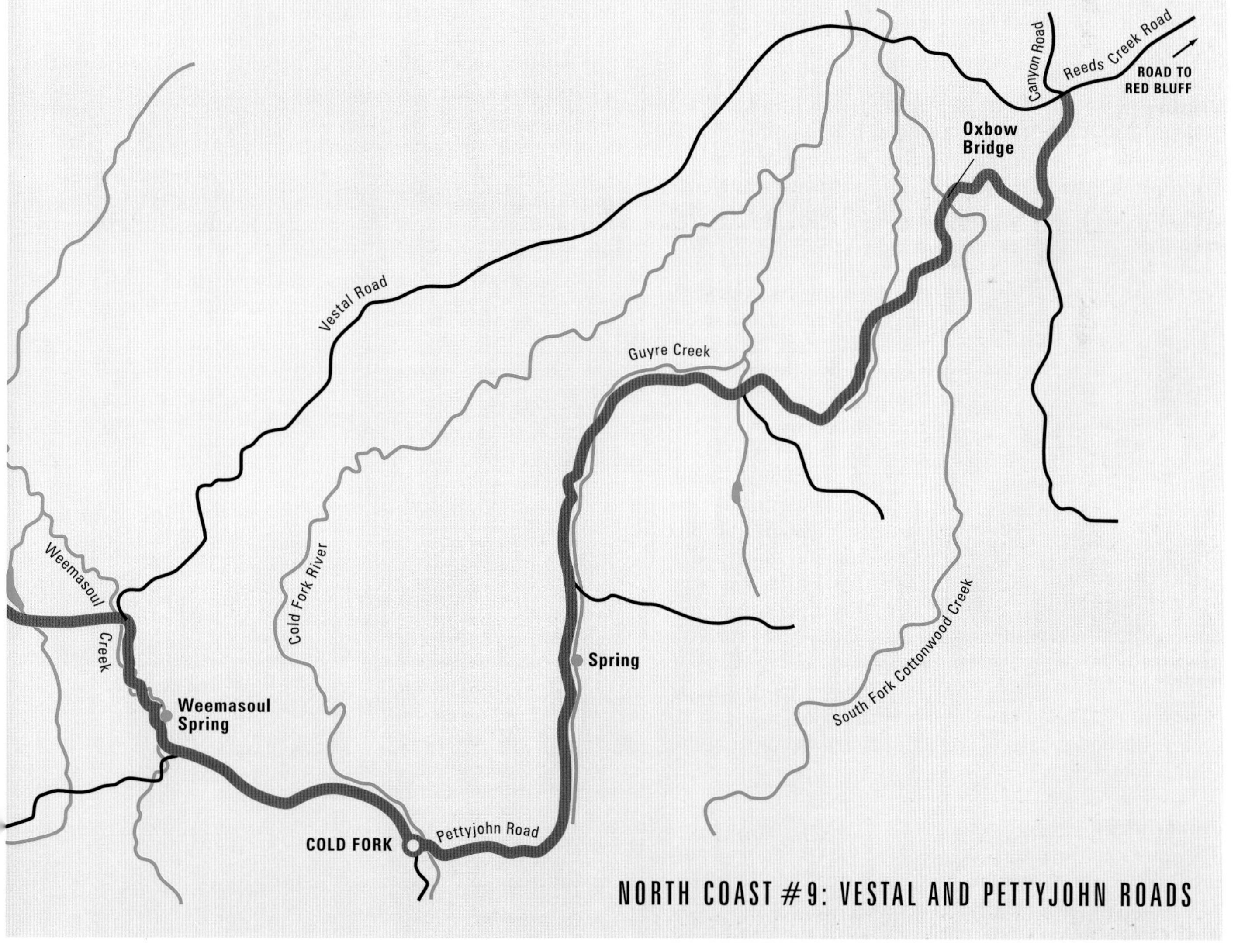

NORTH COAST #9: VESTAL AND PETTYJOHN ROADS

NORTH COAST #10

Beegum Gorge Trail

Starting Point:	**Intersection of California 36 and CR A16 in Platina**
Finishing Point:	**Campsite beside Beegum Creek**
Total Mileage:	**7.5 miles (one-way)**
Unpaved Mileage:	**7.5 miles**
Driving Time:	**1 hour (one-way)**
Elevation Range:	**2,100–3,400 feet**
Usually Open:	**April to December**
Best Time to Travel:	**Dry weather**
Difficulty Rating:	**2**
Scenic Rating:	**9**
Remoteness Rating:	**+0**

Special Attractions

- Remains of the Chrome Mine.
- Views into Beegum Gorge and camping along Beegum Creek.

History

Beegum Gorge is in the Harrison Gulch Mining District, a mining region active around the turn of the twentieth century. Platina, at the start of this trail, was originally known as Noble Station, a stage stop on the wagon road from Red Bluff to the nearby Midas Mine. The rich mine was discovered in 1894 and sparked a small gold rush lasting for the next two decades, until fires and floods doomed this remote find.

Large wooden hopper at the Chrome Mine site at trail's end

In the winter of 1966, a find of a different kind made headlines in this picturesque mountain region. The Hampton family, who lived west of Platina near Little Round Mountain, returned home after a two-day vacation to find the door of their house ripped off its hinges. They also found 18-inch-long footprints in the snow around the house. Tales of Bigfoot instantly resurfaced in the Platina community.

Description

Beegum Gorge Trail leads down a long shelf road that wraps around Beegum Gorge, to finish at a small, undeveloped USFS camping area along Beegum Creek. The first part of the road climbs the rise above Platinum Gulch through private property before entering BLM land. From here, the trail makes a steady descent along a shelf road, which has an adequate number of passing places. Lassen Peak can be seen through the gorge to the east. Beegum Peak, on the east side of the gorge, is made up of pocketed limestone that has some beehives.

Descending toward Beegum Gorge through Zachary Gulch

After crossing Zachary Gulch, the trail passes the turn to a delightful camping area on the banks of Beegum Creek, with plenty of shade and a great swimming hole. The main trail continues for another 1.4 miles to a second, more open camping area beside the creek. A hiking trail to Seeliger Ranch leads out the back of the camping area. Although the trail is shown as continuing on forest maps, most drivers will prefer to stop at the creek. The trail becomes very brushy after the crossing and is mainly used by ATVs. The Chrome Mine is 0.2 miles past the creek crossing. A concrete slab, footings, and remains of a loading hopper can still be seen.

A trail, shown on forest maps as leading to the north, is well used but rated most difficult by the forest service because of

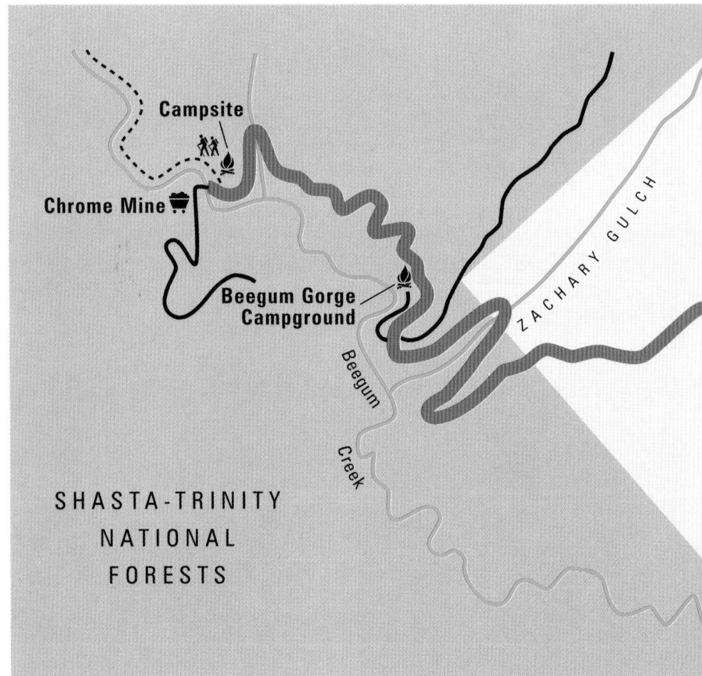

extremely steep, loose-traction climbs up the ridge. The main trail should not be attempted in wet weather; the shelf road becomes treacherously greasy and dangerous when wet.

Current Road Information

Bureau of Land Management
Redding Field Office
355 Hemsted Drive
Redding, CA 96002
(530) 224-2100

Map References

BLM Red Bluff
USFS Shasta-Trinity National Forest
USGS 1:24,000 Beegum
1:100,000 Red Bluff
Maptech CD-ROM: Shasta Lake/Redding
Northern California Atlas & Gazetteer, p. 55
California Road & Recreation Atlas, p. 51

Route Directions

▼ 0.0		From the intersection of California 36 and CR A16 at Platina, 46 miles west of Red Bluff and 9 miles east of Wildwood, zero trip meter and turn south on dirt road 29N06, following the sign to Beegum Gorge Campground.
		GPS: N40°21.68' W122°53.20'
▼ 0.7	SO	Track on left to communication towers.
		GPS: N40°21.21' W122°53.31'
▼ 2.1	BR	Track on left.
▼ 2.2	SO	Track on right. Entering BLM land.
		GPS: N40°20.53' W122°54.41'
▼ 2.5	SO	Track on right. Start of shelf road descent to Beegum Gorge.
▼ 5.2	BL	Turnout on right.
		GPS: N40°18.69' W122°55.62'
▼ 5.7	BL	Cross over Zachary Gulch; then track on right.
		GPS: N40°18.99' W122°55.71'
▼ 6.1	TR	Well-used track continues straight ahead for 0.2 miles to Beegum Gorge USFS Campground. Zero trip meter. End of shelf road.
		GPS:N40°18.70' W122°55.91'
▼ 0.0		Continue to the north. Immediately track on right up hill.
▼ 1.1	SO	Cross over creek.
▼ 1.4		Trail ends at campsite on right beside creek. Trail bears left and fords through Beegum Creek. A hiking trail to Seeliger Ranch leads out the back of the camping area. The trail continues over the creek, but is brushy and mainly used by ATVs.
		GPS: N40°18.66' W122°56.67'

NORTH COAST #11

Knob Peak Trail

Starting Point:	**California 36, 2.5 miles west of Platina**
Finishing Point:	**Knob Peak Fire Lookout**
Total Mileage:	**5.1 miles (one-way)**
Unpaved Mileage:	**4.6 miles**
Driving Time:	**30 minutes (one-way)**
Elevation Range:	**2,800–4,800 feet**
Usually Open:	**May to December**
Best Time to Travel:	**Dry weather**
Difficulty Rating:	**1**
Scenic Rating:	**8**
Remoteness Rating:	**+0**

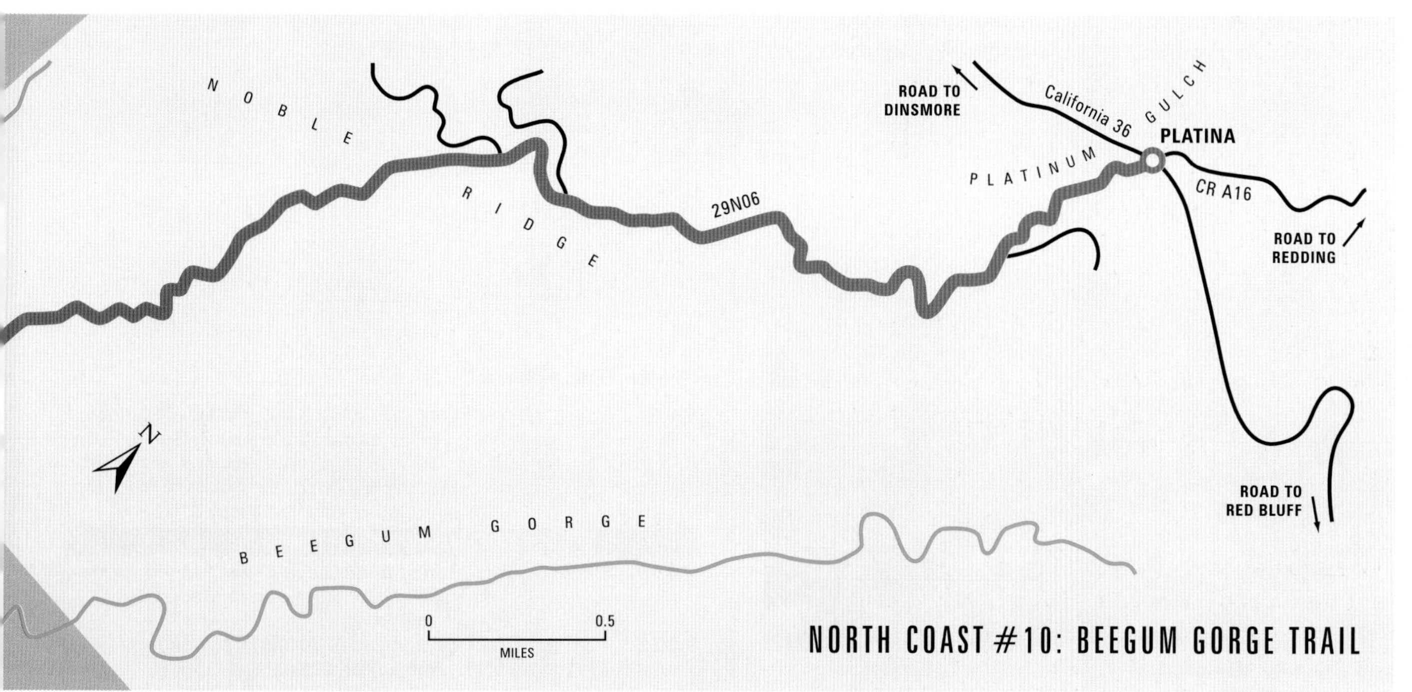

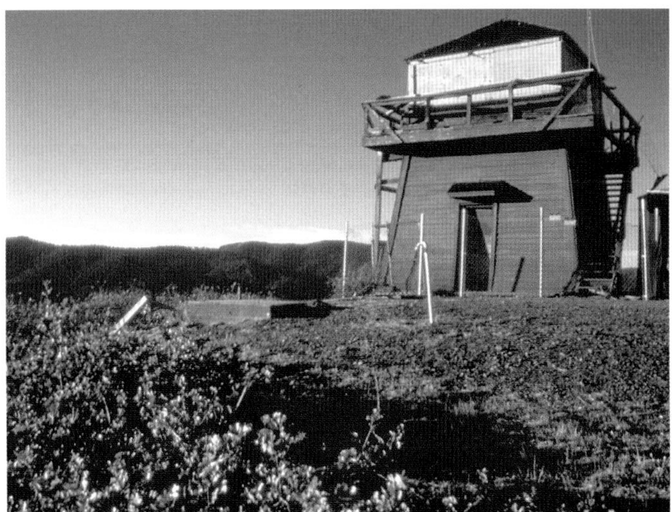

Knob Peak Fire Lookout prior to restoration

Special Attractions

- Excellent views from Knob Peak Fire Lookout.
- Easy shelf road suitable for all vehicles in dry weather.

History

Knob Peak Fire Lookout (4,819 feet) is perched 1,700 feet above and 2 miles west of the Midas Mine, once a hive of activity in Harrison Gulch. This rich gold mining district was named after W. F. Harrison, who settled here in 1852. A number of prospectors, namely Messrs Benton, Fowler, and the Hurst brothers, struck gold here in the mid-1890s and started the Midas Mine, which eventually produced nearly $7 million worth of gold.

Several hundred miners arrived to establish the town of Knob, named for a nearby round hill. Saloons, hotels, trading posts, schools, restaurants, a smelter, and more lined the streets of Knob by the turn of the twentieth century. Although far from Redding and Red Bluff, Knob enjoyed a vibrant social scene with regular plays, musical events, and the ever popular boxing matches. Stagecoaches plied the rough wagon road from Red Bluff to Knob daily. The population approached 2,000 at its peak shortly after the turn of the twentieth century.

Eastern view from the lookout

In 1914, a fire destroyed the timber bracings in the mine, vital water pumps failed, and the shafts flooded. Attempts to get the mine running again failed and the town emptied. Little now remains in the Harrison Gulch Mining District except for foundations of the smelter and some tailings.

The Hayfork Wintun tribe, also known as Nor-el-muk, frequented the surrounding Trinity Mountains. The Nor-el-muk, meaning "southward uphill people," established permanent villages and used the region's abundant foods such as salmon, venison, and acorns. Their spiritual beliefs were closely linked to landscape features. Chanchelulla Peak, meaning "Black Rock" in their language, was the most revered feature in their ancestral territory. Chanchelulla Peak (6,380 feet) rises directly north of Knob Peak.

Description

Although Knob Peak Fire Lookout is only a short distance from California 36, it seems a world away. In dry weather, passenger vehicles can generally reach the lookout. The lookout stopped operating in the 1990s and was restored by the forest service in 2002. It is now available for overnight rentals. Please respect the privacy of people who may be renting the lookout. There is a closure gate 0.2 miles short of the tower. If the gate is closed, it is only a short hike to the top. Panoramic views from the lookout include Mount Shasta to the north, Lassen Peak to the east, the Trinity Alps Wilderness to the northwest, and the Yolla Bolly Middle Eel Wilderness to the south.

Current Road Information

Shasta-Trinity National Forest
Yolla Bolla Ranger District
2555 State Highway 36
Platina, CA 96076
(530) 352-4211

Map References

BLM Red Bluff
USFS Shasta-Trinity National Forests
USGS 1:24,000 Beegum, Chanchelulla Peak
1:100,000 Red Bluff
Maptech CD-ROM: Shasta Lake/Redding
Northern California Atlas & Gazetteer, p. 55
California Road & Recreation Atlas, p. 51

Route Directions

▼ 0.0		From California 36, 2.5 miles west of Platina and 1.8 miles east of the Harrison Gulch Ranger Station, zero trip meter and turn northwest onto 29N02. The turn is marked from the highway. Road is initially paved.
		GPS: N40°22.07' W122°55.86'
▼ 0.3	SO	Track on left under power lines; then track on right is 29N02D. Road turns to graded dirt. Start of shelf road.
▼ 1.7	BL	Track on right; then second track on right is 29N01. Remain on 29N02.

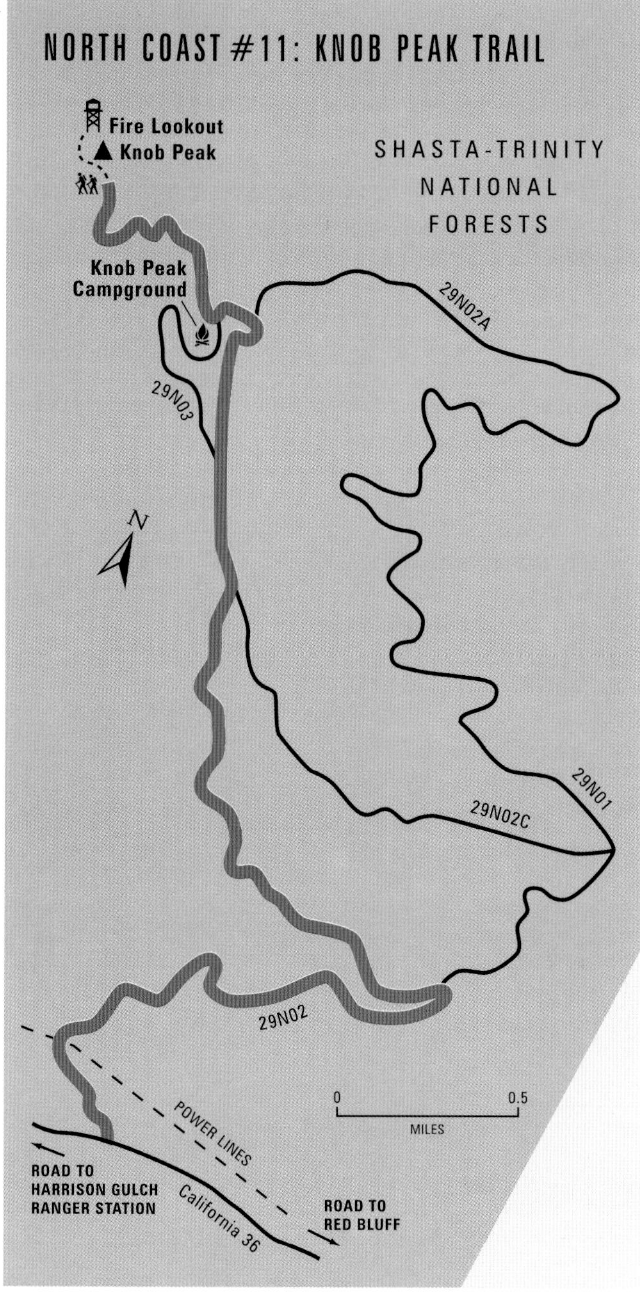

		GPS: N40°22.72' W122°55.16'
▼ 3.4	SO	Track on right is 29N02C.
▼ 3.7	BR	Track on right is 29N02B; then track on left is 29N03. Bear right, remaining on 29N02. Zero trip meter.
		GPS: N40°23.51' W122°56.53'
▼ 0.0		Continue to the northwest.
▼ 0.4	SO	Track on right is 29N02A.
▼ 0.6	BR	Track on left is 29N03 rejoining. Undeveloped Knob Peak USFS Campground on left.
		GPS: N40°23.81' W122°56.75'
▼ 1.2		Track on right; then small track on left; then trail ends at gate. Main trail continues 0.2 miles to Knob Peak Fire Lookout. The lookout is generally gated all year.
		GPS: N40°23.93' W122°57.17'

NORTH COAST #12

Hall City Cave Trail

Starting Point:	**Wildwood Road in Wildwood**
Finishing Point:	**California 36, 0.3 miles east of the intersection with Wildwood Road**
Total Mileage:	**5.6 miles**
Unpaved Mileage:	**5.6 miles**
Driving Time:	**30 minutes, not including the hike to the cave**
Elevation Range:	**3,400–4,100 feet**
Usually Open:	**April to January**
Best Time to Travel:	**April to January**
Difficulty Rating:	**1**
Scenic Rating:	**9**
Remoteness Rating:	**+0**

Special Attractions

- Hall City Cave.
- Harrison Gulch mining ruins close to the trail.

History

Hall City Cave Trail travels along an old twisting county road from Wildwood to Platina. Wildwood was a stage stop on the early wagon road to the Midas Mine, near the end of this trail. In the 1890s, Ed Landis built a sawmill with a water-driven circular saw near the trading post and inn on the banks of Hayfork Creek. His name is attached to Landis Gulch, which drains into Hayfork Creek from the west.

The old county road passes near the site of Hall City, which takes its name from the nearby Hall City Cave. A local tale relates how two miners from the vicinity of Hayfork were ambushed by Indians who made off with two sacks of gold, leaving the miners to die by the roadside. A posse pursued them, and the Indians dropped the gold into Hall City Cave. Though the assailants were captured, interrogated as to the location of the gold, and later hanged at Wildwood, the gold was never retrieved from the deep water-filled cavern.

Many ditches, tunnels, tailings, and rockwork remain deep within the forest—testimony to the high activity in the 30 mines around Hall City.

Signpost to Hall City Cave

Description

This short loop passes the trailhead to Hall City Cave. The cave, set beneath a limestone cap, is reached by the easy graded dirt road and then a 0.3-mile hike.

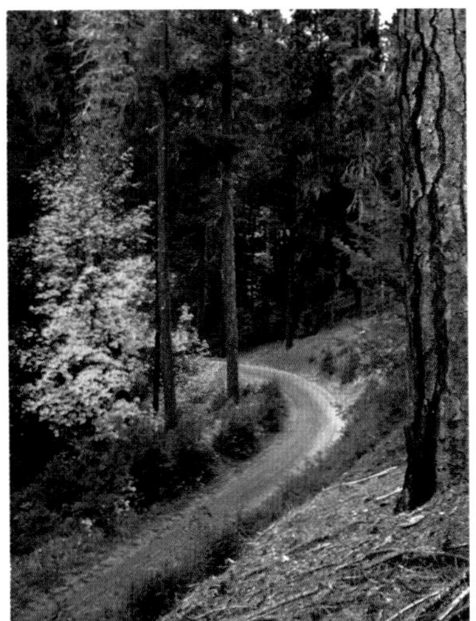

The trail follows an old logging route above Hall City Creek

The trail starts in the small community of Wildwood, a couple miles north of California 36. The cave is well marked as far as the final turnoff; then all markers disappear. Take the side trail and proceed to a parking area for cave visitors. A vehicle trail continues past the parking area, but it is blocked by a closure gate. The hiking trail leads out the back of the informal parking area, runs alongside Hall City Creek for a short distance, then crosses over the creek and switchbacks up the hill to the cave. If, after crossing the creek, you find yourself continuing along the creek instead of climbing up the hill, you have overshot the switchbacks.

A bit of scrambling over boulders is required to reach the cave. From the tall entrance, you will descend a rough wooden ladder into this exciting subterranean world. Inside, the narrow passageway opens up to a small cavern. The cave goes back for about 100 feet, crossing a trickling underground stream, and ending at a pool of deep, clear blue water. To the left of the pool, you can see a deep shaft extending beneath the water; this is supposedly the site of lost gold. The walls and ceilings of the cave have several small limestone formations. If you are planning to enter the cave, boots with good tread will help you cope with the very slippery, rough floor. A good flashlight is also essential. Allow 30 minutes round trip for the hike, plus time to explore the cave. The parking area for the cave is at GPS: N40°24.24' W123°00.59' and the coordinates of the cave are GPS: N40°24.41' W123°00.43'.

The trail can often be traveled year round, but snow is likely to block the road for short periods in January and February. Even if there is no snow, the road can be icy during winter. The trail finishes on California 36.

Current Road Information

Shasta-Trinity National Forest
Yolla Bolla Ranger District
2555 State Highway 36
Platina, CA 96076
(530) 352-4211

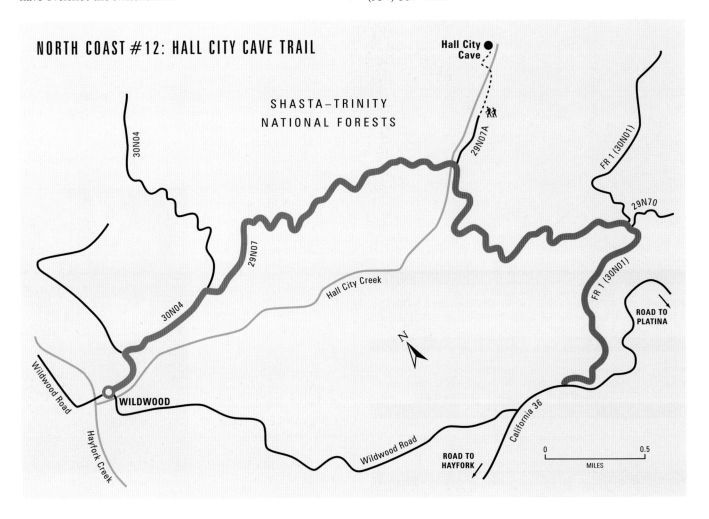

NORTH COAST #12: HALL CITY CAVE TRAIL

Hall City Cave
SHASTA–TRINITY NATIONAL FORESTS
30N04
29N07A
FR 1 (30N01)
29N70
29N07
Hall City Creek
30N04
FR 1 (30N01)
ROAD TO PLATINA
N
Wildwood Road
WILDWOOD
Hayfork Creek
Wildwood Road
California 36
ROAD TO HAYFORK
0
0.5
MILES

Map References

BLM Garberville
USFS Shasta-Trinity National Forests
USGS 1:24,000 Dubakella Mt.
1:100,000 Garberville
Maptech CD-ROM: North Coast/Eureka
Northern California Atlas & Gazetteer, p. 55
California Road & Recreation Atlas, p. 51

Route Directions

Mileage		Directions
▼ 0.0		From Wildwood Road in Wildwood, 2.4 miles north of California 36, zero trip meter and turn northeast on graded dirt road 30N04.
3.0 ▲		Trail ends on Wildwood Road in Wildwood. Turn left for California 36.
		GPS: N40°24.03' W123°03.30'
▼ 0.3	BR	Track on left.
2.7 ▲	BL	Track on right.
▼ 0.8	TR	Trail 30N04 continues straight ahead. Turn right on 29N07, following the sign for Hall City Caves.
2.2 ▲	TL	T-intersection with 30N04.
		GPS: N40°24.19' W123°02.54'
▼ 0.9	SO	Track on left.
2.1 ▲	SO	Track on right.
▼ 2.9	SO	Track on left is 29N07D.
0.1 ▲	SO	Track on right is 29N07D.
▼ 3.0	SO	Cross over Hall City Creek; then track on left is 29N07A, which goes 0.3 miles to the parking area for Hall City Cave. Zero trip meter.
0.0 ▲		Continue to the northwest and cross over Hall City Creek.
		GPS: N40°24.06' W123°00.91'
▼ 0.0		Continue to the southeast.
2.6 ▲	SO	Track on right is 29N07A, which goes 0.3 miles to the parking area for Hall City Cave. Zero trip meter.
▼ 0.6	BR	Track on left is 29N07C.
2.0 ▲	BL	Track on right is 29N07C.
▼ 1.1	BR	Two tracks on left.
1.5 ▲	BL	Two tracks on right.
▼ 1.6	TR	4-way intersection. FR 1 (30N01) crosses. Track straight ahead is 29N70. Turn right onto FR 1 (30N01), following the sign for California 36.
1.0 ▲	TL	4-way intersection. FR 1 (30N01) continues straight ahead. Track on right is 29N70. Turn left onto 29N07, following the sign for Hall City Cave.
		GPS: N40°23.41' W123°00.25'
▼ 2.1	BR	Track on left; then track on right is 29N10.
0.5 ▲	BL	Track on left is 29N10; then track on right.
▼ 2.5	SO	Track on right under power lines.
0.1 ▲	SO	Track on left under power lines.
▼ 2.6		Trail ends at T-intersection with California 36. Turn left for Platina and Red Bluff; turn right for Hayfork.
0.0 ▲		Trail begins on California 36, 0.3 miles east of the Wildwood Store and intersection with Wildwood Road. Zero trip meter and turn northeast on graded road FR 1 (30N01), following the sign to Hall City Cave.
		GPS: N40°23.02' W123°01.01'

NORTH COAST #13

Low Divide Road

Starting Point:	**California 197, 2.2 miles north of intersection with US 199**
Finishing Point:	**US 101 in Smith River**
Total Mileage:	**14.5 miles**
Unpaved Mileage:	**12.5 miles**
Driving Time:	**1.5 hours**
Elevation Range:	**200–2,400 feet**
Usually Open:	**Year-round**
Best Time to Travel:	**Year-round**
Difficulty Rating:	**1**
Scenic Rating:	**8**
Remoteness Rating:	**+0**

Special Attractions

- Views over the Pacific Coast and mouth of the Smith River.
- Easy loop east of US 101.
- A good trail to see coastal vegetation and wildflowers in spring.

History

Northwestern California attracted a number of Chinese immigrants, many of whom worked at the Occident & Oriental Commercial Fish Cannery, established in Del Norte County in 1857. They also worked in the logging industry in this part of the Klamath Mountains and built wagon roads, including most of this trail, over High Divide to the mining settlements of Low Divide, Altaville, and Gasquet.

In the early 1860s, the Occidental Copper Mining Company worked the Copper Creek Mine, just below the high point of the trail. The mine was busiest during the 1860s and '70s. Some of the copper ore was shipped to Swansea, Wales,

Historic Battery Point Lighthouse is a pleasant stop near Crescent City before heading out on the trail

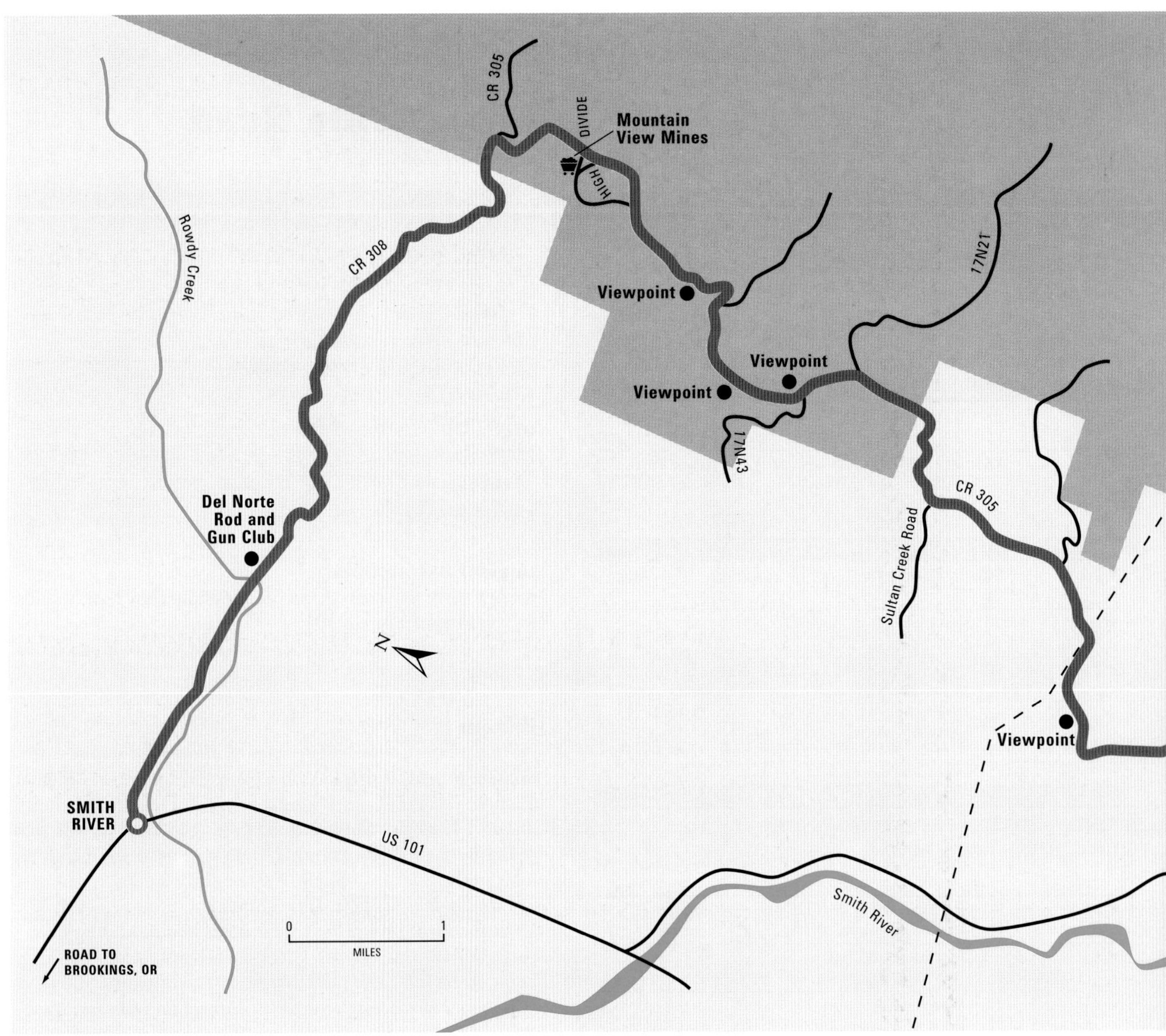

and some to Germany for processing, returning anywhere from $41 to more than $100 per ton.

Logging above Rowdy Creek, at the northern end of Low Divide Road, was in full swing in the early 1920s. The Del Norte Company, based in Smith River, shipped fir and redwood logs to the sawmill in Brookings, just over the state line in Oregon, by way of the newly built North West Railroad. The Del Norte Company's parent organization was the California & Oregon Lumber Company, headquartered in Brookings. Logging crews were based out of Crescent City, California, and Brookings, Oregon, and Smith River boomed as the social half-way point.

Description

Low Divide Road is maintained as CR 305 and loops through the lower elevations of Six Rivers National Forest. The shrubby vegetation is different from other forest drives in this region: Much of it is manzanitas and azaleas, which produce a bright array in spring. The route has a number of views overlooking the mouth of the Smith River and the Pacific Coast.

Much of the road crosses private land—tracks mentioned in the route directions often go to private property and are mentioned only as points of reference for navigation. Workings of the Mountain View Mines at the top of High Divide are privately owned. The road snakes down to meet US 101 via Rowdy Creek Road (CR 308). The southern portion of this route is shown on topographical maps as Wimer Road.

Current Road Information

Smith River National Recreation Area
Six Rivers National Forest
PO Box 228
Gasquet, CA 95543
(707) 457-3131

NORTH COAST #13: LOW DIVIDE ROAD

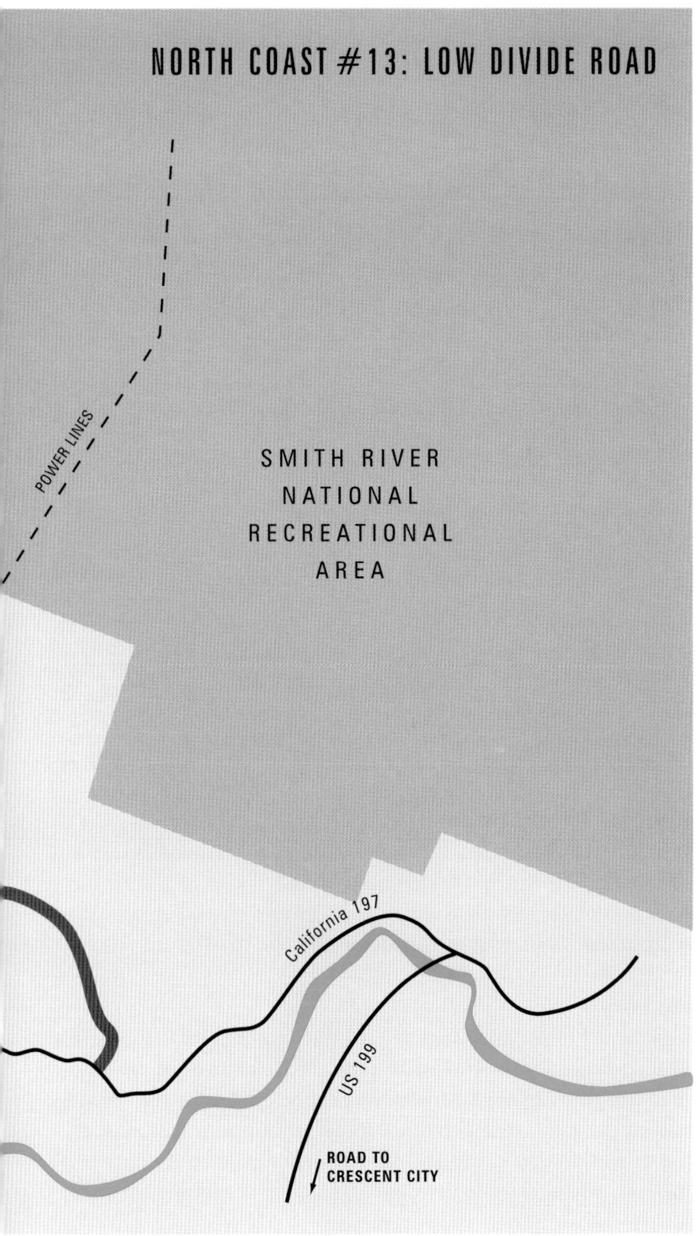

Map References

BLM Crescent City
USFS Six Rivers National Forest, Smith River National Recreation Area
USGS 1:24,000 Hiouchi, High Divide, Smith River
1:100,000 Crescent City
Maptech CD-ROM: North Coast/Eureka
Northern California Atlas & Gazetteer, p. 22
California Road & Recreation Atlas, p. 44
Trails Illustrated, Redwood National Park, North Coast State Parks, Smith River NRA (218)

Route Directions

▼ 0.0 From the intersection of US 199 and California 197, 3.5 miles east of US 101, proceed north on California 197 for 2.2 miles. Zero trip meter and turn east on paved Low Divide Road (CR 305).
5.2 ▲ Trail ends at T-intersection with California 197. Turn left for US 199 and Crescent City; turn right for US 101 northbound.

GPS: N41°49.74' W124°06.16'

▼ 0.3 SO Road turns to graded dirt.
4.9 ▲ SO Road becomes paved.

▼ 1.6 SO Track on left.
3.6 ▲ SO Track on right.

▼ 2.1 SO Coastal viewpoint on left.
3.1 ▲ SO Coastal viewpoint on right.

GPS: N41°51.02' W124°05.47'

▼ 2.3 SO Track on left through seasonal closure gate.
2.9 ▲ SO Track on right through seasonal closure gate.

▼ 2.4 SO Track on left.
2.8 ▲ SO Track on right.

▼ 2.7 SO Track on left and track on right under power lines.
2.5 ▲ SO Track on left and track on right under power lines.

▼ 3.1 SO Track on right.
2.1 ▲ SO Track on left.

▼ 3.4 SO Track on right.
1.8 ▲ SO Track on left.

▼ 4.1 SO Sultan Creek Road on left. Remain on Low Divide Road.
1.1 ▲ SO Sultan Creek Road on right. Remain on Low Divide Road.

GPS: N41°52.16' W124°04.41'

▼ 4.3 SO Track on left.
0.9 ▲ SO Track on right.

▼ 5.2 SO Graded road on right is 17N21. Zero trip meter.
0.0 ▲ Continue to the southeast on Low Divide Road (CR 305).

GPS: N41°52.80' W124°03.75'

▼ 0.0 Continue to the west on Low Divide Road (CR 305).
3.7 ▲ SO Graded road on left is 17N21. Zero trip meter.

▼ 0.3 SO Track on right.
3.4 ▲ SO Track on left.

▼ 0.4 SO Track on left is 17N43.
3.3 ▲ SO Track on right is 17N43.

▼ 0.5 SO Viewpoint on right over Hardscrabble Creek Basin and Gasquet Mountain to the east.
3.2 ▲ SO Viewpoint on left over Hardscrabble Creek Basin and Gasquet Mountain to the east.

▼ 0.7 SO Track on left.
3.0 ▲ SO Track on right.

▼ 0.9 SO Viewpoint on left over mouth of the Smith River, Prince Island, and Hunter Rock to the west.
2.8 ▲ SO Viewpoint on right over mouth of the Smith River, Prince Island, and Hunter Rock to the west.

GPS: N41°53.46' W124°04.11'

▼ 1.4 SO Track on left; then track on right.
2.3 ▲ SO Track on right; then track on left.

▼ 1.8 SO Viewpoint on left over mouth of the Smith River, Prince Island, and Lake Earl State Wildlife Area to the west.
1.9 ▲ SO Viewpoint on right over mouth of the Smith River, Prince Island, and Lake Earl State Wildlife Area to the west.

GPS: N41°53.84' W124°03.54'

▼ 2.4 SO Track on right into active mining claims; then track on left.
1.3 ▲ SO Track on right; then track on left into active mining claims.

▼ 2.9	SO	Track on left.
0.8 ▲	SO	Track on right.
▼ 3.0	SO	High Divide. Graded road on left to Mountain View Mines.
0.7 ▲	BL	High Divide. Graded road on right to Mountain View Mines.
		GPS: N41°54.68′ W124°02.92′
▼ 3.1	SO	Track on right.
0.6 ▲	SO	Track on left.
▼ 3.2	SO	Track on right.
0.5 ▲	SO	Track on left.
▼ 3.5	SO	Track on left.
0.2 ▲	SO	Track on right.
▼ 3.7	SO	Graded road on right is the continuation of CR 305. Zero trip meter.
0.0 ▲		Continue to the south on CR 305.
		GPS: N41°55.16′ W124°03.10′
▼ 0.0		Continue to the west on graded Rowdy Creek Road (CR 308).
5.6 ▲	BR	Graded road on left is CR 305. Zero trip meter and head uphill.
▼ 0.2	SO	Road on right.
5.4 ▲	SO	Road on left.
▼ 0.9	SO	Track on left.
4.7 ▲	SO	Track on right.
▼ 1.3	SO	Track on right.
4.3 ▲	SO	Track on left.
▼ 3.9	SO	Del Norte Rod and Gun Club on right. Road is now paved. Cross over Rowdy Creek. Remain on paved road until the end of the trail.
1.7 ▲	SO	Cross over Rowdy Creek. Del Norte Rod and Gun Club on left. Road turns to graded dirt.
		GPS: N41°55.59′ W124°06.63′
▼ 5.6		Trail ends at T-intersection with US 101 in Smith River. Turn left for Crescent City; turn right for Brookings, OR.
0.0 ▲		Trail commences on US 101 at Smith River. Zero trip meter and turn northeast on Rowdy Creek Road. Remain on paved road for the first 1.7 miles.
		GPS: N41°55.76′ W124°08.58′

NORTH COAST #14

Howland Hill Road

Starting Point:	**Elk Valley Road, 1 mile east of US 101**
Finishing Point:	**US 199, 7 miles east of US 101**
Total Mileage:	**8.4 miles**
Unpaved Mileage:	**5.3 miles**
Driving Time:	**1 hour**
Elevation Range:	**100–500 feet**
Usually Open:	**Year-round**
Best Time to Travel:	**Year-round**
Difficulty Rating:	**1**
Scenic Rating:	**10**
Remoteness Rating:	**+0**

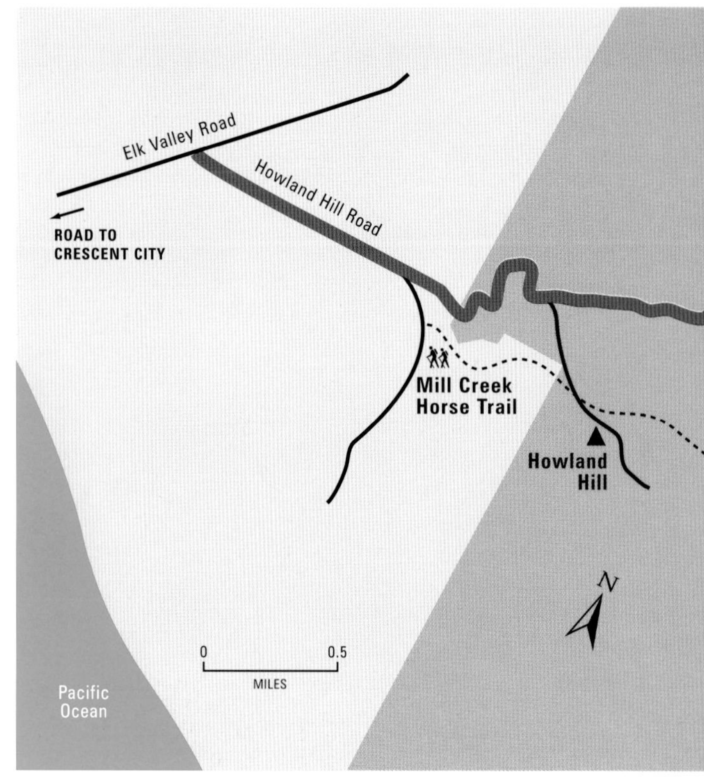

Special Attractions

- Small winding road through giant coast redwoods in the Jedediah Smith Redwoods State Park.
- Access to the Smith River and a number of hiking trails.
- Excellent photo opportunities along the road.

History

Howland Hill Road weaves a path through magnificent stands of redwoods, remnants of the coastal forest traversed by Jedediah Smith in 1828. Smith, whose name graces the river at the end of this trail, was a trapper, trader, mountain man, and explorer in the 1820s. He and his men spent the better part of a month cutting a trail through the dense vegetation of these northwest California mountains.

The community of Hiouchi, near the end of the trail, was in the ancestral homeland of the Yurok and Tolowa Indians. Hiouchi is thought to mean "high clear water." Douglas Park, in the depths of the forest directly opposite Hiouchi, was formerly known as Berteleda, in memory of Bertha Brown, daughter of a Crescent City physician.

Description

On maps, Howland Hill Road appears to be a simple trail. But this easy route is a stunningly beautiful, meandering drive through large groves of moss-hung coast redwoods in Jedediah Smith Redwoods State Park. The single-track road is graded dirt for most of its length, and the surface is often wet and slippery with fallen leaves. The quiet drive is surprisingly beautiful on a wet day, when mist lends it an eerie feel. Take care when it is wet—the trail can be extremely slippery.

The trail climbs steeply from the edge of Crescent City, entering Jedediah Smith Redwoods State Park and then winding

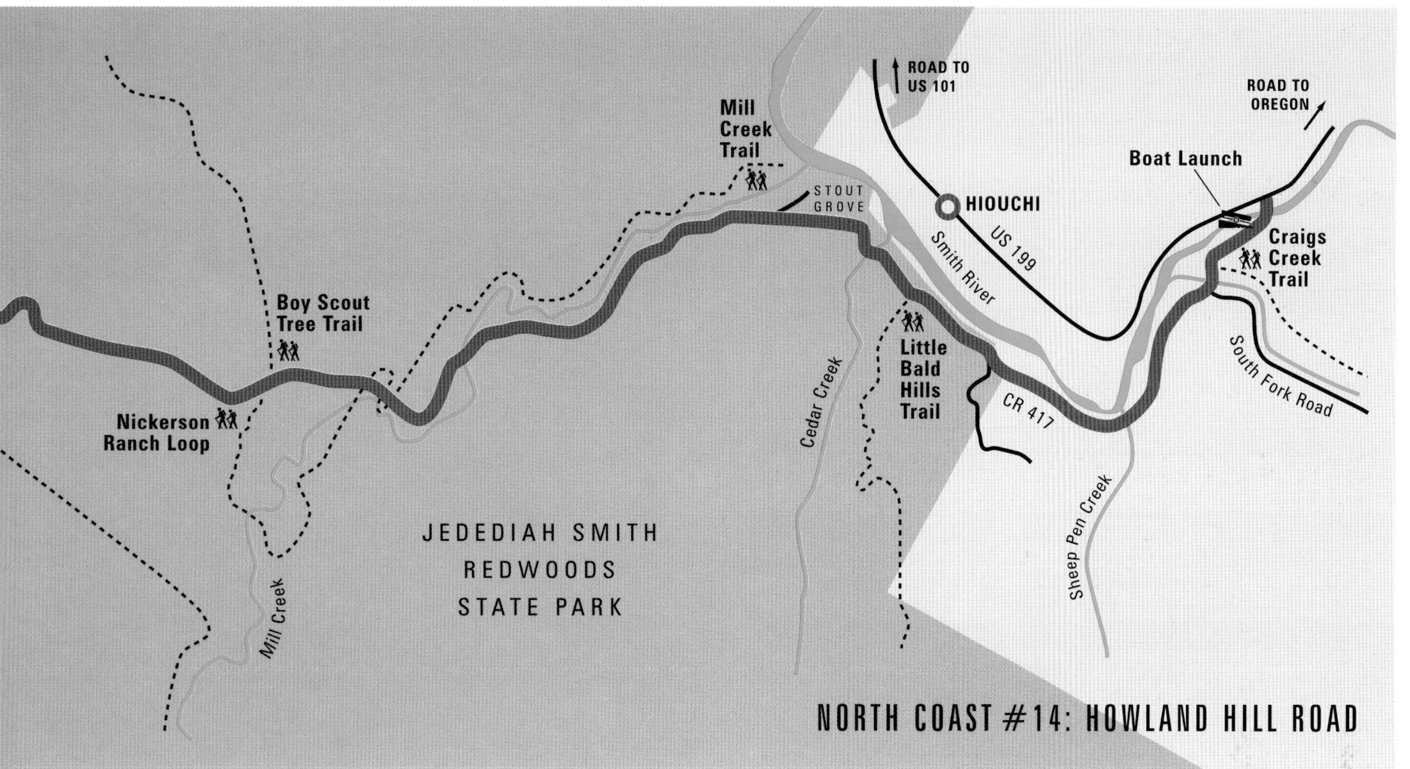

among the large trees. Turnouts allow for safe parking at most of the hiking trails, which lead farther into the groves of giants.

The trail crosses Mill Creek near its halfway point, after which a short spur leads to the Stout Grove of giant redwoods. The road becomes paved after it passes the residential community of Hiouchi, most of which is on the far side of the river. River access points for boaters and anglers can be found at the east end of the trail.

Brilliant yellow banana slugs live in the forest and are valuable to the ecosystem. Try to avoid stepping on them when hiking.

Coastal redwood giants

Current Road Information

Jedediah Smith Redwoods State Park
1375 Elk Valley Road
Crescent City, CA 95531
(707) 464-6101 ext. 5112

Map References

BLM Crescent City
USFS Smith River National Recreation Area, Six Rivers National Forest
USGS 1:24,000 Crescent City, Hiouchi
1:100,000 Crescent City
Maptech CD-ROM: North Coast/Eureka
Northern California Atlas & Gazetteer, p. 22
California Road & Recreation Atlas, p. 44
Trails Illustrated, Redwood National Park, North Coast State Parks, Smith River NRA (218)

Route Directions

Mileage		Direction
▼ 0.0		From Elk Valley Road, 1 mile east of US 101 and Crescent City, zero trip meter and turn east on paved Howland Hill Road, following the sign for Stout Grove.
5.6 ▲		Trail ends at T-intersection with Elk Valley Road. Turn left for US 101 and Crescent City.
		GPS: N41°45.51' W124°09.98'
▼ 0.8	SO	Road on right leads to Mill Creek Horse Trail.
4.8 ▲	SO	Road on left leads to Mill Creek Horse Trail.
▼ 1.1	SO	Entering Jedediah Smith Redwoods State Park.
4.5 ▲	SO	Leaving Jedediah Smith Redwoods State Park.
▼ 1.4	SO	Road turns to graded dirt.
4.2 ▲	SO	Road becomes paved.

▼ 1.7		SO	Closed road on right. Pass through seasonal closure gate, following sign for Stout Grove.
	3.9 ▲	SO	Seasonal closure gate; then closed road on left.
▼ 2.4		SO	Cross over creek. Metcalf Grove plaque on left.
	3.2 ▲	SO	Metcalf Grove plaque on right. Cross over creek.
▼ 3.4		SO	Nickerson Ranch Loop, for hikers, on right.
	2.2 ▲	SO	Nickerson Ranch Loop, for hikers, on left.
			GPS: N41°46.04' W124°06.61'
▼ 3.5		SO	Boy Scout Tree Trail, for hikers, on left.
	2.1 ▲	SO	Boy Scout Tree Trail, for hikers, on right.
▼ 3.8		SO	Mill Creek Trail crosses.
	1.8 ▲	SO	Mill Creek Trail crosses.
			GPS: N41°46.23' W124°06.30'
▼ 4.3		SO	Cross over Mill Creek on bridge.
	1.3 ▲	SO	Cross over Mill Creek on bridge.
			GPS: N41°46.46' W124°05.92'
▼ 5.6		SO	Track on left goes 0.1 miles to Stout Grove. Zero trip meter and follow the sign to US 199.
	0.0 ▲		Continue to the southwest.
			GPS: N41°47.29' W124°05.06'
▼ 0.0			Continue to the northeast.
	2.8 ▲	SO	Track on right goes 0.1 miles to Stout Grove. Zero trip meter and follow the sign to Crescent City.
▼ 0.5		SO	Cross over Cedar Creek.
	2.3 ▲	SO	Cross over Cedar Creek.
▼ 0.8		SO	Track on right goes to Little Bald Hills Trail.
	2.0 ▲	SO	Track on left goes to Little Bald Hills Trail.
▼ 1.1		SO	Closure gate; then closed road on right. Leaving Jedediah Smith Redwoods State Park. Road is now paved.
	1.7 ▲	SO	Road turns to graded dirt. Entering Jedediah Smith Redwoods State Park. Closed road on left; then closure gate.
▼ 1.3		SO	Road is now called Douglas Park Road (CR 417). Remain on paved road, which now follows alongside the Smith River.
	1.5 ▲	SO	Road leaves the Smith River.
▼ 1.7		SO	Cross over Sheep Pen Creek on covered bridge.
	1.1 ▲	SO	Cross over Sheep Pen Creek on covered bridge.
▼ 2.3		TL	Paved road on right is South Fork Road. Turn left and cross over South Fork Smith River on bridge; then Craigs Creek Trail (1E02) on right.
	0.5 ▲	TR	Craigs Creek Trail (1E02) on left; then cross over South Fork Smith River on bridge; then turn right onto Douglas Park Road. Paved road on left is South Fork Road.
▼ 2.5		SO	Smith River access and boat launch on left.
	0.3 ▲	SO	Smith River access and boat launch on right.
▼ 2.7		SO	Cross over Smith River on Neils Christensen Memorial Bridge.
	0.1 ▲	SO	Cross over Smith River on Neils Christensen Memorial Bridge.
▼ 2.8			Trail ends at T-intersection with US 199. Turn left for US 101 and Crescent City; turn right for Oregon.
	0.0 ▲		Trail commences on US 199, 10 miles northeast of Crescent City and 7 miles east of US 101. Zero trip meter and turn southeast on paved South Fork Road, following the sign for the Howland Hill Scenic Drive.
			GPS: N41°48.13' W124°03.17'

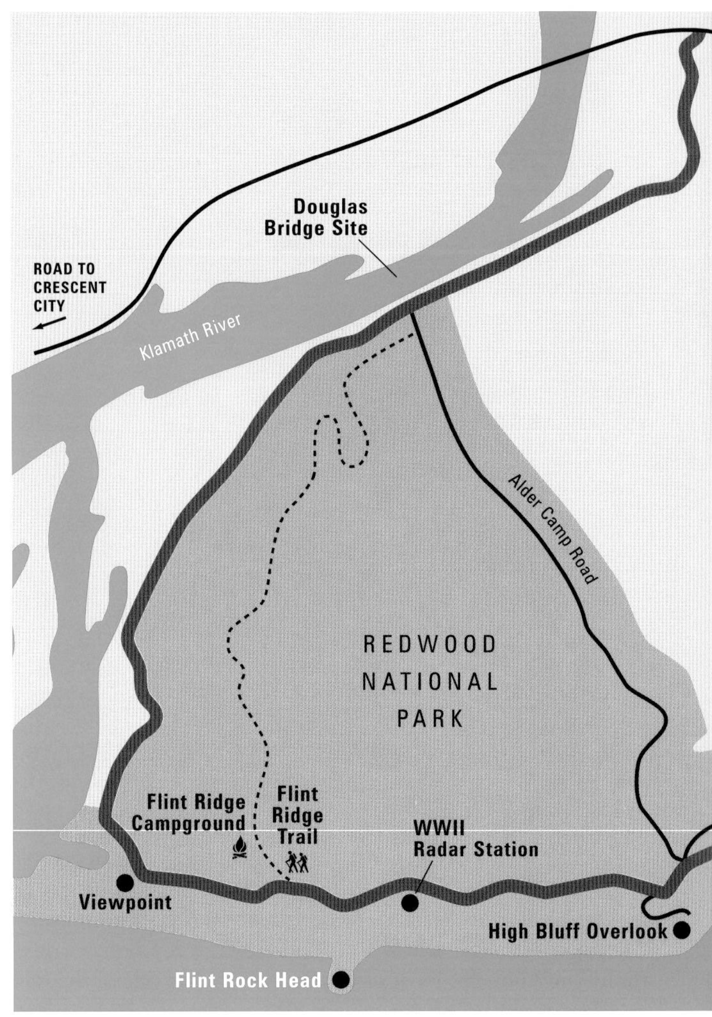

NORTH COAST #15

Redwood National Park Coastal Drive

Starting Point:	**Newton B. Drury Scenic Parkway, 0.8 miles south of its northern intersection with US 101**
Finishing Point:	**US 101 at the Klamath Beach Road, Coastal Drive exit**
Total Mileage:	**9.5 miles**
Unpaved Mileage:	**6 miles**
Driving Time:	**1 hour**
Elevation Range:	**0–600 feet**
Usually Open:	**Year-round**
Best Time to Travel:	**Year-round**
Difficulty Rating:	**1**
Scenic Rating:	**9**
Remoteness Rating:	**+0**

NORTH COAST #15: REDWOOD NATIONAL PARK COASTAL DRIVE

ROAD TO ORICK

US 101

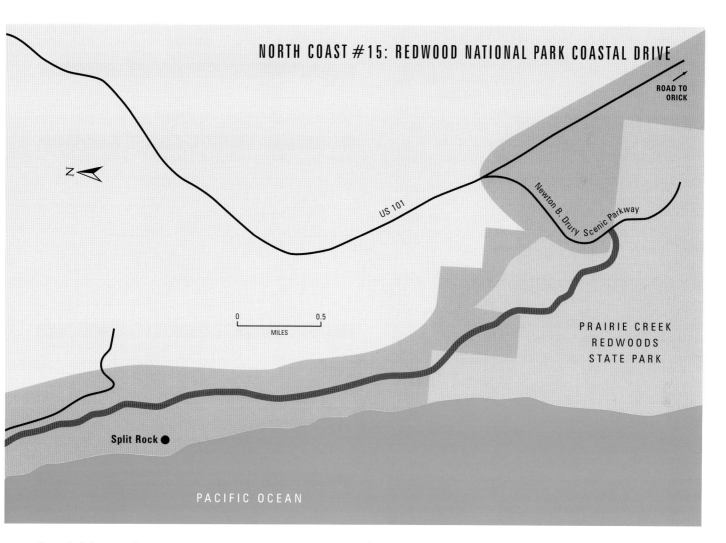

Newton B. Drury Scenic Parkway

0 0.5 MILES

PRAIRIE CREEK REDWOODS STATE PARK

Split Rock

PACIFIC OCEAN

Special Attractions

- Whale watching in season and a chance to see seals along the coast.
- Historic World War II radar station.
- Viewpoints over the coast and mouth of the Klamath River.

History

This coastal drive overlooks the Yurok village of Requa, on the northern side of the Klamath River's mouth. The strategically positioned village once had more than 20 houses and 14 sweat houses and was the meeting point of the coastal and river members of the Yurok. The Yurok hunted sea lions, seals, bears, elk, and deer, as well as fished for salmon and gathered mollusks and other crustaceans.

A World War II radar station is halfway along this scenic drive. The old station, cleverly disguised as a farmhouse, was part of a coastal surveillance operation that watched for a Japanese invasion. The farmhouse, with its false windows and shingled roof, was one of 65 such surveillance stations. A separate silo tower contained the antenna. This high security rural compound had two 50-caliber anti-aircraft machine guns, armed military guards, and a team of patrol dogs. Any movements on the horizon were reported to San Francisco. If the approaching aircraft or vessel was thought to be hostile, fighter planes were dispatched to intercept it.

Description

The coastal drive in Redwood National Park is an easy loop on paved and gravel roads that are suitable for year-round travel. The trail's major attraction is its coastal views, which provide a chance to spot some of the larger marine mammals. Gray

World War II radar station disguised as a farmhouse, part of an early warning system to signal a Japanese invasion

The beach below Redwood National Park Coastal Drive

whales may be seen migrating between the Arctic Circle and Baja California; sea lions bask on the beaches and rocks; and you may be lucky enough to spot a school of dolphins out at sea. Binoculars are a definite help.

The first section of road is paved. Past the turnoff to Alder Camp Road, it becomes a narrow graded dirt road. The High Bluff Overlook, a short distance past the intersection, is one of the most stunning viewpoints along this part of the coast, with views of rocky bays and headlands. There are picnic tables here for day use only. The trail then passes the old World War II radar station. The historic site can be viewed from the road, but it is worth the short scramble down the footpath to see the station up close.

The overlook above the mouth of the Klamath River is excellent, and it is also a good place to spot gray whales. All that remains of Douglas Bridge, near the end of the trail, are the surprisingly ornate stone bears that marked one end of the bridge.

Although rated a 1 for difficulty and suitable for passenger vehicles under normal conditions, this road is closed to trailers and RVs.

Current Road Information

Redwood National and State Parks
1111 Second Street
Crescent City, CA 95531
(707) 464-6101

Map References

BLM Orick, Crescent City
USFS Six Rivers National Forest
USGS 1:24,000 Fern Canyon, Requa
1:100,000 Orick, Crescent City
Maptech CD-ROM: North Coast/Eureka
Northern California Atlas & Gazetteer, pp. 32, 22
California Road & Recreation Atlas, p. 44
Trails Illustrated, Redwood National Park, North Coast State Parks, Smith River NRA (218)

Route Directions

▼ 0.0		From Newton B. Drury Scenic Parkway, 0.8 miles south of its northern intersection with US 101, zero trip meter and turn southwest onto paved road, following the sign for Redwood National and State Parks Coastal Drive.
4.2 ▲		Trail ends at intersection with Newton B. Drury Scenic Parkway. Turn left to join US 101 northbound for Crescent City; turn right to join US 101 southbound for Orick.
		GPS: N41°27.45′ W124°02.66′
▼ 1.2	SO	Road is now a mix of pavement and graded dirt.
3.0 ▲	SO	Road is now paved.
▼ 1.6	SO	Coastal viewpoint on left.
2.6 ▲	SO	Coastal viewpoint on right.
		GPS: N41°28.43′ W124°03.76′
▼ 2.0	SO	Coastal viewpoint on left.
2.2 ▲	SO	Coastal viewpoint on right.
▼ 2.6	SO	Coastal viewpoint on left.
1.6 ▲	SO	Coastal viewpoint on right.
▼ 3.4	SO	Coastal viewpoint on left.
0.8 ▲	SO	Coastal viewpoint on right.
▼ 4.2	TL	Road on right into state prison; then paved road continues around to the right. Zero trip meter and turn left, following the sign for the Coastal Drive North.
0.0 ▲		Continue to the southeast. Road on left goes into state prison. Road is now intermittently paved.
		GPS: N41°30.64′ W124°04.47′
▼ 0.0		Continue to the west. Road is now graded dirt.
5.3 ▲	TR	T-intersection with paved road. Zero trip meter.
▼ 0.1	BR	Track on left goes 0.3 miles to High Bluff Overlook.
5.2 ▲	SO	Track on right goes 0.3 miles to High Bluff Overlook.
▼ 0.9	SO	Hiking trail to the WWII radar station, which can be seen below the trail on the left.
4.4 ▲	SO	Hiking trail to the WWII radar station, which can be seen below the trail on the right.
		GPS: N41°31.29′ W124°04.65′
▼ 1.3	SO	Flint Ridge Hiking Trail on right to Douglas Bridge. Parking on left of trail. Flint Ridge Campground is 0.25 miles up this trail.
4.0 ▲	SO	Flint Ridge Hiking Trail on left to Douglas Bridge. Parking on right of trail. Flint Ridge Campground is 0.25 miles up this trail.
		GPS: N41°31.62′ W124°04.68′
▼ 1.8	SO	Turnout on left is a viewpoint over the mouth of the Klamath River. Road is now paved.
3.5 ▲	SO	Turnout on right is a viewpoint over the mouth of the Klamath River. Road turns to graded dirt.
		GPS: N41°32.03′ W124°04.66′
▼ 3.9	SO	Paved road on right is Alder Camp Road. Old

Sea lions bask on the rocks below the trail

			Douglas Memorial Bridge supports on left.
	1.4 ▲	SO	Paved road on left is Alder Camp Road. Old Douglas Memorial Bridge supports on right.
			GPS: N41°31.45' W124°02.64'
▼ 4.1		SO	Leaving Redwood National Park.
	1.2 ▲	SO	Entering Redwood National Park.
▼ 5.3			Trail ends at intersection with US 101. Turn north for Crescent City; turn south for Eureka.
	0.0 ▲		Trail begins on US 101 at the Klamath Beach Road, Coastal Drive exit. Exit freeway and proceed to the west side. Zero trip meter and turn west on paved road.
			GPS: N41°30.73' W124°01.70'

NORTH COAST #16

Gold Bluffs Trail

Starting Point:	**US 101, 2 miles north of Orick**
Finishing Point:	**Fern Canyon Trailhead**
Total Mileage:	**6.8 miles (one-way)**
Unpaved Mileage:	**6.5 miles**
Driving Time:	**1 hour (one-way)**
Elevation Range:	**0–400 feet**
Usually Open:	**Year-round**
Best Time to Travel:	**Year-round**
Difficulty Rating:	**1**
Scenic Rating:	**10**
Remoteness Rating:	**+0**

Special Attractions

- Chance to see Roosevelt elk.
- Scenic hiking trail through Fern Canyon.
- Trail runs close to the beach and offers beachside picnicking and camping.

History

Arthur Davidson migrated west in the 1880s and worked at the Lower and Upper Gold Bluff Mines and helped out at a nearby dairy. Within a decade he had his own dairy on a flat beside Prairie Creek. He cleared alders and willows to create more pastures. His land and family expanded, and his descendents owned the farm until 1991.

In 1948, a sawmill was built next to the old dairy. The Arcata Redwood Company built miles of logging roads into the surrounding forests. Acres of woodlands were cleared over the next two decades, until the sawmill closed its doors in 1970. The newly established Redwood National Park stepped in to cover the logging scars and established elk habitat on what was once the mill site.

Gold Bluffs Trail ends at Fern Canyon where Home Creek has carved through layers of ancient sediments. Native Americans came to such moist areas to collect black-stemmed five-fingered ferns, valued for use in basket weaving because of their color and fine stems.

Gold Bluffs Beach

Description

Gold Bluffs Trail is an easy drive through a variety of scenery in Redwood National Park and Prairie Creek Redwoods State Park. It starts on US 101 at Elk Meadows, where you have an excellent chance of seeing Roosevelt elk. Although the elk can often be seen close to the highway, it is much safer to park and view the animals at the Elk Meadows parking area near the start of the trail. Although the elk appear to be undisturbed by vehicles and humans, remember that they are wild animals and should not be approached. If you can't see any elk in the meadows, you may be able to see them at a spot farther down the trail, in the dunes along the beach.

The road winds through a lush coastal forest of alders, spruces, and redwoods, with a covering of moss and ferns. It enters Prairie Creek Redwoods State Park, which charges a small fee for day use, and continues close to the beach along the base of Gold Bluffs. There are coastal views and many points where you can park and walk to the beach. No vehicles are allowed on the beach. There is an exposed campground on the foreshore near the beach (additional fee required) and picnic areas for day use only.

Five-fingered ferns grow along the walls of Fern Canyon

Past the campground, low-clearance vehicles will need to take care crossing Squashan Creek. Although low-clearance vehicles often make the crossing in low water, you should walk from this point if there is any doubt.

The trail ends at the Fern Canyon Trailhead. The 0.8-mile loop that sets out

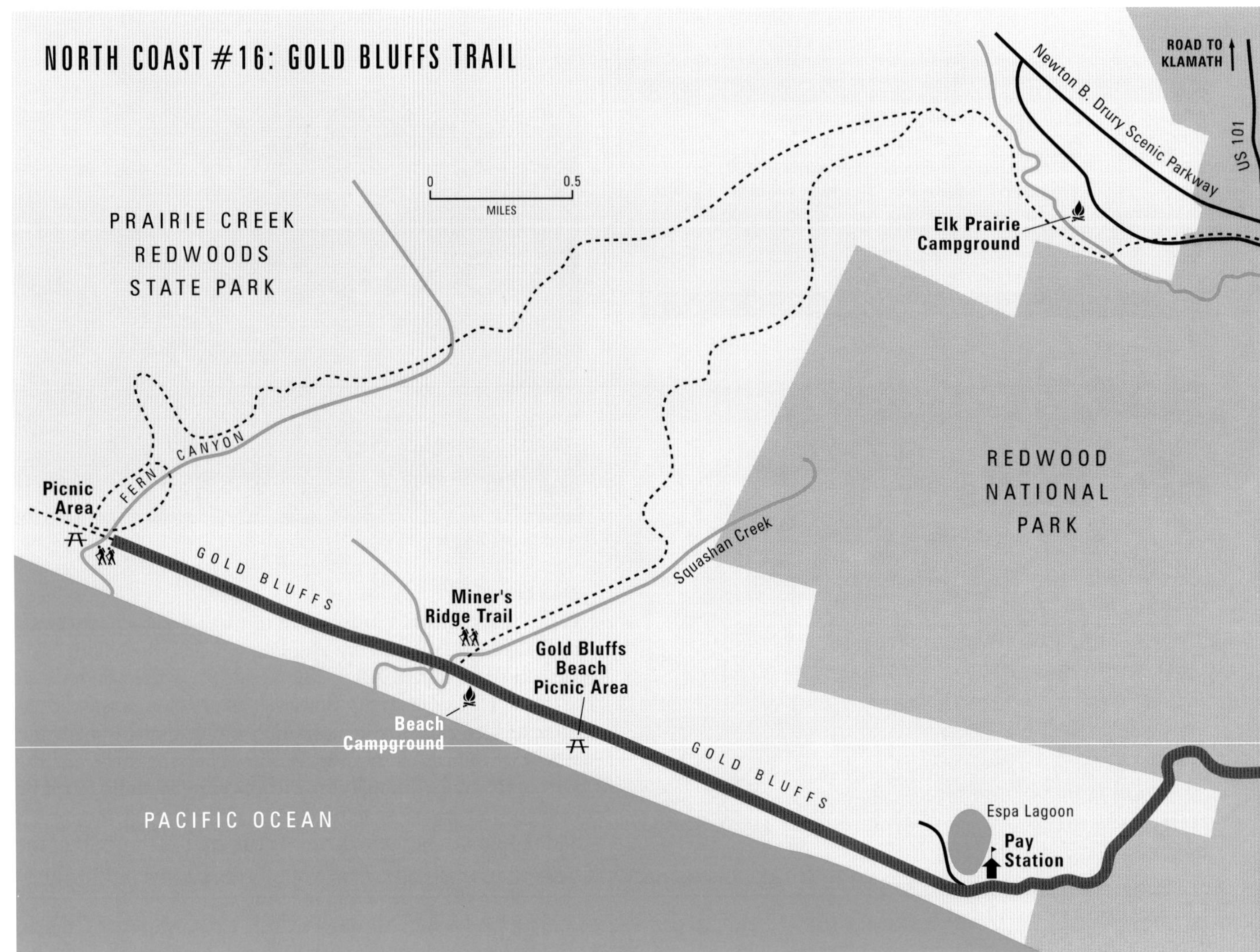

through Fern Canyon is not to be missed. The 50-foot-high canyon walls are covered with ferns, mostly five-fingered ferns, but also lady ferns and sword ferns. The canyon is habitat for eight species in all. Home Creek meanders through the canyon, and hikers have to cross it often so prepare for wet feet. The western red-legged frog and a rare species of tailed frog with a short, stumpy tail live in the canyon. These frogs can often be seen and heard along the damp banks of the creek. The Pacific giant salamander also lives in damp areas of the canyon. The hiking trail climbs out of the canyon and loops back to the parking area.

Current Road Information

Redwood National and State Parks
1111 Second Street
Crescent City, CA 95531
(707) 464-6101

Map References

BLM Orick
USFS Six Rivers National Forest
USGS 1:24,000 Orick, Fern Canyon
1:100,000 Orick
Maptech CD-ROM: North Coast/Eureka
Northern California Atlas & Gazetteer, p. 32
California Road & Recreation Atlas, p.
Trails Illustrated, Redwood National Park, North Coast State Parks, Smith River NRA (218)

Route Directions

▼ 0.0		From US 101, 2 miles north of Orick, zero trip meter and turn east on paved Davidson Road (FR 400), following the sign for Elk Meadows and Gold Bluffs Beach.
		GPS: N41°19.28′ W124°02.29′
▼ 0.1	SO	Elk Meadows parking area for elk viewing.
▼ 0.2	SO	Cross over Prairie Creek on bridge.
▼ 0.3	SO	Elk Meadows Day-use Area on left. Trillium Falls Trail, for hikers, leaves through the day-use area. Road turns to graded dirt. Davison Trail, for hikers, on right to Elk Prairie Campground.
		GPS: N41°19.49′ W124°02.56′
▼ 2.0	SO	Streelow Creek Trail, for hikers and mountain bikers, on right to Elk Prairie Campground.
▼ 2.8	SO	Entering Gold Bluffs Beach—part of Prairie Creek Redwoods State Park.
		GPS: N41°20.96′ W124°03.84′

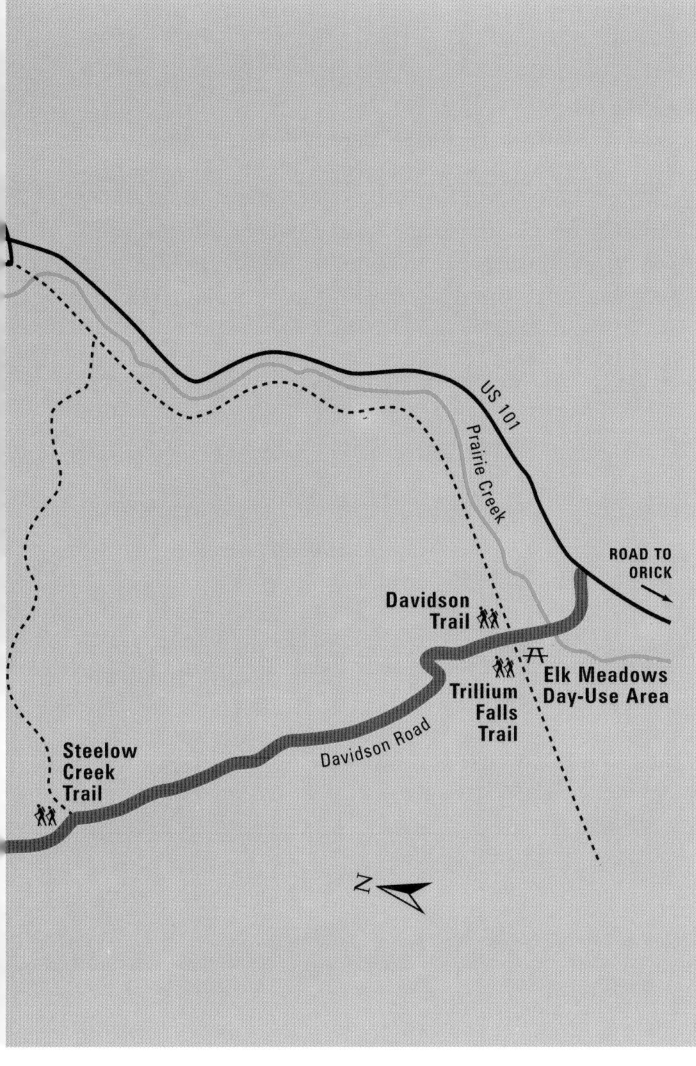

▼ 3.5	SO	Track on right is for authorized vehicles only. Parking area and beach access on left. Zero trip meter at fee station.
		GPS: N41°21.35′ W124°04.35′
▼ 0.0		Continue to the north.
▼ 0.1	BL	Track on right goes to Espa Lagoon. A parking area is immediately off the trail. Bear left following the sign for Beach Overlook.
▼ 0.2	SO	Pass through gate. Trail is now running beneath Gold Bluffs.
▼ 1.5	SO	Gold Bluffs Beach Picnic Area on left.
		GPS: N41°22.65′ W124°04.14′
▼ 2.0	SO	Beach Campground on left.
		GPS: N41°23.03′ W124°04.04′
▼ 2.1	SO	Miner's Ridge Trail on right goes to park headquarters; then cross through Squashan Creek; then pass through gate, which is open from 9 A.M. to 30 minutes after sunset.
▼ 2.2	SO	Cross through creek.
▼ 2.9	SO	Cross through creek.
▼ 3.1	SO	Parking area on left. In the future, the trail will end here and the hiking trail will extend to this point.
▼ 3.3		End of trail at the Fern Canyon trailhead and picnic area.
		GPS: N41°24.22′ W124°03.78

NORTH COAST #17

Bald Hills Road

Starting Point:	**California 169 at Martins Ferry**
Finishing Point:	**US 101, 0.5 miles north of Orick**
Total Mileage:	**30.9 miles**
Unpaved Mileage:	**21.2 miles**
Driving Time:	**3 hours**
Elevation Range:	**100–3,200 feet**
Usually Open:	**Year-round**
Best Time to Travel:	**Year-round**
Difficulty Rating:	**1**
Scenic Rating:	**10**
Remoteness Rating:	**+0**

Special Attractions

- Coast redwoods and Redwood National Park.
- Historic site of Lyons Ranch.
- Schoolhouse Peak Fire Lookout.

History

Bald Hills Road begins on the Klamath River at Martins Ferry. Just upstream is Weitchpec, an important Yurok settlement at the confluence of the Trinity and Klamath Rivers. The banks of the Klamath are within two Indian reservations: the Hoopa Valley Indian Reservation and the Yurok. The forests in the drainages of these two important rivers were valuable for game and collecting seeds and firewood. Villages built by the Yurok on flats along the Klamath include Waseck, formerly called Washekw, Kenek, now spelled Kanick (at the prime fishing spot of the Kenek

Bald Hills Road

Rapids), Kepel, Sa'a, Murekw, and Himetl.

Once over the crest of Schoolhouse Peak, at the southeastern end of the Bald Hills, the road enters Redwood National Park, established in 1968. It passes the historic Lyons Ranch, a cattle ranch started by Jonathon and Amelia Lyons in 1860. By the 1870s, they switched to raising sheep and continued to expand their property. The Lyons entered wool at a show in Paris and won an award that brought them worldwide recognition. As a result, their sheep fetched above average prices and their ranch holdings continued to grow. The family carried on their ranching tradition for more than a century.

Some of the tallest trees in the world can be found in Redwood National Park, in groves at the western end of Bald Hills Road. At 368 feet, an ancient redwood in the Tall Trees Grove is the tallest recorded tree in the world.

Description

This graded dirt road starts at Martins Ferry, on the east side of the Coast Ranges, crosses the Bald Hills into Redwood National Park, and ends near the Pacific Ocean north of Orick. The Humboldt County road is sporadically maintained and is often very washboardy. Drivers should be aware that fast-moving logging trucks use this road at all hours. It snakes up a long, gradually ascending grade to French Camp Ridge and then onto the Bald Hills. From the top of the sparsely vegetated ridge, there are views to the coast and back over the Kla-

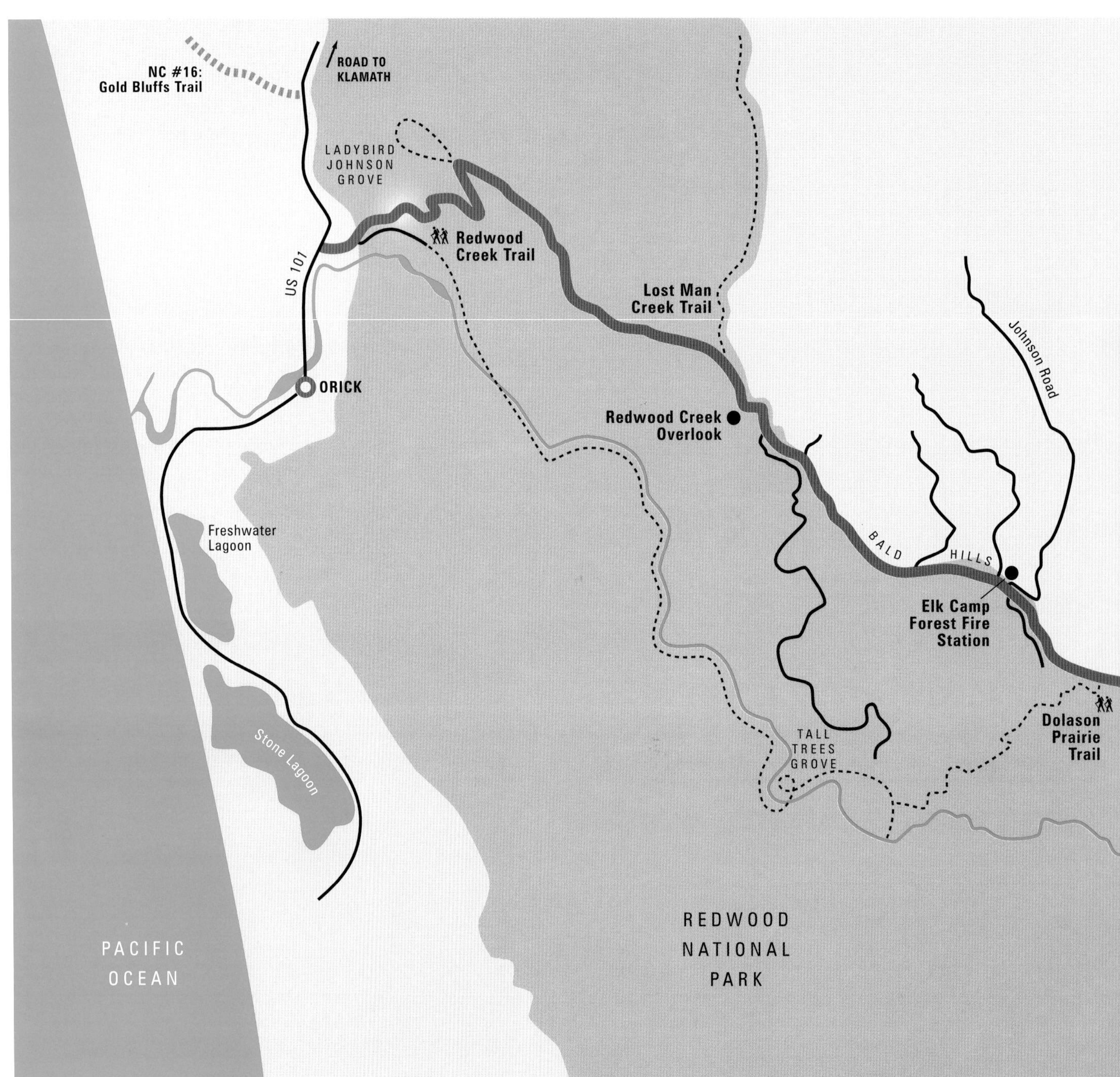

math River Basin toward the Klamath Mountains to the east.

A short, worthwhile side trip goes to the Schoolhouse Peak Fire Lookout (3,097 feet). You can drive the first 0.2 miles, then hike the remaining 0.2 miles to the tower, which sits on a bare peak overlooking the Bald Hills, Redwood Creek Basin, and the coast. The road enters Redwood National Park, passing the hiking trailhead to the Lyons Ranch historical site. A barn and the remains of an old bunkhouse are all that remain at this once sprawling ranch.

Additional hiking trails within the park lead to other points of interest. One popular trail is the Dolason Prairie Trail, a steep 9.5-mile round-trip for experienced hikers. The Lyons Barn is partway along this trail, which eventually connects to the Tall Trees Grove. The Tall Trees Grove can also be accessed by vehicle, but a permit is required from the national park office on the day of travel. The free permit gives the combination to a locked gate.

The trail dips into the lush, damp forest of alders and towering coast redwoods on the west side of the range. Redwoods need a mild, damp climate; coastal fog and the sheltered Redwood Creek Basin create excellent habitat.

The Redwood Creek Overlook views a patchwork of new and old growth forest along Redwood Creek. Interpretive information boards detail past and present restoration projects. The road joins the paved park road and finishes on US 101, just north of Orick.

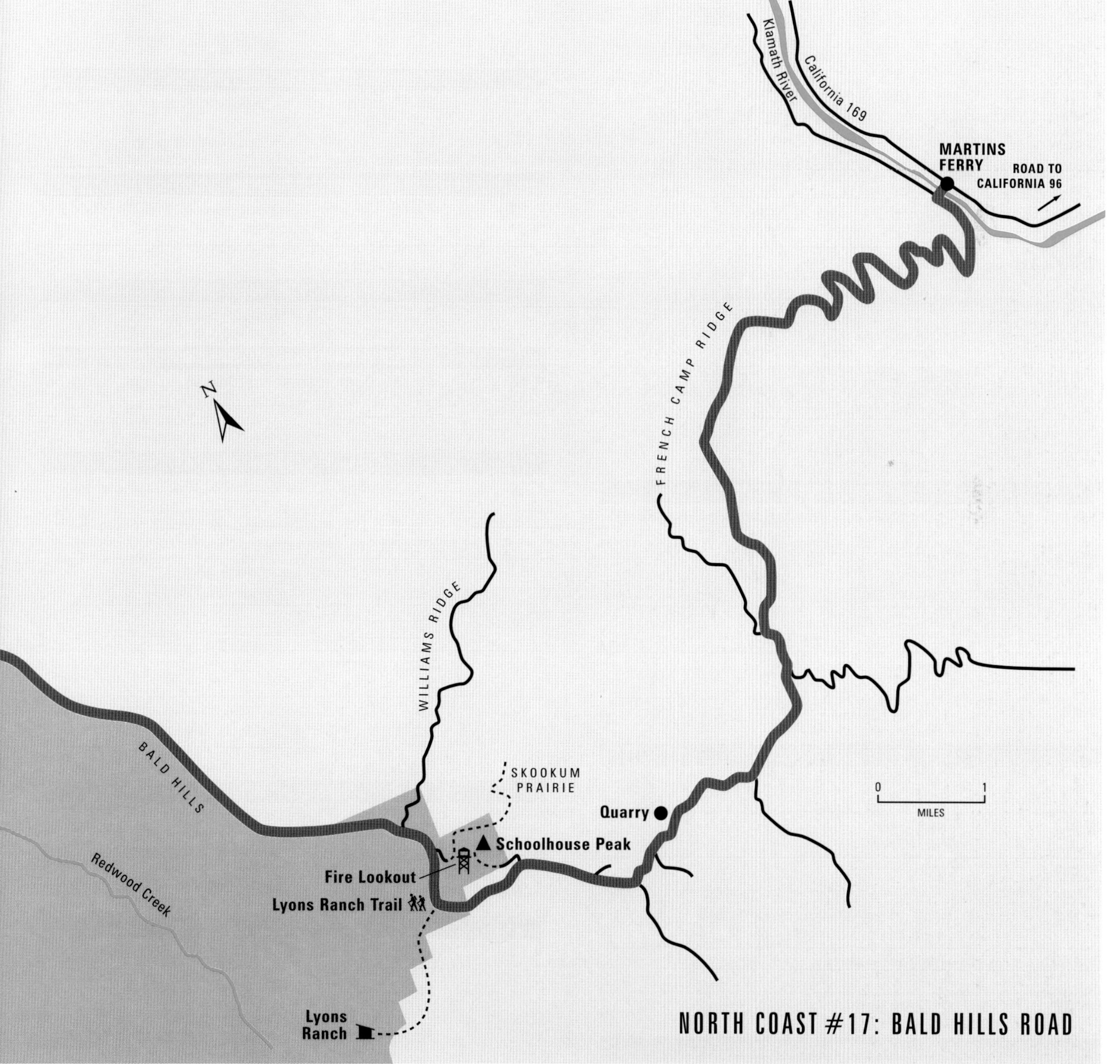

Current Road Information
Redwood National and State Parks
1111 Second Street
Crescent City, CA 95531
(707) 464-6101

Bureau of Land Management
Arcata Field Office
1695 Heindon Road
Arcata, CA 95521
(707) 825-2300

Map References
BLM Hoopa, Orick
USFS Six Rivers National Forest
USGS 1:24,000 French Camp Ridge, Bald Hills, Holter Ridge, Orick
1:100,000 Hoopa, Orick
Maptech CD-ROM: North Coast/Eureka
Northern California Atlas & Gazetteer, pp. 32, 33
California Road & Recreation Atlas, p. 44
Trails Illustrated, Redwood National Park, North Coast State Parks, Smith River NRA (218)
Other: Redwood National Park visitor map

Route Directions

▼ 0.0		From Weitchpec on California 96, at the intersection with California 169, zero trip meter and proceed west on California 169 for 3.4 miles to Martins Ferry. Zero trip meter and turn left (southwest) over the bridge, following sign for US 101 and Orick. Cross over the Klamath River on bridge.
13.7 ▲		Trail ends at T-intersection with paved California 169 at Martins Ferry. Turn right for California 96 and Weitchpec.
		GPS: N41°12.50' W123°45.26'
▼ 0.1	TL	T-intersection. Follow the sign to Orick. Road turns to graded dirt.
13.6 ▲	TR	Road continues straight ahead. Turn right and cross over the Klamath River on the Martins Ferry bridge.
▼ 0.4	SO	Track on left.
13.3 ▲	SO	Track on right.
▼ 1.0	BR	Track on left.
12.7 ▲	BL	Track on right.
▼ 9.3	SO	Track on right.
4.4 ▲	SO	Track on left.
		GPS: N41°09.77' W123°49.08'
▼ 9.7	SO	Track on left.
4.0 ▲	SO	Track on right.
▼ 10.9	SO	Track on left.
2.8 ▲	SO	Track on right.
▼ 11.8	SO	Quarry on right.
1.9 ▲	SO	Quarry on left.
▼ 12.3	SO	Track on left through closure gate.
1.4 ▲	SO	Track on right through closure gate.
▼ 12.6	SO	Two tracks on left.
1.1 ▲	SO	Two tracks on right.
▼ 13.0	SO	Track on right.
0.7 ▲	SO	Track on left.
		GPS: N41°08.61' W123°51.87'
▼ 13.7	SO	Unmarked track on sharp right goes 0.4 miles to the fire lookout on Schoolhouse Peak. There is a locked gate after 0.2 miles. Zero trip meter.
0.0 ▲		Continue to the east.
		GPS: N41°08.90' W123°52.54'
▼ 0.0		Continue to the southwest.
7.5 ▲	BR	Unmarked track on left goes 0.4 miles to the fire lookout on Schoolhouse Peak. There is a locked gate after 0.2 miles. Zero trip meter.
▼ 0.3	SO	Track on left.
7.2 ▲	SO	Track on right.
▼ 0.6	SO	Cattle guard. Entering Redwood National Park. Lyons Barn is downhill to the left.
6.9 ▲	SO	Cattle guard. Leaving Redwood National Park. Lyons Barn is downhill to the right.
		GPS: N41°08.79' W123°53.21'
▼ 0.9	BR	Track on left is the parking area for the Lyons Ranch Trailhead.
6.6 ▲	BL	Track on right is the parking area for the Lyons Ranch Trailhead.
		GPS: N41°08.90' W123°53.52'
▼ 1.5	BL	Track on right to Skookum Prairie—no motor vehicles.
6.0 ▲	BR	Track on left to Skookum Prairie—no motor vehicles.
		GPS: N41°09.36' W123°53.31'
▼ 1.8	SO	Graded road on right goes to Williams Ridge—closed to public use.
5.7 ▲	SO	Graded road on left goes to Williams Ridge—closed to public use.
		GPS: N41°09.55' W123°53.55'
▼ 6.3	SO	Track on left is Dolason Prairie Trail.
1.2 ▲	SO	Track on right is Dolason Prairie Trail.
		GPS: N41°12.35' W123°56.96'
▼ 7.5	SO	Elk Camp Forest Fire Station on right. Johnson Road on right. Zero trip meter.
0.0 ▲		Continue to the southeast. Road is now sporadically paved, turning to graded dirt.
		GPS: N41°13.31' W123°57.48'
▼ 0.0		Continue to the northwest. Road is now paved.
9.7 ▲	SO	Elk Camp Forest Fire Station on left. Johnson Road on left. Zero trip meter and follow the sign to Weitchpec.
▼ 0.1	SO	Track on right and track on left.
9.6 ▲	SO	Track on right and track on left.
▼ 0.8	SO	Track on right.
8.9 ▲	SO	Track on left.
▼ 2.3	SO	Track on right.
7.4 ▲	SO	Track on left.
▼ 2.8	SO	Tall Trees Grove access on left and track on right. Permit required for Tall Trees access road.
4.7 ▲	SO	Tall Trees Grove access on right and track on left. Permit required for Tall Trees access road.
		GPS: N41°15.24' W123°59.18'
▼ 3.3	SO	Redwood Creek Overlook on left.
6.4 ▲	SO	Redwood Creek Overlook on right.
		GPS: N41°15.49' W123°59.27'
▼ 3.7	SO	Lost Man Creek Trail for mountain bikes on right.
6.0 ▲	SO	Lost Man Creek Trail for mountain bikes on left.
		GPS: N41°15.83' W123°59.18'
▼ 7.1	SO	Ladybird Johnson Grove parking area on left; then pass under footbridge.
2.6 ▲	SO	Pass under footbridge; then Ladybird Johnson Grove parking area on right.
▼ 9.2	SO	Exiting Redwood National Park. Road on left to Redwood Creek Trail.

0.5 ▲	SO	Entering the Redwood National Park. Road on right to Redwood Creek Trail.
		GPS: N41°18.02′ W124°02.41′
▼ 9.7		Trail ends at T-intersection with US 101. Turn right for Klamath; turn left for Orick.
0.0 ▲		Trail commences on US 101, 0.5 miles north of Orick. Zero trip meter and turn southeast on paved road at the sign for Bald Hills Road, following sign for Ladybird Johnson Grove.
		GPS: N41°18.11′ W124°02.79′

NORTH COAST #18

Shelton Butte Trail

Starting Point:	**FR 10, 6.5 miles south of Orleans**
Finishing Point:	**Shelton Butte**
Total Mileage:	**9.6 miles (one-way)**
Unpaved Mileage:	**9.4 miles**
Driving Time:	**1 hour (one-way)**
Elevation Range:	**800–3,600 feet**
Usually Open:	**June to December**
Best Time to Travel:	**Dry weather**
Difficulty Rating:	**2**
Scenic Rating:	**9**
Remoteness Rating:	**+0**

Special Attractions

- Views from the old fire lookout site on Shelton Butte.
- Lightly traveled trail in Six Rivers National Forest.

History

Shelton Butte lies on the ancestral boundary of the Karok and Yurok tribal lands. Across the Klamath River from Shelton Butte, Bluff Creek, known as Iiinac in the Karok language, was the southern extent of the Karok's influence. The area downstream from Bluff Creek was considered Yuruk Veezivzaaneen (meaning "downriver country"), the ancestral domain of the Yurok.

The riverside settlement of Orleans, on California 96, is near the start of this trail. The Karok Va-araar, or "Upriver People," once had a village called Panamnik at this site. Although settlers disrupted the culture and natural environment of the Karok and Yurok, tribal members remain in this stunning deep valley country.

Description

Shelton Butte was once the site of a fire lookout tower because of its commanding views. The lookout tower is gone, and communications towers now stand on the butte. The roughly graded road to Shelton Butte's summit is lightly used, and it makes a lovely out-and-back drive for high-clearance vehicles.

Initially, the trail is easygoing, although it can be somewhat washboardy as it travels along a wide shelf road through the lush coastal forests of Six Rivers National Forest. Rockslides are common in this wet region, so be prepared to find boulders and loose rock on the road.

The trail climbing to Shelton Butte

Past the turnoff to Hoopa (10N05), the road becomes a spur and starts the final climb up to the butte. This section is not used as much as the earlier part of the trail and is best traveled in dry weather; the shelf road can become extremely greasy and dangerous when wet. The final section spirals up to the lookout site and offers great views over Six Rivers National Forest and the coastal mountains. Below is the Klamath River and Big Bar river access point.

This trail makes for a beautiful autumn drive, with bigleaf maples providing a radiant golden color.

Current Road Information

Six Rivers National Forest
Orleans Ranger District
Highway 96
Orleans, CA 95556
(530) 627-3291

Map References

BLM Hoopa
USFS Klamath National Forest; Six Rivers National Forest
USGS 1:24,000 Orleans, Hopkins Butte, Weitchpec
1:100,000 Hoopa
Maptech CD-ROM: North Coast/Eureka
Northern California Atlas & Gazetteer, p. 33
California Road & Recreation Atlas, p. 45

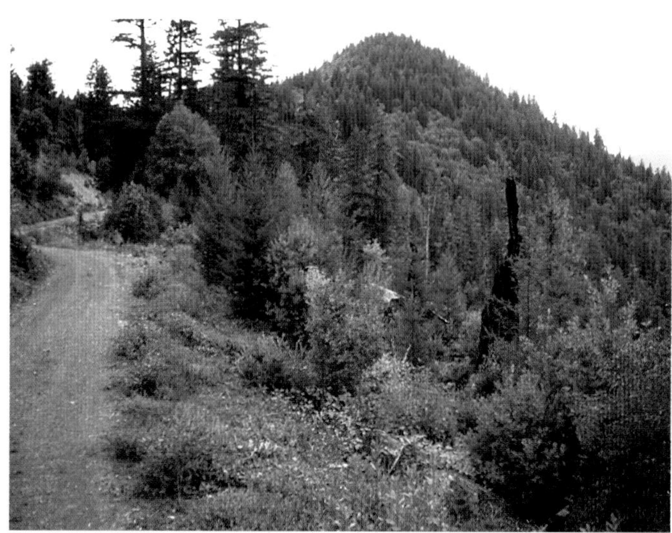
Shelton Butte

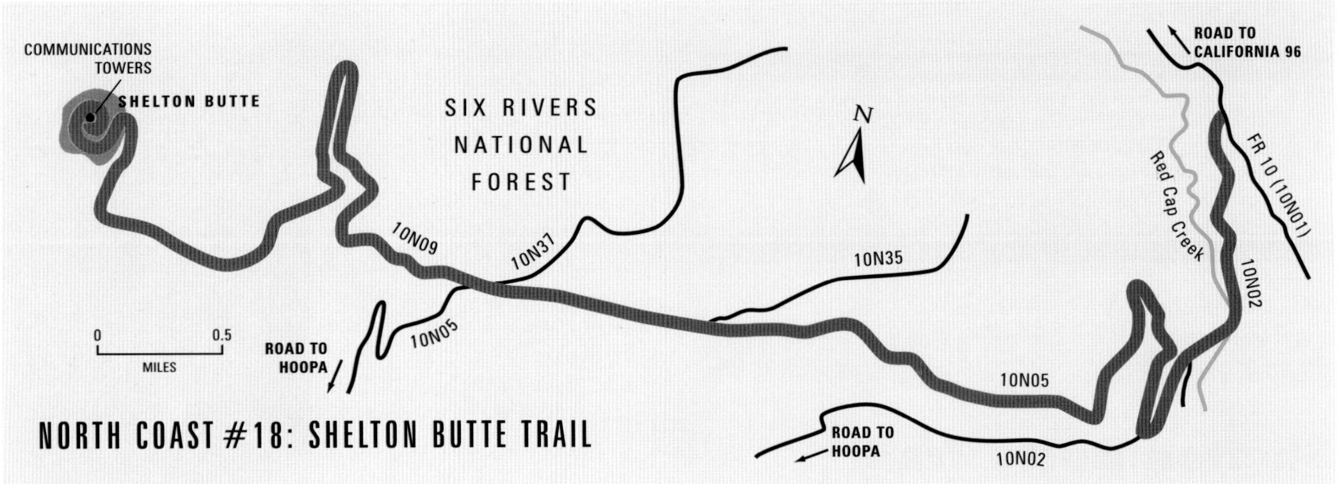

Route Directions

▼ 0.0		From Orleans on California 96, at the north side of the bridge over the Klamath River, zero trip meter and turn southeast on paved Redcap Road and proceed 5 miles. Pass paved road on right and continue straight ahead. The road becomes FR 10 (10N01). Continue straight ahead for another 1.5 miles to the intersection with 10N02. Zero trip meter and turn south onto 10N02, also marked CD12, following the sign to Mill Creek Gap and Hoopa.
1.5 ▲		Trail ends at intersection with paved FR 10 (10N01). Turn left onto this road and proceed 6.5 miles to Orleans and California 96.
		GPS: N41°15.25' W123°32.83'
▼ 0.8	SO	Road becomes paved.
0.7 ▲	SO	Road turns back to graded dirt.
▼ 0.9	SO	Cross over Red Cap Creek on bridge.
0.6 ▲	SO	Cross over Red Cap Creek on bridge.
▼ 1.0	SO	Track on left. Road turns back to graded dirt.
0.5 ▲	SO	Track on right. Road is now paved.
▼ 1.2	SO	Track on left.
0.3 ▲	SO	Track on right.
▼ 1.5	TR	Road 10N02 continues straight ahead to Hoopa. Zero trip meter and turn right onto 10N05, following the sign to Shelton Butte.
0.0 ▲		Continue to the east.
		GPS: N41°14.08' W123°32.85'
▼ 0.0		Continue to the northwest.
4.0 ▲	TL	T-intersection with 10N02. To the right goes to Hoopa. Zero trip meter and follow the sign to Orleans.
▼ 3.1	SO	Track on right is 10N35.
0.9 ▲	SO	Track on left is 10N35.
		GPS: N41°14.08' W123°34.99'
▼ 4.0	BR	Track on right is 10N37; then track on left is the continuation of 10N05 to Hoopa. Zero trip meter and bear right onto 10N09, following the sign to Shelton Butte.
0.0 ▲		Continue to the east.
		GPS: N41°14.05' W123°35.96'
▼ 0.0		Continue to the west.
▼ 2.3	SO	Seasonal closure gate.
		GPS: N41°14.10' W123°36.97'
▼ 3.1	SO	Seasonal closure gate.
▼ 4.1		Communications towers on Shelton Butte.
		GPS: N41°14.30' W123°37.90'

NORTH COAST #19

Patterson Road

Starting Point:	**Ti-Bar Road, 3.8 miles northeast of California 96**
Finishing Point:	**California 96, 8 miles north of Somes Bar**
Total Mileage:	**8.9 miles**
Unpaved Mileage:	**8.9 miles**
Driving Time:	**1 hour**
Elevation Range:	**800–2,800 feet**
Usually Open:	**May to January**
Best Time to Travel:	**Dry weather**
Difficulty Rating:	**2**
Scenic Rating:	**8**
Remoteness Rating:	**+0**

Special Attractions

- Fall color viewing.
- Can be combined with North Coast #20: Ukonom Mountain Trail for a longer trip.
- This region of Klamath National Forest has the most Bigfoot sightings in North America.

History

Patterson Road travels along the eastern slope of the Klamath River Valley. Many Indian camps and villages once dotted the valley. Patterson Road's start near the Ti Bar Forest Service Station is near the site of a former Karok village called Tiih. Persido Bar, north of Ti Bar, was Pasiru Uuvree, another Karok village. The southern end of the trail exits the dense forest at Sandy Bar, the site of Iinpiit. The Karok relied on the Klamath River for fish and as a corridor for travel and trade. Skilled craftsmen carved canoes from redwood, taking many months to create one of the hand-hewn canoes.

Settlers disrupted life in this idyllic valley. Diseases annihilated entire villages. Mountain men who passed through the region on their way to trap beaver were surprised to find villages deserted when they returned. All of the inhabitants had died. Although the trappers moved on as quickly as possible for fear of catching an illness, it seems they themselves may have unknowingly spread the diseases.

This region of California boasts the largest number of Bigfoot (Sasquatch) sightings in North America. Indeed, California 96 is called the Bigfoot Highway, and the nearby town of Happy Camp hosts an annual Bigfoot Festival in summer. Whether or not you believe stories of the giant, keep an eye out as you travel these back roads. You just never know.

Description

Patterson Road travels through Klamath National Forest on the west side of the Marble Mountain Wilderness. The easy trail is a pretty drive and can be combined with North Coast #20: Ukonom Mountain Trail for a longer trip. The wet Pacific Coast forest is dense, with vine-covered trees and blackberry bushes in gullies. Trees here include California Bays, madrones, red alders, and bigleaf maples. Ti Creek, near the start of the trail, flows through a dense thicket of alders.

This trail does not appear in its entirety on topographical maps of the region.

Current Road Information

Six Rivers National Forest
Orleans Ranger District
Highway 96
Orleans, CA 95556
(530) 627-3291

Map References

BLM Happy Camp, Hoopa
USFS Klamath National Forest
USGS 1:24,000 Dillon Mt., Ukonom Mt., Bark Shanty Gulch
1:100,000 Happy Camp, Hoopa
Maptech CD-ROM: North Coast/Eureka
Northern California Atlas & Gazetteer, pp. 23, 24, 33, 34

Ti Creek

California Road & Recreation Atlas, p. 45 (incomplete)
Other: A Guide to the Marble Mountain Wilderness & Russian Wilderness

Route Directions

▼ 0.0		From California 96, 25.5 miles south of Happy Camp at county mile marker 12.18, zero trip meter and turn east onto Ti-Bar Road (13N11), following sign for the Wildlands Fire Station. Proceed 3.8 miles on Ti-Bar Road to the start of the trail. Zero trip meter and turn east on 13N11. Pass through seasonal closure gate.
3.3 ▲		Trail ends at intersection with 14N01. Turn right onto 14N01 for North Coast #20: Ukonom Mountain Trail; turn left onto 13N11 for California 96.
		GPS: N41°32.61′ W123°30.11′
▼ 0.5	SO	Track on right.
2.8 ▲	SO	Track on left.
▼ 1.1	SO	Track on left is 13N11J; then second track on left is 13N15 and track on right is 13N11D.
2.2 ▲	SO	Track on left is 13N11D and track on right is 13N15; then second track on right is 13N11J.
		GPS: N41°32.03′ W123°29.48′
▼ 1.8	SO	Cross over Ti Creek on bridge.
1.5 ▲	SO	Cross over Ti Creek on bridge.
		GPS: N41°31.92′ W123°28.83′

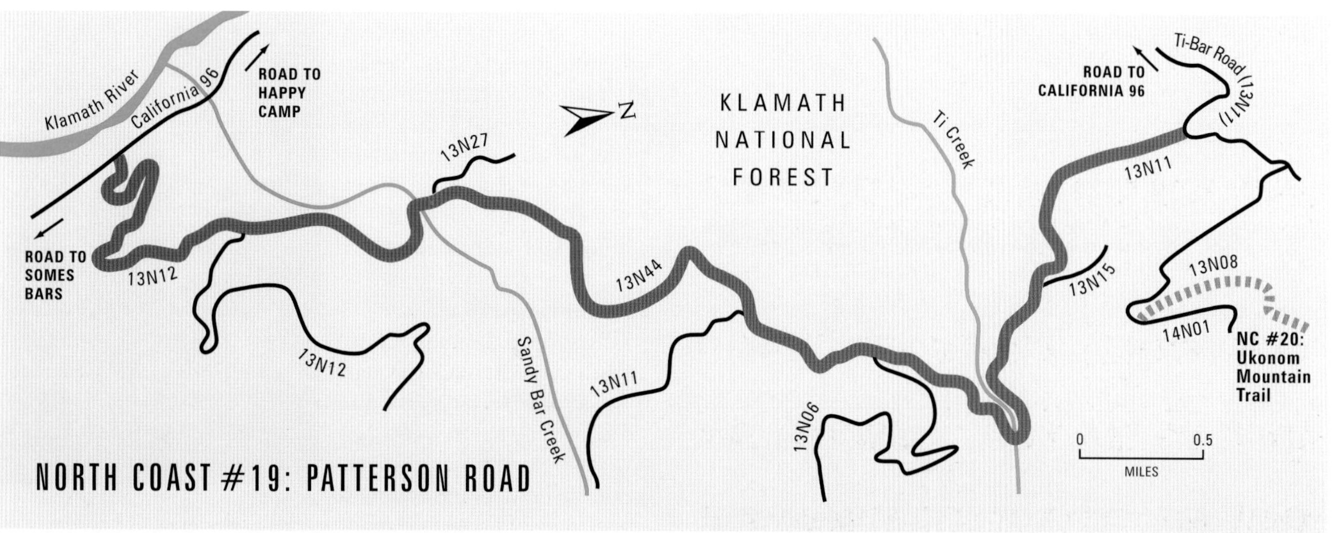

Fall colors along the trail

▼	▲		
▼ 2.7		SO	Track on left is 13N06.
	0.6 ▲	SO	Track on right is 13N06.
			GPS: N41°31.42' W123°29.29'
▼ 3.3		TR	Road 13N11 continues straight ahead. Zero trip meter and turn right onto 13N44.
	0.0 ▲		Continue to the northeast.
			GPS: N41°31.00' W123°29.48'
▼ 0.0			Continue to the northwest.
	5.6 ▲	TL	T-intersection with 13N11. Zero trip meter.
▼ 0.1		SO	Pass through seasonal closure gate.
	5.5 ▲	SO	Pass through seasonal closure gate.
▼ 0.7		SO	Track on left.
	4.9 ▲	SO	Track on right.
▼ 2.4		BL	Seasonal closure gate; then track on right though gate is 13N40.
	3.2 ▲	BR	Track on left through gate is 13N40; then pass through seasonal closure gate.
			GPS: N41°30.10' W123°30.20'
▼ 2.6		TL	T-intersection. Track on right is 13N27. Turn left and cross over Sandy Bar Creek.
	3.0 ▲	TR	Cross over Sandy Bar Creek; then track straight ahead is 13N27. Remain on 13N44.
			GPS: N41°29.96' W123°30.21'
▼ 2.8		SO	Track on left.
	2.8 ▲	SO	Track on right.
▼ 3.0		SO	Track on left to private property.
	2.6 ▲	SO	Track on right to private property.
▼ 3.1		SO	Track on right and track on left to private property.
	2.5 ▲	SO	Track on left and track on right to private property.
▼ 3.8		TR	T-intersection with 13N12.
	1.8 ▲	TL	Turn left onto 13N44. Turn is on a sharp right-hand bend.
			GPS: N41°29.29' W123°30.21'
▼ 4.5		SO	Track on left.
	1.1 ▲	SO	Track on right.
▼ 5.6			Trail ends at T-intersection with California 96. Turn left for Somes Bar; turn right for Happy Camp.
	0.0 ▲		Trail commences on California 96, 8 miles north of Somes Bar, 0.1 miles northwest of county mile marker 8.51. Zero trip meter and turn northeast on graded dirt road, marked Patterson Road (13N12) to Sandy Bar Creek.
			GPS: N41°28.91' W123°30.63'

Ukonom Mountain Trail

Starting Point:	**14N01, 5.4 miles northeast of California 96**
Finishing Point:	**Ukonom Mountain Fire Lookout**
Total Mileage:	**4 miles (one-way)**
Unpaved Mileage:	**4 miles**
Driving Time:	**30 minutes (one-way)**
Elevation Range:	**3,000–4,500 feet**
Usually Open:	**Late May to mid October**
Best Time to Travel:	**May to October**
Difficulty Rating:	**3**
Scenic Rating:	**8**
Remoteness Rating:	**+0**

Special Attractions

- Fall color viewing.
- Ukonom Mountain Fire Lookout.
- Views of the Klamath River Valley and Marble Mountain Wilderness.
- Can be combined with North Coast #19: Patterson Road to make a longer trip.

History

Ukonom Mountain (4,581 feet) was likely named for a nearby Native American village called Yuhnaam. Yuhnaam may have described the Klamath River flat on which the settlement was built. Blue Nose Bluff, another feature on the river, rises above the west bank of the Klamath at the foot of Ukonom Mountain. Nova Scotians, called Blue Noses, arrived in the vicinity in the 1890s. They established the Blue Nose Mine and built the Blue Nose Bridge across the Klamath River below the bluff in 1891.

The Ukonom Mountain Fire Lookout provides views northeast to the Kelsey Range, part of the Siskiyou Mountains. The Kelsey Pack Trail was an early mountain route that connected Crescent City with communities along the Klamath River.

Shelf road around the edge of Ukonom Mountain

Description

This short trail gradually ascends a shelf road through lush coastal forest to the fire lookout at the top of Ukonom Mountain. Vegetation includes alders, birches, madrones, and the verdant undergrowth of the moist forests found on the western, wetter slopes of these mountains. As the trail climbs, the vegetation opens up to give views over the surrounding forest. The trail you see below encircles Ukonom Mountain but does not lead to the lookout.

The concrete block fire lookout on Ukonom Mountain is manned seven days a week during fire season, from late May to mid October. If you are planning to drive the trail at the start or near the end of the fire season, call ahead to see if the gate to the tower is open. The gate is locked in the off-season making the trail inaccessible to vehicles. You are normally able to climb to the tower with permission from the lookout on duty. On a clear day, you will have excellent views of the Klamath River Valley and the Marble Mountain Wilderness. Dillon Creek USFS Campground is directly below the tower on the river.

The trail's 3 rating comes from the steep climb at the end, and the narrow sections of shelf road that have limited passing places. The region has abundant wildlife; look out for black bears, deer, squirrels, and smaller animals.

Current Road Information

Six Rivers National Forest
Orleans Ranger District
Highway 96
Orleans, CA 95556
(530) 627-3291

Map References

BLM Happy Camp
USFS Klamath National Forest
USGS 1:24,000 Ukonom Mt.
1:100,000 Happy Camp
Maptech CD-ROM: North Coast/Eureka
Northern California Atlas & Gazetteer, p. 24
California Road & Recreation Atlas, p. 45
Other: A Guide to the Marble Mountain Wilderness & Russian Wilderness

Ukonom Mountain Fire Lookout

Route Directions

▼ 0.0		From California 96, 25.5 miles south of Happy Camp at county mile marker 12.18, zero trip meter and turn east onto Ti-Bar Road (13N11), following the sign for the Wildlands Fire Station. Turn onto 14N01 after 3.8 miles, following signs for the lookout. Total distance from California 96 to the start of the trail is 5.4 miles. Zero trip meter and turn northwest on graded dirt road 13N08, following the sign to Ukonom Lookout.
		GPS: N41°32.37' W123°29.27'
▼ 0.1	SO	Seasonal closure gate.
▼ 0.5	SO	Viewpoint on left.
▼ 1.5	SO	Track on left is 13N08D—closed to vehicles.
		GPS: N41°33.40' W123°28.72'
▼ 2.2	SO	Track on right is 14N22.
▼ 2.7	SO	Track on left is 13N08B—closed to vehicles.
		GPS: N41°34.08' W123°28.55'
▼ 3.3	SO	Seasonal closure gate.
▼ 4.0		Trail ends at the Ukonom Mountain Fire Lookout.
		GPS: N41°35.04' W123°28.50'

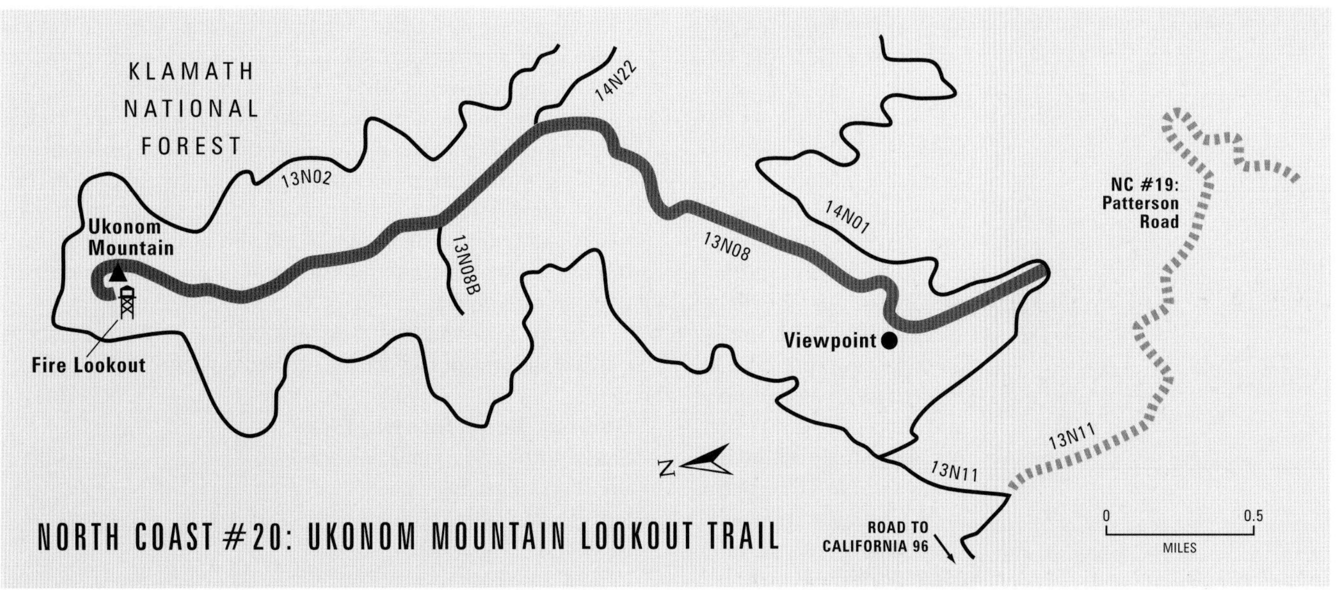

NORTH COAST #21

Hennessy Ridge Road

Starting Point:	**California 299, 2.7 miles north of Burnt Ranch**
Finishing Point:	**California 299 at Burnt Ranch**
Total Mileage:	**11.7 miles, plus 2.7-mile spur along Hennessy Ridge**
Unpaved Mileage:	**9.8 miles, plus 2.7-mile spur**
Driving Time:	**1.25 hours**
Elevation Range:	**900–3,500 feet**
Usually Open:	**May to December**
Best Time to Travel:	**May to December**
Difficulty Rating:	**2**
Scenic Rating:	**8**
Remoteness Rating:	**+0**

Special Attractions

- World's largest tanoak tree.
- Views into the South Fork of the Trinity River Valley.

History

Hennessy Ridge Road parallels a ridge-top pack trail of the late 1800s used by miners working claims along the South Fork of the Trinity River. The trail connected remote mining camps with the towns of Salyer to the north on the Trinity River and Hyampom to the south, on the South Fork of the Trinity. Hennessy Ridge is the watershed between the South Fork of the Trinity and Trinity Rivers.

Hiking trail to the record tree

Salmon from the South Fork of the Trinity River was a significant food source for the Wintun; miners also took advantage of the fish. Mining, however, reduced the number of fish spawning in the river. It wasn't until the 1910s that rivers in this vicinity recovered from the effects of mining projects.

Landslides and unstable soils are common in this region of steep slopes and deep canyons. A major landslide following heavy rains in 1890 swept away Chinese miners who were taking refuge in a cabin at Burnt Ranch.

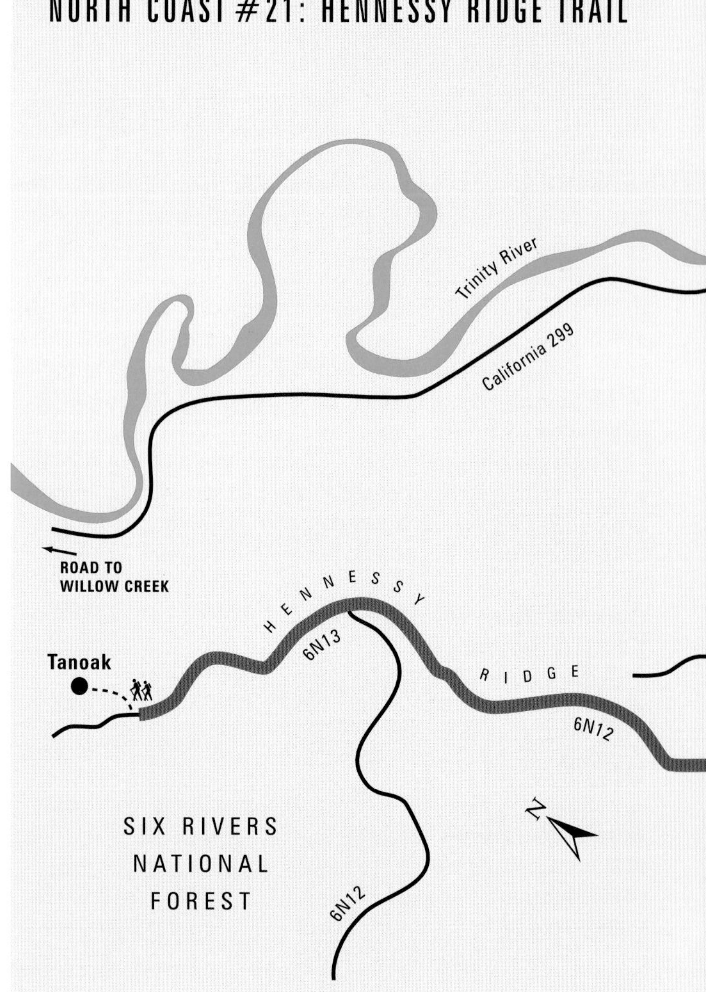

Description

This narrow graded road starts on California 299 near the Six Rivers National Forest's Gray Falls Campground on the Trinity River. The trail is easygoing, but a few rough spots make high-clearance preferable. Much of the trail is single vehicle width shelf road with ample passing places. It ends upstream on the Trinity River, at Burnt Ranch on California 299.

The trees here are predominantly Douglas firs and bigleaf maples, which provide a nice display of golden color in the fall. The world's largest tanoak is near the end of a spur. The massive tree measures more than 22 feet around its girth. The tree is marked by a small sign at the end of the spur trail. You can reach it by hiking about 100 yards or so along a steep path that can be slippery.

The forest service may close this trail during wet weather to prevent the spread of Port Orford cedar root rot.

Current Road Information

Shasta-Trinity National Forests
Big Bar Ranger District
Star Route 1, Box 10
Big Bar, CA 96010
(530) 623-6106

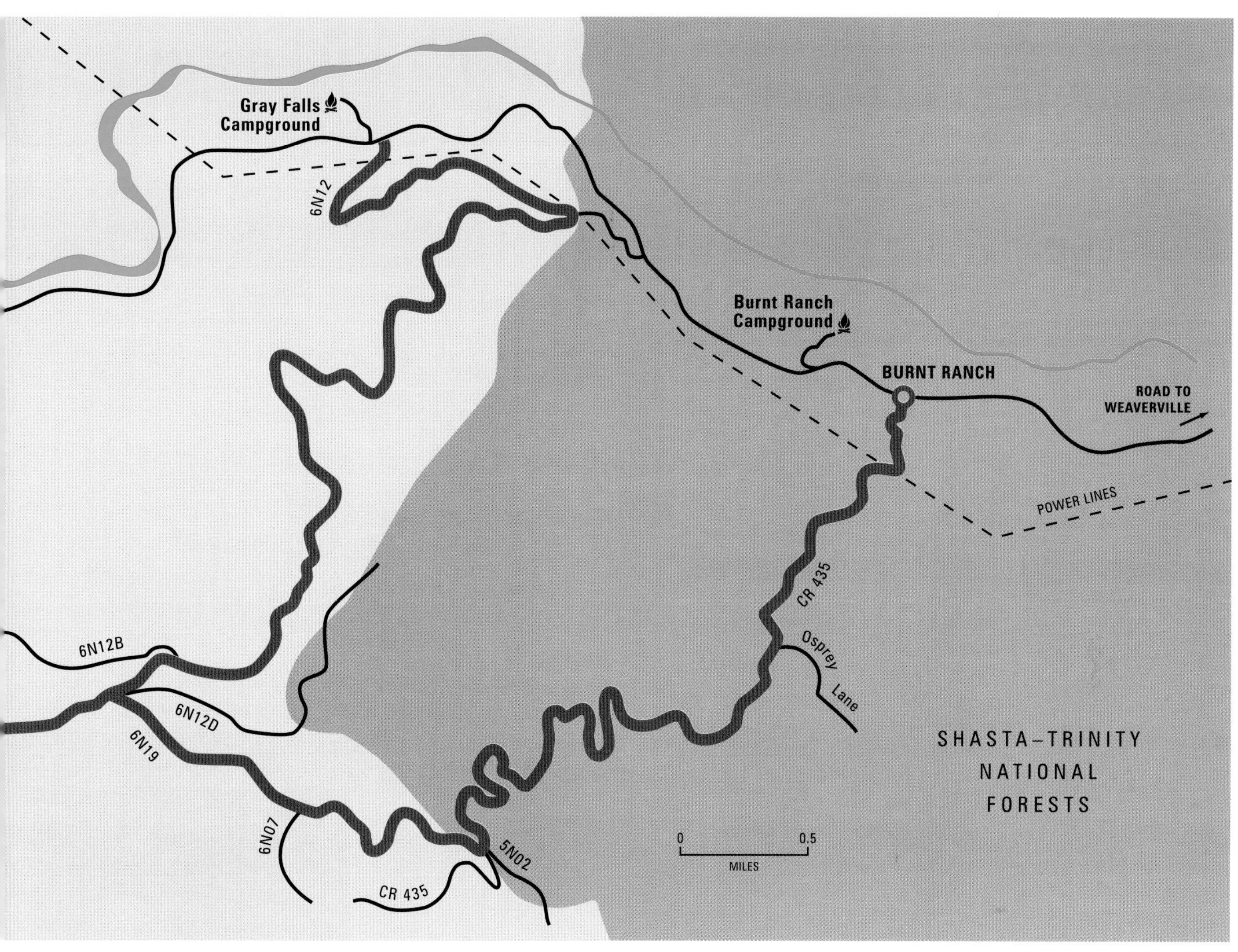

Map References

BLM Hayfork

USFS Six Rivers National Forest; Shasta-Trinity National Forests

USGS 1:24,000 Ironside Mt., Hennessy Peak, Salyer
1:100,000 Hayfork

Maptech CD-ROM: North Coast/Eureka

Northern California Atlas & Gazetteer, pp. 43, 44

California Road & Recreation Atlas, p. 51

Route Directions

▼ 0.0 From the Trinity Scenic Byway (California 299), 2.7 miles north of Burnt Ranch, 11.6 miles southeast of Willow Creek, zero trip meter and turn southwest on graded dirt road 6N12. The turn is immediately east of the Gray Falls USFS Campground at Trinity County mile marker 7.73.

5.5 ▲ Trail ends at T-intersection with the Trinity Scenic Byway (California 299). Turn right for Weaverville; turn left for Willow Creek.

GPS: N40°51.27' W123°29.44'

▼ 0.2 SO Track on left.

5.3 ▲ SO Track on right.

▼ 0.4 SO Track on right.

5.1 ▲ SO Track on left.

▼ 1.4 SO Track on right into quarry; then track on left under power lines.

4.1 ▲ SO Track on right under power lines; then track on left into quarry.

▼ 5.1 BL Track on right is 6N12B.

0.4 ▲ SO Track on left is 6N12B.

GPS: N40°50.73' W123°31.80'

▼ 5.5 TL 5-way intersection. Track on right; then second track on right is the continuation of 6N12 and the spur along Hennessy Ridge. Track on left is 6N12D. Zero trip meter and turn second left onto 6N19, following the sign to Hennessy Peak.

0.0 ▲ Continue to the northeast.

GPS: N40°50.92' W123°32.13'

Spur along Hennessy Ridge

▼ 0.0 Proceed west on 6N12 from the 5-way intersection.

▼ 1.7 SO Track on right.

▼ 1.8 SO 6N12 continues around to the left. Join 6N13.

GPS: N40°52.21' W123°32.83'

▼ 1.9 SO Track on right.

▼ 2.7 Small sign on right points to the record tanoak

tree. Follow the hiking trail for 100 yards to the tree. The vehicle trail continues 0.6 miles past this point to a locked gate.

GPS: N40°52.48' W123°33.73'

Continuation of Main Trail

▼ 0.0		Continue to the southeast.
6.2 ▲	TR	5-way intersection. Track straight ahead is 6N12, the spur along Hennessy Ridge. Track on right is 6N12D; then second track on right is 6N12; then third track on right. Zero trip meter and turn second right onto 6N12, following the sign to California 299.
		GPS: N40°50.92' W123°32.13'
▼ 0.9	BL	Track on right is 6N07; then track on left.
5.3 ▲	BR	Track on right; then track on left is 6N07.
▼ 1.9	TL	Track on left; then 4-way intersection. Straight ahead is 5N02. Track on left and track on right is Hennessy Road (CR 435). Turn left and join this road.
4.3 ▲	TR	4-way intersection. Track on left is 5N02. CR 435 continues straight ahead. Turn right on onto 6N19; then track on right.
		GPS: N40°49.61' W123°31.65'
▼ 3.3	BL	Turnout on right.
2.9 ▲	BR	Turnout on left.
▼ 4.0	SO	Track on left.
2.2 ▲	SO	Track on right.
▼ 4.1	SO	Track on right.
2.1 ▲	SO	Track on left.
▼ 4.3	SO	Road becomes paved; then Osprey Lane on right. Remain on main paved road.
1.9 ▲	SO	Osprey Lane on left. Road turns to graded dirt.
▼ 6.2		Trail ends at T-intersection with California 299 at Burnt Ranch. Turn right for Weaverville; turn left for Willow Creek.
0.0 ▲		Trail commences on California 299 at Burnt Ranch. Zero trip meter and turn southwest on paved Hennessy Road (CR 435). The road is opposite the Burnt Ranch post office.
		GPS: N40°49.32' W123°28.94'

NORTH COAST #22

Hobo Gulch Trail

Starting Point:	**California 299, 8 miles east of Big Bar**
Finishing Point:	**Hobo Gulch USFS Campground**
Total Mileage:	**15.7 miles (one-way)**
Unpaved Mileage:	**11.9 miles**
Driving Time:	**1.5 hours (one-way)**
Elevation Range:	**1,400–4,100 feet**
Usually Open:	**Year-round**
Best Time to Travel:	**Dry weather**
Difficulty Rating:	**2**
Scenic Rating:	**9**
Remoteness Rating:	**+1**

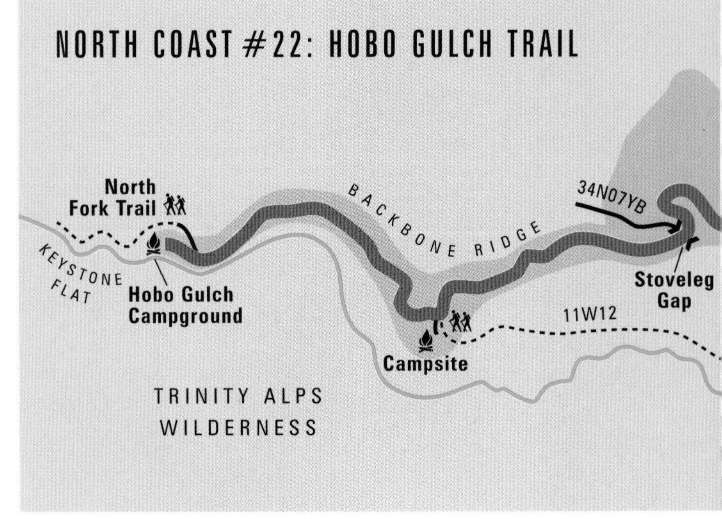

Special Attractions

- Fishing on the North Fork of the Trinity River.
- Fall color viewing.
- Access to hiking trails into the Trinity Alps Wilderness.

History

Many mines were established on the North Fork of the Trinity River in the latter half of the nineteenth century. Helena, known as North Fork until 1891, was a vital supply town for mining camps in the vicinity. This ghost town supported a brewery, hotel, livery stable, trading post, and blacksmith shop in the 1850s. Christian Meckel's red brick hotel, built in 1858, testifies to the town's once thriving past. When North Fork was renamed, it honored Helena, Christian's wife and daughter of the postmaster.

In the 1880s, pack trains from North Fork used the narrow trails across Keystone Flat to supply miners who rushed into the vicinity of the New River deep in the Trinity Mountains. Hydraulic monitors and bucket line dredges were used in mines upstream from old North Fork. Evidence remains in the form of mine tailings along the riverbank.

Hobo Gulch Campground on the North Fork of the Trinity River

Hobo Gulch may have been named for Hobo Dick, a regular at a Junction City bar. Ironically, Dick died after traversing Backbone Ridge on his way to Keystone Flat on a hot day and quenching his thirst too quickly and with too much water from the North Fork of the Trinity River.

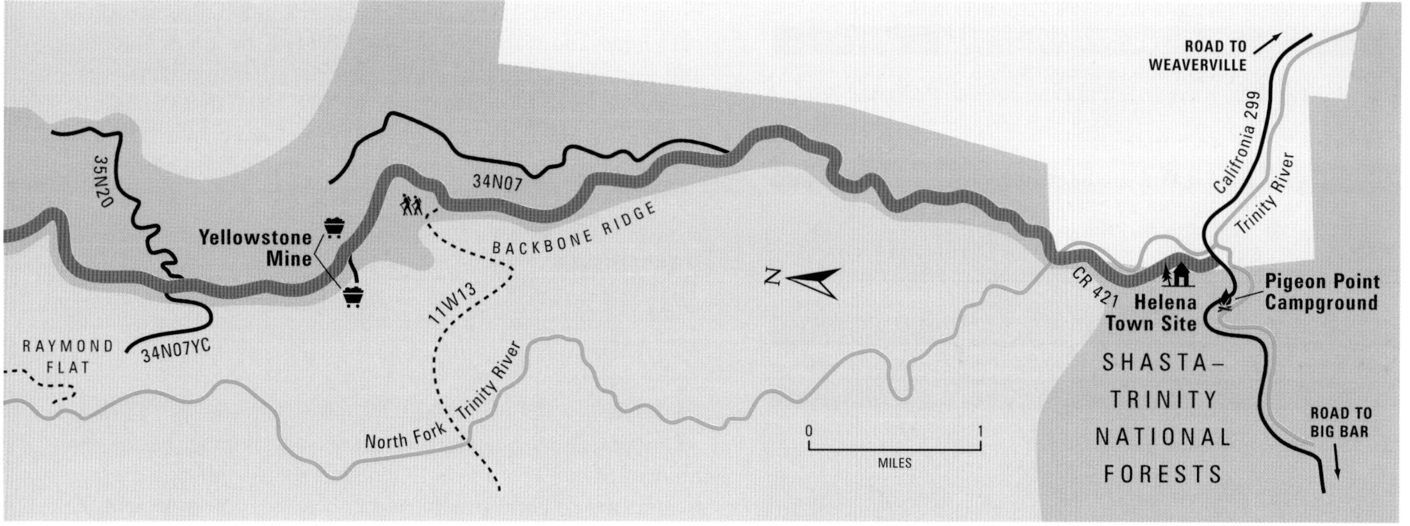

Description

Hobo Gulch Trail travels a vehicle corridor into the Trinity Alps Wilderness and ends at the Hobo Gulch USFS Campground and North Fork Trailhead.

The route starts at the site of Helena on California 299. There are a number of BLM and USFS campgrounds along the Trinity River near the start of this trail with access to rafting and fishing on the river.

North of Helena, the route turns off the paved road to follow a narrow, graded road that winds gradually up toward Backbone Ridge. The trail is spectacular in fall, when bigleaf maples turn to gold and dogwoods become salmon pink. Although trees on the ridge top may obscure some views, there are many opportunities to look down into the North Fork of the Trinity River Valley and west to Limestone Ridge.

The trail finishes at the extremely pretty wooded riverside Hobo Gulch USFS Campground. The semi-developed campground has tables and a pit toilet, but no other facilities. The North Fork Trail for hikers and equestrians leads into the Trinity Alps Wilderness sites of Bear Wallow Meadow and Grizzly Meadow. Horses are not allowed in the main campground, but there are corrals and campsites at the trailhead. A wilderness permit is required for hiking into the Trinity Alps Wilderness.

Current Road Information

Shasta-Trinity National Forests
Big Bar Ranger District
Star Route 1, Box 10
Big Bar, CA 96010
(530) 623-6106

Map References

BLM Hayfork
USFS Shasta-Trinity National Forests
USGS 1:24,000 Helena, Deddrick, Thurston Peaks
1:100,000 Hayfork
Maptech CD-ROM: North Coast/Eureka
Northern California Atlas & Gazetteer, p. 44
California Road & Recreation Atlas, p. 51
Other: A Guide to the Trinity Alps Wilderness (incomplete)

Route Directions

▼ 0.0		From California 299 at the boundary of Shasta-Trinity National Forests, 8 miles east of Big Bar, zero trip meter and turn northwest on paved CR 421, following the sign to Helena.
		GPS: N40°46.19' W123°07.62'
▼ 0.9	SO	River access point on right.
▼ 1.2	SO	Cross over North Fork Trinity River on bridge.
▼ 1.3	SO	Road on right.
▼ 3.8	BL	Paved road continues straight ahead. Zero trip meter and bear left onto dirt road 34N07, following the sign for Hobo Gulch Trailhead.
		GPS: N40°48.80' W123°07.32'
▼ 0.0		Continue to the northwest.
▼ 2.3	SO	Waldorf Crossing Trail (11W13) on left goes 3 miles to North Fork Trinity River.
		GPS: N40°50.41' W123°07.98'
▼ 3.2	SO	Track on left goes to Yellowstone Mine—private property. Diggings for the old mine are below the road to the right.
▼ 4.6	BL	Well-used track on right is 35N20.
▼ 4.9	SO	Track on left is 34N07YC.
		GPS: N40°51.86' W123°08.78'
▼ 7.4	BR	Stoveleg Gap. Track on right on right-hand

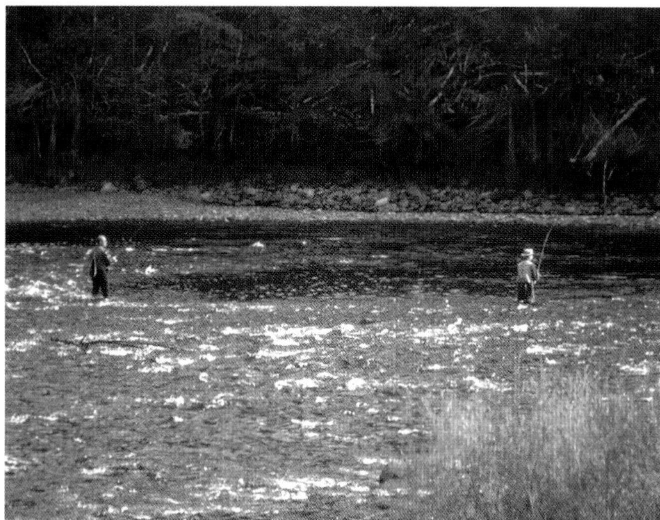

Fishermen in the Trinity River

		bend is 34N07YB. Zero trip meter.
		GPS: N40°52.89' W123°08.69'
▼ 0.0		Continue to the north.
▼ 1.9	BR	Track on left to campsite and Raymond Flat Trail (11W12), which goes 3 miles to North Fork Trinity River.
		GPS: N40°54.17' W123°09.42'
▼ 2.2	SO	Turnout on left gives views up and down North Fork Trinity River.
▼ 4.2	SO	Track on right is 34N07YA to North Fork Trailhead. Follow the sign to Hobo Gulch Campground.
		GPS: N40°55.48' W123°09.26'
▼ 4.5		Trail ends at Hobo Gulch USFS Campground.
		GPS: N40°55.64' W123°09.23'

NORTH COAST #23

Bowerman Ridge Trail

Starting Point:	**California 3, 22 miles north of Weaverville**
Finishing Point:	**California 3, 24.5 miles north of Weaverville**
Total Mileage:	**13.1 miles, plus 4-mile spur along Bowerman Ridge**
Unpaved Mileage:	**10.8 miles, plus 4-mile spur**
Driving Time:	**2 hours**
Elevation Range:	**2,400–4,000 feet**
Usually Open:	**May 1 to October 30**
Best Time to Travel:	**Dry weather**
Difficulty Rating:	**4**
Scenic Rating:	**9**
Remoteness Rating:	**+0**

Special Attractions

- The Bowerman Barn.
- Moderately challenging spur to a beautiful camp or picnic site on a narrow ridge above Trinity Lake.
- Camping, picnicking, boating, and angling at Trinity lake.

History

A barn of hand-hewn timbers on the East Fork of Stuart Creek is all that remains of the Bowerman Ranch, much of which was inundated by Trinity Lake when the Trinity Dam was completed in 1961. Jacob Bowerman, a native of Ohio, made his way west to seek his fortune in the mines. Like many others he wasn't very lucky. So he and his brother John invested in property and established a ranch to supply mining camps with food. Their timing and location at a wagon road junction were keys to their success. The road connected them to markets at Trinity Center to the north, Weaverville to the south, and Minersville, now beneath the waters of Trinity Lake, to the east. Jacob married Anna Tourtellotte, the innkeeper's daughter, at Minersville in 1872. John turned to mining and his sister-in-law established an inn on the ranch for stagecoach passengers and teamsters. Jacob expanded the ranch holdings and sold beef, corn, hay, and barrels of butter to miners.

The restored barn, first built in 1878, is all that remains of this once prosperous ranch. Jacob Bowerman died in 1917, at the age of 83; the main ranch house burned to the ground in the 1920s and Anna passed away in 1931, at the age of 80.

Description

The Central Valley Project, begun in 1935, was conceived to control floods and provide hydroelectric power. Trinity Lake is one of several reservoirs resulting from the long-term project. Trinity Dam, completed in 1961, now holds back the third largest man-made lake in California. When full, it has a shoreline of 145 miles and offers fishing, boating, picnicking, and camping. There are a number of full service marinas along its shore. Although the lake is an extremely popular destination, there are some quiet, out-of-the-way spots accessible only by 4WD.

Bowerman Ridge lies between the East Fork of Stuarts Fork Arm and the southwestern side of Trinity Lake. Bowerman Ridge Trail is a loop with a one-way spur that travels down the ridge, past the site of an old fire lookout, to finish at a wonderful picnic area and campsite near the end of the spur.

The loop starts on a paved road and passes the Bowerman Barn. The trail turns to a narrow dirt road and passes the Alpine View USFS Campground as it begins to climb around the side of the ridge. There are views west over one of the arms of Trinity Lake and toward peaks in the Trinity Alps Wilderness—Granite Peak, Red Mountain, Middle Peak, and Gibson Peak among others.

The main trail joins a graded logging road on top of the ridge to return to California 3. The spur along Bowerman

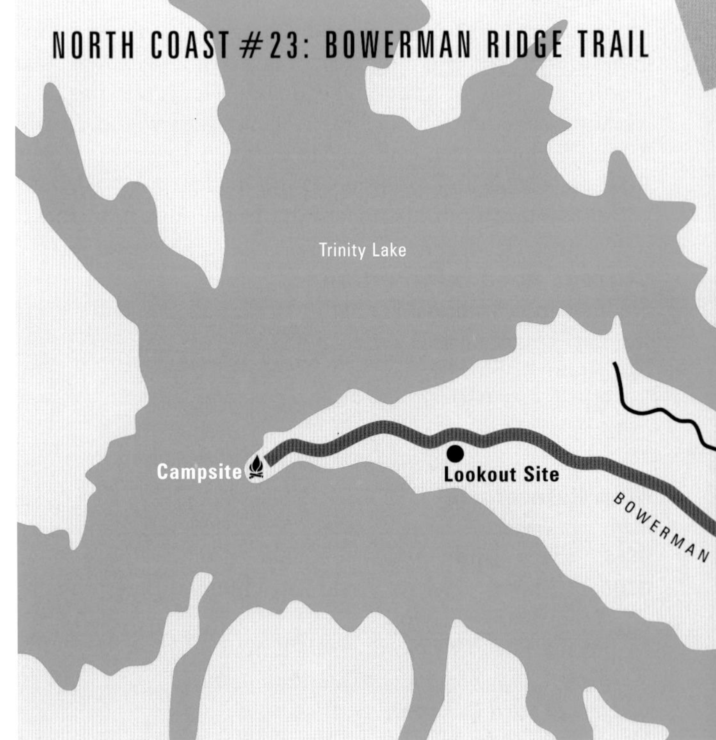

Bowerman Barn

Ridge leads off from here, traveling to the site of an old fire lookout. Past the lookout site, the trail is rated 4 for difficulty and descends steeply along a narrow, formed spur to the turnaround point. The surface can be alternately loose and rocky in places with grades of more than 20 degrees. The turnaround at the bottom is on a narrow spit. A short hike takes you to the tip. The campsite there should be considered a single vehicle site; there is not enough room for more people to pitch a tent or share the space. From the end of the spur, the Fairview boat ramp is visible on the far side of the lake.

The entire trail can be traveled between May 1 and October 30. The section from Alpine View Campground to the ridge top is gated closed to vehicles from October 31 to April 30. However by traveling the trail in reverse, vehicles can access Bowerman Ridge year-round, weather permitting. This trail is not suitable for wet weather travel and should be avoided during rain or snow. This trail is a moderately strenuous mountain-bike route that should be attempted only by riders who are fit and experienced.

Current Road Information

Shasta-Trinity National Forests
Weaverville Ranger District
210 Main Street
Weaverville, CA 96093
(530) 623-2121

Map References

BLM Redding
USFS Shasta-Trinity National Forests
USGS 1:24,000 Covington Mill, Trinity Dam, Papoose Creek, Trinity Center
1:100,000 Redding
Maptech CD-ROM: Shasta Lake/Redding
Northern California Atlas & Gazetteer, p. 45
California Road & Recreation Atlas, p. 52
Other: Trinity Alps Wilderness, Whiskeytown-Shasta-Trinity NRA: Trinity Unit

Route Directions

▼ 0.0	From California 3, 22 miles north of Weaverville, zero trip meter and turn east on paved Guy Covington Drive, following the sign to Alpine View Campground.
2.3 ▲	Trail ends at T-intersection with California 3. Turn left for Weaverville; turn right for Trinity Center.
	GPS: N40°54.89' W122°46.26'

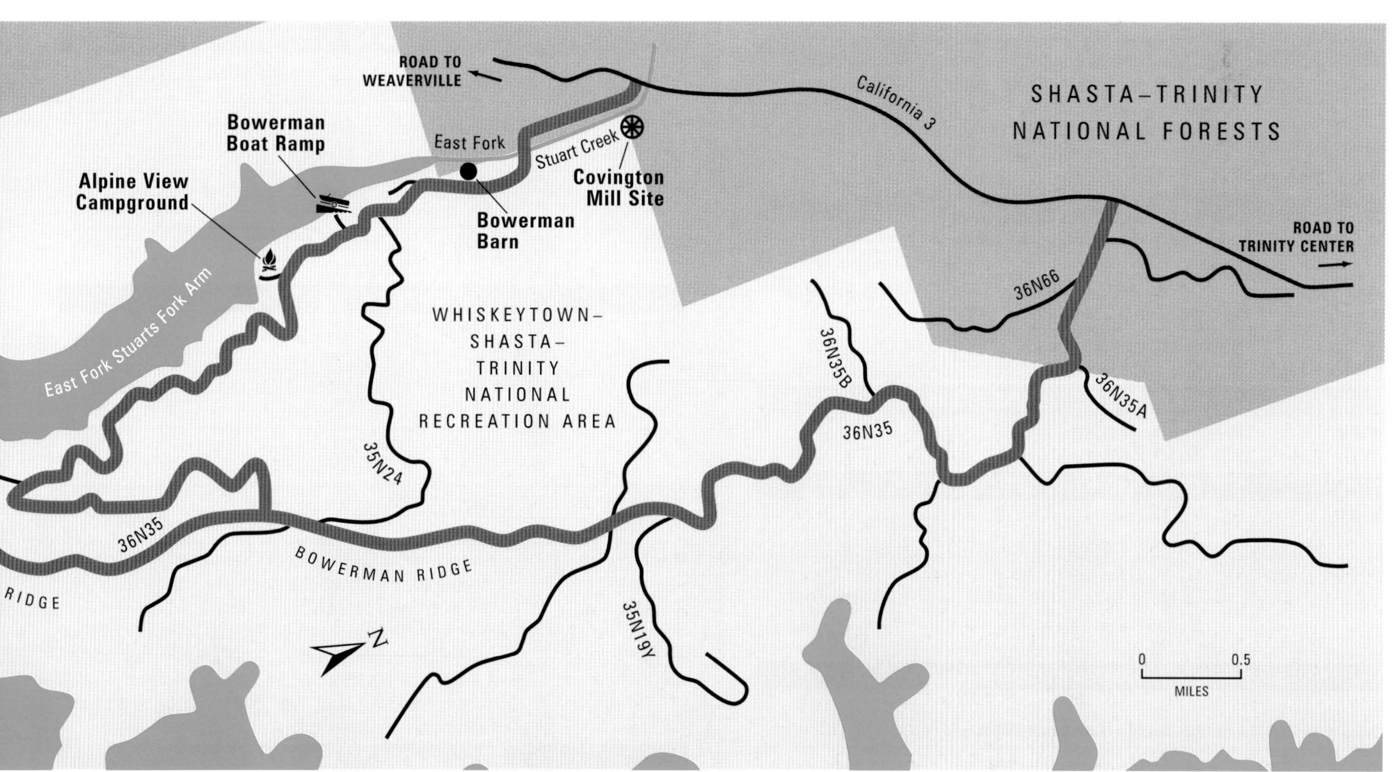

Picnic spot at the end of Bowerman Ridge

▼ 0.2		SO	Covington Mill site on left. The burn cone, also known as the drying kiln, can be seen from the road.
	2.1 ▲	SO	Covington Mill site on right. The burn cone, also known as the drying kiln, can be seen from the road.
▼ 0.7		SO	Cross over East Fork Stuart Fork Creek.
	1.6 ▲	SO	Cross over East Fork Stuart Fork Creek.
▼ 1.1		SO	Bowerman Barn on right.
	1.2 ▲	SO	Bowerman Barn on left.
			GPS: N40°54.00' W122°46.00'
▼ 1.3		SO	Track on right. Road is now marked 35N14Y.
	1.0 ▲	SO	Track on left.
▼ 1.6		SO	Graded road on left is 35N24.
	0.7 ▲	SO	Graded road on right is 35N24.
▼ 1.9		SO	Road on right goes to Bowerman Boat Ramp.
	0.4 ▲	SO	Road on left goes to Bowerman Boat Ramp.
			GPS: N40°53.49' W122°45.91'
▼ 2.3		SO	Road continues to the right into Alpine View USFS Campground. Zero trip meter and pass through seasonal closure gate, remaining on 35N14Y. Road turns to dirt.
	0.0 ▲		Continue to the northwest.
			GPS: N40°53.22' W122°45.88'
▼ 0.0			Continue to the southeast.
	4.6 ▲	SO	Seasonal closure gate; then paved road on left goes into Alpine View USFS Campground. Zero trip meter. Road is now paved.
▼ 0.3		BR	Track on left goes 1.5 miles to a dead end.
	4.3 ▲	SO	Track on right goes 1.5 miles to a dead end.
			GPS: N40°53.16' W122°45.58'
▼ 2.5		BL	Track on right.
	2.1 ▲	BR	Track on left.
			GPS: N40°51.95' W122°45.13'
▼ 2.9		SO	Track on right.
	1.7 ▲	SO	Track on left.
▼ 4.6		TL	Seasonal closure gate; then T-intersection with 36N35. To the right is the spur to Bowerman Ridge Lookout Spit. Zero trip meter.
	0.0 ▲		Continue to the southwest.
			GPS: N40°52.81' W122°44.59'

Spur to Bowerman Ridge Lookout Spit

▼ 0.0			Head south on 36N35.
▼ 1.4		SO	Track on left is 35N15Y; then track on right is 35N38Y.
▼ 2.8		BR	Track on left goes to site of the old Bowerman Ridge lookout, now a viewpoint.
			GPS: N40°50.77' W122°45.75'
▼ 3.7		BR	Track on left.
			GPS: N40°50.11' W122°46.01'
▼ 3.8		SO	Track on left.
			GPS: N40°50.08' W122°46.05'
▼ 4.0		SO	Spur ends at picnic and campsite at the end of the narrow spit. A hiking trail continues a short distance to the lakeshore.
			GPS: N40°49.86' W122°46.00'

Continuation of Main Trail

▼ 0.0			Continue to the north.
	6.2 ▲	TR	Track straight ahead is the continuation of 36N35, spur to Bowerman Ridge Lookout Spit. Zero trip meter and pass through seasonal closure gate onto 35N31Y.
			GPS: N40°52.81' W122°44.59'
▼ 0.1		SO	Graded road on right.
	6.1 ▲	SO	Graded road on left.
▼ 0.3		SO	Track on left is 35N24.
	5.9 ▲	SO	Track on right is 35N24.
▼ 0.4		SO	Track on right is 36N35D.
	5.8 ▲	SO	Track on left is 36N35D.
▼ 0.9		SO	Track on right.
	5.3 ▲	SO	Track on left.
▼ 1.1		SO	Track on left is 36N35C.
	5.1 ▲	SO	Track on right is 36N35C.
▼ 1.9		BR	Track on right into private property; then two tracks on left. Bear right, remaining on major dirt road.
	4.3 ▲	BR	Two tracks on right; then track on left into private property. Bear right, remaining on major dirt road.
			GPS: N40°54.26' W122°43.96'
▼ 2.2		SO	Closed road on right is 35N19Y.
	4.0 ▲	SO	Closed road on left is 35N19Y.
▼ 3.7		SO	Closed road on left is 36N35B.
	2.5 ▲	SO	Closed road on right is 36N35B.
▼ 3.9		SO	Track on left.
	2.3 ▲	SO	Track on right.
▼ 4.4		BL	Three tracks on right.
	1.8 ▲	BR	Three tracks on left.
			GPS: N40°55.65' W122°43.55'
▼ 4.7		SO	Track on right.
	1.5 ▲	SO	Track on left.
▼ 5.4		SO	Track on right is 36N35A and track on left.
	0.8 ▲	SO	Track on left is 36N35A and track on right.
▼ 5.9		SO	Track on left is 36N66.
	0.3 ▲	SO	Track on right is 36N66.
▼ 6.0		SO	Track on right.
	0.2 ▲	SO	Track on left.
▼ 6.2			Trail ends on California 3. Turn right for Trinity Center; turn left for Weaverville.
	0.0 ▲		Trail commences on California 3, 0.3 miles north of mile marker 56, 2.5 miles north of the southern end of the trail, and 24.5 miles north of Weaverville. Zero trip meter and turn east on graded dirt road 36N35, following sign for Bowerman Ridge Road.
			GPS: N40°56.70' W122°44.74'

Deadwood Road

Starting Point:	**CR 105, immediately south of the Trinity River Bridge**
Finishing Point:	**Main Street, at the southern end of French Gulch**
Total Mileage:	**13 miles**
Unpaved Mileage:	**12 miles**
Driving Time:	**1.25 hours**
Elevation Range:	**1,400–4,100 feet**
Usually Open:	**Year-round**
Best Time to Travel:	**Dry weather**
Difficulty Rating:	**2**
Scenic Rating:	**8**
Remoteness Rating:	**+0**

Special Attractions

- Historic mining district along Deadwood Creek.
- Trail connects the interesting settlements of Lewiston and French Gulch.

History

The Deadwood Wagon Road was built in the mid-1800s to connect the emerging mining communities of Lewiston and French Gulch. Lewis Town, named for Ford Lewis who settled there in 1853, evolved as an important supply center during the gold rush. Lewis operated an indispensable ferry on the Trinity River, complimented by his trading post near the present-day site of an old steel bridge. Many of the town's buildings such as churches, school, post office, and stores date from the 1880s. The town's first hotel, the D. B. Nielson Hotel, was built in 1899. A hardware store, printing shop, drugstore, lumberyard, restaurants, blacksmith shop, and many more commercial enterprises had been established by the 1900s. The Central Valley Project of flood control and hydroelectric power facilities was first proposed in 1919, and finally got under way in 1935. The Trinity Dam and Lewiston Dam were built concurrently, with the Trinity Dam being completed in 1961. Lewiston now flourishes as a result of the national recreation area established in 1965.

French Gulch is southeast of Lewiston and was settled by French miners in the late 1840s. Like Lewiston, the town flourished during the gold rush, and it had one of the most productive lode gold deposits in the Klamath Mountains. Charles Camden's toll road brought considerable traffic to this canyon town, which for a while rivaled Shasta. Several impressive gold rush era buildings are in French Gulch: St. Rose Catholic Church was founded in 1856, and the French Gulch Hotel, now listed on the National Register of Historic Places, was built in 1886.

The Deadwood mines brought phenomenal fortune to French Gulch and Lewiston. Several high-grade ore bodies were discovered at the eastern end of Deadwood Road. The Milkmaid and Franklin Mines at the Right Fork of French Gulch Creek yielded a total of $2.5 million worth of gold. Gladstone Mine, east of town in Cline Gulch, produced more than $6 million. Total production for the entire mining district was more than $25 million.

Description

Deadwood Road is an easy run between Lewiston and French Gulch. Initially, the small single-lane road is paved because it accesses some private property, but it quickly turns to roughly graded dirt. There are many blocks of private property along this trail; side tracks given in the directions are not necessarily open for public travel.

There are only a few adits and tailings piles to indicate this was once a thriving mining district. From Deadwood, the trail climbs to a saddle. It becomes rougher and narrower on the east side and is best driven in dry weather. It can become extremely greasy in wet weather. Fall colors along this road are spectacular—predominantly the golden yellow of bigleaf maples and the yellow-brown of oaks along Deadwood Creek.

The Washington Mine, one of the earliest gold mines in the district, is still operating. The mill on the site was built in the 1930s and both the mine and mill are privately owned. There are additional mining remains farther along the trail at the Milkmaid Mine, where an old mill site sits abandoned on the far side of the Right Fork of French Gulch Creek.

The trail ends in the township of French Gulch, a pretty community with many historic buildings.

Current Road Information

Bureau of Land Management
Redding Field Office
355 Hemsted Drive
Redding, CA 96002
(530) 224-2100

Historic general store in Lewiston

Map References

BLM Redding
USFS Shasta-Trinity National Forests
USGS 1:24,000 Lewiston, French Gulch
1:100,000 Redding
Maptech CD-ROM: Shasta Lake/Redding
Northern California Atlas & Gazetteer, p. 45
California Road & Recreation Atlas, p. 52
Other: Whiskeytown-Shasta-Trinity NRA: Trinity Unit

Route Directions

▼ 0.0		From the northern end of Lewiston, immediately south of the Trinity River Bridge at the intersection of CR 105, Trinity Dam Boulevard, and Deadwood Road, zero trip meter and turn northeast on paved road, following sign to the Trinity River Fish Hatchery. Immediately turn right onto the small, paved Deadwood Road.
6.6 ▲		Turn left at T-intersection; then trail ends at intersection with CR 105 in Lewiston. Turn Left for California 299; turn right for Trinity Lake.
		GPS: N40°43.02′ W122°48.04′
▼ 0.8	BR	Track on left. Bear right onto graded dirt road.
5.8 ▲	SO	Track on right. Road is now paved.
▼ 1.5	BL	Track on right.
5.1 ▲	SO	Track on left.
▼ 2.4	BR	Track on left.
4.2 ▲	SO	Track on right.
		GPS: N40°42.90′ W122°45.48′
▼ 3.7	SO	Track on left; then cross over Donnelly Gulch; then track on right.
2.9 ▲	SO	Track on left; then cross over Donnelly Gulch; then track on right.
▼ 4.6	SO	Track on right.
2.0 ▲	SO	Track on left.
		GPS: N40°43.58′ W122°43.83′
▼ 4.7	SO	Cross over Mill Gulch at mine tailings.
1.9 ▲	SO	Cross over Mill Gulch at mine tailings.
▼ 4.9	BL	Track on right.
1.7 ▲	SO	Track on left.
▼ 5.2	SO	Adit on left; cross over creek; mine tailings on right.
1.4 ▲	SO	Mine tailings on left; cross over creek; adit on right.
		GPS: N40°43.70′ W122°43.49′
▼ 5.3	SO	Track on left.
1.3 ▲	SO	Track on right.
▼ 5.4	SO	Track on right; then track on left.
1.2 ▲	SO	Track on right; then track on left.
▼ 5.6	SO	Track on left under power lines.
1.0 ▲	SO	Track on right under power lines.
▼ 6.1	SO	Track on left.
0.5 ▲	SO	Track on right.
		GPS: N40°43.91′ W122°43.04′
▼ 6.2	SO	Cross over creek.
0.4 ▲	SO	Cross over creek.
▼ 6.4	BL	Two tracks on right.

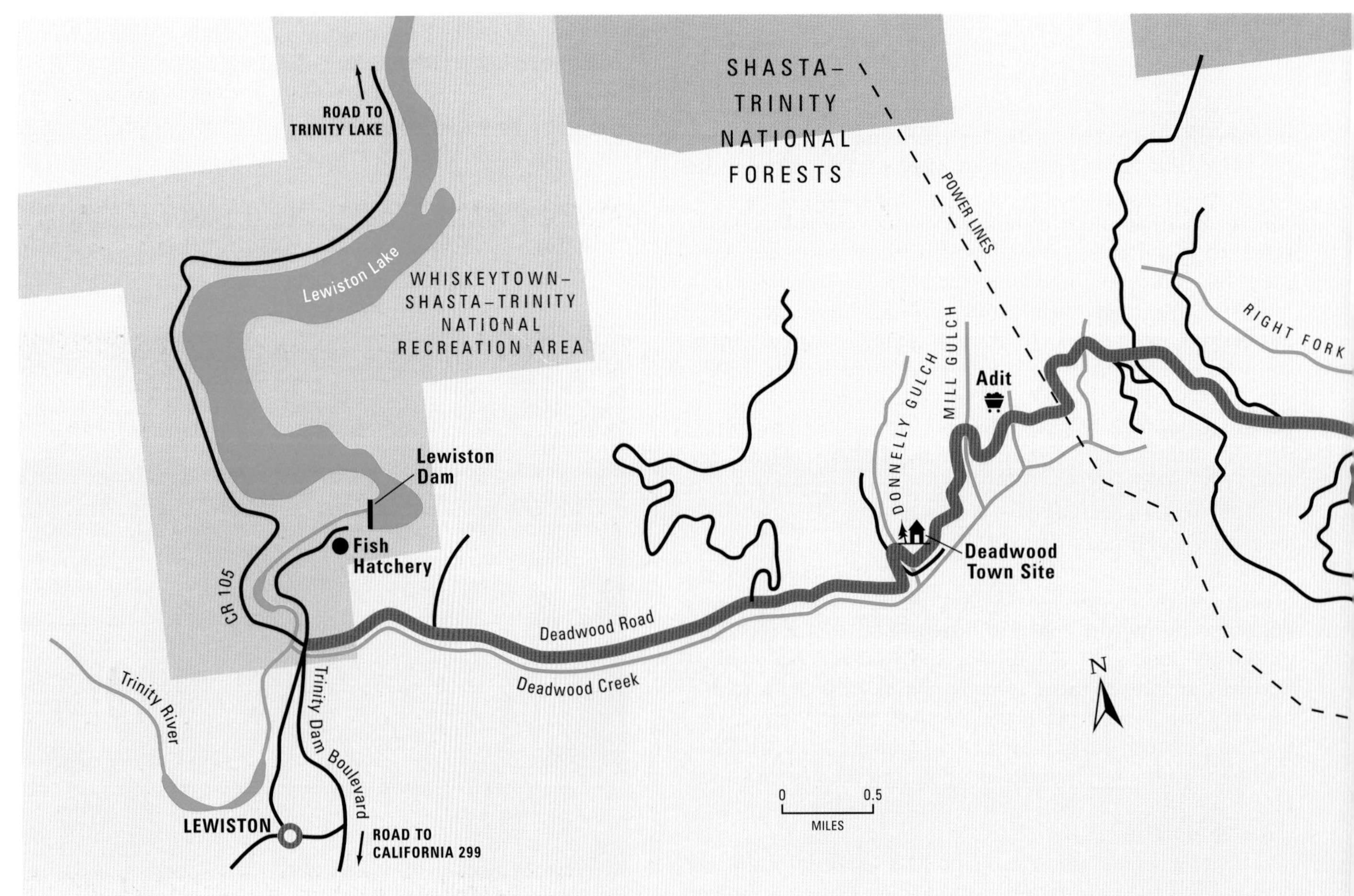

Mileage	Action	Directions
0.2 ▲	BR	Two tracks on left.
▼ 6.6	SO	Unmarked 4-way intersection on saddle. Zero trip meter.
0.0 ▲		Continue to the west on Deadwood Road.
		GPS: N40°43.87′ W122°42.66′
▼ 0.0		Continue to the east on French Gulch Road.
6.4 ▲	SO	Unmarked 4-way intersection on saddle. Zero trip meter.
▼ 0.2	SO	Track on left.
6.2 ▲	BL	Track on right.
▼ 0.7	SO	Track on left.
5.7 ▲	SO	Track on right.
▼ 1.0	SO	Track on left.
5.4 ▲	BL	Track on right.
▼ 1.6	SO	Track on right; then track on left and track on right; then track on left. Remain on main trail.
4.8 ▲	SO	Track on right; then track on left and track on right; then track on left. Remain on main trail.
▼ 2.1	SO	Track on left.
4.3 ▲	SO	Track on right.
▼ 2.2	BL	Two tracks on right.
4.2 ▲	BR	Two tracks on left.
		GPS: N40°43.11′ W122°41.45′
▼ 2.3	SO	Track on right.
4.1 ▲	SO	Track on left.
▼ 2.6	SO	Track on right.
3.8 ▲	SO	Track on left.
▼ 2.7	SO	Track on left.
3.7 ▲	SO	Track on right.

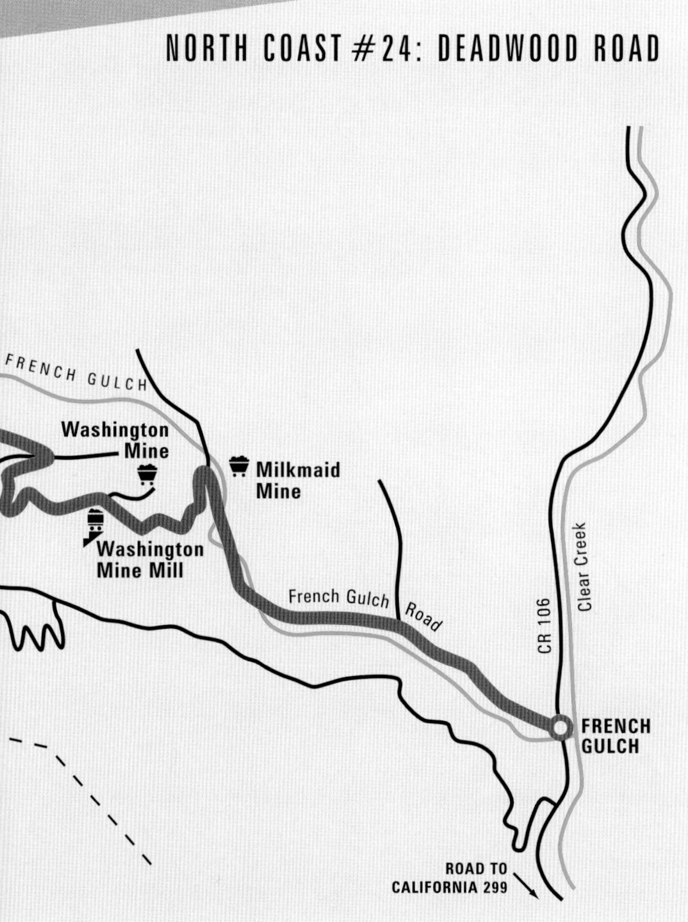

Deadwood Road

Mileage	Action	Directions
▼ 2.8	SO	Track on left; then part of the Washington Mine on right—private property.
3.6 ▲	SO	Part of the Washington Mine on left—private property; then track on right.
		GPS: N40°43.11′ W122°40.85′
▼ 2.9	SO	Track on right is entrance to the Washington Mine's mill.
3.5 ▲	BR	Track on left is entrance to the Washington Mine's mill.
▼ 3.1	SO	Private tracks on left and right.
3.3 ▲	SO	Private tracks on left and right.
▼ 3.5	SO	Track on left.
2.9 ▲	SO	Track on right.
▼ 3.8	TR	Track straight ahead. Turn sharp right and follow along Right Fork French Gulch; then adit of the Milkmaid Mine on far side of creek.
2.6 ▲	TL	Adit of the Milkmaid Mine on far side of creek on right; then track straight ahead. Turn sharp left, leaving the creek.
		GPS: N40°43.22′ W122°40.18′
▼ 4.0	SO	Remains of the Milkmaid Mine's mill on the far side of the creek on left.
2.6 ▲	SO	Remains of the Milkmaid Mine's mill on the far side of the creek on right.
		GPS: N40°43.08′ W122°40.14′
▼ 4.2	SO	Cross over Right Fork French Gulch.
2.2 ▲	SO	Cross over Right Fork French Gulch.
▼ 4.3	SO	Cross over the Right Fork of French Gulch then track on right.
2.1 ▲	SO	Track on left, then cross over the Right Fork of French Gulch.
▼ 4.5	SO	Cross over the Right Fork of French Gulch.
1.9 ▲	SO	Cross over the Right Fork of French Gulch.
▼ 5.4	SO	Track on left.
1.0 ▲	SO	Track on right.
▼ 6.2	SO	Road becomes paved.
0.2 ▲	SO	Road turns to graded dirt.
▼ 6.4		Trail ends at the T-intersection with Main Street in French Gulch. Turn right for California 299 and Redding.
0.0 ▲		Trail commences on Main Street at the south end of French Gulch, at the intersection with French Gulch Road. French Gulch is 3 miles north of California 299. Zero trip meter and turn west on the paved French Gulch Road.
		GPS: N40°41.87′ W122°38.25′

NORTH COAST #25

South Shore Drive

Starting Point:	**California 299, 1 mile east of the Tower House Historic District**
Finishing Point:	**Intersection of J.F. Kennedy Memorial Drive and North Coast #26: Shasta Bally Trail**
Total Mileage:	**6.9 miles**
Unpaved Mileage:	**5.3 miles**
Driving Time:	**45 minutes**
Elevation Range:	**1,200–1,700 feet**
Usually Open:	**Year-round**
Best Time to Travel:	**Year-round**
Difficulty Rating:	**1**
Scenic Rating:	**9**
Remoteness Rating:	**+0**

Special Attractions

- Boating, camping, hiking, mountain biking, and picnicking at Whiskeytown Lake.
- Tower House Historic District.

History

In the mid-1800s, wagon travel in the mountainous Whiskeytown region was far from straightforward. Charles Camden saw a need for a passable route to and from the town of Shasta. The enterprising Camden invested $20,000 to improve his franchised toll road. In 1865, he charged foot travelers 10 cents to cross his toll bridge over Clear Creek, 25 cents for those on horseback, and $1.25 for wagons. Camden complimented earnings from his toll road by extracting approximately $80,000 from a mine on Clear Creek over a 17-year period.

In 1852, Levi Tower built a 21-room hotel north of Camden's bridge. His establishment catered to travelers on the wagon road between Shasta and Weaverville until it burned down in 1919.

Description

South Shore Drive follows the southwestern shore of Whiskeytown Lake, one of the reservoirs included in the Whiskeytown-Shasta-Trinity National Recreation Area. While California 299 runs near the lake's northeastern shore, the southern shore has a quiet, remote feel to it. The graded dirt road is normally suitable for all vehicles in dry weather. It leaves California 299 a mile south of the historic site of Tower House, where you can see Charles Camden's two-story timber house and the site of his toll bridge over Clear Creek.

The main trail is paved as far as the Carr Powerhouse, after which it turns to dirt. Hiking trails access the national recreation area's backcountry, and short spurs lead down to the shore of Whiskeytown Lake. Much of the trail follows a wide shelf road high above the lake, offering great views of its shoreline.

The trail passes a marina on the western shore of the lake and a developed campground for self-contained RV units only. Campgrounds for tent campers can be found along the more difficult North Coast #26: Shasta Bally Trail at Sheep Camp and Brandy Creek; there are also campgrounds on the north shore of the lake. The trail ends at the intersection with

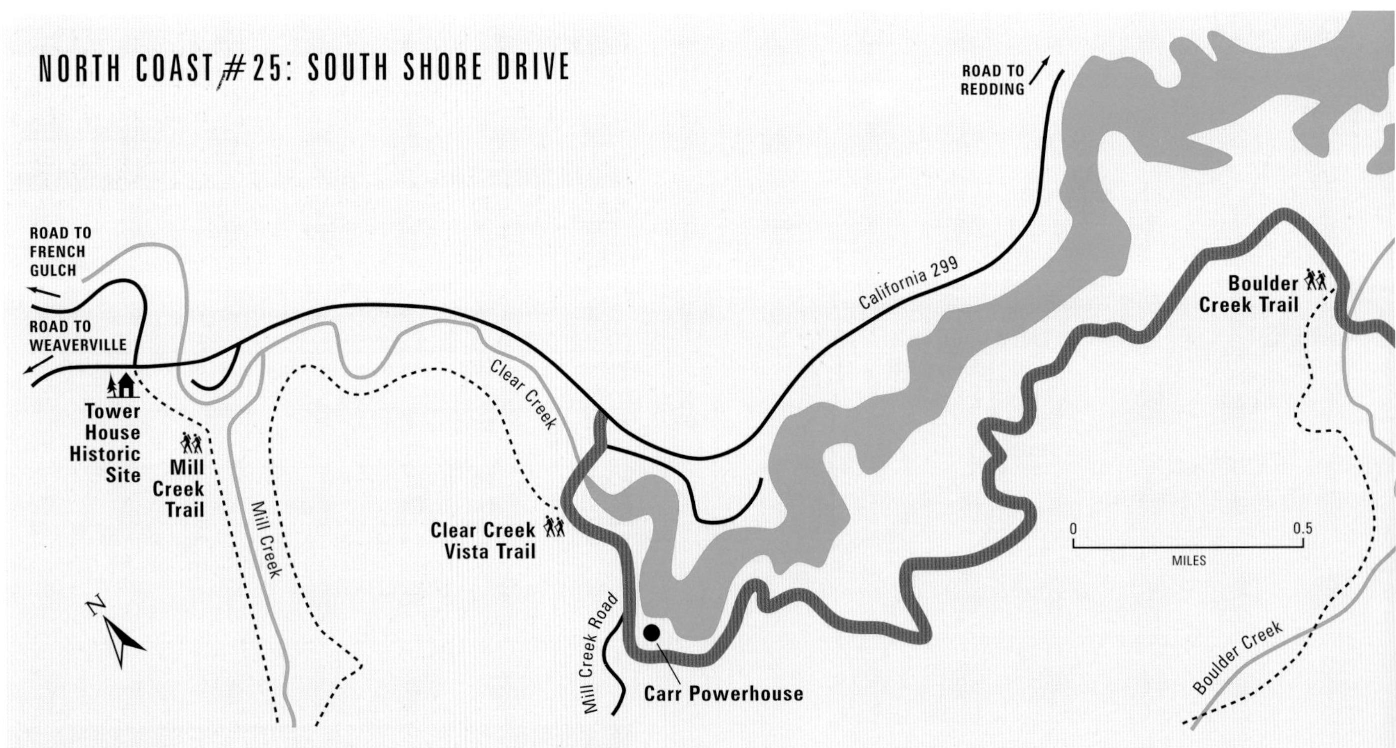

North Coast #26: Shasta Bally Trail, a short distance west of the Whiskeytown Lake Visitor Center.

The Whiskeytown-Shasta-Trinity National Recreation Area is a fee area.

Current Road Information

Whiskeytown National Recreation Area
PO Box 188
Whiskeytown, CA 96095
(530) 246-1225

Map References

BLM Redding
USFS Shasta-Trinity National Forests
USGS 1:24,000 Whiskeytown, French Gulch, Igo
1:100,000 Redding
Maptech CD-ROM: Shasta Lake/Redding
Northern California Atlas & Gazetteer, pp. 45, 46
Other: Whiskeytown-Shasta-Trinity NRA: Whiskeytown Unit

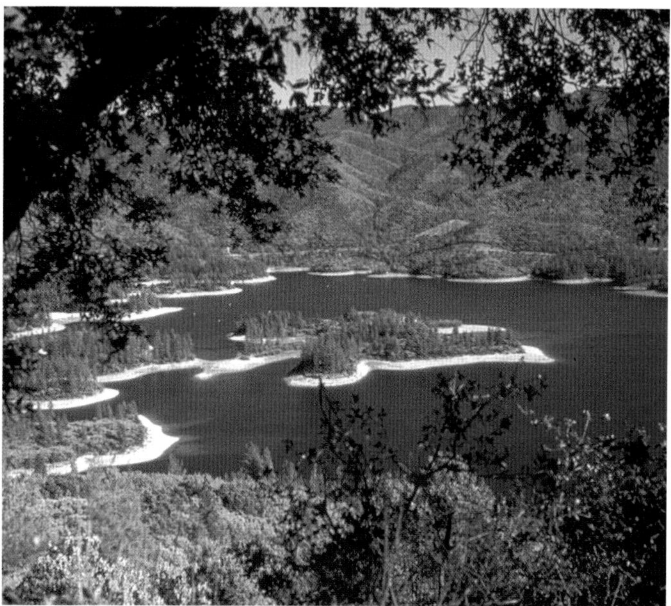

Whiskeytown Lake

Route Directions

▼ 0.0		From California 299 near the northwestern end of Whiskeytown Lake, 1 mile east of the Tower House Historic Site (which is opposite the road to French Gulch), zero trip meter and turn south on paved Carr Powerhouse Road. Remain on paved road for next 1.1 miles.
5.9 ▲		Trail ends at intersection with California 299. Turn right for Redding; turn left for Weaverville.
		GPS: N40°39.28' W122°37.36'
▼ 0.1	BR	Paved road on left.
5.8 ▲	BL	Paved road on right.
▼ 0.2	SO	Cross over Clear Creek on bridge.
5.7 ▲	SO	Cross over Clear Creek on bridge.
▼ 0.3	SO	Clear Creek Vista Trail for hikers on right.
5.6 ▲	SO	Clear Creek Vista Trail for hikers on left.
▼ 0.5	SO	Track on right is Mill Creek Road, which goes to Boulder Creek Trail and Mill Creek Trail, and two tracks on left.
5.4 ▲	SO	Track on left is Mill Creek Road, which goes to Boulder Creek Trail and Mill Creek Trail, and two tracks on right.
▼ 0.6	SO	Carr Powerhouse on left.
5.3 ▲	SO	Carr Powerhouse on right.
		GPS: N40°38.86' W122°37.62'
▼ 1.1	BL	Road turns to graded dirt.

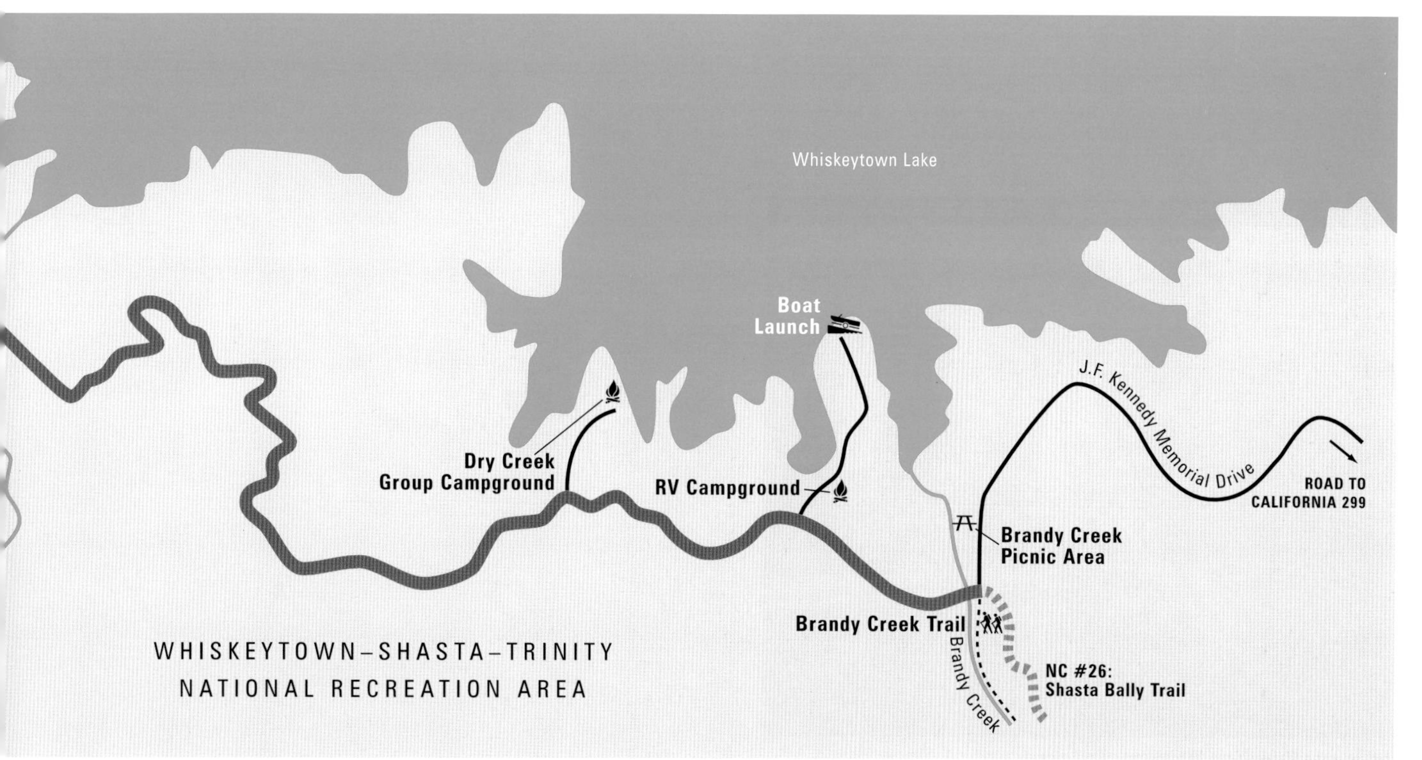

	4.8 ▲	BR	Road becomes paved. Remain on paved road for next 1.1 miles.
▼ 1.2		SO	Track on left.
	4.7 ▲	SO	Track on right.
▼ 3.4		SO	Track on left. Boulder Creek Trail for hikers on right.
	2.5 ▲	SO	Track on right. Boulder Creek Trail for hikers on left.
			GPS: N40°38.50' W122°35.78'
▼ 3.5		SO	Cross over Boulder Creek.
	2.4 ▲	SO	Cross over Boulder Creek.
▼ 5.0		SO	Track on right.
	0.9 ▲	SO	Track on left.
▼ 5.1		SO	Track on right is gated closed.
	0.8 ▲	SO	Track on left is gated closed.
▼ 5.4		SO	Track on left. Service road on right.
	0.5 ▲	SO	Track on right. Service road on left.
			GPS: N40°37.55' W122°35.47'
▼ 5.9		TR	T-intersection with paved road. To the left is the Dry Creek Group Campground (reservations only). Zero trip meter.
	0.0 ▲		Continue to the west.
			GPS: N40°37.42' W122°35.02'
▼ 0.0			Continue to the south.
	1.0 ▲	TL	Paved road continues straight ahead to the Dry Creek Group Campground (reservations only). Zero trip meter and turn left onto graded dirt road, following sign for South Shore Drive.
▼ 0.6		SO	Paved road on left goes to marina, boat launch, and self-contained RV campsites.
	0.4 ▲	SO	Paved road on right goes to marina, boat launch, and self-contained RV campsites.
			GPS: N40°37.10' W122°34.65'
▼ 1.0			Trail ends at intersection with the start of North Coast #26: Shasta Bally Trail. Continue straight ahead to exit to California 299 and Redding. The Brandy Creek Trailhead for hikers is at the intersection.
	0.0 ▲		Trail commences at intersection with J.F. Kennedy Memorial Drive and North Coast #26: Shasta Bally Trail, 4.5 miles west of the Whiskeytown Lake Visitor Center beside California 299. The Brandy Creek Trailhead for hikers is at the intersection. Zero trip meter and continue southwest on paved road.
			GPS: N40°36.78' W122°34.42'

Yachting and fishing on Whiskeytown Lake

NORTH COAST #26

Shasta Bally Trail

Starting Point:	**J.F. Kennedy Memorial Drive, 4.5 miles west of the visitor center on California 299**
Finishing Point:	**Shasta Bally summit**
Total Mileage:	**7.9 miles (one-way)**
Unpaved Mileage:	**7.8 miles**
Driving Time:	**45 minutes (one-way)**
Elevation Range:	**1,400–6,200 feet**
Usually Open:	**May to early December**
Best Time to Travel:	**Dry weather only**
Difficulty Rating:	**4**
Scenic Rating:	**10**
Remoteness Rating:	**+0**

Special Attractions

- Moderately difficult, steep trail that climbs to a summit.
- Panoramic views from Shasta Bally.
- Boating, camping, hiking, mountain biking, and picnicking at Whiskeytown Lake.

History

Shasta Bally (6,209 feet) provides an excellent view over the lands once held by the Wintun Indians, whose territory

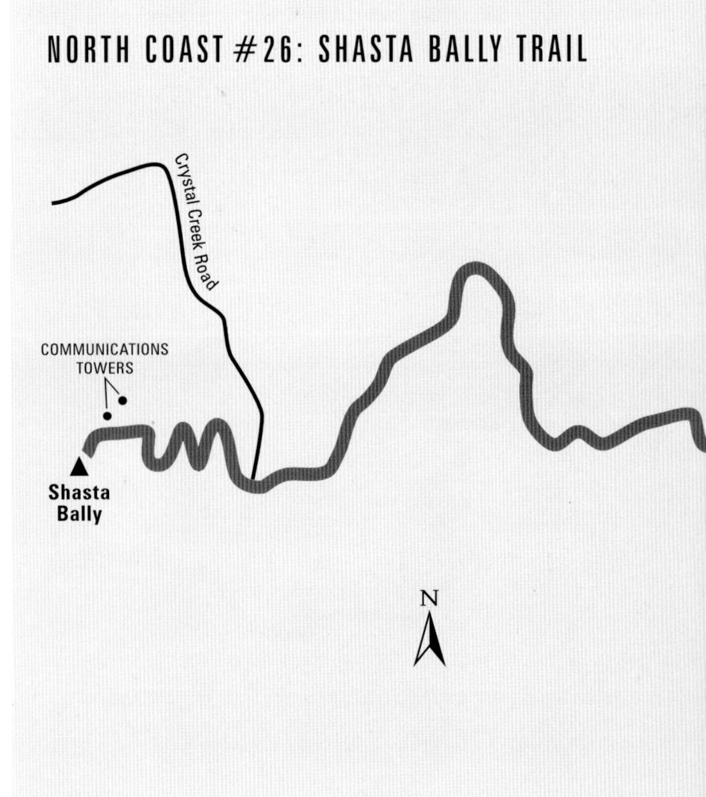

stretched from lands west of Weaverville, east of Redding, north of La Moine (located along I-5), and south to Cottonwood Creek. The region around Shasta Bally—bally is derived from the Wintun word *buli,* meaning "mountain"—had much game and fish, including deer, rabbits, salmon, ducks, and geese. The Indians used acorns to make bread and soups. The Wintun had a strong regard for the landscape in which they lived, believing it was essential to maintain harmony with Mother Earth. Much of their mythology was based on features such as pools, rocks, caves, and mountains like Shasta Bally.

The Wintun's lifestyle came to an abrupt end with the arrival of settlers in the mid-1800s. Diseases swept through villages as miners rushed into the region following the 1848 discovery of gold at Readings Bar, off to the west on the Trinity River. The mining camp of Whiskeytown was established near the base of Shasta Bally in 1849. The town got its unusual name after a keg of whiskey fell into a nearby creek.

Work on the Whiskeytown Dam, part of the Central Valley Project, began in 1959 and ended in 1963. Some of Whiskeytown was torn down, and the rest disappeared as the reservoir filled.

Description

Shasta Bally Trail is a wonderful addition to the easier North Coast #25: South Shore Drive for those with high-clearance 4WDs. The trail winds past Sheep Camp, an undeveloped camping area alongside Brandy Creek (permit required), and then starts to climb a steep and unrelenting 15- to 25-degree grade all the way to the summit of Shasta Bally. The surface is rough in spots and not suitable for wet weather travel. The trail is also narrow and has few passing places. As you approach the summit, the forest gives way to shrubby manzanitas. At the summit, the panorama includes Lassen Peak and the town of Redding to the east. To the north, Mount Shasta dominates the view with the Castle Crags in front. To the northwest is the Trinity Alps Wilderness, and to the south is the Yolla Bolly Middle Eel Wilderness.

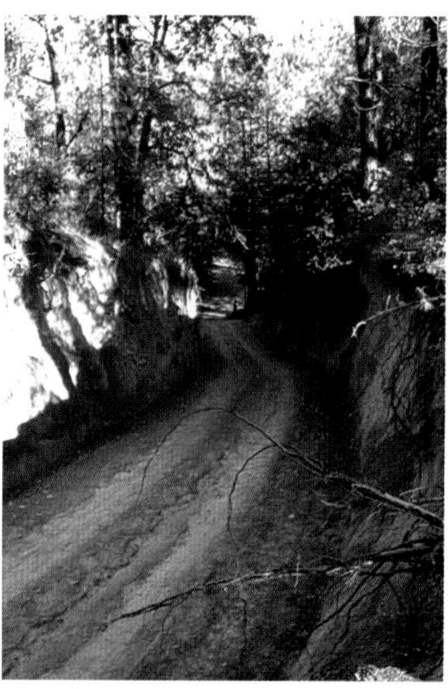
The steep trail climbs grades of up to 22 degrees

Be careful as you descend the steep grade back to Whiskeytown Lake. Judicious use of the transmission will help avoid overheating brakes. Keep in mind that vehicles traveling uphill have the right of way. This may necessitate a quick stop and even an uphill reverse on sections of the single-lane road.

Current Road Information

Whiskeytown National Recreation Area
PO Box 188
Whiskeytown, CA 96095
(530) 246-1225

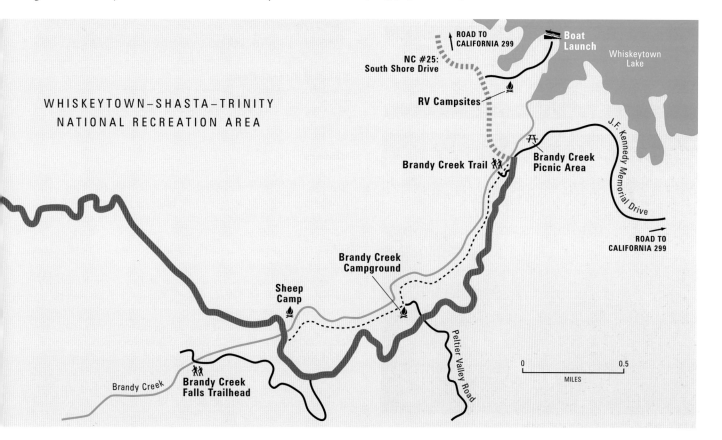

Map References

BLM Redding
USFS Shasta-Trinity National Forests
USGS 1:24,000 Igo, Shasta Bally
1:100,000 Redding
Maptech CD-ROM: Shasta Lake/Redding
Northern California Atlas & Gazetteer, pp. 46, 45
California Road & Recreation Atlas, p. 52
Other: Whiskeytown-Shasta-Trinity NRA: Whiskeytown Unit

Route Directions

▼ 0.0		From paved J.F. Kennedy Memorial Drive on the south side of Whiskeytown Lake, 4.5 miles west of the visitor center on California 299 and 0.1 miles west of the Brandy Creek Picnic Area, zero trip meter and turn south on paved road, following the sign for Sheep Camp and Shasta Bally. Pass through closure gate. The Brandy Creek Trailhead for hikers is at the intersection. Paved road straight ahead to the southwest is North Coast #25: South Shore Drive.
		GPS: N40°36.78' W122°34.42'
▼ 0.1	BL	Road turns to graded dirt. Track on right goes 0.1 miles to Brandy Creek and additional trailhead parking.
▼ 0.2	SO	Track on right.
▼ 1.3	SO	Track on left is Peltier Valley Road. Track on right goes into Brandy Creek Campground. Follow the sign for Shasta Bally.
		GPS: N40°36.08' W122°34.85'
▼ 1.8	SO	Brandy Creek Trail for hikers and mountain bikes on right.
▼ 2.2	BR	Track on left goes 1 mile to Brandy Creek Falls Trailhead. Bear right, following the sign for Shasta Bally.
		GPS: N40°35.77' W122°35.44'
▼ 2.4	SO	Brandy Creek Trail on left; then seasonal closure gate; then cross over Brandy Creek on bridge.
▼ 2.5	BL	Sheep Camp on right (permit required). Zero trip meter. Trail starts to climb.
		GPS: N40°36.01' W122°35.62'

Northerly view of Mount Shasta from the summit of Shasta Bally

▼ 0.0		Continue to the northwest.
▼ 0.2	SO	Seasonal closure gate.
▼ 1.0	SO	Track on right.
▼ 1.8	SO	Turnout on right.
▼ 3.0	SO	Track on left.
▼ 3.7	SO	Turnout on left.
▼ 4.5	SO	Crystal Creek Road on right—closed to motor vehicles.
		GPS: N40°36.01' W122°38.59'
▼ 5.3	SO	Communications towers on right.
▼ 5.4		Trail ends at summit of Shasta Bally.
		GPS: N40°36.05' W122°39.04'

NORTH COAST #27

Backbone Road

Starting Point:	**Dry Creek Road, 0.2 miles north of the intersection with Bear Mountain Road**
Finishing Point:	**California 299, 5 miles southwest of Round Mountain**
Total Mileage:	**17.6 miles**
Unpaved Mileage:	**17.1 miles**
Driving Time:	**2 hours**
Elevation Range:	**1,000–2,200 feet**
Usually Open:	**Year-round**
Best Time to Travel:	**Dry weather**
Difficulty Rating:	**3**
Scenic Rating:	**8**
Remoteness Rating:	**+0**

Special Attractions

- Views of Mount Shasta and Lassen Peak.
- Ridge top trail with spectacular views to the north and south.

History

Clikapudi Creek, near the start of the trail, was the site of a Wintun village and the scene of a battle with the Yana, who moved through this region while hunting and gathering. The Yana attacked the village, claiming it was on their tribal lands. With assistance from other Wintun nearby, the villagers managed to fend off the Yana. The Wintun word for fight, *clikapudi*, survives as the creek's name.

Backbone Road travels the crest of Backbone Ridge, immediately south of Shasta Lake's Pit River Arm. Work on Shasta Dam, another of the great Central Valley Project's dams, began in 1938 and was completed in 1945, with the lake finally filling in 1948. Some 6,000 workers combined to build the dam, which is more than 600 feet high and nearly 900 feet thick at its base. The dam flooded the Pit, Shasta, and McCloud Rivers, and Squaw Creek. The dam at Fenders Flat, at the northeastern end of the Pit River Arm, is one of three dams supplementing Shasta Dam. The great reservoir flooded many mining claims. It also covers much of the right of way of the Sacramento & Eastern Railroad, which was built along the Pit River to the copper mine at Bully Hill Mine. Bully Hill operated from 1901 to 1910. Its smelter was closed by court order in 1919. The sulphur fumes from the smelter were very destructive to forests and fish.

Description

Backbone Road travels through a mix of private land and Shasta-Trinity National Forests south of Shasta Lake and north of California 299. Although marked as forest road 34N02 on maps, much of it travels through private land. Please respect landowners' rights and do not trespass. The best camping is in the developed campgrounds beside Shasta Lake, near the start of the trail.

Backbone Road begins in Jones Valley and immediately starts climbing away from it. The pavement ends after a short distance and the road immediately becomes rough enough to make 4WD preferable. Once on the ridge top, the trail switches from one side of the spine to the other, crossing at saddles. Mount Shasta dominates the view to the north, and Lassen Peak to the east. The trail crosses paved Sugar Pine Camp Road, which serves as access to a state prison. You can usually travel south down this road to California 299. However, the road is private and access should not be relied upon.

The trail gets rougher on the east side of Sugar Pine Camp Road, before once again becoming a graded dirt road. It travels down McCandless Gulch Road to finish on California 299.

Current Road Information

Shasta-Trinity National Forests
Shasta Lake Ranger District
14225 Holiday Road
Redding, CA 96003
(530) 275-1587

Map References

BLM Redding
USFS Shasta-Trinity National Forests
USGS 1:24,000 Bella Vista, Oak Run, Devils Rock
1:100,000 Redding
Maptech CD-ROM: Shasta Lake/Redding
Northern California Atlas & Gazetteer, pp. 46, 47
California Road & Recreation Atlas, pp. 52, 53
Other: Whiskeytown-Shasta-Trinity NRA: Shasta Unit

Route Directions

▼ 0.0		From Dry Creek Road on the southern shore of Shasta Lake in Jones Valley, 0.2 miles north of the intersection with Bear Mountain Road, zero trip meter and turn northeast on paved Backbone Road (34N02). Backbone Road leads off from the general store and is also at the intersection with Hidden Valley Drive. Remain on Backbone Road for 0.5 miles.
5.4 ▲		Trail ends on Dry Creek Road in Jones Valley. Turn right for Shasta Lake; turn left for California 299, I-5, and Redding.
		GPS: N40°43.10' W122°14.39'
▼ 0.5	SO	Road turns to roughly graded dirt; then track on left to water tank.
4.9 ▲	SO	Track on right to water tank; then road becomes paved. Remain on paved Backbone Road for the next 0.5 miles.
▼ 3.4	SO	Track on right.
2.0 ▲	SO	Track on left.
▼ 4.0	SO	Tank and spring on right. Tank was built by the CCC in 1939.
1.4 ▲	SO	Tank and spring on left. Tank was built by the CCC in 1939.
		GPS: N40°43.39' W122°10.90'
▼ 4.1	SO	Private tracks on left and right on saddle.
1.3 ▲	SO	Private tracks on left and right on saddle.
▼ 4.4	SO	Track on right; then cross over Wildcat Gulch.
1.0 ▲	SO	Cross over Wildcat Gulch; then track on left.
▼ 4.8	SO	Two tracks on right.
0.6 ▲	SO	Two tracks on left.
▼ 5.1	BR	Well-used track on left.
0.3 ▲	BL	Well-used track on right.
		GPS: N40°43.59' W122°10.10'
▼ 5.4	TR	Unmarked, well-used T-intersection. Track on left goes to private property. Zero trip meter.
0.0 ▲		Continue to the south.
		GPS: N40°43.74' W122°09.91'
▼ 0.0		Continue to the east.
5.3 ▲	TL	Unmarked intersection. Well-used track continues straight ahead to private property. Zero trip meter.
▼ 0.5	SO	Track on right.
4.8 ▲	SO	Track on left.
▼ 1.1	SO	Track on right is private.
4.2 ▲	SO	Track on left is private.
▼ 2.1	SO	Track on left.
3.2 ▲	SO	Track on right.
▼ 2.2	SO	Track on left.
3.1 ▲	SO	Track on right.
▼ 2.4	SO	Track on right.
2.9 ▲	BR	Track on left.
▼ 2.7	SO	Track on left to private property.
2.6 ▲	BL	Track on right to private property.
		GPS: N40°43.81' W122°07.96'

Manzanitas, oaks, and pines on Backbone Ridge

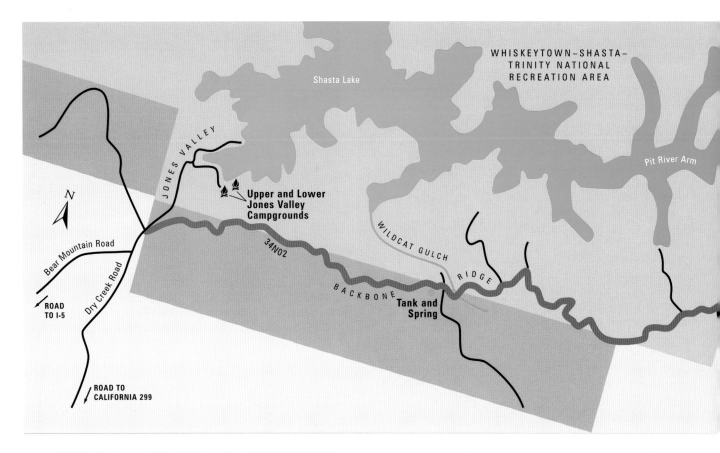

WHISKEYTOWN–SHASTA–
TRINITY NATIONAL
RECREATION AREA
Shasta Lake
Pit River Arm
JONES VALLEY
Upper and Lower
Jones Valley
Campgrounds
N
Bear Mountain Road
Dry Creek Road
ROAD
TO I-5
ROAD TO
CALIFORNIA 299
34N02
WILDCAT GULCH
BACKBONE RIDGE
Tank and
Spring

Mileage		Description
▼ 2.8	SO	Track on right is private.
2.5 ▲	SO	Track on left is private.
▼ 3.1	SO	Two tracks on right are private.
2.2 ▲	SO	Two tracks on left are private.
▼ 5.3	SO	Cross over paved Sugar Pine Camp Road. To the left is the state prison; to the right leads to California 299—the gates on this private road may be locked at any time. Zero trip meter.
0.0 ▲		Continue to the southwest on Backbone Road.
		GPS: N40°44.53' W122°05.65'
▼ 0.0		Continue to the east on Backbone Road.
4.1 ▲	SO	Cross over paved Sugar Pine Camp Road. To the right is the state prison; to the left leads to California 299—the gates on this private road may be locked at any time. Zero trip meter.
▼ 0.3	SO	Track on right.
3.8 ▲	SO	Track on left.
▼ 0.7	SO	Track on left is private.
3.4 ▲	SO	Track on right is private.
▼ 2.3	SO	Track on right is private.
1.8 ▲	SO	Track on left is private.
		GPS: N40°45.76' W122°04.16'
▼ 3.9	SO	Two tracks on left are private.
0.2 ▲	SO	Two tracks on right are private.
▼ 4.1	BR	Graded road on left is the continuation of Backbone Road. Zero trip meter and bear right onto McCandless Gulch Road.
0.0 ▲		Continue to the southwest.
		GPS: N40°46.61' W122°02.98'
▼ 0.0		Continue to the east.
2.8 ▲	SO	Graded road on right is second entrance to Backbone Road. Zero trip meter and join Backbone Road.
▼ 0.1	SO	Second entrance to Backbone Road on left. Remain on McCandless Gulch Road.
2.7 ▲	BL	Track on right is first entrance to Backbone Road.
▼ 0.5	SO	Track on left.
2.3 ▲	SO	Track on right.
▼ 0.7	SO	Two tracks on right, the second is 300-A3.
2.1 ▲	SO	Two tracks on left, the first is 300-A3.
▼ 1.2	SO	Track on right.
1.6 ▲	SO	Track on left.
▼ 2.0	SO	Track on left.
0.8 ▲	BL	Track on right.

Backbone Road

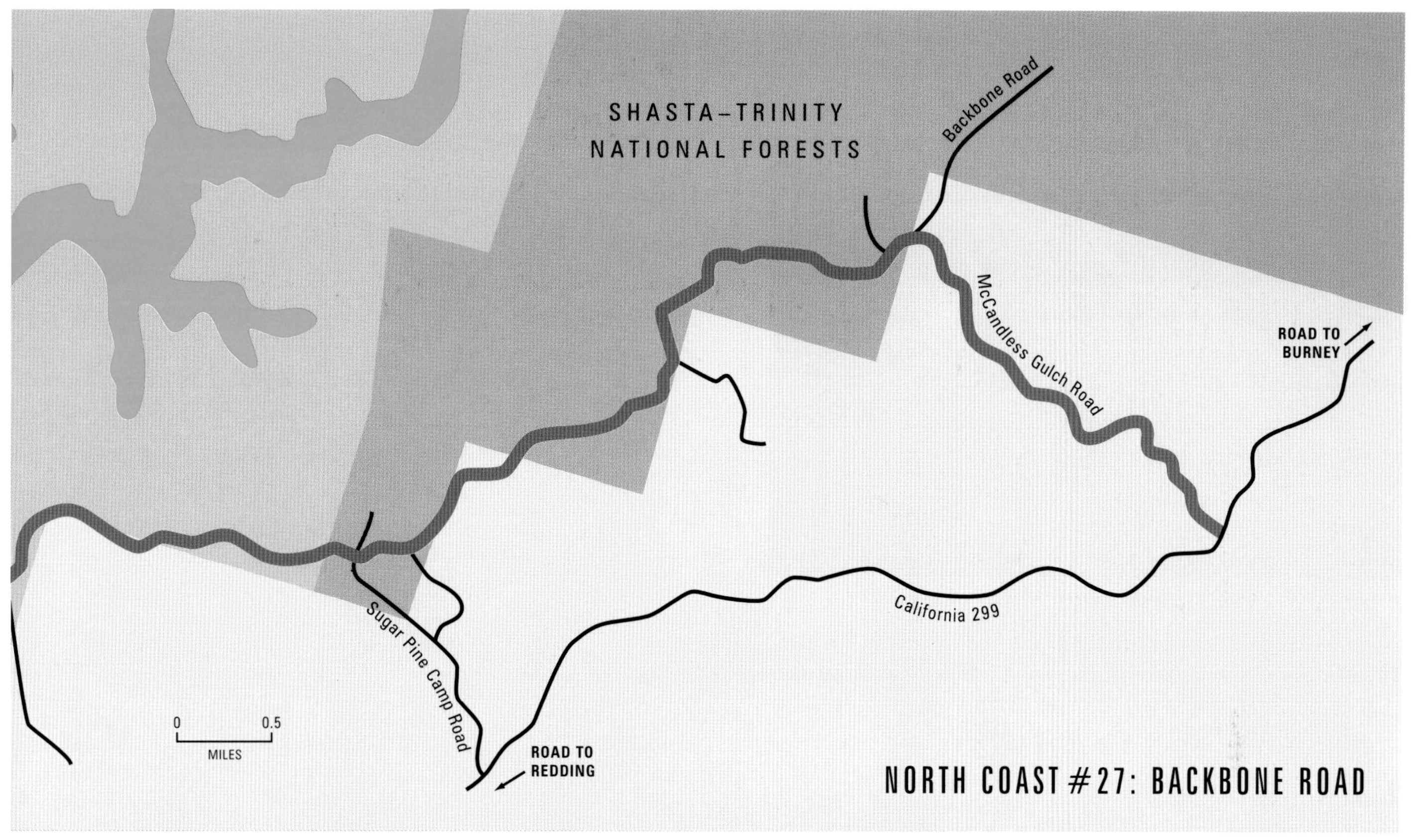

▼ 2.8	Track on left is private; then trail ends at T-intersection with California 299. Turn right for Redding; turn left for Burney.
0.0 ▲	Trail commences on California 299, 5 miles southwest of Round Mountain, 0.2 miles south of Shasta County mile marker 48.00. Zero trip meter and turn west on graded dirt road, marked McCandless Gulch Road (small sign after the turn). Track on right is private.
	GPS: N40°45.71' W122°00.69'

NORTH COAST #28

Backbone Ridge Trail

Starting Point:	**35N08, where the trail turns to graded dirt, 6 miles west of Lakeshore**
Finishing Point:	**Saddle on Backbone Ridge**
Total Mileage:	**8.4 miles (one-way)**
Unpaved Mileage:	**8.4 miles**
Driving Time:	**1 hour (one-way)**
Elevation Range:	**1,200–2,900 feet**
Usually Open:	**May to November**
Best Time to Travel:	**Dry weather**
Difficulty Rating:	**3**
Scenic Rating:	**8**
Remoteness Rating:	**+1**

Special Attractions

- Boating, fishing, camping, and other water-related activities at Shasta Lake.
- Panoramic views from Backbone Ridge.

History

The 370-mile shoreline of Shasta Lake spreads out far below the twisting Backbone Ridge Trail. The lake impounds water from three major river systems: the Sacramento, McCloud, and Pit. Construction of the Shasta Dam commenced in 1938 and was completed in 1945. It took three more years to fill the mammoth reservoir. Many mines, sections of the Central Pacific Railroad and Oregon Trail, and a multitude of historic buildings in the mining town of Kennett, which once supported a population of more than 10,000, lie below the lake's waters.

Elmore Mountain, on the east side of the Sacramento Arm and beyond this trail's route, was on the impressive Elmore Ranch, much of which is now under water. The settlement of Lakehead, passed en route to the start of Backbone Ridge Trail, was named in 1950, five years after Shasta Dam was completed. The hilltop town became a lakeshore town as the waters of Shasta Lake rose to meet it. Initially, the town site was called Pollock Bridge, for a span across the Sacramento River. As the Shasta Dam project continued, the site was moved upriver in 1939 and again in 1940. In 1944, Pollock Bridge was renamed Loftus, to avoid confusion with a town in El Dorado County. Finally, once the waters rose, the site became Lakehead.

Realignment of the Central Pacific Railroad, which later

Shasta Lake lies 2,000 feet below the trail

became the Southern Pacific Railroad, required blasting a series of tunnels to circumvent the rising waters of Shasta Lake. The original railroad, a feat in its own right, was built in 1872. The line followed part of the Oregon Trail.

Description

Backbone Ridge Trail (not to be confused with North Coast #27: Backbone Road on the south side of Shasta Lake, or North Coast #22: Hobo Gulch Trail, which travels along another Backbone Ridge) begins on the western shore of Shasta Lake's Sacramento Arm, south of Lakeshore. There are campgrounds and boat launches along the road from Lakeshore. Anglers will enjoy fishing for rainbow trout, brown trout, and salmon; the best time is in spring and early summer. Bass fishing is good year-round, and crappie and catfish can also be caught.

The trail starts at the end of the paved road and immediately starts to climb a narrow shelf road onto the ridge. The trail runs along the top of Backbone Ridge for a few miles, offering great views over the surrounding area. Passing places are limited, and vehicles must be prepared to back up for oncoming traffic.

The trail enters privately owned forest managed for timber harvesting and has been blocked before it intersects with any other roads.

Current Road Information

Bureau of Land Management
Redding Field Office
355 Hemsted Drive
Redding, CA 96002
(530) 224-2100

Shasta-Trinity National Forests
Shasta Lake Ranger District
14225 Holiday Road
Redding, CA 96003
(530) 275-1587

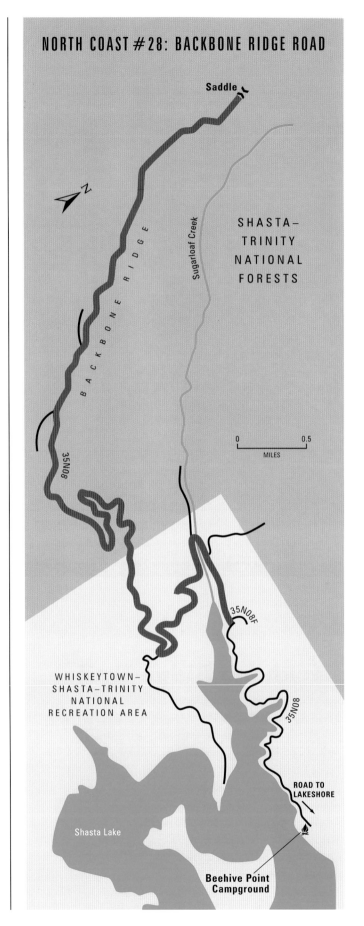

NORTH COAST #28: BACKBONE RIDGE ROAD

Saddle
N
BACKBONE RIDGE
Sugarloaf Creek
SHASTA-TRINITY NATIONAL FORESTS
0 0.5 MILES
35N08
35N08F
WHISKEYTOWN-SHASTA-TRINITY NATIONAL RECREATION AREA
35N08
ROAD TO LAKESHORE
Shasta Lake
Beehive Point Campground

Map References

BLM Redding
USFS Shasta-Trinity National Forests
USGS 1:24,000 Bohemotash Mt., Lamoine
1:100,000 Redding
Maptech CD-ROM: Shasta Lake/Redding
Northern California Atlas & Gazetteer, p. 46
California Road & Recreation Atlas, p. 52
Other: Whiskeytown-Shasta-Trinity NRA: Shasta Unit

Route Directions

▼ 0.0		Trail commences on 35N08, where the road turns to graded dirt, 6 miles west of Lakeshore. Zero trip meter and proceed northwest on 35N08. Immediately track on right is 35N08F.
		GPS: N40°51.12' W122°25.91'
▼ 0.5	SO	Track on right.
▼ 0.6	SO	Cross over Sugarloaf Creek; then track on right.
▼ 1.1	SO	Cross over creek.
▼ 2.0	BR	Track on left on right-hand bend. Zero trip meter.
		GPS: N40°50.68' W122°26.04'
▼ 0.0		Continue to the northwest and start to climb ridge.
▼ 3.7	TR	End of climb. Trail is now on top of Backbone Ridge. Track on left. Zero trip meter.
		GPS: N40°50.94' W122°28.16'
▼ 0.0		Continue to the northwest.
▼ 0.5	BR	Track on left.
▼ 2.7		Road is blocked at saddle where it enters privately owned forest.
		GPS: N40°52.89' W122°29.47'

NORTH COAST #29

Iron Canyon Reservoir Trail

Starting Point:	**FR 11, at the intersection with 38N04Y**
Finishing Point:	**FR 11, at the intersection with 37N78**
Total Mileage:	**13.2 miles**
Unpaved Mileage:	**8.8 miles**
Driving Time:	**1 hour**
Elevation Range:	**2,400–4,100 feet**
Usually Open:	**May to December**
Best Time to Travel:	**May to December**
Difficulty Rating:	**2**
Scenic Rating:	**9**
Remoteness Rating:	**+0**

Special Attractions

- Camping, boating, angling, and picnicking at Lake McCloud and Iron Canyon Reservoir.
- Access to the Pacific Crest National Scenic Trail and a network of dirt roads and 4WD trails.

History

The Pacific Crest National Scenic Trail crosses Iron Canyon Reservoir Trail at the shady Ash Camp and continues to cross a high arched footbridge over the McCloud River on its way to Ah-Di-Na, the site of a Native American village. The Wintun, Pit River, and Okwanuchu people have associations with the riverside site, which was bought by the Whittier family in the late 1890s. They turned it into a hunting camp, planted an orchard, and built guest cabins. The property changed hands in 1919. The new owner William M. Fitzhugh built a cabin; all that remains of a second cabin he built in 1923 is its stone cellar. Little occurred at the riverside property and the buildings eventually fell into disrepair.

Description

This winding trail in Shasta-Trinity National Forests links two very pretty reservoirs. Both offer boating, developed sites for camping and picnicking, and a variety of fishing opportunities. The trail is initially a rough shelf road that follows the McCloud River. Ash Camp, an undeveloped USFS camping area, has a couple of riverside sites. It is a popular place with anglers who fish for rainbow and brown trout in the McCloud River. The Pacific Crest National Scenic Trail crosses this trail at Ash Camp—there is a footbridge to the far side of the river. The trail becomes a narrow paved road for the last couple of miles to Iron Canyon Reservoir. Set in a basin, the multi-armed lake has excellent fishing for rainbow and German brown trout.

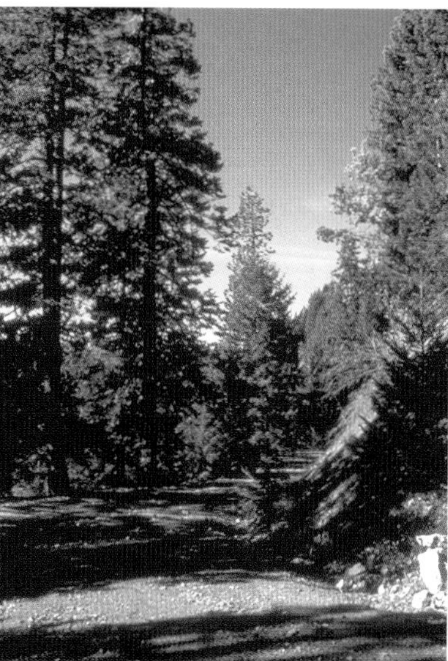

Tall firs line the trail

Many 4WD trails lead off into the forest from this road. One of note is North Coast #30: Grizzly Peak Trail, which can be combined with this route to loop back to California 89.

Current Road Information

Shasta-Trinity National Forests
McCloud Ranger District
2019 Forest Road
McCloud, CA 96057
(530) 964-2184

Map References

BLM Mt. Shasta, McArthur
USFS Shasta-Trinity National Forests
USGS 1:24,000 Lake McCloud, Shoeinhorse Mt., Big Bend
1:100,000 Mt. Shasta, McArthur
Maptech CD-ROM: Shasta-Trinity/Modoc
Northern California Atlas & Gazetteer, p. 37
California Road & Recreation Atlas, p. 53

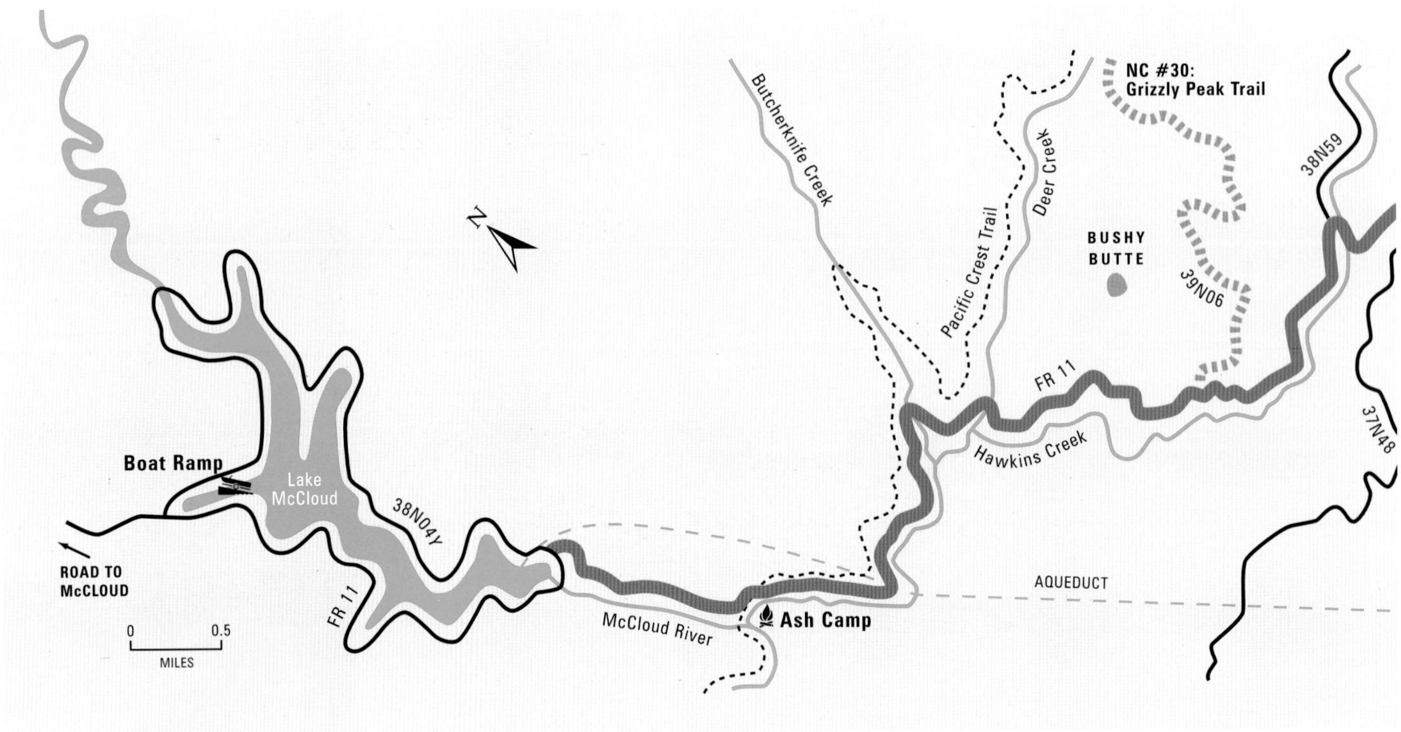

Route Directions

▼ 0.0		From FR 11, at the intersection with 38N04Y at the northeast side of Lake McCloud's dam, 13.5 miles south of McCloud, zero trip meter and turn east on paved FR 11.
5.8 ▲		Trail ends at the intersection with 38N04Y at the northeast side of Lake McCloud's dam. Continue on paved FR 11 to McCloud.
		GPS: N41°07.94' W122°04.16'
▼ 0.3	SO	Track on right.
5.5 ▲	SO	Track on left.
▼ 1.1	BL	Road on right is 38N11H to Ash Camp. Follow sign to Iron Canyon Reservoir. Road turns to graded dirt.
4.7 ▲	SO	Road on left is 38N11H to Ash Camp. Road becomes paved.
		GPS: N41°07.12' W122°03.68'
▼ 1.4	SO	Pacific Crest Trail crosses.
4.4 ▲	SO	Pacific Crest Trail crosses.
▼ 1.9	SO	Track on right.
3.9 ▲	SO	Track on left.
▼ 2.0	SO	Two tracks on right.
3.8 ▲	SO	Two tracks on left.
▼ 2.1	SO	Cross over aqueduct pipeline linking Lake McCloud and Iron Canyon Reservoir.
3.7 ▲	SO	Cross over aqueduct pipeline linking Lake McCloud and Iron Canyon Reservoir.
		GPS: N41°06.55' W122°02.81'
▼ 2.2	SO	Wide track on right.
3.6 ▲	SO	Wide track on left.
▼ 3.4	SO	Cross over Butcherknife Creek.
2.4 ▲	SO	Cross over Butcherknife Creek.
		GPS: N41°07.07' W122°01.88'
▼ 4.0	SO	Cross over Deer Creek.
1.8 ▲	SO	Cross over Deer Creek.
		GPS: N41°06.81' W122°01.53'
▼ 5.8	SO	Track on left is North Coast #30: Grizzly Peak Trail (39N06). Zero trip meter and follow the sign to Iron Canyon Reservoir and California 299.
0.0 ▲		Continue to the west, remaining on FR 11.
		GPS: N41°06.04' W122°00.58'
▼ 0.0		Continue to the north, remaining on FR 11.
7.4 ▲	SO	Track on right is North Coast #30: Grizzly Peak Trail (39N06). Zero trip meter.
▼ 1.1	SO	Cross over creek.
6.3 ▲	SO	Cross over creek.
▼ 1.3	SO	Track on right is 38N11C.
6.1 ▲	SO	Track on left is 38N11C.
▼ 1.5	BR	Graded road on left is 38N59 to Mica Gulch. Follow sign to Iron Canyon

Iron Canyon Reservoir

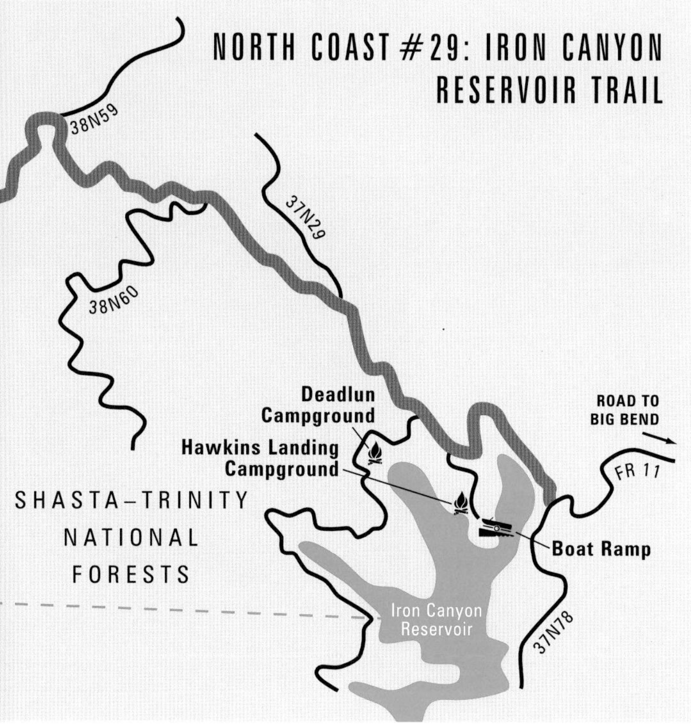

		Reservoir and cross over Hawkins Creek.
5.9 ▲	BL	Cross over Hawkins Creek; then graded road on right is 38N59 to Mica Gulch.
		GPS: N41°06.11' W121°59.25'
▼ 2.2	SO	Track on right is 37N48 to Van Sicklin Butte.
5.2 ▲	SO	Track on left is 37N48 to Van Sicklin Butte.
		GPS: N41°05.90' W121°58.81'
▼ 2.9	SO	Track on left is 38N59.
4.5 ▲	SO	Track on right is 38N59.
▼ 3.1	SO	Road is now paved.
4.3 ▲	SO	Road turns to graded dirt.
▼ 4.1	SO	Track on right is 38N60.
3.3 ▲	SO	Track on left is 38N60.
		GPS: N41°05.13' W121°58.02'
▼ 5.2	SO	Track on left is 37N29.
2.2 ▲	SO	Track on right is 37N29.
▼ 6.1	SO	Paved road on right goes 1 mile to Deadlun USFS Campground. Follow the sign to Big Bend.
1.3 ▲	BR	Paved road on left goes 1 mile to Deadlun USFS Campground. Follow the sign to Lake McCloud.
▼ 6.3	SO	Track on right is 37N66Y to Hawkins Landing USFS Campground and boat ramp.
1.1 ▲	SO	Track on left is 37N66Y into Hawkins Landing USFS Campground and boat ramp.
		GPS: N41°03.47' W121°58.13'
▼ 7.4	SO	Trail ends at intersection with 37N78 to Pit 5 Powerhouse on right. Continue on straight ahead on FR 11 to exit to Big Bend.
0.0 ▲		Trail commences on FR 11 at the intersection with 37N78 to Pit 5 Powerhouse, 5 miles northwest of Big Bend and 21 miles north of California 299. Zero trip meter and proceed north on paved FR 11, following sign to Hawkins Landing and McCloud.
		GPS: N41°02.98' W121°57.95'

NORTH COAST #30

Grizzly Peak Trail

Starting Point:	**North Coast #29: Iron Canyon Reservoir Trail, 5.8 miles from the northern end**
Finishing Point:	**California 89, 13 miles east of McCloud**
Total Mileage:	**19.3 miles**
Unpaved Mileage:	**18.4 miles**
Driving Time:	**2.25 hours**
Elevation Range:	**3,600–6,200 feet**
Usually Open:	**May to November**
Best Time to Travel:	**May to November**
Difficulty Rating:	**3**
Scenic Rating:	**9**
Remoteness Rating:	**+0**

Special Attractions

- Panoramic views from Grizzly Peak.
- Angling in the McCloud River at Algoma USFS Campground.

History

Built in the early 1950s, Grizzly Peak Fire Lookout provides excellent 360-degree views from its lofty perch at 6,275 feet. The twisting course of the McCloud River, some 3,300 feet below, is off to the northwest. The Wyntoon villa estate of William Randolph Hearst, built alongside the river in the 1930s, is just north of Lake McCloud. The elaborate retreat was designed as a Bavarian village by renowned San Francisco architect Julia Morgan. Morgan completed several hundred impressive buildings throughout her working life; many of her commissions followed the San Francisco earthquake of 1906.

Mount Shasta and Konwakiton Glacier from Grizzly Peak

The Wyntoon property had three groups of buildings centered around a green with tennis and croquet courts, a swimming pool, and a variety of entertaining buildings scattered along the McCloud River. The ornate complex was built to showcase Hearst's German art collection. Called "Hearst Castle," the estate was frequented by the Hearst family during World War II because they feared that their coastal San Simeon property would be a target for enemy bombers.

The name Wyntoon comes from Wintun, the Native Americans who inhabited this region.

Description

Grizzly Peak's summit, covered with manzanitas, stands high above the surrounding forests and valleys. However, Mount Shasta dwarfs it because it is nearly twice as high. The trail leaves North Coast #29: Iron Canyon Reservoir Trail and starts to climb through Shasta-Trinity National Forests along a roughly graded road. There are sections of shelf road and enough uneven ground to require a high-clearance vehicle. As you climb, the conifer forest is gradually left behind, and the trail travels across a manzanita-covered ridge. Mount Shasta dominates views to the north. A short 0.1-mile side trail leads to the fire lookout, which is occasionally manned during thunderstorms.

Past Grizzly Peak, the loose, scrabbly trail descends back into the forest. This part of the trail is a good place to see fall colors. Part of the trail travels through privately owned forests managed for timber harvesting. The road is currently open for public travel, but you are not permitted to trespass on the private land off the thoroughfare. Be sure that you are on public land before camping or venturing off the main trail.

Grizzly Peak Fire Lookout

Two old wooden cabins can be seen a short distance off the main trail at Stouts Meadow, along 39N05. These cabins are privately owned. The larger of the two has an ornate veranda and roof. Please admire them from the public road.

Re-entering Shasta-Trinity National Forests, the trail passes Algoma USFS Campground, on the banks of the McCloud River. The river is popular among fishermen, and it contains some brook trout below Lakin Dam (found along North Coast #31: McCloud River Road) and is regularly stocked with rainbow trout.

The trail ends on paved California 89. Watch out for deer, numerous chipmunks, and even black bears along this trail.

Current Road Information

Shasta-Trinity National Forests
McCloud Ranger District
2019 Forest Road
McCloud, CA 96057
(530) 964-2184

ROAD TO McCLOUD
Pacific Crest Trail
38N04
Brushy Butte
39N06
FR 11
38N52
Fire Lookout
Grizzly Peak
Star City Creek
STOUTS MEADOW
39N05
NC #29: Iron Canyon Reservoir Trail
SHASTA–TRINITY NATIONAL FORESTS
ROAD TO IRON CANYON RESERVOIR

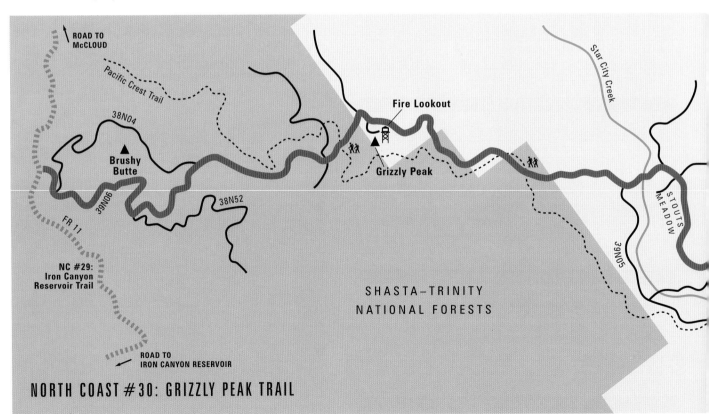

NORTH COAST #30: GRIZZLY PEAK TRAIL

Map References

BLM Mt. Shasta, McArthur
USFS Shasta-Trinity National Forests
USGS 1:24,000 Shoeinhorse Mt., Big Bend, Grizzly Peak, Kinyon
1:100,000 Mt. Shasta, McArthur
Maptech CD-ROM: Shasta-Trinity/Modoc
Northern California Atlas & Gazetteer, p. 37
California Road & Recreation Atlas, pp. 53, 47

Route Directions

Mileage	Direction	Description
▼ 0.0		From FR 11, 19.3 miles south of McCloud and 5.8 miles from the start of North Coast #29: Iron Canyon Reservoir Trail, zero trip meter and turn northwest on graded dirt road 39N06, following sign for Grizzly Peak.
4.8 ▲		Trail ends at T-intersection with North Coast #29: Iron Canyon Reservoir Trail (FR 11). Turn right for McCloud; turn left for Iron Canyon Reservoir and California 299.
		GPS: N41°06.04' W122°00.58'
▼ 0.4	SO	Track on left is 38N04.
4.4 ▲	SO	Track on right is 38N04.
▼ 2.0	BL	Track on right is 38N52.
2.8 ▲	BR	Track on left is 38N52.
		GPS: N41°06.50' W121°59.52'
▼ 2.7	BL	Track on right is 39N06E.
2.1 ▲	SO	Track on left is 39N06E.
▼ 3.1	SO	Track on left is 38N04.
1.7 ▲	SO	Track on right is 38N04.
		GPS: N41°07.19' W121°59.57'
▼ 3.3	SO	Track on left.
1.5 ▲	SO	Track on right.
▼ 3.8	SO	Start of shelf road.
1.0 ▲	SO	End of shelf road.
▼ 4.8	SO	Graded road on right and left under power lines. Zero trip meter.
0.0 ▲		Continue to the southwest.
		GPS: N41°08.14' W121°58.69'
▼ 0.0		Continue to the north.
1.0 ▲	SO	Graded road on right and left under power lines. Zero trip meter.
▼ 0.3	SO	Pacific Crest Trail crosses.
0.7 ▲	SO	Pacific Crest Trail crosses.
▼ 0.6	SO	Track on left.
0.4 ▲	SO	Track on right.
▼ 0.7	BR	Track on left.
0.3 ▲	BL	Track on right.
▼ 0.9	SO	Track on left.
0.1 ▲	SO	Track on right.
▼ 1.0	TL	Track on right is 39N06A, which goes 0.1 miles to Grizzly Peak Fire Lookout. Zero trip meter.
0.0 ▲		Continue to the southwest, remaining on 39N06.
		GPS: N41°08.66' W121°58.73'
▼ 0.0		Continue to the north, remaining on 39N06.
3.3 ▲	TR	Track straight ahead is 39N06A, which goes 0.1 miles to Grizzly Peak Fire Lookout. Zero trip meter.
▼ 0.6	BR	Track on left.
2.7 ▲	BL	Track on right.
▼ 2.3	SO	Pacific Crest Trail crosses.
1.0 ▲	SO	Pacific Crest Trail crosses.
		GPS: N41°09.54' W121°57.11'
▼ 2.8	SO	Cross over creek; then track on right. Trail enters private forest.
0.5 ▲	SO	Track on left; then cross over creek. Trail re-

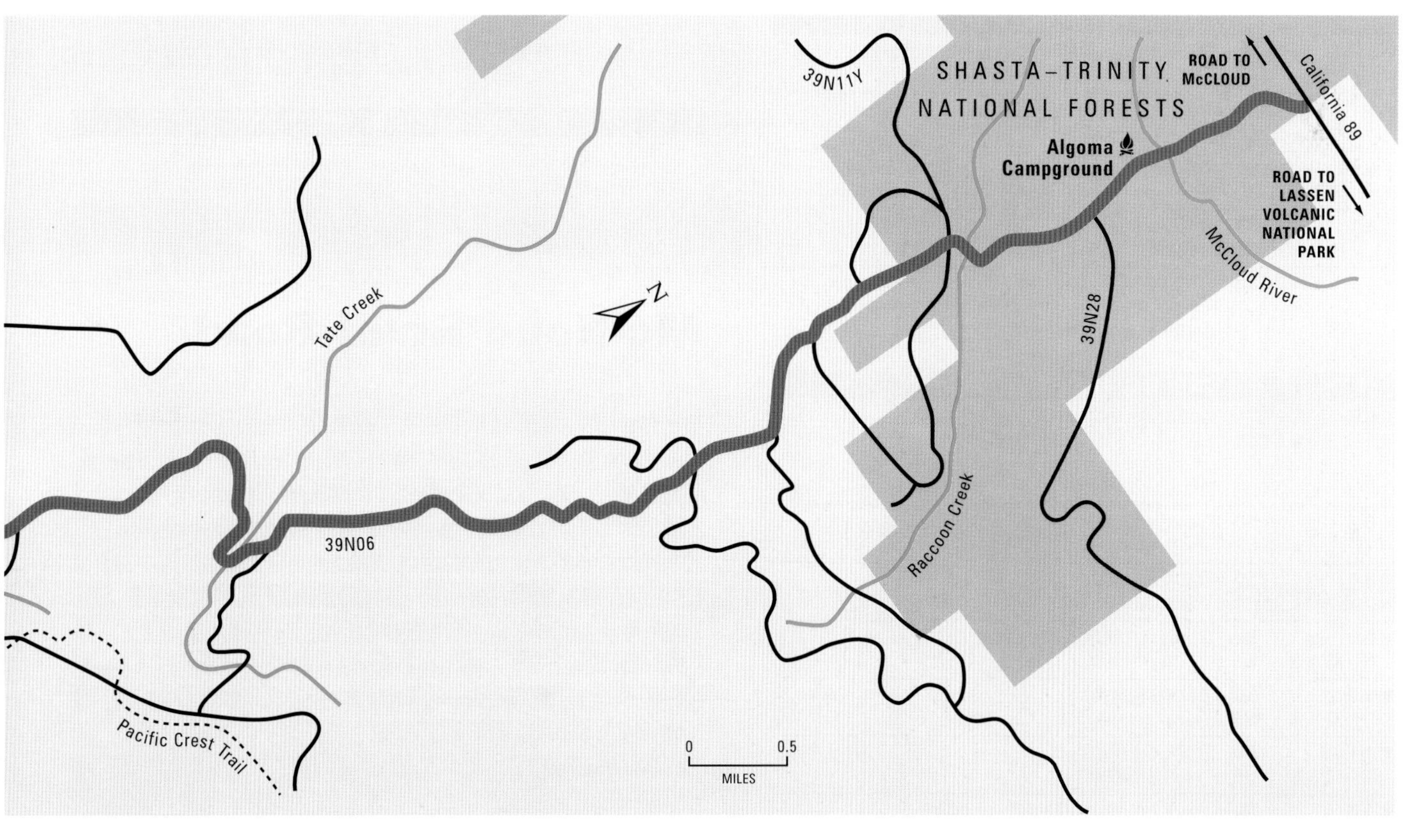

enters Shasta-Trinity National Forests.

▼ 3.3	BL	Stouts Meadow. Track on right is 39N05. Two privately owned cabins are a short distance down this trail on the edge of the meadow. Zero trip meter.
0.0 ▲		Continue to the west, remaining on 39N06.
		GPS: N41°10.14' W121°56.40'
▼ 0.0		Continue to the north, remaining on 39N06. Trail is now marked G Line as well as 39N06.
6.3 ▲	BR	Stouts Meadow. Track on left is 39N05. Two privately owned cabins are a short distance down this trail on the edge of the meadow. Zero trip meter.
▼ 0.2	SO	Cross over Star City Creek; then track on right.
6.1 ▲	SO	Track on left; then cross over Star City Creek.
▼ 0.5	BR	Graded road on left.
5.8 ▲	BL	Graded road on right.
▼ 0.7	SO	4-way intersection. Graded road on left through closure gate. Track on right. Remain on G Line (39N06).
5.6 ▲	SO	4-way intersection. Graded road on right through closure gate. Track on left. Remain on G Line (39N06).
		GPS: N41°10.56' W121°56.11'
▼ 0.9	SO	Track on left.
5.4 ▲	SO	Track on right.
▼ 1.3	SO	Track on left and track on right.
5.0 ▲	SO	Track on left and track on right.
▼ 1.9	SO	Two tracks on right. Remain on 39N06.
4.4 ▲	SO	Two tracks on left. Remain on 39N06.
		GPS: N41°10.38' W121°55.12'
▼ 2.6	SO	Track on right.
3.7 ▲	SO	Track on left.
▼ 3.7	SO	Cross through Tate Creek.
2.6 ▲	SO	Cross through Tate Creek.
		GPS: N41°11.04' W121°54.27'
▼ 4.0	BL	Track on right; then cross over creek.
2.3 ▲	BR	Cross over creek; then track on left.
▼ 4.1	SO	Track on left.
2.2 ▲	SO	Track on right.
▼ 5.6	SO	Cross over creek.
0.7 ▲	SO	Cross over creek.
▼ 6.1	SO	Track on left.
0.2 ▲	SO	Track on right.
▼ 6.3	SO	Well-used track on left passes under power lines. Track on right. Zero trip meter and pass under power lines.
0.0 ▲		Continue to the south.
		GPS: N41°12.89' W121°53.10'
▼ 0.0		Continue to the north.
3.9 ▲	SO	Pass under power lines; then well-used track on right passes under power lines. Track on left. Zero trip meter.
▼ 0.2	SO	Track on left.
3.7 ▲	SO	Track on right.
▼ 0.4	SO	Track on left.
3.5 ▲	SO	Track on right.
▼ 0.5	BL	Graded road on right.
3.4 ▲	BR	Graded road on left.
▼ 1.0	SO	Track on right.
2.9 ▲	SO	Track on left.
▼ 1.1	SO	Track on right.
2.8 ▲	SO	Track on left.
▼ 1.3	SO	Track on left and track on right.
2.6 ▲	SO	Track on left and track on right.
▼ 1.4	SO	Track on left.
2.5 ▲	SO	Track on right.
▼ 1.8	SO	Track on left is 39N11Y and track on right. Re-entering Shasta-Trinity National Forests. Track on right to campsite; then cross over Raccoon Creek.
2.1 ▲	SO	Cross over Raccoon Creek; then track on left to campsite. Entering private forest. Track on left. Track on right is 39N11Y.
		GPS:N41°14.37' W121°53.28'
▼ 2.0	SO	Two tracks on right.
1.9 ▲	SO	Two tracks on left.
▼ 2.1	SO	Track on left.
1.8 ▲	SO	Track on right.
▼ 2.2	SO	Track on right is 39N06B.
1.7 ▲	SO	Track on left is 39N06B.
▼ 2.3	SO	Track on left.
1.6 ▲	SO	Track on right.
▼ 2.6	SO	Track on right is 39N28.
1.3 ▲	SO	Track on left is 39N28.
▼ 3.0	SO	Algoma USFS Campground on left on the McCloud River. Road is now paved. Remain on paved road until the end of the trail.
0.9 ▲	SO	Algoma USFS Campground on right on the McCloud River. Road turns to graded dirt.
▼ 3.1	SO	Cross over McCloud River on bridge.
0.8 ▲	SO	Cross over McCloud River on bridge.
		GPS: N41°15.39' W121°52.92'
▼ 3.9		Trail ends at T-intersection with paved California 89. Turn right for Lassen Volcanic National Park; turn left for McCloud.
0.0 ▲		Trail commences on California 89, 0.1 miles west of county mile marker 11 and 0.2 miles east of Sheephaven Road, 13 miles east of McCloud. Zero trip meter and turn south on paved road, marked Stouts Meadow Road (39N06). Remain on paved road for the next 0.9 miles.
		GPS: N41°15.99' W121°52.69'

NORTH COAST #31

McCloud River Road

Starting Point:	**California 89, 9.8 miles east of McCloud**
Finishing Point:	**California 89, 2.6 miles east of McCloud**
Total Mileage:	**8.3 miles, plus 0.5-mile spur to Lakin Dam and 1.2-mile spur to Lower Falls**
Unpaved Mileage:	**5.9 miles, plus spurs**
Driving Time:	**1 hour**
Elevation Range:	**3,300–3,700 feet**
Usually Open:	**May to December**
Best Time to Travel:	**Spring and fall**
Difficulty Rating:	**1**
Scenic Rating:	**8**
Remoteness Rating:	**+0**

McCloud River Railroad with Mount Shasta behind

Special Attractions

- Many access points for angling, picnicking, swimming, and wildlife watching along the McCloud River.
- Excellent trail for family bicycling.
- Upper, Middle, and Lower Falls and the start of a canoe run to Lake McCloud.

History

In 1854, Ross McCloud purchased land in this area from Harry and Samuel Lockhart, brothers who operated a ferry north of today's Fall River Mills. McCloud built a camp to cater to the passing traffic on the pack trail that led north to Yreka. He went on to become a prominent figure in the community that developed on his land.

In the 1890s, William W. VanArsdale and George W. Scott built a railroad to connect McCloud with Sisson, the original name of the city of Mount Shasta. They also purchased a sawmill in Squaw Valley from A. F. George and began what would evolve into a massive business called the McCloud River Lumber Company. Their railroad network became the McCloud River Railroad Company.

With seemingly endless timber to harvest and a transportation system to reach outside markets, the businesses thrived. Because people could count on finding and keeping a job at McCloud, the town flourished. The railroad network expanded and added passenger service for the public. Steam-powered excursion trains brought many tourists who just wanted to take in the spectacular scenery; guesthouses and hotels in McCloud catered to their needs. McCloud River Road travels a riverside section of the railroad that was built east to Hambone. This river corridor was acquired by the forest service in 1989 in a land exchange deal with Champion International Corporation, then owners of the railroad.

Description

This short easy trail, suitable for all vehicles in dry weather, gives accesses to the McCloud River at a number of points. Although the trail only takes an hour to drive, it is a perfect trail for a full day's outing, allowing time to hike, swim, fish, and view the waterfalls. Campers will find two developed USFS campgrounds: one at the start and one at the end of the trail. There is no camping permitted at any of the picnic areas along the route; this includes Camp 4, which is a group site for day use only.

The route is an easy graded road with short spurs leading to points of interest along the way. Cattle Camp Picnic Area has a wonderful clear blue swimming hole on a bend in the river. This is a great spot to relax, have a picnic, and enjoy a cool dip.

Of the three waterfalls along the trail, Upper Falls, which cuts through black volcanic rock to plunge sharply into the pool below, is the most dramatic and has fewer visitors than the other waterfalls. Middle Falls has a large paved parking area and a short walk to a viewpoint over the falls. Lower Falls has a very popular USFS campground as well as a day use picnic area beside the cascades. A short distance downstream is the put-in for canoes and kayaks. From here, a gentle trip takes paddlers downstream to Lake McCloud. There are short stretches of whitewater, but generally the trip is considered to be easy. The best time of year to make the run is May and June. Around July the water level starts to drop and quickly becomes too low. Anglers will enjoy fishing for rainbow and brook trout below Lakin Dam. This lower section of the river is stocked with rainbow trout. Above the dam, redband trout can be caught.

Handicapped fishing access at Lakin Dam

The final section of the trail follows an old railroad grade, one of the lumber company's many, to finish a short distance east of McCloud back on California 89.

Current Road Information

Shasta-Trinity National Forests
McCloud Ranger District
2019 Forest Road
McCloud, CA 96057
(530) 964-2184

Map References

BLM McArthur, Mt. Shasta
USFS Shasta-Trinity National Forests
USGS 1:24,000 Kinyon, Grizzly Peak, Lake McCloud, Elk Spring
1:100,000 McArthur, Mt. Shasta
Maptech CD-ROM: Shasta-Trinity/Modoc
Northern California Atlas & Gazetteer, p. 37
California Road & Recreation Atlas, p. 47

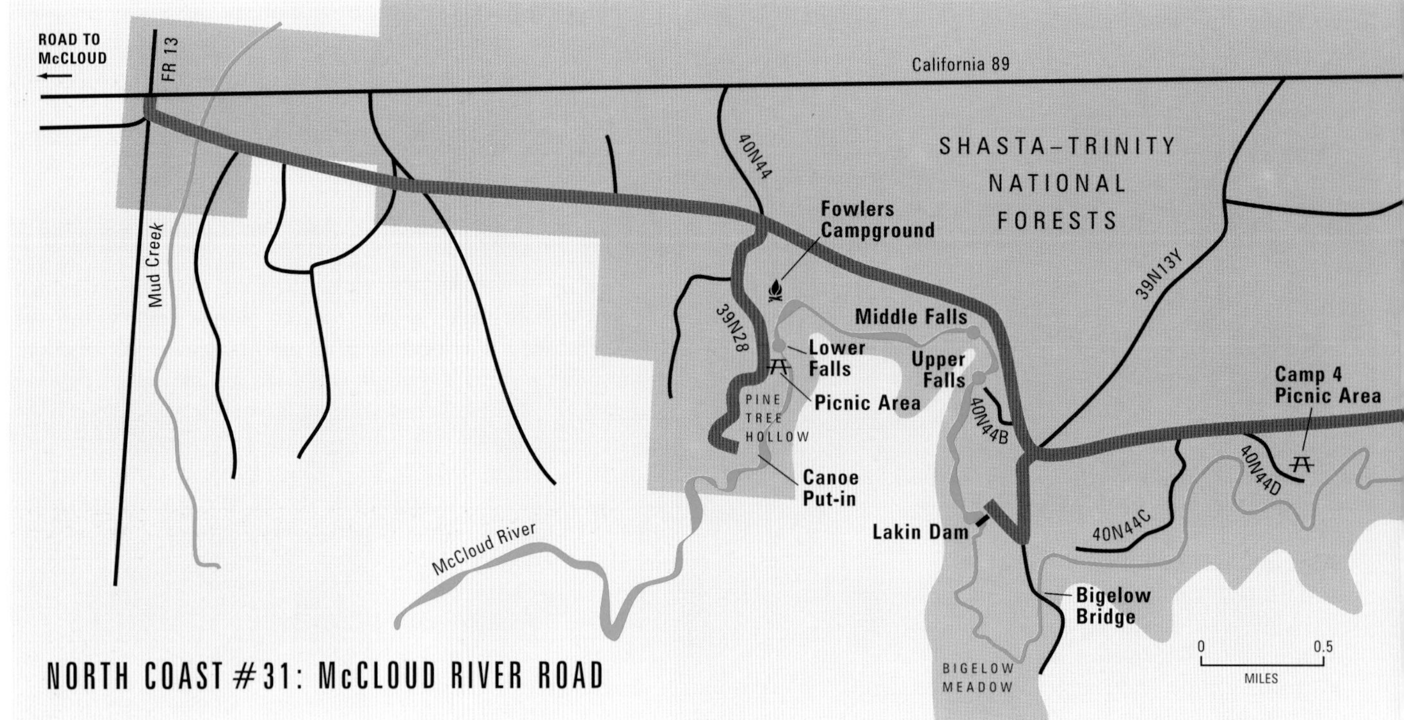

NORTH COAST #31: McCLOUD RIVER ROAD

Route Directions

▼ 0.0		From California 89, 9.8 miles east of McCloud, zero trip meter and turn south onto paved road 40N44, following the sign to McCloud River Loop Road and Cattle Camp USFS Campground.
3.4 ▲		Trail ends back on California 89. Turn left for McCloud; turn right for Lassen Volcanic National Park.
		GPS: N41°15.83' W121°56.49'
▼ 0.1	SO	Track on left is 39N10.
3.3 ▲	SO	Track on right is 39N10.
▼ 0.3	SO	Cattle Camp USFS Campground on left.
3.1 ▲	SO	Cattle Camp USFS Campground on right.
▼ 0.4	SO	Track on right.
3.0 ▲	SO	Track on left.
▼ 0.6	BR	Track on left crosses McCloud River. Remain on paved road.
2.8 ▲	BL	Track on right crosses McCloud River. Remain on paved road.
		GPS: N41°15.32' W121°56.50'
▼ 0.7	SO	Road turns to graded dirt.
2.7 ▲	SO	Road becomes paved.
▼ 0.9	SO	Track on left is 40N44F, which goes 0.2 miles to Cattle Camp Picnic Area, angling point, and swimming hole.
2.5 ▲	SO	Track on right is 40N44F, which goes 0.2 miles to Cattle Camp Picnic Area, angling point, and swimming hole.
		GPS: N41°15.21' W121°56.78'
▼ 1.4	SO	Track on left is 40N44E.
2.0 ▲	SO	Track on right is 40N44E.
▼ 2.1	SO	Track on right.
1.3 ▲	SO	Track on left.
▼ 3.4	SO	Track on left is 40N44D, which goes 0.3 miles to Camp 4 Picnic Area, angling point, and swimming hole. Zero trip meter.
0.0 ▲		Continue to the northeast.
		GPS: N41°14.31' W121°59.26'
▼ 0.0		Continue to the southwest.
0.8 ▲	SO	Track on right is 40N44D, which goes 0.3 miles to Camp 4 Picnic Area, angling point, and swimming hole. Zero trip meter.
▼ 0.2	SO	Track on left is 40N44C.
0.6 ▲	SO	Track on right is 40N44C.
▼ 0.3	SO	Track on right.
0.5 ▲	SO	Track on left.
▼ 0.8	SO	4-way intersection. Graded road on right and left is Bigelow Meadow Road (39N13Y). To the left is the spur to Bigelow Bridge and Lakin Dam. To the right goes to California 89. Zero trip meter.
0.0 ▲		Continue to the east. Road turns to graded dirt.
		GPS: N41°14.16' W122°00.16'

Spur to Bigelow Bridge and Lakin Dam

▼ 0.0		Continue to the south.
▼ 0.3	TR	Road continues ahead for 0.3 miles to Bigelow Bridge, which is blocked to public access. Turn right, following sign to Lakin Dam.
		GPS: N41°13.87' W122°00.22'
▼ 0.5		Lakin Dam.
		GPS: N41°13.99' W122°00.37'

Continuation of Main Trail

▼ 0.0		Continue to the west. Road becomes paved.
1.6 ▲	SO	4-way intersection. Graded road on right and left is Bigelow Meadow Road (39N13Y). To the right is the spur to Bigelow Bridge and Lakin Dam. To the left goes to California 89. Zero trip meter.
		GPS: N41°14.16' W122°00.16'
▼ 0.2	SO	Track on left is 40N44B, which goes 0.3 miles to Upper Falls. Hike 0.1 miles farther downstream to view the falls.

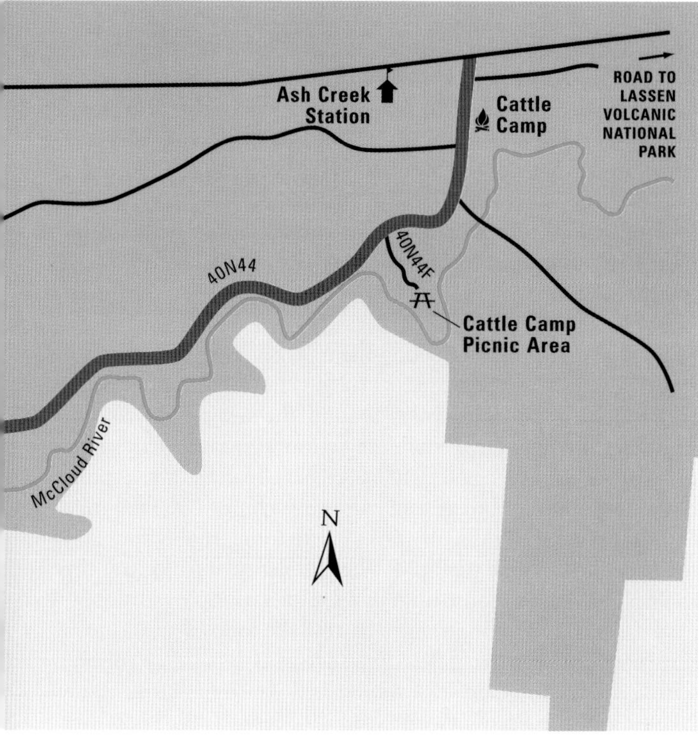

1.4 ▲ SO Track on right is 40N44B, which goes 0.3 miles to Upper Falls. Hike 0.1 miles farther downstream to view the falls.

GPS: N41°14.32′ W122°00.28′

▼ 0.4 SO Upper Falls can be seen between the trees on the left.
1.2 ▲ SO Upper Falls can be seen between the trees on the right.

▼ 0.7 SO Parking area for Middle Falls on left. The falls are a short distance past the parking lot.
0.9 ▲ SO Parking area for Middle Falls on right. The falls are a short distance past the parking lot.

▼ 0.9 SO Track on right.
0.7 ▲ SO Track on left.

▼ 1.5 SO Track on left.
0.1 ▲ SO Track on right.

▼ 1.6 SO Paved road on left is 39N28, spur to Lower Falls. To the right is 40N44, which goes to California 89. Zero trip meter.
0.0 ▲ Continue to the east on paved road.

GPS: N41°14.94′ W122°01.52′

Spur to Lower Falls

▼ 0.0 Proceed south on 39N28.
▼ 0.1 TR Turn right, following sign to Lower Falls.
▼ 0.3 SO Track on right.
▼ 0.6 BR Lower Falls on left; then picnic area on left. Road turns to graded dirt.

GPS: N41°14.44′ W122°01.45′

▼ 1.0 TL Turn left to access Pine Tree Hollow Hiking Trail and canoe put-in.

GPS: N41°14.18′ W122°01.68′

▼ 1.2 Canoe put-in access and hiking trail.

GPS: N41°14.14′W122°01.53′

Continuation of Main Trail

▼ 0.0 Continue to the west on graded dirt road.
2.5 ▲ SO Paved road on right is 39N28, spur to Lower Falls. To the left is 40N44, which goes to California 89. Zero trip meter.

GPS: N41°14.94′ W122°01.52′

▼ 0.6 SO Track on right.
1.9 ▲ SO Track on left.

▼ 1.3 SO Track on left and track on right.
1.2 ▲ SO Track on left and track on right.

▼ 1.5 SO Track on right.
1.0 ▲ SO Track on left.

▼ 1.6 SO Track on left.
0.9 ▲ SO Track on right.

▼ 1.9 SO Track on left and track on right.
0.6 ▲ SO Track on left and track on right.

▼ 2.1 SO Track on left and track on right.
0.4 ▲ SO Track on left and track on right.

▼ 2.2 SO Cross over Mud Creek.
0.3 ▲ SO Cross over Mud Creek.

GPS: N41°15.12′ W122°04.19′

▼ 2.4 TR Paved road on right and left. Track straight ahead.
0.1 ▲ TL Paved road continues ahead. Track on right. Turn left onto dirt road.

▼ 2.5 Trail finishes at intersection with California 89. Pilgrim Creek Road (FR 13) is opposite. Turn left for McCloud; turn right for Lassen Volcanic National Park.
0.0 ▲ Trail starts on California 89, 2.6 miles east of McCloud. Zero trip meter and turn southeast on paved road. The turn is opposite Pilgrim Creek Road (FR 13), which is signed to the snowmobile park and Mount Shasta Wilderness trailheads.

GPS: N41°15.25′ W122°04.43′

NORTH COAST #32

Toad Lake Trail

Starting Point:	**FR 26, 8.1 miles southwest of Mount Shasta**
Finishing Point:	**Hiking trailhead, 0.4 miles east of Toad Lake**
Total Mileage:	**10.4 miles (one-way)**
Unpaved Mileage:	**10.4 miles**
Driving Time:	**1 hour (one-way)**
Elevation Range:	**3,700–6,800 feet**
Usually Open:	**May to November**
Best Time to Travel:	**June to September**
Difficulty Rating:	**3**
Scenic Rating:	**9**
Remoteness Rating:	**+0**

Special Attractions

- Fishing, picnicking, and camping at Toad Lake.
- Views of Mount Shasta from the shelf road.
- Hiking access to the Pacific Crest National Scenic Trail.

Toad Lake

History

Toad Lake, in the Trinity Mountains, is due west of Mount Shasta and the Sacramento Valley. Though Indians used the important north-south corridor of the Sacramento River, it eluded settlers for some time. In 1850, gold was discovered in Scott Valley, to the west of the Trinity Mountains, drawing attention to the region. The site that became the town of Mount Shasta was established in the 1850s. The Central Pacific Railroad reached Mount Shasta in 1887. On June 11, 1903, a Dr. Thompson and Manuel Perry drove the first automobile up the Sacramento Valley to Yreka.

Description

The long climb to Toad Lake follows a snaking path above the South Fork of the Sacramento River, starting at an approximate elevation of 3,700 feet. The trail also crosses the Middle Fork of the Sacramento. As the trail climbs an additional 3,000 feet to Toad Lake, the river corridors come clearly into view.

The trail follows roughly graded forest roads to the trailhead to Toad Lake. The beautiful natural lake is set in a bowl below the ridge top, south of Mount Eddy. Much of the trail is shelf road that travels toward The Eddys, a range of volcanic peaks that is part of the Trinity Mountains. The vegetation is predominantly mixed conifers, but the serpentine soils have a high magnesium content, which is not conducive to plant growth. Because of this, the ridge tops are less vegetated than might be expected.

There are few markers along the trail, but navigation is generally easy because there are few turns. The climbs are gradual, and much of the trail wraps around the mountainside, descending to cross over the Middle Fork of the Sacramento River before ascending again. Landslides have made some sections of the trail uneven, but generally it is easygoing. The final mile earns most of the 3 difficulty rating, with loose, rubbly rocks on the final climb to the trailhead. There is plenty of parking at the trailhead, as well as some undeveloped backcountry campsites.

The 0.4-mile hiking trail to Toad Lake follows an old jeep trail now closed to vehicles. The surface is loose and rubbly, with a moderate grade. The hiking trail continues around the lake to join the Pacific Crest National Scenic Trail. There is a lovely walk-in campsite by the lake beneath some pine trees. The lake offers angling for rainbow and brown trout. It is stocked by air with fingerling trout once or twice a year.

Current Road Information

Shasta-Trinity National Forests
Mount Shasta Ranger District
204 West Alma
Mount Shasta, CA 96067
(530) 926-4511

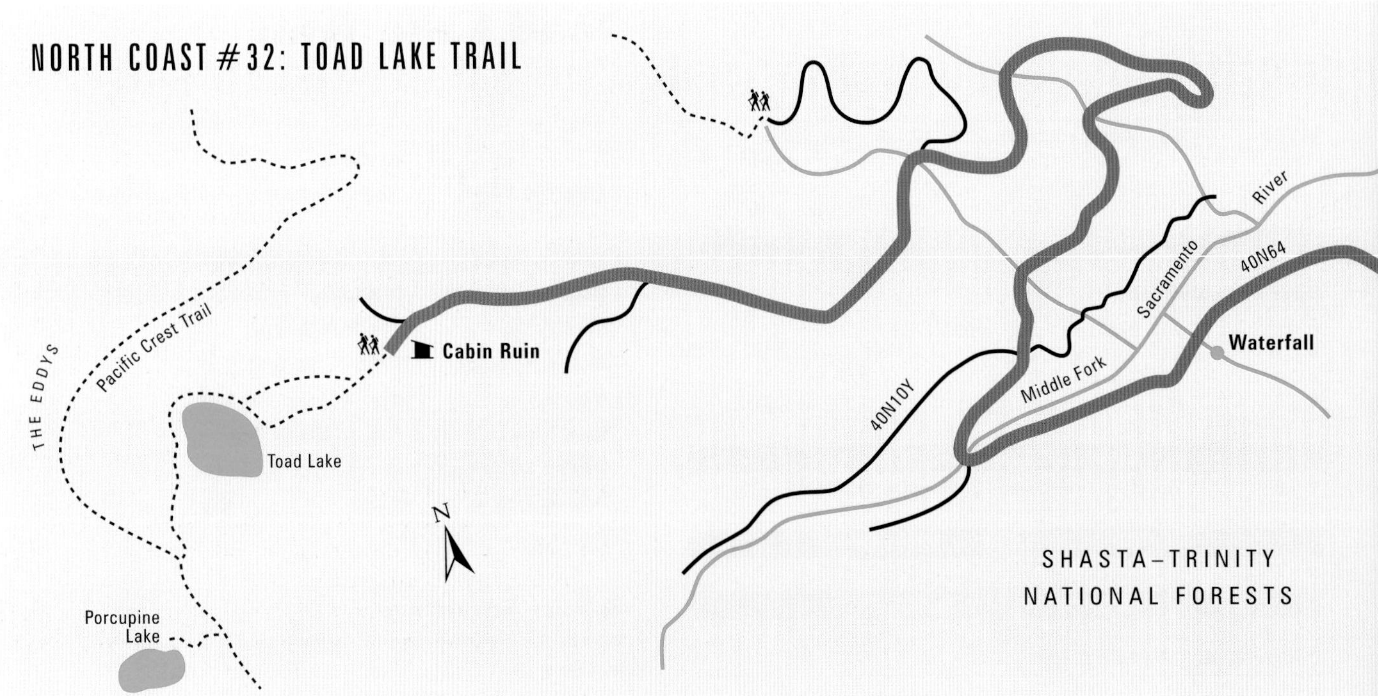

Map References

BLM Mt. Shasta
USFS Shasta-Trinity National Forests
USGS 1:24,000 Mt. Eddy
1:100,000 Mt. Shasta
Maptech CD-ROM: Shasta-Trinity/Modoc
Northern California Atlas & Gazetteer, p. 36
California Road & Recreation Atlas, p. 46

Route Directions

▼ 0.0		From FR 26, 8.1 miles southwest of Mount Shasta, past Siskiyou Lake and 0.1 miles southwest of where the paved road crosses over South Fork Sacramento River on a bridge, zero trip meter and turn north on graded dirt road 41N53.
		GPS: N41°16.25' W122°24.17'
▼ 0.2	BL	Road continues straight ahead. Bear left onto unmarked road.
▼ 1.8	SO	Track on right.
▼ 2.2	BR	Track on left is 39N84.
		GPS: N41°15.76' W122°25.04'
▼ 3.2	SO	Turnout on right with a view of Mount Shasta.
▼ 4.2	SO	Well-used track on left. Track is now marked as 40N64.
		GPS: N41°16.45' W122°26.21'
▼ 4.8	SO	Small waterfall on left.
		GPS: N41°16.39' W122°26.85'
▼ 5.6	SO	Track on left; then cross over Middle Fork Sacramento River on bridge. Zero trip meter.
		GPS: N41°16.29' W122°27.69'
▼ 0.0		Continue to the northwest.
▼ 0.4	SO	Track on left is 40N10Y and track on right.
		GPS: N41°16.49' W122°27.41'
▼ 0.6	SO	Cross over creek.
▼ 1.2	SO	Cross over creek.
▼ 2.6	SO	Track on left.

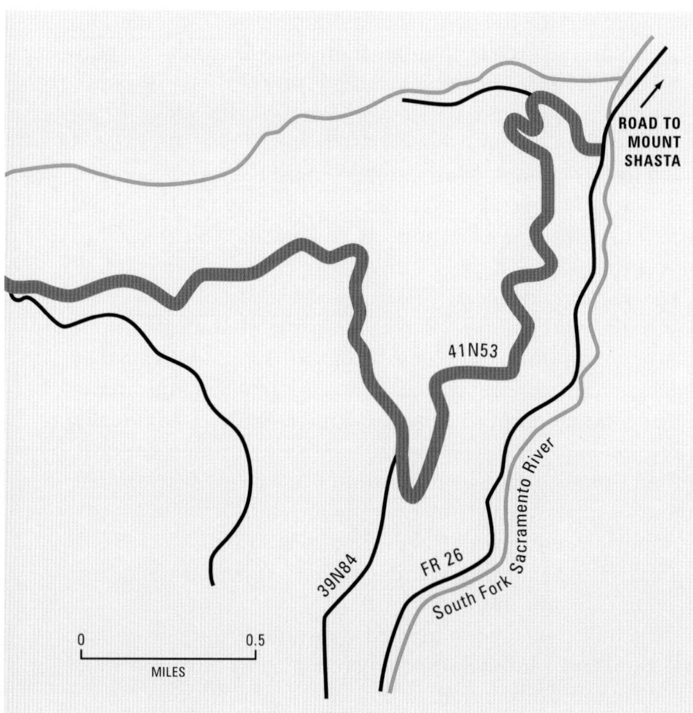

Bridge over the Middle Fork of the Sacramento River

▼ 2.8	SO	Track on right goes to trailhead accessing the Sisson Calahan National Recreation Trail; then cross over creek.
		GPS: N41°17.04' W122°27.47'
▼ 3.9	SO	Track on left.
▼ 4.6	BL	Track on right.
		GPS: N41°17.07' W122°29.30'
▼ 4.7	SO	Track on left to campsite; then collapsed log cabin on left.
▼ 4.8		Hiking trail on left goes 0.4 miles to Toad Lake. The vehicle trail continues another 0.1 miles to a couple of campsites and a turnaround.
		GPS: N41°17.00' W122°29.41'

NORTH COAST #33

Mount Shasta Loop

Starting Point:	**FR 19, 10.5 miles southeast of US 97**
Finishing Point:	**South Mount Shasta Boulevard in the town of Mount Shasta**
Total Mileage:	**31.2 miles**
Unpaved Mileage:	**28.1 miles**
Driving Time:	**3 hours**
Elevation Range:	**3,600–6,400 feet**
Usually Open:	**May to October**
Best Time to Travel:	**May to October**
Difficulty Rating:	**2**
Scenic Rating:	**9**
Remoteness Rating:	**+0**

Special Attractions

- Easy trail around the east and south sides of Mount Shasta.
- Excellent views of the mountain and access to hiking trails that climb to the summit.
- The trail is part of a network of winter snowmobile routes and is close to the Deer Mountain Snowmobile Staging Area.
- Mount Shasta Ski Park and cross-country ski area.

History

Mount Shasta, a volcanic summit in the Cascade Range, rises to 14,162 feet and is the centerpiece of the Mount Shasta Wilderness and Mount Shasta Natural Landmark (see Mount Shasta, page 112). The Konwakiton Glacier, on the south face of Mount Shasta, is subject to mud flows. A particularly devastating flow occurred in 1924.

Mud flows occur when especially warm weather rapidly melts a glacier's ice. Melted water accumulates mud and debris as it flows down its usual channels, but, given the massive amount, Konwakiton's melt overflowed and carried huge rocks and blocks of ice with it. The 1924 flow fanned out of Mud Creek Canyon before it reached the concrete Mud Creek Dam, east of McKenzie Butte, beside the described trail. The flow carried debris nearly 13 miles from the glacier, some 8,000 feet below the mountain's summit. The McCloud River Railroad was engulfed, stalling a train east of McCloud.

Description

This trail travels easy, graded forest roads on the east side of Mount Shasta before swinging around the south side of the mountain to finish in the town of Mount Shasta. Although most of the trail is suitable for passenger vehicles in dry weather, there are a couple of places where high-clearance is preferable: A section of wide shelf road around the south side of the mountain is a little rough for passenger vehicles and the Ash Creek crossing is in a dip on a slight rise. It is impossible to see until you are right on top of it, and vehicles traveling at more than a few miles an hour will risk damage on the sharp dip. Although a small, carefully driven passenger vehicle may be able to negotiate this crossing when the water level is low, high-clearance is definitely preferable. If the water level is high, usually in spring and early summer, the crossing may be impassable to all vehicles.

South end of Mount Shasta Loop

The trail begins on FR 19, a short distance past the end of the pavement. Initially, the trail travels within the Deer Mountain–Whaleback Road Management Area. From August 15 to March 31 each year, motorized travel is restricted to roads and tracks marked with a green arrow on a white background. Side tracks mentioned in the route directions are for navigation purposes only. If you intend to explore the side trails, you should purchase a current forest service map that shows year-round vehicle travel routes.

The trail passes the eastern end of North Coast #34: Military Pass Trail, a 2-rated trail that leads west to US 97 along the north side of Mount Shasta. The main trail remains on FR 19 before turning onto FR 31 at the turnoff to the Brewer Creek Trailhead, which provides access to Mount Shasta's summit. A fee is required to use this trail. Access to the Clear Creek Trailhead is farther south.

The trail passes a wide variety of scenery and a number of exceptional viewpoints along its length. The mountain dominates the landscape, and photographers should be able to get many good shots on a clear day. On the southern part of the trail, the section of shelf road around McKenzie Butte offers views south over McCloud Valley. The trail briefly intersects with paved Ski Park Highway, which leads to the Mount Shasta Ski Park, and passes through the cross-country ski area before joining the paved road to the town of Mount Shasta.

Mount Shasta rises above the trail

Those intending to climb Mount Shasta should be well prepared and not underestimate the mountain. It is essential that you check with the forest service for permits and other related information. The mountain attracts approximately 30,000 climbers a year, many of whom are novices, making it one of the most popular climbs in the United States. A Mount Shasta Summit Pass is required for ascents above 10,000 feet. These are limited and a fee is required. Most climbers make the ascent between May and October and take one to two days for the round trip. The most popular route is Avalanche Gulch, reached from Bunny Flat on the southwest slope. This route is usually covered in two days with a camp at Helen Lake.

Another attraction of this region is the abundance of rare matsutake mushrooms. This valuable cash crop is harvested by Japanese and Koreans who use the very pungent mushroom for ceremonial purposes as well as for seasoning. Traditionally, it is given as a gift of great worth—either a wedding gift or to seal a business deal. The mushroom is harvested between late August and the first frost, typically around October. Matsutake mushrooms grow at high elevations in light, rocky soils typically associated with volcanic regions. A permit is required to collect the mushrooms.

Much of this trail is a marked snowmobile route in winter, and the Deer Mountain Snowmobile Staging Area is a short distance north of the trail.

Current Road Information
Shasta-Trinity National Forests
Mount Shasta Ranger District
204 West Alma
Mount Shasta, CA 96067
(530) 926-4511

Map References
BLM Yreka, Mt. Shasta
USFS Shasta-Trinity National Forests; Klamath National Forest
USGS 1:24,000 West Haight Mt., Ash Creek Butte, Elk Spring, McCloud, City of Mt. Shasta
1:100,000 Yreka, Mt. Shasta
Maptech CD-ROM: Shasta-Trinity/Modoc
Northern California Atlas & Gazetteer, pp. 27, 37, 36
California Road & Recreation Atlas, pp. 46, 47
Other: Mount Shasta Wilderness, Tom Harrison Maps—Mt. Shasta Wilderness Trail Map (incomplete)

Route Directions

▼ 0.0		Trail begins on FR 19 at the intersection with 42N16, which leads to the north and is marked to Butte Creek and Alder Creek. The starting point is a short distance past the end of the paved road, 10.5 miles southeast of US 97 and 6.5 miles south of the Deer Mountain Snowmobile Staging Area. Zero trip meter and proceed northeast, following sign to California 89.
5.2 ▲		Trail finishes at intersection with 42N16. Continue straight ahead on FR 19, which becomes paved, to exit to US 97.
		GPS: N41°30.82' W122°05.50'
▼ 0.9	SO	Track on left.
4.3 ▲	SO	Track on right.
▼ 1.3	SO	Track on right is 42N23 and track on left.
3.9 ▲	SO	Track on left is 42N23 and track on right.
▼ 1.8	SO	Track on left; then cattle guard.
3.4 ▲	SO	Cattle guard; then track on right.
		GPS:N41°30.48' W122°03.89'
▼ 3.0	SO	Track on right.
2.2 ▲	SO	Track on left.
▼ 3.1	SO	Leaving Deer Mountain–Whaleback Road Management Area.
2.1 ▲	SO	Entering Deer Mountain–Whaleback Road Management Area.
▼ 4.6	SO	Track on left is 42N12B.
0.6 ▲	SO	Track on right is 42N12B.
▼ 4.9	SO	Track on right.
0.3 ▲	SO	Track on left.
▼ 5.2	SO	Track on right is North Coast #34: Military Pass Trail (43N19). Track on left is 42N20. Zero trip meter and follow the sign for California 89.
0.0 ▲		Continue to the west, remaining on FR 19.
		GPS: N41°28.61' W122°05.14'
▼ 0.0		Continue to the east, remaining on FR 19.
3.7 ▲	SO	Track on left is North Coast #34: Military Pass Trail (43N19). Track on right is 42N20. Zero trip meter and follow the sign for US 97.
▼ 0.3	SO	Track on right.
3.4 ▲	SO	Track on left.
▼ 0.4	SO	Track on right.
3.3 ▲	SO	Track on left.
▼ 0.6	SO	Track on right and track on left.
3.1 ▲	SO	Track on right and track on left.
▼ 1.0	SO	Track on left is 42N09.
2.7 ▲	SO	Track on right is 42N09.
		GPS: N41°28.03' W122°04.56'
▼ 1.9	BL	Track on right is 43N19X. Follow the sign for California 89.
1.8 ▲	BR	Track on left is 43N19X. Remain on main graded road, following sign for Deer Mountain Snowmobile Park.
▼ 2.2	SO	Track on left is 42N70.
1.5 ▲	SO	Track on right is 42N70.
▼ 2.8	SO	Track on right is 42N05.
0.9 ▲	SO	Track on left is 42N05.
		GPS: N41°26.45' W122°04.92'
▼ 3.0	SO	Track on right; then track on left.
0.7 ▲	SO	Track on right; then track on left.
▼ 3.5	SO	Track on left is 41N19XD.
0.2 ▲	SO	Track on right is 41N19XD.
▼ 3.7	TR	Graded road on right is 42N02 to Brewer Creek Trailhead. Track on left. Then turn right onto FR 31 (41N31) and zero trip meter.
0.0 ▲		Continue to the north.
		GPS: N41°25.85' W122°04.40'
▼ 0.0		Continue to the west.
5.9 ▲	TL	T-intersection with FR 19. Zero trip meter and turn left. Then graded road on left is 42N02 to Brewer Creek Trailhead. Also track on right.
▼ 0.5	SO	Track on right.
5.4 ▲	SO	Track on left.
▼ 1.1	SO	Track on right.
4.8 ▲	SO	Track on left.
▼ 1.4	SO	Track on left.
4.5 ▲	SO	Track on right.
▼ 2.0	SO	Graded road on right is 42N61.
3.9 ▲	SO	Graded road on left is 42N61.
		GPS: N41°24.59' W122°04.83'
▼ 2.2	SO	Cross through Ash Creek. Caution—creek crossing is in a dip and is hard to see, so keep your approach speed slow.
3.7 ▲	SO	Cross through Ash Creek. Caution—creek crossing is in a dip and is hard to see, so keep your approach speed slow.
▼ 2.3	BR	Road on left is 41N16. Remain on FR 31, now marked Sugar Pine Butte Road.
3.6 ▲	SO	Road on right is second entrance to 41N16. Remain on FR 31.
		GPS: N41°24.34' W122°04.87'
▼ 2.5	SO	Track on right and second entrance to 41N16 on left.
3.4 ▲	SO	Track on right is 41N16 and track on left.
▼ 3.5	SO	Cross over Cold Creek; then track on right.
2.4 ▲	SO	Track on left; then cross over Cold Creek.
▼ 3.7	SO	Track on left.
2.2 ▲	SO	Track on right.
▼ 3.8	SO	Track on right is 41N61.
2.1 ▲	SO	Track on left is 41N61.
		GPS: N41°23.34' W122°04.84'
▼ 3.9	SO	Track on right.
2.0 ▲	SO	Track on left.
▼ 4.2	SO	Track on right; then cross over Pilgrim Creek.
1.7 ▲	SO	Cross over Pilgrim Creek; then track on left.
▼ 4.8	SO	Track on left is 41N85.
1.1 ▲	SO	Track on right is 41N85.
▼ 4.9	SO	Track on right.

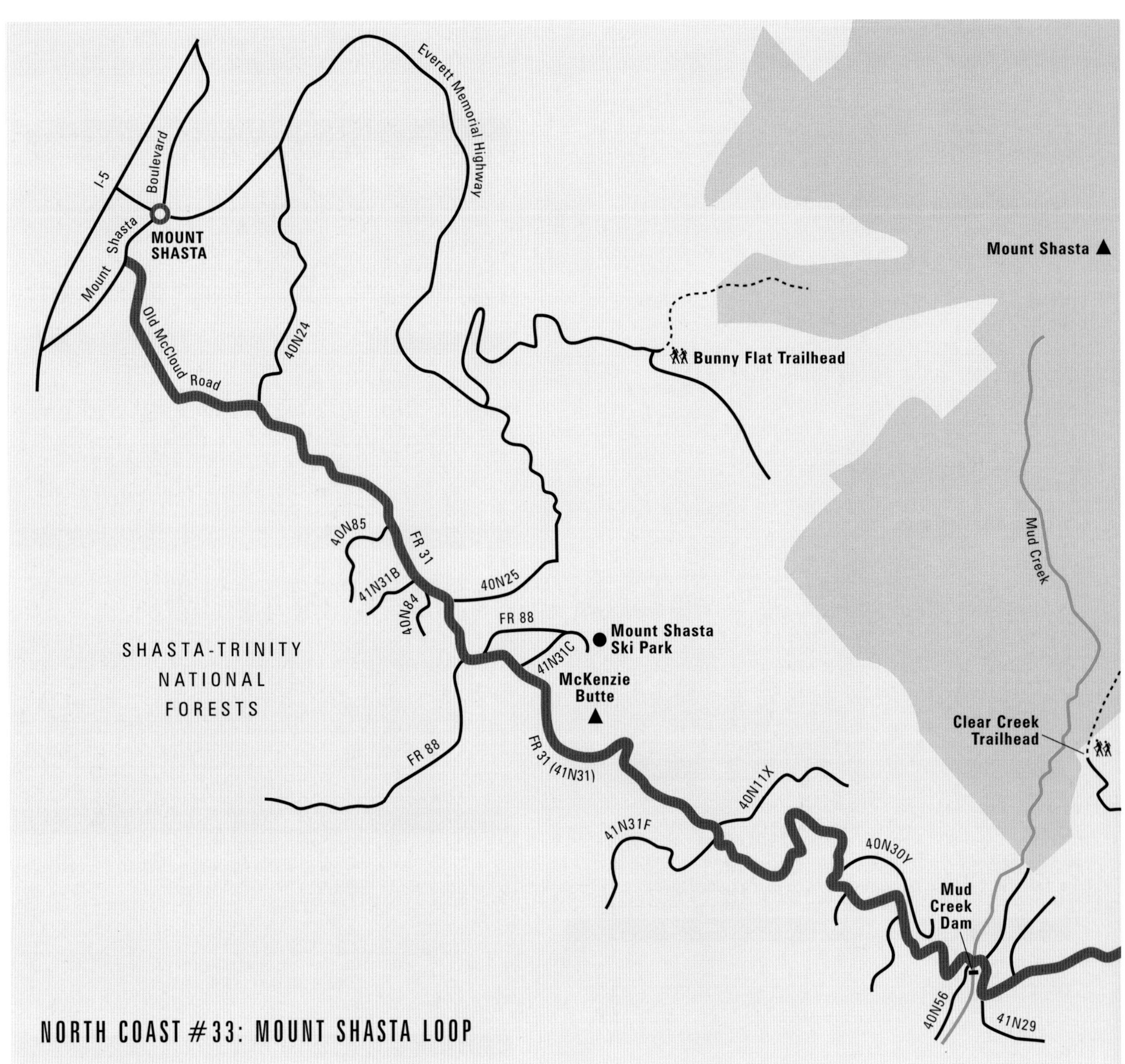

	1.0 ▲	SO	Track on left.
▼ 5.1		SO	Track on right.
	0.8 ▲	SO	Track on left.
▼ 5.3		SO	Cross through wash.
	1.6 ▲	SO	Cross through wash.
▼ 5.4		SO	Track on left.
	0.5 ▲	SO	Track on right.
▼ 5.9		SO	4-way intersection. Graded road on right is 41N61 to Clear Creek Trailhead (fee required). Graded road on left is 41N15. Zero trip meter.
	0.0 ▲		Continue to the north, remaining on FR 31.
			GPS: N41°21.79′ W122°05.15′
▼ 0.0			Continue to the south, remaining on FR 31.
	5.1 ▲	SO	4-way intersection. Graded road on right is 41N15. Graded road on left is 41N61 to Clear Creek Trailhead (fee required). Zero trip meter.
▼ 0.4		SO	Track on right and track on left.
	4.7 ▲	SO	Track on right and track on left.
▼ 1.2		SO	Track on right.
	3.9 ▲	SO	Track on left.
▼ 1.9		SO	Track on right.
	3.2 ▲	SO	Track on left.
▼ 2.1		SO	Track on left.
	3.0 ▲	SO	Track on right.
▼ 2.2		SO	Track on left.
	2.9 ▲	SO	Track on right.
▼ 2.3		TR	T-intersection. Track on left is 41N29. Remain on FR 31.
	2.8 ▲	TL	Track straight ahead is 41N29. Remain on FR 31.
			GPS: N41°20.00′ W122°06.24′
▼ 2.7		SO	Track on right.

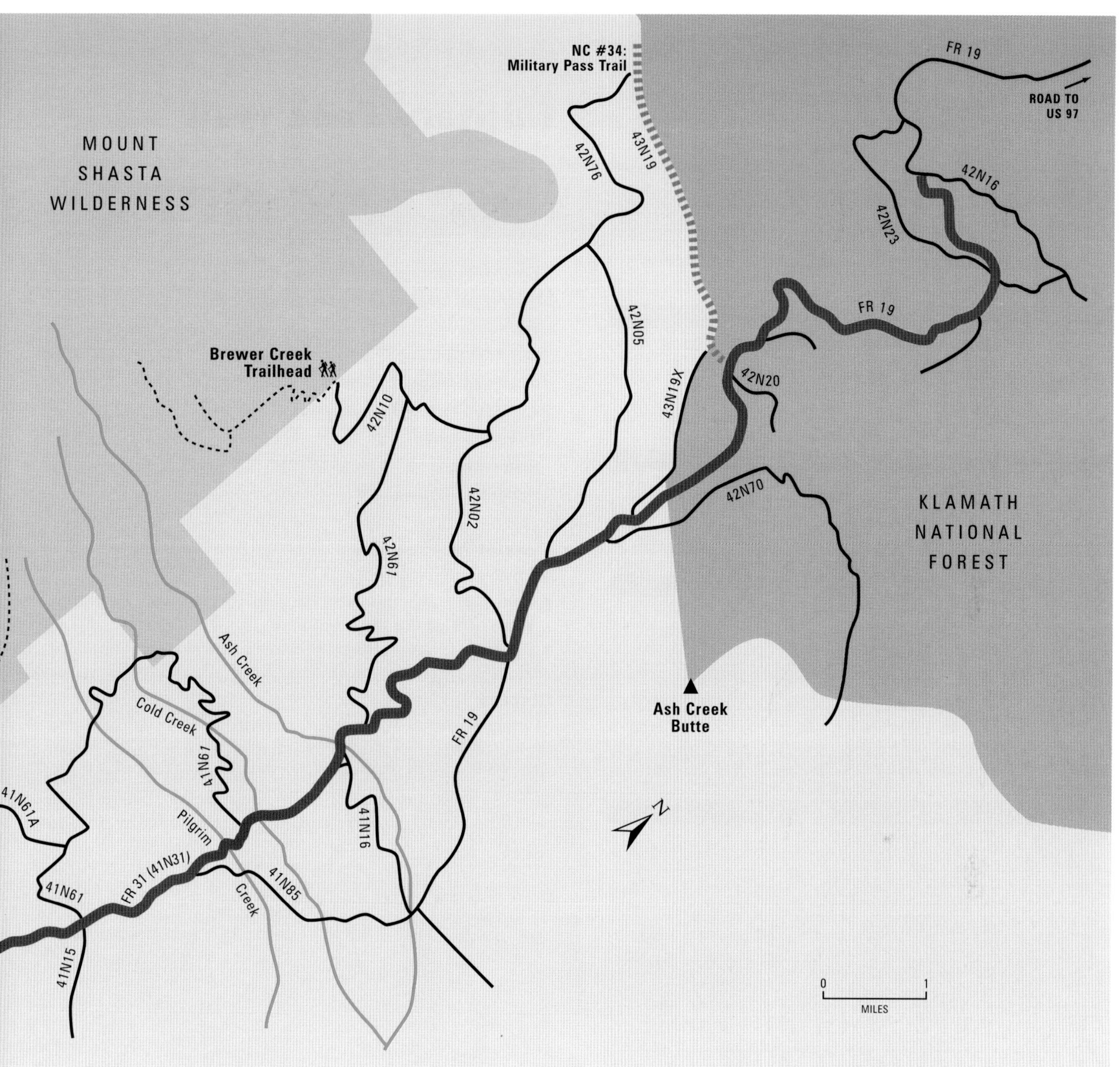

	2.4 ▲	SO	Track on left.
▼ 2.8		SO	Cross over Mud Creek Dam; then track on left is 40N56.
	2.3 ▲	SO	Track on right is 40N56; then cross over Mud Creek Dam.
			GPS: N41°20.10′ W122°06.61′
▼ 3.4		SO	Track on left.
	1.7 ▲	SO	Track on right.
▼ 3.7		SO	Track on right.
	1.4 ▲	SO	Track on left.
▼ 4.1		SO	Track on left.
	1.0 ▲	SO	Track on right.
▼ 4.6		SO	Track on right.
	0.5 ▲	SO	Track on left.
▼ 4.8		SO	Track on left.
	0.3 ▲	SO	Track on right.
▼ 4.9		SO	Track on left is 41N31H.
	0.2 ▲	SO	Track on right is 41N31H.
			GPS: N41°19.69′ W122°08.06′
▼ 5.1		TL	T-intersection. Graded road on right is 40N30Y. Zero trip meter.
	0.0 ▲		Continue to the east, remaining on FR 31.
			GPS: N41°19.70′ W122°08.25′
▼ 0.0			Continue to the south, remaining on FR 31.
	6.3 ▲	TR	Graded road ahead is 40N30Y. Zero trip meter.
▼ 0.5		SO	Track on right is 41N31E and track on left.
	5.8 ▲	SO	Track on left is 41N31E and track on right.
▼ 1.2		SO	Track on right.
	5.1 ▲	SO	Track on left.
▼ 2.0		SO	Track on right; then track on left.

	4.3 ▲	SO	Track on right; then track on left.
▼ 2.5		SO	Track on right.
	3.8 ▲	SO	Track on left.
▼ 2.8		BL	Track on left is 41N31F; then track on right is 40N11X.
	3.5 ▲	BR	Track on left is 40N11X; then track on right is 41N31F.
▼ 3.4		SO	Track on left.
	2.9 ▲	SO	Track on right.
▼ 5.6		SO	Track on left.
	0.7 ▲	SO	Track on right.
▼ 5.8		SO	Track on right is 41N31C.
	0.5 ▲	SO	Track on left is 41N31C.
			GPS: N41°18.75' W122°12.28'
▼ 6.1		TL	Intersection with paved Ski Park Highway (FR 88). To the right goes to Mount Shasta Ski Park. Turn left joining FR 88/31.
	0.2 ▲	TR	Paved FR 88 continues to Mount Shasta Ski Park. Turn right onto graded dirt FR 31. Turn is on a left-hand bend.
			GPS: N41°18.63' W122°12.54'
▼ 6.3		TR	Paved FR 88 continues straight ahead. Turn right onto graded dirt FR 31 at the sign for Mount Shasta Cross Country Ski Center. Zero trip meter.
	0.0 ▲		Continue to the northeast on FR 88/31.
			GPS: N41°18.47' W122°12.67'
▼ 0.0			Continue to the west. Track on right.
	5.0 ▲	TL	Track on left; then T-intersection with paved Ski Park Highway (FR 88). Zero trip meter.
▼ 0.2		SO	Track on right.
	4.8 ▲	SO	Track on left.
▼ 0.4		SO	Track on left.
	4.6 ▲	SO	Track on right.
▼ 0.6		SO	Track on right is 40N25.
	4.4 ▲	SO	Track on left is 40N25.
			GPS: N41°18.65' W122°13.27'
▼ 0.8		SO	Track on left is 40N84.
	4.2 ▲	SO	Track on right is 40N84.
▼ 1.0		SO	Track on left is 41N31B.
	4.0 ▲	SO	Track on right is 41N31B.
▼ 1.4		SO	Track on right.
	3.6 ▲	SO	Track on left.
▼ 1.5		SO	Track on left is 40N85.
	3.5 ▲	SO	Track on right is 40N85.
▼ 1.8		SO	Track on right is 40N01X.
	3.2 ▲	SO	Track on left is 40N01X.
▼ 1.9		SO	Tank on left.
	3.1 ▲	SO	Tank on right.
▼ 2.0		SO	Two tracks on left.
	3.0 ▲	SO	Two tracks on right.
▼ 2.1		SO	Track on right. Road becomes paved. Remain on paved FR 31.
	2.9 ▲	SO	Track on left. Road turns to graded dirt.
▼ 3.5		SO	Track on right is 40N24; then cross over railroad.
	1.5 ▲	SO	Cross over railroad; then track on left is 40N24.
			GPS: N41°18.42' W122°16.31'
▼ 5.0			Trail ends at intersection with South Mount Shasta Boulevard in Mount Shasta.
	0.0 ▲		Trail commences in Mount Shasta at the intersection of South Mount Shasta Boulevard and Old McCloud Road. Zero trip meter and turn east on paved Old McCloud Road. Remain on paved road for 2.9 miles.
			GPS: N41°18.32' W122°18.51'

NORTH COAST #34

Military Pass Trail

Starting Point:	**US 97, 14.3 miles northeast of Weed**
Finishing Point:	**North Coast #33: Mount Shasta Loop, 5.2 miles south of the northern end**
Total Mileage:	**9.9 miles**
Unpaved Mileage:	**9.9 miles**
Driving Time:	**1 hour**
Elevation Range:	**4,400–6,100 feet**
Usually Open:	**June to October**
Best Time to Travel:	**Dry weather**
Difficulty Rating:	**2**
Scenic Rating:	**10**
Remoteness Rating:	**+0**

Special Attractions

- Historic military trail.
- Trail traverses the north slope of Mount Shasta, offering fantastic views of the mountain.
- Access to hiking trails on the north side of the mountain.

History

Military Pass Road follows a route first used by Indians and trappers. Over the years, the pass has been part of many longer trails such as the 1850s Lockhart Wagon Road and Red Bluffs to Yreka Wagon Road, the 1880s Yreka to Fort Crook Road, the 1900s Fall City and Yreka Road, the Shasta Valley Road in

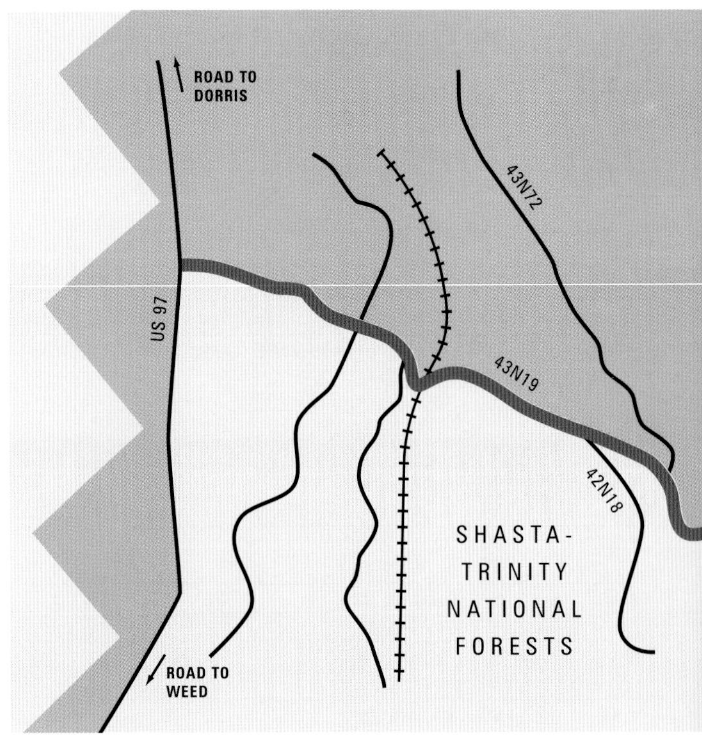

the 1910s, and Sheep Rock–Pilgrim Camp Road for a period in the 1940s. In the mid-1940s it was renamed Military Pass Road on Siskiyou County maps because local information indicated that the army was first to use the route.

Hudson's Bay Company trappers such as John Work may have traveled through this mountain pass in the 1830s. The Lockhart brothers, Harry and Samuel, operated a ferry at today's Fall River Mills in the 1850s and attempted to establish a through road, via their ferry, between Red Bluff and Yreka using this particular pass. Emigrant wagons were noted as passing through the gap in 1855. Teamsters and stagecoaches chose this route on a regular basis, though the California Stage Company eased up on service because of harassment and attacks by Indians in the late 1850s.

Additional skirmishes broke out in the vicinity of the Pit River to the south. One of these resulted in the death of Harry Lockhart, among others, at his ferry in early 1857, apparently at the hands of Pit River Indians. The infantry stationed farther north at Fort Jones patrolled the road through the pass, and troops from Fort Crook were mobilized to forestall raids. These measures brought a level of security to this hazardous route, enabling stages and freighters to once again travel safely through the pass.

Description

The dominant feature of Shasta-Trinity National Forests, and indeed of the region for miles around, is the volcanic cone of Mount Shasta. Towering above the forests at 14,162 feet, Mount Shasta has permanent glaciers and year-round snow on its peak.

Military Pass Trail travels across the mountain's northern slope, passing through mixed conifer forests to join graded North Coast #33: Mount Shasta Loop. The trail leaves US 97 along a roughly graded dirt road. For the first few miles it travels along the border of Klamath National Forest and Shasta-Trinity National Forests. The part of Klamath National Forest (to the north of the trail) is a restricted travel area. From August 15 to March 31, motorized travel is restricted to roads and tracks marked with a green arrow on a white background. Side tracks mentioned in the route directions are for navigation purposes only. If you intend to explore the side trails, you should purchase a current forest service map that shows year-round vehicle travel routes.

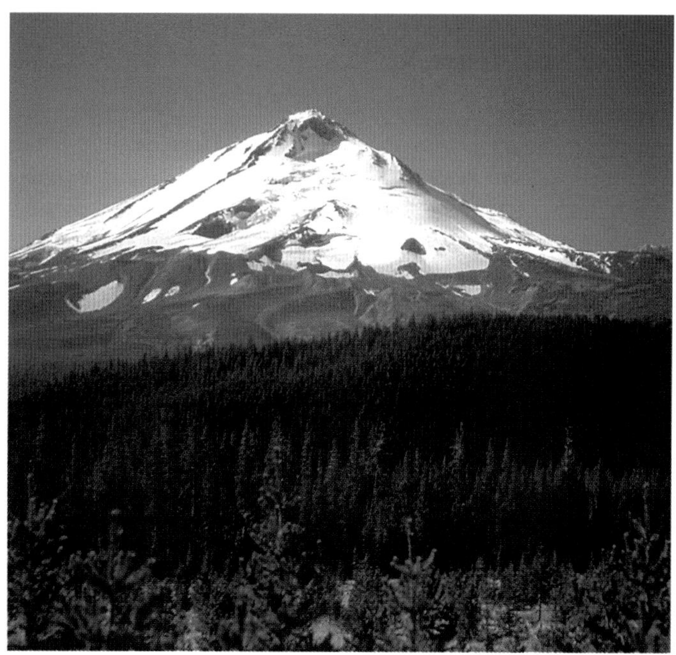

View of Mount Shasta from Military Pass Trail

The graded road sees a lot of use, and it can be very wash-

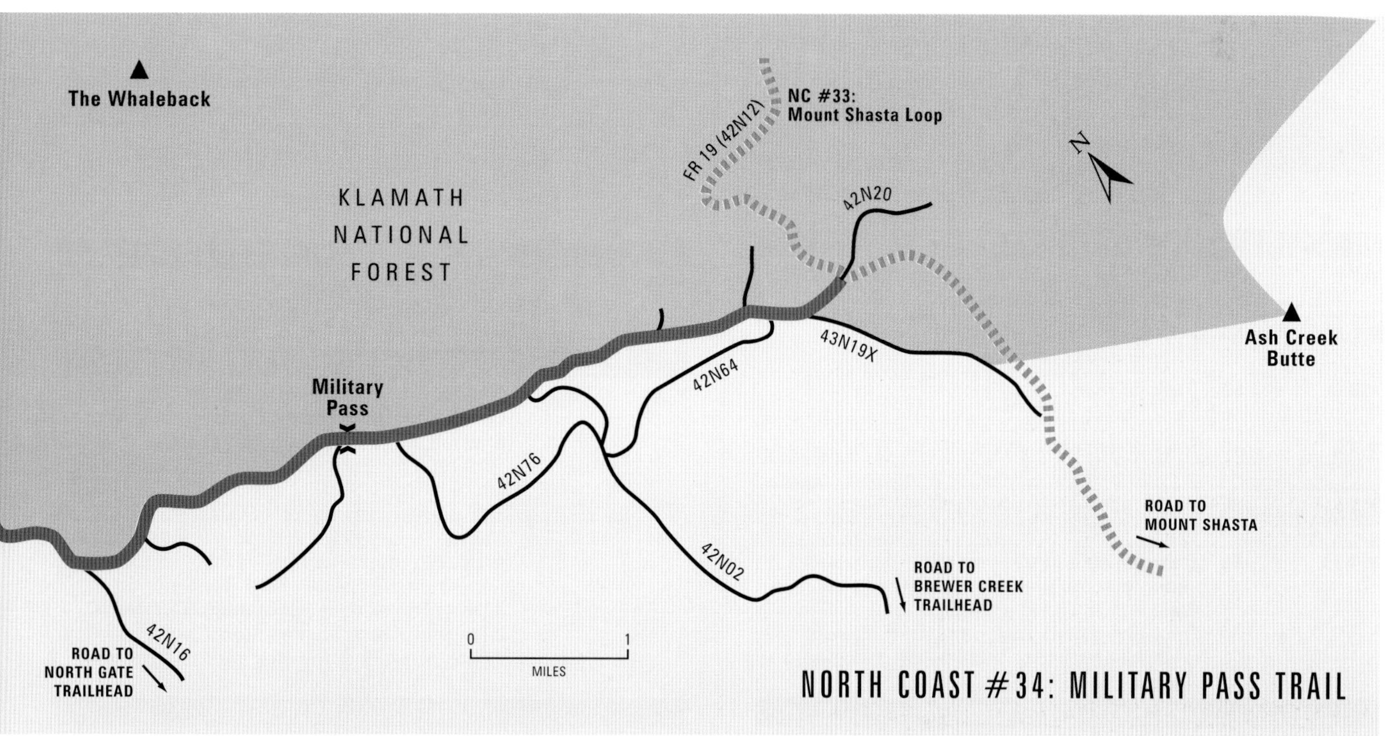

boardy. The climb to the pass is gradual. Military Pass is a long gap between Mount Shasta to the south and The Whaleback to the north. East of the pass, the small, formed trail can be very sandy in dry weather. It travels through sections of privately owned forest managed for timber harvesting.

The trail accesses two hiking trails, North Gate and Brewer Creek, that lead to the summit of Mount Shasta. A fee and permit is required for both. Campers will find many backcountry campsites along this trail.

The trail ends at the intersection with North Coast #33: Mount Shasta Loop.

Current Road Information

Shasta-Trinity National Forests
Mount Shasta Ranger District
204 West Alma
Mount Shasta, CA 96067
(530) 926-4511

Map References

BLM Yreka, Mt. Shasta
USFS Shasta-Trinity National Forest; Klamath National Forest
USGS 1:24,000 The Whaleback, Mt. Shasta, Ash Creek Butte
1:100,000 Yreka, Mt. Shasta
Maptech CD-ROM: Shasta-Trinity/Modoc
Northern California Atlas & Gazetteer, pp. 26, 27, 37
California Road & Recreation Atlas, p. 46
Other: Mount Shasta Wilderness (incomplete), Tom Harrison Maps—Mt. Shasta Wilderness Trail Map (incomplete)

Route Directions

▼	▲		
▼ 0.0			From US 97 on the boundary of Shasta-Trinity and Klamath National Forests, 14.3 miles northeast of Weed and 2.5 miles north of the intersection with CR A12, zero trip meter and turn east on graded dirt Military Pass Road (43N19). Cross cattle guard. Track on left along fence line. There is a sign for Military Pass Road on US 97.
	4.5 ▲		Trail ends at intersection with US 97. Turn left for Weed; turn right for Dorris and Klamath Falls.
			GPS: N41°33.55′ W122°12.49′
▼ 0.1		SO	Track on left at information board.
	4.4 ▲	SO	Track on right at information board.
▼ 0.3		SO	Track on left.
	4.2 ▲	SO	Track on right.
▼ 0.4		SO	Track on right.
	4.1 ▲	SO	Track on left.
▼ 1.2		SO	Track on left and track on right.
	3.3 ▲	SO	Track on left and track on right.
▼ 1.5		SO	Track on left and track on right.
	3.0 ▲	SO	Track on left and track on right.
▼ 1.8		SO	Track on left and track on right; then pass under railroad; then track on left and track on right.
	2.7 ▲	SO	Track on left and track on right; then pass under railroad; then track on left and track on right.
			GPS: N41°32.16′ W122°11.76′
▼ 2.3		SO	Track on left.
	2.2 ▲	SO	Track on right.
▼ 2.9		SO	Track on right is 42N18; then track on left.
	1.6 ▲	SO	Track on right; then track on left is 42N18.
			GPS: N41°31.41′ W122°11.09′
▼ 3.4		SO	Track on left is 43N72.
	1.1 ▲	SO	Track on right is 43N72.
▼ 4.5		BL	Track on right is Andesite Logging Road (42N16) to North Gate Trailhead. Zero trip meter and follow the sign to McCloud.
	0.0 ▲		Continue to the northwest, remaining on 43N19.
			GPS: N41°30.21′ W122°10.73′
▼ 0.0			Continue to the east, remaining on 43N19.
	2.3 ▲	BR	Track on left is Andesite Logging Road (42N16) to North Gate Trailhead. Zero trip meter.
▼ 0.5		SO	Track on right.
	1.8 ▲	SO	Track on left.
▼ 0.7		SO	Leaving motor travel restricted area.
	1.6 ▲	SO	Entering motor travel restricted area.
▼ 2.0		SO	Military Pass. Track on right.
	0.3 ▲	SO	Military Pass. Track on left.
			GPS: N41°29.75′ W122°08.69′
▼ 2.3		SO	Track on right is 42N76 to Brewer Creek Trailhead. Zero trip meter and follow sign to McCloud.
	0.0 ▲		Continue to the west, remaining on 43N19.
			GPS: N41°29.56′ W122°08.41′
▼ 0.0			Continue to the east, remaining on 43N19.
	3.1 ▲	SO	Track on left is 42N76 to Brewer Creek Trailhead. Zero trip meter and follow the sign to US 97.
▼ 0.4		SO	Track on right.
	2.7 ▲	SO	Track on left.
▼ 0.8		SO	Track on right.
	2.3 ▲	SO	Track on left.
▼ 0.9		SO	Track on right.
	2.2 ▲	SO	Track on left.
▼ 1.6		SO	Track on right.
	1.5 ▲	SO	Track on left.
▼ 1.8		SO	Track on left.
	1.3 ▲	SO	Track on right.
▼ 2.3		SO	Track on left.
	0.8 ▲	SO	Track on right.
▼ 2.4		SO	Track on right is 42N64.
	0.7 ▲	SO	Track on left is 42N64.
			GPS: N41°28.77′ W122°05.77′
▼ 2.7		BL	Track on right is 43N19X.
	0.4 ▲	BR	Track on left is 43N19X. Follow sign to Military Pass.
			GPS: N41°28.61′ W122°05.59′
▼ 3.1			Trail ends at 4-way intersection. Graded road on left and right is North Coast #33: Mount Shasta Loop (FR 19). Straight ahead is 42N20. Turn right for the town of Mount Shasta; turn left to exit to US 97.
	0.0 ▲		Trail commences on North Coast #33: Mount Shasta Loop (FR 19), 5.2 miles from the north end. Zero trip meter at 4-way intersection and turn southwest onto 43N19. Track opposite is 42N20. The formed trail is unmarked, but is well-used. There are directional signs on FR 19 to California 89 to the east and US 97 to the west at the intersection.
			GPS: N41°28.61′ W122°05.14′

NORTH COAST #35

Herd Peak Trail

Starting Point:	**US 97, 0.5 miles south of Grass Valley Maintenance Station**
Finishing Point:	**Herd Peak Fire Lookout**
Total Mileage:	**5.5 miles (one-way)**
Unpaved Mileage:	**5.5 miles**
Driving Time:	**30 minutes (one-way)**
Elevation Range:	**5,100–7,000 feet**
Usually Open:	**June to October**
Best Time to Travel:	**Fire season (when the lookout is manned)**
Difficulty Rating:	**1**
Scenic Rating:	**8**
Remoteness Rating:	**+0**

Special Attractions

- Views of Mount Shasta and the surrounding forests.
- Herd Peak Fire Lookout.

History

This short trail to the summit of Herd Peak (7,071 feet) offers spectacular views of nearby Mount Shasta to the east. The trail and peak overlook the route of the Yreka Trail, an emigrant trail developed in 1852 as part of a network that brought gold seekers to California. The Yreka Trail branched off from the Applegate Trail (see page 65) near Oklahoma Flat, just south of Klamath Lake. From there it headed southwest through the Cascade Range to Butte Creek, which is visible from Herd Peak Trail. The wagon road continued west, skirting the southern edge of Grass Lake along a route similar to today's US 97. It passed over the rise at the start of the described vehicle trail. The emigrant trail then swung south, gradually dropping to traverse the southern side of Sheep Rock (5,705 feet) heading due south of Herd Peak. At this point it joined a fur trappers' trail and headed northwest, descending near Yellow Butte to roughly follow the course of the old Cutoff Road, known today as CR A12. Shortly after this, the trail forked: One branch went north to Little Shasta and the other made its way to Yreka.

Easygoing shelf road to the lookout on Herd Peak

Description

This trail follows a graded dirt road through privately owned forest before entering Klamath National Forest for the climb to Herd Peak's summit. Fire spotters occupy the lookout tower during the fire season—normally late May to mid September. During this time, the gate is open and you can visit the lookout in your vehicle. Visiting hours are from 9:30 A.M. to 5:30 P.M. You are normally welcome to climb the tower with permission from the lookout on duty. The gate is closed outside fire season or these hours, in which case it is a 1-mile hike from the locked gate to the lookout tower.

The trail forms part of a loop used by mountain bikers that starts and ends at the start of the vehicle route. It is rated for moderate to advanced riders.

Current Road Information

Bureau of Land Management
Redding Field Office
355 Hemsted Drive
Redding, CA 96002
(530) 224-2100

Klamath National Forest
Goosenest Ranger District
37805 Highway 97
Macdoel, CA 96058
(530) 398-4391

Map References

BLM Yreka
USFS Klamath National Forest
USGS 1:24,000 Grass Lake, The Whaleback
1:100,000 Yreka
Maptech CD-ROM: Shasta-Trinity/Modoc
Northern California Atlas & Gazetteer, p. 26
California Road & Recreation Atlas, p. 46

Grass Lake in the valley below

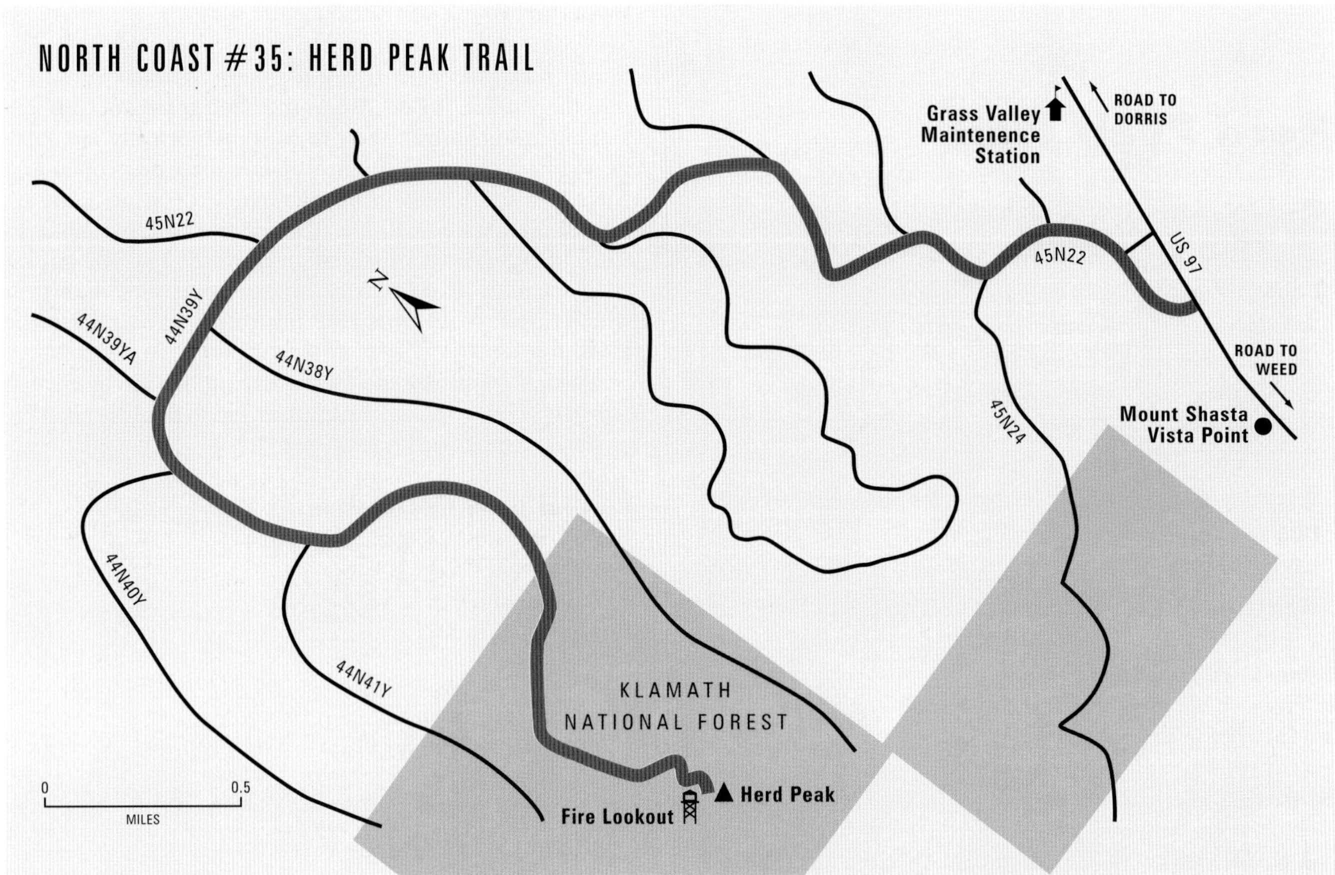

Route Directions

▼ 0.0		From US 97, 0.5 miles south of Grass Valley Maintenance Station and 0.3 miles north of the Mount Shasta Vista Point, zero trip meter and turn east on 45N22. Cross cattle guard.
		GPS: N41°37.47' W122°11.84'
▼ 0.3	SO	Track on right.
▼ 0.4	SO	Track on right.
▼ 0.6	BR	Track on left is 45N24.
		GPS: N41°37.83' W122°12.13'
▼ 0.8	SO	Track on right.
▼ 1.1	SO	Track on left.
▼ 1.4	SO	Track on right.
▼ 1.7	SO	Track on left.
▼ 2.3	SO	Track on left.
▼ 2.5	SO	Track on right.
▼ 2.8	BL	Road straight ahead is continuation of 45N22. Bear left onto 44N39Y, following the sign to Herd Peak. Small track on left. Zero trip meter.
		GPS: N41°39.15' W122°13.30'
▼ 0.0		Continue to the west.
▼ 0.3	SO	Track on left is 44N38Y.
▼ 0.5	SO	Track on right is 44N39YA.
▼ 0.7	SO	Track on right is 44N40Y.
▼ 1.0	SO	Track on right is 44N41Y.
		GPS: N41°38.70' W122°13.94'
▼ 1.7	SO	Gate. Entering Klamath National Forest.
		GPS: N41°38.33' W122°13.53'
▼ 2.7		Trail ends at the Herd Peak Fire Lookout.
		GPS: N41°37.69' W122°13.80'

NORTH COAST #36

Klamath River Road

Starting Point:	**California 96 at Ash Creek Bridge, 1.8 miles west of the intersection with California 263**
Finishing Point:	**California 96 at Walker Bridge, 0.9 miles west of the Klamath River Post Office**
Total Mileage:	**18.1 miles**
Unpaved Mileage:	**16.1 miles**
Driving Time:	**2 hours**
Elevation Range:	**1,700–2,000 feet**
Usually Open:	**Year-round**
Best Time to Travel:	**Year-round**
Difficulty Rating:	**2**
Scenic Rating:	**9**
Remoteness Rating:	**+0**

Special Attractions

- Road parallels the Klamath River and is great for mountain bikes as well as vehicles.
- Excellent fishing in the Klamath River.
- Many raft put-ins.

History

The gold rush to Yreka in 1851 saw miners scouring the entire vicinity in search of a lucky strike. The Klamath River did not escape their scrutiny, and in time camps sprang up along the river. Klamath River Road, also known as Walker Road, passes the site of Walker, long gone from today's maps. The old settlement was at the mouth of Barkhouse Creek, not far from the western end of this road.

In 1851, a rough pack trail was built from the coast up through the river's deep valley. Rocks, boulders, and trees were pushed aside to establish this trail. The earliest wagon road to enter the Klamath River Valley did so from Yreka, north to Hawkinsville, up and over to Humbug, and down along Humbug Creek. Freshour Ferry took wagons across the Klamath near the mouth of Dutch Creek, just east of Gottville. Wagon roads then traveled north up Dutch, Empire, and Lumgrey Creeks before reverting to pack trails that climbed into the Siskiyou Mountains.

The Honolulu School was established just west of Kanaka Bar and Cemetery in 1890. These names reflect the presence of Hawaiian miners in the region. Rather than mine, Chinese settlers started market gardens near Humbug Point. The Trees of Heaven Campground on the north side of the river was the site of one of the gardens that supplied fresh produce to mining camps. The Chinese introduced trees of heaven, also called ailanthus, to California.

The Ash Creek Bridge, at the east end of the road, was built in September 1901, a project supported in part by Abner Weed, a county supervisor and Civil War veteran for whom the town of Weed is named.

Description

For travelers wanting a leisurely drive along the Klamath River, California 96 can be a disappointment. The mostly graded dirt Klamath River Road, on the south side of the river, is a much better alternative. The rougher surface ensures a slow speed, with time to appreciate vibrant colors in fall or to find a perfect fishing spot. Great blue herons and eagles are commonly sighted here.

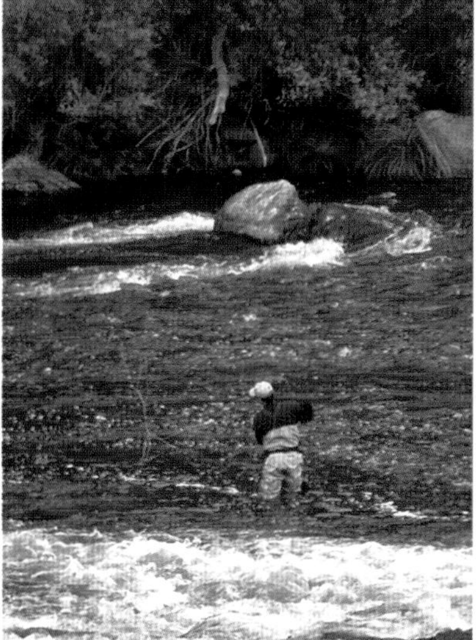
Trout fishing in the Klamath River

The trail starts at Ash Creek Bridge. The road is mainly single vehicle width, and some sections, especially where the road passes around rocky outcroppings high above the river, are rough enough to make high-clearance preferable. Passing places are limited on some of these sections, and there is often quite a drop below the shelf road.

The trail accesses many fishing spots and marked boat put-ins along the river. Campers will enjoy the developed Trees of Heaven USFS Campground on the far side of the river, just west of the start of the trail. Mountain bikers can also take advantage of this easy, scenic riverside route.

The Ash Creek Bridge, built in 1901

The trail ends by crossing the Walker Bridge to rejoin California 96.

Current Road Information

Klamath National Forest
Scott River Ranger District
11263 North Highway 3
Fort Jones, CA 96032
(530) 468-5351

Map References

BLM Yreka
USFS Klamath National Forest
USGS 1:24,000 Hawkinsville, Badger Mt., McKinley Mt.
1:100,000 Yreka
Maptech CD-ROM: Shasta-Trinity/Modoc
Northern California Atlas & Gazetteer, pp. 26, 25
California Road & Recreation Atlas, p. 46

Route Directions

▼ 0.0			From California 96 at the Klamath National Forest boundary, 1.8 miles west of the intersection with California 263 and 9 miles north of Yreka, zero trip meter and turn south. Cross over the Klamath River on Ash Creek Bridge and proceed on CR 8J001.
	3.4 ▲		Cross over Ash Creek Bridge; then trail ends at intersection with California 96. Turn left for Happy Camp; turn right for Yreka and I-5.
			GPS: N41°50.05' W122°37.15'
▼ 0.4		SO	Ash Creek River Access on right.
	3.0 ▲	SO	Ash Creek River Access on left.
▼ 1.8		BL	Track on right to Garvey Bar.
	1.6 ▲	BR	Track on left to Garvey Bar.
			GPS: N41°49.65' W122°38.79'
▼ 2.1		SO	Track on right.

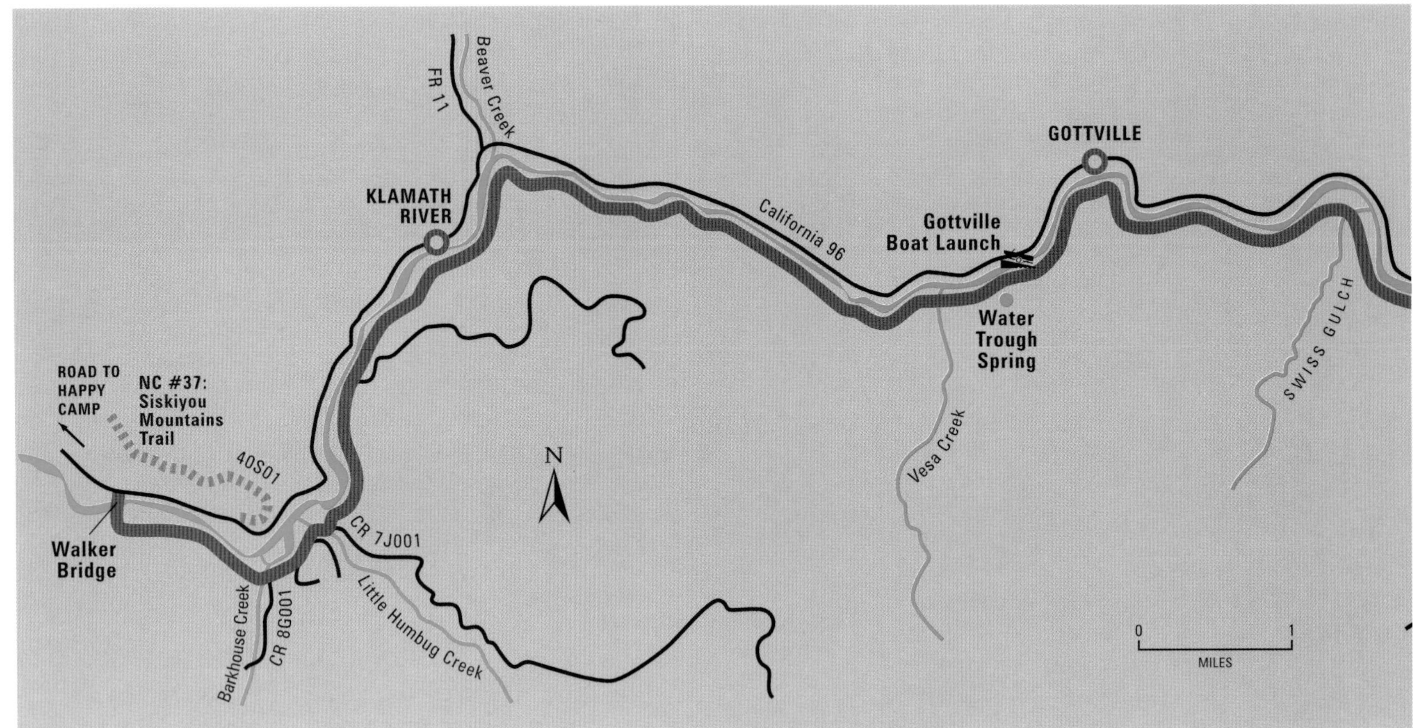

Mileage		Description
1.3 ▲	SO	Track on left.
▼ 2.4	SO	Track on right to river; then track on left; then second track on right.
1.0 ▲	SO	Track on left; then track on right; then second track on left to river.
▼ 3.4	BR	Cross over Humbug Creek on bridge; then graded road on left is CR 7J002. Zero trip meter.
0.0 ▲		Continue to the east and cross over Humbug Creek on bridge.
		GPS: N41°49.97′ W122°39.97′
▼ 0.0		Continue to the north on 46N13Y.
6.3 ▲	BL	Graded road on right is CR 7J002. Zero trip meter.
▼ 0.2	SO	Track on left.
6.1 ▲	SO	Track on right.
▼ 1.0	SO	Track on left.
5.3 ▲	SO	Track on right.
▼ 1.3	SO	Track on right.
5.0 ▲	SO	Track on left.
		GPS: N41°50.58′ W122°41.00′
▼ 2.5	SO	Track on right.
3.8 ▲	SO	Track on left.
▼ 2.6	SO	Track on right.
3.7 ▲	SO	Track on left.
▼ 3.4	SO	Swiss Gulch on left.
2.9 ▲	SO	Swiss Gulch on right.
▼ 5.5	SO	Track on right. Gottville is on the far side of the river.
0.8 ▲	SO	Track on left. Gottville is on the far side of the river.
		GPS: N41°51.91′ W122°44.54′
▼ 6.2	SO	Gottville Boat Launch on far side of the river.
0.1 ▲	SO	Gottville Boat Launch on far side of the river.
		GPS: N41°51.48′ W122°44.93′
▼ 6.3	SO	Track on right; then Water Trough Spring on left. Zero trip meter.
0.0 ▲		Continue to the north. Track on left.
		GPS: N41°51.42′ W122°45.11′
▼ 0.0		Continue to the south. Track on left.
6.5 ▲	SO	Track on right; then Water Trough Spring on right. Zero trip meter.
▼ 0.4	SO	Cross over Vesa Creek; then track on left.
6.1 ▲	SO	Track on right; then cross over Vesa Creek.
▼ 1.2	SO	Track on right.
5.3 ▲	SO	Track on left.
▼ 3.6	SO	Track on right. Beaver Creek is on the far side of the river.
2.9 ▲	SO	Track on left. Beaver Creek is on the far side of the river.
		GPS: N41°52.10′ W122°48.91′
▼ 5.6	SO	Track on left.
0.9 ▲	SO	Track on right.
		GPS: N41°50.85′ W122°50.11′
▼ 6.4	SO	Road becomes paved.
0.1 ▲	SO	Road turns to graded dirt.
▼ 6.5	TR	T-intersection with paved CR 7J001 (45N30). Zero trip meter.
0.0 ▲		Continue to the northwest.
		GPS: N41°50.09′ W122°50.23′
▼ 0.0		Continue to the southwest. Eagles Nest Golf Course on right; then cross over Little Humbug Creek on bridge.
1.9 ▲	TL	Cross over Little Humbug Creek on bridge; then Eagles Nest Golf Course on left. CR 7J001 (45N30) continues straight ahead. Zero trip meter and turn left onto Walker Road (CR 8J001).
▼ 0.2	SO	Lockhaven Drive on left.
1.7 ▲	SO	Lockhaven Drive on right.
▼ 0.3	SO	Barkhouse Court on left.
1.6 ▲	SO	Barkhouse Court on right.
▼ 0.6	BR	Graded road on left is CR 8G001 (46N38); then cross over Barkhouse Creek on bridge.
1.3 ▲	BL	Cross over Barkhouse Creek on bridge; then graded road on right is CR 8G001 (46N38).

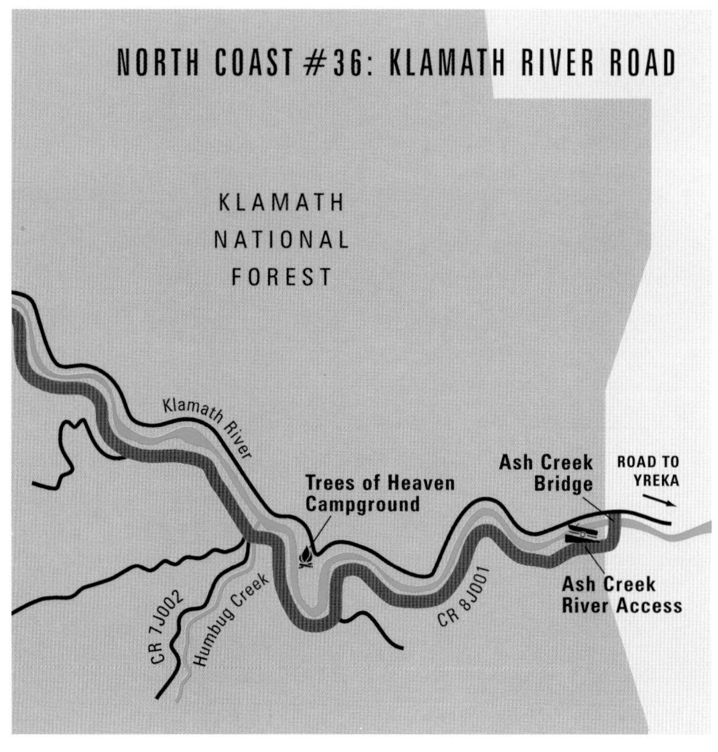

▼ 1.6	TR	Paved road continues ahead.
0.3 ▲	TL	T-intersection.
		GPS: N41°50.11′ W122°51.83′
▼ 1.9		Cross over Klamath River on Walker Bridge; then trail ends at T-intersection with California 96. Turn right for Yreka; turn left for Happy Camp.
0.0 ▲		Trail commences on California 96, 0.9 miles west of Klamath River Post Office. Zero trip meter and turn south on paved road, following the sign for Walker Bridge Road. Immediately cross over the Klamath River on Walker Bridge.
		GPS: N41°50.30′ W122°51.81′

NORTH COAST #37

Siskiyou Mountains Trail

Starting Point:	**California 96, 4.4 miles west of the community of Klamath River**
Finishing Point:	**Beaver Creek Road (FR 11), 5.4 miles north of California 96**
Total Mileage:	**31.6 miles**
Unpaved Mileage:	**30.9 miles**
Driving Time:	**3.5 hours**
Elevation Range:	**1,800–6,900 feet**
Usually Open:	**June to December**
Best Time to Travel:	**June to December**
Difficulty Rating:	**2**
Scenic Rating:	**10**
Remoteness Rating:	**+1**

Special Attractions

- Condrey Mountain Blueschist Geological Area.
- Site of the Dry Lake Fire Lookout.
- Panoramic ridge top views over California and Oregon.
- Access to a network of trails within the Klamath and Rogue River National Forests.

History

Siskiyou Mountains Trail begins in the homeland of the Karok (see page 90). The tribal name Karok means "upriver" and refers to their territory on the upper section of the Klamath River. The river defined the Karok's way of life, providing transportation and abundant salmon and trout. The Karok were exceptional basket makers who wove baskets so tight they were capable of carrying water. Their traditional way of life was disrupted by the arrival of miners in the early 1850s, and their fishing grounds were spoiled with dams, dredging, diversion canals, and hydraulic monitors.

The settlement of Klamath River, near the end of this trail, was a commercial center for the region in the 1920s. In the mid-1920s, Willis Quigley built a riverside store and the Klamath River Lodge. The lodge became a popular fishing destination, and Quigley, also known as Moon, took guests to prime fishing spots along the river.

Description

The Siskiyou Mountains are part of the Klamath Mountains, which straddle the California-Oregon state line. The region is rugged and quiet; the nearest town, Yreka, is a twisting highway away, and most drivers stick to paved California 96. The trail begins on California 96 west of the community of Klamath River. The pavement ends after the Oak Knoll Work Station, and the trail becomes a narrow, roughly graded shelf road that winds into the mountains. The road passes through privately owned forest, maintained for timber harvesting, interspersed with patches of Klamath National Forest. Trail markings are sporadic. Many well-used tracks are unmarked or have signs that have fallen into disrepair. GPS coordinates have been given for these intersections.

Mount Shasta rises above the Condrey Mountain Blueschist Geological Area

As the trail climbs into the range, the views get better and better. Mount Shasta dominates the skyline to the south, and there are fantastic views over the convoluted ridges and mountains of Klamath National Forest to the west.

Deer Camp, a designated undeveloped USFS camping area, is in the shade at the edge of Deer Camp Meadows. Once on the ridge tops, the trees give way to sparser vegetation. The site of an old fire lookout, which operated until 1970, is passed at Dry Lake. As you might expect, views from this spot are tremendous. The lookout site marks the southern end of the Condrey Mountain Blueschist Geological Area, which contains metamorphic blue schist. The rock is flaky and has a high percentage of mica. Twisted ridges of blue schist can be seen along the northwestern end of the trail.

The trail turns northeast near Alex Hole and runs along the crest of a ridge, paralleling the course of the Pacific Crest National Scenic Trail. This part of the trail provides wonderful views into Oregon and California. The Siskiyou Mountains Trail leaves the ridge at Wards Fork Gap and descends a shelf road to the south, traveling above the West Fork of Beaver Creek. Two lonely graves can be found beside the trail near the confluence of Trapper and West Fork Beaver Creeks.

Fall colors along Beaver Creek and the Klamath River are particularly brilliant, making the crisp days of early autumn an excellent time to travel this route. Campers must be sure they are on public land before pitching their tents; Deer Camp is the best site along the trail. Other sites are scarce because of the shelf road and sections of privately owned forest.

Snowmobiles use parts of this route in winter.

Current Road Information

Klamath National Forest
Scott River Ranger District
11263 North Highway 3
Fort Jones, CA 96032
(530) 468-5351

Map References

BLM Yreka
USFS Klamath National Forest, Rogue River National Forest
USGS 1:24,000 McKinley Mt., Horse Creek, Buckhorn Bally, Condrey Mt.
1:100,000 Yreka
Maptech CD-ROM: Shasta-Trinity/Modoc
Northern California Atlas & Gazetteer, p. 25
California Road & Recreation Atlas, p. 46

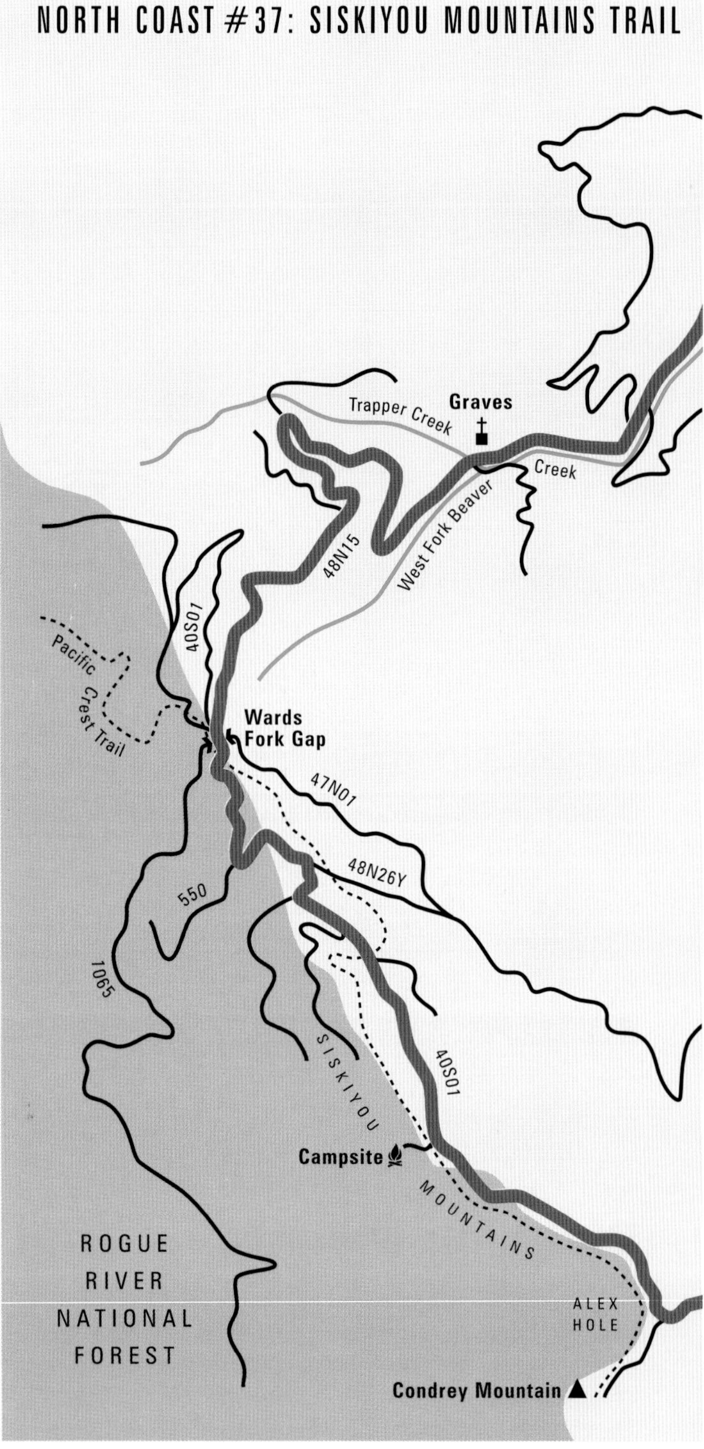

Route Directions

▼ 0.0			From California 96, 4.4 miles west of Klamath River (measured from the bridge over Beaver Creek), zero trip meter and turn northeast on paved road 40S01. The turn is 0.1 miles east of the Klamath River Post Office. Note that this road is shown as FR 20 on the forest map.
	2.3 ▲		Trail ends at T-intersection with paved California 96. Turn left for Yreka; turn right for Happy Camp.
			GPS: N41°50.14' W122°50.90'
▼ 0.6		SO	Pass Oak Knoll USFS Work Station.
	1.7 ▲	SO	Pass Oak Knoll USFS Work Station.
▼ 0.7		SO	Cattle guard. Road turns to graded dirt.
	1.6 ▲	SO	Cattle guard. Road is now paved.
			GPS: N41°50.41' W122°51.04'
▼ 0.8		BL	Track on right is 46N82.
	1.5 ▲	BR	Track on left is 46N82.
▼ 2.3		BR	Graded road on left is 46N42. Zero trip meter.
	0.0 ▲		Continue to the south, remaining on 40S01.
			GPS: N41°51.04' W122°51.97'
▼ 0.0			Continue to the northeast, remaining on 40S01.
	4.9 ▲	SO	Graded road on right is 46N42. Zero trip meter.
▼ 0.1		SO	Track on right.
	4.8 ▲	SO	Track on left.
▼ 2.3		SO	Cross through Salt Lick Gulch.

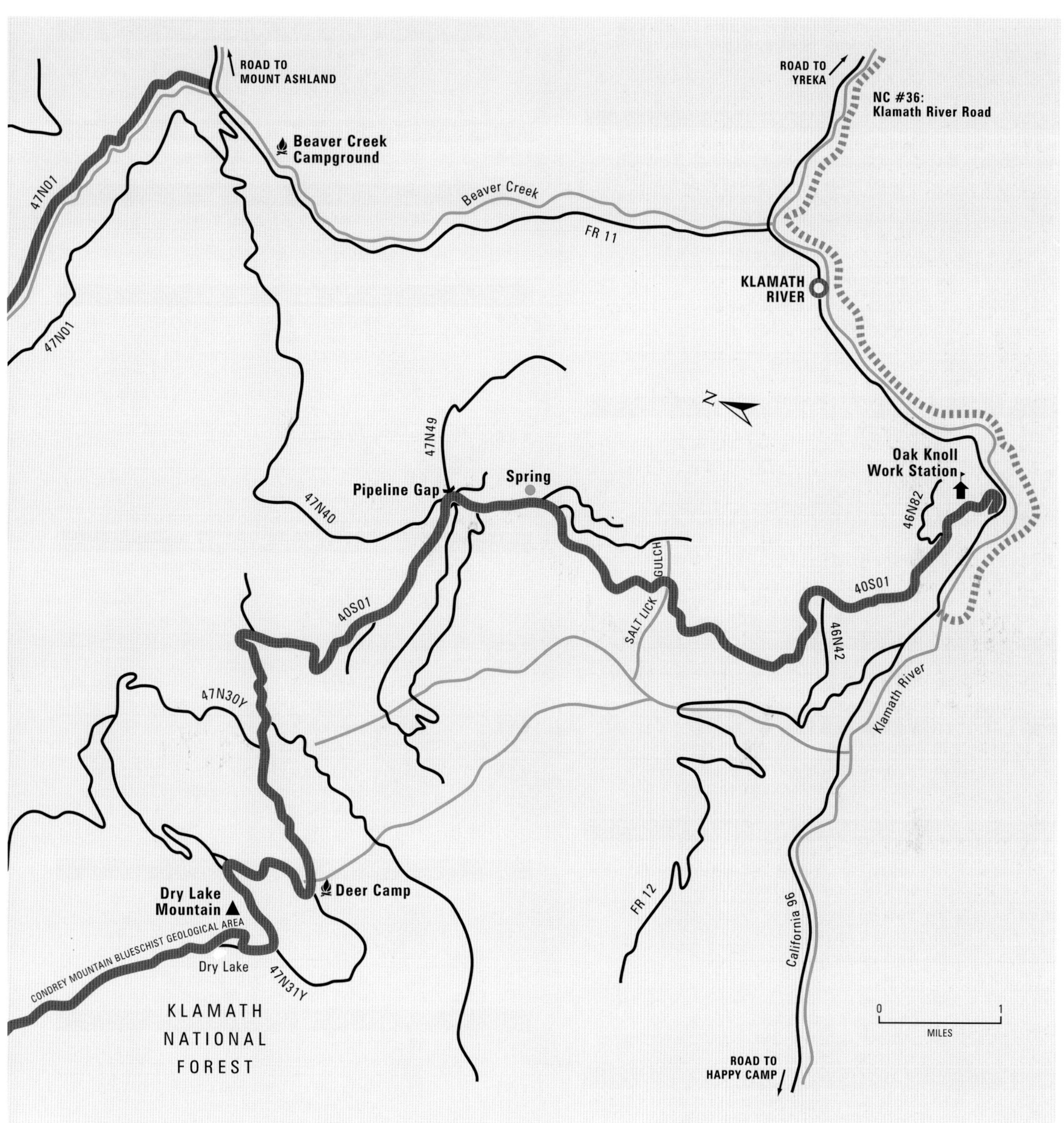

2.6 ▲	SO	Cross through Salt Lick Gulch.
		GPS: N41°52.20' W122°52.26'
▼ 2.9	SO	Track on left is 47N55.
2.0 ▲	SO	Track on right is 47N55.
▼ 3.9	SO	Track on right.
1.0 ▲	BR	Track on left.
▼ 4.1	TL	Turn left at T-intersection. Spring at intersection.
0.8 ▲	TR	Graded road continues straight ahead. Spring at intersection.
		GPS: N41°53.28' W122°51.97'
▼ 4.3	SO	Track on right is 47N55Y.
0.6 ▲	SO	Track on left is 47N55Y.
▼ 4.5	BR	Track on left through gate. Remain on 40S01, following the sign to Deer Camp.
0.4 ▲	SO	Track on right through gate. Remain on 40S01, following the sign to California 96.
		GPS: N41°53.55' W122°52.13'
▼ 4.9	BL	6-way intersection at Pipeline Gap. Track on right, second track on right is 47N49, and graded road on right is 47N40 to Beaver Creek

		USFS Campground. Also track on left. Bear left, following the sign to Deer Camp, and zero trip meter.
0.0 ▲		Continue to the southeast, remaining on 40S01.
		GPS: N41°53.84′ W122°52.12′
▼ 0.0		Continue to the west, remaining on 40S01.
3.8 ▲	BR	6-way intersection at Pipeline Gap. Graded road on left is 47N40 to Beaver Creek USFS Campground, second track on left is 47N49, and third track on left. Also track on right. Bear right, following the sign to Oak Knoll Work Station, and zero trip meter.
▼ 0.5	SO	Track on right.
3.3 ▲	SO	Track on left.
▼ 1.1	SO	Track on left.
2.7 ▲	SO	Track on right.
▼ 1.7	SO	Track on left is 47N59.
2.1 ▲	SO	Track on right is 47N59.
		GPS: N41°54.39′ W122°53.84′
▼ 1.9	SO	Track on left.
1.9 ▲	SO	Track on right.
▼ 2.2	SO	Track on left.
1.6 ▲	SO	Track on right.
▼ 2.4	SO	Track on right.
1.4 ▲	SO	Track on left.
▼ 2.8	SO	Track on right.
1.0 ▲	SO	Track on left.
▼ 2.8	BR	Track on left; then track on right.
1.0 ▲	SO	Track on left; then track on right.
▼ 3.1	SO	Two tracks on right.
0.7 ▲	SO	Two tracks on left.
▼ 3.2	SO	Track on right.
0.6 ▲	SO	Track on left.
▼ 3.4	SO	Track on left.
0.4 ▲	SO	Track on right.
▼ 3.8	SO	Track on right is 47N30Y. Entering travel restricted area. Zero trip meter.
0.0 ▲		Continue to the northeast.
		GPS: N41°54.59′ W122°54.77′
▼ 0.0		Continue to the southwest.
3.6 ▲	SO	Track on left is 47N30Y. Leaving travel restricted area. Zero trip meter.
▼ 0.4	SO	Track on left.
3.2 ▲	SO	Track on right.
▼ 1.0	SO	Track on right.
2.6 ▲	SO	Track on left.
▼ 1.1	BR	Track on left; then smaller track on left into Deer Camp (unmarked).
2.5 ▲	SO	Track on right into Deer Camp (unmarked); then second track on right.
		GPS: N41°54.06′ W122°55.68′
▼ 1.2	SO	Cross over creek; then track on left is 47N31Y. Passing through Deer Camp Meadows.
2.4 ▲	SO	Passing through Deer Camp Meadows. Track on right is 47N31Y; then cross over creek.
▼ 2.2	SO	Track on right.
1.4 ▲	SO	Track on left.
▼ 2.3	SO	Track on right.
1.3 ▲	SO	Track on left.
▼ 2.8	SO	Track on left.
0.8 ▲	SO	Track on right.
▼ 3.0	SO	Track on left is 47N31Y.
0.6 ▲	SO	Track on right is 47N31Y.
		GPS: N41°54.17′ W122°56.42′
▼ 3.3	TR	Track continues straight ahead around Dry Lake. Turn right onto smaller track to pass the site of Dry Lake Fire Lookout.
0.3 ▲	TL	T-intersection with 40S01.
		GPS: N41°54.40′ W122°56.49′
▼ 3.5	SO	Site of Dry Lake Fire Lookout.
0.1 ▲	SO	Site of Dry Lake Fire Lookout.
		GPS: N41°54.48′ W122°56.37′
▼ 3.6	TR	T-intersection. Zero trip meter.
0.0 ▲		Continue to the southeast. Trail leaves Condrey Mountain Blueschist Geological Area.
		GPS: N41°54.56′ W122°56.49′
▼ 0.0		Continue to the northwest, rejoining 40S01. Trail now passes through Condrey Mountain Blueschist Geological Area.
1.9 ▲	TL	Track continues straight ahead. Zero trip meter and turn left onto smaller track to pass the site of Dry Lake Fire Lookout.
▼ 0.6	SO	Track on left.
1.3 ▲	SO	Track on right.
▼ 1.9	BR	Track on left to Alex Hole. Zero trip meter and follow the sign to Mount Ashland.
0.0 ▲		Continue to the east, remaining on 40S01.
		GPS: N41°55.85′ W122°57.85′
▼ 0.0		Continue to the northwest, remaining on 40S01.
5.6 ▲	SO	Track on right to Alex Hole. Zero trip meter and follow the sign to Klamath River.
▼ 0.3	SO	Leaving Condrey Mountain Blueschist Geological Area on right.
5.3 ▲	SO	Passing through Condrey Mountain Blueschist Geological Area on left.
▼ 1.3	SO	Track on left.
4.3 ▲	SO	Track on right.
▼ 2.0	SO	Track on left at campsite. Pacific Crest Trail crosses and now runs parallel to the vehicle route on the north side.
3.6 ▲	SO	Track on right at campsite. Pacific Crest Trail crosses.
		GPS: N41°57.34′ W122°57.19′
▼ 3.2	SO	Track on right.
2.4 ▲	SO	Track on left.
▼ 3.4	SO	Track on left.
2.2 ▲	SO	Track on right.
▼ 3.7	BR	Track on left. Leaving travel restricted area.
1.9 ▲	BL	Track on right. Entering travel restricted area.
		GPS: N41°58.35′ W122°55.90′
▼ 3.9	SO	Track on right is 48N26Y.
1.7 ▲	SO	Track on left is 48N26Y.
▼ 4.5	TR	T-intersection. Track 550 on left goes into Rogue River National Forest.
1.1 ▲	TL	Track 550 continues straight ahead into Rogue River National Forest.
		GPS: N41°58.71′ W122°55.78′
▼ 4.8	SO	Track on left.
0.8 ▲	SO	Track on right.
▼ 5.1	SO	Track on right.
0.5 ▲	BR	Track on left
		GPS: N41°58.89′ W122°55.28′
▼ 5.2	SO	Track on left.
0.4 ▲	BL	Track on right.
▼ 5.4	SO	Pacific Crest Trail crosses on a sharp left-hand bend.

▼	▲		
	0.2 ▲	SO	Pacific Crest Trail crosses on a sharp right-hand bend.
▼ 5.6		BR	6-way intersection at Wards Fork Gap. First track on left is 1065 to Upper Applegate in Rogue River National Forest. Second track on left is 48N16. Straight ahead is 40S01 to Mount Ashland. Track on immediate right is 47N01. Zero trip meter and bear right onto lower shelf road 48N15 to Klamath River. Pacific Crest Trail crosses through this intersection.
	0.0 ▲		Continue to the south.
			GPS: N41°59.03' W122°54.99'
▼ 0.0			Continue to the northeast.
	6.5 ▲	BL	6-way intersection at Wards Fork Gap. Track on immediate right is 40S01 to Mount Ashland. Second track on right is 48N16. Straight ahead is 1065 to Upper Applegate in Rogue River National Forest. First track on left is 47N01. Zero trip meter and bear second left onto 40S01. Pacific Crest Trail crosses through this intersection.
▼ 1.5		SO	Track on left.
	5.0 ▲	SO	Track on right.
▼ 1.8		SO	Track on left through closure gate.
	4.7 ▲	SO	Track on right through closure gate.
▼ 2.6		SO	Track on left.
	3.9 ▲	SO	Track on right.
▼ 2.7		BR	Track on left through closure gate.
	3.8 ▲	BL	Track on right through closure gate.
			GPS: N41°59.11' W122°52.82'
▼ 5.2		SO	Cross over Trapper Creek on bridge; then grave on right of trail.
	1.3 ▲	SO	Grave on left of trail; then cross over Trapper Creek on bridge.
			GPS: N41°58.13' W122°52.72'
▼ 5.4		SO	Graded road on right; then grave surrounded by wooden fence on hillside on left.
	1.1 ▲	BR	Grave surrounded by wooden fence on hillside on right; then graded road on left.
			GPS: N41°57.95' W122°52.66'
▼ 6.1		SO	Track on right.
	0.4 ▲	BR	Track on left.
▼ 6.3		SO	Graded road on left.
	0.2 ▲	SO	Graded road on right.
			GPS: N41°57.32' W122°52.23'
▼ 6.5		SO	Graded road on right is 47N01. Zero trip meter.
	0.0 ▲		Continue to the northwest.
			GPS: N41°57.28' W122°52.00'
▼ 0.0			Continue to the east, joining 47N01.
	3.0 ▲	BR	Graded road on left is the continuation of 47N01. Zero trip meter and bear right onto 48N15, following sign to Wards Fork Gap.
▼ 2.3		SO	Track on left.
	0.7 ▲	SO	Track on right.
▼ 3.0			Trail ends at T-intersection with Beaver Creek Road (FR 11, 48N01). Turn left for Mount Ashland; turn right for California 96.
	0.0 ▲		Trail commences on Beaver Creek Road (FR 11, 48N01) immediately west of the bridge over Beaver Creek, 0.7 miles north of Beaver Creek USFS Campground and 5.4 miles north of California 96. Zero trip meter and turn northwest onto graded dirt road 47N01.
			GPS: N41°56.24' W122°49.23'

NORTH COAST #38

Medicine Lake Trail

Starting Point:	**Modoc Volcanic Scenic Byway (FR 49), 1 mile east of Medicine Lake**
Finishing Point:	**Davis Road (FR 15) at Junction 37**
Total Mileage:	**7.6 miles**
Unpaved Mileage:	**6.8 miles**
Driving Time:	**1 hour**
Elevation Range:	**6,400–7,000 feet**
Usually Open:	**June to November**
Best Time to Travel:	**June to November**
Difficulty Rating:	**2**
Scenic Rating:	**9**
Remoteness Rating:	**+0**

Special Attractions

- Fishing, boating, swimming, camping, and picnicking at Medicine Lake.
- Rockhounding for obsidian at the volcanic lava flow of Little Glass Mountain.
- Little Mount Hoffman Fire Lookout (available for overnight rental).

History

Medicine Lake lies in the center of the collapsed caldera of a massive ancient volcano called Mount Hoffman, whose lava flows are known as the Medicine Lake Highlands. The collapse of Mount Hoffman's summit formed the 25-square-mile caldera. Subsequent eruptions from smaller cones on the caldera's rim have obscured the giant volcano's original shape.

The summit of Little Mount Hoffman has been the site of

Little Mount Hoffman Fire Lookout

Little Medicine Lake

a lookout tower since 1924 and was in use until 1978. The original building was a simple 8- by 8-foot cabin. One fire spotter, George Dunlap, repeatedly walked a portion of the Medicine Lake Trail, from his home at Medicine Lake to the lookout. A larger improved cabin was built in 1930, and a decade later the structure underwent a general overhaul and concrete footings were installed. Little Mount Hoffman was renovated in 1994 as part of the National Forest Lookout rental program. The structure offers basic accommodations in a stunning location, at an elevation of 7,310 feet. The cabin building is not perched on a tower, but it does have a wooden catwalk.

To the west of Little Mount Hoffman, the trail passes the northern rim of Little Glass Mountain, named for the type of lava comprising it: obsidian. Indians used obsidian for arrowheads and other tools. Having such a supply in their hunting grounds was quite an asset.

Description

Medicine Lake, in Modoc National Forest, is a wonderful spot for camping, fishing, and picnicking. In addition, the trail passes short hiking trails, views over the Medicine Lake Lava Flow, and Little Medicine Lake. A hiking trail of less than half a mile takes you to the edge of the Medicine Lake Lava Flow.

The trail immediately enters the Medicine Lake Recreation Area. Camping is permitted in designated sites only, and there are four developed campgrounds to choose from. These are extremely popular in summer and can be very busy on weekends. They are shady, and some sites have lake views. The day-use area has a boat launch and picnic tables on the lakeshore. There is also a beach for swimming. Medicine Lake and Little Medicine Lake are both stocked with trout, and although it is popular, the fishing is generally good.

The trail passes through a restricted area, where travel is permitted year-round on roads and tracks marked with a green arrow on a white background. Other trails are closed to vehicles, and it is your responsibility to know which roads are open. The forest map shows the open network of trails; they are also posted as you enter the restricted area. However, maps become out dated and policies change. Tracks mentioned in the route description are for navigational purposes only. If you plan to explore the region further, you should purchase a current forest map and be sure that the roads you wish to travel are legally open.

The trail enters Klamath National Forest at the turn for Little Mount Hoffman Fire Lookout. The lookout can be rented for overnight use from the forest service. Contact the McCloud Ranger District of Shasta-Trinity National Forests for details. The lookout is situated on the boundaries of three national forests: Shasta-Trinity, Klamath, and Modoc. You can visit the lookout in the daytime, but the forest service requests that you give renters privacy between 8 P.M. and 8 A.M.

The shelf road to the lookout provides fantastic views to the south over Little Glass Mountain, a barren area of jagged lava rock with little vegetation. Rock hounds will find it easy to pick up specimens of obsidian.

As the main trail wraps around the northern edge of Little Glass Mountain, you can see the abrupt halt of the lava, which looks like a cliff beside the trail. Those looking for an undeveloped backcountry campsite will find some pleasant ones

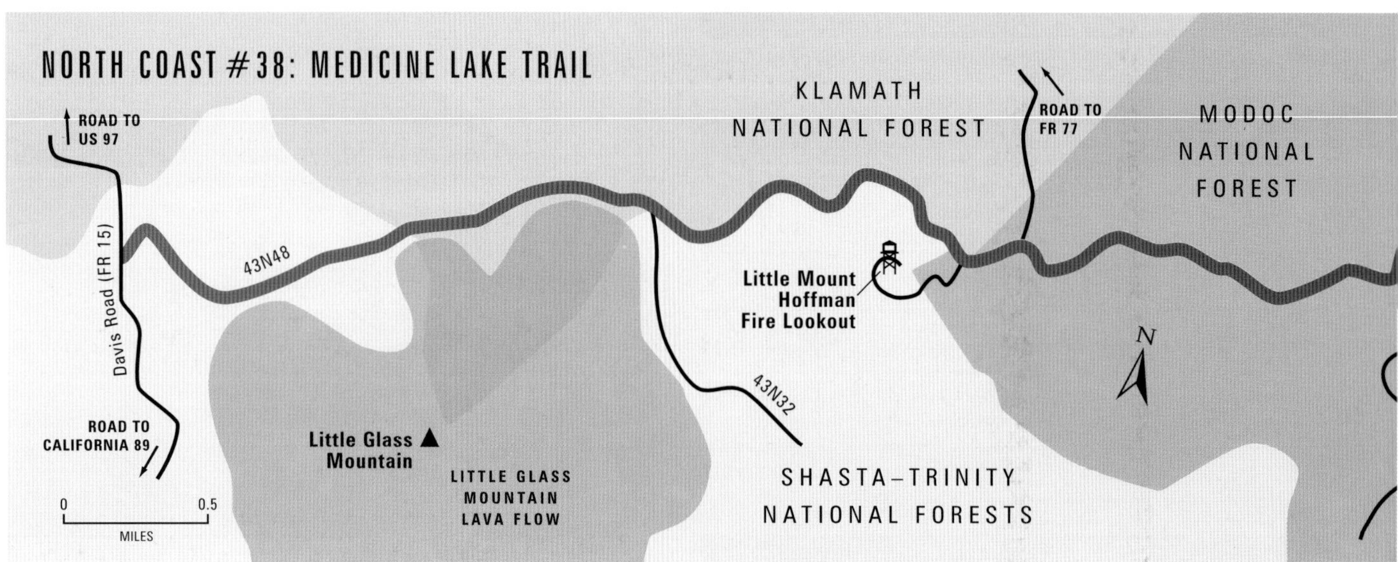

tucked into the trees on the edge of the lava flow.

The trail ends on paved Davis Road (FR 15). The route is marked for snowmobile use in winter.

Current Road Information

Klamath National Forest
Goosenest Ranger District
37805 Highway 97
Macdoel, CA 96058
(530) 398-4391

Map References

BLM Tule Lake
USFS Modoc National Forest; Klamath National Forest; Shasta-Trinity National Forests
USGS 1:24,000 Medicine Lake, Little Glass Mt.
1:100,000 Tule Lake
Maptech CD-ROM: Shasta-Trinity/Modoc
Northern California Atlas & Gazetteer, p. 28
California Road & Recreation Atlas, p. 47
Other: Modoc Country USFS/BLM Map

Route Directions

Mileage		Directions
▼ 0.0		From Modoc Volcanic Scenic Byway (FR 49), 1 mile east of Medicine Lake, zero trip meter and turn west on paved 43N48, following the sign to Medicine Lake. Trail immediately enters the Medicine Lake Recreation Area.
4.2 ▲		Trail ends at T-intersection with paved Modoc Volcanic Scenic Byway (FR 49). Turn left for Lava Beds National Monument; turn right for California 89.
		GPS: N41°35.11' W121°34.83'
▼ 0.3	TR	Turn right, following sign for the campgrounds. To the left goes 0.2 miles to the day-use areas, which include a swimming area and boat ramp.
3.9 ▲	TL	Road straight ahead goes 0.2 miles to the day-use areas, which include a swimming area and boat ramp.
▼ 0.5	SO	Hemlock USFS Campground on left.
4.7 ▲	SO	Hemlock USFS Campground on right.
▼ 0.7	SO	A. H. Hogue USFS Campground on left. Hiking trail on right goes 0.4 miles to the Medicine Lake Lava Flow.
3.5 ▲	SO	A. H. Hogue USFS Campground on right. Hiking trail on left goes 0.4 miles to the Medicine Lake Lava Flow.
		GPS: N41°35.30' W121°35.56'
▼ 0.8	SO	Medicine Lake USFS Campground on left. Hiking trail on right goes 0.8 miles to Little Medicine Lake. Road turns to graded dirt. Follow the sign for Schonchin Springs.
3.4 ▲	SO	Medicine Lake USFS Campground on right. Hiking trail on left goes 0.8 miles to Little Medicine Lake. Road is now paved.
		GPS: N41°35.29' W121°35.74'
▼ 1.1	SO	Hiking trail crosses.
3.1 ▲	SO	Hiking trail crosses.
▼ 1.7	SO	Hiking trail crosses; then Little Medicine Lake on right.
2.5 ▲	SO	Little Medicine Lake on left; then hiking trail crosses.
		GPS: N41°35.30' W121°36.58'
▼ 1.9	SO	Hiking trail on right goes to Little Medicine Lake. Track on left goes to Medicine Lake Guard Station and Headquarters USFS Campground.
2.3 ▲	SO	Hiking trail on left goes to Little Medicine Lake. Track on right goes to Medicine Lake Guard Station and Headquarters USFS Campground.
▼ 2.0	SO	Graded road on right goes to Schonchin Spring. Follow sign to Little Mount Hoffman.
2.2 ▲	SO	Graded road on left goes to Schonchin Spring.
		GPS: N41°35.21' W121°36.88'
▼ 2.6	SO	Track on left.
1.6 ▲	SO	Track on right.
▼ 4.0	SO	Track on right.
0.2 ▲	SO	Track on left.
		GPS: N41°34.86' W121°38.96'
▼ 4.2	TR	Track straight ahead goes 0.6 miles to Little Mount Hoffman Fire Lookout. Zero trip meter and follow the sign for Little Glass Mountain.
0.0 ▲		Continue to the northeast.
		GPS: N41°34.80' W121°39.14'
▼ 0.0		Continue to the northwest.
3.4 ▲	TL	T-intersection. To the right goes 0.6 miles to Little Mount Hoffman Fire Lookout. Zero trip meter and follow the sign to Medicine Lake.
▼ 1.4	SO	Track on left is 43N32. Trail now follows alongside Little Glass Mountain Lava Flow.
2.0 ▲	SO	Track on right is 43N32. Trail leaves Little Glass Mountain Lava Flow.
		GPS: N41°34.77' W121°40.39'
▼ 1.7	SO	Passing alongside Little Glass Mountain.
1.7 ▲	SO	Passing alongside Little Glass Mountain.
▼ 2.8	SO	Track on left. Leaving Little Glass Mountain Lava Flow.
0.6 ▲	SO	Track on right. Trail follows alongside Little Glass Mountain Lava Flow.
▼ 3.4		Trail ends on paved Davis Road (FR 15) at Junction 37. Turn right for Macdoel; turn left for California 89.
0.0 ▲		Trail starts on paved Davis Road (FR 15) at Junction 37. The turn is 2.1 miles south of the intersection with FR 77 and 5 miles south of the Corners Snowmobile Trailhead. Zero trip meter and turn northeast on graded dirt road 43N48.
		GPS: N41°34.33' W121°42.46'

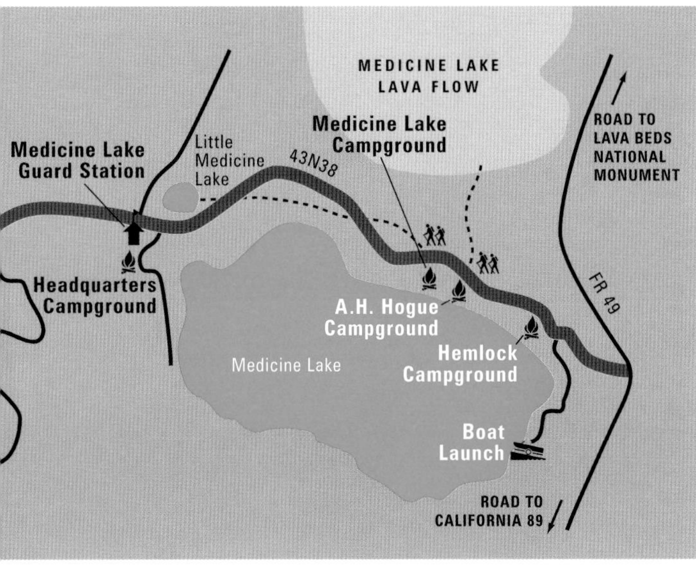

NORTH COAST #39

Tule Lake National Wildlife Refuge Trail

Starting Point:	**Hill Road, 4.7 miles south of the Tule Lake Visitor Center**
Finishing Point:	**California 139 on the southern edge of Newell**
Total Mileage:	**15.4 miles**
Unpaved Mileage:	**10.6 miles**
Driving Time:	**1 hour**
Elevation Range:	**4,000–4,200 feet**
Usually Open:	**Year-round**
Best Time to Travel:	**Year-round**
Difficulty Rating:	**1**
Scenic Rating:	**10**
Remoteness Rating:	**+0**

Special Attractions

- Petroglyphs at Petroglyph Point in Lava Beds National Monument.
- Excellent waterfowl viewing in Tule Lake National Wildlife Refuge.
- Historic sites of Captain Jacks Stronghold, Canby Cross, and the Japanese internment camp at Newell.

History

The Tule Lake Basin has been occupied by humans possibly as early as 11,000 years ago. At an elevation close to 4,000 feet, winter conditions here were more favorable than those in neighboring mountain ranges. The Modoc (see page 90) have lived in the region for generations, and evidence of their habitation includes rock rings, developed depressions, middens, and broken and chipped tools. Tules, or reeds, were used to build shelters and boats.

The volcanic formations on the shores of Tule Lake—Captain Jacks Stronghold

Settlers and miners arrived in the region by the 1850s. Initially, relations were peaceful, but conflicts inevitably arose. The Modoc were eventually removed to a reservation in Oregon, which led to the Modoc War in 1872–73 (see page 107).

The Tule Lake National Wildlife Refuge Trail passes Petroglyph Point, once surrounded by Tule Lake. The people who created symbols here may predate the Modoc. Most of the petroglyphs are geometric shapes; there are very few animal and human figures. The exact date of the petroglyphs is not known, but many are thought to be between 2,500 and 4,500 years old. Many of the petroglyphs have suffered from wind and rain eroding the friable rock surface. The high outcrop is also known as Prisoner Rock, because Japanese detainees from the Tule Lake Relocation Center at Newell left inscriptions, too. More than 19,000 persons of Japanese ancestry were incarcerated here during World War II.

John C. Frémont passed this way in the spring of 1846, on his third western expedition. He named the lake Rhett in honor of his friend Barnwell Rhett of South Carolina. The name Rhett Lake remained until the late 1870s. In 1900, the nearby post office registered the name Tulelake.

The original shallow lake once covered almost 100,000 acres before the land was "reclaimed" and drained from 1912 to 1958. The reclamation effort created a more reliable water source and a massive expanse of fertile land for homesteads and large-scale agriculture. Prior to reclamation, the western edge of the lake was called High Rim, and its northern boundary stretched just over the Oregon state line; to the south, the lake extended to the northern boundary of today's Lava Beds

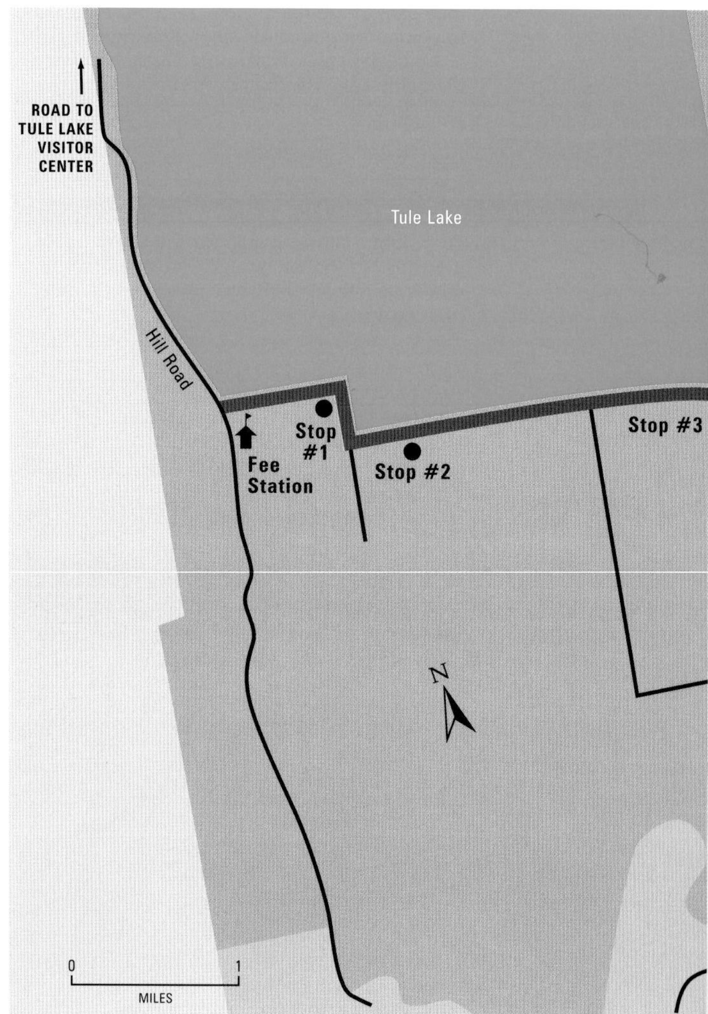

National Monument. Tule Lake today is approximately one sixth its former size. In 1926, the Tule Lake National Wildlife Refuge was established. It is one of six wildlife refuges comprising the Klamath Basin National Refuges Complex.

Description

This easy trail travels a mix of paved and gravel roads past a variety of interesting features in the Tule Lake region. The first section runs along the gravel roads of Tule Lake National Wildlife Refuge. It passes along the south side of Sump 1-A before swinging alongside Sump 1-B. The bird life is prolific; thousands of birds inhabit or migrate through these wetlands. Pheasants live in the grasslands, and mule deer are often spotted near the lake. Photographers may like to take advantage of blinds on the water's edge. Hundreds of species of wildlife have been observed in the Klamath Basin. Fall and spring are excellent times to visit, as migratory flocks of ducks, geese, and other waterfowl pass through the refuge.

The trail exits the refuge at a 4-way intersection. To the right goes to the historical sites of Captain Jacks Stronghold and Canby Cross. There are two hikes at Captain Jacks Stronghold: A 0.5-mile trail loops around the inner stronghold, and a 1.5-mile trail loops to the outer line of defenses. Hikers can reach Captain Jacks Stronghold through the wildlife refuge by following an old vehicle trail that intersects the paved road opposite the trailhead. Please note that tracks mentioned in the refuge are not necessarily open to vehicles; they are mentioned for navigation purposes only.

Tule Lake Relocation Center, a WW II Japanese concentration camp

The main trail turns east and follows a paved road for a short distance before turning off to enter a small section of La-

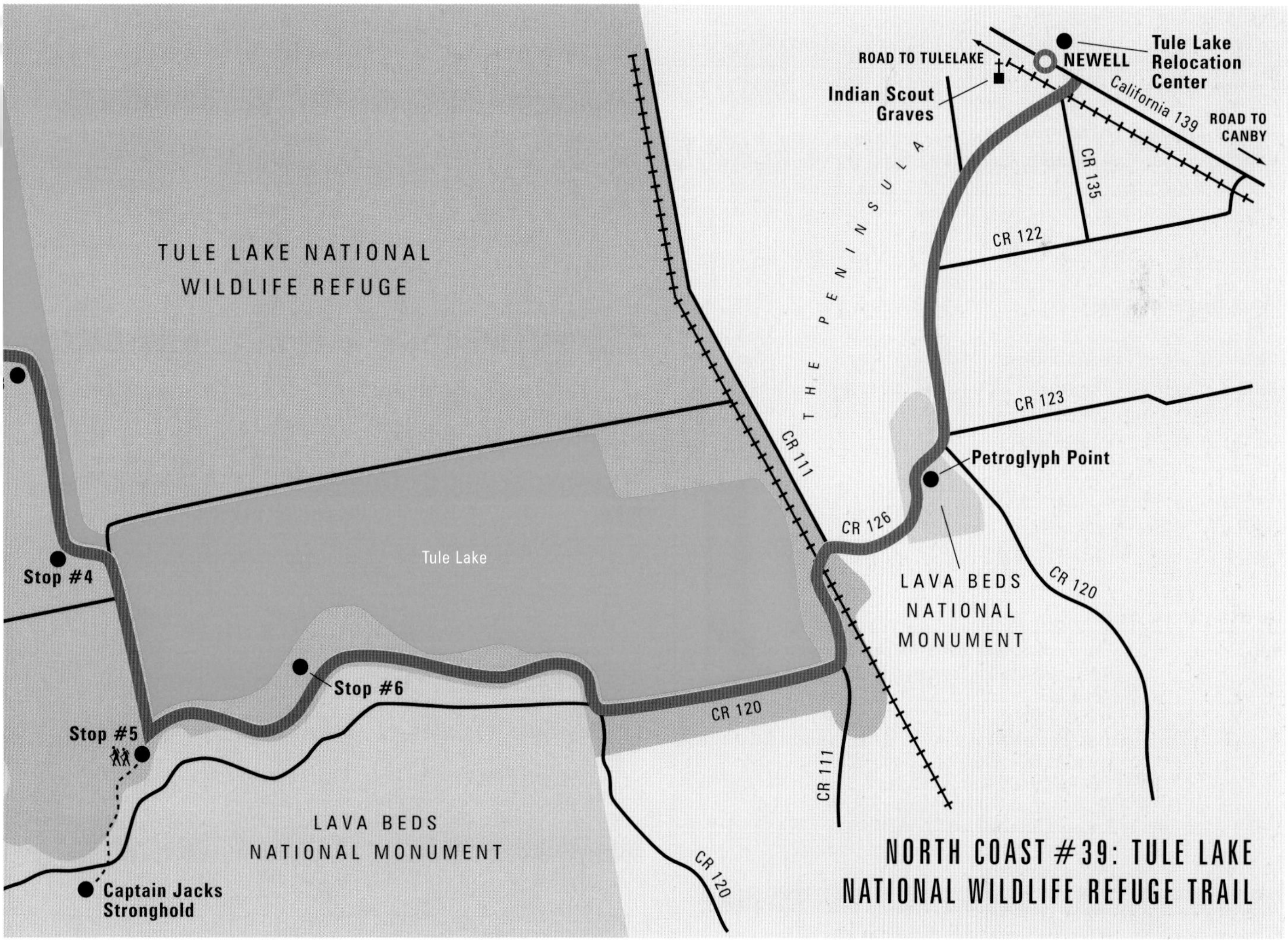

ROAD TO TULELAKE
NEWELL
Tule Lake Relocation Center
California 139
ROAD TO CANBY
Indian Scout Graves
THE PENINSULA
CR 135
CR 122
TULE LAKE NATIONAL WILDLIFE REFUGE
CR 123
CR 111
Petroglyph Point
CR 126
Tule Lake
Stop #4
LAVA BEDS NATIONAL MONUMENT
CR 120
Stop #6
CR 120
Stop #5
CR 111
LAVA BEDS NATIONAL MONUMENT
CR 120
Captain Jacks Stronghold

NORTH COAST #39: TULE LAKE NATIONAL WILDLIFE REFUGE TRAIL

Migratory birds at the Tule Lake National Wildlife Refuge

va Beds National Monument. Here, the promontory of Petroglyph Point rises abruptly from the bed of what was once Lake Modoc. More than 5,000 symbols have been carved into the rock, making this one of the largest concentrations of petroglyphs in North America. Petroglyph Point is also an important nesting site for many species of birds. Sixteen raptor species have been sighted here, including red-tailed hawks, prairie falcons, and kestrels.

The trail ends on California 139 in Newell, a short distance south of the internment camp site.

Current Road Information

Tule Lake National Wildlife Refuge
4009 Hill Road
Tulelake, CA 26134
(530) 667-2231

Map References

BLM Cedarville
USFS Modoc National Forest
USGS 1:24,000 Hatfield, Captain Jacks Stronghold, The Panhandle, Newell
1:100,000 Cedarville
Maptech CD-ROM: Shasta-Trinity/Modoc
Northern California Atlas & Gazetteer, p. 28
California Road & Recreation Atlas, p. 47
Other: Modoc Country USFS/BLM Map

Route Directions

Mileage		Description
▼ 0.0		From paved Hill Road, 4.7 miles south of the Tule Lake Visitor Center and Refuge Headquarters, zero trip meter and turn east on gravel road, following the sign for the auto tour. The visitor center is 5 miles east of the town of Tulelake along East West Road. The trail follows the south side of Sump 1-A.
4.7 ▲		Trail ends at T-intersection with paved Hill Road. Turn right and proceed 4.7 miles for the Tule Lake Visitor Center and Refuge Headquarters.
		GPS: N41°52.73' W121°33.39'
▼ 0.1	SO	Fee station on right. Pay daily fee here.
4.6 ▲	SO	Fee station on left. Pay daily fee here.
▼ 0.6	SO	Auto tour stop #1.
4.1 ▲	SO	Auto tour stop #1.
		GPS: N41°52.73' W121°32.63'
▼ 1.0	TL	Track straight ahead.
3.7 ▲	TR	Track on left.
▼ 1.4	SO	Auto tour stop #2.
3.3 ▲	SO	Auto tour stop #2.
▼ 2.4	SO	Track on right.
2.3 ▲	SO	Track on left.
▼ 2.6	SO	Track on right.
2.1 ▲	SO	Track on left.
▼ 3.2	SO	Auto tour stop #3.
1.5 ▲	SO	Auto tour stop #3.
		GPS: N41°52.31' W121°29.88'
▼ 4.4	SO	Auto tour stop #4.
0.3 ▲	SO	Auto tour stop #4.
▼ 4.7	TR	T-intersection in front of Sump 1-B. Zero trip meter.
0.0 ▲		Continue to the west.
		GPS: N41°51.17' W121°29.50'
▼ 0.0		Continue to the south.
4.6 ▲	TL	Gravel road continues ahead. Zero trip meter.
▼ 0.3	SO	Graded road on right.
4.3 ▲	SO	Graded road on left.
▼ 1.1	TL	Auto tour stop #5. Turn left at T-intersection. Captain Jacks Stronghold is 0.8 miles southwest of this intersection (on foot) along a disused vehicle trail.
3.5 ▲	TR	Track continues straight ahead. Auto tour stop #5.
		GPS: N41°50.15' W121°29.48'
▼ 2.5	SO	Auto tour stop #6.
2.1 ▲	SO	Auto tour stop #6.
▼ 2.6	SO	Track on left is for authorized vehicles only.
2.0 ▲	SO	Track on right is for authorized vehicles only.
▼ 2.9	SO	Track on left is for authorized vehicles only.
1.7 ▲	SO	Track on right is for authorized vehicles only.
▼ 3.4	SO	Boardwalk on left to blind.
1.2 ▲	SO	Boardwalk on right to blind.
		GPS: N41°50.22' W121°27.20'
▼ 4.6	TL	4-way intersection. CR 120 is straight ahead and to the left. Paved road on right goes 3.5 miles to Captain Jacks Stronghold. Zero trip meter.
0.0 ▲		Continue to the northwest on gravel road.
		GPS: N41°49.84' W121°26.11'
▼ 0.0		Continue to the east on paved CR 120.
6.1 ▲	TR	4-way intersection. CR 120 continues to the left. Paved road straight ahead. Zero trip meter.
▼ 1.5	TL	T-intersection with paved road. Remain on CR 120. Road on right is CR 111.
4.6 ▲	TR	Paved road ahead is CR 111. Turn right, remaining on CR 120, following sign to Lava Beds National Monument Visitors Center.
		GPS: N41°49.87' W121°24.25'
▼ 2.2	TR	Cross over railroad; then turn right onto CR 126. Road is now graded dirt.
3.9 ▲	TL	Turn left onto CR 120 at T-intersection; then cross over railroad. Road is now paved.
		GPS: N41°50.50' W121°24.26'
▼ 2.8	SO	Entering Lava Beds National Monument.
3.3 ▲	SO	Leaving Lava Beds National Monument.
▼ 3.1	SO	Petroglyph Point on right.

	3.0 ▲	SO	Petroglyph Point on left.
			GPS: N41°50.73′ W121°23.41′
▼ 3.4		SO	Petroglyph Bluff Hiking Trail on right. Trailhead parking on left.
	2.7 ▲	SO	Petroglyph Bluff Hiking Trail on left. Trailhead parking on right.
			GPS: N41°50.90′ W121°23.30′
▼ 3.5		BL	CR 120 on right. Road becomes paved. Leaving Lava Beds National Monument.
	2.6 ▲	BR	CR 120 continues to the left. Bear right onto CR 126. Road turns to graded dirt. Entering Lava Beds National Monument.
▼ 3.6		SO	CR 123 on right.
	2.5 ▲	SO	CR 123 on left.
▼ 4.6		SO	CR 122 on right.
	1.5 ▲	SO	CR 122 on left.
▼ 5.2		SO	Track on left.
	0.9 ▲	SO	Track on right.
▼ 6.1			CR 135 on right; then cross over railroad; then trail ends at intersection with California 139 on the southern edge of Newell.
	0.0 ▲		Trail commences on California 139 on the southern edge of Newell. Zero trip meter and turn south on paved CR 120, following sign to Captain Jacks Stronghold. Cross over railroad; then CR 135 on left.
			GPS: N41°52.74′ W121°21.79′

NORTH COAST #40

Sand Buttes Trail

Starting Point:	**California 139, 13.7 miles south of Newell**
Finishing Point:	**FR 10, 8.6 miles northwest of Tionesta**
Total Mileage:	**11.7 miles**
Unpaved Mileage:	**10.7 miles**
Driving Time:	**1.5 hours**
Elevation Range:	**4,200–4,500 feet**
Usually Open:	**May to November**
Best Time to Travel:	**Dry weather**
Difficulty Rating:	**3**
Scenic Rating:	**8**
Remoteness Rating:	**+0**

Special Attractions

- Trail passes historic sites from the Modoc War.
- Cinder pits at East Sand Butte.
- Wide-ranging views from an optional 4-rated spur to the top of East Sand Butte.

History

Skirmishes and battles of the Modoc War of 1872–73 (see page 107) took place in the vicinity of Sand Buttes Trail. The trail passes the Battle of Dry Lake site, where a group of Modoc attacked a unit led by Captain Henry Hasbrouck just before dawn on May 10, 1873. Horses stampeded in all directions at the first volley of shots and loud Indian yells. Men arose from sleep and took up arms. Within minutes, they were charging the nearby bluff where the Modoc had positioned themselves during the night. The troops flanked their assailants on three sides. However, the Modoc retreat was so fast that they had escaped to the next volcanic bluff before the troops and Warm River Indian scouts could cut them off. This flank and retreat battle continued all day and crossed nearly 4 miles before the exhausted troops abandoned pursuit.

Twelve of Hasbrouck's men were wounded during this engagement, and one Modoc was found dead at the battle scene. Two Indian scouts working for the U.S. Army were killed in the battle. There is a memorial to them on California 139 at Newell, at the end of North Coast #39: Tule Lake National Wildlife Refuge Trail.

Description

Sand Buttes Trail travels along the south side of a lava field, east of Lava Beds National Monument. The trail is predominantly smooth, with sections of embedded rock. The surface can be uneven, with some deep, fine sand traps in dry weather. In wet weather the trail is likely to be impassable and should not be attempted.

The turnoff for the trail from California 139 is not marked, but it is opposite Modoc County Road 136, so it is easy to find. The rest of the trail is sketchily marked, so pay close attention to the route directions and GPS coordinates to avoid taking a wrong turn. Right away, the trail enters Modoc National Forest; the entrance is unmarked. The site of the old Dry Lake Guard Station is immediately on the left—the new station is located approximately a mile south of the start of the trail on California 139.

The formed sandy trail passes around the northern edge of Dry Lake, which is littered with volcanic rock and covered with sagebrush. This was the site of the Battle of Dry Lake, one of the final battles in the Modoc War. There is no marker for the lakebed battle site.

East Sand Butte

Shelf road climbs along East Sand Butte

The trail continues through open country to join an old railroad grade toward the prominent East Sand Butte. A cinder pit has removed much of the material from the south side of the butte. From the pit, a 4-rated side trail winds around the back of the butte and climbs a rough, narrow shelf road to the top. Hardy curl-leaf mahoganies and windblown junipers grow on top of the butte. The plateau of Devils Garden can be seen to the east.

The main trail turns sharply south and briefly joins the paved road before turning north and heading directly toward Big Sand Butte. Some ruins of stone military fortifications from the Modoc War are at the base of the butte. From here, the trail heads west to rejoin the paved road.

Current Road Information

Modoc National Forest
Double Head Ranger District
PO Box 369
Tulelake, CA 96134
(530) 233-2246

Map References

BLM Tule Lake
USFS Modoc National Forest
USGS 1:24,000 Perez, Caldwell Butte
1:100,000 Tule Lake
Maptech CD-ROM: Shasta-Trinity/Modoc
Northern California Atlas & Gazetteer, pp. 29, 28
California Road & Recreation Atlas, p. 47
Other: Modoc Country USFS/BLM Map

Route Directions

Mileage		Directions
▼ 0.0		From California 139 opposite CR 136, 13.7 miles south of Newell and 0.1 miles south of Modoc County mile marker 30.5, zero trip meter and turn southwest on unmarked formed dirt trail. There is a grave on the southeast corner of the intersection.
3.9 ▲		Trail finishes at intersection of California 139 opposite CR 136. Turn left for Newell; turn right for Canby. There is a grave on the southeast corner of the intersection.
		GPS: N41°42.15' W121°16.79'
▼ 0.1	SO	Pass site of old Dry Lake Guard Station on left.
3.8 ▲	SO	Pass site of old Dry Lake Guard Station on right.
▼ 0.2	SO	Wire gate.
3.7 ▲	SO	Wire gate.
▼ 0.3	TL	Track continues straight ahead along fence line. Turn left onto unmarked trail.
3.6 ▲	TR	T-intersection with track along fence line.
▼ 0.4	BR	Track on left.
3.5 ▲	BL	Track on right.
▼ 1.0	SO	Track on left.
2.9 ▲	SO	Track on right.
		GPS: N41°41.62' W121°17.26'
▼ 1.6	TL	Track on right in front of power lines. This is the site of the Battle of Dry Lake (on the northwest corner of Dry Lake). Immediately track on right.
2.3 ▲	TR	Track on left; then turn right. Trail continues straight ahead. This is the site of the Battle of Dry Lake (on the northwest corner of Dry Lake).
		GPS: N41°41.48' W121°17.87'
▼ 1.7	BR	Track continues straight ahead.

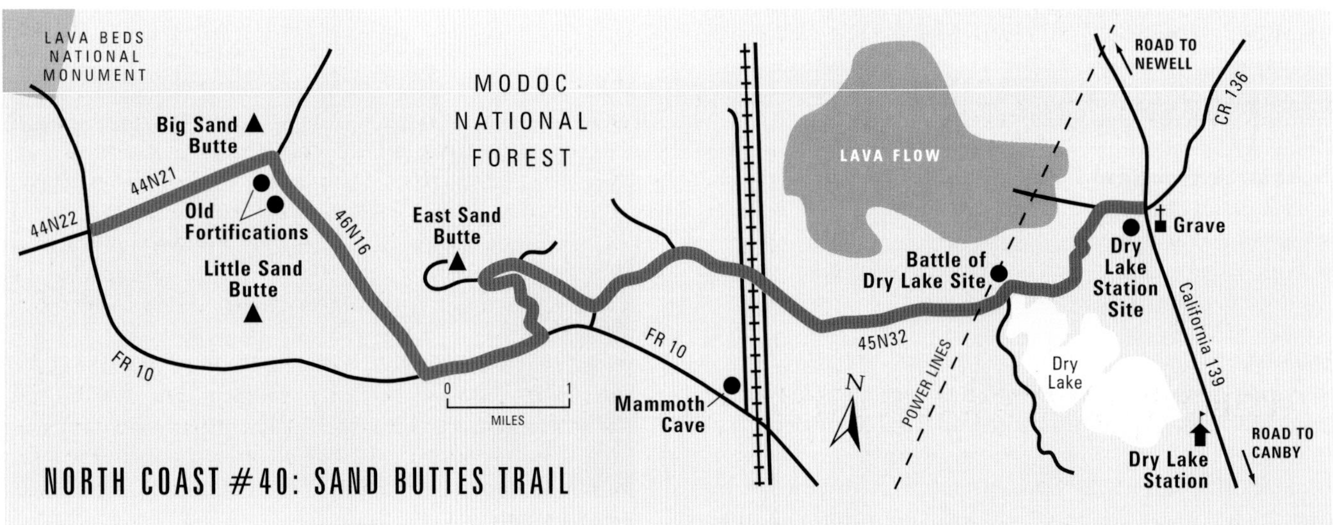

	2.2 ▲	BL	Track on right.
▼ 1.9		SO	Pass under power lines.
	2.0 ▲	SO	Pass under power lines.
▼ 2.0		SO	Track on left and track on right along power lines.
	1.9 ▲	SO	Track on left and track on right along power lines.
			GPS: N41°41.28' W121°18.14'
▼ 3.9		SO	Track on left and track on right. Zero trip meter and cross over railroad.
	0.0 ▲		Continue to the east. Track on left and track on right.
			GPS: N41°41.19' W121°20.20'
▼ 0.0			Continue to the west. Track on left goes 1.1 miles to Mammoth Cave. Also track on right.
	2.4 ▲	SO	Track on left. Track on right goes 1.1 miles to Mammoth Cave. Cross over railroad and zero trip meter.
▼ 0.7		SO	Track on right.
	1.7 ▲	SO	Track on left.
			GPS: N41°41.26' W121°20.97'
▼ 1.4		TR	Track continues straight ahead. Turn right onto raised track of the old railroad grade and pass under power lines.
	1.0 ▲	TL	Pass under power lines; then turn left at T-intersection, leaving the old railroad grade.
			GPS: N41°40.79' W121°21.59'
▼ 2.1		SO	Track on right.
	0.3 ▲	SO	Track on left.
▼ 2.4		TL	Track straight ahead goes into cinder pit of East Sand Butte and continues for 1 mile to the top of the butte. Zero trip meter.
	0.0 ▲		Continue to the northeast.
			GPS: N41°40.83' W121°22.69'
▼ 0.0			Continue to the east.
	1.9 ▲	TR	Track straight ahead goes into cinder pit of East Sand Butte and continues for 1 mile to the top of the butte. Zero trip meter.
▼ 0.1		SO	Track on right.
	1.8 ▲	SO	Track on left.
▼ 0.4		SO	Track on right.
	1.5 ▲	SO	Track on left.
			GPS: N41°40.82' W121°22.29'
▼ 0.9		TR	T-intersection with paved road.
	1.0 ▲	TL	Turn left onto formed trail at sign for East Sand Butte.
			GPS: N41°40.53' W121°22.02'
▼ 1.9		TR	Turn right onto formed trail 46N16 and zero trip meter.
	0.0 ▲		Continue to the northeast.
			GPS: N41°40.12' W121°23.08'
▼ 0.0			Continue to the northwest.
	3.5 ▲	TL	T-intersection with paved road. Zero trip meter.
▼ 1.8		SO	Modoc War fortifications on left.
	1.7 ▲	SO	Modoc War fortifications on right.
▼ 2.0		TL	Track on right. Turn left at the base of Big Sand Butte. On the left is the oblong shape of some military fortifications.
	1.5 ▲	TR	Track on left. Turn right at the base of Big Sand Butte. On the right is the oblong shape of some military fortifications.
			GPS: N41°41.34' W121°24.85'
▼ 2.1		SO	Rock structure on left is military fortification ruin.
	1.4 ▲	SO	Rock structure on right is military fortification ruin.
			GPS: N41°41.32' W121°24.92'
▼ 2.5		SO	Track on right.
	1.0 ▲	SO	Track on left.
▼ 3.5			Trail ends at intersection with paved Lava Beds National Monument Road (FR 10). Turn right for Lava Beds National Monument; turn left for Tionesta and California 139.
	0.0 ▲		Trail commences on Lava Beds National Monument Road (FR 10) opposite 44N22, 8.6 miles northwest of Tionesta. Zero trip meter and turn east on formed trail marked 44N21.
			GPS: N41°40.68' W121°26.37'

NORTH COAST #41

Fairchild Swamp Trail

Starting Point:	**California 299, 3.5 miles west of the intersection with US 395 at Alturas**
Finishing Point:	**California 139, 7 miles northwest of intersection with California 299 at Canby**
Total Mileage:	**36.1 miles**
Unpaved Mileage:	**36.1miles**
Driving Time:	**4 hours**
Elevation Range:	**4,400–5,200 feet**
Usually Open:	**June to November**
Best Time to Travel:	**June to November**
Difficulty Rating:	**1**
Scenic Rating:	**8**
Remoteness Rating:	**+0**

Special Attractions

- Excellent birding opportunities for waterfowl and migratory birds.
- Chance to see pronghorn and wild horses.
- Fairchild Swamp petroglyphs.
- Peaceful fishing and camping at the four reservoirs along the trail.

History

Fairchild Swamp Trail begins in the region known as Devils Garden. This territory was occupied by the Modoc and Northern Paiute; Paleo-Indians may have lived here as much as 6,000 years ago. The Modoc and Northern Paiute had seasonal camps at Devils Garden to take advantage of the area's resources. They also had camps at Fairchild Swamp and Goose Lake, where they would hunt antelope and deer and collect edible roots.

The Modoc established temporary camps across the region during spring and would set up hunting blinds. Occasionally, chips of obsidian and basalt can be found at these campsites; such areas of lithic scatter should be left undisturbed. The Modoc built more permanent villages consisting of pit houses in the vicinity of Clear Lake.

Settlers raised sheep and cattle in this region, but attempts at crop production were seldom successful. The Triangle Ranch holdings were quite extensive, and there are ruins of ranch buildings midway along the trail.

Description

This easy graded road is suitable for passenger vehicles in dry weather. Sections of it follow a Back Country Byways Discovery Trail.

The trail begins a short distance west of Alturas and gradually climbs into the Devils Garden area. This high-elevation volcanic plateau is made up of predominantly flat swamps and plains, littered with volcanic boulders. Vegetation includes junipers, conifers, and, around old homestead sites, white poplars. There are many small reservoirs on the plateau; most have a boat launch, campsites, and picnic areas. The reservoirs may dry up during summer.

A herd of wild horses live at Devils Garden. The forest service manages the herd of about 300. The area is also a prime spot for birders. The region is part of the Pacific Flyway, and the wetlands provides great opportunities to see migratory birds and waterfowl. Birders can look for Canadian geese, mallards, pintails, teals, shorebirds, sandhill cranes, ospreys, and bald eagles. The plains are also habitat for pronghorn; in particular, the Antelope Plains is a wonderful spot for observing these graceful animals.

The graded road passes part of the old Triangle Ranch. A short distance farther, near the man-made wetlands area of Joe Sweet Pond, is an abandoned wooden cabin. Dr. Joe G. Sweet was an enthusiastic supporter of wetlands habitat. The Triangle Ranch Headquarters are 0.6 miles north of the main trail in Round Valley. A wooden cabin remains in a dense stand of white poplars; two cabins built of local stone near a flowing spring also remain. The site is shown on topographical maps as Round Valley Ranch.

The main trail passes near Reservoir C, which has a boat ramp and a pleasant campground with juniper-shaded sites on the shore. Fairchild Swamp is being restored as a wetlands, however, because farmers in Oregon still own the water rights, the project is taking a long time to complete. The forest service is purchasing water rights. This restoration project shows the classic dichotomy between water for humans and water for wildlife. Restoration includes seeding and building a rock nesting island. The rocky cliffs on the western side of Fairchild Swamp have some petroglyphs high up near the rim. Other faint markings can be found on large boulders near the bottom. The petroglyphs are hard to locate; binoculars will help you find the ones high on the cliff. If you walk up for a closer look, be aware that the scrubby vegetation supports a large population of ticks.

Bleached juniper trunks on the shoreline of Reservoir F

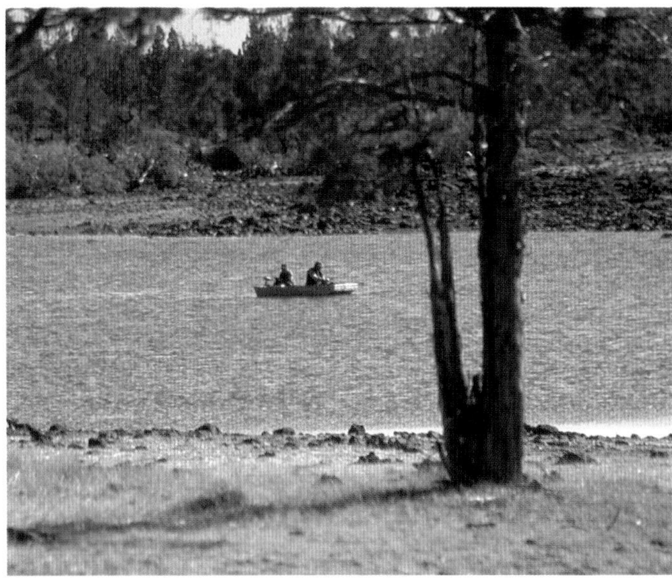

Fishing on the remote Reservoir C

The trail continues past Reservoir F, which also has a shady camping area on its shores, before coming to an end on California 139 west of Canby. Duncan Reservoir, which often dries up after dry seasons, is located a short distance from the trail's end. You can fish for trout and bass on Reservoir C, Reservoir F, and Duncan Reservoir, all of which are stocked by the forest service.

Current Road Information

Modoc National Forest
Devils Garden Ranger District
800 West 12th Street
Alturas, CA 96101
(530) 233-5811

Map References

BLM Cedarville, Alturas
USFS Modoc National Forest
USGS 1:24,000 Alturas, Big Sage Reservoir, Whittemore Ridge, Boles Meadow East, Jacks Butte, Ambrose
1:100,000 Cedarville, Alturas
Maptech CD-ROM: Shasta-Trinity/Modoc
Northern California Atlas & Gazetteer, pp. 40, 30, 29
California Road & Recreation Atlas, p. 48

Route Directions

▼ 0.0			From California 299, 3.5 miles west of the intersection with US 395 in Alturas, zero trip meter and turn northwest on graded dirt CR/FR 73, following the sign to Devils Garden CCC.
	5.9 ▲		Trail ends at T-intersection with California 299. Turn left for Alturas; turn right for Canby.
			GPS: N41°29.78' W120°36.48'
▼ 0.3		SO	Cattle guard.
	5.6 ▲	SO	Cattle guard.
▼ 1.6		SO	Track on right; then track on left; then track on right.
	4.3 ▲	SO	Track on left; then track on right; then track on left.
▼ 1.9		SO	Track on right and track on left.
	4.0 ▲	SO	Track on right and track on left.
▼ 2.0		SO	Graded road on left goes 2 miles to Devils Garden Camp, now a prison.
	3.9 ▲	SO	Graded road on right goes 2 miles to Devils Garden Camp, now a prison.
			GPS: N41°30.51' W120°38.04'
▼ 2.4		SO	Graded road on right.
	3.5 ▲	SO	Graded road on left.
▼ 2.6		SO	Cattle guard. Entering Modoc National Forest. Track on right.
	3.3 ▲	SO	Track on left. Leaving Modoc National Forest. Cattle guard.
			GPS: N41°30.95' W120°38.37'
▼ 2.7		SO	Track on left.
	3.2 ▲	SO	Track on right.
▼ 3.0		SO	Track on left.
	2.9 ▲	SO	Track on right.
▼ 5.1		SO	Track on right and track on left under power lines.
	0.8 ▲	SO	Track on right and track on left under power lines.
▼ 5.9		SO	Graded road on right is CR 180 (44N03), which goes 4 miles to Big Sage Reservoir, boat ramp, and USFS campground. Zero trip meter and follow the sign to Crowder Flat Station.
	0.0 ▲		Continue to the southeast.
			GPS: N41°33.24' W120°40.84'
▼ 0.0			Continue to the northwest.
	3.5 ▲	SO	Graded road on left is CR 180 (44N03), which goes 4 miles to Big Sage Reservoir, boat ramp, and USFS campground. Zero trip meter and follow the sign to California 299.
▼ 1.9		SO	Track on right.
	1.6 ▲	SO	Track on left.
▼ 2.2		SO	Track on left is 43N06. Track on right goes 0.5 miles to the edge of Big Sage Reservoir. Cross over wash.
	1.3 ▲	SO	Cross over wash. Track on right is 43N06. Track on left goes 0.5 miles to the edge of Big Sage Reservoir.
			GPS: N41°34.95' W120°41.87'
▼ 2.8		SO	Track on left to stock tanks.
	0.7 ▲	SO	Track on right to stock tanks.
▼ 3.5		TL	Graded road on right is FR 73. Zero trip meter and turn left onto 43N18, following sign to Fairchild Swamp.
	0.0 ▲		Continue to the south on FR 73.
			GPS: N41°36.11' W120°42.32'
▼ 0.0			Continue to the west.
	5.8 ▲	TR	T-intersection. Graded road on left is FR 73. Zero trip meter and follow sign to California 299.
▼ 1.3		SO	Track on right.
	4.5 ▲	SO	Track on left.
▼ 1.4		SO	Track on left.
	4.4 ▲	SO	Track on right.
▼ 1.6		SO	Track on left.
	4.2 ▲	SO	Track on right.
▼ 1.7		SO	Track on left.
	4.1 ▲	SO	Track on right.
▼ 2.4		SO	Track on right.
	3.4 ▲	SO	Track on left.
▼ 3.8		SO	Track on right.
	2.0 ▲	SO	Track on left.
▼ 4.3		SO	Track on right.
	1.5 ▲	SO	Track on left.
▼ 5.1		SO	Track on left to corral on the edge of the Antelope Plains.
	0.7 ▲	SO	Track on right to corral on the edge of the Antelope Plains.
			GPS: N41°38.79' W120°45.88'
▼ 5.2		SO	Track on right.
	0.6 ▲	SO	Track on left.
▼ 5.3		SO	Track on left through gate goes to an old cabin of the Triangle Ranch.
	0.5 ▲	SO	Track on right through gate goes to an old cabin of the Triangle Ranch.
			GPS: N41°38.88' W120°46.08'
▼ 5.4		SO	Cattle guard.
	0.4 ▲	SO	Cattle guard.
▼ 5.7		SO	Joe Sweet Pond on right.
	0.1 ▲	SO	Joe Sweet Pond on left.
			GPS: N41°39.01' W120°46.43'
▼ 5.8		SO	Graded road on right goes 1.3 miles to Reservoir C. Zero trip meter and follow the sign to Triangle Ranch.
	0.0 ▲		Continue to the east.
			GPS: N41°39.05' W120°46.57'
▼ 0.0			Continue to the west.
	3.5 ▲	SO	Graded road on left goes 1.3 miles to Reservoir C. Zero trip meter and follow the sign to Alturas.
▼ 0.6		SO	Track on left through gate; then track on right.
	2.9 ▲	SO	Track on left; then track on right through gate.
▼ 1.3		SO	Track on left.
	2.2 ▲	SO	Track on right.
▼ 2.3		SO	Track on right.
	1.2 ▲	SO	Track on left.
▼ 2.5		SO	Track on right.
	1.0 ▲	SO	Track on left.
▼ 3.1		SO	Track on right.
	0.4 ▲	SO	Track on left.
▼ 3.4		SO	Cattle guard.
	0.1 ▲	SO	Cattle guard.
▼ 3.5		TL	Round Valley. Straight ahead, 43N18 goes 0.6 miles through Round Valley to the wooden cabin, stone ruins, and spring at Triangle Ranch. Zero trip meter and turn left on 44N33, following the sign to Fairchild Swamp. Spring at the intersection.
	0.0 ▲		Continue to the east.
			GPS: N41°40.25' W120°50.23'
▼ 0.0			Continue to the south and cross cattle guard.
	6.2 ▲	TR	Round Valley. Cattle guard. Straight ahead, 43N18 goes 0.6 miles through Round Valley to the wooden cabin, stone ruins, and spring at

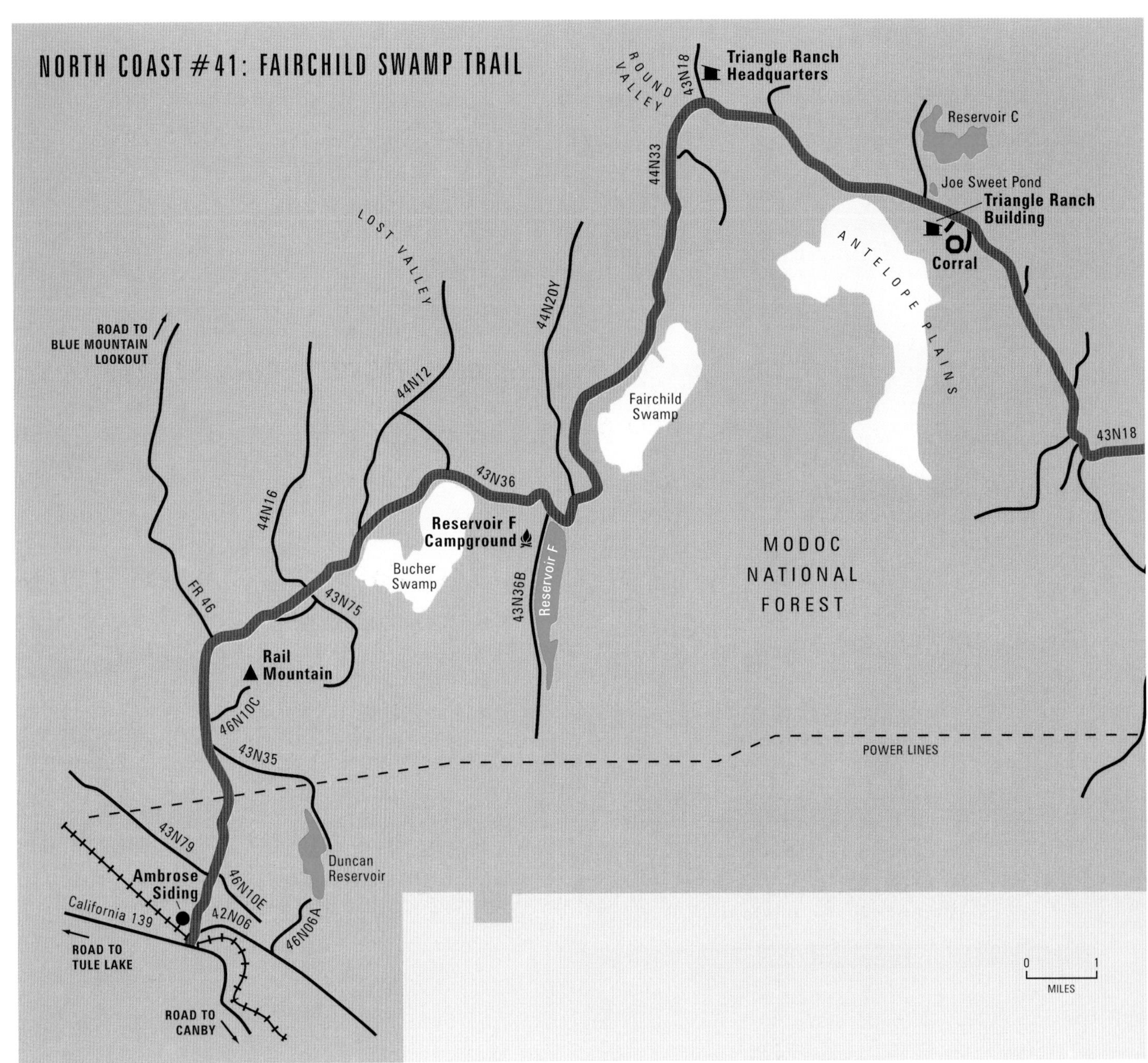

		Triangle Ranch. Zero trip meter and turn right onto 43N18, following the sign for Alturas. Spring at the intersection.
▼ 0.2	SO	Track on right through gate.
6.0 ▲	SO	Track on left through gate.
▼ 0.9	SO	Track on left.
5.3 ▲	SO	Track on right.
▼ 1.6	SO	Cattle guard.
4.6 ▲	SO	Cattle guard.
▼ 1.8	SO	Cross over canal and start to run alongside Fairchild Swamp.
4.4 ▲	SO	Trail leaves Fairchild Swamp. Cross over canal.
▼ 3.1	SO	Cattle guard; then track on left. Cliffs on right.
3.1 ▲	SO	Track on right; then cattle guard. Cliffs on left.
		GPS: N41°37.77′ W120°50.97′
▼ 4.1	SO	Track on left.
2.1 ▲	SO	Track on right.
▼ 6.2	BR	Three tracks on left across swamp. Follow the sign to Reservoir F and zero trip meter.
0.0 ▲		Continue to the northwest around Fairchild Swamp.
		GPS: N41°35.54′ W120°51.95′
▼ 0.0		Continue to the southwest away from Fairchild Swamp. Track on left.
7.0 ▲	BL	Track on right; then three tracks on right across Fairchild Swamp. Follow the sign to Reservoir C and zero trip meter.
▼ 0.4	BL	Track on right is 44N20Y.
6.6 ▲	BR	Track on left is 44N20Y.
▼ 0.7	TR	Track on left goes to Reservoir F. Turn right onto 43N36, following the sign to California 139.
6.3 ▲	TL	Track on right goes to Reservoir F. Turn left onto 44N33, following the sign to Fairchild Swamp

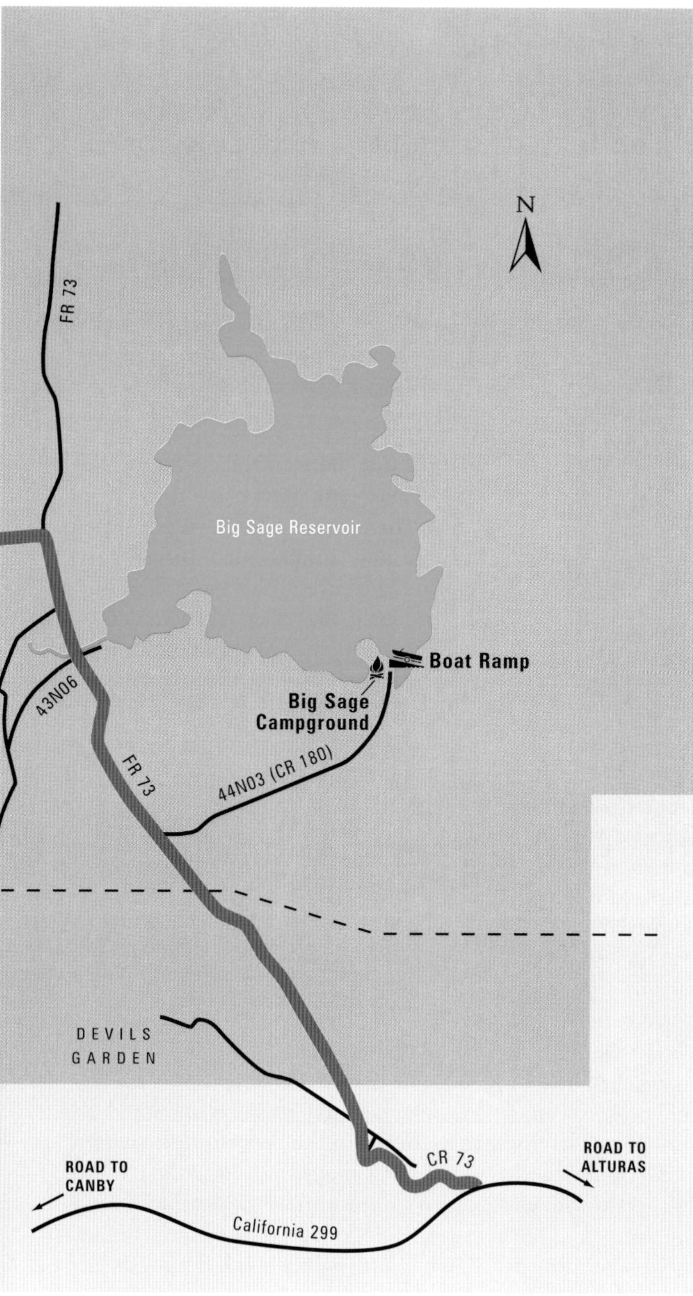

			GPS: N41°35.11′ W120°52.45′
▼ 1.0		SO	Cattle guard.
	6.0 ▲	SO	Cattle guard.
▼ 1.1		SO	Track on left is 44N36B, which goes 0.2 miles to Reservoir F, campground, and boat launch.
	5.9 ▲	SO	Track on right is 44N36B, which goes 0.2 miles to Reservoir F, campground, and boat launch.
			GPS: N41°35.31′ W120°52.74′
▼ 1.2		SO	Track on right.
	5.8 ▲	SO	Track on left.
▼ 2.1		SO	Cattle guard. Bucher Swamp on left.
	4.9 ▲	SO	Cattle guard. Bucher Swamp on right.
▼ 2.8		SO	Track on right.
	4.2 ▲	SO	Track on left.
▼ 4.4		SO	Graded road on right is 44N12 to Lost Valley. Follow the sign to California 139, remaining on 43N36.
	2.6 ▲	SO	Graded road on left is 44N12 to Lost Valley. Follow the sign to Reservoir F, remaining on 43N36.
			GPS: N41°34.87′ W120°55.95′
▼ 4.6		SO	Track on left to remains of log cabin beside Bucher Swamp.
	2.4 ▲	SO	Track on right to remains of log cabin beside Bucher Swamp.
▼ 4.7		SO	Cattle guard; then track on left.
	2.3 ▲	SO	Track on right; then cattle guard.
▼ 5.4		SO	Track on left is 43N75 and track on right is 44N16; then cattle guard.
	1.6 ▲	SO	Cattle guard; then track on right is 43N75 and track on left is 44N16.
			GPS: N41°34.29′ W120°56.79′
▼ 6.3		SO	Track on left.
	0.7 ▲	SO	Track on right.
▼ 6.8		SO	Track on left.
	0.2 ▲	SO	Track on right.
▼ 7.0		TL	T-intersection with FR 46. To the right goes to Blue Mountain Lookout. Zero trip meter and follow the sign to California 139.
	0.0 ▲		Continue to the northeast.
			GPS: N41°33.67′ W120°58.37′
▼ 0.0			Continue to the south.
	4.2 ▲	TR	FR 46 continues straight ahead to Blue Mountain Lookout. Zero trip meter and turn right onto 43N36, following the sign to Fairchild Swamp.
▼ 1.0		SO	Track on left is 46N10C.
	3.2 ▲	SO	Track on right is 46N10C.
			GPS: N41°32.77′ W120°58.53′
▼ 1.1		SO	Track on right.
	3.1 ▲	SO	Track on left.
▼ 1.4		SO	Graded road on left is 43N35 to Duncan Reservoir.
	2.8 ▲	SO	Graded road on right is 43N35 to Duncan Reservoir.
▼ 2.0		SO	Track on right and track on left under power lines.
	2.2 ▲	SO	Track on left and track on right under power lines.
▼ 3.3		SO	Track on left is 46N10E.
	0.9 ▲	SO	Track on right is 46N10E.
▼ 3.4		SO	Track on right is 43N79.
	0.8 ▲	SO	Track on left is 43N79.
▼ 4.1		SO	Track on right; then track on left is 42N06, which goes 2.4 miles to Duncan Reservoir (via a second left turn onto 46N06A after 1.3 miles).
	0.1 ▲	SO	Track on right is 42N06, which goes 2.4 miles to Duncan Reservoir (via a left turn onto 46N06A after 1.3 miles); then track on left.
▼ 4.2			Ambrose Siding. Cross over railroad; then cattle guard. Road is now paved. Trail finishes at T-intersection with California 139. Turn left for Canby and Alturas; turn right for Tule Lake.
	0.0 ▲		Trail commences on California 139 at Ambrose Siding, 7 miles northwest of Canby and California 299, 0.2 miles east of Modoc County mile marker 7.5. Zero trip meter and turn north on paved FR 46 at the sign for Loveness Road. Cross cattle guard; then cross over railroad. Road turns to graded dirt.
			GPS: N41°30.01′ W120°58.72′

NORTH COAST #42

Surprise Valley Trail

Starting Point:	CR 1, 5 miles north of Cedarville
Finishing Point:	CR 8A in Nevada, 2.7 miles east of the California-Nevada state line
Total Mileage:	11.5 miles, plus 3.1-mile spur to Salt Creek
Unpaved Mileage:	11.5 miles, plus 3.1-mile spur
Driving Time:	2 hours
Elevation Range:	4,500–5,500 feet
Usually Open:	Year-round
Best Time to Travel:	Dry weather
Difficulty Rating:	4
Scenic Rating:	8
Remoteness Rating:	+0

Special Attractions

- Hot springs and a warm hot spring creek.
- Chance to see herds of wild horses in Surprise Valley.
- Trail follows a section of the historic Applegate Trail.

History

Surprise Valley, as the name suggests, was just that—a surprise to westbound emigrants who had survived the harsh Black Rock Desert of Nevada. The unexpected sight of this impressive north-south valley was a welcome relief to emigrants. They were in fact looking at the remains of ancient Lake Surprise, which covered the full length of the valley approximately 10,000 years ago.

Archaeologists have detected evidence of Paleo-Indians in this valley. After the last ice age, vegetation was lush and the region supported large mammals such as bison. Excavations indicate that these people lived in communal dwellings by the

Hot spring soaking area beside Warm Creek

Mustang herd in Surprise Valley

lakeshore. As the climate became more arid, Lake Surprise receded. The inhabitants adapted and settled by the marshy shores. Climatic conditions changed over 3,000 years, and the fauna changed, too. People and animals that survived the changing conditions continued to live in this great valley.

The Northern Paiute occupied the valley when settlers arrived in the mid-nineteenth century. The Paiute moved to higher elevations during spring and summer to gather enough seeds, roots, and game to last through the winter, which was spent at lower elevations on the valley floor.

Description

Surprise Valley is a long, arid valley in the northeasternmost corner of California, between the Warner Mountains to the west and the Hayes Range to the east. The valley is known for its dry lakebeds and proliferation of hot springs. Surprise Valley Trail passes a few undeveloped hot springs and follows a section of the Applegate Trail.

The trail leaves Surprise Valley Road (CR 1) north of Cedarville. For the first few miles, it follows a graded county road called Fortynine Lane across the flat Surprise Valley. The trail crosses a small flowing creek, fed by some unnamed hot springs a short distance to the north. The entire creek is warm, and by following an unmarked vehicle trail along the creek to the north, you will come to some informal, undeveloped soaking areas. The farther up the creek you go, the hotter the water. These areas are shallow and lightly used. This side trip crosses land shown on maps as private, but there are no signs posting the property, so access seems to be okay. However, be considerate and should no trespassing signs be posted, respect them. There is an alternate, lesser used trail to the east that accesses the springs by traveling across public lands.

Farther to the east, a spur travels past buttes and abundant sagebrush to a pretty stop along a tributary of Sand Creek. One of the side trails, which leads east to the Nevada state line, offers the best chance to see a wild horse herd. The horses are called Sand Creek duns for their predominant coloring. Many are descended from a quarter horse stallion turned out by a local rancher. The horses carry his color as well as quarter horse confirmation.

The main route diverges from the graded road to follow a section of the Applegate Trail. The California Trail Association has placed several markers along the trail, but these can blend into the background and may be hard to spot. This section gives the trail its difficulty rating of 4. It climbs up and over a rocky ridge, with large embedded boulders that must be negotiated. The smooth valley sections of the trail are impassable in wet weather. These sections break up the slow rocky crawls over the ridges. The trail ends on CR 8A in Nevada, 2.7 miles east of the California state line.

Current Road Information

Bureau of Land Management
Surprise Field Office
602 Cressler Street
Cedarville, CA 96104
(530) 279-6101

Map References

BLM Cedarville, Vya (NV)
USFS Modoc National Forest
USGS 1:24,000 Cedarville, Leonards Hot Springs, Fortynine Mt.
1:100,000 Cedarville, Vya (NV)
Maptech CD-ROM: Shasta-Trinity/Modoc; Northwest Nevada/Winnemucca/Sheldon Wildlife Refuge (NV)
Northern California Atlas & Gazetteer, p. 31
Nevada Atlas & Gazetteer, p. 18
California Road & Recreation Atlas, p. 49
Other: Modoc Country USFS/BLM Map (incomplete)

Route Directions

▼ 0.0		From Surprise Valley Road (CR 1), 5 miles north of Cedarville, 0.2 miles north of Modoc County mile marker 34, zero trip meter and turn east on small paved Fortynine Lane (CR 18).
7.8 ▲		Trail ends at intersection with Surprise Valley Road (CR 1). Turn left for Cedarville; turn right for Lake City.
		GPS: N41°36.15′ W120°10.84′
▼ 0.8	SO	Road turns to graded dirt.
7.0 ▲	SO	Road becomes paved.
▼ 1.2	SO	Cattle guard.
6.6 ▲	SO	Cattle guard.
▼ 1.9	SO	Track on left.
5.9 ▲	SO	Track on right.
▼ 4.1	SO	Track on right. Graded road on left is the Applegate-Lassen Trail. Trail now follows this route.
3.7 ▲	SO	Track on left. Graded road on right is the Applegate-Lassen Trail. Trail now leaves that route.
		GPS: N41°36.11′ W120°05.92′
▼ 4.5	SO	Leonard Hot Springs on private property beside the road on right.
3.3 ▲	SO	Leonard Hot Springs on private property beside the road on left.
▼ 4.6	SO	Track on left; then cross over warm water creek; then track on right. Follow the track on left, west of the crossing, alongside the warm creek to the hot spring soaking areas.
3.2 ▲	SO	Track on left; then cross over warm water creek; then track on right. Follow the track on right, west of the crossing, alongside the warm creek to the hot spring soaking areas.
		GPS: N41°35.89′ W120°05.31′
▼ 4.8	SO	Track on left.
3.0 ▲	SO	Track on right.
▼ 5.0	SO	Small track on left goes to the same hot springs by way of BLM land. Track on right.
2.8 ▲	SO	Small track on right goes to the same hot springs by way of BLM land. Track on left.
▼ 5.8	SO	Track on right.
2.0 ▲	SO	Track on left.
▼ 6.1	SO	Track on right.
1.7 ▲	SO	Track on left.
▼ 7.1	SO	Track on right.
0.7 ▲	SO	Track on left.
▼ 7.3	SO	Track on right.
0.5 ▲	SO	Track on left.
▼ 7.5	SO	Track on left; then cross through Sand Creek.
0.3 ▲	SO	Cross through Sand Creek; then track on right.
		GPS: N41°34.74′ W120°02.59′
▼ 7.8	BR	Unmarked well-used track on left is the spur to Sand Creek. Bear right, remaining on graded road. Zero trip meter.
0.0 ▲		Continue to the southwest.
		GPS: N41°34.82′ W120°02.17′

Spur to Sand Creek

▼ 0.0		Proceed to the northeast.
▼ 0.2	SO	Track on left.
▼ 0.3	SO	Track on right opposite butte.

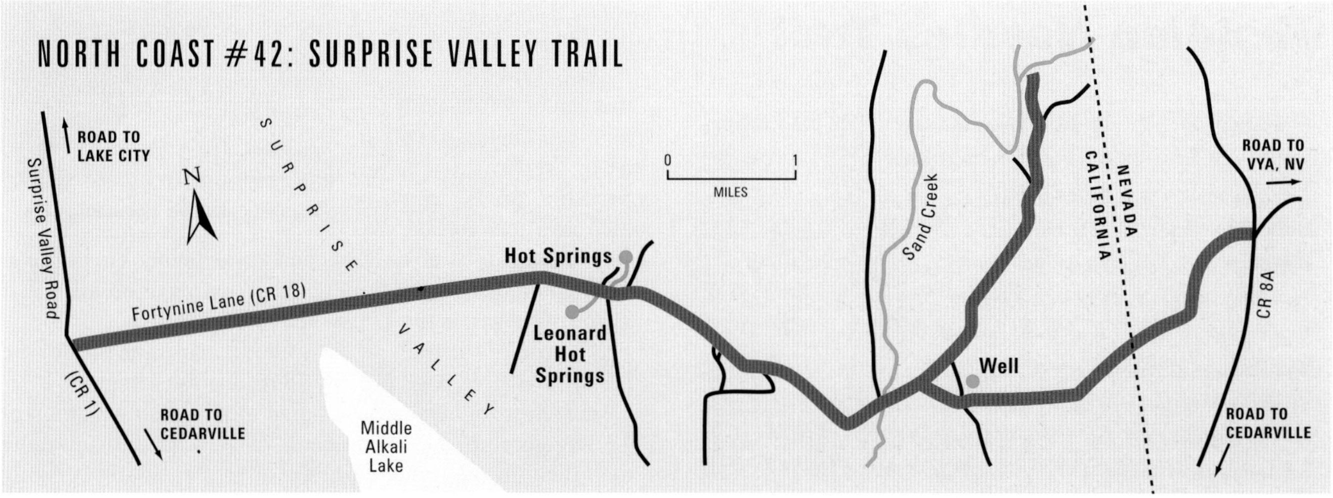

▼ 0.5 SO Track on left.
▼ 1.2 SO Track on left.
▼ 2.0 BR Track on left.

GPS: N41°36.16' W120°00.68'

▼ 2.6 BL Track on right goes 0.6 miles to the Nevada state line.

GPS: N41°36.61' W120°00.54'

▼ 3.0 SO Track on left.
▼ 3.1 Trail ends at a turnaround beside a tributary of Sand Creek.

GPS: N41°37.06' W120°00.53'

Continuation of Main Trail

▼ 0.0 Continue to the southeast.
3.7 ▲ BL Unmarked, well-used track on right is the spur to Sand Creek. Bear left, remaining on graded road. Zero trip meter.

GPS: N41°34.82' W120°02.17'

▼ 0.4 TL Track on left; then well on left; then immediately turn left.
3.3 ▲ TR Well on right; then T-intersection with graded road.

GPS: N41°34.62' W120°01.77'

▼ 0.8 SO Applegate Trail marker on right.
2.9 ▲ SO Applegate Trail marker on left.

▼ 2.1 SO Posts and cairn on either side of the trail mark Nevada state line.
1.6 ▲ SO Post and cairn on either side of the trail marks California state line.

GPS: N41°34.89' W120°00.00'

▼ 3.4 SO Applegate Trail marker on left.
0.3 ▲ SO Applegate Trail marker on right.

▼ 3.7 Trail finishes at T-intersection with CR 8A. Fortynine Mountain is southeast of the trail. Turn right for Cedarville.
0.0 ▲ Trail commences on CR 8A, 2.7 miles east of California-Nevada state line. Zero trip meter and turn west on formed dirt trail. There is an Applegate Trail maker at the intersection, but otherwise the intersection is unmarked. A second track leads north from the same point.

GPS: N41°35.55' W119°58.42'

NORTH COAST #43

Obsidian Needles Trail

Starting Point:	**Surprise Valley Road (CR 1) in Lake City**
Finishing Point:	**US 395 at Davis Creek**
Total Mileage:	**22.9 miles**
Unpaved Mileage:	**21.7 miles**
Driving Time:	**3.5 hours**
Elevation Range:	**4,500–7,700 feet**
Usually Open:	**June to December**
Best Time to Travel:	**Dry weather**
Difficulty Rating:	**3**
Scenic Rating:	**9**
Remoteness Rating:	**+0**

Lake City Flour Mill, built in 1870

Special Attractions

- Rockhounding for obsidian.
- Historic Lake City Flour Mill at the start of trail.
- Long, pretty trail through the Warner Mountains.

History

Obsidian Needles Trail begins in the Surprise Valley town of Lake City, founded in 1857. The town, just east of the Warner Mountains, is near several playa, or dry, lakes in this basin. Water was essential for at least two of the town's businesses: a sawmill built in 1866, and the Lake City Flour Mill, built in 1867. The flour mill consists of hand-hewn timbers with wooden wedged joinery. The mill's owner, John Bucher, produced a variety of desirable flours: wheatgerm, stoneground and graham flour, cornmeal, and unbleached flour. Lake City Flour Mill closed in 1935, swung back into action the following year, and continued to supply surrounding communities until the 1960s. Sadly the innards of the mill have been removed.

Pink Lady obsidian collecting area

The Obsidian Needles that can be found along this trail were highly sought after by the Northern Paiute. Such fine needles could be used as a tool to penetrate animal skin or as arrowheads and spear points for hunting. They could be chipped from the larger pieces of obsidian that are plentiful across this part of the range.

The end of the trail, in Davis Creek, marks the start of the Lassen Trail (see page 66). In 1848, Danish emigrant Peter Lassen left from here to blaze a trail south, leading a group of 12 wagons into the Sacramento Valley. The difficult route took them through the future site of Alturas, southeast along the Pit River, and eventually to the Sacramento Valley. Lassen's route veers off the Applegate Trail at this point, which crossed the lower reaches of Goose Lake and went through Devils Garden toward Tule Lake.

Description

This trail travels from Lake City, on the east side of the Warner Mountains, over to Davis Creek on the west side of the range. It leaves Lake City up South Water Street, passing the old Lake City Flour Mill. The privately owned building is currently in a state of disrepair.

The route travels up Lake City Canyon—a tight, rocky passage along Mill Creek. It is a single-vehicle width shelf road for much of the way, but with plenty of passing places. There are a few scattered campsites sheltered below pine trees beside the creek. The route climbs out of the canyon and across open slopes at the top. There are excellent views east over Surprise Valley toward Nevada. The trail improves slightly when it joins wide, graded FR 30, part of the network of California Back Country Discovery Trails. These trails are marked by distinctive route markers. Obsidian Needles Trail intersects the Discovery trail several times.

Obsidian Needles collected along the trail

A narrow trail leaves FR 30 to travel a smaller, rougher loop that diverges near the edge of the range. There are views here back down to the Surprise Valley. Those not wanting to travel this section can remain on FR 30; the two routes rejoin after a couple of miles.

One of the major features of this part of Modoc National Forest are the rockhounding sites where it is possible to view and collect different types of obsidian. Non-commercial users must obtain a free permit from the forest service to rockhound here. The first of these sites, Pink Lady, is 0.1 miles from the main trail. The collecting area is littered with obsidian. Simply step out of your vehicle and start collecting. The site has a lot of black obsidian and some smoky gray obsidian, lightly tinged with pink. Obsidian of all types is scattered along much of this trail. Note that collecting outside designated areas is not permitted.

The second obsidian collecting area, Obsidian Needles, offers easy rockhounding for the super-fine obsidian needles that give the trail its name. Specimens here are black, clear, and mahogany, found in large pieces as well as the distinctive fine rock needles. This site is right beside the main trail, and once again, specimens are very easy to find. A few minutes of hunting will yield many fine pieces. Remember, recreational collectors must not enter zones reserved for commercial use.

Past Obsidian Needles, the trail winds down the western side of the Warner Mountains on easier graded forest roads. It finishes on US 395 in Davis Creek, where the Applegate and Lassen Trails diverge.

Current Road Information

Modoc National Forest
Warner Mountain Ranger District
PO Box 220
Cedarville, CA 96104
(530) 279-6116

Map References

BLM Cedarville
USFS Modoc National Forest
USGS 1:24,000 Lake City, Sugar Hill, Davis Creek
1:100,000 Cedarville
Maptech CD-ROM: Shasta-Trinity/Modoc
Northern California Atlas & Gazetteer, p. 31
California Road & Recreation Atlas, p. 49
Other: Modoc Country USFS/BLM Map

Route Directions

▼ 0.0		From Surprise Valley Road (CR 1) at Lake City, zero trip meter and turn west on CR 17, following the sign for Benton Meadows and Plum Creek Campground.
0.4 ▲		Trail ends at intersection with Surprise Valley Road (CR 1) in Lake City. Turn left for Fort Bidwell; turn right for Cedarville.
		GPS: N41°38.72' W120°12.72'
▼ 0.2	TL	Turn left onto Main Street.
0.2 ▲	TR	Turn right onto CR 17.
▼ 0.4	TR	Turn right onto formed dirt South Water Street, following the sign for Benton Meadows. Zero trip meter.
0.0 ▲		Continue to the northwest.
		GPS: N41°38.49' W120°12.91'
▼ 0.0		Continue to the southwest.
5.8 ▲	TL	Turn left onto paved Main Street. Zero trip meter.
▼ 0.1	SO	Lake City Flour Mill on left; then cross through creek; then track on left.
5.7 ▲	SO	Track on right; then cross through creek; then Lake City Flour Mill on right.
▼ 0.2	SO	Cattle guard.
5.6 ▲	SO	Cattle guard.
▼ 0.3	SO	Cross over Mill Creek. Start of shelf road.
5.5 ▲	SO	End of shelf road. Cross over Mill Creek.
▼ 0.8	SO	Entering Modoc National Forest at sign.
5.0 ▲	SO	Leaving Modoc National Forest at sign.
		GPS: N41°38.53' W120°13.77'
▼ 0.9	SO	Cattle guard.
4.9 ▲	SO	Cattle guard.
▼ 3.5	SO	Cross over Mill Creek.
2.3 ▲	SO	Cross over Mill Creek.
		GPS: N41°39°19' W120°16.38'
▼ 4.9	SO	End of shelf road. Cross through creek.
0.9 ▲	SO	Cross through creek. Start of shelf road.
▼ 5.3	SO	Track on left.
0.5 ▲	SO	Track on right.
▼ 5.7	SO	Track on left; then cattle guard.
0.1 ▲	SO	Cattle guard; then track on right.
▼ 5.8	TR	4-way intersection. FR 30 goes left to Joseph Creek Basin. Straight ahead is 45N04 (CR 11) to Davis Creek. Zero trip meter and turn right onto FR 30, following the sign to Sugar Hill Lookout.
0.0 ▲		Continue to the southeast.
		GPS: N41°40.55' W120°17.23'

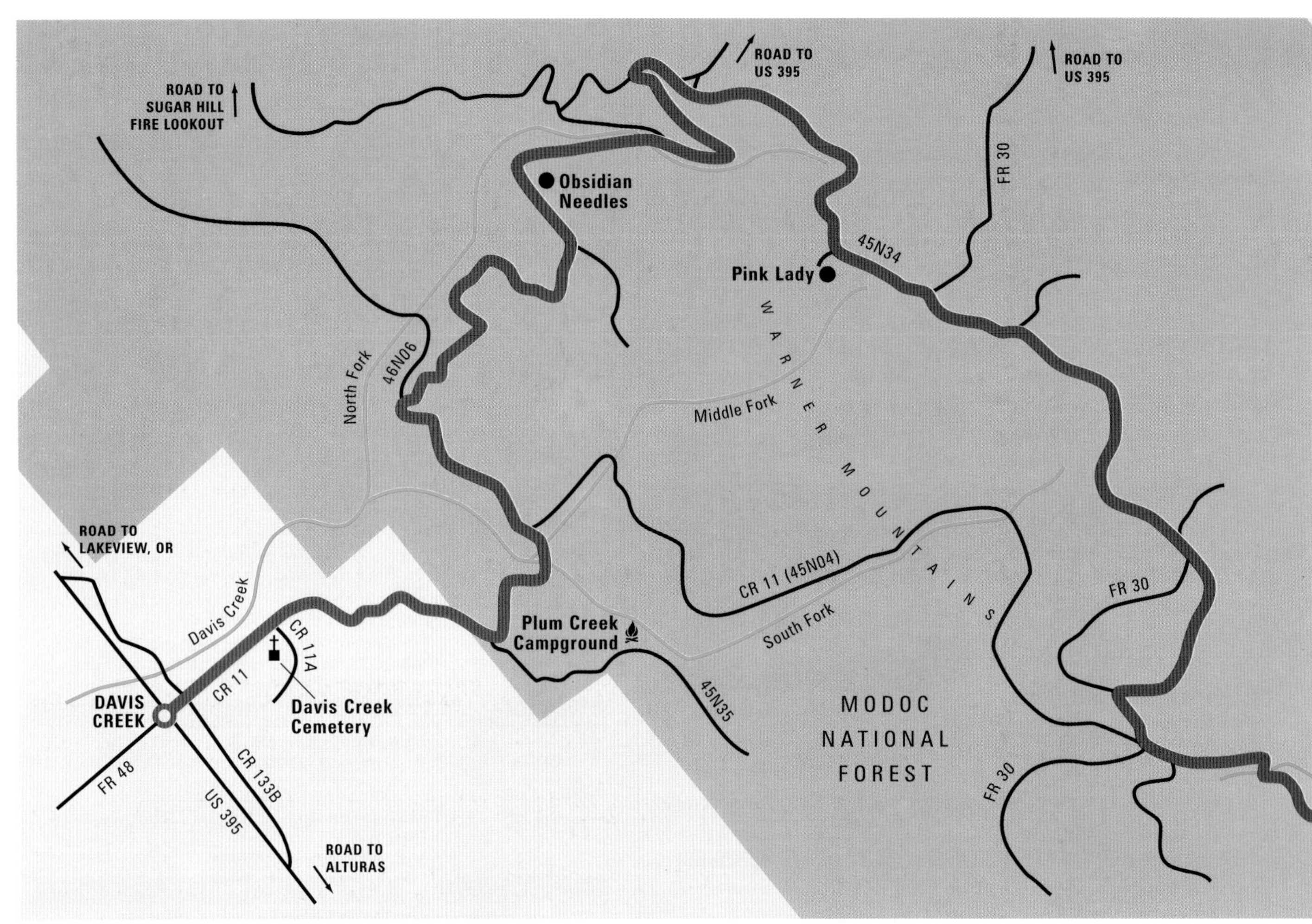

▼ 0.0		Continue to the northeast.
4.2 ▲	TL	4-way intersection. FR 30 continues straight ahead to Joseph Creek Basin. Road on right is 45N04 (CR 11) to Davis Creek. Zero trip meter and turn left onto on 45N34 (CR 11), following the sign to Lake City.
▼ 0.4	TR	Graded road continues straight ahead. Turn right onto small, unmarked trail.
3.8 ▲	TL	T-intersection with graded FR 30.
		GPS: N41°40.87′ W120°17.14′
▼ 1.0	SO	Track on right.
3.2 ▲	SO	Track on left.
▼ 1.4	SO	Track on right.
2.8 ▲	SO	Track on left.
▼ 1.5	SO	Track on right.
2.7 ▲	SO	Track on left.
▼ 1.7	TR	T-intersection with FR 30. Turn right and rejoin this road; then track on right.
2.5 ▲	TL	Track on left; then graded road continues straight ahead. Turn left onto small unmarked trail.
		GPS: N41°41.22′ W120°16.15′
▼ 2.8	SO	Track on right; then track on left.
1.4 ▲	SO	Track on right; then track on left.
▼ 3.5	SO	Track on left.
0.7 ▲	SO	Track on right.
▼ 3.6	SO	Track on right.
0.6 ▲	SO	Track on left.
▼ 4.2	TL	Graded road continues straight ahead to Harris Flat and US 395. Zero trip meter and turn left onto 45N34, following the sign to Sugar Hill Lookout.
0.0 ▲		Continue to the southwest.
		GPS: N41°43.12′ W120°16.39′
▼ 0.0		Continue to the northwest.
0.6 ▲	TR	T-intersection with graded dirt FR 30. To the left goes to Harris Flat and US 395. Zero trip meter and follow the sign to Lake City.
▼ 0.1	SO	Track on right.
0.5 ▲	SO	Track on left.
▼ 0.6	SO	Unmarked track on left goes 0.1 miles to the Pink Lady obsidian collecting site. Zero trip meter.
0.0 ▲		Continue to the southeast.
		GPS: N41°43.58′ W120°16.76′
▼ 0.0		Continue to the northeast.
3.7 ▲	SO	Unmarked track on right goes 0.1 miles to the Pink Lady obsidian collecting site. Zero trip meter.
▼ 0.9	SO	Track on right.
2.8 ▲	BR	Track on left.
		GPS: N41°43.99′ W120°16.27′
▼ 1.2	SO	Track on right.
2.5 ▲	SO	Track on left.
▼ 1.9	SO	Track on right.
1.8 ▲	SO	Track on left.
▼ 2.0	SO	Track on right.
1.7 ▲	SO	Track on left.
▼ 2.4	SO	Track on right.

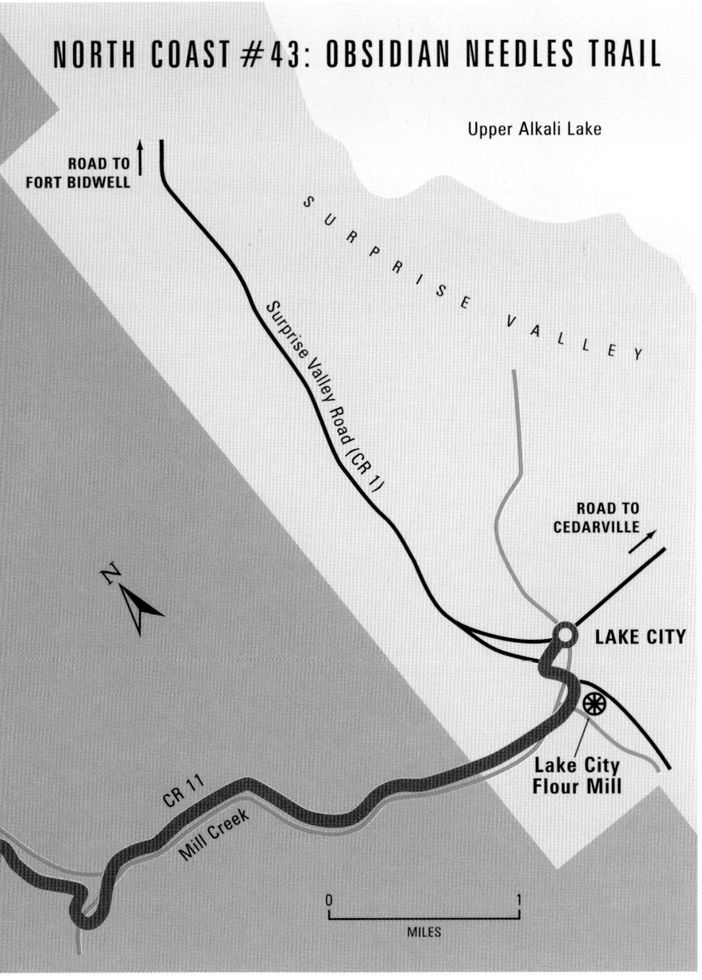

	1.3 ▲	SO	Track on left.
▼ 3.7		TL	Track straight ahead goes to the Sugar Hill Fire Lookout. Zero trip meter.
	0.0 ▲		Continue to the southeast.
			GPS: N41°44.71′ W120°17.23′
▼ 0.0			Cross over North Fork Davis Creek; then track on left is dead end. Continue to the northwest.
	3.6 ▲	TR	Track straight ahead is a dead end; then cross over North Fork Davis Creek; then T-intersection. To the left goes to the Sugar Hill Fire Lookout. Zero trip meter and turn right, following sign to Buck Mountain.
▼ 0.9		SO	Obsidian Needles collecting area on left, marked by a sign.
	2.7 ▲	SO	Obsidian Needles collecting area on right, marked by a sign.
			GPS: N41°44.86′ W120°18.16′
▼ 1.5		BR	Track on left.
	2.1 ▲	BL	Track on right.
▼ 3.6		TL	T-intersection with 46N06. Zero trip meter.
	0.0 ▲		Continue to the east.
			GPS: N41°44.46′ W120°19.81′
▼ 0.0			Continue to the south.
	4.6 ▲	TR	Graded road continues ahead. Zero trip meter and turn right onto 45N34 for 4WDs, ATVs, and motorbikes.
▼ 1.2		SO	Graded road on left is 45N04 (CR 11) to Davis Creek obsidian collecting area and Lake City.
	3.4 ▲	SO	Graded road on right is 45N04 (CR 11) to Davis Creek obsidian collecting area and Lake City. Join 45N04, following sign to Buck Mountain.
			GPS: N41°43.51′ W120°19.67′
▼ 1.4		SO	Cross over Middle Fork Davis Creek.
	3.2 ▲	SO	Cross over Middle Fork Davis Creek.
▼ 1.6		SO	Cross over South Fork Davis Creek.
	3.0 ▲	SO	Cross over South Fork Davis Creek.
▼ 2.4		SO	Graded road on left is 45N35, which goes 1 mile to Plum Creek USFS Campground. Follow sign to Davis Creek.
	2.2 ▲	BL	Graded road on right is 45N35, which goes 1 mile to Plum Creek USFS Campground. Follow sign to Buck Mountain.
▼ 2.5		SO	Cattle guard. Leaving Modoc National Forest.
	2.1 ▲	SO	Cattle guard. Entering Modoc National Forest.
▼ 2.8		SO	Cattle guard.
	1.8 ▲	SO	Cattle guard.
▼ 3.0		SO	Track on right.
	1.6 ▲	SO	Track on left.
▼ 3.5		SO	Track on right.
	1.1 ▲	SO	Track on left.
▼ 3.8		SO	Paved CR 11A on left. Join this road. Davis Creek Cemetery is 0.1 miles to the left.
	0.8 ▲	BL	Paved CR 11A continues straight ahead and goes 0.1 miles to Davis Creek Cemetery. Bear left onto FR 11, following sign to Plum Creek Campground.
			GPS: N41°44.00′ W120°21.53′
▼ 3.9		SO	Davis Creek Cemetery on left; then cattle guard.
	0.7 ▲	SO	Cattle guard; then Davis Creek Cemetery on right.
▼ 4.5		SO	Cross over CR 133B.
	0.1 ▲	SO	Cross over CR 133B.
▼ 4.6			Trail ends on US 395 at Davis Creek, opposite FR 48. Turn right for Lakeview, OR; turn left for Alturas.
	0.0 ▲		Trail commences on US 395 at Davis Creek, opposite FR 48. Zero trip meter and turn east on CR 11, following sign to Plum Creek Campground and the Needle Mines.
			GPS: N41°44.01′ W120°22.45′

NORTH COAST #44

Fandango Pass Trail

Starting Point:	**Surprise Valley Road (CR 1), 10.5 miles north of Lake City**
Finishing Point:	**US 395, 7.5 miles south of New Pine Creek**
Total Mileage:	**14.7 miles, plus 2.3-mile spur to Rainbow Mine**
Unpaved Mileage:	**14 miles, plus 2.3-mile spur**
Driving Time:	**1.5 hours**
Elevation Range:	**4,600–6,200 feet**
Usually Open:	**May to November**
Best Time to Travel:	**Dry weather**
Difficulty Rating:	**1**
Scenic Rating:	**9**
Remoteness Rating:	**+0**

Special Attractions

- Fandango Pass—an important point on the historic Applegate Trail.
- Rockhounding for obsidian at the Rainbow Mine.
- Good trail to see fall colors.

History

Fandango Pass (6,332 feet) is a memorable spot, not only for its beauty and significance as an historic pass, but also for the settlers and miners who lost their lives while traveling this passage through the Warner Mountains.

The Applegate Trail (see page 65), an emigrant trail blazed through this pass in 1846, was an alternative to a difficult section of the Oregon Trail, west of Fort Hall in present-day Idaho. Lindsay Applegate found the route.

Stories behind Fandango Pass's name vary. One explanation is that emigrants believed the pass was their last major climb—that they had crossed to the Pacific slope and were now on their final downhill run. The celebrations as they crested the pass often included dancing the fandango. Another explanation is that forty-niners spent a cold night on the pass and danced around to keep warm. Either way, cresting this ridge, which rises 1,800 feet above Surprise Valley, was a major achievement for emigrants and the oxen pulling their heavy wagons.

Description

Fandango Pass Trail winds up the grade from CR 1 in Surprise Valley to Fandango Pass in approximately 20 minutes. There are great views east as you climb over Upper Alkali Lake, Surprise Valley, and into Nevada.

The top of the pass has an historical marker that describes where the Lassen and Applegate Trails diverged, which is at Davis Creek (at the end of North Coast #43: Obsidian Needles Trail). Those with high-clearance 4WDs might like to take a short, narrow formed side trail that runs 0.6 miles to a

Fandango Pass

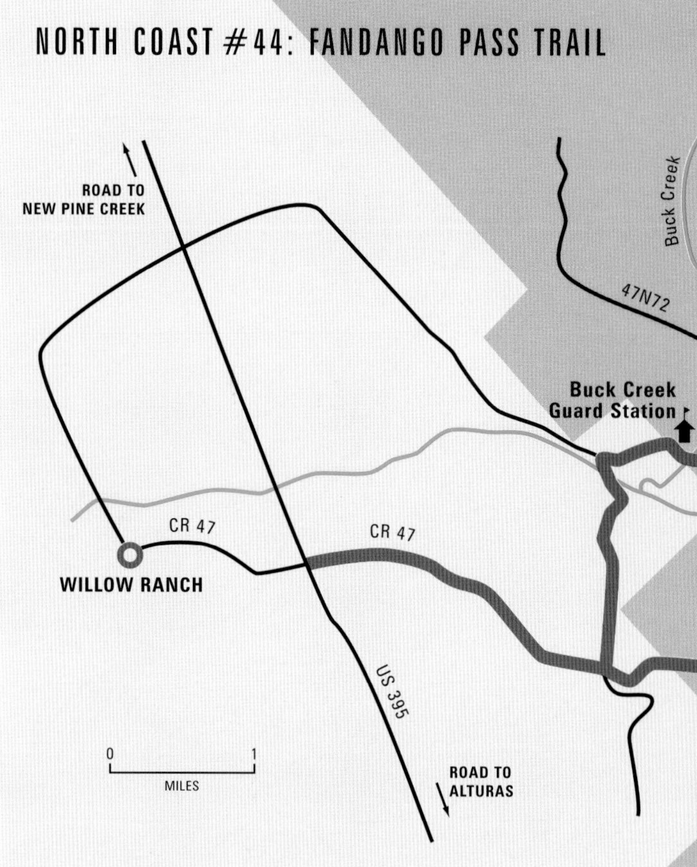

viewpoint over Surprise Valley, Fandango Valley, and Goose Lake. The spur travels a side slope that reaches a tilt of 25 degrees in places and there is limited room for turning. This spur is rated 5 for difficulty.

The main trail descends to Fandango Valley, now private property, and a possible site of the Fandango Massacre; there is no marker. Remain on the county road and please respect property owners' rights. A short distance past the Buck Creek Guard Station, the trail turns southwest. A spur leads to the Rainbow Mine—an obsidian collecting area open to the public. Collectors must have a permit in hand (free) issued at any Modoc National Forest office. The site mainly has black obsidian, which is easy to find. Lassen Creek USFS Campground is a short distance past the collecting site, and has mainly undeveloped sites in a pretty spot beside Lassen Creek. Lassen Creek is habitat for the rare redband trout, which also live in Goose Lake. Catch and release rules apply.

The entire trail follows graded dirt county roads and in dry weather, it is suitable for passenger vehicles. Much of the trail passes through private property, so campers will find Lassen Creek USFS Campground the best option.

Current Road Information

Modoc National Forest
Warner Mountain Ranger District
PO Box 220
Cedarville, CA 96104
(530) 279-6116

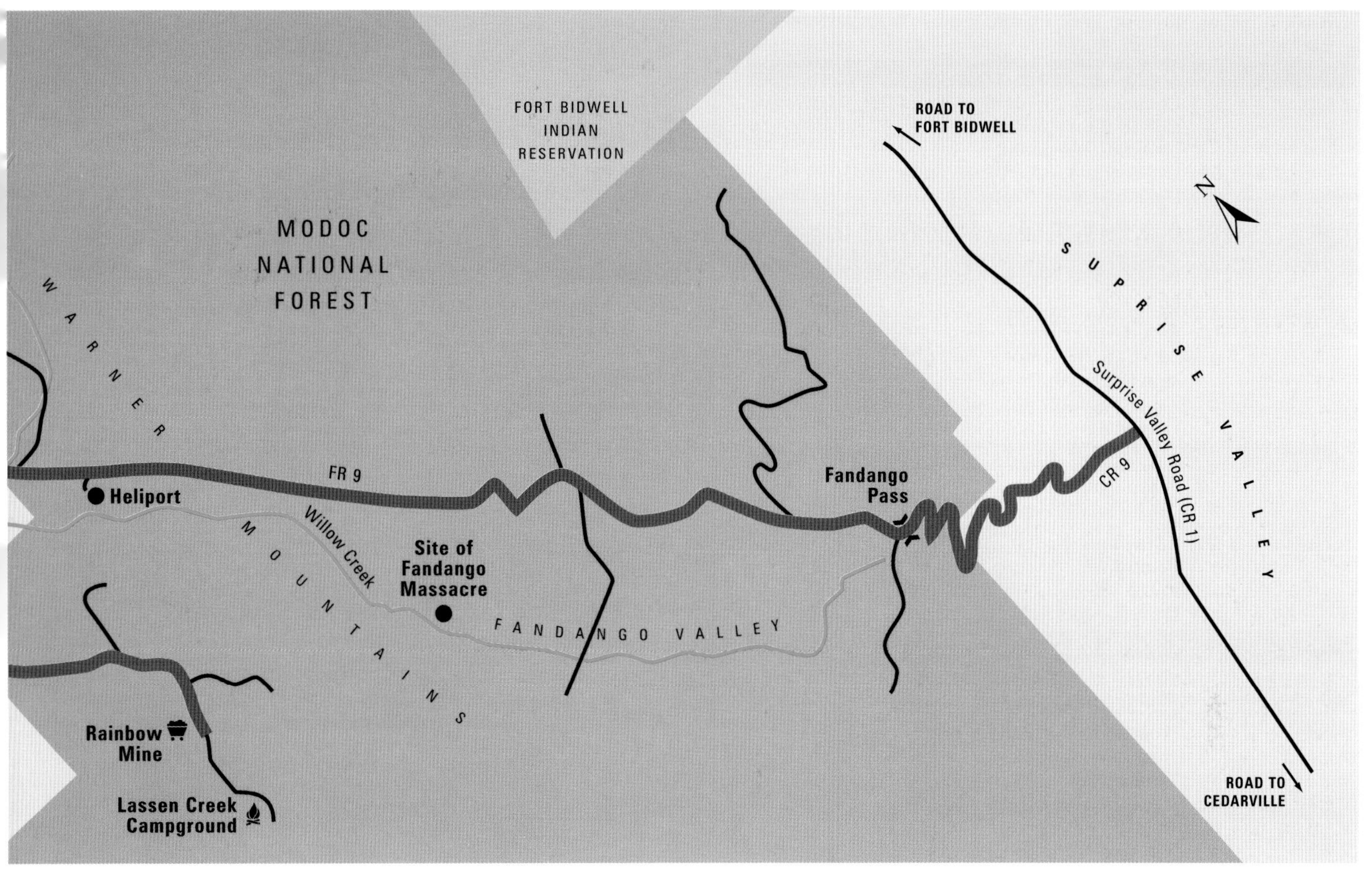

Map References

BLM Cedarville
USFS Modoc National Forest
USGS 1:24,000 Fort Bidwell, Sugar Hill, Willow Ranch
1:100,000 Cedarville
Maptech CD-ROM: Shasta-Trinity/Modoc
Northern California Atlas & Gazetteer, p. 31
California Road & Recreation Atlas, p. 49
Other: Modoc Country USFS/BLM Map

Route Directions

0.0		From Surprise Valley Road (CR 1), 10.5 miles north of Lake City, zero trip meter and turn northwest on graded dirt CR 9 at the sign for FR 9, forest access.
3.6 ▲		Trail ends at T-intersection with paved CR 1. Turn left for Fort Bidwell; turn right for Cedarville.
		GPS: N41°47.49′ W120°10.36′
▼ 0.2	SO	Cattle guard.
3.4 ▲	SO	Cattle guard.
▼ 2.2	SO	Look to the right to see a section of the hand-built military road.
1.4 ▲	SO	Look to the left to see a section of the hand-built military road.
▼ 2.3	SO	Entering Modoc National Forest at sign.
1.3 ▲	SO	Leaving Modoc National Forest at sign.
		GPS: N41°47.78′ W120°12.00′
▼ 2.9	SO	Track on right.
0.7 ▲	SO	Track on left.
▼ 3.6	SO	Fandango Pass. Historical marker at the pass. Zero trip meter.
0.0 ▲		Continue to the east.
		GPS: N41°48.11′ W120°12.27′
▼ 0.0		Continue to the west. Track on left—there is an Applegate Trail marker a short distance down this trail on the right—goes 0.6 miles to an excellent viewpoint over Surprise Valley and Goose Lake. This side trail is rated 5.
6.6 ▲	SO	Track on right—there is an Applegate Trail marker a short distance down this trail on the right—goes 0.6 miles to an excellent viewpoint over Surprise Valley and Goose Lake. This side trail is rated 5. Fandango Pass. Historical marker at the pass. Zero trip meter.
▼ 0.8	SO	Track on right goes to Shinn Spring.
5.8 ▲	SO	Track on left goes to Shinn Spring.
▼ 2.5	SO	Track on left along fence line. Entering Fandango Valley.
4.1 ▲	SO	Track on right along fence line. Leaving Fandango Valley.
▼ 2.7	SO	Track on right; then cattle guard.
3.9 ▲	SO	Cattle guard; then track on left.
▼ 4.8	SO	Track on left to corral.
1.8 ▲	SO	Track on right to corral.
▼ 6.1	SO	Track on left to heliport.
0.5 ▲	SO	Track on right to heliport.
		GPS: N41°51.87′ W120°17.02′
▼ 6.6	SO	Paved road on right is 47N72 to Del Pratt Spring. Zero trip meter.
0.0 ▲		Continue to the southeast on FR 9, following

the sign to Fandango Pass. Road is now graded dirt.

GPS: N41°52.19' W120°17.41'

▼ 0.0 — Continue to the northwest on FR 9, following sign to Buck Creek Guard Station. Road is now paved. Cattle guard.
2.3 ▲ SO Cattle guard. Paved road on left is 47N72 to Del Pratt Spring. Zero trip meter.

▼ 0.1 SO Buck Creek USFS Guard Station on right and left.
2.2 ▲ SO Buck Creek USFS Guard Station on right and left.

▼ 0.7 TL Paved road continues straight ahead to US 395. Turn left onto graded dirt road, following sign to Lassen Creek.
1.6 ▲ TR T-intersection with paved FR 9 (CR 133C). Follow sign to Fandango Pass.

GPS: N41°52.61' W120°18.04'

▼ 0.9 SO Cross over Willow Creek on bridge.
1.4 ▲ SO Cross over Willow Creek on bridge.

▼ 2.3 TR 4-way intersection. Track on left is the spur to Rainbow Mine. Zero trip meter and follow sign to US 395.
0.0 ▲ Continue to the northeast.

GPS: N41°51.65' W120°19.17'

Spur to Rainbow Mine

▼ 0.0 Proceed to the south.
▼ 0.7 SO Track on right.
▼ 1.3 SO Track on left.
▼ 1.7 SO Track on left.
▼ 2.0 SO Track on left.
▼ 2.3 Rainbow Mine—obsidian collecting site—on right, marked by a sign. Two tracks on left. Lassen Creek USFS Campground is 0.5 miles farther along this road.

GPS: N41°50.13' W120°17.75'

Continuation of Main Trail

▼ 0.0 Continue to the northwest and cross cattle guard.
2.2 ▲ TL Cattle guard; then 4-way intersection. Track straight ahead is the spur to the Rainbow Mine. Zero trip meter and turn left onto FR 30.

GPS: N41°51.65' W120°19.17'

▼ 0.8 SO Track on left.
1.4 ▲ SO Track on right.

▼ 1.3 SO Track on left; then cattle guard.
0.9 ▲ SO Cattle guard; then track on right.

▼ 1.9 SO Track on left.
0.3 ▲ SO Track on right.

▼ 2.0 SO Track on left to transfer station.
0.2 ▲ SO Track on right to transfer station.

▼ 2.2 Trail ends at US 395. Turn right for New Pine Creek and Oregon; turn left for Alturas. CR 47 continues straight ahead and travels 1.4 miles to the site of the lumber mills and the settlement of Willow Ranch.
0.0 ▲ From US 395 at Modoc County mile marker 54, 7.5 miles south of New Pine Creek, zero trip meter and turn east on graded dirt FR 30 (CR 47). To the west, CR 47 continues 1.4 miles to the site of lumber mills and the settlement of Willow Ranch.

GPS: N41°53.33' W120°20.39'

NORTH COAST #45

New Pine Creek to Fort Bidwell Trail

Starting Point:	**US 395 at New Pine Creek**
Finishing Point:	**Intersection of CR 1 and CR 6 at Fort Bidwell**
Total Mileage:	**16.5 miles**
Unpaved Mileage:	**15.4 miles**
Driving Time:	**1.5 hours**
Elevation Range:	**5,600–7,500 feet**
Usually Open:	**June to December**
Best Time to Travel:	**June to December**
Difficulty Rating:	**2**
Scenic Rating:	**8**
Remoteness Rating:	**+0**

Special Attractions

- Easy picturesque trail provides access to other 4WD trails in the Warner Mountains.
- Camping and picnicking at Lily Lake.
- Aspen viewing in the fall.

History

New Pine Creek enjoyed a boom period after the 1905 discovery of gold in the nearby Highgrade Mining District. New Pine Creek had a population of about 100 when the initial discovery was made, and by 1911, the population had shot up to nearly 1,000. The stagecoach service changed its route to facilitate the booming mountaintop mining community. The stages had previously crossed the Warner Mountains via the well-formed Fandango Pass route; now they traveled a longer and rougher route. The twisting grade to the settlement of Highgrade was an additional 1,300 feet higher than the more straightforward Fandango Pass. Our trail follows close to the original stagecoach trail.

Stages passed a mill just before the crest of the mountain. The mill was on the south side of the wagon road beside the old Bonanza Mine, only a few hundred yards before the turn for Dismal Swamp. The Big Four, Consolidated, and Custom Mines also operated large stamp mills in the area. The stages stopped off at the Highgrade hotel and continued down the east side of the range to Fort Bidwell.

The fort had been established back in 1866 to protect settlers in Surprise Valley and assure the safe passage of freight wagons to and from Idaho. John Bidwell (see page 82) of the Chico region had vested interests in wagon roads to Idaho and pushed for appropriate military protection in this region. Fort Bidwell, named for the then Congressman, reflected his success. Troops at the new fort were involved in major engagements throughout the late 1860s, lesser so in the 1870s except for the Modoc War of 1872–73. By the late 1870s, Fort Bid-

Small lake near the beginning of the trail

well consisted of an imposing number of buildings on a quadrangle. The officers' quarters were of splendid construction, with front verandas and excellent views of the valley. The impressive general store in the growing town, which still stands, was built in 1874. The fort was abandoned in 1893 and became a non-reservation boarding school for Native Americans until 1930.

The community at Fort Bidwell pursued agriculture and logging industries, and enjoyed the increased trade brought by the gold rush at Highgrade. The Fort Bidwell Hotel and restaurant were constructed during this period. Though mining continued into the 1930s, the boom times of New Pine Creek and Fort Bidwell dwindled after 1913. The stone schoolhouse at the eastern end of the trail was built in 1917.

Description

This trail travels a roughly graded county road from New Pine Creek, up and over the Warner Mountains, to Fort Bidwell in Surprise Valley. The road is rough enough that a high-clearance vehicle is preferable.

Two miles from the start of the trail, you will see a rock house on the left that was built in the early 1900s by a man wanting to please his wife. The house is built in the style of her home country of Ireland, and is listed in Modoc County's historical houses tour. It is privately owned; please respect the occupants' privacy and remain on the road.

Lily Lake, a small natural lake in a basin surrounded by aspens and conifers, is especially picturesque. There is a forest service picnic ground at the lake, which is particularly lovely in fall when the aspens are golden. The best time to see fall colors along this trail is mid-September to mid-October. The Cave Lake USFS Campground is a short way past the lake, and a hiking trail circles the lake and connects the picnic area and the campground.

Historic Fort Bidwell schoolhouse

Two more difficult 4WD trails intersect at the high point of this trail. To the north is North Coast #46: Dismal Swamp Trail; to the south is North Coast #47: Highgrade Trail. Both require high-clearance 4WDs. The old mining shanty town of Highgrade was on the northwest corner of this intersection. Little remains at the privately owned site.

The trail descends the eastern side of the Warner Mountains, passing the remains of the Klondike Mine, and crosses open country with sagebrush and stands of aspens. There are views west to Mount Vida and southeast to the Surprise Valley. The trail ends in the quiet hamlet of Fort Bidwell. Look for the stone schoolhouse on a rise at the end of the trail. Built of local stone by a mason from Scotland, it is one of the few stone buildings to remain, most have been razed. The schoolhouse is privately owned.

Current Road Information

Modoc National Forest
Warner Mountain Ranger District
PO Box 220
Cedarville, CA 96104
(530) 279-6116

Map References

BLM Cedarville
USFS Modoc National Forest
USGS 1:24,000 Willow Ranch, Mt. Bidwell, Fort Bidwell
1:100,000 Cedarville
Maptech CD-ROM: Shasta-Trinity/Modoc
Northern California Atlas & Gazetteer, p. 31
California Road & Recreation Atlas, p. 49
Other: Modoc Country USFS/BLM Map

Route Directions

▼ 0.0		From US 395 at New Pine Creek, 0.5 miles south of the Oregon state line, zero trip meter and turn east on paved FR 2, following the sign for Lily Lake and Cave Lake Campground. Remain on paved road for 0.6 miles.
4.8 ▲		Trail ends at intersection with US 395 at New Pine Creek, opposite CR 44. Turn right for Oregon; turn left for Alturas.
		GPS: N41°59.16' W120°17.82'
▼ 0.6	SO	Track on left. Road turns to graded dirt.
4.2 ▲	SO	Track on right. Road is now paved.
▼ 0.9	SO	Cross over Pine Creek.
3.9 ▲	SO	Cross over Pine Creek.
▼ 1.5	SO	Track on right; then cross over Pine Creek.
3.3 ▲	SO	Cross over Pine Creek; then track on left.
▼ 1.7	SO	Stone house on left is private property.
3.1 ▲	SO	Stone house on right is private property.
▼ 2.6	SO	Track on right.
2.2 ▲	SO	Track on left.
▼ 2.7	SO	Track on right.
2.1 ▲	SO	Track on left.
▼ 2.8	SO	Track on left.

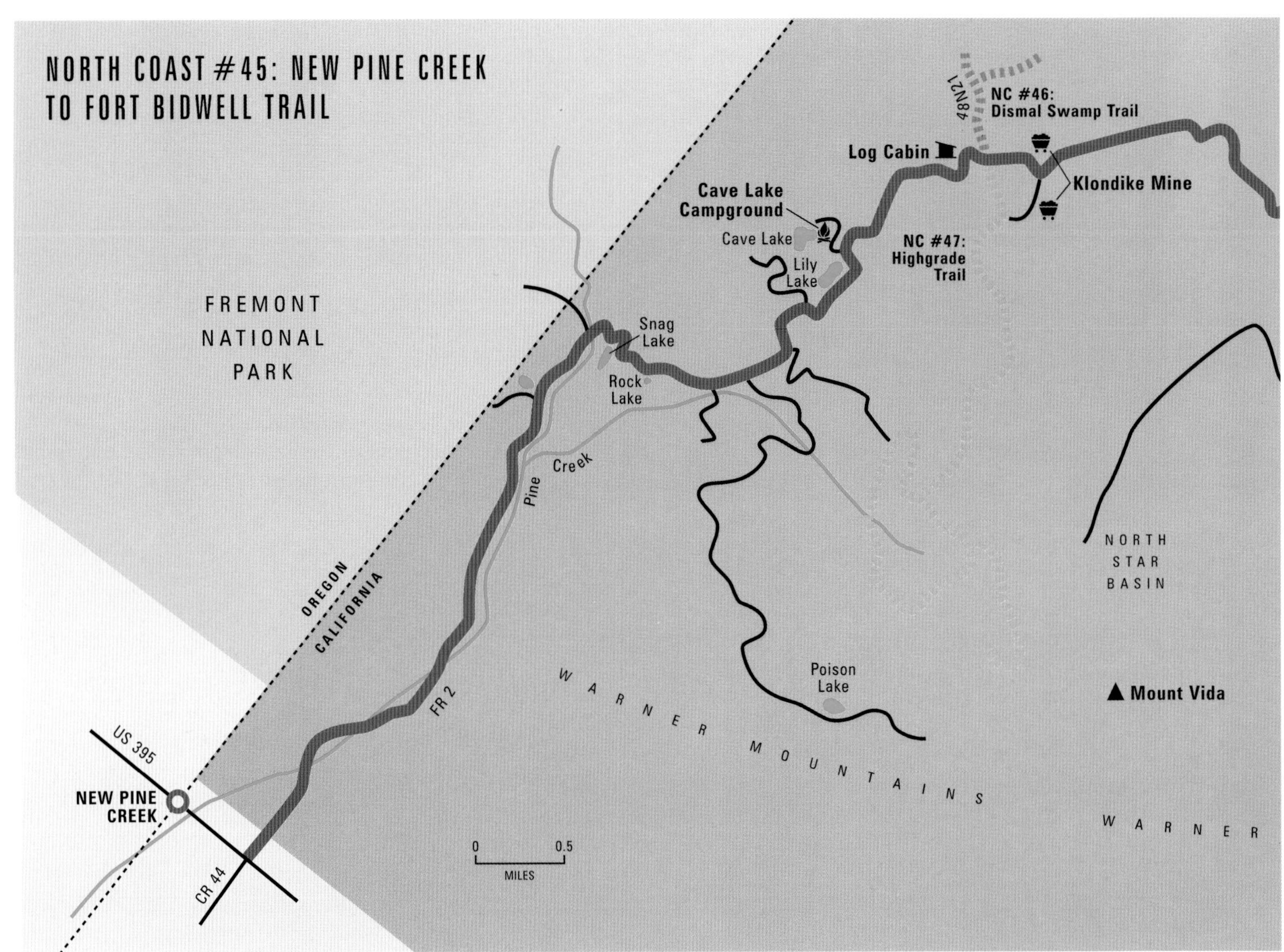

	2.0 ▲	SO	Track on right.
▼ 3.1		SO	Track on left; then small lake on left.
	1.7 ▲	SO	Small lake on right; then track on right.
			GPS: N41°59.39' W120°14.34'
▼ 3.7		SO	Track on left; then cross over creek.
	1.1 ▲	SO	Cross over creek; then track on right.
▼ 3.8		SO	Cross over creek.
	1.0 ▲	SO	Cross over creek.
▼ 3.9		SO	Track on right; then Snag Lake on right (privately owned).
	0.9 ▲	SO	Snag Lake on left (privately owned); then track on left.
▼ 4.4		SO	Track on right; then Rock Lake on right (privately owned); then track on right.
	0.4 ▲	SO	Track on left; then Rock Lake on left (privately owned); then track on left.
▼ 4.6		SO	Track on right is a dead end.
	0.2 ▲	SO	Track on left is a dead end.
			GPS: N41°58.82' W120°13.61'
▼ 4.8		SO	Graded road on right goes to Poison Lake. Follow sign to Cave Lake Campground. Zero trip meter.
	0.0 ▲		Continue to the northwest.
			GPS: N41°58.70' W120°13.46'
▼ 0.0			Continue to the southeast.
	1.2 ▲	SO	Graded road on left goes to Poison Lake. Zero trip meter.

▼ 0.1		SO	Track on left.
	1.1 ▲	SO	Track on right.
▼ 0.2		SO	Track on left.
	1.0 ▲	SO	Track on right.
▼ 0.4		SO	Graded road on right.
	0.8 ▲	SO	Graded road on left.
			GPS: N41°58.57' W120°13.10'
▼ 0.7		BR	Graded road on left.
	0.5 ▲	BL	Graded road on right.
			GPS: N41°58.62' W120°12.80'
▼ 0.9		SO	Graded road on left goes a short distance to Lily Lake Picnic Area.
	0.3 ▲	SO	Graded road on right goes a short distance to Lily Lake Picnic Area.
			GPS: N41°58.55' W120°12.63'
▼ 1.2		BR	Graded road on left goes into Cave Lake USFS Campground and continues 0.3 miles to the lake. Zero trip meter.
	0.0 ▲		Continue to the south.
			GPS: N41°58.64' W120°12.40'
▼ 0.0			Continue to the northeast.
	1.2 ▲	BL	Graded road on right goes into Cave Lake USFS Campground and continues 0.3 miles to the lake. Zero trip meter.
▼ 0.7		SO	Two tracks on right.
	0.5 ▲	SO	Two tracks on left.

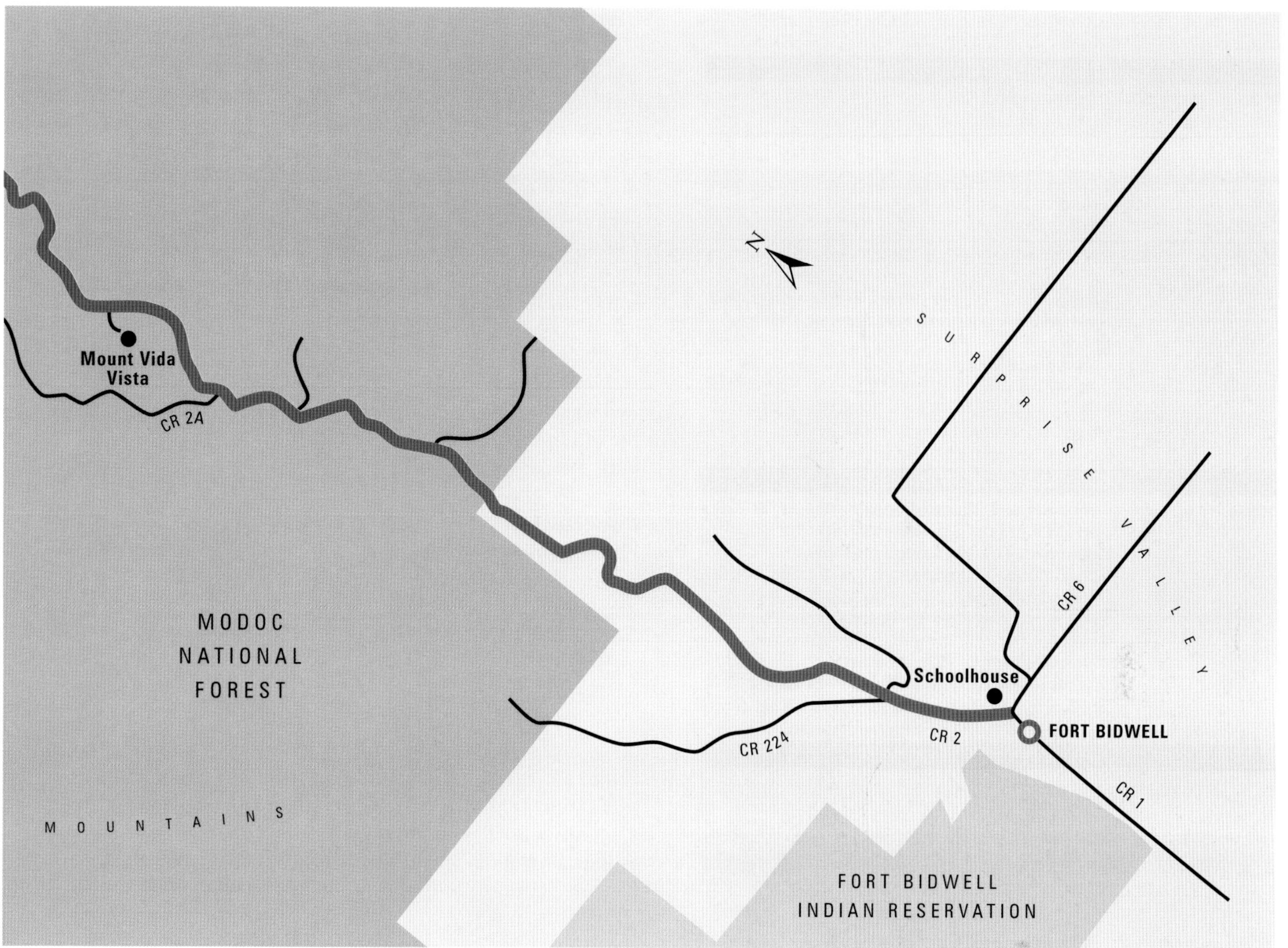

▼ 1.0	SO	Small track on left; then remains of a log cabin on left; then two tracks on right.
0.2 ▲	SO	Two tracks on left; then remains of a log cabin on right; then small track on right.
		GPS: N41°58.41' W120°11.50'
▼ 1.2	SO	4-way intersection on saddle. To the right is North Coast #47: Highgrade Trail. To the left is North Coast #46: Dismal Swamp Trail (48N21). Zero trip meter and follow the sign to Fort Bidwell.
0.0 ▲		Continue to the northwest.
		GPS: N41°58.38' W120°11.37'
▼ 0.0		Continue to the southeast.
4.0 ▲	SO	4-way intersection on saddle. To the left is North Coast #47: Highgrade Trail. To the right is North Coast #46: Dismal Swamp Trail (48N21). Zero trip meter and follow the sign to Lily Lake and US 395.
▼ 0.2	SO	Track on right.
3.8 ▲	SO	Track on left.
▼ 0.4	SO	Klondike Mine on left, track on right, and log cabin on right.
3.6 ▲	SO	Log cabin on left, track on left, and Klondike Mine on right.
		GPS: N41°58.10' W120°11.23'
▼ 0.9	SO	Track on left.
3.1 ▲	SO	Track on right.
▼ 1.6	SO	Track on left.
2.4 ▲	SO	Track on right.
▼ 3.1	SO	Track on right goes 0.1 miles to Mount Vida Vista.
0.9 ▲	SO	Track on left goes 0.1 miles to Mount Vida Vista.
		GPS: N41°56.44' W120°10.65'
▼ 3.6	SO	Track on left.
0.4 ▲	SO	Track on right.
▼ 3.8	SO	Cross over ditch; then track on right.
0.2 ▲	SO	Track on left; then cross over ditch.
▼ 4.0	SO	Graded road on right is CR 2A to North Star Basin. Zero trip meter.
0.0 ▲		Continue to the northwest.
		GPS: N41°55.80' W120°10.62'
▼ 0.0		Continue to the southeast.
5.3 ▲	SO	Graded road on left is CR 2A to North Star Basin. Zero trip meter and follow the sign to Cave and Lily Lakes.
▼ 0.1	SO	Cattle guard.
5.2 ▲	SO	Cattle guard.
▼ 0.5	SO	Track on left.
4.8 ▲	SO	Track on right.
▼ 1.3	SO	Track on left.
4.0 ▲	SO	Track on right.
▼ 1.9	SO	Cattle guard. Leaving Modoc National Forest.

	3.4 ▲	SO	Cattle guard. Entering Modoc National Forest.
			GPS: N41°54.44' W120°10.07'
▼ 2.3		SO	Track on right.
	3.0 ▲	SO	Track on left.
▼ 3.1		SO	Cattle guard.
	2.2 ▲	SO	Cattle guard.
▼ 4.7		SO	Graded road on left.
	0.6 ▲	SO	Graded road on right.
▼ 4.8		SO	Paved road on right is CR 224, which goes to Bidwell Canyon Trail and Mill Creek Access. Road is now paved. Remain on paved road, following sign to Fort Bidwell. Cattle guard.
	0.5 ▲	SO	Cattle guard; then paved road on left is CR 224, which goes to Bidwell Canyon Trail and Mill Creek Access. Road is now graded dirt. Continue straight ahead on CR 2 (FR 2), following sign to Cave and Lily Lakes.
			GPS: N41°52.22' W120°09.36'
▼ 5.3			Trail ends at T-intersection with paved CR 1 and CR 6 in Fort Bidwell. Turn right for Cedarville. The old stone Fort Bidwell Schoolhouse is up on the hill to the left at the intersection.
	0.0 ▲		Trail commences on the north side of Fort Bidwell where CR 1 meets CR 6. Zero trip meter and turn northwest on paved CR 2, following the sign for Mill Creek and US 395. The old stone Fort Bidwell Schoolhouse is up on the hill to the right at the intersection.
			GPS: N41°51.84' W120°09.05'

NORTH COAST #46

Dismal Swamp Trail

Starting Point:	**North Coast #45: New Pine Creek to Fort Bidwell Trail, 7.2 miles east of New Pine Creek**
Finishing Point:	**Moonlight Mine at the end of the loop, 0.4 miles east of North Coast #45: New Pine Creek to Fort Bidwell Trail**
Total Mileage:	**11.4 miles**
Unpaved Mileage:	**11.4 miles**
Driving Time:	**2.5 hours**
Elevation Range:	**7,000–8,200 feet**
Usually Open:	**June to December**
Best Time to Travel:	**Dry weather**
Difficulty Rating:	**6**
Scenic Rating:	**10**
Remoteness Rating:	**+1**

Special Attractions

- Open expanse of the very pretty Dismal Swamp.
- Aspen viewing in the fall.
- Views into three states from Bidwell Mountain.

History

"Dismal" is a misnomer for this picturesque high mountain region, but it probably describes the way settlers felt when their land was appropriated for an army post. Initially, the site for a post was selected just south of Lake City in 1865, but it was changed to the vicinity of what is now Fort Bidwell. Major Robert S. Williamson's choice meant that the government usurped the land held by three settlers. Though letters were written to appropriate authorities, their cries of injustice went unanswered. One settler, a Mr. Disabell, moved north to the wetlands that took on his name. Over the years, however, the name changed from Disabell to Dismal.

Dismal Swamp Trail leaves the old New Pine to Fort Bidwell wagon road at the crest of the Warner Mountains near the site of Highgrade, a mining camp that enjoyed a boom period until 1912.

Description

Don't be fooled by the name of this trail. Dismal Swamp is anything but dismal. The trail leaves North Coast #45: New Pine Creek to Fort Bidwell Trail opposite the start of North Coast #47: Highgrade Trail. The well-used road leads through the forest, passing the site of the still-active Moonlight Mine to enter the Dismal Swamp–Twelvemile Creek Area. This is a sensitive wildlife and vegetation area. Dismal Swamp is an open area, dissected by small creeks and surrounded by conifers and aspens. In fall, the area is a popular base camp for deer hunters. The trail wraps around the edge of the open area and crosses briefly into Fremont National Forest in Oregon. It follows unmarked small formed trails that traverse the open sagebrush areas to Bidwell Mountain. In fall the area is bright with golden aspens.

A short but worthwhile side trail leads 0.4 miles to the top of Bidwell Mountain. From the rocky open summit, there are excellent views toward Oregon and Nevada. To the southeast is small Lake Annie at the foot of Lake Annie Mountain, the seasonal Cow Head Lake, and north end of Surprise Valley. To the west are the Warner Mountains.

The main trail immediately passes small Snow Lake. When dry, large boulders of obsidian can be seen on the lakebed. The trail continues along the ridge top to Mount Bidwell (not to be confused with Bidwell Mountain), and travels across the open top. Mount Vida is to the south, Goose Lake to the west, and North Coast #45: New Pine Creek to Fort Bidwell Trail is below.

The trail becomes more difficult at the descent from Mount Bidwell. As far as the top of the mountain, it is rated a 4 for difficulty. As you descend, the rating increases to a 5. The final section of the trail descends a very steep pinch to exit back to the start of the trail. This final descent is rated 6. Continuing straight ahead past the top of the final descent may enable you to exit via an easier trail that travels through the workings of the Moonlight Mine. This is an active mine, and the owners may impose travel restrictions. Should this happen, please respect their rights and use only the more difficult route to exit.

This trail is lightly used, and you are unlikely to see other travelers except in hunting season. Mountain bikers know the trail as the North Star Basin Trail, rated for novices. Campers will find many suitable backcountry sites along this trail. Some of the best are on the edge of Dismal Swamp, but there are other more exposed sites on top of Mount Bidwell. The trail is best traveled in the direction described below.

Current Road Information

Modoc National Forest
Warner Mountain Ranger District
PO Box 220
Cedarville, CA 96104
(530) 279-6116

Map References

BLM Cedarville
USFS Modoc National Forest
USGS 1:24,000 Mt. Bidwell, Lake Annie
1:100,000 Cedarville
Maptech CD-ROM: Shasta-Trinity/Modoc
Northern California Atlas & Gazetteer, p. 31
California Road & Recreation Atlas, p. 49 (incomplete)
Other: Modoc Country USFS/BLM Map

Route Directions

▼ 0.0		From North Coast #45: New Pine Creek to Fort Bidwell Trail, 7.2 miles east of New Pine Creek, zero trip meter and turn northeast on formed dirt trail 48N21, following the sign to Dismal Swamp. North Coast #47: Highgrade Trail is opposite.
		GPS: N41°58.38' W120°11.37'
▼ 0.3	SO	Track on left; then Moonlight Mine on right. This is the alternate end of the loop.
		GPS: N41°58.56' W120°11.07'
▼ 0.4	SO	Track on right. This is the end of the loop. Continue straight ahead. Trail is best traveled in the direction described.
		GPS: N41°58.63' W120°11.00'
▼ 0.5	SO	Track on right.
▼ 0.7	SO	Track on right.
▼ 0.8	SO	Entering Dismal Swamp–Twelvemile Creek Area.
		GPS: N41°58.78' W120°10.72'
▼ 1.7	TR	Track on left; then cross over Dismal Creek. This is the old dam.
		GPS: N41°59.32' W120°10.34'
▼ 1.8	SO	Track on right.
▼ 2.1	SO	Cross through wash.
▼ 2.2	BL	Track on right.
		GPS: N41°59.40' W120°09.83'

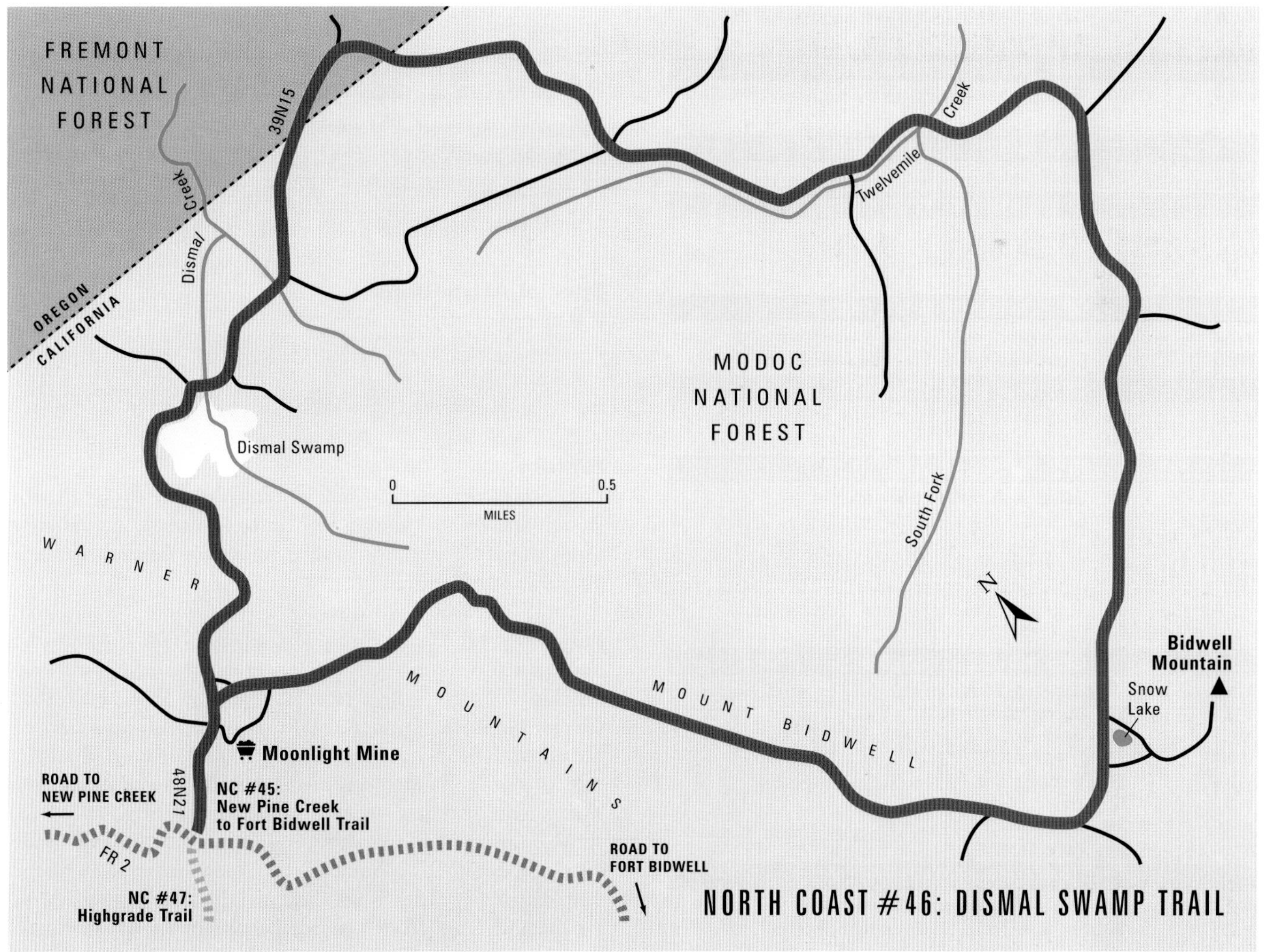

View of Oregon from Bidwell Mountain

▼ 2.6	SO	Cattle guard at Oregon state line. Cross into Oregon and enter Fremont National Forest. Road is now designated 39N15. Zero trip meter.
		GPS: N41°59.67′ W120°09.48′
▼ 0.0		Continue to the northeast.
▼ 0.4	TR	Turn right onto unmarked track and cross through wash.
		GPS: N41°59.80′ W120°09.17′
▼ 0.6	SO	Track on left; then pass through gate. Re-entering California and Modoc National Forest.
		GPS: N41°59.70′ W120°09.06′
▼ 1.0	TR	Track on left.
		GPS: N41°59.49′ W120°08.65′
▼ 1.2	SO	Tank on left.
▼ 1.5	SO	Unmarked 4-way intersection. Continue to the south.
		GPS: N41°59.12′ W120°08.63′
▼ 2.3	SO	Track on right.
▼ 2.6	SO	Cross through South Fork Twelvemile Creek.
		GPS: N41°58.64′ W120°07.65′
▼ 2.7	BL	Track on right.
▼ 3.2	SO	Track on left.
		GPS: N41°58.34′ W120°07.17′
▼ 3.9	SO	Cattle guard; then track on left.
▼ 4.2	SO	Cross through wash.
▼ 4.8	SO	Track on left.
▼ 5.2	TR	Short climb; then T-intersection. Track on left goes 0.4 miles past Snow Lake to Bidwell Mountain. Zero trip meter. Intersection is unmarked.
		GPS: N41°57.01′ W120°08.43′
▼ 0.0		Continue to the west.
▼ 0.1	SO	Snow Lake on left.
▼ 0.2	SO	Track on left.
▼ 0.4	SO	Track on left.
▼ 0.6	BR	Track on left.
▼ 1.2	BL	Track on right.
▼ 2.0	SO	Track on left.
▼ 2.4	SO	Wire gate.
		GPS: N41°58.31′ W120°09.98′
▼ 2.8	SO	Cross through creek.
▼ 2.9	SO	Trail becomes rockier and looser as it descends toward the Moonlight Mine.
		GPS: N41°58.45′ W120°10.43′
▼ 3.3	TR	Turn right onto lesser used trail and descend short steep slope. Track ahead and is an easier alternate exit through the Moonlight Mine.
		GPS: N41°58.54′ W120°10.81′
▼ 3.5		Track on right. Bear left; then end of loop. Turn left to exit back to North Coast #45: New Pine Creek to Fort Bidwell Trail
		GPS: N41°58.63′ W120°11.00′

NORTH COAST #47

Highgrade Trail

Starting Point:	**North Coast #45: New Pine Creek to Fort Bidwell Trail, 7.2 miles east of New Pine Creek**
Finishing Point:	**Mount Vida**
Total Mileage:	**5.3 miles (one-way), plus 1.4-mile spur to Mount Vida**
Unpaved Mileage:	**5.3 miles, plus 1.4-mile spur**
Driving Time:	**1 hour (one-way)**
Elevation Range:	**6,800–8,000 feet**
Usually Open:	**June to December**
Best Time to Travel:	**Dry weather**
Difficulty Rating:	**7**
Scenic Rating:	**9**
Remoteness Rating:	**+0**

Special Attractions

- Remains of Highgrade.
- Views from Mount Vida over Surprise Valley and Goose Lake.
- Challenging steep climb at the end of the trail.

History

Prior to its designation as a mining district, the Northern Paiute knew the Highgrade Mining District, immediately south of the Oregon border, as a source of obsidian for spear points and arrowheads.

In 1905, a shepherd discovered the rumored Hoags gold site, named for Daniel Hoag, a scout from Fort Bidwell who found the site in the 1860s but was killed before he could map his find. A rush to the area ensued and by 1910, New Pine Creek's population neared 1,000. Fort Bidwell also enjoyed the boom. The camp at Highgrade could not meet all of the miners' needs. Branley sprouted up south of the main east-west wagon road, just uphill from Mineral Spring.

More than 70 mines were in operation at the Highgrade district's peak in 1911. Some of the mines you'll pass along the trail, roughly in order as you head south along Alturas Ridge, are Evening Star, White Quartz, Mountain Sheep, Klondike,

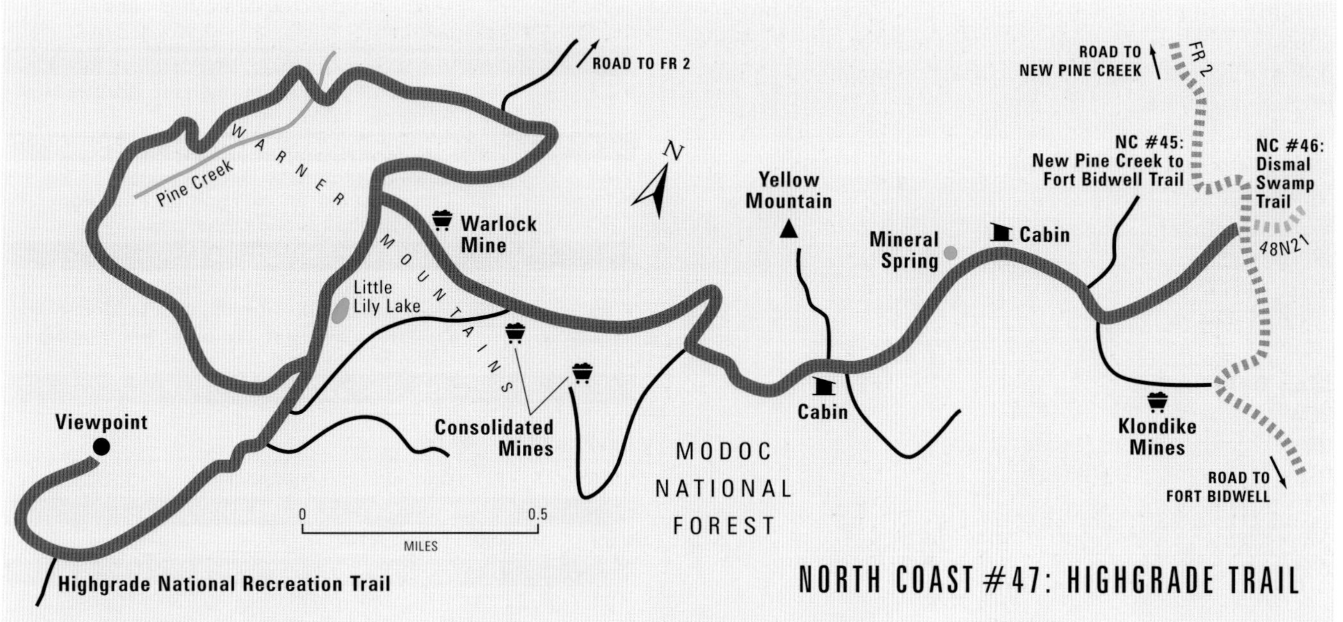

Alturas, Mineral Spring, and Alturas Fraction before you enter the old site of Branley. Beyond Yellow Mountain, mine claims start again: Crown Point, then another Klondike claim, Diamond Fraction, Old Glory, Valley View, Leland, and Uncle Joe, which is close to the spur toward Mount Vida, just below the rise called Discovery Hill.

After the ore played out in the late 1910s, the Highgrade district began to fade away, though mining activity continued into the 1930s, and still continues on a very small scale. The whole area still has the ghostly feel of a mountain community swept up by a gold rush and long abandoned.

Description

This short spur trail partly follows the Highgrade National Recreation Trail through the remains of Highgrade. A very difficult spur also runs 1.4 miles toward Mount Vida, where it turns into a hiking trail. Initially, the trail is lightly graded as it winds through the forest. Many tracks lead off through the forest, some to the remains of mine sites. There are shafts and some old log cabins scattered among the trees.

Remains of Warlock Mine stamp mill

After a short distance, Mineral Spring bubbles up alongside the trail. The trail then passes the remains of the Warlock Mine. Old cabins, two stamp mills, and several old vehicles remain at the site. A spur leads away from the trail and skirts the north side of North Star Basin toward Mount Vida. This spur is rated a 7 for difficulty and should not be underestimated. The rating comes from a 0.3-mile section with a side slope that tilts vehicles toward the drop. The track is also steep and loose, with some sharp, awkward turns. Once on the difficult section, there is nowhere safe to turn until the top of the ridge, visible at the end of the climb. You can see the difficult section ahead, twisting down into a gully and climbing steeply to the ridge. The final climb to the ridge is extremely steep, with a loose, low traction surface. Drivers should be very sure of their ability to make the climb before attempting the stretch. It is not an option to reverse and should be considered a highly dangerous manuever.

Highgrade trail signpost

The spur continues along the ridge to a high point with views over Goose Lake, north into Oregon, east into Nevada, and of Mount Vida and the bald top of Mount Bidwell.

Drivers who do not wish to tackle the 7-rated section should turn at the hiking trail mentioned in the route directions. A short hike west to the top of the ridge will yield the same views. The trail to this point is rated a 4 for difficulty, as is the main loop.

The main loop travels back on small forest roads crossing over Pine Creek and returning to the Warlock Mine. Mule deer are here, and the area is popular with hunters in season. Sections of the 4WD trail are also used by mountain bikers, who can continue along the national recreation trail to the south of Mount Vida. The mountain bike route is rated moderate.

Current Road Information

Modoc National Forest
Warner Mountain Ranger District
PO Box 220
Cedarville, CA 96104
(530) 279-6116

Map References

BLM Cedarville
USFS Modoc National Forest
USGS 1:24,000 Mt. Bidwell
1:100,000 Cedarville
Maptech CD-ROM: Shasta-Trinity/Modoc
Northern California Atlas & Gazetteer, p. 31
California Road & Recreation Atlas, p. 49
Other: Modoc Country USFS/BLM Map

Route Directions

▼ 0.0		From North Coast #45: New Pine Creek to Fort Bidwell Trail, 7.2 miles east of New Pine Creek, zero trip meter and turn south on formed dirt trail marked Highgrade Trail, National Recreation Trail, following sign to Mineral Spring. North Coast #46: Dismal Swamp Trail is opposite the start.
		GPS: N41°58.38' W120°11.37'
▼ 0.4	TR	Track on left goes to the Klondike Mines. Track straight ahead. Follow sign to Mineral Spring, remaining on the national recreation trail.
		GPS: N41°58.09' W120°11.57'
▼ 0.5	SO	Track on right.
▼ 0.6	SO	Mine tailings on right; then track on right.
		GPS: N41°58.14' W120°11.73'
▼ 0.7	SO	Collapsed log cabin on right.
▼ 0.8	BL	Mineral Spring on right; then track on left.
		GPS: N41°58.06' W120°11.95'
▼ 1.1	SO	Track on left; then log cabin on left in the trees; then track on right.
		GPS: N41°57.78' W120°12.12'
▼ 1.5	TR	Track on left into the Consolidated Mines.
		GPS: N41°57.68' W120°12.52'
▼ 2.1	SO	Track left goes 0.1 miles to the Consolidated Mines. National recreation trail goes left at this point.
		GPS: N41°57.58' W120°12.95'
▼ 2.3	SO	Track on right goes through the Warlock Mine workings.
		GPS: N41°57.58' W120°13.14'
▼ 2.4	SO	Second entrance to Warlock Mine.
▼ 2.5	TL	T-intersection. Turn left and start the loop. Track on right is end of the loop.
		GPS: N41°57.63' W120°13.35'
▼ 2.7	SO	Track on left to Little Lily Lake.
▼ 2.9	TR	Track straight ahead is the spur to Mount Vida. Zero trip meter and turn right, following sign to the Sunset Mine.
		GPS: N41°57.30' W120°13.31'

Spur to Mount Vida

▼ 0.0		Continue to the southeast.
		GPS: N41°57.30' W120°13.31'
▼ 0.1	SO	Track on left.
		GPS: N41°57.21' W120°13.29'
▼ 0.7	SO	Track on left with viewpoint over North Star Basin. Track on right.
		GPS: N41°57.12' W120°13.26'
▼ 0.9	SO	Marker for the national recreation trail on right. Drivers not wishing to do the difficult 7-rated section should turn here.
		GPS: N41°57.03' W120°13.44'
▼ 1.0	SO	Start of off-camber section with a difficult twist.
		GPS: N41°56.91' W120°13.52'
▼ 1.2	TR	T-intersection. Track on left.
		GPS: N41°56.75' W120°13.70
▼ 1.4		Spur trail finishes at a high viewpoint.
		GPS: N41°56.93' W120°13.73'

Continuation of Main Trail

▼ 0.0		Continue to the southwest.
		GPS: N41°57.30' W120°13.31'
▼ 1.4	BR	Track on left; then track on right; then cross over Pine Creek.
		GPS: N41°57.75' W120°13.63'
▼ 1.8	TR	T-intersection.
		GPS: N41°57.86' W120°13.20'
▼ 2.0	SO	Track on left.
▼ 2.4		End of loop. Turn left to exit back the way you came.
		GPS: N41°57.63' W120°13.35'

Selected Further Reading

Massey, Peter, and Jeanne Wilson. *4WD Adventures: Colorado.* Castle Rock, Colo.: Swagman Publishing, Inc., 1999.

—. *Backcountry Adventures: Arizona.* Castle Rock, Colo.: Swagman Publishing, Inc., 2001.

—. *Backcountry Adventures: Southern California.* Castle Rock, Colo.: Swagman Publishing, Inc., 2002.

—. *Backcountry Adventures: Utah.* Castle Rock, Colo.: Swagman Publishing, Inc., 2002.

AAA California, Nevada Tour Book, 2001.

Alt, David D., and Donald W. Hyndman. *Roadside Geology of Northern California.* Missoula, Mont.: Mountain Press Publishing Co., 1996.

—. *Roadside Geology of Northern and Central California.* Missoula, Mont.: Mountain Press Publishing Co., 2000.

Bauer, Helen. *California Mission Days.* New York: Doubleday & Company, Inc., 1951.

Beck, Warren A., and Ynez D. Haase. *Historical Atlas of California.* Norman, Okla.: University of Oklahoma Press, 1974.

Belden, L. Burr, and Mary DeDecker. *Death Valley to Yosemite: Frontier Mining Camps & Ghost Towns.* Bishop, Calif.: Spotted Dog Press, Inc., 1998.

Bischoff, Matt C. *Touring California & Nevada Hot Springs.* Helena, Mont.: Falcon Publishing, Inc., 1997.

Blackwell, Laird R. *Wildflowers of the Sierra Nevada and the Central Valley.* Renton, Wash.: Lone Pine Publishing, 1999.

Boessenecker, John. *Gold Dust and Gunsmoke.* New York: John Wiley & Sons, Inc., 1999.

Braasch, Barbara. *California's Gold Rush.* Medina, Wash.: Johnston Associates International, 1996.

Bright, William. *1500 California Place Names, Their Origin and Meaning.* Berkeley, Calif.: University of California Press, 1998.

Broman, Mickey, and Russ Leadabrand. *California Ghost Town Trails.* Baldwin Park, Calif.: Gem Guides Book Company, 1981.

Brown, Ann Marie. *California Waterfalls.* San Francisco: Foghorn Press, 1997.

Brown, Vinson. *The Californian Wildlife Region.* Happy Camp, Calif.: Naturegraph Publishers, Inc., 1999.

Vinson, Brown, Henry Weston Jr., and Jerry Buzzell. *Handbook of California Birds.* Happy Camp, Calif.: Naturegraph Publishers, 1986.

Browning, Peter. *Place Names of the Sierra Nevada.* Berkeley, Calif.: Wilderness Press, 1992.

—. Day Trips: *Roaming the Backroads of Northern California.* San Francisco: Chronicle Books, 1979.

California Historical Landmarks. Sacramento, Calif.: State of California—The Resource Agency, 1996.

Clark, Carol. *Explorers of the West.* Salt Lake City, Utah: Great Mountain West Supply, 1997.

Clark, Lew, and Ginny Lew. *High Mountains & Deep Valleys, The Gold Bonanza Days.* San Luis Obispo, Calif.: Western Trails Publications, 1978.

Crutchfield, James A. *Mountain Men of the American West.* Boise, Idaho: Tamarack Books, Inc., 1997.

DeDecker, Mary. *Mines of the Eastern Sierra.* Glendale, Calif.: La Siesta Press, 1993.

Deverell, William. *Railroad Crossing: Californians and the Railroad, 1850-1910.* Los Angeles: University of California Press, 1996.

Dunn, Jerry Camarillo, Jr. *National Geographic's Driving Guides to America: California and Nevada and Hawaii.* Washington, D.C.: The Book Division National Geographic Society, 1996.

Durham, David L. *Place Names of California's Central Coast.* Clovis, Calif.: Word Dancer Press, 2000.

—. *Place-Names of California's Eastern Sierra, Including Death Valley.* Clovis, Calif.: Word Dancer Press, 2000.

—. *Place-Names of California's Gold Country, Including Yosemite National Park.* Clovis, Calif.: Word Dancer Press, 2000.

—. *Place Names of California's North Coast.* Clovis, Calif.: Word Dancer Press, 2000.

—. *Place-Names of Northeastern California.* Clovis, Calif.: Word Dancer Press, 2000.

—. *Place-Names of California's North Sacramento Valley.* Clovis, Calif.: Word Dancer Press, 2000.

—. *Place-Names of California's North San Joaquin Valley.* Clovis, Calif.: Word Dancer Press, 2000.

—. *Place-Names of California's Desert Counties.* Clovis, Calif.: Word Dancer Press, 2000.

—. *Place-Names of Central California.* Clovis, Calif.: Word Dancer Press, 2000.

—. *Place-Names of the San Francisco Bay Area.* Clovis, Calif.: Word Dancer Press, 2000.

Egan, Ferol. *Frémont.* Reno, Nevada: University of Nevada Press, 1985.

Fix, David, and Andy Bezener. *Birds of Northern California.* Renton, Wash.: Lone Pine Publishing, 2000.

Florin, Lambert. *Ghost Towns of The West.* New York: Promontory Press, 1993.

Gersch-Young, Marjorie. *Hot Springs and Hot Pools of the Southwest.* Santa Cruz, Calif.: Aqua Thermal Access, 2001.

Gray, Mary Taylor. *Watchable Birds of California.* Missoula, Mont.: Mountain Press Publishing, 1999.

Grossi, Mark. *Longstreet Highroad Guide to the California Sierra Nevada.* Atlanta, Georgia: Longstreet Press Inc., 2000.

Gudde, Erwin G. *1000 California Place Names.* Berkeley, Calif.: University of California Press, 1959.

Harris, Edward D. *John Charles Frémont and the Great Western Reconnaissance.* New York: Chelsea House Publishers, 1990.

—. *California Place Names.* Berkeley, Calif.: University of California Press, 1998.

Hart, James D. *A Companion to California.* New York: Oxford University Press, 1978.

Heizer, Robert F., ed. *The Destruction of California Indians.* Lincoln, Nebraska: University of Nebraska Press, 1993.

Heizer, Robert F., and Albert B. Elasser. *The Natural World of the California Indians.* Berkeley, Calif.: University of California Press, 1980.

Helfrich, Devere, Helen Helfrich, and Thomas Hunt. *Emigrant Trails West.* Reno, Nevada: Trails West Inc., 1984.

Hirschfelder, Arlene. *Native Americans.* New York: Dorling Kindersley Publishing, Inc., 2000.

Historical Guide to North American Railroads, The. Waukesha, Wisc.: Kalmbach Publishing, 2000.

Holliday, J.S. *Rush for Riches: Gold Fever and the Making of California.* Berkley, Calif.: University of California Press, 1999.

Holmes, Robert. *California's Best-Loved Driving Tours.* New York: Macmillan Travel, 1999.

Hopkins, Sarah Winnemucca. *Life Among the Piutes.* Reno, Nevada: University of Nevada Press, 1994.

Horn, Elizabeth L. *Coastal Wildflowers of the Pacific Northwest.* Missoula, Mont.: Mountain Press Publishing Company, 1993.

Hoxie, Frederick E., ed. *Encyclopedia of North American Indians.* Boston: Houghton Mifflin Company, 1996.

Huegel, Tony. *California Coastal Byways.* Idaho Falls, Idaho: The Post Company, 1996.

—. *Sierra Nevada Byways.* Idaho Falls, Idaho: The Post Company, 1997.

Indians of California, The. Alexandria, Va.: Time-Life Books, 1994.

Jameson, E. W., Jr., and Hans J. Peeters. *California Mammals.* Berkeley and Los Angeles: University of California Press, 1988.

Jameson, W. C. *Buried Treasures of California.* Little Rock, Ark.: August House Publishers, Inc., 1995.

Johnson, William Weber. *The Old West: The Forty-niners.* New York: Time-Life Books, 1974.

Johnston, Verna R. *California Forests and Woodlands.* Berkeley, Calif.: University of California Press, 1994.

Jones, William R. *Yosemite: The Story Behind the Scenery.* KC Publications, Inc., 1989.

Kavanagh, James, ed. *The Nature of California.* Helena, Mont.: Waterford Press Ltd., 1997.

Keyworth, C.L. *California Indians.* New York: Checkmark Books, 1991.

Klein, James. *Where to Find Gold in Northern California.* Baldwin Park, Calif.: Gem Guides Book Company, 2000.

Kricher, John. *California and Pacific Northwest Forests.* New York: Houghton Mifflin Company, 1998.

Kroeber, A. L. *Handbook of the Indians of California.* New York: Dover Publications, Inc., 1976.

Kyle, Douglas E. *Historic Spots in California.* Stanford, Calif.: Stanford University Press, 1990.

Lamar, Howard R., ed. *The New Encyclopedia of the American West.* New Haven, Conn.: Yale University Press, 1998.

Lewellyn, Harry. *Backroad Trips and Tips.* Costa Mesa, Calif.: Glovebox Publications, 1993.

Lewis, Donovan. *Pioneers of California.* San Francisco: Scottwall Associates, Publishers, 1993.

Marinacci Barbara, and Rudy Marinacci. *California's Spanish Place.* Houston, Texas: Gulf Publishing Company, 1997.

Martin, Don, and Betty Martin. *California-Nevada Roads Less Traveled.* Henderson, Nevada: Pine Cone Press, Inc., 1999.

May, Antoinette. *Haunted Houses of California.* San Carlos, Calif.: Wide World Publishing/Tetra, 1998.

McConnell, Doug. *Bay Area Backroads.* San Francisco: Chronicle Books, 1999.

McDannold, Thomas A. *California's Chinese Heritage: A Legacy of Places.* Stockton, Calif.: Heritage West Books, 2000.

McDermott, John D. *A Guide to the Indian Wars of the West.* Lincoln, Nebraska: University of Nebraska Press, 1998.

McFerrin, Linda Watanabe. *Best Places Northern California.* Seattle, Wash.: Sasquatch Books, 2001.

McGlashan, C.F. *History of the Donner Party.* Stanford, Calif.: Stanford University Press, 1947.

McGrath, Roger D. *Gunfighters Highwaymen & Vigilantes, Violence on the Frontier.* Berkeley, Calif.: University of California Press, 1987.

Milner, Clyde A., II, Carol A. O'Conner, and Martha A. Sandweiss, eds. *The Oxford History of the American West.* Oxford: Oxford University Press, 1996.

Mitchell, James R. *Gem Trails of Northern California.* Baldwin Park, Calif.: Gem Guides Book Company, 1995.

Mitchell, John D. *Lost Mines and Buried Treasures Along the Old Frontier.* Glorieta, N. Mex.: Rio Grande Press Inc., 1995.

Morgan, Dale L. *Jedediah Smith and the Opening of the West.* Lincoln, Nebraska: University of Nebraska Press, 1964.

Munz, Philip A. *California Spring Wildflowers.* Berkley, Calif.: University of California Press, 1961.

Nadeau, Remi. *Ghost Towns & Mining Camps of California.* Santa Barbara, Calif.: Crest Publishers, 1999.

Nash, Jay Robert. *Encyclopedia of Western Lawmen and Outlaws.* New York: Da Capo Press, 1994.

National Audubon Society Field Guide to California. New York: Alfred A. Knopf, Inc., 1998.

National Audubon Society Field Guide to North American Birds: Western Region. New York: Alfred A. Knopf, Inc., 1998.

National Audubon Society Field Guide to North American Trees: Western Region. New York: Alfred A. Knopf, Inc., 1996.

National Audubon Society Field Guide to North American Mammals. New York: Alfred A. Knopf, Inc., 1996.

National Audubon Society Field Guide to North American Wildflowers: Western Region. New York: Alfred A. Knopf, Inc., 1998.

Norris, Robert M., and Robert W. Webb. *Geology of California.* Santa Barbara: John Wiley & Sons, Inc., 1976.

North American Wildlife. New York: Readers Digest Association, Inc., 1982.

Oakeshott, Gordon B. *California's Changing Landscapes.* San Francisco: McGraw-Hill Book Company, 1978.

O'Neal, Bill. *Encyclopedia of Western Gunfighters.* Norman, Okla.: University of Oklahoma Press, 1979.

Paher, Stanley W. *Early Mining Days – California Gold Country: The Story Behind the Scenery.* KC Publications, Inc., 1996.

Patterson, Richard. *Historical Atlas of the Outlaw West.* Boulder, Colo.: Johnson Publishing Company, 1985.

Pearson, David W. *This Was Mining in the West.* Atglen, Penn.: Schiffer Publishing, 1996.

Pierce, L. Kingston. *America's Historic Trails with Tom Bodett.* San Francisco: KQED Books, 1997.

Poshek, Lucy, and Roger Naylor, comps. *California Trivia.* Nashville, Tenn.: Rutledge Hill Press, 1998.

Powell, Jerry A., and Charles L. Hogue. *California Insects.* Berkeley, Calif.: University of California Press, 1979.

Powers, Stephen. *Tribes of California.* Berkeley and Los Angeles: University of California Press, 1976.

Prucha, Francis Paul. *American Indian Treaties.* Berkeley, Calif.: University of California Press, 1994.

Roberts, George, and Jan Roberts. *Discover Historic California.* Baldwin Park, Calif.: Gem Guides Book Co., 1999.

Robertson, Donald B. *Encyclopedia of Western Railroad History, Volume IV: California.* Caldwell, Idaho: The Caxton Printers, Ltd., 1998.

Rolle, Andrew. *California: A History.* Wheeling, Ill.: Harlan Davidson, Inc., 1998.

Sagstetter, Beth, and Bill Sagstetter. *The Mining Camps Speak.* Denver: Benchmark Publishing, 1998.

Seagraves, Anne. *Soiled Doves: Prostitution in the Early West.* Hayden, Idaho: Wesanne Publications, 1994.

Secrest, William B. *California Desperadoes.* Clovis, Calif.: World Dancer Press, 2000.

—. *Lawmen & Desperados.* Spokane, Wash.: The Arthur H. Clark Company, 1994.

Schaffer, Jeffery P., Ben Schifrin, Thomas Winnett, and Ruby Johnson Jenkins. *The Pacific Crest Trail, Volume 1: California.* Berkeley, Calif.: Wilderness Press, 2000.

Schoenherr, Allan A. *A Natural History of California.* Berkeley, Calif.: University of California Press, 1992.

Small, Arnold. *California Birds.* Vista, Calif.: IBIS Publishing Company, 1994.

Smith, Raymond M. *Ten Overnight Trips on the Backroads of Nevada & California.* Minden, Nevada: Mr. Raymond M. Smith, 1994.

Stuart, John D., and John O. Sawyer. *Tress and Shrubs of California.* Berkeley, Calif.: University of California Press, 2001.

Takaki, Ronald. *Journey to Gold Mountain: The Chinese in 19th Century America.* New York: Chelsea House Publishers, 1994.

Taylor, Colin F. *The Native Americans: The Indigenous People of North America.* London: Salamander Books Ltd., 2000.

Tefertiller, Casey. *Wyatt Earp: The Life Behind the Legend.* New York: John Wiley & Sons, Inc., 1997.

Teie, William C. *4 Wheeler's Guide to the Rubicon Trail.* Rescue, Calif.: Deer Valley Press.

Thollander, Earl. *Earl Thollander's Back Roads of California.* Seattle, Wash.: Sasquatch Books, 1994.

Thrap, Dan L. *Encyclopedia of Frontier Biography.* 3 vols. Lincoln, Nebr.: University of Nebraska Press, 1988.

Trafzer, Clifford E., and Joel R. Hyer, eds. *Exterminate Them!* East Lansing, Mich.: Michigan State University Press, 1999.

Twain, Mark. *Roughing It.* New York: New American Library, 1962.

Varney, Philip. *Ghost Towns of Northern California.* Stillwater, Minn.: Voyager Press, Inc., 2001.

Waldman, Carl. *Encyclopedia of Native American Tribes.* New York: Facts on File, 1988.

Wright, Ralph B., ed. *California's Missions.* Los Angeles: The Stirling Press, 1967.

Wyman, David M. *Backroads of Northern California.* Stillwater, Minn.: Voyager Press, Inc., 2000.

Zauner, Lou, and Phyllis Zauner. *California Gold: Story of the Rush to Riches.* Sonoma, Calif.: Zanel Publications, 1997.

Zauner, Phyllis. *Those Legendary Men of the Wild West.* Sonoma, Calif.: Zanel Publications, 1991.

http://bss.sfsu.edu/calstudies/Hoopa.HTM

http://cal-parks.ca.gov/default.asp?page_id=458

http://ceres.ca.gov/geo_area/counties/Lassen/landmarks.html

http://ci.santa-rosa.ca.us/index.asp

http://infodome.sdsu.edu/research/guides/calindians/calinddict.shtml

http://library.humboldt.edu/infoservices/humco/holdings/archives/Cron12-73.htm

http://myclouds.tripod.com/shasta/towns.html

http://www.arcata.com/

http://www.backcountrypages.com/redwoods/redwood2.html

http://www.bushong.net/dawn/about/college/ids100/leaders.shtml

http://www.ca.blm.gov

http://www.cagenweb.com/shasta/shasthis.htm

http://www.chico.ca.us/

http://www.chinadaily.com.cn/star/2001/0322/di24-2.html

http://www.ci.shasta-lake.ca.us/

http://www.cityofukiah.com/

http://www.coastnews.com/nh/nh.htm

http://www.co.humboldt.ca.us/etd/rwpeda/Hoopa8d.htm

http://www.colostate.edu/Orgs/TuleLake/Tule%20Lake%20Menu.html

http://www.fresno-county.com/fresno.html

http://www.fs.fed.us/htnf/laketaho.htm

http://www.geocities.com/ftcrook/

http://www.geocities.com/Heartland/Ridge/5850/josiah.html

http://www.ghosttowns.com

http://www.gorp.com

http://www.highonadventure.com/Hoa99aug/Shasta/shasta.htm

http://www.kachina.net/~alunajoy/shasta.html

http://www.kings.k12.ca.us/kcoe/curric/history/people/ethnic/chinesejj.htm

http://www.lewistonbridgerv.com/attract.htm

http://www.mccloudchamber.com

http://www.mtshastachamber.com

http://www.ncgold.com/Museums_Parks/syrp/henness.html

http://www.nps.gov/prsf/history/hrs/elpresid/elpresid.htm

http://www.nps.gov/whis/

http://www.outdoors.myareaguide.com/redwood/history.html

http://www.over-land.com

http://www.pashnit.com/roads/cal/HennessPassRd.htm

http://www.r5.fs.fed.us/heritage/056.HTM

http://www.r5.fs.fed.us/lassen/ishi_wilderness.htm

http://www.r5.fs.fed.us/shastatrinity/nra/

http://www.r5.pswfs.gov/heritage/miningsites.html

http://www.raken.com/american_wealth/railroad_barons/central_pacific13.asp

http://www.redbluffchamberofcommerce.com/

http://www.redding.com/

http://www.redwoodvisitor.org/

http://www.rh2o.com/modoc/

http://www.roamingtimes.com/chambers/bigfoot.htm

http://www.rvjournal.com/archives/mtshasta.html

http://www.shastacascade.org

http://www.shastahome.org

http://www.shastasunset.com

http://www.shastalake.com/

http://www.sierrahistorical.org/Summer%20at%20Camp%20Ducey.html

http://www.sierratimes.com/archive/files/jul/07/ardca070701.htm

http://www.siskiyous.edu/library/weedhist.htm

http://www.sjyc.org/Articles/Delta/history_of_the_california_delta.htm

http://www.snowcrest.net/whm/Weed3.html

http://www.snowcrest.net/geography/black/butte.htm

http://www.snowcrest.net/wb6fzh/tchist2.html

http://www.srpnet.com/water/lakes/granitereefdam.asp

http://www.tahoevacationguide.com/laketahoe.html

http://www.tcoe.trinity.k12.ca.us/~wmoss/knob.html

http://www.treasurenet.com/westeast/200108/feature/

http://www.trinitycounty.com/

http://www.tulelake.org/

http://www.usbr.gov/cdams/dams/shasta.html

http://www.usparkinfo.com/redwood.html

http://www.virtualtourist.com/m/.128900/4246/?s=n

http://www.weedchamber.com/

http://www.zpub.com/sf/history/harte.html

25 Favorite Trails

	Trail Name	Difficulty rating (Hardest = 10)	Scenic Rating (Best = 10)	Length (miles)
1	High Sierra #18: Shuteye Peak Trail	5	10	6.6
2	Northern Sierra #27: Sierra Buttes Trail	5	10	9
3	Northern Sierra #44: Peligreen-Grapevine Jeepway	6	10	19.8
4	Northern Sierra #29: Gold Valley Trail	6	9	14.2
5	North Coast #16: Gold Bluffs Trail	1	10	6.8
6	Northern Sierra #10: Corral Hollow OHV Route	5	10	12.5
7	Northern Sierra #26: Alleghany Trail	4	10	31.1
8	High Sierra #41: Coyote Creek Trail	3	9	16.2
9	High Sierra #25: Hite Cove Road	6	10	5.1
10	High Sierra #2: Sycamore Springs Trail	3	9	9.1
11	High Sierra #30: Trumbull Peak Trail	3	10	9.9
12	Northern Sierra #30: Poker Flat OHV Trail	5	10	41.5
13	Northern Sierra #12: Red and Blue Lakes Trail	3	9	14.8
14	High Sierra #46: Papoose Flat Trail	4	9	16.3
15	High Sierra #13: Onion Spring OHV Route	4	10	5.7
16	High Sierra #23: Miami Trail	3	9	31.6
17	Northern Sierra #28: Gold Lake Trail	5	9	6.4
18	North Coast #46: Dismal Swamp Trail	6	10	11.4
19	Northern Sierra #16: Angora Lakes Road	1	10	2.8
20	Northern Sierra #1: Clavey Bridge Road	3	9	33.7
21	High Sierra 5: Granite Gorge Overlook Trail	3	10	4.4
22	High Sierra #38: Laurel Lakes Trail	4	10	8.7
23	North Coast #14: Howland Hill Road	1	10	8.4
24	Northern Sierra #55: Payne Peak Trail	3	9	32
25	North Coast #37: Siskiyou Mountains Trail	2	10	31.6

25 Longest Trails

	Trail Name	Length (including spurs) (Miles)	Difficulty Rating (Hardest = 10)	Scenic Rating (Best = 10)
1	High Sierra #45: Saline Valley Road	91.4	2	10
2	Northern Sierra #21: Henness Pass Road	79.6	2	10
3	Northern Sierra #42: Ponderosa Way	63.8	3	10
4	Northern Sierra #9: Calaveras Dome Trail	56.2	2	9
5	Northern Sierra #35: Grizzly Ridge Trail	55.1	2	9
6	Northern Sierra #5: Crandall Peak Trail	50.4	3	9
7	Northern Sierra #52: Buckhorn Backcountry Byway	49.1	1	8
8	Northern Sierra #40: Susan River to Juniper Lake Trail	45	2	9
9	Northern Sierra #48: Burney Mountain Trail	44.2	2	9
10	Northern Sierra #30: Poker Flat OHV Trail	41.5	5	10
11	Northern Sierra #37: Thompson Peak Trail	39.4	2	9
12	North Coast #41: Fairchild Swamp Trail	36.1	1	8
13	Northern Sierra #24: Summit City Loop	35.3	3	9
14	North Coast #3: Bartlett Springs Road	33.7	2	9
15	Northern Sierra #1: Clavey Bridge Road	33.7	3	9
16	Northern Sierra #55: Payne Peak Trail	32	3	9
17	Northern Sierra #53: South Warner Mountains Trail	31.8	3	9
18	High Sierra #23: Miami Trail	31.6	3	9
19	North Coast #37: Siskiyou Mountains Trail	31.6	2	10
20	High Sierra #28: Old Coulterville Road	31.4	3	10
21	North Coast #33: Mount Shasta Loop	31.2	2	9
22	Northern Sierra #26: Alleghany Trail	31.1	4	10
23	North Coast #17: Bald Hills Road	30.9	1	10
24	Northern Sierra #20: Soda Springs Road	29.2	3	9
25	High Sierra #35: Sawmill Meadow Road	28.1	2	8

25 Shortest Trails

	Trail Name	Length (Miles)	Difficulty Rating (Hardest=10)	Scenic Rating (Best=10)
1	High Sierra #12: Bear Diversion Dam OHV Route	2.3	4	10
2	Northern Sierra #31: Chimney Rock OHV Trail	2.4	4	9
3	North Coast #7: Red Mountain Trail	2.4	3	9
4	High Sierra #11: Mount Tom Fire Lookout Trail	2.7	3	10
5	Northern Sierra #16: Angora Lakes Road	2.8	1	10
6	Northern Sierra #47: Murken Bench Trail	3.0	2	8
7	High Sierra #21: Iron Lakes Trail	3.1	5	9
8	HIgh Sierra #7: Bald Mountain OHV Route	3.4	5	9
9	Northern Sierra #18: Blackwood Canyon Trail	3.6	5	8
10	High Sierra #39: Convict Lake Overlook Trail	4.0	3	9
11	North Coast #8: Nome Cult Mountain House Trail	4.0	4	9
12	North Coast #20: Ukonom Mountain Trail	4.0	3	8
13	High Sierra #15: Whiskey Ridge Trail	4.0	4	9
14	High Sierra #29: Crocker Ridge Trail	4.1	3	8
15	High Sierra #8: Brewer Lake OHV Route	4.3	5	9
16	High Sierra #5: Granite Gorge Overlook Trail	4.4	3	10
17	High Sierra #26: Merced River Road	4.9	1	10
18	Northern Sierra #11: Mattley Ridge Trail	5.0	4	8
19	High Sierra #6: Spanish OHV Route	5.0	7	7
20	High Sierra #16: Browns Meadow Trail	5.1	4	9
21	High Sierra #25: Hite Cove Road	5.1	6	10
22	North Coast #11: Knob Peak Trail	5.1	1	8
23	North Coast #35: Herd Peak Trail	5.5	1	8
24	North Coast #12: Hall City Cave Trail	5.6	1	9
25	High Sierra #13: Onion Spring OHV Route	5.7	4	10

25 Hardest Trails

	Trail Name	Difficulty rating (Hardest = 10)	Scenic Rating (Best = 10)	Length (miles)
1	North Coast #47: Highgrade Trail	7	9	9.3
2	North Coast #5: Lovelady Ridge Trail	7	9	8.8
3	High Sierra #6: Spanish OHV Route	7	7	5.0
4	North Coast #46: Dismal Swamp Trail	6	10	11.4
5	Northern Sierra #29: Gold Valley Trail	6	9	15.2
6	High Sierra #25: Hite Cove Road	6	10	5.1
7	Northern Sierra #44: Peligreen-Grapevine Jeepway	6	10	19.8
8	High Sierra #7: Bald Mountain OHV Route	5	9	3.4
9	Northern Sierra #54: Bearcamp Flat Trail	5	10	7.7
10	Northern Sierra #18: Blackwood Canyon Trail	5	8	3.6
11	High Sierra #8: Brewer Lake OHV Route	5	9	4.3
12	Northern Sierra #10: Corral Hollow OHV Route	5	10	12.5
13	Northern Sierra #28: Gold Lake Trail	5	9	6.4
14	High Sierra #48: Harkless Flat Trail	5	9	11.5
15	High Sierra #21: Iron Lakes Trail	5	9	3.1
16	Northern Sierra #30: Poker Flat OHV Trail	5	10	41.5
17	High Sierra #18: Shuteye Peak Trail	5	10	6.6
18	Northern Sierra #27: Sierra Buttes Trail	5	10	9.0
19	High Sierra #50: Sierra View Trail	5	9	14.3
20	Northern Sierra #26: Alleghany Trail	4	10	31.1
21	High Sierra #12: Bear Diversion Dam OHV Route	4	10	2.3
22	Northern Sierra #8: Black Springs Route	4	7	18.4
23	North Coast #23: Bowerman Ridge Trail	4	9	21.1
24	High Sierra #16: Browns Meadow Trail	4	9	5.1
25	Northern Sierra #31: Chimney Rock OHV Trail	4	9	2.4

25 Easiest Trails

	Trail Name	Difficulty rating (Hardest = 10)	Scenic Rating (Best = 10)	Length (miles)
1	Northern Sierra #16: Angora Lakes Road	1	10	2.8
2	Northern Sierra #39 Antelope Mountain and Crater Lake Trail	1	9	26.7
3	North Coast #17: Bald Hills Road	1	10	30.9
4	High Sierra #9: Big Creek Railroad Grade Trail	1	9	12.8
5	Northern Sierra #52: Buckhorn Backcountry Byway	1	8	49.1
6	High Sierra #40: Casa Diablo Road	1	8	27.9
7	High Sierra #17: Central Camp Road	1	8	17.8
8	High Sierra #1: Dinkey-Trimmer Road	1	9	26.7
9	North Coast #41: Fairchild Swamp Trail	1	8	36.1
10	North Coast #44: Fandango Pass Trail	1	9	24.1
11	North Coast #16: Gold Bluffs Trail	1	10	6.8
12	North Coast #12: Hall City Cave Trail	1	9	5.6
13	Northern Sierra #46: Hat Creek Rim Trail	1	8	22.1
14	Northern Sierra #50: Hayden Hill Trail	1	7	16.6
15	North Coast #35: Herd Peak Trail	1	8	5.5
16	North Coast #14: Howland Hill Road	1	10	8.4
17	North Coast #11: Knob Peak Trail	1	8	5.1
18	North Coast #6: Log Spring Ridge Trail	1	9	19.3
19	North Coast #13: Low Divide Road	1	8	14.5
20	North Coast #31: McCloud River Road	1	8	11.7
21	High Sierra #26: Merced River Road	1	10	4.9
22	Northern Sierra #49: Popcorn Cave Trail	1	8	11.1
23	North Coast #15: Redwood National Park Coastal Drive	1	9	9.5
24	High Sierra #4: Sawmill Flat Road	1	10	10.1
25	North Coast #25: South Shore Drive	1	9	6.9

25 Scenic Trails

	Trail Name	Scenic rating (Best = 10)	Difficulty Rating (Hardest = 10)	Length (miles)
1	Northern Sierra #26: Alleghany Trail	10	4	31.1
2	Northern Sierra #16: Angora Lakes Road	10	1	2.8
3	North Coast #17: Bald Hills Road	10	1	30.9
4	High Sierra #12: Bear Diversion Dam OHV Route	10	4	2.3
5	Northern Sierra #54: Bearcamp Flat Road	10	5	7.7
6	Northern Sierra #10: Corral Hollow OHV Route	10	5	12.5
7	North Coast #46: Dismal Swamp Trail	10	6	11.4
8	North Coast #16: Gold Bluffs Trail	10	1	6.8
9	High Sierra #5: Granite Gorge Overlook Trail	10	3	4.4
10	Northern Sierra #21: Henness Pass Road	10	2	79.6
11	High Sierra #25: Hite Cove Road	10	6	5.1
12	North Coast #14: Howland Hill Road	10	1	8.4
13	High Sierra #38: Laurel Lakes Trail	10	4	8.7
14	High Sierra #26: Merced River Road	10	1	4.9
15	North Coast #34: Military Pass Trail	10	2	9.9
16	High Sierra #11: Mount Tom Fire Lookout	10	3	2.7
17	High Sierra #28: Old Coulterville Road	10	3	31.4
18	High Sierra #13: Onion Spring OHV Route	10	4	5.7
19	Northern Sierra #44: Peligreen-Grapevine Jeepway	10	6	19.8
20	Northern Sierra #6: Pinecrest Peak Trail	10	4	7.8
21	Northern Sierra #30: Poker Flat OHV Trail	10	5	41.5
22	Northern Sierra #42: Ponderosa Way	10	3	63.8
23	High Sierra #45: Saline Valley Road	10	2	91.4
24	High Sierra #4: Sawmill Flat Road	10	1	10.1
25	North Coast #26: Shasta Bally Trail	10	4	7.9

Photograph Credits

Unless otherwise indicated in the following list of acknowledgments (which is organized by section and page number), all color photographs were taken by Peter Massey and are copyrighted by Swagman Publishing Inc., or by Peter Massey.

Abbreviations: California Historical Society, San Francisco (CaHS); California Academy of Sciences Special Collections, San Francisco (CalPhotos); Colorado Historical Society (CoHS); Utah State Historical Society (UHS); San Francisco Botanical Gardens, Strybing Arboretum Society (Strybing); Tucson Botanical Gardens (TBG); San Diego Museum of Man (SDMOM); University of Southern California (USC); Huntington Library (Huntington); Arizona State Library (ASL); Brother Alfred Brousseau Project (Brousseau); Cornell Lab of Ornithology (Cornell); The North American Indian, by Edward S. Curtis (NAC); Don Baccus Photography (Baccus); Denver Botanical Garden (DBG); Jim Gratiot, CalFlora (Gratiot); Doug Von Gaussig, NatureSongs.com (NatureSongs); Denver Public Library Western History Collection (DPL); Corel Stock Photo Library (Corel); PhotoDisc (PD).

23 CaHS; **24** CaHS; **25** (left) CaHS; (right) Bushducks; **26-30** CaHS; **31** (left) CaHS; (right) Bushducks; **32** CaHS; **33** CaHS; **34** (left) Bushducks; (right) CaHS; **35-68** CaHS; **69** (left) CaHS; (right) DPL; **70** (upper) UHS; (lower) USC; **71** CaHS; **74** CaHS; **75** UHS; **76** Huntington; **77** (upper) CoHS; (lower) Bushducks; **78** USC; **80-81** CaHS; **83** (right) DPL; (left) CaHS; **84** CaHS; **85** CaHS; **86** CaHS; **89** NAS; **90** (left) NAC; (right) CalPhotos; **91** NAC; **92** (upper left) USC; (lower left) NAC; (right) NAC; **93-97** NAC; **98** (left) NAC; (right) SDMOM; **99** NAC; **100** SDMOM; **103-108** CaHS; **109** Earthquake Engineering Library, National Information Service for Earthquake Engineering **112** Corel; **113** Corel; **115** CaHS; **115** CaHS; **116** CaHS; **118** Corel; **119** (left) Corel; (upper right) Corel; (lower right) PD; **120** Corel; **121** (lower left) Paul Berquest; (others) Corel; **122** Corel; **123** (lower left) PD; (others) Corel; **124** (lower left) Paul Berquest; (others) Corel; **125** Corel; **126** (upper left) Corel; (upper right) PD; (lower right) Corel; **127** (left) Corel; (upper right) PD; (center right) Bushducks; (lower right) Corel; **128** (upper left) Corel; (center left) PD; (lower left) Corel; (upper right) NatureSongs; (lower right) Corel; **129** Corel; **130** (upper left) CalPhotos; (lower left) Corel; (upper right) NatureSongs; (center right) Corel; (lower right) James C. Cokendolpher; **131** (upper left) CalPhotos; (others) Corel; **132** (upper left) Corel; (center left) CalPhotos; (lower left) Earle Robinson; (upper right) CalPhotos; (lower right) Baccus; **133** (left) Corel; (upper right) CalPhotos; (center right) PD; (lower right) PD; **134** (upper left) CalPhotos, H. Vannoy Davis; (lower left) Corel; (upper right) PD; (center right) Corel; (lower right) Earle Robinson; **135** (upper left) CalPhotos; (middle and lower left) PD; (upper right) PD; (upper center right) Baccus; (lower center right) Cornell; (lower right) Corel; **136** (Upper two photos, left) Corel; lower three photos, left) CalPhotos; (upper right) Corel; (lower right) Cornell, photography by Art Biale; **137** (upper left) Corel; (center left) Baccus; (lower left) Earle Robinson; (upper right) Earle Robinson; (center and lower right) Corel; **138** (left) Corel; (upper right) Cornell; (lower right) Corel; **139** (left) Corel; (right) Earle Robinson; **140** (upper left) Corel; (lower left) Baccus; **141** (upper left, four photos) Corel; (lower left) Baccus; **142** (upper left) Strybing; (upper center left) Brousseau; (lower center left) Gratiot; (lower left) Gratiot; (upper and center right) Corel; (lower right) Strybing; **143** (upper left) Bushducks; (center left) Gratiot; (lower left) DGB; (upper right) Gratiot; (upper center right) Gratiot; (lower center right) Strybing; (lower right) Gratiot; **144** (upper left) Strybing; (upper center left) DBG; (lower center left) Strybing; (lower left) Strybing; **145** (upper left) Gratiot; (upper center left) Gratiot; (lower center left) PD; (bottom left, left column) Bushducks; (bottom center, left column) DBG; (bottom right, left column) Gratiot; (upper right) Gratiot; (upper center right) Strybing; (lower center right) Strybing; (lower right) Gratiot; **146** (upper left) TBG; (upper center left) Corel; (lower center left) Gratiot; (lower left) Corel; (upper right) DBG; (center right) Gratiot; (lower right) TBG; **147** (upper and center left) DBG; (lower left) CalPhotos; (upper right) Strybing; (upper center right) Gratiot; (lower center right) Strybing; (lower right) Strybing; **148** (upper left) Strybing; (upper center left) Brousseau; (lower center left) CalPhotos; (lower left) Strybing; (upper right) Bushducks; (upper center right) DBG; (lower center right) Strybing; (lower right) Gratiot; **149** (upper left) Strybing; (center left, two photos) Gratiot; (lower left) Strybing; (upper right) Gratiot; (center right) Corel; (lower right) Bushducks; **150** (upper left) Brousseau; (upper center left) Brousseau; (lower center left) Bushducks; (lower left) Brousseau; (upper center right) Bushducks; (lower center right) Corel; (lower right) Bushducks; **151** (upper center left) Brousseau; (lower center left) Bushducks; (lower left) Bushducks; (upper right) Bushducks; (lower right) Strybing; **152** (upper left) Strybing; (upper center left) Strybing; (middle center left) Strying; (lower center left) Brousseau; (lower left) CalPhotos; (upper right) Bushducks; (upper center right) Bushducks; (middle center right) Strybing; (lower center right) Strybing; **153** (upper center left) Bushducks; (lower center left) Bushducks; (lower left) CalPhotos; (upper right) Cal Photos; (center right) Bushducks; (lower right, four photos) Bushducks **154** (upper left) Strybing; (upper central left) Strybing; (middle center left) Brousseau; (lower center left) Brousseau; (lower left) Bushducks; (upper right) Bushducks; (upper center right) CalPhotos; **155** (upper left) Strybing; (upper center left) Strybing; (lower center left) PD; (lower left) Strybing; (upper and center right) Strybing; (lower right) CalPhotos **156** (top left, left) Strybing, (top right, left) Gratiot; (upper center left) Brousseau; (lower center left) CalPhotos; (lower left) Strybing; (upper and center right) Brousseau; (lower right) Bushducks; **157** (upper left) Bushducks; (lower left) Brousseau; (upper right) Brousseau; (lower right) DBG; **162-619** Bushducks

Front cover photography: (main) Corel; (small) Bushducks

Rear cover photography: (Tidytips) Gratiot; (Black bear) Corel; (Bodie ghost town) Bushducks; (Rafters) Bushducks; (Beckwourth) CaHS

Index

ABOUT THE SERIES OF swagman guides

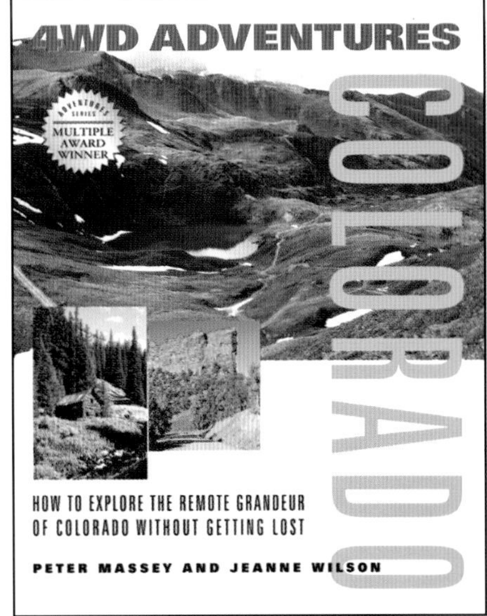

71 TRAILS
232 PAGES
209 PHOTOGRAPHS
PRICE $29.95
ISBN: 0-9665675-5-2

The Adventures series of backcountry guidebooks are the ultimate for both adventurous four-wheelers and scenic sightseers. Each volume in the Adventures series covers an entire state or a distinct region. In addition to meticulously detailed route directions and trail maps, these full-color guides include extensive information on the history of towns, ghost towns, and regions passed along the way, as well as a history of the American Indian tribes who lived in the area prior to Euro-American settlement. The guides also provide wildlife information and photographs to help readers identify the great variety of native birds, plants, and animals they are likely to see. All you need is your SUV and your Adventures book to confidently explore all the best sites in each state's backcountry.

4WD Adventures: Colorado gets you safely to the banks of the beautiful Crystal River or over America's highest pass road, Mosquito Pass. This book guides you to the numerous lost ghost towns that speckle Colorado's mountains. In addition to the enormously detailed trail information, there are hundreds of photos of historic mining operations, old railroad routes, wildflowers, and native animals. Trail history is brought to life through the accounts of sheriffs and gunslingers like Bat Masterson and Doc Holliday; millionaires like Horace Tabor and Thomas Walsh; and American Indian warriors like Chiefs Ouray and Antero.

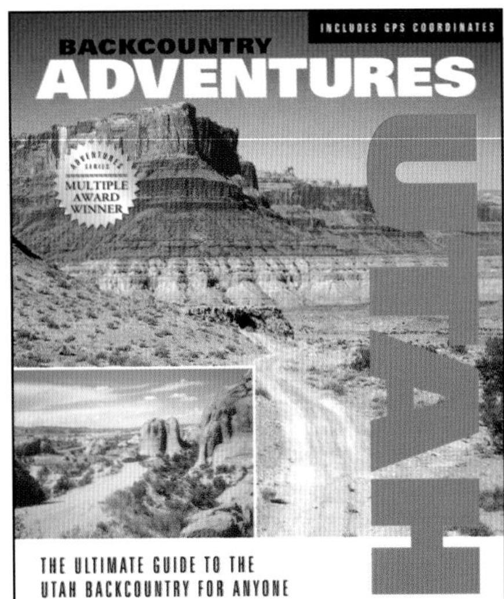

175 TRAILS
544 PAGES
525 PHOTOGRAPHS
PRICE $34.95
ISBN: 1-930193-12-2

Backcountry Adventures: Utah navigates you along 3,721 miles through the spectacular Canyonlands region of Utah, to the top of the Uinta Range, across vast salt flats, and along trails unchanged since the late 19th century when riders of the Pony Express sped from station to station and daring young outlaws wreaked havoc on newly established stage lines, railroads, and frontier towns. In addition to enormously detailed trail information, there are hundreds of photos of frontier towns, historic mining operations, old rail-

157 TRAILS
576 PAGES
524 PHOTOGRAPHS
PRICE $34.95
ISBN: 0-9665675-0-1

153 TRAILS
640 PAGES
645 PHOTOGRAPHS
PRICE $34.95
ISBN: 1-930193-04-1

152 TRAILS
640 PAGES
679 PHOTOGRAPHS
PRICE $34.95
ISBN: 1-930193-08-4

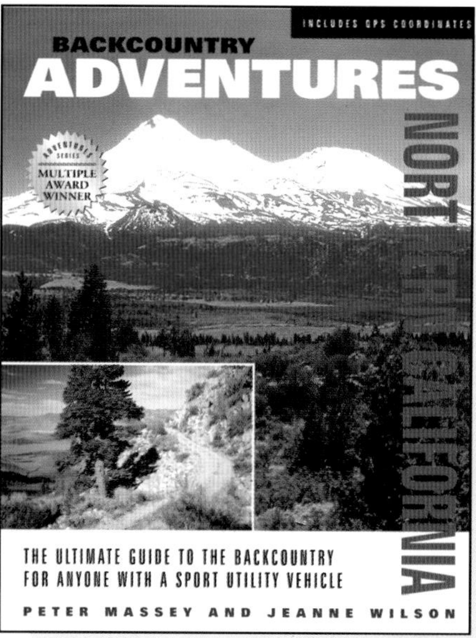

road routes, wildflowers, and native animals. Trail history is brought to life through the accounts of outlaws like Butch Cassidy and his Wild Bunch; explorers and mountain men like Jim Bridger; and early Mormon settlers led by Brigham Young.

Backcountry Adventures: Arizona guides you along the back roads of the state's most remote and scenic regions, from the lowlands of the Yuma Desert to the high plains of the Kaibab Plateau. In addition to the enormously detailed trail information, there are hundreds of photos of frontier towns, historic mining operations, old railroad routes, wildflowers, and native animals. Trail history is brought to life through the accounts of Indian warriors like Cochise and Geronimo; trailblazers like Edward F. Beale; and the famous lawman Wyatt Earp, a survivor of the Shoot-out at the O.K. Corral in Tombstone.

Backcountry Adventures: Southern California takes you from the beautiful mountain regions of Big Sur, through the arid Mojave Desert, and straight into the heart of the aptly named Death Valley. In addition to the enormously detailed trail information, there are hundreds of photos of frontier towns, historic mining operations, old railroad routes, wildflowers, and native animals. Trail history is brought to life through the accounts of Spanish missionaries who first settled the coastal regions of Southern California; eager prospectors looking to cash in during California's gold rush; and legends of lost mines still hidden in the state's expansive backcountry.

Backcountry Adventures: Northern California takes you from the rugged peaks of the Sierra Nevada, through volcanic regions of the Modoc Plateau, to majestic coastal redwood forests. In addition to enormously detailed trail information, there are hundreds of photos of frontier towns, historic mining operations, old railroad routes, wildflowers, and native animals. Trail history comes to life through accounts of outlaws like Rattlesnake Dick and Black Bart; explorers like Ewing Young and James Beckwourth; and the biggest mass migration in America's history, the gold rush.

Additional titles in the series will cover other states with four-wheel driving opportunities. Information on all upcoming books, including special prepublication discount offers, can be found on the Internet at www. 4WD books. com.